Modern Clinical Psychology

MODERN CLINICAL PSYCHOLOGY

Principles of Intervention in the Clinic and Community

SHELDON J. KORCHIN

UNIVERSITY OF CALIFORNIA, BERKELEY

Basic Books, Inc., Publishers

NEW YORK

Permission to reprint excerpts from the following sources is gratefully acknowledged.

Durkin, H. E. *The group in depth.* New York: International Universities Press, 1964. Copyright © 1964, International Universities Press.

Erikson, E. H. Identity and the life cycle. *Psychological Issues,* 1959, *I.* Copyright © 1959, International Universities Press, Inc.

Gill, M. M., Newman, R., & Redlich, F. C. *The initial interview in psychiatric practice.* New York: International Universities Press, 1954. Copyright © 1954, International Universities Press.

Greenson, R. R. *The technique and practice of psychoanalysis.* Vol. 1. New York: International Universities Press, 1967. Copyright © 1967, International Universities Press.

Lazarus, A. A. *Behavior therapy and beyond.* New York: McGraw-Hill, 1971.

Offer, D., & Sabshin, M. *Normality: Theoretical and clinical aspects of mental health.* New York: Basic Books, 1966. Copyright © 1966, 1974, Daniel Offer & Melvin Sabshin.

Perls, F. S. *Gestalt therapy verbatim.* Lafayette, Calif.: Real People Press, 1969.

Patterson, C. H. *Theories of counseling and psychotherapy* (2nd ed.). New York: Harper & Row, 1973.

Rogers, C. R., with the assistance of Coulson, W. R., & Truax, C. In S. Arieti (ed.). *American handbook of psychiatry,* Vol. 3. New York: Basic Books, 1966. Copyright © 1966, Basic Books.

Rogers, C. R. *Carl Rogers on encounter groups.* New York: Harper & Row, 1970. Copyright © 1970 by Carl Rogers.

Satir, V. *Conjoint family therapy* (Rev. Ed.). Palo Alto, Calif.: Science and Behavior Books, 1967.

Streitfeld, H. S. The aureon encounter: An organic process. In L. Blank, G. B. Gottsegen, & M. G. Gottsegen, *Confrontation: Encounters in self and interpersonal awareness.* New York: Macmillan, 1971. Copyright © 1971, Macmillan Publishing Co., Inc.

Watson, J. B. *Behaviorism.* New York: Norton, 1924. Copyright © 1924, 1925, 1930, W. W. Norton & Company, Inc. Copyright renewed 1952, 1953, 1958 by John B. Watson.

Wyatt, F. What is clinical psychology? In A. Z. Guiora & M. A. Brandwin (eds.). *Perspectives in clinical psychology.* Princeton, N.J.: Van Nostrand, 1968. Copyright © 1968, Litton Educational Publishing Inc. Reprinted by permission of D. Van Nostrand and Co.

The author would also like to thank the American Psychological Association and the American Psychiatric Association for permission to either quote or summarize material from their public documents.

Library of Congress Cataloging in Publication Data

Korchin, Sheldon J

Modern clinical psychology.

1. Clinical psychology. 2. Personality assessment. 3. Psychotherapy. I. Title. [DNLM: 1. Psychology, Clinical. 2. Psychology, Social. WM100 K835m]

RC467.K67 157'.9 76-2067

ISBN: 0-465-04638-x

Printed in the United States of America

DESIGNED BY VINCENT TORRE

77 78 79 80 10 9 8 7 6 5 4 3

For Sylvia

ACKNOWLEDGMENTS

In the writing of this book I have cumulated debts to friends, colleagues, and students. My greatest debt is to my friends David Krech and H. A. Witkin, who counseled wisely throughout. Neither, interestingly enough, is a clinician; both are general psychologists in the old and best sense of the term. Perhaps they could see my work in a starker and clearer light because they were not burdened by my professional commitments and pretensions.

Considerable gratitude is also due to my colleagues of the Psychology Clinic at the University of California at Berkeley, faculty and students, who read, argued, and suggested changes in chapter after chapter, as each was drafted. Steve Lerner, Brian Feldman, and Carol Morrison, graduate students, worked closely with me in different phases, abstracting literature, seeking out information, and commenting on drafts. Above all, I am grateful to the late Clementina Kuhlmann Hollenberg who, through what she knew was a terminal illness, read and painstakingly reviewed a number of chapters, returning the last to me just barely before her untimely death. She was a fine teacher and psychologist, a marvelous woman, and a dear friend.

The heavy clerical and secretarial work involved in this book was done by a succession of talented and dedicated people. First, and foremost, was my daughter Ellen Curtis who creatively and meticulously organized our files, references, notes, and—most important—me. She is living proof that, happily, something beyond heredity and environment determines human character. Portions of the manuscript were typed by Belinda Ponsonby, Flo Oakes, Lynda Hammers, Sue Eicher, and Debbie Bucher. My friend Genevieve Marshall Reynolds carefully proofread the entire manuscript. All of them have my sincerest gratitude.

Fred Allen, the radio comedian, once said to a network official who criticized a script of his, "But where were you when the paper was blank?" There was one person who stood by me when the paper was blank. She contributed in numerous specific ways, much as all the people I have just named, but more in that she brought an atmosphere of love which made it possible for me to sustain the loneliness and pain of writing. To my wife Sylvia, this book is dedicated.

TO THE READER

Some years ago, a publisher sent a wise and cleverly written brochure to prospective authors of scholarly and scientific books. It called attention to the curious compulsion of specialists to describe their fields in terms of two overworked cliches. Forewarned, I will resist the temptation to say that clinical psychology has "grown like Topsy" and that it can be thought of in numerous ways "like the elephant described by the blind men." I will avoid these two cliches, though they just happen to be perfectly true of clinical psychology.

In this volume, I have attempted to survey the many concerns of the growing field of clinical psychology, examining its more traditional as well as emergent interests, from a broad conceptual and historical perspective. Just as one knows an individual life better through knowledge of its developmental history, so the evolution of our field becomes clearer if viewed against the movement of ideas and events—in psychology generally, in the mental health fields, and in the larger society. Particularly in Parts 1 and 2, but throughout the volume as well, I have tried to present philosophical, theoretical, and historical contexts for understanding current trends in clinical psychology.

The psychological clinician is motivated by the *clinical attitude*—the desire to understand people in order to help them. It is this emphasis on knowledge to reduce human suffering that most clearly distinguishes clinical psychology from other psychological fields, even those as close as the psychology of personality and psychopathology, which attempt to discover the nature of personality functioning and disorder in general terms.

In this volume, therefore, emphasis is on the concepts and methods of *intervention*—the things clinicians do to help people in psychological distress. Broadly, these fall into three major groups defined by three parts of this book: (1) gaining an understanding of the patient and his problems (Clinical Assessment, discussed in Part 3); (2) effecting desired changes in individual personality and psychological functioning (Psychotherapy and Behavior Modification, Part 4); and (3) altering some of the social determinants of human problems (Community Psychology, Part 5). The many competing concepts and techniques of intervention will be critically examined, but I have tried to avoid simply listing and contrasting alternate approaches. Thus, in Part 4, a general model of individual psychotherapy is presented, which contains elements generic to many approaches, *before* divergent systems are considered. Overall, attention is given to models of intervention which have arisen in the context of psychodynamic, behavioral, humanistic-existential, and community psychological frameworks. The increasingly pluralistic nature of clinical psychology is revealed not only in these competing models but also in the diversity of training programs and professional roles which characterize the contemporary field (Part 5).

Clinical psychology is a science-practice field, as indeed it must be to generate the knowledge necessary for effective intervention. Too often, however, science and practice are conceived as if they were separate from each other, when in actuality each must feed the other. To avoid further polarization, I have chosen not to have a separate chapter on "Research in Clinical Psychology." Instead, in every chapter issues are considered in terms of research evidence, where available and appropriate. Matters of research design and methodology, specific to the problems of clinical psychology, are most fully and explicitly discussed in the context of the study of clinical inference (Chapter 11), the evaluation of psychotherapy (Chapter 16) and community intervention (Chapter 19).

Except for brief consideration in the context of family therapy and of community intervention, the problems of the child are slighted. Similarly, biomedical interventions, particularly the many important developments in the use of psychoactive drugs, have not been discussed. Child clinical psychology and psychopharmocology are specialties in their own right, and authoritative volumes are available in each area. I will be happy, indeed, if the student gains from my book some notion as to what clinicians do (and more important, why) in their psychosocial interventions with adult clients. I will be happier still if the student can come to share with me some of the excitement of being a clinical psychologist.

SHELDON J. KORCHIN

Berkeley, California
August, 1975

CONTENTS

PART 2

THE NATURE OF MENTAL HEALTH

PART 3

CLINICAL ASSESSMENT

PART 4
PSYCHOTHERAPY

PART 5

COMMUNITY PSYCHOLOGY

PART 6

THE PROFESSION OF CLINICAL PSYCHOLOGY

PART 1

ISSUES AND ORIENTATION

CHAPTER 1

People with Problems

Clinical psychology is concerned with understanding and improving human functioning. Along with other fields of psychology and the behavioral sciences, it shares the task of increasing knowledge about the principles of psychological functioning in "people in general," but its unique concern is with the human problems of "persons in particular." As one of the so-called mental health professions, clinical psychology shares responsibility for increasing the well-being of psychologically troubled people. As a clinical field, it is dedicated to improving the lot of individuals in distress, using the best knowledge and techniques available, while striving through research to increase the knowledge and sharpen the techniques needed for improved intervention in the future.

Much of the history of clinical psychology is contained within the twentieth century, with most of the growth of the field occuring in the years following the Second World War. In these three decades, the number of clinical psychologists has grown enormously. The scope of the field expanded in the range of human problems dealt with, the variety of services rendered, and the diversity of roles in which clinicians function. Theory, knowledge, and technique have grown greatly, not always in orderly progression. During these years, public policy and lay acceptance of the goals and methods of clinical psychology have fostered its emergence as an autonomous profession.

But the human issues which engage clinical psychology are as old as the history of mankind. When man emerged as a conscious animal, more particularly as a self-conscious one, the behavior of his own kind was an inevitable source of fascination. To understand and even to change human nature was no less vital than understanding and controlling the physical world. Indeed, survival itself as well as organized social life depends as much on knowledge in the one realm as in the other. Systems of philosophy, religion, and popular psychology evolved to explain why we think, feel, and behave as we do, how disturbed behavior arises, and what can be done to alter psychological growth and human behavior. In the historically recent past, the behavioral sciences emerged as organized attempts to systematize such knowledge and to develop more rational techniques of inducing psychosocial change. Through methods of scholarship, theory development, and empirical research, modern human science has produced a more secure base for understanding and intervening in human affairs. But from prehistoric time to the present, there have been well-developed formulations about the nature of human behavior and the conditions for its change. On analysis, we discover that many of the prescientific ways of altering the behavior of others anticipate the generic processes involved in psychotherapy and behavior change (J. D. Frank, 1973).

What Human Problems Fall Within our Ken?

What are the human problems which concern clinicians? Who defines them as problems, sees them as psychological, and decides that the efforts of a psychological clinician are appropriate? As we shall see, the social definitions involved in declaring a problem to exist, to be psychological, and to necessitate psychological care differ from place to place and from time to time.

All of us, at some time or other in our lives, experience inadequacy, helplessness, or anxiety or we manifest behaviors which to us or to those around us are strange and frightening. When these are personally overwhelming or intensely disturbing to others, some external solution is sought. But whether this involves a psychological clinician or is seen as more appropriate for the police, priests, physicians, lawyers, or other social agents is complexly determined by personal and social values, available resources, laws, and customs. Many human problems which in former times were treated by family or friends, priests or doctors, have now moved into the realm of the psychological clinician. With growing psychological-mindedness, particularly among educated Americans, the range of human problems viewed as psychological has expanded greatly. Issues formerly in the domain of education, criminal justice, and medicine have been reconceived as psychological in nature and amenable to psychological intervention.

Patient and Clinician

In view of the changes that have taken place both in the conception of mental problems and in the role of the helping professional, it is difficult to decide on the terminology to describe the parties in the helping transaction. On the one hand, there is the sufferer, who experiences inadequacy and pain and who seeks help and relief, or whose behavior is so distressing to others that they may seek help for him. Conventionally, he has been called a patient. I will, although with some reluctance, use the term in this volume. It derives from the context of medicine and, as we shall see, there are problems with the medical analogy. Others have used parallel words, such as “client,” to describe the sufferer, but there seems little advantage to such terms. If the medical overtones are lost, "client" picks up the connotations of law or business. On the other side of the transaction, the term "clinician" will be used to refer to anyone who, through systematic intervention, seeks to alter and improve the state of the patient. Such interventions may involve personality study to discover potential sources of psychological malfunction and to program subsequent interventions, or it may involve one of the many kinds of psychotherapeutic activities, or it may involve actions directed toward the patient's social environment, family, classroom, job setting, or the larger community. The greater part of this book will detail the concepts and methods of clinical assessment, psychotherapy, and social and community interventions practiced by clinicians.

We will focus on clinical psychology, as one among the psychological helping professions. However, much of what we discuss will be generic to the helping role and would as well apply to psychiatrists, social workers, counselors, and other mental health professionals and, indeed, to teachers, ministers, and others who as part of their involvement with human well-being must deal with individuals in psychological distress. Rather than becoming involved in circumlocutions or professional-boundary disputes, the term "clinician" will be used simply to refer to the person, of whatever professional training, who performs acts of psychological intervention.

Some Illustrative Human Problems

The range of human problems which engage the clinician is wide and resists simple classification. Here are some illustrative eases, described in brief vignettes intended more to suggest than to illuminate the nature of the problem, its background and history, the interventions involved, and the settings in which they took place.

JOHN D.—A COLLEGE STUDENT

A bright young man came from a small town to the state university. At home, he had been a conforming adolescent, who had done well but not brilliantly in high school. His family was ambitious for him and wanted him to go into a professional career. Without much conviction or personal goals, he left for the university. There, the size of the student body, the many strange-looking people and activities, and the intensity of life left him frightened and isolated during his freshman year. However, he worked hard and received creditable grades. He made no real friends, neither men nor women, nor did he become much involved in extracurricular activities. During his second year, both coursework and college life seemed dull and futile. He became disheartened about the state of American society, although he had seen little of it firsthand. He came to believe that society was corrupt, mistreating minorities at home and aggressing on weaker nations abroad. The university itself, he believed, was bureaucratic and dehumanizing, more concerned with preserving itself and providing privilege for its faculty than in educating students or providing a genuine community. He joined in some student political activities, but had no great sense of commitment or purpose, nor did he take on any leadership roles. He was the cynic rather than the revolutionary. In time, he found companionship in a like-minded subgroup on campus. With them, he had long "rap sessions" and experimented with marijuana and LSD. He felt no guilt nor anxiety, but neither did the drugs produce the transcendent experiences others had described.

On one "bad trip" however, he fell from an apartment window, fortunately on a first floor and over a planted area, and broke his wrist. He was treated at the Student Health Service which recommended that he go to their Psychiatry Department. He accepted the appointment passively, was interviewed, and given some screening psychological tests. These he treated as an amusing game, teasing the examiner with intentionally provocative responses. In a few sessions with the clinician, he denied having any personal problems nor need for psychological treatment, pointing out, without contention and as a self-evident proposition, that the mess lay in society and not in him. Although the clinician suggested that they should continue to discuss these matters, he saw little purpose and ceased coming.

His parents, frightened by his use of drugs and the seeming aimlessness of his life, prevailed on him to go to a psychotherapist in private practice. He went, more "to get them off his back" than out of any felt need. Nor was this experience any more productive or satisfying than the few sessions at the Student Health Service. He resented the therapist-patient relationship, its lack of mutuality, intellectual game quality, one-way communication, and the professional detachment of the therapist, who he felt was well enough intentioned but a stolid, conforming man who could not really understand his thinking. Once again, psychotherapy was terminated.

Although he had a sense of purposelessness and an inchoate discontent, there was no focal distress nor desire for help. Through friends, he learned of "encounter groups" and, with amused curiosity, he joined one. Early, he felt a heightened excitement as he and others engaged in highly charged emotional exchanges, as often of a hostile as compassionate sort, the goal of which was to be fully honest and revealing of one's true and immediate feelings. He felt alive, and began to seek new experiences elsewhere. He would hike in the woods, read poetry, try new foods, often in company with a girl he met in the group. He was eager to have others discover the benefit of encounter groups, and he proselytized among classmates. He discovered an interest in the study of anthropology, in large part through identification with a teacher who was an impassioned and dedicated scholar. He now plans to do graduate work in the field.

MRS. R.—A DEPRESSED WOMAN

Mrs. R. is fifty-seven years old, though depending on her state at the time, either looks younger or older. She has had a comfortable life and, by her own standards and those of her friends, it has been a good one. Immediately after college graduation, she married a competent and considerate man, who has provided both financial security and true affection. He has had a good position in a stable company and has provided them with a comfortable home. Furnishing the home, tending the garden, entertaining friends, many of them business associates and their families, were satisfying activities. With neighbors, she has joined in local campaigns for better schools, additional hospital facilities, and other community-improvement projects.

For the first fourteen years of their marriage, the couple could not have a child, which was an acute disappointment to them. In many medical consultations no physical reasons were found for the apparent sterility. Finally, they adopted an infant boy, although Mrs. R. would have preferred a girl. About a year later, she did become pregnant. The months of pregnancy were filled with the fear that she might lose the baby. Following a healthy birth, Mrs. R. had a severe depressive episode and it was felt best to keep her in the hospital. She was consumed by fantasies that she might do the baby harm and she had unfounded beliefs that her husband was unfaithful. After a few weeks in the hospital, which included treatment with antidepressant drugs, she apparently recovered completely and returned home.

Throughout their childhood, Mrs. R. invested great love and concern in the two children. Their growth and achievements were a source of deep pride and satisfaction. When, in time, they left for college and subsequently to marry, there was a void in her life. At that time, she began to alternate between vague feelings of emptiness and worthlessness and sporadic and futile attempts to find new commitments. Guilt feelings were pervasive—she had wasted her life, been a poor wife and mother, neglected the children's welfare, and most particularly the adopted son whom she believed she had slighted in favor of the natural daughter. These beliefs were not shaken by the reassurances of her husband and children. Although she is able to run her home on a day-to-day basis, she has been continuously depressed. Sometimes, she is tearfully agitated and self-recriminatory, at other times more profoundly depressed, dry-eyed, and unresponsive.

During the past three or four years she started psychotherapy on a couple of occasions. These experiences have been unsatisfying and unproductive, and they were soon terminated. There has been little change in her state, and family and friends have been concerned that she might even attempt suicide. Mr. R. has talked with her about the possibility of going to a good psychiatric hospital, but neither is convinced that it is absolutely necessary. Meanwhile, family and friends have tried to make her life at home as comfortable as possible.

HENRY L.—A "RETARDED" BLACK CHILD

Henry is a ten-year-old black boy in an inner-city school in a large northern city. The family is poor and lives in a tenement apartment. Henry is the youngest of three boys, who with their mother and father live with the mother's mother. The three boys probably have more contact with the grandmother than with their own parents. She is a domineering woman, who is impatient with their misbehaviors. The mother works long hours as a domestic in a distant part of the city. The father is sporadically employed as a day laborer.

The family migrated north from a southern farm area twelve years ago and, until two years ago, returned almost every summer to work in the harvest. When they came back to the city, they usually found a different apartment, as often as not in a new school district. The movement in and out of the city disrupted the children's education. The oldest brother, now fifteen, has been arrested for delinquent behavior; the father, on several occasions, for drunkenness. Although the father is kind to the mother and boys, he is not a strong or positive parent. He tends either to ignore the boys or, when sufficiently provoked, to punish them.

In school, Henry has done poorly. He is now in a special class for retarded children. He is often truant, preferring to wander alone in the parks and alleys of the city. In class, he daydreams, doodles and draws during class assignments, and appears sullen and unresponsive. On the playground, he occasionally flares in anger and hits out aggressively at other children. When in the third grade, he was the particular scapegoat of an older white woman teacher, who had been in the school from a time when the neighborhood had no blacks. She is envious of colleagues who are able to transfer to "better" schools, and resents having to teach "unteachable" children. This teacher requested that Henry be transfered to the special class.

A school psychologist tested Henry and noted that although his overall IQ, as assessed by standard tests, was sufficiently low to warrant placement in the special class, there were peaks in some of the performance tests, particularly those involving special relations and visual imagery, which were suggestive of greater ability. Despite his surliness, she found him an appealing boy whose alertness when involved belied the low test scores. She discussed Henry with Mrs. M., a black "mental health worker" recently assigned to the school, to see whether some special help might not be available in the community.

Mrs. M.'s job is part of a new community mental health program for which women were chosen because of their considerable human-relations skills; even though they lacked formal education, they were trained to work with problem children. Living in the community and knowing its particular customs and problems, it was felt that they could serve as a bridge between the school and the social and clinical resources of the community. Mrs. M. introduced Henry to an after-school program, run largely by black college students, which included tutoring in specific skills (spelling, reading, arithmetic), as well as organized sport and outdoor activities for the boys. Along with the subtle opportunities to identify with older blacks, the project was also consciously preoccupied with strengthening black identity through discussions of black history, culture, and customs.

At the same time, Mrs. M. took Henry to the Child Guidance Clinic at the Community Mental Health Center. There he was observed, interviewed, and tested by clinicians, who supported the view of the briefer school examination. Henry did seem to have considerable potential ability, although it was not revealed in school work, standard achievement nor intelligence tests. His tendency toward surly withdrawal or, contrariwise, angry attack when aroused, went along with a defensive disinterest in the alien school environment. At the same time, it was discovered that Henry had difficulty in focusing attention, delaying gratification, and controlling impulse, qualities suggestive of a lower level of ego development than was appropriate for his age. A member of the Center staff (a social worker by background) discussed Henry's problems and talents with his mother, and encouraged her to continue bringing him to the Clinic. On three or four subsequent occasions, Henry visited the clinician "to chat." An effort was made to start a course of psychotherapy which would involve puppet play intended to externalize and release pent-up feelings. However, the Clinic staff decided that participation in the afterschool program was probably more important and relevant to Henry's needs than treatment in the Clinic. Through Mrs. M., the principal of the school was asked to reassign Henry out of the stigmatized "retarded class."

After a few months, Henry has changed visibly. He looks and acts more mature, proud, and competent. He has developed interest in school work, and is drawing abreast of his age mates.

MR. G.—A HOSPITALIZED SCHIZOPHRENIC PATIENT

Mr. G. is a thirty-five-year-old engineer, who is completely engrossed in his work in electronics. He has never married and since leaving his family home to go to college, has lived alone. He has always been seclusive and prefers the company of books and mechanical projects to that of people. In a large engineering firm, he has been a dependable and thorough worker, although colleagues find him somewhat secretive. He sometimes alludes to radical new ideas he is developing, but carefully gives little specific information. What he does reveal is not always understandable, even to equally trained technical people. One of his associates said, "It is as though he talked in code, part of which we know and part of which is secret." About a year ago, he confided to some fellow workers that company officials were exploiting his ideas without his consent.

Late one night, the police were called to a bar where he had gotten into a fight with another man. He was incoherent and shouted obscenities, which seemed to suggest that he believed the man was making homosexual advances to him. The police took him to the emergency service of the city hospital and he was committed the following day to the nearby state mental hospital. There, his agitated, irrational, and emotional behavior continued for some days, after which he became lethargic, staying in a corner of his room. He said little, either to staff or other patients, except to repeat the demand that he be released since he was being held against his will and there was nothing wrong with him. He slept little, paced his room in a repetitive and mechanical way, sometimes masturbating openly. He ate erratically and neglected his appearance completely. He alternated between periods of apathetic withdrawal and emotional storms. During these days he was given drugs to reduce the agitation, although sometimes he had to be actively restrained.

After a week he was sufficiently calm to be interviewed and given a battery of psychological tests, in order to assess the degree and type of disturbance and to plan future clinical interventions. In reviewing the time just prior to the bar-room incident, he said that he was on the verge of a major discovery and knew that "enemy forces" were eager to get his invention. He could hear the voices of their agents and, although not clearly recognizable, he knew they were accusing him of unpatriotic as well as immoral acts. He also felt that he was rotting away inside and that portions of his body were separated from his control "as if amputated." He was very frightened and would carefully avoid strange or dark streets. Every evening he locked his room with great care.

In psychological testing, his knowledge, intelligence, and technical training were clearly evident, although thought processes were fragmented, either being inappropriately abstract or inappropriately concrete. Thus he might define a word correctly, but go on to a stilted and unnecessary discussion of its many meanings. Associations were distant and difficult to follow. Explosive affect was revealed, both in test responses and in behavior with the examiner. Much of the time he was crafty in giving information. Compared to his first days in the hospital, he had calmed down considerably and was willing to cooperate in hospital activities. He denied that he was "insane" but agreed (though with uncertain conviction) that he had acted irrationally, which he thought was probably due to overwork and fatigue.

He has now been in the hospital for almost a year. He has psychotherapy sessions twice weekly with a woman clinician who has great tolerance and genuine fondness for such patients. Much of the time is spent without overt communication, but in a warm and comforting relationship. He has talked openly with her about some of the more painful episodes of his childhood and of his feelings of estrangement as an adult. Though his behavior is less bizarre, his peculiar mode of thinking is still evident. Socially, he has become involved in two important hospital activities. The hospital has a closed circuit TV system and its own studio, which broadcasts films and patient-produced shows including a popular staff-patient interview program. Mr. G. has virtually taken over responsibility for the maintenance of the television equipment and he has been of great help to the staff in the technical problems of making and broadcasting TV programs. He has also joined in patient-government groups, which combine group therapeutic and administrative functions. Patients meet regularly and discuss their mutual concerns and problems, where possible attempting to change hospital practices. In these sessions Mr. G. makes incisive and perceptive observations about the feelings and motives of others—often disconcertingly so! Still, he has gained the respect of a number of people and is taking some pride in being instrumental in effecting changes in the hospital.

At this point, the hospital staff is discussing the possibility of discharging Mr. G. Psychological testing has been repeated and reveals a more integrated person, with considerably augmented ability to control impulse and affect. Much of the same type of thought process earlier revealed is still present, but in less florid form. There is concern, however, that without an available family home and supporting people, Mr. G. might slip back and need to be rehospitalized. At the same time, some express the view that he is "adjusting too well" in the hospital and might slip into a passive patient role if allowed to stay indefinitely. They believe that the best solution would be a halfway house or night hospital where he could be in a protected environment for part of the time, while working and reengaging himself with the real community. Unfortunately, no such facilities are readily available.

Human Problems and Clinical Interventions

John D., Mrs. R., Henry L., and Mr. G., though differing in numerous ways, barely illustrate the enormous diversity of problems which engage the professional concern of clinicians. Though brief, these vignettes depict some of the kinds of people, types of human distress, varieties of clinical interventions, institutional settings, and professional issues with which clinicians work. Complete cataloguing is both impossible and unnecessary, but we can now look in more general terms at the varieties of *persons, problems, interventions,* and *settings* with which clinicians work.

PERSONS

Anyone can have a psychological problem, though the type may well differ as a function of the age, personality organization, or social background of the person. From earliest childhood to the most advanced age there are potential problems, some of which are related to transitional crises such as puberty, marriage, or retirement. Some forms of psychological problems are more common among men, others among women. Similarly, black and white people differ, as well as city dwellers and farmers, rich and poor, or people in different occupations. But no person, by virtue of any of these qualities, is either exempt from or guaranteed human problems. Ultimately, it is in the individual personality that healthy growth or disability occurs, and it is in the individual personality that all orders of determinants—biological, psychological, and social—converge. In a statistical sense, there are "high-risk" groups for particular conditions, just as public health epidemiologists have long shown to be true for medical ailments. Thus children are more likely to get measles, and some types of metal and mining workers are prone to respiratory diseases. "Base rates" for certain psychological conditions differ among social groups. Similarly, people of different backgrounds and values differ as well in their attitudes toward psychological help, their readiness to seek it, and their responsiveness to different forms of intervention. Meaningful psychological intervention thus depends on knowledge of the incidence and prevalence of psychological conditions in different sectors of the population and on understanding the group values and attitudes which affect exposure and response to intervention.

PSYCHOLOGICAL PROBLEMS

A problem comes to light when someone is distressed, either the person himself, his immediate family or friends, or the larger society. As psychologists, we describe criteria for impaired, adequate, and optimal functioning, and we may help people interpret their status by these criteria, but in a typical situation help is not sought unless the individual or those about him are disturbed by his condition. For a problem to be called "psychological," the primary manifestations (symptoms) should be of a psychological sort; for example, a sense of inadequacy, anxiety, or depression, impaired psychological functioning (e.g., inability to concentrate, to work effectively, to solve problems), or aberrant needs or behaviors (e.g., intense aggressiveness, compulsive acts). However, psychological problems may or may not have their origins in psychological conditions, nor for that matter need they be altered only by psychological interventions.

For convenience, we distinguish the physiological, psychological, and social realms in considering the determinants of a condition, its manifestations, and the treatments which may alter it, but these distinctions are in fair measure arbitrary. There are no necessary relations between the origins of a problem, its symptoms, and the mode of treatment which can best serve to alter it. For example, a person may feel anxious and inadequate after failure in school (a psychological stress), or following a heart attack (a medical condition), or unemployment (a social problem). Yet in all of these cases the person may experience personal weakness for which the relationship and self-exploration of psychotherapy may provide relief. Similarly, anxiety which is deeply rooted in the psychological history of the individual may be relieved by drugs, on the one hand, or change in the social environment, on the other. Social stress can result in physiological symptoms which in turn yield to psychological interventions. Thus it has been remarked that the incidence of gastric ulcers among tax accountants rises as the day for filing income tax returns draws closer, then it falls sharply. Psychosomatic conditions, such as ulcers, have been found to benefit from psychotherapy as well as from medical treatment. From the vantage of the psychological clinician, therefore, a psychological problem is one which engages the human personality, regardless of its origins or potential treatments.

Human problems differ in their inclusiveness as well as severity. Some are relatively focalized and engage only a portion of the person's life. Others, such as the severe neuroses and psychoses, encompass all facets of living. Problems vary too in their duration and their situation-specificity. Some are short-lived and occur at a particular time and place. They may be reactions to the death of a loved one or changes in life circumstances such as occur when one enters a new school, gets married, or retires. Other problems, however, are built into the fabric of the personality, and although they may peak and retreat, they reflect continuously maladaptive behavior patterns existing over much, if not all, of the life span. Problems which persist are called chronic, in distinction to acute episodes in which problem manifestations and disability are intense but short-lived.

INTERVENTIONS

All clinical interventions have as their goal increasing the well-being and effectiveness of individuals in distress. Viewed broadly, clinical intervention includes efforts to (1) understand the state of the person, i.e., the assessment process; (2) alter the personality and functioning of the person, i.e., the therapeutic process; and (3) alter the influences acting upon him which produce or exacerbate his problems, i.e., the environmental control process. The *locus* of intervention may be the person himself (as in individual psychotherapy or behavior modification), the small groups in which he functions (as in family or group therapy), or the larger community in which he lives (social and community intervention).

There are numerous *modes* of intervention. Much of this volume will be concerned with the varying conceptions and techniques of intervention. As we will examine in some detail, systems of intervention depend on how one conceives personality and human problems. Thus interventions differ in the degree to which they stress reeducation, personality exploration and self-understanding, emotional release, reconditioning of aberrant behaviors, or alteration of the social factors which impinge on the individual.

SETTINGS

Clinicians work in a variety of settings: psychiatric hospitals and clinics, general hospitals, community mental health centers, nonmedical human service agencies, private-practice offices, and nonclinical organizations such as schools, prisons, businesses, and churches. Both the variety of settings and the diversity of services offered have grown greatly in recent years. In principle, there is a division of labor among settings: the most severely disturbed patients are treated in hospitals; painful and disabling but not incapacitating neurotic and character problems are seen in clinics and private practice; more minor problems get the attention of school counselors and guidance workers; problems related to medical diseases are seen in medical settings; social problems are dealt with in social service agencies; and so on. In actuality, things are not so neatly arranged. The same problem may be treated in different settings, for reasons which, from the clinician's view, are irrelevant. The poor person is more likely to be hospitalized; the affluent one to receive outpatient care from a private practitioner (Hollingshead and Redlich, 1958). Though intended for students with personal difficulties related to academic studies, university counseling services frequently deal with as intense emotional problems as do psychiatric clinics. Family service and other social agencies see multiproblem families who, in addition to severe social and economic problems, may have equally severe behavioral problems. What setting is chosen, indeed whether a problem comes to clinical attention at all, is complexly determined by what resources are available, attitudes toward their use, and their cost and accessibility, among other factors. Moreover, patterns of use are changing, particularly as part of the movement toward bringing mental health care closer to community life.

The Mental Hospital. Both private and state-supported hospitals are used for the inpatient treatment of psychiatric patients. Some of the best private hospitals provide excellent care in a humane environment. Many private hospitals, however, are little better than the average state facility. In any case, private hospitalization is exceedingly expensive and, over any period of time, drains the resources of all but the richest families. The great majority of Americans, therefore, have to depend on the large state hospitals. These are often overcrowded and understaffed and located at distances from population centers. Thus patients are far from their homes and families and the staff is far from sources of professional stimulation. Much of the day-to-day care of patients falls to technicians and aides, often undertrained and underqualified. In an atmosphere which may be more custodial than therapeutic, the conditions of hospital living can themselves contribute to the deterioration rather than cure of many patients. In recent years, there have been significant moves both toward changing the hospitals themselves and toward developing alternatives to hospitalization, as we will consider more fully in Chapter 17.

Clinics. In clinics, patients may be seen on one or a few occasions or come in for regularly scheduled psychotherapy sessions over many months, but during other times they live and work in the world outside. Clinics may be units of general or psychiatric hospitals, provide services on university campuses, or be free-standing organizations. Some attempt to cover the wide range of human problems and patients; others are specialized. Thus, there are Child Guidance and Child Psychiatric Clinics, units for the special problems of drug addicts, alcoholics, and for those convicted of crimes. Clinicians work in medical clinics of various types, including neurology, speech and hearing, pediatrics, and physical therapy and rehabilitation, to help with the psychological problems associated with the disorders treated. Although they are usually not termed clinics, social agencies provide help with a variety of human problems. As part of the trend toward the further development of community mental health services, crisis clinics, emergency services, and suicide prevention centers have been developed to provide immediate, focussed help. Many clinic services are tax-supported and minimal fees are charged.

Most clinics are staffed by psychiatrists, clinical psychologists, and social workers; in medical settings, they are usually administered by psychiatrists.

There are relatively few clinics primarily managed and staffed by psychologists. Most conspicuous are the university training clinics.

Community Mental Health Centers. To increase the quality and availability of clinical services, particularly in the poorer urban ghettos, federal legislation in the early 1960s encouraged the growth of community mental health centers (see Chapter 17 for a fuller description). These centers draw on and extend existing facilities for inpatient and outpatient care, providing hospitalization, clinic treatment, emergency and crisis intervention, rehabilitation and aftercare services, and consultative help to other community agencies. They are intended to give more integrated and coordinated service, greater "continuity of care," so that people in need do not "slip between the cracks." A unique feature is community participation in the development and management of these centers.

Private Practice. A large number of American mental health professionals are in private practice; this includes the majority of psychiatrists and a sizeable minority of psychologists (see Chapter 20). In most cases, private-practice clinicians specialize in intensive psychotherapy. Full-scale psychoanalysis is almost invariably done in private practice. For the practitioner, office practice is both financially rewarding and professionally gratifying. Most usually, he works with educated and psychologically minded people who understand, seek out, and value his services. Although they may be intensely distressed, they often function effectively in many activities. Not least, they are likely to be relatively well off. Fees are high and therapy can extend over months or years.

Herein lies a problem. To the extent that limited manpower is invested in office psychotherapy, it is not available in clinic, hospital, and community services. A small minority of people receive the largest proportion of professional time. Like their therapists, they tend to be urban, educated and affluent, sick but not too sick. Although it is easy to sympathize with the desire of practitioners for an autonomous vocation, good income, and "interesting patients," the resultant social problem has lead many thoughtful leaders of psychiatry and clinical psychology to urge that professional values and training be reevaluated in order to assure more services in the public domain.

Nonclinical Settings. Thus far we have considered what are ordinarily conceived to be "mental health settings." In addition, however, clinicians work in schools and universities, businesses and churches, courts and prisons, institutions for the aged, for orphaned or handicapped children, in military units and governmental agencies. In some cases, they offer direct services to people in distress; in others, their role is consultative and their effort directed toward altering institutional practices in order to facilitate human functioning and well-being. The development of social interventions, of potential value in nonclinical settings and even in the larger community itself, is an important theme in the emerging community psychology.

Becoming a Patient

Human problems vary enormously (1) in their manifestations (symptoms, diagnoses); (2) in the degree to which they are distressing or disabling; (3) in the likelihood that they will come to clinical attention; (4) in the relevance of such attention, and (5) in the probability that it may relieve the patient's suffering. In this section, let us look more closely at the question of how someone becomes the object of psychological intervention. How is it decided that there is a human problem? How is it decided that it is psychological in nature? And how, among available alternatives, is it decided that the help of a psychological clinician is needed? In short, how does one become a patient?

For a problem to be said to exist at all, some one has to be distressed by the state of the patient-to-be—either the person himself, immediate friends, family or advisors, or formal agencies of social control. Thus recognized, for the problem then to come to clinical attention one or another of these parties must decide that it is a psychological problem for which the unique talents of a psychological clinician are required. Clinicians have described what they believe constitutes psychological problems, as I will in Chapter 3, and have offered more or less objective criteria by which such problems can be recognized. Ultimately, however, the decision depends on the patient and relevant others in his social environment, influenced only in part by the judgment of clinicians. Decision is made in terms of deeply held attitudes, some shared with, but others opposed to, those of professional clinicians.

In some regards, seeking psychological help is no different than seeking help with, for example, an automobile or medical problem. The need to depend on the judgment and skills of experts is a daily experience in a complex and technological society.

How do I decide that I have an "automobile problem" and should take my car to a garage? It is easy if the car simply does not run. But suppose that there are some unaccustomed noises or the steering seems vague, or it was serviced some time ago and I fear that some problem, perhaps unnoticed, has developed? Obviously, the decision to go to a mechanic depends upon how important a well-functioning car is to me, how sensitive I am to minor symptoms, how prepared I am to spend money, and whether I can be without a car for some time, among other considerations. Whether the car is just another possession, useful but not particularly valued, whether my livelihood depends on it, or whether it is symbolically an extension of my manhood, would figure in the decision. Having decided that there is a problem, I then have to choose among alternate repair shops, perhaps seeking advice from more informed associates. I present myself and the automobile, explain its "complaints," try to evaluate the mechanic's opinion as to the need for repair; if convinced, I turn the job over to him.

In essence, we go through a similar decision process in going to a physician. If symptoms are sufficiently disturbing, there may be little question, but at less intense levels we have to decide whether professional attention is warranted, whether we can doctor ourselves, or best simply ignore the problem. Cultural groups and individuals differ greatly in their tolerance of pain, concern with bodily functions, and faith in medicine. Economic factors, knowledge and availability of medical services, among other factors, play inevitable roles. If a problem is recognized, there still is the matter of choosing among different types of physicians in different settings. For some conditions, medical treatment may be forced on us, as in the quarantine and treatment of contagious diseases which endanger others. Usually, however, we are free to choose whether or not we wish medical care.

Despite all these complexities, people recognize and seek help for malfunctioning automobiles and human bodies in terms of generally shared social criteria and knowledge, at least in comparison to their thinking about psychological problems. We know what mechanics and doctors do, though we are perhaps ignorant of the technical details of their work. We have faith in their expertness. Most importantly, we regard our automobiles and bodies with some detachment; recognizing a problem and seeking help is not usually accompanied by shame.

Recognizing and seeking help for psychological problems is different in a number of critical respects. By their nature, such problems are intrinsic to the personality, and it is virtually impossible for the sufferer to be detached in their diagnosis. They reflect directly on the adequacy of the self, and their recognition can therefore be a source of shame. Moreover, in distinction to medical and automotive problems, criteria of diagnosis are far less certain. What constitutes a problem, how intense and disabling it must be to warrant outside intervention, criteria for optimal as well as disturbed functioning, are issues which elude precise definition among professionals; they are even more uncertain to laymen.

People become patients in one of three general ways:

1. By Self-initiated Action. A problem is recognized, the patient knows of the existence of psychological clinicians and has faith in their expertness. In psychotherapy practice, clinicians have usually viewed such patients as the best prospects since they start informed and motivated. The probability of seeking psychotherapy is greatest if one lives among people who know and value psychotherapy (Kadushin, 1969).

2. On the Advice of Others. A problem may be recognized, but not defined as psychological, or the patient may not be informed as to available resources. In the simplest case, the person wants help but has to be told where to find it. The situation is more complex where the potential patient sees the problem in other terms and has it redefined for him by advisors. Thus, some one may visit a physician and be told that "there is nothing medically wrong" with him, and therefore he should go to a psychiatrist. Priests and ministers, lawyers and school teachers, often serve this intermediate role between the recognition of a problem and viewing it as needing psychological help. The move toward clinical services can be tortuous, with professional advisors retarding as well as facilitating progress (Lichtenberg, Kohrman, and MacGregor, 1960). Thus, concerned parents may be advised by the school psychologist to take their child to a clinician, only to be told by their pediatrician that he will "outgrow his problem." Decisions are sometimes influenced by adventitious events and seemingly irrelevant agents. Lichtenberg and his colleagues report the case of a woman who over many months had been advised by teachers, social workers, and physicians to take her child to a clinic, but found numerous reasons not to. One day, the child had a tantrum on the street. At that moment, a drunken, skid-row derelict lurched by, looked down and said, "If that was my kid, lady, I would take him to a psychiatrist." Minutes later, she did.

3. By Coercion. Particularly in the so-called psychotic and sociopathic conditions, patients often come to clinical care neither on their own initiative nor on the recommendation of others, but because they are required to do so by legal authority. If judged to be dangerous to himself or others, a person can be restrained in a psychiatric hospital. Involuntary commitment usually starts with complaints by neighbors, relatives, or the police, and involves examination by qualified psychiatrists as well as judicial action. There has been great concern with the civil-rights implications of legal commitment among both psychiatric and legal minds. In the

United States the trend has been toward restricting the use of legal commitment and limiting the lengths of involuntary hospital stays. Still, many people are held on court orders, sometimes after only cursory examination. Related is the common practice of judges to require psychological treatment as an alternative to criminal prosecution. The judgment that a clinic might do more than a jail to redirect the future life of the defendant often reflects humane concern with his welfare. At the same time, it coerces an act which many clinicians believe should be an informed and voluntary choice. In a less extreme sense, business organizations or schools sometimes require psychological treatment as a condition of continuing in the organization. Without the sanction of a court order, these are also instances of social coercion.

Need and Demand

There has been a decided growth of psychological-mindedness in recent years, particularly among the more educated, affluent, and urban segments of society. The language and concepts of clinicians are familiar to many educated people. They accept the notion of psychological causation and understand the value of psychological intervention. Hence when distressed they readily seek psychological help. For them, there is little sense of stigma or shame in looking for assistance. There is wide acceptance of the technical skill of psychological clinicians. Many others, of course, do not share these views, as we will consider in a moment.

The broad base of acceptance of psychological thinking and psychological intervention reflects, I believe, an important theme in the American democratic ethos. We see human character as maleable, expect people to change and improve over time, and we applaud efforts at self-improvement. Thus, formal education, freely available to all who would take advantage of it, is highly valued in American society as a way of improving the human condition. Individualism and achievement are highly regarded. There is basic optimism about the possibility of social as well as personal change, if people only apply themselves and use knowledge wisely. These values contrast with those of more traditional societies which assume that people as well as society itself remain unchanging. It is not surprising, therefore, that clinical psychology and allied fields have found widest popular acceptance in the United States and the more open societies of Western Europe.

Nonetheless, a great part of the American population is not psychologically minded. Emotional problems are viewed as moral depravity, unalterable results of bad heredity, or spiritual matters requiring confession and prayer. Many who have psychological problems do not view them as such, nor take them to psychological clinicians. In a national survey Gurin, Veroff, and Feld (1960) found that fewer than 20 percent of those who saw themselves as needing help with emotional problems went to clinicians; the remainder sought the counsel of ministers, friends, or other advisors. Notably among the poor and uneducated, the concepts, practices, and settings of the clinical field are alien. In these communities, there are many distressed people, some needing help urgently.

Thus there is a great difference between the *demand* and the *need* fror psychological services. Schofield (1964) has used the apt phrases "the countable thousands" as against the "hidden millions" to highlight the important distinction between those who seek psychological help (demand) and those whose problems may be no less acute, but who are unwilling or unable to find psychological help (need). Demand may be estimated from the caseload statistics of clinical practitioners. Estimating need is far more difficult. It has been the subject of many epidemiological surveys in which mental health researchers have gone into communities to assess the probable numbers of people suffering from psychological dysfunctions. In Chapter 19, we will consider some of these findings in more detail, but for now we should note that it has been estimated from field surveys that psychological help would be of value to as much as 60 percent of the population who have not sought it. There are many difficult methodological and theoretical issues involved in assessing need, most particularly in deciding the criteria for defining psychological problems. Whatever the actual level of need, however, it is clear enough that it cannot be served with presently available resources and methods. Even future demand, projecting present caseloads and population growth, cannot be met by the manpower likely to be available in the major mental health professions (see Chapter 17). These issues have spurred the quest for alternate approaches to mental health care.

The Mental Health Professions

Psychiatry, clinical psychology, and psychiatric social work have been described as the three major mental health professions, for they are most centrally involved in providing care for psychologically disturbed patients. Their work is supplemented, particularly in hospital settings, by psychiatric nurses, occupational and rehabilitation therapists, and psychiatric technicians and aides.

The field of mental health stands at the crossroads of the biomedical, psychological, and social sciences. Consequently, research of relevance to improving the care of psychological patients has engaged the efforts of scientists from many disciplines, in addition to psychiatrists, clinical psychologists, and psychiatric social workers. Among the many involved in the effort to increase understanding of mental disorder and therapeutic change are physiologists, biochemists, geneticists, and neurologists, among other biological scientists; sociologists, anthropologists, and nonclinical psychologists, among behavioral scientists. In addition, there are many human helping professions whose work overlaps that of psychological clinicians, such as lawyers, physicians, educators, clergymen, and public health and community workers. The core mental health professions need to work closely with specialists in all these areas both to provide service and to advance knowledge.

PSYCHIATRY

Psychiatry is the oldest of the mental health professions and the one with greatest status and major responsibility for mental health problems, both in the eyes of the public and of policy makers. The psychiatrist is trained as a physician. Typical specialty training involves a three-year residency in a psychiatric training center after completing the MD degree and the general internship expected of all physicians. A number of specialties have developed within the general field of psychiatry, in some cases requiring special training or accreditation. The most distinct subspecialty is child psychiatry. Others, less sharply defined, are military, geriatric, forensic (concerned with legal issues), school, college, industrial, and community psychiatry. Psychiatrists may also be grouped by the nature of their work and the settings in which it occurs. Thus, there are hospital and clinic psychiatrists, private practitioners, and academic psychiatrists who teach and do research in universities or research hospitals. In general, psychiatrists can be distinguished as being biologically, psychologically, or socially oriented (Strauss, Schatzman, Bucher, Erlich, and Sabshin, 1964).

Among the psychologically oriented, the most noteworthy are psychoanalysts. Psychoanalysis is, simultaneously, a theoretical system, a form of psychotherapy, a method of clinical observation, and also a professional movement. It originated in the work of Sigmund Freud, who felt that the theoretical and philosophical contributions of his creation might outlive the clinical technique. Freud himself felt that psychoanalytic training and practice need not be limited to physicians, and many of his early students as well as his distinguished daughter Anna were not medically trained. In the United States at present, however, with few exceptions only physicians with psychiatric training are accepted for advanced study of psychoanalysis.

Psychoanalysis is taught in independent institutes, usually separate from academic medical centers. There is considerable emphasis on the learning of theory and on the personal psychoanalytic therapy of candidates, in order to increase their self-knowledge and reduce the possibility that neurotic trends in their own characters will make them unable to deal with those in others. Psychoanalysis is the most complete, refined, and self-contained theoretical system in the mental health field; only slowly has it incorporated ideas from other sources. Until recent years it was the dominant influence in psychiatry. Its influence has now been reduced under the impact of vigorous developments in biological, existential, behavioral, and social psychiatry, each of which provides a systematic alternative to the psychoanalytic approach.

CLINICAL PSYCHOLOGY

The clinical psychologist is usually trained in an academic psychology department. Graduate training typically consists of four or five years of coursework, research, and internship experience; the last most often takes place in an independent internship program in a hospital or clinic. At the end, the graduate student in clinical psychology earns a doctorate, most usually a PhD in psychology though other doctoral degrees are emerging. Some continue in specialized postdoctoral training programs, but most enter into clinical, research, or teaching positions immediately after completing the doctorate. American psychology views clinical psychology as a "science-profession," whose graduates are equally qualified for scholarly and service careers. Many clinicians seek opportunities for combining research, teaching, and clinical service. However, the majority are in full-time practice, though more usually in institutional settings than in private practice. The trend of recent years, however, has been toward increasing numbers of clinicians moving into part- or full-time private practice.

Among the mental health professions, the unique competence and contribution of clinical psychology has been in the areas of diagnostic testing and research. Clinical psychologists are distinctive for having been trained in research methods. Because of their special interests in theory and methodology, psychologists are often centrally involved in the research programs of mental health institutions. Although less focal than in former times, clinical testing remains a basic part of the work of the clinician. However, increasingly large numbers of clinical psychologists are involved, largely or exclusively, in psychological treatment, including various forms of counseling, psychotherapy, and behavior modification, with individuals, groups, and families.

The relation between psychologists and psychiatrists is often close and cooperative. However, there are strains between the two professions, particularly because of the opposition of many psychiatrists to psychologists going into the independent practice of psychotherapy. Some of the pros and cons of this issue will be examined later on. Suffice it to note now that the arguments on both sides, though couched in terms of patient welfare and social good, as often reflect issues of professional power, pride, prestige, and economic self-interest.

PSYCHIATRIC SOCIAL WORK

The third major mental health profession consists of social workers especially trained to deal with the psychosocial problems of emotionally disturbed people. In principle, though not always in actuality, their concern is more with the familial and social environment than with the identified patient himself. In many clinics there is a "team" approach. For example, in a child clinic, the psychiatric social worker typically works with the parents, while the child is seen therapeutically by a child psychiatrist or perhaps a child clinical psychologist, who may in addition have the responsibility for testing the child. In clinics and hospitals for adults, the psychiatric social workers have traditionally been concerned with issues such as the family's reactions to the patient's condition, the patient's social and vocational adjustment, planning environmental changes that might facilitate rehabilitation, and maintaining liaison with community agencies and other resources which are available toward that end. The psychiatric social worker, it is often said, differs from other mental health colleagues in being more oriented toward social reality than toward the internal psychological problems of the patient.

However, psychiatric social workers are often directly involved in psychotherapy with patients as well as families. Although called "casework," their interventions are not significantly distinguishable from those of other psychotherapists. Casework practice has been deeply influenced by psychoanalysis and has tended to focus on intrapsychic processes to the relative neglect of the external social environment. Although in its origins social work was directed toward helping the human casualties of social problems, in time it became more concerned with psychodynamic than with sociological issues. In the present era, however, there is a resurgence of concern with the impact of social forces. Significant numbers of future social workers will likely be involved in social and community interventions, more in line with their more distant heritage than with their existing clinical roles. Like psychiatry and clinical psychology, the field is in change.

The training of social workers, compared both to psychiatrists and clinical psychologists, is both shorter and more highly focused. The field typically attracts people who have profound interest in helping those in distress, with less interest in theoretical or research issues. Training consists of a two-year master's program, and one or two years of supervised fieldwork. Learning through supervised practice is basic to the training of all clinicians, but it is more highly developed and systematically used by social workers.

A number of social-work schools have developed doctoral programs which emphasize research training and scholarly achievement as well as clinical proficiency. It seems likely, however, that the great majority of social workers will continue to be on the master's level, trained and competent to provide direct services in helping agencies. With few exceptions, psychiatric social workers have not gone into private practice. They are mainly to be found in salaried positions in clinics, hospitals, and social agencies. In some community agencies, psychiatric social workers administer and staff the entire program, with psychiatrists and clinical psychologists being available only on a consultant basis.

OTHER MENTAL HEALTH WORKERS

Psychiatric nurses are centrally involved in caring for hospitalized patients. In addition to basic nursing courses and experiences, they receive psychiatric courses and supervised experience on a psychiatric unit. In the usual hospital, patients spend only a few hours a week, at most, in scheduled therapeutic activities with psychiatrists or clinical psychologists, but they are in constant contact with the nursing staff. Nurses are responsible for ward management, housekeeping, and recreational activities, as well as more conventional nursing duties. Consequently, nurses have a major role in fostering a therapeutic social environment; they may also be in an essentially psychotherapeutic relation to the patients. Nurses are assisted by nurses aides and psychiatric technicians in often poorly paid positions, requiring little training or personal qualification. Efforts have been made to upgrade such positions in order to attract persons with human-relation skills. Volunteers, many of them college students, further supplement the work of the nursing staff, in some cases by providing personal companionship, tutoring, or other forms of personal attention not otherwise available in an understaffed hospital.

Valuable contribution to the treatment and rehabilitation of patients is made by a variety of trained workers who have special skills in work-related, hobby, or recreational realms. In many hospitals and some clinics, there are occupational, art, and educational therapists, music and dance therapists, and recreational workers of various sorts. They not only train patients in useful skills and help them pass the time, but they can provide a setting for the expression of personal problems and the development of psychosocial skills. Thus, a schizophrenic patient who is unable to put his feelings into words may be able to express them in paintings, under the guidance of an art therapist. A dance therapist can help patients come into contact with their blocked feelings through motor expression. In their various realms, occupational and recreational workers increase the sense of competence, well-being, and useful occupation in patients who might otherwise stagnate in the hospital. In clinics and rehabilitation centers they can also help prepare patients for useful employment in the outside world.

CHAPTER 2

What Is Clinical Psychology?

THE PERSPECTIVE OF CLINICAL PSYCHOLOGY

The Clinical Attitude

The clinical psychologist can be described in terms of his training, the techniques he uses and the problems he deals with, the clients he serves, the settings in which he works, and the social issues he confronts. What best distinguishes the clinician from fellow psychologists, I would propose, is more a way of thinking—the *clinical attitude*—than emphasis on particular subject matters or techniques.

Many other psychologists are as much concerned with personality development and malformation, the assessment of personality, and in the workings of many of the separately distinguishable facets of psychological functioning, such as cognition, aggression, anxiety, conscience, or fantasy, to name a few, and in their measurement. The phenomena of psychopathology, interpersonal behavior, group processes, and learning and development, all of these are the common property of all psychologists, indeed of all behavioral scientists. As preparation for his work, the clinician should be learned in these and cognate areas. As consequence of his work, he brings new knowledge to these fields. Indeed, study guided by the clinical attitude has made available understanding of human psychology which could not have been gained by other means (Klein, 1949; Ruesch, 1967).

However, it is in the import of psychological knowledge to the lives of *persons in particular* that the clinical attitude is uniquely revealed. Clinicians are concerned with *understanding* and *helping* individuals in psychological distress. In this pursuit, they engage directly with particular persons in their actual functioning, in their natural life situations, or more usually in the miniaturized life situations of the clinic. They intervene in individual human lives, respecting their complexity and uniqueness. Although clinicians assess and conceptualize part processes, it is the whole individual with whom they work clinically. Their approach is necessarily *personological,* considering psychological and personality variables as they converge in individual persons. Nor can clinicians neglect those factors, in a technical sense external to the person, but which determine his functioning and psychological well-being. Thus, the impact of relevant others, the small groups in which the patient lives, and the larger social institutions which act upon him are all important to the full understanding of the individual patient's life and problems. But it is as they come to focus on, and have meaning for, the particular person that they are most relevant to the clinician. Ultimately, the clinical attitude centers on the unique person.

Essentially the same concept of a clinical attitude was expressed by Wyatt (1968):

> The essence of the clinical attitude, I submit, is its concern with actual behavior and with the actual urges, interests, and apprehensions of people in on-going life. The emphasis is on the importance of the stream of experience, in its affective as well as cognitive aspects; an emphasis which includes the plurality of experience (several things going on simultaneously), the changes in self-awareness, the metaphorical and symbolic quality of thought and, especially, the important consequences of the mind's capacity for creating meaning. The term *clinical,* furthermore, suggests the psychologist's willingness to study the behavior of people through direct observation, frequently in transactional settings involving varying degrees of participation and interaction. Finally, implied in the concept *clinical* is a clear transition and distinction, but no absolutist separation, between observation, understanding, and acting in the service of re-adaptive goals. The ideal of "doing something about it" is indigenous to clinical psychology; it denotes a more inclusive and diffuse concept than that of research, which is indeed more exclusive, specific and self-limiting . . . a psychological approach is *clinical* to the extent that it attempts to understand people in their natural complexity and in their continuous adaptive transformations. . . . [Wyatt, 1968, pp. 235–236] (Emphasis in original).

Similarly, Watson notes that "the clinician, psychologist or otherwise, steadfastly considers the individual for the sake of that individual" (1951, p. 3).

As is so often true in the history of language, the term "clinical" evolved from ancient roots and changed its meaning with time. Deriving from the Greek word for "bed," its medical connotation was only later attached. In medical usage, clinical first described care at the sickbed but later generalized to include any setting. Indeed, clinics today treat ambulatory outpatients in contrast to hospitals where bedridden inpatients are to be found. But the constant core of meaning, in medicine or in psychology, is on direct engagement with and concern for an individual. As adjective in expressions such as "clinical training," "clinical intervention," and "clinical science" the term is appropriately used to characterize the learning experiences, therapeutic activities, and requisite knowledge of the clinician. "Clinical judgment" and "clinical responsibility" describe the thinking and values of the clinician, who may be required to take actions on behalf of his patient even if based on incomplete knowledge. In medical diagnosis, clinical tests are distinguished from laboratory tests, depending on whether diagnosis depends primarily on direct observation and evaluation by the clinician or whether laboratory procedures and technicians are involved. By contrast, in psychology, the term "clinical assessment" is used inclusively regardless of the procedures involved provided that its aim is the understanding of the individual sufferer.

The Problem of Individuality

Every person is unique. His personality is as distinctive as his fingerprints. In genetic endowment and in bodily functions, as in psychological activities, appearance or character, the distinctiveness of the individual is supported by the findings of science as well as by the evidence of our senses. We recognize each of our friends and reasonably predict his behavior. When we look inward, we see a *me* unlike any other person's. Surely, we resemble others in particular regards, and psychologists have abstracted numerous dimensions along which individuals can be compared. The science of psychology has dedicated itself to the discovery of general laws—laws of learning, of perception, of motivation—in the course of which "individual differences" may be conceived as "error variance." But the fact of individuality is inescapable and of central concern to clinical psychology. Guided by the *clinical attitude,* the clinician is necessarily focussed on the particular person and his uniqueness.

Gordon W. Allport (1937, 1961) stands out among American psychologists for his efforts to bring the problem of individuality to the concern of American psychology. Against a dominant positivistic and behavioristic psychology in the 1930s, he defended the need for supplementing the prevailing *nomothetic* approach, which is concerned with the *generalized* human being, with an *idiographic* approach, which focusses on the understanding of *particular* persons. Science, it was claimed, has no room for the uniquely patterned individual. It is concerned with general law, and is necessarily a nomothetic discipline. Idiographic understanding is the business of art, biography, or history. Allport could not accept this exclusion of individuality from the science of psychology, nor could he accept a "separate but equal" doctrine which would hold that there should be two unrelated sciences—one idiographic and the other nomothetic—as suggested by German philosophers in the early part of the century (cf. Allport, 1961, p. 12). In his own view, a unitary psychology should treat respectfully both the generalized and the individual. But his concern ultimately was with the patterned uniqueness of the individual. Thus, in commenting on the usual textbook chapter on "personality," Allport notes: ". . . . often we find that the picture of personality offered is that of an uncemented mosaic of elements or test scores, or of fragmentary processes, never vitally interrelated. Such a lifeless picture is jarring to one who feels that the individuality of man, the future-pointed thrust of his living, and the systematic interlacing of his key qualities, are the central features of his personality" (1961, p. 21).

Allport's distinction between the nomothetic and the idiographic, and his persuasive defense of the idiographic, became the focus of a whirlpool of polemic which brought out many of the key issues which still bedevil clinical psychology (e.g., Sarbin, 1943; Beck, 1953; Stephenson, 1953; Eysenck, 1954; Rosenzweig, 1958; and many others). In Chapter 11 we will consider in further detail one facet of this controversy which is expressed in the problems of clinical inference and the relative merits of statistical versus clinical prediction (Meehl, 1954; Holt, 1958; Sarbin, Taft, and Bailey, 1960; Gough, 1962). But, for now, let us consider further some general issues which emerged in the idiographic-nomothetic controversy.*

In the sense that it is concerned with general laws, all science is by definition nomothetic. But the simple, mechanistic model against which the originators of the idiographic viewpoint contended has very much changed over the past fifty years. Simple notions of mechanistic causation have been supplanted or at least supplemented by field-theoretical concepts. Multivariate and configurational analyses, increasingly more subtle and manageable as computers evolve, replace univariate analyses in experimental and psychometric research in psychology. Warren Weaver, a distinguished scientist, talking about physics and biology affirms that modern science should and can move from the study of "organized simplicity" and "disorganized complexity" (the probabilistic expectation of events in a population) to "organized complexity," that is, the determination of the fate of particular individual events (Weaver, 1948). In this climate, it is far easier to visualize the middle ground in which clinical and personological psychology can stand. Within the framework of a *scientific* psychology, one can assert that while knowledge of general psychological processes is necessary, it cannot be a sufficient basis for understanding the individual.

It is certainly true that many psychologists still hold views of science in terms of which a "personological science" is—to quote a wit in another realm—a contradiction in terms. Those who see psychology as a science of behavior (objective, observable, external) based on experimental evidence would hold that personology is art, not science. They would find ready agreement among those clinicians who are similarly convinced that each person is a law unto himself, a unique and indivisible whole, which can be apprehended intuitively but not analyzed nor studied. But the two groups would surely differ in whether "artist" or "scientist" is to be taken as compliment or insult. Through the history of psychology there has always been a contention between the "tough-minded" and the "tender-minded" in William James' famous terms or those of the "right" and those of the "left" (Tomkins, 1963). The difficult but critical task is to make per-

* These awkward terms were borrowed by Allport from Windelband, a turn-of-the-century German philosopher, and were anchored in what Holt (1962) has called the "romantic movement in science." *Nomothetic* derives from the Greek work for the giving or enacting of laws. *Idiographic* has its root in the Greek for "one's own," and connotes that which is private, personal, and particular to the individual. Despite widespread use, a common error is to substitute *ideo* (Greek for "idea," as in ideology) for *idio* (Allport, 1961a; Holt, 1962). Partly for this reason, Allport has more recently suggested the dual terms *dimensional* and *morphogenic*, at least to characterize methods of study. Dimensional methods are those which study the individual in terms of comparisons with others, while morphogenic characterizes attempts in understanding the unique organization of the person (Allport, 1962).

sonological science more rigorous without, at the same time, losing the phenomenon which most concerns us and with which clinicians daily work—the individual human being.

The idiographic-nomothetic distinction is not only overdrawn, but it is also confusing, for it perpetuates either-or dichotomies of an archaic sort in terms of the concepts of modern science (Holt, 1962). For example, the tenet that nomothetic science is concerned only with prediction and control, while an idiographic personology aims at understanding is too simplified a distinction. While many positivistic psychologists have indeed seized on prediction and control as the hallmarks of science, others recognize that mature science is concerned with understanding, even when prediction or control are not possible. Thus Robert MacLeod (1947) states: "The goal of science is not prediction and control but understanding. Prediction is merely the test of understanding and control the practical reward." Ideally, scientists in any field seek to predict and alter *through* understanding of the essential principles involved. Also, the firm insistence on a holistic approach, namely, that the totality of a person is more than the simple sum of parts,* made more sense when psychology was more elementaristic. The assumption that any analysis is destructive of the essential nature of the whole person, which can only be apprehended and appreciated empathically but not dissected, does not take account of the more subtle approaches to the study of human personality and functioning available to contemporary clinical psychology. Although the extreme idiographic position was a necessary antidote to the reductionistic and elementaristic psychology of the past, there is now an ample base for a personology which is both scientific and humanistic.

Variables, Individual Differences, and Persons

The phenomena of psychology can be viewed from three vantage points:

1. General psychology †
2. Differential psychology (individual differences, psychometrics)
3. Personological psychology (clinical)

At points the positions fade into each other, but it is of heuristic value to distinguish them. In distinguishing between these three orientations, we can note the distinctive qualities of the personological or clinical approach. However, the knowledge gained in each mode supplements that gained in the other. The clinical approach utilizes while it extends the knowledge gained in the other modes.

Take, for example, the concept of "anxiety," a variable which has deeply concerned workers within each of the three orientations. One can ask:

1. What physiological reactions characterize the anxiety state? (General orientation.)
2. Do different kinds of people (e.g., men vs. women, schizophrenics vs. normals)

* "Take a watch to pieces and examine, however carefully its separate parts in turn, and you will never come across the principles by which a watch keeps time." (Polanyi, 1964, p. 47.)

† The term "general psychology" is used here in the meaning suggested by Drever (1952): "A systematic discussion of general principles and laws holding of the mental life in general, as distinct from peculiarities characteristic of the individual."

show different physiological reactions to the same stress? (Differential orientation.)

3. What symptoms does our patient, John Doe, show when *he* is anxious? What conditions make *him* anxious? What relieves *his* anxiety? (Personological or clinical orientation.)

The vast literature on anxiety supports general, differential, and personological propositions about the nature of anxiety. It is well established, for example, that there is a wide range of physiological responses which people generally show when anxious, whether measurement is made in naturally stressful circumstances, under conditions of laboratory stress, or in clinical states. Thus, pulse is quickened, breathing is faster, galvanic skin response is accentuated. However, groups differ not only in the extent and pattern of these responses but also in their subjective counterparts. Thus, women more commonly report cold hands or feet, while men more often mention heart palpitations or breathing difficulties when asked to describe typical anxiety responses (Korchin and Heath, 1961). Moreover, Lacey, Bateman, and van Lehn (1953) have described "autonomic response specificity," individualized patterns of physiological responses when several are measured simultaneously. Thus, one person more typically shows an elevated pulse rate, while another may breathe more rapidly, as his typical response to an anxiety-producing situation. For example, Basowitz, Korchin, Oken, and Gussack (1957) tested people on two occasions. In one session, they were interviewed to discover their characteristic psychological and bodily reactions in situations of extreme emotion. In the other session, they were given small doses of adrenalin and asked to report any subjective changes. Typically, the bodily symptoms they mentioned were the same ones they had described as usually occurring in real-life stress. What emerges in these illustrations is that even those physiological manifestations of anxiety, which are mediated by a primitive part of the nervous system, can reflect general, differential, or personological principles. How much more true when we raise questions such as: What life conditions and early experiences dispose to anxiety? What determines the threshold for anxiety-disrupted behavior? How long does the state endure; how far does it generalize? When might anxiety facilitate as well as disturb performance? Which psychological functions are altered in the anxiety state? How is anxiety defended against?

From the vantage point of general psychology, individuals are taken to represent humanity in general and general principles are sought to account for their behavior. In principle, a study could therefore use just one "experimental subject." In practice, however, many subjects are studied even though the differences among them are not the focus of concern. Sampling a number of individuals allows the investigator to assess the reliability of the procedures and to determine sampling or error variation against which the "main effects" of the study can be evaluated. Where possible, the general psychologist prefers the experimental method, in which one or a few variables are systematically varied while others are systematically controlled, in order to discover the effect of a critical independent variable on the dependent variables assessed. Thus, a general-psychological study of anxiety might involve a test of the hypothesis that in the anxiety state there is a drop in, say, problem-solving ability. To test this hypothesis experimentally, two groups would be contrasted, an experimental and a control group. Both would be given a test of problem-solving skill on two occasions, before and after a period of time which involved, for the Experimental Group, an anxiety-arousing situation (e.g., threat of electric shock), and for the Control Group, a relatively innocuous task. The hypothesis is upheld if the Experimental Group shows a greater drop than the Control Group; the extent of the drop being greater than that which might occur through chance variation (statistical significance). The same experiment would incorporate the *differential viewpoint* if the experimental and control groups were made up of two "kinds" of people (say, men and women) or if the extent of before-and-after change in problem-solving was correlated with some personality factor which theoretically might moderate the extent of anxiety disruption. Thus, there might be a measure of "ego strength" defined in part as the capacity to maintain ordered behavior under stress. Ego-strength scores would then be related to before-and-after changes in problem-solving scores, with the expectations that a negative correlation would be found, that is, persons higher in ego strength would show less of a poststress drop in performance. Finally, the same experiment could take on a *personological* cast if the effort is made to ascertain how individuals interpreted the anticipated electric shock and if the findings are again analyzed in terms of the individual meanings ascribed to it. It may be seen as a challenge to one's fortitude, which might lead to greater effort and better performance, a threat of bodily harm, a punishment for sin, or whatever. In fact, people have been found to make many such idiosyncratic interpretations of electric shocks as used in stress experiments (Tomkins, 1943).

General psychology looks to the laboratory experiment as the ideal model of psychological research. Differential psychology, by contrast, depends more on correlational methods. Unique to the personological approach, particularly in the clinical context, is the case-study method.

In the case study, effort is made to consider as many facets of a particular personality as possible, as they develop over time. Ultimately, findings from all three vantages should converge toward, for example, a greater understanding of the nature of anxiety. The variables (i.e., traits, structures, or processes) are essentially the same in the personological as in the general or differential contexts; what differs is the vantage from which they are studied. Understanding the *variable* (e.g., anxiety) is the task of a general or differential psychology; understanding the *person* who is anxious is the task of clinical psychology. Put another way: *General and differential psychology study variables across individuals; personological psychology studies individuals across variables*. Thus, in the case study, all factors are investigated which might allow one to understand the nature of the patient's condition, the probable effects of clinical interventions, and the possible future course of his life.

It is worth noting, however, that research methods other than case studies have been proposed for personological study. For example, Cattell (1946) distinguished between *ipsative* and *normative* test measures. Normative measures compare individuals along particular variables; by contrast, ipsative measures involve the comparison of a population of variables within single individuals. The normative question would be: How does Harry compare to Joe, Mary, Steve, and others in dependency or achievement needs, anxiety or intelligence? To which the answer might be: He is at the 80th percentile in that population on that variable. By contrast, the ipsative issue is: Is achievement, dependency, or anxiety a more salient quality of Harry's? Stephenson's (1953) Q-methodology involves ratings of different traits according to an observer's (or the subject's own) judgment as to the importance of each trait for the particular person. The correlation of these ratings between two persons tells how similar or dissimilar they are in the pattern of their personality qualities. Typically, the method has been used to describe large numbers of persons, although initially Stephenson proposed it as a uniquely idiographic method. The procedure has been useful in personality and clinical research since it allows quantitative ratings of many variables at once with reference to normative populations (Block, 1961). Allport (1961, 1962) has called attention to other "morphogenic" methods which allow description of principles of personality functioning in particular people.

To visualize better the difference between variable-centered and person-centered analyses, let us consider a hypothetical set of personality measures. In Table 2.1 each row describes one person, identified as I, II, III, IV, and V. Each

TABLE 2.1
Five Persons and Five Variables

	VARIABLES				
PERSON	ECONOMIC STATUS	ANXIETY	INTELLIGENCE	DEPENDENCY	ACHIEVEMENT
I	80	40	65	45	15
II	60	85	75	40	25
III	40	10	90	20	75
IV	20	50	70	60	45
V	10	65	20	25	85

column contains the scores of each person on one of five variables: economic status, anxiety, intelligence, dependency, and achievement motivation. To simplify, suppose that all the scores run on a scale of zero to one hundred, with high values indicating more and lower values less of the characteristic. What can we infer from the information in Table 2.1?

First, we can describe the distribution of each variable separately—over what range does it extend, is it normally distributed or skewed in some fashion, how does this sample differ from the parent population or from another sample, and so on. Thus, it can first be noted that on four of the five variables there is considerable range; however, in intelligence only one person (V) scores low. Second, correlations among the different variables could be discovered: are anxious people more intelligent, dependent, achievement oriented, etc.? In more complex forms of correlative analysis, variables are combined to discover whether there are any "factors" which reduce and simplify the pattern of correlation among variables. In such factor analyses, it might be discovered that the variations in a number of variables simultaneously can be understood in terms of some superordinate factor. Many valuable studies have been done describing personality variables through such correlative and factor analyses. All of these approaches are, in terms of our present concern, variable-centered.

In the clinical approach, emphasis shifts from variables to persons—in Table 2.1, from columns to rows—and our concern is to describe each person. In this effort, we may have to infer the importance of the particular variable in light of the others, and consequently the weights given each may differ from case to case.

Consider Mr. I: Well off financially, less anxious than the average person, yet more intelligent and independent, why might he be so unconcerned about achievement? Right off, he would seem to be a happy-go-lucky playboy type, ready enough to enjoy, without need to increase, his already privileged role. It is harder to suppose that he has suppressed achievement needs either for fear of failure because of insufficient ability or for lack of opportunity. He may, however, have an altruistic value system which abhors striving and competition and actually be, if one inquired, interested in helping others. As alternative, or even as a possible antecedent, he may have negatively identified with a striving and successful father—the source of the family's affluence—and his renunciation of achievement values is a rebellious flaunting of familial values. These speculations obviously run beyond the information in hand, but they are of the sort which, in the clinical situation, would lead to further investigation. Now Miss III would seem to be the most favored of the five—the noblest Roman of them all! Brightest by far, independent, with strong needs to achieve, and unencumbered by anxiety, she would seem to be the most effective, happiest, and productive person here. She would not be likely to be coming into a clinic seeking help. But the suspicious clinician might wonder if her very low dependence and anxiety might not indicate a kind of psychopathic character structure, marked by an unconcern for the welfare of others and willingness to cut ethical corners in selfish pursuit of her own goals. Take Mr. V: poor and disadvantaged, lacking in intellectual ability, but independent and determined to achieve. Might one not assume that his already considerable anxiety is bound to rise further? There would seem to be here the makings of a career of frustration, leading into failure and despair. But there are realms in which dedicated effort and work, rather than intellectual prowess, are required, and with his independence and motivation perhaps he can achieve. Starting so poor, relatively modest successes can lead to material improvement in living standards and freedom from financial cares; this, in turn, feeding back to increase morale and effort, lower anxiety, and encourage future success.

These speculations and predictions, of course, build in considerations beyond the variables contained in Table 2.1. More complete understanding of each case and predictions as to future behavior surely requires not only more knowledge of other personal variables but also information about the actions of relevant others, social conditions, and external events which could alter the course of each life.

At the heart of the personological approach is the consideration of the variables of personality as they interplay in the particular individual. Whether we are concerned with understanding, control (i.e., clinical intervention) or prediction, we need knowledge of the peculiar structure of a particular person which, in turn, requires clinical investigation of how such factors are ordered for him. But this process is not independent of general or differential knowledge; indeed, it is guided by it. Understanding of the ways in which relevant factors relate in general provides a framework for visualizing their relations in the specific case. In this spirit, instruments of personality assessment designed to measure specific personality factors, and which were developed and standardized on large populations, have an important role in studying individual personalities. It is necessary, though not sufficient, to know how a particular person deviates from group norms on such measures. The pattern of deviations along many such variables contributes to a description of the individual, but understanding the particular person depends on discovering the relative importance of deviations in each realm and the ways in which the variables combine for him. This requires the more extensive, intimate, and subjective modes of enquiry which usually characterize clinical assessment.

Persons and Types

In a much-quoted statement, Kluckhohn and Murray (1953, p. 35) remind us that:

> Every man is in certain respects:
> a. like all other men
> b. like some other men
> c. like no other man.

From the clinical vantage point, emphasis is necessarily on the particular person and the ways in which he is "like no other man." But it is necessary to remember that every person is indeed like all other and like some other humans. Many of the determinants of personality are universal in the human species. They derive from common biological heritage, common features of the physical environment, and from life experiences we all share. Everybody is born, matures and dies. We have needs in common, social as well as biological. We learn, think, remember and experience emotions in much the same way because of the brain and nervous system which distinguishes humans from other species. Any human on the face of the earth is more like other humans than like, say, a bird, snake, or insect or even a chimpanzee. The implications of this simple fact are great for a science of psychology.

However, the proposition that each of us is like some other human is equally important. We recognize differences in the psychological attributes of members of different nations, social classes, ethnic groups, and cultures. Despite overlap, one can predict that a sample of Americans will look, act, think, and believe differently than a comparable sample of Chinese. But, as Kluckhohn and Murray note, being "like some men" is by no means limited to membership in social units such as nations, classes, or tribes. People in similar climates or in similar occupations may develop similar character structures, so that fishing folk or farmers of one country may resemble those of another as much or more than they do city people or factory workers in their homeland. Rich people and poor people, those in authority and those subjected to their control, people of the same age, occupation, and sex—any such characteristic which a number share can be the mode to which common personality characteristics are related. Consequently, to the extent that we know something about the qualities of the larger group, we can foretell something about the behavior of the individual member even in the absence of knowledge of his particular personality. Thus, to know that someone is English or Italian, is to be able to predict that he is more likely to be emotionally constrained or expressive; if student or farmer, more likely to be politically liberal or conservative; if young or old, more likely to be vigorous or sedate.

Moreover, knowledge of class characteristics provides a framework against which the specific individuals can be evaluated. Thus, we have frames of reference against which we judge the particular case in hand: She walks well *for* a two-year old; *even* among Harvard students, he is very intelligent; he is remarkably open-minded *for* an old man. All of these statements which we make daily reflect class-related judgments. Often enough they are based on partial facts and unwarranted generalization and do injustice to individuals, but they reflect the actuality that there are class-related commonalities in personality. In judging a patient's condition, the clinician makes use of expectations based on group norms. A story is told about the famous neurologist and neurosurgeon, Harvey Cushing, who worked in Boston about fifty years ago. He was to examine a man suspected of having brain damage in the presence of a class of young physicians. The man entered the amphitheater, accompanied by his wife, but even as he approached the examining table, Cushing told them that they could leave. He then turned to the students and announced that the man did, indeed, have a lesion of the cerebral cortex. In reply to their surprised questions, he explained that he could not otherwise understand why an upper-class, educated Boston gentleman would come through a door ahead of a lady! The event may well be mythical, but the story continues in medical folklore to honor the wisdom of a great clinician.

TYPOLOGICAL PERSONALITY THEORIES

Typological theories of personality can be contrasted with trait theories. Traits are enduring tendencies to act in particular ways across a range of situations. Traits describe diverse aspects of human functioning: motives or needs (sexy, aggressive), abilities or skills (intelligent, musical), temperament or emotions (energetic, anxious), personal styles (careful, adventuresome), cognitive styles (distractible, attentive), or beliefs and values (liberal, religious). Traits are viewed as dimensional attributes which are distributed in the population. An individual can be assessed along each of these dimensions and his personality described in terms of the pattern of traits peculiar to him.

Type concepts, by contrast, assume that a particular pattern of qualities is held in common by a large number of people which distinguishes them from another large number. At the extreme, all humanity can be pigeonholed into two or three types. Typological theories have been discredited for their simplistic thinking, overinclusiveness, disregard for individuality, and the common assumption that type membership is fixed once and for all. Recall the Nazi characterology which distinguished "Nordics" and "Jews," ascribing all human virtues to the one and subhuman failings to the other; in one unbelievable case, describing chickens as either Nordic or Jewish depending on whether they ate their food with constraint or attacked it greedily. This mode of typological thinking has obviously to be rejected by scientific psychology. However, there are more subtle and scientific ways in which personality typologies can be conceived. Let us note first some of the ways in which persons can be typed.

Psychobiological Types. The relation between bodily characteristics and personality has attracted interest throughout recorded history. A classic typology was proposed by Hippocrates, the great Greek philosopher and "father of medicine" in the fifth century, B.C. Hippocrates described the body as containing four "humors" or fluids—blood, black bile, yellow bile, and phlegm. Depending on which of these dominated, one of four temperaments was to be found. With blood went the *sanguine* (hopeful, optimistic) personality; black bile accounted for the *melancholic* (sad, reflective) person; yellow bile led one to be *choleric* (aggressive, irascible); while phlegm determined the *phlegmatic* (slow, apathetic) temperament. Not only temperament, but also disease was to be explained by the actions of these humors, according to Galen, the Roman physician in the second century, A.D. Thus, too much black bile made the normally melancholic into a clinically depressed patient.

Differences in gross constitution have served as the basis for personality typologies in more modern times. Ernst Kretschmer (1925) claimed that disorders of mood and feelings (e.g., manic-depressive psychosis) were more commonly found in people with *pyknic* physiques (soft, rounded people) while those with slim bodies (*asthenic* physique) more often had disorders of thought (e.g., schizophrenia). Measurement was crude, and the relationship reported did not take account of the fact that schizophrenia appears at an earlier age than manic-depressive conditions.

More precise measurements and a more detailed system were evolved by William H. Sheldon (1940, 1942). He identified three constitutional types: (1) the rounded *endomorph,* characterized by large visceral organs but weak in muscular and bony development; (2) the square *mesomorph,* with heavy bones and muscles; and (3) the linear *ectomorph,* long, slender, and fragile, where nervous tissues seem to predominate over viscera or muscle. Related to these body types are three temperament types: (1) the *visceratonic* (going with the endomorphic physique), who is relaxed, amiable, sociable, liking people and seeking their company, slow moving, eating and sleeping well; (2) the *somatotonic* (normally associated with the mesomorph), strong, dominant, noisy, adventuresome, action-oriented, direct, ambitious; and (3) the *cerebrotonic* (related to ectomorphy), intense, anxious, inhibited, introversive, preferring solitude and thought to action or people. In Sheldon's own work, a high order of relationship was reported between the bodily and temperamental types; subsequent research showed a more modest association, but overall Sheldon's formulation of physique-temperament patterns seems to hold up. There is the large issue, of course, of whether such relationships necessarily indicate biological determinants of temperament; they could as well or better be interpreted as resulting from the life history and social reactions which go with one or another physique. That the frail boy might shun sports and seek out intellectual pursuits and that the husky, sturdy lad would be dominant and assertive, are reasonable enough predictions in our culture.

Psychological or Characterological Types. Carl Jung's (1933) distinction between *extraverts* and *introverts* is a classic example of modern psychological typology. Extraverts are oriented toward the outside world and toward other people, introverts toward inner experience. In Jung's view, extraversion and introversion find expression in several realms of psychological function—sensation, intuition, thought, and feeling. It is possible, therefore, to be a feeling extravert although a thinking introvert. In crossing the Atlantic, Jung's theory lost much of its subtlety and became translated too readily to a single polarity expressing primarily sociability versus seclusiveness.

The Freudian distinction between *oral, anal,* and *phallic* character-types derives from the psychoanalytic theory of early psycho-sexual development. At each stage, there is a bodily area (erogenous zone) in which sexual interest and gratification is centered. For the first year or so, this is the lips and mouth (oral stage). During the second and third year, the anal mucosa is more highly sensitized (anal stage). The phallic stage is reached in the fourth and fifth year, though full sexual maturity (the genital stage) is not reached until puberty. Adult character traits represent, in part, derivatives from the history of gratifications and frustrations in the successive libidinal stages. The oral, anal, or phallic character qualities in the adult may result from fixation at any of these stages, so that personality does not properly develop beyond that point, or it may reflect regression back to that level following severe frustration, as in psychopathological states (Fenichel, 1945). In any case, the oral character type is marked by passive dependent relations to others, the anal character by stinginess and obstinancy, the phallic type by immature sexuality in adulthood. The history of libidinal development was the basis not only of character formation but also of the theory of neurosis and psychosis in older psychoanalytic theory.

Psychological typologies are suggested in modern psychoanalytic ego psychologies which join with researches in personality and cognition. Though not tied to libidinal development as such, it has been possible to describe the convergence of personality traits, defensive or coping modes, and cognitive styles which are characteristic of types of people. For example, Shapiro's "Neurotic Styles" (1965) is a subtle exposition of the interplay of modes of interpersonal functioning, problem-solving, perception, memory, and other cognitive processes, and ego-defense and coping mechanisms which characterize the hysteric, obsessive-compulsive, and paranoid personality organizations.

Finally, note should be taken that diagnostic systems can function as psychological typologies, at least for those declared to be mentally ill. To the extent that "schizophrenia" is conceived as a clearly defined and bounded composite of behaviors, it constitutes a type to which an individual does or does not belong. In this sense, diagnostic categorization shares some of the problems implicit in typological thinking.

Social Types. The Boston Gentleman, as we have seen, is a type. As any group shares common conditions of life, values, and culture, it is predictable that they will have personality characteristics in general. Terms like "modal personality" and "national character" describe the common personality characteristics of cultural or national groups. As most often considered, these are not strictly speaking typologies in the sense of the Jungian introversion-extraversion. They are not meant to be inclusive, nor to distinguish one from a contrasting type of humanity, but rather to call attention to the common personality features, though admitting that there are individual variations arising from individual experiences. Sometimes, however, true typologies are developed as in Ruth Benedict's (1934) famous distinction between "Dionysian" and "Appollonian" cultures, discovered in her studies of primitive societies. The "Dionysians" were people whose practices were openly emotional, orgiastic, and gave full play to the appetites, while "Appollonians" were more constrained, sedate, and controlled. It is probably true that the more homogeneous, simpler, and isolated a society the more likely are people to have character traits in common. In a pluralistic society such as ours, with its many subgroupings, between which individuals can move and among which they can choose, there are likely to be more forms and varieties of the "American personality."

In the language of sociologists and social psychologists, role describes the pattern of expected beliefs, attitudes, values, and behaviors which correspond to positions in society. The study of how roles are organized and how they exert their influence on individual behavior is quite complex and beyond our present concern. Suffice it to note that roles may be related to durable group memberships such as race or religious affiliation, to occupational position, to the place in a social system or power structure, or even more temporary, though defined, social positions. Each of us occupies several roles and social identities. One can be a teenager, Quaker, son, student, Democrat, football player, boyfriend, and so on. At a given moment, we are more in one than another role; with father, son; with professor, student; with girlfriend, boyfriend. Obviously, we are expected to behave differently, and we do, in each of these roles, though there is a personal identity which exists throughout. Some roles are more salient, and more central to our self-definitions. There are surely professors who, as students fantasy, must sleep in cap and gown and are "professorial" when being husbands, fathers, lovers, or neighbors; others wear the role lightly and shed it easily.

Role and personality are independent concepts, but they interplay in three important respects. First, role membership shapes behavior directly. Living under particular social conditions, by values and expectations of particular groups, develops particular modes of thinking and acting. The priest, at least in the traditional church, is expected to be and probably becomes pious, compassionate, and obedient to authority. Second, roles mold behavior in an indirect way, by providing frames of reference by which we evaluate our own actions. The role constitutes a "reference group." My actions may be guided importantly by "what will the guys in the Faculty Club think . . . ?," or "the students," or "the Deans," for each are complementary role groups which provide framework for my judgments. Finally, where choice is possible, persons select roles compatible with their personal characteristics. Pious men become priests, scholarly ones, professors, and somber ones, undertakers, though it is probably equally true that the priest becomes more pious, the professor more scholarly, and the undertaker more somber in the pursuit of their calling. A common problem facing clinical and counseling psychologists is the person who, through fate, limited opportunity or coercion, finds himself in roles which match his personal needs poorly.

PROBLEMS IN TYPOLOGICAL THINKING

In pursuit of the proposition that all men are "like some other men," we considered many varieties and principles of grouping people, which differ greatly in form, inclusiveness, scientific status, and utility. The most complete typologies, in effect, visualize humanity as divided into subspecies. They are based on a limited number of highly generalized categories, to which all people are to be fitted. Usually these are conceived as genetic or constitutional in origin, static and unchangeable in nature. There is little room for concepts of change, learning, or growth, either arising from naturally occuring experiences in social learning or in the interventions of psychotherapy or education. Absolute typologies have little place in psychological science because of their simplicity, crudeness, disregard for individuality, and their fixity.

Crude typological thinking is understandable in popular psychology. It is easier to explain behavior by a smaller than a larger number of categories and principles. To try to comprehend diversity is far more difficult than to apply a simple categorical system and judge the particular case by its membership in a class. "If he is black, he must be. . . ." saves one the trouble of discovering the particular qualities of *this* black man. Moreover, it saves worrying about change, "If he is black, he will always be. . . ." As Walter Lippmann pointed out a long time ago (1922), stereotypic thinking saves mental energy; the closed mind exerts itself less than the open mind.

Still, scientific understanding and clinical intervention requires description of the common qualities which characterize groups of individuals. Contemporary personality research seeks to reduce the number of individual traits along which persons can be compared by deriving, often through statistical techniques, a fewer number of more general characteristics which seem to underlie the obtained relationships. Many such studies are empirical, seeking without preconception to discover what factors exist in a particular population. Others are guided by theory, which suggests the selection of variables and predicts particular clusterings. For example, the well-known studies of the "authoritarian personality" were conceived within a generally psychoanalytic framework (Adorno, Frenkel-Brunswik, Levinson, and Sanford, 1950). Whether empirical or theoretical, however, the guiding notion is that every man is *in certain respects* like some other men, not that everyone is *in every respect* like some others, as implied by absolute typologies of the past. Correlations are never perfect, and hence no individual precisely fits the types described. The personality patterns obtained in modern personality research can best be visualized as *ideal types* which can serve as hypothetical models with which individuals can be compared.

Types can become stereotypes, in clinical practice as well as in ordinary social life. In the final analysis, Dr. Cushing's clever diagnostic feat may have been wrong. Some, if only a few, Boston Gentlemen may be rude to ladies, if only their wives. The good clinician must ascertain the actual state of this Boston Gentleman's personality and nervous system. Labelling patients in pat diagnostic categories with minimum regard for their individual problems parallels the dangers of labelling people "Blacks," "Jews," "typical students," or "typical businessmen."

At the same time, there are equally real dangers in the overly individualistic approach which denies the existence, or minimizes the importance, of groupings. Though such a view might seem more democratic and imply greater respect for the individual, it may have just the reverse effect. Groups *do* differ and an individual should be known in terms of norms appropriate to his group. Psychological tests developed on white Americans may unfairly judge black Americans. Clinical settings and methods oriented to values of the white community may fit poorly the values and needs of the black community. A major trend in modern clinical psychology is toward reconceptualizing personality concepts and methods of intervention in terms of the qualities and problems which are common to social groups. This community-oriented emphasis supplements and extends the clinician's traditional concern with the unique individual.

Persons and Environments

It is a simple truth that "no man is an island unto himself." We all live in environments, both physical and social, some more enduring and others transient, which affect and shape our behavior. Whether adaptive or maladaptive, behavior has to be viewed in the perspective of transactions with environmental stimuli and events. No one would deny these propositions, but psychologists differ greatly in their conceptions of person-environmental transactions. They differ in their views as to the nature of environmental stimuli, whether they are to be conceived as objective and external or whether their importance for human psychology lies in their subjective meanings. Psychologists disagree as to the relative importance of intrapersonal factors (needs, drives, traits) as against environmental or situational factors (stimulus demands, reinforcement) in the determination of personality functioning. Though differing in other respects, both dynamic (e.g., psychoanalytic) and phenomenological (humanistic, existential) theories focus on the person while behavioristic theories emphasize the external situation. Intermediate are field-theoretical views which attempt to describe the person-in-the-environment as the proper unit of study. Ultimately, these different orientations reflect profound differences in conceptions of the nature of man and they link with metaphysical questions—does the world exist independent of man and determine his cognition of it or is there no world except as we perceive and know it?

Behavioristic theories start with a faith in the reality and importance of external stimuli. Behavior consists of stimulus-response (S-R) sequences. Learning, of central concern to behaviorists, involves the association of particular responses with particular stimuli, so that the probability of future occurrence increases with the degree of past association between stimulus and response. Different behaviorist views differ in the role ascribed to reinforcement (reward), but in all the core process in learning consists of stimulus-response pairing. Personality consists of the habituated reactions acquired in response to stimuli through the learning process. Minimal assumptions are made about intrapersonal dispositions to behavior, particularly those which might be assumed to be innate. Except for biological drives and some unconditioned reflexes, behaviorists assume that the organism starts life only with the general plasticity needed for later adaptation and learning. Thereafter, the growth of personality is the history of learning, of the cumulating associations between stimuli and responses. Concern is with observable behavior, if not visible then at least measurable in terms of objective indexes. Except as they can be represented in behavioral terms, concepts such as thought, fantasy, unconscious wishes and feelings are usually dismissed as mentalistic and unscientific. At the extreme "man is . . . a hyphen within an S-R process" (Koch, 1969, p. 14). Overall, the behavioristic approach is nomothetic in emphasis, molecular rather than molar or holistic, empirical rather than theoretical or philosophic. In the clinical realm, behaviorists are concerned with the behavioral symptoms of malfunction rather than with hypothesized underlying causes or determining states. Since maladaptive habits are learned in the first place, behaviorists hold, they can be extinguished or unlearned in the second. Thus, clinical intervention ("behavior modification," in this view) consists of applying learning principles to alter or replace maladaptive reaction patterns.

Phenomenological theorists are diametrically opposed to behaviorists in their view of the relation of the person and the environment. Psychologically, the physically defined stimulus is irrelevant, for it is only through perception and mental processing that we know it. What we are responding to, therefore, is the phenomenological (experienced) rather than the objective (physical) world. Psychologists must seek to explain behavior by interpreting the workings of the mediating processes, internal to the individual, which create his private and personal concepts. Of greatest importance are those factors which determine personal meanings and which underlie the differences among individuals in the ways in which they conceive themselves and their worlds. The *self* as that portion of the personality which is central to its organization and the seat of personal experience is most often the focus of theoretical concern.

Nobody would deny that there may be unknown and unknowable factors in the surrounding environment, such as radiation, which can vitally affect our lives. What matters of the physical environment are those facets represented in consciousness. We live in a "behavioral world," as Koffka (1935) reminded us years ago. To make this point he recounted the story of a man who arrived at the back door of a Swiss inn during a blinding snowstorm after riding his horse through an impenetrable fog. From the surprised comments of the innkeeper the man learned for the first time that he had just come across the thin ice of Lake Constance. The "objective" danger was now past, but as the physical world was transformed into a behavioral world, anxiety swept over the man and he died of shock. Though the response might seem a bit extreme, the distinction between the "real" and the "experienced" is well taken.

Psychoanalysis and other *dynamic theories* share with phenomenology concern with the person rather than the environment. However, their concern is less with conscious experience than with its hidden determinants. Focus is on the drives, memories, and wishes of the individual, many of the most important of which are repressed or dynamically unconscious (unknowable to the person without special efforts). There is no denial of an external reality definable in its own terms, either in classic psychoanalysis or in more modern "ego psychology." In the course of development, there is movement from a primitive "pleasure principle" to a more mature "reality principle" as the major determinant of psychological activity. Through the growth of "reality testing" the child comes to know the properties of the external world and their potential effects on him. Paralleling the turning of interest from drive processes to ego processes in the recent history of psychoanalytic thinking, there has been increasing concern with those psychological (ego) processes which function relatively autonomously of intrapersonal drives and unconscious conflicts to assure more adaptive reality contact. Similarly, there has been a shifting of concern from early life to more current experiences. Still, it is certainly true that the primary emphasis of psychoanalysis has been and remains on the intrapersonal rather than the environmental determinants of human functioning.

Dynamic psychologists have been properly criticized for overweighing the intrapersonal and underemphasizing the situational and environmental determinants of human behavior. Such imbalance can lead to misinterpretations. Thus, double-checking locks, jumping at unexpected sounds, being fearful at the approach of a stranger may well indicate a phobic state derived from unconscious wishes and neurotic conflicts; however, this interpretation is more likely if these behaviors occur in a secure suburban home than in a crime-ridden slum. At the same time, it is equally true that situational and environmental factors are not sufficient to explain behavior. People can be neurotically fearful in a slum as well as a suburb. An old aphorism reminds clinicians that "even paranoids can have real enemies"; equally true would be the reverse proposition: "even people with real enemies can be paranoid."

Ultimately, whether one emphasizes *persons* or *environments*, whether one believes that the world as *conceived* or the world as it *exists* is more important, depends on profound philosophic differences which have long divided schools of psychology. In all, however, human functioning can best be understood in terms of person-environment transactions; exclusive emphasis on either pole limits understanding. Many of the determinants of a patient's adaptive or maladaptive functioning are to be found in his character organization, skills and abilities, and enduring personality traits, which, in turn, reflect the history of his drive satisfactions and frustrations, identifications and learnings, group memberships and socializing experiences. All of these, however, emerge in transactions between the person and his social and physical environments. The individual's present functioning, similarly, reflects the external forces which continue to act on him. Though the person in distress remains the focus of clinical concern, his behavior cannot be fully understood apart from the context in which it occurs.

Persons and Social Systems

As people cannot truly be understood outside of the environments in which they function, neither can they be abstracted from the social systems of which they are a part. The personality system of the individual is in constant interplay with social systems. Hence, change in a desired direction can be brought about by changing the social forces acting on the individual, as well as by changing the individual personality itself.

Rather than discussing these propositions in abstract terms, let us consider a specific case. In School A classes are small and teaching is personal. Desks are movable. Teachers are young and concerned. They have a considerable voice in deciding school programs and communication between teachers and administrators flows easily in both directions. The children help decide the material to be learned and the pace of lessons. By contrast, in School B classes are large and crowded, desks are fixed, and teachers are aloof and formal. Teachers have little opportunity to express views about the curriculum; decisions are made by administrators. The children themselves participate even less in deciding school programs. They are expected to do the required work in a uniform way. In the classic studies of Lewin, Lippitt, and White (1939) it was found that children were more docile in the "authoritarian atmosphere" of a school like B and less orderly in the "democratic atmosphere" of A. However, they also noted that when the teacher left the room, children in the authoritarian system became more destructively aggressive while those in the democratic system had greater capacity for self-discipline. In School A, the motility and curiosity of children is not frustrated and conditions are right for more effective learning. The higher morale of teachers is reflected in more satisfied children.

Despite the apparent advantages of School A over School B, we can visualize a particularly shy or constricted youngster who might be out of place in School A, for whom the freedom of choice and movement might be threatening. The same child in the more structured environment of B might not only be more comfortable but perhaps learn more. On the other hand, a particularly motile or rebellious child might find School B onerous, and be a constant irritant and object of discipline. In School A, he could more readily be tolerated and he might, possibly, have more opportunity to find his own way and learn in his own fashion, or at least, to suffer less.

The clinician, concerned with these contrasting children, is obviously well advised to know the social systems of the two schools and their impacts on the children. One strategy of intervention might involve transferring the children between the schools. This would have the immediate effect of relieving pressure on both the rebel and the recluse, perhaps even contributing to longer-term resolution of their problems. Individual psychotherapy of one or another sort might still be necessary, but changing the school environments could have immediate and tangible effects. It is a common error to suppose that clinicians work only with the personal experiences of patients, ignoring or taking as unalterable the environments acting on them. Such "environmental manipulation" has long been an alternative for clinicians.

It is true, however, that only in the recent past has there been systematic interest in the social system as a primary target of intervention. In the main, mental health workers have operated with patient-centered rather than system-centered methods. The case of School A and School B points up the challenge of a system approach. If, as the illustration suggests, School A provides more of the basic social conditions which might facilitate individual growth and "positive mental health," could we not try to make School B more like School A? Such an approach aims at creating optimal conditions, at least for the modal person, by altering the social system itself. It holds out the promise of being able to prevent emotional problems, thus extending the clinician's contribution beyond the care of the already disturbed. The concepts, methods, and problems involved in efforts to produce health-enhancing social changes will be considered in detail in later chapters on community psychology.

The Perspective of Clinical Psychology: A Recapitulation

Clinical psychology is most distinctly defined by the *clinical attitude,* that is, a concern with understanding and helping individuals in psychological distress. The clinician works directly with troubled people in the effort to help them toward more satisfying and effective lives. Through the clinical process, knowledge is gained which increases understanding of the dynamics, development, and disturbances of personality in *general.* Similarly, knowledge about people in general is applicable to the understanding and treatment of the *particular* individual. Clinical psychology is concerned with generating and utilizing knowledge about the structure and functioning of human personality. But in his most distinctive role, the clinician works within a *personological* framework. He tries to understand the way psychological variables and personality traits converge in the functioning of particular persons. This contrasts with the approach of *general psychology,* which seeks uniform principles of behavior characteristic of all people, and with *differential psychology,* which examines the ways groups of persons differ along particular variables. In the broad field of psychology, the general, differential, and personological approaches complement and feed into one another, but for clinical psychology, the personological framework is the most relevant.

Each person is unique, and the clinician works with that uniqueness. Defenders of an idiographic point of view have correctly challenged a *nomothetic* science which ignores individuality. At the same time, the case can be overstated and the conclusion suggested that a science of personology is impossible to attain. I have argued instead that this conclusion depends on an overly narrow view of science, and that the essential concerns of the idiographer can be encompassed in a systematic and scientific personological psychology. Such a science emphasizes understanding, as well as prediction and control, as scientific goals; it can deal with empathy and intuition, with human values and subjective meanings, and with structural as well as elementalistic features of personality. A scientific personology provides the appropriate framework for clinical psychology.

Although ultimately unique, each person shares qualities with other persons, often importantly related to common experience, group memberships, or social roles. Personality-type concepts are useful for providing models against which individuals can be compared. Inclusive typologies, however, which attempt to force all people into two or a few categories are, at the least, overly simplistic and, at the worst, conducive to stereotypic thinking, labelling, and social injustice. Proper understanding of the axiom that "all men are in some respects like some other men" would emphasize the "in some respects." Modal personality characteristics shared by people of the same culture are still distinctively organized in each individual. Social types, however, are real and denial of this fact—either by emphasizing the universalistic qualities of all humans or by insisting on the individuality of every person—reduces our ability to help those who differ from us.

Individuals live in environments and in social systems, and behavior is importantly determined by them. Personality psychologists and clinicians have, on the whole, located the major determinants of human functioning within the person. The current emphases on ecological psychology and on system-oriented community psychology are welcome antidotes. Interactional concepts are necessary to put into proper perspective the interplay of forces within and outside the person. In professional polemics, the one or the other realm is likely to be overemphasized, as they have been in the polarization of phenomenological and behavioristic views. In fact, it is as true that objective outside events shape our behavior as it is that intrapersonal factors give meaning to external events. The implications of these contrasting viewpoints for clinical intervention will be considered in later chapters.

A BRIEF HISTORY OF CLINICAL PSYCHOLOGY

Origins

Clinical psychology has roots in both the psychometric and dynamic traditions of psychology. The psychometric tradition, emphasizing measurement and individual differences mainly in intellectual processes, was of greater prominence in the earlier history of the field, when emphasis was largely on mental testing. The dynamic tradition, with concern focussed on motivation, adaptation, and personality change, had its greatest impact at a later date and is represented in the concern of clinicians with personality dynamics, development, and psychotherapy. However, the two trends coexisted over the short history of psychology and intertwine in the development of clinical psychology. Both traditions are rooted in nineteenth-century European psychology, but they moved readily and flourished in the intellectual climate of America of the 1890s. Indeed, the functionalist orientation which came soon to characterize American psychology made particularly fertile soil for the nascent clinical field. In the United States, there was little patience for a psychology which either dissects into minute detail the structures of the mind or for one which speculates philosophically about its ultimate nature. Emphasizing what could be empirically studied and measured, American psychology had an early and continuing concern with altering and improving human functioning. Applied psychologies, addressing problems of industry, education, and social behavior, as well as psychological growth and personality dysfunctioning, had an early and prominent place in American psychology. By 1896, the first psychological clinic was founded at the University of Pennsylvania by Lightner Witmer.

The Psychometric Tradition

Not many years after Weber, Fechner, and the mid-nineteenth-century founders of the science of psychology had developed laboratory techniques for measuring psychological processes, Sir Francis Galton's studies of differences among people were laying the groundwork of differential psychology. By 1890, James McKeen Cattell coined the term "mental tests." Shortly afterwards, statistical procedures were being applied to tests in many realms and considerable effort was being put into developing test norms and standardized procedures. An event of great moment occurred in 1904 when the Minister of Public Instruction of Paris sought the help of the French psychologist Alfred Binet in order to distinguish mentally defective children who could better be taught in special rather than regular classes. To develop an objective means of examining intelligence, Binet and his collaborator developed the famous Binet-Simon scale. Drawing on his earlier work (1896) with Henri, a series of tests for measuring attention, memory, imagery, motor skills, comprehension, and other psychological variables were assembled. It is noteworthy that an essential notion in this earliest of intelligence tests was that intelligence had to be measured by assaying a number of functions and could not be judged from any single measure. Binet's procedure yielded "mental-age" scores. Years later in Germany, William Stern suggested that these be evaluated in terms of actual or chronological age to yield a stable "intelligence quotient" (IQ). Through successive revisions, notably by Lewis Terman in America, the original procedure evolved into the present Stanford-Binet test. For many years, establishing the IQ of children by administering the Stanford-Binet was a major task of clinical psychologists.

Drawing on the methods of the new experimental laboratories, Witmer's psychological clinic studied children with learning or school problems. He was the first to use the term "clinical psychology" and to describe the "clinical method in psychology." In a talk before the American Psychological Association in 1896 Witmer, according to his friend Joseph Collins, pointed out that "clinical psychology is derived from the results of an examination of many human beings, one at a time, and the analytic method of discriminating mental abilities and defects develops an ordered classification of observed behavior, by means of postanalytic generalization. He put forth the claim that the psychological clinic is an institution for social and public service, for original research, and for the instruction of students in psychological orthogenics which includes vocational, educational, correctional, hygienic, industrial, and social guidance." And, his friend continued, "The only reaction he got from the audience was slight elevation of the eyebrows on the part of a few of the older members" (Collins, quoted by Brotemarkle, 1947). Eyebrows and all, the ideas and the situation seem remarkably fresh to those of us who have described the ideals of clinical psychology to academic audiences over the years since then. However, Witmer's approach was within the general scope of the "structural" psychology of the time, focussing on specific mental processes, though concerned with their measurement and treatment in the cases of specific individual patients. In important regards, his differed from the clinics of today, mainly for not sharing the input of the "dynamic tradition."

The Dynamic Tradition

In the same years as Cattell, Binet, and Witmer were taking the procedures of the "new" experimental laboratories into studies of individual differences and clinical testing, students of abnormal behavior were germinating the core ideas about motivation, psychopathology, and psychotherapy which were to profoundly affect clinical psychology and psychiatry. The French psychopathologists, notably Charcot and Janet, were studying hypnosis, hysteria, and the phenomena of dissociation, and laying the groundwork for the investigation of conflict in the unconscious as well as conscious mind. Influenced by them, Freud moved forward to what still remains the most extensive and coherent theory of human motivation and personality disturbance. Freud's thoroughgoing "psychic determinism," attention to early childhood, and his conceptualization of the unconscious and repression were keystones of a way of visualizing human behavior which profoundly altered psychology, general as well as clinical. In 1909, William James was to say: "The future of psychology belongs to your work." Freud's *Studies in Hysteria* (with Breuer) was first published in 1895; within the next decade appeared the *Interpretation of Dreams* (1899), *Psychopathology of Everyday Life* (1904), *Jokes and Their Connection with the Unconscious* (1905), and *Three Essays on the Theory of Sexuality* (1904). Although a small and loyal group gathered around the Viennese sage, these works made small impact on "establishment" thinking in European psychology or psychiatry.

Indeed, it was through the efforts of two giants of American academic psychology—G. Stanley Hall and William James—that the dynamic tradition entered American psychology. James was the renaissance man of early American psychology. His own *Principles of Psychology* (1890) and *Varieties of Religious Experience* (1902) delved into the nature of the self and ego, the stream of consciousness, human values, and psychopathology, in contrast to which the writings of contemporary "structuralists" seem barren and irrelevant to the developing clinical psychology. His philosophy of pragmatism encouraged concern with the utility of ideas, which were to be tested in actual experiences. James' devotion to human well-being was reflected in his later support of the nascent Mental Hygiene movement, through encouragement of Clifford Beers, whose description of his own experiences as a hospital patient spurred reforms.

G. Stanley Hall had a similar influence in the first decades of American psychology. In his own writings, he emphasized developmental processes, understanding of sexuality, and of adolescence. He taught and encouraged students to go into clinical practice and research, sponsored work on tests of clinical importance, and founded journals which were to be major carriers of clinical theory and knowledge. In 1909, he brought Freud and many of his coterie to America, to present their ideas to American scholars and psychologists. This famous meeting at Clark Univeristy left an indelible impact on the future development of American clinical psychology, though for some years thereafter clinical psychology continued in the tradition of Witmer. It is noteworthy that it was a psychology department rather than a medical institution which first brought psychoanalysis to these shores. Indeed, until 1913 the only outlet for psychoanalytic publications in the United States was the *Journal of Abnormal Psychology*, founded and edited by Morton Prince who later founded the Harvard Psychological Clinic. At the meetings in 1909, Carl Jung described his studies of word association as a way of discovering unconscious complexes or conflicts. Along with Freud's analysis of dreams, this was an important forerunner of projective testing. The projective test, which involves the analysis of fantasy produced in response to unstructured stimuli, as an agent for clinical assessment, represents a major confluence of the dynamic and psychometric traditions in American clinical psychology, though it was not to occur for another thirty years.

The First Fifty Years of Clinical Psychology

During the first decades of the twentieth century, new psychological clinics were launched on university campuses; there were twenty by 1914 (R. I. Watson, 1953). Psychologists moved out into mental hospitals and clinics and into specialized settings for the mentally retarded and physically handicapped. In hospitals, considerable research was done describing psychological functioning of psychotic patients, using the techniques, concepts, and measures of the experimental laboratory. Psychologists continue to develop, perfect, and use mental tests. In clinical centers, some became "mental testers," applying and reporting test findings to medical superiors. Few held doctorates in psychology, which was to remain true up through World War II.

World War I spurred the growth of clinical psychology. The military services faced the problem of differentiating among men of differing abilities. A number of psychologists, mainly distinguished experimentalists, took on the challenge and developed group intelligence tests. The Army Alpha was a verbal test, which sampled such abilities as arithmetic, following directions, judgment, and vocabulary. Paralleling it was the Army Beta, which was nonverbal and intended for illiterate or non-English speaking recruits. Woodworth's Psychoneurotic Inventory (labelled "Personal Data Sheet" out of respect for the sensibilities of those taking it) was developed to diagnose and screen soldiers with emotional problems. It is the prototype of the numerous paper-and-pencil inventories which have proliferated since 1917. Indeed, some of the Woodworth items moved from test to test over the years, so that many contemporary questionnaires have a trace of original Woodworth, much as today's sherry has a bit of the primeval wine carried forth in diminishing amounts in the solera processing of the Spanish vintners. By the end of the war, it was estimated that 1,726,000 men were group-tested and 83,000 individually examined (Reisman, 1966). Published findings which showed racial differences, a high order of illiteracy, and an average "mental age" of the American soldier to be 13.5 years led to widespread and understandable public and professional reaction.

During the twenties and thirties clinicians continued to work in clinical settings, in the main assessing intellectual and educational functioning of children. With the growth of the Child Guidance Movement, many new clinics were established and the "team approach" evolved. Under the leadership of the medically trained psychiatrist, who was responsible for most of the clinical decisions and for therapy, the psychologist was primarily involved in psychological testing and in applying educational and remedial therapies. The third member of the team was a social worker, who took care of intake and social-history interviews, did casework with parents, and worked in liaison with other social agencies to better the child's social environment. This basic pattern was to continue into the years following World War II, even as psychologists moved from child clinics to adult psychiatric institutions.

From World War II to the Present

During World War II large numbers of psychologists, many with minimal clinical background, found themselves in military psychiatric units working shoulder to shoulder with psychiatrists and social workers. They left service, determined to continue in the field. Discharged with them were thousands of men who were emotionally impaired and entitled to the services of the rapidly expanding Veterans Administration (VA). By 1945, the VA launched a major program to support training in the mental health disciplines. Substantial stipends were provided to students and internship opportunities were made available in VA hospitals and mental hygiene clinics. In a description of the role of the clinical psychologist in the VA, a 1946 circular notes that he is expected to do diagnosis, psychotherapy, and research (the holy trinity of postwar clinical psychology). The clinical psychologist, it also stated, was one trained to the PhD. By 1950, about half of the PhDs given in psychology were to persons going through the newly developed *Graduate Programs in Clinical Psychology* (E. L. Kelly, 1961). Growing concern with the mental health needs of the nation led to further federal support through the United States Public Health Service and its new National Institute of Mental Health (NIMH), which continues to be a major supporter of clinical psychological training and research.

The postwar skyrocketing of interest in, and support for, clinical psychology forced the body politic of psychology to consider the proper training of psychologists and the relation of the clinical profession to the remainder of psychology. Throughout the 1920s and 1930s there had been value conflicts between applied professionals and academic psychologists, but these were sharpened in the postwar boom. Many psychology professors had misgivings about the newly emerging clinical psychology, for it represented to them a commitment not only to an alien subject matter but to an even more alien professional role and values. Most, at least in the postwar years, were willing and even eager to help the fledgling field grow.

Shortly after the war, the American Psychological Association (APA) set up a committee, under the chairmanship of David Shakow, which laid down the philosophy and a proposed model of clinical training time (APA, Committee on Training in Clinical Psychology, 1947). In 1949, at a conference at Boulder, Colorado, leaders of American psychology, from universities, clinical centers, and federal agencies (VA and NIMH), and members of allied professions considered the broad issues of clinical training and largely affirmed the position of the Shakow Committee (Raimy, 1950).

Broadly stated, the new clinical psychologist was to be a "scientist-professional," trained to a PhD in a university psychology department, with internship in a clinical setting. First a psychologist and only then a clinician, the clinical student was expected to be broadly grounded in the major areas of psychological theory, knowledge, and research, more specifically in the fields of personality, social psychology, and psychopathology, and to learn the competencies needed for clinical intervention. The fully trained clinical psychologist should be able and motivated to function fully and autonomously in psychological diagnosis, psychotherapy, and research. Practicum and internship training, within the PhD program, were viewed as essential. To provide the necessary range of academic and clinical experiences, a partnership was visualized between universities and field-training centers, at that time primarily psychiatric hospitals and clinics; the latter to provide the internship resources. In whatever professional role, it was hoped that the clinician would be a scholar and researcher, in order to increase knowledge about the nature of human distress and its treatment. Finally, procedures were developed for the evaluation and accreditation of both university graduate programs and internship programs in clinical centers, the so-called "APA-approved" programs. In 1948, twenty universities were given full approval (another twenty-three were put on interim approval); by 1975, there were 101 fully approved doctoral programs.

Since the Boulder conference, the APA sponsored a sequence of other national conferences which reaffirmed the PhD scientist-professional concept of clinical psychology (Strother, 1956; Roe, Gustad, Moore, Ross, and Skodak, 1959; Hoch, Ross, and Winder, 1966). Only in the most recent of these, at Vail, Colorado, during the summer of 1973, did the participants vote to legitimize an alternate route for graduate training, to a new professional degree to be awarded without a research thesis to students being trained to be clinical practitioners.

During the 1950s and 1960s, clinical psychology continued to grow, diversify, and excite controversy. Ethical standards were developed by the APA. A system of examination and accreditation of mature clinicians was instituted, somewhat after the model of medical specialty boards, under the auspices of the American Board of Examiners in Professional Psychology (ABEPP), later to become the American Board of Professional Psychology (ABPP). One state after another passed certification or licensure laws governing the practice of psychology, so that today in most states practicing clinicians are examined and certified by state agencies as well as by ABPP. Where before and immediately following World War II most clinicians worked as members of a "psychiatric team" in mental hospitals, increasing numbers found greater satisfaction in new roles in university teaching, psychological clinics, group and individual private practice, clinical research units, and, most recently, community mental health centers and other community agencies. Although still a minority, perhaps 25 percent of clinical psychologists today are in full-time private practice, mainly of individual psychotherapy.

Not only in professional status and training patterns, but also in theoretical and practice orientations, clinical psychology has become increasingly diversified. In the days of the Shakow Committee, clinical intervention consisted largely of testing and psychotherapy, guided mainly by psychoanalytic thinking and the tradition of psychometric testing. Rogers' client-centered therapy was new and exciting to many psychologists, and provided the only major alternative to psychoanalytic psychotherapy. Today, these contend with approaches deriving from existentialistic, ego-psychological, conditioning and social-learning, and community-psychological positions. Many favor the small group rather than the individual as the locus of clinical intervention, and many forms of group and family therapy have evolved. Other psychologists are seeking ways of intervening in the social ecology and institutions which deeply affect people's lives in the quest for methods of preventing rather than simply treating human problems. Through most of the remainder of this volume, we will consider the variety of approaches, both traditional and innovative, which are used by contemporary clinical psychologists in their efforts to understand and reduce human malfunction and misery.

CHAPTER 3

A Conceptual Framework for Clinical Psychology

The Need for Theory

Boldly carved in the stone of Harvard's Emerson Hall, which once housed philosophy and psychology, is the motto "What is man that thou art mindful of him?" This is a proper though humbling question for students of the human condition. There is of course no simple answer, and Gordon Allport warned generations of Emerson Hall students against seeking or accepting "simple and sovereign" explanations for the complexity of human behavior. The many general theories of personality are manifestly diverse, though each has contributed understanding of some phenomena. Similarly, in the separate areas of psychological functioning—perception, learning, cognition, emotion—theoretical formulations of relevance to clinicians have been developed and should be incorporated into their thinking. In their work with particular people in distress, clinicians need a theoretical framework to guide understanding and intervention. Wisdom not cowardice suggests a *healthy eclecticism,* a willingness to incorporate the ideas, techniques, and knowledge of different orientations as they prove their value. Ideally, in the mature clinician, these should be personally integrated within a more comprehensive view. A flexible conceptual framework is necessary; both dogmatic adherence to a single view or uncritical openmindedness are limitations. In the present chapter, I will briefly present some concepts which are important to the understanding of personality functioning and dysfunctioning and which provide a basis for clinical intervention. The context and relevance of these concepts should emerge in later chapters which examine modes of intervention. For now, the purpose is to introduce these concepts, at the same time defining a technical vocabulary which will be used in later sections.

The story of personality and clinical psychology can be told from the vantage of the many ways psychologists have responded to the question "What is man . . . ?" The student is already familiar with "theories of personality," from which differing conceptions of personality, psychopathology, assessment, and psychotherapy derive. Textbooks usually contain chapters discussing schools (e.g., psychoanalysis), classes of theory (e.g., phenomenological views, behavioristic theories), or the ideas of creative men (e.g., Freud, Skinner, or Lewin). Thus, Mischel (1975) groups (1) trait or type theories; (2) psychodynamic theories; (3) psychodynamic behavior theories (e.g., Dollard and Miller); (4) social behavior theories (e.g., Skinner, Rotter, or Bandura); and (5) phenomenological theories. Other groupings and extended lists could be made to include, say, biological views, role-theoretical models, organismic theories, or others. What is clear, however, is that each school differs not only in its basic concepts as to the nature and development of personality, but simultaneously and necessarily in its view of disordered behavior and of the proper modes of clinical assessment and psychotherapy. Thus, in clinical assessment, trait approaches favor psychometric techniques, "objective" personality tests, and correlational methods; psychodynamic approaches emphasize depth interviewing and projective personality testing; phenomenological views are self-ratings and descriptions of subjective experience; while behavioral psychologists depend on direct measurement of observable behavior. Similarly, conceptualizing the necessary conditions for therapeutic change, the psychodynamically oriented depend on depth exploration to achieve insight into disabling and often unconscious conflicts; the behavioristically inclined attempt to affect relearning by altering reinforcement contingencies in the current situation; while phenomenological therapists encourage examination of contemporary self- and world-views to foster new guiding orientations. Clearly, such diverse viewpoints and the approaches derived from them cannot readily be brought into a more unitary framework. But each has contributed to understanding, and their tenets and techniques should be known to clinicians.

Theory consists of a web of constructs, assumptions, and hypotheses, within which knowledge is cumulated and systematized. Theory guides investigation, whether of a phenomenon in general or an event in particular, by suggesting where and how to look for explanation. In research and clinical practice, the clinician needs a theoretical framework within which to search for and interpret evidence. Albeit incomplete and eclectic, theoretical concepts must be explicit and communicable. Without such framework, the clinician risks bumbling ineffectually or perhaps worse yet, acting on implicit assumptions about the nature of man which reflect more his own personal needs and biases than the qualities of his patient.

No person—bartender, mother, nor clinician-as-layman—is without "theories" about the nature of human nature. Some are cultural beliefs, and so widely held as to seem axiomatic. They are reflected in our folk sayings and conversational platitudes. While some reflect psychological truths of some generality, others are deceptive caricatures. Some beliefs are "simple and sovereign" explanations of wide ranges of behavior, such as "All men are inherently aggressive; thus, violence, war, and crime are inevitable." Others are limited to presumed types or groups of people. Some theories are idiosyncratic and derive from the personal history of their owners, whether dependent on generalizations from actual experiences or outward manifestations of psychopathological conflicts. At extremes, such personalized belief systems reveal their pathological origins. The person with the conviction that "everybody is out to get me" can be diagnosed as paranoid. But the aphorism "You can't trust anyone these days," comes close to being a folk myth, unhappily. But, however generated and of whatever origin or degree of truth, we each have an assumptive system in terms of which we judge and respond to the behavior of others.

It would be foolish to expect that psychologists, despite knowledge and skill, would be without naive psychological assumptions, whether shared or idiosyncratic. We would certainly expect that they would be free of those which flout readily available evidence or which are demonstrably projections of own inner problems. There are two basic safeguards which clinicians have at their disposal. The first we have already noted: they can guide their thinking by explicit psychological theory which derives from scientific (i.e., systematic) evidence and can be tested against further evidence. Theories exist of all degrees of elegance, quantitative expression, and inclusiveness; for present purposes, what matters is explicitness and communicability. The availability of such theory is one safeguard against naive assumptions.

The second safeguard lies in the clinician's commitment continuously to examine and test his assumptions whatever their origin. He must turn on himself the same investigatory attitude which he uses with his patient. The question "Why is *he* acting this way? What belief-system underlies his behavior?" must as well be asked with *I* substituted for *he*. Questioning and explaining, as we will discover when we discuss psychotherapy, do not necessarily change assumptions, but they reveal them, which is a necessary first step. One of the arguments for personal therapy for clinicians is that it gives opportunity for examining and testing (perhaps, changing) beliefs and values, while perhaps more profoundly altering neurotic character qualities which further limit understanding and distort behavior toward patients. In clinical supervision, of central importance in clinical training, the senior clinician attempts to help the clinician-in-training to understand his own premises, reasons for actions, and hitherto unexamined assumptions. The mature clinician carries on the same dialogue, internally.

The same issues arise in the related realm of personal values. Just as the clinician holds assumptions in terms of which he *understands* human behavior, he also holds values in terms of which he *evaluates* it. The line between belief and value is tenuous. The notion that clinical psychology is a science without values is indefensible. Many core issues, the nature of mental illness itself, require a position on what human behavior is believed desirable. In all dealings with patients, the clinician's values are of critical importance, for they affirm or deny the "rightness" of the patient's beliefs or actions. The clinician's values, like his assumptions, must be made explicit. In no sense am I suggesting that the clinician be without values—an idea as inconceivable as it is undesirable—nor that he act "as if" he had no values. Sometimes, the term "clinical detachment" is used to suggest such a stance in medical practice. In the psychoclinical situation, however, it is probably impossible and certainly undesirable for the clinician to deny or dissimulate his value judgments. It is necessary for them to be fully known to the clinician (and patient, too, I believe), rather than acting as silent and invisible determiners of his actions.

A conceptual framework is clearly necessary for the clinician. But now we come to a paradox. Although theory sharpens vision it can also blind it. A well-articulated and securely held theoretical position can make one insensitive to a phenomenon visible to the naive eye. Contradictory evidence is hard to assimilate to a view which would have led to contrary predictions. Moreover, a conceptual system involves a network of constructs and the technical vocabularies that necessarily go with them. While this may facilitate communication between like-minded scientists, it can also lead to pseudocommunication, where the same words carry different meanings. Certainly, communication with patients is limited if the clinician uses the words in which he thinks and talks in professional settings. In addition, however, the theoretical system can be a barrier to the acute observation of actual human events. Persons are lost; in their place are oedipal complexes, negative reinforcements, self-concepts, repetition compulsions, and a host of other constructs which may characterize but not describe human actions. It would seem, therefore, that theory can limit and deceive, and that the naive vision which saw the emperor as naked is just as necessary in clinical study. We seem trapped between the one possibility of having a framework which gives meaning to events, but perhaps erroneously, and the other possibility of being engulfed in immediate behaviors and having no frame of reference for understanding them, except our naive and unverbalized beliefs.

The dilemma is real; both dangers are present. The actual task of the clinician is the difficult one of finding, developing, extending, and utilizing a theoretical system to guide his understanding and interventions and, at the same time, preserving an openness of mind to conceive and consider alternate explanations, *and* all the while, remaining open to the raw data of his field, the statements, actions, and feelings of the patient. In principle, all scientists face the same dilemma, but it is greater for the clinician whose constructs are usually less articulated and whose data are both more complex and more immediately relevant. Ultimately, the clinician is his own most important instrument, for tests and intervention techniques merely extend the range of human skills without substituting for them. The present issue is another face of the same problem. Remaining open to experience in its own terms, comprehending the patient's meaning in his terms, yet comprehending them in a theoretically relevant context is the hard but necessary job of the clinician. Clinical psychology, as a field, needs theory to guide research and the improvement of intervention techniques. Individual clinicians similarly need theory to guide their understanding and treatment of individual patients. Ultimately, as Kurt Lewin noted, "There is nothing as practical as a good theory."

A Framework for Viewing Human Functioning and Disorder

I will start with some simple, but I believe central, propositions about the nature of human beings which can guide our understanding of personality and clinical intervention. For the remainder of this chapter, these basic propositions will be elaborated in terms of six perspectives—the motivational, structural, developmental, adaptational, ecological, and biological. Together, the simply stated propositions and the more developed perspectives are intended as a framework for understanding personality functioning and disorder of relevance to clinical intervention. They are themes around which theory can be built; in no serious sense do they represent a theory of personality.

Some Orienting Assumptions

1. All behavior is *determined,* both in the sense of having roots in the individual's history and in the sense of being explicable in terms of personality needs, structures, and situational determinants. The determinants may be unknown to the actor and/or dynamically repressed. They may be directly observable or only to be discovered through inference from available cues.

2. Behavior has *plasticity.* Though dependent on his past, man's needs, skills, knowledge, and other facets of psychological functioning change in response to life circumstances and experience. Thus, learning is a major principle of psychological life. However, there is no single mode of learning, but many different types, each operating in different realms. In the ordinary course of life and in therapeutic intervention, behavior changes through conditioning, reinforcement, modeling, identification, and cognitive restructuration.

3. Man is *reactive* to external and internal stimuli, but he is also *proactive.* He not only responds and adjusts, but he acts upon the world, fashioning it according to his concepts and needs.

4. Each person is ultimately *unique* and must be understood in his own terms, but the *principles* of psychological functioning and organization are common to all men. Moreover, in consequence of common experiences, groups of people have characteristics in common.

5. Behavior is *motivated* and *goal-directed.* There are various needs, of greater and lesser importance in the life of particular persons and of greater and lesser salience at a given moment. Needs drive behavior toward goals. They may arise in internal states of the person, deprivations or excesses, or be aroused by environmental stimuli. Needs may be contradictory and in *conflict.* Conflict can be resolved in ways that are either more beneficial or more destructive of the integrity and well-being of the person.

6. Behavior is *centrally regulated,* more so in the mature and effectively functioning individual. Both needs and environmental pressures are mediated by structures of central importance. These include the executive functions of the Ego and the values of the Self.

7. Personality *develops* in patterned sequences. In general, the trend is toward greater differentiation, integration, and self-regulation. Psychological growth spurts and plateaus, moves through critical periods and through discernible stages, but it is continuous through life.

8. Behavior is *adaptive.* It tends toward problem-solving, growth and optimal functioning, even in the face of stress. *Defensive* and *coping* mechanisms, to avert harm and to facilitate positive solutions, preserve stability and further the

ends of the person. Adaptive functioning can be discerned even in the most disturbed behavior.

9. Man is a *biological* and *social,* as well as *psychological,* organism. For his purposes, the psychologist must focus on and start out from the psychological frame of reference. Behavior, however, is determined by a continuous and interlocked series of systems, from the genetic to the social-institutional. Behavior has both causes and expressions in various conceptually distinct biosocial systems. Complete knowledge of human functioning requires understanding of their transactions.

Perspectives

With these orienting hypotheses in hand, let us consider their import from the vantage of six distinct, though—as we shall see—overlapping, perspectives.

THE MOTIVATIONAL PERSPECTIVE

Psychologists' conceptualization of human motivation has been dominated by two related views: (1) there are *primary* or basic motives, usually related to physiological needs, from which *secondary* or *acquired* motives are derived through learning and maturation, and (2) that motivation moves toward *tension reduction* by the attainment of goal objects which satisfy the aroused drive (motive, instinct, need for now; these theoretically distinct concepts can be used interchangeably). These propositions are true, as far as they go, but they limit understanding of motivation in its full extension. For one thing, emphasis on physiological needs neglects evidence for a wide range of other equally primary motives which can be conceptualized as spontaneous expressions of the functioning of the nervous system. Along with hunger, thirst, and the like are needs for activity, exploration, mastery, and curiosity, which R. W. White (1959) has incorporated within an overarching need for *effectance.* Such needs cannot be conceptualized in a need-reduction scheme, for they require seeking of tension, arousal, or stimuli in the environment. Despite the conceptual unification that resulted from Freud's motivational theory with its assumption of two basic instincts—sex and aggression—and the view of development in terms of their evolution, the rich variety of motives which characterize adult behavior cannot easily be understood in terms of a system which locates primary motives within the biology of the organism and sees subsequent motives as direct derivatives of them.

Krech et al. (1969) suggested the distinction between *deficiency* and *abundancy* motivation, the former related to survival and security and operating by principles of tension-reduction, the latter serving ends of satisfaction and stimulation often in the form of increasing tension. These two types of motives can be seen in all realms of human functioning, from the biological to the social. Table 3.1, borrowed from their volume, lists some principal motives according to their distinction. Man's potential for *proactivity* is best seen in his abundancy motives. Deficiency rather than abundancy motives dominate the functioning of psychologically disturbed persons.

TABLE 3.1
The Human Motives *

	SURVIVAL AND SECURITY (DEFICIENCY MOTIVES)	SATISFACTION AND STIMULATION (ABUNDANCY MOTIVES)
Pertaining to the body	Avoiding of hunger, thirst, oxygen lack, excess heat and cold, pain, overfull bladder and colon, fatigue, overtense muscles, illness and other disagreeable bodily states, etc.	Attaining pleasurable sensory experiences of tastes, smells, sounds, etc.; sexual pleasure; bodily comfort; exercise of muscles, rhythmical body movements, etc.
Pertaining to relations with environment	Avoiding of dangerous objects and horrible, ugly, and disgusting objects; seeking objects necessary to future survival and security; maintaining a stable, clear, certain environment, etc.	Attaining enjoyable possessions; constructing and inventing objects; understanding the environment; solving problems; playing games; seeking environmental novelty and change, etc.
Pertaining to relations with other people	Avoiding interpersonal conflict and hostility; maintaining group membership, prestige, and status; being taken care of by others; conforming to group standards and values; gaining power and dominance over others, etc.	Attaining love and positive identification with people and groups; enjoying other people's company; helping and understanding other people; being independent, etc.
Pertaining to the self	Avoiding feelings of inferiority and failure in comparing the self with others or with the ideal self; avoiding loss of identity; avoiding feelings of shame, guilt, fear, anxiety, sadness, etc.	Attaining feelings of self-respect and self-confidence; expressing oneself; feeling sense of achievement; establishing moral and other values; discovering meaningful place of self in the universe.

* From Krech, D., Crutchfield, R. S., & Livson, N. *Elements of psychology*. New York: Knopf, 1974, p. 459. Copyright © 1974 by Alfred A. Knopf, Inc. Reprinted by permission.

A related view has been proposed by Maslow (1954, 1962). He conceived a hierarchy of motives, at the peak of which is a need for *self-actualization,* a notion derived from K. Goldstein (1939). Most fundamental of man's needs is to realize his full potentials in their most complete and effective form. Within this conception, many of the specific abundancy motives would be early or partial expression of self-actualization, which in its full extension is nothing less than the realization of full creativity, autonomy, and mastery. Though often more a vision and goal than an achieved actuality, the state is reflected in *peak experiences* in most lives and seen more enduringly in a small number of highly creative persons.

Self-actualization stands at the top of a conceptual sequence moving from "lower" to "higher" needs. Those lower in the sequence appear earlier in psychological development, are more closely related to biological requirements, and tend to be narrower in scope. The sequence includes:

1. Physiological needs, including hunger, thirst, and pain avoidance.
2. Safety needs, including security and stability.
3. Belongingness and love needs, including affection, conformity, and identification.
4. Esteem needs, including prestige and self-respect.
5. The need for self-actualization.

Central to Maslow's view is the thesis that "lower" needs must be satisfied before one can move to "higher" needs. It is pointless to search for self-actualization in a starving man. But neither can one express safety needs until basic physiological needs are met, nor esteem needs until one is secure in his sense of belonging and affection. Distorted or insufficient gratification at any level blocks normal personality growth and the attainment of higher needs.

Biological deficiency concepts of motivation often use Cannon's (1939) principle of homeostasis, which describes the finely tuned physiological mechanisms which restores balance when there has been physiological deprivation or stress. The capacity for homeostasis is critically important for the maintenance of health and life. However, using homeostasis as a model for all motivated behavior, as some theorists have, suggests too limited a view of human behavior. Humans strive toward goals beyond the maintenance of bodily integrity and psychological well-being. Claude Bernard, grandsire of the theory of homeostasis, wisely observed that achieving constancy in the internal environment of the organism is the condition for freedom in the external world. Thus, homeostasis and tension reduction, at any biosocial level, are not ends in themselves but are conditions for further growth.

Motives and their associated ideas, wishes, and fantasies, may be *unconscious* as well as known to the person. The conceptualization and exploration of the dynamic unconscious was probably the greatest of Freud's achievements. Needs may be unconscious because they existed prior to the child's capacity for symbolic representation and hence we have no "vocabulary" in which to express them. Such cases reflect the operation of what Freud termed "primary repression." Though fully conscious at the time, events which were too painful, conflicted, or dissonant with one's self-concept are excluded from later memory. However, neither the secondarily or primarily repressed necessarily lose motive power; indeed, it can be intensified by being out of communication with present experiences. The existence of the unconscious is witnessed by derivatives escaping into overt behavior, as Freud demonstrated, in slips of the tongue, humor, and in dreams. A central thesis of psychoanalytic theory is that the maintenance of repression requires energy. Continuous effort has to be expended in excluding the unwanted impulse or thought. Maintenance of repression can be viewed as a major "survival-security" motive which depletes energy otherwise available for "stimulation-satisfaction" ends. This notion is of profound importance in understanding human functioning, even if a simple concept of a closed-energy system is discarded.

It is also true that what seems functionally unconscious may simply be so much out of context that, as ground to the figure in perception, we have no cognizance of it. Thus, returning to old surroundings and recalling contingent events may lead to the recovery of memories which might be thought repressed. Freud himself distinguished a *preconscious* state, neither conscious nor unconscious, from which memories can be recovered when attention is turned to it. Thus, you surely do not know the name of your eighth-grade English teacher, though with some effort you can recall it, particularly if you return to your home town, meet an old school friend, or run into the lady herself on the street. But there might have been another teacher associated with a happening too shameful to recall (plug in your own fantasy!) which in later years might have deprived you of the pleasure of reading literature, kept you from visiting your home town, or having a sense of panic when chalk dust is in the air, all without knowing why. The reconstruction and recall of the repressed is a central aim of psychoanalytic therapy. However, there is more in the unconscious realm than unwanted and dangerous impulses; it is also the source of artistic and creative ideas, as Jung emphasized in his view of the *creative unconscious*. The fully functioning person, Jung noted in his concept of *individuation*, comes to realize his human potential through increased access to these hidden sources.

There has been a resurgence of interest in the working of the unconscious mind, a realm which fascinated William James but was relegated to limbo by scientific psychology. Unconscious processes are being studied in investigations of altered states of consciousness, dreaming, and fantasy, "cognition without awareness," and as a necessary part ("preattentive processes") of normal cognitive functioning (e.g., Neisser, 1967). As the scope of modern psychology broadens, new knowledge is emerging on the role of unconscious factors in cognition and motivation, from laboratory as well as clinical studies.

Conflict is a basic fact of motivational life. Even in simple choices, there are coexisting motives and action that satisfies one but may automatically frustrate the other. Lewin (1931) distinguished three patterns of conflict: (1) approach-approach, (2) avoidance-avoidance, and (3) approach-avoidance. The *approach-approach* conflict involves two desired goal objects, but where the attainment of one involves the loss of the other. The more balanced the desirability of the two goals, the more difficult is the decision; at the extreme is Buridan's ass of mythology, who starved to death halfway between two precisely equal piles of oats. The *avoidance-avoidance* conflict consists of choice between two negative alternatives, without the option of leaving the problem entirely. We have to take an unpleasant course *or* leave school; the child must eat spinach *or* suffer punishment. In such cases, decision may be put off as long as possible. Vacillation occurs until some third factor forces action. The *approach-avoidance* conflict is the most familiar and distressing. It can result from the same goal having both repelling and attractive features; a well-paying job offer involves distasteful work. The phenomenon of *ambivalence* describes the simultaneously invested love and hate in the same person, act or goal. Approach-avoidance conflicts often occur in sequential goal-directed acts—to reach a positive goal one must first traverse, in Lewin's terms, a negative region; dessert always seems to follow spinach for the child. Similarly, presently positive outcomes may have predictably unpleasant consequences. The movie tonight can mean failing tomorrow's examination. Obviously, these simple examples do not reflect the real complexity of motivational conflicts, particularly where unconscious motives are involved. Typically, there are more than two goals, two directions to take, or two motives operative at the same moment, nor are all issues seen and understood at the same moment. In actuality, goals can be delayed and gratifications postponed. The full analysis of conflict behavior, particularly as it is relevant to clinical understanding, depends too on the *structural aspects* of personality (as we will consider them in a few pages). These include the capacities for defining alternatives, fantasying consequences, delaying gratification, and establishing plans. Involved too are the mechanisms of ego defense through which motivational choices are construed or distorted, in order to allow action while preserving the integrity of the self. Rationalized as well as rational choice makes decisions. Related are the ego controls which, for example, allow some of us to tolerate ambiguity while others must have things in black and white. Thus, the "neurotic indecision" of patients may as well indicate "ego weakness" such that they cannot analyze, choose, and make commitments as well as the coexistence of powerful but opposed motives or feelings. The task of psychotherapy is, at one time, developing the capacity for decision, defining the alternatives and consequences of choices, and making visible the motives involved.

Conflict and frustration while usually painful are not necessarily destructive. Under the impetus of frustration there may be renewed striving, reconceptualization of goals, discovery of new routes to favored ends, and a reordering of motivational priorities. The arousal of strong affect may facilitiate performance, much as a sudden cold draft can make us more alert at our desks, though still higher levels can disorganize and disrupt organized and adaptive behavior. The facilitory effects of conflict and anxiety have been well demonstrated in laboratory, life, and clinical studies, but the more disruptive consequences are perhaps more vivid and have engaged the concerns of psychologists and laymen even more. Hence, we sometimes hear the ideally healthy state described as though it were one free of conflict. Whether one does or does not have conflicts is only part of the story; of greater importance are the mechanisms available for the healthy resolution of conflict. Even if it were possible to conceive a person, or for that matter, a society, entirely free of conflict, it would inevitably be bought at the cost of diversity and choice. Some years ago, mistaken reading of psychoanalytic theory led parents and teachers to seek a minimizing of frustration in the rearing of children, so as not to develop inhibitions believed central to neuroses. In fact, the consequence was often that such children, denied the struggle with the minor frustrations of childhood, failed to develop the coping mechanisms necessary for effective functioning in adulthood.

The destructive consequences of frustration, when they exceed tolerance limits, are clear enough, however. Aggression is the most prominent; in one well-known view, frustration is the necessary and sufficient condition for all aggression (Dollard, Doob, Miller, Mowrer, and Sears, 1939). There are other conditions for aggression and other consequences of frustration (e.g., escape and other defensive maneuvers), but aggression is a common and destructive consequence of frustration. It may be directed at persons viewed as barriers to one's goals, more diffusely toward the world, or turned back on the self. Conflict and frustration cue into operation the mechanisms of defense, which have the twin purpose of reducing anxiety while allowing oblique and partial satisfaction of needs. More about the nature and operation of defense mechanisms is discussed below. But first let us consider anxiety and emotional life in general.

For the understanding of personality functioning and disorder, *anxiety* is the most central of human emotions. It describes the state of apprehension and dread cued by threat to essential personal values, the integrity of the personality, or to life itself. When intensely anxious, there is a foreshortening of time perspective, and immediacy of behavior, and no view of a future solution. There is no defined danger, only an encompassing dread. Not only can one not locate danger in space or time, but there is a general inability to distinguish relevant and irrelevant, safe and unsafe; in general, a diffusion of cognitive organization. Fear has sometimes been distinguished as a less intense affect, occasioned by a definable and realistic danger, for which the organism is mobilized for "fight or flight." For our purposes, a continuum can be visualized, ranging from slight activation to intense anxiety of panic proportions. At lowest levels, anxiety serves as an alerting response, akin to Pavlov's "What is it?" or orienting reflex. This facilitates adaptive behavior. But at intense levels, immobilization, panic behavior, and incapacitating confusion are seen. Viewed as a continuum, anxiety acts to narrow and focus attention, thus facilitating performance; with continued increase, attention is diffused and behavior disorganized (Korchin, 1964).

In his final theory of anxiety, Freud (1926) viewed anxiety as both *signal* and *symptom,* a concept which has become central to the theory of neuroses. In its signal function, anxiety is cued by threats, arising either in external stress or internal conflict, and, in turn, brings ego-defense mechanisms into play. These protect the person from further anxiety, though in the process limiting flexibility and adaptability. Overly used and rigidified, defensive maneuvers become the symptoms of neurosis. Adaptive functions become frozen in maladaptive structures and the person is crippled in his growth, albeit safe. However, should defenses not work effectively ("decompensate") free anxiety itself emerges. In its most dramatic form, this is seen in the traumatic neuroses and in the episodes of "catastrophic anxiety" which Kurt Goldstein (1939) described in brain-damaged persons who do not have sufficient resources to cope with complex demands.

Anxiety originates in the earliest experiences and helplessness of infancy; indeed, Otto Rank proposed, in the trauma of birth. The powerlessness to avoid, understand, or master painful threats is the prototype of later anxiety attacks. Related to anxiety are other "negative affects," notably depression, shame, and guilt. Depression is the sense of unworthiness, loss of feelings and purpose, inertia, hopelessness, and, finally, disinterest in life itself. Shame is experienced when one feels exposed to ridicule and contempt, when one falls short of a personal ideal, or fails to attain a desired end. Guilt, by contrast, is felt in connection with moral transgression, particularly if harm is caused another. It is the "pangs of conscience." Shame and guilt have been studied and distinguished not only in terms of their phenomenology and motivational functions, but as they enter differently into socialization and neurosis (e.g., Piers and Singer, 1953; Lynd, 1958; Lewis, 1971). Collectively, the "negative affects" contrast with the "positive affects." Love, excitement, hope, and joy are feeling states which mark the well-functioning person.

The border between *affect* and *motive* is not at all clear, and different theories postulate different relationships. The feeling state can be viewed as the consequence of motivated behavior. We are happy and contented when motivated goals are reached; when they are thwarted, we are downcast or angry. Or, feelings can be described themselves as motives or concomitant with them: I hate someone; I strike out and hurt him; I feel guilty and attempt restitution. This sequence of motives/feelings and actions illustrates the difficulty in attempting sharp distinction. Affects clearly motivate behavior. We work to gain pleasure and avoid pain, to be joyful, to avert shame, to feel competent. Affects also accompany and guide the perception of success and failure in goal-directed strivings.

In a far-reaching theoretical analysis, Tomkins (1962; 1963) proposed that affects may be primary motives. In his view, the biological drives have motivational strength only to the extent that they are *amplified* by the emotions. Hunger leads one to search for food, but if there were a prospect of severe shortage, the resulting anxiety would make the search frantic. In this sense, amplification occurs; we are more responsive to the anxiety than to the bodily deprivation. At birth, the child has inherent positive and negative affects: joy or excitement, fear and pain. Sudden sounds or discomforts cue the negative affects, satisfactions or stimulation, the positive. With development, the child learns and seeks conditions for positive, and avoids those which produce negative affects. According to Tomkins, affect is communicated through facial expressions, not only to others but as well to oneself. The full development of this provocative and important theory and the supporting evidence should be studied in Tomkins' original writings.

Emotions include both conscious experience and bodily changes. Along with the experienced tension and dread, the anxiety state includes accelerated pulse and respiration, flushing and gastric reactions, muscle tension and changes in metabolic and endocrine functions. These, in turn, reflect a complex set of neurophysiological mechanisms, involving midbrain structures, the autonomic nervous system and hormonal regulation. Some have emphasized the somatic systems and their measurable symptoms, and minimized the phenomenological experience. In a commonly held physiological theory of emotion, a single dimension of arousal or activation, varying in intensity, is proposed as the central issue in the understanding of emotional behavior (Duffy, 1962; Malmo, 1959; among others). Whether consciously experienced emotion is prior to physiological change or dependent upon it has been the focus of long controversy, dating from James' proposal in 1884 (the James-Lange theory) that stimulating circumstances evoke physiological responses, which we then perceive and experience as conscious emotions. This view was, it was thought, effectively demolished by the classic researches of Cannon and Bard, but it has returned in the theory of Schacter and Singer (1962). The issues are many and complex. For our purposes, it is sufficient only to realize that both experience and physiological states coexist, probably related in different ways, dependent on different feedback systems. Surely, we recognize affective states in ourselves and others by noting and measuring physiological change (e.g., as in lie detection). It is also true that the range and variety of experienced emotions is not matched by measures of psychophysiologists, though patterns of physiological response give greater promise of showing personologically distinct emotional states. Finally, we should also note that intense and continuing emotions can lead to irreversible physiological changes, which have been called the psychosomatic diseases.

THE STRUCTURAL PERSPECTIVE: EGO, SELF, CONSCIENCE, AND VALUES

What best distinguishes man from lower animals, and the mature person from the newborn child, lies in what might be termed the "central structures" of personality, which guide and direct behavior. These mediate between inner impulse and action, on the one hand, and between external stimulation and action, on the other. They provide both the *capacities* to choose among alternatives (the executive functions of the ego) and the *basis* on which to do so (self and conscience). The behavior of the child is immediate, reactive, oriented mainly to need gratification, diffuse and limited in diversity; that of the adult controlled, organized, capable of deferring gratification, oriented to long-term goals and values, guided by moral strictures and values, planful and self-regulated. The movement from one state to the other reflects the development of the ego and its related structures.

The concept of the *ego* includes two related but distinguishable aspects. On the one hand, there are those capacities or functions which underlie *regulated behavior*. On the other hand, there is the experienced *self*, the individual's identity, values, self-concepts, aspirations, and the like which form the core of personality. These develop together and are mutually dependent. For example, the identity of the person depends on a sense of where he has come from (the past represented in memory), who he is in the present, and where he is going (his ideals and expectations). For such identity to exist, one must suppose a capacity for time-binding, an ability to causally relate past, present, and future. If experience existed only in the present moment, with no memory and no fantasy, there could be no personal identity. Similarly, if there were no concept of self, then there would be no base from which temporally distant events could be related. The statement "I had better not go to the movies tonight, because there is an examination tomorrow, and if I fail it, I may not be able to go to graduate school," simultaneously tells us that the person has the capacity for time-binding and something about the content of his self-concept. These two facets of the ego concept have sometimes been distinguished as ego and self or as ego-executive-functions and ego-identity. The terms used are less important than an appreciation of two types of issues involved in the broad concept of ego, both of which are critical to the understanding of personality functioning, disorder, and change. I will use the terms "ego" and "self," though occasionally using the term "ego" to incorporate both aspects as in the phrase "ego development."

In the classic Freudian view, the ego was conceived as growing out of the inevitable conflicts in infancy between the biological drives (the Id) and the constraints of reality. Drives press for immediate discharge; if not immediately satisfied, pain results. In this phase, behavior is dominated entirely by the pleasure-pain principle. Similarly, the infant is *stimulus-bound*. He is immediately responsive to stimulation, which he can neither anticipate nor control. This passive and helpless condition is intolerable. The beginning of ego control is seen in the barriers to stimulation ("Reizschutz" in Freud's term) which block the painful overload of stimulation. This is the prototype of the later ego-defense mechanisms: the protective sleep of the infant evolves into the capacity for denial, avoidance, projection, and, with the development of rational thought, rationalization and intellectualization.

Even with the most nurturant mother, needs can never be satisfied immediately. Frustration is inevitable. To manage such frustration, the ego develops. The basic requirement is for delay between drive arousal and discharge into action. As delay of gratification becomes possible, there can be interposed fantasy, directed attention, and problem-solving thought, in brief the ego. With the development of perception, memory, and the cognitive apparatus, the infant can await satisfaction, seek appropriate goal objects, avoid those things found painful in the past, and begin to test possible consequences of present actions (reality-testing). With the growing knowledge of what rewards and what punishes, behavior moves from domination of the *pleasure principle* to control by the *reality principle*. Events are now seen by the child as they are, not as it would wish them. Acts which had harmful consequences are avoided. The conditions for satisfying needs are learned.

Recent ego psychologists within the Freudian tradition have called attention to the limitations of a conflict-based concept of ego development. For one thing, as we have already noted, there are needs for stimulation, exploration, and effectance as early and as basic as those for food and physical comfort. Furthermore, there are the autonomously developing apparatuses of perception, memory, motility, and cognitive functioning in general, which develop in the maturation of the nervous system and the interplay of the child with his environment. As Heinz Hartmann (1939) noted, the ego is not merely the result of drive-reality conflict, it results too from the evolution of innate or autonomous functions. They are part of the adaptive potential of the person from birth, and in later development are, in Hartmann's term, the basis of the "ego apparatus of primary autonomy." These aspects of the ego function develop, in the main, independent of conflict as the "conflict-free sphere of the ego." These views have broadened the concept of the ego to focus on its adaptive as well as defensive properties; in terms of our earlier discussion, its role in abundancy as well as deficiency motivation. The *mechanisms of ego defense,* which arise in development to avert anxiety and protect the integrity of ego functioning and the self-concept, will be discussed in the context of the adaptational perspective. In that context, coping as well as defensive functions of the ego can be considered together to discover how similar processes can serve growth as well as security needs.

Ego strength describes the effectiveness with which ego functions are carried out, how well the personality is governed. Included in the concept are such qualities as the capacity to judge external events objectively, to have an undistorted view of oneself, to concentrate and direct attention willfully, to inhibit irrelevant thoughts and feelings and to think logically, to make and retain resolves, to have a long-time perspective, to evaluate alternatives and resolve conflicts, to be self-reliant and to choose among social demands, resisting those contrary to fundamental values, to take responsibility for one's actions, and to work toward goals. Implied is a sturdy sense of personal identity. In general, the ego-strong personality is self-governed (characterized by self-control and self-determination), rather than being dominated by inner drives or environmental pressures, whether physical or social. Phrased another way, the strong-weak ego concept parallels Rotter's (1966) concept of "expectation of inner control" versus "expectation of outer control," which was developed within a social learning context.

In actuality, the functional ego strength of a person has to be assessed in terms of the strength of momentary or continuing drives and/or external coercions. Severely deprived needs strain the resources for delaying their gratification. Powerful needs press more urgently for discharge and can determine or disorganize behavior even where ego strength is sufficient to modulate more moderate needs. So too, external situations can be more or less coercive. The weak ego succumbs to temptation, the strong ego resists. But there are all grades of temptation. I may be able to forego a movie . . . but a date with Jane Fonda? Obviously, the outcome to be predicted would depend on the interplay between the capacities of the person for ego control and the strength of the impinging forces. Finally, we should note that ego strength depends on the physical state of the person. When drugged, fatigued, or sick, the person is less capable of governing his own behavior.

The concept of ego strength emphasizes the self-regulatory, rational, and controlled aspects of human behavior which, certainly compared to their opposites, index effective personality functioning. However, rich and fulfilling human experiences sometimes depend on the relaxation of ego controls, intentional release from reality-appropriate thinking, even loss of the sense of self. Artistic creation, play, love, creative fantasy, and religious and spiritual experiences are illustrative. These are among the most important and creative of human accomplishments. But they cannot be encompassed within a simple notion of ego strength. Kris (1950) described such experiences as depending on "regression in the service of the ego." This phrasing is intended to distinguish between the inability to be rational, as occurs in severe psychopathology, and the willing renunciation of rational thought in order to explore new realms of experience. It is ego-strong to be able to inhibit day dreaming, but only if the task at hand requires focussed, reality-attentive concentration. It requires as much or more strength to be able to relinquish reality, relax into day dreaming, and even use the free flow of consciousness to problem-solving ends (J. L. Singer, 1975). Creative people, whether in the arts or sciences, describe the use of subrational thought as a central part of the creative process. What distinguishes the creative from the psychotic, of course, is the capacity to move back to reality-appropriate thinking as necessary. To be able to be both arational and rational, it could be said, indicates the highest order of personality functioning and ego strength. By contrast, both the undercontrolled-disorganized and the overcontrolled-overorganized person, fearful of relaxing his grip on the real and manageable, represent lower levels of ego strength.

The *self* is the experienced core of the personality. It consists of one's "assumptions about, judgments of, and feelings toward oneself as a person—a part of his subjective, experiential life" (Keen, 1970, p. 13). It includes those experiences which Allport (1955) called *propriate,* which have a special, personal relevance. Or, in James' (1895) famous dictum, the self is "all that a person is tempted to call *me* or *mine*." In many personality research studies, psychologists have investigated the *self-concept* (the "assumptions-about" aspect) and *self-esteem* (the "judgments of, and feelings toward" aspect) (e.g., Wylie, 1974). The self-concept ("identity" is a popular alternate term) describes the qualities by which we know ourselves and distinguish ourselves from others. It is the answer to the question "What am I?" As seen by the outsider, the person's self-conceptualization may or may not concur with observable behaviors, and this may be important to our evaluation of him. But the concept of the self must be defined from the vantage of the person himself, as he experiences himself. So too, his self-esteem reflects his appraisal of himself ("I am great" or "I am worthless"). It is true, of course, that self-esteem as well as self-concepts may reflect the perception and acceptance of the views of others. As George Herbert Mead (1934) suggested long ago, the self arises out of transactions with significant others and consists of the internalized integration of the views of us held by others. From the standpoint of clinical assessment and intervention, we are often confronted with disparities between the person's self-definitions and our view of him, the beautiful woman who sees herself as ugly, the intelligent man who believes himself stupid. Neither a mirror nor an IQ report will keep them from acting in accord with their self-concept rather than their "objective" characteristics. Exploring and unravelling such discrepancies and contributing to the reconception of self-concepts, is an essential part of the clinical process.

We not only have an experience of *what* we are, but also an experience *that* we are, what Erikson called a "sense of identity" (1959; 1968). From the vantage point of an existential psychology, Keen (1970) distinguishes the "what I am" experiences as the *self-as-object* and the "that I am" as the *self-as-subject*. The self-as-object has qualities like other objects; it is defined by "essences." But the self-as-subject is a pure existential experience. "Rather than being experienced as a fixed entity, the 'I' is experienced as a dynamic, open-ended activity without the stability of me-as-object, e.g., without an essence. The 'I' is pure experience, noteworthy because it *is*, not because it is *such and such*" (p. 14). Loss of the "I" experience, Keen proposes along with Laing and other existential psychiatrists, is the focus of psychotic disorganization. The schizophrenic, in this view, not only has deviant characteristics, and sees himself deviantly (self-as-object) but he also has a basic existential problem, a massive disturbance in the sense "*that* I am." The self-as-subject serves as a center for experiencing and understanding the world, the behavior of others, and underlies the sense of control or power to act upon the world, rather than submitting passively to it. From other contexts, concepts of "alienation," "anomie," and "identity crises" carry similar meanings.

An important part of the self-system is what Rogers (1942) termed the "ideal self" and psychoanalysts call the "ego-ideal." We not only see ourselves as having qualities and existence, but we have a vision of a better self to which we aspire. Whether one is contented or distressed can depend less on present accomplishments than on their valuation in terms of an ideal self. To be second best in the world, as the wise William James noted, may be a great frustration for the man whose heart is set on being world champion, though a great satisfaction to the rest of us.

The self, as the ego, emerges in the development of the child. Milestones involve the characteristic negativism of the two and a half year old. Then, as later, an independent self is asserted through a resounding "NO!" The development of language and the importance attaching to one's own name mark other stages. The child, it is interesting to note, first refers to himself as others do; he describes himself as "he" or "Johnny" and only later as "I." However, full identity does not emerge until the adolescent years, and is dependent on resolving earlier crises and establishing a base of emotional attitudes, as we shall discuss in terms of Erikson's (1963) concept of psychosocial development.

The third among the central structures of personality is the conscience, the set of moral values which define "what I ought to be or do," what is morally right and wrong. In his classic tripartite view of personality, Freud distinguished the *id*, the unconscious reservoir of instinctual needs, the *ego*, the largely conscious executive, and the *superego*, the partly unconscious, partly conscious, internalized representation of societal constraints and prohibitions. The ego moderates between the necessary conflicts of the amoral drives and the socially derived prohibitions; anxiety and guilt are the painful prices of ineffectual resolutions. Freud saw the superego as the last of the three institutions to evolve, and viewed the process as involving internalization of the proscriptions of the both loved and feared parents through identification. Where prior to the formation of the superego the child was restrained by fear of punishment from without, following it, the restraints are within his own character structure.

No organized society can exist without the internalization of social constraints and the *self-suppression* of individual needs; Freud was correct in seeing that civilization is built on the denial of basic drives (Freud, 1930). But in opposing the social and individual, the Freudian thesis also implies the profound concept that attaining individual well-being and expression may necessarily involve conflict with social institutions. The ancient injunction "To thine own self be true" has become a keystone in the philosophy underlying a concept of positive mental health.

As a general schema, the Freudian view calls proper attention to the major forces within the personality and their potential for conflict, and it explicates an important (if not exclusive) principle of moral development. Moreover, it conceptualizes the strains between the needs of the person and societal pressures. However, the three-way split better characterizes the experience of the neurotic than that of the well-integrated and well-functioning person. The latter does not feel his drives or moral precepts to be "ego-alien" and threatening, but rather acceptable (i.e., ego-syntonic) to his conscious purposes and self-concept. The term "conscience" is preferred as an overall concept which would include both the coercive, alien forces of the superego and the self-chosen values by which we guide our lives. Except for definitional niceties, there are no clear boundaries between self, ideal self, and conscience and, when the person is harmoniously functioning, no important phenomenological distinctions. But we are all familiar with the intense problems and painful affects which arise when "what *I* ought to be" and "what *they* want me to be," come into conflict. This is particularly true when the battleground is within the personality.

Modern thinking and research on moral development has revealed some of the detailed ways in which it parallels and is part of the ego development moving through stages as cognitive processes mature and experience accrues (e.g., Kohlberg, 1969).

THE DEVELOPMENTAL PERSPECTIVE

That the human organism moves from the relatively simple structures, needs, affects, and behaviors of childhood to the complexities of adulthood is among the most evident and basic facts of psychology, yet how and why development occurs is vigorously argued. Langer (1969) suggested that competing theories can be grouped in three major classes:

1. "Mechanical Mirror" Views. These emphasize the impact of environmental events on a plastic but passive organism, which initially has few if any built-in behaviors or growth principles. Behavior is modified through stimulation and reinforcement, acting through learning principles which are basically the same in animals and man and throughout human life.

2. "Organic Lamp" Views. Here emphasis is on active, self-constructive human acts. Concern is with the processes underlying psychological acts, which move development through sequential stages, each of which emerges from and is dependent on earlier stages. The most prominent theorists are Piaget (e.g., 1952) and Werner (1948).

3. Psychoanalytic Theory. Psychoanalysis, particularly in its classic form, emphasized the instinctual drives and their development, the universality of conflict and the mechanisms, healthy and pathological, for its resolution, and the consequent evolution of structures for guiding behavior and managing conflict. In modern "ego psychology" there is relatively more concern with conflict-free functions, coping and cognitive processes and, similar to organic lamp views, a concern with self-constructive acts and stage sequences (e.g., Erikson, 1963; R. W. White, 1963a; Loevinger, 1969).

The clinical student should be well grounded in the developmental concepts of each orientation. In this brief section, I will call attention to some of the issues which seem of importance to me. These are drawn mainly from the convergence of "organic lamp" and psychoanalytic theories. Specific learnings are of course important, but understanding development requires principles emphasizing organismic properties rather than environmental learning influences per se. Moreover, development must be seen in terms of the necessary movement from lower to higher stages of function.

Overall, development moves from primitive, global, functionally isolated action of simple structures to the more differentiated, centralized and integrative organization of the adult, as expressed in Werner's (1948) *orthogenetic principle.** In this view, development has two faces: the *differentiation* and specialization of functions and structures, and the *integration* of the differentiated parts into larger and more organized wholes. Early in the differentiation process, separate functions are either fused (syncretic), have no functional relation to each other (segregated), and are rigidly fixed or unstable (rigidity/lability). In development, the parts become more specialized, articulated, and internally integrated.

Witkin and his colleagues (1954, 1962), in an extensive body of research, have described the coordinate changes in perception, cognition, and personal and social behavior which characterize psychological differentiation. The younger child is more "field dependent" than "field independent." His percepts are more determined by external stimuli than by inner, self-determined cues. He can less well segregate related intellectual themes, as in problem-solving. As a person, his "sense of separate identity" is less developed, and he looks to others for deciding the direction of his behavior. These and related qualities describe the degree of differentiation, which generally increases with age, though differing among children and adults at any age.

With differentiation, there is opportunity and need for integration, bringing the parts into proper relation with each other. However, more than coordination is involved. Werner has called attention to *hierarchic integration* as the second major aspect of development. Such integration involves the subordination of less developed and more primitive systems in hierarchies in which more developed systems are in more central positions. In this fashion, developmentally lower-order systems are still present, though subordinated and normally controlled by more evolved systems. At any life stage, we can function at one or another developmental level; lower functions can be used, for example, if more advanced ones are not available. Thus, we can count on our fingers if more conceptual means of calculation are not available. The child at the "sensorimotor developmental stage," as Piaget terms it, can only count on his fingers. Similarly, those who have attained the "abstract attitude" can conceptualize the world of objects in terms of either general principles or in terms of immediate, concrete attributes; those limited to the "concrete attitude," as children or brain-damaged adults, can only do the latter (K. Goldstein, 1939). Under grave stress, injury to the nervous system, or in psychopathological conditions, there is regression toward more primitive, dedifferentiated, and less centrally integrated behaviors. Less enduring and less ex-

* Orthogenesis was originally used in biology to describe the view that tissues tend to evolve under the control of internal conditions along a patterned course. The prefix has been adopted in terms characterizing growth toward a desired end. Thus, orthopsychiatry is concerned with early preventative interventions aimed at averting later emotional problems and, thus, facilitating healthy psychological growth. Orthodonture, as a branch of dentistry, involves guiding teeth toward a straighter, prettier, and healthier future.

tensive regression occurs in drugged, fatigued, and intense emotional states. The concept of regression, as the obverse of developmental progression, is central to the understanding of disturbed behavior in both the "organic lamp" and psychoanalytic theories, though in importantly different forms.

Development, though continuous, is not a simple linear process involving quantitative changes but rather moves through discrete qualitative stages. Moreover, there are critical periods during which particular events affect growth in ways not possible at earlier and later moments. Vivid illustration of the importance of critical periods is best seen in the studies of imprinting in birds by ethologically oriented students of animal behavior (e.g., Hess, 1964). Imprinting involves the development of deep attachment to an object by relatively brief experience. In experimental studies, for example, a duckling at the critical age of about fourteen hours if exposed to a wooden decoy of a grown mallard for as little as ten minutes will be imprinted on it permanently, follow it about as it would its mother even after the duckling is brought into contact with live and more appropriate objects. After a couple of days, imprinting is not possible. Similarly, it has been found that baby dogs who have no contact with other dogs during their critical period are thereafter isolated animals unable to relate naturally to other dogs. In human development, there is no simple imprinting, and critical periods are less sharply defined. In physiological as well as psychological growth there are times of heightened activity of particular biological systems during which an illness, for example, can have unusually severe consequences.

The concept of stage rather than linear development, where progression depends on the resolution and incorporation of lower-level tasks in successive stages, is shared by diverse developmental theories; the essential concept exists, for example, in Piaget's far-reaching theory of development, which centers on cognitive growth, and in Freud's basic developmental theory, focussed on the evolution of the sexual drive, which viewed later character development and neurosis in terms of the satisfactions and frustrations during the oral, anal, and genital stages of libidinal development. Though manifestly different, these views share emphasis on step-wise, qualitative stages in growth.

Erikson's (1963; 1959) view of psychosocial development, or ego epigenesis, brings together a number of important ideas for the understanding of personality growth. Though building on Freudian psychosexual stages, Erikson brings into conjunction with them ego development, i.e., the role of sensorimotor and cognitive capacities, and interpersonal interactions. In this fashion, concepts of dynamic motivation, ego functioning and social behavior converge in a unitary schema of personality development. At each stage, the maturing person faces new and important encounters with his world (developmental tasks) in which his growing abilities are tested. The resolution of each task provides a base for further growth; unsolved developmental crises block further development and/or leave neurotic residuals in the later character structure. Thus, for example, the first stage, during nursing in infancy, lays the base for the individual's basic sense of trust or distrust; the conflicts over retention and elimination, in the second stage, determine whether the individual develops a sense of autonomy or of shame and doubt; and so on until the last stage of adult life where the issue is integrity versus despair and disgust. At this point the question is whether the person can fully and responsibly accept himself and others or whether he is depressed and bitter over his own life and the values of others. Table 3.2 represents a schematic outline of Erikson's eight stages of epigenesis.

TABLE 3.2

Erikson's Eight Stages of Epigenesis *

LIFE STAGE	PSYCHOSOCIAL CRISES	SIGNIFICANT RELATIONS	PSYCHOSOCIAL MODALITIES AND TASKS	PSYCHOSEXUAL STAGES (FREUDIAN)
1. Infancy	Trust vs. mistrust	Maternal person	To get; to give in return	Oral-respiratory, sensory-kinaesthetic (incorporative modes)
2. Early Childhood	Autonomy vs. shame and doubt	Parental persons	To hold (on); to let (go)	Anal-urethral, muscular (retentive-eliminative)
3. Play Age	Initiative vs. guilt	Basic family	To make (go after); to "make like" (play)	Infantile-genital, locomotor (intrusive, inclusive)
4. School age	Industry vs. inferiority	Neighborhood, school	To make (complete) things; to make things together	Latency
5. Adolescence	Identity vs. identity diffusion	Peer groups and outgroups; models of leadership	To be oneself (or not to be); to share being oneself	Puberty
6. Young Adult	Intimacy vs. isolation	Partners in friendship, sex, competition, cooperation	To lose and find oneself in another	Genitality
7. Adulthood	Generativity vs. self-absorption	Divided labor and shared household	To make be; to take care of	
8. Mature age	Integrity vs. despair	"Mankind," "my kind"	To be, through having been; to face not being	

* Adapted from Erikson, E. H. *Identity and the life cycle.* New York: International Universities Press, 1959, p. 166. Reprinted by permission.

As development progresses, so can it *regress* and along the same conceptual dimensions. The concept of regression is central in developmental theories, particularly in the interpretation of disturbed behavior and pathological states. Regression can occur in two related senses: a primitivization of the *form* (structure, organization) of psychological activity or a regression in the *content* of behavior, returning to actual, earlier behaviors. Kurt Lewin suggested that the term "retrogression" be used to describe the behavior of a person who copes with a presently unsatisfying situation by using behaviors found more satisfying at earlier life stages, and that the term "regression" itself be reserved for simpler and less mature forms of behavior. In a general way, "organic lamp" theorists have emphasized the regression in form and psychoanalytic thinkers have emphasized the regression in content, though attentive to the formal qualities as well. It is probably true that regression in both modes occurs and is related. Thus, the frightened child can begin again to bed-wet or dig out a long-forgotten "security blanket" and/or manifest more childish (i.e., dedifferentiated, diffuse, syncretic, etc.) modes of behavior. The regressed schizophrenic shows more primitive modes of thought—e.g., thinking in overinclusive terms, confabulating, or losing abstract language referents—or very literally take on fetal positions or reenact the memories of a happier, lost childhood. Even as we emphasize regression in form, it must be realized that the adult, albeit senile, schizophrenic, or brain-damaged, cannot again be a child even though he acts childishly.

In terms of the orthogenetic principle, regression is marked by increased dedifferentiation and disintegration of higher organization of the psychological system. Werner follows the Jacksonian principle that the most highly evolved functions dissolve first in the backward course of development (J. H. Jackson, 1931). Thus, in the language disturbance (aphasia) which follows brain injury connective and referential words are lost, though nouns referable to concrete objects remain. The relation of developmental progression and regression can be illustrated by reference to a small part of the extensive research of Werner and his coworkers. The young child has a diffuse perception of himself and the boundaries between himself and the world outside. Thus, if asked to indicate the size of his head with eyes closed a five-year-old will overestimate (Wapner and Werner, 1965). With increased differentiation, the estimate greatly decreases. Wapner (1964) then tested the hypotheses that in arrested development and in regression, there should be overestimation of head size. Such an outcome occurred in a group of retarded children compared to age equals, in schizophrenics compared to normals, and in aged people and in adults given LSD, a drug viewed as regression-producing. The convergence of findings from these various groups is evidence for the continuity in process, development, and regression.

The concept of *fixation* parallels that of regression, and is important in the psychoanalytic view. Development through the psychosexual stages may not proceed uniformly and part of the energy of the sexual drive (libido), Freud suggested, can remain fixed at earlier levels related to earlier drive aims or objects. In consequence, if at a later point in development there is severe frustration, there will then be regression to the point of fixation. The importance of the concept of fixation is that it describes a mechanism that determines the extent of regression by predicting the level at which it will stabilize. Fixation itself can be a consequence of unresolved conflicts at the lower developmental stage, of overgratification, or of overfrustration or trauma. Thus, if a woman had been excessively rewarded for "pretty-little-girl" behaviors in childhood, she may continue on to apparently adult heterosexual adjustment in marriage, but at the time of marital crises or the birth of a baby, which tests her ability to truly take on adult responsibilities, she may revert to the childlike pattern. Fixation may be so intense and complete that the person does not advance beyond the fixated stage, but the more usual pattern involves partial arrest of the sort just described. The twin concepts of fixation and regression are of basic importance in the Freudian theory of psychopathology. It is clear too that although developed in the context of libido theory, the essential notions are applicable to any need system or behavior. Indeed, the concept of fixation can be readily recast in learning theory terms.

The mechanisms of fixation and regression are revealed in much more trivial ways than usually concern clinicians, as illustrated in the story of the, say, Albanian in New York. With no knowledge of English, the poor man went hungry until he met a compatriot who volunteered to teach him a few necessary words, "Cheese sandwich and coffee." With this knowledge he could get himself fed, but after some weeks found the diet boring. Fortunately, he again met his fellow countryman, who this time taught him "Bacon and eggs, salad, and milk." The first time he tried his new phrase the clerk asked, "How do you want them? Fried over, sunnyside up, scrambled? Salad with French, Russian, or Roquefort dressing?" To which the Albanian sadly replied, "Cheese sandwich and coffee."

Knowledge of developmental theory and findings is of particular importance to clinical psychology for at least three different reasons:

1. Understanding of psychological growth and deviations of the developmental process are basic to theories of personality, psychopathology, and the conception of clinical intervention. How the person came to be, the evolution of his personality problems, and what one can do to alter and improve his present state require a developmental perspective.

2. Less broadly, clinical intervention techniques must be geared to the developmental level of the patient. Obviously, one would not talk to a five-year-old in the vocabulary of a PhD, but it may be wise not to use language at all to explore the child's experiences and concerns. Child therapists, as we will discuss later, often use play techniques. Similarly, over the entire developmental range, knowledge of the developmentally related modes of thought and behavior, growth crises, and experiences furnish the base for clinical transactions. With the adolescent, the issue may be personal identity and commitment to life goals, with the postretirement adult, disengagement from life interests.

3. Particularly as psychologists become more concerned with prevention rather than just with treatment the developmental orientation and increased knowledge of conditions which may facilitate or block growth become centrally important. Let a single illustration suffice. It now seems clear that even in the earliest days of life an infant needs, along with satisfaction of more obvious biological needs, a level of "stimulus nutriment" (Rapaport, 1958; Piaget, 1952). Deprivation can lead to long-term behavioral and neurological deficits. An enriched environment, contrariwise, leads to changes in brain chemistry and learning (Diamond et al., 1966). If animals are deprived of stimulation, they are less well able to learn, they are more emotional, they show deficits of social adaptation, activity, and curiosity (e.g., Beach and Jaynes, 1954; Newton and Levine, 1968). Young rats handled for even a few minutes a day, indeed, even roughly, learn far better in adult life than unhandled litter-mates. Although some of the specific evi-

dence has been argued, overall it seems clear that human infants deprived of stimulation by early caretakers can be retarded in development, and may later be unable to form human relationships and manifest severe apathy and depression (Bowlby, 1952; Goldfarb, 1955, among others). A broad-scaled effort to reduce human misery might well seek ways of providing optimal stimulation and mothering for infants in danger of deprivation.

THE ADAPTATIONAL PERSPECTIVE

The history of evolution, in its broad sweep, can be told in terms of the disappearance, survival, or modification of species as they cope successfully or unsuccessfully with adaptational demands. Similarly, in the history of the individual personality growth involves changes in functions and structures as individuals face successive crises and stress. From this vantage point, personality malfunctioning and mental illness can be viewed as the emergent of a history of excessive stress and maladaptive solutions. Knowledge of the conditions that produce stress, its consequences, the resources people develop for coping and defense are essential to the understanding of personality functioning and distortion.

A state of *stress* exists when unusual or excessive demands threaten a person's well-being or integrity. Extraordinary efforts are needed to master the situation and there is the danger that coping capacities will be overwhelmed with the consequence of disturbed functioning, pain or anxiety, illness or even death. Stress is defined neither by the conditions acting on the person (the stressor), nor by the state of the person (coping resources, ego strength, etc.), nor by his reactions (stress responses), but rather by the interplay of the three. It is obvious that one man's stress is another's play. The well-conditioned athlete can take in stride a five-mile run which is stressful to a sedentary academic. The forthcoming examination is stressful to the ill-prepared but ambitious student; of no great moment to either the well-prepared or the unconcerned student. In the psychological realm, it is clear that the meaning of the stressor and its relevance to the needs and self-concept of the person determine its impact. Students of stress psychology have called attention to the importance of acts of *cognitive appraisal* which determine threat-value (e.g., Lazarus, 1966).

Stress can originate in physiological, psychological, and social conditions and threaten the integrity of the body, the personality, or the social system. To the extent that the threat can disturb psychological well-being and psychological functioning, it is of concern to us, regardless of its origin and effects in other systems. Thus, a major economic depression obviously puts great strain on economic, political, and social systems, but it affects individual human life as well. Not only are people left hungry and cold, but they can be stripped of their pride as self-sufficient workers and providers for their families. Not surprisingly, unemployed workers during economic crises are found to become depressed and apathetic. In more subtle ways, social institutions produce psychological stress. The university which emphasizes achievement and evaluation—perhaps at the expense of learning and personal growth—keeps students in a more intense stress state than does a more relaxed setting.

On the biological side, we should note that many of the mechanisms which have evolved to manage physiological stress are as much responsive to psychological threats. Thus, following infection, injury, physical exertion, and other physiological stressors there is a characteristic sequence of stress responses, importantly involving the activation of the pituitary-adrenal hormonal system. But adrenal activation occurs as well in response to anxiety and other psychological conditions which involve no direct insult to the body, and indexes psychological stress as well as biological. The linkage between systems and some of the subtleties of relationship are illustrated in a study of the adrenocortical output of crew members during races. It was found that in intercollegiate racing levels were elevated in all crew members, but much more so for the coxswain than for the oarsmen (Hill et al., 1956). The oarsmen were clearly more physically stressed, but the coxswain had the "executive" responsibilities and hence the greater psychological stress.

In laboratory, field, and clinical studies, students of psychological stress have investigated the effects of numerous stressors. Some general classes of stressful situations can be distinguished (Korchin, 1965):

1. Uncertainty and Understimulation. Particularly if the person is highly motivated or anxious, ambiguous and vague situations are a powerful source of stress. Coming into a new and unknown situation, whether or not danger is present, has been found to be disturbing to animals as well as men. At the extreme, a complete lack of stimulation, as in studies of sensory deprivation, can lead to gross emotional and behavioral disorganization. That we become disturbed, even when in womb-like comfort, points up the basic fact that optimal functioning and comfort depend on constant input, neither too much or too little.

2. Information Overload. Flooding an organism with many intense, competing, and demanding stimuli is stressful. However large our capacities to process information and to act discriminatively, we are still limited. Conditions of distraction, time pressure, excessive stimulation, or multiple tasks are all illustrations of information overload. Recall that Freudians view the prototypic trauma as the overwhelming flood of excitation which the infant can neither avoid or master.

3. Danger. Danger, existing or anticipated, either to physical well-being or the satisfaction of central needs is an obvious source of threat.

4. Ego-control Failure. An important function of the ego system is the control of primitive impulses. Threat to the capacity for control, as for example in situations of temptation or drive arousal, is therefore stressful. Situations in which the individual is forced into passivity, powerlessness, or impotence, and where he has no sense of control over his fate is similarly distressing.

5. Ego-mastery Failure. "Control" suggests holding the line; "mastery" intends moving forward. In a view of personality which emphasizes the exercise of competence (R. W. White, 1959) or the movement toward self-actualization (K. Goldstein, 1939; Maslow, 1962) it is worth taking separate note of mastery, in addition to control, failure. Thus, being blocked from mastering new goals, developing and exercising new talents, even without threat to present control or well-being, can be an important source of stress.

6. Self-esteem Danger. Though related, the importance of self-esteem suggests separate emphasis for situations which lower a person's view of himself. In experimental studies of stress, there are often contrived failures in seemingly important tests.

7. "Other" Esteem Danger. A parallel source of stress is threat of losing the affection and esteem of others, losing status or love, being ridiculed, being rejected, or thought unworthy. The love and esteem of others may of course be the

source of one's self-esteem, but the situations of self-esteem threats and other-esteem threats are manifestly different.

In Table 3.3 the major factors in the analysis of stress are sketched. These include:

1. The *stressor,* which in general can be distinguished as to its origin (e.g., physiological, psychological, or social), type (e.g., overload, underload, fear-arousing, etc.), intensity (judged from its expectable effects on people in general), and duration.

2. The act of *cognitive appraisal,* by which the extent of personal threat is judged. Such appraisal is often—but need not always be—consciously made.

3. The factors within the *personality* which determine the importance of the stressor and those which determine the sensitivity or tolerance of the person to

TABLE 3.3

A Schematic Analysis of the Stress State

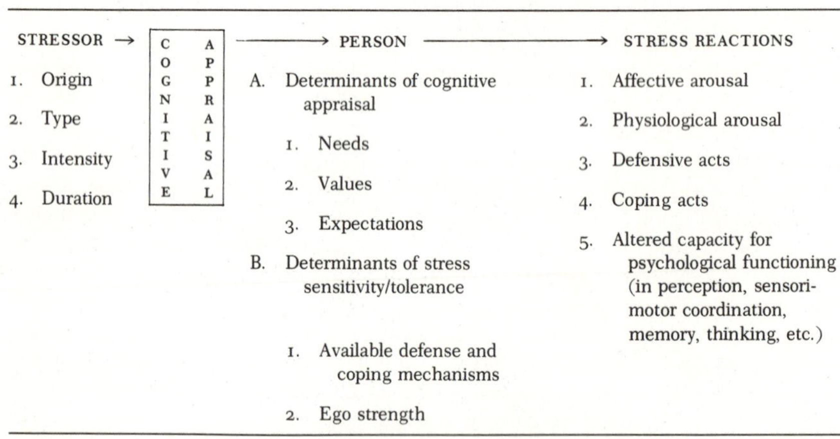

STRESSOR →	COGNITIVE APPRAISAL	→ PERSON →	STRESS REACTIONS
1. Origin 2. Type 3. Intensity 4. Duration		A. Determinants of cognitive appraisal 1. Needs 2. Values 3. Expectations B. Determinants of stress sensitivity/tolerance 1. Available defense and coping mechanisms 2. Ego strength	1. Affective arousal 2. Physiological arousal 3. Defensive acts 4. Coping acts 5. Altered capacity for psychological functioning (in perception, sensorimotor coordination, memory, thinking, etc.)

stress in general. The cognitive appraisal depends on the needs which are currently active, the personal values to which the stress is related, and the person's expectations as to the impact of the situation and its probable outcome, based in fair measure on his history of past encounters with comparable situations. The second realm of personality factors consists of those qualities which determine the person's stress tolerance in general, but are not specific to the appraisal of the present threat. This includes ego strength, as earlier discussed, and the repertory of defensive and coping mechanisms.

4. The range of *stress reactions* includes those defensive and/or coping maneuvers by which the threat is modulated and efforts made for mastery and need satisfaction. Depending on the effectiveness of these mechanisms, more or less negative affect is then aroused. Correspondingly, there are changes in the physiological state, particularly in the activation of the pituitary-adrenal system, which Selye (1956) used as the sine qua non of stress response, and in the autonomic responses which have provided the major indices of stress response to psychophysiologists. Where stress effects are not modulated or blocked, deficit in the capacity for organized psychological functioning is typically found over a wide range. There is less good sensorimotor coordination, more diffuse perception,

poorer memory, and learning, less effective problem-solving, etc.; in general, a primitivization or regression of functions, as described in Werner's orthogenetic principles. In less intense states, stress-induced changes can be adaptive, as in the more focused attention found at lower levels of anxiety.

The mechanisms of defense and coping figure prominently in the understanding of personality adaptation, neurosis, and psychotherapy. The concepts of *ego defense* mechanisms were first described in the writings of Sigmund Freud (e.g., 1926) and Anna Freud (1936), and developed by their followers in psychoanalysis. They include repression, isolation, reaction formation, projection, introjection, rationalization, regression, and the other particular ways in which we avert the painful anxiety and threat of personality disintegration attendant upon conflict, stress, drive arousal or frustration, and other dangers. They protect self-esteem and provide some satisfaction for active needs, albeit indirect and incomplete. They allow the person to continue functioning, though typically in more limited and inflexible ways. In crystallized forms, the defenses are the symptoms of psychopathology; thus, repression is associated with hysteria, projection with paranoia. Though adaptive in the sense of averting greater calamity, the defenses are related to security needs and the more pathological aspects of behavior.

The parallel concept of *coping* calls attention to growth-related and more effective functioning. Not only do we avert and avoid danger (defense) but we confront and master it (coping). Both defensive and coping mechanisms arise in ego development, and may be conceptualized as alternate uses of the same ego functions (Haan, 1963; Kroeber, 1963). Thus, the capacity for selective attention, required for organized cognition, can subserve *concentration* on the problem in hand (coping) or *denial* of its importance or relevance (defense). The discrimination between objects and their contexts underlies both *objectivity* (coping) and the separation of ideas from their emotional referents (isolation = defense). The study of coping behavior in general and the relation of coping mechanisms to the better-known defense mechanisms is still in an early phase but of great potential for clinically relevant theory.

Defenses operate automatically and usually without awareness. Coping mechanisms, by contrast, are more likely to be under voluntary control and conscious. Though sharing a common protective purpose, the different mechanisms operate on different aspects of the threatening situation; some are directed toward the external danger (e.g., avoidance, denial), others toward relevant persons (e.g., identification), others toward unacceptable drives and affects (e.g., repression, isolation, sublimation), some toward the post hoc interpretation of our intent and action (e.g., rationalization, projection).

In a brief account, it is impossible to describe the genesis, action, and interrelations among the several defense mechanisms in any detail. At best, only a few can be characterized.

1. *Repression* was viewed as the prototype and most basic of the mechanisms by Freud. It involves the blockage of a drive into behavior and the exclusion from consciousness and memory of associated thoughts. The "recovery of the repressed" was the primary goal of classical psychoanalytic therapy.

2. *Denial* is an inability to recognize that an experience occurred. It might involve the blocking or distorting of perception and in the extreme be related to delusionary beliefs or hallucinations. Related are *escape* or *avoidance* mecha-

nisms, in which one retreats from an unpleasant situation or refuses to have contact with it.

3. *Projection* involves not only a refusal to recognize one's own motives, but an ascription of them to another. "I don't hate him, he hates me." On this basis, one is not only relieved of responsibility for an unacceptable impulse, but gains justification for actions against the other person.

4. *Identification with the aggressor.* Anna Freud called attention to this mechanism as a particular distortion of normal identification in childhood. By modeling on a threatening person, one thereby feels less in danger from him. A pathetic illustration of this was described by Bettelheim (1943) in the behavior of some concentration-camp inmates who took on the beliefs, behaviors, and even scraps of uniform of their Nazi tormentors.

5. *Reaction formation* is taking on behaviors opposite to a denied drive or affect; the hostile person can appear to be excessively kind and considerate. It is in the exaggerated appearance of an otherwise desirable trait that the mechanism is seen. Related is the mechanism of *negation,* the direct assertion that one is *not,* say, angry or hostile. When, with Shakespeare, we feel "Me thinks, he protests too much" we are sensing negation.

6. *Isolation* consists of separating the thought from the related drives and feelings, which normally converge in unitary experiences. Either the thoughts (e.g., sexual images or fantasies) or the feelings (experienced as a detached, cold impulse) exist at the moment, but not together and naturally related. Related is *intellectualization,* a minimization of the emotional component and exaggerated emphasis on the intellectual activity and logic. Isolating, intellectualizing people will talk about sexual, destructive, or other urges but without feeling or consequent action. It is safer that way!

7. *Regression,* though itself the breakdown product of conflict, can also be a defense against further disorganization and distress. Conceived as a strategic retreat, regression can allow some satisfaction at a lower level and avert the full impact of the present stress. Remember our Albanian friend? At least he could eat a cheese sandwich and coffee, which is better than an ineffectual temper tantrum or other more grossly regressed behavior.

8. *Sublimation* allows for the expression of unacceptable drives and affects by rechanneling them (displacement) into more acceptable outlets. It was conceived as the most normal of the defenses and the basis for developmentally adaptive actions (Anna Freud, 1936).

These illustrate some of the variety of defenses. They can be conceptualized along a hierarchy from more primitive to more sophisticated, which parallels the general development of ego functioning. Blatant denial is more gross than, say, intellectualization, which requires more evolved cognition. Thus, in the child denial, avoidance, and similar mechanisms are expectable; they should be supplanted by more intellectual defenses in adulthood. Within the individual personality organization, defenses are also hierarchically integrated. Some are more readily available, come into play more rapidly and over a wider range of situations, others only after preferred defenses are found ineffectual. The personological description of an individual should include his unique organization of defenses as it does his needs, values, and other attributes.

From an adaptational viewpoint, defenses both protect and limit at the same time. To be "well-defended" can either connote a smoothly functioning person who handles conflict and stress easily, or one whose defensive behavior dominates and who, therefore, is incapable of reality-appropriate coping functions. To be "undefended" could connote helpless inadequacy or the full maturity of a self-actualizing person. Defensive mechanisms are necessary for growth and effective functioning, though disturbed behavior can be characterized, in fair measure by their over- and misuse. As ego functions are freed and turned to coping ends, the person is able to live more fully, happily, and productively.

THE ECOLOGICAL PERSPECTIVE

Human adaptation depends not only on processes within the individual, nor those which arise in interpersonal transactions, but it also requires coping with forces of the larger social and physical environment. As with animals in nature, man's functioning and well-being depend ultimately on the qualities of the ecological systems (ecosystems) within which he lives. Concern with human ecology has grown as clinicians are turning attention to the challenge of improving mental health in large populations. It joins with widespread concern, professional and public, with the deteriorating conditions of life—paradoxically, many are unintended by-products of earlier gains in industry, medicine, education, and social justice—in the problems of pollution, overcrowding, population growth, poverty, social unrest, disaffection, and violence. That "no man is an island unto himself" is more poignantly true as the sea around and air above become polluted, both literally and figuratively. Because of the particular relevance of the ecological perspective to community mental health, fuller discussion will be held for that context in Chapter 19. At this point, some general issues will be introduced.

Both the orienting ideas and their applications to mental health issues are still in a nascent stage. They indicate intent more than accomplishment, but they are of growing importance to a social-clinical psychology. In sociology and in anthropology there has been long-standing interest in social ecology and in the impact of community factors on human behavior. Social epidemiological studies of mental illness, crime, suicide, and other social problems date back to the pioneering work of the Chicago sociological school of "social ecology" of the 1920s. Investigating differences in the distribution of particular problems between areas of a city has shown that both the amount and type of problem is related to the nature of the community; thus, more schizophrenics are found in center-city areas (Faris and Dunham, 1939), and are hospitalized if lower-class (Hollingshead and Redlich, 1958). Similarly, more pathology was found in disorganized than better organized small towns by the Leightons and their co-workers (1963). Though well-known, such findings were not integrated into clinicians' concepts of the origin, course, or treatment of psychological disturbance, which centered mainly on processes within the individual. Even now, we lack clear concepts for joining individual-centered and community-centered approaches. At present, the ecological perspective only suggests a way of thinking which calls attention to the following relatively neglected issues.

Interrelatedness in the Ecosystem. Biological ecologists have described the ways in which organisms adapt to their habitat and to each other in ways which maintain the ecosystem in a dynamically balanced state. The balanced home aquarium is a simple, if artificially created, ecosystem which illustrates principles found in the wild. Ecosystems tend toward stability, through a series of changes or stages. If any important element changes, through natural cause or human intervention, the system as a whole changes and if possible a new equilibrium is reached. Thus, should a particular type of plant not continue to grow in the forest, animals that feed on it may die or leave; other species dependent on the first would then not be able to survive, still other species might move in, and so on. Detail aside, the important principle is that all life is interdependent, among individuals and species and on the resources of the environment. Students of ecology call the interlocked network of organisms and environmental resources a community. Human communities can also be characterized as ecosystems, though they obviously reflect the far greater power man has developed to make his own environment. In addition to structures of stone and concrete, transportation, agriculture, and manufacturing, man has also created social institutions by which life in communities is regulated. Though vastly more complex, there are nonetheless ecosystems which are balanced or disturbed as parts change (qualities of persons, cultural rules, social institutions, technology, physical and natural environment). Among more primitive peoples, the relation between social custom and the conditions of the natural ecology, with its animal and plant forms, and weather and geography, are more immediately visible, and have encouraged many anthropologists to view cultural forms as direct evidence of environmental adaptation. But in the most complex as well as simple of human communities, the fact of interrelatedness in human ecology is clear.

The Importance of the Physical Environment. On the whole, psychologists have been relatively unconcerned with the ways in which the physical environment might affect human behavior. In recent years, there has been a growing interest in "environmental psychology," which sometimes joins the work of psychologists and other behavioral scientists with that of architects, engineers, and city planners. Inspired by an ecological orientation, factors of climate and geography, the use of space, and the design of man-made structures are being investigated to understand how they may affect psychological functioning and well-being. The progress of a hospitalized patient may depend not only on the individual therapy he receives and the social environment in which he functions but also the physical environment within which he lives, whether it provides stimulation, color, spaces for different activities, privacy, and the like. Similarly, efforts to create better communities have to be attentive to such matters as open spaces, recreational facilities, and esthetically pleasing surroundings.

The Importance of the Immediate Social Environment. Though closer to traditional concerns of psychologists, the ecological emphasis has strengthened interest in the immediate "life space" of people, in its psychosocial as well as physical aspects. Sometimes these fuse in their effects. We can better understand the surliness of a clerk in a New York department store when we have shared his commute to work on the New York subway during rush hours. Social situations have "demand qualities" which determine individual behavior; we act in accordance with the rules, expectations and customs of the particular setting in which we are. We are quiet in church, raucous in a ballpark. The importance of the behavior setting has been emphasized by ecologically oriented psychologists.

The Need for Naturalistic Studies. Ecological principles have been developed, in fair measure, through unobtrusive observation in field settings. Laboratory or clinical studies, ecologists claim, necessarily involve artificial simplifications of the behaviors observable in real life. Consequently, attention has been turned toward the perfection of naturalistic and field methods (e.g., Willems and Raush, 1969; Moos and Insel, 1974), some of which parallel the approaches of the field biologist, naturalist, and cultural anthropologist. For the clinician, an ecological emphasis means greater attention to the "other twenty-three hours," that is, the patient's life when he is not in contact with the clinician but involved in the natural settings of home, work, and community.

THE BIOLOGICAL PERSPECTIVE

It may seem odd, having reached the grand scale of human ecosystems, to turn now to the biological substrata of human functioning. We are so conditioned to think in terms of a stepwise progression of the sciences, moving from the molecular to the molar, from simple to complex, that we might have expected that the biological basis of human life should be considered first; building on that the psychological, social, and ecological would then follow. I have chosen, instead, to discuss the biological realm last, mainly to put it into the context of the psychosocial factors which are the center of our concern in this volume.

The noted neurophysiologist Ralph Gerard once said, "Behind every twisted thought there is a twisted molecule." And, presumably, straight thinking depends on straight molecules. Looked at one way, this can be taken as a simple statement of faith, of the sort which has inspired important neuropsychological research seeking correlates of thinking disorders in brain dysfunctions. However, Gerard's statement may also suggest that psychological study is futile, on the assumption that the explanation of thinking disorder can only be found in the study of neurological processes. This type of *reductionism* is dangerous in psychology, for it runs the risk of losing the phenomenon we are concerned to understand. Psychological phenomena must be understood in their own terms; psychological data cannot be replaced by biological knowledge. Krech (1964) reminds neuropsychologists of two important issues in conceptualizing the relation of psychological and neurological findings: First, it is the psychological data, in the last analysis, which must provide the test of adequacy of any theory of brain action; and second, a unified point of view will not be achieved by reducing psychological principles to neurological ones and neurological ones to physical ones, but rather by making each congruent with the other.

Students with specific interest in the biology of personality development and functioning (motivation, affect, learning, ego functioning, etc.), mental disorders, and treatment, are well-advised to read more deeply in the literature of psychophysiology, physiological psychology, neuropsychology, biological psychiatry, and psychopharmacology. These composite terms indicate the rich diversity of the field. In the present context, and elsewhere in this volume, I will touch most lightly on these topics. Instead, some general principles to guide a psychological clinician in his understanding of biological factors will be briefly stated.

1. The unity of man as a *bio-psycho-social organism* is expressed in parallel theoretical principles which are manifested at each level. Orthogenesis, discussed earlier, is of this nature. So too, the dynamics of stress-defense-coping-adaptation can be conceptualized in biological, psychological, and social systems in coordinate terms. Knowledge at one level facilitates theory development at another, a process which has figured importantly in theoretical analysis, particu-

larly in system-theoretical positions (e.g., Grinker, 1956). Danger lies in analogistic thinking, which is tempting, easy, and dangerous. Thus, the biological advances of the nineteenth century seduced some social theorists into describing society as a social organism, with communications systems equated to the nervous system, transportation to blood flow, etc.

2. Biological factors deeply affect personality development. The growing field of behavior genetics leaves little doubt that many characteristics are transmitted genetically; considerable evidence has accumulated for a genetic basis for schizophrenia. Very early in life, individual differences in gross behavior and biological functioning are visible, from which later temperamental characteristics can be reliably predicted. Thus, infants differ in activity level, sensory thresholds, autonomic system reactivity, apparent drive levels, and intensity of response; as they grow, active infants are more decisive and vigorous children. In contrast to more placid infants, they act on their environment rather than placidly receiving it (Escalona and Heider, 1959; Escalona, 1968; Murphy et al., 1962). These authors, among others, call attention to the fact that biologically based individual differences from earliest life interplay with learning situations. Having certain characteristics, the child seeks complementary situations, gains experiences, and so on.

Psychological functioning is obviously dependent on biological qualities—in the fine words of a Berkeley friend—which are "built-in at the factory"; at the first level are those which distinguish us from other animals. Unaided, we cannot fly, as Icarus learned so painfully. There are also gross anatomical and morphological factors within men which are reflected in behavior. The round, fat man may be jollier; the long, lean one more seclusive. But, often the personality consequences of morphological differences depend more on the secondary rather than primary effects of the differences, i.e., the experiences they dispose to and the social valuation of the characteristics. Even the most palpable (perhaps better to say, visible) division of humanity, men and women, gains its full psychosocial meaning only in terms of sex roles and specialized experiences which are socially determined, differ between societies, and over time. That "anatomy is destiny," as Freud once said about female psychology, is properly protested by women seeking social equality.

In thousands of more subtle ways, there are differences in the functioning of the nervous system, endocrine regulation, metabolism, and other aspects of human biology which determine psychological functioning.

3. Psychological functioning depends on the intact state of the physical organism, particularly the nervous system. Obviously, the blind man must depend on different perceptual modes than the sighted. The brain-damaged individual has less capacity to adapt intellectually. Lesions in different parts of the brain have different consequences in behavior. From the clinician's vantage point important issues lie in the distinction between primary loss (reduced capacity) from the secondary reactions (compensations, shame, and fear). Thus, as K. Goldstein (1939) pointed out, the reduced intellectual capacity of the brain-damaged patient is further reduced by the anxiety he experiences when he recognizes his inadequacy. The clinician has the important task of distinguishing what portion of the deficit is attributable to the primary loss and which to the secondary reaction, perhaps utilizing psychological interventions to alter the latter, though the former may be unchangeable.

4. Psychological states and physiological reactions are correlated, even

though views as to cause and effect may differ. Our anxiety is revealed to others by rapid breathing, tremulous hands, sweaty palms, among other bodily signs; overall tension, by muscular contraction. For the clinician, these and more idiosyncratic symptoms index the emotional state and can guide the process of clinical intervention. In psychophysiological research, they become measured variables.

5. Altered psychological states alter physiological functioning, often profoundly. Chronic emotional conflicts can result in somatic diseases, such as gastric ulcers and essential hypertension. Although the evidence is still contested, there is a long-standing view that each such psychosomatic disease is determined by a specific conflict theme (ulcers = autonomy vs. dependence). Whether the specificity hypothesis is ultimately confirmed, the existence of psychosomatic diseases, over a wide range of conditions, is of clear importance both to the physician and the psychological clinician. At the extreme, instances of "voodoo death" show that belief in malicious magic and the consequent anxiety can have fatal consequences (G. L. Engel, 1970). In a Broadway musical some years ago, an unloved girl voiced the "psychosomatic hypothesis" in a song "A Person Could Develop a Cold." A lot worse can happen.

6. Contrariwise, alterations in the physiological state can alter psychological functioning. Not only gross damage, but temporary and more minor bodily changes are reflected in psychological activities. If oxygen supply is reduced, we first feel euphoric, lose psychological coordination, often without realizing it, before becoming unconscious. In fevered states, there is the possibility of delirium, but more subtly our time sense speeds up, and if tested, we count faster. A wit has said that "the superego is soluble in alcohol." The literally thousands of "psychoactive drugs" available can change countless aspects of feelings, thought processes, competencies, or ego functions. Indeed, we are now in a process of "mystification" over the use of drugs, such that there is the widespread faith among both physicians and amateur drug users that psychological life can be manipulated in any desired direction by the proper pill (Lennard, Epstein, Bernstein, and Ransom, 1971).

Even though focused on the psychosocial level of personality organization and clinical intervention, the clinician should be well grounded in the human biological sciences. As we have seen, the biological realm contributes to the development of broad-scaled psychological theory (and vice versa). Clinical problems reside in the relation between physiological, neurological, and psychological functioning. Both clinical assessment and therapeutic intervention depend on knowledge of biopsychological relationships, though the focus of clinical concern should properly be the psychological person.

"What *is* man . . . ?" So many and contradictory things. A tension-reducer, a stimulation-seeker, a biological organism, a creature of and producer of culture, controlled by unconscious impulses, a self-knowing and self-regulating person, a unique identity, interlocked with others in communities. All these, and many more, assertions are perfectly true, yet each is limited. The clinician with his twin goal of understanding and facilitating human functioning must be guided by theory. Out of available knowledge and ideas he must develop the guiding principles necessary for his work. Some principles of potential value have been considered in this chapter.

PART 2

THE NATURE OF MENTAL HEALTH

CHAPTER 4

Concepts of Normality and Pathology

Psychopathology in Historical Perspective

In the present-day field of mental health, clinicians are concerned with disturbed behavior of all sorts, severity, and duration. At the one extreme are grossly and visibly deranged people, once called insane, mad or lunatic, and now diagnosed as psychotic. At the other are unhappy people, unable to cope effectively with life demands, limited in their ability to love, work, or find meaning in their lives, either over extended periods or in brief, stress-related episodes. Against standards of mental health or normality, which we will examine in this chapter, these are all described as forms of mental disorder or psychopathology; it is the task of the clinician to study and to treat them. Included too are conditions of psychological dysfunction resulting from injury to the nervous system (brain syndromes), emotional problems resulting in somatic diseases (psychosomatic conditions), forms of delinquency and social deviance (alcoholism, drug addiction, criminality, etc.), as well as the great variety of lesser psychosocial problems (maladjustments, immaturity reactions, and the like) which plague so many people. All of these are described in texts of abnormal psychology, psychiatry, or psychopathology. Despite manifest differences among these conditions, they are all visualized as types of disordered or disturbed behavior. In what ways are these various modes of psychological functioning similar? Is it proper to consider all of them forms of psychopathology, properly within the concern of the clinician? What defines psychological normality and abnormality? In this chapter, we will address these questions. To anticipate the answers: there are serious theoretical, ethical, and pragmatic issues embedded in each of these questions; some would reject the concept of "mental illness" entirely, others give diverse meanings to mental health or normality. The best we can do is examine the issues honestly and seek a position consonant with available evidence on human functioning and dysfunctioning and which has utility for improving the well-being of people in distress. To start, let us look at the way concepts of mental illness have changed historically.

Considering more minor personality malfunctioning within the scope of abnormal psychology and as warranting professional intervention is a recent development in social history and still suspect among all but the most educated, urbanized, and industrialized societies today. Surely, there have always been people who were painfully shy or fearful, unable to work productively, to relate warmly with friends and family, who drank excessively, were self-centered, immature, and impulsive, who were needlessly rigid, moralistic, and intolerant of others, or who felt inadequate, defeated, and worthless, or in a thousand other ways, lived joyless lives burdening others. For those immediately involved these were personal problems, reflecting defects in character and will, requiring greater effort, self-examination and self-control, or the sage counsel of friends or religious advisors. Sensitive and literate men understood the intricacies and distortions of human character; modern clinical descriptions are pale beside the writings of a Shakespeare. But until recent times, there was little scientific concern with personality development and functioning nor were there specialists to alter their course.

THE INSANE AS POSSESSED OF DEMONS

The history of man's view of mental illness is best told in terms of the more severe psychological abnormalities. The madman claimed public and medical interest from earliest times. Hippocrates, the father of medicine, described insanity as a disease of the brain in the fifth century, B.C., though the popular belief from ages past and centuries to come saw the madman as possessed of demons. The Roman physicians Asclepiades and later Galen sought naturalistic explanations for psychotic behavior and supported humane treatment and hospitalization. Although some of the scientific and humanistic thinking of the Graeco-Roman world continued in Arab realms, the Christian world slid back to belief in possession and maltreatment of the insane from the fall of Rome to the age of enlightenment.

Until the end of the eighteenth century, there were no real hospitals for the mentally ill in western Europe. Instead, they were treated as social outcasts. They were objects of morbid curiosity or contempt. If believed harmless, they roamed free, surviving as best they could. If thought dangerous, they were incarcerated in prisons with criminals, paupers, heretics, and other unwanted people. There, they lived in intolerable misery and filth, subject to caprices of the guards, tortured and treated as subhuman. The prevailing view was that they were mindless beasts who could be controlled only by chains and physical discipline. In 1547, Henry VIII built London's Hospital of St. Mary of Bethlehem to house lunatics. In short order, it became a public amusement (for a fee!) to visit Bethlehem (pronounced Bedlam) to taunt and watch the weird behavior of the inmates, a practice which was allowed for over two centuries. The word "bedlam" remains in our language to describe chaotic confusion.

Throughout history, the bizarre and irrational behavior of the insane could only be taken as evidence that they were possessed of evil spirits who controlled their acts and thoughts from within or without. In some centuries, this belief led to more or less kindly efforts to purge these spirits by monks or physicians. But in the middle ages, when medieval Europe was overrun by plague, religious and political dissension, and the authority of the Church wavered, the insane became hapless scapegoats in the revival of witchcraft. Women were singled out because their presumed lustful natures made them easy preys of the devil. Heretics, Jews, and other disbelievers, along with the insane, were brought before tribunals, accused of bartering with the devil to do his work, tortured to extract confessions, and put to painful deaths. The spirit of the time was represented in the infamous *Malleus Maleficarum* ("The Witches' Hammer," 1487), which detailed ways of discovering, trying, and punishing witches. Against this spirit, Johann Weyer, a sixteenth-century physician, tried heroically to have insanity conceived as illness and distinguished from possession. His is a special place in the history of psychiatry as one among the few voices to stand for science and compassion against the bigotry and superstition of the age. Even after the era of witchcraft and inquisition abated, the mentally ill remained social outcasts, imprisoned under miserable conditions. Weyer's plea was not to be realized for 230 years, until the end of the eighteenth century.

THE INSANE AS SICK

A new concept of mental illness emerged at the time of the French and American Revolutions as part of the renaissance of rationalism, humanism, and political democracy. The insane were coming to be viewed as *sick* people. Chiarugi in Italy and Müller in Germany spoke out for humane hospital treatment. But it is mainly in the reforms instituted by Phillipe Pinel (1745–1826) in Paris that the new conception was expressed. A scholarly, humane man, he removed the shackles and chains from his patients. Although they did not withhold consent, it is worth noting that the revolutionary government of the Paris commune was anything but enthused about his action. But he was convinced that dignity and freedom could restore the sanity of his charges and indeed it did in many cases. "The mentally sick," he said, "far from being guilty people deserving of punishment are sick people whose miserable state deserves all the consideration that is due to suffering humanity. One should try with the most simple methods to restore their reason" (quoted by Zilboorg, 1941, pp. 323–324). It is an ironic comment that a drunkard whom he had released from ten years in chains saved him from lynching by an angry crowd who thought he harbored political subversives in his hospital!

In his *Treatise (Traité Médico-philosophique sur la Manie,* 1801) Pinel defended the thesis that the hospital should be a place of treatment, not of imprisonment. It spoke out against bloodletting, punishment, and purging. Pinel argued for scientific study and the categorizing of mental diseases, for case records and life histories, and for the study of treatment methods. Finally, he proposed that some psychotic conditions might have psychogenic origins.

The spirit of Pinel continued in the work of British Quakers who established "asylums for the insane"; now a word with ugly connotations, but originally with the literal meaning of places of refuge and rest. Early in the nineteenth century, American and British hospitals emphasized "moral treatment" to restore mental health through spiritual inspiration, study, and benevolent care. Mid-twentieth-century concern with developing "therapeutic milieus" and transforming the hospital from a custodial to a therapeutic agency recapitulate these themes. In between, however, hospital care regressed to conditions virtually as dehumanizing as those decried by Pinel. The abuses exposed by Dorothy Dix and Clifford Beers in the early decades of this century and by Deutsch (1949) and others more recently show the readiness of society to reject and maltreat its deranged members in any time. In many state hospitals today, Bedlam lives on. Similarly, in public attitudes the view of the "insane as sick" may be explicitly stated, but the "insane as subhuman and/or possessed" is as often revealed.

THE MEDICAL APPROACH TO MENTAL ILLNESS

Overall, however, the concept of mental illness as a disease, with natural causes, scientifically understandable and treatable, has been the dominant view during the past two and a half centuries. Admitted to the domain of medicine, physicians have sought to describe the forms and varieties of mental illness, to discover their causes, typical course, and outcome, and to develop methods of treatment. Though historical antecedents go back to Hippocrates, from the time of Pinel to the present the search for organic bases and medical treatments of mental diseases has gone on vigorously. As an orienting philosophy, many psychiatrists hold that all behavior pathology, or at the least the more severe forms, must reflect diseases of the nervous system. Thousands of studies, many fruitless and others productive, have been done under the guidance of this point of view. However, a major form of psychosis, general paresis (*dementia paralytica*, first described in 1798), has almost been completely eradicated in the western world. Through clinical and experimental studies, it was determined that the condition was a later stage of syphilis, occurring when the syphilitic baccilus invades the nervous system and brain. Today, through prevention of infection in the first place or by early treatment of infection if it does occur, few patients reach the psychotic state characteristic of general paresis. Through the application of medical thinking and investigatory methods, shock treatment, a variety of drugs and other medical therapeutic methods have been developed of value in the treatment of conditions for which there is no known organic etiology.

The tradition of medical psychiatry is perhaps best represented in Emil Kraepelin (1855–1926). His is the classic textbook of psychiatry, going through many editions from 1883 to 1927. With extraordinary patience and energy, he attempted to sort out the many manifest symptoms of mental dysfunctioning, to classify mental patients according to symptom patterns, and thus to identify and classify mental diseases. He looked for patterns in the precipitating circumstances, the course of the condition, and its outcome. Behind his work lay the faith that if forms of mental illness could be properly distinguished and classified (i.e., a proper *nosological* scheme developed), then systematic medical research could discover the agents which produced the disease and methods for its cure, as had indeed occurred in the case of general paresis. Kraepelin used the methods of the physiological and the new psychological laboratory to describe specific functions which might be deranged in his patients. He poured over numerous case histories to discover common patterns in the earlier histories, behavior in the hospital, and posthospitalization follow-up information.

Kraepelin defined and labelled the two most common forms of severe mental illness—*dementia praecox* (now better known by Eugen Bleuler's term, "schizophrenia") and *manic-depressive psychosis*. In each case, Kraepelin synthesized observations of seemingly diverse behaviors to describe the disease entities. What characterized dementia praecox was its onset early in life (hence, praecox) and progression to an incurable and apparently irreversible dementia. The various symptom patterns, hebephrenic, paranoid, catatonic, and simple, were viewed as subvarieties of the disease. Overall, Kraepelin postulated biological defect in the functioning of the sex glands which, in turn, affected the central nervous system. In describing the manic-depressive psychosis, he brought together the manifestly different states of agitated, elated excitement (mania) and the retarded melancholy (depression). These, he noted, were related so that patients would move from one to the other pole, often in cyclical fashion. The onset tended to be sudden rather than gradual. There were long periods of apparently normal functioning between episodic crises and no overall deterioration. To explain this disease, he proposed a hereditary metabolic defect.

Among contemporary psychosocially oriented clinicians, "Kraepelinian" is a pejorative term, characterizing a form of psychiatry which overstresses nosology and diagnosis—mainly with regard to the severe mental disorders—and centers mainly on biomedical explanation and treatment, to the neglect of the psychosocial realm. The "psychogenic hypothesis" was not to come into its own until attention turned to the nonhospitalized neurotic patient. However, even within hospital psychiatry, strong voices tempered the Kraepelinian tradition in his own lifetime. Thus, the American Adolf Meyer (1886–1950) described the major mental disorders not as diseases but as "psychobiological reactions" to life stress. In the atmosphere of functional psychology, he emphasized the developmental, life-historical factors which determined abnormal behavior. The Swiss psychiatrist, Eugen Bleuler (1856–1935) noted the important disharmony between intellectual and emotional life of the dementia praecox patient and coined the term "schizophrenia" to characterize the "split" between them. Though contested from many quarters the spirit of Kraepelin lives on in contemporary psychiatric nomenclature and in the practice of many hospital clinicians.

THE PSYCHOLOGICAL APPROACH TO MENTAL DISORDER

Psychopathology, conceived not only as diseases *of* psychological functioning but also as disorders *caused by* psychological factors, emerged later in scientific and medical history. The psychogenic orientation arose in the study of hysteria, a neurotic condition which often included bodily symptoms such as paralyses, anaesthesias, or blindness, as well as behavioral symptoms such as loss of memory, double personality, and emotional storms. Converging with the study of hysteria was an interest in hypnosis, stemming from Franz Anton Mesmer's (1734–1815) demonstrations of "animal magnetism." Under hypnosis, hysterialike symptoms could be newly produced and established symptoms of hysterical patients could be removed. That particular behaviors could be induced without voluntary participation and knowledge provided evidence for unconscious processes and psychological determination. Hypnosis became an important method of psychological treatment in the clinics of the French psychopathologists and in the first stage of psychoanalysis, though it was shortly to be supplanted by more familiar methods (free association and dream analysis) for exploring the unconscious mind. The psychodynamic tradition evolved through the work of the French physician-psychologists, including Charcot (1825–1893), Bernheim (1840–1914), and Janet (1859–1947), during the last half of the nineteenth century. It reached its culmination in Sigmund Freud (1856–1939). Psychoanalysis was deeply influenced by the physiological energy theories of Freud's medical teachers, by Darwinian evolutionary concepts, particularly as expressed in Jackson's neuropsychological notions of progression and regression, and by the studies of hypnosis and hysteria of Freud's French contemporaries. But Freud's genius was to transcend these origins and to create a thoroughly psychological theory of human motivation and psychopathology, bridging normal and abnormal behavior, and with it, a *psycho*therapy which might reorganize basic character structure and relieve neurotic suffering through the rooting out of nuclear conflicts. Over the past seventy-five years, the history of psychoanalysis is a complex tale of refinement and extension and of the development of deviant psychodynamic viewpoints. With Freud the psychological approach to mental illness was firmly established. Whether pro or con, contending views in the current mental health scene often take positions with regard to psychoanalysis. Community-oriented and sociological-psychiatric clinicians, those of existentialist and humanistic persuasion, behavioral and learning-theory proponents, the biomedically oriented as well as Jungians, Sullivanians, Adlerians, and Horneyians, all argue their positions in reference to psychoanalysis. Even among vigorous critics, basic Freudian concepts have entered the fabric of normal and abnormal psychology; too often, Freudian scholars fear, losing their essential meaning in the process (Shakow and Rapaport, 1964).

CURRENT ORIENTATIONS TO MENTAL ILLNESS AND HEALTH

Thus, over the centuries, there has been a steady growth of scientific and medical concern with the nature and treatment of mental illness. Where formerly the mentally ill were looked on as sinful people possessed of demons, they are now conceived as sick people, deserving of treatment and humane care. As we have seen, there have been two major trends in scientific psychopathology, the one oriented to mental illness as a *biomedical* state and the other to the *psychological and social* nature and treatment of abnormal behavior. By and large, the biomedical orientation has been anchored in the study of grossly disturbed (psychotic) and hospitalized patients while the psychosocial orientation arose and prevails in the outpatient care of less distressed persons (neurotics, character disorders, etc.). But this is true only in an overall sense. There are psychological theories and therapies of schizophrenia and simutaneously concern with the biology of mood disorders and their alteration through drugs. An easy and not inappropriate generalization is that psychological disturbance is a function of factors which range from the biochemical to sociological spheres, and that scientific understanding is necessary in all of these realms for the reduction of human misery. While true enough, in actuality the current field of mental health is organized around three contrasting and sometimes conflicting orientations: (1) the *biomedical*, in the tradition of Kraepelin, but now involving the vastly more sophisticated methods of medical science; (2) the *psychological*, following Freud, though now including many divergent and even antagonistic points of view which, however, all focus on the individual personality; and (3) an emerging *psychosocial* orientation which directs attention to the impact of social systems and underlies community mental health approaches. As we shall discuss in the next chapter, and elsewhere in this volume, the three orientations determine not only the way psychological disorder is conceived, but how it should be studied and treated, the professional roles of clinicians, the institutional settings, etc. The three positions coexist; although historically they emerged in sequence, one has not superseded the other. M. Brewster Smith (1968) argued that the biomedical viewpoint was a great step forward from the demonological concept and appropriate for work with hospitalized psychotics. The psychological orientation, he notes, arose in the context of psychotherapy with neurotics, but sincere attention to the human needs of large groups of disadvantaged and powerless people, as in community mental health, requires emphasis on the development of psychosocial competencies necessary for coping with an often overwhelming society. Toward this end, he argues, earlier concepts of mental illness and health are inadequate. We will return to this issue again shortly.

Meanwhile, however, we should note that there has been a steady increase in the range of human problems which have come within the ken of the mental health fields. With growing psychological-mindedness and the reduced stigma for seeking professional help, clinicians of today are seeing a wide range of "minor maladjustments." The development of the psychodynamic and psychosocial frameworks, over the past century, have provided concepts and techniques for dealing with the confusion, worries, and anxieties and personality problems of people who could hardly be called or would see themselves as demented or insane. In illness terms, clinicians are now treating the psychological colds and sore throats where previously only pneumonia and tuberculosis came to their attention. Consequently, the borders of normal and pathological are becoming increasingly hard to define, nor what is and should be in the purview of mental health workers and what is properly outside. Increasingly, the borders expand, as professionals reconceptualize their roles and competencies and the public and social institutions reach out for their help. The continuity between normal and abnormal personality processes, first emphasized by psychoanalysis, is clearly illustrated. At the same time, some have argued, the distinction itself is needless if not mischievous in these times.

Overall, there has been a shifting of emphasis from psychological illness to psychological health. In part, this reflects an optimistic attitude toward the possibility of cure and in part reluctance to stigmatize the mentally ill. Thus, what were once *asylums for the insane* became *psychiatric hospitals* many of which, in turn, evolved into *mental health centers*. Thus, the famous Boston Psychopathic Hospital of colonial days was transformed into the Massachusetts Mental Health Center in the 1950s. New outpatient clinical services are sometimes not called "clinics," but rather "centers for special problems"; so too in schools, where classes for "retarded children" now teach "exceptional children." We have talked repeatedly in the preceding pages of "mental *health* specialists." The Mental Hygiene movement in the United States, following the pioneering efforts of Clifford Beers, was an effort to reduce stigma, to improve hospital care, and work toward the prevention of mental disorders, reflected and fostered the shift from an illness to health emphasis. Under their aegis, child guidance clinics were founded, to treat early emotional problems and hopefully to avert more extensive disability in later life. Focus on health rather than illness should not be taken as a cynical public relations play with words—to get the "I'm not crazy, just confused" trade. Rather it reflects genuine change in public and professional attitudes, reflecting humane concern and hope for the future of patients, with an increasingly wide range of human problems.

The "Medical Model" of Mental Illness

Along with the new conceptualization of human problems and of modes of mental health care, there is considerable controversy around the "medical or disease model." Continuing to think of psychologically disturbed behavior in disease terms limits attention to essential ethical and social questions and keeps intervention within the institutions of medicine. Psychiatrists, psychologists, sociologists, and social critics have argued that the use of medical metaphors block proper understanding and treatment of psychosocial problems and should be abandoned (Szasz, 1961; Sarbin, 1969; Scheff, 1966, among others). Often these attacks occur from different vantage points, themselves contradictory, and on different issues loosely united within a notion of the "medical model," different aspects of which have been emphasized in each polemic. Here are some of the elements ascribed to a medical conception of psychological dysfunction which have been attacked from one or another viewpoint: (1) There are disease entities, which have etiology, course, and outcome; (2) These diseases are of organic origin; (3) Even if conceived as psychological diseases, they are viewed in analogy with physical ailments. There is an underlying state which is manifested in surface symptoms. Disease is to be inferred from symptoms; changing symptoms will not cure the disease; (4) People get these diseases through no fault of their own; (5) Cure depends on professional intervention, preferably by people with medical training; and (6) The diseases are in the person and, although they may have culturally distinct manifestations, the essential disease process is universal and not culturally specific.

An early and vigorous attack on the "myth of mental illness" was launched by the psychiatrist Thomas Szasz (1960; 1961). By now, he asserted, the concept of mental illness is nothing but a convenient myth. Most mental symptoms cannot be related to lesions of the nervous system. Rather, they are communications the patient offers which characterize his beliefs about himself and the world. They are necessarily parts of his social and ethical context, and should be treated accordingly. The patient should have the right to determine how and why his behavior should change, and he should also be responsible for his acts (see also Mowrer, 1960). Under the guise of medical care deviants are punished and incarcerated. Medicine cannot and should not judge ethical and social issues. And so Szasz argues that psychological disturbances should be ". . . regarded as the expression of man's struggle with the problem of how he should live." And again: "Mental illness is a myth whose function it is to disguise and thus render more palatable the bitter pill of moral conflicts in human relations."

From a quite different vantage point behavioristic clinicians center their attack on the issue of disease and symptom (Krasner and Ullman, 1965). They argue that the visible symptom is the disease and that there is neither need nor justification for assuming underlying disease states. Their approach to therapy, as we will discuss further in Chapter 14, consists of attempts to remove symptoms or to substitute new behaviors through the application of learning principles. They have less quarrel with other aspects of the medical model. By contrast, existentialistic and humanistic clinicians, at complete variance with the behavioristic group, oppose the deterministic theme in the disease model, and the emphasis on historical and unconscious factors. Far more important, they believe, is the patient's phenomenal experience, his quest for meaning, and his striving to realize his potential. From yet another perspective socially oriented clinicians are unhappy at the focus on the individual patient and on intrapersonal factors, whether organic or psychological, which divert attention from the social systems within which people live and function, well or poorly. Keeping human problems within the scope of medical concepts and institutions, they further argue, limits the innovations (e.g., use of nonprofessionals, new settings, etc.) necessary for comprehensive community care. A more extreme view is represented by those sociological theorists who would see mental illness as another form of social deviance, like criminal behavior, sexual aberrations, immorality, or drug use, which is defined by social values. What is most critical, they contend (e.g., Scheff, 1966) is the valuation society places on the behavior, whether it defines it as sick, dangerous, sinful, or acceptable. In this view, the patient is given a role ("crazy man"), which he can accept and act accordingly. In its full expression, this thesis sees mental disturbance as being determined wholly or primarily by being the recipient and actor of a social role, and in that form it can hardly be accepted. Nonetheless, the importance of labeling and role-ascription as one among other factors which supports disturbed behavior is clearly seen in hospitalized patients, from Pinel to the present (Goffman, 1961). Finally, there are psychologists who contend with the medical model out of status rather than conceptual concerns. Within the medical model, the physician is necessarily in the dominant role while other professions are viewed as ancillary, a term which derives from the Latin for "handmaiden."

The many issues that have emerged in the flow of arguments pro and con are too numerous and complex to review in any detail. Suffice it to note that, in the polemics, medical thinking amd medical practice in areas outside as well as in psychiatry are too often caricatured and straw men are attacked. Particularly as preventative and public health medicine have evolved, with their emphasis on fostering health and development, many of the concepts of modern medicine are quite consonant with the conceptualization of psychological health programs (Dubos, 1959). Moreover, the understanding of psychological functioning has been greatly facilitated by the study of principles of broad generality, such as stress and defense, which figure in biological as well as psychological adaptation. Still, overdependence on medical metaphors for the conceptualization and treatment of psychological problems presents distinct dangers, such as:

1. Both implicitly and explicitly, biological rather than psychological or social factors are stressed. This is true of the patient's conception of his problem, as well as the professional's. "If I have a disease then there must be something wrong with my body. Cut it out or dose it, and I will be well again." Or "If I am sick, what good is it to sit here talking?"

2. The view of the patient as passive recipient of expert care is fostered. It is true of course that in many medical conditions the cooperation of the patient is of

critical importance, but in psychotherapy the patient is, in a significant sense, a coequal partner without whose collaboration therapy is impossible.

3. Medical role models are perpetuated. Too often, these have an authoritarian cast. "The doctor knows best. Follow his prescriptions and you will be well." Needless to say, the "authoritarian doctor and passive patient" relationship can exist if the doctor is a PhD as well as MD. Indeed, psychologically minded psychiatrists, notably psychoanalysts, often go to lengths to dissociate the psychotherapist role from the physician role. The white coat is eschewed for the business suit and the nurse for a receptionist. Thus, the psychological rather than medical aspect of the relationship is emphasized and with it there is greater role equality.

4. The disease model does suggest the importance of medical qualifications. Historically, in the United States, physicians have controlled the mental health field. In all their ramifications, questions of interprofessional relationship, division of labor, the proper training of psychological clinicians, whether in or out of medicine, have given rise to some of the most difficult and exasperating controversies in our field. A psychosocial concept of psychological disturbance does not prejudge the issue and automatically make mental health a problem primarily for physicians. There should be opportunity for qualified professionals of diverse backgrounds to make their best contributions, particularly in a time of manpower shortages in all fields.

5. Emphasis on disease directs attention to a search for specific etiologies, therapies, and prognoses. It can lead to an overemphasis on the diagnostic phase of the clinical process. To my mind, good clinical practice requires clearly describing and understanding a patient's condition (though some clinician might argue the proposition). But overemphasis on diagnosis can divert concern from the ultimate purpose of fostering change.

6. With diagnosis, there are the dangers of labeling and stigmatizing. As noted, calling someone sick rather than bewitched was a historic step forward. But in the present scheme of things a label such as "schizophrenic" may have the effect of casting out the sufferer and consigning him to banishment in a mental hospital. While the label does not create the condition, as some role-theoretical views hold, it does matter greatly. It has social import for the patient, contributes to his self-concept, and the actions of people toward him.

7. The disease model emphasizes the pathological themes in life and neglects the sources of competence and strength in personality development. Professional activity is too often directed toward discovering personality weaknesses rather than strengths. If a person comes to a clinic, he and we view him as ill and being ill needing to be restored to health. The disease model encourages, though by no means does it require, emphasis on pathology.

There is need for vocabulary and ways of thinking which conceives psychological problems in terms other than those traditional in medicine. To argue this point, critics have too often simplified modern medical thinking, though probably not much out of line with common usage. To sophisticated medical thinkers, health is not simply the absence of disease. Thus, the charter of the World Health Organization defines health as "a state of complete physical, mental, and social well-being and not merely the absence of disease or infirmity." Similarly, issues like discrete disease entities, patient passivity, dangers of labeling, doctor authoritarianism, and other matters just discussed have been given thoughtful attention in medicine, and need not be intrinsic to a "medical model." However, they do represent the kinds of attitudes and distortions which are commonly held and which from the vantage point of psychological health, limit our and the public's understanding of the problem. The words and concepts of medicine, at least as understood by the average man, can block progress. Not unlikely they will remain with us for a good long time but the literal application of medical metaphors should be resisted.

The Meaning of Normality

What we consider normal and what we consider abnormal, disturbed or psychopathological obviously has great import for clinical psychology and psychiatry. Yet, there is no clear consensus as to a definition of normality against which particular types of deviant or disordered behavior can be considered abnormal. Discussions of normality and abnormality, mental health and illness, are inevitably filled with value-laden terms (Jahoda, 1958; M. B. Smith, 1961). It seems impossible, nor do I believe it desirable, to avoid values in conceiving mental health. What is necessary is that the value framework be made explicit.

Offer and Sabshin (1966) have surveyed the many meanings of normality which have arisen in psychology, psychiatry, sociology, and anthropology. Building on their analysis let us consider alternate views of normality.

NORMALITY AS HEALTH

In this meaning, common to both traditional medical-psychiatric and lay usage, normality simply means "not sick." If no gross pathology is present, behavior is said to be normal. Normality is then the wide range of functioning which has in common that it does not represent a disease state. In this context, Offer and Sabshin note, health refers to a *reasonable* rather than an *optimal* state. Reflected in clinical practice, this view would go along with efforts to reduce symptoms and restore adequate functioning. In research, this perspective provides a relatively straightforward criterion and avoids some of the difficulties of assessing degree of positive health. Thus, numerous studies have been made in which the behavior of clinical groups, defined by symptoms, hospitalization, or clinic attendance, are contrasted with "normals," persons who do not have symptoms and are not hospitalized or treated. Implicit in this view is the notion that the great mass of people are normal, while some few are abnormal.

NORMALITY AS IDEAL (UTOPIA)

By contrast, a second perspective seeks a definition of normality in terms of a desirable or ideal state, which describes optimal rather than reasonable or average personality functioning. Views of *positive* mental health (e.g., Jahoda, 1958) or those which emphasize the goal of psychological development as self-actualization (Maslow, 1954; K. Goldstein, 1939), becoming a "fully functioning person" (Rogers, 1963), or attaining the "mature personality" (Allport, 1961) are of this class. Such definitions of normality often emerge in discussions of the ideal goals of psychotherapy. This is in contrast to a view of treatment as removing symptoms and restoring comfort (achieving normality as health). In actuality, however, the ideal normal may be represented in few if any living mortals. It is in this sense that Freud once characterized normality as an ideal fiction. Clearly, the criteria by which an ideal state is to be defined are more difficult to establish and assess and more dependent on the values of the investigator than those which describe a not-sick or an average man. However, it is a necessary perspective, particularly as we are concerned with prevention of pathology and optimizing the personality functioning of large numbers of adequate but limited people.

NORMALITY AS AVERAGE

A third perspective derives from the statistics of measurement. If any human attribute is measured, values fall along a "normal" or bell-shaped curve; most will cluster near the center and increasingly fewer cases will be found the farther out one goes. In many areas of psychological and medical measurement extensive normative data exist which define the average and describe the distribution of numerous characteristics, such as height, intelligence, blood pressure, reading skill, aggressiveness, and so on. Within a statistical conception, it should be noted that the average is normal, while *both* extremes are abnormal. A physician may speak of blood pressure as abnormally high or low; we commonly use the same phrase in describing, say, a person's height. It is worth noting, however, that although description along statistical lines is often described as scientific (i.e., value-free), where characteristics are clearly desirable, we rarely use the term abnormal to characterize one extreme. Thus, the person with an IQ of 150 is not likely to be called abnormally intelligent, nor is the perfect body described as abnormally beautiful. The statistical concept of normality has, nonetheless, considerable utility for describing the empirical distribution of human characteristics and is widely used in clinical research and practice.

NORMALITY AS SOCIALLY ACCEPTABLE

A related view of normality is based on the premise that behavior can only be judged in terms of the social context within which it occurs. If it conforms with the normative expectations of the society, it is normal; if it does not, it is deviant or abnormal. Some social scientists have defended the view that what clinicians conceive as personality aberrations should be understood as social deviance and that universalistic definitions of health and illness are misguided. Ralph Linton (1956, p. 637) says "The tests of absolute normalcy are the individual's ability to apprehend reality, as understood by his society, to act in terms of this reality, and to be effectively shaped by his society during his developmental period. The test of relative normalcy is the extent to which the individual's experience has given him a personality conforming to the basic personality of his society." The *cultural relativism* of anthropologists in the 1930s was an extreme of this point of view (e.g., Benedict, 1934). The evidence they drew on was of three sorts: (1) There are some behaviors considered normal in our society which are abnormal in others. Thus, Benedict points out, the normally expected initiative and drive of the white American is looked on as severely disordered behavior among the Zuni Indians; (2) some behaviors considered abnormal in our society are normal elsewhere. The northwest American Indians, Benedict reports, have institutionalized paranoid behavior; and (3) it is noted that there are forms of psychological disturbance found in other cultures which are not known in our own, such as going "amok" among the Malaysians. It is certainly true that even between subcultures of a complex society such as ours there are vast differences in social norms, which would make a particular behavior expectable and approved in one place, condemned in another. It is equally true that the clinician must know and interpret the social context of his patient if he is to understand his personality functioning and problems. But does this mean that there are no general culture-free criteria by which behavior can be defined as normal and abnormal? Critics of cultural relativism (e.g., Wegrocki, 1939) point out that too often the evidence for a cultural concept of abnormality rests on behavioral data alone and does not take into account the meaning of the behavior for the economy of the personality. A culturally determined act of another society may look like a psychopathological symptom of our own society, and vice versa, but on examination it is not accompanied by the anxiety, defensive properties, ego-alien, and compulsive experiences which are the proper marks of pathology.

One of the difficulties of conceiving normality from a cultural or statistical vantage point is the danger of identifying normality with conformity and conversely, abnormality with nonconformity, originality, or individuality. While it is true that the acts of mentally disturbed people often flout social norms, it is equally true that rigid adherence to norms can indicate pathology. Weak and uncertain people find security in being just like everyone else; to stand out in any respect is to be vulnerable.* Alberto Moravia's novel *The Conformist* graphically depicts the pathetic situation of a man who wants nothing more than to be average during the era of Italian Fascism, in the hope that he can thus erase the guilt of his childhood. By contrast, experimental studies have shown that leaders compared to more average men more often held fast to their points of view even when they seemed to be in disagreement with their group (Crutchfield, 1955). Erratic and unpredictable behavior can as well go with creativity as with mental illness. From the standpoint of psychological health, what matters is the motivation of the act rather than the degree to which it conforms to social expectation. Many psychotic individuals would want to conform, but they cannot comprehend the norm or they cannot control their actions sufficiently well to do so. Indeed, in small ways within their control, grossly disturbed people are often remarkable conformists, being eager not to offend. On the other hand, voluntary nonconformity—even to the extent of civil disobedience—may be the mark of a healthy personality, acting with conviction on his own values.

NORMALITY AS PROCESS

Some theories attempt to characterize normality in terms of processes over time rather than in cross-sectional perspective. They emphasize the evolutional nature of biological or psychological systems, so that the valuation of a particular

* In this connection, I must express a strongly held prejudice against the use of the term "adjustment" in mental health. The image it brings to mind, mine at least, is of accommodation of the person to the social norm, with little concern for his individuality. When I hear the phrase, "a well-adjusted child," I have a slight chill, expecting to see a colorless youngster, harmless I suppose, who has been compressed in a common mold. If I use the word anywhere in this book, it will be an oversight.

behavior may alter depending on the phase of the life process. Thus, Erikson (1963) as earlier noted, views the epigenesis of personality development in terms of the successful mastery of successive stages of development, which leads to adult functioning and normality. It is the temporal process, rather than status at points along the way, that defines normality. For theoretical analysis, this distinction is important, though for our present survey process positions can be considered together with those that stress status.

A Concept of Psychological Health and Abnormality

Clearly, a person can be called normal if he is not sick, if he is average, if he conforms to social norms, or if he approximates an ideally mature, healthy, or fully functioning personality. Indeed, one can view a kind of continuum ranging from the grossly disturbed to the conventionally adequate to the creatively mature, and we often do this in clinical practice as in ordinary social life. Is there value in striving for a general definition of psychological health and, if so, where should it position among these alternatives and how does one decide?

It is necessary, I believe, for the individual clinician, and for the field as a whole, to have a distinct concept of psychological health. For the concept of health that is held guides thinking about emotional disorders, modes and goals of treatment, and in general the planning of mental health services. I also believe that the concept of psychological health must focus on the *ideal* state, emphasize the "positive well-being" of the WHO charter, rather than on disease, statistical, or conformity criteria. This does depend on a statement of values and in that sense an ethical rather than scientific position is required. As Allport (1958) noted there is an important distinction between statistical norms (what people *are* like) and ethical norms (what the healthy person *should be* like). The latter can only be decided on ethical grounds. The views presented here, including my own, arise out of the matrix of a democratic ideology, with its emphasis on the autonomy and integrity of the individual human being. While an ideal concept oriented to ethical norms is clearly based on value judgments, it also seems true that the seemingly most objective criteria may disguise, but as much depend on, other value judgments.

There have been many attempts to describe mental health in ideal terms, which have generally led to lists of qualities which characterize the mature, healthy, fully functioning, self-actualizing person; often enough, the terms are used interchangeably. On analysis, there is considerable agreement among the proposed conceptions. At least in western society, general themes emerge.

THE HEALTHY PERSONALITY

From her analysis of many definitions Jahoda (1958) gives the following as criteria of positive mental health:

1. Attitudes toward the self; they include the accessibility of the self to consciousness; the correctness of the self-concept; its relation to the sense of identity and the acceptance by the individual of his own self.

2. Growth, development, and self-actualization; the extent the individual utilizes his abilities; his orientation toward the future and his investment in living.
3. Integration; the extent to which the psychic forces are balanced; a unifying outlook on life and a resistance to stress.
4. Autonomy; the aim here is to ascertain whether the self-reliant person is able to decide with relative ease and speed what suits his own needs best.
5. Perception of reality; a relative freedom from need-distortion and the existence of empathy.
6. Environmental mastery; under this heading is listed: ability to love, work, and play; adequacy in interpersonal relationships; meeting situational requirements; adaptation and adjustment; and efficiency in problem solving.

Shoben (1957) proposes a model of "integrative adjustment" which is characterized by "self-control, personal responsibility, social responsibility, democratic social interest, and ideals." Behavior according to Shoben is normal to the extent that it expresses man's most unique capacities for symbolization and social involvement. Among his criteria of the fully functioning person Rogers (1963) emphasizes the capacity for awareness and openness to experience. Offer and Sabshin (1966), Jahoda (1958), and Allport (1961) list other characteristics described for the healthy personality. In the context of many of these same characteristics, Maslow (1954) notes that "self-actualizing" people also are invariably creative, in the sense of giving whatever they do a personal and distinctive quality.

Gordon Allport (1961) describes the "mature personality," for him synonymous with soundness of health, as having six salient qualities: (1) Extension of the sense of self. This involves authentic participation in important spheres of human endeavor, beyond immediate self-interest; (2) Warm relating to others. Because of self-extension, the mature person is more capable of intimacy but also of respect and compassion; (3) Emotional security (self-acceptance). This is reflected both in frustration tolerance and in trust; (4) Realistic perception, skills, and assignments. This includes not only accurate judgment, but the capacity to be problem-centered and to lose oneself in one's work; (5) Self-objectification, i.e., insight and humor. To know oneself and to laugh at oneself requires mature detachment; and (6) A unifying philosophy of life. The mature person has a sense of direction and purpose and a broad personal philosophy.

Overall, then, through the overlapping concepts and alternate terms, a coherent picture of the healthy, mature personality emerges. Developmentally, the healthy person is highly differentiated and well integrated. He is more motivated by abundancy than deficiency needs. There is a strong sense of personal identity, realistic self-esteem, detachment, and sensitivity to the self and others. He has a sense of competence and actual competencies in psychological functioning (i.e., learning, memory, problem-solving). His ego is strong, his behavior is flexible and adaptable and there is considerable stress tolerance. Coping devices are more evident than defenses. Within ecological possibilities, he is an autonomous agent, mastering problems rather than being the passive object of the forces of the environment, the social order, or inner drives. With a secure sense of being and value, he can be compassionate, sympathetic, and loving toward others. Conscience and values are coherent, conscious, and well integrated. Finally, the healthy personality is comfortable with himself and valued by others.

This is not to suggest that such a person is without conflicts, worries, or anxiety. Because of high ideals and self-confidence, he can overreach and know failure and frustration. He can hurt others and know guilt. As anyone, he is capable of foolish, thoughtless, and self-defeating acts. In his spontaneity and desire for experience, in a readiness to accept challenges "because it's there," defeat and despair are predictable risks. But what distinguishes the healthy personality is that these do not lead to defensive retreat, hostile anger, or face-saving maneuvers. Instead, adversity is counteracted as possible, but above all it is the basis for further learning and wisdom. It is in the capacity to continue growth, rather than being without pain or suffering, that the healthy person is best defined.

The definition of psychological health given here is, admittedly, in general terms. It is intended to depict the positive state which can serve as an ideal model against which the disability of a patient can be viewed and, more important, to describe the state toward which we, as clinicians, should want to see him grow. It focusses on positive attributes, to the intentional neglect of pathological, statistical, or cultural criteria. In practice, the conceptual criteria require restatement in terms of the actual behaviors of particular persons living under particular life circumstances. But I have wanted to avoid a concept of normality which suggests that there is a particular behavioral mold which describes *the* normal person. In fact, there are many alternate behaviors which could as well fit the hypothetical model, provided that they reflect the functional and structural properties suggested by the general concepts. In principle, at least, these transcend particular social roles and national differences. Whether carpenter or business executive, Finn or Spaniard, man or woman, a firm sense of personal identity, for example, bespeaks health, though its content and the conditions under which it develops may indeed differ widely. Surely, there are manifest differences in the behaviors and, too, their social acceptability of Finnish carpenters and Spanish women; what is appropriate for the one might well be deviant for the other. It is importantly true that cultures differ too in the stresses they put on individuals and there are changes as well in a particular society over time. Thus, the Spanish woman, say, may be more beset by identity conflicts as her society becomes more open and egalitarian and she has more choice than in the earlier traditional society which sharply defined her role and actions. However, this is talking about the factors which influence personality and test the strength of the mature person rather than about the qualities which define maturity itself.*

THE PATHOLOGICAL PERSONALITY

In general, the disturbed person can be characterized by the obverse of the traits which describe psychological health. Depending on the extent and type of disturbance, the person lacks voluntary control, ego strength, flexibility, and adaptability. He experiences himself as weak among powerful and uncontrollable forces. His self-concept is distorted and unrealistic; he lacks self-esteem or has a vastly exaggerated notion of his worth. He is driven by deficiency motives. Basic drives are either acted out in raw and impulsive actions or inhibited and blocked. Powerful and painful negative affects are more usually his lot than experiences of

* In the case of the child, which we have thus far not considered, the criteria of psychological health do, of course, have to be adjusted to age-specific development. In terms of the developmental framework considered earlier, there is steady change along a general dimension of increased differentiation and integration as the child masters age-specific tasks. The health of the child has to be viewed against the developmental sequence, although the general criteria just discussed still serve as an ideal, if more distant, model of health.

joy, love, or accomplishment. Despite frequent and rigid defensive maneuvers, crystallized into symptoms, threat is always present and with it, anxiety, actual or potential. His knowledge of himself is poor and self-deceiving; similarly, he is unable to be genuinely empathic or sympathetic to others. Others, in turn, see him as dangerous and incomprehensible, as demanding and intrusive, as isolative and hostile, and perhaps pathetic but not worthy of respect. Basic psychological functions may be disturbed; perception, learning, and memory may be need-determined rather than reality appropriate or they may reflect forms (e.g., syncretism) more characteristic of lower developmental levels. All told, he is miserable himself and disturbing to others.

However, we must recall again that there is a continuum from the abnormal to normal and that boundaries are indeed hard to define. In terms of the general state of the personality, individuals can be positioned from one pole of complete disorganization and pathology to the other of heroic health. But it is also true that in different situations, in different realms of behavior, and at different moments any of us, or most patients, could appear more or less abnormal. There are few acts which, as such, are unequivocally pathological. The healthy person, fatigued or irritated, may express intense rage or other grossly inappropriate feelings or behavior. In such states, we can even approximate schizophrenic thought processes, the analog of which we have all experienced, for example, in the brief period between sleep and waking. Conversely, even severely disordered people may have long periods in which they function adequately, or particular situations which allow ordered behavior. In general, it is under conditions of stress, when extreme or unusual demands are made, that the strengths or weaknesses of the personality organization appear most vividly. For this reason, G. L. Freeman (1939) once suggested the term "psychiatric Plimsoll mark," to characterize the point of dangerous overload for an individual, in analogy to the line drawn on the hull of a ship to indicate how much cargo it can take and still ride safely in the water. Finally, we should recognize that functioning can be impaired in one realm though normal in another. The story is told of the man who had a flat tire in front of a state hospital. While he changed it, a patient looked on curiously. As he was about to put on the spare, he accidently kicked the hubcap into which he had put the lugs for mounting the wheel, sending them spinning into a nearby sewer drain. In complete perplexity, he looked helplessly at the car. After a discrete while, the patient called out, "Why don't you borrow one lug from each of the other three wheels? They'll be secure enough and you'll be able to mount the fourth wheel." The man did so and in thanking the patient couldn't help but express surprise at his creative solution. Said the patient, "I may be crazy but I'm not stupid." We are all too ready to assume that undesirable traits cluster together.

Perhaps the quality which most clearly describes the abnormal person is his lack of voluntary control. At the extreme are the violent emotional storms, bizarre acts, and seemingly irrational behaviors of the psychotic. Not only do they appear to others as if he is possessed of some demonic force, that he has "gone out of his mind," but so are they experienced by the patient himself. The neurotic cannot contain the obsessive thoughts, the driven behaviors, the constant doubts and anxieties, even though he knows them to be groundless and would rather perform differently. An ultimate threat for both the psychotic and neurotic is still further loss of control, experienced as disintegrative anxiety. In defense, inhibitions are strengthened, activities avoided; overall, gaining some security but at the cost of further rigidity. This, in turn, further limits choice and freedom.

Among psychoanalysts, Kubie (e.g., 1954) has most clearly developed the thesis that the essential difference between normal and neurotic lies in whether behavior is under conscious control or whether it is automatically determined by unconscious processes. He says:

> The essence of normality is flexibility, in contrast to the freezing of behavior into patterns of unalterability that characterizes every manifestation of the neurotic process, whether in impulses, purposes, acts, thoughts, or feelings. *Whether or not a behavioral event is free to change depends not upon the quality of the act itself, but upon the nature of the constellation of forces which has produced it. No moment of behavior can be looked upon as neurotic unless the processes that have set it in motion predetermine its automatic repetition irrespective of the situation, the utility, or the consequences of the act.* This may be the most basic lesson about human conduct that has been learned from psychoanalysis [1954, pp. 182–183] (emphasis in original).

The unconsciously determined act is repetitive, insatiable, and impervious to conscious experience because, says Kubie further, it is directed toward unconscious symbols and goals which by their nature are unattainable. Generalizing these concepts, Kubie argues that a person can be called normal to the extent that his actions are determined by conscious motives. ". . . we may say that a state of greater health is achieved whenever those areas of life that are dominated by inaccessible unconscious forces are shrunk, so that a larger area of life is dominated by conscious or preconscious forces, which can come to awareness when necessary. This is a reasonable concept of health and a reasonable formulation of the goal of therapy. . . ." [1954, p. 184].

Forms of Mental Disorder: Psychiatric Nomenclature

In 1968, the American Psychiatric Association published the *Diagnostic and Statistical Manual of Mental Disorders* (DSM-II), which revised their 1952 standards (DSM-I) for recording and reporting the diagnoses of psychiatric patients. DSM-II attempted to bring American usage more in line with international practice and the release of DSM-II coincided with the publication of an *International Classification of Diseases* by the World Health Organization. Comparison of the incidence and prevalence of psychiatric conditions and international communication should in principle at least be facilitated by DSM-II. The manual assigns a three-digit number to each condition, which is qualified as necessary by additional digits following a decimal point. Thus, the diagnosis of *schizophrenia* is 295; *schizophrenia, catatonic type* is indicated by 295.2, and *schizophrenia, catatonic type, excited* by 295.23. Patients can be given multiple diagnoses; other conventions allow for indicating severity of impairment and whether the condition is acute, chronic, or in remission. Although considerable controversy has surrounded DSM-II, indeed the concept of standardized diagnosis itself, DSM-II is now the standard for case reporting in the United States.

The major, and some of the minor, diagnostic categories of DSM-II are listed below, without troubling to indicate their code numbers. In parentheses are included some explanatory comments, drawn mainly directly from the *Manual.*

THE DSM-II DIAGNOSTIC NOMENCLATURE OF PSYCHIATRIC CONDITIONS

I. Mental Retardation

(Mental retardation refers to subnormal intellectual functioning which arises during development. The subdiagnoses—borderline, mild, moderate, severe, and profound—are defined in terms of IQ ranges. Diagnoses further specify the apparent etiological factors involved.)

II. Organic Brain Syndromes

(These reflect impairment of brain-tissue function. Conditions may be acute-reversible or chronic-permanent. In general, organic brain syndromes involve impairments of orientation, memory, judgment, and other intellectual functions, as well as changes in personality and emotional functioning. In addition, however, they may or may not involve psychotic states, which provides the major basis for classification.)

A. Psychoses associated with organic brain syndromes

1. senile and presenile dementia
2. alcoholic psychoses
3. psychoses associated with intracranial infection
4. psychoses associated with other cerebral conditions (e.g., arteriosclerosis, epilepsy, tumor)
5. psychoses associated with other physical conditions (e.g., endocrine, metabolic, or nutritional disorder; infection or poisoning; during childbirth)

B. Nonpsychotic organic brain syndromes

III. Psychoses Not Attributed to Physical Conditions Listed Previously

(This category includes the major psychotic conditions such as schizophrenia and manic-depressive psychoses, which are of greatest concern to psychological clincians. However, whether related to organic brain disease or not, patients are said to be psychotic "when their mental functioning is sufficiently impaired to interfere grossly with their capacity to meet the ordinary demands of life" [DSM-II, p. 23]. In the present diagnostic system, such gross behavioral and thought disorder must be present for psychosis to be diagnosed. It is possible therefore to diagnose one of the "psychotic" conditions as "without psychosis" if the patient is presently functioning adequately although the basic diagnosis may still seem to be clinically justified. Thus, 295.26 is *Schizophrenia, catatonic type, without psychosis.)*

A. Schizophrenia

Type:
1. simple
2. hebephrenic
3. catatonic
4. paranoid
5. acute schizophrenic episode
6. latent
7. residual
8. schizo-affective
9. childhood
10. chronic undifferentiated

B. Major affective disorders

1. involutional melancholia
   (This is a disorder of the involutional, i.e., "change-of-life," period, marked by anxiety, insomnia, agitation, and guilt.)

2. manic-depressive illnesses
(Subcategories include manic, depressed, and circular type, marked by both manic and depressed episodes.)

C. Paranoid states

D. Other psychoses

IV. Neuroses

(In contrast to the psychoses, there is neither gross distortion of external reality, nor major personality disorganization. Anxiety and the symptomatic evidence of excessive defensive activities are the prime characteristics).

A. Anxiety neurosis

B. Hysterical neurosis

Type: 1. conversion

2. dissociative

(The latter includes symptoms of amnesia, multiple personality, or somnambulism, rather than the organiclike symptoms of the conversion state.)

C. Phobic neurosis

D. Obsessive compulsive neurosis

E. Depressive neurosis

F. Neurasthenic neurosis

G. Depersonalization neurosis

H. Hypochondriacal neurosis

J. Other neuroses

V. Personality Disorders and Certain Other Nonpsychotic Mental Disorders

A. Personality disorders

(These are long-standing maladaptive behavior patterns without the specific symptoms and, usually, without the disability of neuroses or psychoses.)

1. paranoid personality
2. cyclothymic personality
(characterized by alternating moods of depression and elation)
3. schizoid personality
4. explosive personality
5. obsessive-compulsive personality
6. hysterical personality
7. asthenic personality
8. antisocial personality
9. passive-aggressive personality
10. inadequate personality
11. other specified types (e.g., immature personality)
12. other unspecified types

B. Sexual deviations

(Included among others are homosexuality, fetishism, exhibitionism, sadism, etc. It is interesting to note that within five years of the publication of DSM-II, the American Psychiatric Association voted to delete homosexuality, accepting the argument of the homosexual community that homosexuality represented an alternate life-style but should not be considered a "mental disorder.")

C. Alcoholism

D. Drug dependence

(Catalogued in terms of particular drugs, e.g., opium and derivatives, barbiturates, sedatives, cocaine, etc.)

VI. Psychophysiological Disorders

(Included here are physical diseases of presumably psychogenic origin, often called psychosomatic diseases. They are grouped in terms of the physiological system or organs involved; thus, psychophysiological skin disorder, cardiovascular disorder, gastrointestinal disorder, etc.)

VII. Special Symptoms
(Here are included symptoms not elsewhere classified which do not result from other organic or mental disorders. Illustrations would include speech disturbances, learning disabilities, sleep disturbances, among others.)

VIII. Transient Situational Disturbances
(These are acute reactions which occur in otherwise well-functioning individuals in the face of overwhelming environmental stress. They are expected to recede as the stress reduces. They are grouped by the patient's developmental level; thus, the types include adjustment reaction of infancy, childhood, adolescence, adult life, and late life.)

IX. Behavior Disorders of Childhood or Adolescence
(These are conditions of childhood [or adolescence] which are more stable and persistent than transient situational disturbances but less so than psychoses, neuroses, or personality disorders. The types are diagnosed in terms of characteristic manifestations such as overactivity, withdrawal, overanxiety, unsocialized aggression, or delinquency.)

X. Conditions Without Manifest Psychiatric Disorder and Nonspecific Disorders
- A. Social maladjustments without manifest psychiatric disorder
(Here included are problems for which consultation may be sought by people who are "psychiatrically normal.")
  1. marital maladjustment
  2. social maladjustment
  3. occupational maladjustment
  4. dyssocial behavior
  (This describes people who are not classifiable as antisocial personalities, but who "follow more or less criminal pursuits.")
- B. Nonspecific conditions
(Describes conditions which cannot be classified in any of the foregoing categories.)

The DSM-II list suggests the variety of conditions with which clinicians work in hospital, clinic, community, and private-practice settings. Obviously, they differ enormously in terms of severity, extent, and duration of impairment, discomfort to the patient and those in contact with him, and in the causative factors which determine them. As we have already discussed, serious issue has been taken with the enterprise of diagnosis in general. Human psychological problems cannot be cataloged in simple analogy to medical diseases and, in any case, such labelling not only may not be helpful to the treatment of the patient but may itself be the cause of deviant behavior. Others have noted that, even if the term "psychiatric disorder" is appropriate for cases of brain damage, psychosis, or neurosis, it is inappropriate to include situational stress reactions, occupational maladjustments, and other psychosocial problems within even the most general definition of disease.

Without considering these issues again, the diagnostic nomenclature can be viewed simply as descriptive categories characterizing, somewhat loosely and incompletely, problems which society or the sufferers themselves bring to professional attention. For clinicians, particularly those working in psychiatric hospitals, it is important that the terms be understood, for hospital practice and records use them extensively. Often enough, the terms have administrative or legal consequences, rather than simply serving to guide description or treatment. Depending on diagnosis, patients can be involuntarily committed or released from hospitals, be paid pensions, be held responsible or not for criminal activities, and similarly important life decisions be made on their behalf.

It is interesting to note some of the changes in the diagnostic system between 1952 (DSM-I) and 1968 (DSM-II): (1) In DSM-II, mental retardation (then called mental deficiency) has been given a much more prominent place in psychiatric thinking, no doubt reflecting the concern of the Kennedy Administration and the National Institute of Mental Health with the relative neglect of this problem; (2) The range of conditions listed in DSM-II has been increased greatly over that of DSM-I, notably by the inclusion of categories IX and X, describing conditions of childhood and adolescence and the variety of social maladjustments; (3) DSM-I used the traditional psychiatric terms in adjectival form along with the term "reaction," while DSM-II reverts to the older usage of simply stating the condition in nominative form. Thus, prior to 1952, it was *schizophrenia;* DSM-I used the term *schizophrenic reaction;* in DSM-II, it is again *schizophrenia.* The *reaction* form had the advantage of suggesting that disturbed behavior arises in the interplay between the person and conditions acting upon him and is reversible through intervention, rather than suggesting a permanent and unchangeable condition. Logically, however, *reaction* should be followed by *to,* if it is to have any real meaning; thus, allergic reaction to, say, strawberries extends the meaning of allergy, but *pneumonia reaction* says no more than *pneumonia.* In any case, following DSM-I, neither professionals nor the public changed their thinking about mental disorders nor did the *reaction* form gain much usage. Unfortunately, word changes do not necessarily alter attitudes nor create scientific knowledge.

A number of problems are built into the DSM-II classificatory scheme.

1. Categories are loosely *empirical* and *descriptive.* They are not oriented to a particular theoretical position, nor refer to etiological causes nor treatment consequences of the disorder. Moreover, the categories are of distinctly different "widths." Some describe a relatively well-defined condition, e.g., anxiety neurosis, while others loosely group a variety of problems, e.g., marital maladjustment.

2. As in any typology, the diagnosis better fits a hypothetical "textbook case" rather than real individuals and there is the danger of stereotyping. In pathology as well as in health, individuals are unique and differ along numerous dimensions. At least, the diagnostic rubric must be qualified greatly to describe the individual case, which is ultimately the clinician's concern. Early in this century, the distinguished American psychiatrist Adolph Meyer summed up the view of many good clinicians, then and since: "We understand this case; we don't need any diagnosis." (Quoted by R. I. Watson, 1951.)

3. Logically and scientifically, the scheme is less than elegant. The principles of classification are mixed so that some conditions are defined by behavioral symptoms, (e.g., low IQ, hallucination, or anxiety), others by originating conditions (e.g., brain damage) and still others by patient characteristics (e.g., age). Understandably, workers in the field have argued the need for a classificatory system which is based only on one type of criterion, such as behavioral symptoms (e.g., Kanfer and Saslow, 1965).

4. Not only are different types of concepts involved, but the particular symptoms for specific diagnoses are insufficiently specified. Zigler and Phillips (1961) have shown in an extensive statistical study that there is great overlap between the symptoms actually manifested by differently diagnosed patients. In principle,

this should lead to considerable unreliability of diagnosis, which is commonly enough reported. However, in view of the vagueness of the concepts, the subjectivity of psychiatric diagnosis, and the many distorting influences which might act on examiners, there is an impressive amount of reliability in psychiatric diagnoses, both in interrater and repeat-reliability studies (cf., for example, Schmidt and Fonda, 1956; Sandifer et al., 1964; Babigan, 1965).

5. Despite the extended range of conditions included in DSM-II, it still does not cover many of the problems with which clinicians work. This is particularly true of the existential neuroses which have become a commonplace of clinical practice, manifested by feelings of emptiness, a loss of meaning, and identity problems. In other realms, DSM-II assigns only gross categories to wide ranges of problems which deserve more differentiated consideration. Thus, the problems of children and adolescents are compacted into a few diagnostic entities. Clinicians working with children and youth have attempted independently to develop diagnostic schemes for the particular needs of child practice (e.g., Group for the Advancement of Psychiatry, 1966). Similarly, the psychological problems of the aged are slighted. In the main, the scheme is most explicit when dealing with the more defined and major conditions of adulthood, particularly those related to brain damage, psychoses, and the symptom neuroses, and less useful as it refers to other age groups, specific disabilities (e.g., as in the learning problems of children), or diffuse psychosocial or existential problems.

Despite all of these criticisms, and the dangers inherent in its use, psychiatric diagnosis as represented in DSM-II can be valuable to clinicians. It helps to organize, although it should not be allowed to bind, the clinician's thinking. The diagnostic entities have persisted over so many decades because they do represent general classes of behaviors which differ one from the other. However inexact and however much they overlap, they give a basis for discussing forms of psychopathology and for seeking relevant causal conditions and intervention procedures. It is not inappropriate to ask "How do schizophrenics differ from brain-damaged or neurotic patients?" for these are general classes of personality functioning differentiable one from the other. Obviously, clinical intervention does not end with diagnosis, nor in the present state of knowledge can any but the most general assumptions about etiology or treatment be derived from diagnosis. There are the real issues and dangers of stereotypy and of stigmatization and the clinician has the obligation to seek understanding of each patient individually. Nevertheless, classification systems will persist and have heuristic value.

One effort to improve classification has involved empirical studies in which many specific forms of behavior are measured and intercorrelated in order to derive statistically defined clusters. Though methods of factor analysis or similar statistical techniques, groupings of traits or measures which go together and are relatively independent of other such groupings are derived. Factorial studies have been made on children's behavior problems (Dreger et al., 1964), depressed patients (Grinker et al., 1961), borderline patients (Grinker et al., 1968), psychotics (Wittenborn, 1964), schizophrenic Rorschach patterns (Beck, 1954), among many others. The studies of Lorr and his colleagues (Lorr, Klett, and McNair, 1963; Lorr and Klett, 1969a; 1969b; Lorr, Klett, and Cave, 1967) are illustrative of this approach and show its potential value. They developed a scale of some seventy-five items describing the behavior of hospitalized patients, which are rated by a clinical examiner following interview and observation. From the intercorrelations of these items, Lorr and his associates have distinguished ten psychotic syndromes: excitement, hostile belligerence, paranoid projection, grandiose expansiveness, perceptual distortion, anxious intropunitiveness, retardation and apathy, disorientation, motor disturbances, and conceptual disorganization. More recently, Lorr, Klett, and Cave (1967) have proposed that the ten syndromes could be reduced to five higher-order constructs, representing disorganized hyperactivity, schizophrenic disorganization, paranoid process, hostile paranoia, and anxious depression. Although first described in American patients, essentially the same syndromes were found in Japanese patients and those of five European nations (Lorr and Klett, 1969). It is noteworthy that the syndromes derived from statistical analyses are relatively similar to those traditional in clinical practice. However, the work of Lorr's group allows for more precise rating of each patient on a number of variables, each treated as a separable dimension of personality functioning. Thus, the patient can be characterized by a pattern of scores rather than simply being included or excluded from a given diagnostic category. Empirical-statistical studies can expand and specify the criteria of diagnostic classification.

Toward a Unitary Concept of Mental Health and Mental Illness

The official psychiatric diagnostic classification suggests a view of mental disorders as separate and discrete disease entities, which patients contract and which mental health workers must differentially diagnose. Although clearly more sophisticated, DSM-II is heir to a tradition descending from antiquity in which lists have been generated cataloging endlessly the varieties of deviant and bizarre behaviors known to psychiatry. Against this tradition, for many years clinical theorists have sought unifying concepts which would allow mental health and illness to be conceptualized within a unitary framework. As early as 1874, Hughlings Jackson proposed that mental diseases could be classified according to the degree of dissolution of psychological functions. The notion of a continuum from effective functioning to gross dysfunction is intrinsic to many contemporary theories of psychopathology. Such views build on the developmental and adaptational perspectives, as discussed in Chapter 3, to characterize progressive and regressive development as individuals cope successfully or unsuccessfully with life demands. Emphasis is shifted from static disease states to the processes which move human adaptation from a pole of mental health toward one of mental illness. Illustrative are the views of Engel (1962) and K. A. Menninger, Mayman, and Pruyser (1963), which build on a theoretical framework in which dynamic, developmental, and adaptational (stress) concepts converge.

Opposing a discrete disease orientation, Menninger and his colleagues propose that all psychological diseases are the same in quality though differing in quantity. They represent positions toward the end of health or toward that of illness along a single scale; at the extremes, between life and death. Position is determined by the stresses, internal and external, acting upon the person and on his coping resources. Neither is there a fixed state of mental health nor fixed disease entities, but rather degrees of effectiveness (or, contrariwise, dysfunction, dyscontrol, or "dysorganization") of the adaptational processes. At any level, symptomatic behaviors represent the best possible adaptation, and regression can be viewed as "adaptive retreat." Symptoms follow from the action of emergency mechanisms, called into play by threats to the person, which function to attain or restore equilibria. If the threat is too great, or the resources too weak, adaptation moves to a lower level. Each step down brings into play more extreme defensive actions, reveals more disturbed behaviors, and is more deviant from the adaptations of everyday life.

Everyday life, Menninger et al. note, is not without its tensions and threats and a variety of coping devices are normally called into play. But these operate smoothly, mainly during emergencies, for brief times and without disrupting daily activities. They are rarely sources of discomfort, nor experienced by the individual himself as ego-alien, nor are they viewd by clinicians or others as symptoms of disease. Such coping devices include, among others, seeking comfort in contact with others, in food or alcohol, self-discipline, laughing, swearing, crying, boasting, fantasy and dreaming, and other techniques which avert tension and maintain stability. By contrast, the phenomena of psychopathology can be described in terms of five levels of dysfunction, each further removed from the behaviors of everyday life.

1. The First Order of Dysfunction. When threat exceeds the coping capacity of everyday mechanisms, some degree of dyscontrol and dysorganization becomes evident. More extreme mechanisms come into play. At this level, the behavioral effectiveness and relative comfort are largely maintained, but at a cost. Most visible is "nervousness." With it are exaggerated evidences of inhibition, hyperemotionalism, restlessness, worry, some somatic and sexual dysfunctions, and conscious efforts at self-control.

2. The Second Order of Dysfunction. At this level there is some detachment from reality and distinct subjective discomfort. Such symptoms appear as fainting, dissociations, phobias, hysterical conversions, compulsions, sexual perversions, addictions, and "frozen emergency reactions" (i.e., personality deformities). In general, this level includes much of what has been described as the symptom neuroses and character neuroses in the past. However, Menninger sees them as at the same level of dysfunction in terms of their being alternate ways in which aggressive discharge is blocked from consciousness (e.g., fainting), or displaced to the body (e.g., somatic symptoms), or symbolically or magically averted (e.g., obsessive thoughts).

3. The Third Order of Dysfunction. This level is characterized by the escape of naked aggression, leading to repetitive or episodic acts of violence. These are manifestations of much more gross ego failures than at the second level. Included too would be the convulsions and seizures of epileptic patients and the catastrophic reactions of the brain-damaged. However, the functional episodic dyscontrol, whether acute or chronic, is viewed as adaptive since it averts the even more catastrophic disintegration of the person, ultimately represented at the fifth level.

4. The Fourth Order of Dysfunction. Here are the extreme states of disorganization, repudiation of reality, and regression which have classically been identified as psychoses. Particular syndromes include despondency, disorganized

excitement, self-absorption, mannerisms and bizarre delusions, persecutory preoccupations, disorientation, and confusion.

5. The Fifth Order of Dysfunction. This involves the ultimate disintegration of the person, complete deterioration, "psychogenic death," out of despair or hopelessness, and suicide. All adaptive efforts, even those of a psychotic adjustment, have failed.

In this fashion, Menninger, Mayman, and Pruyser conceive a continuum from psychological health to illness, which emphasizes the processes of stress and adaptation, particularly with regard to destructive impulses.

> The various orders of dyscontrol which we have described and illustrated are not pigeonholes into which people may be fitted; they are only still photographs of a moving picture of human life. In every individual are potentialities for destructiveness and self-destructiveness and in every individual there are potentialities for salvage, concern, growth, and creativity. The ceaseless struggle between these opposing trends occupies all the energies of our lives. One could say there were all degrees of failure, but one could also see these as all degrees of success. . . . If the phenomena of human life are looked at in this way, psychiatry passes from being a science of classifying and name-calling into a discipline of counsel for the maximizing of the potentialities of the individual and the improvement of social happiness [1963, p. 272].

As an alternative to descriptive psychiatry, Menninger's thesis is a praiseworthy attempt to understand the ebb and flow of health-supporting and distress-producing processes in individual lives as well as between individuals manifesting different types and severity of pathology. It encourages further quest for the common processes of pathology, rather than seeking disease-specific determinants. As a framework for research and clinical practice, this view is bold and far-reaching.

At the same time, it is clear that the basic premises on which it rests have yet to be proven. There is no clear evidence for a linear continuum from personality disturbances to neuroses and psychoses. It has not been demonstrated that patients have at one time disorders of, say, the second order and at another, of the fourth order. Nor, as psychotic patients improve do they necessarily go through a neurotic phase. The notion that neuroses and psychoses are alternate rather than sequential conditions, as expressed in Eysenck's (1960b) independent dimensions of psychoticism and neuroticism, is an equally creditable concept. It has been found for example that personal and social stress increases the occurrence of first, second, and even third order dysfunction, but they seem less related to the incidence of psychotic conditions. There is growing evidence for genetic factors which dispose to schizophrenia (e.g., D. Rosenthal and Kety, 1968), though there is no comparable evidence for the *lower*-order conditions. It may well be, as Meehl (1962) suggests, that there must be some neural defect probably of genetic origin to account for the "cognitive slippage" of schizophrenics, though the emergence of clinical symptoms may depend on additional environmental stress. It is beyond our present needs to examine the enormous amount of research and theoretical controversy which underlie these few comments. Suffice it to note, in its present form the continuum proposed by Menninger, Mayman, and Pruyser cannot be taken as a literal representation of the progress and regress in movement between health and illness, but rather as a valuable heuristic device for understanding the apparent diversity of psychopathology.

CHAPTER 5

Models of Mental Health Intervention

Prospect and Retrospect

In the remainder of this volume, we will be considering the interventions practiced by clinicians, the things they do to understand and help people with problems, particularly in the realms of clinical assessment, psychotherapy, and community psychology. Before going on, however, it is well to note that the concepts and methods in each of these areas arose in terms of broader conceptualizations of the mental health field. These orientations determine how mental health and illness are viewed and, hence, what kinds of interventions are selected to relieve or avert such problems. Such "models" of mental health thinking are the focus of the present chapter. Some of the ideas have been anticipated in earlier chapters and others will be further developed in later ones. At this point, a brief overview of alternate models can serve as a map to guide further discussion.

Five Models of Mental Health

For analytic purposes, mental health orientations can be described in terms of five distinct models, which, in turn, fall into three major groups. Like any analytic scheme, these categories are somewhat arbitrary and admittedly gross, but they can be helpful to comprehend contrasting views. The five models are:

I. Clinical Models
   A. Custodial
   B. Therapeutic
II. Community Models
   A. Clinical pole
   B. Public health pole
III. Social action model

The clinical models span the entire field of mental health as it existed, with relative minor exceptions, until the mid-1950s. Emphasis is on the *individual* in distress. At the custodial pole, thinking is anchored firmly in a medical concept of psychiatric illness; in the therapeutic position, psychological understanding and psychotherapy are emphasized. The therapeutic pole encompasses a wide variety of conceptions of personality, psychopathology, and psychological interventions (as we will consider in Parts III and IV); what they have in common is a concern with the well-being of the individual patient.

The community models, by contrast, shift emphasis from the individual toward the social setting. There is a growing trend, in the community mental health movement, to provide early and immediately available care to all parts of the population, hopefully in ways that might prevent as well as treat psychological disturbances, in settings as integrated as possible with community life. These concepts and methods are still very much in a developmental phase, as we will discuss in Part V. Interventions at the clinical pole, like those of the therapeutic model to which it is closely related, still focus largely on the individual in need, although there is more explicit concern with the social context of intervention. By contrast, the public health pole of the community-orientation centers concern more directly on the social influences which affect individual lives. The analogy, and hence the term, is to the public health physician's efforts to discover and eradicate the sources of disease to which a "population-at-risk" is exposed. A classic illustration, unfortunately impossible to parallel in the realm of mental health, is the discovery and eradication of the breeding grounds of the malaria-carrying mosquito. While a clinical approach is concerned with the diseased individual, a public health approach is aimed at prevention through the elimination of disease-causing conditions.

Finally, the social action model is presented for contrast, since it represents the view, in line with but more extreme than the public health model, that ultimately human problems are reflections of the strains in society. Hence, broad-scaled reorganization of social institutions is absolutely essential in order to achieve full and lasting relief of human problems.

Overall, the progression among the five models represents a number of related trends as one moves down the list from (1) historically older to more recent conceptions; (2) medical to psychological to social assumptions about the nature of psychological disturbance and treament; (3) a person-centered to a society-centered emphasis; (4) more direct to more indirect modes of intervention; and (5) more to less sharply defined and exclusive professional roles.

Table 5.1 characterizes some of the salient features of each model, illustrating underlying values in each case. The different orientations are pictured in terms of their positions on a number of issues, posed in the sixteen questions of Table 5.1, which bear on the conception of the patient, his role in seeking ("contracting") help, the nature of his problem, the conditions under which intervention occurs, its goals and likely outcome, and the roles of mental health professionals and relevant others in the process. The brief responses to these questions at best suggest rather than describe the alternate positions. In some cases, as yet undefined terms are used; hopefully, their meanings can be inferred in context, though they will become clearer in later chapters. Moreover, some words are used for their connotation rather than their literal usage in each model. Thus, the recipient of service is described as a "person" rather than a "patient" in the therapeutic and community models, though the term "patient" is commonly used by workers in both clinical and community models. However, its explicitly "medical model" connotation is more clearly seen in custodial usage.

With Table 5.1 before you, let us consider each model in somewhat greater detail.

CLINICAL MODELS

Custodial. At the heart of this orientation is the view that the patient is the victim of a psychiatric condition, that he has limited if any capacity to manage his own life, and that therefore professional care must be imposed by society, for his sake and the welfare of others. It is in this sense that the model is described as custodial. It is best exemplified in traditional psychiatric hospitals. Patients are often committed involuntarily, but even if admitted at their own request, the hospital takes over the major responsibility for their lives. The patient's condition is usually viewed as a disease, likely of biological origin. Patients are given drugs, electroshock, and other somatic therapies; psychological and social interventions are either not available or believed to be of minor importance. Psychiatric diagnosis is valued, though more often used for administrative and record-keeping purposes than to guide treatment. Authority and responsibility are vested in physicians, with other professionals viewed as "paramedical" and ancillary. The medical model dominates work in the traditional hospital.

Therapeutic. This is by far the largest, most evolved, and internally differentiated category, for it encompasses most of the activities of clinicians from positions as diverse as psychoanalysis, existentialism, and behaviorism. The various interventions involved will be described and contrasted in Parts III and IV of this volume. What is common to all the approaches within a "therapeutic" model is faith in the efficacy of psychological intervention, of one or another sort, for bringing about desirable changes in patients. Patients are viewed as disturbed individuals, whose conditions have psychological roots and who can voluntarily contract for professional services. In this model, the clinician works directly with the patient, and only secondarily or not at all with relevant others in his social environment. Thus, the hallmarks of this orientation are a primary concern with a person in distress, respect for his needs and desires, personally contracted interventions, which usually occur in a professional setting (hospital, clinic, or private practice) and are offered by a professionally trained mental health worker.

COMMUNITY MODELS

Clinical Emphasis. The community orientation emphasizes the role of social factors as determinants of human problems. Patient care is brought into the context of community values and institutions; as far as possible, in innovative set-

TABLE 5.1

Models of Mental Health Intervention

ISSUE	CLINICAL MODELS		COMMUNITY MODELS		SOCIAL ACTION MODEL
	CUSTODIAL	THERAPEUTIC	CLINICAL POLE	PUBLIC HEALTH POLE	
Who is recipient (R) of service?	A patient	A person	A person (and relevant others)	A population-at-risk or everyone	A population-at-risk or everyone
How is individual R's state conceived?	Diseased; unable to care for self	Psychologically disturbed; worthy of sympathy, respect and professional effort	In psychosocial crisis; worthy of sympathy, respect and assistance	In present crisis or potential danger; respect-worthy, but may not be motivated to change	Under present or potential social stress; all worthy of benefits of "great society"
Locus of problem?	In R (probably biologically)	In R (probably psychologically)	In R and his psychosocial situation	There, or more importantly, in social system	In social and political systems
Is it likely to change?	Probably not	Yes, with professional help	Yes, with help	Yes, with a change in social conditions	Yes, with a change in institutions
What is done?	Custodial care and medication	Individual, group, and family psychotherapy; milieu therapy	Crisis intervention, brief therapy, counseling and/or direct help with jobs, school, economic and similar problems	Various actions intended for secondary, tertiary, and primary prevention	If possible, actions directed to broad-scaled social change
Importance and purpose of clinical assessment?	Important, for diagnostic categorization	Very important, for broad-scaled personalistic understanding of R, for therapy planning, and evaluation	Important, for assessing R's focal problem, strengths and liabilities, but time-consuming and costly	Important, but mainly for survey and epidemiological purposes	Irrelevant, except in survey role as evidence of social problem
Who initiates?	Courts, family, and professionals	R, preferably self-motivated	R or family	R, social agency, health authority	Social authorities

ISSUE	CLINICAL MODELS		COMMUNITY MODELS		SOCIAL ACTION MODEL
	CUSTODIAL	THERAPEUTIC	CLINICAL POLE	PUBLIC HEALTH POLE	
Under what contract?	Involuntary, when need is established	Voluntary, on demand	Usually voluntary, on demand	Involuntary or voluntary, when needed	Involuntary for individual, decision controlled by political process
At what time?	When "doctor" decides	When R requests	When R needs it (in crisis)	Whenever possible; in advance of need	All the time
Who conducts intervention?	"Doctor"	Mental health professional	Professional with nonprofessional assistance	Professionals in collaboration with nonprofessionals, other professional caretakers	Professional in collaboration with policy makers
Who else is involved?	Paramedical staff	No one, or "psychiatric team"	Team, community caretakers and nonprofessionals	Same and community agents and leaders	Policy makers
How does the professional function?	Administratively, medically	Directly, as therapist	Directly and through supervision of nonprofessionals	Indirectly, through consultation	Indirectly, through advising policy makers
Specific role of the psychologist?	Diagnostic tester	Psychotherapist and/or clinical assessor	Therapist, counselor, community/clinician	Community change agent, organizational consultant	No specific role
Place of intervention?	Hospital	Hospital, clinic, private office	Community mental health center, day hospitals, half-way houses, community settings	In community institutions (schools, church, etc.)	In political arena, social-planning institutions
Goal of intervention?	Discharge or remission of symptoms	Personality change, positive mental health	Strengthening of coping potential, relief of distress	Reduction of social stress	An improved society
What realm of knowledge is necessary for intervention?	Descriptive and medical psychiatry	Individual psychodynamics, personality theory, psychotherapy	Personality theory, social psychology of primary institutions, organizational psychology	Social psychology, community organization, epidemiology, sociology	Sociology, policy sciences, urban planning

tings which are more flexible than traditional mental health institutions. A major aim is to make clinical services immediately and easily accessible to all portions of the populations, particularly the poor and disadvantaged who had previously been denied adequate services.

At the clinical pole, intervention methods are generally of the same type as in the therapeutic model, though adapted to the special needs and life styles of particular communities. Service is offered in settings that are less professional (e.g., storefront clinics), frequently in collaboration with family members and community "caretakers," sometimes with the help of specially trained community members ("indigenous nonprofessionals"). The immediate goal is to carry patients through life crises and to foster social competencies. There is relatively less concern with attempting to bring about major personality changes of the sort sought by psychotherapists. Therapy is briefer and more focussed. In community-oriented practice, the clinician is necessarily more involved with the daily life and social problems of his client, particularly in work with poor and minority populations and his role is less distinguishable from those of other helping professionals (e.g., social welfare workers, employment counselors, etc.). The present problems of the client and his immediate social behavior are more the focus of concern than his life history, personality organization and functioning, values and attitudes. In order to serve as large a population as possible as effectively as possible, shorter and less costly modes of psychological intervention are sought and valued. Because the well-being of the patient is intimately connected with the behavior of family members and relevant others in the community, the clinician works with them. In other ways he also becomes directly involved in efforts to alter the patient's environment in order to alleviate psychosocial stress. Extensive personality evaluation, through interviews or psychological testing, are a luxury in community clinical service.

Public Health Emphasis. Here the shift is from direct involvement with the human problems of particular people toward efforts to alter some of the social conditions which affect whole communities. In principle, prevention is the major goal. Toward this end, there is a shift from person-centered to population-centered or social-system-centered interventions. The family, school, police, factory, and social ecology in which the person lives are more an issue than the thinking, feeling, or actions of that person. To reduce stressful qualities in those systems, it is argued, would have the ultimate effect of advancing the well-being of large groups of people as well as helping the particular individual in distress.

Any social institution can, in principle, be the target of community psychological intervention, but most typically community psychologists focus on those which are most immediately involved with the lives of community members and which may be most accessible to change. This is perhaps best illustrated in interventions in the schools. Through consultation with teachers, community psychologists attempt to sharpen teachers' sensitivities to the learning and emotional needs of children, particularly if they are from differing social backgrounds. At the same time, they may work with school administrators, teachers, and community people in the effort to alter the educational system itself—curriculum, teaching methods, communication patterns within the system, and the way it relates to other portions of the community—all to the end of increasing the likelihood that the school experience will be more growth-enhancing. Relevant research for understanding social and community processes and for developing programs of community intervention is more in the model of social-science research than that of psychological investigation.

SOCIAL ACTION MODEL

This model represents the extreme social-oriented position. It rests on the fundamental assumption that society, not the patient, is disturbed and needs change. Activities of mental health professionals, even if community oriented, are seen as palliative at best (Leifer, 1969). At its most literal, this position not only denies the value of clinical intervention but sees it as a positive barrier to effecting radical change. Human problems lie in the fabric of society itself and change in its fundamental structures is needed if human well-being is truly to be achieved.

Within this model are located the most vigorous critics of "medical-model" thinking; some arguing that the medical conception of psychiatry disguises its role as an instrument of social control in a repressive society and thereby limits its potential for contributing to social change. Commenting on the present state of psychiatry, Leifer (1970) notes that "Psychiatry is social action disguised as medical treatment," (p. 19), and again, ". . . community psychiatry is a quasipolitical movement supported by state-sanctioned power and money" (p. 19). Within this view, therapeutic and community approaches are both used to influence and control the individual in accordance with the dominant ideology of the state, industry, and other centers of power in our society. In varying form, radical social critics have restated the same theme.

A less radical version of a social action position argues that the goals of mental health might be best achieved by influencing major social programs, and that the target of "intervention" should be less the individual or community institutions than the political and social policy makers in the highest possible positions of authority. The premise is the same, that change must proceed from the largest and most basic social institutions on down to the smaller, but the role of social-action agent is conceived more as consultant to, and friendly critic of, those in power rather than being their revolutionary antagonist.

Some Cautionary Comments

The scheme just presented attempts to map major orientations in the field of mental health, though in broad and probably overinclusive terms. Thus, the therapeutic model contains strange bedfellows, which by many other criteria would be sharply distinguished (see Chapter 14). There are very real differences in theory and practice among, for example, psychoanalysts, behavior therapists, and humanistic psychotherapists, although for present purposes they are grouped together in terms of their common faith in the importance of *psychological* factors in the genesis and change of personality disorders.

At the same time, the boundaries between categories are vague. Differences are suggested where actually the transitions between models may be minor. Thus, the psychotherapist in the "traditional clinic" who sees someone in an acute crisis and works with the family and others as well as with the patient to reduce stress is doing much the same thing that his colleague in a community mental health center calls "crisis intervention." The clinical activity is the same; what separates them is the setting in which they occur and their ideological context, how they are conceived in the framework of a therapeutic or community approach. Active involvement with the patient in crisis may be looked on, by the psychotherapist, as a minor episode which may even divert him from his more central interest in effecting extensive personality changes through long-term psychotherapy; for the community clinician, crisis intervention is a central and valued activity which has sometimes been conceived as a route toward the prevention of emotional disorders.

The setting alone does not define the model of intervention. Although a certain type of hospital exemplifies the custodial model, there are hospitals organized along therapeutic or even community lines. Overall, however, as one goes from positions on the left to those on the right of Table 5.1, there is increasing objection to hospitalization of any sort. Indeed, at the extreme, are positions such as that of a former president of the American Psychological Association who proposed, at a meeting of the American Psychiatric Association, no less, that state hospitals be closed, torn down, plowed under, and then, like Carthage in antiquity, sowed with salt! (Albee, 1968a).

A community mental health center, built under federal programs oriented to a community ideology, may also be actually organized and run along therapeutic or custodial lines. Because of the availability of financial support and public approval, new settings have been created and labelled community programs, although in fact they are slightly if at all altered from older forms. In this realm, as we will consider more fully in Part V, the differences between ideal and actual have to be carefully distinguished.

Moreover, even where a setting can be readily identified with a dominant ideology, particular professionals may hold and attempt to work with different views. In a custodial hospital, there are likely to be individual psychiatrists and psychologists oriented to a therapeutic model and perhaps even advocates of a social action position—if only in off-duty hours as socially conscious citizens.

Finally, it should be realized that there is no necessary relation between intervention model and disciplinary identification; members of all disciplines are to be found over the entire spectrum. It is probably true that medical psychiatrists are more likely to be to the left (as Table 5.1 is laid out), dynamic psychiatrists and clinical psychologists to the center, and social-science-oriented clinicians and community psychologists to the right. But it should be remembered that some of the sharpest attacks on the "medical model" have come from medically trained psychiatrists (e.g., Szasz, 1961; Dumont, 1968; Leifer, 1969) and that the community mental health field was largely developed and conceptualized by psychiatrists. Thus, the simple identification of MD's with one emphasis and PhD's with the other, and the "good guys versus bad guys" significance of all such polarizations, not only misrepresents the historical development of these models but it maliciously perpetuates interprofessional strains.

Models of Intervention and Psychiatric Ideologies

The models discussed here clearly overlap the concerns of those who have attempted, in empirical studies, to describe the value orientations of psychiatric workers. Hollingshead and Redlich (1958) described and measured two major attitude patterns among psychiatrists, what they termed the "analytic-psychotherapeutic" and the "directive-organic." The former includes part of what has just been called "therapeutic" while the latter corresponds to our use of the term "custodial." Gilbert and Levinson contrasted psychotherapeutic and sociotherapeutic orientations among psychiatric hospital staff (Gilbert and Levinson, 1956; Sharaf and Levinson, 1957). Building on this work Strauss and his associates developed a three-way analysis of ideologies toward mental health problems, termed "somatotherapeutic, psychotherapeutic, and sociotherapeutic" (Strauss, Schatzman, Bucher, Ehrlich, and Sabshin, 1964).

It is interesting to note that the sociotherapeutic ideology described in these studies was conceived in the 1950s largely within the scope of hospital practice. At that time there was considerable interest in the potential of milieu therapy, patient-government programs, and other alterations of the social environment which might facilitate patient autonomy and responsibility. Protagonists of this approach contrasted with those committed to medical or psychotherapeutic positions. In terms of the mental health models of the 1970s, the sociotherapeutic orientation would likely be reflected in adherence to concepts of community and social intervention in the larger context. A decade after the Gilbert and Levinson studies, Baker and Schulberg (1967) developed a scale of "community mental health ideology" to assess the sociotherapeutic values of mental health workers at the time.

The Role and Contribution of the Clinical Psychologist

Contemporary clinical psychology evolved mainly within a therapeutic model of mental health. The knowledge and talents of the clinicians are oriented to understanding and helping particular people in psychological distress. Their training involves the study of personality processes and psychopathology, learning the concepts and methods of assessment and psychological intervention, and developing the research skills to advance knowledge further in these areas. As clinicians, psychologists have come to function as autonomous professionals, whether in private practice or in multidisciplinary clinical settings. They may work as consultants with special competencies or as peers, carrying parallel responsibilities in the same realms as their coprofessionals. When duties are divided, the psychologist is likely to carry responsibility for clinical assessment and research. Within the scope of the mental health field, clinical psychologists most clearly represent a behavioral science orientation, although some psychiatrists are coming to view their field in similar terms (Hamburg et al., 1971).

This situation contrasts with the older role of the psychologists in the custodial model, where they were cast more as technicians to the dominant psychiatrist. As a "mental tester," the psychologist contributed test findings to be interpreted and used by a physician for diagnostic purposes. In general, the psychologist had little role in therapeutic interventions which, whatever their nature, were viewed as involving "medical responsibility." Many psychologists continue working in custodial settings, under such limitations. In the main, however, the ideal of the autonomously functioning professional is being realized in most job settings. Even in the traditional area of clinical testing, the psychologist has moved toward the role of a "diagnostic consultant" to coprofessionals who have direct responsibility for the care of the patient (Matarazzo, 1965a). The psychotherapeutic role of the modern clinical psychologist is well established. All in all, the trend from custodial to therapeutic orientations has allowed psychologists to make more diverse and personally satisfying contributions to the needs of people in psychological distress.

The more recent emergence of the community and social-action models has further increased the potential contribution as well as the range of activities of psychologists. The term "clinical psychologist" itself, some have argued, is too identified with the therapeutic model and terms such as "community/clinical psychologist" or "community psychologist" (Bennett et al., 1966) have been offered to characterize workers within this orientation. As there is greater concern with system-centered rather than person-centered interventions, the community clinicians need knowledge of more than human personality, psychopathology, and the techniques of clinical intervention. In addition, they should be well grounded in organizational and social psychology, understand group processes, and the social determinants of individual behavior. The human relations skills which underlie the clinician's empathic understanding of another human have to be supplemented with those social skills needed for working with groups and organizations. In consequence, community psychologists have argued for new models of training, extending beyond those traditional to clinical psychology (e.g., Iscoe and Spielberger, 1970).

Clinical psychology is now, and promises to become increasingly, a pluralistic field. Perhaps it could as well be viewed as a family of fields, each defined by the substantive concerns and tasks of the psychologists involved. Thus, there are "clinicians" primarily oriented to neuropsychology, childrens' problems, psychotherapy, clinical assessment, psychopharmocology, problems of the aged, schizophrenia, sensitivity training, psychodynamic theory, and community psychology, nor need the list end there. So too, "clinicians" work in hospitals, clinics, laboratories, community agencies, field projects, and private offices. None of these settings is in serious danger of disappearing or of being supplanted by altogether new settings; despite dire forebodings and/or enthusiastic anticipation, hospitals will not likely be plowed under, much less salted over, though the trend toward community-based care is likely to continue. Within each type of setting and each kind of approach, contribution to human well-being is possible. Each of the many approaches in the therapeutic and community models has potential value for some patients under some circumstances. To polarize arguments over which is *the* best is dangerous. More important, at this point, is the need to examine contending claims, in order to discover for whom, under which circumstances, with which consequences, each works.

Working in any subfield requires particular knowledge, skills, and attitudes.

The psychologist who would seriously contribute in the community area must understand the particular culture of the people he would serve. Parenthetically, one could equally well argue that any clinician, however individual and personal his interventions, is equally obliged to know the situational, role, and cultural determinants of his patient's behavior as well as its intrapersonal sources. However, the community psychologist must have special knowledge of the social systems which affect, for good or for bad, the lives of his clients. But his effectiveness as a community psychologist depends on his understanding of the personalistic functioning of individuals; understanding which is best developed through the study and treatment of unique individuals in the direct clinical process. In training and in subsequent professional life, the community psychologist along with other clinicians is guided by the clinical attitude (see Chapter 2). Educational philosophers, school sociologists, and others know the workings of school systems and can propose organizational changes as well or better than most community-oriented psychologists. The unique contribution of psychologists in school intervention programs derives from their knowledge of child behavior and their ability to understand and deal with the problems of individual children. The danger in the community model is that the psychologist can become an amateur sociologist or politician, with no special competence or power.

At the broader reaches of the social orientation this problem becomes even clearer. For one thing, psychologists and other social scientists do not have any special authority to determine major social policies, which in our society depend on complex political processes in which technical expertise is not particularly valued. Also, the specifically human problems with which psychologists are best qualified to deal fuse with broader issues of human welfare, as represented for example in racism, unemployment, or crime. Often, the "mental health component" cannot readily be disentangled. Policy decisions have to be made in which psychologists' concerns are pitted against other desirable social ends: Will this community benefit more from new jobs in a public works program or from a new mental health center? In this arena the psychologist can contribute, but more as an informed citizen than as a responsible professional.

While a society free of war, racism, poverty, social injustice, and hate would surely be desirable, and might indeed foster positive mental health in its members, there is need for action in the spirit of "lighting a single candle rather than cursing the darkness." A thoughtful black colleague reminds our students that when asked for help by a poor black woman whose child is failing, frightened, and disturbed in his classroom, it helps little to tell her about the evils of racist schools. With sympathetic understanding of the child and his culture, his particular competencies and personality, one can work within available options to advance the competencies and self-esteem of *this* child. To that end, the community clinician may be effective.

None of what has been said should be construed as suggesting that the psychologist, as concerned and informed citizen, should not be fully involved in pressing for social change. However, the simple version of a social action approach, which denies the value of clinical intervention and would substitute political action, runs the risk of diffusing the possible contribution of psychologists to human welfare.

Psychologists, however, can potentially have an important impact on the political process and help bring about valued social changes through research and consultation to guide policy makers. By virtue of technical knowledge about the nature of human behavior and problems and expertise in methods of assembling data in scientifically convincing ways, needed information can be made available to guide decision making, whether at a local or societal level. An ideal illustration is the analysis prepared for the Supreme Court by a group of concerned psychologists who examined the effects of school segregation; they came to the conclusion that segregated schools adversely affected both white and minority students. Taking the report into account, the Court reached its famous decision in 1954 integrating the nation's schools. Less dramatic but important illustrations are to be found in the many research-and-consultation contributions made to national commissions studying violence, drug abuse, and pornography, among other social problems.

PART 3

CLINICAL ASSESSMENT

CHAPTER 6

The Nature and Purpose of Clinical Assessment

What Is Clinical Assessment?

DIAGNOSIS AND CLINICAL ASSESSMENT

We would readily agree that in order to solve a problem it is necessary (if not sufficient) to "diagnose" it correctly. Whether we are considering a malfunctioning TV, a person in distress, or nations in conflict, the route to solution starts with knowledge of the problem's nature and causes. In this broad and commonsensical meaning, diagnosis is as necessary to mental health intervention as to action in any other realm. It is an inevitable part of the clinical process, whether or not special procedures are involved. Diagnosis often involves a systematic study of the patient through the use of specially designed interviews, tests, and observations in a differentiated stage of the clinical process (formal assessment). It may, however, be part of the fabric of psychotherapy or other interventions, in which the clinician in less intentional ways is sensitive to, notes, and judges qualities of his patient (informal assessment). Whatever its form and the techniques involved, however, diagnosis goes on, and serves the clinician's constant need to make decisions about his patient. He must decide whether and how the problem can be treated, what might occur if no intervention took place or if there were particular changes in the patient's life circumstances. Some judgments required of clinicians are momentous—should a patient be admitted to a hospital or released from one? Should an accused murderer be tried for homicide or acquitted for "reasons of insanity?" Should a child with a learning problem be transferred to a special school or can remedial work be done in the present setting? Other decisions have constantly to be made in the ongoing work of psychotherapy, such as:

Is the patient ready to explore a particular problem area? Is that area central or peripheral to his neurotic conflict? Should therapy hours be increased or therapy terminated? The variety of judgments clinicians must make is virtually limitless. *Clinical assessment is the process by which clinicians gain understanding of the patient necessary for making informed decisions.*

Diagnosis, in its broad meaning, is thus both inevitable and necessary. However, in the narrower sense of characterizing the patient in terms of one or another nosological entity (psychiatric disease), it is of limited value, as we have already considered. The task of the clinician is to describe the patient's personality structure and dynamics, his assets as well as failings, the demands on him and his coping resources; what Holt (1968) has described as "characterological diagnosis" rather than "symptomatic diagnosis."

For this reason, the term "clinical assessment" seems preferable to others in common use, such as "psychodiagnosis," "diagnostic psychological testing," or "psychiatric evaluation." Although the broad as well as narrow concept of diagnosis can be intended by each of those terms, it seems better to reserve the word "diagnosis" for the particular act of specifying a psychiatric nosological label. On the other hand, terms such as "psychological assessment" (or "evaluation" or "measurement") or "personality assessment" are overly broad. They do not suggest the unique purpose of *clinical* assessment, to gain understanding of an individual *in order to act on his behalf.* It is true of course that concepts and methods have been shared and interchanged between clinical assessment and psychological measurement in general. Measures developed in the context of general psychology, as well as differential psychology, have contributed much to clinical testing. Thus, the perceptual demonstrations of Gestalt organizational principles became the basis of Bender's (1938) famous test for organic brain damage. In the other direction, word association tests developed originally for discovering conflict areas (e.g., Jung, 1909; Kent and Rosanoff, 1910) have been widely used in the study of verbal association generally. For purposes of clinical assessment, many procedures developed in a framework of differential psychology for the study of abilities, intelligence, or personality traits have found wide applicability in clinical psychology. Contrariwise, the Rorschach test and other projective techniques developed in the clinical framework have been widely utilized in the study of personality processes in well-functioning people.

Clinical assessment describes any act by which the clinician gains information of value about (and to) his patient. It may include only measures of a specific variable, using a well-validated test, or it may involve a full-scale effort to construct a "working image or model of the person" (Sundberg and Tyler, 1962). It is in the latter case that the unique qualities of clinical assessment can best be seen, which bring it most into contrast with the psychometric tradition in psychology. Many procedures are used, tapping multiple levels of functioning, in historical as well as contemporaneous perspective. Above all, this orientation puts the clinician rather than the test at the center of the assessment process. The clinician conceptualizes the questions to be answered, the techniques to use, and finally has to integrate the many findings into a coherent whole. At all stages, clinical judgment and inference are required and the effectiveness of the assessment depends on the skill and wisdom of the clinician. Hence, clinical assessment is and probably will remain as much art as science, though grounded in disciplined thinking and knowledge.

HISTORICAL ASPECTS OF ASSESSMENT CONCEPTS

The model of clinical assessment described here has its roots in two related bodies of work, that of Henry A. Murray and his colleagues of the Harvard Psychological Clinic and that of David Rapaport and his co-workers at the Menninger Clinic. Though differing in important regards, both exemplified intensive clinical assessment using many methods to assess multiple facets and levels of functioning, where findings could be combined through skilled clinical inference into a theoretically consistent model of the person.

From the 1930s to the 1950s, the Harvard Clinic psychologists studied intensively small groups of people, usually normals and often students. Their intent was to understand the individual human life, where possible over extended periods of time and as holistically as possible. They were concerned to discover the sources of creative and adaptive personality functioning, rather than centering on pathological trends. Although generating their own theory of personality (e.g., H. A. Murray, 1938; 1959), their thinking was influenced by the convergence of the dynamic psychologies of Freud and Jung, the emphasis on integrative and holistic functioning of organismic theorists (e.g., K. Goldstein, 1939), and Allport's (e.g., 1937) stress on individuality and uniqueness of the human personality.

In a "study of lives" (as Robert W. White aptly titled a volume of essays honoring Murray's 70th birthday) a small group of subjects was studied intensively over time. A series of interviews explored such areas as early development, school history, sexual development, family relations, and childhood memories, as well as the range of current experiences, present problems, desires, and goals. Each subject wrote an autobiography. A wide variety of objective and projective personality procedures, tests of various abilities, interests, attitudes, and values were administered. The subject's behavior was observed in natural and contrived situations, including experimental procedures designed to assess such dimensions as level of aspiration, reactions to failure and stress, and other variables which might be of concern in the particular study. During World War II, Murray and his colleagues developed an assessment program for the Office of Strategic Services (OSS) which applied the same basic strategy to an effort to select men for delicate and secret intelligence work (OSS Staff, 1948). OSS officers had to function in dangerous situations, often behind enemy lines, and the OSS staff had the difficult task of judging whether a particular man had the personal qualities which might reasonably predict effective service. In this work, many situational tests were introduced which mimicked military stresses. The intent, however, was to predict whether the officer had personality strengths believed to be important in actual duty rather than to sample actual behaviors which might later be relevant. Whether dealing with interview, standard or situational tests, the predictions depended on the inferences of clinicians.

A central and unique feature of the assessment approach lies in the group process involved. Each of a number of assessors collects and analyzes data in a particular area or of a particular procedure which are then brought together and integrated into a composite, consensual picture of an individual in a staff conference or "diagnostic council." The complex use of multiple assessors and the diagnostic council method rarely occur in actual clinical practice, though the collective thinking and problem solving involved is sometimes approximated in case conferences in fine clinical centers.

Murray's assessment approach inspired postwar efforts to predict success in clinical psychological training (E. L. Kelly and Fiske, 1951) and in psychiatric training (Holt and Luborsky, 1958). The spirit and much of the methodology continue in the work of R. W. White (1966), R. W. Smith, Bruner, and R. W. White (1956), Stern, Stein, and Bloom (1956), Kenniston (1960, 1965, 1968), and at the Institute for Personality Assessment and Research (IPAR) at Berkeley (MacKinnon, 1975).

Murray's personological theory and the thinking it inspired is well depicted in a volume of essays written by his students and colleagues (White, 1963b). White's introductory essays convey particularly well the nature and influence of this position in American psychology, which is further discussed in a review (Korchin, 1964).

Unlike Murray's group with its emphasis on the healthy personality, Rapaport's concerns were firmly centered in the study of psychopathology, within the framework of Freudian psychoanalysis. Perhaps more than any other contemporary psychoanalyst, however, he focused on the workings of cognitive and ego processes, particularly to understand their distortions in pathology and relation to drive dynamics. He was a systematizer and scholar, dedicated to the effort to explicate psychoanalysis as a general psychological theory, as much concerned with thinking, memory, and problem-solving as with drive, affect, and unconscious processes; overall, his writings are a rich contribution to psychoanalytic ego psychology (Gill, 1967).

Patients' performance on standard psychological tests provided, in Rapaport's view, primary data supplementing those of free association and depth interviewing (Rapaport, Gill, and Shafer, 1945). Central to his assessment methodology was the use of a battery of tests intended to tap different levels and areas of psychological functioning. The same basic battery was used with all patients and the psychological findings combined with those of psychiatrists, social workers, and other staff members in case conferences. The battery included tests of general intelligence, conceptual thinking, association, and, importantly, the projective personality tests, particularly the Rorschach and Thematic Apperception Test. Rapaport contributed to the conceptualization of the "projective hypothesis," namely, that we reveal ourselves in the way we deal with unstructured stimuli, and probably contributed more than any other psychologist to the postwar popularity of projective procedures. The "projective orientation" is reflected as well in the interpretation of objective (structured) tests. Thus, intelligence test items are not only scored as correct/incorrect to yield a total score which can then be transformed into an intelligence quotient according to preestablished norms, but they are also interpreted as reflecting the subject's unique personality dynamics or psychological disturbance. The comprehension subtest of the Wechsler Adult Intelligence Scale (Wechsler, 1958) starts with the question: "What would you do if you found an addressed, sealed, and stamped letter on the street?" You would receive no credit if you said either: "Gee, I don't know" or "I'd open it to see if there was any money in it." In the latter case, however, a lack of social morality can be inferred; at the extreme, psychopathy.

In more standardized as well as projective procedures, Rapaport was less interested in test scores as such than in item-by-item or scale-by-scale analyses which could uncover the underlying processes by which a patient's thinking, feeling, motives and behavior could be coherently understood. This necessarily put great weight on the clinician's ability to make inference, which for Rapaport involved the disciplined use of theory and clinical experience, though for colleagues wed to the psychometric tradition it seemed unbridled speculation from the data in hand. In the years following World War II, the Rapaport approach to diagnostic testing deeply influenced assessment in clinical practice; in our discussion of test methods in later chapters, this influence will be amply illustrated. A good recent demonstration of the Rapaport tradition is contained in Allison, Blatt, and Zimet (1968).

CONFLICTING ORIENTATIONS TO CLINICAL ASSESSMENT

"Clinical assessment," as we are now using the term, unfortunately, carries two meanings. First, there is a *generic sense*, that is, *any* act of any nature which furthers understanding and helps the patient. But as I will use the term, and as it is commonly used in the literature, there is a *particular* meaning: "clinical assessment" describes a mode or approach that depends heavily on clinical judgment and inference and uses batteries rather than single tests to tap different levels and facets of the person with the goal of yielding a full-bodied personalistic analysis. What (for this one sentence only!) might be called "clinical" clinical assessment derives, as noted in Chapter 2, from the convergence of the dynamic with the psychometric tradition in clinical psychology. However, the two traditions still coexist and provide conflicting orientations to clinical assessment (in the generic sense). Common usage contrasts clinical assessment (in the particular sense) with the psychometric (or objective) approach and we will consequently use the term in both senses, distinguishing where necessary. The most vivid confrontation between the two orientations is seen in the controversy over "clinical versus statistical prediction" (see Chapter 11). The essential question is whether behavior can be better predicted by objective test scores combined into prediction formulas from correlative studies or whether a clinician can better integrate the diverse data available to him and better predict the outcome.

For now, however, let us simply take cognizance of the difference in orientations and some of their implications; both have served clinical assessment (in the generic sense). The psychometric approach is more related to differential than personolistic or dynamic psychology. It is concerned with the comparison of individuals along trait dimensions, which are well defined empirically. Standardized and objective tests are valued. Objectivity is sought both in the acts required of the patient and of the clinician. Ideally, subjects need only check one of a limited number of alternate responses to well-structured questions; forms can then be mechanically scored and interpretation of test findings depends on comparison of individual scores with well-developed norms. Judgment and inference are minimized, both in test taking and interpreting. Test reliability and validity, confirmed by statistical methods, are highly valued. Intelligence tests, tests of particular abilities, and personality inventories have derived from the psychometric approach; interview and projective techniques are the unique products of the clinical orientation. In subsequent chapters, both types of technique will be considered. However, in clinical assessment (now in the more particular sense) "wide-spectrum" if less objective procedures (e.g., interviews, projective techniques, etc.) are of central importance. The value of assessment findings derived from such procedures depends less on the technique as such, than on the interpretative skills of the clinician.

In contemporary clinical psychology two additional and contrasting orientations are of increasing importance, namely, the *behavioral* and the *phenomenological* (existential). Though clearly opposed to each other, they share antagonism toward traditional assessment concepts and methods, in either the psychometric or clinical model. Behavioral psychologists minimize the importance of dispositional characteristics of the person, whether conceived as manifest traits, drives, or unconscious wishes; observable behaviors rather than personality constructs are the focus of their concern (Mischel, 1968; Goldfried and Kent, 1972). Human problems are viewed as the derivatives of the learning history of the person to be understood in terms of general learning principles and change is seen as dependent on extinction of old habits and on new learning. Emphasis is on current stimulus conditions that control current behavior. Assessment is therefore limited to the study of observable behavior, to discover the conditions under which it is maintained and might be therapeutically varied by altering reinforcement contingencies. At the other extreme, phenomenological clinicians are less concerned with behavior as such or with personality constructs of an intrapsychic sort, than with the meanings people give to their own lives and to the world about them. Roger's (1942) argument against formal assessment was predicated on the notion that such meanings have to become known to clients themselves in the course of psychotherapy; it matters little to have the clinician discover them or for that matter other qualities of the patient through formal assessment. At most, phenomenologically oriented clinicians use the interview and some forms of self-rating; performance on objective or projective tests and overt behavioral measure are of minor concern to them. In Chapter 15 we will consider these contrasting theoretical orientations in greater detail in terms of the therapeutic approaches they have engendered.

THE DECLINE OF PSYCHODIAGNOSIS IN CLINICAL PRACTICE

Psychodiagnosis (clinical testing) has been the oldest, best established, and most respected tool of the clinical psychologist. In the years immediately following World War II, clinicians were excited by the then new concepts and methods of psychodiagnosis, and devoted great effort to perfecting and practicing diagnostic skills. They held the respect of psychiatric colleagues, particularly those who, within the therapeutic orientation, saw diagnostic testing as a necessary and vital prelude to therapy. More recently, however, there has been a decided decline of interest and commitment and growing criticism of the work of testing, both in and outside the mental health professions. In one survey, only 17 percent of 168 psychotherapists, of all persuasions and disciplines, reported that prior knowledge of the patient's personality "greatly speeds therapy" (Meehl, 1960). Meehl counsels that young clinicians would do better to fix their identities as therapists or researchers than as diagnosticians; advice which many clinical students and their academic elders are quite willing to accept. There is little question but that diagnostic testing is occupying an increasingly less important role in the work of the clinician. Whereas in 1960, a national sample of clinical psychologists in mental health agencies reported spending 44 percent of their professional time in testing, by 1969 the proportion was reduced to 28 percent (Lubin and Lubin, 1972). Breger (1968) argued that continuing pretreatment testing because it was a traditional role of the psychologist is no more defensible than that barbers continue to bleed their customers. Indeed, he contends further that testing might be a positive barrier to establishing a therapeutic encounter. Such arguments have been countered by psychologists who believe that not only testing but diagnosis itself is still of great value in the clinical process and an important contribution of the psychologist (e.g., Gough, 1971; Holt, 1967, 1968). But the decline of interest and involvement is clear. Professional psychologists often look on clinical testing as menial and assign it to junior staff and students. ". . . the teaching of diagnostic techniques in graduate training programs is often regarded as a chore by the instructor and as a bore by the students" (Rosenwald, 1963). What accounts for this decline in the status of psychodiagnosis?

A number of diverse trends probably explain the decline of diagnostic testing. In a deft and detailed analysis, Holt (1967,1968) proposes a variety of hypotheses, many of which are contained in the following points.

1. Many new roles have opened for clinical psychologists, once limited to clinical testing, and it is inevitable that less time and effort is spent in psychodiagnosis. Thus, clinicians work as psychotherapists, ward administrators, in teaching and research, and in community activities. Many of these are more gratifying, lucrative, and professionally rewarding.

2. Not only are there new roles, but some of the new approaches and ideologies are theoretically or pragmatically opposed to testing. Thus, as already noted, behavioral and existential therapies have little need for diagnostic testing. In the community mental health movement, the emphasis is on immediate and brief intervention; extended assessment, and for that matter, intensive psychotherapy, are seen as needlessly expensive and time-consuming. Moreover, concern is shifted to social systems and away from the individual personality, on which traditional testing necessarily focuses.

3. Because of the rapid growth of the field, there were not sufficient experienced and masterful testers to teach testing to and provide role models for students. The slow process of apprenticeship was short-circuited and many young clinicians went on to teach others before their own competence and skills had matured.

4. Psychodiagnosis was initially oversold, and clothed in oracular mystique. Inevitably it could not live up to these promises; some disappointment was bound to follow as research results failed to support many of the claims of testers. Critics argue too quickly, however, that little if any validity has been demonstrated. In any case, Rosenwald (1963) notes, psychologists in training are embarrassed by the artistic facet of psychodiagnosis, which threatens their scientific conscience. It is hard for them to learn the disciplined use of empathy, intuition, and inference, which with empirical knowledge and technical skill is required of the expert.

5. The nature of psychodiagnostic work is inherently difficult and stresses the clinician's identity. Schafer (1954), Rosenwald (1963), and Appelbaum and Siegal (1965) have done excellent analyses of the dynamics of the testing role. In the clinic, the psychologist has to prove his worth in the eyes of psychiatrists (often residents in training) who are his professional rivals. He may be the victim

of negative preconceptions or exaggerated expectations, undervalued and ignored, or overvalued and made anxious, grandiose, or defensive. Too often, he has no knowledge as to the consequences of his work, what difference it made in the treatment of the patient and, indeed, whether his predictions are confirmed. There are constants in the testing role, Schafer notes, which strain both tester and patient: it is voyeuristic, autocratic, oracular (he sees into hidden meanings and predicts the future), and saintly. There is, however, as Rosenwald (1963) emphasizes, a unique quality in the saintly, nurturant role, for it is one step removed from direct intervention. In consequence, the tester helps but in a passive role, unlike the therapist, who is a more direct and active helper. The strong desire to help others which brings psychologists into clinical service can thus be frustrated in testing. Not only the act of testing, but the subsequent contemplative intellectual study, focused on test protocols rather than direct engagement with the patient is a further face of the passivity involved. Then, too, it is an essentially one-way relationship, in which the tester asks much from the patient but gives little. Where he would be a helper, he is pushed into ". . . the waiting stereotype of the schizoid intellectual who is interested in people only as objects of his dispassionate scrutiny and scientific dissection" (Holt, 1968, p.29). Holt adds further "Testing does, typically, appeal to and satisfy intellectual curiosity, as research does. But the latter allows the investigator to be his own boss . . . All in all, diagnostic testing is not an emotionally and motivationally satisfying activity for the full-time endeavors of the kind of person who is likely to be best at it" (p. 29).

6. Although directed mainly against personality inventories as used in personnel selection, civil libertarian concern about the misuses of personality testing has probably rubbed off on clinical testing. Tests have been attacked as unscientific instruments used against the best interests of the person; they invade privacy and enforce conformity. After Congressional hearings on the subject in 1965, the use of personality tests was forbidden in selecting employees for the Federal government (cf., *American Psychologist,* 1965, 20, whole issue). More recently, testing has come under a cloud by virtue of the criticism of minority psychologists that tests developed and standardized on white, largely middle-class populations unfairly appraise the competencies of minority people. In this case, the target has mainly been intelligence tests used in school placement. But these, largely justified, attacks on the social evils of testing have inevitably put psychologists on the defensive and reduced their enthusiasm for testing of any sort.

7. Finally, diagnostic testing exemplifies the concepts and role-relations of the "medical model" and is avoided by many on that score.

In view of these considerations it is surprising how much clinical testing is done. In medical settings, where most clinical psychologists work, it is still a major function of psychologists and is in constant need and demand, despite the emergence of new modes of practice. Even if it were demonstrable that the time and cost of testing are prohibitive, or that tests too often lead to incorrect clinical decisions, there are still strong arguments for learning and using clinical tests. They are still one of the best ways we have to learn about the inner workings of human beings for research, personality study, or to sharpen the understanding of clinicians.

What is Assessed? Variables and Techniques

BROAD AND NARROW FOCUS ASSESSMENT

The purpose of assessment is, as it is sometimes stated, "understanding the whole person." Under any circumstances, such a goal is probably unattainable. But in actual practice, assessment necessarily has to serve more modest ends. Even the most ambitious program, using many assessors and many techniques, can only attempt to approximate full understanding of a person in all his individuality and complexity. The very intricacies of the human personality, let alone the limitations in our techniques, time, and skill, limit the reach of assessment. More realistically, we are guided by a conceptual framework (as detailed in Chapter 3) within which we sample personality functioning in order to construct a model of the particular person, from which hypotheses can be derived and tested as to how and why he acts, thinks, and feels as he does. Particular variables, such as abilities, needs, skills, and the like, are studied, both in a comparative framework, to see how the individual compares with others, and in a personalistic framework, to discover how the variables interrelate in the functioning of the individual himself.

In actual clinical situations, the aims and methods of assessment are determined in fair measure by the needs of clinical decision-making expressed in "referral questions," which we will consider in further detail below. Such questions can be narrower or broader in scope. Thus, the question "How anxious is this patient?" is relatively straightforward. The focus of assessment increasingly broadens as additional questions are added: "And under what circumstances is the patient likely to become more (less) anxious?" "When threatened what defense mechanisms come into play?" "How?" "Is the patient able to carry on the normal requirements of his job under such conditions?" to finally "And what kind of person is he anyway?" As Levy (1963) noted, the issues which draw most on the interpretative skills of the clinician are "unbounded" questions; those more familiar to psychometric measurement are "bounded" questions.

TYPES OF ASSESSMENT TECHNIQUES

In principle, there are four ways one can gain information about another person: (1) ask the person himself; (2) ask someone who knows the person; (3) observe the person as he behaves naturally; and (4) observe the person in standardized test situations. The many different techniques used in formal clinical assessment depend on one or another, sometimes combinations, of these modes of information gathering.

1. Ask the Person Himself: The *interview* is the backbone of clinical assessment. In fair measure, it involves putting questions to the patient to which, if he can and will, he gives direct replies. Most obvious are those which seek specific facts, such as age, number of siblings, place of birth, social status, and the like. However, even in addressing personal needs and characteristics, the intent and relevance of the question is usually clear, though it may be more or less specific. Thus, we ask "Are you anxious when you approach the boss for a raise" or more generally "Do you feel inadequate with older and more powerful people?" or even

more general, "Tell me about situations in which you feel inadequate and anxious." In the normal process of clinical interviewing, the flow of statement and response is relatively free, as the interviewer follows the patient into areas which concern him. But interviews may be more structured, following a more or less specific line of questions. One type of *personality inventory* is essentially a structured interview in written form. Other techniques which approximate the structured interview involve lists of adjectives from which patients choose those most characteristic of them or statements which are to be sorted along a similar dimension. It is true, of course, that interviews and personality inventories often involve questions whose apparent meaning does not indicate their relevance or interpretation; in such cases, the patient reveals rather than describes himself in his responses. It is further true that an interview provides opportunity for observing of nonverbal behavior. The patient is not only describing himself but living and acting in the situation, revealing characteristic behaviors. From the clinician's standpoint, the disparity between the patient's assertions ("I'm at ease in any social situation") and his visible behavior (say, tremulous voice, sweaty palms, fidgiting) provides important information about personality trends. Overall, however, the interview and related self-descriptive techniques are vehicles par excellence for the patient to characterize himself and his views of relevant others and of his world, in his own terms.

2. Ask Someone Who Knows the Person: Friends, parents, spouse or lover, teachers, colleagues, and employers, who know a great deal about a person in various settings, are potentially rich sources of information. In a clinical study of reasonably competent adults, they are only infrequently interviewed. A major barrier arises out of concern with confidentiality in the clinical relationship, but a second reason lies in the wish to understand the patient's problems from his vantage point. Thus, the question "Do you believe your teacher thinks you are intelligent?" is valued over directly asking the teacher, "Do you think he is intelligent?" However, in working with less competent or articulate patients, information from relevant others is almost invariably sought. Thus, the treatment of children, grossly psychotic patients, the aged and neurologically damaged required interviews with persons who can describe the patient's behavior, personality characteristics, development, and so forth. Similarly, in assessment studies of normal subjects, systematic information is often sought from friends and others. Peer ratings, supervisory ratings, or sociometric ratings as well as open interviews provide basic information as to how the patient is seen and judged by others. Where clinical assessment occurs after a period of psychotherapy, or after termination to assess change, the therapist himself becomes an "informant" in the manner of a friend or teacher, though his knowledge of the patient is of course limited to the transactions between them in the situation of therapy.

3. Observe the Person as He Behaves Naturally: For full understanding, direct observations of the patient in critical life situations would obviously be desirable, but under most circumstances they are unobtainable. Full clinical assessment may involve a "home visit" by a staff member who can then report on observations of the physical environment and something of the spontaneous interplay among family members, but even though obtained in the home the information is primarily based on a quasi-clinical interview. With hospitalized patients, nurses and other staff members have ample opportunity to observe the patient in the "life situations" of the hospital and their judgments are grist for the

mill of clinical assessment. Similarly, the behavior of the patient in the clinic, while in the waiting room, or in exchanges with the elevator operator or receptionist, provides some but limited observational data. In assessment studies of normal subjects, psychologists have been ingenious in developing quasi-natural conditions (in effect, situational tests) for observing subjects. Ingenious techniques have been used; for example, Soskin (1966) had cooperating subjects carry miniature radio transmitters with them for days on end so that naturally occurring social interplay could be recorded and studied. Nevertheless, in psychology generally as well as in clinical assessment, psychologists remain committed to experimental and test measures.

4. Observe the Person in Standardized Test Situations: Whatever their limitations, tests of numerous sorts remain the major instruments of assessment for clinicians as well as other psychologists. They represent the unique contribution of the psychologist, both as behavioral scientists and in clinical practice. The principal qualities of tests are: (1) observations can be made under standard conditions; (2) when needed; (3) in ways that reduce subjective bias; (4) so that quantitative measures (of varying type and precision) can describe psychological functions, and (5) in ways that different individuals can be compared. In later sections, we will describe from many perspectives tests used in clinical practice. Let us note here that they can be grouped as *objective* or *projective*, as measures of specific variables or broad areas of functioning (e.g., immediate memory, general intelligence, aggression, anxiety, personality dynamics), and according to the particular area of human functioning they are presumed to assess (e.g., intelligence, social values, personality needs, cognitive styles, etc.).

LEVELS OF PERSONALITY FUNCTIONING

The techniques of clinical assessment tap different levels of personality functioning. Some relevant information is readily available, in that the individual both knows and is quite willing to describe that facet of himself. At another extreme is unconscious material, which he neither knows nor can express. Considering the interplay of communicability and awareness, Zubin (1950) has suggested that assessment techniques can be characterized as yielding information in one of four possible cells (Table 6.1).

Table 6.1 indicates the realms of personality with regard to the person's knowledge and capacity/willingness to express, which different techniques are intended to sample. It should not be read too literally. Thus, projective procedures often yield information which the subject is perfectly aware of and able to describe, though it has the particular capacity for revealing suppressed or repressed material. Similarly, behavioral observation can also reveal perfectly conscious material, as well as that of which one is unaware. My tremulous hands and quaking voice, as we talk, indicate my anxiety, of which however I may be quite aware and express a moment later in words. Observable behavior itself also contains signs from which unconscious material can be inferred; a classic instance are the slips of the tongue which Freud early realized were determined errors expressing repressed attitudes or wishes. The message comes through when we describe a general as a "bottle-scarred veteran;" it becomes loud and clear when we embarrassedly add "No, no, I meant 'battle-scared'!"

Rosenzweig (1950) notes that test responses to procedures typically used in

TABLE 6.1
Level of Personality Tapped by Different Types of Assessment Techniques *

INWARDLY ACCESSIBLE (AWARENESS)	OUTWARDLY REPORTABLE (COMMUNICABILITY): YES	OUTWARDLY REPORTABLE (COMMUNICABILITY): NO
YES	*Conscious Material* Interview Questionnaires Self ratings	*Suppressed Material* Projective techniques Rorschach
NO	*Overt Behavior* Observation of behavior Situational tests Ratings by others	*Repressed Material* Projective techniques Free Association Rorschach and TAT

* From Zubin, J. Tests, construction and methodology. In R. E. Harris, J. G. Miller, G. A. Muench, L. J. Stone, H. L. Teuber, & J. Zubin (Eds.), *Recent advances in diagnostic psychological testing.* Springfield, Ill.: Charles C. Thomas, 1950. Reprinted by permission.

personality assessment consist either of "opinion behavior" (the subject's view of himself as he would communicate it), "overt behavior" (his characteristic modes of behavior as they would appear to an observer), or "implicit behavior" (revealing unconscious motives and feelings). Corresponding to these levels of personality expression, assessment techniques can be grouped as *subjective, objective,* or *projective*. The schema suggested by Rosenzweig for relating level of personality, diagnostic method, type of test behavior, and the process involved in subsequent predictions is pictured in Table 6.2.

REFERRAL QUESTIONS

Assessment is always undertaken because someone wants and needs to know more about the patient. It may be initiated by the patient himself, by a school or employer, by a court or legal agency, the patient's physician, or another mental health clinician. In each of these cases, there are particular issues—referral questions—which bring the patient to the clinician and which should guide the course of assessment. Obviously, the questions are of very different types, as is the professional and ethical relationship of the assessing clinician to the referring source and to the patient. For simplicity, and because it is the most typical case in practice, let us consider only the particular instance of a referral from a fellow mental health clinician. In the practice of many clinics, there is division of labor between the clinician entrusted with the treatment of a patient and the clinical psychologist who provides assessment information and consultation.

Particular referral questions group around the five major purposes of clinical assessment:

1. To Provide Baseline Information: Research on the effectiveness of one or another therapeutic intervention obviously requires "before" data against which "after" can be compared. But even in the treatment of the individual case, it is im-

TABLE 6.2

Levels of Response in Typical Methods of Personality Appraisal *

LEVEL	PSYCHODIAGNOSTIC METHODS	BEHAVIOR ELICITED IN TEST SITUATION	MODE OF PREDICTION
1.	Subjective: Subject takes self as direct object of observation; e.g., inventory or questionnaire, opinion or attitude poll, autobiography.	Opinion: Subject gives self-critical or censored responses in keeping with his concepts of what is right or proper, intelligent or socially acceptable.	Extrapolation to other self-consciously critical situations.
2.	Objective: Examiner takes subject as object of observation; e.g., time-sampling observations, miniature life situations, physiological measures, some rating scales.	Overt: Subject functions as he observably would in the corresponding actual situations of everyday life, thus providing a sample of his gross behavior.	Extrapolation to similar externally defined situations.
3.	Projective: Both subject and examiner "look the other way" at some ego-neutral object; e.g., Rorschach, TAT, word association, play technique; expressive movement (handwriting, gait, voice).	Implicit: Subject responds impersonally in terms of unconscious or latent attitudes, feelings or thoughts.	Interpretation from manifest content to underlying factors.

* Rosenzweig, S. Levels of behavior in psychodiagnosis with special reference to the Picture-Frustration Study. *American Journal of Orthopsychiatry*, 1950, 20, p. 64. Reprinted by permission.

portant to understand the patient's condition at the outset in order to assess his later progress.

2. To Evaluate the Patient's Status after Treatment: This is the obvious corollary of the first purpose. Not only does posttreatment assessment evaluate the effects of the therapeutic program, but it describes the state of the patient should he later return to the same or another clinic for further therapy at a later date. Clinical practice makes much less use of posttreatment than of pretreatment assessment; systematic posttreatment evaluation is usually made in the context of therapy research.

3. To Plan and Guide Therapeutic Intervention: This is the major purpose for assessment in the therapeutic model of mental health. Assessment is intended to yield an overall description of the patient's character structure, major needs and conflicts, defenses, and personality assets and liabilities. This information is used for planning therapeutic goals and strategies and for making specific decisions as, e.g., choice of therapist, frequency of therapeutic hours, areas to be focussed on, and so forth. Normally, such assessment occurs before therapy begins; less commonly but occasionally, when problems arise in the course of the therapy process.

4. For Diagnosis: Particularly within the custodial model of mental health, clinical assessment often has a primary function of assigning the patient to a diagnostic entity. This is often for record-keeping, legal or administrative purposes, but sometimes is related to subsequent therapy. The full array of assess-

ment procedures, including clinical tests, are generally used when the patient cannot be clearly diagnosed from clinical interviews and overt behavior. Thus, the clinician is likely to have borderline cases referred, where the primary problem is one of differential diagnosis to distinguish between two or more equally likely diagnostic categories. Referral questions often focus on particular facets of the person, necessary to assign to a particular diagnosis. Thus, the psychologist may be asked: "Is there evidence of thought disorder of the sort that would suggest schizophrenia?" "Is the general level sufficiently low so that the patient can be considered retarded rather than schizophrenic?" "Are there deficits in intellectual functioning of the sort following organic brain damage?"

5. To Predict Future Behavior: Aside from the particular needs of therapy, it is often important to make informed predictions about possible future behaviors. "Is it possible that the patient will become more depressed and possibly suicidal?" "Can he now leave the hospital, work, and care for himself?" "If he does this or that, is he likely to be successful?" Whether predictions turn out to be true or not depends not only on the accuracy of the present assessment but on the circumstances of the later time. A series of lucky breaks, new friends, even an upturn in the national economy may make it possible for a discharged patient to function effectively and well; inadvertent stresses might have returned him to the hospital. Consequently, predictions must necessarily be made conditionally and, if possible, take account of forseeable future influences on the patient. Studies of normals as well as patients have shown that accurate prediction depends on knowledge in three realms: (1) the characteristics of the psychosocial situations into which the person is going; (2) the personal qualities required for coping with it; and (3) the personality characteristics of the person, as presently assessed. Prediction involves matching the qualities of the person, as we are now able to know him, with those required by the future situation (Stern, Stein, and Bloom, 1956). Thus, if our patient is impulsive, short-tempered, and hypersensitive to criticism, we would hardly predict a happy future for him at the complaint counter of a department store.

Ideally, the particular referral questions which are to be answered by assessment arise out of a collaborative examination by the referring and assessing clinician of the issues in the particular case. In a good working relationship, both clinicians review together areas of knowledge and ignorance, what more needs to be known, what information formal assessment might yield, and what options are available and future courses possible. Communication and decision-making are facilitated to the extent that they operate within the same conceptual framework, sharing vocabulary and concepts for describing personality dysfunctioning. Between them, then, they can decide the scope and focus of assessment and forsee the possible uses of the data developed. However, in actuality, there is too often minimal communication, and the referring clinician has only vague ideas as to what information he needs or can use. The referral phrased as "Psychologicals, please," with little or no amplification or justification reflects this state of affairs. In his turn, the assessing clinician has to guess the motives and needs of the referrer. He may return a report far more (or less) detailed than expected which speaks to issues other than those the referrer had (implicitly) in mind or is phrased in concepts alien to him. Assessment under these circumstances does little for the patient's welfare and can only be frustrating to both clinicians involved. A major task of the assessing clinician involves clarification of the issues and problems in the particular case, as necessary reconceptualizing and redefining the referral questions.

In principle, assessment should build on and extend existing knowledge about the patient. Some have argued, however, in favor of minimizing prior communication between referring and assessing clinicians in order for the assessment to be independent and unbiased. Knowledge of the referring clinician's observations and clinical findings and his concerns and hypotheses, it is noted, might wittingly or otherwise prejudice the inferences made by the assessor from his particular data. This logic has justified "blind testing," a practice more common in the past than at present. Under such circumstances, a standard test battery was generally used. Findings are organized around the same general framework, producing in effect case studies with the same outline. In the hands of masters like Samuel Beck and David Rapaport, blind testing often led to elegant and clinically useful personality analyses. It should be noted, however, that they worked in settings in which shared conceptual thinking had evolved over years and where the major concerns and practices of colleagues were mutually known and respected. In a sense, one might say that the "referral questions" were implicitly known, although specific facts and hypotheses might be withheld. Moreover, though testing itself was done "blind," findings were subsequently coordinated with other clinical data in case conferences in which the entire clinical staff was intensely involved. In that process, communication and joint problem-solving were much in evidence.

In less-experienced hands, blind testing can deteriorate into a competitive and wasteful game. Surely, there is the danger that prior knowledge can bias the clinician's judgment, but it is only one among many distorting influences which the skillful clinician must avoid so that assessment can be maximally valid and useful. Working without such information, however, involves the equal or greater risk of turning up irrelevant or redundant findings. Prior knowledge of the patient, along with carefully articulated referral questions, is a primary base for structuring the assessment program. Ultimately, by information of whatever source—the referring clinician, the patient's own statements, his appearance, and test or interview responses. Interpreting each in its own right and integrating them all into a meaningful and consistent picture of the individual personality is the hard work of assessment.

Stages in the Assessment Process

Sundberg and Tyler (1962) described the course of clinical assessment as a flow through four major stages: (1) preparation: in which the clinician learns of the patient's problem, "negotiates" the referral questions, and plans further steps in assessment; (2) input: during which data about the patient and his situation are collected; (3) processing: during which the material collected is organized, analyzed and interpreted; and (4) output: during which the resulting study of the person is communicated and decisions as to further clinical actions made. Pictured in Figure 6.1 are specific actions within each of these stages; in actual practice some might be bypassed or others added. Thus, there might not be an intake conference or a case conference. Depending on whether the clinician favors a psychometric or clinical orientation, as noted previously, there will be greater or lesser use of statistical prediction or of clinical interpretation.

Sundberg and Tyler reveal admirably well the two types of actions which are necessarily involved at each stage in the assessment process. On the one hand, there are clearly specifiable and objective actions; these are named in rectangles in Figure 6.1. On the other hand, there are cognitive acts, named in ovals, which describe the clinician's interpretations, hypotheses, judgments, and decisions. The controversy over clinical versus statistical prediction, which will be considered in some detail later on, depends on whether "rectangle" or "oval" acts are considered of greater merit. What is clear from this diagram, however, is that clinical interpretation does not appear at one moment, e.g., after data are collected, as a basis for final judgment; wise and thoughtful decisions are required in all stages. In fact, assessment requires statistical and clinical prediction throughout. While improved techniques and better modes of statistical analysis and prediction should be sought in continuing assessment research, they have ultimately to be utilized by thinking and decision-making clinicians.

Outline for a Case Study

The "output" of a particular assessment program depends, of course, on the questions originally raised and the consequent focus or breadth of the assessment activities undertaken. At the extreme is the full-bodied case study, describing the patient's functioning, personality structure and dynamics, strengths and weaknesses, the developmental antecedents and possible future course of the patient's condition, and recommendations for further clinical intervention. In more or less detail, the clinician typically presents this analysis ("formulation of a case") at a case conference and/or in written form in a psychological report (see Chapter 2). An outline which can guide making and reporting clinical case studies is sketched below. Though it goes beyond our present concern, it should be recalled that the case method is a basic approach, not only in clinical and personality psychology, but in the many areas of the behavioral and social sciences where general principles can be illuminated through the intensive study of particular lives (Allport, 1942; R. W. White, 1966; Bolgar, 1965).

Ideally, the complete case study describes the patient's personality and functioning from each of the six basic perspectives discussed in Chapter 3, namely, the motivational, structural, developmental, adaptational, ecological, and biological. The case study addresses such questions as: What problems are troubling and/or incapacitating the patient? What kind of a person is he? Why does he function as he does? How did he come to be? How does he relate to his social environment? What are the major stresses in his life and what resources does he have to cope with them? What accounts for his present distress and the decision to seek help? What interventions are possible? What can be done, to what ends, and with what hope of success? What is the likely outcome (prognosis)?

FIGURE 6.1.

The Course of Clinical Assessment *

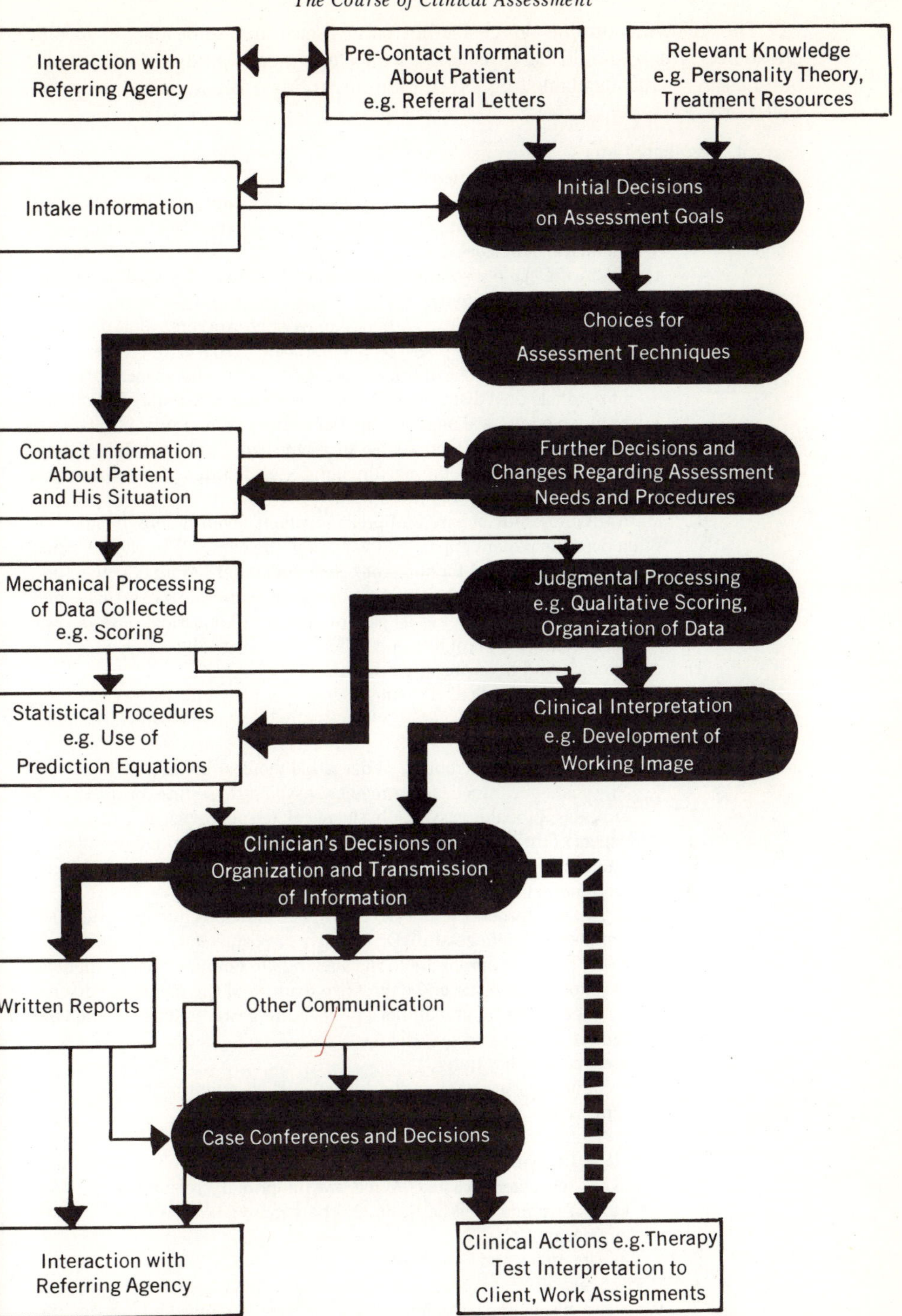

* Adapted from Sundberg, N. & Tyler, L. E., *Clinical psychology*. New York: Appleton-Century-Crofts, 1962, p. 87. Reprinted by permission of the authors and Prentice-Hall, Inc., Englewood Cliffs, New Jersey.

The following outline suggests the major areas, and some of the specific questions, which should be considered in a clinical case study. More detailed outlines are readily available (e.g., K. A. Menninger, Mayman, and Pruyser, 1962; Beller, 1962; Huber, 1961).

I. Present Status
  A. Adaptation in life situations
     What are the major tasks in the patient's life (work, school, family) and how well is he functioning? Does he seem to be at or below optimum?
  B. Symptomatic behaviors
     1. From the patient's standpoint, what is troubling him? What are his "presenting symptoms?"
     2. As viewed by concerned others, family or co-workers, what deviant or disturbed behaviors does the patient show? What bothers them?
     3. From the perspective of the assessing clinician, what evidence is there of psychological disturbance? Are there thought disorders or failure of reality testing? Are negative emotions overly strong, uncontrollable, or painful? Anxiety? Depression? Are distressing conflicts visible? Obsessive thoughts? Specific dysfunctions, e.g., failures of memory, inept problem-solving, concrete thinking?
  C. Motivation for clinical care and preconceptions about mental health
     What does the patient expect will happen in the clinic? Why did he come? What is the hoped-for outcome? Symptom relief? More effective functioning? Personality change? Change in distressing external conditions? What does being a "patient" mean to him? How does he view mental illness, mental health? Is he psychologically minded?
  D. Appearance and behavior in clinic
     Is he anxious? Guarded? Trusting? Uncooperative and resistant?

II. The Manifest Personality
  A. Biological features
     Is the patient healthy, robust? What is his medical history? Somatotype? Physical appearance? (In a medical-psychiatric setting, or if the problem has probable psychophysiological or neurological causes, this aspect of the case study would be expanded by appropriate medical examinations and tests.)
  B. Temperament
     Is the patient energetic, lethargic, active? Are emotions intense, controlled, impulsive? Is life zestful? Do negative or positive emotions dominate? Are emotions appropriate to his age and life circumstances? Included here too are stylistic and expressive features of the manifest personality such as: Is he graceful or clumsy? Are gestures tense, open, compulsive?
  C. Manifest personality traits
     How might the patient describe himself? How might others who know him well?
  D. Interpersonal behavior
     How does the patient appear to others? What is his "stimulus value?" Is he liked, respected, trusted? What are his primary relationships? What kind of friends does he have, and how many? Is he isolated, gregarious? A joiner?

III. Personality Dynamics and Structure
  A. Motives and affects
     What are his major conscious and unconscious motives? How are they related? Where do they conflict? What are the sources of characteristic

affects? To what are anxiety, hostile feelings, guilt, and shame related? What gives pleasure? What are his fantasies and wishes, concealed as well as revealed?

B. Moral principles, social values, and attitudes

What are the major precepts by which the patient lives? Is his conscience stern, rigid, corruptible, nonexistent? Are there mature ideals, flexibly held, or childlike imperatives?

C. Ego functions and identity

1. Ego strength. Is behavior self-initiated and internally controlled? Are impulses modulated? Does he work toward goals? Preserve objectivity and perspective?
2. Defenses and coping mechanisms. What are the salient defenses? Are they paralleled by effective, positive coping mechanisms? Are more primitive defenses called into play too soon?
3. Thought organization, cognitive controls, and styles. What are the characteristic ways the subject approaches cognitive problems (by reducing or perhaps increasing complexity)? Can he tolerate ambiguity? Does he scan broadly or focus narrowly? Delay appropriately before decision?
4. Intelligence, abilities, competencies. What are the patient's skills, talents, hobbies, and vocational competencies, and his intellectual resources?
5. Identity and self-concept. How does the patient view himself? What kind of person does he see himself to be? What are his aspirations? How much self-esteem does he have? On what does it rest?

IV. Social Determinants and Current Life Situation

A. Group memberships and roles

To what social groups does the patient belong? Which of these are most important in defining his social identity; which serve as "reference groups?" What roles are similarly central for the patient— "doctor", "union man", etc? Are social and personal identity congruent? Does the patient feel that he shares class characteristics with others?

B. Family

What are the relationships between patient and spouse, parents, or children? How does the present family system work? Is it like or unlike that of "family of origin?"

C. Education and work

School and work history. Is the patient satisfied with his work achievements, income, conditions of work? Is leisure available? How is it used? Hobbies?

D. Social ecology

In what kind of community (physical and social) does the patient live? Is it "home" or alien? Does he identify his welfare with community goals? Does he participate in community affairs, work for community improvement? Is the environment crowded, noisy, safe, ugly? Does he commute or live close to work? Are desired facilities available?

V. Major Stresses and Coping Potential

What are the major stresses in the patient's current life? Do they consist of social problems, realistically beyond his control, e.g., unemployment, poverty? Are there excessive demands in his job or school situation, intense competition, long hours, and too heavy workload? Do strains result from interpersonal, marital, or love relationships? To what extent can the person reduce or avoid stress through his own efforts? What personality or social resources are available to him?

VI. Personality Development

Here the question is "How did this personality come to be?" The answer necessarily involves analysis of early life experiences, relationships to significant others, parents, and peers. The critical identifications throughout life and major learning experiences. The history and sequence of social and interpersonal influences on the person. Of particular importance is the way in which the patient coped with successive developmental tasks. What alternatives were available to the subject? How did he deal with new experiences and challenges? Did he hold to safe and established modes of behavior? Could he take on new roles?

VII. Formulation of the Case

A. Synthetic interpretation of the personality

All told, how can the person be conceived and understood. What are the major themes—descriptive, dynamic, structural, and genetic—which allow us to describe a "whole person?" Within this context, how can the patient's psychological disturbance be understood? What functions do his symptoms have in the economy of the personality, how do they prevent greater disintegration of psychological distress (primary gain)? Is there evidence that the patient is gaining further reward from his pathology (secondary gain)?

B. Overall diagnostic impression (if necessary)

In terms of standard nomenclature, what should the patient's condition be called? What other psychiatric diagnoses have to be considered (differential diagnosis)?

C. Specific dysfunctions

In terms of the many specific psychological functions which can be assessed, in which realms does the patient function adequately and in which are there evidences of malfunction? For example, are there speech problems, memory deficit, impaired abstract thinking, intense neurotic drives, etc., which can be separately described without regard for formal diagnosis?

VIII. Recommendations and Predictions

A. Desired outcomes

What qualities of the person and/or his situation requires change if the patient is to function in a more effective and comfortable way? What are his major growth needs which could provide goals for therapeutic intervention?

B. Possible interventions

1. Environmental and social. Can the patient's life conditions be changed in ways to reduce stress and facilitate growth? For example, change of home living conditions, taking leave from school, new job, etc. Can counseling be done with relevant others, e.g., parents or friends, who might change their impact on the patient? Might new social activities be of benefit, perhaps in conjunction with people with similar problems?
2. Psychotherapy. Might psychotherapy be helpful? Of what sort, with what kind of therapist, for how long, to what goals? Should it be individual, group, or family? Might other forms of psychological intervention be useful, instead of or in addition to psychotherapy; e.g., vocational or educational counseling, occupational therapy, music, dance, or other activities?
3. Other therapeutic interventions. Is hospitalization necessary? Are drugs required? Which? For what purpose? What idiosyncratic psychological effects to drugs might be predicted for this patient? Electroshock or other somatic therapies? Is treatment needed for ancillary conditions, e.g., hearing loss, speech defect, reading disability.

C. Course of the future life
Following intervention (and/or without any) what predictions can be made about the patient's future life history? Extrapolating from his present character structure and life situation what intensifications and/or reductions in his problems might be expected? Are any events in the offing (e.g., leaving school, marriage, birth of a child) which might have predictable consequences? What kind of psychological or social intervention might be needed in the future?

As drawn up, this outline is intended to guide case study before systematic clinical interventions. At later points, such case analyses would include material which emerged during the course of psychotherapy, description of hospital behavior, and follow-up studies. Case studies reporting the entire sequence of clinical encounters, as well as the full assessment of the patient's personality, would necessarily include more categories. Correspondingly, the final section on Recommendations and Predictions would be oriented to the future beyond the clinical process.

CHAPTER 7

Informal Assessment and the Clinical Relationship

Informal Assessment and Person Perception

Whether as psychologists or as laymen, each of us each day engages in informal assessment. We judge other persons, friends, or strangers, as angry or happy, trustworthy or dishonest, intelligent or stupid, friendly or hostile, and we adjust our behavior accordingly. In interplay with others, we discern their motives, attitudes, emotions, and intentions, much as we perceive objects of the physical world. In his daily work, the clinician depends heavily on informal assessment. *Formal assessment*, involving interviews, tests, and systematic observation, builds on, extends, and sharpens informal assessment, but it does not replace it. This is true for two basic reasons. First of all, clinical practice necessarily involves a mixture of informal and formal assessment activities. While interviewing or testing, the clinician remains alert to the visible behaviors, words, or gestures, which amplify or contradict the meaning of test responses. Second, and more important, is the fact that many of the same psychological processes—as determinants of *clinical judgment*—are ultimately involved in all assessment decisions, whether based on formal or informal data. For example, if one has a stereotyped conception as to how all people of a particular class behave (e.g., all blondes are stupid), then obviously one can "see" a particular person of that class as having the stereotyped characteristics. However, the same stereotype can prejudice, if more subtly, recording, scoring, and interpreting test responses. Indeed, it may influence the response given by the subject in the first instance. The black child, believed stupid by a biased white examiner, may indeed perform less well on an intelligence test (Sattler, 1970).

We noted in the previous chapter that even the most objective of tests cannot be applied or evaluated mechanically. Judgments required of clinicians in the evaluation of test findings are conceptually akin to those involved in direct observation of the patient. For these reasons, it is important to understand the processes underlying informal assessment before going on to further consideration of the interview and test methods used by clinicians.

In this chapter, we will first consider the general case of person perception, drawing on the extensive literature of social psychology, to discover how we judge the personal qualities of others, what factors reduce accuracy of such judgments, whether some persons are better judges of people than others, and whether some subjects are more easily judged than others. Within this context, we will examine the qualities of the good clinician, those which can make him a more sensitive and accurate observer of the qualities of others. Finally, we will look more closely at the specific qualities of the clinical situation to see the particular ways it determines clinical judgment.

The Study of Person Perception

Much of our knowledge of how we apprehend the qualities of another person (person perception) comes from the study of two related phenomena: (1) the judgment of emotions, and (2) the formation of first impressions of personality. In the earlier phase of this research, the emphasis was largely on the *accuracy* of person perception and particularly on the factors which lead to distortion and inaccuracy. More recently, interest has shifted to the study of the *process* rather than the outcome of person perception, to discern the ways in which judgments are made, cues used, and perceptual and inferential processes involved. Although any thorough examination of this literature is well beyond our present purposes, some characteristics might be noted before drawing from it material of relevance to the understanding of informal assessment in the clinical situation.*

Scientific concern with the process of apprehending the emotions of others dates from the publication of Charles Darwin's *The Expression of the Emotions in Man and Animals* (1872). In the century since, numerous studies have led to inconclusive and contradictory findings as to the extent to which emotions can be recognized and differentiated from facial expressions. In the main, earlier studies depended upon the matching of photographs, often posed, with preset lists of descriptive terms. In real life, of course, we rarely—if ever—judge from the momentary expression of another, much less a photograph, and it is not surprising that under these conditions subjects are less than accurate. Still, it is worth noting that extreme emotions are not confused; one might take surprise to be fear but not joy. Over the years, more subtle stimuli have been used in such studies, including motion pictures rather than stills, taped voices, candid photos of naturally occuring emotions, and live actors. In more recent years, there is the growing conviction that emotions can be accurately recognized, although accuracy

* Extensive discussions of the research and the theory of person perception can be found in Sarbin, Taft, and Bailey (1960); Allport (1961, particularly Chapters 20 and 21); Cline (1964); Vernon (1964); Bieri et al. (1966); Warr and Knapper (1968); Taguiri (1969) and Cook (1971).

varies with the emotion judged, the age, sex, and intelligence of the observer, and the amount of information available. The overall conclusion of many studies is that the more information available, the more accurately can one judge another's emotional state (Taguiri, 1969). Thus, the face alone is a less adequate stimulus than the entire body, a longer time sample is better than a shorter one, adding sound to a motion picture increases accuracy; in addition, knowledge of the surrounding situation further facilitates recognition. In general, although it has been shown that different people express the same emotion differently (Davitz, 1964), there has been relatively little study of individual differences in emotional expression. More is known about cultural differences in emotional expression; there is little question that the oriental may be inscrutable to us because of culturally required modes of affect expression. Still, a remarkable amount of evidence has been found for transcultural recognition of emotional states. Such evidence, along with findings that young children and animals recognize and respond appropriately to expressions of affect, is offered in support of a nativistic concept of affect recognition, which would minimize learning or experience in the perception of emotional states.

Paralleling the study of the recognition of emotion, research on impression formation stemming largely from the studies of Asch (1946) and Heider (1958; Heider and Simmel, 1944) gave further impetus to the psychological study of person perception. In his original study, Asch described a hypothetical person to two groups of subjects, after which they were to write a sketch of the person and check off which of a number of adjectives might characterize him. To each of the groups, Asch described the person to be judged as intelligent, skillful, industrious, determined, practical, and cautious, but for one of the experimental groups the term "warm," and for the other "cold," was added. In the consequent sketches and adjective ratings the two groups described the person as having essentially different personality pictures, rather than differing only in the specific qualities connoted by warm or cold. The perception of another, Asch argued, is thus the apprehension of a *Gestalt*, in which parts are organized in a totality, defined by central rather than peripheral qualities of the personality. Thus, in a subsequent experiment he showed that changing a more peripheral characteristic (polite versus blunt, instead of warm versus cold) made rather little difference in the later ratings. In a more lifelike situation, Kelley (1950) introduced an unknown guest lecturer to a class of students. Before coming, Kelley had distributed one of two written descriptions of him which were identical except for the terms "rather cold" and "very warm." After a twenty-minute discussion meeting, the guest left and the students were asked to characterize him. The findings were substantially the same as Asch's. Moreover, Kelley found that students entered into discussion more fully with the "warm" than with the "cold" lecturer. Building on experiments such as these, an extensive research literature evolved exploring both the accuracy and process of person perception.

First impressions of personality tend, on the whole, to be vague and global. We usually have little sense of individual characteristics, but rather an overall evaluative or emotional reaction. Research as well as common experience has shown that goodness versus badness or like versus dislike figure more prominently in first impressions than does knowledge of specific traits. Such reactions are often hard to verbalize or justify and we find ourselves saying: "I don't know what there is about him, but I just don't trust him" or "He seems ordinary enough, but I find him fascinating." Only over time do we differentiate out a more complete and detailed picture of the person, which often amplifies, though sometimes contradicts, the original reaction. But from the first, the response is to a whole person rather than to individual or randomly assembled traits. Nor does the emergence of a fuller picture depend on the collection of information about specific characteristics so much as on differentiation of the originally global concepts.

From the outset, the observer's concern centers on knowing determining tendencies (motives, intentions, attitudes) *within* the observed person (Heider, 1958). People have a particular interest to us and perceiving another person is to that degree different from perceiving objects of the physical environment. We are primarily attentive to the person's intentions or motives—"out there" in him—which might make his behavior toward us understandable and predictable. Because we perceive others as the origins and responsible agents of actions, Heider notes, we need to understand them at that level. Indeed, Heider and Simmel (1944) showed that the tendency to see actions as internally determined is so profound that we even attribute intentions to geometric figures in motion in experimental films; thus, a circle is seen as *chasing* a square, rather than simply moving in the same plane at different speeds.

In trying to understand how judgments of personality are formed, two basically different models have been proposed; one emphasizing the *immediate* and *intuitive* and the other the *inferential* nature of person perception. Phenomenological and Gestalt psychologists have pointed to the fact that perception of another is immediate, organized, direct, and apparently based more on innate than learned mechanisms (e.g., Allport, 1937, 1961). Advocates of an inference view, by contrast, believe that judgments of personality are built up from the cues available and from general principles about human behavior (e.g., Sarbin, Taft, and Bailey, 1960). The inferences can be considered as syllogisms, in which the qualities of the particular person are judged in terms of general postulates (schemata, constructs), as for example:

> All college students are intelligent;
> this person is a college student;
> therefore he is intelligent.

The major premise is part of the "postulate-system" of the observer, the set of beliefs he holds about the nature of human behavior in terms of which he judges the particular case. Such postulates, Sarbin et al. propose, arise by (1) *induction*, from experiences; (2) *construction*, i.e., developing an organized set of beliefs which constitute in effect a personality theory; (3) *analogy* to other phenomena (emphasized is the "as if" nature of the behavior), and (4) *authority*, the uncritical acceptance of principles from teachers, parents, or the culture generally.

The second proposition ("This person is a college student") involves *instantiation;* in Sarbin's term, classifying the particular case as an instance of a class. This may involve, in turn, the examination of many cues to establish class membership. With the case instantiated in terms of an existing postulate, the person is then able to arrive at a judgment and make subsequent predictions. Although as just described many nuances have been left out, in essence this inference model has been proposed to describe not only the personality judgments we all make as laymen, but the professional behavior of clinicians as well. In the latter case, the postulate-system is expectably more explicit, complex, and articulated; hopefully too, it derives from a broader and more accurate base of scientific research and clinical experience. In addition, the clinician has more precise methods for gathering the data necessary for instantiation. However, the quasi-syllogistic process is presumed to characterize person perception, lay or professional, whether using methods of informal or formal assessment.

Immediate objection to the inference model can be made by noting the fact that it does not accord with our experience. "When we form impressions and pass judgments of other people, we are not always aware of going through the quasi-syllogistic procedure described above. We do not approach social encounters as if we were a combination of a detective seeking clues and a logician drawing inferences. We 'just know' that the other person is angry or that he is aggressive." (Cook, 1971, p. 23). Proponents of inference can dismiss such objection out of general distaste for introspective data, or by admitting that inferences may actually occur rapidly and apparently unconsciously. They might even admit that one might take "intuitive judgments" to be those for which the observer is unaware of his postulates and of the behavioral evidence that led to his judgment. The inference position, however, emphasizes the conscious, empirical, and logical qualities of perception.

The evidence for innate, immediate, and global processes in perception is too compelling to dismiss, as Allport (1961) and others have shown. Thus, we know that facial expressions of basic emotional states are similar in many cultures and that children born blind have recognizable expressions (Ekman, 1969). Despite cultural variations, expressions can be recognized by members of different cultures (Ekman, Sorenson, and Friesen, 1969). Doubtless, however, judgments of others' behaviors can be learned and their expression in the first instance differs between groups and societies.

The inference view has great value for facilitating the study of person perception by drawing attention to relevant facets such as the source of postulates and the modes of instantiation. The danger, however, lies in the effort to dismiss the processes of intuition and empathy (more about this essential concept later) as trivial or unreal. I would agree with Allport (1961) that we cannot know how we understand other persons without respectful attention to both *inferential* and *intuitional* (immediate, empathic) processes. For the clinician, fuller understanding of the patient has to involve the disciplined use of subtle empathic processes ("listening with the third ear"); all the while making explicit and critically examining the inferential postulates and syllogistic stages through which conscious, rational decisions are reached.

The Nature of Empathy

The original German word "Einfühlung," carrying the meaning of "feeling oneself into," is more expressive than the English translation "empathy." At the turn of the century, Lipps introduced the concept to explain both esthetic experience and the understanding of people. The original emphasis was on motor mimicry, the slight movements induced in us by objects outside. Contemplating a Gothic spire, our bodies lift responsively and we experience it as soaring and inspiring; the Greek temple and massive office block require us to stand firm and erect as we view the linear surfaces. The smooth and effortless movements of the skilled athlete give us pleasure; awkward, strained, and uncertain actions discomfort us. In the ballet, the pathos of death is understood as we capture in ourselves the drooping, fading, and falling movements of the ballerina. In such cases, our many small movements and postural strains are largely involuntary and unknown to us. The qualities evoked are perceived in the object or person "out there," though it is through our kinesthetic sensations that we know them.

The concept of empathy encompasses a variety of related phenomena. Feelings can spread contagiously from one person to another in groups or crowds, even though those "infected" may lack the original stimulus. An infant lying quietly beside another will start to cry moments after the second becomes disturbed. A profitable application of "emotional contagion" is the theater claque, i.e., hired stooges spread through the audience who applaud or laugh uproariously on cue, a practice technologically advanced to taped laughter by TV. Still another form of empathic mimicry is evident in the attempt, as it were, to influence magically the behavior of persons or objects through our involuntary actions. It is almost impossible for a mother not to open her own mouth as she brings a spoon toward her child's. The bowler and his watching friends urge the ball down the alley by tensing their bodies forward; from the game of pool, such movements have been called "body English." Indeed, if all the muscular effort expended had effect, every batted baseball would clear the centerfield fence! In all such instances of empathy, whether in primitive or more mature forms, there is a "feeling oneself into," an unintended transmission of experience, largely but not wholly through motoric mechanisms.

Thus through empathy, Lipps and other theorists proposed, we put ourselves in the place of the other and thereby understand his experience and character. In the psychoanalytic view, empathy is part of the important process of identification, through which the self develops. We take as models persons of particularly great emotional relevance—typically in childhood the parent of the same sex—and through empathy and imitation we internalize behaviors and characteristics. At an early stage, the process of identification is passive and nondiscriminating; with the development of personal identity, it becomes more active and selective. Early empathic behavior, like the emotional contagion of infancy, is similarly passive and automatic.

In the mature adult, empathic understanding of another personality, work of art, or nature, supposes a well-developed sense of self so that the qualities perceived can be properly localized "out there" not "in here." Moreover, it supposes a fair range of experience, for we cannot truly conceive and name feelings we have not known ourselves. The grief of another at the death of a loved one may distress us, but we can appreciate it as grief only as we too have suffered loss. The person who is shut off from his own feelings, as by obsessive-compulsive neurotic defenses, cannot afford to be cognizant of those of others. Many of the qualities of someone who is a good judge of personality—as we will discuss shortly—are those which allow contact with one's own, and hence other's, inner life and, at the same time, provide a degree of detachment and insight.

It may seem paradoxical that empathy, as an effective mechanism of informal assessment, requires both closeness and distance; indeed, a balance between them. For empathy to exist at all there must be identification, a fusion of the self and other, but such identification must be partial and temporary, lest the self merge with the other (Schafer, 1959). We sometimes use the term *over*identification to characterize the common behavior of young clinicians who, so to speak, cannot distinguish their patients' feelings from their own. To simply have the feelings of the other aroused in ourselves, to cry when he does, does not constitute understanding of his feelings. True understanding requires some distance, so that we can perceive the qualities of the other in their own terms. *Under*identification, contrariwise, blocks the sharing of experience entirely.

The concept of empathy, as noted, figures prominently in views of person perception which emphasize the immediate, global, and structured nature of perception in contrast to the empirical sequential information processing presumed by inference theories. There is sufficient evidence that both types of processes exist, and it seems futile to argue whether one can be reduced to the other or which is more important. Nor should it be supposed that some people know others only through empathy while others are "inferencers," though it is likely to be true that people differ in this regard as in other cognitive orientations toward the world of objects. From the standpoint of advancing clinical assessment both processes have to be understood, including the ways in which they may interact. It is a common enough experience that an empathic reaction supplies the hypotheses and clues which then lead us to seek out appropriate data and test our understanding by inferential rules.

In the following sections, we will consider some of the factors in person perception which facilitate or block accurate judgments and some of the personal attributes which characterize more adept judges without particular concern as to whether empathic or inferential processes are involved. Often it is impossible to tell, except as an act of faith; as often, both are visible.

The Accuracy of Person Perception

Our judgments of others, even in brief encounters, are often remarkably full and accurate. Often, however, they are incomplete, distorted and inaccurate. Much of the research in the field has focused on sources of inaccuracy in order to discover their nature and locus. In general, they include conditions in the *observer*, in the *person* being judged, and in the *context* in which the judgment is made.

SOURCES OF ERROR IN THE OBSERVER

Oversimplification. We simply cannot process the amount of information available when perceiving another person. Inevitably, there is selection and condensation from the available input and the resulting percept is as much a caricature as a photograph of the stimulus person. There are more facets to any personality than we can hold simultaneously in mind. Hence, simplification is inevitable and reflects the limits of human cognition. But along with reducing the amount of information we also tend to shape it into a more meaningful whole than in fact exists. Whether perceiving man or objects, there is the universal tendency toward attaining the most meaningful, unitary, and comprehensive concept possible—in Bartlett's (1932) classic phrase, an "effort after meaning." Consequently, confronted with the complexities of another person, we tend to see his personality as more unitary, formed, and structured than it may in fact be (Allport, 1961). In the process of oversimplification, some characteristics may be more salient and determine our picture of the whole person. Thus—recall Asch's experiment—whether a person was "warm" or "cold" colored the total judgment.

A common characteristic of personality judgments, the so-called "halo effect," reflects this same process. If one generally likes the person being observed, then all complimentary traits are rated high while those which might be negatively valued are rated low. Again, an unnaturally consistent picture emerges defined by immediate liking or disliking of the person. On the whole, however, studies of judging strangers have shown a *leniency effect*. By and large, we tend to rate others (ourselves as well) high on favorable traits and lower on unfavorable ones.

In the same spirit, *stereotypes* and *popular theories of personality* organize and bias person perception. If the stranger differs from the observer in some clear way, then that difference is first noted and immediately calls to mind the set of preconceptions which defines "people like that." Stereotypes exist, of course, around most of the dimensions of group membership—race, ethnicity, nationality, social class, sex, or age—or are related to salient physical qualities (height, weight, hair coloring, facial characteristics) or handicaps and deformities. Stereotypes project the social prejudices and values of society. They assume a set of highly correlated traits characteristic of all persons in the group; to know one is to know them all. In person perception, stereotypes function as inferential rules. Thus, if the man before us is, say, Italian, then infer that he is emotionally expressive, warm, loves music and spaghetti, etc. As Walter Lippman (1922) noted long ago, stereotypes conserve mental energy; it is far simpler to have one preconceived picture in the head for fifty million people than to trouble to consider each in his own right. Social life is simplified by having and holding stereotyped conceptions, even if social injustice is created.

The obvious dangers of stereotyped thinking should not, however, blind us to the fact that popular theories about the nature of people often contain germs of truth. Members of the same social group, sharing the same values and conditions of life, do have personality characteristics in common, as discussed in Chapter 2. In the absence of information about the particular person, traits more or less common to a culture can supply a base for prediction about the individual. If an unkown Italian were coming to your home for dinner, it would probably be wiser to prepare spaghetti than borscht. Danger lies in the overspecificity and inaccuracy of the beliefs held and in the inflexibility of an "all . . . are . . ." way of thinking.

Emotional and Motivational States. Moods and needs of the observer influence his judgments of the other. Whether we ascribe our own feelings, or search out conditions appropriate to their arousal, we distort the perception of the actual qualities of the other person. Thus, the anxious person may see others as anxious (like himself) or as threatening (to justify his anxiety), but either way it is *his* state not *theirs* which determines his view. The happy person sees a happy world;

the sad person tints it blue. In a classic experiment, H. A. Murray (1933) had his daughter and her guests judge the pictures of men just after they had played a frightening game of "murder." Compared to a more relaxed occasion, the faces were rated as significantly more malicious and threatening. Similarly, Feshbach and Singer (1957) aroused fear in observers by the threat of electric shock and found that they rated photographs as both more fearful and more aggressive.

Any strongly aroused and unsatisfied need can determine the perception of others. As the hungry person is alert to the sight or smell of food, so the sexually frustrated person is more tuned to the sexual appeals of the other. Under conditions of strong arousal the person is not only alerted to the presence of appropriate objects of gratification but he can hallucinate them. Thus, the hungry man "sees" a distant object as food; while driving on a dark, dreary night shadows of trees take on frightening, animate forms. What we judge another person to be is in part at least a function of the motivational and emotional state we are in.

Projection and Other Defenses. Not only needs and emotions themselves, but defensive maneuvers to guard against their expression or recognition distort person perception. Projection has been of special concern. In the sense originally intended by Freud in his explanation of paranoia, projection involves seeing in another a need denied in the self because it conflicts with moral principles and is incompatible with one's self-concept. The projecting person is thus protected from confronting the distasteful motive in himself. More broadly, the term has been used to describe alterations or distortions of perception in many forms related to inner states of the person. But regardless of whether projection is taken in its literal and limited meaning, i.e., as defensive distortion, or in a more general sense, it functions importantly in person perception.

Projection can be viewed as the opposite of empathy (Haan, 1969; Holt, 1968). In both, boundaries between self and other are weakened. There is "confusion" as to the locus of experience and the other is judged in terms of the self. However, in empathy, the observer perceives feelings which are properly another's by allowing them to be aroused, in a measure, within himself. Sensing the feeling within himself, he can then better understand its nature "out there." By contrast, in projection, as the feeling grows within the observer, he attributes it to the other, in order to avoid recognition of a quality judged evil by his moral and rational nature. In fullest and most dramatic form, projection is seen in paranoids, whose distortions of reality can be on a grand scale. Not surprisingly, paranoids can be flagrantly wrong in judging other people. However, the very intensity of their need to deny evil in themselves and see it in others often makes them capable of detecting defects in character, invisible to healthier eyes, with penetrating if highly selective acumen. Holt (1968) contrasts projection and empathy as follows:

> Projection and empathy are two forms of one basic process in the perception and judgment of other people, but projection distorts the accuracy and depth of understanding, whereas empathy enhances it. The basic process might be called subjectivity, or egocentricity; whatever name we give it, it is the almost universal tendency to judge everyone else in relation to the self-concept. A person inevitably compares everyone else to himself. He himself is, after all, the person he knows best and longest and for whose welfare he makes the most continuous efforts [p. 596].

A particular type of projection that has bedeviled empirical research in person perception has been named "assumed similarity." Particularly if the person judged is like us, we tend to rate him as we would ourselves. Obviously, this would have the effect of making one observer seem more accurate if in fact there were actual similarity between the judge and the person judged (Bender and Hastorf, 1950; 1953). Assumed similarity, along with some of the other response sets noted, such as leniency, halo effect, and oversimplification, have posed major methodological problems for researchers in the area.

Defenses other than projection can also, if differently, distort judgment. Thus, the hysterical person who denies or represses hostile impulses in himself sees a bland and conflict-free world and consequently cannot see hostility or other strong negative feelings in others. The rationalizer is not likely to trust the explanations of others. The person who defensively must protect an uncertain self-concept is predictably limited in his capacity to judge others in their own terms.

Other Characteristics. Good judges of personality, it has been noted, possess a variety of intellectual and personality qualities, as we will discuss further presently. A lack in such abilities limits the accuracy of person perception. Some of the more salient traits are intelligence, cognitive complexity, intraceptiveness (psychological mindedness), personal insight, and breadth of experience. In general, the more intellectually limited the observer is or the more restricted in depth and breadth of personality, the more likely is he to lack skill in judging another person.

SOURCES OF ERROR IN THE PERSON BEING JUDGED

Open and Closed Personalities. Some people are simply more difficult to know than others. Some are more *opaque*, others are more *transparent*. Some are willing to share their feelings and experiences. Others stay behind a defensive shield, whether out of shyness or defensive mistrust, letting only surface qualities be known but otherwise remaining closed to the viewer. The degree to which we voluntarily reveal or conceal our inner feelings varies, of course, with circumstances, with the people we are with, whether friends or strangers, and the like. But some people are persistently more transparent or opaque, as Allport (1961) noted. Cultural groups differ in their accessibility. Lewin (1935–1936) claimed that Americans are more open to strangers than Germans and more readily disclose personal feelings and experiences. By contrast, he suggests, the German allows penetration to the very core of personality once friendship is established, while Americans retain barriers around the innermost regions of personality even with intimates. Other evidence quoted by Allport shows persistent individual differences in social accessibility within our own culture; people differ in the amount of information and the range of people they are willing to confide in. Experimental studies show that extroverted, adaptable, and dominant people can be more easily judged. To start with, then, the nature of the personality being judged, particularly its open or closed quality, affects the completeness and accuracy of judgment.

Presentation of the Self. We not only make impressions on others, but we intend to give impressions to others. Personal qualities are not only revealed, they are also presented (Goffman, 1956). Commonly enough, people try to influence first impressions positively be acting in a friendly, cordial way, by smiling, being neatly dressed, and the like. However, should it serve his purposes, the person may present other faces. Thus, in a study of habituated and satisfied psychiatric patients, who—in the authors' clever phrase—found the state hospital "a last resort," answers were given to personality tests which showed them to be more mentally disturbed than, in fact, they were (Braginsky, Braginsky, and Ring, 1969). This parallels the condition called "malingering" in clinical fields, in which the patient, perhaps to avoid a more unpleasant fate, consciously fakes the symptoms of a disease. More usually, however, patients and normals both attempt to present themselves in the best light possible, concealing consciously or unconsciously facets of themselves which might engender scorn, ridicule, or disgust in the viewer. "Faking positive" whether out of the unconscious action of defense, or through conscious deception, is the usual order of the day.

The ways in which people present themselves usually are determined by role concepts from which expectations are generated as to probable responses by the observer. Thus, someone aspiring to a salesman's job wants to appear hearty and genial but persistent. Such aspects of his behavior as can be controlled will be altered so as to project the desired image. An applicant to a highly favored psychiatric training program confessed to the author (after selection interviews were completed!) that he had spent an hour that morning buying a necktie, a tie which would show him to be a "promising young psychiatrist." He realized, of course, that the tie was a trivial symbol, nor could he predict what criteria might actually be used by interviewers concerned to find the best future psychiatrists. Nonetheless, hunting for *the* tie gave him some sense of control and self-determination, hence alleviated anxiety, in an inherently important, ambiguous, and stressful situation. In another vein, friends tell the charming story of how they met and fell in love on a trans-Atlantic ship. She did not want to be bothered by amorous men. Consequently, she went about with a copy of *The Decline and Fall of the Roman Empire* conspicuously tucked under her arm—only thereby to catch the eye of a young scholar coming to teach in the United States! Today, she is happily married to a professor. How one presents oneself clearly affects the judgments and actions of others.

Deception, whatever its source and whether conscious or not, is a barrier to the accurate understanding of another person. Whether in informal or in formal assessment, the skills of the clinician are tested in efforts to penetrate the facade presented by the patient. However, it should also be realized that understanding *what* the patient is attempting to convey and *why* is often as important as knowing the *real* person who lies behind.

SOURCES OF ERROR IN THE CONTEXT OF JUDGMENT

Normally, we know people in life contexts and our judgments of their feelings, traits, and intentions depend on cues coming both from the person and from the situational context. We judge someone to be in pain not only because he exclaims or looks pained, but also because we have just seen him hit his thumb with a hammer. By combining information from both situation and subject, we are ordinarily more accurate in understanding the state of the subject. A grimacing face in a still photograph may suggest either *disgust* or *determination;* if we knew that the picture was taken as the subject observed a surgical operation or, alternately, just taken as he spurted toward the finish line in a race, the choice would be easy.

Not only does a particular behavior gain meaning from the momentary situational forces acting on the subject, but also from its position in an on-going sequence of activities. Thus, Taguiri (1969, p. 420) notes: " 'The boy *began to sob,* then he hit his playmate in the face' gives the act of beginning to sob a different meaning from 'The boy hit his playmate in the face, then he *began to sob.*' " In the first case, we can infer frustration and rage; in the second, guilt may be more likely. Despite the fact that such temporal sequences are normal and natural in real life, experimental studies are more commonly limited to momentary situations in which the judge has little knowledge of circumstances surrounding and preceding the behavior to be judged. It is worth noting, too, that we judge intimates in terms of longer temporal units, which supply a baseline against which present states are assessed. When talking of a friend, we say "Compared to his *usual* calm, he really is agitated *today*. I wonder what touched him off?" Implied in these statements is the possibility that our friend's agitated state is only moderately high on some absolute scale, but so uncharacteristic of his prevailing mood that special explanation need be sought. In formal clinical assessment, we try to gain such understanding through interviews exploring the patient's history of characteristic responses to recurrent situations; in psychotherapy, we come to know baselines as the relationship evolves hour after hour.

It is self-evidently true, and was noted earlier, that behavior is determined not only by internal states of the person but also by situational demands. Situations require certain behaviors and inhibit others; we are put in momentary roles in which certain acts and feelings are expected and normally occur. Not only are we likely to feel sad at a funeral, but even if some humorous thought perversely crosses our mind, we are unlikely to laugh openly. Contrariwise, to appear sad at a cocktail party is virtually as forbidden a deviant act. Situational roles, just as more durable social roles, determine actions and feelings. To act accordingly indexes the extent to which we have accepted and internalized social rules and tells little therefore about the individual personality. However, even in well-structured situations, individuals act differently. The task in assessment is to subtract, so to speak, the situational baseline from the observed behavior of the individual; "He looks awfully sad for someone at a cocktail party." Indeed, it is precisely in the difference between the expected and the actual that diagnosis can be made clinically. The compulsive and preemptive drives of the neurotic do not brook situational constraints. The "inappropriate affect" characteristic of schizophrenics is seen in situations where there are compelling expectations for one feeling, yet another is shown; laughing when informed of the death of a loved one.

The meaning of another's behavior can readily be misconstrued if we are ignorant of, or misinformed about, the social and temporal contexts in which he acts. However, correct and complete knowledge of the situation alone allows at best predicting the state or behavior of an average, socialized person; the more readily where there are well-defined, consistent and widely accepted social rules. Understanding individual behavior requires simultaneous consideration of both person and situation.

The Good Judge of Personality

We all know people who seem to have an uncanny understanding of the feelings and motives of others, who are, in the German word, "*Menschenkenner*," translated "people-knowers." There are others, incapable of understanding people, who are grossly insensitive to our needs and feelings. The immediate answer most of us would give to the question, "Are there good and bad judges of personality?" is "of course." Yet the psychological research literature is equivocal; there is no secure evidence that (1) people-knowing is a general trait and (2) there are distinct qualities which characterize a good judge. Overall, however, there is sufficient evidence to argue for generality, rather than specificity, in the ability to judge, and from which we can identify some of the qualities found to characterize better judges.

Studies have compared the accuracy of judges over different tasks, over different variables of personality, with different types of subjects and over time. In a number of cases, no correlations are found (e.g., Crow and Hammond, 1957) across a variety of tasks, variables, and subject groups, but other careful studies have shown considerable correlation (e.g., Cline and Richards, 1960), though sometimes of a complex sort (Bronfenbrenner, Harding, and Gallway, 1958). A finding of some significance, which we will consider in more detail shortly, is that we judge more accurately people who are like us in age, sex, and social background (Taft, 1955), though one can wonder how much of this effect involves "assumed similarity" which happens to be correct.

More recent studies have supported a suggestion of Gordon Allport (1937) that accuracy of prediction for the *average* of a group should be distinguished from predictions for *individual* persons. The ability to judge the generalized other (sometimes called *stereotype* accuracy) and sensitivity to individual differences (*differential* accuracy) have been found to be relatively unrelated and indeed, in one study, negatively related (Stone, Gage, and Leavitt, 1957). So much of the research is limited by methodological questions, and the resulting evidence so uncertain, that it would probably be wisest to suspend judgment as to whether the ability to judge others is a general or specific trait. Still, I am inclined to go along with Allport's conclusion (1937) that we would err more to "consider the ability entirely specific than to consider it entirely general" (p. 512).

Whether people-knowing is a unitary characteristic or a composite of multiple traits, there do seem to be a number of qualities which distinguish the superior judge of personality (Taft, 1955; Shrauger and Altrocchi, 1964; Allport, 1961; Taguiri, 1969). Among these, Allport (1961) notes are breadth of personal experience, similarity, intelligence, cognitive complexity, self-insight, social skill and adjustment, detachment, esthetic attitude, and intraceptiveness. Let us consider these and related factors.

EXPERIENCE

A good judge is not only mature in the sense of having a well-differentiated and integrated personality, but he also must have had extensive life experiences bringing him into meaningful contact with people of different age, sex, class, race, and life style. Where experience is limited, we are more likely to fall back on stereotypic conceptions. Proponents of the inference theory note that experience is one base of an extensive and differentiated postulate system, of a type to guide correct judgments.

SIMILARITY

We know best those who are most like us. Similarity is thus a special case of experience; the emphasis here is on depth rather than breadth. We know ourselves best and by extension those who share our physical and social attributes, and who have developed and live under the same life circumstances. Note, again, that *assumed* similarity tends to limit accuracy, as *actual* similarity enhances it. In the present era, there is considerable concern with similarity of judge to judged, in large measure out of a more embracing concern with making mental health service more responsive to the needs of minority populations. Thus, it is argued that Blacks, Chicanos, Indians and also young people and women, can best be served by clinicians of their own communities, who share their identities, experiences, and problems. While it is certainly true that *dis*similarity, particularly if accompanied by dislike and distrust as well as ignorance, negates communication, it still need not follow that nonminority clinicians cannot understand or serve minority people. The range of experience with many kinds of people and similarity with some are balancing factors in determining how well one can understand another person.

INTELLIGENCE

In general, research shows that more intelligent people are better judges of others (Taft, 1955). The sensitivity to subtle cues, the capacity to integrate information, to generalize, to retain and utilize past experience, and other facets of general intelligence, are as much involved in attaining a concept of another person as in solving intellectual problems.

COGNITIVE COMPLEXITY

Related is the fact that people who are themselves complex and subtle in cognitive style are better judges of personality (Bieri, 1955; 1966).

SELF-INSIGHT

The person who knows himself tends to be a better judge of others. For one thing, he is better able to avoid the pitfalls of projection, oversimplification, and other response sets which operate best when one is blind to his own qualities. Moreover, experiencing oneself as being richly differentiated, albeit with some undesirable qualities, allows one to respect the complexity and uniqueness of others.

SOCIAL SKILL

Studies show that good judges are usually skilled socially and emotionally stable. They tend generally to be rated higher in popularity, leadership, outgoingness, and interest in others; by contrast, the poor judge is more often seen as neurotic, aggressive, dependent, and awkward in social encounters.

DETACHMENT

While the good judge is usually outgoing and warm, he also must be able to be detached from others. Perspective and impartiality require a degree of distance; the overly nurturant, social, affiliative, sympathetic, and loving person cannot readily see objectively qualities, particularly faults, of the other. A good judge despite the general findings just noted, is often reserved and introversive. Overall, however, neither extreme ideally characterizes him; too close and one merges with the other, too distant and one cannot make contact with his experience. The good clinician has to be able to change distance, to come close or withdraw, in order to understand and help his patient. Psychotherapy often involves the interposition of a "therapeutic barrier" between therapist and patient.

ESTHETIC ATTITUDE

Allport notes that a gifted judge is highly esthetic. "The esthetic attitude seeks always to comprehend the intrinsic harmony of any object that is the center of attention . . . The object may be as trivial as an ornament or as substantial as a human being" (1961, p. 509). This quality he considers foremost among the qualifications of the good judge, and indeed, when highly enough developed, it may offset limitations in experience, similarity, intelligence, insight, and complexity.

INTRACEPTIVENESS

Murray et al. (1938) first used the term "intraception" to describe an orientation toward the inner workings of one's mind and personality, involving ". . . the dominance of feelings, fantasies, speculations, aspirations. An imaginative, subjective human outlook. Romantic action." By contrast, the extraceptive person is disposed to stay with the obvious facts of the real world; he is practical and down-to-earth. Related to the general quality of intraception, in Murray's view, are the specific attributes of psychological-mindedness, self-awareness, and empathy. Being attentive to fantasy, internal feelings and wishes, and personal meanings in himself, the intraceptive person is more likely to understand their meanings in other lives as well.

Anti-intraception characterizes the authoritarian personality (Adorno et al., 1950; D. J. Levinson, Sharaf, and Gilbert, 1966), who denies his own internal states and is insensitive to those of others. In an excellent study, Scodel and Mussen (1953) demonstrated how authoritarianism is related to distortion of person perception. They tested a large number of students on the F Scale, a major instrument in research on authoritarianism. For twenty minutes, each pair was to chat informally about radio, movies, or television. Following this, each member of the pair was asked to fill out the F Scale again as he believed his partner had done. The results showed that the high authoritarians thought their partners (all lows) had responded as they had, and therefore gave significantly higher scores than the "lows" actually had had. The low authoritarian subjects, on the other hand, were much more accurate in their estimates of the scores of their mates, judging them to be higher in authoritarianism (though not as extreme as they actually were). Thus, the authoritarian subjects tended to ascribe their own values to others who in fact were quite different.

CARING FOR OTHERS

The capacity to understand others is clearly related to concern and affection for others. The sympathetic and interested person is the empathic person. To be grossly self-centered, misanthropic, or continuously suspicious of other's motives is to be isolated from understanding them, except perhaps as potential objects to be used for one's own ends. A primary quality of the amoral, manipulative, and often criminal psychopath is his incapacity to understand the feelings of others and hence to predict their behavior correctly (Gough, 1948; Gough and Petersen, 1952).

FEMALENESS

Although the evidence from research studies is far from conclusive, and such differences as are found tend to be small, women are generally reported to be better judges of emotional and personality qualities than men (Taft, 1955; Taguiri, 1969). This accords, of course, with the popular belief which views women as more "intuitive" and hence more perceptive of the inner states, needs, and feelings of others. Not unlikely, the superiority of women in this respect reflects their traditional social role. Women have primary responsibility for care and nurturance, particularly of children, while men are expected to move in the "real" world of ideas and work. With her life focused in human relationships, a woman would predictably be more sensitive to nuances of feelings and attitudes. Men are expected to be work- and problem-oriented, hard-headed and rational; tender feelings, sympathetic involvement with others, fantasy, beauty, and the nonutilitarian facets of life are largely left to women. But some of the qualities already noted as characterizing the good judge, notably the esthetic attitude and intraception, are related to precisely these nonreality-oriented dispositions. With the present move toward greater sexual equality, we might well expect that sex differences in interest in and ability to understand others will diminish. Just as women have become less tolerant of inferior social status, men are increasingly able to recognize tenderness, sympathy, playful fantasy, and the like in themselves, which bodes well for freer use of empathic abilities.

Can Interpersonal Sensitivity Be Increased?

Some studies have found that specific training in a person perception task can increase accuracy. Davitz (1964) found that subjects who were given "correct" answers in practice sessions were then more accurate in identifying emotions expressed in faces and voices. Similarly, Jecker, Maccoby, and Breitrose (1965) showed that feedback improved teachers' judgments of their pupils' behavior. Other supportive findings have been reported, although often in studies with dubious criteria of accuracy. Overall, however, the evidence available supports the notion that specific training in the realm in which judgment is required can increase the accuracy of that judgment.

Of potentially greater interest are nonspecific procedures, intended to have the general effect of facilitating social behavior, and with it, more accurate person perception. Since the 1940s, many types of "sensitivity training" groups have been developed including the well-known T (for training) group. In Chapter 15, we will consider in detail T-group and other procedures designed to increase personal sensitivity and effective social behavior. In the main, they depend on having participants become more attentive to their own and others' patterns of communication and interaction in face-to-face group encounters. Unlike therapy groups (but often difficult to distinguish from them) the T-group is more concerned with the social process between persons than with the conflicts and personality distress within each. Protagonists of T-group and related methods claim that they result in considerable personal growth, heightened cognizance of the needs and feelings of others, and more effective use of group processes for communication and problem-solving. Evidence that such goals are reached is at best partial, but the continued enthusiasm and testimony of both group leaders and participants suggest that these group methods may have powerful effects.

In the same spirit, clinical training is a vehicle for increasing interpersonal sensitivity. Central to this end is the painstaking and critical examination by the clinician in training and his supervisor of the transactions between clinician and patient. Other facets of clinical training—study of theory and research methods, of the cumulated knowledge of personality and psychopathology, of practice in assessment and therapy, indeed, reading a book such as this—all have the effect of extending the base of knowledge and sharpening the intellectual skills required for clinical inference and intervention. We would like to think that the consequence is a more personally sensitive as well as knowledgeable and technically adept psychologist; research studies as well as direct experience usually support this belief. Yet, contrary evidence of both sorts exist. Thus, Crow (1957) found that clinical training did not visibly improve the accuracy of young psychiatrists' judgments on a trait-rating test. While they differentiated more among people, these more subtle judgments did not correspond better with criterion scores and hence accuracy was lower than among less-trained persons. Such experiments often put clinicians in artificial judgmental situations quite dissimilar to the conditions under which real clinical judgments are made. However, it is fair enough to conclude that clinical training—just as sensitivity training, or, for that matter, education itself—does not guarantee heightened interpersonal sensitivity. That some people "just naturally" seem to excel is an obvious fact, which should perhaps lead clinical faculties to more concerted efforts to find, as well as develop, people-knowers.

In principle, however, anything which can be done to reduce those conditions, discussed earlier, which distort the process of person perception should of course increase its accuracy. To understand potential sources of distortion is a start at least; awareness of tendencies toward oversimplification, halo effect, stereotypy, assumed similarity, and similar processes can be the beginning of relatively bias-free perception. Similarly, knowledge of how and why people present themselves, information about expectable behaviors in socially defined situations, and the like, contribute to the same end. The base of personal experience from which we view others can surely be extended, though other personality and intellectual attributes of the good judge may be too durable to be readily altered. It is hard to see how we can make ourselves more intelligent, cognitively complex, esthetic, or intraceptive. But while we may not be able to create or extend these positive traits, we can reduce in some degree barriers against their expression. The frightened, defensive person, clinging securely to concrete realities, lacks the personal freedom necessary for empathic understanding. Factors which block the clear and correct perception of others can be reduced through critical self-examination, clinical supervision, sensitivity training, and personal psychotherapy in anyone, clinicians included.

It is easy to state why clinicians *should* be better judges of others, at least in comparison to the average person if not the creative poet or novelist. Factors can be readily identified in three realms: (1) knowledge and experience; (2) personality qualities; and (3) state or attitudinal factors, characterizing his behavior in the clinical encounter. Some of these have already been noted; others will be discussed in greater length later.

1. Knowledge and Experience. While a broad base of life experience may or may not be characteristic, clinicians have a spectrum of systematic encounters with patients and normals in the course of training. Learning the organized knowledge of research and the organized concepts of psychological theory, are the essence of graduate training; importantly involved is the critical examination of fact and theory. All of this militates against simplistic concepts and stereotypy. It is probably true that knowledge and experience, as gained in academic and clinical training centers, are more conducive to the ability "to judge the generalized other" than to produce "sensitivity to individual differences" (Allport, 1937). And, again, we can note that formal knowledge, theoretical commitment, and scientific hypercriticalness can bind as well as free clinical judgment. But we should note that they are the very foundations of expert professional functioning; without them, we grope and flounder, although with unpredictable flashes of intuitive understanding.

2. Personality Qualities. Clinical training attracts people who have a sympathetic concern to help others and a firm affection for people. Those entering the field are likely to be of above-average intelligence, esthetically oriented, and cognitively complex and intraceptive. These qualities may well combine into neurotic self-doubt and painful self-searching, though more usually underlying a compelling interest to know oneself in order to know others. Wheelis (1958) with poetic beauty tells of his own *Quest for Identity* as a clinician. While there are few like him, most clinicians are far from being simple, complacent, self-certain Archie Bunkers.

3. State (Attitudinal) Factors in the Clinical Role. Derived from knowledge and theory, and certainly dependent on personal qualities, but separately conceptualizable in themselves are those attitudes of the practicing clinician which collectively can be described as "clinical technique." In the clinical encounter, the clinician maintains a relaxed and alert, but not aroused state. He is schooled to listen, as Reik put it, with a third ear; in Freud's phrase to maintain "free-floating attention." There is a willingness to sustain ambiguity, remain uncertain while hearing out the patient and trying to make the parts of a puzzle fit. The clinician is calm, appropriately detached, appropriately warm if not promiscuously accepting; while he must be a real person, his own needs and feelings are in relative

abeyance as he attends to those of the patient. He inspires trust and encourages openness. These and similar qualities facilitate understanding of others; they are not characteristic of ordinary social intercourse. Indeed, the self-same clinician outside the consulting room may shout at his wife or kick his dog; I do not mean to suggest that he is a paragon of patience, self-denial, and wisdom. But, in the professional role, he listens attentively and sympathetically and delays action and feeling. In principle at least, such attitudes facilitate understanding the patient's personality and concerns.

Are clinicians actually better judges of personality? The research literature is at best equivocal and overall suggests that there is no great advantage to psychological education generally, or clinical training specifically. Sarbin, Taft, and Bailey surveyed fourteen relevant studies up to 1961 and noted that three showed psychologists to be worse judges of personality than laymen, six found them equal, and in only five were they superior. Elsewhere, Taft (1955) concludes "Physical scientists and possibly other nonpsychologists, e.g., personnel workers, appear to be more capable of judging others accurately than are either psychology students or clinical psychologists." While some studies show clinicians off to advantage (e.g., Cline, 1955), the overall picture is not heartening. It is true of course that most of these studies involved person-perception tasks which do not parallel the realities of assessment in clinical settings; from the standpoint of the clinicians involved they were put in an artificial situation. Moreover, studies of the type cited involved mainly young and relatively inexperienced clinicians.

Still, these findings are cause for thoughtful concern. Allport (1961) reading these same results expresses concern that psychologists are trained in ways which give them *knowledge about* rather than *acquaintance with* (in William James' terms) human nature as it is directly realized. Other studies show, too, that clinicians tend too readily to make overinclusive generalizations, and particularly those which emphasize pathological trends in the person. Where the layman would use the same data to predict more moderate and conventional behavior, the clinician is perhaps too ready to interpret the extreme and aberrant.

Studies are needed which include judgmental tasks and conditions more similar to those with which clinicians work. Yet, available evidence however incomplete and biased should challenge clinical psychology to train (again, perhaps select) its novices in ways which maximize those factors noted earlier which should make them more sensitive and accurate in understanding other human beings.

The Clinical Relationship

Informal assessment, that is, judging the personal qualities of others, occurs wherever and whenever two or more persons interact. It may be: 1. incidental to ordinary social intercourse ("Gee, that lady in the store seems unhappy."); 2. instrumental to life decisions ("Should I buy a used car from him?"); or 3. more or less systematically involved in any of a multitude of professional decisions ("If I give him a failing grade, will he stop fooling around and start studying, or perhaps get discouraged and drop out?"). Obviously enough, the particular participants involved, the types and meanings of decisions made, and the social contexts in which they occur determine the particular ways in which assessment and decision-making is arrived at, the process, and accuracy. Let us therefore now examine the particular qualities of the clinical relationship within which clinical assessment is made.

Clinical psychologists work in a variety of institutional contexts, each of which colors the clinician-patient relationship in particular and predictable ways. The referral questions asked and the clinical options available, are obviously different if one is, say, a clinician working for the Juvenile Court, a state hospital, a public school, or a university-based psychological clinic. (For a more detailed analysis of the social constraints on clinical assessment in a number of such settings, see Levine, 1968.) For present purposes, let us take the prototypic situation of the psychological or psychiatric clinic oriented to psychotherapy. In this case, the client is typically self-referred, or he comes voluntarily at the suggestion of family or professional advisors. His problems would ordinarily be diagnosed within the spectrum of neurotic or characterological conditions. A fee is typically involved. On his part, the clinician is an autonomous professional, acting neither as technician nor consultant, though he may collaborate with other staff members. He is part of the clinic's treatment staff and importantly involved in the clinic's decision-making.

THE SITUATION FROM THE PATIENT'S VIEWPOINT

The patient is suffering personal distress and made the decision to seek help. Feelings of shame and inadequacy are predictable, because coming to the clinic is an admission to himself that he has problems which he cannot deal with alone. In most communities, some social stigma may also be attached to going to a psychiatrist or psychologist. At the same time, having made the decision, he experiences relief and hope, for he can now look forward to professional help in lifting the burden. He may be more or less psychologically minded and willing to see the sources of his problems in himself or inclined to see the world around him as putting undue pressures on him, but at the moment he has agreed that talking about his concerns and personal feelings may do some good. He may have a rather limited idea of how psychological clinics work, but he is ready to do whatever is asked of him. He expects the clinician to be a technically competent and knowledgeable professional, but also a trustworthy, considerate, and sympathetic person. In the absence of a clear concept of the clinician's role and functions, the patient projects role expectations from other helper-client relations he has known. Most usually he sees the clinician as "physician," though of the head rather than the body, and he expects to have prescribed "medicines" which, if he dutifully takes, will remove the pain and allow healthier functioning. Alternative role ascriptions are those of a "spiritual advisor" (like a priest), "counselor," "friend," "seer," or even "magician." Approaching assessment, the patient has evaluation anxiety, for the clinician may find him to be incurably disturbed—in fantasy, at least, a hopeless madman. Despite our assurances that "there are no right or wrong answers," deep down the patient is convinced that there are. Many of his questions are directed at comparing himself with other people along some dimension of normality—"Do many people have such symptoms?" "Are such feelings normal?" and so on. As he enters the clinical process, the patient is likely to be (1) in psychological distress; (2) both relieved and shamed for bringing it to professional attention; (3) uncertain as to what will happen; (4) frightened at what might emerge; (5) resolved to cooperate, usually in a rather passive sense, in whatever will transpire; (6) trustful and hopeful, and (7) ready to invest the clinician with extraordinary wisdom, skill, and humanity.

How the patient behaves and hence what he reveals of himself in initial clinical encounters is determined both by enduring personal qualities which he brings in with him and by his expectations and perception of the clinician and setting. The anxious patient looks and acts anxiously, and talks of conditions under which feelings become more intense and incapacitating. He may be garrulous or reserved, confused or well-organized, impulsive or controlled, depending on his usual style and emotional state at the moment. It hardly needs saying that we see in the consulting room a personality which preexisted the present moment. At the same time, the patient's behavior and self-presentation are tempered by factors in the current situation, namely, his prior expectations and his present perception of the clinician and the clinic. Although not explicitly involved in informal assessment, the patient is responsive to all of the cues normally involved in forming percepts of people in other social situations. The clinician's age, sex, race, physical appearance, gestures, clothing, hair length, and mode of communicating, as well as what is said, all contribute to the patient's view of him. Information given by others and already held preconceptions fill out the patient's image of the clinician and the clinic. However, the patient's concerns center on his problems and it is in reference to them that judgments of the clinician emerge. Thus, a young married woman seeing a woman clinician in a university clinic might think to herself: "She seems about thirty-five and the receptionist called her 'doctor.' But she's not wearing a wedding ring; I wonder if she's a liberated woman or just not married. Either way, can she really understand the problems of relating to a husband who's a student, when we've got two kids and no money? I'll bet she didn't have trouble in school like I did. I wonder what it takes to be a professor at this university? I noticed it said the clinic was for 'research and training.' Do they really want to help me or just to use me for a guinea pig? But it's better than going to a psychiatric clinic, where they treat you like you were crazy and might put you in a hospital. She does look kind and understanding. . . ." and so on. Such thoughts may be quite conscious and result in equally conscious decisions, such as continuing at the clinic. They need not however be consciously represented in order to affect the patient's behavior and feelings. Whether recognized by the patient or not, qualities of the clinician and situation importantly influence the information about the patient available to us as clinicians, in formal as well as informal assessment (see, e.g., Sarason, 1954, and Masling, 1966).

THE CLINICAL SITUATION FROM THE CLINICIAN'S VIEWPOINT

The clinician's most salient need is to understand and thereby help the patient. Unlike the patient whose need to know the clinician is secondary to obtaining help from him, developing a meaningful picture of the patient is the clinician's explicit concern. He may blush at the patient's notion that as a skilled clinician he can immediately and confidently look through and behind the surface and make psychological sense out of apparent chaos, but he believes that he does have greater knowledge, personal sensitivity, and skill with assessment techniques and therefore can comprehend the intricacies of human personality more expertly than the layman. Whatever his conceptual orientation, he believes that the personality and behavior of another is knowable and that it derives from lawful psychological antecedents. The layman can simply dismiss complexity ("What's with that guy? What a nut!"); the clinician must explain it. To do so he needs information, which the patient must supply. The clinician therefore values sensitivity, articulateness, insight, openness, and self-searching in the patient. For him to do his job, the patient must do his. Consequently, the "good patient" often turns out to be someone rather like the clinician, only moderately disturbed, who can ally himself with the clinician in the quest for understanding.

The clinical process lacks the normal reciprocity of ordinary social encounters. Particularly in the assessment phase, communication flows mainly from patient to clinician. The interaction is controlled by the clinician, who asks questions or suggests topics, who listens attentively and sympathetically but often says little in return. Direct response to patient concerns is averted, while further information is sought. Giving information, interpretations, or advice is minimized while the clinician explores to discover what makes the patient tick and what might be the sources of his problems. While gaining considerable information about his patient, the clinician tells little about himself. These facets of the clinical relationship strain the identity and integrity of the clinician; they present him with temptations and pitfalls which must be guarded against. As we noted in the preceding chapter, Schafer (1954) described four "psychological constants" of the clinical role which bedevil the clinician, particularly as diagnostic tester. The clinical role, notes Schafer, has built into it these aspects: (1) It is *voyeuristic*. We observe without revealing ourselves; we peep into the hidden lives of others; (2) It is *autocratic*. We control the situation, lay down the rules for communication; (3) It is *oracular*. We nod wisely and seem to understand everything; and (4) It is *saintly*. We convey that all of this is to the ultimate benefit of the patient, who indeed is an ingrate if he does not cooperate fully. As we recognize their effects, the voyeuristic, autocratic, oracular, and saintly components can readily arouse guilt and anxiety. Worse yet, they can tempt us to satisfy our own irrational and primitive needs at the patient's expense. Who is not tempted to be a voyeur, autocrat, oracle, or saint, at least once in a while? Nor, Schafer also cautions, can the clinician escape these aspects of his role; instead, he must cope with them adaptively. To do so requires a sense of personal and professional self-esteem and identity, personal insight, competence, humility, and compassion; the hard-won products of personal growth and professional training.

For the clinician to admit uncertainty and confusion is a sign of professional maturity; to continue to be confused and uncertain tokens ineffectiveness as a clinician. Just as the patient suffers evaluation anxiety in the clinical relationship, so can the clinician. The clinician tests his understanding of the patient's personality and problems first by his own standards: Do things seem to fall in place? Are the factors which seem to exist sensibly related to each other? So too, understanding is tested in further clinical interactions, as in therapy where hypotheses are tested by the patient's response to our interpretative explanations. The clinician's understanding of his patient is also tested by colleagues in the clinic to whom he may report assessment findings. But whether he accounts only to his professional conscience or to the review of his colleagues, the clinician is properly concerned that his work be as competent as possible. Understandably, he is anxious over the prospect of seeing his own faults. The anxiety of clinicians is illustrated in the common reaction to audio or video recording of clinical interviews. When recording equipment first became available, many clinicians expressed the fear that recording would frighten, inhibit, or destroy the trust of the patients. Instead, it has been confirmed repeatedly that most patients accept recording as a matter-of-fact part of a procedure which they are already accepting on faith. It is the clinician, however, who is more usually distressed, for the microphone or camera make his work public and requires him to confront his own inadequacies as well as achievements.

Although to his patient the clinician may appear assured, relaxed, sympathetically attentive, and eager and competent to help, the clinician himself may subjectively experience confusion, annoyance, boredom, ineptness, and other similarly undesirable reactions. His need to know can readily lead him, as well as the layman, to oversimplification, projections, and other distortions. Threats to his vanity, along with the inherent temptations in the role, can seduce him into acting the oracle or saint. The clinical role is an intrinsically difficult one, and full of pitfalls for the novice. To perform well in it requires consummate self-control and self-knowledge.

SOME SALIENT QUALITIES OF THE CLINICAL RELATIONSHIP

Note can now be taken of some of the specific qualities of the clinical relationship which distinguish it from other professional and social relationships.

1. It is a *unique* relationship. Although similar in particular ways to other relationships, the clinical relationship differs importantly from that of doctor-patient, priest-parishioner, parent-child, or friends. The roles of clinician and patient as noted are complementary, but the relationship is *asymmetrical.* Information flows mainly in one direction. Although controlled largely by the clinician, the patient must participate voluntarily with at least some understanding of the process. The purpose, shared by patient and clinician, is understanding the patient and thereby effecting change toward desired ends. The particular goals of such a change are set primarily by the patient.

2. The relationship is based on *trust.* The patient believes (and the clinician agrees) that the clinician is competent to understand and help him. Such faith, it has been argued (e.g., J. D. Frank, 1973), may indeed be the ultimate cause of therapeutic change. The patient believes, moreover, that the clinician would not willingly harm, use, or degrade him. Consequently, he is willing to entrust hitherto concealed wishes, embarrassing fantasies, and evidences of immaturity and incompetence to the clinician. As one evidence that his trust will not be abused, the clinician assures the patient of complete *confidentiality;* whatever is revealed will not be told others without the patient's complete and informed consent. The term "rapport" is often used to describe a relaxed and nondefensive relationship based on mutual confidence.

3. The relationship is one of *collaborative problem-solving.* The patient is allied with the clinician in the common task of understanding and advancing the well-being of the patient. The patient is thus both subject and object of concern; in the former case, working as a partner with the clinician. In other cases, for ex-

ample, physician and patient, it may be necessary for the patient to cooperate, but the treatment is performed by the physician. In the psychological realm, however, there can be no treatment process without full collaboration.

4. A clinical *contract* defines the mutual responsibilities and obligations of patient and clinician. The understanding of both parties as to the purposes, procedures, and goals of clinical interaction should, ideally, evolve in open discussion and constitute an explicit contract. Not unlikely, some part of the understanding remains implicit. The clinical contract specifies, at the first level, agreements as to schedule, fees, availability in emergencies, and the like. It defines mutual obligations: among the more fundamental is the precept: "You talk fully and honestly and I'll listen with undivided attention." The contract also delimits the relationship and distinguishes it from others: "However intimate the topics we consider, we will not eat, sleep, or socialize together."

CHAPTER 8

The Interview

The Interview in Clinical Practice

The interview is the clinician's basic technique for both assessment and psychotherapy. Indeed, in current clinical practice the formerly sharp distinction between assessment and therapeutic interviewing has evolved more into a matter of emphasis than of kind of procedure. Assessment-oriented interviews more typically occur early in the patient's contact with the clinic and have as their major but by no means exclusive purpose to clarify the clinician's understanding of the patient's problems in order to plan further therapeutic intervention. Therapeutic interviews, in contrast, are designed to facilitate the patient's understanding of himself so as to effect desirable changes in his feelings and behavior. In both, however, the patient's problems and needs are the focus of both parties' concern. Whether in therapeutic or assessment interviews, the clinician is necessarily complementing his understanding of the patient; so too, even in the earliest assessment interview the clinician is already acting in the therapeutic role. He is attentive to the effects of the transaction for relieving the patient's distress and facilitating problem-solving. Learning about the patient's problems and efforts to solve them are thus two interlocking phases of a continuous process. Both require sincere collaboration of patient and clinician.

In the traditional clinic, the patient gains entry into psychological treatment through a series of assessment procedures, which may include an intake interview, diagnostic interview, social-history interview, and psychological testing. The findings are then combined in decisions about the further therapeutic program. For most patients, it is less trying as well as clinically more effective to consolidate most of these procedures in a single initial interview which launches the entire clinical process (Gill, Newman, and Redlich, 1954). The initial interview, so conceived, has assessment as only one among at least four explicit purposes: (1) to establish the interpersonal relationship (rapport, trust, etc.) necessary for this and any further clinical transactions; (2) to gain information about the patient and his problems (assessment proper); (3) to give information about the workings of the clinic, possible future program, conditions of therapy, fees, and the like; while (4) bolstering the patient's resolve to improve, if necessary through further therapy. In form, as well as purpose and content, the initial interview is less focused and stylized than the older diagnostic interview. There is less compulsion to cover particular areas and less dependency on a question-answer format. Instead, it is a more free-flowing exchange between clinician and patient. Though guided by the clinician, the concerns of the patient emerge in his own terms.*

In its role in assessment, the interview is the major vehicle for exploring the conscious concerns, feelings, and problems of the patient as he experiences them. He talks about his life situation, meaningful relationships, achievements and failures, and the gratifying and frustrating facets of his own personality and of the attitudes of others toward him. This information, much of which could have been discovered in other ways, emerges in terms of its personal meaning to the patient. He pictures his phenomenal world, the personal values and conceptions, hopes and fears, in which he lives. Material emerges spontaneously or in response to the interviewer's inquiries. Either way, the patient does more than simply tell about himself, describing feelings and behavior in his usual life circumstances. All the while, he is living and acting in the here-and-now of the interview itself. What the patient says and does is determined in fair part by the fact of being in the clinic, in terms of his expectations and perceptions of the clinical relationship. He is also responding to the real presence of the interviewer, whose personal qualities and actions shape the patient's behavior. What topics he chooses, where emphasis is put, what emotions are expressed all reflect the stimulating qualities of the clinician. Unlike testing which requires the patient to interact with passive and nonhuman test stimuli, the interview necessarily reflects the encounter of real people, albeit in roles of clinician and patient. From his perspective the clinician is a "participant-observer;" at the same time and inextricably, both actor and observer.

The assessment data thus yielded by the interview include: (1) statements by the patient himself, describing characteristic feelings of his current and past life ("I have always been shy with girls"); (2) accompanying behaviors, some unintended and outside of awareness (e.g., tremulous voice); and (3) reactions inspired by the clinician, whether based on real or fantasied acts (e.g., annoyance at a seemingly unsympathetic response). The difficult task of the clinician is to note and remember the content of the patient's utterances, observe his behavior, and assess the contribution of his own actions to what he hears and sees. It is a task which requires considerable skill, sensitivity, and flexibility.

The interview, clinical or otherwise, is "a conversation with a purpose" (Bingham and Moore, 1924). But as the purposes differ widely so do the areas covered and the form of the interview. Thus, census-takers ask precisely the same factual questions in precisely the same order; somewhat more flexible schedules, open-ended questions, and "probes" are typically used in survey research; all of these are quite structured compared to the free-ranging clinical interview. It is possible, however, to describe general principles, dealing mainly

* For more detailed discussion of the principles and practices of the initial interview, see Gill, Newman, and Redlich (1954); Sullivan (1954); Stevenson (1959); Group for the Advancement of Psychiatry (1967, Chap. 1); Wolberg (1967, pp. 445–569); and MacKinnon and Michels (1971).

with the interpersonal transaction and the processes of communication, that characterize interviews with varied purposes. In particular, valuable principles have been derived from extensive experience and research in survey interviewing (e.g., Kahn and Cannell, 1957) some of which will be discussed in later parts of this chapter. The social research interview has gained from ideas developed in the clinic and the clinician in turn benefits from study of the research interview. In one important respect, however, clinical interviews differ from those done in social research (or for that matter, clinical research). In a research study, the need is to reliably obtain comparable and valid information from a number of individuals for purposes of the investigator. The form and content of the interview are determined by the research goals, not the individual respondent's needs. The respondent must of course be motivated to cooperate, but he does not necessarily have to understand or concur in the purpose of the study. By contrast, the purpose of the clinical interview is to understand a particular person toward the end of relieving his distress. While it is surely true that many patients act the part of a passive respondent ("Just tell me what you want to know, Doc."), in principle at least the quest for understanding is a collaborative effort toward a common goal.

Kinds of Interviews

Later on, in considering the process of the interview, we will have the general initial interview in mind. The tendency in current practice is to reduce the number and variety of pretreatment assessment interviews, which were often conducted by different professionals in different roles and might or might not include the person who would then take on therapeutic responsibilities. The initial interview, as we visualize it, covers many of the areas of the more specialized interviews albeit in less detail. It is conducted by the person likely to continue as the patient's therapist. Not only is clinical practice thus streamlined but some of the indignity of being passed from hand to hand, often to repeat matters previously discussed, is averted. From his standpoint, the patient who came to the clinic for help is immediately in the helping process without feeling that he had first to pass entrance examinations.

Specialized interviews, however, are still common and we should consider the various types to be found in clinical practice. There are circumstances in which a division of labor among professionals with particular skills is desirable and cases in which the more detailed information of specially designed interviews are needed for good clinical care or research. The clinician should be able, as necessary, to interview in a focused way to any of the purposes of the traditional special interviews.

THE DIAGNOSTIC INTERVIEW

This is the core of the traditional psychiatric examination modeled on the diagnostic evaluations common to, and more relevant to, medicine. The diagnostic interview developed mainly in hospital practice in the Kraepelinian tradition.

Such interviews are still more commonly used with psychotic patients. The interview focuses mainly on the patient's symptoms, in order to describe as precisely as possible the type, extent, duration, past history, and future course of the patient's psychiatric illness. Often the format of the interview is rigid, with particular areas investigated in preset sequence. The absurd extreme possible is illustrated in an anecdote told by Gill, Newman, and Redlich (1954).

> This can reach the preposterous heights of an instance we once saw while examining for the American Board of Psychiatry. The candidate was asked to interview a patient. His first remark to the patient was to ask him whether he had been a full-term normal delivery. Contrast this with the patient's remark to the candidate at the end of the interview, "Doctor, I hope you pass!" The patient was responding to what was emotionally relevant to the doctor, while the doctor was treating the patient like an inanimate object to be thumped at will according to some predetermined routine of his profession [pp. 76–77].

The complete psychiatric examination often includes a *mental-status examination*. The areas generally covered include: (1) intellect and thought processes, i.e., the capacity for accurate, swift, and complex thinking as indexed by extensive vocabulary, considerable information, good recent and long-term memory, fast and accurate problem-solving and the like; (2) disorders of perception, i.e., hallucinations, illusions, or more simple misperceptions; (3) attention and orientation, i.e., distractibility, knowledge of time, identity, and place, and capacity to maintain focal attention; (4) emotional expression, i.e., dominant affects, appropriateness and strength of emotions, capacity for control; (5) insight and self-concept, i.e., the patient's capacity to understand the extent and possible causes of his illness, his view of himself, exaggerated or realistic, "not himself," etc., and (6) behavior and appearance, i.e., the patient's facial expression, expressive movements, visible physiological reactions, dress. In addition to direct observation and questioning, the examination usually includes brief and simple test items. Thus, the patient is asked "Do you have trouble remembering things?" and then he may be asked to hold in mind and repeat back increasingly long lists of digits as a direct test of short-term memory. A standard task for assessing concentration involves subtracting 7s serially from 100. Explaining the meaning of proverbs can reveal thought disorders and the capacity for abstract reasoning. Detailed interview outline and test items can be found in Wells and Ruesch (1945), Stevenson and Sheppe (1959), and in most textbooks of psychiatry. This type of examination is of use in evaluating psychotic patients. It is of less relevance to understanding the personality or status of neurotic patients.

THE INTAKE INTERVIEW

This is designed to introduce the patient to the clinic, while judging whether its facilities are appropriate to his needs. The interview focuses on the patient's desires, motivation for treatment, expectations from the clinic, and alternative courses of action. The patient is given information about the clinic's procedures, fees, schedules, and other matters which might clarify his thinking about further contact. Intake interviewing is a traditional function of the psychiatric social worker, who has special knowledge of clinic organization and of alternate community resources. In this first contact, plans are made for further visits to the clinic or, if it seems mutually advantageous, referral to another agency, perhaps for services the clinic cannot provide. Although focusing on the present needs and desires of the patient, and the relevance of clinic resources to serve them, inevitably the social worker crosses over into the domain of diagnostic and/or social-history interviews.

Most people telephone before coming to a clinic. Usually this is just a convenient way to arrange a first interview, but the telephone can also serve the tentative patient uncertainly reaching out for help. Every clinician has lifted the phone to hear "Could you tell me what you do in your clinic?" or "What would you think of a person who . . . ?" On the phone, a person can reveal fears and preoccupations while concealing his name and face. The clinician is deprived of many of the cues usually available in clinical encounters. The *telephone interview* takes considerable skill and patience to identify and respond to the patient's major concerns and to guide him, if necessary and feasible, to venture into the clinic.

THE SOCIAL-HISTORY OR CASE-HISTORY INTERVIEW

In the multidisciplinary clinic, another common function of the social worker is to obtain a history of the patient. This is less with regard to his symptoms and focal problems (explored in the diagnostic interview) than to obtain an overall view of the evolution of his life and of his current personal and social situation. In as much detail as possible, usually in chronological sequences, the patient is encouraged to talk about his early childhood experiences, parents, siblings, education, hobby activities, job history, dating and sexual relations, present social life, marriage, work and interests—much of the material outlined in Chapter 6. Overall, the emphasis is on consciously remembered and objectively reportable events; less on searching out emotionally important experiences relatable to the patient's focal problems. Knowing the history of a person is important to the understanding of his current personality structure and functioning. Similarly important is knowledge of his current life situations, the stresses and realities within which he lives.

INTERVIEWS WITH INFORMANTS

Supplementing the history are interviews with the spouse, parents, or perhaps others with whom the patient is intimately involved. Such information is most likely to be sought where the patient himself is incapable or unwilling to talk, notably in the cases of severely psychotic, grossly depressed, or mute adults, or very young children. Most clinicians in the dynamic tradition, save of course child guidance workers, have strong clinical and ethical objections to interviews with informants. The world of the patient as he sees it, including the reactions of others as he perceives them, is the primary focus of the clinician's concern; the "real facts" as they might be recounted by others are largely irrelevant. What might be of central interest to the historian, press reporter, or FBI agent is not the concern of the clinician. Under no circumstances, of course, should such information be sought without the express agreement of the patient. There are conditions, however, where clinician and patient see the value of a session with a relevant other, say, spouse or parent, often to give as well as receive information. Such sessions should occur well into the context of an ongoing therapeutic relationship; rarely is it justifiable in the assessment phase, except for the severely incapacitated or very young person.

OTHER CLINICAL INTERVIEWS

Sometimes it is valuable to have a patient (or the clinician himself) seen by a more experienced consultant, always with the patient's consent and sometimes at his request. The form of the *consultation interview* varies, of course, depending on the issues raised; in the older tradition it was likely to be a diagnostic interview by the "professor." Although consultation has been deemphasized in the "therapeutic model," there has been a resurgence in community-oriented work, where the clinician often works consultatively through a person such as a teacher who is in immediate contact with the "patient" (see Chapter 18).

Various forms of brief interviews have evolved in different aspects of clinical work: *screening interviews*, where a number of people have to be examined in short order as in the military; *transfer*, *furlough*, or *discharge interviews*, when hospitalized patients are to be moved to another unit, given off-hospital privileges, or are ready to go home.

Finally, there is the *pretesting interview* conducted by psychologists in multidisciplinary settings where diagnostic, history-taking, and other interviews are likely to be taken care of by other professionals. A primary purpose of such an interview is to establish the necessary clinician-patient relationship; in principle, no different in kind from that required for assessment interviewing, but with the special considerations related to the mysterious and sometimes frightening nature of testing. The clinician should inform the patient as to the nature and purpose of the tests, the kinds of activities involved, the use to which the findings will be put. The patient should be assured as to the confidentiality of his findings and report. Included in this process is the essential task of discovering any personal or situational factors which need consideration in the interpretation of the test findings. All too often, psychologists convinced of the "objectivity" of their tests make a cursory and trivial affair of this pretesting period.

> "Mr. Jones? I'm Dr. Smith. How are you today? Fine! I've been asked to test you. Now, here are some inkblots. Just tell me what you see. There are no right or wrong answers. By the way, do you have your glasses with you?" (At least he is spared having all form-determined Rorschach responses dissolve in myopic blurs!) Insert a few grunts from the patient and the dialogue is complete.

Such a test-centered psychologist joins Gill's diagnosis-happy psychiatrist in the annals of clinical insensitivity.

THE RESEARCH INTERVIEW

Compared to ordinary clinic procedures, interviews specifically designed to gather research data are usually more structured and focused. Both form and content are determined mainly by the purposes of the study rather than by the needs of the particular patient. While the research interviewer should be neither mechanical nor callous, his task involves obtaining the same sort of information about and from each of the patients studied. To insure comparability, there is the same sequence of topics and identical questions are asked in much the same way, often of all patients by the same interviewer. The free flow of the clinical interview is necessarily reduced in the interests of uniformity and quantification. As in social research, investigators must be attentive to the many methodological issues, such as question wording and sequence, form and condition of probing, and mode of recording, on which reliability and validity depend (Kahn and Cannell, 1957; Cannell and Kahn, 1969).

Research ethics require that no subject be exposed to harm or humiliation and that no research procedure ever be conducted without the subject's clear understanding and voluntary agreement ("informed consent"), whatever the setting and kind of subject involved. These principles have particular relevance in the clinic because of the sensitivity and vulnerability of patients who can readily (be led to) believe that the research procedure is part of a treatment program and/or that their continued clinic treatment depends on participation. Hence, investigators have a strong obligation to explain to the fullest the purposes and nature of the study and to assure patients of their complete freedom of choice.

Arrangements for the Interview

All that is needed is a quiet, comfortable room free of distractions. Furnishings need not be lavish, but they should allow for relaxed conversation. Patient and clinician should have comparable chairs of the same height and similar style, neither so close as to intrude on each other's personal space nor so distant as to suggest fear of contagion. It is hard to relate openly to someone in an oversized and overstuffed swivel chair, particularly with a massive desk in between, if you are sitting on a small, hard sidechair. Nor is it pleasant to be sunk into a low armchair with someone hovering over you. Some clinicians prefer interviewing across a desk or table for elbow-resting and note-taking; others, myself included, prefer lower chairs with perhaps a coffee table available for an ashtray. Some clinics have special rooms for interviewing, but they usually look a bit barren. Many clinicians interview in the same office they use for other professional purposes; the setting is necessarily more personal and more comfortable for being so. Although some prefer an anonymous environment, I see no good reason why personal books, favorite paintings, mementos, hobby items, or family pictures should not be in view. Obviously, personal letters or patient files should not be left lying about. The limit as to what is visible in the room is set by common sense and good taste. If you have built a ship in a bottle, by all means keep it in the office; your collection of shrunken heads had better be displayed elsewhere.

It is critical that the room be private and free of distractions. If the patient can hear voices in an adjoining room, he can reasonably enough suppose that he too can be overheard. Arrangements should be made that no one can walk in during the interview, nor even knock at the door. Outside street noises or a jangling telephone are irritating and reduce the necessary concentration of both patient and clinician. Overall, the physical setting should bear out the clinician's assurance of confidentiality.

It is important for the clinician to be able to later recall accurately the major themes, affects expressed, and the flow of topics discussed during the interview. There has been much controversy, however, about taking notes during the interview itself. Everyone would agree that it is not only impossible, but grossly inappropriate, even to attempt to record the session verbatim. Under no circumstances should the clinician act or appear as the court stenographer. However, some clinicians feel strongly that any note taking should be avoided, in the belief that it necessarily diverts full attention from the patient's words and face while suggesting a breach of confidentiality. I myself believe that jotting down a few key words or phrases now and then is perfectly appropriate, provided one does not lose eye contact for long and provided that one's own listening and thinking is not disturbed. True, brief occasional notes can signal to the patient topics of particular interest to the clinician; but so too can minimal gestures such as raising an eyebrow, leaning forward, or saying "uh-huh." As a general rule, the clinician should be sufficiently disciplined to intentionally guide the flow of the interview ("Tell me more;" "That's interesting") when he wishes to do so and avoid, whatever the means of communication, unintentionally shaping the patient's behavior.

Particularly in training and research clinics, magnetic tape recording of interviews has become quite common. Where it is desirable to have as full a record as possible for later study, tape recording is certainly preferable to the detailed "process notes" which used to be taken by clinicians in training. Since recording will leave a permanent and identifiable record of the patient's statements, he should be free to refuse to have the interview taped. Under no circumstances should any recording be made without his knowledge; in every case the patient should be informed in advance and feel free to consent or refuse. However, since consent in advance constitutes, so to speak, a blank check, the patient should be offered the option of having the tape erased at the end of the session if, knowing what went onto it, he has any reservations. Except for a few suspicious patients, most people have no objections to having interviews recorded.

In my judgment, the microphone should always be in full view. When hidden, it too readily suggests that at other times and with other patients recording is made secretly. But scruples aside, concealed microphones seem to lead inevitably to recordings of poor quality; they may be too far from the patient or too close to air ducts and other sources of extraneous noise. It should simply be placed where it produces the best recording. Seeing the microphone itself seems not to have any direct effect on patients. Indeed, it is the interviewer rather than the patient who is more likely to be disturbed by the matter of recording. The patient usually accepts it matter-of-factly as part of a generally strange procedure. By contrast, the interviewer is threatened by having his work preserved and open to later criticism by himself and colleagues. While the patient is communicating to the interviewer and the tape recorder usually becomes an incidental appurtenance, the interviewer has to resist acting for an outside audience through the tape recorder.

The tape recorder itself should be somewhat to the side, only because we become fascinated too easily with the whirling spools and jumping needle or flickering light of the sound-level meter; nor can we resist watching intently as the tape nears the end of a spool. All preparation should be made in advance, so that one only needs to throw a switch when the interview starts. Similarly, tapes of sufficient length should be used to minimize the time for changing spools.

With the increased availability of low-cost, good-quality equipment, videotape is coming into more common use in clinical training, research, and psychotherapy for immediate feedback and discussion (for some recent developments, see Berger, 1970, and Geertsma, 1971). Videotape is a considerable advance in recording the detail of the clinical interchange, in nonverbal as well as verbal communication. By the same token, it is more penetrating and revealing and hence potentially more threatening to patient and clinician. Overall, however, these are differences in extent rather than kind, and the same general rules should govern video as audio recording.

Although we have emphasized the setting of a consultation room, it is well to recall that information of importance is also transmitted in hallways and waiting rooms, in accidental encounters as well as scheduled interviews. The clinical process does not start with the closing of a soundproof door behind the patient, nor does it depend on having two comfortable chairs, privacy, and quiet. Clinically meaningful communication can occur under any and all circumstances in which patient and clinician meet.

Stages in the Initial (Assessment) Interview

The initial interview, we have already noted, has four major purposes which generally emerge sequentially during the session: (1) a clinical relationship is established; (2) information about the patient is gained; (3) information about the clinic is given; and (4) the patient's resolve to change is bolstered. In a similarly general way, the session moves from emphasis on *present* feelings, toward concern with the patient's *past* experiences, and ends oriented toward *future* plans and actions. Let us now consider the interview process as it evolves in time.

THE OPENING PHASE

The clinician is host, the patient his guest, and the first few minutes are spent in the usual amenities of settling someone comfortably in a strange setting. Comments about finding the clinic, the inevitable difficulties of parking and the like are made as chairs are drawn up, an ashtray offered, and introductions made. More by manner than by words, the clinician communicates from the very first moment concern about the patient's comfort and well-being and a sympathetic understanding of his uncertainty and apprehension at being in the clinic

An opening question such as "Tell me what brings you here?" is sufficient. In his own fashion, the patient may start to talk quite fully and freely about present problems and difficulties. However, he may also emphasize instead the way in which he came to this particular clinic at this time. From either starting point, with encouraging questions we can learn something about his view of his immediate difficulties, the extent to which he accepts responsibility for them, whether he conceives them in psychological terms or feels manipulated by outside persons or circumstances. Not unlikely, some crisis occurred in the recent past which propelled him to the present decision to seek help, though he may recognize himself that his problems are long-standing. Exploring the conditions of his decision to come is an early task of the interview. We are all too prone, for obvious reasons, to assume that the very fact that the patient is before us is prima facie evidence that he recognizes that he is a troubled person and wants to better himself with our help; it is far better to give him every opportunity to say right off "Frankly, the only reason I'm here is because my wife insisted. . . ."

Particularly at the outset, the clinician's questions are few and brief, and intended mainly to encourage the patient to develop themes relevant to him in his own fashion. Particular comments may pique our curiosity, but it is well to hold off any inquiry in depth until the patient has ranged freely over matters most urgent and important to him. We can mentally file and hold for later exploration seemingly important themes which are touched on and passed over. Questions such as "When did that happen?" or "Where was that?" and the like, which would give the story greater coherence as to time, place, and circumstance should be resisted in order to discover the patient's own meanings and his own ways of expression. This does not mean that the clinician does not guide the flow of the interview through strategic questions, particularly as the patient blocks or becomes repetitive. However, the patient should be allowed as much freedom as he wants and can use in telling his story in his way. It is sometimes true that such freedom is confusing to an already anxious person and questions such as "Is that the sort of thing you wanted to know?" or "What would you like me to tell you now?" are not uncommon. Although encouraging a free-flowing presentation, the clinician has to be ready to relieve anxiety in the momentary situation by comments like "That's fine, but why don't you tell me more about . . ." Neither interrogation nor passive listening is advisable; brief comments to clarify somewhat but mostly to encourage the flow of the transaction are preferable.

The patient is likely to be anxious for various reasons. The situation is novel and he is not certain how to behave. He is fearful at revealing his weaknesses to a stranger, even though he has sought out his help. Telling about his troubles inevitably means reliving them, and the interview reinstates painful feelings which might be averted in daily routine. And the patient is uncertain as to the outcome, how seriously disturbed the clinician will find him to be, perhaps even to believing him to be a "hopeless case." To all of these sources of anxiety the clinician must be responsive. At the most fundamental level, the clinician must communicate sincere respect for the patient, attentive interest and concern with his problems, nonjudgmental acceptance, and a warm though detached understanding. In the immediate situation of the first interview, the clinician supports and encourages the patient as necessary. The clinician must help the patient to understand the clinical relationship and his role in it. This can be accomplished better by example than by explanations. In addition, the clinician must be attentive to painful affects the patient is suffering right in his presence. Appropriate sympathy and understanding are necessary; excessive commiseration is to be avoided. "It *is* hard to talk about . . ." takes sympathetic note of the patient's pain. Gratuitous comforting can as readily offend as relieve the patient. Hear the difference between "I can imagine how you feel" and "Don't worry. Lots of people feel that way." The former shows empathy and concern; the latter may seem to depreciate an intensely personal feeling.

The patient understandably wants to know more about the clinic and the clinician and likely has specific questions in mind. If possible, discussion of such matters should wait until the latter part of the interview. If the patient raises direct questions (in this realm or for that matter in any other) they should of course be answered directly if briefly. Overall, however, the first portion of the interview is meant to convey "First tell me something about yourself, your present problems, and reasons for coming." In this phase, the interpersonal and emotional climate is set for the patient to reveal, in terms meaningful to him, the nature of his concerns.

THE MIDDLE PORTION

The body of the interview is concerned with gathering information necessary for at least a tentative formulation of the nature of the patient's problems and character. In general, the clinician seeks to learn: (1) What are the patient's current complaints and symptoms ("presenting problems")? Why has he sought help at this time? What is the nature of his present crisis? What are his present life circumstances? (2) Were there recent stressful events which might have dislocated adaptive mechanisms and led to the present crisis? (3) What kind of a person is he? What are his talents, strengths and competencies as well as personality defects? What are his most important character traits, affects, defenses, conflicts, particularly those which seem relevant to his present problems? Have there been any important changes in this behavior in the recent past? Are there early experiences which might make his present character or problems more explicable? (4) Are there any relevant organic factors? Might medical consultation or treatment be necessary?

All of these areas cannot be explored in depth and the clinician has to be satisfied with information sufficient to make reasonable hypotheses. Further assessment-oriented interviews and psychological testing may have to be scheduled in order to develop the firmer understanding needed for planning subsequent therapy.

In general, the clinician works out from discussion of the patient's present concerns to consideration of surrounding and past events. After the patient has told about his immediate predicament and distress, it seems reasonable to inquire "How long has this been going on?" "What was your life like before that?" "Did anything else change at about that time?" Exploring possible precipitating events often yields critical information about the person's present problems. Often the patient can report meaningful changes, sometimes tragic events such as the loss of a loved one, sometimes seemingly happy events, such as the birth of a child or graduation, but in either case sufficiently profound as to upset established patterns of adaptation. In listening to the patient's history, the clinician should be specially attentive to note whether there is evidence that current stress is reactivating old conflicts. By asking questions like "Were there other times when you felt like you do now?" it is possible to explore selectively aspects of the person's past which can illuminate his present dilemmas.

There is no set scenario, sequence of topics, or questions to be covered in the interview. The clinician takes his cues from the patient and pursues those themes which seem most important. He is attentive to repetitive references, the order in which the patient presents issues, the emotional emphasis he gives different topics, and indeed the areas he avoids or passes over too lightly. It is not only what the patient says, and how he says it, but what he does not say that gives information about him. Some material is avoided because of repression; in other cases, it might just be too painful for the patient to speak about it at this time. The clinician notes critical references and recalls them under more appropriate conditions. Thus, after the patient has talked for some while about his family, we might say "Though you mentioned a brother, you said very little about him. Could you tell me more?" In another context, the clinician might say, in place of the last sentence, "I wonder why?" This challenges the patient to examine his possible motives though it may threaten him this early in the clinical relationship; the former question simply seeks more information, though the perceptive patient may sense an implicit question.

Even after a fairly lengthy interview (or set of interviews) with a cooperative and articulate patient we can feel ignorant and confused. This is true even with the most systematic diagnostic and history interview technique, as well as with the type of initial interview we are now considering. The patient may have gone on at length about apparently trivial matters and barely mentioned areas of considerable importance. He may be confused or inconsistent even as to simple facts; at one moment giving the impression that "it" occurred in Akron in 1971 and then again, in Calgary in 1968. The interviewer may easily become frustrated and wish for a simple, coherent, well worked out story, easy to follow, and easy to retell. In fact, few lives are so orderly and few people can characterize their inner experiences, thoughts, feelings, and life events in a straightforward and readily comprehensible fashion. This, of course, is all the more true of a disturbed patient at the time of his first contact with the clinic. Indeed, if he did understand himself and could communicate clearly he would not be there in the first place. We must expect confusion and uncertainty, jumbled memories, and material too painful to discuss, defensive reconstructions and efforts to impress the clinician even as he confesses to inadequacies. For all of this is the expectable state of the patient whom we are trying to understand. The clinician's task is to appreciate the patient's state and to develop a reasonable picture of a human being in trouble from whatever he hears and sees. Needless to say, he should not compound the patient's troubles by adding his own confusion.

By the end of the interview the clinician should have at least a provisional formulation in mind. This should include knowledge of the patient's current problem, physical state, and social environment, precipitating stresses and habitual coping mechanisms and their current efficacy. There should be some notion of historical antecedents of his present conflicts. In general terms, he should be able to characterize the major facets of the patient's personality, talents and intelligence, capacity for work, and satisfying relations with relevant others. The patient's self-concept, identity, characteristic affects and defenses, his ego strength and capacities for self-determined as well as pathological functioning. Obviously, the "working image" of the person will be incomplete, but it is the necessary basis for further clinical interaction. The subsequent task of the clinician is to decide whether and what form of treatment is indicated, and to formulate provisional treatment goals. Toward this end, the clinician must judge the patient's accessibility or resistance to psychotherapy, the depth of his desire to change, self-awareness and psychological mindedness, as well as other personal and social factors which might recommend for or against further contact with the clinic, referral to another agency, or perhaps some emergency measure as in the case of a depressed and potentially suicidal person. The clinician has such alternatives in mind and reaches tentative formulations and decisions as the interview nears an end.

THE FINAL PHASE

Before the interview is ended, there is need to restore the patient's calm, give him information, and plan with him the next steps. Though not oriented to assessment, further information about the patient can readily be revealed in this as in earlier phases.

The interview has been a difficult experience for the patient. He has recalled painful experiences and revealed embarrassing feelings to a virtual stranger. Anxiety and other negative affects were likely aroused. Before terminating, it is necessary to restore the patient's composure and, if possible, have him leave with some sense of accomplishment and hope. This cannot be done through blanket reassurances or trite generalizations which would seem to minimize the severity or importance of his problems. As earlier in the session, the clinician communicates empathic understanding of the difficult task of talking in the interview, appreciation of the profundity of the patient's problems, and hope for the future. Concern and sympathy can be openly expressed; simple remedies can be suggested. "This hour has been difficult for you. You've been crying a lot. Perhaps you can take the rest of the afternoon off and go home and rest?" However, if the patient seeks unqualified approval, absolution from guilt, or authoritative pronouncements, such pressure is to be resisted. The patient may well ask: "Now that you have all the facts, doctor, don't you agree that my wife should stop bugging me?" The most appropriate reply is usually something like: "Well, it's clear enough that there's a real conflict between the two of you that needs working out." While the clinician is sympathetically attentive to the realistic needs and pained feelings of the patient, he should strictly avoid serving infantile wishes and neurotic demands. Blanket approval or unconditional affection usually do more harm than good, and hardly prepare the patient for the painful self-examination of psychotherapy.

As fully and honestly as possible, the clinician should share his present, albeit tentative, understanding of the patient's problems and needs, and work with him toward planning future interventions. Viewing the psychological consultation in analogy to medical consultation, the patient may well ask about diagnosis, prognosis, treatment alternatives, and the like and expect to be told authoritatively that he has "something-with-a-Latin-name," which will get worse/better, unless this particular "medicine" is taken. The clinician must resist the oracular role and simply explain the differences between the psychological and medical realms. Without implying excessive certainty, the clinician summarizes the situation as he sees it, the options available, and his best judgment as to a preferred course. Here is a hypothetical statement:

> These anxiety attacks do seem to be related to long-standing conflicts about whether you can risk committing yourself to new ventures or would rather stay with the safe and familiar. We just don't know the sources of the conflicts or how exactly they can be resolved. But as long as you have as much anxiety as you described, it's clear that you just won't be able to work effectively in your courses, even though you seem intelligent enough to do well otherwise. At this rate, your grades will likely get even worse in the next quarter, when you go into the more difficult major sequence. You

> could, as you've considered, drop out and do less demanding work. That might relieve some of the immediate pressure, but with your goals and values I don't think you'd be happy in the long run. I think it would be worthy your trying psychotherapy first. You'd then have a chance to talk with a clinician and maybe discover why you get so anxious. . . .

The ultimate choice is of course the patient's and he should have as much information as possible on which to make it. He may have misconceptions or simply lack information about the nature, availability, cost, and procedures of psychotherapy. The clinician should give as much information as possible, in all of these areas, without overselling his own clinic or procedure. One common alternative is that no form of psychological intervention is indicated. The patient may be facing a temporary, situational stress and his behavior may predictably change as the situation alters. Or he may be locked into a chronic social problem, which psychological intervention can neither remedy nor compensate. Much of human suffering is beyond the power of psychological clinicians to avert or alleviate. The clinician should be wise enough to know, and honest enough to admit, when such boundaries are reached.

After the patient leaves, time should be allowed for thinking back over the events of the session. In assembling our memories, we often see relationships which escape us in the give and take of the interview proper. Parts fall into place as we can recall without simultaneously thinking about our own next response. Notes are scanned and a more detailed account written or dictated. In the process, we reconceptualize and focus major themes and bring them into the framework of our theoretical thinking. Moving away somewhat from the primary data of the interview to a higher level of abstraction increases our understanding, though one has to guard against losing the distinctive detail of the individual life in the process.

An Illustrative Initial Interview

In their study, Gill, Newman, and Redlich (1954) present the transcripts of three recorded initial interviews in complete detail, along with running critical commentary by the authors. The recorded interviews themselves are also available for study by professional students. In their technique, the interview focuses mainly on the patient's current problems, his motivation for treatment, and relationship with the clinician; there is relatively less emphasis on history or diagnosis. The recordings, transcripts, and analytic comments of the authors are a rich source of material for the student interested in clinical interviewing. For our present purposes, we will reproduce parts of their first interview with a thirty-year-old woman. The statements of the patient (P) and clinician (T, therapist) are numbered sequentially. Unfortunately, there is not space enough to reproduce the detailed, self-critical, line-by-line comments of the authors, which in the original volume appear on facing pages. The first five minutes of this interview, it might be noted, have also been analyzed in microscopic detail in an entire book (Pittenger et. al., 1960).

The patient is a thirty-year-old married woman who telephoned the clinic for an appointment and was seen four days later. The interview begins as patient and clinician enter the interviewing room.

T.1: Will you sit there. (*Softly.*)

P.1: (*Sits down.*)

T.2: (*Closes doors.*) What brings you here? (*Sits down.*)

P.2: (*Sighs.*) Everything's wrong I guess. Irritable, tense, depressed. (*Sighs.*) Jus' . . . just everything and everybody gets on my nerves.

T.3: Nyeah.

P.3: I don't feel like talking right now.

T.4: You don't? (*Short pause.*) Do you sometimes?

P.4: That's the trouble. I get too wound up. If I get started I'm all right.

T.5: Nyeah? Well perhaps you will.

P.5: May I smoke?

T.6: Sure. (*Pushes ashtray toward patient.*) What do you do?

P.6: (*Sighs; takes cigarettes out of pocketbook and lights one.*) I'm a nurse, but my husband won't let me work.

T.7: How old are you?

P.7: Thirty-one this December. (*Exhales smoke forcefully.*)

T.8: What do you mean "he won't let you work?" (*Clears throat.*)

P.8: Well (*Clears throat.*) for instance I . . . ah . . . I'm supposed to do some relief duty two weeks (*Sighs.*) this month . . . next month, September, and he makes it so miserable for me that I'm in a constant stew. (*Sighs.*)

P.8: And he says that my place is home with the children. I agree, but I wa . . . I need a rest. I need to get away from them. I need to be with . . . oh with people. I can't stay closeted up in the house all the time.

T.9: How many kids are there?

P.9: Two.

T.10: How old are they? (*Clears throat.*)

P.10: Three . . . five months.

T.11: Mmmhnn.

P.11: (*Sighs.*) Oh it isn't only that. It's a million things.

T.12: Tell me some of them.

P.12: (*Sighs.*) Well to begin with, there are a lot of things I didn't know about him before we got married that I should have known—at least I feel I should have.

T.13: You've been married about four or five years?

P.13: Four years . . .

T.14: Mmm.

P.14: . . . in November. And (*Sighs.*) I think he's a chronic alcoholic. He drinks every day, and he just can't seem to let the stuff alone. He says he can, but he can't. He never has been able to except (*Sighs.*) the one time the doctor had him on a diet (*Half-sigh.*) and then he ate candy bars. Candy bars, I suppose he had to have sugar. But it's just (*Half-sigh.*) I feel that it's . . . it's either going to ruin me or the kids or all of us. It . . .

T.15: What does he do?

P.15: He's a truck driver.

T.16: One of these long-distance hauls or what?

P.16: No. He used to do it. He doesn't now. They just do (*Sighs.*) . . . ah . . . hauling within the state. And about (*Sighs.*) mm . . . five or six months ago he went on trailers. Well I know it's hard, but he comes home and he takes it out on all of us. He starts nagging the minute he gets in the house.

T.17: Is he away a good deal?

P.17: (*Sighs.*) He eats and he sleeps in the house, and that's all there is to it. And it's an insult to me naturally.

T.18: Mmmhnn. (*Short pause.*)

P.18: (*Sighs.*) Once in a while he's decent. (*Pause; sighs.*) I keep thinking of divorce, but (*Half-sigh.*) that's another emotional death. And I don't want to do it with the kids right now. They're too young.

T.19: Divorce is an emotional death?

P.19: (*Sighs.*) I think so.

T.20: I don't quite understand what you mean. (*Short pause.*)

P.20: (*Sighs.*) Well it's . . . I think it's a . . . worse than death. If he died I think I'd be happy. I honestly would. (*Tearful.*)

T.21: Mmmhnn. I didn't understand . . .

P.21: (*Interrupting.*) And he won't get help. That's the trouble. He won't admit that it's any problem.

T.22: I would like to hear more about that, but first I . . . I didn't quite understand about divorce being an emotional death.

P.22: (*Wearily.*) I don't know whether I can explain it. (*Sighs.*) (*Short pause.*)

Comment. Up to this point the patient is complaining about her husband and the clinician can rightfully wonder whether that is her only purpose or whether she feels she has some problem herself. He has picked up her curious statement "divorce is an emotional death," and wants to explore further. However, after her comment (P.22) he drops the question though continuing to talk about divorce. She reveals that she cannot consider divorce because of the children. She is talking about them in the following exchange.

T.35: If they were in school then you would consider a divorce?

P.35: Yes. And then I wouldn't . . . (*Simultaneously with T.35.*) Then I would.

T.36: I see.

P.36: But I'm still generally opposed to it . . .

T.37: Yes.

P.37: . . . because I think that . . . that I can be straightened out.

T.38: That you can be straightened out?

P.38: Yes.

T.39: I didn't get the impression that you thought it was . . . ah . . . your problem.

P.39: Well it's affecting me. It's making me unstable. I never used to be like this.

T.40: Yes?

P.40: Things didn't used to bother me this way. I used to be depressed. Occasionally. Sure! Who isn't? But not the way I am now. Not so that I wanted to turn on gas and jump out the window. (*Tearful.*)

T.41: How long have you been feeling that way? (*Clears throat.*)

P.41: Ever since I've been married. And on the honeymoon (*Voice breaks.*) he drank every night. He didn't want to go anywhere. All he wanted to do was sit in and drink. And I couldn't see that.

Comment. In P.37, it seemed as if the patient was contradicting her earlier position, that her husband was solely responsible for her problems. However, note P.39, as she backs away from the implications of her earlier remark. During the next period of the interview she talks a good deal more about her husband and family and about their problems with their landlord. The clinician brings her to the issue of why she has come to the clinic, and what relevance psychotherapy might have for her.

T.95: Has anything happened recently that makes it . . . you feel that . . . ah . . . you're sort of coming to the end of your rope? I mean I wondered what led you . . .

P.95: (*Interrupting.*) It's nothing special. It's just everything in general.

T.96: What led you to come to a . . .

P.96: (*Interrupting.*) It's just that I . . .

T.97: . . . a psychiatrist just now?

P.97: Because I felt that the older girl was getting tense as a result of . . . of my being stewed up all the time.

T.98: Mmmhnn.

P.98: Not having much patience with her.

T.99: Mmmhnn. (*Short pause.*) Mmm. And how had you imagined that a psychiatrist could help with this? (*Short pause.*)

P.99: Mmm . . . maybe I could sort of get straightened out . . . straighten things out in my own mind. I'm confused. Sometimes I can't remember things that I've done, whether I've done 'em or not or whether they happened.

T.100: What is it that you want to straighten out? (*Pause.*)

P.100: I think I seem mixed up.

T.101: Yeah? You see that, it seems to me, is something that we really should talk about because . . . ah . . . from a certain point of view somebody might say, "Well now, it's all very simple. She's unhappy and disturbed because her husband is behaving this way, and unless something can be done about that how could she expect to feel any other way." But, instead of that, you come to the psychiatrist, and you say that you think there's something about you that needs straightening out. I don't quite get it. Can you explain that to me? (*Short pause.*)

P.101: I sometimes wonder if I'm emotionally grown up.

T.102: By which you mean what?

P.102: When you're married you should have one mate. You shouldn't go around and look at other men.

T.103: You've been looking at other men?

P.103: I look at them, but that's all.

T.104: Mmmhnn. What you mean . . . you mean a grown-up person should accept the marital situation whatever it happens to be?

P.104: That was the way I was brought up. Yes. (*Sighs.*)

T.105: You think that would be a sign of emotional maturity?

P.105: No.

T.106: No. So?

P.106: Well, if you rebel against the laws of society you have to take the consequences.

T.107: Yes?

P.107: And it's just that I . . . I'm not willing to take the consequences. I . . . I don't think it's worth it.

T.108: Mmmhnn. So in the meantime then while you're in this very difficult situation, you find yourself reacting in a way that you don't like and that you think is . . . ah . . . damaging to your children and yourself? Now what can be done about that?

P.108: (*Sniffs; sighs.*) I dunno. That's why I came to see you.

T.109: Yes. I was just wondering what you had in mind. Did you think a psychiatrist could . . . ah . . . help you face this kind of situation calmly and easily and maturely? Is that it?

P.109: More or less. I need somebody to talk to who isn't emotionally involved with the family. I have a few friends, but I don't like to bore them. I don't think they should know . . . ah . . . all the intimate details of what goes on.

T.110: Yeah?

P.110: It becomes food for gossip.

T.111: Mmmhnn.

P.111: Besides they're in . . . they're emotionally involved because they're my friends. They tell me not to stand for it, but they don't understand that if I put my foot down it'll only get stepped on.

T.112: Yeah.

P.112: That he can make it miserable for me in other ways . . .

T.113: Mmm.

P.113: . . . which he does.

T.114: Mmmhnn. In other words, you find yourself in a situation and don't know how to cope with it really.

P.114: I don't.

T.115: You'd like to be able to talk that through and come to understand it better and learn how to cope with it or deal with it in some way. Is that right?

P.115: I'd like to know how to deal with it more effectively.

Comment. By this point, the clinician is working with the patient to clarify what she might expect in the clinic. They are now focusing on her psychological state and on the possibility that she can change and deal better with her problems. This is the turning point in the interview. In the remaining half, the patient talks about earlier difficulties with men and other facets of her problem. The basis for a therapeutic alliance is set.

In their synopsis of the entire interview, Gill, Newman, and Redlich (1954), describe the content and process in these terms:

> The patient begins the interview by saying that she is irritable and depressed and that she blames this on her husband. She has thought of a divorce but refrains because of her children. The therapist questions these statements but the patient continues to ascribe her difficulties to outside circumstances. He then begins an inventory of her background and present situation and returns to confront her with her attitude (that her difficulties are external or situational) and asks what she expects from a psychiatrist. He tries to find out why she seeks help now and what she expects from treatment. The patient begins to realize the contradiction between the stated cause of her trouble (external circumstances) and her own role in possibly causing her difficulties. She realizes that she is confused about this and that it might be helpful to clear up the confusion by talking about it. About the middle of the interview (T.101) the therapist summarizes this and presents it to the patient, evoking feelings which come from this confusion and an inner source of disturbance: her premarital sexual behavior. The therapist tries to clarify the patient's feelings in a forceful but kindly, sympathetic manner. He accepts her use of psychiatric terms, as he earlier accepted her expressed hostility to her husband and landlord, and asks her what she thinks is the trouble. She then, with some difficulty, tells of her early feelings about boys, leaving home, her subsequent behavior and her affair with a married man which led to pregnancy and then to marriage to another man (with considerable feeling she tells the therapist a secret). The therapist says that he sees she needs help and that he will arrange it. The patient cries, the therapist comforts her and promises help.

> The patient, pushed by we know not what or why at the time (the children—somebody to talk to) comes for help apparently for what she thinks of as help with her external situation (her husband's behavior as she sees it). The therapist does not respond to this but seeks her role and how it is that she plays such a role. Listening to the recording it sounds as if the therapist is at first bored and disinterested and the patient defensive. He gets down to work and keeps asking, "What is it all about?" Then he becomes more interested and sympathetic and at the same time very active (participating) and demanding. It sounds as if she keeps saying, "This is the trouble." He says, "No! Tell me the trouble." She says, "This is it!" He says, "No, tell me," until the patient finally says, "Well I'll tell you." Then the therapist says, "Good! I'll help you" [pp. 132–133].

Communication and Language

The interview, whatever its purpose or form, is a particular type of interpersonal communication in which messages, both intended and unintended, are passed back and forth between the two participants. Understanding another person, accurate clinical assessment, depends on the clarity and effectiveness of this communication. Communication can be distorted or limited by reasons of *motivation,* i.e., the patient wishes to conceal, distrusts the interviewer, is frightened, etc., or for *lack of cognitive ability,* i.e., he has forgotten or repressed the relevant material, has difficulty conceptualizing experience or organizing his thoughts. Furthermore, there are problems which reside in language itself.

Philosophers and linguists tell us that language is a relatively crude system of representation for the variety of percepts and concepts available in direct experience. Think how difficult it is to characterize in words nuances of emotion so as to communicate your feelings of the moment. Not only must the sender have the necessary words but the receiver must attach the same meanings to them. Interactive communication is further limited by the lack of shared vocabulary. It has been said that the average person knows about ten percent of the half million words of the English language. Nor are they the same ten percent, since each social subgroup has a somewhat different sample of the total pool. There are differences in vocabulary between social classes, ethnic groups, regions of the country, and occupational and age groups. Emotions aside, if I want round, hot, doughy things to put maple syrup on for breakfast, I best know that they can be called hotcakes, pancakes, flapjacks, or wheat cakes, depending on where I am. To make matters even more complicated, there is good evidence of extensive individual differences in vocabulary and language styles, so that the speech of each of us is to some fair degree distinctive. In general, the closer two people are in social characteristics the more likely will they have a common vocabulary.

In the interview, questions should be couched as far as possible in the vocabulary common to both clinician and patient. The alternative of trying to teach the patient the clinician's words is both difficult and often offensive. Contrariwise, attempts to use the patient's vocabulary are likely to be ludicrous. Understanding the patient's words as he uses them spontaneously is important; the good clinician, we noted earlier, is one with a breadth of experience with different people in different settings, a by-product of which is a more extensive vocabulary. Patients often choose their words in terms of their notions as to proprieties and requirements of the clinic, whether to say "sexual intercourse" instead of a simpler word or to make comments like ". . . what you call paranoia. Right, doc?" As a general rule, the atmosphere of the interview should be such that the patient feels free to use his natural vocabulary, as he faces a clinician concerned to understand and able to appreciate his experiences and to know the words by which he communicates them. In turn, the clinician must resist the temptation of using his own technical terms or of patronizing the patient by affecting the patient's idiom. As far as possible, the clinician should use language natural to him selecting from within the vocabulary he shares with the patient.

For communication to be effective, not only must words themselves be known but the frame of reference of the speaker must be understood. If someone says, "I was offered a good job," we simply do not know, without further information, if he means that it involves interesting duties, socially valuable work, short hours and easy tasks, contact with compatible people, or good pay, or for that matter what "good" is in dollar terms. Visualize the confusion inherent in "She is an interesting woman" or "He is one of the most intelligent people I know." Frames of reference may be wholly idiosyncratic or shared with others of like experience and background. To farmers, Buffalo may be a "big town;" to New Yorkers, a "hick town." Whatever the case, the framework of meaning and judgment within which the patient is operating must be known. This is often discovered through sequences of questions which explore the particular meaning of the message: "In what sense is it a good job? Do you mean in terms of duties, hours, salary, or what?" Where specific information is being sought, the frame of reference can sometimes be controlled through question-wordings which specify context. Thus, we can ask "In terms of earnings, is it a good job?"

On the whole, the clinician tends to use relatively neutral, direct, and open-ended questions, particularly in the early exploration of a topic, in order to give the patient maximal opportunity to present his concerns in his own terms. Thus, in enquiring about marital relations, it seems better to ask "Tell me something about your marriage" or "What kind of person is your husband?" than to open with "Do you and your husband get along well?" or "Is your marriage happy?" Later on, should the patient go on at length telling how idyllic his married life is, it may be useful to ask an intentionally provocative and leading question of the sort, "Do you mean you *never* argue about *anything*?" However, in general, leading questions—which imply their answers in the asking—should be avoided, along with those which require an abrupt change of reference, or those which fuse a number of issues together (double-barrelled questions). Anything the interviewer says which confuses or needs further explanation, is provocative or insulting, or makes the patient feel stupid or foolish is of course to be avoided.

In addition to direct questions, whether of an open-ended or more focused sort, it is sometimes valuable to use more indirect (projective) questions, particularly to explore areas in which the patient is reluctant or unable to speak directly. A question phrased in terms of the behavior of "other people" is less threatening and yet it may reveal the patient's own feelings. To discover, say, whether a patient has suicidal thoughts, rather than putting direct questions to him, one can ask, "What might make a person consider suicide?" The same hypothetical question, incidentally, put by the patient to the clinician could as well reveal the patient's suicidal concerns.

Nonverbal Communication

Information is conveyed by nonverbal behavior as well as by words. A gesture can serve as an intentional act of communication: a finger to the lips says "quiet!" But gestures, along with body movements, posture, gait, facial expression, and nonverbal speech patterns can unintentionally yield information about a person. They all provide cues for informal assessment, as we considered in the last chapter. In the main, clinicians have been more concerned with the verbal productions of patients, but sensitive clinicians have always been attentive to the bodily behavior of their patients. In 1905, Freud noted: "He that has eyes to see and ears to hear may convince himself that no mortal can keep a secret. If his lips are silent, he chatters with his finger-tips; betrayal oozes out of him at every pore" (Freud, 1905, pp. 77–78). Behavior patterns can reveal the enduring personality or clinical condition of the patient or they may communicate his momentary state. Recall Harvey Cushing's diagnosis of brain damage in the Boston gentleman who pushed through a door ahead of his wife (Chapter 3). Reich (1958) has described the tensed musculature of the severely constricted person as rigidified "body armor." Very depressed patients move and talk in a characteristically slow and lethargic way. Momentary bodily behaviors as well reveal immediate and fleeting states of the person. Most of us readily recognize the fidgeting or stammering of embarrassment, the tremulous hands or voice of anxiety, or the clenched fists and flushed face in anger. Some expressive behaviors seem universal, in some cases because they reflect physiological changes common to us all (e.g., flushing or trembling), others are culturally shared gestures (e.g., the no-no wagging finger), while some are wholly individual. Whatever their origin, they provide cues to the clinician.

In a study of gestures during initial interviews, Mahl (1968) found that personally meaningful gestures reappeared periodically during interviews. In Figure 8.1 are pictured two gestures of "Mrs. B.," turning her palms up and out and playing with one or the other of her rings, and the frequency with which they occurred in each minute of the interview. When matched with on-going verbal utterances and interpersonal exchanges, Mahl noted four types of relationship: (1) Some of the movements had the same meaning and occurred simultaneously with verbal material. Thus, when describing her helplessness, Mrs. B. turned her palms up-out. This gesture is a communicative act with a culturally shared meaning. (2) While not appearing to be related to the manifest verbal content, some gestures foretell later implications of current themes. Thus, while Mrs. B. was talking about her symptoms, with little mention of her husband, she played with her wedding ring. When she came to verbalize her complaints against her husband, this gesture ceased. (3) Some gestures betray meaning contrary to concurrent verbal content. Mahl describes an apprentice machinist who deftly manipulated a pencil throughout the interview, only to drop it precisely when he was defensively claiming that his work on the job was absolutely perfect. (4) Some bodily activity seems directly related to the interplay with the interviewer. The drop in Mrs. B.'s palms out-up activity in the eighth minute of the interview (note graph in Figure 8.1) occurred immediately after the interviewer showed considerable empathic understanding and sympathy, which might be supposed to have gratified for the time at least her desire for help in her helplessness.

FIGURE 8.1.

The Frequency of Two of Mrs. B.'s Gestures During an Initial Interview

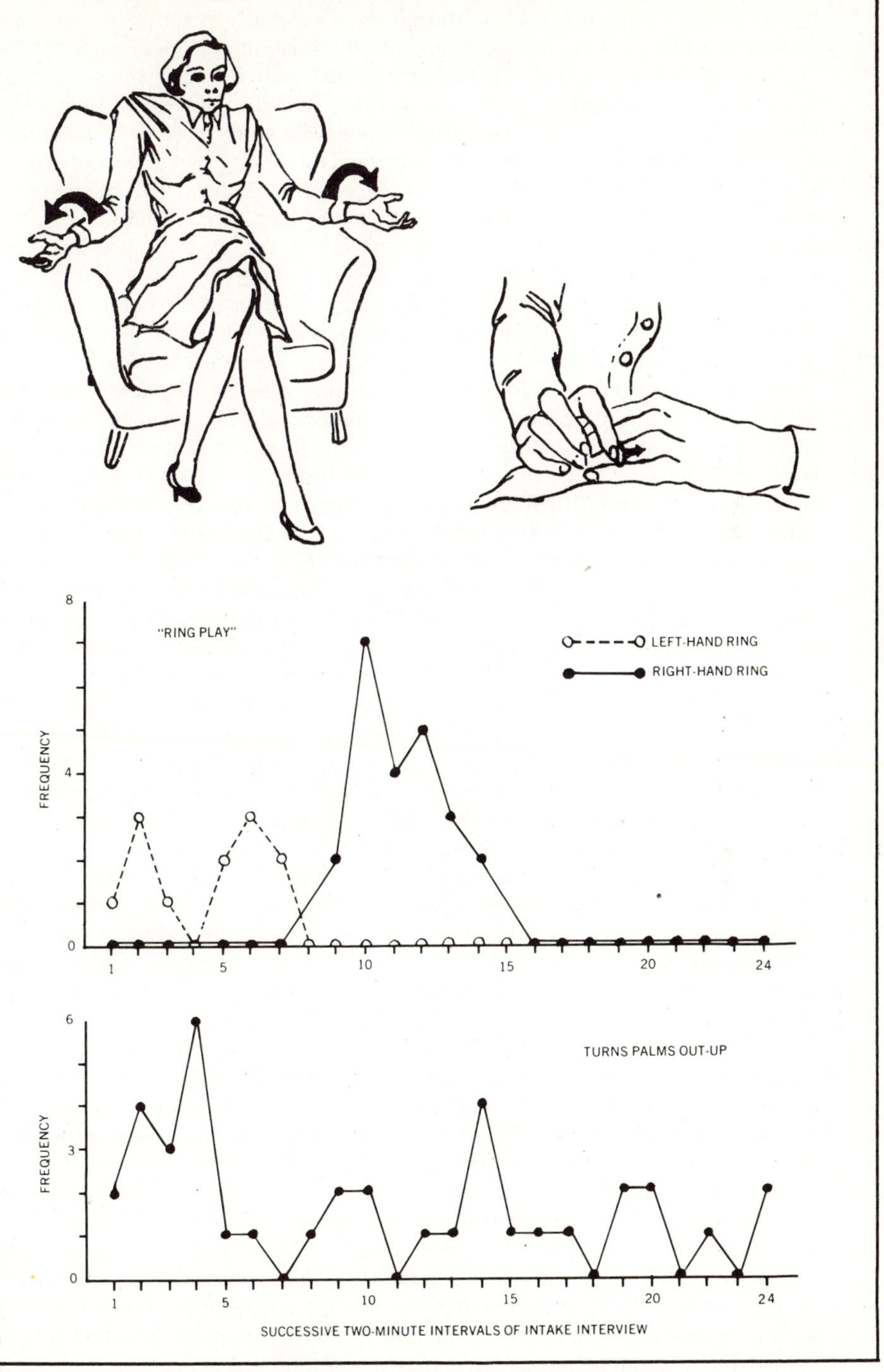

* Mahl, G. F. Gestures and body movements in interviews. In J. M. Shlien (Ed.), *Research in psychotherapy*, Vol. 3. Washington, D.C.: American Psychological Association, 1968. Copyright 1968 by the American Psychological Association. Reprinted by permission.

There has been an upswing of interest in research on nonverbal communication. In part, this reflects the greater availability of film and videotape equipment, though it parallels growing interest in communication generally, including nonverbal facets, in the behavioral and mental health sciences (e.g., Ruesch and his co-workers, 1951, 1956, 1957; Birdwhistell, 1952). Among the many facets of interview behavior which have been studied are the relation between emotional states and speech disturbances (Mahl, 1956; Boomer, 1963; Dittman and Wynne, 1961) and facial expression, gesture, movement (e.g., Sainsbury, 1955; Ekman, 1964; Ekman and Friesen, 1968; Dittman, 1963), and posture (e.g., Scheflen, 1964) as indexes of the patient's psychological states.

Research on the interview has moved in a number of directions not concerned directly with the content of the messages exchanged. There have been extensive psycholinguistic analyses of the language structure used (e.g., Gottschalk, 1961). In another realm, simultaneous physiological measurements have been made on both interviewer and patient, and parallel and complementary reactions are found in autonomic measures; empathy exists as it were at the gut level (DiMascio et al., 1955; Lacey, 1959). Research has been done on the "anatomy" of the interview in which verbal interaction patterns are objectively measured in terms of the frequency and duration of verbal utterances made. Thus, in the course of a more extensive study of therapeutic communication, Lennard and Bernstein (1961) report that for each therapist-patient pair there is a characteristic balance such that the proportion of time each talks remains at a relatively constant ratio from hour to hour. However, within these stable ratios there is a tendency for the output of the therapist to go up if the patient's goes down, and vice versa. When questioned after the session, patients tended to express greater satisfaction with sessions in which the therapist output was relatively high.

Matarazzo, Saslow, and their colleagues at the University of Oregon Medical School have conducted a number of studies of the structural or content-free dimensions of the interview, in which the frequency and duration of periods of speech and silence were measured (for reviews, see Matarazzo, 1965b; Matarazzo and Weins, 1972). Even when interviewed by different clinicians, patients had approximately the same speech durations. On the whole, the duration of each speech unit tends to be quite short, as is the reaction time to the interviewer's preceding comment. However, the sicker the patient the briefer are his average speech units. Thus, the median unit for hospitalized schizophrenics was about 20 hundredths of a minute while for normal subjects it was about 90, with neurotic patients positioning in between. In another study, the investigators attempted to alter the interaction patterns experimentally by having interviewers intentionally increase or decrease the length of their speech units. It was found that when interviewers doubled or halved their own speech durations the subjects' speech units changed accordingly. This experiment suggests that it might be possible to induce depressed patients to speak more fully, or manic patients to talk more briefly, by the clinician's control of his own behavior. In still other studies, the effects of interpretative versus nondirective statements were assessed (the former shortened interviewee replies). When interviewers nodded their heads each time interviewees spoke, the average length of interviewee speech units increased. These and similar findings are illustrative of the kind of objective study which can increase our understanding of interview processes.

The Reliability and Validity of Clinical Interviews

To be useful, any assessment technique should yield both reliable and valid measures and it is fair to evaluate the interview in these terms. It is true that the initial interview, in the form discussed earlier, has purposes beyond assessment, for example, to develop a working relationship with the patient, to give him information as to available alternatives, and to support his motivation for change. In comparison, the traditional diagnostic interview, the interviews of social and clinical research, or an interview specifically designed to assess a particular personality variable—say, achievement needs or anxiety—are primarily assessment techniques and can therefore be more readily evaluated as instruments of measurement. Although interviews obviously vary enormously in purpose and form and simple generalizations are clearly impossible, it is still fair to ask whether they produce valid and reliable information.

In a later chapter, when considering psychological testing, we will give more detailed attention to the twin concepts of *reliability* and *validity* in psychological measurement. For now, let us take validity to mean that an instrument measures whatever it purports to measure. A test is valid to the extent that it approximates "true" values, usually as defined by an external and accepted criterion. Thus, my watch is a valid time-measurer if its readings correspond to Naval Observatory time. Reliability, on the other hand, describes the consistency of measures, whether valid or not. My watch is reliable if every hour is of the same length, even though a "validity check" would tell me that my "hour" contains seventy minutes of the navy's time. The issues of reliability and validity are obviously more complex in psychological measurement, for we are dealing with variables more ambiguous than time and instruments far less standardized than clocks.

The interview could be said to yield reliable data if two clinicians interviewing the same patient reached the same judgments about him. In principle, any of numerous types of judgments commonly made in clinics could be compared, such as the patient's degree of anxiety, type of defense, motivation for treatment, or the like; in actuality, much of the published research centers on the reliability of psychiatric diagnoses, usually in terms of describing patients in the categories of standard psychiatric nomenclature. Some of these studies have already been discussed in Chapter 4. In that context, my own reservations about both the scientific merit and clinical utility of psychiatric diagnosis were made amply clear.

Matarazzo (1965) reviewed the literature on the reliability of interview-based psychiatric diagnosis in considerable detail. Findings range widely, from evidence of considerable unreliability to studies reporting a high order of agreement between independent clinicians. As one might readily expect, there is greater "inter-judge reliability" when broader categories are used and less when finer discriminations are needed. Thus, for example, in a study in a state hospital (Schmidt and Fonda, 1956), 426 patients were each seen by a pair of psychiatrists. When placing them in one of three major categories (organic, psychotic, or character disorder) they agreed in 84 percent of the cases. When diagnosing in terms of eleven subtypes, however, agreement fell to 55 percent. In other studies, it is found that agreement tends to be greater when clinicians are better trained and in greater accord as to the definitions of the diagnostic groupings. Where more detailed personality analyses rather than simple diagnoses are required, clinicians can selectively perceive and emphasize different qualities of the same patients (e.g., studies of Raines and Rohrer, cited by Matarazzo).

The issue of validity is even more complex; the few studies available understandably yield even more diverse findings. For one, there is the persistent "criterion problem"; by what standard do we decide whether a judgment is valid or not? Then too, different estimates of validity are found depending on the purpose of the interview, its form, the information sought, the skill and training of the interviewer, the type of patient, and not unlikely numerous other factors as well. Findings can be found as often contradicting as supporting the common assertion that interview-based judgments are of limited validity. For example, in studies which followed the subsequent careers of 944 men seen earlier in their enlistments Wittson and Hunt (1951) found that diagnoses made in early screening interviews predicted quite accurately whether navy men would later function well or be given psychiatric discharges. Despite the known fallibility of judgments made in job interviews, Vernon (1963) calls attention to evidence of considerable success in predicting later performance. In still another realm, studies of survey interviews show similar discrepancies, depending on how the validity question is phrased. An interesting illustration is given by a study in which respondents were asked a number of factual questions which could be independently verified (Parry and Crossley, 1950; reported in a review by Cannell and Kahn, 1969). Only 2 percent of 900 respondents incorrectly reported owning a telephone, 3 percent incorrectly reported auto ownership and 4 percent home ownership. However, 17 percent inaccurately reported their age, 25 percent registering and voting, and 40 percent contributing to the Community Chest. Clearly, where the issue of social acceptability was involved the likelihood of inaccurate reporting went up. In a similar vein, and closer to the clinical situation, Wenar (1963) found that mothers' accounts of their children's developmental histories tended to be distorted in the direction of making the children appear more precocious.

As a method of assessment, interviews are fallible and subject to bias from various sources. Many of the factors discussed in the preceding chapter which limit the accuracy of person perception in informal assessment operate as well in the clinical interview. There is ample evidence that interviewers can intentionally or otherwise bias the information given to them by respondents in social research interviewing (H. H. Hyman, 1954; Cannell and Kahn, 1969). What respondents report is a function of the age, sex, and other social characteristics of the interviewer, the relationship he establishes and his personal qualities, as well as the topics he inquires into and the particular questions he asks. As more is learned about sources of bias, better methods can be developed to eliminate them. Further studies of interview process can further sharpen our understanding of where and how distortion can occur. Through training and practice, the interviewer can function more effectively. For some purposes, greater standardization can make the interview a sharper and more dependable tool. However, as in the case of the initial interview, standardization which might make for greater reliability can at the same time limit the flexibility needed to discover the most relevant and valid information.

The interview remains the most basic, most commonly used, and most powerful technique of clinical assessment. Compared to any standardized test, it is an instrument of great flexibility and breadth. It can potentially cover a greater range of information and as individually relevant themes emerge the course of inquiry, can be redirected and refocused. Language and question form can accommodate to the patient's communication style; so too the pace, intensity, and duration of the transaction to his emotional needs. For most people, the interview is a natural situation, for it resembles the conversations of ordinary social life and, unlike psychological tests, entails no apparatus nor artificial tasks, nor does it as readily suggest the pass/fail evaluation of school testing. As participant-observer, the interviewer both stimulates and records the behavior of the patient; though enmeshed in the situation, he has control over it. Finally, as we have already repeatedly observed, the interview serves nonassessment purposes vital to the clinical process.

The very strengths of the interview are also its weaknesses, when considered as a method of psychological measurement. Flexibility and breadth allow unreliability and bias. Although there have been many salutary efforts to develop standardized procedures for special purposes, in daily clinical use the lack of standardization, which confounds the psychometrically minded psychologist, is a prime source of value. Undoubtedly, assessment interviewing will continue to be a major tool of the clinician; his obligation is to sharpen his understanding of the essential processes involved and of his own contribution to the (in)validity of the resultant findings. Because the clinician is at one time stimulus to, observer of, and interpreter of the patient's state, the interview is the most difficult of assessment methods.

CHAPTER 9

Psychological Testing: I. General Principles

Testing in Clinical Practice, Research, and Training

Psychological testing was once the primary, if not sole, activity of clinical psychologists. Although increasingly involved in other clinical activities, testing remains a central function of psychologists, particularly in psychiatric settings (Lubin and Lubin, 1972; Wellner, 1968). Psychologists entered the clinical field through their expertise in the development and application of test methods, which still represents their most distinctive contribution to the study and treatment of mental health problems. As part of clinical assessment, test findings are joined with interview, observation, and other assessment data to form the basis for clinical planning, diagnosis, and evaluation. In principle, they add standardized and objective measures by which a particular patient can be better understood, his treatment planned, and change evaluated, and by which different patients can be compared. Although controversy still surrounds the proper use of testing in clinical decision-making, skillfully applied test information can increase the effectiveness of clinical service. But regardless of their direct value to the patient, the study of test behavior is of prime importance for extending the clinician's understanding of psychological adaptation and pathology. Similarly, research of clinical relevance requires test measures which allow quantitative comparison as, for example, to assess the effectiveness of a particularly therapeutic approach. Such research can utilize existing standard tests or require the development of new ones, but in either case knowledge of testing principles is essential. Thus, for purposes of clinical practice, research, and training, psychological tests are basic tools of clinicians. They should be well schooled in their use and sensitive to their potential abuse.

To add to his knowledge of psychological testing, the student is advised to read further in the literature of psychometric theory and methods, psychological testing generally, and personality and clinical assessment specifically. Psychometric theory is a highly technical field, rooted in statistics and mathematics, but the clinical student should have appreciation of the problems with which, for example, workers such as Ghiselli (1964) and Nunnally (1967) deal. For a broad overview of psychological testing, Cronbach (1970) and Anastasi (1968) provide fine surveys of the issues of test development, application, and evaluation. They each describe in some detail a number of tests in each of the several realms of psychological measurement (e.g., intelligence, abilities, personality). Of great value are the reference volumes edited by O. K. Buros—*Seventh Mental Measurements Yearbook* (1972); *Tests in Print, II* (1974); *Personality Tests and Reviews, II* (1975) are most relevant—which are periodically updated. In these volumes appear critical reviews of the literature on several hundred tests. Before using any psychological test, the student, or professional clinician for that matter, is well advised to read the reviews in Buros as well as the *Test Manual,* usually prepared by the author of the test. A brief though highly informative overview of issues of test development, distribution, use, and evaluation can be found in the American Psychological Association's *Standards for Educational and Psychological Tests and Manuals* (APA, 1974). Good surveys of the general field of clinical assessment and of available test methods are contained in Holt (1968), Lanyon and Goodstein (1971), and Kleinmuntz (1967). Holt's introductory volume, as his other writings on assessment, are in the tradition of Murray and Rapaport's ego-psychological approach to testing (cf. Chapter 6). More detailed expositions in this tradition are to be found in Rapaport, Gill, and Mayman (revised edition by Holt, 1968); Schafer (1948, 1954); and Allison, Blatt, and Zimet (1968).

To use tests wisely in clinical assessment, the student should be well versed in this literature. Clinical training further involves observation of experienced testers and supervised practice, in order to develop a fund of personal knowledge. Being tested oneself makes it possible to learn what the test "feels like" for the subject and gives a futher basis for empathic understanding of the patient's experience. Experienced testers get more information through the use of their procedures, not only more than the novice but also more than the literature would suggest. They develop internal standards and personal norms, become sensitized to minor cues, and finely tuned to their own contributions to the testing transaction. They develop a secure sense of how and when to alter standard procedures, to conceive, modify, and test hypotheses during testing, and to temper interpretation according to the particular issues of the case. The expert "Rorschacher" or MMPI authority, like the astute psychotherapist, "listens with a third ear." Such expertise comes with years of experience focused on a particular technique. By the same token, the expert may be overcommitted to a particular test and lose perspective on its limitations. It may be used even where another procedure might be preferable. To guard against such rigidification the test expert is obliged to study his test constantly, both in the sense of formal research and in the sense of checking his interpretations against those of other clinicians and other procedures. To verify predictions made, the future progress of patients should be followed.

What Is a Psychological Test?

Everyone knows what a test is, yet it is curiously difficult to offer an inclusive definition. In school, we did better or worse on tests of arithmetic, history, and, more recently, psychology. Our IQs were measured, drum-playing skill assessed, and football potential tested. To find a job, we may be given tests of secretarial skills, manual dexterity, leadership or social skills, or knowledge of a particular field. Attitudes toward social issues are tested by polling organizations. The state tests us for a driver's license. When we seek vocational guidance, interests and abilities are tested. Finally—in despair at all this testing?—we arrive in a psychological clinic, only to be clinically tested. What is common to all these activities?

In most general terms, *a test is a standardized situation in which a person's behavior is sampled, observed, and described*. Often, but not always, the result is stated in numerical values. Many tests yield scores which indicate the individual's position in respect to others along a quantitative continuum, for example: IQ = 110; B + in psychology; 85th percentile in neuroticism. Other procedures place the individual into one of two or more categories (color-blind or not; psychotic or not). The output of a test is often a group or *profile* of scores, which can be evaluated psychometrically or clinically. Finally, there are tests which are not scored in the usual sense but instead provide a pool of observations or indicators, gathered under reasonably constant conditions, which have to be evaluated by the assessing clinician. Indeed, the same test can be used in all of these ways. Thus, the Wechsler Adult Intelligence Scale (WAIS) provides the psychologist with (1) an overall IQ; (2) a profile of subscale scores; and (3) responses to particular items from which he can infer characteristic modes of intellectual functioning.

Although the clinician is usually concerned with the qualities of individuals, we can note that psychological tests need not focus on the particular person but can assess the attributes of groups, organizations, or even environments. Tests have been developed for describing the psychological qualities of groups or families as a psychological whole (Loveland, Singer, and Wynne, 1962), and of social systems such as a school or hospital (Moos, 1974). In fact, in the current interest in ecology, attention is being turned to the psychological assessment of the physical environment as well.

GROUP AND INDIVIDUAL TESTS

Many terms are commonly used to describe types of tests. *Group tests* differ from *individual tests* in allowing a number of people to be tested simultaneously. They are usually *self-administered tests*. In addition to procedures specifically designed for that purpose, individual tests have been adapted for group administration. Normally, the Rorschach or Thematic Apperception Test (TAT) involves considerable discussion, inquiry, and exploration as subjects are shown inkblots or pictures and asked to interpret their meaning. The individual relationship is necessary, most clinicians feel, to get fully interpretable responses. However, it is possible to project the test stimuli and have patients in a group write down their responses in test booklets. Information is lost, but time and cost are reduced. Other tests, such as the Minnesota Multiphasic Personality Inventory (MMPI), are available in both individual and group forms. Since the MMPI is less dependent on personal interaction with a tester, the two forms are generally considered equivalent. In clinical settings, group procedures are usually reserved for screening or research purposes, where relatively large numbers of patients have to be examined over a relatively short time. In educational, vocational, and selection testing, group testing is the usual procedure.

PERFORMANCE AND VERBAL TESTS

Tests differ widely in the materials used and in the acts required of the subject. Thus, there are paper-and-pencil tests, questionnaires, apparatus tests, visual tests, multiple-choice tests, and other terms whose meanings are fairly obvious. While all tests involve performance of one or another sort, the term "performance test" is usually reserved for procedures involving motor activity or manipulation of materials. Illustrative of the tasks used in performance tests are drawing a picture of a person, copying geometric designs, placing pieces in a formboard, repairing a piece of mechanical equipment, tying shoelaces or stringing beads. Such tests contrast with *verbal tests*, which directly involve the use of language.

STRUCTURED AND UNSTRUCTURED TESTS

Tests differ in definiteness of the task put before the subject and the range of responses available to him. An essay examination is an unstructured test; a true-false examination is more structured. The unstructured test allows the subject greater freedom and consequently greater opportunity to bring forth his individual concerns. However, it is more difficult to score and to standardize. The structured test requires more effort in item selection and design in order to assure proper sampling of the domain being assessed, understandability, and the like. The unstructured test, by contrast, demands greater effort in interpretation, since there is more room for bias and unreliability in evaluating responses. The term "objective test" is often used synonymously with structured.

SELF-REPORT AND PERFORMANCE TESTS OF PERSONALITY

In the domain of personality assessment, most structured procedures are *self-report tests* in which a subject knowingly describes himself, as for example by making self-ratings, or checking adjectives or endorsing statements which characterize him. These procedures contrast with tests in which the subject reveals himself through the ways he manipulates or responds to relatively impersonal stimuli. Such procedures might be called "performance tests of personality," except for the possible confusion with the term "performance test," as just noted, in the field of ability testing. *Projective tests*, such as the Rorschach or TAT, are performance measures of personality in the sense used here. What is most typical of projective techniques, however, is their dependence on indirect rather than direct indicators.

DIRECT AND INDIRECT MEASURES

On some tests, the tasks required of the subject are self-evidently related to the variable being assessed; in other cases, the test items and responses serve as *indirect* indicators. Most measures of intellectual functioning and ability depend on *direct* indicators. Thus, we discover the breadth and maturity of a child's vocabulary by asking him to define a list of words; achievement in school subjects is tested by seeing how much of the subject the student knows; typing skill, by timing someone typing a standard passage. In the same way, self-report responses on an adjective or symptom check list are direct indicators of personality traits or clinical status. On the other hand, having subjects respond to Rorschach inkblots provides indirect indicators of the personality variables being studied. As such, the psychologist is not concerned with the perceptual task or the responses they yield, but rather with what they reveal about the subject's personality. The interpretative value of an indirect indicator is established ultimately by demonstrating its relationship with more direct evidence of the variable about which judgments are made.

The patient can better understand a test involving direct measures. He is better able to predict the use the psychologist will make of his responses and correspondingly better able to control them if he wishes. In contrast, when taking projective tests he is presented with mysterious tasks, whose meaning or interpretation is by no means obvious. Where indirect indicators are involved, the subject is less able intentionally to project a desired image.

However, while many self-report techniques are direct measures, they are sometimes designed to serve as indirect indicators. In inventories such as the MMPI, items are *empirically keyed*, and the evident meaning of the item does not reveal its interpretative meaning. Scoring and interpretation is based on the correlation of responses with outside criteria. Thus, if subjects of a particular type consistently endorse an item in a particular way, this fact can be used to diagnose that attribute, regardless of its content. Suppose, as a fictitious example, that it was discovered in some fashion that aggressive people prefer blue bathing suits while nonviolent souls would rather wear red ones. Thus, on an inventory measuring aggressiveness, the item "Do you prefer red or blue bathing suits?" can serve as an indirect indicator of aggressiveness. (In a market survey by a bathing suit company, the same item would of course be a direct indicator.) Failure to distinguish between the face meaning and the interpretative use of inventory items underlies at least some of the public antagonism against personality inventories (Hathaway, 1964).

TESTS OF MAXIMUM AND OF TYPICAL PERFORMANCE

Cronbach (1970) places tests in one of two broad classes. Some tests seek to measure the maximum performance of the subject; others seek to determine his typical performance. The first class is typified by tests of ability; the second by tests of personality, interests, mood, and the like. Both types of procedures are important in clinical assessment, often as part of the same battery. To some degree, the distinction between maximum and typical performance is unclear, for even in the most precise test of ability a subject can achieve the same end product in individual ways. The person's individual style provides data of considerable moment to the psychologist.

Overall, however, ability tests are intended to discover how well the subject can function at his best; they get at optimal rather than typical functioning. The subject is urged to do well and precise instructions are given which include criteria for a high score (say, maximal accuracy or speed). It is assumed that the person wants to do well and will reach for the highest possible score. Tests of general intelligence, specific mental abilities, psychological deficit of the type resulting from brain damage, particular skills and past achievement in learning, are all instances of maximum-performance tests.

By contrast, tests of typical performance seek to discover "not what the person can do but what he does" (Cronbach, 1970, p. 38). Personality measures and tests of interests and social attitudes are in this class. The subject does not aim to attain a maximal score on a defined dimension, for in principle no particular response is better or worse. Indeed, personality tests are often introduced with the statement: "This is not a test. There are no right and wrong answers . . ." The first sentence seems contradictory, until we realize that for most people, psychologists included, the word "test" itself implies evaluation of an ability, a measure of maximum performance. The implication of doing better or worse, passing or failing, is built into the popular image of testing, nor are we likely to change it by assurances or circumlocutions.

Three Strategies of Personality Test Development

There are three major approaches to the construction of personality measures: (1) Rational-theoretical; (2) empirical; and (3) internal consistency (Lanyon and Goodstein, 1971). These are not mutually exclusive and some procedures may in their development even involve all three approaches. They do, however, represent alternate orientations.

RATIONAL-THEORETICAL

A test can derive from commonsensical or rational considerations. In ability testing it is self-evident that, say, on a test of typing proficiency a subject should be asked to type a standard passage or that driving skill should be measured in the laboratory by speed and accuracy of response in an auto simulator. So too, a scale of characteristic emotional states would contain items such as "I am often frightened," "I tend to lose my temper easily," or "Often, I'm too depressed to work." Rationally developed tests thus use stimulus materials which, in the judgment of the test developer, tap the behavior which concerns him. The materials used may be obviously and directly related to the variables to be assessed, or they may derive from a theoretical approach to personality. Thus, in developing the TAT, Morgan and Murray (1935) started with the assumption that in telling stories about ambiguous pictures subjects would represent their own needs and expectations about the behavior of others. The task of test development then becomes one of choosing pictures which would best sample the range of personality characteristics, needs, expectations ("press"), affects and the like, in order to describe the structure and dynamics of the individual personality as completely as possible. A similar procedure, the Blacky Picture Test (Blum, 1950), is derived directly from Freud's theory of psychosexual development. Each picture represents a little dog, Blacky, his family and friends, in scenes depicting crises at each psychosexual level; the subject's responses are scored and interpreted as to the amount and type of conflict revealed. We can visualize a rational-theoretical continuum from procedures based on a commonsensical choice of test materials, as in questionnaires and symptom checklists, to more subtle and theoretically based tasks; all of which, however, share the common property of depending on the test developer's logical or theoretical analysis of the area rather than empirical or statistical determination.

EMPIRICAL

Empirically based tests depend on evidence that the test indicators are related to the variable to be assessed. Test items are chosen according to their power to discriminate between criterion groups. Thus, if we wished to predict leadership potential among college students, we might enlist two groups: one of club presidents, team captains, and student council officers and the other of nonleaders, but otherwise comparable students. To each group, we might give a very large number of items and retain those which discriminated and reject the rest—regardless of their nature. The MMPI is a well-known illustration of the empirical approach. Meehl (1945) gave the classic defense of the empirical method. The essential consideration is that the test does what it is supposed to do; whether it makes sense or not is secondary. The rational-theoretical approach starts from the opposite position, that is, to be useful, it should make sense. Not infrequently, as in the original standardization of the MMPI, the original pool of items are chosen on rational grounds, but their retention depends on empirical standards. Some, however, have argued that the rational content of test stimuli literally does not matter, provided only they are allowed enough variability to discover empirical relationships (e.g., Berg, 1959). However, L. R. Goldberg and Slovic (1967) have shown that items in personality inventories which have higher face or content validity (i.e., which seem to be sensibly related to the variable being assessed) do actually have higher empirical validity.

It is possible for some items to be included by chance alone in the empirical approach. For example, an item may be included if it correlates with the criterion at the .05 level of confidence, but this can mean that 5 percent of the total number of items are erroneously included. To guard against this possibility, the test should be *cross-validated*. The items should be administered to other, closely comparable but independent, criterion groups. Those items which survive cross-validation can more confidently be included.

Still, we have to be cautious in interpreting the variable that an empirical scale is supposed to measure, since the obtained correlations might reflect the operation of other, extraneous variables. Suppose, in our leadership illustration, that ability to define esoteric words distinguished leader from nonleader students. This might only be evidence of the fact that more intelligent and verbal students are chosen for leadership positions; the test might actually be measuring an intellectual ability related to choosing leaders rather than the personality qualities required for leadership. From a strict operationist or pragmatic view, this consideration might be deemed quite irrelevant, for we do now have a test which might quite well predict potential college leaders among entering freshmen. Empirically developed scales may be of practical use, but at the same time yield little help in understanding the nature or operation of personality variables.

INTERNAL CONSISTENCY

Still another approach to the construction of personality tests is based on the statistical study of the internal consistency of test items. Here the effort is to define, from inside as it were, the variables being assessed, rather than establishing them either in a rational-theoretical way or by reference to behavior of criterion group. In this model, a large pool of items, usually chosen rationally to cover a broad domain of concern, is administered to a large number of subjects. The responses are then intercorrelated and through the complex statistical technique of *factor analysis* the clustering patterns (factors) are discovered. Thus, scoring high on one variable or item goes along with scoring high on another. Since they draw consistent responses, the factor or grouping of items which has been extracted is assumed to indicate a particular psychological variable. Researchers working with factor analysis differ in their interpretation of the psychological meaning of statistically defined factors. Cattell (e.g., 1965) holds that factors indicate "source" traits, which are to the domain of personality what the atomic elements are to physics and chemistry. Based on many factorial studies of self-report inventories, the Sixteen Personality Factor Questionnaire (16PF) was developed to provide measures of source traits (Cattell and Stice, 1957). Guilford (e.g., 1949, 1959), Thurstone (1949), and Eysenck (e.g., 1960a) developed factor analytic tests of personality on other premises. The concepts and methods of factor analysis originated in the study of mental abilities and some of the basic work on intelligence testing involves their use.

Factor analytic methods may be used to study and reconceptualize existing tests, however they were originally derived. Thus, there have been analyses of Rorschach response patterns, patient behavioral ratings, and symptom checklists, and of many empirically derived personality inventories such as the MMPI. Factor analytic studies of the MMPI (cf., Lanyon and Goodstein, 1971; Kleinmuntz, 1967) have led to general agreement in reporting two major independent (orthogonal) factors. There is general agreement in naming these "extroversion" and "neuroticism," which are the two factors described by Eysenck (1960a) as central to his theory of personality.

Criteria for Judging Tests

STANDARDIZATION

Tests provide, as we have noted, standard conditions for sampling, observing, and describing a person's behavior. In what respects and to what degree are conditions standardized, compared for example to the circumstances of informal assessment and interviewing? What advantages lie in standardization?

Standardization refers to *uniformity of testing procedure*. The term is sometimes used to include *uniformity of test interpretation*, particularly in terms of having available appropriate norms (scores of reference groups) against which the responses and scores of the individual can be compared. The issues of norms will be considered separately. Thus, a test is said to be standardized if test-administration procedures, materials and apparatus, instructions to subjects, and recording and scoring are as constant as possible at all times. Although rarely achieved in reality, the aim is to control all possible sources of variation, save the one the psychologist wishes to measure. Standardization in testing is analogous to the scientific ideal of experimental control. To the extent that extraneous—from the standpoint of the particular experiment—variables are controlled, we can be more secure in interpreting the obtained results. Another researcher on another occasion using the same experimental conditions and controls should replicate our findings. However, in psychological testing, as indeed in human experimentation, it is rarely possible to know and control all "irrelevant" variables. Along with regulating the controllable variables, the tester needs to understand the potential impact of the uncontrollable ones in order to minimize error in interpretation.

The first quality of a standard test is that the same items or test stimuli are given to all subjects in the same order, with the same instructions and time limits. Overall, the testing environment is reasonably constant with regard to privacy, quiet, lighting, and the like, though differing in other ways. The basic instructions given the subject are identical or nearly so; in group and self-administered procedures they are usually printed on the test forms. The attitude of the examiner is usually relatively neutral; he projects a warm interest, an air of concerned curiosity, but the basic transaction is between patient and test materials rather than patient and tester. The psychologist tries, as far as possible, to say and do about the same things with each patient without becoming a mechanical robot. The examiner attempts to induce attitudes appropriate to the test; to work as efficiently as possible on a test of mental ability; to be as frank as possible on a personality inventory, and to fantasy as freely as possible on a picture-telling technique. Where possible, recording is done in fixed ways and scoring by the established rules.

Obviously, tests differ greatly in the degree to which they allow standard procedure. The more structured the test task, the easier it is to follow fixed procedures of administration, recording, and scoring. Those techniques which give the subject greater freedom in response, necessarily allow more variation in recording and processing material given by the patient. The ideally standardized test, in the minds of some psychologists, would be one which would obviate completely the need for a human, hence fallible, mediator between the subject and the test tasks. This ideal is barely approximated by the most standardized tests in clinical practice; many, such as the projective tests of personality, involve the tester's judgment not only in their administration, but also in the recording, analysis, and interpretation of the resulting responses. Indeed, some psychologists (e.g., Zubin, Eron, and Schumer, 1965) have suggested that it would be better to view projective tests more as interviews than as tests, properly speaking. However, in the actual comparison it is clear that even projective tests are far more standardized than interviews, wherein lies their strength. It appears that standardization, like virtue and unlike virginity, is more a relative than an absolute state.

Of greater importance is the fact that although we can control many relevant factors in the testing situation, others elude our control. The tester may say the same words, but patients filter them through different histories and expectations. We can try to establish "rapport," induce cooperation, and act in a friendly, warm manner, but the patient may still be threatened by us, and respond positively or negatively to qualities we might deem irrelevant, such as our age, sex, or skin color. Despite our intent and overt motives, the dynamics of the testing situation, as Schafer (1954) noted, draws on our unconscious motives and problems. Test standardization reduces, but hardly removes, the range of factors which can influence test performance. Hence our ability to describe with some accuracy the patient's characteristics depends on our knowledge as well as our control of the assessment situation.

NORMS

In psychological testing, the performance of an individual can be described by comparing his scores with those obtained by others. Test developers are advised to publish norms describing the frequency distribution of scores obtained in as broad a sample as possible of the relevant population (APA, 1974). On many tests, the actual ("raw") score obtained matters little, for items could have been more or less difficult; what defines a person's ability is his relative position with regard to others. To describe the individual's score in relation to normative groups, psychometric workers have developed a variety of scoring methods, including standard scores, T-scores, and percentile scores (for discussion of these and other methods, see Ghiselli, 1964, or Cronbach, 1970). An individual is called "average" if he scores at or close to the group mean, "superior" if above, and "inferior" if below. Obviously, norms must be appropriately representative. Particularly as critical decisions such as hiring, placement in retarded classes, entry to school, and the like are made on the basis of "cutoff scores" the appropriateness of the norms that define them becomes a vital issue. Much of the current controversy, it might be noted, about the use of standard tests with minority people revolves on the question of whether the normative samples in terms of which the tests are scored and consequently test-related decisions made, represent them fairly.

Test makers often cannot anticipate the variety of populations with which tests will be used and it is necessary for test users to develop local norms. In a less formal sense, each tester develops personal norms as he cumulates experience with particular procedures. Before using a test, a psychologist should study the published norms to discover their appropriateness to his own work, and extend them through a more-or-less systematic collection of data in his own setting.

Developing norms for personality and clinical tests is vastly more complicated than for ability tests. Usually there is no single score, but rather a profile of scores or a set of indicators. Other facets of test performance require subjective judgment and clinical interpretation to arrive at the "test results." MMPI workers have carefully tabulated the distribution of different profiles as they appear in different populations; similarly, Rorschach workers have calculated the frequency with which particular classes of responses are given by reference groups. Such norms guide, but do not decide, the interpretation of personality test results. Interpreting particular scores, patterns of scores, or the meaning of particular responses is facilitated by the availability of norms, but judgment as to the nature of the patient's personality necessarily involves interpretative steps beyond comparison with normative samples. However, all possible normative data, both systematically gathered and, as it were, in the clinician's head, are valuable in this as in all realms of testing.

RELIABILITY

Reliability refers to the repeatability and precision of measurement. If a measure were ideally reliable, then any change in test score should reflect a change in the attribute being assessed. A test is unreliable to the extent that its scores are determined by chance factors. If one visualizes a hypothetically "true" value, then the reliable measure is the one which comes closest to approximating it. There are both systematic and random sources of error in virtually all measurement, particularly in psychology; the quest for reliability is to reduce the range of error within which the hypothetically true value lies. There is no single respect in which a test can be described as reliable or not. The study of reliability involves various attempts to describe agreement among measurement acts.

The concept of reliability has two major facets expressed in the terms "stability" and "consistency." Stability refers to the reproducibility of the measure over time. If the test is given on two occasions, the same results should be obtained, provided that the attribute being measured has not changed in the meanwhile. This is the familiar test-retest reliability, usually expressed as a coefficient of correlation between successive testing of the same subjects. Consistency refers to agreement between measurements taken simultaneously, usually involving equivalent forms of the test. Where possible, psychologists have attempted to develop parallel tests (equivalent-forms reliability) or correlated half of the items with the remaining half (split-half reliability). In procedures requiring judgment as to the scoring of items, the ratings made by two or more scorers are correlated to establish consistency in the procedure.

In principle, tests should be reliable by standards of both stability and consistency. Sometimes test developers lean more heavily on one or the other approach, because of the nature of the phenomenon being studied or the form of the test. Thus, where subjects could learn the particular answers to items, retest reliability would be deceptive. Similarly, personality processes such as, for example, emotional state predictably change over time and repeat measures would give a false picture of unreliability. Testing for reliability by equivalent-forms or split-half is difficult in the case of procedures with few and complex test stimuli, such as the Rorschach. On the whole, projective tests have fared poorly in reliability studies by the standards of psychometric research. Where the purpose of measurement is a global personality description, as is most usually the case in clinical practice, then emphasis on reliability and validity at the level of items, test scores, scales, and score profiles has to be supplanted by study of the total process including the clinician's ability to synthesize data from all levels. Thus, Holzberg (1960) among others, has suggested that the proper study of the reliability of the Rorschach should involve having clinicians independently prepare personality descriptions and then matching them for correspondence or difference. The essential questions of stability and consistency remain, but the locus of analysis moves from the more microscopic level of test items and scores to the macroscopic level of clinical judgment and interpretation. This logic holds as well for the study of validity in clinical assessment.

VALIDITY

Stated broadly, the term "validity" describes the utility of a test or assessment procedure and how well it achieves its aims (APA, 1974). The issue of validity brings us to the most central of the psychologist's concerns: What do the test results mean? Can they help us do our job better? What can the test be used for? Do they improve our ability to make clinical decisions? As a concept in measurement, validity carries us beyond the test itself—unlike reliability—to the relation with the phenomenon being studied. The question of validity must always be qualified by "for what?" and often "by whom?" and "under what circumstances?" We can speak of a procedure as being valid for differential diagnosis, for predicting discharge, or for identifying thought disorder. The commonly heard statement that "a test is valid if it measures what it is supposed to," is too simple a proposition.

As there are many possible purposes of tests, there are different possible approaches to study validity. The APA Standards (1974) distinguish four major approaches.

Content Validity. Content validity is concerned with showing that the test items cover the range of behaviors which we are trying to assess. The concept has special significance for achievement and aptitude tests, where items are in the nature of a work sample of the behavior being studied. Since test items can only be a sampling of the larger domain, we should want to be sure that all relevant facets are included. Thus, a behavior checklist intended to describe patients' anxiety should contain behavioral, verbal, and psychophysiological items, it should inquire into defensive acts, evidence of disorganization, cognitive dysfunctioning, and the like, just as a general history test should sample all nations and periods rather than being restricted, say, to American colonial history. The term "face validity" is sometimes used as roughly synonymous with content validity, to indicate the fact that the procedure would appear to be in the right territory. This, as we have noted, is a characteristic of rationally derived procedures, which may or may not be valid by other standards. Here, as elsewhere, appearances can be deceiving. However, as noted earlier, content validity may be a necessary if not altogether sufficient condition for the usefulness of a personality inventory.

Concurrent and Predictive Validity. Concurrent and predictive validity both depend on the relationship between test measures and some independent *criterion;* the difference between them lies in whether the criterial data are presently available or to be gathered at some future point. In both cases, a *validity coefficient* expresses the magnitude of the correlation between test and criterion measures. Where there is considerable information already available and it would be time-consuming and costly to gather further data, concurrent validation is likely to be done. Often this involves the use of other tests, judges' ratings, or behavioral observations, presumed to measure the same variable. Predictive validation, as the name suggests, depends on predicting from the present test to future behaviors. Thus, if one wished to develop a new intelligence test for children, test items could be given to a large group and scores correlated with the Stanford-Binet, or with teacher ratings, or school grades (concurrent validation). Alternatively, one could predict future performance, correlating present test scores with grades as they become available (predictive validation). Obviously, the two approaches could be used successively. In principle, if the ultimate purpose of the test is to predict performance (e.g., selection), then a predictive test is more appropriate. Concurrent criteria can be used if the intent is to develop a better measure for which there are already existing standards.

A critical issue immediately becomes apparent. By what criteria is the criterion to be decided? If the new test is to improve on existing methods, then to validate it by correlation with these tests is contradictory. In principle, the validity criterion should be a better, truer, or more accurate measure, or there would be little point in using it. Yet it is not uncommon to find new test scores correlated, for example, with psychiatric diagnoses, supervisor ratings, or school grades, which, indeed, the test is expected to eventually supplant. If a test fails to predict such a rating, one is hard put to decide whether the fault lies in the test or in the rating. In future predictive studies, there is not only the problem of deciding what and how to assess, but when measurement should be made and whether extraneous rather than test-relevant factors have not decided the outcome. For example, if a measure is proposed to predict hospital improvement, using discharge as a criterion, one should want to be quite sure, at the least, that the hospital does not change discharge policies in the meanwhile.

Construct Validity. Construct validity describes a strategy for establishing measures of theoretically defined concepts for which there are no simple, definite, or commonly accepted criterion measures for the characteristic to be assessed. For many of the concepts by which we understand personality functioning, construct validation is both necessary and a method of choice. It depends on the gradual accumulation of evidence from diverse research studies showing a network of relationships between the particular measure and other, theoretically relevant concepts. "Nomological net" is the term used by Cronbach and Meehl (1955) who first named and elaborated the concept of construct validity. Such relationships should be deducible from the theoretical context of the concept being studied. Thus, if one wishes to validate a measure of anxiety, research should be undertaken to discover whether the measure is elevated under conditions of experimental stress, when people are in life crises, when there is weakening of defenses, whether it correlates with psychophysiological measures such as heart rate and galvanic skin response and with stress-related endocrine changes, whether it relates to self-reported mood changes and observers' ratings, whether it distinguishes phobic from hysteric patients, and whether values decrease after taking tranquilizing drugs or following appropriate psychological intervention. Furthermore, one should demonstrate that the measure is *not* related to theoretically irrelevant variables. Obviously, this can be a long and arduous process without a finite end, resulting only in stepwise gains in confidence. For many of the subtle, yet conceptually important indicators of clinical assessment, construct-validity studies are clearly desirable. In a seminal paper, D. T. Campbell and Fiske (1959) proposed a method for establishing construct validity which they termed the "multitrait-multimethod matrix."

In evaluating the practical utility of a test, it is important to discover the extent to which it adds information above that already known. It is the *incremental validity* of a procedure that proves its worth, particularly if other information is more cheaply or readily available. To justify the test it should add precision or certainty to predictions which can be made without it. To be correct in its own right is not sufficient.

Similarly, where there is knowledge as to the frequency of a certain outcome (characteristic, diagnosis, etc.), then the validity of the test has to be shown as exceeding predictions that could be made from knowledge of the *base-rate* itself (Meehl and Rosen, 1955). If for example it is known that all patients considered, 70 percent improve in psychotherapy, then a prediction that each patient would improve (with no other information or measurement) would be correct 70 percent of the time. If a test is to be useful in predicting therapeutic outcome, it would have to be correct in excess of 70 percent.

The issue of validity is nowhere near as simple as it might appear at first glance. There is no single sense in which a test is or is not valid; it is more useful for some purposes and not others, in some hands, under some conditions. There are alternate strategies for studying validity and there is the persistent "criterion problem." Indeed, for the philosophic and scientific ambiguities in the concept, based as it is on the notion that there is an ideally "true" measure independent of measurement operations and conditions, Ebel (1964) has proposed that the concept be abandoned. Instead, he proposes that the quality of an assessment measure depends on (1) the importance of the inferences which can be made from its scores; (2) the "meaningfulness" of its scores; and (3) its convenience. Meaningfulness, his core notion, in turn depends on operational understanding of the measurements made, knowledge of relationships between the measure and other relevant variables (including, thus, validity coefficients of a predictive or concurrent sort and the network of relationships of the sort which describes construct validity), as well as reliability and appropriate norms. These criteria, it seems to me, amply incorporate the qualities which should ideally be found in psychological tests.

Should THIS Patient Be Tested?

In principle, a patient should be tested if so doing adds usable information for clinical treatment or decision-making. The time, effort, and cost of testing should be avoided if the test gives us unusable or uncertain information or if it duplicates what is already known. To be able to confidently decide whether it is advantageous to test a particular patient depends on assessing what is known and needs to be known about the patient, his current state, the alternatives available for his future treatment, as well as the properties of available tests. To wisely integrate these considerations is the measure of an experienced and skillful clinician.

A number of practical as well as conceptual issues enter into the decision to test a particular patient.

1. The more important the issues at stake, the greater the need for additional information. If decisions have to be made about hospitalization, criminal prosecution, or costly or potentially dangerous treatments, all available contributions to decision-making should be sought. If a patient is potentially suicidal, it is more

critical to discover the sources and extent of his depression than, for example, to explore the mood swings of an adolescent suffering existential malaise. When long-term psychotherapy is contemplated, extensive personality testing is more relevant than if the patient can only be seen for short-term intervention.

2. Testing is less valuable where there is already most or all of the information necessary for answering the referral questions. If the purpose of assessment is diagnosis and the patient has clearly manifested "textbook symptoms" in clinical interviews and observation, then testing is not likely to add much. In point of fact, such cases are rarely referred in actual clinical practice. The confusing, opaque, defensive patient, the borderline patient, or one with mixed symptoms is more likely to be referred for psychological testing.

3. Test data are more desirable if they can add specific information not available in other ways. Thus, for example, in the diagnosis of organic brain pathology, test findings indicating particular types of intellectual deficit supplement what can be known from clinical interviews and neurological measures.

4. Testing is costly, and its value has to be balanced against the expense of materials and the time and effort involved. Some critics have suggested that more time is spent in testing than is justified by the contribution made and that psychologists should reduce testing time by perhaps 40 percent (Hathaway, 1959). Whether such an estimate is accurate or not is less important than that we realize that testing is costly and should be used judiciously. Not only does testing consume valuable professional time, it also requires time and effort from patients. Using paper-and-pencil, self-administered and objectively scored tests, where applicable, can save the time required for individual clinical testing. Still, the patient has to invest his time in what may be a fairly dull or even threatening activity.

5. The meaning of testing to the patient and its potential impact on the clinical relationship has always to be carefully considered. For some, taking psychological tests is a strange, artificial, and possibly threatening experience. The guarded and suspicious person sees tests as penetrating, against his will, to his innermost and hidden secrets. He is frightened of the prospect at being found stupid, inadequate, or crazy. Clinical testing recalls school examinations and evaluation anxiety and resentment are often aroused. Others see the test tasks as trivial and childish, unrelated to their concerns, and as having little face validity. Ideally, tests should be administered when and as the patient understands their purpose, need, and potential contribution; at the least, tests should be accepted in the same faith as interviews and other clinical activities. Consequently, even if test findings are desirable from our vantage point, testing should be held off if it would realistically endanger the ongoing clinical relationship. Sometimes, it should be noted, the situation is reversed; the patient finds testing more comfortable than talking about himself and his problems. The relative impersonality and artificiality of the testing transaction can allow, as well as block, communication. Either way, the advisability of testing depends on the meaning of testing to the patient within the larger clinical context.

Choice of Test

Procedures used in the assessment of a particular patient should, ideally, be those best suited to answer specifically the referral questions, as these emerge from earlier assessment and are clarified by the referring and testing clinicians. Such questions may be of a focused sort, for which a single, standardized test may be sufficient. More usually, however, initial interviews and clinical observation may have located some salient issues, but the need remains for these to be explored and understood in terms of a broad-scaled analysis of psychological functioning, personality structure, and dynamics. The referral questions narrow down, but rarely bring to sharp focus, the problems for which further information is required. Clinical testing, thus, continues the initial survey, and itself may define questions which can then be studied by more limited and often more precise procedures in a second round of testing.

In consequence, a *test battery* is more often used than any single procedure. A test battery consists of a group of tests, which together give a broader and firmer base for assessment than is possible with individual tests. The battery should be chosen to be as responsive as possible to the particular needs of the individual patient. In the psychodynamic tradition, a common battery for testing adults for therapy planning includes, as a nucleus, the Wechsler Adult Intelligence Scale, Rorschach, and TAT. Although the same basic battery may be used, such procedures are interpretable toward different ends. Thus, the individualization of a psychological examination involves varying one's orientation toward the analysis and interpretation of data yielded by the *same* battery of broad-gauged tests as well as putting together a unique package of different procedures for each patient. In practice, the two alternatives are often combined; a common nucleus is used with procedures added to answer specific questions.

Sometimes a battery is used in much the same way with each patient, providing the referring clinician with a broad-scaled personality analysis, whether he wants it or not. In some cases, this results in a kind of "information overkill," for the referring clinician may only need to know or be able to use responses to quite specific questions. (The situation is not unlike the anxious parent who replies to the child's question "Did the stork bring me?" with a long lecture on sex.) Needless to say, overloading, just as vagueness and lack of appropriate detail, frustrates the responsible clinician, as well as the assessor who has invested much time and skill to little purpose.

Routine test batteries are sometimes used in clinics or hospitals for the clinical screening of incoming patients or to provide a base for evaluation research. Ordinarily, such batteries include briefer, self-administered procedures, perhaps group tests, including self-report inventories, paper-and-pencil group intelligence measures, or projective tests, such as a sentence-completion test. There is advantage to having uniform data available on all patients, although routine testing may supplement but cannot substitute for individualized referral testing. Routine testing carries the danger too of being insensitive to the patient's concerns and fears in coming to the clinic. It can too readily be interpreted as a kind of bureaucratic "entrance exam," mechanically imposed on the patient to test his worthiness to obtain help. When routine screening tests are administered, the clinic must also convey to the patient why this procedure is necessary for his care. Such tests should always follow, never precede, a first interview.

Tests are to be selected in accordance with the patient's general attributes as well as the specific referral questions. Obviously, a child should be given tests designed for children; women should be tested on the "woman's form," and scored to women's norms; a Rorschach should not be administered to a blind man, nor a written test to an illiterate; a spastic child cannot be expected to assemble block designs on a timed test. All of this is self-evident, but we need to remind ourselves that individual needs and personal qualities must constantly be foremost in the clinician's mind in designing testing programs. Many procedures have been developed and standardized for patients with particular handicaps and limitations. There are tests for the blind, deaf, motor-handicapped, and illiterate and it is the task of the psychologist to know of their existence and call on them when necessary. Sometimes, however, the issues are more subtle, as in the case of people from particular subcultures. Thus, for example, if a Chicano child must be tested in English, special care has to be taken in simplifying or rephrasing instructions and test items, choosing performance rather than verbal tests, and the like. Groups and individuals have their own vocabularies, in both a limited and extended sense, and, as already noted in the case of interviewing, the testing transaction must be in terms of shared vocabulary for it to be at all meaningful.

These considerations make clear that the clinician must be sensitive, ingenious, and inventive. It is sometimes necessary to improvise new procedures or alter standard tests even on the spur of the moment. Clinical wisdom may dictate calling a halt to a test which is disturbing to a patient, perhaps returning to it when he has gained composure. Some years ago it was shown that children taking the Stanford-Binet may do better overall by alternating easy and difficult subtests, for proceeding up a scale of difficulty until failure is reached may lead to blocking or loss of motivation under a cumulating sense of inadequacy (Hutt, 1947). When dealing with a frightened child, it can make good sense to vary standard procedure in such a way. An alternative would be to complete the test in standard fashion and then return to particular items to see if the child, now more relaxed, can handle them. At this point, the child can be encouraged, given hints, items can be simplified, all to the end of exploring the child's abilities under the most favoring circumstances. Variation from standard procedure means, of course, that available norms may be inapplicable. However, the gain in personologically useful information can offset the loss of standardization and norms.

The testing relationship is dynamic and changing. The clinician is constantly alert to the patient's behavior and comments. Any cues from the patient's general behavior, as well as the specific test responses, provide information valuable for later analyses and interpretation. In the process of testing and observing the patient, the clinician develops and changes his hypotheses and, as necessary, adds new procedures, alters existing ones, or even invents new ones. Wanton variation amounts to unreliability and leads to findings which cannot be interpreted. On the other hand, intentional variation to test hypotheses yields valuable, if not standardized, findings. The experienced tester should have sufficiently broad experience with his tests to know the probable consequences of procedural variation, and to account for it in later interpretations. It is precisely along these lines that an expert clinician differs from a psychometric technician. The clinician has (1) greater knowledge of what determines test responses; (2) greater sensitivity to subtle clues which can lead him to temper future interpretations and/or alter his present procedure; and (3) a more extensive framework within which to predict the probable consequences of his acts.

Determinants of Test Performance

Clearly, the test performance of a patient is determined by many more factors than the attributes we mean to assess. If the procedure is completely unreliable and the performance is more determined by unintended than intended variables, it should not be used. However, expecting psychological tests to function as, for example, a ruler does in the measurement of length is an unrealizable hope. At their best, psychological tests can be more appropriately compared to medical procedures, like the X-ray and electrocardiogram, where variables of many sorts, relevant and extraneous, determine test findings, and a skilled clinician has to disentangle and interpret their meaning.

In developing and using psychological tests, the psychologist's task is to control as many of the performance-determining factors as possible and to understand and be able to account for the action of others. Only then can we with some certainty learn something about the personal attributes we intended to assess. In earlier discussions of the clinical relationship, test standardization, validation, and interviewing, note has already been taken of the variety of determinants of a patient's behavior in assessment. At this point, we can summarize the major classes of such determinants, commenting on some of them briefly. The schema which follows is intended to orient the student, and to caution him against overly simple assumptions as to the meaning of test responses.

For simplicity, we can divide test-performance determinants into those which, in a general sense, are in the *test*, in the *examiner*, in the *situation*, and in the *patient*. Among the patient variables, we can further distinguish those related to the patient's *attitude toward testing in general. toward this particular test*, *state factors* (see below), and the *personal attributes* with which we are ultimately most concerned. Such categorization is admittedly arbitrary, but it can help to visualize the range of relevant factors.

An Outline of Factors Which Determine Test Performance

TEST VARIABLES

1. Stimuli and Test Items. The patient's test responses depend directly on the stimuli to which he is responding. Changes in stimuli, gross or subtle, can consequently affect response. If the MMPI were reprinted daily by newspapers, we could never compare the responses of different patients for we could never be

sure they were reading the same items. In more subtle ways, ink-blot qualities, the number of response categories in inventories, the form of questions—whether stated affirmatively or negatively—and many similar factors influence response.

2. Sequence of Items or Subtests Within a Test and Order of Tests in a Battery. Earlier items can induce expectations or alter the state of the subject so that later portions of the test or later tests in a battery are influenced.

3. Clarity of Instructions. The instructions should make clear the subject's task in understandable terms. He should be able to ask clarifying questions. In ability tests, scoring criteria should be known to the patient, whether speed, accuracy, and neatness are required.

4. Method of Administration. Is a clock visible? Are one or a number of items before the patient at the same time? Is the test individually or group administered? Together with how many and what kind of people is the patient tested?

EXAMINER VARIABLES

1. Characteristics. The examiner's age, sex, race or ethnic background, social class, cultural similarity or dissimilarity, are all of consequence in terms of their meaning to the patient.

2. Attitudes Toward the Patient. Does the examiner like, respect, feel warmly or coldly toward the patient? What preconceptions and expectations does he have about the patient? What attitudes does he project in relation to his own self-concept as "clinician"? An extensive research literature has grown in recent years documenting "examiner" or "experimenter effects" on the subject's performance in testing and psychological experimental situations (see Masling, 1960, 1966; R. R. Rosenthal, 1966, 1967, for reviews).

SITUATIONAL VARIABLES

1. Physical Context. Illumination, size and type of room, furnishings, distractions, and the like all can affect test results.

2. Social Context. Whether the testing is done in a hospital, clinic, court, university classroom, or other setting carries different social meanings for patients, which may be reflected in test performance.

3. The Clinical Relationship. Has the tester previously interviewed the patient? Has trust been established? Does the patient expect to continue seeing the clinician in a therapeutic role or is this a one-time encounter?

PATIENT VARIABLES

Attitudes Toward Being Tested in General

1. Previous Experience with "Tests." The meaning of testing to the patient. Is he "test-wise," knowledgeable about how tests are constructed and how they are to be taken?

2. Sociocultural Attitudes Toward Testing. The story is told that a class of Hopi children were given a group intelligence test with instructions to turn papers face down when each had finished, so that individual time scores could be recorded. Instead, they all turned their papers over when the last had finished, which reflected the Hopi emphasis on cooperative rather than competitive

achievement. It is considered improper to assert superiority at the expense of others. In less dramatic forms, other subcultural groups have other values which affect the ways in which they approach and perform on tests.

Attitudes in the Particular Testing Session or Related to Particular Procedures

1. Motivation. Is the patient trying to impress the examiner, do well on tests, is he eager and concerned or lackadaisical, trying to prove his innocence or show how badly disturbed he is? Are the test tasks inherently interesting or seemingly trivial? An important finding in the study of schizophrenia is that the typically poor and erratic performance on tests of mental ability may be more a function of the patient's disinterest and lack of cooperation than of any real deficit in ability. In constructing tests for schizophrenics it is wise, therefore, to compare performance in different realms and assess relative deficit, rather than using unidimensional scales to evaluate absolute levels of ability. Moreover, the less one can suppose that the patient (whether schizophrenic, criminal, or college student) approaches testing with the expected set, the more necessary is it for the clinician to know what the patient's motivation actually is, as well as to encourage an appropriate level of cooperation and commitment.

2. Test-Taking Attitudes ("Response Styles" or "Response Sets"). A related issue, of particular importance in interpreting personality inventories, has been termed "response style" or "response set." These describe the orientations patients set themselves, consciously or unconsciously, which leads them to consistently choose one kind of response rather than another. In discussing person perception, we have already noted tendencies toward leniency, reluctance to use extreme categories, the "halo effect" and similar processes. Even in psychophysical judgments—for example, in judging the loudness of two tones—subjects differ in their readiness to say "louder" or "softer" and consequently give more or less "equal" judgments. In research on personality inventories, a number of response attitudes have been identified and studied extensively. Among others (1) *acquiescence,* the tendency to respond "true" on true-false items; (2) *deviation,* the tendency to choose the extreme response; (3) *social desirability,* to endorse items in a socially acceptable direction, and (4) *defensiveness,* to deny inadequacies. Efforts have been made to control response sets by altering the form of items. Thus, items can be stated in negative as well as positive form as a control on acquiescence. Edwards (1953, 1957) launched the concern with social desirability and designed his own Personal Preference Schedule in a fashion intended to avert its effects. Instead of subjects endorsing self-report items as true or false, pairs of items were matched for social desirability, and subjects are required to choose between them (Edwards, 1959). Vigorous controversy continues over the importance of attitudes such as social desirability and acquiescence, some holding that they impugn the validity of inventories, while others, notably Block (1965) in a tightly reasoned argument, defend the view that their importance has been greatly overrated.

3. Sociocultural Interpretations of Test Items. Test items have to make sense in terms of the patient's particular cultural or group experiences. The intelligence test item "If lost in a forest, how would you find your way out?" is obviously meaningless to a youngster brought up in a Brooklyn slum, where at most there is the one proverbial tree. More subtle, and as important, is the fact that the

individual draws on social frames of reference in responding to any novel situation, tests included. Thus, the self-report item prefixed by "often" or "sometimes" is judged by the patient's standards, dependent on what he knows to be common or occasional in his social world, which may be quite different from the test developer's or interpreter's.

The Patient's State

If our concern is to assess enduring attirbutes of the individual, rather than his momentary state, it is important to distinguish the effects of such state variables on our "trait" measures. *State factors* are important in their own right and can properly be the focus of assessment.

1. Physiological State. Fatigue, hunger, physical pain, recent drug use, and similar factors can all have profound effects on test findings.

2. Psychological State. Similarly, the patient's present emotional condition, whether he is anxious, angry, depressed, or relaxed, matters greatly. For example, we can seriously misread the potential intellectual ability of a severely depressed patient if a timed test is given and evaluated by normal standards. A prime characteristic of such patients is a distinct slowing of activities and response.

3. Capacity to Understand Instructions and Carry out Task Activities. If the language is strange and too complexly worded, or the patient too confused, distractible or preoccupied, he may function poorly even though he has requisite abilities. Necessary instrumental skills must be available. An elderly patient with gross tremor of the hands cannot be expected to function on a test requiring writing or fine motor coordination.

Personal Attributes

Finally we come to the personal attributes, which testing is primarily intended to assess, that is, the patient's needs, motives, values, traits, abilities, conflicts, defenses, and the like.

In view of all that *can* determine test behavior, how can we ever be sure we are assessing these personal attributes? Strictly speaking, we cannot. Clinical testing strains the clinician's ability to withstand frustration and tolerate uncertainty. Indeed, some psychologists have despaired at the possibility of ever having dependable assessment techniques of any general utility, except perhaps for narrowly defined psychological variables. A more hopeful attitude, shared by most students of personality and clinical assessment, is based on the faith that it is possible to identify many or most of the performance-determining factors and then to develop new tests, or interpret existing ones, in ways which limit the role of "extraneous" variables. Our capacity to control, as noted earlier, is necessarily limited. The task, then, becomes one of knowing and accounting for the potential contribution of the many factors involved. Our measures of human personality and psychological functioning are necessarily overdetermined; our task is to know and disentangle the contributions of variables of all sorts and to temper interpretations accordingly. This requires study of the research literature and cumulating experience in testing patients. With this background, clinicians can use imperfect techniques wisely.

There is a danger in being overdependent on psychological tests to answer clinical assessment questions and of losing the person in the test findings. Test-derived hypotheses have constantly to be checked against clinical observation and interview. Test findings should never be treated as if they were self-evidently "true" measures, a belief too common among the clients and coprofessionals of clinical psychologists. Ultimately, the value and power of tests lie in the skill and knowledge of the clinician who uses them. They are tools of great potential, but like other tools depend on the hand of the craftsman.

With all their limitations, clinical tests provide standard conditions for assessing relevant behavior, particularly when compared to available alternatives. They can increase the objectivity, scope, and depth of clinical assessment. They complement, extend, and provide checks on clinical findings. In a later chapter, we will further consider issues in the interpretation, synthesis, and communication of assessment findings, which increase the value of psychological tests. First, however, we shall examine in closer detail some of the procedures most commonly used in clinical practice.

CHAPTER 10

Psychological Testing: II. Tests in Clinical Use

Tests Used by Clinicians

In 1969, 251 agencies which had clinical psychologists on their staffs replied to a questionnaire concerning psychological testing (Lubin, Wallis, and Paine, 1971). Although clinicians in private practice and university psychological clinics were not included, the sample covered a wide range of state psychiatric hospitals, state institutions for the mentally retarded, Veterans' Administration psychiatric hospital and clinic services, outpatient psychiatric clinics, community clinics and comprehensive community mental health centers, and counseling centers. In similar surveys, Sundberg (1961) reported test usage in 1959, and Louttit and Browne (1947) described usage in 1946 and in 1935. Hence, it is possible to observe trends over virtually the entire modern history of clinical psychology. Although styles change, new procedures enter and old ones are dropped, the Stanford-Binet, the basic standby of prewar clinicians, has remained in the "top ten" over the four decades. Since the time the Wechsler Intelligence Scales were published, each has been heavily used. From the postwar era on down to the present, the major projective techniques have maintained their preeminent positions, although there is indication of growing interest in objective personality inventories.

In all, 72 different tests were mentioned by at least 10 percent of the responding institutions. The ten most commonly used tests included three general intelligence scales (Wechsler Adult Intelligence Scale [WAIS], Wechsler Intelligence Scale for Children [WISC], and the Stanford-Binet); five projective techniques (Rorschach, Thematic Apperception Test [TAT], Machover Draw-A-Person, House-Tree-Person, and Rotter Incomplete Sentences Blank); one personality inventory [MMPI]; and the Bender-Gestalt Visual Motor Test. The counseling centers differed from the hospitals and clinics in their proportionately greater use of vocational interest tests and objective personality inventories, and correspondingly less reliance on individual than group procedures.

The tests clinicians use can be grouped into a number of broad classes, according to the area assessed and the form of the test. These classes are briefly described below, illustrated by particular tests. For more detailed description of particular procedures and references to the often extensive research literature, Buros (1972, 1974, 1975), Cronbach (1970) or similar volumes on psychological testing should be consulted. Later in this chapter some of the more important and commonly used procedures will be discussed individually.

GENERAL INTELLECTUAL FUNCTIONING

These tests are designed to tap a variety of intellectual functions and give an overall estimate of general intelligence or ability. They often consist of a variety of subtests, the scores on which combine to an IQ. Tests are usually standardized either for children (e.g., WISC or Stanford-Binet) or adults (WAIS). Efforts have been made to develop nonverbal tests, of value in testing the foreign-born, illiterate, or handicapped (e.g., Revised Beta, Progressive Matrices, Leiter International Performance Scale). The Porteus Mazes, which require only that a patient trace a path through a printed maze, has been widely used in clinics because it assesses deficit due to psychopathology. Picture-vocabulary tests require only that subjects name the objects depicted.

SPECIFIC COGNITIVE FUNCTIONS, PSYCHOLOGICAL DEFICIT, AND THOUGHT DISTURBANCE

In principle, any procedure designed to evaluate perception, memory, problem solving, information processing, language, and other cognitive functioning in the laboratory, can serve in the clinic and many have, particularly in research on deficit or thought disorders in severely disturbed patients. Specific perceptual procedures, such as Witkin's measures of field independence and field dependence (1954, 1962), have considerable potential utility. Chief among the procedures more commonly used is Bender's Visual-Motor Gestalt Test (or Bender-Gestalt) which requires that the subject copy nine designs presented sequentially. Distortions in the reproductions are indicative of brain damage and psychological deficit and at the same time reveal personality trends. Another commonly used procedure of the same general type is the Memory-for-Designs test. A general test of orientation, learning, and recall is the Wechsler Memory Scale. A variety of procedures have been developed to test the subject's ability to conceptualize and abstract by requiring him, for example, to group objects of the same category (e.g., Hanfmann-Kasanin or Vigotsky Concept Formation Test and Goldstein-Scheerer Tests of Abstract and Concrete Thinking). Because the thinking deficit due to organic pathology or functional conditions is often best seen in the differential loss of conceptual functioning, when compared to a more stable measure of intellectual attainment such as vocabulary, performance of the Hanfmann-Kasanin or Goldstein-Scheerer is often compared with a vocabulary test or general IQ scores. The Shipley-Institute-for-Living Scale contains both a vocabulary and concept-formation portion, with the comparison between them yielding an estimate of potential deficit.

EARLY INTELLIGENCE AND PSYCHOLOGICAL DEVELOPMENT

A number of procedures exist for the study of infants and very young children. The more commonly used include the Cattell Infant Intelligence Scale, Bayley Scale, and Gesell Developmental Schedule. These procedures involve observations of the child which yield ratings of development in perceptual, motoric, language, personality, and social functioning. Of particular value in the study of mental retardation is the Vineland Social Maturity Scale which uses information obtained from the parents or other informants to assess developing competencies or defects.

ABILITIES, APTITUDES, AND ACHIEVEMENT

For specific purposes, for example, to assess specific skills, deficits, or knowledge for vocational counseling, clinicians can call on the large array of procedures developed for educational or vocational measurement. Among the more commonly used are broad-scaled procedures such as the Differential Aptitude Tests, Wide Range Achievement Tests, and Metropolitan Achievement Test. Others include the Minnesota Clerical, California Achievement Tests, and Cooperative School and College Ability Tests.

INTERESTS, VALUES, AND SOCIAL ATTITUDES

Related are those procedures which assess the subject's interests and orientations toward, rather than particular aptitudes for, occupational roles. Two well-known procedures are the Kuder Preference and the Strong Vocational Interest Blank (SVIB), which ask the subject to express preferences for particular types of activities. In standardization, the patterns of preference of people established in a number of fields were established and the subject's responses are scored against these norms. The SVIB was an early instance of empirical keying. More general orientations toward social values are measured by the Allport-Vernon-Lindzey Study of Values. This test derives from Spranger's system which describes six basic value orientations, namely, the theoretical, economic, esthetic, social, religious, and political. Morris' Paths of Life is a similar attempt to get at basic value orientations. Although not yet widely used in clinics, there have been recent attempts to assess the sense of meaning and purpose (e.g., Crumbaugh and Maholick's Purpose-in-Life Test, or McClosky and Schaar's Test of Anomia) which are of central importance in existential psychology.

PERSONALITY ASSESSMENT, BROAD FOCUS

As a convenience, we can distinguish between those procedures which attempt a reasonably broad picture of the individual personality from those which assess specific personality variables. In general, clinicians work more with broad-scaled, multivariable procedures, although increasing use is being made of specific-variable procedures, particularly in personality and clinical research. For the problems with which the clinician deals, personality assessment rather than the study of intelligence, aptitudes, or values, is the core of his concern. Personality tests are of central importance for the assessment of neurotic patients and those with personality or behavior problems and in the planning and evaluation of psychotherapy. In general, they are of two types: (1) self-report measures and inventories, which are typically more standardized, structured, and objective; and (2) projective techniques, which are less structured and depend more on clinical judgment.

Self-report measures and inventories. By far the most commonly used inventory is the MMPI. A related technique, developed for the assessment of normals and more tuned to the healthy dimensions of personality, is Gough's California Psychological Inventory. Other widely used inventories include the Sixteen Personality Factor Questionnaire (16PF), developed through factor analysis, the Edwards Personal Preference Schedule (EPPS), and the Guilford-Zimmerman Temperament Survey. Commonly used in the past, though less so today, are Bell's Adjustment Inventory and Bernreuter's Personality Inventory. These have been largely replaced by the MMPI, but references to them will often be found in the older literature. More direct self-description is obtained in symptom checklists, such as the Cornell Index or the Mooney Problem Check List. Adjective self-reports have been used in many forms, including the evaluation of emotional state (e.g., Clyde and Zuckerman), but their use in the assessment of personality characteristics is best exemplified by Gough and Heilbrun's Adjective Check List (ACL). A related procedure is the Q-sort, consisting of a large number of statements, which the subject sorts into piles from the one extreme of "most characteristic" to the other of "least characteristic." The number in each category is controlled to approximate a normal curve. The self-ratings can then be processed statistically. A thoroughly researched Q-sort deck has been developed by Block (1961). Both ACL and Q-sort can be used equally well for self-report or to describe a patient.

Projective techniques. Along with the interview, projective techniques —discussed in detail later on—are the clinician's major instruments for the study of the structure, mechanisms, and dynamics of the patient's personality. Among them, the Rorschach remains the most employed and studied. Increasing use is being made of Holtzman's inkblot technique derived from the Rorschach. It is better structured and psychometrically developed and allows for group administration. The TAT is the primary instrument for exploring a patient's needs, expectations, concerns, and conflicts. It has been adapted for use with children in the Childrens Apperception Test (CAT) by substituting drawings of animals which better stimulate children's fantasies. A do-it-yourself TAT was developed by Shneidman in his Make-A-Picture-Story test (MAPS), in which a variety of cardboard figures can be placed in different stage-settings. Having constructed his own stimulus picture, the subject then tells a story about it. The Tomkins-Horn Picture Arrangement Test (PAT), more objectively, gives the subject sets of three pictures which he has to arrange in meaningful sequence. Two popular procedures depend on interpretations of the subject's drawings. Machover's Draw-A-Person has the subject draw a person, after which he is asked to draw one of the opposite sex. The House-Tree-Person test, as the name suggests, requires drawings of the three objects. The Word Association test asks subjects to give the first word that comes to mind in response to a stimulus word. It was first used in clinical assessment early in this century. Various lists of words have been used, but most often they are those described by Kent and Rosanoff (1910) in their study of psychotic thinking. Similarly, the Sentence Completion Test is a procedure which has been used in many forms; at present the most popular is that proposed by Rotter and Rafferty. In the Sentence Completion Test, as its name implies, the patient is given the first part of a sentence and has to fill in the remainder.

SPECIFIC PERSONALITY VARIABLES

For research on personality processes, it is often advantageous to have measures of more limited scope, specifically aimed at the assessment of particular personality variables. Research in the field has led to the development of many such procedures, some of which have already come into general clinical use, while others would seem to have future usefulness. Tests of specific variables, like broader-gauged procedures, are either inventories or projective devices. Indeed, some are derived directly from "parent" tests through empirical or rational analysis. Thus, the popular Taylor Manifest Anxiety Scale and Barron's Ego Strength Scale are subsets of items drawn from the MMPI. The MMPI has fathered many such specific scales. Using the TAT, McClelland and his associates have developed a specific measure of "need achievement," which has been extensively investigated. A brief and relatively structured projective procedure is Rosenzweig's Picture Frustration Study (P-F). The subject is shown a series of cartoons showing frustrating social situations and he is to fill in the response of the frustrated person. The extent and direction of aggression is scored according to well-developed criteria. Blum's Blacky Pictures are designed to reveal psychosexual conflicts, as predicted from the Freudian theory of psychosexual development. Widely used inventories assessing important personality variables include the F scale of authoritarianism and Rotter's Locus of Control measure. Locus of Control describes the subject's experience as being master of his own fate or the victim of outside influences. It is impossible to name all the many variables for which new devices have been developed or standard tests adapted. Few, excepting those named here, have gained much usage in clinical assessment. It would probably be well if clinicians were familiar with and used such procedures in order to bring more specific findings to bear on particular referral questions.

OTHER ASSESSMENT MEASURES

Finally, attention should be drawn to other procedures of value to clinical assessment which are not tests, in the usual sense. The patient does not describe himself or perform test tasks in a standard situation. Instead, objective and quantified descriptions of the patient are derived from the observations of others as he behaves in his usual social environment or, in some cases, in clinical interviews. A number of scales have been developed to assess the extent and type of pathology of psychiatric patients based on the observations and ratings of clinicians and other hospital personnel. These include the Lorr and Klett Inpatient Multidimensional Psychiatric Scale, Wittenborn Psychiatric Rating Scales, Spitzer's Psychiatric Status Scale, and his Current and Past Psychopathology Scales, to name the most commonly used. To describe patients' roles and behavior in groups, the Bales Interpersonal Checklist has been used productively with patients as with normals in group interaction. *Peer ratings,* having patients comment on each other's behavior and personal characteristics, can yield important understanding of how the patient is viewed by others as well as how he sees them. The same sort of result, in a more complicated form, is expressed in *sociometric ratings.* The network of relationships in a group, for example, on a psychiatric ward or in a college class, are plotted by gathering the stated preferences of members for interaction with each other. For example, if each patient on a ward were asked, "With whom would you like most to go to the movies? . . . . share a room? . . . . be in the same work group?" patterns of leadership, respect, and alienation emerge. "Stars" and "isolates" are identified. Such ratings can describe the present stimulus value of each patient; they can also be used as a measure of the patient's improvement in the hospital. These illustrations are mentioned only to indicate the range of techniques available, and to note that formal assessment does not end with interviews and standard tests administered directly to the patient.

The Wechsler Adult Intelligence Scale (WAIS)

The Wechsler Intelligence Scales, which in addition to the WAIS include the Preschool-Primary Scale (WPPSI) for ages four to six-and-a-half and the Wechsler Intelligence Scale for Children (WISC) for children from seven to sixteen, are the leading tests of general ability or intelligence in use today. In 1955 the WAIS replaced the earlier Wechsler-Bellevue Scale in its secure place in the basic battery of tests for adults used by many clinicians. All of the Wechsler tests have the same basic structure. To sample a broad range of intellectual functions they consist of a number of subtests, which are administered in sequence. Within each test, items are of increasing difficulty. The WAIS includes six verbal tests, which together yield a Verbal IQ, and five performance tests which produce a Performance IQ. The Full Scale IQ is based on all eleven. These point scores are converted to IQs in terms of the distribution of scores obtained for people of the same age. Thus, although the point scores decrease for older people, the IQ remains relatively constant over the life span for adults. Taking as denominator the average point scores of the subjects' age group, rather than making the mental-age conversion used by the Stanford-Binet and similar procedures, is a better procedure for assessing adult intelligence.*

The standardization samples were chosen with care, including in the initial

* The Stanford-Binet defined IQ in terms of the equation: Mental Age ÷ Chronological Age = Intelligence Quotient. It is beyond our present purpose to consider the theory and measurement of intelligence, around which an extensive and fascinating literature has grown. For a brief overview of the major issues, Tuddenham (1962) is recommended. Wechsler (1958) should be read for more detailed discussion of the rationale, development, and standardization of the WAIS. General texts, such as Cronbach (1970) and Anastasi (1968), discuss the WAIS and other measures of general ability within a broad context of psychometric research.

studies over 1700 people, representing the American population along dimensions of age, sex, rural-urban residence, race, occupation, and education. Reliability coefficients have been calculated and published for each of the tests separately and for the Verbal, Performance, and Full Scale IQs for a number of separate age groups. The Performance IQs had reliability coefficients (odd-even) of .93 and .94; the Verbal IQs, .96; and the Full Scale IQs yield coefficients of .97 in each age sample. Considerable validation data are available. At the first level, content validity, of particular concern to Wechsler and most clinicians, is supported by the range of functions assessed and their importance in studies of normal and disturbed cognition. Empirical findings on concurrent validity is provided by studies of occupational and educational groups and of mental retardates as well as other patient groups. The WAIS correlates well with the Stanford-Binet (about .80 in various groups) and other individual and group measures. The study of relations among subtests, factor analyses, and experimental studies of people differing in WAIS scores have all contributed to its construct validity.

The importance of the WAIS in clinical testing extends beyond its capacity to supply reliable and valid estimates of general intelligence. Not only the principal scores, but the ways they pattern and the performance of the subject on individual scales are of interpretative significance. The behavior of the patient in testing, qualitative characteristics of his test responses, and evidences of stylistic and pathology-based impediments to functioning all enter importantly. The understanding of adaptive cognitive functioning depends on discovering *how* not only *whether* patients can reach solutions for test problems (Scheerer, 1946). The WAIS is often included in a battery which otherwise includes mainly projective techniques and self-report measures. Compared, for example, to other "performance" measures such as the Rorschach and TAT, it emphasizes logical and reality-appropriate thought processes. The patient's ability to function rationally with neutral tasks, paralleling the demands of everyday life, is under study. Thus, "A major role of the WAIS is to assess for the individual the characteristic and unique patterns of ego processes which he uses to integrate and adapt to reality demands" (Allison, Blatt, and Zimet, 1968, p. 22.) Within this ego-psychological framework, the interpretation of the WAIS was developed largely from the work of Rapaport and his colleagues (e.g., Rapaport, Gill, and Schafer, 1945, [rev. ed. 1968]; Schafer, 1948; Mayman, Schafer, and Rapaport, 1951), who extend the interpretation of the scales given by Wechsler himself (1958). For an overview of the current status of the Wechsler Scales, see Matarazzo (1972).

The Subtests and Their Interpretative Rationale

VERBAL SCALE

1. *Information* consists of twenty-nine questions covering a variety of topics which adults should know about by virtue of having lived in our culture. Specialized and technical information is avoided. Along with Vocabulary, the Information Test is one of those less affected by aging or pathology. Still, the repressive person will often do poorly while the pedantic and obsessive individual will score high, often giving pretentious responses.

2. *Comprehension* includes fourteen items in which the subject is asked to explain why certain practices are followed, to interpret proverbs, and to tell what should be done under certain circumstances (for example, if one finds a stamped, addressed envelope on the street). It is a measure of conventional knowledge and social appropriateness. The psychotic who is impaired in social judgment or the psychopath who flouts convention might both do poorly.

3. *Arithmetic* requires the subject to solve fourteen problems of the sort found in grade-school arithmetic texts. Problems are orally presented and paper and pencil cannot be used. Unlike the preceding tests which depend on previously acquired knowledge, arithmetic requires mental work at the time of the test. Successful solutions demand concentration and the effective use of previously learned principles within the time limits of the item.

4. *Similarities* consists of thirteen items which require the subject to state how two things are alike. This is a measure of verbal concept formation, in which different levels of abstract thinking can be revealed. Two objects can be likened in terms of their visible attributes, their functional properties, or in terms of more abstract concepts. The loss of abstract ability of the type found in brain damage and some acute schizophrenic states can result in low test scores.

5. *Digit Span* tests short-term memory for lists of digits, going from three to nine digits which are orally presented and must be immediately repeated back. This is followed by a second portion in which the subject must say the digits in reversed order. This procedure requires close, though relatively passive, attention. Predictably, therefore, if the subject is distractible, preoccupied, or anxious, he will fare poorly.

6. *Vocabulary* requires the subject to define forty words of increasing difficulty. Vocabulary is the best single measure of general intelligence. It correlates most highly with Full Scale IQ. It is the most stable of subtest scores over time and the most resistant to neurological damage and emotional disturbance. For this reason, the Vocabulary score is often used as the baseline against which to evaluate other tests. It is also the test most frequently used in short forms of the WAIS for quick screening or research. The Vocabulary level, like Comprehension but more so because moral principles are not involved, reflects the breadth of experiences and ideas developed over the years. Lack of educational opportunity and of early intellectual stimulation can lead to disproportionately low scores; hence, other baseline measures (total IQ, Performance scores, etc.) may have to be used in interpreting the intellectual functioning of many economically or culturally deprived subjects.

PERFORMANCE SCALE

7. *Digit Symbol* is a code-substitution test which has often been used in nonverbal test procedures. There are nine symbols paired with nine numbers. With the key before him, the subject must fill in as many of the blanks on the answer sheet as he can in one-and-a-half minutes (see Figure 10.1). There is relatively little learning, memory, problem-solving, or more abstract ability involved in this task. Rather, it taps the subject's capacity to muster energy and work in a concerted fashion on a rote task. Thus, a low Digit Symbol score, along with high Vocabulary, often accompanies depression. Because the Digit Symbol test, along with Digit Span and Block Design, is essentially neutral in content, some schizo-

FIGURE 10.1.
Some Items Similar to Those Used in the Wechsler Performance Subtests.
Reprinted by permission of The Psychological Corporation.

OBJECT ASSEMBLY

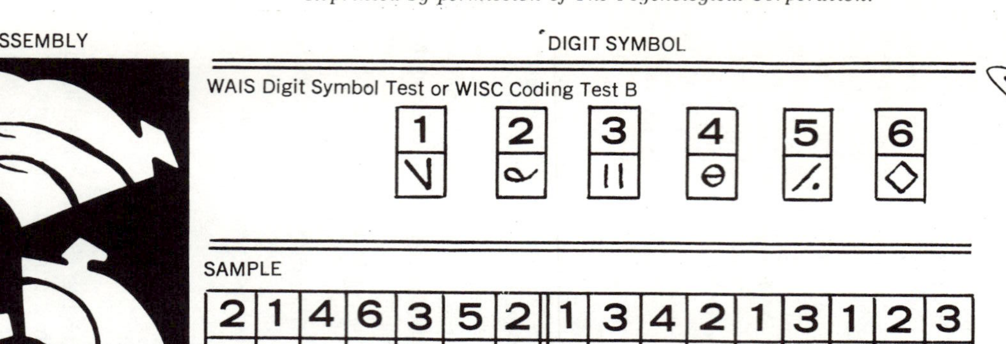

PICTURE COMPLETION

PICTURE ARRANGEMENT

FIGURE 10.2.
The Block Design Test of the WAIS, reprinted by permission of The Psychological Corporation. Photo by Jon Korchin reprinted by permission.

phrenics may function reasonably well on these tasks though doing poorly on tests with more social material.

8. *Picture Completion.* The subject must tell what part is missing in each of a series of twenty-one drawings (see Figure 10.1). Close attention is required to discover and note incongruities of the picture. As in Arithmetic, concentration is required, but of a more passive sort. Scores will sometimes be high in hypervigilant, paranoid patients, who are generally quick to note minor and trivial details of their world.

9. *Block Design* is similar to the Kohs Block Design Test and the block design portion of the Goldstein-Scheerer scales (see Figure 10.2). The subject has to reproduce designs, printed on cards, by using a set of children's blocks, whose sides are red, white, or half-red and half-white. To solve these problems, the subject must analyze the pictured pattern into block-sized units and then reconstruct it. It is a concept-formation task, with both analysis and synthesis involved. The visual-conceptual-motoric integration necessary for solution is often impaired in brain damage, though poor functioning can result as well from intense, disruptive affects.

10. *Picture Arrangement* consists of sets of cartoon drawings on separate cards which the subject must arrange in story-telling sequences (see Figure 10.1). There are eight items. This task reflects the subject's ability to grasp causal sequences in temporally related events. Hence, Rapaport and his colleagues noted, it can serve as an index of a person's capacity to judge, anticipate, and plan for future events.

11. *Object Assembly.* Fragmented objects have to be assembled (see Figure 10.1) into their original wholes. On easier items the subject may be able to visualize the whole and work smoothly toward attaining it. In the more complex items, the process by which the subject builds up to the solution, often by creating and discarding hypotheses, is discernible. Visual-motor coordination as well as planfulness of problem-solving is revealed in the process.

The entire WAIS can be administered in about one hour. The order of subtests can be altered to keep up the subject's interest. Several tests are timed, including Arithmetic, Digit Symbol, Block Design, Picture Arrangement, and Object Assembly. In some cases all items are given, in others the examiner stops in the series after a number of failures. Scoring is rather straightforward, although sometimes, notably on the Verbal tests, the examiner has to make delicate judgments as to the correctness of an item. Final judgment may depend on asking more information as to what the subject intended by his response.

THE PATTERN OF WAIS SCORES

Analysis of the pattern (scatter) of subtest scores reveals the unique organization of cognitive-personality functions. Considered separately, each score describes the individual patient's standing relative to his age peers in the normative population, as do the Full Scale IQ, Verbal IQ, and Performance IQ. The way in which the subtest scores pattern allows the clinician to infer the particular patient's mode of ego functioning, his adaptive and defensive strengths and limitations. This depends in turn on assumptions about the differences in psychological functions assessed by each subtest. Some of the guiding hypotheses used have just been mentioned; more extensive discussions can be found in Rapaport et al. (1968); Wechsler (1958); Allison et al. (1968); Guertin et al. (1956, 1962, and 1966), and Matarazzo (1972). Pattern analysis requires that individual subtest scores be viewed as deviations from a baseline, since it is not the absolute but rather the relative level of each which defines a pattern. Most usually, the Vocabulary Score provides such a baseline measure, for it is the most stable and reliable single measure of general ability. Under special conditions, if for example the patient is foreign born or raised under conditions of extreme cultural deprivation, the overall mean of weighted subtest scores may be preferable. In addition to the particular patterning of scores, clinicians are concerned with the overall scatter, the total variance between tests, intratest scatter, the relation of Verbal to Performance IQ, and the relation of "Hold" to "Don't Hold" tests which Wechsler (1958) proposed as a measure of deterioration.

The "Don't Hold" tests (Digit Span, Similarities, Digit Symbol, and Block Design) are those which normally decline with age, while the "Hold" tests (Vocabulary, Information, Object Assembly, and Picture Completion) tend to remain stable. Since the scales scores are adjusted to age norms, the levels of the two groups of tests should be the same, regardless of the subject's age. Thus, Wechsler argues, disproportionately lower "Don't Hold" scores can be interpreted as indicative of pathology-related deficit. His *Deterioration Index* is calculated by subtracting the sum of the four "Don't Hold" tests from the sum of the four "Hold" tests, and dividing by the sum of the "Hold" tests. Thus,

$$DI = \frac{\text{Hold} - \text{Don't Hold.}}{\text{Hold}}$$

Another comparison between subtest scores is the overall *scatter*, the total amount of variation among the eleven subtests, regardless of which are up and which down. If the patient did about equally well on each, the plot of his profile should be a relatively flat line; a high degree of scatter would result in a jagged profile. Wechsler proposed that scatter increases with pathology and gives evidence for a high degree of scatter in schizophrenic patients. Considerable scatter has sometimes been found in normal records, but it is more likely true that the erratic performance of schizophrenics will be reflected in high scatter scores.

Related to *between-test scatter* is *within-test scatter*. Since the items are arranged in increasing difficulty, one should expect that patients would be able to perform correctly up to a point and fail consistently thereafter. Sometimes, however, individuals do poorly on one or more easier items and then pass more difficult ones or they may fluctuate between passes and failures all along the way. Considerable within-test scatter usually reflects temporary deficit such as results from anxiety or more severe and permanent loss as in brain-damaged patients.

Another focus of interpretation is the difference between Verbal and Performance IQs. Depressed people often have distinctly higher (fifteen or more points) Verbal IQs. By contrast "action-oriented" people, who have difficulty delaying sufficiently to deal with problems requiring concentration, thought, and internal elaboration, are more comfortable with tasks requiring action and manipulation and thus have proportionately higher Performance IQs (Allison, Blatt, and Zimet, 1968). This would include narcissistic characters, and psychopathic and hysterical patients. However, it is known that Verbal-Performance IQ differences relate to general ability and to subcultural factors as well as to pathology and individual personality differences. Generally, the higher the Full Scale IQ, the more likely is the Verbal IQ to exceed the Performance IQ. Laborers, on the whole, tend to have higher Performance IQs, as do lower-class people and those with less education. Among ethnic groups, Jews are consistently found to have significantly higher Verbal than Performance IQs, which has also, interestingly, been found to increase with age (B. M. Levinson, 1959). Further analyses suggest that the discrepancy is greatest among those most tied to traditional values, and decreases with education and contact with the majority culture (Levinson, 1963). Such findings make clear the continuous need for the clinician, in interpreting WAIS patterns (indeed, all assessment data) never to neglect the contribution of cultural and background factors in the effort to discover personolistic and clinical determinants of test performance.

Considerable controversy has waged over the validity of pattern analyses in any of its forms, even among those who would accept the Wechsler IQ as a valid measure of general ability. It has been argued that the reliabilities of the individual tests are insufficiently high and that they are too correlated for secure pattern analyses. Some of the diagnostic signs proposed by Wechsler and others have been found to characterize almost equally well unintended patient groups or normals. Statistical limitations in subtest scores must temper the certainty of profile interpretations in tests like the WAIS or MMPI. Nor is there sufficiently unequivocal evidence of correlations between test patterns and diagnosis to justify a simple "diagnostic-sign" approach. However, this does not deny the value of interpreting score patterns, indeed individual responses, in terms of theoretically meaningful determinants, many of which have been found to relate to Wechsler performance in construct-validity-like studies (Blatt and Allison, 1968).

The Minnesota Multiphasic Personality Inventory (MMPI)

The MMPI was originally developed by Hathaway and McKinley (1940; 1951) as an aid to psychiatric diagnosis. A large pool of potential items was developed, drawn from older inventories, mental-status-examination forms, and the diagnostic clues used by psychiatrists. These were presented to psychiatric patients and normals in self-report form, as simple affirmative statements, to which subjects were to respond "True", "False", or "?". The items ranged widely in content, describing overt behaviors—current or past—attitudes, beliefs, symptoms, traits, and feelings. Illustrative items include:

> I have used alcohol excessively.
> My sex life is satisfactory.
> I am afraid of losing my mind.
> Most of the time I wish I were dead.
> I sometimes tease animals.
> At times I am full of energy.
> I pray several times a week.

After revisions, the number of items was reduced to 550. These are now given to subjects either in a printed booklet with the responses to be checked or individually printed on cards which he sorts into the three response categories. The test is scored for ten or more clinical or personality scales and for three "validity" scales.

The MMPI scales were empirically developed by contrasting the responses of over 800 diagnosed psychiatric patients with about twice as many normals. There were fifty or fewer patients in each of the diagnostic criterion groups. Items were retained and keyed to a particular scale, if they showed a statistically significant difference in the frequency with which they were endorsed by the particular diagnostic group as against the normal population. Items might then be excluded if they were endorsed just too frequently or too infrequently to be useful, if the responses seemed determined by some extraneous variable, such as sex or age, or if they did not differentiate sufficiently well among the diagnostic groups. However, no item was discarded from a scale because its face content appeared meaningless or irrelevant to the condition or trait being diagnosed. This is central to the principle of empirical criterion keying. It should be noted, of course, that at first items were chosen rationally in terms of their presumed relevance to psychiatric diagnosis. The authors did not include just *any* conceivable statement about human behavior as later writings by both defenders and detractors seem sometimes to suggest.*

The ten "clinical scales" of the MMPI include:

1.	Hs:	Hypochondriasis	6.	Pa:	Paranoia
2.	D:	Depression	7.	Pt:	Psychasthenia
3.	Hy:	Hysteria	8.	Sc:	Schizophrenia
4.	Pd:	Psychopathic Deviate	9.	Ma:	Hypomania
5.	Mf:	Masculinity-Femininity	10.	Si:	Social Introversion

Except for Mf and Si, the other eight scales consist of those items that distinguished each of the named diagnostic groups from normal controls. The Masculinity-Femininity scale includes those items in which the responses of men and women differed. A high score indicates interests more like those of the opposite than of one's own sex. The Social Introversion scale was later added to the MMPI. It was derived from the constrasting item responses of college students who had scored at the extremes on a test of introversion-extroversion

A special feature of the MMPI is its so-called validity scales. These attempt to check on sloppiness, misunderstanding, falsification, or the operation of response sets which might limit the interpretation of the basic scores. Included are:

Question Scale (?), the number of items marked "cannot say."

Lie Scale (*L*) reflects the subject's frankness. It consists of items which describe socially desirable, but quite improbable behaviors. For example, saying "False" to "I sometimes put off for tomorrow what I might do today."

Validity Scale (*F*) indicates carelessness, scoring errors, or effort to deceive. It consists of items which normally are responded to in the same way by most people, and counts the frequency of deviant responses.

* The logic and use of empirical keying has led to both controversy among psychologists, as well as public misunderstanding (Hathaway, 1964). It also invites parody of a sort not likely to be appreciated in Minnesota. The columnist and humorist, Art Buchwald, among others, has spoofed the MMPI, offering items such as "I salivate at the sight of mittens," "Spinach makes me feel alone," "I am never startled by a fish," and "I would enjoy the work of a chicken flicker." In the same vein, Walker and Walsh (1969) jokingly propose a Medieval Multi-Purpose Inquiry. Their MMPI includes the items "Sometimes my sword is too heavy to lift," and "I can joust as well as the next knight." So far they are prepared only to score for Renaissance Resistance!

Correction Score (*K*). This is another and more subtle measure of test-taking attitude which gets at defensiveness or "faking good." At the other extreme, the K scale is used to discover people who are excessively self-deprecatory (faking bad). Unlike the other control scores, which simply indicate whether or not the test protocol is trustworthy, the K score is used as a correction factor in adjusting clinical-scale scores.

On the basis of the responses of the original normal sample of about 700 people, norms are expressed in terms of standard scores which have a mean of fifty and a standard deviation of ten. The particular individual's scores are plotted to obtain a profile.

It soon became evident that the MMPI did not serve well its original purpose, which was to classify patients into one or another of the clinical categories on the basis of elevated scores on particular scales. Patients clearly diagnosable by other criteria often did not score high on the particular scale and vice versa. Moreover, normals were found to have high scores on some of the pathology dimensions, although, by and large, psychiatric patients do have more extreme scores. Consequently, the approach to the MMPI has shifted. In present use skilled interpreters are concerned with the *pattern* of scores from which they can describe personality and psychopathology in general terms, rather than simply allocating the patient to one or another diagnostic category. In pattern (profile) analysis the individual scale scores are interpreted as indicative of broad dimensions of personality, which may or may not be particularly characteristic of the diagnostic entity named. Thus, for example, a high Hy score is taken to reveal general immaturity, naivete, excessive need for affection and support, and readiness to deny problems. The specific meaning of any score is tempered by its relative elevation in the profile. Considerable validational and other research has been done to discover empirically the meanings of different profiles, as such. Systems have been developed for coding and comparing profiles according to the relative positions of scale scores in the profile. Thus, MMPI authorities will describe a patient as being 13″2′—79 045/68LK-F? This would indicate that the "neurotic triad" (Hypochondriasis, Depression, and Hysteria) stands highest in the profile, with scale 1(Hs) and 3 (Hy) only a point apart and scale 2(D) a full ten points lower, with the remaining variables ranging on down. The particular illustration shows the "conversion V" of the neurotic triad (1 and 3 above 2), found to be characteristic of conversion hysteria.

To facilitate clinical interpretation, Hathaway and Meehl (1951) developed an *Atlas* which provides coded profiles with accompanying case descriptions for almost a thousand patients. Similar handbooks have been prepared for the counseling of high-school students (Hathaway and Monachesi, 1961) and college students (Carkhuff, Barnett, and McCall, 1965), as well as for clinical and personality assessment. Such volumes can serve for a "cookbook" interpretation of the MMPI, by giving psychologists standards against which to match their cases (Marks and Seeman, 1963; Gilberstadt and Duker, 1965; Dahlstrom, Welsh, and Dahlstrom, 1972). Indeed, profile analysis of the MMPI has been carried another step forward by psychologists who have worked out computer programs based on these interpretative rules which produce completely automated reports (Kleinmuntz, 1963, 1969; Finney, 1965; Pearson and Swenson, 1967). Such computer analyses are now commercially available and are gaining increasing use particularly for screening and some large-scale research purposes. They can facilitate the work of the clinician, but not substitute for the judgment of a sophisticated and experienced clinician.

Since the original publication of the MMPI, at least 300 new scales have been developed, in most cases out of the empirical relationship of MMPI items to outside criteria or through factor-analytic studies (Dahlstrom, Welsh, and Dahlstrom, 1972, 1975). A number of these have been created in normal populations to assess nonpathological personality traits. Among the more widely studied are the scales of Ego Strength, Manifest Anxiety, Dominance, Prejudice, and Maladjustment.

The MMPI is open to criticism on many counts: (1) Despite the fact that scales are now referred to by number rather than the older diagnostic terms, the test derives from and is still anchored conceptually in a psychiatric system of dubious value; (2) The size and representativeness of the original normative sample is insufficient. The profile codes are based on some 700 Minneapolis adults of the late 1930s, with inadequate representation of subcultural groups as well as other regions. It has been suggested that it might be better to view the original sample as a "nonnormative fixed reference group" to determine scale scores and not as a true standardization sample (Anastasi, 1968); (3) Some of the scales are highly correlated, which limits the independence of profiles; (4) So too, some of the scales are of limited reliability; hence profiles may combine scores each of which is too dependent on chance factors; (5) Responses may be too much determined by response sets, beyond those accounted for by the validity scales. As noted in the last chapter, the problem of response sets has been the bugaboo of personality inventories. While their importance may have been overestimated, they do raise some important issues in inventory assessment; (6) The test is overly long, with too many redundant items, and (7) The manifest content of some items, regardless of their interpretative significance, particularly those pertaining to religion and sex, can understandably offend some people. The most severe limitation of the MMPI, however, lies in its relative insensitivity to differences within psychiatric groups and within the normal population, as critics have noted repeatedly (e.g., Lingoes, 1965). The test arose and gained its popularity as an instrument for distinguishing abnormal from normal people. For that it has proven valuable, as well as for discriminating between the gross nosological entities, particularly neurotic and psychotic. But the test remains weak in making finer discriminations within any one of these groups.

Nevertheless, the MMPI remains the most used and studied self-report inventory in clinical practice and personality research. It has served as a model for empirically keyed inventories some of which have improved upon the MMPI, in terms of one or another of the above criticisms and are rivaling the parent in their popularity. Foremost among these is the California Psychological Inventory (CPI). The CPI was developed by Gough (1957, 1964) specifically to measure personality characteristics of relevance in a normal population. About half of the items were drawn from the MMPI and the rest created by the author to form fifteen scales such as Responsibility, Achievement-via-conformance, Achievement-via-independence, Sociability, Dominance, Self-control, etc. The CPI includes three thoughtfully developed validity scales to assess possible response-set influences. By now, a considerable amount of validational and other psychometric research has been done showing the value of the test and detailed criteria are available for test interpretation (Megargee, 1971). It already has an established position in clinics as well as in personality research and is likely to continue to grow in popularity.

Projective Techniques

The most distinctive feature of the techniques called "projective," when compared to other kinds of psychological tests, is that they maximize the person's freedom to respond in unique ways. Confronted with relatively plastic materials, in a generally uncertain situation, the subject imposes his own organization and meanings on them. By presenting many people with the *same* tasks and materials under relatively standard conditions the differences among them in their characteristic modes of thinking, feeling, and behaving are highlighted. Unlike direct measures, projective methods are less dependent on the subject's willingness or ability to give personal information. He is unaware of the purposes of the test and unable to judge how particular responses are interpreted. The subject reveals rather than describes himself in his test performance. In the process, facets of his personality of which he is unaware, and of which he may be unconscious, become accessible for study. It is a mistake to think of projective techniques as a kind of personality X-ray, for we know that characteristics may be revealed which are perfectly visible to the subject himself and to observers. Moreover, projective-test responses, as has been well documented, are determined by many factors quite aside from the individual personality, either in its overt or covert qualities. Still, because of the response variety they allow and their relative resistance to conscious control, projective techniques are the clinician's most effective tools for discovering subtle and hidden aspects of personality. At the same time, the strengths of projective techniques are their weaknesses as well. The unstructured nature of the tasks and the variety of response possibilities puts the burden of interpretation on the psychologist's clinical judgment. He has guidelines but few explicit rules for evaluating test protocols. He has to organize and synthesize a considerable amount of diverse data, generating hypotheses which can give a coherent and internally consistent account of the patient. Ultimately, his task is to create a personalistic theory to describe the particular patient. All along the way, there are pitfalls in administration, analysis, interpretation, and theory-building, for it is all too easy for the clinician to project himself in the study of his patient's "projections."

Lindzey (1961) has offered a definition of projective techniques which synthesizes the major elements described in the literature.

> A projective technique is an instrument that is considered especially sensitive to covert or unconscious aspects of behavior, it permits or encourages a wide variety of subject responses, is highly multidimensional, and it evokes unusually rich or profuse response data with a minimum of subject awareness concerning the purpose of the test. Further, it is very often true that the stimulus material presented by the projective test is ambiguous, interpreters depend upon holistic analysis, the test evokes fantasy responses, and there are no correct or incorrect responses to the test [p. 45].

With characteristic wit, George Kelly once noted: "When the subject is asked to guess what the examiner is thinking, we call it an objective test; when the examiner tries to guess what the subject is thinking, we call it a projective device" (1958, p. 19).

The term "projective test" was popularized by L. K. Frank (1939), although H. A. Murray had earlier (1938) described the Rorschach, TAT, and other procedures used in Harvard Psychological Clinic studies as "projection tests." The term is, in a way, unfortunate, for it invites confusion with the Freudian defense mechanism. Projection, as defense mechanism, involves a veritable misbelief or delusion, in which the subject ascribes some centrally important, but unacceptable, attribute of his own to another and in the process denies its existence and thus maintains his self-esteem and averts anxiety (H. A. Murray, 1951). Only part of this process is found in projective testing; there is externalization and attribution of one's needs and feelings, but not only unacceptable ones, which serve as a basis for perceiving and judging external stimuli. There is neither denial of their existence in the self, nor is self-esteem served in the process. Because of the possibility of semantic confusion, psychologists have suggested a number of alternative terms, but it seems that after more than three decades "projective techniques" are here to stay.

Depending on the type of task involved, projective techniques are of five types (Lindzey, 1961):

1. *Association techniques* ask the subject to tell what is suggested by a verbal, visual, or auditory stimulus (e.g., Word Association, Rorschach).
2. *Construction techniques* involve the creating of an imaginal production for which the test materials provide a framework (e.g., TAT, Make-A-Picture Story, Blacky).
3. *Completion techniques* require that subjects complete a statement or story; they are a more structured construction procedure (e.g., Rosenzweig Picture-Frustration Study, Sentence Completion tests).
4. *Choice or ordering techniques* involve arranging materials in story-telling sequences, in order of choice, etc., often with no verbal elaboration (Tomkins-Horn Picture Arrangement Test, Szondi).
5. *Expressive techniques* do not depend on test stimuli, but rather ask the subject to perform an artistic or creative act (Draw-A-Person, Finger Painting, Play, Psychodrama).

Literally thousands of books and articles have appeared since the mid-1930s in the field of projective testing. It is impossible, and needless in this context, to even attempt to indicate the variety of theoretical, clinical, and research issues which have been addressed, nor to try to survey very many of the findings which have emerged. Needless to say, the literature is confusing, marked by controversy between those who—since Murray, Frank, and Rapaport—see projective techniques as a major route to a new dynamic psychology of the person and those who see the whole enterprise as an affront to science. The same polarity exists in views as to the clinical utility of the methods, from unswerving faith to complete rejection. In large measure, points of view toward projective testing reflect temperamental differences and ideological commitments among psychologists, which are not likely to be swayed by argument or evidence.

In getting his own bearings in the field, the student should read some of the literature which considers the history, rationale, and variety of projective techniques, issues in their creation and validation, their use in the study of personality mechanisms and psychopathology, and their value in clinical assessment. General references which can be recommended include R. W. White (1944), H. H. Anderson and G. L. Anderson (1951), Lindzey (1961), Shneidman (1965), Zubin, Eron and Schumer (1965), and Rabin (1968). Other references, more specific to the Rorschach and TAT, will be mentioned later in this chapter as we consider these techniques.

The Rorschach Test

Origin. Projective testing, indeed modern clinical psychology, starts with the Rorschach, which remains the most studied, used, and argued-over technique of clinical assessment. Although inkblots as a vehicle for psychological study were first used in the mid-1800s, and Binet of intelligence-testing fame suggested their value in 1895, it was not until Rorschach that they were systematically studied. In 1921, Hermann Rorschach, a Swiss psychiatrist, published his classic monograph *Psychodiagnostik,* subtitled (in somewhat rough translation) "Methods and results of diagnosis-through-perception (*Wahrnehmungsdiagnosen*) experiments." Although anchored in Jungian and psychoanalytic thinking, the work has a strongly empirical flavor. By comparing the responses of different types of patients and people he knew, he tried to discover important personality dimensions in inkblot responses and to find patterns which could be used in the diagnosis of patients.

Rorschach was never to continue his program. He died only a year later in 1922. But others were captured by his ideas and the research was carried forward in Europe and, by the late 1920s, due to David M. Levy and Samuel J. Beck, in the United States. Since then, there has been continuous and vigorous interest.

Test Materials and Administration. The test consists of ten symmetrical inkblots. These are shown one at a time in the same order. The subject is asked to tell what they might represent. After the first exposure—the "free-association" period—there is an "inquiry" in which all of the responses are reviewed to clarify in each case the what, where, and why of each response, on which scoring and interpretation depends—*what* precisely was intended, *where* in the blot it was seen, and *why,* what aspect of the stimulus contributed to the response. Many examiners then enter a third phase, following Klopfer's suggestion (Klopfer and Davidson, 1962), of "testing the limits" to discover whether the subject is capable of other sorts of responses by calling attention to particular areas, hinting or asking outright "Might it also be. . . . ?" There is no limit on the number of responses the subject can give.

Of the ten blots, five are printed in black ink, two add red areas, and three are multicolored (see Figure 10.3). The examiner records as fully as possible the initial responses and later elaboration. Time until the first response and total time for each card is noted. Gross and subtle behavior, incidental comments, and visible

FIGURE 10.3
An inkblot, similar to those used in the Rorschach test.

feelings are carefully observed. The average record has about twenty-five responses. The figure tends to be higher among brighter people with a broad range of interests. However, a larger number of responses, though usually of more banal or contrived sorts, can be produced by an intellectually ambitious person wanting to show himself off. A smaller number may indicate a low intellectual level, inhibition or retardation as in a depressed person, or meticulous concern that each response be perfectly "correct." In each case, the quality of the responses would differ.

Scoring and Interpreting Rorschach Responses. Each response can be described by its "what, where, and why" characteristics and it is at this point that Rorschach analysis and interpretation begins. Many specific scoring systems have evolved from Rorschach's original categories; a compact tabular comparison of their similarities and differences can be found in Toomey and Rickers-Ovsiankiana (1960). The two most commonly used are those of Samuel J. Beck and Bruno Klopfer. The subtle differences among systems cannot concern us here (see Exner, 1969, for review). In discussing some of the more important scores and their meanings, we will be attending mainly to those common to all systems. Where conventions differ, Klopfer's notation will be used.

Following Rorschach's lead, all systems score each response in terms of (1) its location; (2) the determinants used in forming the response; (3) the level of accuracy of the percept; and (4) its content, including the conventionality or originality shown. Thus, if a patient says "bat" to Card 1, it is scored "W F+ A P" to show that (1) it involves the **W**hole blot (location); (2) it depends on the ***F***orm quality (determinant); (3) which is appropriately (+) used (accuracy); and (4) it depicts an **A**nimal (content), which in this case is a ***P***opular response. Each response is scored along these dimensions and totals are obtained for each category. Although each score represents a particular aspect of psychological functioning, their interpretation depends on how they relate to and balance with each other. In general, the first three categories (location, determinants, and accuracy) represent the formal structure of the protocol, and describe the more stable personality-cognitive characteristics of the patient. They depend on spontaneous and automatic response characteristics and are less open to conscious control than the content of the response.

Location. The subject can respond to the whole blot (W), to large and commonly segregated areas (D), to smaller but usual detail (d), or to tiny or rare details (e.g., dd), or the subject can reverse figure and ground and respond to the white spaces instead of the inked areas (S). The area chosen indicates, in general, the subject's cognitive orientation, i.e., whether he integrates or segregates experiences, deals in more abstract or is limited to conventional categories, or whether he is drawn to the trivial and unusual. Thus, many W responses, if of sufficient complexity and accuracy, are usually said to show a capacity for abstraction and integration. Staying with D is the mark of conventional thought. However, a reasonably short record made up largely of "easy" or vague W's is often given by the mentally retarded. Here, as in all aspects of Rorschach analysis, interpretation depends not only on the particular score, but its relation to other variables and the qualities of the response, among other considerations. The S response—seeing the hole instead of the doughnut—is intrinsically interesting. More than one or two in a record (above 5 percent) often indicates oppositional or negativistic tendencies and is found in passive-aggressive people; they may however also be found in creative and original thinkers.

A healthy record should show an overall balance among the location scores. Often this is paralleled by orderly sequences of response on most cards, in which the subject moves from whole to larger to smaller details. A shift in the subject's style of approach may token particular emotional response to a particular card. Similarly, selectively nonattending to particular portions, if of affective or sexual significance, allows interpretation of particular areas of conflict. Gross thinking disorder can be seen in confabulated responses (called DW by Rapaport) or position (Po) responses. In the former, the person generalizes unjustifiedly from the part to the whole: "The whole thing is a woman." "Why?" "Here is her vagina." In itself, the vagina response may be a perfectly appropriate D, but *therefore* calling the entire blot a woman reveals the kind of impulsive and arbitrary generalization usually found only in schizophrenia. Defining a response solely by its position on the card: "This is hell." "Why?" "Because it's at the bottom," reveals similar thought disturbance.

Determinants. The determinant scores indicate whether form, color, movement, or shading, alone or in combination, underlie the response. These are the aspects of the stimulus subjects often point to when justifying their responses: "It's shaped like a heart." "The colors suggested flowers." "The shades of black make it look furry." The major categories are *movement* (M, if human; FM, if animal; m if inanimate), *shading* (c, for texture; K, for vista or three-dimensional effects), *form* (F), and *color* (C). Since form can be involved, in varying degree, in color and shading responses, this is indicated by the addition of F: thus, a "pure" color response ("sunset") is scored C; if some form is involved, but color is more important, it is CF ("a garden"), if the shape is relatively more important ("a red Darwin tulip"), it is scored FC. The accuracy of form responses is shown by adding + or −. Many specific categories and scoring conventions have been suggested for scoring determinants; it is in this realm that scoring systems are most diverse, and that the clinician's judgment is most taxed.

Form represents the individual's concern with external realities. In a general sense, it indexes ego control. A very high proportion of F responses indicates someone who is literal and factual, a "colorless" person with little capacity for spontaneity, emotional warmth, or fantasy; at the extreme, rigid and unfeeling. At the other extreme, a very low proportion of F (particularly if these are of poor quality, F−) goes with impulsivity, emotional dominance, and low capacity for logical thinking. In the well-integrated person, perhaps three-quarters of the F responses should be F+ (accurate forms), leaving some room for "regression in the service of the ego" (Korchin, 1960).

Color responses are related to the emotional life of the individual, his responsivity and readiness to discharge rather than delay tension into action. In the FC response, the affects are modulated and socialized; the person is warm, able to relate to others, without intruding egocentric needs. Pure C, however, shows a lack of intellectual control and correspondingly readiness for intensely impulsive acts, hyperstimulatibility, and minimal thought or logic "before leaping." The balance between the FC, CF, and C is the focus of interpretation, as well as the relative proportion of all C responses to F and M. Rorschach early noted that neurotics seemed to be particularly prone to "color shock," to be disconcerted and disorganized when first confronted with colored blots. Shading responses often signal anxiety and the use of "achromatic color" ("blackbird") often goes with depressive trends.

Movement responses are of particular interest because, of course, the blots are immobile. M is scored when the subject experiences "kinaesthetically" a living, moving human being; that is, when some order of empathy can be inferred. In seeing movement in static stimuli, the subject is going beyond the given. For these reasons, we can consider M as a measure of the capacity for fantasy and inner reflection; if +, of the sort required in creative thinking; if −, of the kind of which delusion is made. High M people are imaginative, well-endowed intellectually, and, as interpreted by Rapaport and other psychoanalytic ego psychologists, capable of delaying action and affective expression by substituting thought and fantasy (J. L. Singer, 1960). Important to Rorschach himself, as well as to later workers, is the "experience-type" score, which relates the proportion of M to C. The resulting ratio describes a continuum conceptually similar to Jung's introversion-extraversion.

Content. Here the scores describe what the subject reports in categories such as human, part of human, animal, part of animal, nature, object, clothing, anatomy, sex, food, clothing, etc. To the layman, content is the most obvious and seemingly most important quality of the response; by contrast, for many Rorschach workers, it is of the least concern. Content scores obviously reflect educational, cultural, vocational, and other background factors and interpretation must be tempered in their terms. However, the analysis of content adds considerable information about personality structure, as well as personal interests, concerns, and conflicts. At the first level, sheer variety shows the richness of the subject's ideas and interests. Stereotyped records, on the other hand, can result from limited intelligence or experience, considerable anxiety, inhibition or rigidity, or conflict-laden preoccupation in particular realms. (Remember the old joke? Patient to Rorschach examiner: "Why are you showing me all these dirty pictures?") Thus, many anatomy, X-ray, sexual, and human-part responses may reflect preoccupation with intactness of the body. Few human responses can indicate alienation and inability to relate to others. What kinds of people are shown, in what kinds of actions, is often taken as a basis for inferences about the subject's own self-concept. Animal responses are easy to give and more common in children's records; consequently, they indicate stereotyped thinking, conventionality, or social immaturity. Stereotypy is also seen in an excessive number of popular responses. In any average-length record, the percentage of P is about twenty.

Some Rorschach systems have focused considerable attention on the symbolic interpretation of Rorschach content as a route to the understanding of personality dynamics (e.g., Phillips and Smith, 1953; Schafer, 1954). To investigate particular dimensions of personality, special scoring has been developed, for example, for hostility and anxiety (Elizur, 1949), body image boundaries (Fisher and Cleveland, 1958) and primary and secondary process thinking (Holt and Havel, 1960).

Other Aspects of Rorschach Interpretation. A further aspect of Rorschach interpretation involves *sequence analysis,* changes in the behavior of the subject over time as he copes with the Rorschach task. The importance of response sequences in terms of location has already been noted. Whether the subject moves from whole to part responses in an organized way, builds up from small to larger details, or flits haphazardly about suggests analogous modes of intellectual analysis and problem-solving. Both within a particular card and between cards, sequence can be studied in other terms as well. After giving a particular disturbed or affect-laden response, does the subject then reinstate control with a well-organized F+ response or does his performance deteriorate further? Over the entire test, does the accuracy of form go down or up? Are there repeated sequences of particular content areas, to suggest associatively related conflicts? When presented with novel experiences, for example, color or a particularly complex blot, can he maintain his pace? Sometimes the subject is simply unable to produce a response to a particular card (card rejection), which may be relatable to the characteristics of that card or to distress aroused by earlier responses.

Supplementing the interpretation of Rorschach scores and variables are the *behaviors* of the subject during the testing session, whether he seems to be enjoying the task, frightened by it, playful, guarded, or what. Similarly, the specific response *verbalizations* yield further information. Percepts can be named in simple, direct terms ("a woman") or in convoluted language ("a person of the opposite sex") which can further be personalized (". . . like my wife Mary. What a . . . !") and even extend into bizarre associations (". . . she's twenty-eight today, so this here must be a birthday candle . . ."). The basic response might be scored the same way, but obviously the comments made tell a good deal more about the subject.

Evaluation of the Rorschach. The Rorschach can be conceived as a perceptual-cognitive task, a structured interview, or a stimulus to fantasy productions (Goldfried, Stricker, and Weiner, 1971). These are not exclusive conceptions; most psychologists operate in all three realms, but one or another can be emphasized. (1) As a perceptual-cognitive task, concern is focused on the ways in which the subject structures and organizes the stimulus material. From such data, inferences can be made to conceptually comparable personality-cognitive variables. Thus low F + percent can be taken as representing the impaired reality testing of the schizophrenic. (2) Viewed as a structured interview, there is more concern with the subject's behavior in the situation, his language and speech and expressed concerns than with formal responses as such. From such behaviors inferences can be made about typical expressive modes, language patterns, and interpersonal behaviors. The subject may show himself to be hesitant, verbose, businesslike, of limited and ungrammatical vocabulary, and so on. (3) However, when conceived as a source of fantasy, emphasis shifts to the content of the response, i.e., *what* he sees rather than *how* he sees it or how he *expresses* himself. Here the Rorschach becomes kin to dream analysis and other modes of exploring symbolic process to reveal unconscious needs and conflicts. As perceptual-cognitive task or interview, Rorschach scores or behaviors more directly represent variables with which we are concerned; in the latter case, however, they are symbolically related. Interpretation is necessarily more complex and subjective. More distinct inferences have to be made in deciding symbolic meanings than in the interpretation of perceptual responses or interview transactions. After reviewing an extensive clinical and research literature, Goldfried, Stricker, and Weiner (1971) conclude that there is greater validity for Rorschach indices which represent than for those which symbolize behavior. In clinical use, the interpretation of symbolism always contains the danger of what Freud in another context called "wild analysis."

However viewed, the Rorschach is manifestly different from the usual standard psychometric test though it shares common qualities. The test stimuli are absolutely standard. Administration proceeds in much the same fashion from subject to subject. There is considerable standardization in the recording and, within each of the scoring systems, in the scoring of responses. A great deal of effort has gone into the development of norms for the evaluation of particular scores, as for example in Beck's norms for form-level. Many volumes have been published which describe the distributions of individual scores, ratios and profiles for groups of all ages, differing social characteristics and forms of psychopathology. Special scores have been developed to assess, for example, developmental level, hostility and anxiety, and diagnostic signs of neurosis, schizophrenia, organicity, and suicide risk. (For an up-to-date and complete review of work in these and related areas, see Goldfried, Stricker, and Weiner, 1971.) However, this important body of work provides the clinician only with guidelines for the interpretation of the individual protocol. Unlike a psychometric test, the examiner cannot simply refer the particular patient's scores to normative standards and reach conclusions about him directly. The analysis of the individual protocol depends on the clinician's synthesis of the considerable amount of data available into a coherent picture of the individual. Normative data provide standards for judgment; knowledge of personality theory gives the framework; but ultimately the clinician must integrate the many clues in the record into personolistic hypotheses which can be further sharpened and tested.

How to study the reliability and validity of the Rorschach has perplexed psychologists for many years (for analyses of the problems involved, see MacFarlane and Tuddenham, 1951; Ainsworth, 1954; Holzberg, 1960; Zubin, Eron, and Schumer, 1965; Goldfried et al., 1971). For all tests, but particularly for a procedure like the Rorschach, these questions have to be rephrased as "Reliability and validity for whom? Under what circumstances? In whose hands? To what ends?" To add measurably, clinical research has to refocus on questions such as "Does Klopfer's Prognostic Rating Scale predict outcome of psychotherapy for patients treated by . . ?" and so on. Out of many answers to such questions the utility and limitations of the technique emerge. The bald questions of "Is it reliable?" "Is it valid?" contribute little and encourage needless polemic.

Some 3000 Rorschach studies have been published. With no effort at all, anyone can draw subsets which either prove or disprove the claims of the Rorschach. The findings are indeed mixed and they elude easy generalization.* In general, studies show a fairly high degree of inter-scorer reliability, more so if they share the same scoring conventions and conceptual framework. Split-half and alternate-forms reliability are of questionable applicability to the Rorschach because of the unique set of blots, but studies have been done in both modes. Similarly, retest reliability studies have shown high to modest correlations. Stability over time, it should be recalled again, should only be expected if the personality quality being assessed can be assumed to remain constant.

Validity has been studied in terms of content validity, criterion-related (both concurrent and predictive) validity, and construct validity. In each mode there are studies supportive of and contradictory to Rorschach hypotheses. Thus, Piotrowski (1965) cites some 250 studies to show dependable differences among diagnostic groups, while other reviews indicate far less clinical differentiation.

Research of a construct-validity sort has yielded some of the most consistent and intriguing findings. Where there is a theoretical framework to guide the research, studies of some facet of Rorschach performance have shown meaningful patterns of relationships in clinical, correlational, and experimental studies. As one illustration, Friedman (1952, 1953) developed a scoring system to measure developmental levels in terms of Werner's orthogenetic principle (see Chapter 3). As predicted, the scores differentiated among children of different ages, mental defectives, brain-damaged and schizophrenic adults, among others (cf. Goldfried et al. 1971, Chapter 2, for review of this research). Over a number of studies, J. L. Singer, Meltzoff and their colleagues have traced out the implications of the concept of M responses as a measure of internalized fantasy as a substitute for overt action, in line with ego-psychoanalytic theory. In the first of these studies, it was found that high M people were better able to delay action in an experimental situation and further that periods of motor inhibition (being required to write as slowly as possible) raised a number of M responses from pre- to post-testing (Meltzoff, Singer, and Korchin, 1953; for reviews of the later research and theory, cf. Singer, 1960, 1968). Still other illustrations worth detailed study include the work of Holt on primary and secondary process thinking (e.g., Holt and Havel, 1960) and Levine and Spivak on repressive style (1965).

When all is said and done (and it never is!) the Rorschach surely leaves much to be desired by psychometric standards. At the same time, a substantial research literature as well as the informed opinions of many committed clinicians attest to the utility of Rorschach's test. It remains true that some psychologists are believers and some are disbelievers and that emotional commitment rather than evidence determines conviction. In general, clinicians who have worked with the Rorschach tend to have their faith sustained by first-hand, if selective, evidence

* Note, however, Zubin et al. (1965): "No other technique has captured the attention of so many on such little evidence" [p. 251].

of confirmable personality descriptions or predictions. Critics, often academic students of personality measurement, note the number of research studies which do not support Rorschach claims. Such research, clinicians in turn note, does not test the Rorschach in the way and under the conditions it is used clinically. And so the arguments continue.

Such contrasting orientations, it has been found, are even reflected in the type of research done in the two camps and the resultant findings. Levy and Orr (1959) surveyed all the validity studies they could find in the four most relevant psychological journals for the period 1951–1955. In all, there were 168 studies. For each they noted and related three variables: (1) the type of institutional setting (academic or nonacademic); (2) the type of validity study (construct or criterion); and (3) whether the outcome was favorable or unfavorable to the Rorschach. Their findings tell an interesting story (see Table 10.1).

TABLE 10.1.
Distribution of Studies Among Variables of Setting, Type of Study, and Outcome *

	ACADEMIC		NONACADEMIC	
	CONSTRUCT	CRITERION	CONSTRUCT	CRITERION
Favorable	51	12	14	19
Unfavorable	22	23	14	13

* From Levy, L. H., & Orr, T. B. The social psychology of Rorschach validity research. *Journal of Abnormal and Social Psychology*, 1959, p. 82. Reprinted by permission.

Right off, it is clear that academics are more concerned with theoretical dimensions and nonacademics with empirical studies of diagnostic and predictive validity. Of particular interest is the interaction between the three variables. Academics were more than twice as likely to obtain positive findings in a theoretical (construct validity) study, and twice as likely to get negative results in a criterion study. Contrariwise, clinicians not only more frequently did criterion studies, but were proportionately more likely to obtain positive results when they did. Overall, it is clear that there is sufficient evidence both in academic and clinical settings which support and reject Rorschach claims.

THE THEMATIC APPERCEPTION TEST (TAT)

Origin and Method. The TAT is the most widely used "constructive" projective method. Unlike the Rorschach with its roots in European psychiatry, the TAT is a product of American university psychology. It was developed by H. A. Murray and his Harvard colleagues (Morgan and Murray, 1935; Murray, 1938, 1943) as an instrument for the study of normal personalities and it has remained a major technique in personality research over the years since its birth in 1935. Among projective techniques, it is second only to the Rorschach in popularity and volume of published research. It is commonly used along with the Rorschach and WAIS as part of a basic test battery. The TAT presents patients with a less structured and reality-oriented task than the WAIS, though one which is more structured than the Rorschach. Commonly, though only in part correctly, the TAT is said to add information about the "content" of personality to the knowledge of its structure and organization gained from the Rorschach. The TAT is also often described as a "test of fantasy," although as Holt (1961) has persuasively argued, the stories told to TAT pictures differ in numerous important respects from naturally occurring fantasies.

The test materials consist of thirty-one cards, one of which is blank and the others depicting scenes or interpersonal events. Thus, the first card shows a boy looking down somewhat pensively at a violin before him. In the recommended administration, twenty cards are used, selected according to the patient's age and sex, half of which are shown on one occasion and the other half at a later time (H. A. Murray, 1943). In actual practice, clinicians typically use less than twenty cards and limit testing to one hour-long session. Subjects are told, in essence: "I will show you a series of pictures and would like you to make up a story for each one. The stories should be as dramatic and imaginative as possible. Tell me what is happening in each picture, what led up to it, and what the outcome will be. Describe as fully as you can the thoughts and feelings of the characters." With the blank card, the subject is asked further to imagine and describe a picture, then to tell a story about it. To encourage the flow of the stories, the examiner asks nonleading questions of the sort: "What happens then?" "How does it turn out?" and the like. At the end, some inquire further as to the sources of the stories, whether they reflect personal experiences, whether they were suggested by movies, books, or TV, or whether they were just "made up." As they are being told, the stories are recorded verbatim, including the examiner's probes.

Mode of Analysis. Unlike the Rorschach, there are no generally accepted systems of TAT scoring and interpretation. There have been a number of efforts to develop specific scoring systems, in terms of which major themes, feelings expressed, nature of outcome, and other story qualities are catalogued and counted (for reviews of a number of these systems, see Harrison (1965), Murstein (1963), and Zubin, Eron, and Schumer (1965). In the main, however, clinicians proceed in a more impressionistic way, following the guidelines of H. A. Murray himself (1943), Tomkins (1947), Stein (1955), Henry (1956), and Rapaport et al. (1968), among others, who have developed systems of TAT analysis and interpretation, usually within a psychodynamic framework. In general terms, this usually involves careful reading and rereading of the set of story productions, noting repetitive themes, characteristic ways in which the hero (usually taken to represent the patient himself) and others are described, the range of feelings expressed, how stories are resolved, whether outcomes tend to be happy or not and reasonably related to story plots. The clinician approaches the protocol with whatever knowledge he has about the patient which can provide guiding hypotheses as to the most salient needs and conflict areas. In analyzing the TAT protocol, the clinician's task is, ultimately, to construct a set of hypotheses which can best explain why these particular stories were told and what kind of person lies behind the story productions.

The skilled interpreter brings to the task a framework of expectations, based on cumulated experience with the stories told by others and to some extent on formal normative data such as those published by Eron (1965) and Murstein (1972), against which he compares the stories in hand. Divergences from such expectancies are noted. Particularly noteworthy for clinical inference are stories containing unusual or peculiar plots, which seem to have a personal flavor and are intensely told perhaps with visible signs of emotion, or which contain repetitive themes, particularly where the picture provides little justification. In addition to noting how the subject differs from people in general, the clinician is quick to note deviation from the subject's own baseline patterns. Suppose, for example, that virtually all stories are resolved in happy endings, suggesting a bland optimism. In some cases, however, there is failure or frustration. The question then becomes one of discovering what other qualities distinguish these particular stories. It might then be possible, for example, to infer that this person expects the best *except* when in conflict with older, stronger males. In analyzing story elements and attempting to discover functional relations among them, the examiner operates implicitly if not explicitly according to established rules of logical analysis, as expressed, for example, in Mills' canons of inference (Tomkins, 1947).

In the process of interpretation, psychologists use *empathic perception, statistical (empirical) inference,* or *inference based on theory* (Holt, 1968) to differing degrees depending on their bent. Stories are read with minimal preconception to sense empathically their personally important meanings. In contrast, the interpretative value of story elements can be inferred from past evidence of empirical association. Lindzey, Bradford, Tejessy, and Davids (1959) have assembled an interpretative lexicon of various TAT characteristics of different psychiatric groups to facilitate diagnostic testing. Interpretation in this case depends on demonstrated association between the story element and some characteristic of the story teller, whether or not the relationship seems sensible. Finally, clinical inferences can derive from a wider frame of personality theory, which would make understandable the way a particular aspect of test performance is determined by a particular facet of personality. These forms of inference are not incompatible; they converge in the work of skilled clinicians.

The Structural Aspects of the TAT. Interpretation, particularly in the earlier development of the TAT, focused mainly on story content to discover the subject's major needs, concerns, feelings, and conflicts. Increasingly, a parallel concern has arisen with the structural aspects of TAT performance, namely, *how* the stories are told as well as *what* they contain (e.g., Schafer, 1958; Holt, 1958). Information about the subject can be obtained from observation of ways the subject copes with the story-telling task, the degree to which he follows the instructions, his manner and language, how he perceives or misperceives the picture material, and how the stories are organized as literary products. These facets of performance often allow more direct inferences about the subject's characteristic behaviors and ego processes than those about his motivational determinants made from story content.

The TAT requires imagination. Stories produced can be original and creative or they can be banal and trite; they can indeed be dramatic and engrossing or dull and limited. Subjects can range freely from the pictured scene or cling closely to it, with the "story" being little more than a description of the card. Thus, the subject reveals creative intelligence and capacity for imaginative play at one extreme, or inability to detach himself from the concrete realities of the picture, limited intelligence and imagination at the other.

The instructions ask that stories extend over time, telling "what led up" and "what will happen" as well as "what is now going on." Subjects who limit their production to the visually present also tend to hold to the temporally present and there is minimal time perspective. Others, in contrast, cover an extended time span with past, present, and future events integrated as in a well-turned novel. A depressed patient predictably emphasizes the past, with only minor concern with the present and virtually none with the future. Repressive people, such as hysteric patients, stay primarily in the present, with vague and artificially happy events forecast ahead. Schizophrenics are likely to shift arbitrarily between past, present, and future events (Allison, Blatt, and Zimet, 1968). Not only the span of time perspective, but the organization of causal sequences, "means-ends relationships" in Tomkins' phrase, are important in interpretation.

Although the TAT is not a perceptual task and the subject has poetic license to depart from the picture in hand, the accuracy with which the picture elements is described is of considerable importance and parallels conceptually the form-level of Rorschach responses. There may be gross or minor misperceptions of the objects pictured; the sex of characters can be misidentified; objects visible to most subjects ignored; and still others introduced. The patient can lose himself in the stories and personalize them to the extent that an autobiographical episode is told. The subject can put greater or lesser distance between himself and the story told by describing the events in more exotic or familiar times or places. Indeed, Tomkins (1947) first offered the intriguing hypothesis that distanced themes more likely reflected unconscious needs than the same material set closer in time, place, or character. Thus, if a college student describes a present-day scene in a local restaurant in which a young man is eating gluttonously, we might infer actual concern with (over) eating of which, however, the subject may be quite consciously aware. On the other hand, if the student describes Henry VIII in sixteenth-century England, deeper and perhaps more guilt-associated oral conflicts are suggested.

As in the Rorschach, the subject can approach the story-telling task in an orderly way or flit from element to element. I once tested a minor government official whose ways of telling TAT stories precisely reflected his characteristic approach to life and work tasks. Each story was written in identically numbered and labelled paragraphs:

1. Now happening: ....
2. Led up: ....
3. Will happen next: ....

and so on, to reveal a meticulous but dull man at work.

Still other facets of the patient's behavior of similar interest include the range of vocabulary, clarity of verbal expression, singular verbalizations and other aspects of the patient's communication, gross behavior during testing, and reactions to his own stories ("Boy, that's a weird one!"). Sequence analysis as in the Rorschach reveals coping patterns over time and underscores interpretations based on single stories. Thus, having told a harsh and aggressive story, the patient may defensively deny hostile feelings by making the next story bland and optimistic. It is impossible, of course, to characterize all the ways in which the structure of performance can be interpreted; some of the more salient dimensions have been touched on in this section.

The Content of TAT Stories. The major elements of the story include: (1) the hero; (2) the needs, strivings, and characteristics of the hero; (3) the environmental forces acting on him; (4) the themes (press-need-outcome combinations); (5) affective tone, of the story generally and of the major actors; and (6) the outcome. The "hero assumption" is pivotal, in that the subject identifies with the central figure and represents in him, directly or symbolically, his own needs, values, and expectations (Lindzey, 1952). Lindzey and Kalnins (1958) brought forth evidence supporting the hero assumption, though others have argued that any (and all) characters can represent the subject. Generally, however, interpretation proceeds from the notion that the hero represents the subject.

One patient told the following story to Card 1 (Boy and Violin):

> This boy's parents want him to practice so that he can appreciate music better. At this point, he would rather be out playing with the other boys. He is angry and resentful that they are forcing him to do something he doesn't want to do, but they have told him that he would be punished if he doesn't practice for an hour. He finally does. As time goes by, however, he becomes better and better at the violin, and comes to enjoy playing it. In fact, he has great talent, and would rather play the violin than do almost anything else. Finally, he becomes a great violinist. He now remembers sadly how much he resented his parents pushing him. Now he knows that they somehow recognized his talent and wanted him to develop it for his own sake.

In this brief story, which is a variant on the most common theme, the needs of the hero are, first, to avoid practice and to resist parental coercion (press) which, following compliance and intrinsic mastery, shift to self-motivated effort, achievement strivings, and success. In the process, warm feelings toward the parents and some guilt are discovered. Implicit is the moral "parents know best."

Is this a literal representation of the patient's present or historic relation to his parents? It may or may not be. A common error in TAT interpretation is to project isomorphically story themes to the patient's life ("When he was a child, he. . . .") as if the relationship between stories and life were invariant. It is equally possible that the story represents themes which are wished for, feared, defensive projections, or unconscious denials. In this particular case, the patient may actually have felt that the parents were unconcerned about him and that he would have fared better if they had been more controlling; the story then representing the wish "if only. . . ." Which of these or alternate interpretations can be made depends on evidence from other TAT stories and other assessment data. What is immediately known, however, is that the patient is capable of fulfilling the obligations of the task, telling a well-organized story in reasonably good prose, spanning an appropriate time perspective, with realistic means-ends relationships; in all, evidence of intact ego functioning.

The question of how TAT themes relate to overt behavior has perplexed and intrigued psychologists and a sizeable body of research has emerged. Under some conditions, TAT performance clearly parallels and predicts overt behavior. A generally held view is that such parallelism is more likely to occur if expression of the need is socially approved, less so if there are cultural prohibitions. In the extensive body of research on "*n*eed *Ach*ievement" by McClelland and his colleagues (McClelland et al., 1953; Atkinson, 1958; McClelland, 1961) and later workers, significant correlations are generally found between TAT-scored *n Ach* and achieving behavior. Similarly, Kagan and Mussen (1956) found that students with considerable evidences of dependency in TAT protocols were more likely to be "yielders" in a conformity experiment. Considerable research has been developed to study the relation between fantasied and actual aggression with varying findings, some negative and some positive. Positive relationship is more likely to be found when evidences of the inhibitory effects of anxiety and guilt are considered along with scoring of aggressives themes.

Studies have attempted to arouse drives experimentally and investigate consequent changes in TAT stories. R. A. Clark (1952) found that young male students who were either first shown slides of nude women or tested by an attractive and seductive (but dressed!) woman showed both a *decrease* of erotic imagery and of sex-related guilt in their TAT stories. However, when the same slides were shown after students were drinking at a beer party, there was an *increase* of sexual material and correspondingly of sexual guilt. Apparently, sexual stimulation—without the benefit of alcohol—aroused sufficient guilt that the expression of sex was inhibited and along with it guilt was lowered. However, the disinhibiting effect of alcohol acted to reduce potential guilt over sexual arousal and therefore permitted the expression of sexual themes *and* expressed guilt in the TAT.

These studies indicate too that TAT productions can reflect current states as well as more enduring traits of the individual. An extensive literature (see Harrison, 1965; Murstein, 1963; Zubin et al., 1965, for reviews) clearly shows the importance of current situational determinants. The way the test is administered, variations in stimulus materials and in instructions, characteristics of the examiner, among other factors, all influence performance.

An even larger literature shows systematic and sensible differences among age groups, between men and women, among ethnic and national groups, among socioeconomic and occupational groups, patients of different diagnoses, and among individuals differing in intelligence. Thus, in a number of studies correlations are reported between TAT IQ estimates and tests of general ability ranging in the .70's and .80's, about as high as those found between different intelligence tests. Lower-class and less-educated subjects were found to give shorter and less complete stories (Veroff, 1961; Korchin, Mitchell, and Meltzoff, 1950) with different language patterns (Mason and Ammons, 1956) and more violent themes (Harrison, 1953; Ruess, 1958). Predictable differences in sociopsychological patterns were found between ethnic groups, class groups, and natives of different nations (Harrison, 1965; Lindzey, 1961).

Reliability and Validity. The study of reliability and validity is even more complex than in the case of the Rorschach because of the lack of commonly agreed-upon scoring and analysis systems. In a pioneering study, Shneidman (1951) gave the same patient's protocol to fifteen TAT authorities, each of whom analyzed it without knowledge about the patient. Shneidman presents each psychologist's report along with his work notes, scores, and analytic considerations. It is instructive to read through the entire book, for there are manifest differences in the conclusions reached, yet, considerable areas of agreement exist, particularly for those working in the same general conceptual climate.

Harrison (1965) assembled findings from almost 100 studies of interjudge reliability, where some sort of quantitative rating was made. Of those which reported correlations (sixty-two studies), four-fifths were .70 or above, with most in the .80's and .90's, although some low coefficients were also found. In the thirty-five studies where percentage of agreement, rather than correlation, between raters was reported, the agreement was usually between 80 and 90 percent.

There were fewer studies and less consistency in studies of reliability based on global analyses. That reliability can be quite high, if the examiners are well trained and share the same conceptual system, is attested by correlations in the .90's found in the Murray group (Tomkins, 1947).

Other approaches to the study of reliability, including split-half and retest, have reported more variable and generally less convincing findings. Whether such methods are applicable is itself questionable. To ask whether a person will tell the same stories when retested is somewhat like asking whether he will laugh again when the same joke is retold (Tomkins, 1961). Tomkins himself (1942), incidentaly, has conducted one of the most interesting personolistic studies of TAT retesting. Over a ten-month period a single subject was tested repeatedly. A different card was administered on each of five days of the week. The entire test was also given at three-month intervals and on one occasion when the subject was drunk. The major themes, Tomkins found, all appeared in the first administration and reappeared, despite efforts of the subject to vary the stories, on later occasions.

The story of validity is even more complex; the literature includes flatly contradictory opinions and findings. Numerous studies have been done in every mode. After reviewing a sizeable number, Harrison (1965, p. 597) concludes: "To summarize TAT validity, there is impressive evidence that the technique possesses intrinsic validity. When on occasion empirical findings suggest otherwise, the explanation is usually to be found in methods of analysis, criteria, or experimental conditions that are inappropriate. The clinician or experimenter is and probably will continue to be an inseparable part of what is not too aptly called the Thematic Apperception Test. The 'test' is still a test of the tester." The last observation is worth underscoring, as we have previously done in other contexts. Ultimately, the utility of any wideband method and of clinical assessment itself, depends on the skill, knowledge, and self-constraint of the clinician.

One issue is worth special note. Critics and protagonists use the *same* findings as evidence against and for the TAT. Thus, the fact that the TAT reflects situationally aroused needs (as in Clark's study of sexual arousal, mentioned earlier) has been taken as evidence of invalidity on the assumption that the TAT does not, therefore, measure (only) durable personality dispositions. Protagonists—this author included—would point to the same data and note that the fact that the TAT changed sensibly when subjects were aroused shows that it can capture state changes *as well as* durable personality dispositions. Similarly, findings of stimulus and examiner effects, or for that matter differences between age, sex, educational, occupational, and cultural groups, are occasion for consternation (or glee, depending on one's commitments) only if it is assumed that "personality" is only a deeply buried, eternally constant set of dispositions determined only in the personal history of the individual. Personality properly includes both state and trait variables, momentary and enduring, individually determined and of social origin. The stethoscope is not invalidated because I arrive breathlessly at my doctor's office and my pulse is abnormally high. The hard, but necessary, task for the physician is to ascertain what is situationally determined and what might be a symptom of a heart condition. Similarly, the psychological clinician has to be able to judge what is test-related, situation-related, and psychosocially determined as well as what reflects the individual personality, in the more limited sense.

CHAPTER 11

Interpreting, Synthesizing, and Communicating Assessment Findings

The Purpose and Methods of Assessment

Clinical assessment, it was noted in Chapter 6, is the process by which clinicians gain understanding of the patient necessary for informed decisions. Evidence as to the patient's personality and psychological functioning is gathered both informally and formally. On the one hand, there are the direct data of informal assessment, akin to person perception in ordinary social life; on the other hand, there are clinical interviews, psychological tests, and systematic observation. Formal assessment builds on, extends, and sharpens, but does not replace, informal assessment. Psychological tests are the principal and most distinctive tools of the assessing clinician. Their great value lies in the fact that they allow focused observation under standard conditions in ways that reduce subjective bias, so that different individuals can be compared in more quantitative ways along relevant dimensions of psychological functioning. We have given some attention (Chapter 9) to the principles which guide test development and standardization and the study of their reliability and validity. In the preceding chapter, we considered some of the particular tests most commonly used in clinical practice.

How are assessment findings interpreted, synthesized, and communicated? How accurate and useful are the resulting analyses? Each procedure, in its own right, can be studied for its reliability and validity. Particularly in the case of "wideband" procedures, such as clinical interviews and projective techniques, it is difficult to speak of the validity of the test as such. Instead, the study of validity becomes essentially an evaluation of the accuracy and effectiveness of the interpreting clinician. This principle becomes even more true when attention is turned to clinical assessment as a whole and away from particular procedures. The issue of clinical judgment now becomes central. In this chapter we will look at problems in the interpretation, synthesis, and communication of assessment findings.

From Psychological Data to Clinical Decisions—the Role of Interpretation

WAYS OF VIEWING ASSESSMENT DATA

Each datum gathered about an individual can be conceived in three ways: (1) as a *sample* of the larger population of the patient's typical behaviors; (2) as a *correlate* of something else, and (3) as a *sign* of underlying, theoretically relevant characteristics (Sundberg and Tyler, 1962). At the first level, our observations, the patient's statements, test scores, and the like are recognized as limited samples from which the psychologist can extrapolate to similar populations outside of the clinic. Thus, if the patient does poorly on an arithmetic test, the clinician judges that he may be generally limited in his ability to handle mathematical tasks; if he appears in worn and sloppy clothing, it can be supposed that he is unconcerned about his appearance.

However, the available data may be taken as a *correlate* of a more relevant characteristic. From cumulated clinical experience or empirical research studies, manifest observations or scores have been found to indicate another trait or condition, although the relationship may not be evident to the untutored eye. Indeed, it may not even seem to be sensible. Thus, a depressed state may be indicated by the tattered appearance of the patient, for depressed people often let their appearance go, or by a pattern of MMPI scores which have been found to be given by depressed people.

Finally, the information in hand can be taken as a *sign* of underlying states or determinants. Hesitance, slowness, tears, and other visible behaviors may indicate a state of depression, reflecting a deep-lying sense of futility and guilt resulting from internal conflict. The clinician is led to find other evidences—say, black cloud responses in the Rorschach, TAT themes of defeat—which might support the depression hypothesis. Furthermore, his inferences would be checked against other types of data in the effort to locate the essential conflicts, major motive and frustrations, life circumstances and situational stresses, which within a theoretical frame of reference would make the patient's present condition explicable.

While all psychologists consider some data as sample, correlate, or sign and correspondingly operate at lower or higher levels of interpretation, there are clear differences in the orienting philosophy of psychologists in terms of which they favor one or another level of analysis. What tests are used, how they should be validated, how clinical inference should procede, how indeed personality, psychopathology, and psychotherapy should be conceived are all related issues. In general, as I noted in Chapter 6 and will again discuss later in this chapter, they cluster in two broad orientations which have been called the "psychometric" and the "clinical." In general, proponents of the first orientation favor staying closer to the data in hand—in the interests of scientific parsimony as they see it—while those of the latter persuasion see the need "to go beyond the given," in the interest of gaining more meaningful understanding.

LEVELS OF INTERPRETATION

In arriving at clinical decisions, the clinician may function with greater or lesser amounts, as well as different kinds, of interpretation. In general, three levels can be distinguished (Sundberg and Tyler, 1962).

Level 1. At this level there is a minimal amount of any sort of interpretation. The information gathered is as simply and directly related to the outcome decision as possible and there is minimal concern with intervening processes. Data are primarily treated in a sampling or correlate way, never as "signs" for there is no concern with underlying constructs to explain why "input" and "output" events are related. Suffice to know that they are, and from known relations to be able to make reasonably good predictions. The purest instances of such an approach are found in large-scale selection testing where, for example, people are given a validated aptitude test and jobs are offered to those above a critical score and denied to those who fall below it. Similarly, psychiatric screening as in the military service may involve a symptom checklist, inventory of emotional adjustment, or at most a brief structured interview. In such cases, little or no skilled clinical data collection or interpretation is needed; a clerk or computer program could function just as well and much more cheaply. For certain purposes, notably "institutional decision-making" (Cronbach and Gleser, 1965), the Level 1 process is attractive for its efficiency, standardization, and utility. What is lost along the way is the ability to consider those factors which may be of particular relevance to the individual case.

On philosophic as well as pragmatic grounds, psychologists of an atheoretical bent have argued for staying at the level of inputs and outputs, with minimal concern with intervening constructs. With B. F. Skinner, they would treat the organism as a "black box"; the relationships between antecedent events and consequent actions are the focus of their concern. Such an orientation offends the intellectual curiosity of most of us, who want very much to know what goes on in-between and who believe moreover that full understanding of psychological principles cannot exist without intervening theoretical constructs.

Level 2. At the next higher level, Sundberg and Tyler (1962) note, there are two kinds of interpretations. The first of these are *descriptive generalizations.* From the particular behaviors observed, we generalize to more inclusive, although still largely behavioral and descriptive categories. Thus, they note, a clinician might observe instances of slow bodily movements and excessive delays in answering questions and from this infer that the patient is "retarded motorically." With the further discovery that the patient eats and sleeps poorly, cries easily, reports a constant sense of futility and discouragement, and shows characteristic test behaviors, the generalization is broadened to a view of the patient as "depressed." This secondary interpretation approaches a *hypothetical construct,* i.e., the assumption of an inner state which goes logically beyond the description of visible behavior. Such constructs imply causal conditions, related personality traits and behaviors, and allow prediction of future events. According to Levy (1963), it is the movement from description to "construction" which is the essence of clinical interpretation. With interpretations at this level, whether more in the nature of descriptive generalizations or hypothetical constructs, the clinician can deductively arrive at decisions as to the further needs and treatment of the patient.

Level 3. Here the effort is to develop a coherent and inclusive *theory of the individual life,* what Sundberg and Tyler have called a "theory of the person-situation" or in somewhat less ambitious form, a "working image" of the patient. In terms of a general theoretical orientation, the clinician attempts a full-scale exploration of the individual's personality, psychosocial situation, and developmental history; in all, the various facets of the individual which were earlier described in the outline for a case study (see Chapter 6). At the fullest, the output would be a psychobiography of a sort that would make clear what the patient is, how he came to be, how he might act under specifiable conditions, and how he might change, particularly in terms of available clinical interventions. It is certainly true, as Sundberg and Tyler state, that in the contingencies of actual clinical assessment situations, we approach but do not attain this ideal theory, and settle instead for a good "working image." This consists of a looser set of hunches and hypotheses, that are generated during successive stages of gathering and analyzing clinical assessment material. In the process, certain constructs emerge that serve as "organizers" (M. Engel and Blatt, 1963) and which we will discuss in greater detail later on.

The Psychometric and Clinical Traditions in Assessment

Clinical psychology is heir to the traditions of psychometric and dynamic psychology. In principle, its strengths and potential contribution lie in the fusion of these manifestly diverse ways of thinking. In actuality, the objective and subjective orientations do not readily fuse and psychologists tend to align with one or the other tradition and the conflict between them continues. The two traditions are derivatives of long-standing and conflicting ideologies reflected in differing theories of personality, methodology of research and measurement, and approaches to psychological intervention. With specific regard to assessment, proponents of the psychometric, objective tradition would minimize interpretation and indeed, if possible, eliminate the clinician in assessment entirely; those in the clinical tradition see clinical judgment as essential for understanding and helping patients. The necessarily subjective processes by which the clinician observes, empathizes, judges, conceptualizes information, and forms theories of the person are at the core of clinical assessment. The conflict between the psychometric and clinical approaches came to a head in the issue of the relative merits of "statistical versus clinical prediction," which we will examine shortly.

First, however, let us look at some of the differences between the clinical and psychometric traditions in more detail. The comparison, along a number of dimensions, is given in Table 11.1, which reveals the many ways in which the two orientations differ. Nonetheless, there has been and should be cross-fertilization.

TABLE 11.1
The Differences Between the Psychometric and Clinical Approaches to Human Assessment

ISSUE	PSYCHOMETRIC	CLINICAL
Role of assessor	Detached observer in standardized situation; records responses; eschews empathy	Participant observer in changing interpersonal situation; values empathy
Data conceived as:	Sample or correlate of behavior	Correlate or sign
Psychological variables of typical concern	Abilities, interests, personality traits	Motives, needs, conflicts, adaptive capacities
Preferred assessment techniques	Favors "narrow-band, high-fidelity" measures; objective in form and scoring; univariate; minimizes interpretation	Favors "wide-band, lower-fidelity" techniques; projective in form; judgmental in scoring; multivariate; depends on interpretation
Preferred mode of test development	Empirical or internal-consistency (factor analytic)	Rational-theoretical
Approach to validation	Content and criterion	Construct
Mode of data combination	Statistical (actuarial)	Judgmental
Level of interpretation	Level 1 to 2	Level 2 to 3
Type of decision-making	Oriented to institutional decision-making	Oriented to individual decision-making
Ideals of assessment	Accuracy of measurement; prediction of criteria; understanding of psychological variables as they differ between persons	Fullness of description; theoretical relatedness; understanding of psychological variables as they interplay within a person
Role of prediction	Central	Secondary to understanding

Clinical assessment requires the objective and statistical tools of psychometric science, not to substitute for but to sharpen its traditional approaches. The criticism and research attacks on the clinical method, generated by those of psychometric bent, can serve as challenge to discipline the thinking of workers in the clinical tradition. It is not easy, but it is necessary, to blend the best of both traditions.

Statistical Methods in Clinical Decision-Making

The techniques developed by students of psychological measurement are not substitutes for clinical judgment, but they provide valuable tools for the clinician. They can be of distinct help in the process of interpretation.

ORGANIZING AND QUANTIFYING CLINICAL DATA

For any statistical analysis, the fundamental need is for reliable classification of the phenomena being studied. In the clinic, there is first the necessary task of recording, grouping, and classifying clinical statistics in organized and consistent form. Such quantification properly includes dichotomous data, such as male-female, psychotic-neurotic, and accepted-refused therapy, as well as continuous scores, such as age, IQ, length of hospitalization, etc. In general, records should include: (1) information about the *patient,* in terms of social characteristics, life circumstances, and symptoms and, as well, the specific scores and inferences of assessment; (2) information about *clinical decisions,* e.g., to offer psychotherapy or hospitalization; and (3) measures of *outcome*—How long did the patient stay in psychotherapy? What were the results? Evidences of psychological change?—and so on.

Data of these types are obviously needed for research or evaluation studies. Investigations of test validity, correlates of psychotherapy, therapy outcome determinants, among others, start with such measures. In the same way, "program-evaluation" studies of the particular clinic depend on reliable and accessible clinical statistics. In addition, of course, any particular research study is likely to require specially designed measures, statistical comparisons, and analyses. With such data one can answer general questions about the clinical process or about the functioning of the particular clinic. However, the same sort of material can also facilitate decisions in the individual case. Thus, for example, clinic statistics used to discover whether in general adolescent boys fare better in psychotherapy with women than with men therapists can also help decide whether eighteen-year-old Joe Winkowski might better be assigned to Dr. Colleen O'Flaherty or to Dr. David Greenberg.

EXPERIENCE TABLES AS A BASIS FOR PREDICTION

An experience table, also called "actuarial" from the practice of life-insurance statisticians, records the relationship between a result and one or more predictor variables which have been discovered in many cases. It has been used successfully in sociological research, for example, in the prediction of parole violation. Thus, Burgess (1928, cited by Gough, 1962) in a classic study developed an experience table to predict parole violation, which incorporated a number of variables found to be meaningfully related to the criterion. Whereas 28.4 percent of all parolees from an Illinois prison violated parole (this is the base rate), the group with no work record prior to prison had 44.4 percent violators; with casual work, 30.3 percent; with irregular work history, 24.3 percent; and with regular work records, 12.2 percent. When this variable is combined with a number of others, a composite score is obtained which at the high end corresponds to an expectancy rate of 99 percent nonviolators and at the low end, 24 percent. There are many logical and statistical problems in such experience tables, as Gough (1962) shows. Among others, it should be noted that there is a tendency for the relations found in the original group to become reduced in cross-validation on another population. Moreover, account has to be taken of the base rate, because it is against this standard that the accuracy of prediction has to be judged. When the base rate departs considerably from 50–50, it becomes increasingly difficult to improve base-rate predictions (Meehl and Rosen, 1955). Thus, if 90 percent of former prisoners actually succeed on parole, one would obviously be making very few errors by predicting that *all* would succeed. Even when the base rate was as high as in Burgess' sample, Gough shows that the experience-table prediction is not significantly above the base-rate prediction. A relatively crude predictor might be useful if we wanted to release only the very best prospects, thereby running the risk of keeping many in prison who might well succeed on parole. However, in the case where we want to minimize both types of prediction errors—both false positives and false negatives—then knowledge of the base rate is critical, for the predictor has to improve on it.

Clinical judgment can be strengthened by cumulating base-rate data and generating experience tables for the work of the clinic or hospital. These would record the types of patients seen, by such characteristics as age, sex, and the like, diagnoses made, types of treatment, outcomes, and other relevant information. For example, if it is discovered that eighteen-year-old boys, regardless of the therapist's sex, typically break off psychotherapy within ten hours, this might well figure into our decision about Joe Winkowski.

NORMS FOR TEST SCORES AND PROFILES

An important statistical aid to interpretation is provided by test norms. As we have already discussed in Chapter 9, these describe the distribution of scores on a particular test or subtest found in a normative sample; the individual patient's performance is evaluated by reference to his relative position in the table of norms. The score itself may be transformed, as in the case of IQs, to percentile or standard scores, so that the individual's position is immediately evident. Earlier, we noted the importance of checking the relevance of the normative sample for the evaluation of the particular patient's record. Local norms, just as local base rates, should be collected by clinicians working with tests. If, for example, a particular child tests out at a Stanford-Binet IQ of 100, but in his particular class in this particular community, the mean is 115, he may in fact act and feel dumb and suffer the emotional consequences. It matters little that he stands at the mean of the national normative group.

Test norms do not, in themselves, tell anything about the validity of the test for particular decisions. Too often, we and our patients take test results too literally. I remember all too well my first "case" when I was a starting graduate student in psychology. An undergraduate came to me with the story that he had been given a vocational interest test and had been told that he had the interest pattern and abilities for a medical career. At the moment, he was fighting a heroic but losing fight with the premedical curriculum, while discovering interests in political science and law. Though miserable, he was willing to continue to go on to his test-determined future, but needed help. In going over the test findings, it was clear enough that he had ample ability for any of a number of fields and, that in any case, he would do better and be happier if he pursued his real interests. It took a few minutes to say just this and he left relieved and happy. Sometime later, I learned that he was a dedicated and successful lawyer. I wish that I could say that all our psychological interventions are as quick or effective. This case illustrates how the literal reading of test scores and norms can create problems which in this case could easily be reversed.

A more vital illustration of the harm testing can do is becoming increasingly evident. Social critics and psychological theorists (McClelland, 1973) are insisting that present standardized intelligence tests can perpetuate social injustice by labeling poor and minority people inadequate and then further reducing job and educational opportunities for them by using test scores in selection. The direct evidence that IQ scores relate to capacity for achievement is scanty, except insofar as both are related to social class. What is needed, McClelland argues, are direct measures of the relevant competencies rather than the present class-biased measures of so-called general intelligence.

Where tests involve a number of subtests or separate scores, more complex norms have been developed to code and compare score profiles. In the preceding chapter, we noted that virtually all of the major tests used by clinicians are multifaceted and in the case of the Rorschach, WAIS, and, notably, the MMPI more complex statistics have been developed to compare score profiles.

THE USE OF MULTIPLE REGRESSION

If a number of variables correlate with a criterion, then, through the statistical method of multiple regression, an equation can be written which will allow the best estimate of the criterion from known values on the predictor measures. The equation is of the form $y = a + bx + cz$ (and so on) for the number of variables involved; it is called a "regression equation" where there is only one predictor variable. Suppose, as a hypothetical instance, that we wished to predict students' freshman college grades. It might have been discovered that high-school grades correlate highly with college freshman performance, but so too do teacher's ratings of "energy" and "conscientiousness," and test scores on "self-esteem." These may correlate in differing degrees with each other. In fact, if the intercorrelations among the predictor variables are all rather low, though each relates well with the criterion (freshman college grades), this would indicate that separate traits are involved which, taken together, allow a more powerful prediction. Multiple regression is thus a statistical method which draws from the matrix of intercorrelations among predictors and criterion a set of weights for each score and produces an equation for combining them into a prediction formula. Although many stages of theoretical and empirical analysis may have been involved in finding the best set of predictor variables, once the formula exists it can be applied mechanically. No psychological knowledge or skill is then required.

Other methods of statistical (or actuarial or mechanical) prediction include the discriminant function and methods which have attempted to treat the combining of variables in more configural or patterned ways. Regression analysis, it can be seen, involves the linear combination of variables; $y = a + bx$ is the formula for a straight line. Sometimes, however, curvilinear relationships exist; above a point, more is not necessarily better. Perhaps with too much "self-esteem," one can be cocky, not study sufficiently and hence do poorly in school; thus, above a particular value the weight given the "self-esteem" score may reverse. To account for phenomena such as these, more sophisticated statistical techniques have been developed.

Under optimum conditions, regression analysis and kindred methods of statistical prediction are powerful tools and have served well, but these are not usually the conditions under which clinicians work. Ideally, large numbers of subjects should be involved. There should be clear, quantitative criteria (such as passing or failing courses, typing speed or other measures of job skills or output), available measures should be reliable, and preferably simple and inexpensive to use. Conditions should be stable, for the prediction formula—unlike the human judge—cannot accommodate to changing circumstances.

In the main, statistical prediction methods are better suited for large-scale selection and placement testing in industrial, military, or educational settings than in dealing with the typical problems of clinical decision-making. The matter of predictive efficiency aside, the clinician works within a value system which makes it difficult—if not impossible—to turn aside a prospective client as easily as an applicant for a position can be rejected. Often the decision takes on a life-or-death quality; sometimes literally, if one is trying to predict whether a particular patient may be suicidal. We know that the base rate for suicide in the general population is very low and not much higher among psychiatric patients. Test data may suggest depressive trends, inwardly turned aggression, but no conclusive evidence of the signs sometimes found in suicidal persons. Thus, in terms of base-rate and test predictors, the "smart-money" bet would be that the patient will not commit suicide. But, with a human life involved, and any reasonable basis for concern, the necessary clinical decision is to take all possible precautions to guard the patient from self-inflicted harm. Whatever the actual odds, a wrong guess is too tragic to risk.

Clinical Versus Statistical Prediction

Statistical methods are clearly of value to clinical practice and research. But the question has been vigorously argued whether they are not to be preferred to clinical judgment. Some critics of clinical assessment have proposed that statistical methods are scientifically more valid, useful, and economical tools which can and should wherever possible substitute for the judgmental methods of the clinician. To support this view, evidence is presented to show the relative merit of a statistical (actuarial, mechanical, formal) approach over a clinical (judgmental) approach to the prediction of behavior.

Right off, it should be noted that joining the issue in the realm of prediction reflects both a limited view of clinical assessment and of the nature of science generally. It is based on the disputable assumption that the capacity to predict is the fundamental proof of scientific knowledge. As noted earlier (Chapter 2), this is a limited and particular view of science, for it is as or more logical to argue that the basic goal of science is *understanding* of lawfully determined phenomena, with both *prediction* and *control* being fortunate but not essential by-products. In any case, making specific predictions about future behavior is only a limited part of the actual work of the clinician, whose greater concern is describing and understanding the patient's character and problems. Moreover, the specific sorts of predictive tasks put to clinicians in empirical studies intended to contrast the two approaches rarely parallel the real-life concerns of clinicians but instead put them in the wholly anomalous role of guessing at future grades, success in military or occupational training, and other matters about which they have little knowledge and which bear little resemblance to their usual tasks.

Sarbin's (1943) was the first study specifically designed to contrast and evaluate statistical and clinical predictions. Entering university students were studied and the task was to predict academic success in the freshman year. Statistical predictions were made by a clerk using a previously developed multiple-regression equation. The two predictor variables involved were high-school percentile rank and the score on a college aptitude test. By contrast, the clinical predictions were made by five staff members of the university's student-counseling center. At their disposal were not only the two scores (though, of course, without knowledge of the regression weights), but also scores on vocational interest and personality inventories, aptitude and achievement tests, biographical information, and an interview before the start of classes.

At the end of the fall quarter, the two sets of predictions were correlated with the grades actually obtained by the student subjects. No significant differences were found between the two methods, as shown by the following correlations:

	MEN	WOMEN
Clinical	.35	.69
Statistical	.45	.70

Here, it seemed, was clear evidence that case analyses, with all the additional information available, did not improve on predictions which could be made more efficiently by a regression equation previously developed empirically from the correlations of two predictor variables with the criterion measure. Indeed, Sarbin suggests, and argues more extensively later (Sarbin, Taft, and Bailey, 1960), that the clinician uses the same data but less accurately and efficiently. Clinical inference, as he sees it, is essentially an imprecise form of statistical inference.

Meehl's famous volume *Clinical Versus Statistical Prediction* (1954) polarized the issue for many psychologists. Along with thoughtful and sensitive analysis of the processes involved in each and of the special requirements and advantages of both the statistical and clinical approaches, Meehl surveyed a number of empirical studies which compared them. He concluded:

> In spite of the defects and ambiguities present, let me emphasize the brute fact that we have here, depending upon one's standards for admission as relevant, from sixteen to twenty studies involving a comparison of clinical and actuarial methods, *in all but one of which the predictions made actuarially were either approximately equal or superior to those made by a clinician* [p. 119].

In a scholarly, historically oriented review of the issues and methods involved, Gough (1962) also surveyed a number of predictive studies. In general, he concludes that neither approach has fared particularly well but that the available evidence would favor the statistical. However, he notes further "No fully adequate study of the clinician's forecasting skills has been carried out" (p. 573). In a later paper, Meehl (1965) stated that he had by then collected some fifty studies and his earlier conclusion remained unaltered. He noted however that one good instance of clinicians surpassing statistical methods had been found in a study by Lindzey (1965). In that experiment it was found that two expert clinical interpreters could better distinguish heterosexual from homosexual TAT stories than could an actuarial system based on earlier correlative analyses. However, L. R. Goldberg (1968) reanalyzed Lindzey's data and claims that the clear superiority of clinical judges is not demonstrated.

Sawyer (1966) broadened the scope of the problem by distinguishing clinical and statistical measurement as well as prediction methods. Both Meehl and Gough defined the controversy in terms of alternate ways of combining data, whether mechnically by the techniques of the statistician or in the clinician's head; what data were used and how they were originally obtained, i.e., by judgmental or by quantitative means, was intentionally ignored. To compare along the two dimensions, Sawyer surveyed forty-five studies which represented differing combinations of clinical and statistical measurement and of clinical and statistical prediction. He concludes that "The present analysis finds the mechanical mode of combination always equal or superior to the clinical mode; moreover, this is true whether data were collected clinically or mechanically," (p. 192). Matters are not so clear, however, in the comparison of clinical and statistical measurement. Indeed, the best results were obtained when both were used together to provide the data from which a mechanical combination was made. Thus, Sawyer concludes further that "This suggests that the clinician may be able to contribute most not by direct prediction, but rather by providing, in objective form, judgments to be combined mechanically," (p. 193). The clinician is thus relegated to an instrumental role. While he may contribute some usable ratings along the way, he is less to be trusted in the final synthesis and prediction. Sawyer's survey, as well as Meehl's earlier writings, supported many psychologists in their conviction that clinical assessment is an uncertain and perhaps worthless enterprise.

The reasons why such a conclusion is unjustified are best revealed in a series of incisive and scholarly papers by Holt (1958, 1969, 1970). He calls attention to the methodological and logical errors in the design and selection of studies in these reviews and shows, overall, that they give a grossly unfair view of the state of clinical assessment. First of all, there is more evidence in the research literature favoring the clinical side than is usually included in such surveys. The Lindzey study has been noted; Holt also calls attention to the greater efficacy of clinical than actuarial in his own studies of psychiatric residents (Holt and Luborsky, 1958) and to a survey by Korman (1968). Over much the same period as Sawyer, Korman studied forty attempts to predict managerial performance. He concludes:

> Perhaps the most intriguing finding that emerges from this review is the relative usefulness of the "judgmental prediction" methods, as exemplified by executive assessment procedures and peer ratings. While allowance must be made for the generally small samples involved and for the general paucity of research overall, it would seem that there is no basis for assuming any superiority of the "actuarial" over the "clinical" method at this time. In fact, the evidence is to the contrary [Korman, 1968, p. 316, cited by Holt, 1970, p. 338].

Some other limitations in the research literature comparing clinical and statistical prediction are briefly noted here:

1. The criteria being predicted are often inadequately conceived or defined and are usually of a type quite unlike the behaviors ordinarily assessed by clinicians. Thus, predictions are required of future grades, occupational success, hos-

pital discharge, and the like. In some of these cases the prediction criterion may not even depend on the qualities of the person of the type clinicians are trained to assess, but instead depend on the acts of unknown others in unknown future situations. In one study where clinicians collaborated with the investigator in developing scales that made sense to them, reliable and valid inferences from psychological test interpretations were reported (Lewisohn et al., 1963).

2. In about one-third of the studies Sawyer surveyed, Holt (1970) notes that the prediction formula is applied to the same sample from which it was originally derived rather than to a new (cross-validational) sample of subjects. It is well known that correlations tend to shrink in cross-validation.

3. In only about half of the studies reviewed by Sawyer were the "clinicians" actually trained professionals; in the remainder, they were students, military officers, or the subjects themselves. The implied reasoning is: "If clinicians use judgment, then anyone using judgment is a clinician." This is a patent fallacy. However, even when trained clinicians are used, the implicit question usually is "Can the average clinical psychologist predict some criterion better than the best statistical formula that can be devised?" There are certainly considerable differences among judges, and one would hope that individual judges would be treated as respectfully as individual formulas. It is important to know what clinicians at their best can do, much as one would wish to study the best statistical techniques. Indeed, L. R. Goldberg (1970) argues that the behavior of the best clinical judges should be used as a basis for developing better actuarial equations which can then replace their human progenitors.

5. In many studies, the only data available to the clinical judges were quantitative scores, usually MMPI profiles. With such a constraint the clinician can only apply an informal actuarial method, which might then predictably be less efficient than an empirically derived formula. A fair test of clinical judgment has to allow access to relevant, qualitative data as well as to test scores.

Virtually all of the published studies oppose *pure actuarial* against *naive clinical* methods, without testing the power of *sophisticated clinical* prediction (Holt, 1958, 1969, 1970). Although interest has focused on the final stage of the prediction process involving the combination of obtained data by judgmental or by mechanical means, it should be noted that there are at least five earlier steps in the process. The pure actuarial approach uses psychometric techniques and concepts, minimizing judgment all along the way in order finally to use objective data to predict statistically an objective criterion at the end. By contrast, a naive clinical prediction involves intuitive processing of qualitative data by whatever rules experience or whim dictate without study of the criterion or the relevance of the assessment data to it. Through the entire process, clinical judgment is used, not simply to integrate data and make predictions but as an alternative to discovering relevant facts.

But, as Holt notes, there is another course, the sophisticated clinical prediction, which can combine the best of both traditions. As in the actuarial approach, job analyses, pilot studies, item analyses, and successive cross-validational trials can be undertaken, but at the same time the clinician uses qualitative information and his personal judgment. "It would be a perverse clinician indeed who claimed that a casual, informal, uncontrolled approach was necessarily better than a disciplined, unbiased one. It is not being 'more clinical' to give tests in a slipshod manner than to do so precisely and carefully. Why, therefore, should it be assumed that prediction is clinical only when the person doing the predicting does not have the benefit of well-organized procedures?" (Holt, 1969, p. 788). As yet, there are no studies which clearly oppose statistical procedures to sophisticated clinical prediction.

When all is said and done, Meehl (1957) notes, we still have to "use our heads instead of the formula." Clinical judgment is required because, with rare exceptions, formulas simply do not exist. This is true in most areas in which clinicians have to make decisions, but it is even more clearly evident where the prediction is about events which have not occurred or are so infrequent that no experience tables could possibly have been developed. Moreover, even if there were an actuarial formula which predicted with fair accuracy, infrequent or unforeseen contingencies could negate the prediction. An actuarial approach works best when we are dealing with regularly recurrent events in their more usual forms. Thus, in the limited case of formal diagnosis, an actuarial analysis would be most useful in the diagnosis of the usual, average, or "textbook case." But it is precisely this type of person who is least likely to be referred to the psychologist; the clinician is more commonly asked to see the patient with confusing and contradictory signs. For pragmatic as well as theoretical reasons the methods of the actuary are of limited value in the clinic.

Research to date simply does not constitute a proper test of the adequacy of clinical assessment. It does show that, under particular circumstances, actuarial methods can indeed predict individual behavior, thus contradicting the extreme idiographic position. At the same time, it does not support the position (e.g., Sarbin, 1943, 1960) that clinical inference is nothing but informal and relatively crude statistical inference. Depending on the problem on hand, either statistical or clinical prediction is better adapted to its solution.

What emerges is the realization that systematic, organized, and disciplined judgment and inquiry are essential to either a statistical or clinical approach. A naive clinical approach is surely worse than either a sophisticated clinical or pure actuarial, but the choice between the latter two has to be made in terms of the particular task requirements—whether, for example, institutional or individual decision-making is primarily involved, whether there are large numbers of subjects, a stable criterion, more usual than idiosyncratic conditions, and the like—and not because of ideological commitment.

Let us now go on to examine the process of interpretation as it is used in clinical assessment and consider further some of the ways in which it can be disciplined and improved.

The Process of Interpretation

An often-cited illustration of skillful clinical interpretation was originally described by Theodore Reik (1948):

> One session at this time took the following course. After a few sentences about the uneventful day, the patient fell into a long silence. She assured me that nothing was in her thoughts. Silence from me. After many minutes she complained about a toothache. She told me that she had been to the dentist yesterday. He had given her an in-

> jection and then had pulled a wisdom tooth. The spot was hurting again. New and longer silence. She pointed to my bookcase in the corner and said, "There's a book standing on its head." Without the slightest hesitation and in a reproachful voice I said, "But why did you not tell me that you had had an abortion?" [p. 263].

His inference was correct. Reik's own analysis of how he arrived at it is well worth studying; important cues included the tooth extraction as a symbol of forcible birth and the image of the book on its head suggesting the fetus. Whatever the reasoning, however, clearly it is of a sort which cannot be programmed for actuarial analysis and prediction.

Similarly, blind analysis of projective test records sometimes reveal strikingly accurate inferences, though they can also be grossly mistaken. Commenting on clinical assessment, Cronbach (1970) notes:

> Nearly every clinical tester can point to cases where projective techniques gave him insight into unique features of individuals. Features so rare that they could not possibly be attributed to chance. George DeVos once analyzed the Rorschach record of a research worker he had never met and, in reporting on the inferred personality structure, commented, "This man ought to be a historian. He'd be completely happy down in Washington digging minute details out of the Lincoln archives" (these being a set of century-old documents that had just been opened to scholars). The man was a specialist in a field in which historical research is most uncommon—but he actually was in Washington at the time the analysis was made, extracting detailed information from 50-year-old files of a Congressional committee! Such "hits" cannot be explained away, and constitute the most persuasive evidence of the value of projective methods [pp. 680–682].

In the same vein, two studies by Margaret T. Singer illustrate what an astute clinician can do with Rorschach protocols in clinical research (cited by Harris, 1968). The first case concerned the differentiation of ulcer patients from those with ulcerative colitis, two medical conditions for which psychodynamic correlates have been proposed. An earlier research study had reported that of the many individual Rorschach scores only the total number of responses reliably distinguished the two groups (Krasner and Kornreich, 1954). In the face of these negative findings, Singer did a blind sorting of the same protocols, on the basis of her extensive experience both with psychosomatic patients and with the Rorschach. She predicted correctly in fifty out of fifty-four cases. Moreover, she was then able to describe the cues which determined her judgments and other psychologists were able to discriminate between the groups with better-than-chance accuracy. The second illustration derives from Singer's extensive work with schizophrenic patients and their parents. Here, she has been able to distinguish the Rorschach records of schizophrenics (both patients and parents) from those of both normal and neurotic patients and families with a high degree of precision. Again, she has been able to make explicit her interpretative criteria and to provide analytic standards that can readily be applied by others (M. T. Singer and Wynne, 1965).

The essential task facing the clinician is the synthesis of diverse and sometimes fragmentary bits of information into a coherent picture of the individual. Toward this end, interpretation is needed to fit the given facts together into a meaningful and useful conceptual scheme that can account for the patient's thoughts, feelings, and actions. In the multiprocedure, multilevel model of clinical assessment, the available "raw data" include the clinician's first-hand observations, impressions, and empathic reactions, the reactions of others as viewed by the patient and/or reported to the clinician, the patient's self-description in interviews and tests, his performance in test situations, both in terms of idiosyncratic responses and scores or profiles which allow comparison with others. With all this before him, the clinician must develop hypotheses which encompass and make sense of as much of the information as possible. The process is guided by more-or-less formulated theory and more-or-less systematized knowledge, but in large measure concepts arise inductively from the evidence in hand. Along the way, the psychologist moves from a simple description to descriptive generalizations, then to secondary inferences about intervening variables and constructs, and finally to a more total view of the particular person; generally from a lower to a higher level of interpretation. But, at the same time, there is movement "down" as well as "up," for as ideas are formed available material is again reviewed and additional information sought to test emergent hypotheses. In all, therefore, interpretation involves the continuous interplay of hypothesis-forming and hypothesis-testing acts toward the end of formulating the best possible theory of the person.

In the experience of the clinician, understanding of the patient develops somewhat like a photographic print emerging in the developing bath. Broad but vague outlines become more articulated; small separate areas of clear detail emerge and join as connecting portions clarify. M. Engel and Blatt (1962) studied their own inferences and later those of six experienced colleagues, as they analyzed the protocols of a test battery. By thinking aloud, they could externalize and record what usually goes on in the clinician's head. They were able to catalog a number of types of inferences: (1) The earliest statements could be called *preinferential*. Curious items were noted, slight peculiarities noticed and underscored, as it were, but left uninterpreted; (2) *Descriptive inferences* were made—of the sort "he is anxious"—that correctly described a trait of the patient though not notably distinguishing him from others; (3) *Conditional inferences* were made, both of a sort which suggest but do not state a condition for the expression of a personality quality (e.g., this patient is excit*able*) and those which clearly state the contingencies (he is excitable *when* . . .); and finally (4) *Conjunctive inferences* in which at least two concepts are linked with some features of the test data. They give as illustration a statement such as: "His fantasies terrorize him and he constantly tries to degrade this terror by attempts at logical thinking." Such a proposition is related to the theoretical propositions that one's fantasies can be terrifying, that terror instigates defense, and that logical thought can have a defensive function. It opens new issues and suggests inferences which can be further checked in the data.

The emerging picture, M. Engel and Blatt note, is less gradual than the photographic analogy might suggest, for there are turning points in the process as hypotheses crystallize. Prior to these points, ideas are generated freely; afterwards, some are clearly excluded and confirmation for other inferences is actively sought. What enters at these points they term "organizers." These are concepts which link the observations to a relatively cohesive personality theory. They exist at a higher level of abstraction than the inferences they organize; they have considerable salience and importance for understanding the organization of the personality. The organizer, they note, is not sought for, rather it emerges, though once in view, it suggests further inferences. What kind of "organizers" are used depends on the conceptual framework or the psychologist. They could derive from psychiatric nosology, e.g., "schizophrenic"; Engel and Blatt draw on the richer conceptual system of psychoanalytic ego psychology.

Many psychologists, as we have seen, believe that interpretation in this mode is needlessly complex and subjective and of dubious validity. They prefer to work at a lower level of interpretation and, indeed, question the need for understanding the individual personality as a condition for clinical decision-making in the first place. From such an orientation, the necessary inference process has been viewed more in hypothesis-testing than in hypothesis-forming terms. Thus, Sarbin and his co-workers (1960) have conceptualized clinical inference as akin to the syllogistic reasoning processes described by logicians. They use the term "taxonomic sorting" to describe a series of stages during which, in effect, hypotheses about the particular patient are made. First, there is a *postulate system,* based in the cumulated experience, beliefs, and knowledge of the clinician from which he develops a *major premise:* "Patients with good prior work histories, intact families, and no visible thought disturbance are likely to fare well after hospital discharge." From the assessment of the particular patient, the clinician forms a *minor premise:* "Smith is one of that class of patients who earlier had a good job, is married, and now performs well on a Proverb Test." The minor premise is reached through acts of *instantiation;* that is, matching the patient's characteristics to those required for class membership. With these two premises in hand, the conclusion follows: "Smith will probably do well in the community and should therefore be discharged." Unlike the logician, the psychologist works in probabilistic rather than absolute statements, but the essential task is the same—to reach a logical conclusion (or here, clinical decision). Even though the clinician may have no sense of proceeding through such a logical sequence, Sarbin argues that he in fact does. Recall, in this same connection, our earlier discussion of empathy in which attention was called to Sarbin's argument that what has been called empathic is simply unverbalized and often inaccurate inference (Chapter 7). Whether gathering or interpreting data, the process of clinical inference should be made explicit and always utilize the best empirical and quantitative data. In the end, therefore, statistical means could then be created which could either fully substitute for, or at least markedly improve, the clinician's judgments.

There is little doubt that some questions of formal diagnosis and clinical decision-making could be cast in this model and indeed computerized decision-programs have been evolved in some cases. But in one critical respect Sarbin's model cannot substitute for clinical interpretation. In its essence it describes a process of hypothesis-testing, where the central question is of the type "Is Smith the sort of person who has the characteristics of persons already known to be good risks for discharge?" Instead, as earlier noted, the critical issue in personological interpretation is essentially of a hypothesis-generating sort: "What kind of a person is Smith? How can we best understand his behavior? Does he have resources to cope effectively with forseeable posthospital demands?" We not only test to see if Smith's attributes fit existing categories, but indeed we may have the task of discovering the variables which best fit Smith. In the process, we work inductively, most of the time, up from the data in hand not down from premises and decision rules. The personolistic theory which emerges and which then allows further deductions and predictions involves an essentially creative process which cannot be described by processes of instantiation and taxonomic sorting alone.

What then is involved? The term "clinical intuition" is sometimes used, either admiringly or disparagingly depending on one's bent, to describe one facet of interpretation. The term has at least two meanings. The clinician may not know the cues on which his judgment is based. The old clinician's "he just smells schizy" or his young colleague's "the vibes are bad" may well reflect sensitive empathic responses to relevant but unidentified qualities of the patient. Empathic perception of subtle cues is a necessary and powerful tool of the clinician, but this is not to say that the unidentified stimulus is necessarily unidentifiable, as is sometimes implied by clinicians. For clinical skill to be transmittable, as in the illustration of Margaret Singer's Rorschach analyses, it is the essential task of the clinician to identify the cues involved.

A second meaning of intuition is more pertinent to our present concern: The clinical interpreter may not know the way he reached a particular conclusion, although he can be quite aware of the cues involved. At the interpretative moment, the parts seem simply to fit together though why this is so cannot then, nor perhaps later, be explained. In subsequent examination, the skillful clinician, as in Reik's case, can reconstruct the pattern of inference, discovering too where logical leaps were made. The good clinician is not only one who is more likely to be accurate in the first instance, but he is also more capable of later reconstruction and explication of the reasoning process involved. Clinical interpretation necessarily involves going beyond the immediately obvious, combining informational cues in novel ways, often not knowing in the particular moment why a given conclusion seems right. These are qualities, of course, of everyday thinking as well; in more dramatic forms, they are the essence of creative thinking.

The often-raised question of whether the clinician functions as artist or scientist confuses matters, for science itself is both "art" and "science." This is particularly true in that phase of the scientific process which Reichenbach (1938) called the "context of discovery," during which organizing concepts and understanding of the essential issues emerge and hypotheses are formed. This is in contrast to the later "context of justification" in which evidence is systematically sought to test the validity of one or another thesis. Meehl thus notes: ". . . high-level clinical hypothesizing partakes to some degree of that kind of psychological process which is involved in the creation of scientific theory" (1954, p. 65). In this process, intuition or what Reik has called "conjecture" figure prominently. This is not to deny, of course, that conjecture can be inept and inaccurate, nor that "intuition" cannot cloak ignorance. But these processes in their disciplined and "high-level" forms are necessary and creative parts of clinical interpretation as well as of science generally. Science requires the evolution of guiding concepts arrived at inductively from exploration of and speculation about the phenomena in hand, as well as the more commonly recognized process of formal testing of propositions deduced from more general theoretical principles. Sarbin's position and his attack on clinical interpretation as unscientific is based on the mistaken equation of the nondeductive and nonformal with the nonrational.

Some Sources of Error in Clinical Interpretation

Let us consider now some of the dangers and pitfalls in clinical interpretation and some ways they can be minimized or avoided. To some extent, we will be recalling the earlier discussion of the sources of bias and distortion in person perception (Chapter 7). Although the clinician's techniques should, and to some extent do, reduce some of the problems inherent in informal assessment, at heart they still depend on the psychological judgment of one person made by another. Thus, for example, stereotypic thinking in the clinician, deception by the subject, and "demand characteristics" of the situation could distort judgments of personality in formal as well as informal assessment. There are, of course, some issues particular to the clinician's interpretation and synthesis of test and interview data which are a step removed from direct observation and interaction, but in important respects the processes and difficulties of interpretation are similar in the two cases.

Clinical experience and research point up a number of difficulties in interpretation and allow us to make some cautionary comments.

SCHEMATIZATION

All humans, unhappily including clinicians, have a limited capacity to process information and to form concepts. Consequently, the resulting picture of the individual can be schematized and simplified, perhaps centering on one or a few salient and dramatic (too often, pathological) characteristics. The resulting interpretations are too organized and consistent and the person emerges a two-dimensional caricature. The clinical interpreter has to be able to tolerate complexity and deal at one time with more data than he can comfortably handle.

INFORMATION-OVERLOAD

At the same time, there can be too much material and the clinician is overwhelmed. Studies have shown that clinical judges typically use less information than is available to them. The need usually is to gather an optimal, rather than maximal, amount of information of a sort digestible by the particular clinician. Obviously, familiarity with the tests involved, type of patient, referral questions, and the like figure in deciding how much of what kind of material is collected and how extensively it can be interpreted. However, a smaller amount may be as justified as a larger amount, with the additional benefit of reducing time and cost, if as has been suggested by some experiments (e.g., Kostlan, 1954; Golden, 1964) additional procedures do not add appreciably to the inferences that can be drawn from a more limited battery.

INSUFFICIENT INTERNAL EVIDENCE FOR INTERPRETATION

Ideally, interpretations should emerge as evidence converges from many sources, such as different responses and scores of the same test, responses of different tests, self-report, observation, etc. Particularly for interpretations at higher levels supportive evidence is required. It is at best risky, at worst foolhardy, to interpret important personality themes from one or a few indicators. There is no simple formula for deciding how much evidence is enough evidence. Certainty is gained as information of different sources come together to support the same inference. In a general way, the process is similar to the work of the detective or law court in discovering "truth."

OVERINTERPRETATION

Related is the temptation to overinterpret assessment material in pursuit of a dramatic or encompasing formulation. Deep interpretations, seeking for unconscious motives and nuclear conflicts, or those which attempt genetic reconstruction of the personality are always to be made cautiously and only on the basis of convincing evidence. Interpreting symbols in terms of fixed meanings is a cheap and usually inaccurate attempt at psychoanalytic interpretation; recall that Freud himself reminded overzealous followers that "sometimes a cigar *is* a cigar" and elsewhere warned against the dangers of "wild analysis." At all times, the skillful clinician should be able to indicate the relationship between the interpreted hypothetical variable and its referents in overt behavior.

INSUFFICIENT EXTERNAL VERIFICATION OF INTERPRETATION

Too often clinicians interpret assessment material and report on the patients without further checking on the accuracy of their statements. What might be called "personal validation studies" have constantly to be made in at least these regards: (1) opportunity should be sought to match one's own view of the patient with those of fellow-clinicians who have observed the patient from different perspectives, e.g., as therapist, ward-nurse, etc. A good case conference is invaluable in this regard; (2) the assessing clinician should follow-up the patient, to discover what in fact happens later in his life, whether predictions made at the point of assessment hold up, what unforeseen events might make apparently erroneous predictions understandable; and (3) in general, the clinician should keep tabs on his "hits" and "misses" as he cumulates experience, to discover in retrospect at least with what kind of patient he seems best to function, where he might have particular blind spots, where he tends to over- or underinterpret and so on. Such self-study is in the same class with the clinician's need to generate local base-rates, test norms, and other information of a statistical sort. In all these instances, the clinician tests his work against criteria external to himself.

LACK OF INDIVIDUALIZATION

It is perfectly possible to make correct statements which are entirely worthless, because they could as well apply to anyone under most conditions, for example: "In the initial interview, the patient was nervous." Few patients are calm; more important would be an estimate, even in only roughly quantitative terms, of the extent and type of the anxiety, the conditions which accentuated or attenuated it, the needs and conflicts to which it is related. To the extent that qualities of the patient can be characterized in intensive, conditional, and relational terms we are approaching personolistic assessment and moving away from what Tallent (1958) once called "Aunt Fanny" descriptions, those that might apply to anyone's Aunt Fanny as well as the patient.

LACK OF INTEGRATION

A related problem is seen in the novice clinician's tendency to note trait on trait, as if putting beads on a string, without conceptualizing how they are related to each other. Human personality is organized and integrated, usually in hierarchical systems. It is of central importance to understand which facets of the personality are most central and which are peripheral, which needs subserve others, and how defensive, coping, and ego functions are organized, if understanding of the personality is to be achieved. Over-cautiousness, insufficient knowledge, or a lack of a theoretical framework are sometimes revealed in contradictory interpretations made side by side. On the face of it, a person could not be called both, say, domineering and submissive. A theoretically relevant higher-order concept is needed—say, authoritarian character structure—if both qualities are to coexist.

OVERPATHOLOGIZING

The bizarre and disturbed are more vivid than the commonplace and expected and psychologists are all too quick to note the pathological in assessment records (Soskin, 1954, 1959). Indeed, this may be one reason why untrained people are sometimes found to be more accurate in their judgments of normals. A heritage of concern with psychiatric diagnosis further tunes the clinician selectively to pathological themes. Understanding the patient demands attention to the adaptive as well as pathological trends in the personality. Indeed, the same aspect of personality, for example, ego defense mechanisms, can be utilized to both healthy and disturbed ends, and it is important that they be conceived from both points of view. Clinicians are prone, however, to see the pathological and, in general, to emphasize the subject's weaknesses rather than his strengths.

OVER-"PSYCHOLOGIZING"

The focus of the clinician's concern is with the enduring qualities of the personality. Consequently, he may be insufficiently attentive to the determinants of behavior that reside both in the immediate psychological situation and in the social-cultural conditions of the patient's life. It has already been noted that a major source of error in "naive-clinical" predictions lies precisely in ignorance of the circumstances under which predicted behaviors will occur, for these as surely as personality dispositions will determine future behavior. It is self-evident, but sometimes overlooked, that a patient's fidgeting during an interview may as well reflect a hard chair or uncomfortable underwear as emotional discomfort at the emerging material. The more serious consequences of not knowing the social values and experiences of members of other subcultural groups can lead to gross misinterpretation. A ready illustration is what is currently being called "cultural paranoia." It is understandable that a minority person, with a history of hostile rejection by the majority society, is slow to invest trust in a white clinician; indeed, in the larger scene, such suspiciousness may be quite adaptive. A black woman's report that she fears attack while waiting for a bus on a ghetto street corner has simply to be interpreted differently from the same fear expressed by a white, middle-class woman at a suburban bus stop. In the first case, the fears may well be reality-appropriate and adaptive; in the second, they may be reflections of neurotic sexual fantasies. Anything that increases the range of the clinician's sympathetic understanding of life in segments of society different from his own reduces the likelihood of culturally specific misinterpretations. More immediately, he should ask help from minority clinicians, who from first-hand experience can test the appropriateness of his interpretations. This extends the principle, noted under *Insufficient Verification* above, that ideas about any patient should be tested against those of other clinicians in order to reduce what might be called "egocentric errors"; in the present case, the need is to reduce *ethnocentric* errors as well.

Research on the Process of Clinical Judgment

Research, in the main, centers on the outcome or result of the process of clinical judgment. As we have seen in our examination of the clinical-statistical controversy, and earlier in the much larger literature on test validation, the core question is how accurate and useful are the judgments made. By contrast, there has been much less research on the process itself, investigating how clinicians actually utilize and synthesize available information in order to reach their decisions, whether ultimately correct or incorrect. In recent years, there has been a growing interest in the judgmental processes as such. So far, too little is known but alternate approaches and some findings are well worth examining.

THE NATURALISTIC STUDY OF CLINICAL JUDGMENT CONCEIVED AS CREATIVE PROBLEM-SOLVING

Synthesizing clinical information can be viewed as a special case of creative thinking, involving processes of the type described by psychologists and creative workers in many fields. Although hardly as dramatic as creating a scientific theory or a work of art, in important regards the process of developing understanding of the individual patient seems to move through similar stages. First, there is a stage of *preparation,* in which one becomes acquainted with the problem and plays with ideas. This is followed by *incubation,* during which no conscious work is done, attention may be diverted elsewhere, but advance is made nonetheless toward solution. Scientists and artists have given dramatic testimony of suddenly and inexplicably achieving solutions, even where the problem was apparently ignored for days or months. The next stage is one of *insight,* where the parts fall in place and a satisfying solution seems attained. Finally, there is *verification.* The details of the solution are worked out and its applicability to the problem tested against further evidence. Clinical judgment conceived in this framework is an emergent process of concept formation.

The work of M. Engel and Blatt, described a few pages back, illustrates the value of an introspective, naturalistic study of clinical judgment. By having clinicians think aloud while studying the full variety of material they normally use in clinical assessment they were able to catalog types and levels of inferences and to describe the progression from preinferential "noticings" to complex, theory-related formulations. Such research is in the tradition of Duncker's (1945) classic studies of creative problem-solving, in which subjects were similarly asked to verbalize their thoughts as they worked toward solutions of conceptual problems. What is intrinsic to this approach is that inference or problem-solving is studied as it naturally occurs, with the subject able to range freely through the available material and to assemble and test ideas in his own fashion. Although there have been many observations and considerable speculation, so far there have been few systematic studies of clinical judgment in this mode, despite their potential contribution.

MATHEMATICAL MODELS OF CLINICAL JUDGMENT

An alternate approach to the study of clinical judgment has grown with the increasing interest in the quantitative study of decision-making processes generally. An early illustration is the study of Hoffman (1960) in which he attempted to represent judgmental process statistically. Each of a number of judges was given the same set of quantitative data about a number of subjects and asked to rate each on a criterion variable. By studying their actual decisions, he could reconstruct the weights given by the judges to each of the variables. He could thus create a prediction formula which mimicked their judgmental behavior.

Such research requires that each judge have available the same set of quantified cues (MMPI profiles are often used) for each subject and that judgments be made in quantitative terms. With such data, a set of regression weights, one for each predictor variable, can be derived. Hoffman described the resulting formula as a "model" of clinical judgment. While such models cannot explain how clinicians combine cues to make decisions, they do reproduce the process and hence can predict the judges' behavior, at least under the particular constraints of these judgmental tasks. The model thus duplicates human clinical judgment and may indeed be able to improve on it, since the model unlike its human prototype does not fatigue, become bored or otherwise become less reliable (Goldberg, 1970).

One of the primary questions studied in this mode is whether clinical judgment is best described in linear or nonlinear (configural) terms. In the context of the statistical-actuarial controversy, Meehl (1959) maintained that one potential advantage of the human judge over the prediction formula is that clinicians can combine cues in complex, configural ways, that cannot readily be reproduced in prediction formulas which are typically linear. To see whether clinical judges use simple, additive combinations of data or combine the data in more complex ways, statistical analyses have been made to separate the amount of linear and nonlinear processing involved (see Goldberg, 1968 for a description of the methodology and findings of this work). Overall, it seems that linear-regression equations can represent the greater part of the judgments of most clinicians, though studies show that some do use configural combinations of cues in reaching their conclusions. L. R. Goldberg (1965) and Wiggins and Hoffman (1968) showed by different methods that the MMPI profiles of neurotic and psychotic patients could be distinguished by linear rules about as well as by the more complex configural rules proposed by Meehl and Dahlstrom (1960).

Mathematical models have been developed in the hope of finding substitutes for human judgment which are less costly and more accurate and reliable, i.e., to improve on the outcome of judgment. My reservations about this goal have been amply revealed in earlier sections of this chapter, though it may well happen that in particular areas such as formal diagnosis or the prediction of particular behaviors clinically useful prediction formulas will be developed. However, the quest for mathematical models can increase knowledge of judgmental process by providing a paradigm for studying, for example, different kinds of judges, working with different kinds of materials, toward different kinds of predictions. Studies have already shown that information is used inconsistently, that irrelevant cues cannot readily be ignored and that relatively untrained judges given basic decision rules do not function noticeably differently than more skilled clinicians in these situations. Professionals are, however, more cautious and have less confidence in their judgments.

Whether conceived as creative problem-solving and studied by naturalistic means or treated as mathematically representable decision processes, there is clear need for the further study of clinical judgment. With the present vigorous interest in mathematical models of human thought and their obvious successes in, for example, medical diagnosis and executive decision-making, there may well be developments of more visible relevance to the problems with which clinicians struggle. It behooves the clinician to understand these developments, even if he believes, as I do, that the human clinician is not likely to be displaced by computerized decision formulas.

Computers and Clinicians

The importance of electronic computers in contemporary life can hardly be overstated. With their capacity to store and retrieve vast amounts of data and to process them according to complex rules at extraordinary speeds, they have been able to take over many human functions. But computers are engaged in tasks well beyond those of statistical computation. They have been programmed to play games, solve problems, mimic learning and perception, and to simulate human intelligence at work. Ultimately, of course, the computer can do no more than it is programmed for by its human inventor but as the complexity of technology and application grows, it is hard to avoid the science-fiction fantasy of superhuman machines running the affairs of men.

In 1960, Wayne Holtzman published an article entitled "Can the computer supplant the clinician?" His reply was "Yes, but only in part." Analysis of the clinician's tasks suggested that the computer could do little as a *collector* of information which could not better be done by a clinician, particularly in view of his empathic sensitivity and flexibility. As a *processer* of information, once collected and coded, the machine can greatly improve on the human. As *interpreter* and decision-maker, however, the clinician again has a decided edge, at least until more research defining better decision criteria is done. Faith in the potential importance of computers depends, Holtzman notes, on where one stands philosophically on the clinical-statistical issue. These general conclusions seem just as valid today, although great progress has been made in computer design and applications.

Since 1960, computers have proved their worth mainly by reducing the human labor involved in processing and analyzing quantitative data. They can free the psychologist for other work, particularly those parts of the clinical process requiring interpersonal sensitivity, affective interaction, and creative intelligence. The extent to which the computer is seen as substituting for the clinician's work, now or in the future, depends in large measure on how that role is conceived.

At the simplest level, computers can save considerable time in the *scoring* and *analysis* of objective tests. Techniques are now available which "read" and score subject's responses on special answer sheets of self-report inventories, such as the MMPI, CPI, and Adjective Check List, plotting out the profiles of scale scores immediately. However, in addition to the usual scores, programs are being developed for complex configural scoring, which would be very arduous to do manually. Thus, in addition to simply adding up the number of items marked according to the scale key, the computer can consider two or more items simultaneously. If, for example, the subject responds "true" to a particular item, "false" to another, and "true" to still a third, this pattern is recorded but only if all three conditions exist.

Programs have also been developed for interpreting the MMPI and CPI and computer-written assessment reports are already available commercially from mail-order firms. MMPI authorities generated interpretative statements corresponding to particular scale scores, profiles, and distinctive item responses, which are stored in the capacious memory system of the computer. At low cost, these mail-order-service agencies return a profile of scale scores and a narrative account of the subject's personality, calling attention to idiosyncratic item responses as well. A number of alternate computer MMPI interpretation programs are now available. The most complex has been developed by Finney (1965) which uses the MMPI or CPI together or each alone. It scores out 123 different scales as well as indexes based on two or more scales and "composes a lengthy, detailed, and highly organized psychological report" (1965, p. 1, quoted by Lanyon and Goodstein, 1971, p. 214). Finney has attempted to write rules which reduce the conflict between descriptive statements and to make reports read more sensibly. Still, most computer reports read like the fledgling efforts of clinicians who apply interpretative rules one by one and have insufficient understanding of personality theory to note contradictory interpretations flatly stated side by side.

Computer interpretation is being developed for the Rorschach test by Piotrowski (Lanyon and Goodstein, 1971). In this case, the scoring and precoding of responses is still the hard work of the clinician, but with this step past, some 800 scoring units can be examined according to 937 interpretative rules. On the whole, these emphasize the structural rather than content-related aspects of the test.

Computerized psychiatric records now provide vast storehouses of information on patient symptoms, life-history data, demographic and social characteristics, and other material of considerable potential value to epidemiological and clinical studies as well as to the diagnosis and evaluation of the individual patient. Their role in mental health and psychotherapy is increasingly recognized (American Psychiatric Association, 1971). In the main, the input consists of ratings made by psychiatrists as to the current status, major symptoms, mental-status examinations, history, diagnosis, and the like on standardized recording forms. One program is already in effect recording data on psychiatric patients in seven states and the District of Columbia (Spitzer and Endicott, 1970–1971, 1971).

Still more recent is the *computerized interview* in which the patient himself gives information directly to the computer. The patient sits before a TV-like computer terminal on which questions appear. He in turn operates a typewriter on which he replies either in yes-or-no, multiple-choice, or even narrative form. The programs allow sophisticated "branching," so that the reply to a particular question determines which question is asked next. So far, the interviews developed are similar in type to psychiatric diagnostic interviews, with emphasis on symptoms and complaints. However, it is worth noting that some workers have been experimenting with computer-patient "conversations" which mimic the therapeutic process as well. In early reports, it seems that structured diagnostic interviews can be carried out, that patients find the procedure interesting, and that they willingly give detailed and reliable information (Greist, Klein, and Van Cura, 1973). There is little question, however, that in most important respects such interviews cannot duplicate the sensitive flexibility of the skillful clinician, either in discovering or interpreting the patient's concerns.

Thus, computers interview patients, score and interpret tests, amass and analyze clinical data, and finally have been used to facilitate clinical decision-making. Computer diagnosis is well along in the field of medicine (Lusted, 1968) and programs for psychiatric diagnosis have been developed (e.g., Spitzer and Endicott, 1968; Nathan, 1967). In medicine, computer-assisted programs have been developed for a number of specific diseases and more are being developed all the time. In many hospitals in the course of a general physical examination information is immediately coded and fed to computers which can analyze and within minutes call a potential problem to the attention of the physician, diagnose a disease, or recommend further testing. The situation is different, of course, in psychiatry, for diagnosis in and of itself has little relevance to further clinical care; at this point, diagnosis by man or computer is mainly of interest to clinical record keeping and certain kinds of research.

In principle, the logic of computerized diagnosis applies to clinical decision-making phrased in other terms as well. Take, for example, the question as to whether a patient should be discharged from a psychiatric hospital or not. If all the relevant considerations could be discovered and all the relevant assessment data collected and computerized, then the decision rules could be given to the machine and decisions then made, more rapidly and consistently than could be done by humans. However, note the "ifs." They are the same as those earlier discussed in the controversy over actuarial prediction. Indeed, in making judgments of any sort, whether in the interpretation of tests, diagnosis, or predictions the computer is only a more efficient instrument for developing and applying actuarial equations. True, it allows simultaneous consideration of many more variables and more complex ways of combining them than was possible earlier, but it still cannot replace skilled human judgment. It functions best in the general case, with quantified data, and where the prediction criterion is clear and consistent; least well, in the uniquely organized individual case, where qualitative information may be most relevant and where the options are many and novel. As statistical aids to interpretation, as noted earlier, the computer is of inestimable value which is likely to grow as new machines and programs are developed. As processors of data, computers are invaluable. For particular clinical purposes, say, screening tests or selection studies, computerized testing and interviewing can have a distinct role. But, as Holtzman noted in 1960, for the essential tasks of the clinician, we will still have to use our heads instead of a machine.

The new computer methods have raised a number of ethical questions for the mental health professions as for society generally. The storage and ready availability of vast quantities of personal data endanger the clinical tradition of patient-clinician confidentiality and privacy. Employers, schools, or government agencies, more concerned with their own purposes than with the patient's welfare, may be able to gain access to information in well-organized and compact form that used to be available only in the clinician's files or, more likely, in his head. Similarly, the commercially available tests scored and interpreted by computer, as noted earlier, raise the spectre of employers by-passing the sensitive concern of a testing psychologist for his client. It is of course true that handwritten clinical records and human-interpreted tests can, and have, been used stupidly or maliciously, but at least they were within the control of professionals guided by an ethical concern for the individual client. In the present era, the problem of abusing psychological information has increased enormously, as great quantities can be stored, assembled from different sources, and easily retrieved, all outside of the immediate and protective confines of the clinical relationship. Clinicians and their professional organizations (e.g., American Psychiatric Association, 1971) are justifiably concerned with the potential social dangers which accompany the potential contribution computers can make to their work.

Communicating Assessment Findings: The Psychological Report

PURPOSE OF THE REPORT

Assessment is made to guide the clinician's work with the patient, to advise a colleague who will be responsible for the patient's continued care, perhaps as his therapist, or at the request of some other agency concerned with the patient's well-being. Whether to facilitate his own work or as a consultant to others, the clinician typically reports his findings and recommendations in written form. Traditionally, when prepared by psychologists, this has been called a "psychological report." Often the main themes are communicated verbally to the therapist, a case conference, or the representative of another agency, but a written account is usually required. This report joins other documents in the patient's *clinical or case record,* for example, reports of the psychiatric and medical examinations, social history, nursing notes, psychotherapy progress notes, case conference reports, therapy termination summary, or discharge statement. In many clinics or hospitals, quite a bit of paper can cumulate this way and there sometimes seems to be more concern with writing and keeping records than with helping patients. However, there are good and necessary reasons for complete clinical records, to record the patient's basal state changes during therapy, and final status, and to guide on-going and facilitate later work if the patient returns to this or another clinic. Clinical records are obviously necessary too for clinical research or program evaluation, even where they may have little visible relation to the patient's immediate treatment.

Psychological reports gain their immediate focus from the referral questions raised. These define the primary purpose of the report. Inevitably, other questions arise in the process of assessment and potentially relevant information appears, which should of course be reported. However, the value of the report in the first instance lies in the degree to which they respond to the immediate issues raised in the referral. At the same time, reports have secondary purposes as part of a continuing clinical record. Today's pretherapy assessment is basal data for tomorrow's posttherapy evaluation, although the need may not be immediately obvious at the time of the referral. Consequently, the report should contain information of relevance to foreseeable future questions, though first responding to the issues in hand.

Above all, the psychological report has to clarify and explain, as fully and precisely as necessary and possible. In this sense, it is a scientific document recording the results of an inquiry. It is not a literary product, though happily truth and beauty are not antagonistic goals. Nor is it a legal brief, intended to convince and "make a case," nor an effort to sell, defend, or otherwise present someone in a particular light as one might, for example, in a letter of recommendation. The report should not be used to instruct the reader in assessment methods, personality theory, or principles of psychopathology. However much you want to share your knowledge and ideas about these general fields, it is inappropriate when the task is to convey a personolistic understanding of the particular patient.

The report should transmit the interpretations of the clinician in words that communicate clearly and economically. As the end-product of the interpretative process, it should ideally exemplify the best thinking of the clinician. An assessment report is inadequate, therefore, to the extent that it reflects the sources of error, earlier discussed, in clinical interpretation; specifically, schematization, information overload, insufficient internal evidence, insufficient external verification, overinterpretation, lack of individualization, lack of integration, overpathologizing, and overpsychologizing. We will reconsider some facets of these principles as they apply particularly to the written report.

FORM AND STYLE

There is no single form in which a report should be written. The topics covered, emphases, and amount and type of detail should all reflect the purpose and importance of the referral questions, the interests and background of the referring clinician, and the amount of information gained. Reports are appropriately longer in a teaching clinic if they are intended for study by a student clinician and his supervisor as well as by the referring clinician. The more open-ended the question(s) raised and the more critical the resulting clinical actions, the fuller and more complex the analyses should be. Thus, the most detailed reports are usually required where a potential psychotherapist needs to know the general structure and workings of the personality in order to guide long-term therapy. On the other hand, it may be as short as "Don't," if the essential question is, for example, whether a young person, presently anxious and agitated perhaps for understandable situational reasons, should be given electroshock treatments.

A general outline for the psychological report has already been suggested in the proposed outline for a case history although in the working situations of the clinic, reports may well be shorter and more concise. Moreover, if the psychological report is made in a team-assessment context, where a psychiatrist may contribute a "diagnostic interview" and a social worker a "social history," the report would focus on the particular findings yielded by psychological tests and the accompanying interview and observation.

OUTLINE FOR A FULL-SCALE ASSESSMENT REPORT*

I. Purpose and Procedure of Assessment
   A. Referral question
   B. Techniques used
   C. Particular conditions under which assessment made
   D. Patient's attitudes toward assessment procedures
II. Patient's Present Staus
   A. Adaptation in life situations
   B. Symptomatic behaviors
   C. Motivation for and attitudes toward clinic help
   D. Appearance and behavior in clinic
III. The Manifest Personality
   A. Biological
   B. Temperament
   C. Manifest personality traits
   D. Interpersonal behavior
IV. Personality Dynamics and Structure
   A. Motives and affects
   B. Moral principles, social values, and attitudes
   C. Ego functions and identity
      1. Ego strength
      2. Defenses and coping mechanisms
      3. Thought organization, cognitive controls, and styles
      4. Intelligence, abilities, and competencies
V. Social Determinants and Current Life Situation
   A. Group membership and roles
   B. Family
   C. Education and work
   D. Social ecology
VI. Major Stress and Coping Potential
VII. Personality Development
VIII. Formulation of the Personality
   A. Synthetic interpretation
   B. Overall diagnostic impression (if necessary)
   C. Specific dysfunction
IX. Recommendations and Predictions
   A. Desired outcomes
   B. Possible interventions
      1. Environmental and social
      2. Psychotherapy
      3. Other therapeutic interventions (drugs, hospitalization, etc.)
X. Course of the Future Life, With or Without Further Clinical Intervention

As communication, the value of a psychological report depends on the clarity of its language. It is beautiful indeed to find a psychologist who conveys his essential ideas with both precision and elegance, but few of us are so blessed. In the choice, let simple and clear if less than beautiful prose prevail. Attempts at dramatic exposition, literary references, humor (worse so, if at the expense of the patient), metaphor, the bon mot (i.e., the well-chosen word), foreign words (particularly if you then feel the urge to translate: vide supra bon mot!) are more likely to

* See Chapter 6, pp. 140–143, for more detailed explanations of the headings.

confuse than help. Use simple words and syntax. I once read a report in which a relation was described between the patient and another "whose room was juxtaposed to his." How much simpler to say "next door" or "across the hall," though one should wonder in the first place whether it makes any difference at all to know the location of the friend's room. All the rules of good writing are entirely relevant to report writing.

Reports should be written in the language of the educated layman. The constructs and special terms of the clinician are valuable only in so far as their meanings and referents are clear. To the extent that the consulting and referring clinicians share the same theoretical orientation and know each other's thinking personally, conceptual terms, even idiosyncratic phrases, can convey ideas well and avoid the need for lengthier explanations. The purpose of technical terms is, after all, to describe phenomena more economically. Too often, however, jargon and theoretical constructs can mask ignorance and make for pseudocommunication. Try to describe the patient's "oedipal conflict," "inferiority complex," or "aperiodic reinforcement schedule" in ordinary words; it will test your understanding of both theory and the particular patient. Mayman (1959) lists a number of terms, such as "compulsivity," "malignant," "decompensating," which are often abused in psychological reports.

The report should contain statements at all levels of interpretation, from immediately visible behaviors ("he wore a black hat") to lower-level inferences ("because his wife died, and that is the custom of his group, but that was almost a year ago"), to more distant inferences ("he is still guilty at the hostility he felt toward her during her last illness"). It is necessary to indicate the evidence for the inferences and the certainty with which they are made. However, it helps little to fill a report with endless qualifying terms. Phrases like "may be," "appears to," "it is believed," "apparently," more usually express indecision than scientific caution. Qualify only when necessary, particularly to indicate quantitative ("marked," or "some") degree, or for emphasis. Particularly where qualifiers suggest value judgments ("good," or "adequate") it is necessary to spell out the criteria involved. To say that a patient will make a "good job adjustment" does not tell the reader by what standards the prediction is made.

The report represents a professional opinion, i.e., an integrative conceptualization of available evidence oriented toward usable recommendations. The raw data of assessment, such as test scores, item responses, interview quotes, or the like should only be cited to accent an interpretation. Normally it is inappropriate to fill a report with actual scores, particularly if the reader is unfamiliar with the tests involved. To say that the patient obtained a raw score of x corresponding to a standard score of y, which puts him in the nth percentile, is the task of a testing technician to report to a clinician, who in turn has to tell a professional colleague what it all means, in terms meaningful to him.

Where there is contradictory evidence or a striking bit of information which just does not fit in and the clinician is simply confused, the first cardinal rule is to admit it. To deny confusion or pretend omniscience in human assessment is, at the very least, arrogant. Where information cannot readily be integrated and interpreted, the contradictory themes and alternate possible explanations should be put forth openly, thus sharing the interpretative dilemma with the reader. In this case, considerable detail is warranted. Perhaps the reader, from his vantage point, may have further evidence that can clarify the issue. If not, the issue can be held open to be resolved in further contacts with the patient. At the end of an assessment program, the Harvard Psychological Clinic used to leave time for a "loose-ends interview." Loose ends are the fate of the clinician who would understand human personality in its proper complexity and individuality.

PORTRAYING THE INDIVIDUAL

With a few salient facts, it is perfectly possible to write a report about a person you have never seen by making general statements that might apply to anyone of the same age, sex, and life circumstances. Indeed, such cliché reports have been presented to staff conferences in some clinics and apparently were accepted without comment. This tells more, perhaps, about the average level of clinical work in these settings than about the skill of the writer of the simulated report.

Here is part of a hypothetical report on a male college student, age twenty, who comes to a university Psychological Clinic.

> Joe is a bright student who sometimes doubts his intellectual ability. Though he does reasonably well in his courses, he is fearful at examination time. When studying, he sometimes feels that he is not learning anything, though later on he realizes that a fair amount of material was retained. He is uncertain in his relations with women classmates for fear that he cannot please them. He hesitates before making dates, though usually things turn out all right. Toward his family, he holds ambivalent attitudes; often welcoming their concern, other times wanting to be free from their control. At present, he is in an identity crisis. His future seems vague, and he is not sure what is really important. He is looking for meaning, in philosophy, in rap sessions with friends, and by going to meetings of campus political groups. He has a conflict between hostile and dependent needs, sometimes acting aggressively, sometimes passively. He feels he is not assertive enough, but feels guilty when he takes advantage of someone. He should do well in psychotherapy with a sympathetic therapist, provided that a proper relationship develops. And so on.

This picture may not describe every last student on campus, but it would certainly apply to a large number. At best, it describes a type, but the individual, Joe, is lost. Most of the statements are simple clichés. Anyone would do better with a "sympathetic therapist"; in every case, the value of therapy depends on the relationship formed. To be sometimes aggressive, sometimes passive, is the lot of all of us. To have an "identity crisis" in college these days is about as distinctive as having acne in high school.

Here are some principles of value in writing an individualized report.

1. Avoid mentioning general characteristics which could describe almost anyone, unless the particular importance in the given case is made clear. One would not mention, for example, that the patient had two feet; one or none is worth comment. This is not to suggest that only the idiosyncratic or bizarre is distinctive. There are modal personality qualities, reflecting common group memberships. Indeed, the individual can sometimes best be pictured in comparison to reference groups; "Like many college students today, Joe . . . , but unlike most, he . . ."

2. Describe the particular attributes of the individual fully, using as distinctive terms as possible. The value of the report grows as the clinician can specify the conditions under which traits are manifested, the sequences of behavior then likely to occur, the strengths of impulses and the particular conditions for arousal.

To say that Joe is "sometimes aggressive" tells little; a great deal more is told by "Joe is so short-tempered that he readily blows up if a stranger steps in front of him in a movie line. For hours afterward, though he tries to dismiss it, he cannot help but think of the event, dwelling endlessly on what still nastier things he could have said or done."

3. Simple listing of characteristics is not helpful; tell how they are related and organized in the personality. It is particularly important to show which traits are central and which peripheral, which are manifest and which covert, and whether conflicts are conscious or unconscious. To discover the hierarchical organization of the person is a key task of the clinician. Noting isolated characteristics of the person without showing how they are interrelated yields a disjointed and fragmented picture of the individual.

4. Information should be organized developmentally with respect to the time line of the individual life. To know emergent trends and past experiences increases knowledge of present characteristics. "Joe hopes to make the football team and finally to overcome a sense of puny inadequacy carried over from high school. Consequently, he is greatly concerned with proper diet and exercise."

5. Many of the problems of poor reports, such as vague generalizations, overqualification, clinging to the immediate data, stating the obvious, and describing stereotypes are understandable but undesirable reactions to uncertainty. Describing no one or describing anyone may be a defensive reaction to the fear of being wrong; characterizing the unique individual necessarily involves more risk than sketching the modal person. Good clinical interpretation and report writing require a degree of risk-taking as well as creative intelligence, knowledge, and experience. Caution is surely necessary. The clinician should always be ready to acknowledge the shortcomings of his knowledge and techniques in general and, in the particular case, the limitations on his findings and understanding of the individual. But overcautiousness can limit the utility and individuality of the case study, just as unbridled speculation can produce dramatic but grossly inaccurate portraits. In-between is the necessary disciplined imagination for which no sure formula can be offered.

PART 4

PSYCHOTHERAPY

CHAPTER 12

What Is Psychotherapy?

The Talking Cure

Anna O.—whose treatment launched psychoanalysis—called it "the talking cure" (Breuer and Freud, 1895). Psychotherapy might thus be termed "a conversation with a therapeutic purpose," extending the definition of an interview noted earlier. True, psychotherapy is not always therapeutic and therapeutic changes in a patient's life can occur without psychotherapy. Then too, "talking" is only part—though usually the essential part—of the process. Still, these brief phrases convey what we usually have in mind when we visualize psychotherapy. At its core is a unique relationship between the clinician and the patient within which there is communication which can relieve distress and set conditions for relearning and personal growth.

More broadly, and closer to the literal meaning of "psychological treatment," psychotherapy describes any intentional application of psychological techniques by a clinician to the end of effecting sought-after personality or behavioral changes. Within this more inclusive meaning, we will examine many types of intervention, such as family and group psychotherapy, play therapy, and various forms of behavior modification, as well as the one-to-one therapeutic conversations between the therapist and an individual adult patient. Using the term "psychotherapy" in so inclusive a sense would surely displease many clinicians. Those in the behavioral tradition distinguish their approach from "verbal psychotherapy" to emphasize its concern with observable behavior in what they hold to be a more scientific framework. To them, psychotherapy carries the unwanted connotation of being both mentalistic and medical, as well as unscientific. Many psychoanalysts, on the other hand, want psychoanalysis kept distinct from psychotherapy, which they view as, at best, a cheapened and diluted form of Freud's technique for discovering the root causes of an individual's neurosis and thereby reconstructing the human personality. Surely, there are profound differences among the many contending approaches to psychotherapy, and we will consider them in Chapter 14. They differ not only in the goals sought and the techniques used, but ultimately in their fundamental assumptions about the nature of man and the causes of human dysfunction. But before comparing and contrasting schools and theories of psychotherapy it is well to ask what general qualities they all share and to what extent these might account for the efficacy of therapy, whatever its specific forms. This will be our major task in the present chapter.

Over the years, the field of psychotherapy has expanded greatly—not only in the number of contending approaches and theories, but also in the range of people treated, the variety of professionals involved, and in the more recent past, the amount of research devoted to the study of its processes and effects. Originally conceived as a method of treatment of patients with symptom neuroses—hysteria in the first instance—it has come to be used with people who are both more and less disturbed. By now, forms of psychotherapy have been used with patients with brain damage or psychosomatic problems, with psychotics, drug addicts, alchohics, the aged and the very young, and with patients formerly believed to have too little ego strength to collaborate in self-exploration. On the other hand, people seek help in coping with the distressing but less devastating problems of living. People seek psychotherapy because of painful dependence or inferiority feelings, inability to work effectively, identity crises, a sense of futility, guilt, or inadequacy, or spiritual malaise. For many it is viewed more in terms of opportunity for personal growth and a better future than as relief from a presently painful state. With the growth of psychological-mindedness and the corresponding reduction in shame at being known to visit a psychotherapist, increasing numbers of people are seeking their help. Indeed, in some circles, it is quite fashionable to talk lightly about "my shrink."

Over the past twenty or so years, clinical psychologists have become increasingly involved in the practice of psychotherapy to the point where it is today their most common professional activity. A survey of the commitments of clinical psychologists shows that while assessment, consulting, teaching, research, and administration are important facets of their work, they spent the greatest amount of time in psychotherapy (Goldschmid, et al, 1969). Once the exclusive province of psychiatry, today, psychologists and social workers share the therapy caseload with the consent—if not always with the unqualified blessings—of their psychiatric colleagues.

General Conditions of Psychotherapy

PSYCHOTHERAPY AS OPPORTUNITY FOR RELEARNING

However different their particular concepts and practices, all systems of psychotherapy start from the fundamental assumption that human behavior can be changed. The personality of the individual and his capacities for coping, whether adaptive or maladaptive, represent the residuals of a lifetime of learning. His feelings toward himself and others, his attitudes, values, skills, habits, competencies and inadequacies, which together comprise the present personality, were learned in earlier interplay with others. Many were necessary, if neurotic, adaptations to earlier conditions which, however, remained fixed and are not dysfunctional as circumstances have changed. Symptomatic behaviors, now personally painful or socially destructive, may earlier in life have served to manage problems adequately. Though patently undesirable, such behaviors continue and block successful functioning and new learning in the patient's current life. He is dissatisfied with himself and likely distressing to others. Along with painful affects, anxiety, guilt, depression, and the like, he experiences himself as inadequate and powerless and buffeted about rather than being master of his own life. He seeks both relief from suffering and further development in the direction of autonomy and self-control. These, in the broadest sense, are the goals of psychotherapy.

As neurotic problems develop through learning, so we believe they can be undone through unlearning and relearning in psychotherapy. Positive personality changes can, of course, occur without psychotherapy and regularly do as people develop new relationships, face new challenges or changed life circumstances. Disturbed behaviors can, in this sense, be "outgrown." "Spontaneous" remission or cure is a fact of clinical life and, as we shall see, a factor to be taken seriously into account in the evaluation of intentional therapeutic efforts. Still, disturbed behaviors can be remarkably tenacious, even though they are inappropriate, not only as seen by the outside observer but to the person himself. "I know I shouldn't feel this way, but I just can't help it," has been said by virtually every patient entering therapy. Whether the tenacity is due to the disturbed behavior being rooted in unconscious conflict, being the result of excessive reinforcement, or because it is part of an inclusive meaning-system is controversial, but the fact itself is visible to patient and clinician alike. That psychotherapy can provide conditions for relearning is the faith on which therapists operate. Ideally, the patient shares this faith which, combined with his discontent and desire for change, is the basic force toward therapeutic improvement. Specific interventions build on this motivational base.

EXPERIENCING VERSUS "TALKING ABOUT"

What kind of learning goes on in psychotherapy and why does it take place? Looking in on a therapy session, one would see the patient talking about his problems, experiences, attitudes, and feelings; the therapist, in turn, inquires, comments, clarifies, and perhaps advises. From this, we expect the patient better to understand and control his impulses, thoughts, and actions, to resolve problems, and to develop more effective ways of coping with future problems. The visible surface of psychotherapy does not reveal its essential process. Thus, the naive onlooker can fairly ask "Why should talking about one's problems, even if greater self-understanding does result, lead to any essential change in a person's character or behavior?" "Don't we talk about our interests, concerns, and problems all the time with friends; what's so different about telling them to a psychotherapist?"

It oversimplifies to see psychotherapy as only "talking about" and gaining understanding. This puts the emphasis on intellectual exchange and clarification, which are part of the therapeutic dialogue but not the essential process. The relearning which occurs in therapy is not intellectual, as when we acquire new knowledge in an area where we were formerly ignorant. For therapeutic change to occur, the process must also include new, personally meaningful and emotionally important *experiencing* in the therapy relationship itself. What Alexander and French (1946) once termed the "corrective emotional experience" must take place. Under the particularly favorable conditions of therapy, the patient has to be reexperiencing emotions which he has been unable to cope with in the past. Coming to know his problems better, including knowledge of their origin, is secondary. Affective rather than intellectual learning is central. As Frieda Fromm-Reichmann once put it, "The patient needs an experience, not an explanation."

The emphasis on gaining *insight,* of considerable importance in psychoanalysis, suggests a more intellectual process. In fact, at first Freud believed that recapturing repressed memories and bringing them to the light of consciousness was the essence of therapeutic cure. But it is by now widely recognized by psychoanalysts as well as therapists of other persuasions that insight—in its narrow meaning—is insufficient. Thus, psychoanalysts often distinguish between "emotional insight" and "intellectual insight." The same distinction is implied in "I *know* there's nothing to be afraid of, but I'm still afraid." Therapeutic change occurs as the patient learns how not to be afraid, rather than of what and why he is afraid, through repetitive and controlled emotional experiences in therapy. In the behavioral model, for example, a phobic person may literally be put in contact with the feared object, through moving in graded doses from fantasy visualization to actual confrontation, which allows him to discover that his fears are now groundless whatever their origin. Similarly, in psychoanalytic psychotherapy, the neurotic is led by the therapist to reexamine and reexperience painful impulses, fixed defenses, and maladaptive behaviors. In doing so, he suffers the pain of self-confrontation and feels again anxiety, guilt, shame, and other negative affects sometimes directed toward the therapist himself.

Because change depends on experiential and emotional learning, it necessarily takes time and the patient's active participation. Unfortunately, it suffices little to tell a patient that he has an irrational fear or to explain how it came about; he has to discover it for himself. Unlike the surgeon or the lawyer, we have no dramatic interventions which solve the patient's problems with one stroke. Arduous and painful work is required of the patient, which he must be sufficiently motivated to undertake and continue. All the therapist can do is provide conditions which facilitate therapeutic relearning—his task is more that of the educator than of the physician—many of which reside in the unique interpersonal relationship of therapy. Indeed, many have argued that it is this very particular relationship, rather than the specific interventions of the therapist, that is the major if not sole source of therapeutic change.

THE PSYCHOTHERAPEUTIC RELATIONSHIP

What does the therapist do? Above all, he listens with unswerving attention, sympathetic concern, and continuous effort to understand the patient's personal meanings. The capacity to listen without responding in terms of one's own needs and feelings or the demands of social convention is, according to Fromm-Reichmann (1950), the fundamental requisite of effective psychotherapy. At appropriate moments, the therapist communicates his understandings to the patient or otherwise acts to relieve the patient's suffering. The clinician values the patient's integrity as a person and his striving for self-betterment, nor does he fault the patient for his inadequacies. At the same time, he maintains necessary objectivity and detachment. The therapist is simultaneously compassionate and dispassionate. His one goal is to advance the well-being of his patient by using his trained knowledge, intelligence, and empathy to understand and help the patient. The blend of these characteristics gives the psychotherapeutic relationship its special character as a setting within which emotional relearning can take place. After thorough and scholarly review of the concepts and methods of psychotherapy, Reisman (1971) concludes that the essential definition of psychotherapy must rest not on what therapists *intend* nor on what they *accomplish* but rather on what they *do* and includes most centrally ". . . the communication of person-related understanding, respect, and a wish to be of help" (p. 66).

Though similar in some respects, psychotherapy differs importantly from other human and professional relationships. In some regards, it is like that between any expert and his client, teacher and pupil, or pastor and parishioner; in other regards, it more resembles the interplay between friends, intimates, or relatives. While like and unlike each, it is ultimately distinctive. The client can, and probably has, taken his troubles to friends and loved ones. They may offer solace or material help, but they are too close to him to view his troubles with any detachment, nor do they have the knowledge or perspective to do so. Their lives are too much affected by his behavior for them to suspend judgment while patiently hearing him out. They properly expect a reciprocal relation within which they can as much depend on his advice and support as he on theirs. Indeed, this very fact and the continued intertwining of his life with theirs may effectively bar his sharing his shameful feelings and personal inadequacies with them in the first instance. The minister and lawyer may be too identified with established morality. The doctor is expert in diseases of the body, but human problems are manifestly different. In any case, most psychotherapists see the expert-client relationship as intrinsically too authoritarian for the necessary work of psychotherapy. The patient with psychological problems cannot be *given* treatment; improvement depends on willing collaboration in an on-going learning process. On the other hand, neither is the therapeutic relationship egalitarian and symmetrical in the ideal of friendship and love.

Psychotherapy is a professional relationship. Patently, it involves an expert offering a service to a needful person for which in return he receives a salary or fee. The recipient is a "client," one of many in the therapist's workweek, each of whom is equally deserving of his professional attention and concern. (This is a simple reality of clinical practice many patients wishfully deny!) As an honest professional, he sets his fee properly, sees the patient at appointed times, and otherwise keeps to the obligations of the clinical contract. The patient is assured of privacy, confidentiality, and moral neutrality. Within the therapeutic session, the therapist gives his full attention to understanding the patient's communications putting aside any personal concerns. Above all, he does not manipulate the patient to serve his own needs, whether financial, sexual, ideological, or power-related. The therapist's singular goal is to advance the well-being, autonomy, and personality competence of his patient. Nor is this goal put aside except momentarily because of the patient's suffering, though the therapist is perceptive of and sympathetic toward the patient. Simply to comfort is not the work of psychotherapy; a sympathetic ear and warm shoulder are not the requisites of therapeutic change. Characterizing psychotherapy as "the purchase of friendship," as some critics have, distorts the essential relation of therapist and patient.

It is of course true that psychotherapists can slip from this ideal role model into more typically human reactions. Psychotherapy is an intense and intimate human relationship, even framed within a professional role. We become bored; we find some patients irritating, others we are overly fond of; personal preoccupations become too insistent and we lose the patient's words; an additional session is scheduled more because of our unpaid bills than of the patient's need; we become angry at the patient for not changing; and so on. Any therapist can multiply the list. However, every skillful therapist works hard to avoid such "all-too-human" behaviors. The well-trained therapist, who—in the opinion of many—should undergo psychotherapy himself, knows the dangers well and is tuned to the early warning signs in himself. Indeed, many clinicians wisely know that there are types of people with whom they cannot work at all and therefore they do not take them on in the first place. At the extreme, it is sometimes necessary for a therapist to discontinue seeing a patient or to suggest another therapist, if he feels that he has lost the balance of attachment and detachment required for giving the patient understanding, respect, and help.

THE PATIENT'S MOTIVATION, FAITH, AND EXPECTATIONS

The patient approaches psychotherapy both frightened and hopeful. He is not quite sure what will happen, but he knows it will take time and money and is likely to involve painful revelations. The clinician may find him to be even worse off than he feels; may indeed find him to be "crazy." Even among the sophisticated, there is some sense of stigma. Friends, relatives, and employers may think the less of him for needing professional help; to himself, it is painful admission that he has not been able to manage his life effectively.

At the same time, he is filled with hope. Seeking treatment is, in the first instance, a positive behavior. There is conscious recognition of a psychological problem with which the patient cannot cope unaided. It betokens, for many, emergence from despair, isolation, or denial of the realities of one's own situation. The decision is not at all easy to make and often enough there are mixed feelings, but once made there is an understandable surge of positive affect. With a history of self-defeating behavior, the patient is now doing something which can make an important difference.

Moreover, the patient is seeking the help of an *expert* knowledgeable in how human problems arise and how they can be disentangled. Friends may have commiserated, encouraged him, or minimized his problems, urged or threatened him to "shape up," but *this* person will understand and respect his misery and undo his troubles, though at the moment he may not be sure how. He has faith in the technical training and scientific knowledge of the therapist; others may have meant well, but they did not know how to modify feelings and behavior. The therapist is surely invested with undue power and magic, both out of the need for relief and to validate the patient's decision to enter therapy. The prospective patient knows that he can confide in this authority and his confidences will be treated with respect. He can speak his mind freely, without risking condemnation or rejection. Though he has been told that he must work hard to express his thoughts and feelings fully and clearly in a collaborative venture with much of the outcome depending on his sincerity and effort he may still believe that it is the therapist's acts rather than his own that make the difference. Though few therapists make any such promise, many patients start with the assumption that if they only do what is expected, as the therapist dictates, they will immediately feel better. And, indeed, many do. Early in therapy there is often a great sense of relief and some functional improvement and many clinic patients terminate therapy at this point.

Many students of psychotherapy, notably Jerome Frank (e.g., 1973), have pointed to the great importance of the patient's faith and trust in the therapist as a major, if not primary, determinant of therapeutic change. Because of his belief in the therapist, the patient develops hope and an expectancy that he will be bettered by the treatment. This is viewed as a common denominator to all professional efforts to change behavior, which indeed is shared with shamans and other folk healers. Thus, at one point, Frank notes (1959):

> A patient's expectancy of benefit from treatment in itself may have enduring and profound effects on his physical and mental state. It seems plausible, furthermore, that the successful effects of all forms of psychotherapy depend in part on their ability to foster such attitudes in the patient [p. 36].

Concern with "expectancy effects" in psychotherapy is related to a long-standing interest in "placebo effects" in medical research. It is well known that response to a drug may depend on belief as to the drug's action, faith in the doctor, and other psychological factors unrelated to the specific physiological action of the drug. Hence, to distinguish the specific drug action from nonspecific attitudinal and expectancy effects, response to a placebo is used as a control condition. The placebo is an inert substance which resembles the experimental drug in form, color, and taste, and which is administered in as close a manner as possible to the drug. Under these conditions, considerable improvement in physical symptoms has been found. Indeed, it has been argued that many of the compounds prescribed by physicians may have a positive effect mainly because of the faith invested in them by the physician and the patient rather than because of their physiological value. "The history of medical treatment until relatively recently is the history of the placebo effect" (A. K. Shapiro, 1959, p. 303). The considerable literature on placebo and expectancy effects in psychotherapy has been well surveyed in recent years (e.g., A. P. Goldstein, 1962; Shapiro, 1971; Wilkins, 1973; and J. D. Frank, 1973). There is hardly any doubt but that generalized expectancy or placebo effects alleviate anxiety and induce improvement, but recent research suggests that more subtle analyses are necessary. What matters for example, is the congruence between the patient's particular expectations and what goes on in therapy, which can either facilitate or block the therapeutic process.

Faith is important in different ways and at different times in psychotherapy. In the first instance, the patient would not enter therapy without belief in its curative powers nor, in the second, would he continue. Although he may have started hopeful and even enthusiastic, the patient is typically unprepared for the long road ahead. He can readily become disheartened with the plodding, day-to-day work of therapy which requires him to reconfront old anxieties and to move out from accustomed, hence safe if inadequate, behaviors to new ones. In part, his motivation is sustained by his need to please the therapist. However, this is no longer based on blind faith, but increasingly derives from evidences of understanding and respect communicated in their earlier encounters. To the extent that the patient has felt that the therapist is making efforts to understand him, values him as a person, and is sincerely concerned to help, he in turn sustains his faith in the process, despite the effort, pain and, at times, simple boredom involved. As he feels important to the therapist, in return he respects the therapist and is willing to work for him. Motivation is thus sustained by the evolving therapeutic relationship, though anchored originally in a general and relatively undefined "expectancy of benefit."

Differences Among Therapeutic Approaches

To this point, we have considered what is generally common to all therapeutic approaches, emphasizing those factors that are inherent in the therapeutic relationship. All therapists aim to reduce suffering and increase their patients' well-being and effectiveness, but they differ widely in how these goals are specified. All would agree on the importance of relearning, but disagree as to what is to be learned and how such learning occurs and can be facilitated. There is considerable controversy among competing theories and systems of psychotherapy. Schools are associated with the names of Freud, Jung, Adler, Rogers, Sullivan, Wolpe, Skinner, Perls, Fromm, May, and Bandura, among many others, and their proponents engage in vigorous polemics. These views can be grouped as *psychodynamic, behavioral,* or *existential-humanistic,* but these are broad entities with considerable variation within each. Books comparing and contrasting the various systems can give the student a sense of the premises and methods of the major approaches (e.g., Ford and Urban, 1963; C. H. Patterson, 1973). In one such volume (Harper, 1959), thirty-six systems of psychotherapy are described. This number is not exhaustive, nor has it decreased as the field has matured. In fact, the number of approaches has increased decidedly since 1959. Indeed, it is almost fair to say that there may be as many distinct approaches to psychotherapy as there are psychotherapists, for each impresses his personal style and unique techniques on the framework within which he works.

Psychotherapists differ more in their stated principles than in their practices. When describing and defending their particular viewpoints clinicians strive to bring out what is most distinct in their theory and tend to minimize ways in which it overlaps with other views. To the student the publications of different therapists suggest more profound differences than he would see if he were actually observing their work. Thus, the oft-quoted studies of Fiedler (1950, 1951) showed that psychoanalysts, client-centered, and Adlerian therapists were more alike than would have been supposed from their theoretical positions. This was more true with more experienced therapists than with novices of each school who were, so to speak, staying closer to the book.

All good therapists practice what Alexander and French (1946) once termed the "principle of flexibility," adjusting their methods to the needs of a particular patient rather than staying firmly with one or another therapeutic approach. The psychoanalyst does not always use free association, dream analysis, and the like, nor does the behavioral psychologist stick to the selective application of reinforcement in order to shape behavior. As the situation requires, each may give explicit advice on an urgent problem or sympathetically console an overwrought patient, though this might not be predictable from reading "principles of psychoanalysis" or "principles of behavior modification." This is not to minimize the very real differences among these and other therapeutic theories, but to note that there is, on the whole fortunately, more eclecticism in practice than in theory.

Before considering systems as such (cf. Chapter 14), let us look at some of the dimensions along which diverse approaches differ.

GOALS AND STRATEGIES

Psychotherapists differ both in their *ultimate* and in their *mediate* goals (Parloff, 1967). Ultimate goals derive from views as to the nature of man and the desired state of mental health. Often, they can be stated only in broad and abstract terms, which elude specification when one wishes to compare therapeutic outcomes of different systems. Thus, the goal of therapy has been put in terms of removing symptoms, restoring earlier levels of functioning, freeing the person to be self-actualizing (in Rogers' term, "a fully functioning person"), helping the patient find personal meaning and values, or reconstructing defenses and character. Of equal or greater importance are the mediate goals which define the means felt necessary to move the patient toward ultimate goals. Included among these would be releasing pent-up feelings, conditioning or reconditioning of particular responses, examining one's values and concepts, muscular relaxation, and becoming aware of unconscious impulses, among others. The mediate goals of therapy, and the techniques related to them, reflect the major differences among systems of psychotherapy.

A related way of contrasting therapeutic approaches has been suggested by Sundberg and Tyler (1962) who compare the work of different therapists in terms of the major purposes which therapeutic intervention is said to serve. Such purposes include, in their words: (1) strengthening the patient's motivation to do the right things; (2) reducing emotional pressure by facilitating the expression of feeling; (3) releasing the potential for growth; (4) changing habits; (5) modifying the cognitive structure of the person; (6) gaining self-knowledge; and (7) facilitating interpersonal relations and communication. In addition, to extend and update the list, I would add: (8) gaining knowledge and facilitating decision-making; (9) altering bodily states; (10) altering states of consciousness; and (11) changing the social environment. It is helpful to view therapeutic approaches in these terms before considering psychoanalysis, client-centered therapy, and other systems *as* systems. These purposes do not correspond in any one-to-one fashion with the approaches of different schools. Rather, they are themes which run through different therapeutic systems, though one or another may be emphasized in each case. They also describe different strategies that the same therapist might use with different patients or with the same patient at different points in the therapeutic process. Thus, a therapist attempting to alter the cognitive structures of a person in order for him to rectify distorted perceptions and beliefs may still find it necessary to encourage emotional release and/or enter directly into attempts to change the patient's social environment. Let us consider each of these therapeutic purposes separately.

1. The first has been named by Sundberg and Tyler *strengthening the patient's motivation to do the right thing*. It is the oldest and most enduring of ther-

apeutic aims and is reflected in *directive* and *supportive* psychotherapies as well as in the work of evangelistic prophets. Persuasion of all types, from simple advice to exhortation and hypnosis, are used to induce people to act in more desirable ways. Long before (and since!) professional therapists appeared on the scene, troubled people were encouraged to strive to be better than they are or were given inspirational books or sermons to point up the errors of their present ways and redirect them to a better life. The essential idea is that change depends on motivated striving and that, with persuasion, a person can willfully move in the right direction. The theme is important in self-help philosophies and evangelistic religions. It figures prominently in the work of Alcoholics Anonymous and Synanon, organizations which attempt to keep former alcoholics and drug addicts from slipping back into their addictions largely through persuasion combined with social pressure.

2. The second therapeutic purpose involves efforts *to reduce emotional pressure by facilitating the expression of intense feelings.* Freud called this process *catharsis* from the Greek term for the emotional release which can be experienced when viewing great drama. Particularly in the early treatment of hysteria, cure was seen to occur when the patient dramatically recovered a repressed memory in a flood of emotion. Except perhaps in cases of traumatic anxiety neuroses, such as might result from the stress of combat, psychotherapy rarely involves such intense and curative cathartic experiences. Catharsis in such cases is often facilitated by hypnosis or drugs. However, in lesser forms, releasing pent-up feelings figures importantly in many types of therapy, notably in some of the newer methods which encourage patients to express strong affects toward fantasied persons by, for example, pounding a pillow, doll, or punching bag, screaming and the like. Among the newer therapeutic approaches (e.g., primal therapy, Gestalt therapy) there has been a renewed interest in direct emotional expression rather than talking about feelings and experiences.

3. Another purpose of psychotherapy emphasizes *releasing the patient's potential for growth.* Central to this view is the notion that life proceeds along developmental lines and that neurosis represents a blocking of normal growth tendencies toward integration and autonomy. In the psychoanalytic system, such blocks reflect fixations resulting from unresolved and repressed earlier conflicts. In therapy, these are revealed in transference reactions of the patient toward the therapist onto whom he projects (or transfers) childish attitudes and wishes. These earlier emotional attitudes are thus brought into the present relationship and become accessible for conscious examination. The person can then more likely be freed from symptomatic and compulsive behaviors, crippling defenses, and immature character traits. The developmental theme is also important to the humanistic psychotherapies, though in a quite different form. Rogers and Maslow, among others, postulate a primary tendency for growth and self-actualization. They are less concerned with the deterministic effects of early life experiences, and emphasize more the modifiableness and human potential of adults. Even with this faith, however, they recognize that the growth process can be delayed or distorted. The task of the therapist is to release and facilitate the basic potential for growth that exists in all humans. "The psychotherapist should not be thought of as a mechanic, locating and repairing defects in a piece of equipment, but rather as more of a gardener, removing weeds, providing light, nutrients, and moisture to stimulate a plant intrinsically disposed to grow" (Sundberg and Tyler, 1961, p. 289).

4. Still another way of viewing the purpose of therapy is in terms of *habit change*. Although all therapies, as we have noted, can be conceived as learning, in this context learning is intended in the particular and narrow sense of the word. Neurotic symptoms are seen as learned behaviors, albeit inadequate and undesirable, which were acquired in the patient's past. The therapeutic task is to set up new learning situations which can alter or replace these troublesome habits, mainly by use of the general principles of conditioning and learning, involving principally the selective application of reinforcement. For many years, direct conditioned response methods have been used to remove unwanted responses. Thus, the Mowrers (1938) had bedwetting children sleep on a specially designed pad which when moistened would set off a loud bell, waking the child. In time, this noxious stimulus became associated with the cues preceding urination and the child should then wake in ample time to go to the toilet. In more recent years, increasingly sophisticated methods have evolved, as we shall consider shortly, which however share the basic premise that disturbed behaviors can be conceived as learned responses which can be modified through the application of basic learning principles.

5. A fifth purpose of therapy involves *modification of the cognitive structure of the person*, that is, his ideas about the nature of the world, others, and himself. Theorists in this vein see the person's basic problems as reflecting distorted preconceptions, "personal constructs" (G. A. Kelly, 1955) or "assumptive systems" (J. D. Frank, 1973). He is unaware of these assumptions and acts as if they were inevitable and unchangeable facts of life. Many therapists have pointed to the importance of differentiated, reality-appropriate cognitions as a fundamental characteristic of healthy functioning. Thus, therapeutic change involves having patients become aware of their cognitive structures and the incongruencies among their constructs and between their beliefs and external criteria.

6. A related therapeutic purpose involves *increasing the patient's knowledge and his capacity for effective life decisions*. Here is the border area between psychotherapy and counseling, two modes of psychological intervention which cannot readily be distinguished. In principle, the psychotherapist deals with problems of sufficient intensity and extensity to dislocate the patient's life over a broad spectrum, while counselors facilitate decision-making where there are more focused conflicts, typically, for example, in deciding vocational commitments, choice of a school or a major. Toward this end, the counselor tries to achieve the best combination of the client's abilities and interests with opportunities in the field. The client is interviewed and tested to discover where his talents and interests lie. He is given information about opportunities; the pros and cons of different alternatives are discussed in order that the client can make the wisest and most satisfying decision. At points in most any psychotherapy similar exploration to aid in reality-related decisions goes on.

7. A seventh, commonly stated, purpose of psychotherapy is to *increase self-knowledge or insight*. The notion that therapy should lead to increasing awareness and understanding of how and why we act as we do is fundamental to many therapeutic approaches. It is expressed in the classic psychoanalytic principle that the task of the analyst is to make the unconscious conscious, or as Freud noted at one point "Where id is, let ego be." It is surely true that bringing hidden motives to conscious critical examination reduces their potential for compulsive, maladaptive action. However, as noted earlier, the process involved is not one of intellectual mastery but rather involves emotional learning. The ancient philoso-

phers' maxim "know thyself" is true only in an extended meaning of "knowing." In psychotherapy, there can be extensive changes in the patient's behavior and functioning without insight, without, that is, the patient coming to understand hitherto unknown motives. Nor, as noted, does understanding when it does occur automatically lead to personality or behavior change. Still, the concept of insight has an important position in psychotherapy.

8. Another therapeutic orientation emphasizes *interpersonal relationships* rather than those psychological processes which reside, so to speak, within the individual. From earliest infancy on, we develop and are socialized in constant contact with others, and disturbed as well as healthy functioning reflects the patterns laid down in earlier relationships. Some interpersonal theorists focus on the earliest primary relationships within the family of origin, while others are more concerned with contemporary relations with spouse, lover, children, parents, boss, and colleagues. Whether historic or current or both, therapy aims at clarifying how the patient's functioning depends on the ways he was and is interdependent with others. Considerable emphasis is placed on patterns of communication between the patient and relevant others, which make for satisfying or alienating relationships. It should be noted that therapy itself involves a new interpersonal relationship, which contrasts with those to which the patient is accustomed. The interplay between the therapist and patient can be made the focus of therapeutic examination, for it is an immediately available arena for observing and studying characteristic modes of communication, feelings, and expectation. The emphasis is on the therapist as a real person in interaction with the patient, rather than a screen for the projection of internal fantasies. Methods of group and family therapy carry the logic of an interpersonal approach still further. Such methods bring into the therapy room not only the patient's *accounts* of his relations with others but the *actual social interplay* with real people. Thus, modes of social functioning are directly available for observation and interpretation and can, it is believed, thereby be changed.

9. Still another form of intervention, which in a sense extends this logic further, sees the need for *effecting changes in the patient's social environment*. The well-being of a patient rests importantly on the effects of outside persons or social institutions whose actions are beyond his control. This is hardly a novel observation and clinicians have known for a long time that extensive and durable changes in a patient's status can often not be made without simultaneously altering social forces acting upon the patient. Thus, traditionally child psychotherapists want to see one or both parents in psychotherapy at the same time as the child. In more extreme cases, the child may be placed in a foster home or school to relieve the pressures of his usual family environment. In psychiatric institutions programs designed to create a "therapeutic milieu" have been worked out. In the more recent past, as part of the growing interest in preventive interventions within a community framework (cf. Chapter 5 and Part 5), there is increased concern with altering social forces affecting the patient. This may be at the simple direct level of aiding the patient in finding suitable housing or a job, tasks ordinarily outside the ken of psychotherapists. Beyond this, however, there are serious efforts to conceptualize "system-oriented" rather than "person-oriented" interventions which would have the effect, for example, of producing an emotionally healthier school environment for all of the children involved rather than dealing with the problems of particular disturbed children. In full extension,

such system-oriented interventions are of course beyond the limits of "psychotherapy," however broadly defined. In less ambitious form, however, attempting to alter the behavior of relevant others or change some aspect of the patient's current life circumstances may be a necessary if adjunctive part of the psychological treatment of the individual patient.

10. At another extreme, there is an emphasis on *altering somatic processes in order to reduce painful feelings and/or increase body awareness.* As our awareness of man as a social organism has grown, psychological clinicians have also become increasingly impressed with his biological nature. On the one hand, there has been vigorous development of psychopharmacological agents which can directly reduce anxiety, depression, agitation or other painful states. Such drugs must of course be administered by physicians, with whom however psychologists can collaborate both in a prediagnostic and postevaluative way. But aside from their direct therapeutic effects, psychoactive drugs can be important adjuncts to psychotherapy. By reducing gross distress, the patient may then be more amenable to psychotherapeutic transactions. Similarly, relaxation training as a device to reduce tension and anxiety is of major importance in some approaches to behavior therapy as a first and necessary step to counterconditioning. "Relax and tell me your problems" is more than a polite figure of speech in therapy.

In a more extensive sense, some therapists have focused on the interdependence of bodily and mental processes. Reasoning that one facet of pathology involves undue separation of bodily and psychological experiences, techniques have been developed for explicitly increasing "body awareness." These may involve focusing attention on particular muscular or somatic sensations, or they may make use of exercises, some derived from Indian Yoga, or of massage or dance. They are all intended to increase the range of experience by bringing to conscious awareness and control sensory experiences which normally occur outside of awareness. The value of such motoric and somatic experiences has been conceptualized in a variety of ways but specially emphasized are the sense of self-mastery of bodily activity, and thoughts, feelings, and actions as necessary facets of psychological health. In these approaches, we see a new meaning to the ancient Greek ideal of the "clean mind in a clean body."

11. Finally, a last therapeutic purpose involves *altering states of consciousness in order to extend self-awareness, control, and creativity.* Paralleling the exploration of hitherto unknown somatic experience is a concern with normally inaccessible psychological experiences of the sort which, for example, occur in dreams and other "altered states of consciousness." Psychoanalysis and other dynamic therapies have always emphasized the importance of reducing the constraints on conscious thought, as in free association, in order to make accessible unconscious wishes and impulses. But the purpose was largely instrumental; one departed from rational, reality-appropriate thought processes in order to make fantasies available for *rational* examination and conscious control. The present concern is more in line with Jung's "creative unconscious," which expressed the belief that therein lay not the destructive and primitive in man's nature but essentially his highest potential. Oriental philosophies have long emphasized the importance of inner experience in distinction to the western concern with rational thought and conscious, goal-directed action. People are honored who can shut themselves off from ordinary stimuli and meditate on internal experience. Thus, isolation, meditation, and other techniques are used to facilitate a reduction of at-

tention to the external, "real" world and a corresponding inward turning of attention toward a realm of experience which is viewed as equally "real" and perhaps more important, particularly in a time when "the world is too much with us." Profound and mystic experiences are reported which lead the person to emotional peace and heightened self-awareness. As with body awareness, different rationales are used to justify different methods of "consciousness expansion," but here too a common theme points to an increased sense of self-mastery and self-knowledge. Compared to conventional psychotherapies, such approaches minimize the importance of conscious communication and discussion of experience in favor of extending the range of experience itself.

These *eleven purposes* of psychotherapy and their associated techniques are obviously not exclusive nor most probably is the list inclusive. When one turns attention to systems of therapy as such, it is clear that each includes a pattern of particular purposes, with some more central and valued than others. Thus, Rogerian client-centered therapy puts primary emphasis on the potential for growth (No. 3); of importance are self-knowledge (No. 7), modifying cognitive structures (No. 5), the interpersonal relationship (No. 8), and to a lesser degree catharsis (No. 2); of no importance or specifically disavowed are social manipulation (No. 9), methods of persuasion (No. 1), or behavior modification (No. 4). Too, emphases change over time. The Rogerian therapy of the early fifties, for example, laid more weight on examining the conscious content of the patient's beliefs and feelings (No. 7), then it moved toward greater emphasis on the interpersonal process (No. 8) and, most recently, to an interest in the nonverbal, bodily (No. 10) and altered states of consciousness (No. 11) processes. Other systems can be examined in a similar manner, which can be of some help in characterizing different approaches.

As noted earlier, the flexible therapist should be able to work in several modalities, depending on the patient's needs and circumstances, and many do. However, by predilection or training, many therapists are limited to a particular approach, and act in much the same way with each patient. The particular treatment a patient gets is more likely to be a function of the therapist he goes to than what problem he brings. Nor, it must also be admitted, are there clear and generally accepted criteria for what kind of intervention best suits what kind of person or problem, despite many valuable opinions in the clinical literature. It seems that all sorts of patients have been helped by therapists of all persuasions. This may, in part at least, result from the general factors discussed earlier in this chapter. Along with their relative inflexibility is the fact that most therapists are sincerely and deeply committed to their work which, when communicated to the patient, is itself therapeutic.

OTHER DIMENSIONS ALONG WHICH PSYCHOTHERAPIES VARY

Considering the various purposes psychotherapy is presumed to serve has given us one way of understanding the diverse activities of psychotherapists. We can now view other facets of the process and content of psychotherapy, related to but conceptually independent of its purposes, in which approaches differ. These are in the realms of the therapeutic relationship, the role of the therapist, the type of communication, and the realms of experience and behavior felt most important for therapeutic emphasis. In this section, I will briefly suggest and discuss some dimensions which can serve as a conceptual framework for describing various therapeutic systems.

Client-determined versus therapist-directed. The activities and emphases of therapy can be largely decided by the patient or determined by the therapist. In some systems, notably Rogers' "client-centered therapy," the therapist is expected to take his lead from the patient who brings forth his problems in his own fashion and at his own pace, while the therapist responds to them and clarifies their meaning as they appear. An authoritarian role is explicitly shunned. At the opposite pole, the activities of therapy are programmed primarily or solely by the therapist. Some therapists not only direct the patient's activities within the therapy hour, but outside as well by assigning him "homework." The therapist role has often been described as more *active* in therapist-directed therapies, for it involves advising, encouraging, demanding specific behaviors, and the like in contrast to the more *passive* role of listening and interpreting which is characteristic of more client-determined therapies.

Therapist as friend versus therapist as investigator. At one pole, some therapists see themselves mainly warm and compassionate, empathically understanding the patients' communications. They prefer to see themselves more as an equal to the patient than as an expert and they try to minimize therapist–patient status differences. For example, first names may be used and the therapist may not hesitate to reveal facets of his own personal life as he expects the patient to be open and unguarded. By contrast, particularly in the psychoanalytic tradition, the therapist is an analyst or "investigator" (Chessick, 1969) whose job it is to remain sufficiently detached to be able to inquire incisively and work out the riddles of the patient's messages. He sees himself in a less egalitarian and in more of an authoritative (expert) role, though wishing to avoid an authoritarian stance. In still other modes, however, therapists act in distinctly directive and manipulative roles.

Past, present, or future orientation. Systems of therapy differ distinctly in the relative emphasis put on past, present, or future events of the patient's life. Typically, psychodynamic views emphasize the role of early life events in forming the present personality, and consequently expend much effort in discovering their historic determinants. By contrast, humanistic-existential views focus in sharply on the present concerns, beliefs, and feelings of the patient in his current life. Still other therapists give major attention to the patient's hopes and expectations of the future, in the belief—as Allport once put it—that man is more pulled by the future than pushed by the past.

Conscious versus unconscious. A parallel dimension concerns belief in the relative importance of unconscious wishes and impulses in the original determination of the patient's neurosis and the importance, therefore, of their discovery and analysis. This is, of course, a central emphasis in standard psychoanalysis, though relatively less critical in more modern forms of ego-psychological psychoanalytic psychotherapy. Other therapies, by contrast, emphasize the patient's conscious experience, perceptions, and conceptions of himself and the world, and deny the existence or the importance of unconscious material.

Experience versus behavior. Whether emphasizing more the conscious or the unconscious material, both psychodynamic and humanistic therapists are concerned with psychological experience, that is, the patient's personal meanings and motives. On the other hand, behavioral therapists are concerned mainly with overt and observable behavior, namely, what the patient does or says rather than what he believes or feels, and the situational conditions rather than internal psychological conditions, which control his behavior. From the behavioral viewpoint, the question of whether the patient is aware or unaware of the meaning of his behavior is of little importance, for behavioral therapists are concerned with the behavior itself and not its phenomenological status. Issues of awareness or meaning fall within a realm they see as "mentalistic" and beyond what can be understood and controlled scientifically.

Verbal versus motoric. Many therapists, those oriented to the experiential as well as behavioral frameworks, see the need for less emphasis on therapeutic conversations and more on physical actions. We have noted the growing emphasis on nonverbal communication (facial expression and body language) as an alternative for people to express themselves, accompanied by efforts to develop interventions specifically designed to alter bodily states, for example as in massage, exercise, or dance. In recent years, such approaches along with the behavioral have much extended the traditional realm of psychological intervention beyond the boundaries of verbal transaction.

The psychological realm emphasized. It is possible to define psychotherapeutic approaches in terms of whether greater or lesser importance is given to (1) drives and emotions—the motivational realm; (2) concepts, beliefs, judgments, and values—the cognitive realm; (3) dreams, hopes, wishes, imagination—the fantasy realm; or (4) actions and behavior—the behavioral realm. In some cases, activities in one realm are used as a route for investigating or altering variables of another. Thus, for example, dreams and fantasies are important in the psychoanalyst's effort to discover hidden motives and feelings, while for the behavioral therapist fantasying situations related to phobic feelings has been used to eliminate them through a process of desensitization. Counseling, client-centered psychotherapy, personal-construct therapy, and related methods focus more on the cognitive realm.

DIFFERENCES AMONG PSYCHOTHERAPIES IN FORMAL ARRANGEMENTS

Finally, we should note briefly some of the different ways in which psychotherapies are organized, such as the number of people involved, scheduling, duration, and the like. In this area too there is great and increasing diversity from the classic vision of psychotherapy as a one-to-one encounter of the patient and therapist talking and listening in the privacy of a "fifty-minute hour."

The number of patients. The one-to-one relationship of *individual psychotherapy* is the oldest and most basic form of psychotherapy, but more than one patient can be seen at the same time. Often these are naturally related people who bring into the therapeutic sessions their characteristic modes of interaction, which as such can then be the focus of therapeutic exploration. The participants may be husband and wife or lovers, as in *marital* or *couples psychotherapy*, or parents and children, as in *family psychotherapy*. This has been called "conjoint family therapy," to distinguish it from "collaborative psychotherapy," in which a child is seen by one therapist and one or both parents by another therapist, who try to combine their efforts with the needs of the child in mind.

Group psychotherapy in any of its many forms involves working simultaneously with anywhere from six to twelve people, usually previously unknown to each other. In recent years, group methods have become much more commonplace with the realization that they are not just economic but watered-down versions of individual therapy, but have their special qualities. The therapeutic advantages and disadvantages of group and family methods will be considered in some detail in Chapter 15.

The number of therapists. In principle, more than one therapist could treat a patient. The advantages of such an arrangement have been proposed in terms of each therapist fulfilling a somewhat different role, for example in the model of father and mother or as interpreter and observer. But in practice, multiple therapists with one patient are obviously too costly and cumbersome. This is less true in family, couples or group therapy, where multiple therapists are as much the rule as the exception.

Methods of *indirect psychotherapy* have been developed which reduce the involvement of the therapist by allowing him to work through another agent (Riesman, 1971). A classic illustration was Freud's treatment of "Little Hans" (Freud, 1909). The boy actually saw only his father, who then wrote to Freud and was advised as to how to proceed further. Today, there is renewed interest in using parents as intermediaries to take advantage of the strength of their relationship to the child rather than, as it appeared to Freud, as an expediency. Thus, Guerney (1964) taught a kind of client-centered method of play therapy to parents which he calls "filial therapy." Similarly, one of the principle methods of the growing community mental health movement involves consultation between the clinician and others in direct contact with the patient. Such methods of indirect therapy have the potential advantage of extending the reach of clinicians to greater numbers of patients, some of whom might otherwise be inaccessible.

Indirect therapy has been done in various other ways as well, including by correspondence, telephone, two-way closed-circuit television, or recorded tapes; indeed, in principle through any medium that people can communicate. In recent experiments, therapeutic gains have been furthered by having patients later view and study videotapes of their own therapy sessions. Seeing their more bizarre behaviors on videotape has also been reported as improving the behavior of hospital patients. Perhaps the most ambitious and potentially valuable form of indirect psychotherapy involves the programming of computers to interact directly with patients in a therapeutic conversation (Colby, Watt, and Gilbert, 1966). These experiments point up intriguing directions both for research on the therapy process (e.g., Is the face-to-face human relationship really essential, as we now believe?) and on ways of making psychological intervention more economical and widely available.

Length and frequency of therapy session. The fifty-minute hour is clearly the mode for individual psychotherapy. However, there is nothing sacred about this unit; it undoubtedly reflects the fact that desk calendars are marked in hour units and we are accustomed to scheduling on the hour, and that psychotherapists need a few minutes between patients to gather their wits, make phone calls, record some notes, attend to less intellectual needs, or simply relax. However, therapy is sometimes done in smaller or larger time units. It is not uncommon in hospitals and crowded clinics for patients to be seen for ten or fifteen minutes at a time. On the other hand, some therapists stay on with a patient well over an hour at least on special occasions if they feel that the patient greatly needs the additional attention. Except in special settings, however, most therapists schedules do not allow such flexibility. Though there is little logical or empirical argument for it, the "hour" remains the basic unit of individual therapy.

Group psychotherapy more typically runs to ninety-minute or two-hour units, which is justified in terms of the greater need for warm-up time and the diffusion of effort among a number of people. "Marathon groups," so named by George Bach (Stoller, 1968a), may go on for twenty-four, forty-eight or even more hours.

Typically in clinics, and usually in office practice, appointments for individual, family, and group therapy are scheduled on a once-a-week basis, except for psychoanalysis. Analytic sessions average about three hours a week, which is a distinct reduction from the older ideal of five or six. Despite many different opinions, there is no solid evidence that one schedule is better than another, although it is commonly agreed that less than one session a week makes it very difficult to carry on psychotherapy.

In psychotherapy of all sorts the frequency as well as length of sessions usually reflects pragmatic considerations and customs and tends to be relatively inflexible. Good clinical arguments can be advanced for varying the amount of the therapeutic contact, increasing it when the patient is in a crisis, severely disturbed, or suicidal, and decreasing it during stable periods or if the patient has become overly dependent on the therapist. While clinicians are sensitive to such issues and try to adapt their schedules accordingly, generally a particular schedule of appointments is maintained.

Duration of psychotherapy. Psychotherapy can run from one to dozens, hundreds, or even thousands of hours. How long it should take has been a source of endless arguments, with positions defined in fair measure by the way ultimate goals are visualized. If seen as involving dramatic changes in basic character structure, then long courses of therapy are proposed; if relief of present distress is emphasized, then shorter programs are described. It is clear, however, that important changes in the patient can occur in one or a few sessions and that time in therapy and the degree of change are by no means perfectly correlated. Methods of crisis intervention, even single consultative sessions, as well as a limited number of weeks of "brief psychotherapy" have been of considerable help to patients, and have become standard procedures in some clinics.

A common attitude, however, is that important and lasting changes must involve considerable time and therapeutic effort. The term "intensive psychotherapy" is used by many (e.g., Fromm-Reichmann, 1950; Chessick, 1969) to characterize psychotherapy aimed at effecting major personality changes, related to but not in the precise model of standard psychoanalysis. Wolberg (1967) uses the term "reconstructive" to characterize such therapies in contrast to "reeducative" and "supportive" approaches. In this view, brief therapies are often seen as superficial, aimed at reducing discomfort, giving advice, or helping with the solution of some immediate and limited problem. More so in the past than now, "the more the better" was the prevailing belief. Patients who dropped out of treatment after a relatively short time were seen as resistive, even if they felt distinctly better and grateful for the therapist's help. This was sometimes described as "a flight into health," a defensive tactic to lessen the effort of working toward more profound changes. This surely can happen, but it is also possible that the patient genuinely improved and, by his standards and with his personal priorities, he has correctly decided that he has adequately solved his problem and now should use his time and money for other needs.

The field of psychotherapy has changed considerably over the years, and continues to do so. Terms such as "long-term," "intensive," and "brief" are only relative; indeed, what was "brief" in 1946 is "long-term" in 1976. Diversity of methods and ideas is characteristic of the field today, and also a greater willingness of practitioners to examine their goals, conceptual assumptions, and techniques, in order to better serve the needs of their patients. Growing apace is an enlarging body of research, much of it admittedly limited in scope and methodologically inadequate, but which nonetheless brings evidence forward on the process and outcome of therapy of potential value for improving future practice. Conceptual issues and research findings will be considered in detail in later chapters, but first, to give context to that discussion, the actual process of individual psychotherapy will be examined in some depth from the perspective of a particular approach.

CHAPTER 13

The Process of Psychotherapy: A General Model

One Model of Psychotherapy

All psychotherapists work to alleviate human distress and foster more effective functioning. They all build on the same basic elements in the therapeutic relation and in the patient's expectations which, in fair measure, may account for the successes reported by all approaches. But, as we have seen, along with these common elements, psychotherapies differ greatly in their purposes, concepts, and methods. In the present chapter, we will consider one approach, in order to have a better idea of what actually goes on in therapy. For now, we shall put aside concern with how systems of psychotherapy differ in order to know one in depth. Later, we will return to a comparative framework.

The form of psychotherapy we will consider is clearly among the approaches described as "evocative" rather than "directive" by J. D. Frank (1973), or "insight-oriented" rather than "action-oriented" by London (1964), and more in the nature of "reconstructive" than "reeducative" or "supportive" in Wolberg's terms (1967). This approach depends primarily on verbal communication aiming at increasing self-awareness and with it autonomy and control. Historically and conceptually, this form of therapy derives from psychoanalysis, though tempered importantly by the ideas of client-centered, interpersonal, and cognitive theorists. Though concerned with drives, affects, and the unconscious residues of early experiences, attention is more focused on the more or less conscious wishes, values, and feelings of the person in his current life. Particular interest is given to ego processes and defenses in order to understand the ways the person construes and organizes experience and the concepts he holds of himself, relevant others, and the world in general, in both coping as well as defensive aspects. Adaptive strivings and personality competencies as well as pathological defects concern us. Within the context of psychoanalysis, such an approach has been described as ego-psychological.

The vantage point is that of individual adult psychotherapy with patients who have distressing but not disabling problems. They are neither so disorganized and helpless that they cannot voluntarily seek a helping relationship nor, on the other hand, are their problems so limited that some information, advice, or encouragement can suffice. In diagnostic terms, most would be called neurotic, character disorder, or perhaps borderline patients. Typically, the patients are seen for one, or perhaps two, one-hour sessions a week over a period of not more than forty or fifty weeks. This model is possibly the most commonly used by clinicians, whether psychologists, psychiatrists, or psychiatric social workers and, in its general form, is the model within which most clinicians are trained.

Within this broad and somewhat eclectic framework, we can now look more closely at what goes on in individual psychotherapy.*

Starting Psychotherapy

THE INITIAL INTERVIEW

Psychotherapy starts with the very first contact between the clinician and the patient, even when the initial interview is intended mainly for the purpose of clinical assessment. The explicit purposes of the initial interview, as noted in Chapter 8, include: (1) establishing the interpersonal relation, i.e., rapport, trust, etc., necessary for this and any further clinical transaction; (2) gaining information about the patient and his problems; (3) giving information about the clinic, its policies, the nature of therapy, and fees, appointments, and the like; and (4) bolstering the patient's resolve to change. The first phase of psychotherapy necessarily involves both parties coming to understand what the other is like and what the conditions of their relation can be. It necessarily covers a number of sessions, which may also include other assessment activities such as psychological testing, interviews with members of the family, etc. But from the beginning, the conditions of psychotherapy exist, namely, a communication of understanding, respect, and a desire to help. During this phase, the therapist learns about the patient, but more important, the patient learns, in general terms at least, what will happen and what is expected of him.

THE THERAPEUTIC ALLIANCE

For therapy to proceed, the patient must be motivated and willing to exert the needed effort. There are powerful resistances, both overtly in terms of the pain of confronting one's less admirable qualities and covertly since the neurotic adapta-

* Much of the material to be discussed in this chapter has been anticipated in earlier chapters on clinical assessment, particularly in discussions of informal assessment (Chapter 7), interviewing (Chapter 8), and interpretation (Chapter 11). This points up the artificiality of the distinction between assessment and therapy, which are continuous stages of the helping process, occurring within the same basic relationship and involving essentially similar processes of communication and understanding. I will try not to be overly repetitive, but will necessarily repeat points made earlier as they are now relevant to the understanding of psychotherapy.

tion, however uncomfortable, is still familiar and secure and change of any sort is potentially dangerous. The patient falters continuously in his resolve, being torn between hope and fear, between the wish to change and the wish to remain the way he is. Therapy depends on the development of a therapeutic alliance between the therapist and the more rational, health-seeking part of the patient's personality.

The patient can be viewed as if he were two distinct people. One is compulsively driven by neurotic needs, distrustful of proferred help, hopeless and self-defeating, and quite unable to see himself and his problems with any detachment. Yet, within the same person is another one, who *knows* himself to be in pain, driven and irrational, but by that very token he *is* rational. He has hope and a vision, however vague, of a better future of greater maturity and health. The irrational, sick self may be quite willing to continue that way; the rational, health-seeking, self-critical self strives for growth. These facets of the person are in conflict along many fronts, witnessed most immediately by the ambivalent feelings at undertaking therapy.

A therapeutic alliance has to be formed between the therapist and the more rational self. Together they take on the task of uncovering and altering the patient's irrational and sick self, until the whole personality becomes more of one piece, as a rational, integrated, and self-regulating self. This metaphor is of course not meant to suggest a Jeckyl-and-Hyde splitting of the personality into two discrete selves, though phenomenologically the experience of many disturbed people is almost literally of being a battleground between contending forces. Psychological well-being, indeed, is often experienced as being unitary, in harmony with oneself, or, in the current phrase, "together."

Therapy requires the voluntary participation of the patient and a readiness to sacrifice necessary time, effort, and money. It depends on a high level of motivation, both to start and to continue, for there are inevitable trials along the way. At the outset, the patient is sustained by hope and trust, though he may have little notion of what specifically is required of him. Early in the formation of the therapeutic alliance is the necessary task of discovering and accepting what I will call the "fundamental commitment" of psychotherapy; in essence, a willingness to look at oneself fully and honestly. This is the essential part of the patient's contribution to the "therapeutic contract" which defines the mutual obligations of therapist and patient. Let us consider these related matters in turn.

THE FUNDAMENTAL COMMITMENT

Psychoanalysts have used the term "the basic rule" to describe the fundamental requirement that the patient allow himself to say anything that enters his mind, without censoring or selecting and without thought as to its possible meaning, the impression it might convey, or whether it is logical or silly. By reducing conscious review, it is hoped that unconscious impulses will emerge in the patient's free associations. The patient who truly will not, or cannot, fulfill the basic rule cannot, in principle at least, be psychoanalyzed. The basic rule requires a peculiarly passive cognitive attitude, akin to the relaxation of controls during sleep, rather than the active processes of normal cognition.

The term "fundamental commitment" shares some meaning with the Freudian "basic rule" though differing importantly in other regards. Essential to both is the notion that the patient is not commited to therapy if he would consciously screen communication. Difficult as it is, the patient must be willing to verbalize thoughts and experiences openly, fully, and nondefensively. It is true, of course, that there are formidable barriers, both of social convention and unconscious resistances, to such openness and these are the proper focus of therapeutic intervention. But, from the outset, he must be willing to *try* to be completely honest in telling what is *on* his mind, as well as what *enters* it in the momentary situation. Obviously, conscious deceit is the most patent abuse of the "fundamental commitment."

Beyond a readiness to communicate feelings and experience, the patient must voluntarily examine them. This involves taking the perspective of others, notably and in the first instance the therapist's, and trying to understand what meanings his behavior conveys. The more passive mental attitude, central to the "basic rule" of classical psychoanalysis, is not required. The distinction between a more active and more passive cognitive orientation is important but it can too easily be overstated. Even in classical psychoanalysis active and collaborative efforts are required of the patient, but mainly in order to comprehend and integrate the meanings of his behavior as they emerge through the therapist's interpretations. In the type of therapy being described here, which does not emphasize retrieval of unconscious material, the psychological process is more akin to that required of the analysand in dealing with the interpretation rather than the production of therapeutic material. The essential quality is the conscious intention to relax defenses against viewing and describing one's inner feelings and experiences. Total honesty is beyond the reach of most of us, before or after therapy, but it is the ideal which defines the fundamental commitment.

THE THERAPEUTIC CONTRACT

The mutual obligations and understandings between patient and therapist can be described as a "therapeutic contract." In effect, it consists of "If you do this-I'll do that" clauses. Ideally, terms are mutually understood, openly discussed, and freely negotiated by both parties; in fact, there may be unstated expectations, implied conditions and "small-type" clauses. To the extent that understandings differ there will be conflict and ill will in psychotherapy as in any other relation. Where therapy proceeds from unvoiced and contradictory expectations, a "corrupt contract" exists which can be destructive of therapeutic ends (Beall, 1972). It is important, therefore, that clear agreements which can be lived up to by both parties be reached early in therapy. Usually, however, the contract is formed over several sessions and may be renegotiated and changed later on. It is rarely possible, of course, to state in all details the necessary actions and obligations of patient and therapist. But it is necessary that the basic framework of therapy be openly communicated and understood.

The first and easiest conditions to specify are those concerned with scheduling and fees. An appointment time is set, the fee established, and the frequency of visits decided. The patient agrees to come promptly at these hours, to call sufficiently ahead of time if an appointment must be cancelled, and to pay his bill in some mutually agreeable way. The therapist, on his part, is to be available in the scheduled hours and reachable by phone at other times if there is an emergency. He is to arrange for uninterrupted privacy during the therapy session and protect the patient's confidences later on.

Therapy usually starts with a conditional and open agreement as to the length of the process. Except in some forms of time-limited therapy, the therapist's reply to the patient's understandable concern can only be an honest "I don't know how long it will take," though from experience a possible range can be indicated. Usually, however, arrangements are left tentative in the first session(s), for the essential understanding is that it is a time of assessment and mutual exploration. In effect it is a provisional contract: "Let's get together for a few sessions so that I can get a sense of the problem and see whether I can help and you meanwhile discover whether you really want to work with me." Only after this first phase is the contract for therapy decided.

Other than agreeing to schedule, fee, and the like, which provide the outer structure of the relation the patient's primary obligation is to the fundamental commitment, that without conscious reservation and to the best of his ability he will communicate his feelings and experiences openly and honestly wherever that inquiry might lead. What is actually involved in the process can only be known as time goes by, but the patient has to start with the intent to cooperate in the therapeutic dialogue and with the realization that the process may be painful and time-consuming. This essential facet of the contract is poetically encapsulated in the title of Hannah Green's account of her own treatment, "I never promised you a rose garden."

What does the therapist promise? He agrees to give undivided attention to the patient during the therapy session, to avoid prejudgment, particularly of a moralistic sort, and to use his full knowledge, best judgment, and empathic ability on the patient's behalf. Beyond this, he assures the patient of privacy and confidentiality and that he will not otherwise abuse the patient's trust. The therapist communicates, in general terms at least, his adherence to the ethical principles of his profession.

What does the therapist not promise? Most important, he cannot and does not assure a particular outcome. He will try, he will work toward goals, but he cannot guarantee accomplishment. At best, the outcome can only be conjectured—"Many people find after therapy . . ."

The unsophisticated patient may say outright, "Doctor, after ten sessions will I lose my fear of heights and be able to go mountain-climbing?" The more psychologically minded patient, cognizant of the ways of psychotherapy, phrases it more subtly. But the message is essentially the same—can I expect to improve for the effort, time, and money I'm investing?—nor is the question at all unreasonable. Our sympathy, professional pride, and indeed guilt, induce us too frequently to promise more than we can ultimately deliver and the consequences are predictable. The hope and power with which the patient invests us makes it easy indeed to act omnipotent in return. Any suggestion of a sure return on the therapeutic dollar—"Ten sessions with me and you can be a champion flagpole sitter!"—is not only arrogant and ignores the evidence known to all therapists about the uncertainty of therapeutic outcomes, but obviously contains the seeds of disillusionment.

Honesty, in this as in other facets of the therapeutic contract, is essential. The realities and uncertainties of therapy have to be communicated. At the same time, the therapist must convey his willingness to work and his faith in the patient's potential for growth, if indeed he believes it. If he does not, then he should not take on the patient. Whether rationalized as "it can't do any harm" or justified in any other fashion, the therapist who undertakes psychotherapy under these circumstances is acting cynically and ultimately against the best interests of the patient. He, as the arrogant over-optimist, is operating under a dishonest contract. In between, and difficult to define, is that balance of realistic caution and optimism necessary for a workable and moral therapeutic contract.

SETTING GOALS

An essential part of the therapeutic contract and of considerable importance in planning the future course of therapy are the goals set up early, even though they may be modified as therapy progresses. Broadly, of course, we strive to relieve distress and foster personal growth. However, these general aims can only be concretely specified in collaboration with the patient. The essential starting point is the patient's view of what should and can be accomplished. He starts with a notion, more or less sharply articulated, of what he wants and expects of therapy, and it is imperative for the psychotherapist to recognize these expectations as early as possible. They may be represented in aims as diverse as "to be happier," "to be more effective in my work," "to get rid of my fear so I can climb mountains," "to get over my hangups and go to graduate school," "to discover what I really want to do with my life," "to straighten out my marriage," and a thousand similar phrases. Sometimes the purpose is more external and does not reflect any wish on the patient's part to change but rather reflects a response to an external demand, such as "because my boss said he'd fire me if I don't shape up," "because the probation officer insisted," and the like. The stated motives may be mixed, containing different and sometimes contradictory aims; sometimes the manifest reason barely conceals a more vital and urgent motive. And, as commonly happens, the patient may have an undefined sense of distress and inadequacy with no clear vision of a desired future. Whatever the case, however, the therapist's first task is to understand the patient's needs and desires.

Danger lies in the therapist assuming or projecting his own goals and values on the patient. Sooner or later the therapist conveys his view of the patient's problems, the desirable ends toward which they might work together, and his own values as to psychological health. But it is a dangerous deceit for him to assume at the outset that they share values and that the patient comes wanting what he, were he the patient, would want of therapy. Typically, it has been found that patients' goals tend to be more immediate and modest ("to improve my home life and get a better job") than therapists' goals for them ("to become a creative, fully functioning individual"). It is true, of course, that patients can have extravagant expectations ("a *new* man") compared to those of the therapist ("the same person, but a little less anxious.") Whatever the disparity, the therapist can find himself too readily in the position of the artist who accepts a commission for a painting assuming a mandate for a masterpiece depicting, say, man's repugnance for war, when all the client had in mind was a pleasant piece in mauve, coral, and green to fit the space over the fireplace.

This does not mean, of course, that the therapist or the artist must accept any commission precisely as the client defines it. On the contrary, the therapist is obliged to say which goals he feels are worthy, realistic, and within the scope of his technique. Open discussion is necessary to arrive at mutually agreeable goals, some of which may be more immediate and others more distant, some more feasible and others less likely of attainment.

How do we know what goals are realistic? The most honest answer is that we cannot, for we cannot know the future of a human life. But the clinician can predict, within wide limits, probable trends and the likelihood that one or another therapeutic intervention might alter them. Such predictions proceed from knowledge gained in assessment, whether involving prior interviewing and testing or emerging in the early sessions of therapy. The clinician must integrate information about the particular person with knowledge of general principles of personality functioning and psychotherapy and temper his judgments by reasonable expectations as to probable situational events. As we have seen in earlier chapters, it is far from easy to gain the necessary personalistic understanding, and the resulting predictions are at best risky. Suppose a college senior seeks my help because he wants to go to a professional school, but he is severely anxious and feels profoundly inadequate. At the outset we must discover as much as possible about the nature and possible sources of the anxiety, the student's self-concept and coping resources and his intellectual capacities, interests, and school history. If his history shows marginal grades and perhaps limited abilities, coupled with a tendency to buckle under stress and retreat into emotional despair, it might be quite unrealistic to suppose that he could enter a professional school, with or without therapy, particularly in view of the limited number of applicants now being accepted. Still, therapy could be undertaken in the effort to reduce the painful emotions and strengthen coping mechanisms by discovering some of the conditions and conflicts which might underlie his disturbed feelings and behavior. This, rather than the specific and probably unattainable goal of gaining admittance to a professional school, is a feasible goal.

How one proceeds in therapy derives from the goals sought. If, for example, solving a marital problem is primary, then therapeutic conversations at least initially must focus on the husband-wife relationship. In this case, it might even be advantageous to suggest conjoint sessions rather than individual therapy, if both parties are willing. If a person is in acute despair, then a first task is to reduce the painful affect so that the person can give more attention to other facets of his life. It seems self-evident to say that the destination desired defines the route to be taken. Where therapists differ is in their notions as to how early, on what basis, and how firmly goals and consequently therapeutic strategies are to be defined. Some hold that therapy should start with as open a contract as possible and find its directions as issues arise spontaneously. Such clinicians would minimize the importance of prior assessment information, goal-setting, and planning in therapy, lest the therapist work mechanically to predetermined ends. My view is that the therapist must gain, in collaboration with the patient, a clear though not fixed sense of the end sought and the approach that will be taken. Without such a plan in mind, there is the risk of contradictory expectations and confused wandering. The plan should be open to change as new understandings emerge or conditions change, but at any point the therapist should have a fair sense of where he is at, what he is doing, and why.

SETTING LIMITS

The therapeutic relation is often characterized as permissive, as indeed it is in the sense of allowing the patient a unique opportunity for revealing personal feelings without fear of ridicule, censure, or exposure. However, this does not mean that the patient can do anything he pleases as impulse moves him. There are definite limits. Most obvious are those deriving from the initial terms of the therapeutic contract. The patient is simply not free to arbitrarily break appointments, come or leave at whim, not pay bills, and the like.

Beyond this, the patient must respect the person and property of the therapist. He is free, indeed encouraged, to vent angry feelings, but only verbally. Physical assault on the therapist or damage to office furniture cannot be tolerated. Similarly, feelings of admiration, affection, or love can be openly expressed, but sexual contact is forbidden. The therapeutic alliance differs importantly from the relation between friends, lovers, business partners, a physician and patient, or a priest and parishioner, and its value is reduced as it moves in any of those directions.

Nor is the patient truly free to say anything at all he pleases. Communication is to be directed toward the exploration and understanding of the patient's experiences and feelings. Should he want to chat idly about a recent movie, a baseball game, or such other topic, or indeed remain entirely silent, the patient is reminded that he is avoiding the therapeutic task. Such avoidance is understandable to provide respite from the difficult task of self-confrontation and may reflect involuntary blocks as the patient moves toward painful areas. Inevitably too there may be short periods in any hour that the patient will need and want to take "time out" by commenting on some impersonal topic. But continuing in this way has to be averted.

Now we come to the knottier issue of whether the therapist should limit and control the patient's behavior *outside* of the therapeutic session. The issue here is not whether he should attempt to *influence,* which is a proper and inevitable part of therapy, but directly *require* or *prohibit* behavior. Thus, a patient may feel that he has gained sufficient certainty to approach his boss for a raise and he explores possible strategies with the therapist; it is entirely appropriate for the therapist to say, "If you feel confident enough, why don't you try it?" But some therapists feel it important to require specific activities or to prohibit others. One notion is that the patient should give his full energy to working on a problem in therapy and hence, as necessary, remove himself from living in it in real life. Thus, therapists have required that husband and wife separate for a period or cease sexual relations. People have been required not to drink, smoke, gamble, and the like as a condition for undertaking therapy for these problems. Whatever reasons are given, I believe that therapists should not limit or determine the patient's outside activities. Clinicians have a clear obligation, of course, to help patients understand the meaning, consequences, and potential dangers of their actions. But prohibition as such, which, if meaningful must be backed by the threat of discontinuing therapy, is rarely if ever justified.

Essential Processes in Psychotherapy

THE FLOW OF COMMUNICATION

The patient talks about his experiences and feelings, wishes and fantasies, problems he is now facing and memories of the past, anticipated events and plans. Words, silences, and gestures carry his messages, some of which are intended and others unintended. The therapist listens with "evenly hovering attention," trying to comprehend the patient's meanings, noting themes, repetitions, and omissions. He then comments, in ways intended to clarify, extend, or relate (interpret) the patient's communications or simply to stimulate or guide their flow. Thus, there is a continuous communicational transaction between the two. In earlier discussion of assessment interviewing, we considered the need for shared vocabulary, common frames of reference, attention to nonverbal behavior, and a variety of other factors which facilitate communication. All of these are equally relevant in the therapeutic interview, although there is a shift in purpose and correspondingly in form. Perhaps "therapeutic dialogue" is a better term to describe the on-going conversations of psychotherapy, if "interview" suggests the meaning of one person gaining information from the other toward his own ends.

The therapist acts to encourage the flow of communication in different ways. He attempts to *reduce inhibition* and blocks to free expression by, for example, encouraging relaxation, or calming emotional states—"It is painful to talk about . . . but why don't you try to go on?" More explicitly, the therapist can *suggest topics* for discussion—"You've talked a good deal about your sister, but haven't mentioned your brother. Could you tell me something about him?" Under some circumstances the therapist not only suggests a focus but he may ask the patient to limit his attention to it. "A number of times, you've started to tell me about resentment at . . . but each time you got off on another issue. Why don't you tell me everything about . . . and don't think about anything else for this hour?" In less direct ways, the therapist can *steer the conversation,* intentionally or unintentionally. Leaning forward, raising an eyebrow, jotting down a note conveys "tell me more" as well as the words themselves. Experimental studies have shown that speech can be conditioned in interviewlike situations even though the subject may be unaware of the reinforcing cues (e.g., Greenspoon, 1955). Krasner (1962) has not inappropriately described the therapist as a social reinforcement machine. In psychotherapy, as in any human encounter, the therapist cannot avoid communicating his own feelings and reactions to the patient's behaviors, despite efforts at neutrality and permissiveness; hence, conditioning of the patient's speech is bound to occur. In principle, however, the therapist should know his own feelings and what he is communicating sufficiently well so that he minimizes inadvertently guiding the patient along lines which more reflect his own needs than the patient's concerns. However, even experienced therapists have heard patients say "I didn't tell you more about . . . because I somehow thought it didn't interest you."

Of greatest importance, however, are the comments of the therapist intended to *recognize, clarify,* or *interpret* the patient's meanings. This is the major contribution of the therapist and we will consider it further later, but for now we should note that interpretive comments of any form guide the therapeutic conversation toward particular areas, both in content and emphasis. The comment "that made you feel angry, didn't it?" not only underscores the importance of "that" but also encourages the patient to dwell on the subjective experience rather than only the objective description of an event.

Central to the therapeutic dialogue is the communication of such personal meanings. In an earlier paragraph, I used the phrase "convey information" to describe what goes on in a communicative act. The term is not inappropriate, but it is important to note that the information conveyed is of a rather different sort than is usually intended by this phrase by students of human cognition or language. The sentence "The next train leaves at 4 o'clock," conveys an important bit of information for me when I am travelling; the patient's "I arrived at my girl-friend's apartment at 4 o'clock," is relatively trivial unless accompanied by modifiers such as "enthusiastically" or "dreading another confrontation." In general, our concern is less with the "facts" as such but with the meaning they have for the patient in the context of his personal feelings, attitudes, and motives which make them relevant and understandable.

Comprehending such communications requires more than listening to the person with our usual reality-oriented, logical attitudes. Processing the informational bit "4 o'clock" is the same in both illustrations, but it is the essence of the message in the station and a trivial portion in the therapy room. It may well be that the railway employee *also* has in mind "Oh God, how I hate to say the same stupid things over and over. Can't he read the sign? How I wish *I* was getting away from all this on the 4 o'clock train!" But unless he forces it on me, all of that message goes unreceived.

As therapist, however, one has to hear beyond the manifest statement and to be able to grasp half-stated, unverbalized, and even unknown meanings. In part, this requires a kind of "empathic listening" which picks up more than is carried by the message content. As any empathic act (recall Chapter 7), it involves sensing in oneself cues aroused by the patient's words and gestures which make it possible to know his experience as he does.

It is difficult here, as in our earlier discussion, to convey fully what is meant by "empathic understanding." In the psychotherapeutic theory of Harry Stack Sullivan (1953) the concept of empathy figured prominently. However, at one point he said:

> I have had a good deal of trouble at times with people of a certain type of educational history; since they cannot refer empathy to vision, hearing, or some other special sense receptor, and since they do not know whether it is transmitted by the ether waves or air waves or whatnot, they find it hard to accept the idea of empathy. . . . So although empathy may sound mysterious, remember that there is much that sounds mysterious in the universe, only we have gotten used to it; and perhaps you will get used to empathy.

As we continue to work with a particular patient, we internalize a broader and deeper base for knowing his experience not only from the information he directly conveys, nor even from our inferences based on other material, but directly in terms of our empathic responses. Whatever the mechanism, however, the therapist uses this understanding as a base for interpretative comments which in turn serve as hypotheses for further exploration and ultimately lead, we hope, to increased self-awareness.

EXAMINING EXPERIENCE

Overall, the therapeutic dialogue centers on the patient's *present* needs, problems, and life experiences. In the first phase of therapy, much attention is given to the patient's symptoms and problems, to picture fully what is troubling him and why he has sought therapeutic help. In these sessions, the patient describes the circumstances under which his problems are intensified and those which relieve him, when he feels happy and when he feels distressed, in what contexts he feels adequate and when inept; in general, the framework of contingent circumstances which seem to govern his well-being. As time goes on, the emphasis usually broadens from discussion of his focal complaints to wider-ranging considerations of his current life. The patient talks about his family, friends, and colleagues, the interpersonal network within which he lives. The patient describes his work, hobby and recreational interests and his social and political concerns; in general, the full range of matters in which he is involved. Some may be long-standing concerns, others are stimulated by immediate experiences ("Strange, on the way over here I noticed . . . and it made me think . . ."). The patient will talk about his wishes and expectations of the future as well as his memories of the past as they give context to his present experience ("Y'know, it wasn't always like this . . . I used to . . ."). It is literally impossible, of course, to catalog all of the sorts of issues which might be considered even in a brief course of therapy. Many topics are wholly idiosyncratic reflecting the particular patient's unique interests, others bear on the common experiences and concerns of all of us, whether related to sexual love, job ethics, or national security. But whatever the focus, the amount and intensity of attention given it reflect what most concerns the patient in his current life. The examination of such experiences is to understand what meanings they have for the patient and why, in terms of motives, character structures, beliefs, and the like, they occurred. The basic material of the therapeutic dialogue consists of the patient's phenomenal experiences of his present life.

In picturing his current experience, the patient reveals his characteristic attitudes and feelings. He also reveals modes of thinking, cognitive styles, characteristic defenses, and other ego processes. Let us examine, for example, the following exchange with a patient in therapy.

Therapist: You look sort of downcast today.

Patient: Yes, I feel miserable. Yesterday was my first day on the new job. Everything was wrong. I couldn't even sleep last night. I may not even go back tomorrow.

Therapist: What happened?

Patient: Everybody ignored me. Nobody seemed to care that I was there; they barely said "hello." I suppose I can do the work OK, and I certainly need the money, but who wants to work in such a place. The vibes were all bad. I don't think there's one person there I could relate to.

Therapist: Can you be sure? You were only there one day.

Patient: Well, I suppose I could give it another try. I didn't really get to meet everyone. But they all looked the same, as if they didn't like me and didn't give a damm about me.

Therapist: You said you didn't sleep last night?

Patient: Yeah, I got to thinking about it, and got to wondering if I had done something wrong. Maybe I gave them the impression that I thought they were a bunch of clods. Anyway, I kept thinking about it, feeling miserable, thinking that maybe I had acted pretty snotty. Aw, the hell with it, I'm not going back. . . .

Even in this brief exchange, we can develop a number of reasonable hypotheses about the person's needs, cognitive style, emotional responsivity, and defenses. The patient greatly wants to feel warmly accepted, even in a work situation which might serve other needs and even before there is a reasonable basis for relationships to be formed. He is quick to sense rejection, though also realizing that he may provoke it. Intellectually, he is quick to overgeneralize and, emotionally, to overreact. As defense, he retreats from a potentially threatening situation, but not before he has dwelt on it and allowed it to make him miserable. In the course of therapy each of these themes would be explored, not once but likely several times, the therapist encouraging the patient to examine and view himself from different perspectives by offering interpretative hypotheses. In the present episode, attention was called, and quietly at that, only to the tendency to overgeneralize.

Suppose, one might ask, the patient actually was snubbed by his new co-workers; suppose, for example, he was the first long-haired student in an office of conservative crewcuts. This fact would, of course, temper our understanding of the event, though it still seems true that he overreacted and did not allow the possibility that a warmer and more pleasant relation could evolve. From the isolated episode, we simply do not know whether there were situational provocations or whether the patient was seriously misconstruing an innocent situation. In general, characteristic needs, defenses, and other personality qualities only become clear as we explore with the patient a broad range of his experiences. Overall, however, we are concerned with the patient's understanding and feelings and only secondarily with "what actually occurred." If by contrast we were to look at the same situation with the eyes of an organizational psychologist, we might note that the patient's office tends to be a closed club which receives newcomers most reluctantly, and this has implications for office morale and productivity; however, as the individual's therapist, our concern is with his oversensitivity and, as seems evident in the particular case, maladaptive way of dealing with new social experiences.

EXPLORING THE PAST

In the particular case we have been discussing, it is obviously relevant to know that over years the patient has acted in much the same way on many analogous occasions, or perhaps that, until some particular point, he was less consumed with social acceptance or rejection, readier to absorb social rebuff or better able to stay with and work through potentially awkward relationships. Reviewing the past gives context to understanding the patient's current life and problems. In this sense, historical exploration is a necessary part of the therapeutic process, even though concern centers on the patient's contemporary state.

Kurt Lewin took an essentially *ahistorical* view, declaring that what was relevant of the past still exists in the present. Hence, full analysis of the current "life space" of the person can provide ample base for understanding contemporary behavior. At the other extreme, faith in *historical determinism* was best defended by classical psychoanalysis. Personality was believed to be formed in the emotional transactions of the earliest years; by the age of five or six, and certainly by adolescence, the personality has its adult qualities. Consequently, profound changes in character organization and genuine alteration of neurotic behaviors require delving into the distant, now unconscious, past to locate the root causes of present symptoms and behavior.

From our present perspective, both positions are too extreme. We can never know the current life space with such microscopic accuracy that knowledge is not extended by discovering historical antecedents. It is true that much that happened in the past is irrelevant; past events as such, in the life of a person or a nation, are not a sufficient base for predicting future history. Moreover, personality is a constantly evolving process, always capable of change, although early emotional experiences are surely of great importance. Indeed, if psychotherapy is effective it is direct evidence of the possibility of new learning in a contemporary relation with another person.

Psychotherapy does not depend, as I have already noted, simply on the recovery of repressed memories. Indeed, much of what is conceived as repressed and unconscious may well be more properly viewed as material which belongs to another, now irrelevant, context and hence cannot be retrieved. Thus, if you ask me to name the streets, landmarks, and events I experienced in a town in which I lived twenty years ago, I may well have very limited recall. But should I visit the place, suddenly memories "come back." I can walk along a street and know, without searching my memory, the name of the next street; I can pick up a phone and dial a number I did not "know" for years. Lost memories need not reflect repression, nor does their recovery necessarily indicate a breaking down of repressive, defensive barriers; it may as well indicate the reinstatement of an earlier context.

In the concept being developed here, early emotional experiences are seen as important but by no means exclusive determinants of adult functioning, nor does therapeutic change depend on discovering their original nature. Even if a particular facet of personality is clearly rooted in traumatic or conflict-laden early experiences, subsequent change can occur without necessarily bringing those experiences to light. Neurotic patterns are rooted in the past, but they are sustained through present forces.

Historical events, therefore, are to be studied from the vantage point of the contemporary personality. What matters most is how such events are remembered and how the patient now understands them; what actually occurred in the past and what meaning it had then we may be able to infer but that is of lesser importance. Thus, the patient who felt rejected on his first day on the new job, may report that his parents "always" favored his older brother, and treated him as an unworthy and unlovable appendage to the family. He recalls incidents showing how he was neglected and he feels again the resulting hurt. Today, he still resents his brother and his parents and he cannot relate to them without angry feelings, not however unmixed with envy and a plaintive hope that they will come to appreciate and love him. His readiness to expect social rebuff may be a generalized expectation derived from his sense of unworthiness in the earlier family constellation. In further exploration of early memories, the patient may recall incidents in which he was treated with loving consideration. The patient may dismiss such incidents as atypical, but the therapist can use them to challenge his "always" concept. However, what is ultimately needed is a break in the belief system— "I am an unworthy little boy and people have always and will always treat me as insignificant and unlovable." In therapy, this may occur as a consequence of one or more of the following conditions: (1) The patient recovers hitherto repressed feelings and memories which can be relived in the present therapeutic relationship; (2) He can reconceptualize earlier experiences, whether repressed, distorted, or accurately remembered. ("Yes, I guess there were other times when I was treated fairly," or more radically, "Whatever happened in the past, I can now lead a new life."); or (3) He can be encouraged to discover new, relevant sources of competence and worth in his present life, including importantly the therapeutic relation itself which gives immediate and living evidence of his worth. While all of these processes may occur, the third is ultimately the most important for producing the corrective emotional experiences of therapy.

EXPLORING THE THERAPIST-PATIENT RELATIONSHIP

The relation between the therapist and the patient sets the basic emotional climate within which the patient is willing to undertake self-exploration. In the on-going process of psychotherapy, the relation serves three further functions, as it provides (1) a microcosm of social behavior generally; (2) an opportunity for examining transference feelings; and (3) an opportunity for learning through identification and modeling.

A microcosm of other social relations. However special the transactions between patient and therapist, in some respects it is like other social relations in the patient's life. Behavior varies in different social roles, hence the patient-therapist interplay is predictably different from, for example, the patient-spouse or patient (as student)-teacher interactions. Still, there are consistencies across roles which reflect personality traits. Thus, the submissive person hesitates to express opinions to his spouse, to his teacher and to his therapist, while the assertive person is more ready to speak his mind to all three. Hence, while a considerable part of therapy focuses on events occurring outside of the session, there is in the session itself a constant, on-going flow between the two participants within which the patient, and so too the therapist, reveal characteristic interpersonal attitudes. The immediate information contained in the here-and-now situations of therapy therefore provides a framework for understanding the patient's problems and personality. They provide illustrations of more or less typical behaviors, against which the patient's descriptions of "life" behaviors can be viewed. Thus, the patient who says "I always stutter when I talk about myself," yet at the moment is speaking with perfect clarity. This contradiction can be called to his attention. Either he exaggerates the extent of his distress or it occurs only when speaking with certain kinds of people in some kinds of situations; whatever the case, the present behavior gives context for understanding outside behavior. In addition, of considerable importance are those feelings directed toward the therapist himself as the relation develops. The patient can feel resentment, affection, dependence, respect, or any of numerous other feelings which are more or less appropriate and predictable in such an intimate situation.

The role of transference feelings. Among the reactions to the therapist are those which Freud described as "transference." These are attitudes carried over from early experiences which are now projected onto the therapist, who has not, so to speak, earned them himself. While one might readily feel warmly respectful toward a kind and wise therapist, and even wish to have further contact with him as a friend, it is inappropriate to feel intense love and to yearn for a sexual relationship. Such feelings, psychoanalysts propose, are carry-overs from blocked needs in early life, particularly in relation to one's own parents. The analysis of transference feelings is of central importance to the psychoanalytic process for they bring into present consciousness critical, usually repressed, conflicts of the past. It should be noted that the conditions of psychoanalytic therapy, such as frequent sessions over a long period, encouragement of unconscious fantasy, and the impersonality of the therapist, particularly encourage the development of transference. However, the phenomenon of transferred or projected feelings occurs in any form of therapy and the therapist should be prepared for the onslaught of feelings which are disproportionate to present realities. So too, the good therapist has to be able to distinguish "earned" from "transferred" feelings and know his own contribution to the patient's state. If I yawn repeatedly as the patient talks about matters of great importance to him and he then tells me that I must think him unworthy of my concern, it is at least insensitive to suggest that he is recalling his sense of inferiority in the presence of his father. The fact is that I yawned, which correctly enough he can interpret as boredom, and that fact has to be faced first. The line between realistic, appropriate feelings anchored in the present encounter and unrealistic, exaggerated feelings rooted in historically determined neurotic needs of the patient is surely a difficult one to draw. Both types of feelings are important in therapy; transference reactions, however, have the special quality of revealing what may be critically important and deeply rooted attitudes toward major figures in the patient's earlier life.

Learning through identification and modeling. The relation between therapist and patient figures in still another way in psychotherapy. It provides opportunity for the patient to observe and take on the behaviors of the therapist through an identificational and/or modeling process. Bandura (1971) has called particular attention to the importance of modeling, particularly when working with children. However, in all forms of therapeutic intervention, patients tend to adopt the therapist's ways of thinking, feeling, and acting, sometimes by intent but as often unwittingly through a process of identification and internalization. This may be seen in trivial and not particularly desirable ways, as for example by the patient taking on the therapist's mannerisms or taste in clothing. Some finish therapy not much changed except for a Van Dyke beard, tweedy sport coat, and saying "So?" with a slightly Viennese accent. The gain is more substantial, however, if the patient has learned to plan actions instead of acting impulsively, to remain calm under stress, and to face his own inadequacies rather than denying them, in part at least inspired by observing these qualities in his therapist.

RECOGNIZING, CLARIFYING AND INTERPRETING THE PATIENT'S FEELINGS AND MEANINGS

The therapist listens intently and at various times offers *interpretive comments* on what the patient says. Through these interjections, the therapist calls attention to the patient's feelings and beliefs, identifies and clarifies them, puts them into the context of other aspects of his personality, fosters awareness of their possible antecedents, and ultimately, one hopes, provides opportunity for the patient to alter his behavior in terms of the increased self-awareness. Interpretation focuses both on the *what* and the *why* of behavior, in order to increase awareness of what the patient is presently feeling and what impact it may have on others and as well as to discover why, in terms of the patient's needs, character structure, and determining experiences, he has come to feel, believe, or act in this particular way. In general, in the earlier stages of the therapy process emphasis is on what and only later on why. Whatever their focus, and however simple or complex, the intended effect of interpretation is to alter the patient's cognitions of himself and his world.

At the simplest level, interpretations may involve repeating or restating something the patient has said, perhaps altering the emphasis, to make him more aware of its import. Thus, in reply to the patient's "Nothing went right today," the therapist might reply "Nothing?" Even the simple "Tell me more," carries the meaning that the issue is important and more information desirable. More complex interpretations, involving increasing degrees of inference, include those which attempt to identify and name the feeling state behind the patient's comments, those which summarize a number of parallel productions in order to draw attention to common themes, and those which call to the patient's awareness attitudes of which he seems unaware or may actively be denying. Illustrative interpretive comments in these modes might include: "You seem to be very angry when you talk about him." "It seems that when you get into a frustrating situation, you feel like quitting and giving up." "You say you respect him, but I keep hearing you make disparaging remarks about him." Still more complex and inferential are those interpretations which attempt to show linkages between the patient's feelings toward important figures of the past and those in his current life, including the therapist himself (transference reactions). Finally, there are those interpretations directed toward possible symbolic meanings or theoretical constructs.

The concept of interpretation originates in psychoanalysis, where it usually refers to the more complex forms of inferences, particularly those which seek to explain current personality characteristics in terms of repressed and unconscious conflicts and needs. Classically the effort was directed at divining ultimate causes of the patient's symptoms in terms of their originating experiences. Interpretation is now made of defensive strategies, resistance, and transference reactions in therapy, and of current fantasies, impulses, and behavior, not only to discover their origins but to understand their dynamics in contemporary functioning. Thus, Fromm-Reichmann states:

> The purpose of interpretation and of interpretive questions is to bring dissociated and repressed experiences and motivations to awareness and to show patients how, unknown to themselves, repressed and dissociated material finds its expression in and colors verbalized communications and behavior patterns such as their actions, attitudes, and gestures [1950, p. 70].

The concept of interpretation as used here is intended in a broader meaning, not limited to discovering and revealing "dissociated and repressed experiences and motivations," whether in a historic or contemporary framework. Rather the term, it seems to me, can properly be used to describe any intentional act by the therapist which attempts to foster understanding by calling attention to unknown or ignored factors, by bringing together hitherto unrelated materials and by proposing explanations for feelings and actions, whether or not in terms of unconscious determinants. Thus, included would be "recognizing and clarifying feelings" in the sense used by Carl Rogers, who properly describes his psychotherapy as "noninterpretive" when the term is limited to the psychoanalytic usage. While it might be well to use several terms to describe different levels, complexity, and targets of interpretive acts, they all have in common the effort to reconceptualize the meanings of the patient's communications.

In this conception, therapeutic interpretation can be visualized as ranging from lower-order judgments of a simple, more descriptive type to higher-order inferences of a more conceptual or abstract nature, along much the same type of continuum previously used to describe the interpretive acts of clinical assessment (cf. Chapter 11). Viewed in terms of the clinician's thought processes, interpreting the "data" of therapeutic encounters and those of assessment interviews and tests are quite analogous enterprises. Both require careful observation and disciplined clinical judgment, anchored in extensive knowledge of personality mechanisms and theory. In both cases, there must be a blending of inferential and intuitive processes; on the one hand, the painstaking gathering, processing and generalization of relevant information and on the other, the use of creative imagination and divergent thinking required to create as well as to test hypotheses. In both cases, judgment can be flawed by the operation of many factors, such as schematization, lack of individualization, overinterpretation, and the like considered earlier.

There are, of course, critical differences between interpretation in assessment and in therapy. In assessment, standardized procedures can be used for which there are norms and hence opportunity for statistical inference. Moreover, the clinician has all his material before him, which he can study and restudy and as necessary gather further information before reaching conclusions. In therapy, by contrast, he is in the midst of a flowing stream and interpretive comments have to be made with minimum forethought. But, by the same token, the clinician is dealing with decidedly smaller units at each moment. Moreover, should he miss one opportunity, there are repeated occasions to call attention to the same theme. Most important is the fact that in therapy the clinician has immediate feedback and, by virtue of the therapeutic alliance, collaboration in judging the patient's productions. The patient's immediate reaction advises the therapist as to the credibility of the interpretation and guides his further comments. The patient not only responds to the therapist's interpretations, but he himself actively generates hypotheses about his behavior.

Much has been written about the correctness of interpretation, but the issue is more the plausibility and working value of the interpretation, rather than its literal truth. They are hypotheses as to what is going on; the best guess under the circumstances and they are meant to be tentatively held and considered. They are valuable to the extent that they define issues and move the therapeutic dialogue forward. A gratifying response is "Y'know, I never thought of it that way, maybe that's why . . ." or "I've been thinking about what you said last week and I decided to try it out by acting differently with my wife." Rarely if ever does a single interpretation, or even a series over time, lead to a radical reconceptualization of the patient's problem in a blinding flash of insight.

Interpretations achieve a number of effects in addition to facilitating the recognition, clarification, and understanding of the patient's feelings. They imply acceptance or rejection of the patient's concerns. Labeling a feeling state, for example, reveals to the patient that the feeling is acceptable to the therapist, though the patient may have felt that he would be repelled by it. On the other hand, interpretations suggesting the inappropriateness or maladaptive nature of some act imply criticism and suggest directions for change. Correspondingly, interpretations can alter the patient's emotional state as wall as rousing specific affects. Some interpretations increase the patient's sense of mastery or his faith in the therapist and lead to a reduction of tension; others reveal his inadequacies or bring into view hitherto unknown fantasies or feelings and heighten distress.

Thus, a patient can feel more guilty at the realization that he holds feelings more vicious than he had imagined, but again a patient's guilt might be alleviated by the discovery that others share such feelings. Finally, it should be noted that interpretations convey a conceptual scheme for understanding one's own and the behavior of others. At the very least, the patient comes to understand that behavior is explicable and hence meaningful, even when seemingly determined by powerful forces beyond his understanding and control.

Early in therapy, the therapist focuses mainly on clarifying present feelings and attitudes as they are immediately revealed in the sessions. Much of the emphasis is on his current concerns including his motivation for therapy. Only later are more far-reaching interpretations possible. This is partly because more information is needed of the sort which emerges only with time and growing confidence in the therapist. Moreover, a firm relation is needed to absorb the potentially damaging effects of an inept or inopportune interpretation. The higher the level of inference involved, the greater is the risk that the interpretation will be erroneous and be more painful than helpful to the patient. Too often, interpretations offered seem more intended to show off the therapist's intellectual agility at contriving an all-inclusive view of the patient in favored theoretical terms, than to organize the experiences of the patient in ways meaningful to him. Harry Stack Sullivan, the eminently sensitive and sensible interpersonal psychiatrist, cautioned his students that "The supply of interpretations, like that of advice, greatly exceeds the need for them." (1947, p. 92.) In his own work, he tried to understand the patient as if from inside and generally limited his comments to those most likely to make the patient more fully aware of what he was actually experiencing.

In general, interpretative comments should be close to where the patient is at in his evolving self-awareness. Though few general rules can be made, it seems true that an interpretation is most effective when it anticipates, but not by much, an emerging consciousness of an issue; when a notion is, as it were, on the tip of the patient's mental tongue but not yet consciously available. It is all too easy to know after the fact when an interpretive comment misfires or is premature, or even when it has been delayed too long, but to know the opportune moment as it arises is one of the most difficult tasks of the psychotherapist. One thing is certain, however, just because a hypothesis occurs to the therapist is no reason for him to immediately verbalize it to the patient. Most often such interpretations are simply to be held in mind, developed in the therapist's thinking as more evidence cumulates, and offered to the patient only when the time seems right for him to absorb and use it. In the ensuing dialogue, the ramifications and value of the hypothesis are tested conjointly with the patient, toward the end of extending, altering, or rejecting it as necessary. Although there are dramatic accounts of important symptoms of psychological changes following interpretive acts even in a single interview, much more usually, the linked processes of examining experience, seeking relations, and offering and testing clarificatory concepts require numerous therapeutic transactions in which many of the same issues are discussed repeatedly, if from differing points of view.

From Understanding to Action

In general terms, psychotherapy can be viewed as consisting of three major phases: (1) *Establishing the therapeutic relationship,* with the necessary motivation and trust, fundamental commitment and therapeutic alliance, and a workable contract from which therapy can proceed; (2) *Seeking understanding* of the nature and sources of personality characteristics and defects. This is the major task of therapy and typically involves relentless examination and interpretation of current feelings, attitudes, and behaviors and their historical antecedents and of the patient's relation with relevant others, including the therapist; and (3) *Translating insights into actions and new life patterns.* Failure can occur at any level, but if successful, the patient passes through all three. Thus far, we have considered the first two stages; at this point let us look at the third.

The self-knowledge of the second phase is painfully and arduously, if at all, won. Nor can progress be plotted on a smooth, ascending curve. There are setbacks as new problems arise, life conditions change, or the patient meets defeats in halting efforts at more positive behaviors. Neurotic patterns are not easily shed and patients move back to safer ground after seeming advances. Hence, there is constant need to reexamine, reinterpret, and reanalyze emotional patterns, time and again, in order to consolidate the gains of earlier therapeutic dialogues. This process has been called "working through" and it merges with the more positive activities of the third phase. However, to the extent that the patient has discovered underlying patterns in his behavior, has greater understanding of what he does and to an extent why, and has become aware of the functional roles played by out-moded and self-defeating defenses and character traits, dissatisfaction with them grows apace and with it resolve to change and willingness to try new behaviors. With self-awareness, there is an increased sense of emotional security, self-esteem, and mastery. The patient is more ready to discard old habits and values and to experiment with new actions; he has been liberated to seek more autonomous and constructive behaviors. Throughout, but particularly in this phase, as the patient has been able to master emotional conflicts in the therapeutic relation, he can venture out to try his new skills in "real life." As Alexander (1946) put it:

> Like the adage "Nothing succeeds like success," there is no more powerful therapeutic factor than the performance of activities which were formerly neurotically impaired or inhibited. No insight, no emotional discharge, no recollection can be as reassuring as accomplishment in the actual life situation in which the individual failed. Thus the ego regains that confidence which is the fundamental condition, the prerequisite, of mental health. Every success encourages new trials and decreases inferiority feelings, resentments, and their sequelae—fear, guilt, and resulting inhibitions. Successful attempts at productive work, love, self-assertion, or competition will change the vicious circle to a benign one; as they are repeated, they become habitual and thus eventually bring about a complete change in the personality [p. 40].

In the third and last phase, therapeutic conversations generally turn from (1) consideration of *neurotic* patterns to discussion of *adaptive* potentials; (2) *inner* feelings, fantasies, and memories to *outside* social realities; and (3) from *past* history and present problems to *future* prospects. In fair measure, the basic activity of therapy continues, that is, the patient talks about his concerns and the therapist attempts to clarify and advance understanding. However, there are important changes in the therapy process. The relation between therapist and patient becomes more that of equals. The patient has learned a therapeutic mode of thinking and he is more likely to volunteer interpretations, introduce topics, pose questions and seek advice. As emotional tensions are reduced, he is able to reason more logically. Freer of neurotic resistances and defenses, he can more readily formulate, and is more open to accept, alternate interpretations of his behavior. Increasingly, therefore, the therapist and patient are partners in a joint problem-solving task.

On his part, the therapist paradoxically is freer to act in more directive ways. He can encourage specific actions, offer direct advice, suggest one rather than another alternative. Earlier in therapy such interventions are avoided lest the patient passively obey out of excessive fear, dependence, or awe. But once the patient is better able to make up his own mind, and defend his own positions, the therapist is able to state his own more positively. Where earlier persuasive efforts might seem manipulations of the patient's weakness, they are now more tributes to his strength. Consequently, the therapist can urge particular actions and openly compliment or criticize his efforts. This is not at all to suggest that the therapist has given up the investigatory role in favor of a directive one; major effort still goes into trying to discover the meanings of the patient's wishes and actions. But now, meanings can be tested against direct as well as more indirect reactions. The apparently simple statement "Why do you think that will work?" should now draw from the patient "for the following reasons, a . . . b . . . c . . . ," whereas it might have evoked "maybe I better not try . . ." earlier. In this phase, too, there is need to encourage exploratory activities in previously avoided realms. To this end, supportive encouragement can be valuable without being coercive.

With the patient directing more attention to future activities in the outside world, the therapist can facilitate decision making by vicariously testing alternative possibilities with him. "Well, suppose you went back to school . . . how would that affect your way of life . . . relations with friends . . . your wife . . . etc.?" "If you go into business for yourself, you would have more independence to run things your way, but you'd have less free time . . . more responsibility . . . maybe less income, at first at least? Are you willing to make the trade off?" In some ways, the task is more like that of a psychological consultant facilitating the rational decision-making of an executive than that of a therapist disentangling the confused emotions of a distressed person. Role playing may be a valuable technique for discovering what may be involved in a hitherto untried social situation. Thus, if the patient is fearful at the prospect of a job interview, he and the therapist can enact the roles of applicant and personnel man. In the course of the pretended job interview, the patient reveals his expectations, how he would present himself, his ways of acting, reacting to challenges, and the like. The therapist meanwhile can by playing his role in different ways more or less vigorously test the patient. At the end, they can examine the episode together toward discovering ways in which the patient might improve his chances in a future real-life job interview. Similarly, the therapist might assist the patient frame a letter of application, review with him information on the job market, help him focus vocational or educational goals, or otherwise help him find a more satisfying place for increased talents and personality resources.

Terminating Psychotherapy

A cynic has said that psychotherapy ends when the patient becomes as bored listening to himself as the therapist has been all along. Actually, there is a partial truth here. It is a sign of health for a patient to become less consumed with his problems, to see them as more managable and less important, and hence to prefer putting his energies into seeking new experiences rather than in licking old wounds. The error lies in the implication that the patient was all along self-indulgently dwelling on trivial matters, which depreciates both his pain and the therapist's potential contribution to its relief.

When should psychotherapy end? In one sense, never. There is no limit to personal development and hence therapy, in the essential meaning of the conscious examination, understanding, and perfecting of behavior, is similarly a lifelong process. Psychotherapy is a desirable way of life, which may but does not necessarily involve more than one's own efforts within a therapeutic way of thinking. Such a therapeutic attitude, though a natural part of mature behavior, can be learned in sessions with a professional, and then hopefully carried over to guide future life.

In the more usual and limited sense, psychotherapy should be terminated when the stated goals are reached. The more precisely these were originally phrased, the more certain therapist and patient can be that they have been attained. Thus, we can know with some certainty that presenting symptoms have disappeared or that work can be resumed, but with decidedly less confidence that the patient has developed "emotional maturity" or "resources for creative living." Moreover, new vistas open and goals change as therapy progresses; also, therapist and patient may all along have had different notions of what was expected at the end. Whatever the case, however, the terminal phase necessarily begins with therapist and patient taking stock of the patient's current status and future prospects and deciding whether goals are closely enough approached.

With this decision it is well to set a particular final date, approximately six weeks later, and even to taper off in the final weeks by reducing the frequency or length of sessions. Emphasis in this phase is on the meaning of discontinuing therapy as well as on the patient's plans for the future. There are predictable emotional problems which may have to be dealt with. Just as there are resistances to making commitments to the therapy in the first place, there can be resistances to leaving it at the end. For some patients, being in therapy becomes a way of life, rather than a proper means to an end. Though completing therapy is an achievement, and betokens movement to a more mature level of self-management, it may still be experienced as rejection. There is often a surge of dependent feelings. The patient is suddenly afraid to venture out on his own, and "Wouldn't a few more sessions help . . . ?" There may be a resurgence of earlier symptoms, as if to prove the point, or just generalized distress and anxiety. In some ways, the situation is not unlike the adolescent who may have been rebelliously proclaiming his right to autonomy and yet feels strangely fearful as he leaves the family for college. Uncertainty is an understandable enough feeling when one moves from one life phase to another, but so too is excitement and hope. The effort in the last phase is to accentuate the latter and minimize the former feelings. It is important to assure the patient that, if there are setbacks in the future, additional sessions can be scheduled, even if expressing the hope that they will not be needed.

It is a paradox of psychotherapy that it is a *dependent* relation—the patient seeks and obtains "help"—the goal of which is *independent* functioning. In the nondirective mode described in this chapter, the patient is given maximal respect and autonomy throughout and he collaborates with increasing responsibility in the process. Hence, the transition to still greater freedom after therapy should be, and usually is, an occasion for joy. In more directive modes, which build on the patient's dependency, termination can be a harsher experience. However, in this or any form of psychotherapy, problems of the type discussed can arise in the final weeks. Indeed, it is a measure of the success of psychotherapy that the patient can move smoothly into an autonomous life in which he is, so to speak, his own therapist. Termination is, as graduation speakers remind us, a "commencement," the beginning of a new and better era.

Termination of course can, and often does, occur before goals are reached and with little or no sense of accomplishment. Therapy may have come to an impasse and with the best efforts of patient and therapist, all that can be visualized is a long and futile plateau. Despite earlier resolve, the patient may now be confronting neurotic mechanisms which he cannot or will not change. On the other hand, the patient may terminate therapy "prematurely" because he feels his goals have been reached, even though it may seem obvious to the therapist or onlooker that there are still many outstanding problems. Earlier, note was taken of the fact that therapists not infrequently expect more for their patients than do the patients themselves. From the patient's view, therefore, termination in such cases may not be at all premature. In research on the outcome of therapy the patient's unilateral decision to discontinue is often taken as a sign of failure, when actually it may be success from the patient's point of view. However, walking out in anger or disgust, with a sense of futility and that time and effort were wasted, is another matter. Still, even under these circumstances, the decision to quit sometimes leads to reconsideration and recommitment to therapy.

A funny-sad illustration concerns an old friend who, though a competent professional, was an impulsive, readily arousable person with little tolerance of disappointment or delay. Impatient with the plodding pace of therapy, he simply announced one day that he'd had enough, without failing, however, to accuse his therapist of incompetence. The therapist's last words, as my friend left, were "Please be careful going home." To celebrate his new-found freedom and wealth, now that he would no longer be paying for therapy, he decided to stop and buy glasses and dishes to replace his old mismatched and chipped ones. Loosely wrapped bags were put on the back seat and he took off for home. Only a few blocks later, he carelessly ran into the rear of a car at a stoplight, dumping his glasses and dishes all over himself and the floor of the car. He showed up at the time of the next scheduled therapy session contrite and now ready to get down to work.

Therapy may also be discontinued because the therapist feels that he is no longer capable of working with the patient. Either he recognizes that he lacks sufficient knowledge, experience, or skill to treat this particular kind of patient or problem or he discovers that he has lost the necessary therapeutic detachment by developing overly strong personal feelings, some of which reflect countertransference in the psychoanalytic sense. Just as the patient can project onto the therapist out-moded and inappropriate attitudes, the therapist can do the same to the patient. Such feelings may also be stimulated by salient qualities of the patient, who may, in fact, hold despicable social attitudes or be extraordinarily attractive.

In principle, the well-disciplined therapist should have sufficient self-knowledge, control, and tolerance to continue with this patient despite the arousal of hate or lust. Such feelings can be honestly discussed with the patient, or to advantage reviewed with a colleague or supervisor, but if they become sufficiently demanding, termination may be the only responsible solution. If therapy is discontinued because of the therapist's inadequacies, he has a special obligation to make this clear to the patient, lest the patient be left with a sense of guilt and the feeling that he is a hopeless case. Wherever appropriate, effort should be made to help him find another therapist.

Finally, therapy can be brought to an end for adventitious reasons. The patient or therapist may have to move from the area or one or the other may become too ill to continue. Jobs can change, and the patient may not be able to schedule the therapy hours; perhaps his new position requires him to travel continuously. In training clinics, psychotherapy is usually limited to the academic year, at the end of which student clinicians move on to new assignments. Under all such circumstances, therapy should be brought to as useful a close as possible. Even if not a natural ending point, the last weeks can be used profitably in reviewing the progress and status of the patient, considering the import of termination, and planning for the future.

In this chapter some of the more important considerations in the process of psychotherapy, from the perspective of a particular model, have been discussed. With this as background, we can now examine alternate models of psychotherapy.

CHAPTER 14

Psychoanalysis, Behavior Therapy, and Humanistic-Existential Psychotherapy

Contemporary psychotherapy is dominated by three major orientations: the psychoanalytic, the behavioral, and the humanistic-existential. The numerous distinct forms of psychotherapy currently being practiced can be viewed in terms of belonging to one or another of these major groups, though any cataloging is necessarily arbitrary. Psychoanalytic therapies, behavior therapies, and the humanistic-existential approaches differ not only in their techniques but in their very concepts as to the nature of man, the development of personality and of psychopathology, and in their values as to the desired state of mental health. These differences will be surveyed in the present chapter, starting with consideration of the oldest, most articulated and influential approach—psychoanalysis.

PSYCHOANALYSIS

History and Background

The history of modern psychotherapy begins with the work of Sigmund Freud. In the 1880s, Freud became acquainted with Joseph Breuer, a distinguished Viennese physician, who was then treating a young woman with conversion hysteria. When Breuer hypnotized "Miss Anna O." she could recall emotional experiences of which she was normally unaware. As she expressed these feelings under hypnosis, she was relieved when returning to normal consciousness. Eventually, her bodily symptoms, which included among others anaesthesia in her arm and leg, and visual field defects, disappeared. Freud and Breuer formulated a theory of hysteria and psychotherapy in rather simple terms: Normally, they reasoned, the strong emotions accompanying intense experiences are expressed and discharged, but if direct expression is blocked, the affect takes a more devious route and can give rise to hysterical symptoms. Under hypnosis, the process is reversed and with the recall of the earlier experience and its associated and painful affects (a process they called "abreaction"), the symptom disappears. The cure of hysteria, conceived as a *psychological* disease, thus depends on *catharsis,* the draining off of bottled-up emotional energies.

From Anna O.'s "talking cure" to his death in 1939, Freud experimented and observed his patients closely while advancing hypotheses as to the structure and dynamics of human personality and social behavior, the nature of psychopathology, and of psychological treatment. In time, these formed the body of the most comprehensive and influential psychological theory of our age. Not only did Freud leave a deep impress on psychological science and clinical practice, but he also profoundly affected the course of Western thought and literature, social customs, and human relations. During Freud's lifetime and since, a worldwide community of psychoanalytic scholars, theorists, and clinicians—more or less faithful to Freud's views—carried forward his work. Psychoanalysis evolved and changed—indeed, Freud himself never wrote a definitive account of psychoanalysis—though many of the basic tenets were laid down early.

Even in the *Studies in Hysteria* (Breuer and Freud, 1895) some of these were visible. Neurosis, even when involving physical symptoms, has psychological roots in early emotional experiences. These often involve *sexual* feelings, going back to early childhood. Of particular importance are those feelings of which the patient is *unconscious*. There seem to be forces within the personality which exclude such feelings from awareness (later to be named *repression*) and similar forces which prevent the later recognition of painful affects (*defenses,* and in therapy, *resistances*). The interplay among these forces is the source of *intrapsychic conflicts,* which determine the patient's manifest behaviors. Indeed, there was even an emerging recognition of the importance of the patient-therapist relation. Though in his original account, Breuer mentioned only Anna O.'s trusting attitude, he later confessed to Freud that at the end of treatment she expressed some sexually tinged feelings toward him. This appearance of "transference," as Freud later named it, apparently speeded Breuer's decision to return to the safer territory of traditional medical practice. Happily, however, Freud persevered, though himself discomfited by his patients' unladylike and ungentlemanly feelings, until he fully conceptualized their critical role in psychotherapy.

For forty-seven of his most productive years Freud lived and worked in the same apartment in Vienna, only to be forced to emigrate to England in 1938 by the Nazis. Pictures of his study and consultation room taken in the period reveal a good deal about Freud. On his desk were many pieces from his collection of Egyptian and Oriental art. A shy man, Freud looked at them constantly while talking with his patients. His rooms were overflowing with books, personal mementos, and art objects; hardly the austere setting people often suppose a psychoanalyst's office to be.

Standard Psychoanalysis

In practice today, Freudian analysts work in diverse ways depending on their personal styles and on the needs of their patients. Still, it is fair to describe as *standard psychoanalysis* that procedure which (1) takes as its aim the reconstruction of the personality and relief of symptoms by bringing to light and resolving central emotional problems of the patient's childhood; (2) accomplishes this task through the systematic use of free association, dream analysis, interpretation, and the transference neurosis; and (3) extends over a long period of frequent sessions. It is particularly the intensity and duration of therapeutic contacts which most visibly distinguishes standard psychoanalysis from what is often called "psychoanalytically oriented" brief psychotherapy.

Standard psychoanalysis may involve four to five one-hour appointments a week for two or three years, although four or five years is not uncommon. For many reasons, not least the cost involved, many patients are seen for shorter periods and toward more limited ends. Concerned psychoanalytic leaders (e.g., Alexander and French, 1946) early recognized the need for, and have worked assiduously at, reducing the length of standard psychoanalysis, without losing its unique properties.

Still, most therapists feel that inducing profound changes in personality patterns, which have evolved and been reinforced from earliest childhood, is a necessarily long and arduous task. Though patently inadequate, neurotic adaptations represent at least partial solutions to the patient's problems. Not only must they be unlearned, but new modes have to be developed in their place. Despite conscious efforts, the patient often resists changes which are painful and confusing though ultimately beneficial. The process of character reorganization, some have noted, is about on a par with learning a new language to replace one's native tongue, particularly if the student is ambivalent in his motivation, fighting the new experience while seeking it. In addition, psychoanalysts believe it essential that patients find their own solutions to life problems. Hence, directive and supportive maneuvers, which might be time-saving, are avoided in the belief that the patient must struggle and work at self-exploration and sustain the inevitable frustration and disillusionments, if he is truly to make his way from childlike dependency to adult autonomy. With these goals and values, it is understandable why considerable time and effort is needed for psychoanalytic psychotherapy.

The Aim of Psychoanalytic Therapy

At one point, Freud gave as the purpose of psychoanalysis to help the patient attain greater self-knowledge and hence self-control ("Where id was, let ego be"). Elsewhere he spoke of facilitating the patient's capacity "to love and work." In these and other phrasings an essential theme emerges, namely, the purpose of therapy is to undo the neurotic process and thus allow the patient to move further toward psychological maturity. But what is maturity in Freudian theory?

From infancy onward, development involves increasingly greater freedom from the pressures of primitive drives, notably sex and aggression, and consequently greater self-regulation. From the beginning, there is a clash between biological urges and the demands of social reality—the pleasure principle versus the reality principle—and compromises are required, first for survival and then for civilized living. Mechanisms develop by which the child is able to delay gratification and control impulse. In time, parental and social expectations are internalized. Thus, ego, superego, and associated mechanisms of defense form and guide behavior. Neurosis, however, results from childhood experiences which weaken the effectiveness of these controls and/or intensify instinctual demands. The most visible sign of a neurotic problem is the existence of anxiety, which signals the faulty operation of control mechanisms and the potential flooding of the personality with dangerous impulses. In this view, the essential task of therapy is to increase ego strength and/or reduce the pressure of denied impulses, so that the patient will be free to run his own life.

It is notable that Freud, who most made modern psychology cognizant of the unconscious and irrational in human affairs was himself a rationalist and, indeed, something of a puritan. If man can know and direct his inner needs, he will be happier and society the better for it. The concept of "insight" was central to Freud's notion of therapeutic change. Although in his early work on hysteria, as we have just noted, his initial emphasis was on emotional abreaction and catharsis, as his thinking matured, insight supplanted catharsis as the vehicle of cure. Today, there is widespread appreciation of the critical necessity for patients to relive emotional experiences (the "corrective emotional experience," in Alexander's [1946] phrase). Still, self-knowledge remains high in the values of psychoanalysts, often as a necessary if not sufficient condition of therapeutic change.

In one of his last writings, Freud (1937) made his point of view clear when discussing the conditions under which psychoanalysis could be terminated.

> An analysis is ended when the analyst and the patient cease to meet each other for the analytic session. This happens when two conditions have been approximately fulfilled: first, that the patient shall no longer be suffering from his symptoms and shall have overcome his anxieties and his inhibitions; and secondly, that the analyst shall judge that so much repressed material has been made conscious, so much that was unintelligible has been explained, and so much internal resistance conquered, that there is no need to fear a repetition of the pathological processes concerned [p. 219].

The Process of Psychoanalytic Therapy

FREE ASSOCIATION

A central task of psychoanalysis is to bring out the hidden, unconscious wishes and conflicts which underlie present symptoms and behavior. An important tool toward this end is *free association*. The patient has to accept the *basic rule,* that he will minimize conscious control and without selection or censorship he will tell everything that comes to mind. To facilitate free association, distracting stimuli are minimized and relaxation is encouraged. The patient typically lies on the couch with the therapist out of view. Indeed, at first Freud had patients close their eyes in addition, only to discover that this too much removed the patient from the necessary contact with the therapist. Still, compared to most forms of psychotherapy, classic psychoanalysis involves conditions which minimize response to present physical and social stimulation in order to encourage the emergence of internal fantasies and wishes. Under these conditions, the patient's communications are more likely to follow the dictates of emotional and unconscious logic rather than that of more conventional rational thought; to be closer to the "primary process" of infantile cognition, dreams, and psychotic thought than to the "secondary-process" thinking of the normal adult when alert and reality-oriented. In the sometimes chaotic ramblings of the patient are clues which can make his repressed motives and hidden meanings known to both analyst and patient.

"To tell everything that comes to mind," would seem an easy task. On the contrary, it can be exceedingly difficult. One cannot readily wipe away years of commitment to logical thought nor easily bypass the conventions and inhibitions which guide ordinary social intercourse. Even with the best intentions, we are loathe to speak about things that seem trivial, illogical, embarrassing, or irrelevant. Some issues are consciously avoided, others kept from awareness by the operation of unconscious defenses such as are involved in the neurotic process itself. Blocks, periods of silence, dwelling on trivia, avoidance of topics, and similar behaviors reflect resistance in the treatment process, as do more gross behaviors such as forgetting or coming late for appointments. Resistance represents a counterforce to therapeutic improvement, the tendency to oppose change, even when seeking it, and to maintain the neurotic status quo. As early as 1912, Freud recognized the ubiquity and importance of resistance: "The resistance accompanies the treatment step by step. Every single association, every act of the person under treatment must reckon with the resistance and represents a compromise between the forces that are striving toward recovery and the opposing ones" (Freud, 1912,

p. 103). Analyzing and overcoming resistance is thus a major task of analytic therapy.

THE ANALYSIS OF DREAMS

During sleep, there is more profound relaxation of normal ego controls than is possible in free association and hence unconscious processes are more free to operate in sleeping than in waking thought. Consequently dreams provide a potentially rich source of information about unconscious needs; Freud once described dreams as a "royal road to the unconscious." Patients in standard psychoanalysis are encouraged to recall and recount their dreams and these are discussed and analyzed in the analytic sessions. Often, the themes and images of these dreams are further explored by using them as stimuli for further free association.

However royal the road, it is hardly a freeway with unlimited visibility, nor do hidden meanings roll forth with simple clarity. Meanings, as with material of free association, have to be extricated through inquiry, inference, and interpretation. What is visible in the reported dream, Freud noted in his classic study *The Interpretation of Dreams* (1900), is the *manifest* rather than its *latent* content (the hidden unconscious material). If the latent material were to emerge undisguised, we would be unable to sleep, hence a censoring process works to transform the unconscious wishes and conflicts into more innocent appearing images. The "dreamwork" responsible for these changes involves a complex series of mental operations, such as displacement, condensation, and symbolization. Many of these symbols are personally unique, though others are more universal. Thus, an elongated object may represent a penis. However, even where symbols would seem to represent widespread human experiences and have the generality of symbols of mythology, art, or poetry, in clinical work they must be explored for their personal meanings in each case.

Dreams reveal not only deep-lying and long-standing emotional problems, but also the strains and conflicts of current life. During the course of therapy, the patient is stirred by emerging feelings which are neither understood nor resolved. Of central importance among these are the transference feelings, either loving or hostile, directed toward the analyst. Well before these can be openly expressed, or even emerge indirectly in free association, they may be represented in dreams. Dreams can thus index developments in therapy, and indeed may provide the earliest indications of dramatic developments which only later appear in waking fantasy, free association, or overt behavior.

TRANSFERENCE

The analysis of transference is the core of psychoanalytic therapy. Freud early realized, though with some surprise and embarrassment, that patients held strong, personal feelings toward the analyst which simply could not be understood in terms of the actual event of therapy or the analyst's character or present behavior. Admiration, respect, and love (positive transference) or their opposite, i.e., hate, contempt, or anger (negative transference) would appear in excessive amounts. These were often expressed in childlike and primitive ways, quite out of keeping with the adult status and professional relation of the patient and analyst. Freud reasoned that such feelings were not generated in the present, but rather were brought forward (transferred) from childhood experiences with key persons, notably the parents. The patient was now acting *as if* the analyst were his father or mother, on his part acting out feelings, wishes, and fantasies of his childhood, most of which have been repressed in the years since and even suppressed in the first instance. To Freud's credit, he conceived the idea that such reactions were not only not barriers to therapy but they might indeed be the major vehicle of therapeutic change. The essential fact about transference is that it brings hidden and repressed feelings and conflicts into the present where they can be examined, understood, and resolved.

To construe present encounters in terms of past experiences and expectations is a common-enough tendency. But this tendency to perceive projectively is intensified among neurotics and particularly so under the special conditions of psychoanalysis. The neurotic person is driven by intense, fixed, and archaic needs which determine his behavior regardless of present realities. Thus, convinced that he is unlovable, he sees a stranger as rejecting him before anything has actually occurred. The conditions of psychoanalysis, moreover, foster such projection. The patient lies on a couch, with the analyst out of view. The analyst remains relatively anonymous, just so that the patient can treat him as a blank screen onto which to project. He does not react, as people normally do in everyday life, with emotional reactions to emotional provocation. He shares little of his personal life, but remains a nonintrusive, shadowy entity. Thus, a patient with demanding needs and a reduced capacity for reality-appropriate judgment encounters a therapist who intentionally minimizes ordinary human interplay in an intimate, intense yet detached relation—and transference understandably results. Rarely, if ever, in normal social intercourse between adult humans would similar behavior emerge. "The transference neurosis is an artifact of the analytic situation; it can be undone only by the analytic work. It serves as a transition from illness to health" (Greenson, 1967, p. 35).

In its most acute and intense form a *transference neurosis* is said to exist. Current concerns and problems fade into relative insignificance, as the patient struggles with the analyst to achieve frustrated childhood needs. His behavior may regress to childlike ways. In all, Freud believed, there is a virtual recapitulation of the childhood neurosis, but now acted out in the arena of the therapist's office. In classical analysis, a fullfledged transference neurosis was felt to be necessary to complete cure, but in more recent times psychoanalysts feel more able to work productively with less intense transference reactions.

Though perhaps to a lesser extent, transference reactions can arise in any form of psychotherapy. Nonanalytic therapists, psychoanalysts believe, are prone to misunderstand and misuse transference. Thus, the patient might be told implicitly: "If indeed you respect and love me so much, then you'll do as I say to preserve my love." By thus coercing or suggesting, a therapist might effect "transference cures," which are viewed as impermanent and antithetical to the development of true autonomy and maturity. Instead, the analyst must confront and interpret these behaviors and by acts as well as words demonstrate their neurotic origins and their irrelevance to the patient's present needs and life.

INTERPRETATION

The fundamental tool in analysing a patient's production is interpretation which, along with free association, is the hallmark of psychoanalytic technique. It figures prominently in any dynamically oriented psychotherapy, and we have already discussed interpretation at some length in the context of the general model of therapy presented in the preceding chapter. In psychoanalysis, however, interpretation has the specific meaning of making the unconscious conscious. More particularly, it means bringing into awareness the unconscious meanings, origins, causes, and modes of functioning of the patient's feelings, beliefs, or other psychological events. The analytic process involves other interventions, for example, efforts to confront the patient with his own actions ("Do you realize you have avoided talking about . . . for months?") or to clarify and specify his meanings ("Do you really mean that all teachers are obnoxious?"). But psychoanalytic interpretations, as such, focus more on what is unsaid than what is said, in order to bring out its hidden significance. Not inappropriately, Freud himself and later analysts likened interpretation to the work of the archeologist or detective who attempts to reconstruct a past era or event through inferences from available fragments. Such interpretation is viewed as the major tool for increasing self-awareness and inducing the corrective emotional experiences necessary for therapeutic change.

A primary target of interpretation is the patient's resistances, the defensive maneuvers by which he averts self-knowledge and personal growth. At first, emphasis may be mainly on his characteristic behaviors, steretyped beliefs, repetitive acts, and other facets of his functional personality as it is manifested in his life situations. With growing knowledge of his personality dynamics, attention is turned more to examining his major needs and conflicts, delving into their early origins. When transference reactions occur, these become the central focus of the analytic process, as we have seen. Nor is the work of analysis finished with one or even a few interpretations, however penetrating and insight-producing they may be. Typically, the same areas have to be worked over and over again, approaching the same issues from various directions before the full impact is felt. This is called the process of "working through." In fair measure, this involves continued explorations of the resistances which block insights from being translated into personality and behavioral change.

At all levels, however, interpretations have to be appropriate in depth and scope and properly timed. An elaborate formulation, even if both elegant and true, will have little impact if it seems grossly irrelevant to the issue at hand. Moreover, the patient must be ready to deal with a particular impulse or defense for an interpretation to have the desired effect. If premature, interpretations can rouse anger or anxiety and slow down or break off therapy. It is properly timed if the impulse of defense is close to awareness and the patient has already dealt with derivative issues. In this case, the analyst's intervention seems explanatory; it engenders a sense of understanding and relief. The defense can then be relaxed or the impulse acknowledged.

AN EPISODE IN PSYCHOANALYSIS

To illustrate some of the principles involved, we can examine a brief episode in a patient's psychoanalysis, as reported by Greenson (1967). He presents this vignette to illustrate the process of interpretation and to show how this inference can be validated. One can see evidences, too, of transference reactions, the use of dream analysis, and the role of symbols in psychoanalytic inference.

Mr. N. reports a fragment of a dream. All he can remember is that he is waiting for a red traffic light to change when he feels that someone has bumped into him from behind. He rushes out in fury and finds out, with relief, it was only a boy on a bicycle. There was no damage to his car. The associations led to Mr. N.'s love of cars, especially sport cars. He loved the sensation, in particular, of whizzing by those fat old expensive cars. The expensive cars seem so sturdy, but they fall apart in a few years. The little sports car of his can outrun, outclimb, outlast the Cadillacs, the Lincolns, and the Rolls Royces. He knows this is an exaggeration, but he likes to think so. It tickles him. This must be a carry-over from his athletic days when he loved to be the underdog who defeated the favorite. His father was a sports fan who always belittled my patient's achievements. His father always hinted that he had been a great athlete, but he never substantiated it. He was an exhibitionist, but Mr. N. doubted whether his father really could perform. His father would flirt with a waitress in a café or make sexual remarks about women passing by, but he seemed to be showing off. If he were really sexual, he wouldn't resort to that.

It is clear that the patient's material concerns comparing himself with his father in terms of sexual ability. It also deals with people who pretend to be what they are not. The strongest affect in his associations was the moment when he said he was "tickled" by the fantasy of beating out the big cars. He knew this was a distortion, but he liked imagining it. In the dream his fury changes to relief when he discovers he has been bumped by "only a boy on a bicycle." It seemed to me that these two affect-laden elements must contain the key to the meaning of the dream and the analytic hour.

I interpreted to *myself* that the boy on the bicycle means a boy masturbating. The red light probably refers to prostitution since "red-light district" is a common term for those areas where prostitutes congregate. I knew my patient claimed to love his wife but preferred sex with prostitutes. Up until this point in the analysis the patient had no memories concerning the sexual life of his parents. However, he often mentioned his father's flirtations with waitresses, which I took to be screen memories. I therefore felt that I would point my interpretation in the direction of his adult attitude of superiority versus his childhood concern with the sexual life of his father. (I deliberately neglected, for the time being, all the references to bumping, behind, anger, etc.)

I said to Mr. N. toward the end of the hour that I felt he was struggling with his feelings about his father's sexual life. He seemed to be saying his father was sexually not a very potent man, but I wondered if he had always thought so. The patient responded rather quickly, in fact, a bit too quickly. In essence he was in haste to agree that his father always seemed to him to be arrogant, boastful, and pretentious. He didn't know what his sex life was like with his mother, but he is quite sure it couldn't have been very satisfactory. His mother was sickly and unhappy. She spent most of her life complaining to him about his father. Mr. N. was quite sure his mother disliked sex, although he couldn't prove it.

I intervened at this point and said that I supposed the idea that his mother rejected sex with his father tickled him. The patient said that it didn't tickle him, but he had to admit it gave him a sense of satisfaction, a sense of triumph over the "old boy." In fact, he now recalls finding some "girlie magazines" (magazines with photos of nude women) hidden in his father's bedroom. He also recalls that he once found a packet of condoms under his father's pillow when he was an adolescent and he thought, "My father must be going to prostitutes."

I then intervened and pointed out that the condoms under the father's pillow seemed to indicate more obviously that his father used the condoms with his mother, who slept in the same bed. However, Mr. N. *wanted* to believe his wish-fulfilling fantasy: mother doesn't want sex with father and father is not very potent. The patient was silent and the hour ended.

The next day he began by telling me that he was furious with me as he left my office. As he drove away he drove wildly, trying to pass all the cars on the freeway, especially the expensive ones. Then he got the sudden impulse to race against a Rolls Royce if he could only find one. A fleeting thought crossed his mind. On the front of the Rolls Royce are the initials R. R. Those are Dr. Greenson's initials, he suddenly realized. With that he began to laugh, all by himself in the car. "The old boy is probably right," he thought, "it does tickle me to imagine that my mother preferred me and I could beat out my father. Later I wondered whether this had something to do with my own screwed-up sex life with my wife" [pp. 40–41].

Critical Evaluation of Psychoanalysis

AS A PSYCHOLOGICAL THEORY

Psychoanalysis is the most comprehensive and far-reaching conceptualization of personality, psychopathology, and psychotherapy in existence. It has had profound effects on literature and the social sciences as well as on many facets of psychological science and clinical practice. Within a unitary perspective, there is consideration of the historical, developmental, and unconscious aspects of human life, along with emphasis on the defensive and adaptive. Though firmly deterministic in seeing behavior as being rooted in earlier experiences, there is considerable respect for man's capacity for rational and self-regulatory action. Still, many of the basic constructs, for example the central role given sexual development and conflict, seem more applicable to turn-of-the-century Vienna than to present society. Much of what Freud considered biologically based and universal among all humans has proved to be more culturally and individually specific. Intrapsychic determinants have been overemphasized at the expense of psychosocial and cultural influences. Despite its comprehensiveness, psychoanalysis has remained a relatively closed conceptual system dependent for its primary data on the productions of neurotics during psychoanalytic therapy. Overall, psychoanalysis has been resistant to ideas and findings generated in other intellectual climates and by other research methods. In relatively recent years, there has been increased communication between psychoanalysts and other behavioral scientists to their mutual advantage, but considerable isolation remains.

AS A SYSTEM OF PSYCHOTHERAPY

Psychoanalysis sets itself the highest and most difficult goal, the reconstruction of the total personality in order to free patients for an autonomous and productive life. The reduction of distress and the removal of presenting symptoms are subsidiary goals, not viewed as worthy in their own right. Evaluative studies, as we will see in a later chapter, have yet to show convincing evidence that these goals are commonly enough reached to justify the effort and cost. Yet there is ample evidence of the therapeutic value of psychoanalytic technique and that favorable outcomes are reached in a majority of cases treated. At the extreme, there are dramatic instances of therapeutic improvement, and, for many who have undergone psychoanalysis, a life-long change in their capacity to understand and regulate their own lives. It is true, however, that standard psychoanalysis is best adapted to the needs of certain kinds of people, notably those who are relatively young, intelligent, capable of a fair degree of detachment and self-examination, highly motivated to change, and already reasonably successful in facing life stress. For others, which would include those beset by reality problems, the psychotic and retarded, and those neurotics who cannot form transference neuroses, other treatment modes are clearly necessary. Of considerable concern is the fact that the painstaking and time-consuming process of psychoanalysis is necessarily costly, hence, under our present system of private practice, limited to the well-to-do. While a large part of the population in need of mental health care may not benefit from psychoanalysis, for those that it can help, there is no intrinsic reason why economic status should be the determining factor. Higher education, once limited to the rich, has now become increasingly available to qualified and motivated people, regardless of economic background; by the same token, intensive psychotherapy could be provided for those who particularly needed it, even if they could not afford it under present arrangements. George S. Klein (1970) has advanced an even more radical argument. Because of its potential for generating knowledge about human psychology and its importance in the training of psychotherapists, in addition to its value to particular patients, society should underwrite psychoanalytic therapy as a contribution to the continued development of the mental health sciences, much as we now support major laboratories in, for example, atomic research, primatology, or costly facets of medicine.

AS A PROFESSION

Psychoanalysts pioneered in establishing high standards for the training of therapists and for the ethics of clinical practice. Extensive theoretical studies, though limited to psychoanalysis, are required, as is extensive and close supervision of work with patients. They have been willing to turn their own concepts on themselves; because of the central importance given to transference and countertransference, they are insistent that psychoanalysts first know and correct their own emotional flaws before attending to those of their patients. Hence, candidates are selected with great concern for their own personality functioning and personal psychoanalysis is required of them. This can have the unhappy side effect, Edward Glover, a distinguished psychoanalytic educator, once cautioned, of so convincing the candidate of the value of analysis—if only to justify his trouble and expense—that he is thereafter incapable of being a sincere critic of the psychoanalytic approach. The fact that so much of the recent criticism of psychoanalysis comes from people orthodoxly trained would argue against the pervasiveness of this brain washing. Still, it is unhappily true that psychoanalysis has too much become a precious and isolated enterprise, much against the spirit and example of its founder. Particularly in its American history, organized psychoan alysis has become a professional guild, more concerned to limit and protect its members than to extend its knowledge or therapeutic contribution. Independent psychoanalytic institutes, with limited intercourse with university, medical, and mental health centers, are in effect exclusive clubs. Despite Freud's explicit desire to see psychoanalysis used as widely as possible (Freud, 1926), with precious few exceptions official psychoanalytic training is offered only to medically trained people. Much of the current disenchantment of other mental health professionals is reaction to psychoanalysis' guild attitudes, which severely threaten, I believe, its own future growth and influence.

Variations on a Theme by Freud

Over its long history psychoanalysis has developed a number of variants and offshoots, some closer and some further from the main trends of Freudian psychoanalysis. Adler and Jung, two of Freud's earliest and closest associates, left the master to move in somewhat opposed directions. Alfred Adler, in his "individual psychology," turned from drives and unconscious processes to a greater concern with the person's conscious intentions, adaptive behavior, and life style. On the other hand, Carl G. Jung, who developed what came to be called "analytical psychology," looked even further inward, at the unconscious fantasies and symbols which are not only unique to the individual history but continuous with the myths and religions of social history. To Jung, the unconscious was a reservoir of creative tendencies rather than only the primitive impulses Freud described. Otto Rank emphasized interpersonal relationships and his ideas influenced the later development of social casework and Rogerian therapy. Wilhelm Reich anchored his concern in the blocking or expression of libidinal drive, particularly as controlled by the bodily musculature. His views have gained renewed interest to clinicians interested in nonverbal interventions, in the nature of relaxation, massage, and body awareness.

In a later era, a group of *neo-Freudian* psychoanalysts emerged. They took issue primarily with Freud's biological stance as represented particularly in his theory of instinctual drives. Instead, they called attention to the importance of psychosocial and cultural determinants of human behavior, and expressed dissatisfaction with Freud's neglect of such factors in his theories regarding the development of personality and neurosis. They questioned the universality and primacy of sexual strivings and conflict, as represented for example in the oedipal complex. Instead, they were concerned with human values, as socially conditioned, and the adaptive functioning of the individual. American born or emigrés from Hitler's holocaust, they were closer to American functionalism with its emphasis on plasticity, individuality, and change than to the traditional and European concern of psychoanalysis with the biological, universal, and unchanging facets of man. The more important of the neo-Freudians included Karen Horney, Clara Thompson, Abram Kardiner, Harry Stack Sullivan, Frieda Fromm-Reichmann, and Erich Fromm.

A parallel development, though closer to the mainstream of Freudian psychoanalysis, is seen in the work of the "ego psychologists." They too see classic psychoanalysis overemphasizing the instinctual and unconscious at the expense of the study of ego functioning. The ego, Heinz Hartman (1939) noted, has its origins not only in the effort to reduce conflict between the id and the environment but also in "conflict-free" functions, such as perception, memory, and other processes of traditional concern to general psychology. The ego in its adaptive as well as defensive roles concerns them; man is motivated to explore and master his world and to display competence, as well as to reach instinctual goals or reduce painful affects. Discovering the ways in which behavior is regulated and steered, as well as the unconscious forces which push it, is the purpose of therapy. The ego-psychological group includes Heinz Hartman, Rudolph Lowenstein, Ernst Kris, David Rapaport, George Klein, Robert R. Holt, and Robert W. White. Related is the important work of Anna Freud and Erik Erikson.

A major impetus toward shorter and more efficient psychoanalysis emerged from the work of the Chicago group led by Alexander and French (1946). In time, concepts of the ego psychologists and the neo-Freudians were combined so that a *psychoanalytically oriented psychotherapy* has emerged. The therapist works within the general framework of psychoanalytic theory with knowledge of the workings of unconscious motives, defenses, resistance, and transference. However, many of the techniques of standard psychoanalysis are bypassed—there is no couch, little free association or dream analysis, and no effort to systematically encourage and interpret the transference neurosis. Even shorter *brief psychotherapies* (i.e., Malan, 1963; Bellak and Small, 1965; and Barton, 1971) and forms of *crisis intervention* (e.g., Caplan, 1964; and Sifneos, 1972) have evolved along psychoanalytic principles. The hope of total personality reconstruction is put aside in favor of dealing with more focal and acute problems, but these therapists feel that their work is facilitated by training in and sensitivity to psychoanalytic principles. A large part of the work of current psychoanalysts is in these briefer forms of therapy; few practice standard psychoanalysis exclusively.

BEHAVIOR THERAPY

Behavior therapy is, in the words of one of its principal proponents, "the use of experimentally established principles of learning for the purpose of changing unadaptive behavior. Unadaptive habits are weakened and eliminated; adaptive habits are initiated and strengthened" (Wolpe, 1969, p. vii). Within the past two decades, there has been a vigorous growth of interest in behavior therapy or—as many prefer to call it—behavior modification, particularly in the English-speaking world. Experimental psychologists have joined clinicians in the quest for interventions which they view as rigorous applications of laboratory-based concepts and techniques to problems of human distress. Disturbed behavior is conceived as the resultant of learning; its modification therefore requires relearning. So stated, therapists of all persuasions might subscribe to this proposition, but modern behavior therapists intend it in its most literal meaning. Observable behavior itself is the focus of their interest; there is little concern with subjective feelings, internal states, or unconscious determinants. If one can manipulate the environmental conditions which shape and maintain behavior, then one can alter behavior in men as well as in animals and through the same general principles. Chief among these are the concepts and methods of conditioning, both in its classical (Pavlovian) and operant (Skinnerian) forms.

History and Background

During the 1920s, John B. Watson in the United States and Ivan Pavlov in the Soviet Union reported some applications of conditioning methods to behavior disorders. In 1938, the Mowrers published their account of a classical conditioning approach to the treatment of bed-wetting and in 1949 Salter published a volume on *Conditioned Reflex Therapy*. Over the years, there have been many efforts to conceptualize psychotherapy in learning terms (e.g., Dollard and Miller, 1950; Rotter, 1954; Shoben, 1949; Bandura, 1961). However, it was not until the 1950s that concerted interest was directed to behavioral methods as an approach to clinical problems. The term "behavior therapy" itself was coined in the early 1950s by Lindsley and Skinner in their efforts to modify psychotic behavior, although the term was used independently by A. A. Lazarus and by Eysenck later in the decade. Contemporary behavior therapy can be traced from the work of Wolpe and his students in South Africa, M. B. Shapiro and associates at the Maudsley Hospital near London, and Skinner and his students in the United States (Yates, 1970). In a relatively short span of years, their ideas and methods have become known to most clinicians and have captured the loyalty of increasingly large numbers of practitioners and researchers (Brady, 1971).

The roots of the behavioral approach lie deep in American behaviorism. After criticizing the mentalistic errors of then-contemporary psychopathologists, John B. Watson (1924) predicted a hopeful future for his orientation which many latterday behaviorists now see as upon us.

> I venture to predict that 20 years from now an analyst using Freudian concepts and Freudian terminology will be placed upon the same plane as a phrenologist. *And yet analysis based upon behavioristic principles is here to stay and is a necessary profession in society–to be placed upon a par with internal medicine and surgery.* By analysis I mean studying the cross section of personality in some such way as I have outlined it. This will be the equivalent of diagnosis. Combined with this will go *unconditioning* and then *conditioning*. These will constitute the *curative* side. Analysis as such has no virtue—no curative value. New habits, verbal, manual and visceral, of such and such kinds, will be the prescriptions the psychopathologist will write.

To clinch his argument, Watson gives the fictional case study of his "psychopathological dog." This is reproduced in its entirety in the following extract from *Behaviorism* (1924) to give the full flavor of his thinking.

> To show the needlessness of introducing the "concept of mind" in so-called mental diseases, I offer you a fanciful picture of a psychopathological dog (I use the dog because I am not a physician and have no right to use a human illustration—I hope the veterinarians will pardon me!). Without taking anyone into my counsel, suppose I once trained a dog so that he would walk away from nicely ground, fresh hamburger steak and would eat only decayed fish (true examples of this are now at hand). I trained him (by use of electric shock) to avoid smelling the female dog in the usual canine way—he would circle around her but would come no closer than ten feet (J. J. B. Morgan has done something very close to this on the rat). Again, by letting him play only with male puppies and dogs and punishing him when he tried to mount a female, I made a homosexual out of him (F. A. Moss has done something closely akin to this in rats). Instead of licking my hands and becoming lively and playful when I go to him in the morning, he hides or cowers, whines and shows his teeth. Instead of going after

rats and other small animals in the way of hunting, he runs away from them and shows the most pronounced fears. He sleeps in the ash can—he fouls his own bed, he urinates every half hour and anywhere. Instead of smelling every tree trunk, he growls and fights and paws the earth but will not come within two feet of the tree. He sleeps only two hours per day and sleeps these two hours leaning up against a wall rather than lying down with head and rump touching. He is thin and emaciated because he will eat no fats. He salivates constantly (because I have conditioned him to salivate to hundreds of objects). This interferes with his digestion. Then I take him to the dog psychopathologist. His physiological reflexes are normal. No organic lesions are to be found anywhere. The dog, so the psychopathologist claims, is mentally sick, actually insane; his mental condition has led to the various organic difficulties such as lack of digestion; it has "caused" his poor physical condition. Everything that a dog should do as compared with what dogs of his type usually do—he does not do. And everything that seems foreign for a dog to do he does. The psychopathologist says I must commit the dog to an institution for the care of insane dogs; that if he is not restrained he will jump from a ten-story building, or walk into fire without hesitation.

I tell the dog psychopathologist that he doesn't know anything about my dog; that, from the standpoint of the environment in which the dog has been brought up (the way I have trained him) he is the most normal dog in the world; that the reason he calls the dog "insane" or mentally sick is because of his own absurd system of classification.

I then take the psychopathologist into my confidence. By this time he is disgusted and says, "Since you've brought this on, go cure him." I attempt then to correct my dog's behavior difficulties, at least up to the point where he can begin to associate with the nice dogs in the neighborhood. If he is very old or if things have gone too far, I just keep him confined; but if he is fairly young and he learns easily, I undertake to retrain him. I use all the methods you now know so well, in unconditioning him and then conditioning him. Soon I get him to eat fresh meat by getting him hungry, closing up his nose and feeding him in the dark. This gives me a good start. I have something basal to use in my further work. I keep him hungry and feed him only when I open his cage in the morning; the whip is thrown away; soon he jumps for joy when he hears my step. In a few months time I not only have cleared out the old but also have built in the new. The next time there is a dog show I proudly exhibit him, and his general behavior is such an asset to his sleek, perfect body that he walks off with the blue ribbon.

All this is an exaggeration—almost sacrilege, you say! Surely there is no connection between this and the poor sick souls we see in the psychopathic wards in every hospital! Yes, I admit the exaggeration, but I am after elementals here. I am pleading for simplicity and ruggedness in the building stones of our science of behavior. I am trying to show by this homely illustration *that you can by conditioning not only build up the behavior complications, patterns and conflicts in diseased personalities, but also by the same process lay the foundations for the onset of actual organic changes which result finally in infections and lesions*—all without introducing the concept of the mind-body relation ("influence of mind over the body") or even without leaving the realm of natural science. In other words, as behaviorists, even in 'mental diseases' we deal with the same material and the same laws that the neurologists and physiologists deal with [pp. 244–246].

In concluding this parable Watson notes that effecting change in a sick personality is the work of physicians. Consequently, if he were himself to develop psychopathological symptoms for which there were no organic causes, then "I should hasten to my psychoanalytic friends and say: 'Please, in spite of all the mean things I've said about you, help me out of this mess' " (p. 246). Today, of course, Watson could be spared the indignity, for mending sick personalities is as much the domain of the psychologist as of the psychiatrist. Indeed, he can now readily find conditioning therapists within either group, who would, an analyst might add cynically, treat him with as much understanding and compassion as he did his dog, after which he would still be turning to psychoanalysis for help.

In an often-quoted study, Watson and Rayner (1920) gave the first laboratory demonstration of an experimental neurosis in a human. Albert, an eleven-month infant, was offered a white rat to play with. Each time the rat was presented to him, a loud noise was simultaneously made. Though previously a neutral stimulus, after five trials the rat alone evoked an emotional response. Thus, it seemed that conditioning of the sort that Pavlov had demonstrated with laboratory animals had occurred. Moreover, the fear generalized to other furry objects and animals. When tested four months later, the fears persisted. Indeed, Watson opined, in some distant future a psychoanalyst might try to discover the origin of Albert's fear in an infantile interest in his mother's pubic hair. More important, Watson and Raynor suggested a possible therapeutic strategy for removing such conditioned emotional reactions. This would involve presenting fear stimuli in conjunction with pleasant stimulation, so that the response could be "reconditioned." This is, in effect, the procedure that Wolpe (1958) later elaborated as reciprocal inhibition therapy.

Mary Cover Jones (1924) attempted to apply Watson's therapeutic concepts to remove existing fears in young children. Peter, three years old, was frightened of rats, rabbits, and other furry objects. To recondition him, she slowly brought a caged rabbit near him while he was eating, on each occasion a bit closer. When thus associated with the pleasant stimulus of food, Peter's fear of the rabbit declined and disappeared within two months. Jones notes that care must be taken to balance the strength of the two stimuli in such a manipulation, lest the fear generalize to the positive stimulus (food) rather than the pleasure to the negative one (rabbit). Watson's and Jones' studies illustrate the essential model, concepts, and techniques of contemporary behavior therapy which, however, was still thirty years in the future.

The Behavioral Orientation

Behavioristic psychologists vigorously oppose the essential concepts and methods of psychoanalysis and related dynamic therapies at virtually every level. As a theory of human psychology, they argue that its concepts are speculative and mentalistic (e.g., the unconscious, the id, ego, etc.) which lack a scientifically verifiable, empirical base. As therapy, psychoanalysis and other "verbal" approaches have failed to show that they are any more effective than less costly therapies, or indeed no treatment at all (Eysenck, 1952). Moreover, psychoanalysis is time-consuming and arduous, requiring the expensive time of a professional practitioner. At best, it is only suited to the needs and abilities of the well-educated, verbal, and affluent and, among these, primarily those with defined symptom neuroses (e.g., hysteria, obsessive-compulsive conditions, phobias, etc.). "Traditional" psychotherapies, as they are often termed in the behavioral literature, are little suited to the vast majority of people needing help or to the broad range of behavior disorders for which they seek it. By contrast, the behavioral approaches are more efficient and more broadly applicable. In fair measure, the behavioral therapies represent a reaction to psychoanalysis; its defenders often present their views in contradistinction to those of psychoanalysis. Thus, Salter (1949) begins his book with the statement:

> It is high time that psychoanalysis, like the elephant of fable, dragged itself off to some distant jungle graveyard and died. Psychoanalysis has outlived its usefulness. Its methods are vague, its treatment is long drawn out, and more often than not, its results are insipid and unimpressive.

Similar sentiments echo through the literature since then. Needless to say, psychoanalysts are no more kindly in their views of behavior therapy, though more inclined to ignore than contend with their opponents.

Behaviorists oppose a "disease model" of neurosis. Central to psychoanalysis is the notion that all behavior is determined and that neurotic symptoms represent the surface, behavioral manifestations of underlying intrapsychic conflicts. Altering a neurotic condition depends on removing basic causes; efforts to change symptoms are at best palliative. Behavior therapists reject this view. To them the symptom is the problem which requires modification. They are minimally concerned with historic origins and hypothesized underlying causes. If the manifest behavior is maladaptive, change that and the patient is cured. According to a disease concept, they argue, removing a symptom should have no effect on the underlying disease process, and hence one should expect recurrence or symptom substitution. A cooling compress may lower the fever but it does not cure malaria. In fact, after behavioral treatment little evidence of symptom substitution has been reported, and this is taken as support of their view that disordered behaviors are better conceived in learning than in dynamic ("disease") terms. Whether described as normal or abnormal, all behavior is learned. Moreover, the principles of learning are the same and are as much evidenced in laboratory studies of both animals and humans as in human development in real life. What the behavior therapist deals with are ineffective or faulty habits, which can be inhibited or extinguished just as any others. The origins are of no particular interest. What matters are the conditions which maintain the behavior. If these can be modified so that disturbed behaviors disappear and/or more functional behaviors are substituted, the job of the therapist is done. Despite differences in particular theoretical orientations and methods, this is the essential faith of the behavioral approach.

Pavlovian and Skinnerian Approaches

Modern behavior-therapy methods derive mainly from one of two primary sources, the classical conditioning theory of Pavlov or the more recent operant conditioning theory of Skinner. The former, best illustrated by the work of Wolpe, has been used most successfully in the treatment of phobias, sexual problems, and social inhibitions, generally of a neurotic sort. The Skinnerian approach has gained greatest application in the treatment of hospitalized psychotics, and autistic and retarded children, though increasingly it is being used to alter less extreme behaviors. In general, workers in the Pavlov tradition have been concerned with involuntary, emotional behaviors, related to the functioning of the autonomic nervous system. Skinner's followers, by contrast, emphasized voluntary (operant) behaviors, controlled by the central nervous system.

Pavlovian or classical conditioning occurs when a previously neutral stimulus becomes associated with a stimulus which normally evokes a particular response, so that in time the neutral stimulus can alone call forth the same or a similar response. Thus, as Pavlov demonstrated in early experiments, if a bell is rung just as food is presented to a dog, the bell alone will come to evoke the salivary response previously elicited by the food. The conditioned stimulus (bell) and unconditioned stimulus (food) must be repeatedly paired for the conditioned response (bell—food) to be established and maintained. Should there not be reinforcement, the conditioned response weakens and becomes extinguished. Conditioned stimuli tend to generalize, so that the animal will give the conditioned response to a bell of another frequency. Similarly, a child frightened by a fall off a bicycle might generalize that fear to cars and other wheeled vehicles. This, it is proposed, is how phobias are formed. To undo such a phobic reaction counterconditioning is required. The feared object, or an imagined representation in Wolpe's method, must be reexperienced in association with a pleasure-producing stimulus. Thus, a strong positive response which is incompatible with the original negative (neurotic) response is conditioned to the same stimulus, which weakens the neurotic response. This Wolpe termed "reciprocal inhibition."

Skinner's theory is concerned mainly with voluntary or operant behavior. The organism emits response; he "operates" on his environment. Those responses become established which lead to positive reinforcement or avoidance of painful consequences. In the Skinner Box, for example, the rat may do many things. However, when he pushes a lever, a pellet of food is released. As such reinforcement recurs the rate at which the operant response (lever press) is emitted increases. The change of rate is thus a simple objective measure of learning, which makes no assumptions about intervening mental activities. To develop more complex behaviors, the experimenter *shapes* behavior. This consists of reinforcing responses which approximate successively the particular ones desired by the experimenter. Thus, as the organism emits responses which resemble or are in the direction of the target response, reinforcement is given until these partial behaviors are shaped into the desired sequence. In the clinical situation, the Skinnerian behavior modifier watches for those behaviors he wishes to encourage and reinforces them selectively. Similarly, he may negatively reinforce (punish) behaviors believed undesirable. Thus, a psychotic child may be given a piece of candy whenever he performs a prosocial act, say, combing his hair, and given an electric shock when he soils himself. Token economy programs, which will be discussed shortly, are a recent application of Skinnerian principles to the treatment of long-term hospitalized psychotic patients.

Although Skinner is heir to the tradition of Watson and other behaviorists, his form of behaviorism is more strictly empirical and behavioral. Rather than seeking or proposing intervening variables of hypothetical constructs, he would limit the science of psychology precisely to the study of the relationship between objectively measured input and output events. Motivational, dynamic or personality variables are shunned; theory in general is considered unnecessary and unscientific. Skinnerian thinking has had great impact on contemporary American psychology, both in and out of the clinical field.

Techniques of Behavior Therapy

SYSTEMATIC DESENSITIZATION

This is the best known and most widely used application of Wolpe's reciprocal inhibition principle for the treatment of phobic reactions. It is based on the simple principle that one cannot be both relaxed and anxious at the same time. Consequently, if increasingly more anxiety-provoking stimuli are experienced while the patient is in a deeply relaxed state, the relaxation response will be substituted for the anxiety response. He will thus be desensitized to the original anxiety-inducing stimuli.

Therapy starts with one or a few interviews and the administration of some personality questionnaires, mainly intended to discover the patient's major sources of anxiety. Before desensitization proper begins, the patient is first trained in relaxation and an anxiety hierarchy is created. The patient is taught the methods of progressive deep relaxation, based on the work of Jacobson (1938). By tensing and relaxing particular muscle groups, the patient comes to distinguish the sensations of tension and relaxation. He practices at home as well as with the therapist. Other techniques involve hypnosis, the imagining of very relaxed situations, and attending to breathing patterns. Although some are simply unable to master the technique, most patients can, after training, relax their whole body in a few minutes.

Along with relaxation training, the therapist and patient explore the patient's history and experiences and construct an anxiety hierarchy. First, major themes are identified (e.g., fear of heights, of dogs, etc.), then particular situations are described which could produce anxiety reactions, ranging from the most moderate to the most extreme. Normally, the hierarchy consists of some twenty to twenty-five items in roughly equal steps. Thus, the person who is fearful of heights might list, at the lowest end, "taking the first step up on a ladder" and at the highest, "standing on the rim of the Grand Canyon."

An illustration of anxiety hierarchies of a patient who had a variety of related social fears is provided by the case of Miss C. (Wolpe and Lazarus, 1966, p. 74) who was an art student who came into therapy because anxiety at examinations had led to repeated failures. Investigation revealed other areas of anxiety, as noted below, none of which however were classical Greek-name-bearing phobias. After seventeen desensitization sessions, she could imagine the highest item in each hierarchy without anxiety. Four months later she took and passed her examinations.

Hierarchies of Miss C.

A. *Examination Series*
1. On the way to the university on the day of an examination
2. In the process of answering an examination paper

3. Before the unopened doors of the examination room
4. Awaiting the distribution of examination papers
5. The examination paper lies face down before her
6. The night before an examination
7. On the day before an examination
8. Two days before an examination
9. Three days before an examination
10. Four days before an examination
11. Five days before an examination
12. A week before an examination
13. Two weeks before an examination
14. A month before an examination

B. *Scrutiny Series*

1. Being watched working (especially drawing) by ten people
2. Being watched working by six people
3. Being watched working by three people
4. Being watched working by one expert in the field. (Anxiety begins when observer is 10 ft. away and increases as he draws closer).
5. Being watched working by a nonexpert. (Anxiety begins at a distance of 4 ft.)

C. *Devaluation Series*

1. An argument she raises in a discussion is ignored by the group
2. She is not recognized by a person she has briefly met three times
3. Her mother says she is selfish because she is not helping in the house (studying instead)
4. She is not recognized by a person she has briefly met twice
5. Her mother calls her lazy
6. She is not recognized by a person she has briefly met once

D. *Discord between other people*

1. Her mother shouts at a servant
2. Her young sister whines to her mother
3. Her sister engages in a dispute with her father
4. Her mother shouts at her sister
5. She sees two strangers quarrel

In the desensitization sessions, the patient is first asked to visualize the least intense item and simultaneously to relax completely. The therapist describes the scene and for some ten or fifteen seconds the patient imagines himself in it. As long as the tension produced is less strong than the relaxation response, relaxation will dominate. Thus, the patient imagines the scene a number of times; the amount of anxiety is successively reduced as no ill effects are experienced. After some minutes of relaxation, the therapist then moves on to the next more disturbing stimulus on the hierarchy, and the procedure is repeated. If at any point, the image produces too great a rush of anxiety, the therapist moves back to the lower level, until the patient is ready to start upward again. After several sessions, the patient should be able to visualize stimuli at the highest level without anxiety being aroused. More details of procedure and case illustrations can be found in A. A. Lazarus (1964, 1971), Wolpe and Lazarus (1966), Wolpe (1969) and Yates (1975).

Here, for example, is a portion of a session with Miss C., the art student whose four anxiety hierarchies were just described. When she was well relaxed, the therapist said:

> I am now going to ask you to imagine a number of scenes. You will imagine them clearly and they will generally interfere little, if at all, with your state of relaxation. If, however, at any time you feel disturbed or worried and want to attract my attention, you will be able to do so by raising your left index finger. First I want you to imagine that you are standing at a familiar street corner on a pleasant morning watching the traffic go by. You see cars, motorcycles, trucks, bicycles, people and traffic lights; and you can hear the sounds associated with all these things. (*Pause of about 15 sec.*) Now stop imagining that scene and give all your attention once again to relaxing. If the scene you imagine disturbed you even in the slightest degree I want you to raise your left index finger *now*. (*Patient does not raise finger.*) Now imagine that you are at home studying in the evening. It is the 20th of May, exactly a month before your examination. (*Pause of 5 sec.*) Now stop imagining the scene. Go on relaxing. (*Pause of 10 sec.*) Now imagine the same scene again—a month before your examination. (*Pause of 5 sec.*) Stop imagining the scene and just think of your muscles. Let go, and enjoy your state of calm. (*Pause of 15 sec.*) Now again imagine that you are studying at home a month before your examination. (*Pause of 5 sec.*) Stop the scene, and now think of nothing but your own body. (*Pause of 5 sec.*) If you felt any disturbance whatsoever to the last scene raise your left index finger now. (*Patient raises finger.*) If the amount of disturbance decreased from the first presentation to the third do nothing, otherwise again raise your finger. (*Patient does not raise finger.*) Just keep on relaxing. (*Pause of 15 sec.*) Imagine that you are sitting on a bench at a bus stop and across the road are two strange men whose voices are raised in argument. (*Pause of 10 sec.*) Stop imagining the scene and just relax. (*Pause of 10 sec.*) Now again imagine the scene of these two men arguing across the road. (*Pause of 10 sec.*) Stop the scene and relax. Now I am going to count up to 5 and you will open your eyes, feeling very calm and refreshed [Wolpe and Lazarus, 1966, p. 81].

Successful treatment requires, of course, that patients should be free of fears in real as well as imagined situations. Wolpe (1961) claimed that as many as 91 percent of phobic patients treated by his technique were cured or markedly improved. Others have made more modest claims. Some have argued that desensitization to be truly effective must involve concurrent and systematic exposure to real-life as well as imagined threats (Sherman, 1972). An intriguing question has also been raised as to whether relaxation is a necessary or incidental part of desensitization (Folkins, Lawson, Opton, and Lazarus, 1968; Folkins, Evans, Opton, and Lazarus, 1969; Davison, 1968, 1969). The theoretical issue here is whether counterconditioning (reciprocal inhibition) is essential or whether the process is simply one of extinction; visualizing anxiety-producing stimuli without dire consequences reduces the potential for anxiety. All therapy, as we noted in Chapter 12, requires patients to "think the unthinkable." Doing this in the safety of the therapeutic relationship, without feared consequences materializing, may be a generic factor in all therapies, regardless of the particular theory or techniques involved. Viewed this way Wolpe's desensitization may just be a special case of this more general principle.

In interesting contrast to systematic desensitization is the procedure of "implosive therapy" (Stampl and Levis, 1967). While Wolpe moves from least to most disturbing stimuli, so that all along the way the patient should suffer minimal anxiety, implosive therapy operates in precisely the reverse way, starting as it were at the top. The therapist describes the most frightening event the patient can conceive, dwelling in the most vivid detail on the worst possible consequences of the experience, in order to bring out the greatest amount of anxiety.

This is done in a number of sessions, and in between the patient must visualize these situations at home. The fundamental assumption is that anxiety is extinguished to the extent that the patient can reinstate, as literally and graphically as possible, the cues to which the anxiety response had originally been conditioned, but now without primary reinforcement. The situation is analogous to catharsis in Freud's early treatment of hysteria, though without requiring the recapture of repressed memories. Stampl and Levis, as well as others, claim good results in relatively few sessions with a wide variety of patients. Others, including Wolpe (1969), have pointed to harmful effects of emotional "flooding." Further research will show the value and limitations of the technique, but for now it is worth noting that Stampl and Levis working within the same general learning-theory framework as Wolpe arrived at the exactly opposite principle.

ASSERTIVE TRAINING

A variety of techniques have been used by behavior therapists to help people overcome social anxieties and inhibitions and to aid in the development of greater interpersonal skills and more effective and spontaneous social behaviors. Teaching assertive responses is conceptualized by Wolpe as another illustration of the reciprocal inhibition principle, for one cannot be assertive and timorous at the same time. Thus, practicing more assertive behaviors in a situation which formerly aroused anxiety and inhibition reduces the strength of the anxiety-related response.

Treatment starts with discussion of threatening interpersonal situations and the patient is aided in identifying the appropriate expressive responses. First in more mild, later in more intense situations the patient is encouraged to try out new behaviors. He is asked to keep notes of the significant interplays with others, what happened, how he acted, what consequence it had, and the like. This both makes the patient more attentive to his own behavior and gives the therapist information about specific problems needing attention. In time, the patient should develop an increased sense of control and adequacy.

To assist in the development of the necessary skills, considerable use is made of *behavior rehearsal*, a technique similar to psychodrama, role-playing or social modeling. The patient has to reenact past experiences or anticipated difficulties of the future, with the therapist playing a complementary role. Roles may then be reversed, with the therapist acting the patient's part and the patient now the antagonist. This procedure gives the patient the opportunity to understand social interactions better, discover the skills needed, practice them in the presence of a nonthreatening therapist, rehearse them in role-playing, get feedback on their effectiveness and guidance on their use in real life. This type of program and many of the specific therapeutic procedures are used, of course, by therapists of other theoretical persuasion.

AVERSIVE CONDITIONING

If a response is followed by pain or punishment, its strength should be weakened. Thus, behavior change can be achieved by conditioning an aversive response to an undesirable behavior, a principle applied by every parent who has ever spanked a child. In clinical practice, aversive techniques have been applied mainly in the effort to eliminate addictions and destructive or deviant behaviors. The best known illustration of such an approach is in the management of chronic alcoholism. An emetic (a nausea-producing drug) is mixed into an alcoholic drink, so that drinking leads to sickness and vomiting. After a number of such occasions, the sight of the drink alone may lead to nausea. The treatment has not been notably successful with chronic alcoholics who tend to backslide once they are out of the hospital and of the control of the therapist. Similar procedures have been used, to better advantage, with more motivated patients suffering from heavy smoking, obesity, or sexual problems. Electric shock, rather than drugs, is being used more commonly by behavioral clinicians. The painful stimuli can be more readily graded and controlled, in some cases by the patient himself. Indeed, punishments can be self-inflicted outside of the immediate clinical situation. Thus, in an ingenious application, people who want to give up smoking are given a portable shock generator, which is activated through a timing circuit whenever a cigarette case is open. A strong shock is given to the forearm about a minute and a half after the subject takes out a cigarette and starts to smoke (Whaley, 1966, discussed by Kushner, 1970).

Aversion therapy has, in recent years, been used mainly with sexual problems. In a typical study, Feldman and MacCulloch (1965) showed slides of partially or fully nude men and women to male homosexuals. When a male picture was on the screen the subject had to signal quickly for another slide or he got a painful shock. Following shock, a picture of a woman was shown. After about fifteen 20-minute sessions, the study was terminated. The authors report that homosexual behavior was eliminated in about half the cases when they were checked up to fourteen months later.

This study also illustrates the principle of *aversion-relief conditioning,* that a stimulus associated with the termination of pain can be positively reinforced. A. A. Lazarus (1971) tells of treating a man who was having an extramarital affair but wanted to return to his wife. When the "other woman's" picture was shown, a shock was given and continued until he looked at his wife's picture, at which point the current stopped. After some sessions, his affection for the girl friend declined markedly while that for his wife increased apace, and he finally returned to the marital bed. In considering this case, Lazarus—a "broad-spectrum" behavior therapist who is concerned with motivational, cognitive, and personalistic as well as behavioral principles—calls our attention to the complexities of human life which are beyond the ken of conditioning theory. Shortly after the "cure," the therapist received an abusive call from the girl friend. It seems that in breaking off with her the patient professed great love but said that he could not continue because he had been brain-washed by the therapist. Perhaps the shocks strengthened his resolve or perhaps they gave him the excuse for acting on a decision already made?

Noxious stimulation can prick the therapist's conscience as well as the patient's body. One effort has been to substitute noxious imagery rather than using actual painful stimulation. Called "covert sensitization" by Cautela (1966) this requires that the patient imagine as vividly as possible the painful consequences of his acts. Thus, a drinker might have to visualize being drunk, stumbling about, becoming painfully sick, and being jeered at and ridiculed.

Though in fact aversive methods are being used increasingly (Rachman and Teasdale, 1969), many concerned behavior therapists (e.g., A. A. Lazarus, 1971) consider them a last resort. Much of the public and professional distaste for behavior therapy stems from this facet. While all behavior modification may seem simplistic, mechanistic, and unsympathetic to human values, aversive methods come off as decidedly inhuman. But there are psychological as well as ethical and humanistic objections to the use of punishment. For one, unless alternative behaviors are readily available, simply suppressing an undesirable response is not likely to be lasting once one has left the training situation. Moreover, punishment may condition a negative attitude toward the punisher, the child toward the mother, or the patient toward his therapist; therapy may be broken off. Not least, it sets a model for social control, where punitive action is accepted as the proper means of influencing other people. The punished child too readily hits out at other children.

However, when the patient is, for example, an autistic child who is tearing at his own flesh and who has not been reached by other means, to stop such behavior by electric shock seems justifiable (Lovaas, Freitag, Gold, and Kassorla, 1965). In such cases, reducing self-destructive behaviors by aversive means is a clear contribution to the patient's welfare. But aversive stimulation can too readily be used in the treatment of less disturbed people, for whom alternative if more costly methods exist. The simplicity and methodological advantages of electrical stimulation (Kushner, 1970) make it appealing, particularly to psychologists whose thinking is more related to animal experimentation and training than to the psychological needs of human beings in distress.

THE TOKEN ECONOMY

One of the more recent and promising applications of the operant conditioning approach is the token-economy programs used to modify the behavior of institutionalized psychotic patients (Ayllon and Azrin, 1968; Atthowe and Krasner, 1968). As in other Skinnerian methods, emphasis is on the therapist's control of the environmental reinforcement contingencies to the patient's behaviors, toward the end of reducing the probability of disturbed behaviors and increasing the frequency of desired ones. In the totally controlled environment of a hospital ward, the clinician is best able to apply these concepts.

There are three issues to consider in developing a contingent reinforcement program in a token-economy study (Krasner, 1971a). (1) The staff of the institution should designate the patient *behaviors* felt to be desirable, and hence to be reinforced; (2) A *medium of exchange* is established, a token that stands for something else (the back-up reinforcers). These are often poker chips, small cards, imitation coins, or even trading stamps; and (3) The *back-up reinforcers* themselves are decided. These are the special privileges and pleasures for which the tokens can be traded and might include weekend passes, movie shows, TV time, special foods, or a private room. Each of these is given a price, so that more tokens are required for the more desirable and fewer for the less wanted items. Similarly, "wages" are set so that more reinforcement is given for greater accomplishments. When the patient acts in desired ways, he receives the proper number of tokens which he can save or spend as he wishes on a greater or lesser reward.

The purpose of using tokens rather than primary reinforcers is that they bridge the delay between the occurrence of the desired behavior and the ultimate reinforcement. Thus, as the patient makes his bed, sweeps the floor, or takes on a job responsibility, he immediately receives the requisite tokens. In some programs (e.g., Atthowe and Krasner, 1968) each time a token is given a social reinforcement accompanies it. The patient is complimented on doing a fine job. Explicit statement is also made as to the contingencies between his behaviors and their reinforcement: "Because you came to lunch on time, you get one token." "Your supervisor said you worked well on your job today, so here are three tokens." The immediate effects of such programs have been clearly demonstrated in a number of experimental studies. As long as tokens are given, reinforced behaviors are strengthened; when they are withdrawn, these behaviors decline.

Proponents of token-economy programs see them as serving broad purposes:

> The goals of a token program are to develop behaviors that will lead to social reinforcement from others, to enhance the skills necessary for the individual to take a responsible social role in the institution and eventually, to live successfully outside the institution. Basically, the individual learns that he can control his own environment in such a way that he will elicit positive reinforcement from others [Krasner, 1971a, p. 637].

In a number of studies, enduring positive effects have been observed. After years of apathy and withdrawal, patients have a livelier interest in their environment. They are willing to groom themselves, keep their room neat and clean, take on job responsibilities, and relate to other patients in ward meetings. Some have been able to return to the outside world and function effectively, though it is still early to say how enduring the effects are once the patient is away from the experimental ward and in the real world of stress and unpredictable reinforcement. A notable consequence is a distinct rise in staff morale, as they realize that they can have immediate and beneficial effects on their patients. Token programs have reduced the demoralization of staff as well as patients, which is all too common in psychiatric hospitals. Not unlikely, this is in part due to the general excitement, enthusiasm, and interest in patients which accompanies any new therapeutic endeavor, as has also been found repeatedly when new and promising drugs are introduced. This does not diminish the importance of the specific learnings accomplished through contingent reinforcement, nor the possibility that they can generalize to a range of desirable behaviors not specifically reinforced. Token programs have also been used effectively in working with mental retardates, delinquents, and disturbed school children.

MODELING

Particularly for children, an important part of learning is based on watching and imitating others. Bandura (e.g., 1969, 1971) developed a form of behavior modification based on social modeling. In earlier work, he had found that a child observing an adult acting aggressively is more likely to be aggressive himself than a child not exposed to such a model. As a therapeutic measure, Bandura points to three ways in which modeling can influence behavior: (1) It can serve as a basis for learning new skills and behavior. The apprentice watching the master learns in this fashion. So too, withdrawn children shown a film of children interacting harmoniously subsequently showed more mature social behavior; (2) it can serve to eliminate fears and inhibitions. Observing another child playing happily with a dog can reduce the subject's fear of the animal; and (3) finally, it can facilitate preexisting behavior patterns. Seeing others remove their hats as they enter a building encourages us to do the same. Some of the effects of token-economy programs might be explained in modeling terms.

In clinical practice, modeling has been found useful for the reduction of unrealistic fears. In treating phobias, Bandura (1971) recommends *participant modeling.* This involves having the patient first watch the model in contact with the phobic object in a series of successively more threatening ways, for example, first touching, then holding, and finally allowing a snake to crawl over one's body. In the next phase, *guided participation,* the therapist encourages the subject to try out the same graded activities. The therapist may guide the patient's hand and praise him for his efforts. In time, there is progressive reduction of the amount of demonstration, protection, and guidance until the patient can, alone and unaided, confront the feared experience. The efficacy of such an approach was demonstrated by Bandura, Blanchard, and Ritter (1969) in the treatment of snake phobias. Four treatment groups were contrasted: (1) *live modeling with participation,* the procedure just described; (2) *symbolic modeling,* in which subjects watched a film rather than a live model in interplay with a snake; (3) *systematic desensitization,* in the manner of Wolpe, involving imagined contact with snakes coupled with deep relaxation; and (4) *no treatment.* While all three treatment groups showed marked reductions of fear compared to the untreated group who did not change, the method of live participant modeling was clearly superior to the others.

Critical Evaluation of Behavior Therapy

Behaviorist psychologists see their methods as scientific, efficient, and broadly applicable derivatives of laboratory-proven learning principles. Joining the efforts of experimentalists and clinicians, without a burdensome superstructure of speculative theory, they view human distress as maladaptive habits which can be unlearned through relatively simple behavioral manipulations. Their opponents, whether of dynamic or humanistic persuasion, see behavior therapy as a mechanistic and dehumanizing orientation to human problems, reflecting at worst an authoritarian ideology. They see its concepts as naive, reductionistic, and simplistic, and its aims of behavior change as trivial and palliative in the light of man's most essential human needs for self-development and creativity. Controversy, at all levels, will continue, for much of it reflects profound philosophic differences in conceiving the nature of man.

In this section, let us consider briefly some of the advantages and limitations of the behavioral approach, which is already a vital part of clinical psychology and likely to continue to grow in importance.

SIMPLICITY, EASE, AND ECONOMY

The procedures of behavior therapy are brief, direct, and pragmatic; they rarely if ever involve the time and effort of traditional psychotherapies. The goals of behavior change are clear and shared by both the patient and therapist.

Progress is visible and there are objective signs of movement. With concrete goals therapy can be terminated when the patient loses the symptoms for which he sought help. While therapists require training in behavioral principles and methods, they do not need the extensive understanding of psychological theory, human relations, and social science, biological or medical knowledge, broad life experience or personal therapy, envisaged as essential to other therapists. Indeed, much of the work of behavior modification can be done by technical assistants or other caretakers (nurses, parents, or teachers), saving professional time for program development and research. The simplicity, relative ease, and economy of behavior therapy are compelling arguments for its use, particularly in a time when social needs far outrun professional resources. The same factors, however, increase the danger of its being applied in superficial and mechanical ways. Thus, Bachrach and Quigley, long-time contributors to behavior modification, note: "It is undoubtedly true that the field of behavior therapy, with its worthy social goals, its theoretical simplicity (deceptive though it may be), and its empirical success (under certain circumstances), will attract many psychotechnicians. It is, therefore, a field in danger of being ruined by amateurs" (1969, p. 510).

RANGE OF APPLICABILITY

To benefit from behavioral treatment, the patient need not be as verbal, introspective, or affluent or even as highly motivated as patients entering verbal psychotherapies. Behavioral interventions, its defenders hold (e.g., A. P. Goldstein, 1973), are ideally suited to the needs of the poor and uneducated, the large part of the population who are not reached by traditional approaches. At another pole, behavior therapies are of demonstrated utility in the treatment of some severely disturbed hospitalized psychotics and autistic and retarded children and adults, who cannot readily be reached by other methods. However distasteful the manipulations may seem, particularly when involving painful punishment, to the extent that they reduce self-destructive behaviors and induce greater socialization, they have to be given a place in the treatment of the most severely regressed patients. In general, then, behavioral therapy has increased the range of psychological intervention, in the direction both of the unsophisticated and the severely disturbed.

However, to argue that behavior therapy is best suited to the treatment of all psychological problems is simply pretentious. It does not address the existential neurosis, depressions, vague but pervasive and disabling anxieties, moral and value dilemmas, problems of finding identity and commitment, and the like which plague many persons. Phobic reactions to specific stimuli may be relieved, but how about grief at the loss of a loved one, shame at failures, guilt whether real or fancied over moral transgressions, a pervasive sense of impotence, and other negative affects? Likening human to animal behavior, and focusing on visible behavior rather than inner states, minimizes precisely those values, feelings, fantasies, and motives which most distinguish and trouble human life.

Behavioral methods are at their best under conditions where the psychologist has greatest control, as in the laboratory or the hospital ward. Under these conditions, behaviors essential to basic social living have been shaped in the severely disturbed, and focal and isolated anxiety reactions have been alleviated in more normal people. Behavioral approaches are less applicable to relatively mature people, moving with some freedom in a natural social world, though pained and made ineffective by emotional problems. It is hard to see how a woman torn between the demands of family and career, searching for greater meaning in her life, can be helped by behavior therapies.

SCIENCE, THEORY, AND PRACTICE

The simple, direct, and pragmatic formulations of the behaviorists are often in refreshing contrast to the sometimes heavy-handed and opaque concepts of psychoanalytic and existential psychotherapies. Behavior therapists have performed a real service by calling into question some of the cherished beliefs of traditional therapies, such as "No real change can be effected in a short time," "Without insight there is no real therapeutic change," "Symptomatic treatment inevitably leads to remission or symptom substitution." Each of these beliefs have had to be qualified by the findings of the behavior therapists. Their insistence on having empirical referents for explanatory concepts and on the need for systematic research to determine and evaluate therapeutic interventions are of great value in a field not noted for the rigor of its ideas or findings. Their investigative skills have been turned on their own therapeutic methods and a large and valuable literature is emerging. Inspired by Skinnerian methodology, many of these reports are individual case studies. Thus, a traditional clinical research method has reemerged in the behavioral tradition, although such reports more usually focus on quantitative measures of precisely defined variables as the individual changes in treatment. The critical and scientific challenges of behavior therapy have sharpened the issues in the field of psychotherapy and, overall, helped elevate the level of research and conceptualization. However, it is fair to ask how secure the behavior therapies are in terms of their own theory and research.

A constant assertion is that behavior therapy rests on the "use of experimentally established principles of learning" as Wolpe was quoted as saying at the beginning of this section. In fact, critics point out, there are few established principles of learning for explaining the simpler phenomena of the laboratory, leave alone the complexities of neurosis and therapeutic change. Moreover, the essential concepts used are vague, sometimes circularly defined, and sometimes used more in a metaphoric than precise meaning. Thus, *stimulus, response, reinforcement*, and *behavior* are loosely and inconsistently applied to describe psychological phenomena which cannot be contained within such a simple terminological system. A lever press is a response, but so too is an imagined fearful scene. Finally, the reluctance of stimulus-response theorists to consider mediational and "mentalistic" central processes forces them to exclude alternate explanations in terms of other, more complex cognitive, motivational, and learning principles. For extended discussion of these and similar criticisms of the theoretical framework of behavior theory, see Breger and McGaugh (1965), Weitzman (1967), Wilkins (1971), A. A. Lazarus (1971, Chapter 1), and E. J. Murray and Jacobson (1971).

After reviewing a recent and very thorough analysis of the learning foundations of behavior therapy (Kanfer and Phillips, 1970), C. H. Patterson (1973) concludes:

> Certainly, the reading of Kanfer and Phillips does not support the repeated claim that behavior therapy is based upon the results of laboratory experiments. The repetition of this claim, without supporting evidence, by so many behavior therapists suggests that its very repetition is being used as a method of conditioning the reader

> (and perhaps the writer as well) to accept behavior therapy as more scientific than other methods. Such terms as "scientific research," "laboratory-based," "experimentally derived," "modern learning theory," "experimentally established" appear to be used for their prestige value by many behavior therapists. As a matter of fact, it seems clear that the methods and techniques are more clearly empirical than based on experimental (or nonexperimental) research results. Many behavior therapists seem unaware that (1) other methods are supported by research; (2) the procedures used by behaviorists are not always based upon prior research demonstrating their effectiveness (not that this should necessarily be the case) but are often developed on the basis of clinical experience; (3) the research evidence for the validity of their method is far from conclusive, and in fact, as more research data have accumulated, the more complex the apparently simple methods appear to be; and (4) the methods are not necessarily explainable only by so-called modern learning theory (whatever that is) but can be rationalized in other ways [p. 210].

THE FUTURE

The behavior therapies have provided simple, direct, and relatively inexpensive help to many people, including some for whom other approaches are inapplicable or unavailable. With the amount of dedicated interest, many clinicians and experimentalists will surely continue to investigate and sharpen techniques and concepts. At present, evidence of their value rests on a relatively narrow base of individual case studies, clinical surveys, and some analog experiments, but the amount and quality of research is bound to increase. As the field matures, hopefully some of the present polarization between behaviorists and dynamic or humanistic psychologists will diminish. Clinicians of other persuasions can then utilize behavioral methods for those problems for which it is best suited, while behavior therapists can focus their activities with these same patients and, at the same time, expand their understanding of clinical process and human personality; ultimately, with the patient's needs rather than the clinician's bias determining the interventive approach.

A. A. Lazarus' "broad spectrum" behavior therapy is a move in this direction, as evidenced in the following passage:

> The achievement of profound insights will frequently fail to eliminate tics, phobias, compulsions, or perversions, whereas operant conditioning, desensitization, or straightforward hypnotic suggestion may often quell these "symptoms" with neither relapse or substitution. Should we then abandon the quest for self-knowledge in favor of conditioning techniques? Indeed, if one's goal is to overcome enuresis or to teach an autistic child to speak, or to instigate prosocial behaviors among schizophrenic inmates, the clinical and research evidence suggests that it would be foolhardy to bypass direct behavioral approaches. While even here, more attention to the patient's interpersonal relationships may well enhance the effects of specific reconditioning, it is obvious that instruction or training in a specific area will probably lead to improved performance in that area. Stutterers will usually find fluency exercises more helpful than introspection for their speech; phobic patients will usually respond better to desensitization than to psychoanalysis; social skills are more readily acquired through behavior rehearsal (modelling and role playing) than through advice or nondirective interviews. Since it is not always so easy to determine when limited problems of function or dysfunction become entagled with far-reaching problems of meaning, therapists should try to determine what they are dealing with before plunging ahead with deconditioning or reconditioning techniques. The basic question to be asked is whether one

is dealing with a *problem* or a *symptom*. To desensitize a phobic patient, for instance, without first establishing whether his phobia is a straightforward avoidance response, or a psychotic manifestation, or a symbolic retreat, or a face-saving or attention-seeking device, or a weapon in family or marital strife violates the cardinal rule—"diagnosis before therapy." It may seem ridiculous to keep asserting the obvious. After all, what self-respecting therapist would apply desensitization (or any other technique) without first conducting a thorough evaluation of the patient's problem? The answer, regrettably, is all too many [A. A. Lazarus, 1971, pp. 218–219; bibliographic references deleted].

HUMANISTIC-EXISTENTIAL PSYCHOTHERAPY

Humanistic Psychology

Abraham Maslow spoke of a "third force" in psychology, opposed to the dominant traditions of both psychoanalysis and behaviorism. In both, man's behavior is seen as determined and constrained, in one case by unconscious instincts and in the other by environmental conditioning. Both view man as less than fully human. Humanistic psychology, by contrast, sees man as having purpose, values, options, and the right and capacity for self-determination, rather than being the hapless victim of his unconscious or of environmental reinforcement. Of his free will, he can maximize his potential for growth and happiness. The highest of human motives is the drive for self-actualization.

The task of the therapist is to release this potential from limiting neurotic forces by (1) empathically coming to understand the unique, personal world-view and self-concept of the patient; (2) fostering full self-awareness by encouraging the patient to experience all facets of himself, including those previously denied; (3) encouraging full acceptance of his unique self and of his freedom and responsibility in acting on his choices; and (4) thus actualizing his full potential as a person. Above all else, therapy involves an authentic encounter between two real individuals, free of sham and role-playing, rather than technical acts of an interpretive, advising, or conditioning sort. The goal of therapy is to move one from being a *deficiency-motivated* person, dependent on the world about to provide him with gratification and to affirm his value as a person, to a *growth motivated* person, striving to enrich and enlarge his experiences, knowing joy and true autonomy (Maslow, 1962). Truly self-actualizing people are rare, but all of us have the capacity for being more spontaneous and natural, free of anxiety, self-doubt, and feelings of alienation and unworth, and at least in *peak experiences*, to exist fully and vividly, to be completely absorbed and centered in experiences which transcend the self (Maslow, 1967). The vision of man contained in this view and the promise that it can be approached through "growth-producing experiences," not therapy which aims no higher than repairing past inadequacies or removing symptoms, underlies the "human-potential" movement. Thousands of normal people seeking further personal growth go into encounter groups or to "growth centers," such as Esalen in California. Since many of their methods are related to group therapy, I will hold discussion of the human-potential movement to the next chapter. Suffice to note now that it is one of the most visible and important facets of humanistic psychology.

As an approach to psychology, humanistic psychology is as yet more a set of orienting values than a systematic theory of personality or psychotherapy. Among its major tenets are: (1) To understand personality, we must study the person as a whole, i.e., *holism;* (2) Of central importance is his direct experience rather than his behavior as viewed from outside, i.e., *phenomenology;* (3) Moreover, scientific method requires participation by the investigator in the experiential field, not detachment from it. Valued are intuitive and empathic understandings, not only empirical knowledge; (4) Personal uniqueness should always be in focus, i.e., the *ideographic approach;* (5) Goals, values, aspirations, and the future matter more than historical or environmental determinants; (6) Human behavior should not be viewed in mechanistic or reductionistic terms, but rather distinctly human qualities should be emphasized, such as choice, creativity, valuation, and self-actualization; and (7) Man is proactive as well as reactive, capable of positive striving as well as adjusting to demands on him. The positive in human behavior needs emphasis; the sick has been overemphasized. These and related principles are reviewed in Bühler (1971), Bühler and Allen (1972), and Bugenthal (1965, 1971).

In present form, humanistic psychology has been in existence for a scant fifteen years. However, its antecedents run deep into the history of psychology and philosophy. It has roots in the earlier philosophy of humanism, European phenomenology and existentialism, and Anglo-American political liberalism. Among psychologists, core ideas were defended by William James, Kurt Goldstein, Carl Rogers, Gordon Allport, and Henry A. Murray among others who resisted the positivistic psychology of their day in favor of a more human psychology. In a number of important regards, it represents an Americanization of European existentialism, which in crossing the Atlantic lost some of its grimmer concepts and was transformed into an optimistic philosophy of growth and self-perfection. Thus, while European thinkers note that existence gets its meaning from the inescapable reality of death, contemporary American humanists focus on the expansion of experience, joy, and fulfillment in the life process. The essential optimism in humanistic psychology may explain its appeal to many American students, who confront a confusing and frightening world which they feel powerless to change. Modern humanism is also a reaction to the excesses of scientific and technological development with their potential for dehumanizing social life. The principles and values of humanistic psychology seem humane and relevant, understandable in terms of our everyday experiences and consonant with visions of a better life.

There is no single theory or method of therapy in the broad realm which is being here called "humanistic-existentialistic psychotherapy." In later sections we will examine three of the best-known and fully developed systems which illustrate the diversity in the area, namely, Rogers' client-centered psychotherapy, Frankl's logotherapy, and Perls' Gestalt therapy. First, however, we should consider further concepts from phenomenology and existentialism which underlie these and related therapies.

The Phenomenological Framework

What we are and what we do is a reflection of our experience of the world and ourselves. Our consciousness of ourselves as sensate beings, memories of our past and visions of our future, give identity, continuity and purpose to our lives. We know "reality" out there only through the inside "reality" of personal and subjective experience which give it meaning and substance. To most of us, when we are not thinking like psychologists, these are simple and almost self-evident propositions; their philosophic elaboration has been called "phenomenology."

Despite the self-evident importance of phenomenal experience, the science of psychology has on the whole tended to ignore it. To achieve scientific objectivity, attention was turned to overt behavior, responses to known stimuli, test behaviors, and other externally visible and measurable events, about which hypothetical variables, such as traits or needs, might then be constructed in order to achieve more inclusive and abstract explanatory concepts. But scientific psychology looked askance at direct and immediate phenomenal experience as a primary data source. Even in the *introspective psychology* of Wundt and Titchener, emphasis was on the highly disciplined judgments of skilled and trained subjects (then properly called observers) who were required to abstract the sensation, feeling, or thought from its ordinary context of personal meaning in the interest of a scientific analysis of conscious mental contents. But even this approach to inner experience was pushed aside in the onrush of behaviorism as being too subjective and mentalistic; what mattered and had scientific status were observable and measurable stimulus-response patterns. Intervening mental process, including the subject's conscious experience, were suspect and minimized. Psychoanalysis, over its long history, preserved a profound concern with subjective experience, but understanding conscious experience as such was, until relatively recent years, considered of secondary importance to the discovery of its unconscious and hidden determinants. In fair measure, the person's own conception as to how and why he feels and thinks as he does was viewed as a surface manifestation of the action of unconscious drives and defenses. Thus in its fashion, psychoanalysis just as behaviorism excluded phenomenal experience as the proper domain of psychology. The phenomenological tradition was sustained mainly in the writings of a relatively small but articulate group who believed that disregard of conscious experience lost to psychology its richest and most relevant data. In American psychology, these include Combs and Snygg (1959), Gordon Allport (1962), Rogers (1942, 1951), G. A. Kelly (1955), Maslow (1954, 1962), and MacLeod (1947), among others.

Such psychologists argued that not only is the personal experience of the subject the relevant and critical data of psychology but the study of psychological events must include as well the "personal knowledge" (Polyani, 1958) of the investigator. Behaviorism strove for objectification of experimental procedures and observation; at the extreme, reducing the experimenter to an efficient, detached, and rational data collecting and processing machine. Feelings and intuition of the experimenter were ruled out as inappropriate to the scientific method, though Polyani and others have shown their importance in the mental life of scientists as they create theory and do research. In Chapter 11 we considered one manifestation of the objective-subjective controversy as it appeared in clinical psychology, i.e., the conflict over clinical versus statistical approaches to clinical inference. There we saw the necessity and value of depending on the clinician's judgments in arriving at valid and useful clinical inferences. A wealth of social psychological research has accumulated showing that, even in relatively simple experimental situations, the expectations and personal meanings of both subject and experimenter are critical determinants of the eventual findings (R. Rosenthal, 1966). For many reasons, including the growth within psychoanalysis of ego psychology and the increased interest of behaviorists in mediational processes, psychology today is far more ready to deal with subjective aspects of human experience, though controversy still swirls on the objective-subjective axis. In the current scene, humanistic and existential psychologists are the strongest defenders of phenomenal experience, giving it central if not exclusive importance in human psychology. As they accuse behaviorists of a "nothing-but" attitude, seeing human behavior as essentially similar to the actions of a machine or an animal, they can in turn be accused of seeing it as nothing but the consciously held beliefs, feelings, and purposes of man with scant attention to dynamic and behavioral phenomena.

Experience is of course important to most if not all psychotherapies, but it is centrally emphasized in the systems of Rogers and Perls which we will consider shortly, G. A. Kelly's (1955) psychotherapy, based on his psychology of personal constructs, is still another expression of the phenomenological orientation, as are those approaches which stress the *transactional* interplay between patient and therapist as they view and understand each other. Illustrative are Grinker's (1961) *transactional psychotherapy* and Berne's (1961) *transactional analysis*. The systems of Kelly, Grinker, and Berne are surveyed in Patterson (1973).

Existentialism

Existentialism arose in European thought in protest against the dominance of rationalism and empirical science, against what Maritain called Hegel's "totalitarianism of reason." It represented an "endeavor to understand man by cutting below the cleavage between subject and object which has bedeviled Western thought and science since shortly after the Renaissance" (R. May, 1958, p. 11). While science would look on him as a substance ("essence") or mechanism, man must be understood as an "existence," in its literal meaning of a coming to be. As such, man is inseparable from the observed object. He is a "being-in-the-world," and the meaning of objective reality is given by man's involvement with his world. Thus, human experience should properly be the center of concern for a philosophy of human life. Influenced by Husserl's phenomenology and the spirit of the romantic movement, existential philosophy emerged in the writings of Kierkegaard and Jaspers and the later contributions of Heidegger, Sartre, and others. A number of European psychiatrists (e.g., Binswanger, Boss, and Frankl) and Rollo May in this country have carried the existential view into psychotherapy. There is no single existential philosophy, nor for that matter a unique psychotherapy related to it. Rather, existentialism is more an orientation toward understanding the nature and meaning of man's existence. For historical surveys of existential philosophy and psychotherapy, see R. May, Angel, and Ellenberger (1958) and van Kaam (1966).

Some of the major themes in contemporary existentialism include: (1) Man is free and has choice. This derives from the distinctly human capacity for consciousness and self-consciousness; (2) Man is inextricably related to others and to his world. Concepts of "participation," "presence," and "encounter" figure prominently; (3) Existence implies nonexistence. The inescapable reality of death gives meaning to existence. It is also the source of "existential" or normal anxiety; (4) Through encounter, man can grow and develop. He is not static. Moreover, he can transcend his immediate situation, go beyond his past, visualize and symbolize, and therefore optimize his future choices; and (5) But modern man is also alienated from the world of nature and man. Increasingly, he feels detached and lonely, isolated and a stranger, as the existentialist novelist Camus expressed so vividly. Today, patients complain less frequently of specific neurotic symptoms than of an "existential neurosis," the sense of isolation and discontent resulting from a lack of meaning in one's life. Many live, in Frankl's (1963) phrase in an "existential vacuum."

At heart, therapy is an encounter. The therapist must be able to relate to the patient, as Binswanger put it, as "one existence communicating to another." The ideal of the authentic encounter is often put in terms of Martin Buber's ideas as expressed in his masterpiece *I and Thou*. It is a relationship founded on trust, openness, and respect for the other's subjectivity; above all, it is a state of communion. As the therapist views him as an existential partner rather than as a subject for investigation (an object to be viewed with detachment) the patient himself no longer sees himself as an object controlled by forces beyond his ken. Various techniques may be used, some of psychoanalytic origin, but these are secondary to the effort to understand the existential realities of the patient's life. The goal ultimately is to foster the patient's experiencing his own existence as real. With this, he can then be free to exert choice and make commitments, to become rather than simply to be, as he discovers meaning in his life.

This brief section can at best give only a flavor of existential philosophy and psychotherapy. However, even more extensive reading of the existential, or the related humanistic, literature leaves one in doubt as to the precise meaning of their concepts of the particular operations of their therapy. What does it really mean to be an authentic psychotherapist or to discover a patient's being-in-the-world? On the whole, existential thinkers tend to reject theory and the systematization of their approaches. In part, this follows from the fear that conceptualization itself can be a barrier to direct understanding of another human and that emphasis on technique necessarily reduces the authenticity of the encounter. The antirationalism tradition remains as a distaste for theoretical ordering of concepts and methods.

Existential psychotherapists would agree with Rollo May (1961, pp. 18–19) that existential therapy "is not a system of therapy, but an attitude toward therapy, not a set of new techniques but a concern with the understanding of the structure of the human being and his experience that must underlie all techniques." Basic emphases are clear, e.g., the importance of direct, personal experience and of the therapist-patient relation, and they have influenced thinking in psychotherapy generally, whether called existential or not. Contemporary client-centered therapy, as compared to earlier forms, shows the clear impact of these ideas, as indeed do many of the dynamic therapies and some of the broader-gauged behavioral approaches. It may be argued that these ideas antedate and are essentially independent of existential philosophy, but their current popularity surely reflects the impact of existential thought on American psychotherapists.

Client-Centered Psychotherapy

HISTORY AND ORIENTATION

Since the late 1930s, client-centered psychotherapy has been an evolving system, largely the creation of the psychologist Carl R. Rogers. Originally called "nondirective counseling" to call attention to the fact that the client, rather than the therapist, sets the pace and decides the issues and goals of therapy, his initial volume focused largely on techniques for accepting, recognizing, and clarifying feelings (Rogers, 1942). In 1951, the name was changed and a broader conceptual base given to "client-centered therapy" (Rogers, 1951). From the outset, Rogers and his students studied the process and effects of this approach and a considerable body of empirical research has been published (e.g., Rogers and Dymond, 1954). Through 1960, Rogers worked mainly in academic settings, notably at the Counseling Center of the University of Chicago, and his methods developed mainly in work with relatively well-integrated college students. Many felt that they were limited to such people; consequently, Rogers was eager to show their applicability to severely disturbed psychotics and he moved to a psychiatric center where he studied schizophrenics in treatment (Rogers, Gendlin, Kiesler, and Truax, 1967). Although always concerned principally with psychotherapy and the processes of personality change, Rogers has also written extensively about his concepts of personality and philosophical orientation to human needs (e.g., 1959, 1961). In recent years, Rogers' interests have turned from individual to group therapy and he is today a leading figure in the human-potential movement (1970).

In the 1940s and 1950s client-centered psychotherapy achieved considerable popularity among psychologists and other nonmedical workers who, along with Rogers, resented the medical domination of psychotherapy. Recipients of help were *clients* not *patients*. The proper therapeutic relation is seen as egalitarian, requiring permissiveness and nondirectiveness, unlike the more formal and authoritarian relation between doctor and patient. Diagnosis is specifically avoided, for it casts the therapist in the role of expert who could discover and tell the patient, conceived as a sick and inadequate person, what was wrong and what to do. Not only does diagnosis foster dependence in the patient but also a non-therapeutic detachment in the therapist and a readiness to deal with the client in categorical rather than individual terms. Similarly, interpretation just as reassurance, advice, or manipulation, is seen as a directive technique and to be avoided. Such acts all imply that the therapist knows, better than the client, why the client acts as he does and what is good for him.

What is required for therapeutic change, Rogers proposed, is that the therapist be accepting, permissive, and nonjudgmental, so that he and the client can together explore the client's phenomenal world and personal meanings. Emphasis is on current experience, delving into past history in quest of hidden causes is of little concern. Given this atmosphere, the client is able to reveal feelings. The task of the therapist is to accept, reflect, and help the patient clarify their meaning. The reflection of feelings often puts the therapist in a curiously passive role, sometimes merely repeating the client's words, which to the non-Rogerian observer can seem absurdly evasive. (Client: "I hate him." Therapist: "You feel that you hate him?" Client: "Yes, I hate him.") However, understanding develops in the process as, first, the client realizes that the therapist maintains respect despite his expression of ugly feelings and, second, as he is able to see and evaluate his acts from the vantage point of another. Rogers proposes that, as therapy proceeds, important changes occur in the client's perception of himself (his self-concept) and of the world about him. With more secure self-regard, he can try new behaviors and move closer to being a "fully functioning person." Ultimately, however, the force behind therapeutic change (indeed, all personal growth) is the client's inherent tendency toward growth or self-actualization. "Contrary to those therapists who see depravity at men's core, who see men's deepest instincts as destructive, I have found that when man is truly free to become what he most deeply is, free to actualize his nature as an organism capable of awareness, then he clearly appears to move toward wholeness and integration" (Rogers, 1966, p. 193). The essential task of the clinician is to release this potential by providing appropriate conditions.

THERAPIST CONDITIONS REQUIRED FOR EFFECTIVE THERAPY

Particularly in his later writing, Rogers places primary emphasis on those *attitudes* of the therapist which are the "necessary and sufficient conditions" for therapeutic change (1957). The particular techniques the therapist uses, his training, technical knowledge, and skills are entirely secondary, compared to these basic qualities of the therapist. Success in therapy depends on the therapist communicating and the patient perceiving (1) the therapist's own congruence; (2) his unconditional positive regard for the patient, and (3) his accurate empathic understanding.

Therapist's congruence. Congruence or genuineness is the first and primary requisite, for nobody can respect others or be empathic unless he is himself open to experience, free of facade, and self-deceit. The therapist should be aware of his full experience and feelings, and able to communicate them openly. This does not mean that the therapist necessarily burdens the client with his personal feelings at every turn, but he should know them himself and be willing and able to share them when necessary. Therapy depends on the readiness of the client to share his deepest and most intimate feelings; it is hard enough to do this under any circumstances, the more difficult if the therapist is not a real person himself.

Unconditional positive regard. The therapist must communicate to the client a deep and genuine caring for him as a human being, with faith in his potential. This means making no judgments about the patient, approving some but not all of his actions or feelings. There are no conditions on the therapist's acceptance or warmth. He is as ready to accept negative as positive feeling from the client. "It is an unpossessive caring for the client as a separate person, which allows the client freely to have his own feelings and his own experiencing." (Rogers, 1966, p. 186.) In his later work with schizophrenics, Rogers came to realize that grossly immature or regressed clients may require more conditional regard—"I'd like you better if you acted in a more mature way." However, with most clients, unconditional positive regard remains one of the essential requirements of therapy.

Accurate empathic understanding. Progress in therapy requires the therapist to perceive feelings and experiences sensitively and accurately and to understand their meanings to the client during the therapeutic encounters. Accurate empathic understanding means that the therapist can sense the client's inner world as if it were his own. In addition, accurate empathic understanding involves the ability to then communicate this experience to the client in words and concepts meaningful to him so that he can gain further awareness of his experience. In this fashion, the client can recognize where his experience is incongruous with his self-concept, and work toward bringing denied feelings into greater congruence with his self.

In fair measure, the success of therapy depends on the communication, and perception, of these therapist attitudes. Growth in the patient involves, in effect, his incorporation and utilization of these attitudes as part of himself. Therapy should, therefore, make him more congruent, be better able to give others unconditional positive regard, and be more accurately empathic in viewing himself as others. These three conditions describe the essence of client-centered therapy, and figure prominently in Rogers' theory of personality and social philosophy. He and his co-workers have done several studies to demonstrate the importance of these three attitudes as conditions of therapeutic progress. These have been recently reviewed by Truax and Mitchel (1971).

A CLIENT-CENTERED INTERVIEW WITH A SCHIZOPHRENIC

The functioning of a client-centered therapist can be illustrated by a fragment of an interview with a deeply disturbed, inarticulate hospitalized male schizophrenic, Mr. Vac. With a better integrated patient there would of course be a more equal exchange, but Rogers (1966) uses this case to illustrate how the therapist, under these extreme conditions, uses his own experiencing as a basis for communication and to build a meaningful relationship.

Therapist. And I guess your silence is saying to me that either you don't wish to or can't come out right now and that's okay. So I won't pester you but I just want you to know, I'm here.

A very long silence of seventeen minutes.

T. I see I'm going to have to stop in a few minutes.
Brief silence.

T. It's hard for me to know how you've been feeling, but it looks as though part of the time maybe you'd rather I didn't know how you were feeling. Anyway it looks as though part of the time it just feels very good to let down and .... relax the tension. But as I say I don't really know .... how you feel. It's just the way it looks to me. Have things been pretty bad lately?
Brief silence.

T. Maybe this morning you just wish I'd shut up .... and maybe I should but I just keep feeling I'd like to, I don't know, be in touch with you in some way.
Silence of two minutes. Mr. Vac yawns.

T. Sound discouraged or tired.
Silence of forty seconds.

Client. No, just lousy.

T. Everything's lousy, huh? You feel lousy?
Silence of forty seconds.

T. Want to come in Friday at twelve at the usual time?

C. *Yawns and mutters something unintelligible.*
Silence of forty-eight seconds.

T. Just kind of feel sunk way down deep in these lousy, lousy feelings, huh? Is that something like it?

C. No.

T. No?
Silence of twenty seconds.

C. No. I just ain't no good to nobody, never was, and never will be.

T. Feeling that now, huh? That you're just no good to yourself, no good to anybody. Never will be any good to anybody. Just that you're completely worthless, huh? .... Those really are lousy feelings. Just feel that you're no good at *all*, huh?

C. Yeah. That's what this guy I went to town with just the other day told me.

T. This guy that you went to town with really told you that you were no good? Is that what you're saying? Did I hear that right?

C. Uh, hum.

T. I guess the meaning of that, if I get it right, is that here's somebody that meant something to you and what does he think of you? Why, he's told you that he thinks you're no good at all. And that just really knocks the props out from you. (*Vac weeps quietly.*) It just brings the tears.
Silence of twenty seconds.

C. I don't care though.

T. You tell yourself that you don't care at all, but somehow I guess some part of you cares because some part of you weeps over it [pp. 189–190].

THE ROLE OF RESEARCH

A distinctive and praiseworthy aspect of the Rogerian approach has been an insistent interest in empirical research. Rogers was first among students of psychotherapy to record therapy hours and to study their content closely. Despite the fact that critics have viewed some of the concepts as vague or superficial, the Rogerians themselves have made every effort to give them operational measurement and to explicitly test hypotheses of the system. Thus, in earlier research, the Rogers group developed as an index of therapeutic outcome a measure relating the client's ratings (by Q-sort method) of his present and of his ideal self-concept (Rogers and Dymond, 1954). As the gap between the two closed, therapeutic improvement can be inferred. More recently, extensive studies have been reported on the therapeutic relationship and the essential therapist conditions (e.g., Snyder, 1961; Truax and Carkhuff, 1967; Truax and Mitchell, 1971) and on the work with schizophrenics (Rogers, et al., 1967), among other areas.

The client-centered viewpoint has been expanded to work with children and families, and most notably in the recent past with encounter groups. From the beginning, Rogerian therapy was opposed to the psychoanalytic orientation and later to the behavioral, as it developed. In time, the existential orientation has influenced Rogerian thinking and been incorporated into it. Today, it is an essential part of the humanistic psychology movement.

Logotherapy

Like Freud, Viktor E. Frankl was a child of Vienna. Schooled in psychoanalysis, his existential views of man and of therapy emerged during, and largely because of, three hellish years in Auschwitz and other Nazi concentration camps. His father, mother, brother, and his wife died in the camps or were sent to the gas ovens. Himself stripped to naked existence, he realized the profound truth in Nietzche's words, "He who has a *why* to live for can bear with almost any *how,*" which remains a guiding principle in his thinking. After the war, Frankl developed logotherapy (logos = meaning), his version of existential analysis. He returned to Vienna eventually to become professor of psychiatry and neurology at the University and the leading figure in contemporary Viennese psychotherapy. His theories and methods are described in three books available in English: *Man's Search for Meaning* (Rev. ed., 1963); *The Doctor and the Soul* (2nd ed., 1965), and *Psychotherapy and Existentialism* (1967). Though differing in a number of regards from other existential therapies, his system has the advantage of greater clarity and simplicity as well as intrinsic interest which allows it to be considered here in a few pages.

Logotherapy aids the individual with problems of a spiritual or philosophical nature, problems related to the meaning of life and death, of work, suffering, and love. The most basic of human motives is the *will-to-meaning,* which is more fundamental than pleasure or tension-reduction, power or self-actualization. *Existential frustration* exists when this need is thwarted. The resulting sense of meaninglessness in life Frankl describes as an *existential vacuum.* Such feelings are widespread, particularly in these complex and confused times, and they may or may not accompany neuroses and psychoses as usually considered. Thus, logotherapy complements, but is not intended to substitute for, psychotherapy which deals with a man's psychological problems. It is the spiritual aspect of life with which Frankl is most concerned, and this he distinguishes from the biological and psychological realms which more usually concern clinicians. Where existential frustration is sufficiently intense and wide-spread, it can lead to neurotic symptoms. This condition Frankl calls a *noögenic neurosis.* It represents not a conflict between drives or instincts but rather a clash of moral principles, and it is to such problems, reflecting existential frustration, that logotherapy is primarily aimed. The goal, ultimately, is to help patients find an aim and purpose in their existence.

Logotherapy strives to make people conscious of their responsibility, since this is an essential of human existence. But such responsibility implies obligations, and these in turn derive from one's understanding of the meaning of life. A person's uniqueness, destiny, and heritage all contribute to the meaning of his life. Similarly, the inevitability of death gives life meaning. For if life were endless, there would be no need for choices or decisions, and hence no responsibility, since actions could be postponed indefinitely. The emphasis on responsibility is reflected in the categorical imperative of logotherapy: "So live as if you were living already for the second time and as if you had acted the first time as wrongly as you are about to act now!" (Frankl, 1963, p. 173.)

In working with people suffering existential frustration, the primary emphasis of logotherapy is on their value or philosophical conflicts, mainly to the end of having them experience their own responsibility for their beliefs and actions. The therapist does not try to impose his own value system, though he must know and stand ready to affirm his own values as necessary. Emphasis is not on the historical reconstruction of the patient's character or philosophy, but rather on the contemporary spiritual problems and, as important, on their future course. Logotherapy is also valuable for dealing with neurotics or psychotics, with particular regard for their spiritual dilemmas. In this case, however, logotherapy is a nonspecific rather than a symptomatic approach. To the extent that the logotherapist is concerned with the patient's symptoms, it is to the end of altering the patient's attitude toward them rather than in curing the symptoms themselves. Two logotherapeutic techniques designed for dealing with obsessive-compulsive and phobic behaviors have been termed "paradoxical intention" and "de-reflection." (Frankl, 1960.)

In order to break the vicious cycle of the phobic patient whose anticipatory anxiety is amplified as he dreads a feared encounter and struggles to avoid it, Frankl encourages him to intend or wish, even momentarily, precisely for that which he fears (paradoxical intention). This is done with as much humor and self-detachment as possible, for laughing at oneself and one's foibles is an important step toward overcoming them. Thus, a young medical student who was afraid that she would tremble when the instructor entered the anatomy laboratory and soon the fear actually caused a tremor tells Frankl: . . . , "remembering what you had told us in the lecture that dealt with this very situation, I said to myself whenever the instructor entered the dissecting room, 'Oh, here is the instructor! Now I'll show him what a good trembler I am—I'll really show him how to tremble!' But whenever I deliberately tried to tremble, I was unable to do so!" (Frankl, 1960, p. 148.) Similarly, "de-reflection" involves having the patient ignore, rather than attend paradoxically and humorously, that which is troubling him. To be effective, he must be de-reflected from the anticipatory anxiety to some more positive striving.

In sum, Frankl's approach deals squarely with problems of meaning, philosophy, and existence, realms which are often skirted by other therapists. He tries to lead the patient toward awareness and responsibility. Although the approach is far from systematic and some of the concepts are difficult to comprehend, there is no doubt that he is pointing the way toward dealing with the existential problems of human beings, which in contemporary society are an increasingly important source of spiritual and psychological distress.

Gestalt Therapy

HISTORY AND BACKGROUND

Gestalt therapy is the brainchild of Frederick (Fritz) S. Perls. Born in Germany, he was educated in medicine and psychoanalysis. With the rise of Hitler, he emigrated to South Africa in 1934, where he established a psychoanalytic institute in Johannesburg. Basic ideas that were to develop into Gestalt therapy were published in *Ego, Hunger and Aggression* (1947 in England, republished in the USA in 1969). In 1946, he moved to the United States and, in 1951, wrote *Gestalt Therapy* in collaboration with Hefferline and Goodman. Later volumes included *Gestalt Therapy Verbatim* (1969) and his autobiographical *In and Out of the Garbage Pail* (1969). *Gestalt Therapy Now* (1970), edited by Fagan and Sheperd, contains a number of contributions by Perls and his colleagues which give an overview of current theory, techniques, and applications. Fritz Perls founded a number of institutes for Gestalt therapy and, for many years, was associated with the Esalen Institute at Big Sur, California. At the time of his death in 1970 at age 77, he was living in Vancouver where he had founded an institute for Gestalt therapy. A forceful and dramatic personality, Perls found devout followers both among laymen and professionals. As it evolved, Gestalt therapy is more geared to work with groups than with individuals. Much of the case material Perls presents is drawn from workshops attended by groups of normal people seeking personal growth experiences. There is increasing interest, however, in the concepts and methods of Gestalt therapy for work with clinical populations, in individual and in group therapy, as well as with normals in encounter and personality-growth groups.

BASIC TENETS

Perls was influenced by the thinking of the Gestalt psychologists, Wertheimer, Koffka, Kohler, and Lewin and particularly by Kurt Goldstein. From the 1920s, originally in Germany and later in the United States, the Gestalt psychologists emphasized organization and relatedness in the perceptual field—a whole, they noted, is more than the sum of its parts—and opposed the atomistic approaches of both Wundt's structuralism and Watson's behaviorism. Gestalt psychology, though focused in the study of perception and cognition, had considerable impact on psychology generally. Perls attempts to view the full life and functioning of humans, thus including motoric, emotional, and social behaviors as well as cognitions, in terms of Gestalt organization. In this endeavor, he draws on Goldstein's holistic concepts, emphasizing the need for balance and integration of part functions in the interest of organismic adaptation. In the detailed development of his theory and therapy, however, Perls incorporates important aspects of both psychoanalysis and existentialism. Though some concepts are rephrased and reconceptualized, Perls depends heavily on psychoanalytic dynamics for understanding motivation and defense. At the same time, his emphasis on the immediate experiential field makes his thinking kin to other existential therapists. Indeed, Perls himself identified Gestalt therapy as one of the three major forms of existential psychotherapy, along with Binswanger's existential analysis and Frankl's logotherapy.

The organism has an inherent capacity for growth, which occurs through leaps of insight and meaningful closures with the environment. Getting in touch with new, meaningful needs means that the environment must be contacted in creative ways. Through the development of awareness, imbalances in the organism are perceived along with the need to correct those imbalances. With full awareness one can achieve "organismic self-regulation," which is the basic mechanism of the organism.

The goal of Gestalt therapy is to restore the self-regulatory mechanism of the organism so that potentialities can be realized and the individual can reach wholeness. The curative factor is awareness—a realization of one's needs along with realization that they need fulfillment. The Gestalt therapist tries to help the patient become what he really is, to get behind the games he plays, his facades, and defenses. It is a process of unfolding potentialities, releasing and expressing feeling. The search for the natural state of the organism is the motivating force. Perls sums up the quest in his dictum, "lose your mind and come to your senses."

For growth to occur, both in life and in therapy, there must be increasing *awareness* in the *here and now* and greater readiness to accept *responsibility* for one's actions. In these three concepts are contained the major precepts of Gestalt therapy, which are as much moral injunctions for the good life as definers of the ends and methods of therapy (Naranjo, 1970). Gestalt therapy values (1) the *actual,* in the temporal sense, i.e., present versus past or future; the *spatial,* i.e., present versus absent; and *substantial,* i.e., act versus symbol or fantasy; (2) *awareness* and the acceptance of experience; and (3) *responsibility* or wholeness. Perhaps the most central theme is the insistence on living-in-the-moment. Perls starts his lectures on Gestalt therapy (1970) with the statement: "In my lectures in Gestalt therapy, I have one aim only; to impart a fraction of the meaning of the word *now.* To me, nothing exists except the now. Now = experience = awareness = reality. The past is no more and the future not yet. Only the *now* exists" (Perls, 1970, p. 14).

THE ROLE OF THE THERAPIST

The therapist's task is to help the patient overcome barriers to awareness, that is, to direct and immediate experiences. The issue is not insight as such or understanding, nor conceptualizing the meaning or origins of feelings or motives, but rather confronting the actual experience in the immediate moment. Thus, the therapist asks "what" and "how" questions, rarely "why," "how come," or "what for." The nonverbal and motoric is as important as the verbal communication. The therapist does not interpret but rather draws awareness to the patient's acts, as illustrated in this example from Enright (1970).

> A woman in individual therapy is going over, in a very complaining voice, some examples of how she was recently mistreated by her mother-in-law. I am impressed in her account by her lack of awareness of how much she invited this, and how she underperceives her capacity to interrupt this behavior but said nothing. My attention is caught by a rapid repetitive movement of her hand against her other arm, though I can't make the movement out.
>
> T.: What are you doing with your hand?
>
> P.: (*slightly startled*) Uh, making a cross.

T.: A cross?
P.: Yes. (*pause*)
T.: What might you do with a cross?
P.: Well, I certainly hung myself on one this weekend, didn't I?
She returns to her account, but with more awareness of her martyr attitude and its contribution to events [p. 109].

THE TECHNIQUES OF GESTALT THERAPY

The techniques of Gestalt therapy involve two sets of guidelines which have been called "rules" and "games" (Levitsky and Perls, 1970). The basic rules are: (1) *the principle of the now,* which requires, for example, communicating in the present tense, avoiding reminiscence or future anticipations; (2) *I and thou,* the mainteinance of a flow of communication between equals, talking to rather than at someone; (3) *Using "I" language rather than "it" language,* in order to see oneself as the responsible actor rather than passive recipient of experience. For example (Levitsky and Perls, 1970):

T.: What do you hear in your voice?
P.: My voice sounds like it is crying.
T.: Can you take responsibility for that by saying, "I am crying?" [p. 142].

(4) The *awareness continuum.* This involves requiring the patient to focus constantly on the content of his immediate experience by questions such as "What are you aware of now?" or "How do you experience the anger?" In this way, the effort is made to implement Perls' dictum to "lose your mind and come to your senses;" (5) *No gossiping,* that is, talking about a person rather than to him, and (6) *Asking questions.* The patient is discouraged from asking questions which are less true requests for information than timid and passive ways of expressing opinions.

Characteristic of Gestalt therapy are the numerous *games* or exercises developed by Perls and his colleagues. There are *role-playing games,* in which the patient has to enact different roles or parts of himself. Thus, where there seems to be conflict between the "top-dog" (i.e., superego or "shoulds") and the "under-dog" (the depreciated self), the patient has to act out each portion in turn, presenting the top-dog's then the under-dog's point of view. Other "splits" in the personality, as for example between masculine and feminine components, are similarly externalized and dramatized. In the game of "I take responsibility" the patient must keep adding the phrase "and I take responsibility for it" after comments on facets of his behavior. Thus, "I am aware that my arm is moving . . . and I take responsibility for it." In "Exaggeration" the patient amplifies and exaggerates a minor, perhaps incomplete or abortive, movement so that he can feel its full import. Related is a game in which the patient is asked to repeat over and over and often louder and louder a comment the therapist identifies as significant. In "I have a secret" each member of a group thinks of a personal secret and then tries to imagine how others would react to knowing it. Still without revealing it, members may then be asked to boast about how terrible their secrets are. In this fashion, Perls proposes, feelings of guilt and shame can be explored. These and comparable games are discussed by Levitsky and Perls (1970).

THE USE OF DREAMS

Dreams are used by Gestalt therapists, but in a quite different way from psychoanalysts. Perls assumes that each element in the dream, nonhuman as well as human, represents some portion, often an alienated part, of the patient's personality. In the therapy session, the patient has to retell and reexperience the dream repeatedly, telling it in the present tense and from the vantage point of each image. He is asked to imagine himself, for example, the dog or the tree. By enacting and becoming the dream element, the patient is expected to reclaim and accept those fragments of his self. As illustration of the technique, we can consider portions of a dream by Jean who volunteered to share her experience with Perls in a Gestalt workshop (Perls, 1969). She tells a dream in which she and her mother are going down into a tunnel. With her mother behind her on a sheet of cardboard, they slide down a chute into the depths of the earth, only to find it a sunlit, everglades-like place. When she tells the complete dream, Perls talks for some minutes telling her (and the others in the room) that dreams represent "unfinished business" of the person's life and he expounds some of his philosophy of growth. He then says:

Fritz: So, let's switch back to Jean. Jean, would you talk again, tell again the dream, live it through as if this was your existence, as if you live it now, see if you can understand more about your life. . . .

Jean: I don't—it doesn't really seem clear until I find myself—the place has become kind of a top of the chute. I don't remember whether at first I was afraid or not, possibly—oh, I should say this is now?

F: You are now on the chute. Are you afraid to go down?

J: (*Laughs*) I guess I am a little afraid to go down. But then it seems like. . .

F: So the existential message is, "You've got to go down."

J: I guess I'm afraid to find out what's there.

F: This points to false ambitions, that you're too high up.

J: That's true.

F: So the existential message says, "Go down." Again our mentality says, "High up is better than down." You must always be somewhere higher.

J: Anyway, I seem a little afraid to go down.

F: Talk to the chute.

J: Why are you muddy? You're slippery and slidy and I might fall on you and slip.

F: Now play the chute. "I'm slippery and. . ."

J: I'm slippery and muddy, the better to slide and faster to get down on. (*Laughs*)

F: Ahah, well, what's the joke?

J: (*Continues laughing*) I'm just laughing.

F: Can you accept yourself as slippery?

J: Hm. I guess so. Yes. I can never seem to. . . . Yeah, you know, always just when I think I'm about to, you know, say, "Aha! I've caught you now!" it slips away—you know, rationalization. I'm slippery and slidy. Hm. Anyway, I'm going because it looks like it would be fun, and I want to find out where this goes and what's going to be at the end of it. And it seems, perhaps only now, I'm turning around and looking to see what I could use to kind of protect my clothes (*laughs*) or maybe make a better slide. I discover the cardboard. . . .

F: Can you play this cardboard? If you were this cardboard . . . what's your function?

J: I'm just—to make things easier. I'm just kind of lying around and left-over, and aha, I have a use for it.

F: Oh—you can be useful.

J: I can be useful. I'm not just left-over and lying around, and we can make it easier to get down.
F: Is it important for you to be useful?
J: (*Quietly*) Yes. I want to be an advantage to somebody. . . . Is that enough for being the cardboard? . . . Maybe I also want to be sat upon. (*Laughter*) [F: Oh!] What is the part in the book about who wants to kick who? I want to be pitied, I want to be scrunched down. [F: Say this again.] (*Laughing*) I want to be sat upon and scrunched down.
F: Say this to the group.
J: Well, that's hard to do. (*Loudly*) I want to be sat upon and scrunched down. . . . Hm. (*Loudly*) I want to be sat upon and scrunched down. (*Pounds her thigh with fist.*)
F: Who are you hitting? [J: Me.] Besides you?
J: I think my mother, who's turning, who's behind me and I look around and see her.
F: Good. Now hit her.
J: (*Loudly*) Mother, I'm scrunching down upon—(hits thigh) ouch!—you (*laughs*) and I am going to take you for a ride (*laughter*) instead of you telling me to go,and taking me whenever you want to. I'm taking you along for a ride with me.
F: Did you notice anything in your behavior with your mother?
J: Just now? (*Laughs*)
F: I had the impression it was too much to be convincing. . . . It was spoken with anger, not with firmness.
J: Mmm. I think I'm still a little afraid of her.
F: That's it. You tell her that [pp. 148–150].

In the remainder of the session, Jean further reveals her feelings toward her mother. Reading this fragment and other case materials in *Gestalt Therapy Verbatim* leaves little doubt that Perls' approach to dream analysis brings into awareness intense and important themes in the person's life. It is also clear that the claim that the method is noninterpretive is hardly accurate. What we see is an active, structuring, and interpreting therapist who stage manages the dialogue with the patient. It is hardly a nondirective encounter, either in the Rogerian or psychoanalytic sense, though Perls puts its purpose (fostering awareness) in terms quite like Rogers. Indeed, critics have argued that the Gestalt therapist is distinctly manipulative, that he as much plays games on as with the patient.

THE FUTURE

As yet, no systematic account has been written of Gestalt therapy. There is virtually no research evidence of its effectiveness or the value of particular techniques. Case illustrations are drawn largely from work with normals in Gestalt workshops. It seems likely that the method is best suited for educated and intelligent adults, suffering existential problems but relatively free of gross disorder, who are somewhat constricted and unable to express feelings freely. It also seems likely that severely neurotic or borderline patients, those with more fragile defenses or those with a propensity to act out rather than inhibit impulses might be more harmed than helped by this approach. There is as yet little direct evidence to support these guesses; in a later context, we will look at some of the available studies of encounter groups run in the spirit of Gestalt therapy.

Particularly in California and other places where the presence of Fritz Perls was directly felt, the Gestalt approach has captured the interest of many mental health workers. Its brevity and group application give promise of helping many more people than can be reached by individual dynamic therapies. It is a refreshing alternative to the elitist and rationalist tendencies in psychoanalysis. Its anti-intellectuality has endeared it to those seeking a way to experience their lives more fully without journeying laboriously through the depths of the unconscious.

Gestalt therapy seems to be both product and answer to the problems of our time. Its emphasis on experiencing the natural flow of emotion and action, stifled by a technological society, promises surcease from the artificiality and alienation of modern life. Immediacy and vitality in experience are glorified; rationality, future-orientation, the "shoulds" of collective morality are denied. Gestalt therapy is essentially a hedonistic philosophy in the spirit of "eat, drink, and be merry, for tomorrow we die"; it is an understandable product of the anxiety and despair of an atomic age. The hedonistic life view is already dominant in the youth counterculture, and increasingly more appealing to overburdened and oversocialized adults.

That it appeals is clear, but whether the philosophy of life of Gestalt therapy is of enduring value in our time is much less clear. The Gestalt therapist seems unconcerned with fundamental questions as to the meaning and purpose of life, in marked contrast to Frankl's logotherapy. The need to reflect upon and to understand the human condition—to ask "why" questions—is as fundamental a human need as the desire for spontaneous expression and pleasure. To know is as basic a drive as to experience. In a time of absurdity, one can give up the quest for meaning or one can intensify it. Granted that the intelligence of man and his capacity for objectivity and detachment have created serious social problems, yet it is precisely through these functions that he can hope to know and control his life and the world about him. In their perfection, rather than in their denial, lies the hope of a better life.

Critical Evaluation of Humanistic-Existential Psychotherapies

Still more in the nature of an orientation rather than a systematic view(s) of psychology or psychotherapy, humanistic-existential clinicians have directed needed attention toward the importance of human experience as the proper center of psychologists' concerns. Protesting the determinism of both the dynamic and behavioral psychologies, they have asserted the freedom of the individual to grow in his own fashion. The various forms of humanistic-existential psychotherapy differ importantly among themselves in their concepts and methods, though sharing a common emphasis on current phenomenal experience and the importance of the therapist-patient encounter. The active, interpretive interventions of the Gestalt therapist are in marked distinction to the nondirective mode of the Rogerian therapist. So too, while the logotherapist directs attention toward man's values and hopes of the future, the Gestalt therapist insistently emphasizes living-in-the-moment, effectively denying the future as well as the past. Such differences aside, let us look closely at some of the major themes of the humanistic-existential orientation.

THE PHENOMENAL WORLD

Man differs from all other creatures in his capacity for awareness and self-consciousness. We each have a unique and distinctive view of reality. As we conceive others, we also conceptualize ourselves, and have hopes, aspirations and values for an as-yet nonexistent future. Our perceptions, expectations, fantasies, and personal meanings give direction and purpose to our external and visible behaviors. Only by knowing the inner experiences of a person can a clinician truly understand and help his patient. A science of psychology which excludes such inner experience is at best limited and cannot account for man's most uniquely human characteristics. Phenomenal reality must be the core of psychological concern and the center of clinical intervention. Understanding a person's perception of his world and his self is a necessary starting point, if not the exclusive goal, of psychological investigation.

Moreover, human beings are not mechanical objects, governed by hidden drives or environmental forces. Humans have an inherent capacity for growth; they can change, make choices, and determine their own destinies. Consequently, the clinician cannot treat a human being as an object to be studied and manipulated, but instead must enter with him in an authentic encounter in which they share their existences one with the other.

These views of the humanistic-existential psychologists provide a healthy balance to the prevailing scientific objectivity, determinism, and professional detachment of American psychology. There is little doubt that clinicians have underemphasized the importance of phenomenal reality and immediate experience and, as well, of the patient's capacity for self-regulation and conscious decision-making. But there is also little doubt that one can overstate the capacity for self-determination, particularly in distressed people seeking psychological help. Whether human behavior is, in some ultimate and philosophic sense, free or determined, the fact is that the neurotic experiences himself as the victim of unknown inner impulses or of external forces, both of which are outside of his control. The goal of any psychotherapy is to increase the patient's ability to regulate his own life, a necessary corollary of which is a sense of personal freedom and autonomy. The question, however, is whether the forces which block such autonomy can be conceived and dealt with within the patient's current and conscious perceptual field or whether important determinants lie in the realm of unconscious and historical experiences. While classical psychoanalysis surely overemphasized the unconscious and historical, humanistic psychology runs the risk of overstating the case for conscious and contemporary experience. To ignore history is to risk repeating it; Santayana's famous caution applies as well to individual as to social evolution. The insistent ahistorical bias of humanistic-existential therapists ignores the fact that what a person is, at any moment in time, reflects where he has come from and where he is going. Understanding what crises he has faced and how he has managed them makes clearer how he is dealing with current problems and how his adaptive techniques might be sharpened and improved. While insight, as such, may not be sufficient, it is often a necessary step toward personality and behavioral change.

THE THERAPEUTIC RELATION

In contrast to both psychoanalysis and behavior therapy, humanistic-existential therapists emphasize the relation between therapist and patient and downgrade the importance of techniques as such. The authentic encounter, one in which each enters and shares the experiential field of the other, is deemed more important than specific acts, whether of interpretation or conditioning. Research as well as clinical experience, as noted in Chapter 12, supports a view of psychotherapy as resting importantly on the psychological environment provided by the therapist. A proper relation, one in which the patient can safely trust his experience to an understanding therapist, is surely critical. The issue here, however, is whether it is a sufficient base for therapeutic change.

Rogers' therapist congruence, unconditional positive regard, and empathy may represent proper ideals for all therapists. But they should be recognized as ideals, for all therapists may not like some clients, be unsympathetic to their values and unable to empathize with the patient's concerns. Still, it is surely true that no psychotherapy could be effective if the therapist himself were confused and conflicted, judgmental and rejecting, and rigid and obtuse. To develop the proper attitudes and avert their negative counterparts, is an important facet of the work and training of all therapists. In the Rogerian view, these attitudes should be expressed authentically and spontaneously and should not themselves be turned into therapeutic techniques. In other words, the therapist should not *learn to act* empathically; instead he should *be* empathic. There is an unresolved dilemma here. Taken at face value, it would seem as if therapists could not at all be trained, for any effort to produce therapeutic attitudes would deprive them of their necessary genuineness and spontaneity. In some writings, there is indeed the suggestion that "therapists are born, not made," yet while depreciating technical skills and professional training, Rogers and other humanistic-existential therapists seek to develop practitioners in their model.

However, even with congruence, unconditional positive regard, and empathy how does this assure therapeutic change? ". . . the client's view of himself and the world, while undeniably possessing a reality of its own, cannot be accepted at face value, and the therapist, as a professional, cannot escape being an outside observer. As such, he must evaluate, judge, and at times oppose the client's phenomenal world. The client, by definition, distorts aspects of himself and the outer world. How can the therapist, simply by being genuine and by empathizing with the client's feelings, correct these distortions?" (Strupp, 1971, p. 49). The therapist has necessarily to confront and interpret (as indeed Gestalt therapists do) the patient's experience. Encounter, like love, is not enough. It seems fair to say that the qualities of the relation are a necessary condition for therapy, but they are not sufficient for assuring full and durable change.

HEALTH NOT SICKNESS

Rather than repairing past inadequacies, achieving symptom-relief or replacing maladaptive habits, humanistic-existential therapists stress man's potential for growth and self-actualization. The goal is increasing awareness, freedom, choice, and a person's options for a better life. Therapy is oriented to healthy strivings rather than pathological trends. This orientation is a welcome antidote to the overpathologizing of many clinicians who imply if not affirm that psychological health is a state of not-sickness.

At the same time, the cavalier disregard of diagnostic issues, as the minimization of historical and unconscious determinants, contains clinical risks. Patients do suffer a wide variety of psychological conditions, ranging from relatively mild to severe dysfunctions. Some are psychosomatic and require medical as well as psychological attention; some of the psychotic conditions have known genetic and biochemical as well as psychological antecedents. Meaningful planning for therapy requires knowledge of such factors, as well as more detailed understanding of the patient's life history and character structure. It may be true that formal diagnosis is gross and that any diagnosis runs the risk of labeling and stigmatizing the patient. But proceeding in ignorance contains equal or greater risks. In general, the bias of humanistic-existential therapists (particularly the Rogerians) is to come to know patients only as information is volunteered in the therapeutic encounter, but not to seek it in advance particularly not through formal assessment methods. Clinical assessment is looked on as the judgmental, detached, and nonreciprocal acts of a clinician acting on rather than with his patient. Assessment can surely be abused but it can also serve to inform and enrich the process of therapy.

On the whole, it is probably true that the humanistic-existential approaches are best adapted to the problems of relatively well-integrated and functional people, who are seeking greater meaning and fulfillment in their lives. For less educated and articulate people, those suffering gross psychological disabilities or severe environmental stress, children, psychotics, and the mentally retarded, the aims and methods of humanistic-existential therapies are less appropriate. The approach addresses best existential problems and in such cases issues of diagnosis and psychopathology are actually of lesser importance.

The currently popular quest for rapid personal improvement in encounter groups and related activities brings out some of the problems inherent in the humanistic-existential position. Numerous growth centers have sprung up which in weekend or other brief programs promise self-development through expanding awareness, getting in touch with one's real feelings or inner self, or gaining intimacy with others through encounter. Leaders may or may not be trained clinicians, but they are valued for their human rather than professional competence. Little or no screening of participants takes place, for prior personality or history is deemed irrelevant.

As yet, we know little about the consequences of such experiences, for encounter leaders are not inclined to study and evaluate their work. Infused with the humanistic growth ideology, they stress the positive and minimize the hazards. For most people, it may well be an emotionally exciting experience but one which leaves little enduring personality or behavior change. However, for some few lonely, sensitive, and fragile people, the experience may be distinctly painful and even more permanently damaging. Recent findings document the harm done in encounter groups, as well as the benefits which some receive; in all, Lieberman, Yalom, and Miles (1973) show that encounter groups are more potent, for good and bad, than most clinicians might have predicted.

THEORY AND TERMINOLOGY

In the effort to describe human experiences, often ignored in traditional psychology, humanistic-existential psychologists have developed a great variety of concepts and terms. Some are common words (encounter, presence, being), others are newly created (Dasein, peak experiences, B-values), but whether familiar or new their meaning often eludes easy understanding or precise definition. Reading the works of the European existentialists can be downright painful. Gordon Allport who saw in the movement the hope for a true "psychology of mankind" still stated: "But, first, if we are candid, most of us will admit that we are repelled by much of the writing and theorizing of our European colleagues. Some of it seems to us turgid, verbalistic, and reckless. A few of the ideas are as bright and as illuminating as the dawn; but often these are then drowned in a sea of darkness." (Allport 1961b, p. 94). He expresses the hope that as American scholars extended and made more precise the contributions of Pavlov, Freud, Binet and Rorschach in earlier eras, they can now perform a like service for Heidegger, Jaspers, and Binswanger. This is happening, as existential ideas have excited American psychologists. However, even in the writings of Americans such as Maslow and Rogers, essential terms seem vague and resistant to precise definition. In part, this reflects the movement's distaste for the insistence of "scientific psychology" upon precision and quantification and on the exclusive use of behaviorally and operationally definable concepts. Characterizing human experience and the human condition may well require more complex and subtle terms but hopefully they should be fully understandable to the human mind.

OPPOSITION TO RATIONALITY, INTELLECTUALITY, AND SCIENCE

Echoes of the revolt against the "totalitarianism of reason" remain in contemporary humanistic-existential psychology. There is a basic distrust of the scientific approach, certainly as conventionally defined. Rather than seeking a new human science which can encompass uniquely human and subjective phenomena, they are instead more prone to disavow the relevance of any scientific inquiry for human psychology. With the notable exception of the Rogers group, concepts and methods are rarely put to research tests. Instead, vague and romantic generalizations are put forth which cannot be ordered systematically or tested empirically. Some have seen the challenge of creating a new and broadened human science, breaking through the limits imposed by positivism and behaviorism, but the more general posture is simply antiscientific.

The is part of a more encompassing anti-intellectual ideology. The distrust of reason is reflected as well in the therapeutic emphasis on sensory and bodily awareness and subjective experience. "Insight," "understanding," and "knowledge" are subordinated to "awareness," pure and nonreflective experiencing. Indeed, the intellect often comes off as the natural enemy of all that is good in human nature. While psychology needs to be reminded that "man lives not by head alone," let us also recall that he doesn't do so well without one either. It is a strange paradox that a school which focuses on that which is most uniquely human should neglect what most of us view as the highest accomplishment of the human mind—its ability to reason, create symbols and fantasy, and project into an invisible future.

The ideas and methods of humanistic-existential psychotherapy are still in a formative period, though many have already enlivened and challenged the clinical field and gained many adherents. At this stage, it is necessary to test and sharpen these ideas, in order to preserve the essential and discard the superficial. True advance must depend on searching and self-critical scrutiny, within the principles of science, although broadly rather than narrowly defined.

Comparisons Among the Psychoanalytic, Behavioral, and Humanistic-Existential Approaches to Psychotherapy

I would like to share with you a series of humorous caricatures of patient-therapist dialogues which appeared in the irreverent *Journal of Irreproducible Results*. Though satirizing, Robert S. Hoffman (1973) captures the flavor of some current approaches. His imaginary dialogues are reproduced below.

TABLE 14.1.
The Varieties of Psychotherapeutic Experience *

1. FREUDIAN
   P: I could use a ham on rye, hold the mustard.
   T: It's evident that a quantity of libidinal striving has been displaced to a regressive object with relative fixation in the anal-sadistic mode.
   P: What do you suggest?
   T: Perhaps a valve job and tune-up.

2. ROGERIAN
   P: Shit! Do I feel shitty!
   T: Sounds like you feel shitty.
   P: Why are you parroting me?
   T: You seem concerned about my parroting you.
   P: What the hell is going on here?
   T: You sound confused.

3. EXISTENTIAL
   P: Sorry I'm late today.
   T: Can you get more in touch with that sorrow?
   P: I hope it didn't inconvenience you.
   T: Let's focus on your capacity for choice rather than on my expectations.
   P: But I didn't mean to be late.
   T: I hear you, and I don't put it down. But where we need to be is the immanence of the I-Thou relationship (in Buber's sense) emanating from the here-and-now, and from there into a consciousness of the tension between be-ing and non-be-ing, and eventually into the transcendence of be-ing itself, through to a cosmic awareness of the oceanic I-dentity of Self and the space-time continuum.
   P: Gotcha.

4. BEHAVIORAL
   P: I feel depressed.
   T: Okay. First, I want you to look at this list of depressing phrases, order them by ascending depression-potential and match them with these postcards. Then I want you to step over to these electrodes—don't worry—and put your head in this vise and your left foot in this clamp. Then, when I count to ten, I want you to . . .

TABLE 14.1 (*continued*)

5. GESTALT
   P: I feel somehow that life just isn't worth living.
   T: Don't give me that shit!
   P: What do you mean? I'm really concerned that . . .
   T: Real hell! You're trying to mind-screw me. Come off it.
   P: You shmuck—what are you trying to do with me?
   T: Attaboy! Play me—play the shmuck. I'll play you.
   P: What's going on?
   T: Not shmucky enough—try again, louder.
   P: I've never met a therapist like this.
   T: No good—you gotta stay in the here-and-now. Again.
   P: (gets up to leave)
   T: Okay, now we're getting somewhere. Stand up on that table and do it again.
   P: (exits)
   T: Good. Now I'll play the angry patient and walk out the door. "You shmuck—I'm leaving."

6. CONFRONTATION
   P: Hello.
   T: Pretty anxious about the amenities, eh?
   P: Not very.
   T: Don't try to wiggle out of it.
   P: I'm not. I just . . .
   T: Trying to deny it?
   P: Okay, you're right.
   T: Don't agree just for agreement's sake.
   P: As a matter of fact, I don't agree . . .
   T: Sounds a bit hostile.
   P: Have it your way. I'm hostile.
   T: That's pretty dependent, that statement.
   P: Okay, I'm EVERYTHING.
   T: God, what modesty!

7. PRIMAL
   P: Can you help me stop cracking my knuckles, Doctor?
   T: Okay. You're three years old—you're hungry—REALLY hungry—you want to suckle—you reach for your mother's bosom—what happens?—she pulls away—SHE PULLS AWAY!—SHE ISN'T GOING TO LET YOU HAVE IT—FEEL THAT!—WHAT DO YOU FEEL??—WHAT DO YOU WANT???—Get down on that mat there or you'll hurt yourself—YOU *WANT*, YOU REALLY WANT THAT MILK!—YOU WANT YOUR MOMMY!—YOU AREN'T GOING TO GET YOUR MONEY, I MEAN MOMMY!!—CRY OUT TO HER!—TELL HER YOU WANT HER!—CRY, YOU SONOFABITCH!!!!
   P: But I'm allergic to milk products.

8. PHARMACOLOGIC
   P: I've been having this feeling that people treat me like an object, that they don't see me as a person in my own right, in all my uniqueness.
   T: NURSE! Get me 500 mg. of Thorazine STAT!

---

* Hoffman, Robert S. The varieties of psychotherapeutic experience, *Journal of Irreproducible Results*, 1973, 19, 76–77. Reprinted by permission.

In a more serious vein, I have tried in Table 14.1 to picture the position of each of the major approaches in terms of a number of basic issues or dimensions, some of which were discussed in Chapter 12. Necessarily, these brief characterizations are overly simple. They cannot adequately depict the variety of viewpoints within each of the major orientations. However, this analysis can serve as a ready summary of the main premises and approaches of psychoanalysis, behavior therapy, and humanistic-existential psychotherapy.

TABLE 14.2.

Comparison of Psychoanalytic, Behavioral and Humanistic-Existential Approaches to Psychotherapy

ISSUE	PSYCHOANALYSIS	BEHAVIOR THERAPY	HUMANISTIC-EXISTENTIAL THERAPY
Basic human nature	Biological instincts, primarily sexual and aggressive, press for immediate release, bringing man into conflict with social reality.	Like other animals, man is born only with the capacity for learning, which develops in terms of the same basic principles in all species.	Man has free will, choice, and purpose; he has the capacity for self-determination and self-actualization.
Normal human development	Growth occurs through resolution of conflicts during successive developmental crises and psychosexual stages. Through identification and internalization, more mature ego controls and character structures emerge.	Adaptive behaviors are learned through reinforcement and imitation.	A unique self-system develops from birth on. The individual develops his personally characteristic modes of perceiving, feeling, etc.
Nature of psychopathology	Pathology reflects inadequate conflict resolutions and fixations in earlier development, which leave overly strong impulses and/or weak controls. Symptoms are partial adaptations or substitute gratifications, defensive responses to anxiety.	Symptomatic behavior derives from faulty learning of maladaptive behaviors. The symptom *is* the problem, there is no "underlying disease."	Incongruence exists between the depreciated self and the potential, desired self. The person is overly dependent on others for gratification and self-esteem. There is a sense of purposelessness and meaninglessness.
Goal of therapy	Attainment of psychosexual maturity, strengthened ego functions, reduced control by unconscious and repressed impulses.	Relieving symptomatic behavior by suppressing or replacing maladaptive behaviors.	Fostering self-determination, authenticity, and integration by releasing human potential and expanding awareness.
Role of therapist	An *investigator*, searching out root conflicts and resistances; detached, neutral, and nondirective, to facilitate transference reactions.	A *trainer*, helping patient unlearn old behaviors and/or learn new ones. Control of reinforcement is important; interpersonal relation is of minor concern.	An *authentic person* in true encounter with patient, sharing experience. Facilitates patient's growth potential. Transference discounted or minimized.
Necessary qualifications and skills	Highly trained in theory and supervised practice; much technical and professional knowledge. Must have firm self-knowledge, to avert dangers of countertransference.	Knowledge of learning principles primary; understanding of personality theory and psychopathology secondary; no concern with self-knowledge. Actual interventions can be done by nonprofessional assistant.	Personal integrity and empathy valued over professional training and formal knowledge.

TABLE 14.2 (*Continued*)

ISSUE	PSYCHOANALYSIS	BEHAVIOR THERAPY	HUMANISTIC-EXISTENTIAL THERAPY
Time orientation	Oriented to discovering and interpreting past conflicts and repressed feelings, to examine them in light of present situation.	Little or no concern with past history or etiology. Present behavior is examined and treated.	Focus on present phenomenal experience; the here-and-now.
Role of unconscious material	Primary in classical psychoanalysis, less emphasized by neo-Freudians and ego psychologists. To all, of great conceptual importance.	No concern with unconscious processes or, indeed, with subjective experience even in conscious realm. Subjective experience shunned as unscientific.	Though recognized by some, emphasis is on conscious experience.
Psychological realm emphasized	Motives and feelings, fantasies and cognitions; minimum concern with motor behavior and action outside of therapy.	Behavior and observable feelings and actions. Emphasis on extratherapeutic actions.	Perceptions, meanings, values. For some, sensory and motor processes.
Role of insight	Central, though conceived not just as intellectual understanding but as it emerges in "corrective emotional experiences."	Irrelevant and/or unnecessary.	More emphasis on awareness, the "how" and "what" questions rather than the "why."

CHAPTER 15

Family Therapy, Group Therapy, and the Encounter Movement

Humans are born, live, and die within social groups. They grow, learn, and work in the company of others. Human problems develop in the interplay among individuals and, in the mind of many clinicians, can best be understood and resolved in the same context. There is a growing tendency to conceptualize clinical problems as residing more in interpersonal and social factors than in intrapersonal conflicts and dysfunctions. Concern has thus shifted from the person to those social systems, both small and large, within which people live and which determine their well-being. Correspondingly, methods of clinical intervention have evolved which focus less on the isolated patient, as in individual psychotherapy, but rather on the social system as such. At the first level, these include methods of working with small, face-to-face groups. These will be considered in this chapter. On a broader scale are those social interventions aimed at altering institutional and community determinants of mental health, which will be discussed in later chapters. In all, these emerging methods of system-centered, rather than individual-centered, intervention represent concrete realization of the poet's truism that "no man is an island unto himself."

FAMILY THERAPY

Treating the Disturbed Child

Many forms of individual psychotherapy for the problems of children have evolved, including child psychoanalysis, client-centered child psychotherapy, and many forms of behavior modification. Necessarily, such therapies can only approximate their adult forms, for not only do the problems and symptoms of the child differ but they are living at a different developmental level. Along with, or instead of, therapeutic conversations, communication between therapist and child patient depends on free play, games, or activities of various sorts. The floor of the playroom rather than the couch or armchair is the arena of the child therapist, whose tools include puppets and sandbox, Bobo doll and finger paints, checkers and other games. In her office, Anna Freud who works with children can hardly display cherished art objects as her father did in his study in Vienna. Not only does the child think, communicate, and express feelings in modes different than the adult, but his life conditions obviously differ as well. He is dependent on the family for sustenance, in the most literal as well as figurative sense. Indeed, his being in therapy at all typically reflects the parents' belief that his behavior is disturbed and that he needs psychological help. On his part, the child is a "reluctant client," who has neither chosen, arranged, nor paid for psychotherapy. Above all, the child is in a process of development, the formative influences of the family are acting upon him right now, not as with the adult are they matters of an historic past.

Early in the child guidance movement it became amply clear that the child should not be treated apart from the family. Without altering, in some degree at least, the forces acting upon the child there seemed little promise for improvement in attempts to influence the child's development alone. Consequently, efforts were made to include the parent(s) within a more broadly conceived treatment program. Most typically, this was the mother who was more available and concerned. Moreover, theory of the time emphasized mothering, to the relative neglect of fathering or "familying," in the development of the young child. The parent's involvement in the treatment process might be quite minimal, involving an initial session mainly intended to discuss the child's problem and the potential family contribution to it, and later sessions to consider the child's progress, to help the family accommodate to changes in the child's behavior and to provide necessary conditions for further growth. Sometimes, but rarely, the parent and child might be seen together in occasional joint sessions. More usually the effort was made to bring the mother into personal psychotherapy so that she could be a more effective person in her own right as well as a better influence on the child. This might take place in *concomitant psychotherapy* in which child and mother each have their own therapist operating independently of each other or in *collaborative psychotherapy* in which the two therapists cooperate closely in the effort to synchronize their therapeutic endeavors. Occasionally, the same therapist might see both mother and child.

The shift in child guidance thinking and the move from one-to-one therapy to two-to-two therapy laid the groundwork for the present *conjoint family therapy,* in which all members of the family are seen together by the same therapist. With the capture of the elusive father, and the growing realization that a *troubled family* rather than of a *troubled individual in a family* must be treated, father, mother, and siblings along with the "identified patient" participate together in a process which focuses on distress and malfunction in the family system itself.*

Pathology and Communication in Families

A major impetus for the present interest in family therapy arose from the studies of psychopathology and communication in the families of schizophrenic patients. In the early 1950s, in Palo Alto, California, a group under the leadership of the anthropologist Gregory Bateson began their studies of communication patterns in such families. Within a few years, other active researchers included a group at the National Institute of Mental Health (Bowen, Wynne, M.T. Singer, and others) and at Yale University (Lidz, Cornelson, Fleck, and others) were contributing importantly to the study of the schizophrenic family. In England, R. D. Laing was developing the view that schizophrenia, rather than being thought of as sick or disturbed, should be looked on as a reasonable accommodation to living in a chaotic world. Within a decade, a vigorous body of research had developed exploring the origins of schizophrenia in disturbed family interactions (e.g., G. H. Frank, 1965; Mishler and Waxler, 1966).

Two concepts are central in the Palo Alto group's understanding of family pathology and therapy: (1) the double bind and (2) family homeostasis (D. D. Jackson and Weakland, 1961). The concept of family homeostasis arose from observations in family therapy in which it was noted that disturbance might appear elsewhere in a family if one member's condition improved. They may act in ways which seem designed to maintain a steady state, even if it may involve blocking the therapeutic progress of one member. Thus, the Palo Alto group came to look on the family as a dynamic homeostatic system which tends to maintain stability when threatened (Jackson, 1959). Hence, to bring about a better level of func-

* Understanding and treating problems of the child is a broad field and an important specialty within clinical psychology. In this volume, I have emphasized in the main assessment, psychotherapy, and community intervention with the problems of the adult in mind. For the reader more specifically interested in clinical work with children, Williams and Gordon (1974) is recommended for an overview of the current field. The textbooks by Ross (1974) and M. Engel (1974) are also valuable; the former is written from a behavioral point of view and the latter from a psychodynamic. The volumes sponsored by the Joint Commission on the Mental Health of Children give a broad view of the child clinical field.

tioning in family members, the family system must be influenced, as a whole rather than its component members.

Central to their notion of how schizophrenia is determined by disturbed family communication is the Palo Alto group's concept of the *double bind* (Bateson, Jackson, Haley and Weakland, 1956). This occurs when the "victim" in the family receives contradictory messages which make it impossible for him to act in consistent and satisfying ways. Whatever course he takes, he loses. The young boy may be told that he should be more assertive and stand up for his rights; at the same time, he discovers that he is expected to respect the parents, not challenge their wishes, and conform unquestioningly to their demands. The mother may express love and affection, but as the child approaches, draw away. Such contradictory messages often involve different levels and modes of communication. What is said in words can be contradicted in gesture. Nor is the incongruence evident. It is masked and hidden, so that the victim may never quite discover and be able to confront the sources of his confusion. When such double-bind communications occur repetitively within the important emotional context of the family in which messages cannot be ignored or avoided, the victim can, in time, participate in the disturbed process by accepting and internalizing the incongruence without question. This, Bateson, Jackson and their coworkers argue, may result in enduring schizophrenic behavior. In a comparable concept, Wynne et al. (1958) describe the "pseudomutuality" which can exist between members of a schizophrenic family. There continues to be much controversy over the explanatory value of the double-bind theory, particularly in the light of evidence for both genetic and sociological causes of schizophrenia, but it has inspired much research and fostered the development of family therapy. The system-centered approach to the family is most fully developed in the work of Satir (2nd ed. 1967) and Haley (1963, 1967, 1971). Independently, in other settings, other workers developed therapeutic methods for working with whole families (Bell, 1961; Ackerman, 1958, 1966). The range of concepts and methods which characterize the current field can be found in volumes edited by Haley and Hoffman (1967), Ackerman, Lieb, and Pearce (1970), Haley (1971), Ferber, Mendelsohn, and Napier (1972), and Sager and Kaplan (1972). In 1961, the journal *Family Process* was started as a vehicle for presenting the ideas and research of workers in the field.

Indications and Contraindications for Family Therapy

Family therapy is usually undertaken where the identified patient, usually an adolescent, is so enmeshed in pathology-producing family processes that he cannot sensibly be treated alone. Earlier individual therapy may have come to an impasse because of resistances within the family to changes in the patient, even to the extent of terminating or at least undermining the work of the therapist. Family homeostasis may have become disturbed by changes in the patient's personality or behavior, with other members showing symptomatic behaviors as the identified patient improved. Where possible, the treatment of young schizophrenic or borderline patients along with available family members is a valuable use of family therapy. Therapy usually starts focused on the problems of the identified patient though dealing increasingly with strains in the family system as members come to appreciate their own contribution. Though families can come seeking help "for the family," more typically they are motivated to change the symptomatic member. Indeed, an early and essential task for the system-oriented family therapist is to encourage all members to see themselves as equally involved in the problem.

Family therapy is particularly indicated where there are: (1) family crises which affect all members, such as a move to a new city, death of a family member, unemployment, and the like: (2) marital or sexual disharmony; and (3) family conflicts along value or generational lines, where the adults may be in controversy with the adolescents over their life styles, goals, or social values. Family therapy seems particularly useful where the focal problem involves an adolescent separating from the family.

There are many circumstances where family therapy cannot be used or may be ill-advised (Ackerman, 1970; Wynne, 1965). Family therapy is contraindicated if it is impossible to establish or maintain a working relationship with key family members. Therapy cannot proceed if, say, the father simply refuses to come; it is no better if he is cajoled, participates reluctantly, and is a constant source of resistance and disruption. But even if all members would participate, some family systems are too fragile to undertake conjoint therapy. There may be an apparently irreversible trend toward the breakup of the family, too late to reverse. Similarly, if one person, particularly a parent, is too grossly disturbed, paranoid, destructive, deceitful, or rigidly defended, wisdom may lie in working separately with a troubled adolescent. Where there may be unyielding religious or cultural values or a valid family secret that has to be kept, the openness and freedom of communication required in any psychotherapy cannot be realized.

It is not clear how young a child can be included, and what risks or benefits there may be. Family therapists often include young siblings of the identified patient, if there is one, even though he may get lost in the adult talk, become restive, and contribute little. There is the realistic danger that he can be overwhelmed in the swirl of intense emotions, and wise family therapists proceed cautiously with young children. Recently, the importance of including the young child in family sessions has been stressed and play methods proposed through which he can participate more fully (Zilbach, Bergel, and Gass, 1972). If, however, the focal problem centers on the youngster himself, most child clinicians prefer individual, concomitant, or collaborative therapy, reserving conjoint family therapy for teen-age and older patients.

Goals of Family Therapy

The first goal of the family therapist is to discover how the presenting problem is related to the network of relations in the family and, consequently, in what way and how family members might participate. It is often necessary to discover who

TABLE 15.1.
Primary Goals Stated by Therapist with Families Actually in Treatment (N = 290) *

PRIMARY GOALS	WITH ALL FAMILIES %	WITH CERTAIN FAMILIES %	TOTAL %
1. Improved communication	85	5	90
2. Improved autonomy and individuation	56	31	87
3. Improved empathy	56	15	71
4. More flexible leadership	34	32	66
5. Improved role agreement	32	32	64
6. Reduced conflict	23	37	60
7. Individual symptomatic improvement	23	33	56
8. Improved individual task performance	12	38	50

* From Group for the Advancement of Psychiatry, *The Field of Family Therapy*. GAP Report #78, 1970, p. 553. Reprinted by Permission.

TABLE 15.2.
Secondary Goals Stated by Therapist with Families Actually in Treatment (N = 290) *

SECONDARY GOALS	WITH ALL FAMILIES %	WITH CERTAIN FAMILIES %	TOTAL %
1. Improved individual task performance	16	29	45
2. Individual symptomatic improvement	23	15	38
3. Reduced conflict	17	18	35
4. Improved role agreement	17	15	32
5. More flexible leadership	11	19	30
6. Improved empathy	17	8	25
7. Improved autonomy and individuation	7	5	12
8. Improved communication	8	1	9

* From Group for the Advancement of Psychiatry, *The Field of Family Therapy*. GAP Report #78, 1970, p. 553. Reprinted by Permission.

is actually involved, and hence should join in group sessions, for relevant participants might include a neighbor, grandparent, or collateral relative who is vitally involved in the family life. In the earliest phase of therapy, family therapists make an effort to involve all of the family members by pointing out ways in which they interact within the family session itself. Satir, in addition, may ask all members of the family to state their personal goals, what they hope to gain for themselves as well as for the identified patient, in order to consolidate their commitment to therapy.

Longer-term goals depend on the orientation of the particular family therapist, whether he is committed mainly to improving the status of the identified patient, clarifying communication patterns in the family, facilitating open expression of emotions, or other ends. In a survey of clinicians who practice family therapy, respondents were asked to indicate their *primary* and *secondary* goals, for all families and for certain families, in terms of eight classes of possible goals

(Group for the Advancement of Psychiatry, 1970). The responses of the 290 therapists who replied are shown in Tables 15.1 and 15.2. Over 90 percent of the therapists said that all eight of the purposes were either primary or secondary goals for at least some families. However, the relative importance of each clearly emerged. The goal most commonly endorsed as primary for *all* families was "improved communication," with "improved autonomy and individuation" a rather distant second. The fewest number chose "individual symptomatic improvement" and "improved individual task performance," though these were well accepted as secondary goals. It is worth noting that reducing symptoms and facilitating individual functioning are central purposes of individual therapy, but family therapists see them as distinctly secondary to changing family-wide processes, notably the communication system and the individuation of family members with respect to each other. The later purpose, Bowen (1966) has described in terms of extracting individuals from the "undifferentiated ego mass of the family."

Elsewhere in the survey, however, it becomes clear that family therapists are hardly of one mind in their concepts and methods of family treatment. Virtually all, in 1970, were originally trained as individual therapists and many still see family treatment as essentially patient-centered. The other family members, in this view, give information as to the context in which the patient lives and the stresses acting upon him. Changing their behavior has relevance insofar as it affects the well-being of the identified patient. At the other extreme are those firmly committed to a system-oriented approach, for example, Satir and Haley. They see the process from beginning to end as focusing on the family as a whole with hoped-for changes in the family process expected to lead to healthier lives for all its members, regardless of who is initially identifed as the patient. In actuality, a goodly number of practitioners position somewhere in-between. They emphasize family process along with individual psychodynamics, with their concern centered on the identified patient.

The Process of Family Therapy

In addition to differing along a dimension of individual-oriented to system-oriented thinking, family therapists can be described as more in the nature of *reactors* or *conductors* (Beels and Ferber, 1972). The former tend to be more nondirective and passive, reacting to issues as they arise. Conductors, by contrast, tend to program and organize the proceedings, setting agenda, assigning tasks, and actively interrogating and teaching. In the case of Ackerman, this may be in order to cut through hypocrisy and denial, requiring family members to be more open with him and with themselves. He has them face sexual, aggressive, and dependent feelings, and "tickles" their defenses against them. His manner is hearty, confident, and honest, and he instills these qualities in group interaction. Satir, on the other hand, presents herself as a resource person and teacher and expert in communication. She gives direction to the discussions, pointing out communicational problems. She sets herself as a model of clear communication, using simple and clear words, and explains her principles to the family. Though concerned with other facets of human feelings and interaction, she is basically a teacher and exemplar of communicational clarity. However, whether more reactor or conductor, as Ackerman and Satir, all family therapists necessarily have to play a more active role than is usual in individual therapy. In the swirl of often heated family interplay, the therapist has to be more vigorous in exerting controls, moderating arguments, and guiding discussions.

Family therapy puts the therapist in an essentially different relation with his clients than exists in either individual or group therapy. He does not start from the shared base of mutual ignorance. The family members come in with a mass of common experience; the therapist is the outsider, in his own office. In order even to make sense out of their allusions to shared experience, he has to learn the family culture, rules, and language. Why does everyone laugh when Johnny says that Dad is getting to be more like Uncle Joe? The therapist has to get within the family system to understand and work with it. Yet he cannot become a "regulated part of the system," caught up in its cliques and power struggles, for he must also stand apart from it in order to understand its workings and guide its changes. Thus, the balance between involvement and detachment becomes more critical in family therapy than in other forms of psychotherapy. In other ways, the family therapist shares the general task of all therapists, to provide a safe and supportive atmosphere for confronting painful experiences.

Therapy usually begins with an effort to discover what is troubling the family and what they hope to achieve through therapy. The first session or two may involve only the marital pair, who as leaders of the family establish the initial relationship and, at the same time, give some indication as to the nature of the marital relationship. Typically enough, the presenting problem is couched in terms of the disturbed behavior of the identified patient. "Johnny won't go to school, loafs all day, and uses drugs." It is virtually a truism that all members of the family do not share the same notion as to what is wrong, why they have come, or how important it is to be in treatment together. To clarify the composite of motives and perceptions is an important early task. In the same process, the therapist tries to communicate some of the ground rules, that all members will be treated as individuals, they will each be expected to participate, and their points of view will be respected.

An example from an early session of a family with Virginia Satir (1967, 143–145) can make this process clearer. The family consists of Joe and Mary and their children, Johnny (10) and Patty (7). The parents had sought help for Johnny's poor work and misbehavior in school. At this point in the interview Satir had discovered that Johnny thought the family was going for a ride while Patty thought they were going to someone to talk about the family. Satir now asks the children where they got their ideas as to what was going to happen.

Patty: Mother said we were going to talk about family problems.
Therapist: What about Dad? Did he tell you the same thing?
P: No.
T: What did Dad say?
P: He said we were going for a ride.
T: I see. So you got some information from Mother and some information from Dad. What about you, Johnny: Where did you get your information?
Johnny: I don't remember.
T: You don't remember who told you?

Mother: I don't think I said anything to him, come to think of it. He wasn't around at the time, I guess.

T: How about you, Dad? Did you say anything to Johnny?

Father: No, I thought Mary had told him.

T: *(to Johnny)* Well, then, how could you remember if nothing was said.

J: Patty said we were going to see a lady about the family.

T: I see. So you got your information from your sister, whereas Patty got a clear message from both Mother and Dad.

[The therapist continues, asking the children how they handle differences in messages from the parents. She then asks the parents what they remember saying.]

T: How about that, Mother? Were you and Dad able to work this out together—what you would tell the children?

M: Well, you know, I think this is one of our problems. He does things with them and I do another.

F: I think this is a pretty unimportant thing to worry about.

T: Of course it is, in one sense. But then we can use it, you know, to see how messages get across in the family. One of the things we work on in families is how family members communicate—how clearly they get their messages across. We will have to see how Mother and Dad can get together so that Johnny and Patty can get a clear message.

[Shortly, she adds:]

T: Well, then, I'll tell you why Mother and Dad have come here. They have come here because they were unhappy about how things were going in the family and they want to work out ways so that everyone can get more pleasure from family life.

In this brief episode we see Satir introducing the family to communication concepts, while exploring their understanding of therapy. In her technique, each member is encouraged to speak for himself and to make his own position known; the therapist may interrupt if one person tries to represent the views of another. Thus, she fosters a sense of worth and distinctness in each person.

Early in the family session, an extensive family history is taken. This starts with the marriage of the parental couple (the "architects of the family," in Satir's term), which conveys to the children the somewhat startling notion that a family existed before their entry into it. The story is brought down to the present and carried back to the early life of the parents in their families of origin. The therapist thus gets a notion of the cast of relevant characters in the family's life and of possible antecedents and continuities in their behavior. The children may discover that indeed their parents were once children and suffered many of the same resentments and conflicts with their parents. By extending the view of the family over generations, rather than in keeping it in the frozen moment, present problems are given perspective and may be more manageable. In the process, family myths can be revealed and perhaps laid to rest. Though they have often heard their father say to the mother, "Well, he does have your Uncle Max's blood," the children can now come finally to know that Uncle Max's 1925 psychiatric hospitalization has nothing to do with Johnny's present transgressions except to serve as an excuse for family distrust.

Family rules are also discovered and discussed. As in the larger society, the microcosm of the family develops regulatory principles which prescribe actions of its members. Many are shared with other families of the general culture such as "girls should help their mother in the kitchen," "unless you do your chores, you don't get an allowance," and represent general societal values. Others however are more specific to the particular family—"Don't disturb Dad, tell your problems to Mother." Many such rules are less than clear and they may be inconsistently applied or interpreted. A constant problem arises, for example, in the application of rules that are age-related. "A child should be home by 10 p.m." may be sensible for a twelve-year-old but an onerous imposition on a seventeen-year-old.

In general, the therapist preserves the neutral role of inside-outsider, moderator of conflict, interpreter of family process, and teacher of more effective interpersonal relations. However, families are given to forming cliques, whether on age lines, sex, or perceived similarity and compatibility. All too frequently there is scapegoating of one member, often the identified patient, with all of the others projecting onto him all of their problems. Though usually neutral and attempting to be fair to all sides, the therapist sometimes has to be a more active "side-taker" (Zuk, 1967). In fact, however neutral a therapist's behavior may seem to him, he will likely be seen as siding with one or another party in a controversy, and indeed he may. What Zuk proposes, therefore, is that the therapist intentionally cast his weight to one or another side if it tips the balance in favor of more productive and less pathological relating in the family. Though this may be useful for bolstering the esteem of a scapegoated member, and perhaps lead the others to see the destructiveness in their behavior, side-taking in general runs the risk of alienating the family and reducing their faith in the fairness of the therapist. Where the therapist unwittingly takes sides by accepting one person's view of the problem and ignoring another, a corrupt contract exists which ultimately reduces the value of therapy (Beall, 1972).

Family therapy has grown rapidly in the last decade, with many clinicians entering the field who previously had practiced individual or group therapy. The base of family theory and therapeutic method is still incomplete, with few systematic views yet developed. There is considerable faith in the efficacy and efficiency of the family approach, both among therapists and their patients, but as of this time there are virtually no published studies of the outcome of family therapy nor sufficient basis for judging the relative value of one rather than another approach. At the same time, the notion of intervening in the family system as such makes intrinsic sense. If as a consequence of such intervention families in which pathology festers can know and confront their feelings, disentangle their lives, and communicate clearly and directly, then it is indeed a promising approach. Minuchin (1974) gives an overview of recent work on family dynamics and family therapy. It is especially recommended for the extensive transcripts of actual interviews with families.

Related Forms of Therapy

MARRIAGE COUNSELING

Marriage counseling can be looked on as a special case of family therapy, where the focus is on the relation between husband and wife and problems with children, if any, are secondary. People whose marriages are foundering have often sought individual psychotherapy, only to discover that life with the mate worsened as their view of the marriage changed in therapy. Similarly, individual-oriented clinicians, viewing marital problems as reflecting only the neurotic state of one partner, have discovered that therapeutic changes in their patients can make the marital balance even more precarious. For this reason, it is often advisable for the therapeutic effort to focus directly on the interplay between husband and wife, rather than the individual lives of either, and the pair are best seen conjointly. Marital counseling of husband and wife together was developed earlier than family therapy, and has been widely used by counseling as well as clinical psychologists, psychiatrists, and social workers. In recent years, the term "couples therapy" is coming into wider usage to describe the conjoint treatment of couples living together whether married or not.

A common source of marital problems lies in divergent role expectations between the spouses. Each carries into the marriage expectations as to how the other is to act and feel, often conditioned by the example of their own parents. Though the marriage vow promises equality, the man may remember too well how his mother waited on his father or the woman how her father treated his wife as a precious doll to be cared for and protected from effort and harm. In fact, the partner may not at all act in the expected way; disappointment and frustration result. Conflicts of expectations regarding responsibility, dominance-submission, autonomy, affection, and respect, among others, lie at the root of many marriage problems. The needs of each partner may be complementary; as each meets the other's needs a stable marriage results. However, a less harmonious state of affairs exists where the needs of each cannot be simultaneously met and the amount of compromise required is great. Where, for example, both husband and wife are overly dependent and fearful, they may compete for the cared-for role and resent the other for forcing responsibility on him or her. The intimacy of marriage not only fosters deep feelings of love but all too often of hostility, anger, and anxiety. Managing the hostility which arises in the inevitable conflicts of marriage is the focus of George Bach's approach to marriage counseling (Bach and Wyden, 1969). In the effort to substitute constructive rather than destructive forms of aggression between mates, he puts them through "fight training" in which they learn, for example, to use verbal rather than physical attack, to focus on reality rather than imaginary problems, and in other ways to stress the constructive rather than destructive elements inherent in any conflict. The goal is not doing away with conflict, but rather encouraging fights which result not in one winning over the other but mutual gain.

In the present era, traditional sex roles are being called into question. Wives are seeking a more equal place in the world of work and expect husbands to contribute proportionately more to the management of the home and family. Marriages which were structured in terms of male dominance come under increasing strain as women seek more liberated social roles. Marital counseling can sometimes help ease the transition to a more egalitarian mode where the couple cannot themselves resolve their differing views as to their marital arrangements.

CONJOINT SEXUAL THERAPY

Marital problems often center on unsatisfying sexual relations. Based on their research on human sexuality, Masters and Johnson (1966, 1970) have developed a form of brief sexual therapy aimed at making the couple's sexual life more exciting and satisfying. While it is certainly true that sexual disharmony may well reflect conflicts in other realms, a truly happy marriage should rest on both partners experiencing sexual satisfaction. Whatever the sexual inadequacy which may exist—premature ejaculation in the man or lack of orgasm in the woman—Masters and Johnson argue that it reflects tension between them and that both partners should therefore participate simultaneously in the treatment program.

The Masters and Johnson technique has the couple spend as much as two weeks at a center away from their own home. It is felt important that they disentangle themselves from their usual obligations, work, responsibilities, children, and friends. Husband and wife each work with the like-sexed member of the male-female cotherapist team. For the first couple of days, each pair meets separately, delving deeply into sexual attitudes, expectations, and performance and into the history of sexual relations both in and outside of the marriage. By the third day, the husband and wife and their two therapists come together for joint sessions, to review the material that has been gathered in the individual sessions, in order to see how the individual and marital histories might be related to present sexual difficulties. Much of the conjoint process is of an educational sort. The partners are taught how satisfying sexual functioning occurs. Effort is made to clarify sexual misunderstandings, myths, excessive expectations, and to improve communication between husband and wife. The couple is instructed in methods of heightening sexual responsiveness and minimizing anxiety over sexual adequacy. On later days, further instruction is given specifically to overcome the particular sexual problem for which they originally sought help. Physical and psychological techniques are taught which can help reduce the symptomatic problem—e.g., inability to maintain erection or to achieve orgasm—and in general to make the sexual relationship more satisfying and comfortable. So far, good results have been reported, though long-term evidence of benefit is still lacking. Not unlikely, the gain results as much from the husband and wife's willingness to openly confront their problem and to collaborate in its solution as from the ingenious techniques Masters and Johnson have evolved for teaching how to facilitate sexual effectiveness and pleasure. The Masters and Johnson program, in many variant forms, is coming into increasing use.

BEHAVIORAL APPROACHES TO MARITAL AND FAMILY PROBLEMS

Learning-oriented therapists have carried over the principles of behavior therapy to the realm of marital and family interventions (e.g., Liberman, 1970; G. R. Patterson et al., 1967, 1971; Stuart, 1969). In their view, the way family members deal with each other can be reconceptualized in terms of contingencies of reinforcement, each acting on the others. Consequently, the therapeutic task is to induce family members to reinforce desired behaviors rather than rewarding maladaptive behavior with attention, concern, and other secondary reinforcements. The behaviorally oriented therapist starts by making a behavioral analysis of the family problems to discover which behaviors they want to augment or decrease. In the same process, he ascertains what reward contingencies might be supporting both problem and desired behaviors. The process of therapy then consists of guiding the marital pair, or members of the family, toward intentionally altering reinforcement contingencies. Some (e.g., Stuart, 1969) have used tokens, somewhat in the style of hospital token economies. Thus, a husband may earn a token from his wife if he, for example, volunteers to help with the dishes. She, in turn, is reinforced by him for having supper prepared on time. Much of the behavioral work so far has been concerned mainly with socializing the disturbed behavior of a child in a family, rather than working with the family as a total system, by "reprogramming the social environment" (G. R. Patterson et al., 1967). Such a therapy program involves teaching social learning principles directly to the parents. The therapeutic work often goes on in the family home.

OTHER APPROACHES

Network therapy. The logic of family therapy is extended by working simultaneously with all available members of the kinship system, friends and neighbors, and anyone else of importance to the nuclear family who has the presenting problem (Speck and Attneave, 1971). As many as forty people may be gathered in meetings in the home in a reconstruction of the ancient custom of gathering in of a clan at the time of crisis. The aim is to strengthen the bonds within the extended family so that they are better able to help solve their problems.

Multiple-impact therapy. Families with a disturbed adolescent child in a crisis situation may be helped by multiple-impact therapy (MacGregor et al., 1964). A mental health team works with the family during two days of intensive sessions. After a brief family conference, different members of the team pair off with one or more members of the family in various combinations. Thus, mother and daughter may work with one therapist, while the father sees someone individually as does the son. As necessary, these combinations regroup to allow maximum exploration of the family's problems particularly with the identified patient. The effort, overall, is to so reorganize the family system that it can break loose from its fixed and repetitive malfunctioning to become a more open system capable of continued adaptive change. Therapy usually continues into a follow-up period.

Multiple-family and multiple-couple group therapy. Multiple-family and multiple-couple group therapy bring into group sessions a number of families (or couples) previously unrelated, except for their common desire for help with emotional problems (e.g., Laqueur, 1972). In this fashion, participants can not only examine transactions within their own family unit but experience simultaneously the manifest ways problems are expressed by the other families and couples. Thus, the advantages of group therapy are brought to bear on family or couple treatment.

GROUP PSYCHOTHERAPY

The Growth of Group Methods

Though group methods have existed since the beginning of this century, it was not until clinicians were faced with the vastly increased pressure for clinical services during and following World War II that group therapy came into common use. Therapists trained in one-to-one methods adapted their techniques to the treatment of many people simultaneously. To many, group therapy was a necessary but inferior substitute for individual therapy, valued mainly for its economy. In time, however, there has been growing realization that group therapy is distinctive, valuable in its own right, involving change mechanisms of different order, and perhaps better adapted to the needs of particular patients. Ideas from group dynamics interpenetrated those of personality dynamics and psychotherapy and new therapeutic concepts emerged. New training developed specifically to prepare clinicians for group therapy. Membership in the American Group Psychotherapy Association, which requires professional education and training qualifications, has grown from less than twenty in 1942 to well over 2000 members today.

Over these years, group methods also evolved intended less to reduce emotional problems than to facilitate personal and organizational effectiveness. The most recent expression of this trend can be seen in the proliferation of encounter groups and kindred methods of the human-potential movement. Consequently, today vast numbers of people—both those seeking relief from emotional pain and those seeking enhanced sensitivity, internal harmony, and effectiveness—participate in group activities of all types. The boundary between "therapy" and "growth" groups is less than clear, both in terms of the clients served or the types of intervention used.

Compared to individual therapy, the emphasis in group methods of all types is more on system properties (group process) than on the individual himself and the patient-therapist dyad, although unlike family therapy it is a more temporary social system. For the period of the group sessions, however, participants are intimate strangers interlocked in a small social system which has change-producing properties. These properties, the "curative factors," may ultimately be the same in all groups (Yalom, 1975), though they differ in the kinds of clients served, the problems and goals of the participants, and the techniques of the leader.

In its broad extension, the contemporary field of group therapy encompasses a wide variety of disparate activities, including ward meetings of psychotic patients, people with neurotic and character disorders discussing their problems with a group therapist in a clinic or private office, self-help groups such as Alcoholics Anonymous, Recovery, Inc., or Synanon, psychoanalytic groups, transactional analysis groups, Gestalt therapy groups, T-groups, encounter groups of numerous sorts including marathon and nude encounter groups, couples' groups, women's consciousness-raising groups, sensory-awareness groups, dance and body-movement groups, among many others. In this section we will consider the nature of group intervention and the factors which may induce therapeutic change within the context of the more traditional group therapeutic methods designed to help people in emotional distress; in the next section, emphasis will be shifted to the new group methods which aim as much at personal growth.

Some History and Background

Group therapy seems to have originated with the work of Joseph Hershey Pratt, a Boston internist, who worked with advanced tubercular patients. He was cognizant of the importance of psychological as well as medical factors in determining both their morale and medical status. In 1905, he arranged regular sessions with a class of twenty-five patients to discuss diaries they kept of their experiences, their weight loss or gain, and in general the state of their lives. Bolstered by patients' reports of successful experiences, and tutored by Pratt, an important degree of group cohesiveness and mutual support developed which helped stave off the isolation and depression common to tubercular patients.

During the next three decades, a number of psychiatrists independently experimented with group methods in hospitals and clinics. Many of their efforts were also of a didactic sort, involving lectures, assigned homework, and group advising. By the 1930s, however, Burrows (1927), Schilder (1939), and Slavson (1940), among others, were applying psychological concepts, mainly psychoanalytic, to group-therapeutic procedures. During a time when most psychiatrists saw group therapy as a poor substitute for individual therapy, Slavson (1964) advocated it vigorously. He worked mainly with disturbed children and adolescents in activity (play) groups, based on notions from psychoanalysis, education, and group work. He organized the American Group Psychotherapy Association and was for years editor of its journal. Through his teaching and writing he exerted considerable influence on the field and was its major spokesman from the 1930s to the 1960s.

Independently of American developments, Jacob Moreno, a Viennese psychiatrist, conceived an alternate way of working with people in groups which has influenced group therapy and the encounter movement. In 1921, he founded the *Stehgreiftheater* (the Theater of Spontaneity) in Vienna, and in 1925 he brought psychodrama to the United States. Its essential principle is to stimulate the free expression of feelings through unrehearsed, spontaneous acting. The chief participants in a therapeutic psychodrama are the protagonist or subject, the director or therapist, auxiliary egos (other patients playing other parts), and with still others (patients and observers) as audience. Though Moreno's conceptual framework (Moreno, 1946, 1953, 1959) is difficult to follow and often grandiose, the essential ideas are straightforward. Drama stands midway between reality and fantasy. In acting roles, one can see one's own and others feelings in perspective; acting is thus equivalent to free association though closer to social reality. Hidden feelings, unknown conflicts, distorted perceptions can emerge, new attitudes and behavior can be tried, all in the relative security of play-acting. Although some clinicians continue to practice psychodrama in relatively pure form, the greater impact of Moreno's work has resulted from the adoption and use in other therapeutic systems of many of his specific techniques, such as role-playing, role-reversal, and the enactment of dreams, among others. It might also be noted that Moreno was the first person to use the term group psychotherapy. In psychodrama, however, one person is treated in a group rather than a number of individuals through group process.

The developments we have scanned thus far arose largely in the clinical context. They were intended as treatment for pathological emotional conditions to be given by professional clinicians. In the postwar period however there was a parallel development, within a more educational context, of group methods intended to increase interpersonal sensitivity and skills among already well-functioning people. Much of this trend followed from the work of Kurt Lewin and his students who developed the science of group dynamics and with it methods for facilitating interpersonal functioning. The best-known of their methods is the T-group, with T standing for "training" (not "therapy") as in "human relations training group" or "interpersonal sensitivity training group." We will consider the T-group further in the next section, for it is the ancestor of the many forms of encounter and growth groups which exist today.

Kurt Lewin was a German psychologist who emigrated to the United States after the rise of Hitler. He was dedicated to the simultaneous advancement of human welfare and psychological science in part through "action research" which seeks to derive general psychological principles in the course of efforts to alter and improve human behavior. Hence, he was responsive to the request of the director of the Connecticut Interracial Commission in 1946 to help train leaders to work with intergroup tensions. That June he organized a workshop for community leaders (businessmen, educators, labor leaders). The training groups were led by Leland Bradford, Kenneth Benne, and Ronald Lippitt, an educator, philosopher, and social psychologist, respectively, while Lewin and a group of social psychologists studied the process and accomplishments of the conference. Lewin died that year, but Bradford, Benne, and Lippitt together with colleagues from Lewin's Center for Group Dynamics at MIT carried the work forward. The following summer a more extensive program was run in a small school in Bethel, Maine, for people in responsible roles seeking greater knowledge of group process and heightened human-relations skills. Subsequent conferences have been held there every year since. By 1950, the National Training Laboratory (NTL) was officially formed, and its work quickly extended over the entire country. Many thousands of people, in time including many clinicians, have been delegates to the NTL conferences at Bethel and elsewhere. Though other procedures evolved, the T-group was the dominant function in the NTL programs. Theory and research on group dynamics proceeded apace at the MIT center and, after its move, at the University of Michigan. The early history of NTL and the development of group dynamics has been chronicled by Marrow (1967), Bradford (1967), Bradford, Gibb, and Benne (1964), and Back (1972).

However, despite the vitality of the NTL movement and the vigorous spread of T-group activities, there was relatively little impact on clinical group therapy. Group therapists knew relatively little about T-group methods or the growing field of group-dynamics theory, with a few exceptions (e.g., Bach, 1954). On their part, NTL psychologists were quick to point out that their methods were not intended to root out individual emotional problems, though even in the 1950s some described their work as "group therapy for normals." Group dynamics principles were little known to therapeutic workers. What was most visible to the professional and lay public was the widespread growth of "sensitivity training" in nonclinical settings, with groups run by nonclinical leaders, who indeed sometimes preferred the title "facilitator" to express their egalitarian ideology.

In time, the situation shifted in two respects. On the one hand, some NTL people and those under their influence saw their role as more therapeutic, though for the essentially healthy rather than the sick, and the focus moved from task-oriented personal and organizational effectiveness to personal well-being. On the other hand, many students of group therapy exposed themselves to the science of group dynamics and to T-group methods, and built these concepts into their thinking about group therapy. Thus, modern systems of group therapy such as those of Whitaker and Lieberman (1964) and Yalom (1975) blend the clinical and group dynamic traditions to good advantage.

Models of Group Therapy

In general terms we can distinguish forms of group therapy which focus on the individual patients from those which focus on the group process. On the one hand, there are those methods which are in effect adaptations of individual therapy; group therapy is then essentially multiple-individual therapy. At the other extreme are methods which attempt to identify, develop and use forces indigenous to groups to facilitate treatment. Parloff (1968) describes this spectrum in terms of approaches which are (1) intrapersonalist, (2) transactionalist (or interpersonalist), and (3) integralist.

Intrapersonalist. Intrapersonalist therapists working in the psychoanalytic mode may encourage association, delve into personal histories, and encourage and interpret transference reactions between individual patients and the therapist. However, individual-centered group therapy can exist as well within a client-centered or behavioral framework; some behavior therapists, for example, gather groups of individuals with common phobic problems into group desensitization procedures.

Transactionalist. Transactionalists tend to focus more on interpersonal relationships between dyads or subgroups. Such therapists, which would include positions as diverse as those of J. D. Frank (1973), Berne (1966), and Bach (1957), realize the importance of the group as a source of stimuli for the individual to reveal his unique ways of relating and responding to a variety of other people. The interrelations among patients as well as those between each member and the therapist are viewed as having therapeutic potential. Thus, for example, they stress the importance of cohesiveness—the attractiveness of being a group member—as a factor in altering individual behavior. Most group therapists fall within this broad class.

Integralist. Integralist therapies place major emphasis on the group process as such. They hold that the study of the group as a social entity reveals in its full complexity the functioning of each of its members. The group as a unit acts in ways which give the individual experiences which differ in degree and perhaps in kind from those which operate in the dyad. In their view, a person's problem may lie in his inability to mesh with others in effective solving of group problems. In treating the group as a unity, integralists sometimes ascribe to it qualities of an individual, transforming it into a superperson, as it were. Central to the thinking of many integralistic therapists is the work of Bion (1959), developed at the Tavistock Clinic in England. Though anchored in psychoanalysis, Bion and his followers reject the distinction between individual and group dynamics, seeing them as essentially two faces of the same process. Bion's ideas of therapy have been developed by Ezriel (1950) and Sutherland (1952) in England; they have greatly influenced the position of Whitaker and Lieberman (1964), who probably have the most decisively group-centered approach in the United States. Overall, the field of group psychotherapy seems to be moving more toward a group-oriented, and certainly away from an individual-oriented, philosophy.

The Process of Group Therapy

Putting these theoretical positions aside for the moment, let us look at what happens in group therapy as it is commonly practiced. In general, this description will be more in line with a transactionalistic than either an intrapersonalistic or a thoroughgoing integralistic approach.

FORMAL ARRANGEMENTS

Groups typically consist of six to ten participants, with eight being an optimal number in the mind of many group therapists. Sessions are usually one and one-half to two hours long, often scheduled in evenings, and meetings may be held once or twice weekly. Participants are seated in an open circle, in a living-room-like setting, so that all members can see each other and the leader equally well. Though many group therapists work alone, having a co-therapist is not unusual. This may be a younger clinician collaborating with a senior clinician while learning his craft, or a man-woman team so as to be more responsive of the particular concerns of each sex or to constitute a familylike group structure. Male-female cotherapists are also used where the focus is on marital problems, as in couples group therapy. Groups may either be closed, continuing with only those who started initially, or open, admitting new members as they become available.

COMPOSITION OF THE GROUP

Many clinicians accept all but a few patients to group therapy, often with minimal preassessment. Others, however, prefer to see each candidate individually and decide in each case if group treatment is the method of choice. Traditionally, clinicians agree that certain classes of patients are less fit for outpatient-group meetings; these include the brain-damaged, extremely narcissistic or paranoid, sociopathic, hypochondriacal or suicidal, or the grossly psychotic. Such patients are unable to accept the tasks and functions of the group and may be continuing sources of disruption; in time they may become scapegoated deviants by the others. In more general terms, those who are painfully shy or private people may be overwhelmed by the group and retreat from it into quiet isolation or by leaving the group; yet many such people, who cannot stand the intensity of individual therapy, may fare quite well in groups if the procedure is such that their boundaries can be respected for long periods. The question of whether group therapy works better with homogeneous groups—in age, sex, cultural background, or clinical condition—or heterogeneous ones remains an open and argued issue. The more homogeneous the group the more likely are they to focus on their common quality, whether women's problems in an all female group, racial issues in an all black group, or educational problems if all are students. Indeed, homogeneous groups are often formed precisely to work in the area of their common concern. However, if the effort is to maximize the exploration and resolution of each individual's human problems, then too much homogeneity can limit the group's effectiveness.

In actuality, in ordinary clinical practice, it is rarely possible to constitute very homogeneous groups. As patients become available while a group is being formed, there obviously has to be an oldest and a youngest member, a most and least educated, a most and least affluent, people of differing occupations, life styles and kind and degree of distress; on the whole, this is to the good, for it opens each person to the range of experiences and perspectives of the others. In the usual case, the therapist's problem is less in selecting suitable members than in sometimes keeping out the extreme patient who might predictably disrupt the group process or be overwhelmed by it. In the last analysis, the "good group" is the one that crystalizes into a working unit, with reasonable cohesiveness among the members, but this often cannot be predicted in advance. Whether the group works well or not depends, in fair measure, on the group atmosphere and norms engendered by the therapist, as much or more than on the prior characteristics of the patients.

THE ROLE OF THE THERAPIST

Group therapists are as distinctive in their styles and different in their conceptual systems as are individual psychotherapists, but in one important respect they all function alike compared to their colleagues in one-to-one therapy. "In the individual format the therapist functions as the sole and direct agent of change; in the group therapeutic format he functions far more indirectly. The curative factors in group therapy are primarily mediated not by the therapist but by the other members, who provide the acceptance and support, the hope, the experience of universality, the opportunities for altruistic behavior, and the interpersonal feedback, testing, and learning. It is the therapist's task to help the group develop into a cohesive unit with an atmosphere maximally conducive to the operation of these curative factors" (Yalom, 1975, p. 107).

The role of the therapist, particularly initially, focuses on creating, building, and maintaining the group culture. As strangers to each other, the members look to the leader for defining the basic rules of therapy. He, in turn, lays down by example as well as precept the basic principles by which the group is to function, though these may change over time as a group culture and norms emerge. The therapist must be alert to potentially disruptive factors and be prepared to intervene as necessary. A group process can be threatened by continued absences or lateness, by clique formations or scapegoating, and it is the therapist's task to minimize them.

Group norms ("Everyone has a chance to say his piece," "All persons' problems are important," "We can be critical but not destructive of each other," etc.) arise in time largely by the agreement of all participants, but the therapist has the special task of guiding the group toward more therapeutic norms. Norms form relatively early in group life and are notably difficult to change later on.

Depending on his concepts and style, the leader can function directively or more nondirectively. Some clearly remain the center of the group process, with communication flowing from each member up and back to the therapist. He asks and answers questions, may occasionally ask other members to comment on a particular person's concerns, but he tends to discourage free interchanges among the members themselves. At points, he may openly advise or lecture individuals or the entire group. By contrast, other therapists function in more discreet and egalitarian ways, much of the time being one among many participants in the group discussions. They allow and encourage all members to participate, commenting on each other's concerns as well as their own. Overall, such therapists are more in the role of participant-observer than of an authority-teaching-novices. Rarely, however, is the leader "just another participant" for he continues to hold responsibility for steering the group process and intervening interpretatively to clarify both what is going on in individual lives and what is happening in the group in the given moment. As in individual therapy, the group therapist must be authoritative without being authoritarian, centrally involved without manipulating the members, being expert without playing the expert.

The therapist's comments, indeed those of the members themselves, can either focus more on individual needs and problems or more on the here-and-now transactions of the group. In actuality, the focus often shifts from moment to moment, as illustrated in the following exchange:

> Joe: My wife never seems to understand what's bothering me. She seems to be hearing something different than what I'm meaning to say.
>
> Mike: Well, in a way, I understand. Sometimes I have difficulty understanding you too, and I'm not married to you. You sometimes make confusing and kind of vague statements.
>
> Roger: (*to group*): I don't think we're being fair to Joe. I've noticed that we're much too ready to jump on each other and tell people what's wrong with them. Maybe Joe's wife doesn't want to understand him; maybe she's got her hangups and can't hear what's clear enough.
>
> Therapist: It would be wrong if we were just putting each other down, but I don't feel that that's happening here. If Mike, who isn't so emotionally involved, feels that he also has some difficulty understanding Joe, maybe Joe has some problem in communicating. Do you think there's any sense in Mike's comment, Joe?

As a general rule, an issue or problem that seems crucial for the existence or continued functioning of the group takes precedence over one that is relevant only to a personal or interpersonal relation. Hence, if the therapist felt that Roger's concerns were widely shared and that an antitherapeutic atmosphere, hypercritical and hostile, was arising, then he should have directed attention to that issue and put aside, for the moment at least, Joe's particular problem in communicating with his wife.

Even when focusing on particular personal behavior or problems, these can be viewed in terms of current or recent behavior in the group. Unlike individual therapy where the therapist must depend largely on the patient's account of his feelings and experiences, as he now recalls and conceives them, the group therapist directly observes the patient's social behavior in the group. If indeed Joe's thinking and speech are muddled enough to confuse Mike, this is known to the therapist who can then relate this fact to Joe's belief that his wife is maliciously misunderstanding him. Consequently, group therapy is often useful for people who tend to externalize or deny their problems. If they accept little responsibility for their troubles, perhaps seeing them as burdens of an unkind world, the individual therapist has difficulty in confronting the problem. In the group, however, such evasion is more difficult, for there is the immediate evidence of discrepancy between the patient's actual and fantasied behavior. Though related to external and past events, meaning is given through analysis in terms of the here-and-now processes of group therapy.

In group therapy, interpretive comments are not the exclusive prerogative of the therapist. By his example, the therapist inculcates in the group an inquiring concern with the how and why of people's actions and a positive valuation of self-knowledge. In time, participants look more closely at themselves and at each other, including the therapist. The therapist cannot avoid, nor should he, having his behaviors questioned. Group therapy requires a high order of personal honesty, willingness to admit fallibility, to openly express affects, and to share experience. The aloof, constrained, or defensive person fares poorly as a group therapist though he might be able to function somewhat better as an individual therapist. To work with groups, one has to be a real and distinct person.

For this reason, among others, transference reactions are much less common in group therapy and, except in the minds of a small group of psychoanalytic group workers, not of central importance in the therapy process. It is surely true that group members can invest the therapist with extraordinary powers, curry his favor, and seek to be the favorite child. Individuals will try to sit close to the leader, address all their comments to him, watch intently for signs of approval or disapproval, linger after meetings, or otherwise seek personal or favored contact with him. Similarly, such reactions may occur between members. As in any emotionally charged relation between people already distressed and uncertain of themselves, there is clearly the possibility of distorted perceptions and unreasonable attributions. As these arise, they must be dealt with by the therapist, particularly as they can endanger the group process. However, the conditions of group therapy make transference reactions less likely than in individual therapy, nor do most group therapists feel that it is necessary to cultivate and analyze them in order to make therapeutic gains. What is therapeutic about group psychotherapy is in fair measure a product of the unique conditions of group life.

The Group as a Vehicle for Change

As a person joins a therapy group he enters a microsociety essentially different from those he knows in his outside life. Fellow members also suffer psychological problems and they have come together to alleviate them. Instead of feeling isolated and shamed in the larger society of apparently well-functioning and happy people, the patient comes to realize vividly that others, at least his fellows in the group, share his inadequacies, self-doubts, and anxieties, which indeed for some are even more disabling. Sometimes months in individual therapy do not reduce a patient's sense of being uniquely stricken as much as a few sessions hearing others describe their lives with feelings as poignant as his own. He can express shamefully hidden feelings, with less fear of ridicule, as he discovers that others hold similar feelings. At the first level, the patient comes to realize that he is not alone in his suffering; indeed, he comes to appreciate the universality of emotional distress. His particular problems can now be viewed in some perspective and, equally important, hope for their relief is generated. Trust and hope, of importance in any therapeutic endeavor, is facilitated in the group by the visible evidence of others striving to improve their own lot; in the first instance by seeking therapeutic help. Later on, as the group becomes more cohesive and develops some sense of common purpose, the accomplishments of any member in mastering his problems are a source of encouragement and support for all. The group thus acts to reduce isolation and to engender hope in its members.

Of considerable importance in understanding the functioning of any group, whether therapeutic or of other sort, is the factor of group cohesiveness. By cohesiveness is meant the sense of solidarity or we-feeling which binds a group together. Cohesiveness has been extensively studied in the literature of group dynamics and group therapy. It has been defined broadly as "the resultant of all forces acting on all members to remain in the group" (D. Cartwright and Zander, 1962, p. 74) or more simply as "the attractiveness of a group for its members" (J. D. Frank, 1957). It has been found that people in cohesive groups (1) are more productive; (2) are more secure; (3) are more open to influence by other group members; (4) are more likely to attempt to influence other members; (5) adhere more closely to group norms; (6) value more and maintain membership longer, and (7) are freer to express hostility, even against the leader (for reviews of this extensive literature, see Yalom and Rand, 1966; A. P. Goldstein, Heller, and Sechrest, 1966; Bednar and Lawlis, 1971). Illustrative of the research in this area is a laboratory study by Pepitone and Reichling (1955). High- and low-cohesion groups of randomly selected college students were formed by informing half of the subjects that they had been specially selected as being particularly compatible; the remaining half were given to understand that they were not well matched and might have difficulty working together. While waiting for the main experiment to begin, each of the groups was insulted and frustrated by a confederate. After he left, the members' discussions in the various groups showed that cohesive groups were significantly better able to express, more intensely and directly, hostility toward the authority figure.

Yalom (1975) proposes the hypothesis that cohesiveness in group therapy is the analogue of "relationship" in individual therapy and that it is one of the primary curative factors. It is a broader concept for it includes not only the relation between individual patients and the therapist, but also the relation of patients to each other and to the group as a whole. Both group therapists and their patients importantly mention cohesiveness when asked to identify factors which matter most in the group process. Thus, when one successful patient looked back over two and a half years of group therapy, he recalled: "The most important thing in it was just having a group there, people that I could talk to, that wouldn't walk out on me. There was so much caring and hating and loving in the group and I was a part of it. I'm better now and have my own life, but it's sad to think that the group's not there any more" (Yalom, 1975, p. 48).

In and of itself, cohesiveness is not a therapeutic factor but it is a necessary precondition for effective therapy. In the cohesive group, individuals are more committed and dedicated to the group tasks. They attend more regularly, adhere to the norms, and concentrate on the work of the group. Hence, they are more ready to reveal and test feelings in the group. Of particular importance is the fact that the group becomes more vital in defining the person's self-esteem. One's feeling of worth, in general, involves the reflected appraisals of others. Not uncommonly, other group members think better of the patient than he does of himself; altruistic and supportive efforts commonly occur in more cohesive groups. The more cohesive the group the more it becomes the standard by which the individual judges himself. As he values the opinions of the group, the more he wants to change so as to be more respected in their eyes. Thus, in more cohesive groups, there is greater opportunity for feelings to be more freely expressed and explored and for social influence to occur. An atmosphere of mutual help and support evolves in which members are free to criticize inadequacy and equally free to applaud change.

Another therapeutic factor of considerable import lies in the fact that the group provides a unique environment for interpersonal learning. Corrective emotional experiences occur as the patient is reexposed to emotional situations which he could not handle in the past but can now under more managable conditions. For example, in a study by J. D. Frank and Ascher (1951) and in findings reported by Yalom (1975), patients were asked to recall a critical incident which had occurred during therapy. Most commonly, the reported incident involved a sudden expression of anger or hatred toward another group member. In every case, however, disaster did not occur, but instead communication continued and the relation was maintained, perhaps strengthened. The patient thus experienced a sense of freedom from inner restraints and simultaneously greater capacity to explore interpersonal relations more deeply and freely. In the process, he came to realize something of the irrational nature of his feelings and the defenses against their expression.

In the group, distortions and self-deceits become vividly apparent, for the therapist and other group members have immediately before them the disparities between the patient's beliefs and his acts. The patient not only describes his characteristic feelings and ways of relating to people but he lives them out in the group. Since our self-concepts and our actions are rarely in accord, and even less so in the neurotic individual, opportunity to recognize and analyze our interpersonal distortions is provided by the group. Thus, group therapy allows for interpersonal learning and psychological health, Yalom notes, as conceived by Harry Stack Sullivan. "One achieves mental health to the extent that one becomes aware of one's interpersonal relationships" (Sullivan, 1947, p. 207). Cure, Sullivan also noted, involves ". . . expanding of the self to such final effect that the patient as known to himself is much the same person as the patient behaving to others" (Sullivan, 1947, p. 237).

Learning in more concrete ways also goes on in group therapy. Some therapists give didactic instruction about personality mechanism, mental health and illness, and advice and guidance concerning life problems, particularly to groups of hospitalized patients or in working with disadvantaged clients. Other patients as well share in imparting information from their own experience, instructing each other in matters as diverse as applying for school, getting a job, methods of contraception, or child care, among numerous others. Not only is specific knowledge transmitted and learned in the group, but more subtle learning takes place through identification and imitation. As in individual therapy, the pipe-smoking therapist may spawn pipe-smoking patients, but in group therapy the number and variety of exemplars is necessarily larger. As one patient successfully manages a life crisis, others learn something of the techniques involved and themselves can develop a sense of competence and hopefulness as to their own future. Imitating the behavior of others may have direct therapeutic effects, as Bandura (1971) has shown. It may seem paradoxical, but imitation can as well foster individuality by giving a person a sense of the variety of possible behaviors and helping to unseat him from fixed modes of thinking and behaving. By trying on the personalities and behaviors of others, we can find what best fits our needs.

An Episode in Group Therapy

The following excerpt is taken from a psychoanalytic therapy group which had been in progress for about a year at the time of this first taperecorded session (Durkin, 1964). Of the group of three men and two women, only four talked in this episode. These are briefly described below:

> Jo's self-assured cool and competent exterior defends against a fear of aggression, her own and that of older women against her. She uses sex as a way of gaining love but is unconsciously driven to make men reject her.
>
> Vi is a sweet, sad, submissive young girl whose friends tend to be strays, whose relationships with men tend to be masochistic, and who is just beginning to be more self-assertive and to accept that good things can happen to her.
>
> Ed is handsome and aggressive. His arrogance defends against his anger at a depriving mother.
>
> Hy is very moral, proper, and ambivalent. His aggressive feelings hide an urge to submit.

The passage has been edited somewhat, mainly to decrease redundancy. The italicized comments in parentheses are Helen Durkin's interpretations of the motives and feelings of the participants, made as asides to the reader not to the participants at the time.

As the episode opens the group is talking about Jo's relation to her boyfriend.

Jo: I'm not very—not passionately drawn to him. I haven't had much to do with him physically. I wasn't initially attracted to him sexually. You know—but it's just the idea that someone is paying attention to me. You know, even if it isn't a good attention, if it isn't a whole thing . . . I suppose I feel something is better than nothing.

Ed: Let's you and me do something instead. (*Again his impulsivity brings the focus to the immediate concrete experience.*)

Jo: From the frying pan into the same (*laughs*). I'm trying to find out why I do these foolish things!

Th: What are you doing with this, Ed? (*Trying to make Ed aware of his resistance here. He wants to play rather than work.*)

Ed: Oh, I don't know (*sighs*). I don't know.

Ed: —In a sense I am—so I can't. I'm not thinking—I mean, I'm sort of watching myself or . . . (*He becomes anxious when he can't go into action.*)

Jo: Well, you said you were very interested in why you do this kind of thing to girls, but—I mean, here you came in and started with the social business and with the physical play. Maybe something else is really on your mind. (*She refers to his having said he turns to sex when he's anxious.*)

Ed: (*Avoids facing his anxiety by acting out verbally*) Well physically often . . . and the idea of your . . . like every time when we leave here and you're going off to your place. . . . Your place would be my escape. And somehow you're alone . . . and I would love to talk intimately with you. It's like goofing off in . . . somewhere in my past or something . . . so I could just feel comfortable for uh . . . for a while . . . like I know it wouldn't have any lasting significance or anything like that. I mean realistically it's impossible. (*He squirms in his seat and gets red.*)

Th: What would you do? For example? (*Trying to get Ed to continue his fantasy. Once a fantasy is fully conscious it tends to lose dynamic force.*)

Ed: What would I do? Well I would . . . (*sighs*) I would go along, you know, to your house, we'd probably stop and have a drink and talk . . . and it would be like the feeling of uh—like rapport, something sympathetic or hungry, going back and forth would be established. And . . . it would be compulsive on my part that—I sleep with you. I mean like we would go and cook dinner and talk all during the cooking—you know, personal things . . . and . . . we'll make love . . . (*sighs*) probably—probably—you know—right after dinner. (*Laughs.*)

(*Group laughs, out of anxiety.*)

Ed: Here we're talking instead of acting.

Th: And you find it so hard to think about things before doing them?

Ed: Yeah, it's difficult sometimes. I mean, you ask me to talk about what I would do. It's hard for me to say what we would do because . . . because—I just do things—I don't talk or think too much about it. I do things compulsively. I mean, I would have to sleep with you (*to Jo*) . . . but here I can't. If I did, I don't think I'd be too aware of you as a person though I would be—terribly aware of you at a purely physical level. (*Here we see a deepening of insight in Ed to which Jo responds. Shortly after this session Ed began to see Jo as a real person. He said he had never had a woman he really talked to before—except me*).

Jo: Yeah (*to herself*). It makes me very sad when Ed talks because this is the kind of thing I have been accepting from men as real feeling. You know, I've been hoping that it's real . . . and of course it isn't . . . (*Getting to the meaning of this behavior helps her recognize the unconscious impulses that she has thought of as realistic before.*)

Ed: It's a feeling, but it's not a feeling which could give you any—well, it's a kind of feeling, but it's not a kind of feeling you can live with.

Jo: Yeah. Well, it's not the kind of feeling that I want. I want to think that men would be in love with me, and would want me permanently and yet I take this kind of thing, you know, hoping that, this was it. But—maybe—it's a good way of not getting it. (*All looked very serious. Their voices are low but intense.*)

Vi: How can you really tell the difference? In the beginning of a relationship?

Jo: Well, I think with somebody like Ed or anybody who acts out a lot, very fast you can . . . you know, begin to suspect that there is something fishy about it because they don't know you. You know, this is the "throwing yourself into it" thing. The girl doesn't mean anything. It could be any girl.

Ed: Yeah, then you can realize you are a symbol for something which isn't quite there or is not quite you.

Jo: Well, I start to carry on before it occurs to me, you know. . . .

Ed: Yeah?

Jo: That it isn't the man.

Ed: Well, then you are just as unaware of me as I am of you. Under that circumstance . . . you are using me! (*He has thought of himself as being aggressive with women. He is just beginning to learn that he is often passively exploited by his counterpart.*)

Jo: (*Laughed*) Yeah.

Th: This is something neither of you usually think of. (*Underlining their growing insight.*)

Ed: About her being unaware of the "me"? In men?

Th: Yes. The fact that she is doing it just as much as the men are doing it.

Jo: Well, it's hard for me to make myself realize that—because it means that I'm not so nice. (*Jo used a good deal of "denial" to preserve her self-image and here began to understand why.*)

Ed: Nice-schmice!

Hy: So where then does the reality begin? (*Hy's ambivalence showed. Made anxious by this sexual stimulation he tried to put us on an intellectual level. He also wants to get into this discussion and does so in the only way he knows.*)

Th: I have a feeling you are all very curious, yet upset, at hearing Ed and Jo talk like this.

Hy: I gather that everyone must be doing something . . . well, playing some sort of role when he does—uh—put his best foot forward toward a young lady—or when a girl does the same sort of thing. So then it's difficult to say just what is reality. Actually I should imagine that this is reality—the fact that people are uncertain of each other and that they don't know what the other person is thinking. Well, that seems to be the reality to me. I don't know what the other thing is.

Vi: I can see where I have a tendency to pretend. I just like the idea of love so much that I force it on that person—even when it isn't there.

Hy: How?

Vi: Well, I mean if I would feel sexually attracted to a man, even if I honestly think—realize—that he hasn't got the real thing—to make me like him . . . I just don't let myself see it . . . or I say it isn't important or it will come, or something.

Th: You're idealizing it? Because plain sex seems wrong to you?

Vi: Yes—So I feel if the sexual part of it is there I feel that the rest of it has to be there as an excuse maybe for feeling that way or . . .

Hy: That sounds a little unrealistic. (*Hy was very tense. He seemed to be warding off sexual stimulation by the group, yet wanting to know and also to reveal his own problems.*)

(*Jo laughs.*)

Ed: Oh, but this is the way she is.

Vi: Just because I want—like I want to be in love so much and I want someone to love me, I do that. And I was thinking that even with J. (*the former sadistic boy friend*) that happened where all these horrible things—I've—I mean I knew that they were happening, but I didn't let myself know that they were so horrible, but they were. Because then I wouldn't be able to—to love him any more, if I recognized them. Or if I could have seen that he really didn't love me (*Growing insight for Vi. There was a silence, full of tension. Hy looked at the therapist.*)

(*After a few minutes:*)

Th: Well—Hy—what is it—what are you feeling? (*He looks upset, angry.*)

Hy: Uh—that's a very nice dress you're wearing (*reaction formation*).

Th: Thank you—but you seem upset.

Hy: Well—I was sort of curious as to when you were going to make some sort of comment. (*He was the spokesman for the "observers" who were puzzled and wanted an answer to their infantile curiosity from me.*)

Th: For instance?

Hy: Well—in general. The fact that our conversation of the last—well—fifteen minutes—(*Hy's tension has been mounting during the talk about sex. Besides being curious, he has also been wanting to talk himself, yet trying to ward off his unacceptable feelings.*)

Th: You feel I should have helped out somehow?

Hy: I was just looking at you, expecting you to say something. (*Hy was probably right. I may have been too much involved with the content of the discussion to sense that the "observers" were not only curious but angry with me for letting it go on. At any rate, I was put off by Hy's use of "what is reality," so that I didn't recognize his resistance. Ordinarily I would have said, "You must be disappointed in me." There are a few minutes of silence. Since I still do not deal with Hy's angry resistance, the whole group becomes rather anxious. They quickly attach it to the presence of the recorder and as they talk about it their feelings about me come through again.*)

Al: There's going to be a whole blank spot on that record there.

Jo: I was thinking of that too.

(*The whole group laughs nervously.*)

Ed: What are you going to do with the record? Erase it or keep it and play it back to us?

Th: What do you imagine I might do? (Durkin, 1964, pp. 224–229).

When Should Individual Therapy Be Used and When Group?

There are no simple guidelines for recommending group over individual therapy or vice versa. Research is minimal and in the main equivocal (Bednar and Lawlis, 1971). In general, the motivation, psychological-mindedness, ability to relate, and other qualities which suit a person for individual therapy are as valuable in group treatment. Many patients who lack the motivation for self-exploration may be moved toward therapeutic change under group influences but it is also true that the skillful individual therapist, giving his full attention to an individual's resistances, may be of greater help to a person who might simply withdraw and be unaffected by group process. The very private or sensitive person, or at another extreme, the more guarded or resistive patient probably does better with an individual therapist. The potentially disruptive patient should generally be kept out of groups; though individual therapy is not much more likely to be helpful, at least he will not be blocking the growth of others.

Group methods are widely used with hospitalized psychotic patients, although for the most severely disturbed patients individual therapy may be necessary. With neurotics, patients with character disorders and lesser problems of living, both group and individual sessions are sometimes recommended, if facilities are available. Each form of therapy has its advantages and, in conjunction, these can complement each other. Where both are used at once, therapy should necessarily involve two different clinicians. Otherwise, the sense of intimacy with the therapist and of holding shared secrets would be disruptive of the group process.

Group methods are coming to be increasingly valued by clinicians. But individual psychotherapy has its unique advantages and is not likely to be replaced by group methods. The group cannot provide the security, intense concentration, and flexibility to follow the patient's lead into deep probing of his unique problems. Altering long-standing defenses and overcoming barriers to personality growth often require the concerted and undivided attention of the individual therapist. Indeed, desired change in many cases may not only not require the group environment, it may be blocked by the presence of other patients. It is often a matter of chance whether a patient is treated in one or another mode; not infrequently, one form of therapy is sought to extend the work of the other. With greater knowledge and research we should be better able to decide when to recommend individual and when group psychotherapy, and when the two might best be combined.

The Therapeutic Milieu

Group methods have come into increasing prominence in the movement for making psychiatric hospitals less custodial and more therapeutic institutions. A large literature has grown in recent years attesting to the fact that mental hospitals, conceived as social systems, can be so structured that all inmates (including staff) can to some degree benefit from membership in it (e.g., M. Jones, 1953; Stanton and Schwartz, 1954; Greenblatt, Levinson, and Williams, 1957; von Mering and King, 1957; Fairweather, 1964; Fairweather et al., 1970; Rossi and Filstead, 1973).

Early moves in this direction included occupational therapy programs that attempted to provide meaningful work for patients, develop skills, and regain interest in the social environment. Similarly, dances, concerts, classes of various sorts, recreation and team sports were programmed so that patients could interact and collaborate in activities that mimicked those of outside life. A more ambitious plan has involved patients in participation in the governance of the hospital. Regular "town meetings" are scheduled or patients elect representatives to work with hospital administrators. In some cases, patients take on extensive responsibilities for organizing and managing recreational and social programs, planning menus and supervising food service, raising money for special equipment and programs, assisting in hospital research and sometimes in therapeutic programs, and orienting new patients to hospital life (e.g., Greenblatt et al., 1957). In addition to formal group therapy meetings, many hospitals now have a variety of patient-led groups concerned as much with hospital management as with personal problems. By becoming vitally involved in these matters patients cease being the dependent wards; their competence, dignity, and morale visibly increase. They take pride in their setting, and their self-esteem grows.

Instituting such programs is never easy. Aside from financial and administrative problems, the move toward greater involvement of patients in the life of their institution requires profound changes in staff thinking. The therapeutic milieu often challenges the preconceptions and status of staff at all levels, and most particularly the attendants, nurses, and other workers most directly in contact with the patients. To many, the maintenance of clean quiet wards of docile patients is too precious to run the risk of noisier if more therapeutic units. Accepting their charges as potentially responsible people and foregoing some of their authority is threatening, particularly since patients can mismanage things, though learning in the process. The problem is not unlike the parent who knows the child should take on increasing responsibility but knows too that he, the parent, is more competent to do the task.

As part of the move toward a more therapeutic environment, lower-level staff have been given more significant roles in the hospital. Aides and attendants outnumber doctors and nurses greatly and in the past often felt little involved in the therapeutic process. Now attendants are often given explicit training so that they can understand the nature of mental illnesses and realize their importance and potential impact on the patients. Attendants often participate with patients as coparticipants or leaders in group discussions. In important respects, some of the therapeutic effects of the "moral treatment" which characterized the smaller and more homogeneous hospitals of colonial times is being recovered.

Projects designed to develop therapeutic environments along social psychological lines (e.g., von Mering and King, 1957; Fairweather, 1964) have been extended to patients in halfway houses and similar settings (Fairweather et al., 1970; Raush and Raush, 1968). Former patients, usually but not necessarily with professional intervention, manage the economic and social affairs of these houses, provide support and encouragement for each other as they venture out into the larger society, and sometimes run small businesses which can help support them.

A parallel development has emerged in the work of self-help groups, particularly of alcoholics and drug abusers. Some are outside of the domain of mental health services, though others collaborate with community mental health agencies and professionals. Synanon is a particularly interesting case of an institution run entirely by former drug addicts which provides a home and a new way of life for other addicts. Within their philosophy, Synanon workers have set up a demanding culture. Applicants must show great motivation to enter and be prepared to humble themselves to group demands and rules. They are given menial jobs and rise slowly, only as they conform to the group's ideals. Through "games," members are harshly confronted with their own shortcomings and reduced in their self-esteem until they fully internalize the self-concept given them by the microsociety. Those who persist frequently stay off drugs entirely and find a new and useful life within Synanon.

The methods of Alcoholics Anonymous are less extreme nor is it as inclusive a society. It does not involve living together. However, members meet regularly, recommitting themselves constantly to helping others and to the philosophy of the movement. This is expressed in part in their "serenity prayer"—"God grant us the serenity to accept the things we cannot change, courage to change the things we can, and wisdom to know the difference." New members are coupled with oldtimers to maintain their resolve to stay off alcohol. If anyone feels the urge to drink, he can call instantly for help and squads of members stand ready to give emergency help and support. Along with the religious flavor, a major theme in Alcoholics Anonymous is that one saves oneself through helping others.

Group-centered approaches of the sort noted briefly here, both within and outside of official mental health services, are of growing importance though their full potential has hardly been realized. Clinicians need to understand the many ways in which altering the social environment can reduce psychological problems, both in and out of clinical settings. Through research, program development, and efforts to utilize group psychological techniques further, considerable contribution can be made to the well-being of large numbers of individuals in distress.

ENCOUNTER GROUPS: GROUP THERAPY FOR NORMALS

Group Therapy, Sensitivity Training, and Encounter Groups

During the 1960s an unprecedented wave of enthusiasm developed for small-group encounters among people in many walks of life. By now numerous Americans have participated in "growth centers" or joined with others in churches, schools, business offices, or homes, for purposes as diverse as extending political awareness, sharpening human relations skills, expanding personal growth, losing weight, stopping smoking, solving organizational problems, or reducing racial tensions. Sometimes viewed as entertainment, an experience in joy or a way of "turning on," more generally such groups aim at personal change—new attitudes or values, greater satisfaction or tranquility, or a new life style.

Some have hailed the current encounter movement as forerunner of a new and liberated consciousness, providng everyman with a readily available route to self-fulfillment in a dehumanizing society. Others have condemned it as a cheap excuse for sensate pleasure, less cure than symptom of a sick society, a dangerous renunciation of rationality, and at the extreme, a Communist plot to undermine the American moral fiber. But, at the same time, increasing numbers of people enter encounter groups of all forms and descriptions. By the end of the 1960s, there were seventy-five growth centers in the United States; Esalen, the oldest and best established, had over 50,000 participants in its programs in 1969, and 200 groups could be counted in the small community of Palo Alto, California (Yalom, 1975). Multiply and update these figures and you have an idea of the scope of the encounter movement.

The encounter movement developed largely outside of traditional help-giving institutions. Participants are not thought of as "patients" nor do they receive "therapy," though the goals of behavior change, increased self-awareness and personal effectiveness often parallel those of group therapy, as do the change-producing group processes involved. The strongly egalitarian and anti-intellectual flavor of the movement represents in part a reaction against established forms of help-giving and the dominance of professional help-givers. Though new in its present form, the encounter movement is heir to the age-old practice of gathering people in small groups to solve collectively their individual and communal problems and to seek a fuller and better life. Religious and spiritual healers have always depended on group processes to inspire faith, sustain hope, increase morale and solidarity, and to give emotional and spiritual support to sufferers from physical and psychological ills. Nor, as we have seen, are these processes insignificant in modern group therapy. The encounter movement represents, from one vantage point, the secularization and popularization of help-giving through group interaction, released from both religious and professional control.

Despite manifest differences, encounter groups have a number of qualities in common. They provide intensive, high-contact, though often short-lived, group experience. Focus is on face-to-face interaction in groups ranging from six to twenty members. Encouraged are self-disclosure, openness, honesty, interpersonal feedback and confrontation, and strong affective expression. Experiencing rather than talking about experience is valued. The here-and-now is stressed; past and outside experiences minimized. Compared to group therapy, there is less structure and sessions span a shorter period of time. Sessions typically involve more nonverbal activities, games or structured exercises (of the sort used in Gestalt therapy), and bodily contact. Members and leader are closer in status than in traditional group therapy; often group leaders have no formal professional training but are themselves alumni of encounter groups who with some further training take on the task of leading others in encounter activities. But whether a trained professional or not, the encounter leader sees himself as more a coequal participant than a technical expert in the group process.

A commonly made distinction is that encounter groups strive to increase man's positive potential while therapy groups aim to reduce his emotional difficulties. The distinction between the healthy-seeking-greater-health, and the sick-seeking-cure, is at best artificial. Clients of both therapy and encounter suffer the loneliness, confusion, and alienation which is an endemic part of the existential malady of our times, and both want growth as much as cure. Recent findings of a study in California show that encounter and therapy groups have a largely overlapping clientele, i.e. people who seek potential-expanding programs and who in other times have often been patients in psychotherapy (Lieberman, personal communication). With increasing psychological-mindedness, at least in a large part of the urban, educated population, therapy is often sought for existential problems; activities of the human potential movement serve these same needs. Whether one goes into psychotherapy or into an encounter group may depend on chance; what goes on in the two settings may be less different than textbook descriptions suggest.

It is true of course that more seriously disabled patients in psychiatric settings will more usually be recommended for and receive psychotherapy with a professional clinician. Many such patients are not sufficiently integrated to withstand the emotional impact of some of the encounter methods, and therapy must be more circumspect and slow-moving. At the same time, patients of all types have gained from the group methods of occupational therapy, the therapeutic community, or self-help groups, as we have recently seen, which are as much akin to encounter as therapeutic group concepts and procedures. In all, the line between group therapy and encounter is tenuous, whether in terms of the problems served or the methods used.

The present encounter group emerged from the T-groups of the late 1940s and 1950s. Under the impetus of the National Training Laboratories (NTL), methods had evolved for sharpening human-relations skills and for sensitivity training. Concepts such as feedback, interpersonal communication, interpersonal perception, and conscious attention to group processes as a participant-observer were stressed. The end was more effective interpersonal functioning, leadership, or organizational development; usually not personal improvement as such. By the early 1960s, however, West Coast workers in the NTL tradition saw their methods also serving as "group therapy for normals." They believed that T-groups need not be limited to the development of interpersonal skills but could, within a humanistic framework, be conceived as vehicles for advancing personal growth and releasing human potential. The ideas of Rogers and Maslow gave conceptual context to the movement; concepts and methods flowed in from Gestalt therapy, transactional analysis, Synanon, and from the youth counterculture. Within the context of the human potential movement, the emphasis shifted from *learning about social behavior in groups* to *learning about oneself*. Spawned in California, the new encounter group movement spread rapidly over the country.

California is to the rest of the country as the United States is to Europe—the cutting edge of social change, for better and for worse. More than elsewhere, the social institutions providing for a sense of intimacy and community have broken down in California, though the situation there is only more so not different than in the rest of the Western world. A highly mobile and dislocated population, lacking generational continuity and tradition, with unstable family, church, neighborhood, and work groups, all in an everchanging physical environment, Californians welcome experiences which promise warm and dependable relations among people. "The encounter group became a social oasis where people could drop the facade of competence demanded by a fast moving, competitive society, and let loose their doubts and fears and disappointments" (Lieberman, Yalom, and Miles, 1973, p. 5). Leaders of the human potential movement suggested in effect that all people were patients. "The disease was the runaway dehumanizing technocratic culture; the remedy was the return to grappling with the human condition; the vehicle of treatment was ideally the small group, 'group therapy for normals.' The differentiation between mental illness and health grew as vague as the distinction between treatment and change. Personal growth leaders claimed simultaneously that patienthood is ubiquitous and that one need not be sick to get better" (Lieberman et al., 1973, p. 6). The flavor of such thinking is illustrated by a quotation from Werner Erhard, developer of "est training," taken from a brochure intended to attract participants: "Sometimes people get the notion that the purpose of est is to make you better. It is not. I happen to think that you are perfect exactly the way you are . . . the problem is that people get stuck acting the way they were, instead of being the way they are."

In the remainder of this chapter we will consider and evaluate some of the methods that have developed within the encounter movement, ranging from the now more staid T-groups to the more swinging, "let it all hang out" types of encounter.

T-Groups and Sensitivity Training

T-groups in the model developed by NTL are learning laboratories in which individuals discover how they and others function and in this way increase their interpersonal sensitivity or human-relations skills. The goals of the T-group experience are either (or both) to increase individual effectiveness or to foster greater organizational efficiency (more about this purpose in the next section), but rarely to effect broad-scaled changes in individual personality of the sort claimed by group therapy or by some of the newer forms of encounter groups. Groups typically consist of ten to twenty participants who come together either locally or in one of the centers such as the National Training Laboratories at Bethel, Maine. The group trainer is mainly a process observer and reporter. He tends to be egalitarian and nondirective, encouraging the group members to make their own agenda and consider matters of their concern. Although relatively inactive, the leader tries to keep attention focused on process rather than content of the group discussions, to keep interactions in the here-and-now, and to deal continually with the interpersonal feelings and perceptions which arise in the group setting itself. Candor and flexibility are encouraged. From its origins in group dynamics and particularly in Lewinian theory, the laboratory method emphasizes a number of processes important to group functioning. Feedback, that is, how individuals respond to each other and communicate that response, is studied. The need to "unfreeze" individuals from their dependence on prior group norms as a condition for learning new ways of relating is also emphasized. A fine illustration of the T-group experience is given by Bradford and Aronson (in press).

The T-group is seen as an educational endeavor, although experiential rather than didactic, and leaders more typically come from academic rather than clinical backgrounds. NTL has attempted to maintain a high level of ethical practice and has defined standards for the training and performance of laboratory trainers (NTL, 1969). Similarly, among all encounter workers T-group people have been the most research-minded and vigorous in evaluating the process and outcome of their work (Gibb, 1970).

A number of reports argue that experience in T-groups produces increased skills in communication, greater autonomy, flexibility, and increased self-awareness and sensitivity to the feelings of others. Not only are these gains visible in the training group, but apparently they can endure in the "back-home" setting. The question remains as to the extent or durability of these changes, particularly when individuals return to organizations in which they have relatively little power. Much of the evidence of change depends on the self-reports of former participants which tend generally to be enthusiastic; judgments by outside observers are more modest. Thus, for example, Miles (1965) reported that of thirty-four high school principals who had participated in NTL programs, 82 percent felt they functioned better afterward. However, their professional colleagues only rated 30 percent as having changed. (For a review of the considerable literature on the effects of T-groups, see Gibb, 1970, 1971; Parloff, 1970; Back, 1972, 1974).

By now, numerous forms of sensitivity training have evolved; see Gibb (1970) for an account of the different forms of groups, their purposes, and procedures. It has been estimated that, by 1970, about three-quarters of a million people had participated in sensitivity training since its inception by NTL in 1947.

The Use of Groups in the Development of Organizations

Laboratory training (T-groups) can be as valuable for an organization as for the personal development of individual participants. Leaders in business, industry, education, and government have responded to the promise of increased organizational effectiveness by sending numerous executives into sensitivity training and related programs. T-groups have become a valued tool of workers in organization development (OD). It is claimed that such training can increase the manager's sensitivity to the ways groups function (e.g., how cliques are formed, how conflicts are resolved, etc.), so that he can better diagnose interpersonal and intergroup relations, and have increased skill in intervening in group situations in ways that improve member satisfaction, effectiveness, and productivity; at the same time, he can increase his own self-awareness, sensitivity to the behavior of others, and personal effectiveness. Such changes could then serve both personal and organizational needs.

Reviewing the sizeable literature on T-groups for business managers, J. P. Campbell and Dunnette (1968) reach a cautious conclusion "The assumption that T-group training has positive utility for organizations must necessarily rest on shaky ground. It has been neither confirmed nor disconfirmed." They do point out, however, that about 30 to 40 percent of the trained individuals were reported as exhibiting some sort of perceptible change. The greatest difficulty is found in terms of change criteria related to job functioning itself; with criteria derived from the goals and methods of the training program, however, there is greater evidence of change. Thus, the executive himself may be more sensitive and understanding, but whether this is reflected in greater organizational efficiency is open to question.

One problem often ignored relates to the organization of power in the company. Exposed to the democratic sensitivity training group, how can the executive exert its lessons in a formal authoritarian system in the office? The problem is less acute the more powerful the executive in his own organization, but with people in less than top-level roles the problems of "reentry" may be too difficult to manage. For this reason, the T-group experience may be more influential in family life than in organizational functioning. One solution of this problem is to encourage two or more executives of the same company to take laboratory training together. A more radical approach, used by workers of the Tavistock Clinic in their work with industrial and other organizations, is to organize training programs for the entire managerial corps of a company at the same time. In this fashion, the distance between laboratory experience and "back home" is removed; if effective, the organization is changed in the laboratory of the T-group.

Another problem which troubles workers in OD is the necessity for keeping T-group participation voluntary (Phares and Campbell, 1971). To avert the unethical and potential harmful effects of coerced participation, which can result from a top manager's enthusiasm, Phares and Campbell propose that, like personal psychotherapy, participation should be entirely voluntary and not directly or indirectly required. Moreover, potential participants should be screened both as to their likelihood for benefitting from the group experience and the possibility of being psychologically injured by it. Some criteria for screening participants have been proposed by Argyris (1964).

Thus far, the value of T-groups for increasing organizational effectiveness has not been proven. However, despite the lack of job-related evidence of change there is considerable evidence that desirable training-related changes do take place, for example in terms of increased empathy, decision-making skill, and self-awareness. The promise and enthusiasm continues and T-group methods will continue to be widely used; hopefully, sharpened and perfected.

Basic Encounter Groups

Basic encounter groups, as viewed by Carl Rogers (1970), use and extend principles from T-groups and Rogers' own client-centered psychotherapy (see Chapter 14) to foster personal growth. Though encounter groups exist in many forms, Rogers (1970) holds that they have a number of guiding assumptions in common:

> A facilitator can develop, in a group which meets intensively, a psychological climate of safety in which freedom of expression and reduction of defensiveness gradually occur.
>
> In such a psychological climate many of the immediate feeling reactions of each member toward others, and of each member toward himself, tend to be expressed.
>
> A climate of mutual trust develops out of this mutual freedom to express real feelings, positive and negative. Each member moves toward greater acceptance of his total being—emotional, intellectual, and physical—as it *is,* including its potential.
>
> With individuals less inhibited by defensive rigidity, the possibility of change in personal attitudes and behavior, in professional methods, in administrative procedures and relationships, becomes less threatening.
>
> With the reduction of defensive rigidity, individuals can hear each other, can learn from each other, to a greater extent.
>
> There is a development of feedback from one person to another, such that each individual learns how he appears to others and what impact he has in interpersonal relationships.
>
> With this greater freedom and improved communication, new ideas, new concepts, new directions emerge. Innovation can become a desirable rather than a threatening possibility.
>
> These learnings in the group experience tend to carry over, temporarily or more permanently, into relationships with spouse, children, students, subordinates, peers, and even superiors following the group experience [pp. 6–7].

This general description of the basic aspects of the encounter experience would be less applicable, Rogers notes further, to Gestalt therapy and other forms of groups in which the leader is more directive and manipulative.

In the typical course of events, according to Rogers, the group is often anxious and irritated at the outset because of the lack of structure and direction. As it becomes evident that all share in the desire to discover ways of relating, they begin to tentatively explore feelings and attitudes toward each other and toward themselves. Initially hiding behind masks and facades, in time they reveal their real selves. As genuine communication grows, so does group cohesiveness. People are ready to reveal concerns as they discover that they are more accepted the more real they become. Hence, negative feelings can be expressed and released. Trust, warmth, and fondness grow; participants often end with a sense of intimacy and closeness which they may not have previously experienced even with a spouse or close friends. Rogers (1970, p. 9) quotes a woman saying after a weekend encounter session: "If anybody had told me Friday evening that by today I would be loving every member of this group I would have told him that he belonged in a nut house."

In the same vein, Streitfeld (1971) quotes a participant saying at the end of the encounter experience:

> The crucial thing about an encounter group is that it's a safe world. You know that within this safe world, people won't fall apart if you let off steam. What happens when we go outside is that we put on some armor. But once you learn what it's like to be in a safe room without the armor, you can become aware when you put it on. It's damm important to realize that the armor is on and to know that it can come off again.
>
> The safe group teaches you about how you can trust people. It does this by showing you what fantastic intuition such a group has. Hal Streitfeld's intuition is special, but everyone in this group has that. The group itself develops a kind of extraordinary wisdom that is dependent on the quality of trust and safeness. In an environment in which it is safe for people to be themselves, beautiful things happen [p. 220].

Such experiences are by no means atypical. Rogers reports the results of a survey he conducted in which the great majority of former participants remember the group as a vital, deeply relevant emotional experience which continued to affect their lives for months afterward. The encounter movement arose in response to man's alienation and it is an antidote for it. To Rogers, it is ". . . perhaps the most significant social invention of this century" (Rogers, 1968). Others, as we will see shortly, have questioned the psychological premises and argued that the beneficial effects may be illusory and for some individuals at least, psychological damage can result. Before considering these arguments, let us look at related but differing forms of encounter groups.

Varying Forms of Encounter Groups

MARATHON GROUPS

Marathon groups are continuous, intense encounters running anywhere from twenty-four hours to a full weekend, with minimal time out for sleeping and eating. Stoller (1968b) calls the process "accelerated interaction," and used it in his work with psychiatric inpatients. Bach (1966) first used the phrase "marathon group therapy" for his application of this method in his clinical practice. Increasingly, however, the approach has been used with normal groups, in its most dramatic form in weekend-long sessions. From Friday evening to Sunday evening all participants are together in continuous group interaction. Food is available, to be eaten as necessary; brief naps are allowed or sleep breaks scheduled; all in the same large room. Isolation, retreat from the group, forming of subgroups are all prohibited. Consequently, a "pressure cooker" atmosphere is generated, which coupled with the inevitable fatigue, is claimed to reduce defensiveness and lead to intense, authentic interaction. Although the group may start in a somewhat uncomfortable and formal way, perhaps each talking about himself in turn, before long the formality breaks down and intense emotions emerge. As participants get unexpected and often unflattering feedback from each other, and without the normal ability to run away, pressure mounts steadily. Much of the period is a succession of crises, of dramatic and frightening exchanges; tears and threats are not uncommon, nor is intense anger and verbal abuse. By keeping people involved and fully immersed in the experience, proponents feel that the very intensity and continuity of the experience requires people to confront themselves. The change process is compressed in the marathon.

As the session draws to a close, there is a heightened sense of intimacy and deeply felt positive feelings among the participants. This final phase has sometimes been called the "love feast." Members experience more deeply their relatedness to each other, as earlier they felt fear, shame, anger, or guilt. A cathartic experience has taken place and been succeeded by relaxed feelings of unity and love. Stoller suggests that the marathons can lead to enduring changes in the participants' lives. As they have come to know themselves in the microcosm of the marathon group, they have come to realize their impact on people and been able to take new responsibility for their actions. For more detailed description of marathon methods, see Stoller (1968b). The entire process of a weekend encounter has been dramatically portrayed by Mann (1970).

NUDE MARATHONS

The philosophy of encounter is advanced a step further, although a controversial one, by having all the participants nude. Nude marathon groups were first described by Bindrim (1968) who argued that physical exposure facilitates emotional disclosure. Clothes are the civilized coverings which define our facade and social class and cover our true selves. Without them, we are stripped to our essential personalities and cannot easily maintain pretense or false self-images. Nude marathon groups operate by the same basic rules as other marathons, except that the first portion is likely to take place in a swimming pool with all the participants naked. After a period of initial embarrassment, participants are said to relate more naturally and to shed inhibitions. While touching or hugging is allowed, overt sexual activity is prohibited. Bindrim claims that nude encounter is particularly useful for people who have sexual problems and for those who have distorted and depreciated body images; for example, those who view themselves as ugly and unlovable. But for everyone the whole process of being more emotionally open and intimate is intensified and quickened by nakedness. Needless to say, nudity in marathon groups has been the focus of controversy, both among professionals and in the press, though the extent of such practice is easily exaggerated. Rogers (1970) estimates that fewer than one-tenth of one percent of encounter groups meet nude.

GESTALT GROUPS

Spurred by the vigorous and charismatic example of Fritz Perls and his workshops at Esalen, the use of Gestalt therapy methods in encounter groups has gained increasing popularity. Gestalt therapy focuses insistently on getting people to be aware and take responsibility for their actions in the here-and-now (cf., Chapter 14). In Perls group technique, each individual in turn occupies the "hot seat" and is the focus of the leader's searching interrogation, while others observe. This person is directed to become aware of his sensations, feelings, and acts in the now, and to put aside conceptualized accounts of his thoughts, expectations and plans. At points, leader and participant engage in role playing. Sometimes, the participant has to interact with an imagined person or a projected facet of himself as if that person or part was in a nearby empty chair. Similarly, as described earlier, portions of a dream have to be acted out. Although more often spectator than actor, all participants in Gestalt groups report intense involvement.

TRANSACTIONAL ANALYSIS GROUPS

Eric Berne (1961, 1966) developed a theory of psychotherapy which has developed into a system of group therapy and been utilized in encounter sessions (Harris, 1967). The term "transactional" refers to the relations between ego states (those related to the roles of child, adult, or parent) within the same person rather than transactions among people. Central importance is given to the "games people play" (Berne, 1964). Games are organized rituals in which people seek concealed ends. Much of ordinary social life consists of game-playing which blocks truly intimate and authentic relations among individuals. Hence, in the group situation, transactional analysis involves uncovering and analyzing the games being played. In general, as in Gestalt groups, the leader is quite directive, questioning, confronting, and interpreting the behavior of individual participants. He acts as a teacher, to the end of having members understand and free themselves from their games. It is not assumed that group process itself exerts much effect, nor that much real intimacy can develop in groups, but rather that through the leader's interventions individuals can achieve a more game-free way of relating.

SYNANON GAMES

Synanon games differ markedly from other encounter techniques in their emphasis on the open, direct, and uninhibited expression of anger and hostility, stopping only at overt violence. They are an integral part of the program at Synanon, a self-help organization for former drug addicts (Enright, 1971). Normally, they occur in the Synanon communities and may involve nonaddict residents and visitors as well as the former addict members. The games consist of leaderless group encounters, of about three hours, in which persons are singled out in turn for intense verbal assault. Participants must be unstintingly honest in describing themselves and others, and to put aside ordinary social conventions. The effort is made to strip away a person's facade and defenses and to expose his weaknesses to ridicule and sarcasm. It is spoken of as a game because once the session is over there is a quick change in the atmosphere to one of warm encouragement and support. The game is seen as a way of helping Synanon residents discharge their hostile feelings directly rather than in more indirect and potentially dangerous ways. Consequently, the sense of solidarity and community necessary to the continued life of Synanon is maintained. Moreover, it is assumed that if a person's weaknesses are exposed and attacked, he can better overcome them. For many former addicts, the more moderate techniques of psychotherapy have been self-defeating; addicts can too easily "con the shrinks," for whom Synanon residents have only contempt. While the games have apparently contributed to the success of Synanon in keeping former addicts away from drugs and giving them a new life style, there are obvious dangers in more extended use, particularly in leaderless groups or under the direction of untrained leaders.

OTHER APPROACHES

It is hard to detail in limited space the numerous forms of group interaction which have arisen in recent years aimed at extending awareness and fostering personal growth. In addition to those noted, the human potential movement in its larger extension includes sensory and body-awareness groups, exercises in meditation, Yoga and Zen, as well as the more formal study of Eastern philosophies and religions. They all share, as noted, an emphasis on the immediate and experiential, distrust of conventional reason, disdain for professional concepts and roles, and overall a vital enthusiasm and commitment to personal and social betterment.

Episodes in Encounter Groups

Rogers demonstrates how an encounter group can pull together to help a member in distress. In this episode (Rogers, 1970) Joe has been telling of the almost complete lack of communication between himself and his wife. Each of the members and the facilitator (leader) are trying to help, each in their own way, in the process showing their affection for Joe. By the end of the session, Joe comes to realize that it would be helpful if he could express his real feelings toward his wife.

Joe: I've got to be real careful when I go somewhere if I know a lot of people and do things, so that my wife just doesn't feel that she's left out; and of course, I—things have changed so in the last year that I have hope, but for a while I *didn't*. I don't know whether we can break through it or not. (Pause.)

John: It comes to me over and over again that she wants very much to get inside—inside you.

Joe: She does.

John: I, I didn't mean in a hurting way, I mean . . .

Joe: No. (Pause.) But it's how to do it. And gosh, I've gotta let her in; but gosh, I've also gotta be so *careful* and the chances don't come very often . . .

Facil.: Do you feel you got somewhere in this group by being careful? (*Pause.*)

Joe: Well, I've been pretty hard the other way here. In other words I think we haven't been careful here at all.

Facil.: I don't either. I think you've taken a lot of risks.

Joe: What I meant by being careful is, I've gotta be careful about how I say anything or it's twisted on me.

Facil.: If—well, I guess I'll be more blunt. If you think she can't tell when you're being very careful, you're *nuts*.

Joe: Yeah, I agree.

Facil.: And if somebody approaches me—and I feel they're moving very gingerly and carefully, then I wonder, what's he trying to put over on me?

Joe: Well, I've tried it the other way—the worst thing is—maybe, to begin with I was too blunt. That's when we got into our arguments.

Facil.: Yeah, but it sounds—I really appreciate the risk you're taking, or the trust you're putting in us to tell us about this kind of situation. Yet you start talking about the elements *outside* of yourself.

John: I keep wanting to ask if you can *feel* her feelings?

Joe: Well, uh, now—feelings, I, yes I'm getting so I can feel her feelings much more and—uh—I—uh—the thing that bothered me was I remembered some feelings that she wanted to come in, and at that time I turned her down. Now that's where I got turned off. And—but I can feel right away when she's upset and so then I—well I don't know—you see then I . . .

Facil.: What does that do to your feelings? Suppose you come home and you find that she's quiet, because you've been away and she's wondering about what has been going on and she's quite upset. What's that going to make *you feel*?

Joe: Uh—a tendency to withdraw.

Marie: What would you be feeling—withdrawal? Or would you be feeling upset, or maybe even anger?

Joe: I did before—not now so much—I can get that pretty much. I've watched that pretty carefully.

Marie: Yes, but that isn't my question, Joe.

Joe: All right.

Marie: I'm not asking if you can control it or push it away. What will the *feeling* be there?

Joe: Uh—I'm pretty much at the place now where it's just sort of withdrawal and wait; and I know if I can get by that evening, it'll be different tomorrow morning.

Fred: Do you feel it might be defensive, and do you express this defense in withdrawing because . . .

Joe: Well, she doesn't like it.

Fred: But you like it *less* this way than getting involved in an argument or disagreement?

Joe: Yeah—because the only thing that might work is—is if I *just expressed the feeling*. And I hope that'll make a difference—that "I resented what you just said" or something like that, because before I would *answer* her, and boy, it was off! *That just didn't work*, and then she would always say I started it—but *with my being so conscious* now of when she's upset—I mean—I've got that real clear, and I just haven't known how to handle it [pp. 22–24].

A second illustration shows other facets of encounter group activity, the powerful pressure to release affect, bodily contact, and the direct involvement of the leader (Hal) in the group process. The episode illustrates Streitfeld's Aureon encounter method, which emphasizes the role of the body and incorporates principles from Gestalt therapy, meditation, and Eastern philosophy (Streitfeld, 1971).

As she continued to speak, I felt a scream rise up in my throat. Suspecting I was feeling Harriet's need to scream, I pressed her to do so. She began to object, but I persisted. "Keep going. Come on. Scream."

Harriet: It doesn't come. I always feel like I'm acting.

Hal: Then act.
Harriet: *(sobs)*
Hal: Now—that's not crying. Scream!
Harriet: *(attempts to scream, sighs, lets out another small scream that ends in a sob)* I really don't feel like it.
Hal: Keep going.
Harriet: *(more sobbing, then screams a little louder)*
(Similar dialogue continues. Harriet, with encouragement, continues to let out small screams, followed by sobbing.)
Harriet: *(bigger scream)* I didn't even scream when I gave birth. I heard the women around me screaming, and I . . .
(I have her lie on her back. As I continue to encourage her, Harriet's screams gradually become louder and deeper.)
Harriet: It's like getting into yourself.
Hal: That's right! *(laughter from the group)*
Harriet: *(more sobbing)*
Hal: We're going to act as your control. Do you think you can give up your control, Harriet?
Andrew: The control's in your face, around your mouth. Your smile is preventing you from screaming. *(Andrew begins kneading her face and keeps this up throughout the rest of this long session. The group draws their circle close around Harriet, holding her hands, massaging her feet, making contact.)*
Harriet: *(fighting against losing control, sobbing, emitting little screams)* Save me, save me! I want to get away from me. I want to let go. I want to get away from it all.
(I keep encouraging her to breathe and scream. Then I ask her to look around at us.)
Harriet: Who'll take care of me?
Hal: You don't let anyone in.
Harriet: *(long sigh, then silence)*
(Leonore, reminded of Harriet's description of her father, suggests she repeat the syllable "da da da")
Harriet: *(repeats syllable, which becomes unsteady with emotion)* My father was so weak. I had to be strong for my father. You make me think of my father. My mother and father . . . I have to be strong for them.
Hal: Let your father go.
(A long dialogue about letting go of her family and finding her own identity takes place between Harriet and the group.)
Hal: Open your eyes and look around.
All: Harriet, Harriet, look at us.
Hal: Harriet, look at us, look at us here, now.
Harriet: There are currents going through my whole body.
Hal: That's right.
Someone: They're in your feet, too.
Harriet: It's like . . . groovy.
Hal: That's it, let it go through you.
Harriet: Oh *(rhythmic sobs)*, it's a real . . .
Hal: It is, it's just the release of all the energy you had bound up in you. Open your eyes now, Harriet.
Harriet: Oh . . . oh . . . (long sigh)
Hal: Open your eyes and look around. Look at Martha's eyes.
Harriet: *(still in rhythmic release)* I was so beautiful. I love. I think everyone is so beautiful. Oh . . . oh . . .
Hal: That's right, just stay with it. Stay with it.

Harriet: Oh, you're working so hard. I always had to work so hard to please.
Hal: Now you don't have to do anything. All you have to do is receive.
Harriet: I can't do that.
(*A kind of duet follows in which Harriet keeps jumping into the past or the future, and the group keeps pulling her back into the here and now.*)
Hal: There's no other moment.
Harriet: How come you're not telling it like it is?
Hal: We're running this show. We're in control, and we're not going to let you tell the way it is.
Harriet: But that's . . .
Martha: We're running it. Don't take it away from us.
Harriet: He hates me.
All: No. No. We're running it. Take it in.
Harriet: (*interrupts again*)
Hal: Harriet, look at us. That word, "us." Are you here? Take it in. How about Andrew's fingers. What do you feel from Andrew? What do you feel from us? Feel Andrew's hand.
Harriet: Oh, my fingers. Oh! Oh!
Hal: That's alright. It's just a release of energy. You're not used to this.
Harriet: I've never made love for real.
Hal: You make love for real now.
Martha: Take in our love. Feel it. Make love to us. (*As she continues, Harriet relaxes.*)
Harriet: (*in weak, uncontrolled voice*) Everybody looks real. (*group laughter*) What will happen to my mother and father? (*laughter*)
Hal: They'll have to take care of themselves. (*laughter*)
Harriet: (*alternating between loud laughter and rhythmic crying. Then, suddenly terrified, she thinks of her children, whom she had forgotten for several minutes.*) Oh my beautiful children. Why didn't I think of them? My beautiful children. (*Realizing that her children are alright without her, Harriet's terror vanishes and she is able to accept their autonomy*) [pp. 205–208].

THE EFFECTS OF ENCOUNTER GROUPS

In numerous statements, proponents and opponents have asserted their faith in or concern with the encounter movement. Until recently, however, there was little evidence of the actual impact of encounter sessions. By and large, participants express satisfaction, even reporting conversionlike experiences. Many are sufficiently moved to themselves get some training in order to lead others in encounter groups. In self-report studies conducted by encounter workers, participants generally report beneficial outcomes.

Typical is Bach's (1967, p. 1147) report that "Ninety per cent of these Marathon Group participants . . . have evaluated their twenty-four-to-forty-hour group encounters as 'one of the most significant and meaningful experiences of their lives.' " Gibbs (1971) reviewing a sizeable number of studies of sensitivity training and similar groups reports a majority of studies showing participant satisfaction.

On the other hand, clinicians have talked of the dangers involved, pointing to instances of serious emotional disturbance precipitated by encounter activities (e.g., Gottschalk and Pattison, 1969). A. A. Lazarus (1971), himself an innovator with behavioral methods, notes that the number of patients seeking help who are "victims of encounter groups is becoming so large as to constitute a new 'clinical entity.'" Encounter workers tend to minimize the risks. Rogers, for example, claims that among the 587 people he has worked with in intensive group sessions, only two showed psychotic reactions (reported by Parloff, 1970). Moreover, within the ideology of the movement, severe emotional distress is not always viewed as necessarily bad. Strong medicine should have strong effects. Some view a transitory psychotic episode as a shaking up of the established personality from which the individual can emerge the better for it.

In a balanced overview of the encounter field, Parloff (1970) concludes that responsible encounter leaders as well as clinicians would agree that already disturbed people should not be in encounter groups. Thus, ". . . participation in encounter groups may be classed as an elective cosmetic operation rather than as an urgent life-saving procedure" (Parloff, 1970, p. 289). Putting together the evidence then available, Parloff (1970) humorously states:

> . . . the circumspect clinician who wishes to advise prospective group participants regarding possible dangers can, with confidence, offer only the following kind of advice: participation in most encounter groups is likely to be more dangerous than attending an office Christmas party and somewhat less dangerous than skiing [p. 289].

The recent publication of the first large-scale experimental study of encounter groups, however, suggests that they have more potent effects, for good and for bad (Lieberman, Yalom, and Miles, 1973).

"ENCOUNTER GROUPS: FIRST FACTS" (LIEBERMAN, YALOM AND MILES, 1973)

In 1968, Lieberman, Yalom, and Miles made it possible for over 200 Stanford students to participate in encounter groups; another sixty-nine served as control subjects. Eighteen groups were created, representing ten major approaches: NTL T-group, Gestalt therapy, transactional analysis, Esalen eclectic (Schutz, 1967), personal growth (NTL, Western Style), Synanon, psychodrama, marathon, psychoanalytically oriented, encounter tapes (leaderless groups), a fair representation of the current field. All groups were limited to thirty hours and were led by qualified and experienced psychologists or psychiatrists. Every session was minutely observed and recorded; participants and observers made numerous ratings. Participants were tested before and after the group experience and at later points for follow-up information; controls were tested at matched points. Information was sought from others who knew the participants in order not to be dependent only on self-report data.

Did participants change after the encounter experience? A surprisingly large number did. The notion that encounter is a harmless diversion is not supported; anyone who believes that the encounter group experience is about in a class with tossing frisbees—no more harmful, no less beneficial, about as pleasant, and similarly motivated—will be shaken by these findings. A full third of the participants made decided gains by a variety of criteria more substantial than enthusiasm and testimonial. Much of the change was in social values, self-concepts, and attitudes, less in observable behavior. These effects were not ephemeral, as some critics suppose, disappearing as the glow wears off. Follow-up studies showed a substantial amount of positive change to be visible months later.

However, encounter groups did harm as well. A sobering finding is that 8 percent of the participants were "psychiatric casualties" by careful and conservative criteria. They suffered actual psychotic episodes, required professional help, or were otherwise greatly discomforted and disabled. An additional 11 percent showed clearly negative, if less pathological, effects. Clearly, encounter groups are not innocuous.

Groups differed greatly in their potency, more as a function of leader qualities and group atmosphere than in terms of their explicit orientations. Thus, of the two transactional analysis groups, one strongly affected its members while the other did not; the same was found true of the two Gestalt therapy groups. In general, positive changes more typically occurred where leaders emphasized caring and cognitive clarification; casualties occurred in groups where leaders were strong, charismatic, and attacking, fostering emotional expression and self-disclosure. It is commonly held in the encounter field that success depends on strong procedures; the findings of this study suggest the reverse.

In fact, the ultimate power of encounter groups, this study suggests, lies precisely in the principles they share with group dynamics and group psychotherapy rather than in the respects in which they dramatically differ. The emphasis on the here-and-now, intense emotional experience, full self-disclosure and feedback, and the much-valued structured exercises, as such, seem to make little difference for effecting positive change. At heart, the effective encounter group provides an involving group experience in which individuals can learn about themselves and affirm themselves through seeing their impact on others in an atmosphere which allows candor and gives support. *Examining* experience as well as *experiencing* is essential.

In its explosive growth, the authors suggest, the encounter movement went from sound basic principles to their caricatures. If freeing people to express emotions is good, then uninhibited release is better. If developing closeness, respect and trust is good, then stripping of privacy and total disclosure is better. In all, "the encounter group scene became like a science-fiction portrayal of basically sound procedures; procedures so misshappen by excess that they no longer served their original function." In these excesses, supported by the belief of practitioner and client alike that therein lies personal and social salvation, are the dangers of the encounter movement.

The Encounter Movement: A Critical Overview

The encounter movement is too new to fairly evaluate its contribution to human well-being or its role as a social movement. Time, thought, and research will be needed to balance the claims and counterclaims of those who see it as a solution to modern human problems versus those who condemn it as a dangerous fad which may deepen rather than alleviate man's plight. At this point certain reservations held by professional clinicians should be noted, for encounter is neither trivial nor harmless.

1. Long-term benefits may be more illusory than real. The "instant intimacy" of encounter groups may produce an emotional high, but it remains questionable whether the feelings carry over to real life.

2. With the mounting interest in encounter, the relatively few clinical professionals involved can only handle a small part of the demand. Many groups are run by enthusiastic but untrained leaders, some messianic and some opportunistic, but all extravagant in their claims. Unethical and high-pressure advertising, which extols encounter with no mention of its limitations, is commonplace. There is little self-discipline or self-criticism, nor interest in submitting their methods to research test, among workers in the human potential movement.

3. The lack of prior screening and the faith that encounter is good for everyone allow sensitive and vulnerable people to be hurt. Defenses can be broken down in encounter without a corresponding building up of coping resources. It is a situation in which the buyer must beware and potential participants are well advised to consider the wisdom of entrusting themselves to encounter groups. Shostrom (1969) wisely recommends that one should not join an encounter group impulsively, for any life crisis warrants careful reflection. Moreover, one should be doubly cautious if ". . . you are sanely suspicious of your grasp on reality" (p. 38).

4. The movement is gimmicky. Methods are quickly conceived and rarely evaluated. Games and exercises abound; their variety is limited only by their creator's ingenuity and daring. The "trust circle" (one person allows himself to fall over passively to be caught by others in a ring about him; thus it is assumed trust is learned) and "crotch eyeballing" (in which all stare fixidly into the open, sometimes naked, crotch of one member, presumably to reduce sexual shame) are but two illustrations.

5. Groups can endorse immature and/or deviant behavior. If spontaneously expressed, any "authentic feeling" may be deemed worthy. Groups support the individual's narcissism; everything is all right if only you get the bear hug at the end from the others.

6. Groups can be coercive and demand conformity (not, as claimed, value individuality) in line with their ideology. Group norms (e.g., of full self-disclosure) are demanded in a manner which more resembles brainwashing than therapy or ordinary social interplay (Koch, 1971; B. Apfelbaum and C. Apfelbaum, 1973). As the Apfelbaums point out, the basic but implicit assumption is that the group is trustworthy and it is for the individual to learn to trust the group. The right to stand apart is lost. Group participation can be an "escape from freedom," while proclaiming personal autonomy as its goal. Ultimately, the dignity of the unique individual is depreciated.

7. The movement is basically anti-intellectual and hedonistic. There is a profound distrust of reason; "head trips" and "mind-fucking" are to be avoided; emotions, the body, and sensory awareness are honored. (Recall our earlier discussion of humanistic psychology in Chapter 14).

8. The movement has fostered faddism, cultism, and fanaticism. Religious fervor substitutes for scientific argument in gaining converts.

Sigmund Koch, who has contended with the reductionism and "scientism" of modern behaviorism, argues as eloquently that the humanistic psychology which arose as protest against it is, in fact, equally reductionist and productive of a distorted and dehumanized image of man. He states (1971):

> The group movement is the most extreme excursion thus far of man's talent for reducing, distorting, evading, and vulgarizing his own reality. It is also the most poignant exercise of that talent, for it seeks and promises to do the very reverse. It is adept

> at the image-making maneuver of evading human reality in the very process of seeking to discover and enhance it. It seeks to court spontaneity and authenticity by artifice; to combat instrumentalism instrumentally; to provide access to experience by reducing it to a packaged commodity; to engineer autonomy by group pressure; to liberate individuality by group shaping. Within the lexicon of its concepts and methods, openness becomes transparency; love, caring, and sharing become a barter of "reinforcements" or perhaps mutual ego-titillation; aesthetic receptivity of immediacy becomes "sensory awareness." It can provide only a grotesque simulacrum of every noble quality it courts. It provides, in effect, a convenient psychic whorehouse for the purchase of a gamut of well-advertized existential "goodies": authenticity, freedom, wholeness, flexibility, community, love, joy. One enters for such liberating consummations but inevitably settles for a psychic striptease [p. 112].

These are strong criticisms and they bring into serious question the philosophy as well as methods of the encounter movement (human-potential movement, humanistic psychology). This is not to suggest that leaders like Rogers and Maslow are not sincere in their desire to humanize psychology and to help unhappy people toward a better life; indeed, the humanistic movement has revived psychology's concern with human experience and reduced some of the professional shibboleths which have limited our help-giving capacity. In fact, many staid group therapists can learn a good deal from encounter as to methods for heightening and quickening group cohesiveness and, increasing emotional exchange in therapy groups; they can discover that people are often better able to tolerate and benefit from confrontation than their clinical conservatism might predict (Parloff, 1970). Nor does this critique deny that many people have been moved by encounter toward more satisfying and productive lives. But it does raise questions for serious thought and empirical research, about the assumptions, limits, and dangers of the encounter movement, particularly in its more simplistic and radical forms.

The encounter movement started, we have speculated, as protest against the growing loss of a sense of psychological community in contemporary America. At its best, it is a groping toward new social institutions and new life styles to replace those which no longer serve our profound needs for intimacy and community. At its worst, however, it perverts and cheapens those needs, a fad which promises much and delivers little, ultimately reducing rather than enhancing human dignity. In a time of deteriorating social values, it may also represent a frenzied quest for individual pleasure and indulgence which serves as an escape from confronting the true problems of the social world; encounter may thus be a new "opiate of the people," at least the affluent and educated (B. Rosenthal, 1971). Hopefully, however, with increasing maturity, growing knowledge and responsible leadership, the encounter movement can come to realize its own better potential.

CHAPTER 16

The Evaluation of Psychotherapy: Issues of Research

Psychotherapy Research: Needs and Problems

THE CURRENT SCENE

Does psychotherapy help? Under what conditions is it most effective, with which patients having which problems, with which therapists using which techniques? What actually goes on in therapy and what aspects of these proceedings makes a difference? These are the questions addressed by psychotherapy research. Over its long history, psychotherapy has evolved through clinical observations and theoretical speculations. Therapists observed their work, reflected on it, reported case studies, and occasionally tallied successes and failures in simple, uncontrolled clinical surveys. Only slowly has the initial naturalistic approach to the study of psychotherapy been supplemented by more systematic research efforts, controlled studies in which relevant variables are isolated, carefully measured, and possibly experimentally altered. Increasing attention is being given to issues of research design and measurement methodology (e.g., Gottschalk and Auerback, 1966; Fiske et al., 1970; Bergin and Strupp, 1972; Kiesler, 1971, 1973; Waskow and Parloff, 1975).

In recent years, therapy research has become more subtle and sophisticated in design and conception. There is increasing concern with the more complex interactions of therapist, patient, interrelational and situational variables as determinants of therapeutic outcome. At the same time, there has been a shifting of interest from an almost exclusive concern with outcome (what is accomplished?) to the study of therapy process (what goes on between therapist and patient?).

Newer studies are also joining process and outcome questions (which aspect of the process makes a therapeutic difference?), though more and better research of this type is still sorely needed. In this chapter, we will review some of the methodological issues as well as the findings of contemporary research in psychotherapy.

How Psychotherapy Research Differs from Medical Research

The first question facing the therapy researcher is deceptively simple: Conceived as an intentional intervention by a trained and skillful professional designed to improve a patient's state, does psychotherapy help? It would seem that investigating the effectiveness of psychotherapy for relieving emotional problems is no different a task than, say, evaluating a drug proposed for the treatment of a biological disease.

The research pharmacologist facing this question would, ideally, form two groups of patients with identical clinical conditions and essentially alike in all other relevant respects (e.g., age, general health, etc.). All members of one group (*experimental* or *treated* subjects) would get carefully measured doses of the drug. Those in the other group (*no-treatment control* subjects) would get no drug or some other treatment (*alternate-treatment controls*), though otherwise all subjects would be treated identically, in terms of nursing care, diet, or other factors which might influence their health. To reduce the possibility that extraneous factors, such as patients' expectations, might influence the comparison between experiment and control groups, a *placebo* control is valuable. Placebos are inert substances, identical to the experimental drug in size, shape, and taste. Then, to guard further against staff treating the two groups differently due to their expectations and attitudes, the staff as well as the patients can be kept ignorant of which person is receiving the drug and which the placebo. This is a *double-blind design;* an ideal of medical research. Identical measurements are made before, during, and after drug administration, and for some *follow-up* period, to discover the speed, extent, and durability of the drug's curative action. Moreover, measurements are not limited only to the signs and symptoms associated with the target disease, but also cover a wider range of functioning to discover the possibility of side-effects, particularly undesirable ones. With a sufficient number of well diagnosed and carefully evaluated patients, using controls of the type described, the pharmacologist should be able to say with some certainty whether his drug is or is not a promising therapeutic agent for the particular disease entity.

We can readily see that the situation of the psychotherapy researcher is at best in rough analogy to that of the pharmacologist, both on conceptual and on practical grounds. Drug research is done within a framework of medical-model thinking which conceives distinct diseases with clear diagnostic criteria from which patients are cured under specifiable conditions. Standards of sickness and health are sharply and objectively defined, and consistently applied by all physicians and patients. By contrast, as we have seen, concepts of mental health and psychological dysfunction are far more subjective and value-laden. Clinicians can disagree widely as to a patient's diagnosis, and indeed as to whether he should be considered to be psychologically "sick" in the first place. At best, psychiatric diagnostic entities are broad and crude descriptive categories. Moreover, unlike their medical counterparts, psychiatric diagnoses do not relate sensibly and consistently to etiological antecedents and prognostic consequences and hence to specific therapies and predictable outcomes.

Research on psychotherapy has been limited, and much needless controversy engendered, because much of it has been conceived within a medical model. Hence, clinical survey studies grade patients as "improved" or "cured" as if these terms had simple and widely accepted meanings. Leaving aside the difficulties of measurement, such terms imply a standard and, even more, one that is one-dimensional. In fact, improvement usually reflects a value judgment of the clinician or the patient (and the two may not be in agreement!).

The outcome of psychotherapy can be better studied in terms of the more neutral concept of "change" rather than "improvement" or "cure." Then the question can be raised: "In what ways, and due to what influences, has the patient changed? Are these changes of a sort which he (and/or the therapist, and/or society) might consider desirable?" Such questions can be investigated empirically without glossing over the value issues wich are hidden within the term "improvement."

THE MYTH OF UNIFORMITY

Medical-model thinking has also encouraged simplistic notions of the elements involved in therapeutic change. Just as diagnostic entities tend to be seen as unitary, so too do patients, therapists, and modes of therapy tend to be viewed as if they were essentially homogeneous categories. Kiesler (1966) has pointed to the difficulties created for therapy research by the "uniformity assumption myth," the belief that patients are essentially alike, that therapists are much the same, and that "psychotherapy" is all of one piece. In fact, of course, there is great variation within each class, and each combination of therapist, patient, method, and setting is unique. The simple question "is therapy effective?" is thus akin to asking "is higher education effective?" without specifying a particular program, university, or the particular faculty and students involved (Hyman and Breger, 1965). Surely, the medical researcher would dismiss as meaningless or impertinent the question "is medicine effective?" yet it is at that level that issues about psychotherapy are sometimes cast. Patients differ greatly, in terms of character, values, attitudes and life conditions and hopes and expectations of therapy even when diagnosed alike. Similarly, therapists differ as widely in these traits, though perhaps sharing common training or credentials. Therapeutic approaches can hardly be distinguished as can be competing drugs. Regardless of what they say they do, two psychoanalysts or two client-centered therapists may actually act quite differently. The same therapist may treat two of his patients quite differently, or the same patient differently on two occasions. These comments are not only meant to point out the intrinsic complexity of the field but also the urgent need to break loose from models which encourage categorical and simplistic thinking.

IS PSYCHOTHERAPY TOO COMPLEX FOR RESEARCH?

These considerations make clear that psychotherapy is indeed a complicated affair. Each therapeutic twosome is ultimately a unique psychosocial event. Some have offered these facts as reasons why systematic research cannot be done without trivializing the phenomena being studied and ending up with meaningless results. There is this danger, as a good part of the published literature attests.

It is tempting, in psychotherapy research as in other fields, to limit oneself to the most accessible and measurable facets of a problem. Like the drunk who lost his keys, it is easier to search "where the light is." Nor is this issue unique to therapy research, it is intrinsic to any scientific endeavor. In a quite different discipline, Daniel Yankelovich cautioned (quoted in Adam Smith, 1972):

> The first step is to measure whatever can be easily measured. This is okay as far as it goes. The second step is to disregard that which can't be measured or give it an arbitrary quantitative value. This is artificial and misleading. The third step is to presume that what can't be measured easily isn't very important. This is blindness. The fourth step is to say that what can't be measured really doesn't exist. This is suicide [p. 286].

Recognizing this danger, however, does not require the conclusion that research cannot be done or is valueless. Rather it emphasizes the need for research designs which can produce scientifically reliable findings while respecting the essential complexity of the phenomenon being studied—granted, a most difficult but necessary task. To acknowledge complexity and uniqueness does not deny the possibility of finding communalities and generalities. In the particular case of psychotherapy research, these concerns underscore the need, on the one hand, for representing as fully as possible the full population of therapists, patients, techniques, and other relevant variables to assure reliable generalizations or, at the other extreme, studying individual cases fully and in depth.

Of necessity, the researcher must reduce and simplify, isolating variables in order to study them. Other variables have necessarily to be ignored, because they are simply too numerous, or appropriate measures are nonexistent or too costly. The task of the researcher is to simplify without distorting, and the psychotherapist should remind him of the variety of considerations which have to be kept in mind. However, to insist that all conditions be perfect and all potentially relevant factors be properly assessed in their full complexity, practically assures that no research will be done. Both clinical complexity and scientific elegance may have to be compromised somewhat in order to do a study that is both feasible and meaningful. The final test is neither perfect inclusiveness nor elegance but whether the potential findings are a valuable addition to knowledge and subsequent practice.

RESISTANCE TO RESEARCH

For the future development and perfection of psychotherapy, there is clear and urgent need for research to separate fact from myth and dogma. Along with this attitude however there is distinct ambivalence and defensiveness. Many see research as a threat to cherished beliefs and to the validity of their training and clinical experience. They have faith in their work, the conviction that it helps clients, and emotional and financial commitment to continue in it, even if hard evidence of its value is sometimes difficult to produce.

Should medical research discredit a particular drug, a clinician's belief and practice may be disturbed but his identity is not challenged. By contrast, the psychotherapist's "medicine" is he himself. He is his own technique. It is his own character and personal actions that help his patients, not an impersonal drug he administers. Consequently, research is a potential threat to the clinician's self-esteem and, as he sees it, the well-being of his patients. At the extreme, ". . . some feel that to contemplate research on psychotherapy is to question it, to question it is to attack it, and to attack it is to be against human welfare." (Meltzoff and Kornreich, 1970, p. 8). Such a view would more likely be held by those who view therapy as essentially a human encounter in the humanistic-existential tradition, than those who see psychotherapy as consisting of informed and intended actions, as do both psychoanalysts and behavior therapists. They too, however, are not without resistance.

DOES RESEARCH DISTORT AND ENDANGER THE PROCESS OF PSYCHOTHERAPY?

Serious issue has been raised as to whether the requirements of research—tape recordings, ratings, the use of special tests, etc.—do not so alter the ordinary conditions of therapy that (1) the resultant findings may not readily be generalized to psychotherapy as it is usually practiced and (2) that there may be breaches of professional ethics.

The relation between patient and therapist is traditionally an intimate, private and confidential one. Both are assured that no third party will know what goes on at least not without their full knowledge and consent. The essence of the therapeutic contract is that the therapist will exert his full knowledge and skill on the patient's behalf and not willfully harm him or use him for any other purpose whatever. A concealed tape recorder abuses the patient's faith in the therapist, without which therapy cannot proceed.

As a fundamental principle of both scientific ethics and wise clinical practice, a patient being recruited into a research study must be completely informed as to the purposes and procedures of that study and have complete freedom to participate or not and to withdraw at any time, particularly if the study requires any unusual efforts, such as being filmed or taking special tests or interviews, or if there are any potential discomforts. Confidentiality of records must be kept by removing names and other identifying features and keeping them in locked files. In publications, individual patients' histories must not be revealed in identifiable form and without consent. Human research, whether on psychotherapy or in any other realm, must always respect subjects' personal rights and well-being in every regard, a principle which is increasingly being understood and enforced by professionals, laymen, and the law.

Fortunately, most patients share the clinical researcher's conviction that scientific knowledge and good clinical practice are not opposed but indeed may be complementary values. Only through the systematic analysis of its successes and failures can a profession develop the base of knowledge necessary for improving future service. Consequently, given the opportunity most patients consent voluntarily to participate in clinical research. Understandably, they resent being "experimented upon" if they are thereby denied adequate treatment or if they feel manipulated in the process.

But even if the investigator is scrupulously ethical, is it not still possible that altering the therapeutic situation for research purposes might produce artificial findings and perhaps even make it less therapeutic? The effects of filming and recording have been investigated in a number of experiments, with somewhat mixed findings. Initially, both therapists and patients may be somewhat anxious, but after a few sessions they become less concerned (e.g., E. D. Watson and Kanter, 1954, 1956; Haggard, Hiken, and Isaacs, 1965). In other studies, no effects are reported while in still others, some differences in the content of the interviews have been noted. For example, Roberts and Renzaglia (1965) found that graduate student counselors were less client-centered when being recorded while their clients, in turn, tended to make more favorable self-reference statements when they were not being recorded. Some therapists feel that they are more attentive and effective when being observed, others report the reverse. Overall, it is my impression that recording and other research procedures do not seriously alter the therapeutic process, provided that the therapists (just as the patients) understand and concur in the purpose of the research, collaborate in the investigation, fully trust the investigators, and are assured of full respect and confidentiality. Nonetheless, the clinical investigator must be attentive to the potential impact of his procedures.

Let us now consider some of the findings of outcome studies, then return in later sections to consider research methodology further, and finally to review some of the recent research on therapeutic process. While many have argued persuasively that the broad question "How effective is psychotherapy?" asked in that form is virtually meaningless, it is well to start at that point. One reason is that contemporary psychotherapy research started with just that broad question and it is worth noting how the controversy got structured. Moreover, the controversy highlights many of the methodological problems and needs of psychotherapy research, which required a solution to reach more definitive results. For these reasons, it is well worth examining in detail the issues raised by Eysenck's attack on psychotherapy in 1952.

The Effectiveness of Psychotherapy

EYSENCK'S CHALLENGE

In 1952, Eysenck startled psychotherapy practitioners and researchers with the claim that there was no good evidence that psychotherapy with neurotics was any more effective than no therapy at all. As evidence, he presented the outcome statistical study of nineteen clinical groups, five psychoanalytic and fourteen "eclectic," covering over 7,000 patients. To obtain a baseline estimate of spontaneous recovery among untreated cases, Eysenck used the discharge rate of hospitalized neurotics from New York State hospitals (Landis, 1937) and the improvement rate among life-insurance claimants treated medically by general practitioners (Denker, 1946). Among these neurotic patients who were given only cutodial or medical care but no psychotherapy, 72 percent were reported as improved. By contrast, Eysenck claimed, only 44 percent of the psychoanalytic patients and 66 percent of those in eclectic psychotherapy were improved. Thus all psychotherapists come off badly in the comparison, especially psychoanalysts.

On several later occasions, Eysenck presented these survey findings again and also included studies which, he felt, further strengthened his position (Eysenck, 1960, 1965, 1966, 1967a). Thus, he states in 1960: "The additional studies which have come to hand since, particularly those making use of a control group, have been so uniformly negative in their outcome that a somewhat stronger conclusion appears warranted. The results do show that whatever effects psychotherapy may have are likely to be extremely small; if they were large as compared with the effects of nonspecific treatments and events, it seems reasonable to suppose that some effects would have been found in the studies quoted. . . . The writer must admit to being somewhat surprised at the uniformly negative results issuing from all of this work." In his later writings, Eysenck argued that while traditional verbal therapies had failed to prove their worth, the emerging behavioral therapies have clear contribution to make to the treatment of neurotic problems (Eysenck and Beech, 1971).

Needless to say, vigorous and often heated objection has been taken to Eysenck's attack on psychotherapy (e.g., Rosenzweig, 1954; Luborsky, 1954; DeCharms, Levy and Wertheimer, 1954; Strupp, 1963; Meltzoff and Kornreich, 1970; Bergin, 1971; Luborsky et al., 1971; Luborsky, 1972, 1975; Malan, 1973), and Eysenck replied in kind (1954, 1955, 1964, 1972).

CRITIQUE OF EYSENCK'S WORK

The following issues emerge in the controversy:

The Criterion Problem. Does it seem reasonable that the same standards of "improvement" were used by all kinds of psychotherapists and by general practitioners as well? While the judgments about treated cases were usually made by the therapists themselves, and one might suppose that they could err on the positive side, still they are practiced clinicians who have had ample opportunity to study their patients thoroughly. By contrast, the amount of information available to hospital psychiatrists or general physicians is decidedly less and, one might guess, their standards may be lower. For the official record, almost any patient discharged from a state psychiatric hospital is likely to be called improved. The insurance physicians similarly deal in fairly gross criteria, such as whether patients have fewer symptom complaints and are able to work or adjust better socially. Psychoanalysts, in terms of their orienting theory and professed goals, may simply demand more of their patients. Behavioral change, if not accompanied by apparently more profound characterological changes, is likely to get less credit in their eyes.

Handling of the Outcome Statistics. Eysenck made a number of arbitrary decisions which had the overall consequence of minimizing the apparent impact of psychotherapy, particularly of psychoanalysis (Bergin, 1971). On equally defensible assumptions, Bergin shows that the improvement rate for psychoanalysis could be calculated at 83 percent instead of Eysenck's 44 percent from the very same data base. Here is how such a marked discrepancy can arise: In order to put the published findings of all clinics on the same scale, Eysenck groups therapy results under four headings: (1) cured or much improved; (2) improved; (3) slightly improved; and (4) not improved, died, left treatment. His improvement rate is based on the first two categories. Thus, "percent improved" is

$$\frac{(1) + (2)}{(1) + (2) + (3) + (4)}$$

Those judged "slightly improved" and those who died or left therapy for any reason as well as those not helped were all on the side of failure.

In the particular case of the Berlin Psychoanalytic Institute data (Fenichel, 1930), the outcomes for completed cases were originally reported in these categories: (1) uncured; (2) improved; (3) very much improved; and (4) cured. For his analysis, Eysenck chose to include Fenichel's "improved" in his own "slightly improved," thus excluding them from the improved groups used in calculating successful treatment. On the basis of Fenichel's description of this group, however, Bergin believes that it is as or more reasonable to put them on the success side of the ledger. Moreover, including all those who died or terminated for whatever reason along with the genuinely unimproved further deflates "percent improved." When Bergin recalculates the box score by (1) eliminating premature dropouts entirely, (2) counting Fenichel's "improved" as improved, and (3) eliminating nonneurotic cases which Eysenck included, he reaches a startling 91 percent improvement rate for the Berlin Psychoanalytic Institute rather than the 39 percent reported by Eysenck. He feels, correctly I believe, that his interpretation of the available information is logical and reasonable. At the very least, this numerical contretemps shows the essential difficulty in dealing with clinical survey statistics. It shows how readily they can be turned to make any point.

Moreover, Bergin also notes that Eysenck applied his own criteria inconsistently. If a therapy survey reported outcome in only three categories, i.e., cured, improved, and not improved, Eysenck divided the "improved" equally into "improved" and "slightly improved," on the assumption that a single category actually encompassed a range. However, in calculating the spontaneous recovery rate in Landis's data (1937), which were originally described as recovered, improved, and not improved, the improved patients are all grouped with the recovered, to yield his reported 72 percent spontaneous remissions. If he treated these control figures as he did the therapy outcome data, then Eysenck's estimate would be 52 not 72 percent. With such corrections in both the base rate and the therapy-improvement rate possible, it is obvious that quite a different story can be told from precisely the same data base.

Selectivity of References. By the time of Eysenck's reports in the 1960s, a sizable number of new and better-controlled studies had become available. From among these, Eysenck described a limited few which, on the whole, cast a poor light on psychotherapy. Considering larger and more representative samples of studies, both Bergin (1971) and Meltzoff and Kornreich (1970) show that a much more favorable judgment of psychotherapy can be drawn.

The Comparability of the Treated and Nontreated Groups. In a good research study, control and treatment groups should be essentially alike in all critical respects except for the independent variable (here, psychotherapy) that is being evaluated. While Eysenck acknowledged that his control groups were imperfect, still he maintained that the control subjects were as seriously disturbed and that the standards of recovery were equally high for the two classes of patients. Both of these assumptions seem unjustified.

It seems highly unlikely that either the hospitalized neurotics or the insurance claimants were comparable to the psychoanalytic patients in such important regards as education, social class, motivation for therapy, or psychological mindedness. Moreover, neurotic patients, even in the years Landis studied, are not ordinarily admitted or kept in state hospitals, except under unusual circumstances. We can probably accept the assertion that they did not receive psychotherapy in a formal sense, but we cannot judge the helpful effects of interpersonal relations with supportive hospital staff members. Similarly, the insurance patients while being seen by medical practitioners and given drugs most likely also received a sympathetic hearing, some reassurance, and advice. We simply do not know what might have gone on which could have hindered or facilitated recovery in the control groups, nor for that matter is there any detail about the therapy process for the treated patients as well. But regardless of the particular influences acting on the two groups, it just seems most unlikely that they were comparable in relevant psychosocial ways.

The Concept and Measurement of Spontaneous Recovery. Eysenck's proof of the ineffectiveness of psychotherapy rests on the high rates of spontaneous recovery in the untreated groups. While some patients surely improve without specific professional intervention or as a consequence of unknown factors operating upon them, seriously disturbed neurotics do not "recover" quite so easily as Eysenck's figures would suggest. Acute symptoms often abate, but extensive clinical experience has shown that recurrences are common and that true improvement in patient's capacities to cope with life stress are much more rare.

All of Eysenck's critics have agreed on the deficiencies in the base line estimates derived from the Landis-Denker data but no alternate figures were proposed. Bergin (1971) points out that a substantial amount of relevant evidence has been available for some years. This material shows several crucial facts: (1) "spontaneous recovery" statistics vary greatly for different types of neuroses, hence any single estimate is arbitrary; (2) generally, rates are lower than the Landis-Denker estimates; and (3) "untreated" neurotics actually seek and receive substantial therapeutic help from professional and nonprofessional workers. In his own survey, Bergin assembled some fourteen studies published between 1942 and 1967 which estimated spontaneous recovery rates. Overall, the median rate seems to be about 30 percent rather than the two-thirds or more claimed by Eysenck. Bergin cautions that "It would be unfortunate if a new 30 percent figure were to be used as a baseline for neuroses, because the number is a mere abstraction that masks a heterogeneous collection of processes" (Bergin, 1971, p. 241). The important issue for clinical research is to study in what ways and how people change with or without psychotherapy. Statistical estimates of "spontaneous recovery," as such, are of little scientific or clinical importance.

It is amazing how much attention, both pro and con, has been given the Eysenck critique of therapeutic effects and for how many years the controversy has raged, particularly in view of the logical and empirical limitations of the study. The debate has continued, in fair measure, because of the intrinsic ambiguity of the original survey data, the firm belief of people as to the worth or worthlessness of traditional psychotherapy, and, besides, the intrinsically critical need to evaluate its effects. At this point, the Eysenck findings can be looked back on as an historic episode. His greatest contribution, in retrospect, is that he stimulated (or irritated) his colleagues to examine their methods and assumptions more rigorously. In consequence, a sizeable and increasingly more valuable body of psychotherapy research has shown the particular conditions under which it is helpful.

MORE RECENT SURVEYS OF THERAPEUTIC OUTCOME

In his own review of the literature, Bergin (1971) surveys forty-eight studies (fifty-two patient groups) of verbal psychotherapy published between 1952 and 1969. Overall, he concludes, there is distinct though modest evidence that psychotherapy works. By and large, more positive effects were found in studies of experienced rather than inexperienced therapists. Those which included control groups and those which were generally better designed also tended more often to show positive outcomes than did uncontrolled and less well constructed studies. Other surveys during the 1960s, examined by Bergin, generally support these findings. In a large but not exhaustive survey Truax and Carkhuff (1967) reach a less hopeful conclusion: "Thus the weight of the evidence, involving very large numbers of clients or therapists, suggests that the average effects of therapeutic intervention (with the average therapist or counselor) are approximately equivalent to the random effects of normal living without treatment. . . ." (p. 12).

In perhaps the most inclusive survey to date, Meltzoff and Kornreich (1970) reach a decidedly more positive evaluation of psychotherapy. Meltzoff and Kornreich consider only controlled studies and assess the findings obtained in terms of the quality of the research involved. They note that the quality as well as the quantity of outcome research has increased markedly since 1950. While the ratio of "adequate" to "questionable" studies (in terms of design, sampling, controls, criteria, etc.) before 1960 was eighteen to twenty-five, since 1960 it shifted to thirty-nine to nineteen in favor of adequate studies. In all, they found 101 studies of reasonable quality covering a broad spectrum including virtually any kind of verbal therapeutic intervention (e.g., hypnosis, group procedures, and lectures as well as conventional psychotherapy) with any kind of patient group (e.g., including children, mental defectives, alcoholics and schizophrenics as well as neurotics). One could surely argue with some of the studies included and with some of their interpretations of findings. Still, the overall picture seems clear. People are helped.

In approximately 80 percent of the studies positive outcomes were found. Moreover, these more commonly occurred in better designed studies (see Table 16.1).

TABLE 16.1.
Summary of Controlled Outcome Studies *

	ADEQUATE STUDIES	QUESTIONABLE STUDIES	TOTAL
Positive	48	33	81
Null	9	11	20
Total	57	44	101

* From Meltzoff, J. & Kornreich, M. *Research in psychotherapy*. Chicago: Aldine Publishing Co. Reprinted by permission. Copyright © 1970 by Atherton Press, Inc.

They note further that about one-half of the adequate studies which gave negative results were failures of verbal therapies to help chronic schizophrenic patients. Another third were failures with delinquency prevention, drug addiction, and enuresis. Moreover, in one-third of the studies that did not yield positive results with verbal therapies, patients who received other forms of treatment (e.g., behavioral methods) still did better than untreated controls. The authors therefore conclude:

> The weight of experimental evidence is sufficient to enable us to reject the null hypothesis (i.e., that psychotherapy is ineffective). Far more often than not, psychotherapy of a wide variety of types and with a broad range of disorders has been demonstrated under controlled conditions to be accompanied by positive changes in adjustment that significantly exceed those that can be accounted for by the passage of time alone [Meltzoff and Kornreich, 1970, p. 175].

They see the different conclusions drawn from other surveys as reflecting either incomplete literature search or misreading of the evidence from the studies surveyed.

> In short, reviews of the literature that have concluded that psychotherapy has, on the average, no demonstrable effect are based upon an incomplete survey of the existing body of research and an insufficiently stringent appraisal of the data. We have encountered no comprehensive review of controlled research on the effects of psychotherapy that has led convincingly to a conclusion in support of the null hypothesis. On the contrary, controlled research has been notably successful in demonstrating significantly more behavioral change in treated patients than in untreated controls. In general, the better the quality of the research, the more positive the results obtained [Meltzoff and Kornreich, 1970, p. 177].

In the most recent overview of the field, Malan (1973) rereviews the reviews from the perspective of dynamic psychotherapy. He notes that the evidence for the effectiveness of psychotherapy is now strong, and that there is considerable evidence for the effectiveness of dynamic psychotherapy with psychosomatic patients. However, "the evidence in favor of dynamic psychotherapy in the ordinary run of neuroses and character disorders—for which, after all, this form of psychotherapy was developed—is weak in the extreme." He examines some of the promising newer work, particularly in the Menninger Clinic and Tavistock studies. He notes the discouragement with therapy-outcome research among therapist researchers, because it has contributed little of definite value to the practice of psychotherapy; a position shared by many clinicians and researchers (Bergin and Strupp, 1972).

Controversy continues as to the conclusions which can be drawn from a quarter century of research and polemic. Anyone with the patience of Job and the mind of a bank auditor is cordially invited to look again at the cumulated mass of material and settle the issue for himself. Meanwhile, it is probably more productive to look for more specific determinants of therapeutic outcome and to study the process of therapy itself.

THE ISSUE OF DETERIORATION

In reexamining some outcome findings, D. S. Cartwright (1956) was the first to note the possibility that an apparent lack of change in a group could conceal the fact that some patients had improved considerably while others had worsened to

FIGURE 16.1.
The Deterioration Effect
Schematic representation of pre- and post-test distributions of criterion scores in psychotherapy outcome studies.*

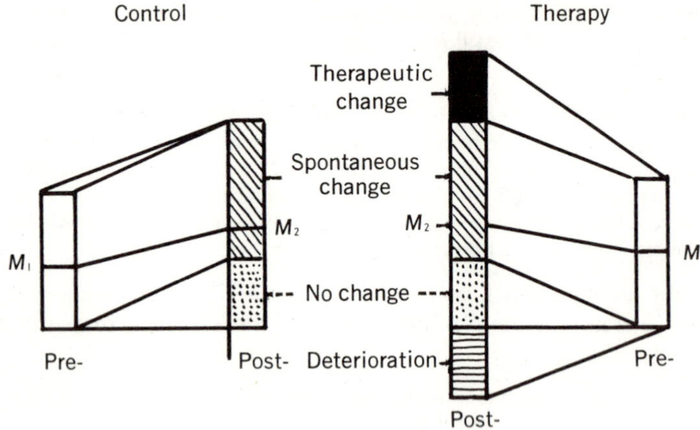

* From Bergin, A. E. Some implications of psychotherapy research for therapeutic practice. *Journal of Abnormal Psychology*, 1966, *71*, 235–246. Copyright © 1966 American Psychological Association. Reprinted by permission.

about the same degree. He showed that although there was no difference in the average improvement level between a treated and a control group, the treated group showed greater variation which must imply that while some had improved significantly others had worsened. Bergin (e.g., 1966, 1971) studied this phenomenon in depth and brought evidence from some thirty studies showing possible deterioration effects. The changes in patients who do and do not receive therapy can be conceptualized in Figure 16.1.

Deterioration effects may either result from the fact that fragile patients already in a deteriorating phase were seen by therapists unable to reverse the process or that the patients may have had a neurotic equilibrium which was disturbed by the therapist. Although the evidence is not definitive, it appears that more fragile and disturbed patients are more likely to worsen in therapy.

The stability and extent of Bergin's deterioration hypothesis has been questioned (e.g., Rachman, 1971; May, 1971). However, his evidence and reasoning seem convincing. Every clinician knows of cases more harmed than helped during psychotherapy, though he may not be certain whether the same patient may not have fared worse during a period without treatment. In the preceding chapter, we saw evidence of a deterioration effect in the study by Lieberman et al. (1973) of the impact of encounter groups.

Finding that treated groups change more, in whatever direction, is important for two basic reasons. For one, it shows that therapy is potent. Like other medicines, it can do harm—hopefully, under identifiable and avoidable conditions—as well as good. At least, psychotherapy is not innocuous, as some critics have contended, though Eysenck (1967b, p. 153) can still comment cynically: "If someone advocated a cure of the common cold on the grounds that while it killed some of the patients, others got well more quickly, I doubt if the medical profession would be as enthusiastic about this discovery as Bergin is about the 'deterioration effect' and its double, the 'improvement effect'—even if these should in fact be shown to exist and have the importance which Bergin attributes to them." Second, and of greater importance, the finding encourages the quest for more specific factors—in the patient, in the therapist, in their interaction, and in the psychosocial context of therapy—which might dispose to positive or negative outcomes. As we will see shortly, a fair number of relevant findings have already accumulated. First, however, we should consider some general methodological issues in psychotherapy research.

Issues of Research Design and Methodology

MODELS OF RESEARCH DESIGN

Knowledge about psychotherapy has been gained in a number of ways, including case studies, clinical surveys, correlational studies, experimental studies, analogue studies and, what I would like to call personalistic designs. A description of the advantages and limitations of each approach follows.

Case Studies. Basic to any clinical science, especially in its early history, is the in-depth study of individual cases. The limitations are clear enough: Case studies are uncontrolled, often unsystematic; generalization is limited and uncertain; observations and conclusions can all too much reflect the subjective judgment and bias of the clinician-observer. Yet in this naturalistic approach the full complexity and uniqueness of the patient-therapist process is best preserved. The astute clinician can guard against bias and temper unwarranted generalization. Case studies have sometimes generated major hypotheses and pointed the way for later, more systematic research (Bolgar, 1965).

In the recent past, there has been renewed interest in the intensive study of individual cases in the natural settings of psychotherapy, though now with less dependence on the clinician's personal observations and judgments. Methods for refining, organizing, and quantifying case studies have been suggested (Chassan, 1967). Methods of audio and video recording have made possible the observation and rating of therapeutic transactions by outside observers. Interestingly, workers in the behavioral tradition have been most receptive to individual studies, conceiving them as N = 1 experiments in the Skinnerian tradition (A. A. Lazarus and Davison, 1971; Leitenberg, 1973).

Clinical Surveys. The simple type of clinical survey, that is recording the patient status as "improved" or "not improved" and then combining the judgments of diverse clinicians in diverse settings, is of limited value, as we have already seen. With better defined criteria and other controls, such data can serve useful epidemiological purposes, though usually more for descriptive than explanatory aims (see Chapter 19). Another type of survey, akin to those of social psychology, has inquired into the values and attitudes of therapists and the perceived problems and needs of patients (e.g., Gurin, Veroff, and Feld, 1960; Henry, Sims, and Spray, 1971).

Correlational Studies. The two basic models of psychological research are correlational and experimental studies (Cronbach, 1957). In the former, there is no effort to manipulate systematically independent variables and then study changes in dependent variables (the experimental method) but rather measurements of the phenomena are taken as they occur naturally. Thereafter, the ways in which variables are associated are discovered through correlation, including more sophisticated methods, such as factor or cluster analysis. The basic requirements of correlational research are that there be a sufficient number of instances and of measures, varying over a sufficient range. The notable advantages of the correlational approach are that it does not require control and manipulation, many more variables can be simultaneously studied, and the possible findings are not limited to the prestudy hypotheses.

Experimental Studies. By contrast, the experimental method is designed to test particular hypotheses, sharply and directly, by setting up contrasting conditions ideally under laboratory control. In the ideal case, all variables other than those being studied are controlled or known and any change in dependent variables can with certainty be attributed to the independent variable(s). Thus, to test the hypothesis that a particular drug systematically reduces, say, blood pressure, the research pharmacologists might get five closely matched (or randomly selected) groups of subjects and give them 0, 1, 2, . . . units of the drug. Measuring blood pressure before and after, he would then generate a precise "dose-response" curve. Obviously, other variables could be studied simultaneously, to pick up side effects and explore possible unforeseen determinants of the curve.

To most psychologists, and scientists generally, the experiment is the zenith of research methods, the purest and most incisive method of gaining knowledge and testing theory. Where possible, the experimental approach is obviously desirable, but it too has limitations. In order to maximize control and the potential for hypothesis testing, the experimenter must often limit the number and range of the variables he studies, perhaps excluding some of prime importance. Moreover, he must be dealing with phenomena which can be controlled and measured in his laboratory. Five doses of drug X can be measured and easily administered to five groups of comparable subjects (particularly if they are laboratory rats), but how can five levels of interpretation be measured? Psychologists who equate experimentation with science should remember that respectable sciences such as meteorology also cannot readily subject their phenomena to laboratory control and variation. Indeed, many wise methodologists (e.g., Bakan, 1968; Koch, 1959) agree with Brentano's view, expressed early in the history of modern psychology, that psychology would be better served to view itself as an *empirical* rather than an *experimental* science. If the experimental model is enthroned as the simple and sovereign route to knowledge, then phenomena of great importance are ignored or made trivial because they do not readily yield to the demands of experimentation. Though honoring the experimental approach above others, most psychologists fortunately use naturalistic and correlational as well as experimental designs as problems require.

Analogue Studies. To circumvent some of the clinical, ethical, and practical difficulties of experimenting with real clinical problems, some investigators have found it useful to use analogue situations. For example, in an analogue design Paul (1966) compared the efficacy of a "modified systematic desensitization" procedure with "insight-oriented psychotherapy" for the alleviation of anxiety. Subjects were college students registered in a public-speaking course. They were asked if they would volunteer for a study evaluating different psychological procedures used to treat anxiety. About half the class volunteered and those judged most anxious were selected. Subjects were assigned to one of the major treatment groups or to one of three control conditions (an "attention-placebo" group and two different no-treatment groups). All "patients" had five individual sessions over a six-week period. Both before and after they were given a speech test under stress conditions. It was found that performance improved most for the desensitization subjects, and then in this order, the insight subjects, attention-placebo group, and finally the no treatment controls. In all, it was a well-designed and carefully done study. But clearly the subjects only approximated persons who actually seek clinical help. They were functioning relatively well and went into "therapy" only at the request of the experimenter. While they were bothered by public-speaking anxiety, we do not know how extensively they suffered nor how central a problem it was. Unlike true patients they did not seek but were offered therapy, with no cost to them whatever. The therapists on their part were experienced clinicians, but hardly functioning in their usual mode. They were working toward the experimenter's goals, not their own. Hence, while under the conditions of the experiment significant differences were found, it is moot whether these can be generalized to the conclusion that behavior therapy is superior to dynamic psychotherapy. The use of similar designs has become relatively common, for example, using normals who express fears of snakes, in the study of behavioral techniques. Findings of considerable interest if limited applicability have been generated.

Another type of analogue situation is illustrated by Strupp's study of therapist behavior (Strupp, 1960). To provide a standard testing situation, Strupp played a film of a patient in an actual therapy situation, stopping the film periodically and asking the clinicians to indicate what they would have said at that point. Again, we simply do not know if they would have acted that way in the actual situation or whether the snatches were not too brief and free of context for meaningful response. Still, it made possible the comparison of a large number of therapists of varying persuasions under relatively controlled conditions.

Personolistic Studies. Of potential importance is a mixed model, combining the advantages of a case-historical and experimental study, which we might call a personolistic design. The basic idea is to study each individual therapist-patient situation in sufficient detail so that criteria of process and change can be individualized while, at the same time, having sufficient numbers of patients treated under sufficiently controlled conditions so that between-group comparisons can reliably be made. Personality research in the Harvard Psychological Clinic was a forerunner of this type of design (H. A. Murray, 1938). A relatively small number of subjects were carefully studied and assessed; their life histories, values, personality development and dynamics were studied from different vantage points by tests and interviews. Only then were they used as subjects in standardized experimental situations. With the background of personal information, individual differences in the mean group differences could be better understood. Alternate interpretations of experimental findings could be deduced from the individualized case-historical information. In therapy research, a particular contribution of a personalistic point of view is that change criteria can be individualized and be made personally relevant, insofar as possible. We will return to this issue in a later section.

THE PROBLEM OF CONTROLS

Good research should produce useful information in terms of which we can choose with confidence between alternate hypotheses or explanations. Poor research leaves us uncertain, with alternate explanations seeming equally reasonable. Many factors contribute to the quality of research, in psychotherapy as in any field. The factors include the adequacy and appropriateness of the sample studied; the number of subjects; the reliability and validity of measures; safeguards against bias; and a study design which provides necessary control groups. Together, these factors have the cumulative value of reducing uncertainty in the interpretation of the obtained data and of allowing choices among alternate explanations; when properly done, we can speak of a well-controlled study. In this brief presentation, I will limit comment to two facets of control in psychotherapy research: (1) control groups and (2) controls of procedure (against bias). The former allow us to know the effects of the experimental intervention; the latter reduce potential bias and error in our measures and judgments.

The need for control groups is illustrated by the exasperating TV-commercial which tries to convince us that Zilch's breakfast cereal is "better." Mr. Zilch hopes you won't ask "than what?" or, worse yet, visualize some of the less appetizing alternatives yourself. While the dangling comparative is offensive and confusing in everyday life, it is anathema in science. Simply discovering that treated subjects have changed does not tell us that it was due to the treatment. To establish that fact a control comparison is necessary.

No-treatment control group. The simplest control would consist of patients, otherwise identical, who receive no treatment at all. They should be equally motivated and essentially similar in relevant clinical and psychosocial respects. Creating such a group would have to involve refusing therapy to clinic applicants, yet asking them to submit to before and after assessment. The ethical and practical barriers are obvious: patients will seek help elsewhere; resent being tested, and hence cooperate poorly if at all; and clinicians are tempted to assign patients to control status who seem less distressed or urgent. In any case, untreated patients do not stay untreated. People seeking help will find it wherever they can. While a true untreated control can be set up in an analogue study where people are offered treatment who are not seeking it, a no-treatment group is almost impossible to visualize in a natural clinical setting.

Waiting-list controls. As an approximation, investigators have taken advantage of the fact that patients often have to wait for a therapist's time to become available. Or a waiting list can be contrived by telling patients that they will be seen when possible but that, meanwhile, their help would be appreciated in taking some tests. Changes can then be measured and compared to other patients who were treated for the same length of time. But whether real or contrived, patients can only be kept on a waiting list for a relatively short time, which may not at all match the therapy being evaluated. Moreover, by the time they arrive on a waiting list, patients have already had intake interviews and other procedures which can relieve some of their distress. Still, waiting-list controls have been useful in therapy research. Asking people to wait is ethically more defensible than denying them treatment altogether.

Placebo controls. To answer the question of whether it is the patient's faith or expectation which is therapeutic rather than the specific procedures, it is desirable to have a condition which imitates psychotherapy. Thus, the patient can meet regularly with someone who has no explicit training for "nontherapeutic conversations." Although, as we noted earlier, all psychotherapies share the same basic relationship conditions and that, in fair measure, the efficacy of any therapy depends on the patient's faith, suggestibility, or the personal attention and support he gets, it is fair to ask whether the particular therapeutic procedures give results beyond these basic effects.

Other-treatment control. Similarly, if the issue is whether a new therapeutic approach is better than an existing one, the latter is an appropriate control condition. In actuality, most control subjects receive some other form of treatment, even when viewed as no-treatment controls, and it is valuable to assess completely whatever other events have gone on which might have affected the patient's state.

The patient as his own control. For some purposes, particularly in process studies, each patient can be used as his own control rather than having an explicit control group. For example, if we wish to know whether supportive rather than nondirective statements facilitate or inhibit the patient's discussing critical areas, some measure of the themes discussed can be made both before and after the therapist increases one or the other type of statement. In any therapy evaluation study, of course, repeated measures are made, whether these are judged only against the patient's own base line or that provided by control subjects. A particular use of "own control" in outcome research is suggested by D. T. Campbell and Stanley's (1963) quasi-experimental design. Measures can be made at four (or more) equally spaced points in time, A, B, C, and D. If the patient is treated between points B and C, then the change between A and B (while on a waiting list, for example) and between C and D can be used as controls to assess the impact of the therapeutic program.

Combining different control groups. In the well-designed study, two or more controls may be used. A no-treatment or waiting-list group can be used to evaluate changes that occur as a function of passing time, a placebo group to control against the effects of suggestion and nonspecific relationship factors, and an other-therapy group to assess the relative merits of one versus another therapeutic approach. The choice of controls in any study should be determined by the question for which an answer is being sought. If the issue is whether this therapy is valuable for anxiety patients, then comparison should be made with a group of, for example, depressed patients given the same treatment, in addition to another group of anxiety patients who are not treated or given alternate treatment. Similarly, if proposed for men, then women become the controls.

Controls of procedure. A second order of research controls are those procedures and safeguards built into the study which insure that the findings obtained are not due to extraneous factors. At the first level, there has to be concern with proper sampling and matching of characteristics of patients, therapists, techniques, and the circumstances under which the therapy is done. Similarly, considerable vigilance is needed to guard against the contaminating effect of bias in collecting and processing of data. The opportunities for bias are countless. The investigator may be so committed to his hypothesis that he may not only design a study in the first instance which stacks the cards in his favor but all along the way he may make small compromising decisions which have the same effect. "This patient didn't terminate because he wasn't being helped. He just lived too far from the clinic. So, let's not include him in the final data." Therapists can be less than objective in describing their efforts and their effects. Even patients can join in the conspiracy by rating an outcome questionnaire in an exaggeratedly positive direction not to disappoint the therapist or clinic or, for that matter, in a negative way if annoyed with the clinic even though he may have been helped. Stein (1971) reports that former patients who voluntarily and fully participate in a follow-up study differ distinctly from those who resist involvement. The more cooperative tend to be more educated, though somewhat less affluent, and to have been in therapy before.

As we have seen, it is rarely if at all possible to use double-blind designs in psychotherapy research to minimize the effects of the hopes and expectations of therapists and patients. However, some bias can be controlled by having dispassionate observers and raters judge clinical change, with minimal knowledge about the patients, therapists, or modes of therapy involved. Thus, all patients treated in a study contrasting methods A and B could be interviewed before and after by the same "evaluating clinician" to judge the extent and type of change, without revealing which treatment method was involved. Moreover, these interviews could be taped and further ratings made "blind" by other evaluaters to establish the reliability of the judgments of change. Bias is further reduced to the extent that the investigators adhere uncompromisingly to the design requirements (e.g., "Alternate subjects coming to the clinic are given treatments A and B") and by the use of appropriate statistical techniques.

THE ASSESSMENT OF CHANGE

Psychotherapy is intended to alter human lives and relieve distress. By what criteria and measures can we assess the type and extent of psychological change? Virtually all of the techniques of clinical assessment have been used, singly or in various combinations, to provide outcome measures in therapy research. The choice of method usually reflects the values and theoretical predilections of the investigator. Thus, Rogerian therapists, with their concern with the patient's self-concept, early developed and extensively used a measure of self-ideal divergence, i.e., the distance between the patient's concepts of what he is (self) and what he would like to be (ideal), as measured by the correlation between Q-sorts of each. The patient is considered to improve as the correlation between the two becomes higher and more positive. On the other hand, behavior therapists use behavioral assessments, more directly focused on the patient's symptomatic complaints and observable behaviors. A phobic patient is considered cured to the extent that he can approach the object of his phobia without anxiety. Workers in the dynamic tradition have, on the whole, used broader and more inclusive criteria of general adaptation and personality integration, including such factors as increased ego strength, capacity for self-regulation, increased personal comfort, and personality competence.

Outcome criteria, therefore, can vary from symptomatic to dynamic, narrowly focused to broad gauged, experiential to behavioral, and one-dimensional to multifactorial. *Outcome measures* include therapist evaluations, patient self-ratings, behavioral observation, assessment interviews, objective personality inventories and other self-report measures, projective techniques, performance tests, physiological tests, and medical examinations.

An important question is whether change is unitary or multidimensional. Is it sufficient to assess "improvement" in a general sense or is it preferable to test for specific changes which might be hypothesized in terms of the goals and procedures of the particular therapy and the needs of the particular patients? To discover whether one or diverse criteria best characterize therapeutic gain, Parloff, Kelman, and Frank (1954) correlated four different measures taken before and after twenty weeks of group psychotherapy. These included a symptom checklist, a staff rating of patient discomfort, and Q-sort measures of self-acceptance and self-awareness. Few significant correlations were found, before or after therapy among these measures. The authors suggest that measures of *comfort, effectiveness,* and *self-awareness* all be used as outcome criteria. In an extensive study, D. S. Cartwright, Kirtner, and Fiske (1963) examined eighty-four change measures made on ninety-three patients in client-centered therapy. Factor analysis revealed a number of factors which, on the whole, were more associated with particular methods of measurement rather than describing general personality attributes. Other studies bear out the general conclusion that therapeutic change is multifactorial rather than unitary (Farnsworth, Lewis, and Walsh, 1971). Such findings point up the need for including as many measures as possible, using different criteria, and taken from different vantage points, in order to describe therapeutic change as fully and accurately as possible.

Increasingly, workers in the field are calling attention to the potential advantages of using personally relevant criteria for each individual patient. Thus, if a patient is excessively anxious, therapeutic gain would clearly involve lowering his anxiety level. By contrast, a stolid, rigidly defended, and constricted person should be considered improved if he became more anxious. Hence, the same anxiety scale could be scored in opposite directions to mark gain in each case. In a more extended way, an entirely unique criterion can be developed for each patient separately, drawing on his and/or the therapist's judgments as to his deficiencies, growth needs, possible goals of therapy, and applicable interventions. In the Menninger Foundation study of psychotherapy (e.g., Robbins and Wallerstein, 1959; Sargent, 1961; Kernberg, Burstein, Coyne, Appelbaum, Horwitz, and Voth, 1972; Horwitz, 1974) such personal predictions were developed for each patient in therapy.

The methods most commonly used in outcome measurement include:

1. *Therapist Judgment.* Therapists have been asked to rate overall improvement and, more commonly in more recent studies, to judge specific facets of change, such as symptom relief, social effectiveness, or ego strength, among others, both as reported by the patient in his outside life and more directly manifested in therapy itself. Therapist's ratings are the most commonly used outcome measure.

2. *Patient Self-evaluations.* Similarly, patients make global estimates of their overall progress or rate more specific characteristics or behavior. Outcome questionnaires of numerous types have been developed; often parallel forms are given

to both the patient and the therapist. Indeed, it has been noted, that agreement may be modest, and that patients sometimes are more convinced of therapeutic gain than are their therapists (Board, 1959). As noted, client-centered therapists have widely used self-ideal Q-sorts. Symptom checklists (e.g., Battle et al., 1966) and clinical self-rating scales (e.g., Lorr, Klett, and McNair, 1963) are commonly used in therapy research.

3. *Assessment Interviews.* Somewhat more objective than the therapist's own evaluations are research interviews by independent clinicians. Standardized interviews have been developed to make comparisons between subjects more valid. One that is widely used in clinical research is the Psychiatric Status Schedule developed by Spitzer and his associates (1967).

4. *Personality Inventories.* The MMPI has been used in many therapy studies; the Pt, D, and Sc scales seem to provide dependable change indices. The California Psychological Inventory and the Gough-Heilbrun Adjective Checklist have also served well in therapy-evaluation research.

5. *Projective Techniques.* The Rorschach test has been used most widely, often as part of a diagnostic battery. The most consistently promising results, however, have been obtained with TAT indicators of particular needs predicted to change with therapy.

6. *Measures Derived from Therapy Process.* On the basis of content analyses of the transactions in therapy, efforts have been made to develop indices of change. Studies have been made of the type of language used, nonverbal behavior, content of self-reference statements, amount and type of interaction with the therapist, affect expression, dream content, and other behaviors which can be judged from interview recordings at different points in the therapy. A classic measure used in a number of studies is the Discomfort Relief Quotient (Dollard and Mowrer, 1947), which consists of the ratio between expressions of discomfort and of relief derived from content analysis of the patient's statements. This was conceived as a general measure of tension level and tension reduction. The changes in the quotient from session to session can be plotted to describe changes in the patient's state.

FOLLOW-UP ASSESSMENT

Ordinarily, measures are made immediately before and immediately after psychotherapy. At the moment of termination, however, the patient may be in a particularly aroused state, excessively hopeful and pleased at the accomplishment or, on the contrary, dismayed at the prospect of venturing forward without therapeutic support. Hence, it is desirable for post-therapy measures to be made when a stable level is reached and it may be necessary to wait before making outcome measures. While it is well to know the patient's status at termination, the stability of the observed changes is of greater importance. Therapeutic gains may evaporate as the patient faces real life problems or they may amplify as he accepts and masters challenges with his newly found confidence and skills. Either way, assessment should be made not only at termination but also at later points, perhaps after three months and after a year, to establish the stability and durability of therapeutic changes.

SOME RECOMMENDATIONS FOR IMPROVING THERAPY RESEARCH

Whether in psychotherapy or any other field, the best research design is the one which most precisely and economically answers the question(s) at issue. There is no one perfect design. The research plan used depends on the particular topic being investigated as well as the resources and facilities available to the investigator. However, certain general principles can be noted. Some of these apply generally to psychological research and will be mentioned here briefly. Others are more pertinent to research in psychotherapy and are worth special attention. More extensive discussion and recommendations can be found in Fiske et al. (1970), Strupp and Bergin (1969), Kiesler (1971), Wallerstein and Sampson (1971), and Waskow and Parloff (1975).

Let us first consider some general issues: (1) Psychotherapy research should be tied to theory and concepts; (2) as far as possible, each new study should coordinate with prior or future studies; (3) wherever possible, standardized measurements should be used in addition to those specially designed for the needs of a particular study; (4) moreover, measures should be developed in terms of the theory underlying the therapeutic approach; (5) foreseeable sources of bias, of the type noted earlier, in the collection and interpretation of findings should be controlled; and (6) as much detail as possible should be reported as to the setting, conditions and type of treatment, patients, therapists, and measures used so that other investigators can, in principle, replicate the study as closely as possible. Ultimately, scientific knowledge grows through replicated findings.

Let us consider now some more specific considerations:

1. Sampling. The more homogeneous the sample, the more precise but also the more limited are the conclusions that can be drawn. For testing certain theoretically relevant questions, homogeneity of the patients and therapists studied is advisable. For other purposes, for example, to describe the state of the art generally, the broadest representation is best. In all, the sample studied determines the population to which the findings can be generalized. It is worth noting that only fifteen of the hundreds of studies performed between 1945 and 1970 was based on the private-practice setting, in which great numbers of patients are seen by the most experienced therapists (Wolff, 1970). Most therapy studies are based on the work of student therapists, usually in training clinic settings. There is great need for more representation of all settings and levels of experience.

2. Controls. "The objective should not be the impossible one of providing controls for every conceivably relevant factor but rather to design a study which can reasonably be expected to tell the field something not now known. As completely as possible, the design should be replicable by others, rather than depending upon the particular personalities of the therapists and of the judges used to provide ratings" (Fiske et al., 1970). A true no-treatment control group is difficult to conceive and raises important clinical and ethical problems. An alternate-treatment control is preferable. The merits of a particular type of therapy should be pitted against another form of treatment. Thus, if one wishes to check the value of a particular short-term therapy, an appropriate control would be long-term therapy in the same mode rather than an untreated group.

3. Knowledge of Potentially Relevant Determinants. Since all factors cannot be controlled, it is incumbent on therapy researchers to record, and analyze the effects of a large variety of potentially relevant factors. These would include char-

acteristics of the therapist, therapy method(s), demographic, clinical and personality qualities of the patients, and social attributes of the treatment environment. In addition, intercurrent events in the life of the patients should be scrupulously recorded. Therapy accounts for only a small fraction of the hours in a patient's life; what occurs in the others can be vitally important.

4. Measures. Because outcome criteria are only poorly correlated, it is important to have as many and *diverse measures* as possible, tapping different facets of functioning and reflecting different observational vantage points. Both internal criteria (e.g., personality characteristics, relation to therapist, etc.) and external criteria (e.g., work adjustment) should be represented. Similarly, behavioral as well as dynamic and experiential factors should be assessed. Views of the patient's character and functioning should be obtained from the vantage point of the clinician, of the patient, and of relevant others in his social environment.

Unobtrusive measures should be used as much as possible. Tests which intrude on the patient's time and privacy or which may arouse negative feelings are to be avoided if possible. A reliable index of the patient's depressed mood, for example, might be obtained by counting the number of times he sighs, the number of self-deprecatory statements he makes, or noting whether he is well-groomed or dishevelled; thus reducing the need for formal testing with, for example, an affect adjective checklist or other assessment procedure.

Wherever possible, however, it is desirable to use *standardized procedures* in order to make possible comparisons between different studies. A conference of authorities on psychotherapy research, sponsored by NIMH, recommended a "core battery," which includes such procedures as the Hopkins Symptom Checklist (Battle et al., 1966; Derogatis et al., 1974), the Psychiatric Status Scale (Spitzer, Endicott, and Cohen, 1967) and the MMPI, among others (Waskow and Parloff, 1975). To the core battery can be added procedures specific to the purposes of the study, including those newly designed for the purpose. The core battery common to all studies, however, would maximize the possibility of meaningful and reliable comparisons among them.

At the same time, greater use should be made of *personolistic measures*. In addition to assessing variables along which all patients can be classified, there is need for idiographic estimates of change for the unique patient. How a patient fares is best described in terms of what troubles him, what life problems confront him, what changes he seeks, and what happens to him in therapy. In the same spirit, careful case studies of individuals in treatment provide valuable N = 1 experiments which can productively supplement large-scale studies.

5. Balancing Naturalistic and Experimental Perspectives. The trend toward more systematic research, particularly in the experimental mode, is laudatory. But we should keep constantly in mind that the advantages of experimentation may be bought at the cost of reducing and simplifying the phenomena we are trying to understand. Recommending personolistic measures and clinical case studies are in the spirit of preserving a more open, if somewhat less exact, research model. The intrinsic complexity of psychotherapy requires the wise investigator to note and record phenomena as they appear naturally rather than hastening too quickly to reduce them to preset variables, measures, and conditions of an experimental design. Ideally too, the investigator should have first-hand acquaintance with the clinical realities of psychotherapy. (By the same token, the collaborating therapist should be able to think "investigatively" and have first-hand knowledge of the

research realities of collecting exact and interpretable data.) The core issue of therapy research (indeed, research in psychology generally) remains balancing a healthy respect for complexity with the needs for systematic and controlled studies. To this end, the investigator must preserve a naturalistic attitude, observing and recording events as they spontaneously occur, while staying with the requirements of systematic measurement and research designs needed to insure replicable findings.

Research on Specific Factors Affecting the Outcome of Psychotherapy

THE SEARCH FOR SPECIFICITY

As we have seen, psychotherapy is not a unitary process applied by the same type of clinician to essentially similar patients under roughly the same conditions. Consequently, the simple question "Does psychotherapy help?" is of limited value. There is growing conviction that the goals of psychotherapy research have to be recast in more specific terms, if further progress is to be made (e.g., Strupp and Bergin, 1969; Paul, 1967). The proper question is "Which therapeutic interventions applied by which therapists to which patients under which circumstances are likely to lead to which results?" To answer such a question, specific research is needed to understand the operation and contribution of the specific variables in psychotherapy—the *patient*, the *therapist*, the *relation* between them, the *therapeutic techniques*, and the general *social situation* in which therapy occurs.

Factors in each of these domains vary in numerous ways, both internally and in interaction with the others. Thus, therapists differ not only in their theoretical orientations, but also in personality, values and attitudes, age and social class, professional training, life experiences, and personal philosophy; each of these may differentially affect his patients. Patients similarly are more than merely phobics or hysterics. They too vary along similar personal and social dimensions, any of which can affect their accessibility to psychotherapy. Moreover, these factors interact, for example, a woman therapist working with a woman patient is in a different situation than the same therapist treating a man. Therapeutic techniques are only roughly classified when we call them psychoanalytic, behavioral, or humanistic. Within each class, there are numerous variations, and, the final therapy process may depend more on the character of the therapist than the precepts of the school. Finally, the social circumstances in which therapy takes place obviously affects its nature and outcome greatly. Treating an adolescent boy as a condition of probation is a predictably different experience than working with another who has voluntarily sought help from a college counseling center. To separate significant and meaningful determinants of therapeutic outcome in this maze of interacting factors is a difficult yet necessary task. A number of clinician-researchers despair at the prospect of evolving a sufficiently broad and sound research base for psychotherapy. As of now, they note, little of the body of therapy research has seriously affected therapeutic practice (Bergin and Strupp, 1972). While probably true, the quest for specific determinants continues.

Some of the studies can now be considered in each of the relevant realms.

THE PATIENT

Working within the medical tradition, Freud and his early co-workers saw their new technique as a treatment for psychological disease, originally hysteria. In time, the treatment was viewed as valuable to all of the so-called "transference neuroses," which included in addition to hysteria, the obsessive-compulsive neuroses and phobic states. Those patients who could not develop transference relations to the therapist, such as schizophrenics, psychopaths, and certain forms of character disorders, were considered poor candidates for psychoanalysis. Moreover, Freud noted that not only clinical status but certain more general characteristics of the analysand affected his suitability for therapy. Ideally, the patient should be young, intelligent and educated, psychologically minded and able to introspect, and have some degree of emotional maturity and control for maximum benefit.

Over the years, the scope of psychoanalysis and related therapies has broadened considerably, so that increasingly they are viewed as general approaches to the alleviation of psychological distress of many sorts in people of all kinds. Consequently, earlier concerns with specific criteria of applicability have been greatly relaxed. At the extreme, the humanistic-existential therapies, reflecting a "growth" rather than "treatment" ideology, see themselves as virtually universal. In the recent past, however, there has been a resurgence of interest in the quest for specific treatments for specific conditions, spurred in good part by the thinking of the behavior therapists (e.g., Paul, 1967). In their own work, they have demonstrated the value of defined behavioral techniques for removing focal symptoms or changing specific behaviors, though there is less evidence of their impact on broader-scaled personality problems.

Research on the patient as a variable in psychotherapy has turned from a central concern with diagnosis and clinical status to an emphasis on either his psychosocial characteristics (e.g., age, sex, class, race) or specific therapy-relevant attitudes and values (attractiveness, expectations, readiness to accept the patient role, accessibility, and the like.) Here are some of the factors which have been found to relate to the patient's progress in psychotherapy.

Degree and Type of Disturbance. Luborsky (1959, p. 324) noted some years ago that "Those who stay in treatment improve; those who improve are better off to begin with than those who do not; and one can predict response to treatment by how well they are to begin with." A substantial number of studies have shown that generally the less rather than more disturbed person is more likely to want and seek therapy, be accepted by therapists, remain in treatment, and benefit in the end (Stone, Frank, Nash, and Imber, 1961; Barron, 1953a; Stephens and Astrup, 1965; Luborsky et al, 1971). Among diagnostic groupings, generally poorer results have been obtained with schizophrenics, mental defectives, and other more grossly disturbed patients than with relatively well integrated and more competent neurotics. Findings are often contradictory and diagnostic criteria are often gross and inexact, but overall Luborsky's wry formulation has held up over the years. Concerned mental health professionals have wondered whether psychotherapy as currently practiced does not help most those who need help least.

Truax and Carkhuff (1967) have noted further that those patients who initially have the greatest experienced disturbance (assessed by self-report and psychological tests) but lesser overt or behavioral disturbance show the greatest therapeutic gains. The more promising patient, it seems, is more anxious, dissatisfied with himself, struggling with painful conflicts, yet managing to meet basic life responsibilities. By contrast, those who are so disorganized and inept socially as to be incapable of handling ordinary life demands are no more capable of seeking therapy or gaining from it.

General Personality Qualities. Related research shows that patients who benefit more from psychotherapy tend to have greater *ego strength* (Barron, 1953b; Kernberg et al., 1972), *anxiety tolerance* (Siegal and Rosen, 1962), and other more positive personality traits. Barron's Ego Strength Scale, derived from the MMPI, and Klopfer's Rorschach Prognostic Scale (1951), also intended as a general index of ego strength, have been used extensively in studies predicting response to therapy, on the whole, quite successfully; see Meltzoff and Kornreich (1970) and Luborsky et al., (1971) for review of this literature. A number of studies have tested the hypothesis that higher *initial anxiety* predicts better outcome. Although results are mixed, it seems overall that while some anxiety is necessary for a person to undertake psychotherapy, it is not clear that it is necessary for a positive outcome. *Suggestibility* was found to be related to staying in therapy by Imber et al., (1956) and J. D. Frank et al., (1957), but in their later work it was not found to be related to improvement. Many other general personality qualities (e.g., hostility, introversion-extroversion, ethnocentrism, authoritarianism, etc.) have been studied, with generally fragmentary and inconsistent findings. More promising is the investigation of those personal attributes more directly relevant to the role demands of psychotherapy.

Personal Qualities Relevant to the Patient Role. Several investigations support the clinician's beliefs that therapeutic progress depends on the patient's *motivation for therapy* and his readiness to *confront* and *communicate* his feelings openly. Some of the more specific factors identified include experiencing guilt and anxiety, acknowledging dependency feelings, wanting help, liking the therapist and his work, accepting personal responsibility for problems, seeing them in psychological rather than medical terms, and kindred qualities. In a number of studies (e.g., A. M. White, Fichtenbaum, and Dollard, 1964; Truax and Carkhuff, 1967; Rogers et al., 1967; Truax and Wittner, 1971) such factors were assessed from patient behavior in the initial interview and were found to predict later outcome. Such variables seem to group into a more general factor which might be termed "openness to therapeutic influences" (Strupp, 1971), or "openness to insight" (Malan, 1973).

Somewhat related to the above factors, another group of studies report that patients regarded by their therapists as more *attractive* had better outcomes (Nash, Hoehn-Saric, Battle, Stone, Imber, and Frank, 1965; Heller and Goldstein, 1961). Similarly, patients rated more *likeable* do better in therapy (Strupp and Williams, 1960). Factors such as likeability or attractiveness, which are in fair measure in the eye of the beholder, probably reflect the presence of other qualities valued by therapists, such as motivation, alertness, and psychological mindedness. Possibly too, they may exert their effect by inspiring the therapist to greater efforts, a warmer relation, or more encouragement.

An effort to assess the patient's capacity to relate was made by Isaacs and Haggard (1966) who derived a measure of "relatability" from the themes in TAT stories told by patients. Patients who scored high had decidedly better outcomes in therapy.

Expectations. The patient's hopes and expectations play a major role in psychotherapy and have been extensively studied (A. P. Goldstein, 1962; Wilkins, 1973). Particularly as developed in the work of J. D. Frank (1973) and his colleagues at Johns Hopkins University, the outcome of therapy is viewed to a large extent dependent on the patient's faith in the therapist and the therapeutic process. As we discussed in an earlier chapter, it is clear that without faith there would be no treatment in the first instance, nor would motivation and effort be obtained. It is surely a necessary condition of therapy, but probably not a sufficient cause of change. Also of importance is the correspondence, i.e., the agreement or disagreement, between the patient's and the therapist's expectations of therapy. With greater congruence, a more favorable outcome can more readily be predicted. We will return to discuss this issue further in considering the interplay of therapist and patient factors as determinants of therapy progress.

Psychosocial Characteristics: Age, Sex, and Intelligence. Along with Freud, many therapists believe that the *younger* person is more malleable and hence more likely to benefit from therapy. In line with this belief, clear preference for younger patients is shown by therapists; the case loads of clinics show disproportionately larger number of younger than older patients accepted and assigned to therapists. However, once accepted, there is less evidence that older people are actually any less likely to continue in or gain from therapy.

There is no clear relationship between the patient's *sex* and the outcome of therapy. Where differences are found, they generally show that women improve more except perhaps in behavior therapy. A striking and consistent fact, however, is that women far more commonly than men seek and are accepted in therapy. Obviously, there are numerous possible explanations—some of which have fueled controversy with the women's rights movement—but the most defensible line of reasoning, it seems to me, is that women are no more psychologically disturbed than men but that they are likely to be more psychologically minded, ready to seek and accept help, less defensive, and better able to communicate; in sum, to have more of the traits which qualify anyone to be a "better" patient.

An interesting incidental fact is that *marital status*, for men or women, has not been found to relate to therapeutic outcome. Epidemiological studies, on the other hand, have shown conclusively that married people (particularly men) have a distinctly lower incidence of severe mental illness, are more likely to be discharged earlier from hospitals, and to fare better in the community (see Chapter 19).

Another firmly entrenched belief is that *intelligence* must be positively related to outcome since the work of therapy, particularly the verbal therapies, involves learning, mastering new concepts, introspection, and conceptualizing and communicating one's thoughts and feelings. In a study of the perceptions of hospital staff held by patients differing in intelligence and education, Keith-Spiegel and Spiegel (1967) found that brighter, better-educated people tended to see psychiatrists as more helpful. A man with an IQ of 83 is quoted as saying: "My doctor was a nice enough guy, but I never knew what the hell he was talking about." Intelligence and education seem to make a difference in the expectations of the patient regarding therapy, his acceptance of it, his continuing in it, and, finally, his gaining from it (Luborsky et al., 1971). Still, useful work has been done with retarded children and adults, particularly by adapting therapeutic techniques by making them less intellectually demanding.

Social Class and Race. There has been great concern with the role of social class and minority racial membership as variables in psychotherapy (e.g., Hollingshead and Redlich, 1958; A. P. Goldstein, 1973; E. E. Jones, 1974). A sizeable body of research suggests that contemporary psychotherapy, particularly as practiced in existing clinical institutions in the main by white, middle-class therapists, falls short of serving the needs of working-class and poor patients, particularly those of minority races.

Specifically, it has been found that: (1) lower-class patients are less likely to be referred for psychotherapy; more commonly, they are sent for medical and organic treatment (Hollingshead and Redlich, 1954); (2) if referred, they are less likely to be accepted for therapy (Rosenthal and Frank, 1958; Cole, Branch and Allison, 1962). This is as true of lower-class patients in Israel as in the United States (Shanan and Moses, 1961); (3) if seen, they are more usually assigned to lower-status and less-experienced therapists (Schaffer and Myers, 1954). Therapists tend to view them as less interesting and cooperative (Carlson, Coleman, Errera, and Harrison, 1965) and more pathological (Lee, 1968); (4) when treated, they are more often given electroshock and drugs than psychotherapy; a consistent finding in many locales and settings (e.g., Hollingshead and Redlich, 1958; Kahn, Pollack, and Fink, 1957; and Gallagher, Sharaf, and Levinson, 1965); (5) if offered psychotherapy, lower-class patients are more likely to refuse such treatment and/or break off prematurely (Rubenstein and Lorr, 1956; Imber, Nash, and Stone, 1955; J. D. Frank, Gliedman, Imber, Nash, and Stone, 1957; Yamamoto and Goin, 1966); and (6) if, however, the lower-class patient persists, the evidence as to outcome is less gloomy. Compared to middle-class counterparts, lower-class patients have been reported as showing less improvement (e.g., Rosenbaum, Friedlander, and Kaplan, 1956; Freeman, 1967). By contrast, D. Rosenthal and Frank (1958) found no significant relation between education, income, or race in the proportion of patients cited by therapists as improved. Though there were more dropouts, the lower-class patients who remained in therapy did as well as middle-class patients (J. D. Frank, Gliedman, Imber, Nash, and Stone, 1957).

Diverse explanations for these findings have also been proposed in a controversial literature. Lower-class patients, some suggest, lack the psychological skills and attitudes necessary for therapy. They are more concerned with external events than with internal experiences, perhaps realistically. They carry into psychotherapy expectations bred in other contacts with "doctors," such as that they will be told what to do and what to take to gain relief. On their part, middle-class therapists approach lower-class patients with misconceptions, trepidation, and bias, being less comfortable because there are fewer shared values and experiences. Moreover, such therapists may in fact be ignorant of the actual life problems of the patient, and hence their concerns can properly seem irrelevant to the lower-class patient. Summing up from the perspective of a community psychiatrist, Dumont (1968, p. 25) says: "Psychotherapy, as generally practiced, requires a patient who is verbal, insightful, and motivated, one who can delay gratification, and who, more or less, shares the values of the therapist, thereby virtually excluding the lower-class person from treatment." Whatever the proper explanation, a problem clearly exists.

Solutions have been proposed along three lines: (1) Abandon individual psychotherapy in favor of community-oriented interventions, which have as their target altering social systems rather than the individual (the community psychological approach, to be discussed in the next and following chapters); (2) abandon verbal psychotherapy in favor of behavioral methods, which are likely to be more comprehensible and effective for the poor (e.g., A. P. Goldstein, 1973). A parallel proposal calls for fuller use of drug and other medical therapies; and (3) adapt psychotherapy so that it is more responsive to the psychosocial skills and needs of the poor. Some possibilities along this line will be considered later in this chapter.

THE THERAPIST

Early in the history of psychotherapy, primary emphasis was on the development of concepts and techniques which could be applied equally well, and generally in the same fashion, by any appropriately trained and qualified professional. Freud saw the role of the therapist as an essentially passive observer-interpreter (analyst) of the patient's mental life and conflicts. His task was to encourage the flow of ideas and associations which, as he apprehended their potential meanings, he was to interpret in order to overcome resistances and facilitate insight. At times, Freud realized, the therapist might serve as an exemplar or teacher, but in the main he tried to minimize personal influence other than through analysis. Conceived as a process apart from suggestion, persuasion, advising, or teaching, the unique work of therapy lay in facilitating communication and interpreting its meaning. To this end, the personality of the therapist was conceived as secondary, his technical skills primary. Hence, it was assumed that all trained analysts should, despite individual differences in other regards, function in much the same way in the therapeutic hour. "The role of the psychotherapist was to be no different from that of a surgeon who applies a well-defined operative procedure and whose personality is of little consequence" (Strupp, 1971, p. 113).

Shortly enough, however, Freud realized that more was involved. The therapist's clinical observations and interpretation could too readily be determined by his emotional reactions to the patient. Such *countertransference* Freud saw as an antitherapeutic barrier which limited good analytic technique. To guard against its unfavorable effects, Freud insisted that all psychoanalysts should themselves be psychoanalyzed. While he realized that countertransference might still arise, Freud viewed the training or didactic analysis as being the therapist's best insurance for objectivity and therapeutic effectiveness. While the training analysis might also have the desirable effect of deepening the psychoanalyst's understanding of his own, and hence others, unconscious processes and defenses, it was justified primarily as a method par excellence for sharpening the therapist's analytic skills. Freud recognized of course that the therapist had to have other human and professional qualities, such as personal integrity and honesty, tact, good adjustment, and the like, but his concern with the therapist's personality centered mainly on the potentially negative effects of countertransference. The issue, ultimately, was to keep the therapist's technical skills sharp, free of emotional encumbrance, and objective.

More recently, there has been growing recognition that it matters greatly who the therapist is as well as what he does. This is true in psychoanalytic circles but even more decisively among students of client-centered therapy and other humanistic-existential therapies. Consequently, considerable research is being devoted to discover which facets of the therapist's personality and background affect psychotherapeutic progress, both positively and negatively. In clinical settings, it is commonplace for therapy to be recommended "with a man, so that the young male patient can work out his male identity problems better" or "with a younger, more active therapist . . ." etc. Because of the central importance given to the personality and attitudes of the therapist by Rogers (e.g., 1957) and his co-workers, many students of therapy are now inclined to the view that the qualities of the therapist may be more vital than the techniques he uses.

In general, research has focused on two types of therapist variables: (1) those qualities which existed before and independently of therapy, and hence can be independently measured (e.g., experience, race, general personality attributes), and (2) those which are manifested and measured in the relation with the patient (e.g., empathy, warmth, countertransference). Though extensive, research on therapist factors has thus far generated fewer major findings than has the study of patient variables.

Professional Background and Training. Surprisingly, there is virtually no research on the effectiveness of therapy as a function of *professional discipline.* Though the relative merits of psychiatrists, clinical psychologists, and psychiatric social workers as psychotherapists have been argued long and hard, there is no empirical evidence supporting or denying any of the claims or counterclaims. Similarly, and just as surprising, is the lack of research evidence supporting the widely held belief that personal therapy and good personality integration increase the therapist's effectiveness. Holt and Luborsky (1958) reported that supervisors' ratings of the competence of psychiatric residents in training did not relate to whether or not, or for how long, they were in personal therapy. In one study in VA clinics, McNair, Lorr, and Callahan (1963) found no relation between the therapist's therapy and patients tendency to quit therapy. Yet in another study (McNair, Lorr, Young, Roth, and Boyd, 1964) there was evidence that those therapists who had had more personal therapy tended to be more effective. On the other side of the ledger is the finding that patients treated by nontreated graduate student therapists have proportionately better outcomes than those being seen by student-therapists who have already completed a moderate (80–175 hours) or a considerable amount (200–450 hours) of personal therapy (Garfield and Bergin, 1971). Though the differences fall short of statistical significance, they show not only that "none" is better than "some," but also that "some" is better than "a whole lot." Patient outcome measures were highest when the therapists had no therapy, intermediate in the moderate group, and lowest in the intensively treated group. Other than the obvious interpretation, explanations could include (1) that perhaps those longest in therapy were the most disturbed people, and the poorer outcome relates to that fact; or (2) that while in therapy, therapists are too consumed with their own problems to attend well to those of others. Perhaps later on the well-therapized therapists will function better than their untreated colleagues. Though incidental to our present concern, it is interesting to note that Wispé and Parloff (1965) found that a sample of fifty-five mature psychologists who had been in long-term therapy, mainly psychoanalysis, did not thereafter increase their rate of publications. Some have interpreted this as a "negative outcome finding," an arguable point!

Evidence for the importance of *experience* is both more available and more positive. Most studies find that more experienced and fully trained professionals tend to do better than less experienced workers in their agencies, regardless of the type of therapy practiced. Patients of the more experienced therapists less commonly terminate prematurely and overall show greater gains by the various indices used. Similarly, in five studies that independently assessed the technical *skills* of therapists, three clearly showed the more skillful to be more helpful to their clients (Luborsky et al., 1971). Kernberg et al. (1972) also reported that therapist skill led to greater improvement in patients. They found therapist skill to be of particular importance if the patient had relatively low ego strength.

There has been considerable interest, in the recent past, in determining whether people without training and credentials could contribute therapy (like) aid to needy patients. Studies have evaluated both college-student volunteers and "indigeneous nonprofessionals," community people sharing the patient's ethnic or cultural background, usually in work with hospitalized patients or in community agencies. Because of the importance of using nonprofessionals in community psychology, we shall discuss these efforts and their evaluation in detail in Chapter 18. Suffice to note here that people without formal training have been found to be of distinct help to their clients, in some cases even in comparison with professionals.

Personality Characteristics. There is no lack of opinion among clinicians (and particularly among those of us who teach them!) about what personal qualities are needed to be a good therapist. Krasner (1962) was able to compile a list of traits, gleaned from several authors, which amounts to a catalog of human virtues, impossible to conceive in the person of any one, flesh-and-blood human. At the same time, empirical findings are few and scattered. Indeed, one can question whether it is even realistic to expect to find a general personality syndrome characterizing the ideal therapist, since different traits would likely be required to work, say, with children or adults, individuals or groups, more hostile or more passive patients, intellectualizing versus repressing individuals, and so on. Of potentially greater importance is the question of whether the matching of therapist and patient characteristics matters; this issue we will consider in the next section.

In their study of psychiatric residents in training, Holt and Luborsky (1958) selected some thirty-two traits generally held to be characteristic of good therapists. Two observers studied the variety of tests and assessment interviews available on each of sixty-four residents and rated each of these traits. These ratings in turn were correlated with supervisors' ratings of therapeutic competence. Overall, the correlations obtained were disappointingly low. There was some evidence that more competent therapists tended to be better socially adjusted, genuine, free from status concerns, self-objective, heterosexually adjusted, and emotionally controlled.

Empathy, Nonpossessive Warmth, and Genuineness. Rogers (1957) argued strongly that the therapist's qualities of accurate empathy, unconditional positive regard, and genuineness serve as necessary and sufficient conditions for therapeutic change (see Chapter 14, pp. 703–705). Considered as "therapist-offered conditions" or more recently as "therapist interpersonal skills," they have been studied extensively (e.g., Barrett-Lennard, 1962; Truax and Carkhuff, 1967; Truax and Mitchell, 1971). In the phrasing of Truax and Mitchell (1971):

> (1) an effective therapist is nonphony, nondefensive, and authentic or *genuine* in his therapeutic encounter; (2) an effective therapist is able to provide a nonthreatening, safe, trusting, or secure atmosphere through his own acceptance, positive regard, love, valuing or *nonpossessive warmth*, for the client; and, (3) an effective therapist is able to understand, "be with," "grasp the meaning of," or have a high degree of *accurate empathic understanding* of the client on a moment-to-moment basis [p. 302].

These characteristics are believed to be the essential ingredients of the psychotherapeutic relation and to cut across the particular concepts and procedures of all schools.

Genuineness, nonpossessive warmth, and accurate empathic understanding are rated directly from the tape recordings of therapy hours. Over many studies these variables, individually and together, have been found to be related to both the course and outcome of therapy. Figure 16.2 gives the findings of a study made in collaboration with the Johns Hopkins group (Truax, Wargo, Frank, Imber, Battle, Hoehn-Saric, Nash, and Stone, 1966). Therapists who provided higher "conditions" (i.e., who had higher composite ratings on the three variables) had patients who improved more in terms of global-improvement ratings made by both the therapists and the patients. On the other hand, patients seen by therapists rated lower in these conditions improved less or actually deteriorated.

However, Garfield and Bergin (1971) were not able to replicate these findings in a study of graduate psychology student therapists. First of all, ratings of the three "conditions" tended to intercorrelate significantly, suggesting that the variables were less independent than hypothesized by the Truax group. Moreover, none of the variables related to outcome. Patients did as well or poorly with therapists at all positions on each of the three scales. Since this group of student therapists inclined more to an eclectic or dynamic model of therapy, Garfield and Bergin propose that the constructs may be limited to a client-centered approach.

Truax and Carkhuff (1967) report that rated warmth, genuineness, and empathy seem to be largely independent of patient characteristics; in other words, they are not simply called forth by patients of particular types, but rather seem to reflect enduring therapist traits. Moreover, though some therapists are more and others less endowed, these are skills which can be developed and sharpened. They seem relevant not only to psychotherapy but other human influence situations, such as teaching. Research in this realm is promising, particularly for the use of process ratings to define therapist qualities, but the findings are far from definitive. Studies have generally used student therapists; it has not yet been shown that measurably effective mature therapists also have these same charac-

FIGURE 16.2.
Patient Change in Relation to Empathy, Warmth, and Genuineness of the Therapist *

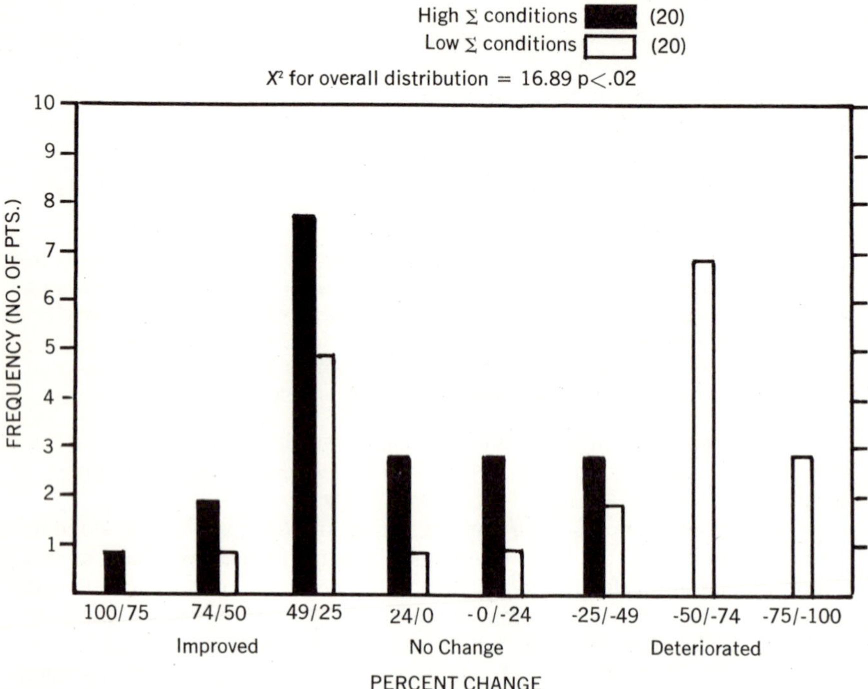

* Data from Truax, Wargo, Frank, Imber, Battle, Hoehn-Saric, Nash and Stone, *Journal of Consulting Psychology*, 1966, 30, 395–401. Figure from A. E. Bergin & S. L. Garfield (Eds.), *Handbook of psychotherapy and behavior change: an empirical analysis.* New York: Wiley, 1971, p. 311. Reprinted by permission.

teristics. Not unlikely, warmth, empathy and genuineness are necessary therapist attributes, but it is at least premature to see them as sufficient conditions of therapeutic change.

Type A and Type B Therapists. Over several years, Whitehorn and Betz (1954, 1960; Betz, 1962) reported evidence that they could distinguish therapists who were particularly effective with hospitalized schizophrenic patients (Type A therapists) from those who were less successful (Type B). Their investigations were based largely on clinical records studied some time after treatment was concluded. Later, they tested the two groups of therapists and found empirically a consistent pattern of scores on the Strong Vocational Interest Blank (SVIB), a widely used test in vocational guidance. Four SVIB scales distinguished the A and B clinicians, namely, Lawyer, Certified Public Accountant, Printer, and Mathematics-Physical Science Teacher. Type A therapists had interests like those of lawyers and accountants and unlike those of printers and mathematics-physical science teachers; Type B therapists more resembled the latter. Extracting the critical distinguishing items, a short A-B scale was constructed. In subsequent studies, it proved to be a useful measure and related to various other facets of therapist personality. An extensive body of research has evolved over the past twenty years (Carson, 1967; Razin, 1971; Chartier, 1971). By and large, the Whitehorn-Betz finding has been sustained, although there is contradictory evidence, and the area has been muddied by a proliferation of different versions of the A-B scale. By now, there are perhaps ten scales all derived from the original Whitehorn-Betz data base, mainly as efforts to simplify, e.g., by factor analysis, the original twenty-three-item scale.

Stephens and Astrup (1965), working in the same setting as Whitehorn and Betz, failed to find A-B scores differentiating better and worse therapists of schizophrenics. They used four different scoring systems but found no significant relationship between the A-B variable and outcome, either at discharge or follow-up. In an effort to see whether the Whitehorn-Betz hypothesis applied as well to the treatment of nonschizophrenic patients McNair, Callahan, and Lorr (1962) studied forty male therapists (twenty As and twenty Bs) who treated forty male patients in seven VA clinics over a four-month period of once-a-week therapy. A variety of assessment procedures were used before and after treatment and at a one-year follow-up. Surprisingly, it was found that the patients of Type B therapists improved significantly more at the end of the four months. The improvement continued at the 12-month follow-up evaluation. Thus, the Whitehorn-Betz finding for schizophrenics was reversed. McNair, Callahan and Lorr speculate that perhaps Type A therapists do better with schizophrenics but Type B therapists with neurotics. A plausible alternate explanation takes account of the fact that the McNair subjects came from distinctly lower social classes than the Whitehorn-Betz group. Their own SVIB scores tended to resemble those of B therapists in emphasizing technical and skilled-labor interests. Hence, the authors speculated that B therapists might have been more successful than Type A therapists with this population because of greater similarity of interests and familiarity with their everyday life and problems. In a later study, McNair, Lorr, and Callahan (1963) found no relation between A-B status and whether patients stayed in or dropped out of treatment.

The results are equivocal, but there continues to be considerable interest in the A-B distinction. Though essentially an empirical typology with no obvious rationale behind it, efforts have been made to explicate its meaning by relating the A-B dimension to other personality characteristics. Thus, in one study (Pollack and Kiev, 1963) A and B subjects were found to differ in cognitive style; the latter were more field independent on the Witkin Rod and Frame test. Still, the meaning of the typology remains elusive, as does its relation to therapeutic outcome, but this may be clarified in further research.

Other Variables. Though the research evidence is contradictory, some studies show that patients liked by their therapists tend to have more favorable outcomes (Strupp, Wallach, Wogan, and Jenkins, 1963) and to remain longer in therapy (Caracena, 1962). However, for each of these studies, contrary evidence can be cited. Still, it seems most unlikely that a therapist could function well with people he strongly disliked.

Direct research evidence for the role of *countertransference* is hard to find, despite its importance as a clinical concept. Surveying the available literature, Strupp (1971) concludes that the evidence in hand suggests that therapist conflicts in regard to dependency, warmth, intimacy, and hostility can adversely affect a patient's progress in therapy.

Although most therapists refrain from directly communicating their political and social values in psychotherapy, nonetheless these somehow become known to patients. D. Rosenthal (1955) found that patients who improved in therapy altered their moral values in the direction of those held by their therapist. Supportive and related evidence has been found in more recent studies (e.g., Parloff, Goldstein, and Iflund, 1960; Parloff, Iflund, and Goldstein, 1958; Bühler, 1962; London, 1964; and Welkowitz, Cohen, and Ortmeyer, 1967). That the therapist, in diverse ways, serves as a model for the patient to emulate is well attested by the work of Bandura (1971).

THE INTERACTION OF PATIENT AND THERAPIST

Distinguishing "patient variables" and "therapist variables" is to an important degree artificial. In actuality, of course, these are in constant interplay, and the importance of any factor may depend on the interaction between patient and therapist qualities. More attractive and likeable patients, we have noted, fare better, but whether a patient is judged attractive and likeable depends on the personal standards of the therapist. Therapeutic gain depends on the patient's trust and faith, but this in turn can be determined by the therapist's communicated trustworthiness and genuineness. That lower-class patients have difficulties in therapy has been demonstrated, but the source of the problem may well derive from the fact that almost without exception they are being treated by therapists of middle-class status and values. Less intelligent patients do more poorly, but how much of what kind of intellectual skill is needed may depend importantly on the cognitive style and intellectuality of the therapist as well as on the particular techniques he uses. Thus, it matters greatly how therapist and patient characteristics mesh. The therapist-patient *relationship,* defined by the unique interplay of the needs, expectations, and values of the two parties, figures prominently in the determination of outcome.

Research on the effects on outcome of the interplay of patient and therapist qualities has centered in three realms: (1) the congruence between patient and therapist expectations; (2) the role of personality similarity; and (3) the role of similarity in cultural-social characteristics.

Congruence Between Patient and Therapist Expectations. Faith in psychotherapy, as already noted, leads patients to seek treatment, stay with it, and generally to benefit. However, if one examines how the patient's particular expectations (as to what will happen, why, and to what end) interact with those of the therapist, it seems that congruence between the two is important for therapeutic progress.

Heine and Trosman (1960) found that patients who viewed therapy in terms of passive cooperation (*guidance orientation,* i.e., taking advice, doing as told) were more likely to drop out than those who shared the therapist's view of therapy as active collaboration (*participation orientation,* i.e., working together toward finding problem solutions). Similar findings were obtained by Overall and Aronson (1963) in a study of lower-class patients. Clemes and D'Andrea (1965) tested the effects of expectation compatibility on anxiety in an initial interview. Patients were divided into participation and guidance groups, according to the Heine-Trosman criteria. Patients in the "compatible interviews" (i.e., where they and their therapists shared the same expectations) showed less anxiety, at least in terms of one of the two measures used. Similarly, therapists found the compatible interviews easier to conduct and less anxiety-arousing for themselves. Lennard and Bernstein (1960) also found that incongruence of expectations went with greater strain in the interview. Other findings support the general conclusion that patients benefit more if they receive therapy consonant with their expectations (Goin, Yamamoto, and Silverman, 1965; Levitt, 1966; Schonfield et al., 1969). Though promising, this line of research has so far been limited to the guidance-participation dimension.

In most studies it is assumed that therapists share equally a participation ideology and, therefore, that differences in congruence are contributed entirely by differences in patient expectations. Moreover, expectations are usually assessed at the outset without studying the way they may change over time; an important part of therapy process in the minds of most clinicians. Further studies are needed to explore other realms of expectations and beliefs, changes over time, and the precise ways in which congruence affects the process and outcome of therapy.

Personality Similarity Between Patient and Therapist. Does "it take one to know one" or do "opposites attract?" Folk wisdom provides us with two reasonable, if contradictory, hypotheses for the study of patient-therapist personality similarity. Greater similarity might make for greater empathy and understanding; dissimilarity might heighten objectivity. In fact, some have proposed that either too much or too little similarity between patient and therapist can interfere. The best outcome would then be predicted from a medium level of similarity between patient and therapist personality. Despite the reasonableness and appeal of the hypothesis, a very mixed picture emerges when one reviews the research literature. Evidence can be found equally well both for and against the assumption that similarity is related to therapeutic progress, in either linear or curvilinear ways.

In a series of studies of client-counselor similarity at the University of California Counseling Center at Berkeley, Mendelsohn and Geller (1963, 1965, 1966, 1967) report limited but persuasive evidence of a relation between similarity and outcome. Client and counselor personality was assessed by means of a measure of Jungian variables; outcome was judged in terms of duration of counseling. In one study, a straightforward linear relation was found between dissimilarity and earlier termination; in other studies, the relation appeared to be curvilinear. However, these findings were neither strong nor consistent. Inexplicable differences were found among various scales of the personality test and for men and women clients. In their 1967 paper, Mendelsohn and Geller report a definite, though contradictory, relation between similarity and terminating or missing appointments. Clients *most like* their therapists more often showed *disinterest* in therapy; the more dissimilar pairs, by contrast, continued working together.

Carson and Heine (1962) used patient-therapist similarity of MMPI scores in a study of clinic patients being given short-term psychotherapy by fourth-year medical students in training. Outcome ratings were based on patient satisfaction, therapist judgment, symptomatic relief, and ratings of work and social adjustment. They found a curvilinear relation between similarity and success. Up to a point, the more dissimilar the pair, the greater the success of treatment. After that point, greater dissimilarity led to poorer results. The authors reason that where the therapist was too similar to the patient, he might overidentify with the patient and his problems and function ineffectively. On the other hand, if too dissimilar he might not be able to understand the patient's concerns. Unfortunately, however, the Carson-Heine findings did not stand up under replication. Using identical procedures and a similar population, Lichtenstein (1966) found no relation whatever between similarity and outcome. In another try, Carson himself was unable to reproduce his 1962 findings (Carson and Llewellyn, 1966). The authors concluded that the originally obtained curvilinear pattern was "at best a rather ephemeral phenomenon."

Another approach was taken by Sapolsky (1965) who tested the hypothesis that patients would improve more who felt they were similar to the therapist, regardless of actual fact. Indeed, he found that those who rated their therapists much as they rated themselves on a series of semantic differential scales showed more improvement.

After critically reviewing some twenty-one studies, Meltzoff and Kornreich (1970, p. 325) conclude: "Looking at all of these studies in the aggregate, we can find no solid evidence that patient-therapist similarity or dissimilarity either aids, abets, or hampers effectiveness. Hopes for matching patients and therapists along personality dimensions dwindle. No strong, consistent effects have been found with a variety of aspects of personality, and some clear failures to find any relation lead us to conclude, pending a truly definitive study, that the null hypothesis is the most tenable." The value of research findings in this area is limited by the fact that most studies have depended on gross and global personality measures and investigated only short-term psychotherapy or counseling, usually performed by inexperienced therapists. Hence, the similarity hypothesis remains plausible and attractive, if not yet empirically established nor even properly tested.

Similarity in Sociocultural Background and Values. A parallel issue concerns the role of similarity, not in terms of personality characteristics, but rather in social class, ethnic identification, and other broad-scaled social characteristics which define the experiences, attitudes, and values of both therapist and patient. Critics point out that we seem most effective in treating people most like ourselves—reasonably healthy, educated, psychologically minded, white, male, and affluent. Articulate spokesmen for the women's liberation movement, the black community, and homosexuals have accused mental health professionals, not without cause, of being at least insensitive if not outright antagonistic to their proper concerns and problems. At the extreme, some argue that if patients are to be fairly and effectively treated they must be seen by a therapist of the same social identity. The notion of the *ideal* therapist has traveled a long way—from Freud's original view of the skilled *psychic surgeon,* through Rogers' insistence on necessary *human* qualities, to the new call, in some quarters, for *social* similarity of therapist and patient!

Certain issues should be put aside quickly in our consideration of the importance of sociocultural similarity.

1. No one would deny that gross dissimilarity cannot produce good psychotherapy. A black man cannot be treated by a Ku Kluxer, nor a male chauvinist by a woman's libber. Patient and therapist must have some (but how much?) shared experience, values, and mutual respect. Therapist and patient must speak the same language, figuratively as well as literally. It would be patently absurd for me

to take my (non-German-speaking) self to Vienna even to be treated by a (non-English-speaking) Freud. So too, it would be equally absurd to expect help from someone who, for ethnic, religious, class, or other reason, could not comprehend nor sympathize with my life style and values.

2. However, if the issue of similarity is pushed to its logical extreme, the only one a therapist could treat is himself, for no one else matches precisely on ethnic, class, sex, education, age, occupation, urbanization, and other potentially relevant variables. The intercept of all these variables, in the limiting case, describes only one person. Realistically, therefore, similarity has to be taken to mean congruence in terms of the patient's principal and most encompassing focus of social identification, whether black or woman or Catholic or, for that matter, professor or psychologist. That this is not always easy to decide was noted, in a simpler era, by William James when he called attention to our several "social selves."

3. Patients should have the full right to choose therapists of compatible qualities, if they so wish. Just as an orthodox Jew should not be forced to go to a Catholic hospital (even if the medical care were identical), so the black person should be free to choose a black therapist, the woman a woman, and so on, regardless of what professional opinion or research evidence says about the effects of such matching. That such choice is now limited is an unhappy consequence of social and professional history and practices which must be changed.

4. Hence, there should be no reservation whatever about the principle that qualified people of all social origins should have equal access to professional training. There is acute need for more minority professionals to improve the service to minority communities.

However, having noted these issues, what is the evidence that social similarity or dissimilarity affects therapy outcome? Let us look at similarity in terms of psychotherapy for the poor, which necessarily also includes ethnic minority status in our society. A body of evidence, already noted, shows that lower-class people, compared to their middle-class counterparts, less commonly seek, are less often referred for, and are less commonly accepted in psychotherapy. They are more likely to be assigned to inexperienced therapists and to discontinue therapy sooner. Whether they actually benefit less remains moot. Even discontinuation, often taken as an index of failure in therapy research, may simply indicate that the patient has realized his goals, if not those of the therapist. For a thorough and critical review of the research literature bearing on psychotherapy for the poor, see E. E. Jones (1974).

It has been claimed that many lower-class patients lack the requisites for psychotherapy; they are insufficiently intelligent, verbal, educated, introspective, and the like. But the available evidence does not demonstrate that these are requisites for therapeutic gain, though they are found to be more distinctly related to continuation. In addition, however, a growing number of therapists and researchers are discovering that lower-class patients are in fact more psychologically minded (Goin, Yamamoto, and Silverman, 1965), verbally expressive (Riessman, 1964; Gould, 1967), and overall, better therapy risks (Riessman and Scribner, 1965) than had been supposed. In some measure, the assumed deficiencies of the poor patient reflect more the bias of clinicians rather than inherent lacks in the patient. The clinician, operating in terms of middle-class ideology and expectations, is inclined to see the lower-class patient as sicker, less adapted for, and less worthy of psychotherapy, as Kingsley Davis (1938) argued long ago.

There is direct evidence of bias. Minority patients are both more likely to be judged as less adequate and also to function more poorly when being evaluated by majority-culture examiners and interviewers as compared to members of their own ethnic group (Sattler, 1970). In a study specifically designed to investigate class-related bias, Haase (1962) constructed eight Rorschach protocols to produce four matched pairs. The members of each pair were equivalent in terms of formal scores and content. Four pairs of social histories were also written, identical except for identifying the "patient" as middle-class in one case and lower-class in the other. Then seventy-five psychologists were asked to analyze the records and make clinical judgments about each of the patients. Significantly more often, the clinicians diagnosed the "lower-class" patients as having a psychosis or character disorder while the "middle-class" patients more commonly ended up as normal or neurotic. Interesting to note, and worth dwelling on, were the further findings that such bias did not relate to the psychologists' own class of origin, experience level, theoretical orientation or type of clientele with which they worked.

We have already noted the fact that the effectiveness of therapy can be limited by incongruence between the patients' and therapists' expectations as to the nature and goals of therapy. Poorer patients, it is reported, expect more directive advice, medical care, and a briefer course of treatment. Since they are less likely to share the typical therapist's "participation" orientation, they are less likely to continue in psychotherapy.

In view of these and related considerations, some have concluded that psychotherapy can be of little help to the lower-class patients with his problems. But before hastening to such a conclusion, some additional facts should be noted:

1. The effects of similarity or dissimilarity along social dimensions have thus far been studied in only limited ways and generalizations have to be tenuous. Invariably, the clients are the poorer and/or minority member of the therapist-patient pair. Moreover, the therapists are usually novices, therapy is brief, the work is done in medical settings or public clinics, and the research analysis is limited to one or a few sessions. There is only one study, to my knowledge, which involves a truly balanced design and attempts to correct some of the deficiencies of the existing literature. Enrico E. Jones in research now in progress in the Psychology Clinic at Berkeley has matched white and black therapists with white and black patients, thus producing white-white, white-black, black-black, and black-white therapist-patient pairings, in order to discover how these different racial combinations might differently affect the process and outcome of therapy. Further and more detailed studies of this type are needed before any definitive conclusions can be drawn.

2. More experienced, mature, and flexible therapists, although middle class and white, work more effectively with lower-class patients than their less well-endowed coprofessionals. Thus, Baum, Felzer, D'Zmura, and Schumaker (1966) found that those therapists who were personally more secure, clinically more experienced, and had had personal therapy, related better to lower-class patients and had a lower dropout rate than those therapists lacking these qualities. Therapists rated as more skillful by their teachers were significantly more successful than less skillful colleagues in treating working-class patients in a psychoanalytic clinic (Terstman, Miller, and Weber, 1974). In the same spirit, Hughes (1972)

found that white therapists who have had personal psychotherapy themselves had more successful outcomes with nonwhite patients than nontreated therapists. Therapists who can be more open and flexible, and modify their procedures in terms of their patients' expectations, can be of greater help to lower-class patients. Gould (1967) in an article appropriately titled "Dr. Strangeclass; Or, how I stopped worrying about the theory and began treating the blue-collar worker," tells how much more successful he became when she became more informal, active, and ready to meet with clients outside the consulting room.

3. Other efforts to modify usual approaches have used instruction and modeling to facilitate patients entering and gaining from therapy. Thus, Hoehn-Saric, Frank, Imber, Nash, Stone, and Battle (1964) have found a "role-induction interview" effective. In this session patients are given a general exposition of therapy, prepared for phenomena like resistance, told that time is required, and how therapist and patient should behave. Truax and Carkhuff (1965, 1967) found that playing a thirty-minute tape of a "good" therapy session to patients positively affected later outcome. Others have experimented with film and videotape to the same end.

4. Matching of therapist and patient, particularly on racial identity, can facilitate therapy. Carkhuff and Pierce (1967) trained two black and two white nonprofessional counselors, one of middle- and one of lower-class origin in each pair, and then assigned them sixteen clients equally distributed along the race and class dimensions. Taped interview segments were scored for "depth of self-exploration," which was found to be greatest when therapist and patient were most closely matched on both race and class.

In all, what emerges is a complex picture. The lower-class patient may gain less in therapy, but the responsibility is as much the therapist's as his. Bias, inflexibility, and narrowness can heighten existing incongruence of values and expectations and block the lower-class patient from therapeutic gain. Under optimal conditions, that is, with a therapist who is open and flexible, personally mature and free of binding prejudice and personal conflict, or where techniques can be creatively altered and/or matching is possible, psychotherapy can clearly be of value to lower-class patients. It may require more effort and creativity, but the ready conclusion, whether from "conservative" or from "radical" premises, that psychotherapy of the poor is futile is not warranted.

It is of course true that the poor have profound psychosocial problems and needs which require more direct forms of intervention than psychotherapy. They have to cope with harsh social reality, and much of their distress relates to marginal budgets, unemployment or work conditions, crime, or inadequacies in housing or schooling, for which material help is needed. They need to be helped to develop social competencies in order to be better prepared to manage their own lives. For the long-term prospect, the mental health of the poor may be more advanced by efforts to alter stressful social institutions rather than by individual therapy of any type, as we will consider in detail in coming chapters. But this does not mean that lower-class people do not have emotional problems or that they are incapable of benefiting from psychotherapy. Psychotherapy is not a panacea for the psychological problems of either the rich or the poor, but it has a proper place in alleviating the human problems of both.

What can we conclude as to the general issue of social similarity between psychotherapist and patient? The determining factors are obviously complex and the empirical evidence is too slight and contradictory for ready general conclusions. The best one can venture are hypotheses. The danger of excessive dissimilarity matching is clear, but neither is too much similarity without hazard. Dissimilarity blocks communication and mutual understanding; excessive similarity encourages overidentification and loss of perspective and projection. While this would argue for some mid-value as being most productive, the actual outcome probably depends on the interaction of these factors: how firmly the patient's identity and problems reside in his social class membership and the professional as well as personal qualities of the therapist. Thus, if a patient's social identity is central to his self-concept, and moreover if his presenting problem centers in that realm as well, then he would probably fare better with a socially similar therapist. A Catholic priest obsessed with sexual thoughts would probably do best to see a Catholic therapist, perhaps one who is himself ordained. On the other hand, a Catholic layman consumed with self-doubt about his adequacy in school or work might as well be treated by a Protestant or Jewish therapist. Finally, the qualifications of the therapist may be the most decisive consideration in deciding who should best treat which patient. The younger person, with narrower life experiences and more limited training, can probably be most helpful to those similar in social class, ethnic origin, sex, and age. With increased maturity, however, and broadened life as well as professional experiences, a therapist should be able to work effectively with a broader spectrum of clients. Ultimately, the essence of a fine clinician lies in his ability to transcend his own experiences, personal or social, so that he can empathically understand those of others.

THERAPEUTIC TECHNIQUES

The outcome of therapy depends obviously not only on the qualities of patients and therapists, separately and in interaction, but also on the specific therapeutic techniques and actions employed. Textbooks and clinical teachers emphasize, as I did in Chapter 13, the many specific technical interventions which therapists can use to influence the feelings, attitudes, and behavior of patients. Depending on the orientation involved, these would include such factors as setting goals and limits, the timing and frequency of sessions, recognizing and reflecting feelings, setting up desensitization hierarchies and the timing, depth, and accuracy of interpretations, among numerous others. Despite the wealth of theory-related precepts drawn from considerable clinical wisdom and experience, there is relatively little empirical research specifically testing the effects on outcome of particular variations in technique.

At the broadest level the issue of technique and outcome is of course the question of the relative efficacy of different schools or approaches to therapy; this subject we considered in some detail earlier in this chapter. As we saw, attempts to compare psychotherapies based on uncontrolled clinical surveys have been notably unfruitful. Even more controlled efforts, as Paul's (1966) analogue comparison of desensitization with "insight-oriented psychotherapy," are questionable on both logical and methodological grounds. Overall, we cannot say, from the research evidence available, that one or another form of psychotherapy is "best," nor is the question particularly meaningful when so broadly phrased.

Interesting information has been obtained on more sharply put questions.

For example, a considerable literature explores the effect of temporal variables in psychotherapy. A greater amount of therapy (i.e., more sessions over a longer period) has most commonly been reported as resulting in greater therapeutic gains. Some studies, however, have found no clear relation between outcome and duration and/or frequency or they report a non-linear relation between amount and outcome. Two contrasting phenomena complicate these studies. On the one hand, many patients who are going to improve make their major gains within the first few sessions. On the other hand, a fair number of patients terminate early as therapeutic failures. These two tendencies could cancel each other in group comparisons of time versus change. A positive relation between amount of therapy and outcome is thus more likely to be obtained where there are more early-failure dropouts than successes. There is no clear evidence that more frequent sessions, e.g., three or four rather than one session per week, has any more beneficial effects, although the literature suggests that less than one session a week may be less useful.

On the twin assumptions that therapy left to go on indefinitely would yield diminishing returns and that given a deadline people tend to work more effectively, studies have investigated the effect of arranging a time limit in advance. In one such study, Henry and Shlien (1958) contrasted a time-limited group (averaging eighteen sessions) with a time-unlimited group (averaging thirty-seven sessions) in client-centered therapy. While both improved significantly in self-ideal Q-sort comparisons, therapists rated the time-limited group as 90 percent successful as against 66 percent for the time-unlimited group. In a more detailed later study, involving Adlerian as well as client-centered therapy, Shlien, Mosak, and Dreikurs (1962) again showed the value of time-limited therapy. In contrast to therapy with no contracted time limit, patients in the time-limited groups showed earlier improvement and rose to a higher final level. Although more studies need to be done, methods of brief psychotherapy and crisis intervention have built on these findings.

In other realms, research relating technique to outcome is much more limited. Efforts to evaluate the relative merits of individual and group procedures come generally to the conclusion that both are valuable though under different conditions. There have also been important research efforts to evaluate the emotional relation between patient and therapist, the therapist's use of interpretation and its depth, and processes of verbal conditioning which alter patient behavior in therapy. However, most of these have not concerned the question of therapeutic outcome; these variables have been investigated in the context of process studies. They will be discussed in a later section reviewing process research.

THE SOCIOCULTURAL DETERMINANTS OF PSYCHOTHERAPY

Much of what we have discussed, though put in terms of characteristics of the therapist, the patient, the interaction between them and the methods of psychotherapy, actually reflects more pervasive social and cultural factors in the larger society. At the broadest level, the fact that psychotherapy exists at all reflects the faith of our society that human nature is malleable, that deviance and human problems result from disturbances of human development and learning, and that they can be undone by the systematic use of technical knowledge. Not all cultures hold such beliefs, and psychotherapy has not gained as extensive acceptance in more traditional, less industrial, and more rigid societies. The system of cultural beliefs within which he operates determines the therapist's orientation and consequently his actions; so too, the patient's beliefs and actions are also culturally determined. Where these differ, as we have noted in the incongruence between the values of middle-class therapists and lower-class patients, the progress of therapy can be hampered.

The more motivated patient gains more in therapy, but motivation in turn depends on the social circumstances of the patient's life. Kadushin (1969) shows that people who seek psychotherapy, compared to those who do not, are more likely to be identified with a social network which he calls "The friends and supporters of psychotherapy." The "friends" tend to be more affluent, educated, culturally sophisticated, and more sensitive to problems of self-valuation, sex, and interpersonal relations. Their attitudes are secular rather than religious. They have sought or considered psychotherapeutic help and see it as a solution to human problems. In their social world, psychotherapy is a significant cultural activity, generally looked on with respect rather than as a source of stigma. By contrast, the greater part of the population, even those with real need for professional service, do not share this system of values, as discovered both in a national survey (Gurin, Veroff, and Feld, 1960) and a more recent study in the Boston area (Ryan, 1969).

At another level, the immediate social system within which psychotherapy is practiced greatly affects its nature and possibly outcome. Such social-system factors include the definitions of professional and patient roles and their accompanying normative expectations (how one should act) and the nature of the setting and its institutional values. Traditionally, psychotherapy was practiced entirely in private offices, clinics, or psychiatric hospitals, paid either on a fee-for-service basis or out of public or philanthropic funds. Today, these have been supplemented by "free clinics" in counterculture communities, psychological clinics, counseling centers and student psychiatric services on campuses, clinical services in church basements and storefronts, community services and crisis centers as parts of community mental health services. Costs are covered by prepaid insurance, union or company benefits, tuition payments, as well as private fees or public funds. Each of these social arrangements suggests different roles, attitudes and self-definitions on the part of the participant. The student who visits the university's psychological clinic rather than the psychiatric clinic of a local hospital may be declaring himself as "disturbed but not crazy." The "street person" who comes into the free clinic is not only getting help he can afford but by people he sees as congenial to his life-style. The psychologist working in the hospital may either feel constrained or supported by the value system of medicine, but he will likely think and act differently than the classmate working in a psychological clinic, though in a technical sense both may be practicing the same form of therapy. In the more extreme case, the prison psychologist may be so torn between the competing values of his institution and of his profession as to be unable to function effectively as a therapist. Is the clinician responsible mainly to the "correctional system" for which he works or to the patient with whom he works? In turn, can the prisoner-patient really be expected to trust and be candid with a person whom he is required to see as a condition of his "rehabilitation" and who then participates in decisions as to the length of his term and conditions of probation?

These few illustrations are briefly mentioned to give some sense of the social and cultural parameters of importance in the understanding of psychotherapy. The complete study of psychotherapy has to include examination of cultural (values, beliefs, and customs) and social (roles, institutional norms, and the social ecology) as well as psychological variables, though the major emphasis in this chapter, as in the field generally, has been on intrapersonal and interpersonal variables (Howard and Orlinsky, 1972).

Research on the Process of Psychotherapy

Process research is concerned with events that transpire within the therapy session in the interaction between the therapist and the patient. An illustrative though simple question might be "if the therapist speaks less, does this induce greater or lesser verbal output from the patient?" Unlike *outcome research,* such a study need not bear immediately or directly on the effectiveness of therapy for bringing about desired changes. Ultimately, however, process and outcome approaches can join in the effort to discover the causes of therapeutic change. The outcome-only study asks, for example, "Do initially more anxious patients gain more from psychotherapy?" Put this way, between the initial measures of anxiety and the final measures of outcome, there is a conceptual black box. An outcome-and-process study would add ". . . and is this likely to be more or less true if therapists more or less structure the therapy hours, talk more or less rapidly, attend more to feelings and less to events, and so on?"

While typical outcome research has used measures taken outside of psychotherapy, process measures may be equally or more meaningful in assessing many of the same variables. For example, a patient's initial and final anxiety level may be evaluated by an independent psychological test or diagnostic interview, but it could as well be measured by ratings of tremulousness, sweating, physiological change, self-deprecatory statements, and the like in the initial interview and at the end. There are two potential advantages to process measures: they may be more unobtrusive and they can more readily be made at repeated points during therapy. Independent measures, by contrast, are more commonly made only before and after therapy, not to tax the good will of patient and therapist, but thereby reducing the possibility of observing change over the entire course of therapy.

Process measures are either direct or indirect. Direct measures use observations or recordings made in the hour from which therapist or patient behaviors are analyzed. Other than consenting to having the session recorded or filmed, no further effort is required from the participants. Indirect process measures, by contrast, require therapists and/or patients to describe what went on or to rate specific variables. The "process notes" made by therapists for supervision or research purposes is a particular instance of an indirect process measure.

An interesting study by Orlinsky and Howard (1967) illustrates the usefulness of indirect process measures for understanding the therapeutic relation. Every therapist and patient has had the experience that some sessions are good, others less satisfying. To explore the meaning of the "good therapy hour,"

Orlinsky and Howard had both patients and therapists complete a questionnaire at the end of each session. They were asked for an overall evaluation of the session and specific questions about the topics covered, feelings experienced, the nature of the relation and the development of the session. Many of these factors correlated in the same way for both patient and therapist with judgments of "goodness" of session; in interesting instances the two differed. Thus, both patients and therapists valued hours in which the patient was emotionally involved and particularly when patients received, generated, and returned positive affects. There was less agreement, however, about the role of negative affect. Patients deemed sessions poor when they felt inadequate, frustrated, or irritable, but therapists did not fully agree that the patients' suffering meant a poor hour. However, both agreed that sessions in which the therapists felt uninvolved and unresponsive were poor. Patients alone judged sessions as good in which the therapists seemed friendly; friendliness seems less important to therapists. Therapists and patients both rated sessions as good when the patients collaborated and sought insight and when mutuality and progress toward goals were seen. The one topic both therapists and patients associated with high marks for the session was the discussion of childhood experiences and feelings. The Orlinsky-Howard study used only indirect process measures (questionnaire responses) but it could as well have used direct measures (based on recordings and judges' ratings) of many of the same factors.

Broadly viewed, the field of process research in psychotherapy lacks the cohesiveness of outcome research. Diverse issues have been addressed by students of social psychology and sociology, anthropology and linguistics, and nonverbal behavior, communication, and psychophysiology, as well as psychiatry and clinical psychology. Many of these people are concerned with the therapy session primarily as an instance of dyadic communication and interpersonal interaction and lack the clinician's concern with its uniquely therapeutic properties. Some have made experimental studies, intentionally altering facets of therapist behavior in order to study consequent changes in the patient. In the main, however, studies are more of a descriptive-correlational type (as the Orlinsky and Howard study just discussed), based on content analyses of the naturally occurring transactions of the interview. The method of content analysis is widely used in many areas of social science (e.g., the analysis of political speeches as efforts to influence attitudes). In therapy research as in other applications, the researcher faces a number of critical methodological issues, related to the size and type of unit for analysis (the word, the sentence, or the "meaning unit;" "lifts finger" or "points accusingly"), the conditions of recording or filming, the reliability of judges, among many others. That such issues matter wherever human communication and interaction is being studied is well illustrated by the arguments that surrounded the accuracy and meaning of recorded (and transcribed) conversations between a recent president and his advisors. Full discussion of the methodological problems in content analysis, and process research in therapy generally, can be found in Kiesler (1973) who also presents in detail seventeen analytic systems which have been used to study therapist-patient interaction as well as relevant aspects of patient and therapist behavior considered separately.

In an earlier discussion of research on the interview (Chapter 8) we have already noted several relevant studies, concerned mainly with verbal and nonverbal facets of communication. Here, in brief summary, are the general areas in which process research has been done, along with some selected findings.

THE DYADIC INTERACTION

Numerous studies have attempted to characterize the interpersonal relation and patient-therapist transactions by both direct and indirect measures of therapist and patient behaviors. There have been efforts to apply Bales' (1950) Interaction Process Analysis method, developed for the study of small groups, which rates the behavior of each participant in such terms as "gives opinion," "agrees," "shows solidarity," "shows tension release," etc. Efforts to develop an analytic system closer to the realities of therapeutic conversations were made by Leary and Gill (1959), Lennard and Bernstein (1960, 1969), and E. J. Murray (1956), among others. Similarly, questionnaires of various types have been used to evaluate patient and therapist attitudes and expectations and their relation to each other.

COMMUNICATION STUDIES

These necessarily overlap with efforts to describe therapist-patient interaction, but many have focused sharply on communication patterns per se. Thus, Matarazzo and his co-workers (Matarazzo and Wiens, 1972) have focused on the temporal characteristics of utterances (pacing, duration, silences, etc.) without regard to their meaning content. A wide variety of findings have been obtained showing consistent individual differences which are highly stable over time. They have found that there is considerable synchrony between the patterns of the two participants and that the interviewer can change the pattern of the person being interviewed by intentionally altering his own speech. Such temporal patterns are also found to differ with the status of the speakers, the area of discussion, and the social conditions of the interview.

In other studies, explicit analyses have been made of the linguistic, paralinguistic, and kinesic (nonverbal, motoric) behaviors in the therapeutic interview. The exquisite detail that can be involved in such studies is illustrated by the fact that Pittenger, Hockett, and Danehy (1960) wrote an entire book analyzing the first five minutes of an initial interview. Gesture, facial expression, and other facets of nonverbal behavior have also fascinated researchers. Movements of both therapists and patients have been classified and counted during therapeutic sessions. It is found, for example, that brief but characteristic facial expressions accompany blocking or denial and that characteristic individualized gestures can appear when important conflicts are touched on (Mahl, 1968).

VERBAL CONDITIONING

An extensive literature shows that the interviewer can reinforce and thereby shape the verbal behavior of the subjects (cf., Kanfer and Phillips, 1970, for review). If, for example, whenever a patient makes a positive self-reference, the therapist says "good," or "mm hmm," or smiles, the probability of such responses thereafter increases. Psychologists of Skinnerian philosophy propose that such verbal conditioning is a major part of all therapy, whether recognized or not as such by the therapist (e.g., Krasner, 1965, 1971b). Some evidence for this claim, in the case of client-centered therapy, has been offered by Truax (1966). Moreover, it has been proposed that such conditioning should be explicitly exploited as a treatment principle in its own right, as has been done by some behavior therapists. That direct verbal conditioning can go on is obvious, even without the patient's or the therapist's knowledge, but whether this can generalize into more widespread behavioral change outside of the therapy situation is doubtful.

PSYCHOPHYSIOLOGICAL STUDIES

Physiological measures such as heart rate, blood pressure, galvanic skin response, respiratory rate, muscle potentials, and the like have been taken during therapy sessions, sometimes of the therapist as well as patient, in the effort to locate physiological correlates of emotional arousal as the emotional climate changes, focal conflicts emerge, or the therapist confronts or threatens the patient. Such measurements are complex and are not simply related to the patient's affective state or the particular transactions of therapy (Lacey, 1959; Averill and Opton, 1968; Lang, 1971). Though most of the studies are small scale and exploratory, some intriguing results have been reported. Thus, DiMascio and Suter (1954), taking continuous measures simultaneously from both patient and therapist, found that during periods of high rapport, their heart rates fluctuated together. During low rapport, however, fluctuations were in opposite directions.

PROCESS STUDIES OF PATIENT VARIABLES

More pertinent are the far more extensive studies of psychological variables of the patient, including emotional state, attitudes, expectations, feelings about therapy, and the like, which have been assessed both through indirect and direct process measures. Kiesler (1973) details numerous questionnaires and content analytic systems which have been used to describe such patient variables. Among the direct measures which have been widely used are: (1) Bordin's (1966) scales assessing capacity for free association; (2) C. S. Hall and Van De Castle's (1966) content analysis of dreams; (3) M. H. Klein, Mathieu, Gendlin, and Kiesler's (1970) experiencing scale; (4) Truax's (Truax and Carkhuff, 1967) depth-of-self-exploration scale; and (5) Gottschalk and Gleser's (1969) content analytic indices of anxiety, hostility, and social alienation-personal disorganization. As the names suggest, these systems assess a number of variables of importance in psychoanalytic and client-centered therapy.

PROCESS STUDIES OF THERAPIST CHARACTERISTICS AND INTERVENTIONS

In the same fashion, extensive work has been done to evaluate qualities of the therapist and of his techniques which affect therapeutic progress. Content analysis methods have been developed to assess (1) the therapist's accurate empathy, nonpossessive warmth, and genuineness (Truax and Carkhuff, 1967; Truax and Mitchell, 1971) that were considered in some detail earlier in this chapter; (2) a depth-of-interpretation measure (Harway, Dittmann, Raush, Bordin, and Rigler, 1955). Using this scale, Speisman (1959) found that overly deep interpretations tend to arouse resistance and reduce self-exploration; shifting to more moderate levels tends to increase the patient's willingness to look at his problems; (3) therapist specificity (versus ambiguity) (Siegman and Pope, 1962); and (4) Strupp's (1957; Strupp, Chassan and Ewing, 1966) multidimensional system for analyzing therapists' behavior and interventions. Using a film-analogue situation, Strupp recorded therapists' statements as to what they would do at each moment that the film is stopped. From their responses, Strupp scores such variables as the type of therapeutic activity (whether clarifying, interpreting, structuring, guiding, etc.), the depth of intervention (amount of inference involved), dynamic focus, initiative (passivity-activity of therapist), and therapeutic climate (cold or warm). In developing his approach, Strupp built on the study of Bellak and Smith (1956), which may have been the first empirical process study of psychoanalysis. Numerous questionnaires and other indirect methods have also been used to characterize therapist behavior.

All told, process research is still scattered and fragmentary. Much effort has been devoted to problems of measurement and scale development, which have still not contributed importantly to our overriding concern—What is therapeutic in psychotherapy? What does therapeutic change depend on? How does it come about? What interventions matter? How do these depend on the qualities of the therapist and the patient which may preexist therapy? Granted these are complex questions, but the methods of process research should help clarify them. Hopefully, this will be more fully realized in the next phase of research on psychotherapy.

PART 5

COMMUNITY PSYCHOLOGY

CHAPTER 17

Community Psychology: Evolution and Orientation

The Third Mental Health Revolution

In the minds of many clinicians, we are entering a new era in the understanding and treatment of mental disorders. Heralded as a "third mental health revolution" (Hobbs, 1964) or a "third psychiatric revolution" (Bellak, 1964), the emergent field of community mental health (community psychology, community psychiatry) is proclaimed as being as radical a change in perspective on human malfunctioning and its alleviation as was wrought in earlier times by Pinel, when he struck the chains from the insane, and by Freud, when he showed that neuroses are psychologically determined and curable through therapeutic conversations. As consequence of the first revolution, the mentally disturbed emerged as sick people worthy of humane concern; from the second, their conditions were conceived as psychologically determined and psychologically treatable. The thrust of the third mental health revolution lies in the quest for the prevention of emotional disorders through social and community interventions aimed at their social determinants. Even when viewed more modestly, the hope of the community movement is that necessary services can be made more effective and available for the total population, including the poor and the alienated who have benefited least from prevailing practices.

Policy makers join with many mental health professionals in the conviction that new models of mental health must evolve if the needs of all of the people are to be served. At the same time, thoughtful critics have cautioned against the dangers of overenthusiastic acceptance of the "newest therapeutic bandwagon" (Dunham, 1965; Kubie, 1968). Work in the field has been motivated largely by pragmatic and idealistic concerns, with the development of the necessary base of theory, systematic knowledge, and program-relevant research thus far lagging behind.

In this and later chapters, we will consider the origins and background of community psychology and the community mental health movement, the emerging conceptual framework and some of the newer developments in mental health practices and techniques conceived within a community framework. Any account at this point is necessarily incomplete as the field is in a state of vigorous growth. Increasing numbers of psychiatrists and psychologists are characterizing themselves with the qualifying adjective "community." A reference guide to papers and books in the field published in 1969 listed 1,500 references which appeared in the 1960s (Golann, 1969); by now, the number has surely more than doubled. In 1965, the *Community Mental Health Journal,* exclusively devoted to work in the field, was started; in 1973, two new journals of community psychology were launched. Also in 1965, a conference was held near Boston to consider issues in the training of psychologists for work in the community mental health field. At that conference, the term "community psychology" emerged to describe the field which included, but also extended beyond, the community mental health roles of clinical psychologists. A Division of Community Psychology was added to the American Psychological Association, which now has over a thousand members. Though containing diverse orientations and activities, a number of broad orienting principles characterize community psychology.

Principles of Community Psychology

Here are some of the major themes which characterize current thinking in community psychology (see M. Levine, 1969; Roen, 1971; Cowen, 1973; Bloom, 1973; Zax and Specter, 1974).

1. Social-environmental factors are critically important in determining and changing behavior.
2. Social and community interventions (*system-oriented* interventions as against *person-oriented* interventions) can be effective for making social institutions (e.g., family, school) more health-enhancing as well as for reducing individual suffering.
3. Such interventions should be aimed at prevention rather than treatment or rehabilitation of emotional disorders. Not only the individual-in-need but the population-at-risk is the proper concern of community psychology.
4. Intervention should have as its goal the enhancement of social competence rather than simply the reduction of psychological distress. Community-oriented programs should stress the adaptive rather than the pathological in social life.
5. Help is most effective when available close to the settings in which problems arise. Therefore, community clinicians should work in familiar settings close to the person in need rather than in socially and geographically alien settings.

6. The community clinician should reach out to clients rather than waiting passively for them to seek his services. Such services should be flexible, readily available at the place and time of need, and offered in an atmosphere which reduces rather than accentuates the social distance between helper and helped. Help should be available to those who need it most, not only to those who seek it.
7. To use available resources and to extend his potential impact, the professional should collaborate with community resource people (caretakers) and use nonprofessional co-workers. His work may involve consultation more than direct services.
8. Traditional role requirements and professional customs have to be relaxed. Community services require imaginative programming and new conceptual models; innovation is to be encouraged.
9. The community should participate in, if not control, the development and operation of programs which are to serve its needs. Program priorities should reflect the needs and concerns of community members.
10. Mental health problems should be broadly rather than narrowly viewed, for they interlock with many other facets of social well-being, such as jobs, housing, and education. To be maximally effective, community mental health programs should deal with as wide a range of social problems as possible.
11. Educating the public to understand the nature and causes of psychosocial problems and the resources available for dealing with them is a valued task.
12. Since many mental health problems relate to broad-scaled social stresses such as poverty, racism, urban density, and alienation, which are beyond the reach of professional interventions, the community psychologist should be oriented toward, and as possible facilitate, social reform.
13. To develop the knowledge necessary for informed intervention, community psychology requires naturalistic and ecological research approaches.

The Field of Community Psychology

Community psychology is oriented toward averting human problems rather than simply repairing those which already exist. The ultimate goal of prevention, community psychologists believe, can best be attained through social and community interventions which alter the social institutions which vitally affect the patient's well-being. Toward this end, emphasis is shifted from intra-individual factors, whether psychodynamic or biological, toward greater attention to the social and institutional determinants of human functioning and disorder. Community psychology represents a "public health" rather than a "treatment" approach to mental health problems; consequently, there is greater concern with populations and prevention than with individuals and cure.

In actuality, however, community psychology covers a broad range of activities. It is more a way of thinking than an explicit set of principles and practices. As we noted in our earlier discussion of alternate models of mental health intervention (Chapter 5), the community approach spans a spectrum from interventions close to the "therapeutic" mode to those of "social action." In surveying a number of community-oriented programs, Schon (1968) notes four groups: (1) those which extend existing practice, aiming at populations for whom treatment has been relatively inaccessible; (2) those which focus on secondary prevention, to identify mentally ill individuals before their illness has reached crisis proportions; (3) those which aim to influence the mental health climate of a community through consultation to key institutions such as courts or schools; and (4) those in which the unit of treatment itself shifts from individuals or families to the community itself, and from the distress of individuals to the sickness of communities. Thus, in practice one community psychologist may work in direct, therapylike services to people presently in distress (as in crisis intervention, suicide prevention, etc.) while another takes as his target the social setting itself, in the interest of people living under its influence. An example of the latter might be an effort to alter the social structure of a school, and hence the behavior of teachers, as to "create a setting" which is more likely to enhance the emotional and intellectual growth of children in it (Sarason, 1972).

The term "community psychology" itself was born in the Boston conference of 1965 (Bennett, 1965; Bennett et al., 1966). The participants were psychologists in community mental health programs, but they saw a new field emerging which extended beyond concern with the mentally ill and therefore required a new name. In their view, community psychology should work toward fostering the adaptive functioning of large groups of people, only a limited number of whom could be considered actual or even potential psychiatric patients. Community psychologists would serve as ". . . change agents, social systems analysts, consultants in community affairs, and students generally of the whole man in relation to all his environments" (Bennett, 1965, p. 833). Some held that community psychologists should go beyond consultation to a social activist role; they should seek to control power as well as influencing those who now wield it. All agreed, however, that the community psychologist was to be a "participant conceptualizer" who could use his scientific skills to generate relevant knowledge and conceive programs within a model of action research. Though most were trained clinicians, community psychology was viewed as a parallel but separate field from clinical psychology, addressing distinct problems, involving different concepts and techniques and requiring separate training. Since the Boston conference, the term "community/clinical psychology" has emerged to characterize the border area, in which clinicians use socially oriented concepts and methods. This is the major area of our concern in this volume, but for simplicity I will use the term community psychology without qualification. In the present context, therefore, community psychology can be viewed as an orientation within the broadly defined field of clinical psychology, though in other respects it is a field in its own right.

Community Psychology, Community Mental Health, and Related Concepts

The term "community psychology" overlaps with the older concepts of community psychiatry, preventive psychiatry, community mental health and social psychiatry, all of which emphasize the importance of the social environment in determining and changing human behavior. Each of these terms has been defined in more conservative or more radical ways, as either being chiefly concerned with the development of new methods for the care of the mentally ill or being oriented to broad-scaled social change of importance to the normal as well as deviant members of society. Some have distinguished a practice field (community psychiatry) from a field of research and theory (social psychiatry) (e.g., Zusman, 1970). The term "social psychiatry," it is interesting to note, dates at least from 1917 when Southard first coined it in analogy to the then new field of social psychology (N. W. Bell and Spiegel, 1966). Just as "social psychology" comes from the conjunction of social and psychological concepts, Southard believed that "social psychiatry" should join social and psychiatric concerns. Terminological complexity is added by the fact that sociologists have had a long-standing interest in the study of the action of social factors on emotional disease. Thus Dunham (1947), reviewing this field for the American Sociological Society, described an already well-developed area of theory and research. "A field of 'social psychiatry' has emerged," he notes, "from the attempt to study certain problems considered as psychiatric from the point of view and with the techniques of the sociologist." However, he is troubled by the "semantic difficulty" in the term since other social and behavioral scientists are much involved in the same area. This fact, he notes further, "questions the proposition that a field of social psychiatry should be regarded as exclusively the product of the sociologist" (Dunham, 1947, p. 183). Indeed, the term "social psychiatry" is widely used by psychiatrists, by some to characterize a focus of practice as well as research (M. Jones, 1968). Thus to avert confusion, Weinberg (1967) urges other sociologists to use Arnold Rose's term "psychiatric sociology" to identify their unique concerns. The same general area has been called the "social psychology of mental health" by psychologists such as Wechsler, Solomon, and Kramer (1970). Clearly, there are no distinct or consistent meanings implied in the various combinations of "social," "community," and "sociological" with "psychiatry," "psychology," and "mental health." In addition, the terms favored often reflect the disciplinary allegiance of the user.*

In this regard, the term "community mental health," which has gained wide usage in recent years, may be the most neutral and inclusive. It can properly include the work of all of the "helping professions," such as clinical psychologists, psychiatrists, psychiatric social workers, group and youth workers, school and counseling psychologists, welfare workers, and criminologists and probation officers. The same term can encompass theory and research as well as practice techniques and programs. Although "community" does not imply as broad a focus as "social," in the present usage the two terms have become essentially synonymous. Community mental health can be narrowly conceived to mean primarily the application of socially oriented treatment techniques to mental patients but it can as much be broadly conceived to include prevention and efforts to foster psychosocial competence and positive mental health. Thus, the staff of the Langley Porter Neuropsychiatric Institute of the University of California in San Francisco defined community mental health as follows:

> The broad, multidisciplined field concerned with the wide variety of forces and structures in a community which affect the emotional stability (positive growth, development, and functioning) of a significant group of its members. It is contrasted with the traditional *clinical* approach which focuses on the particular individual in emotional distress. The attention is directed at social institutions including those concerned with welfare, health, legislation, minority groups, employment, education, church, and their interactions which can in their functioning either enhance or hinder the emo-

* The student interested in the variety of meanings in these terms should read S. E. Goldston (1965), Weinberg (1967), Sabshin (1969), Srole (1968), and Zax and Specter (1974).

> tional growth of a large segment of the population [quoted in S. E. Goldston, 1965, pp. 197–198].

In this statement, "community mental health" is essentially synonymous with "community psychology," as defined earlier in this chapter. For many, however, community mental health has come to mean the provision of psychiatric services in community mental health centers. To preserve the sense of the broader field which concerns us here, the term "community psychology" will be used, although as noted the distinctions between these terms are difficult to maintain.

Some Factors Underlying the Emergence of Community Psychology

Before going on to consider community psychological concepts and interventions in further detail, we should look more closely at the ideological, professional, and social climate which spawned the community orientation and gave it its particular philosophical flavor. Among the more salient issues are the discouragement with existing mental health concepts and functions, the changing concepts of mental illness and health, the manpower shortage, the deterioration of the state hospitals and the quest for alternatives, and the growing interest, in society at large, in problems of poverty and race in a general atmosphere of increasing social concern. Each of these matters will be considered in turn.

DISCOURAGEMENT WITH EXISTING MENTAL HEALTH CONCEPTS, ACTIVITIES, AND ROLES

Community psychology emerged, in fair measure, out of what Hersch (1968, 1969) has termed a "discontent explosion" among clinicians. Established beliefs about the nature of mental disorders and their treatment have been called into question; clinicians have found traditional roles frustrating; they question whether they can contribute significantly to the vast unmet needs of large segments of the population.

Disenchantment with Psychotherapy. Growing criticism from many quarters has shaken the faith of many clinicians in both the effectiveness and efficiency of traditional psychotherapies. Both humanistic and behavioral psychologists, from opposing vantage points, have questioned fundamental premises, as we saw in Chapter 14. More devastating, however, was the claim that psychotherapy had yet to demonstrate its effectiveness even as against no treatment whatever. This argument, launched by Eysenck in 1952, led to considerable controversy over the interpretation of the limited amount of research data available; in time, it inspired more sophisticated research studies. Although the presently available evidence shows psychotherapy to be considerably more effective than Eysenck claimed, as we concluded in Chapter 16, it is still true that it is less than the panacea some thought. However, the same body of research has brought out some genuine issues as to the universal applicability and value of psychotherapy. The ideal patient, it has been noted repeatedly, is someone already on the way to psychological health, with a fair degree of psychosocial competence, intelligence, personality integration, and insight. The more severely disturbed, the mentally retarded, the unmotivated and many of those facing the stresses of poverty or race are less well served.

Even if there were no question of the effectiveness of psychotherapy, it is clearly not an efficient procedure. It is costly in time, effort, and money, and hence most available to the most motivated and affluent. During a professional lifetime, a clinician practicing intensive psychotherapy can see only a very limited number of people. The consciences of many concerned psychoanalysts have long been troubled by this fact, however much they may help the few patients they treat. Particularly in a time of heightened social need and limited professional manpower, the need for increasing the efficiency of treatment becomes more acute. Almost seventy years ago, Freud predicted at the Fifth International Congress of Psychoanalysis in 1918 that the time had arrived for "the conscience of the community" to awaken to the fact that "the poor man has just as much right to help for his mind as he now has to the surgeon's means of saving life. The task will arise," Freud continued, "for us to adapt our technique to the new conditions" (quoted by Galdston, 1971).

Despite many statements of concern and efforts at innovation, the problem of adapting psychotherapy or finding substitutes for it remains with us. Thus, Eisenberg (1962a) speaking out vigorously for a need to shift from a therapeutic to a preventive orientation notes: "The limitations of present therapeutic methods doom us to training caretakers at a rate that ever lags behind the growing legions of the ill, unless we strike out successfully in new directions in the search for cause and treatment. . . . Society can ill afford today's precious overspecialization in which trainees may learn one method even superbly well but remain abysmally unaware of the problems besetting the bulk of the mentally ill" (p. 825).

Changing Concepts of Mental Health and Illness. More broadly, there has been widespread dissatisfaction with traditional "medical" concepts, particularly as reflected in the "custodial" but also in the "therapeutic" approaches to mental problems (see Chapters 4 and 5). From various perspectives, it has been argued that conceiving emotional disorders in analogy to physical diseases limits our understanding of human problems and our effectiveness in alleviating them. Of particular concern is the implication, in the medical model, that mental diseases reside in the individual and hence that intervention must involve treatment of the sick person to the end of removing or altering the pathological processes within him. In opposition to such a view, many have argued the need for a "social," "preventive," "growth-and-development" or in the general term being used here "community psychology" point of view which sees human problems as residing in the interplay between the distressed person and social forces.

At the extreme are those who hold that "mental illness is a myth" (Szasz, 1961) and that mental illness can be conceived essentially as a social role which is adopted by the individual responding to the attributions of relevant others in his social environment (Scheff, 1966, 1974; Sarbin, 1969). This point of view has been described as labeling theory, since the emphasis is shifted from disease-producing factors within the person to the social definitions of his society. A person is "psychologically sick," this view holds, to the extent that his deviant acts are so labeled by relevant and powerful agents of society. In its most simple and direct form, the labeling theory oversimplifies greatly for it negates much of what is known about psychological as well as biological factors in emotional disorders. But it does call attention sharply to those factors in the social environment that, if not causative, are critically important in maintaining and exacerbating mental disorders. As Sanford (1965) and others have pointed out, social forces do not operate in a vacuum; rather they act on an existing personality with its distinctive structures and functions.

Dissatisfaction with Existing Professional Roles. Mental health professionals of all kinds, like their critics, have become concerned with their limited ability to effect important changes in the level of psychological distress in the larger community. Working in clinics, private offices, and hospitals, waiting rather passively for troubled people to present themselves for help, many have come to realize the need for a greater area of influence and for earlier, quicker, and more effective services. Clinical psychologists face the additional problem of feeling unfulfilled in medical settings where primary decisions are made by physicians. The medical environment, many feel, provides too little opportunity to exert their independence and competence; too often, they see themselves as second-class citizens in a mental health enterprise dominated by medical men. The quest for autonomy has led many psychologists into the private practice of psychotherapy. Many others, however, see the new roles emerging in community psychology as providing a better route toward professional autonomy and allowing greater freedom to experiment with uniquely psychological interventions.

THE MANPOWER SHORTAGE

If there is one incontrovertible fact in the field of mental health today, it is that there is a serious and growing gap between manpower resources and the public's needs, at least when the major mental health professions are considered in their present roles and functions. The blatant manpower shortage has been a major impetus to reconceptualize professional roles, to suggest alternate ways of deploying professional time, and to seek new workers in subprofessional roles.

Albee (1959), in one of the major studies of the Joint Commission on Mental Illness and Health, surveyed manpower trends in the major mental health professions. His findings led the author and the Joint Commission to conclude "with frank pessimism, that sufficient professional personnel to eliminate the glaring deficiencies in our care of mental patients will ever become available if present population trend continues without a commensurate increase in the recruitment and training of mental health manpower." And they are not sanguine about such increases taking place. It is pointed out that in medicine itself, the parent field of psychiatry, there is a similar deficit between the number of physicians needed and those being trained. Despite the rapid growth of psychology during the late 1940s and 1950s, particularly in the clinical area, the number of available psychologists also lags behind. The fields of social welfare, psychiatric nursing, and occupational therapy show similar shortages. Private practice was absorbing increasingly large numbers of clinicians, and courts, schools, prisons, and other institutions were making increasing use of them. Career opportunities in college teaching and research centers have also attracted larger numbers of psychologists away from clinical service roles. Thus, relatively few clinicians were available for work in public psychiatric hospitals, an issue which particularly concerned the Joint Commission. At that time, three-quarters of the budgeted positions for psychologists and physicians in state and county hospitals could not be filled. Reviewing the manpower picture some years later left Albee (1967) equally pessimistic about future prospects.

The emerging community mental health centers of the 1960s have had difficulties in finding sufficient numbers of adequately trained personnel. As the hospitals they sought to complement, they have had to compete with a number of attractive alternatives for the already short number of trained professionals. In one projection, the recommended staffing for the new community mental health centers was one psychiatrist, one clinical psychologist, and one psychiatric social worker for every 50,000 people. With our present national population, this would mean that an additional 14,000–15,000 professionals would have to be trained in order to meet current needs.

To make matters worse, manpower authorities call attention to the fact that demand tends to increase with increasing supply (Arnhoff, 1968). It has been shown, for example, that countries differ enormously in the hospital resources available for mental patients, and in every case the beds are fully used. Thus, India had only 0.1 bed per 100,000 population (as of 1959) while, at the other extreme, Ireland and New Zealand had over 450 beds per 100,000 people (Lin, 1968). This hardly means that the Irish and New Zealanders have 4,500 times more psychotics than the Indians. Rather, it reveals the greater economic resources and social concerns of these countries which provides needed beds which are then used. Similarly, the number of psychiatrists, Lin also notes, differs among countries over a range of 250 to 1, between the best endowed and least well endowed nations.

With increased affluence, reduced public resistance, and greater readiness to seek help for less crippling psychological problems, demand for psychotherapy and other mental health services will predictably continue to rise. Moreover, new programs of federal and private health insurance, and contributions by companies and labor unions, will help reduce the financial burden of such care. It is fully predictable that a greater proportion of the population, in the future than in the past, will seek psychological help. Even if the number of professionals could be radically increased, the demand could rise to meet the supply of available time.

In view of present needs, population growth, the disproportionate growth of demand for psychological services, and the limited capacity of training institutions, it is easy to see why the manpower problem has spurred the search for new sources of manpower, more effective utilization of available professional time, and new conceptual models for working with human problems.

POVERTY AND MENTAL HEALTH

When one looks at the problems of the poor and minorities the need for new services comes especially into sharp focus. The life conditions of the poor are pathogenic (Sanua, 1961; Hollingshead and Redlich, 1958; Riessman, Cohen, and Pearl, 1964; Fried, 1964b; Srole et al., 1962; among others). Granted, we still do not know enough about the intervening links between economic deprivation, its sociological expressions, personality development, and subsequent pathology, the overall picture of greater incidence and prevalence of both gross pathology and lessened psychological competence in the culture of poverty is all too well established.

Not only is there greater need but there are also great inequities in the deliveries of services to the poor. Hollingshead and Redlich (1958) showed in their classic study that the poor tended to end up in custodial hospitals while the well-to-do were treated in private psychotherapy. Summing up, M. B. Smith and Hobbs (1966, p. 14) noted that "the more advanced mental health services have tended to be a middle-class luxury; chronic mental hospital custody, a lower-class horror. The relationship between the mental health helper and helped has been governed by an affinity of the clean for the clean, the educated for the educated, the affluent for the affluent." This is not to suggest that mental health workers have maliciously decided to ignore the needs of masses of the population; indeed, most in their personal attitudes would sincerely wish to see the state of the poor improved. But the conditions of clinical work, the settings in which it takes place, the nature of the contract between helper and helped all lead to the likelihood that disproportionately more service will be given to the middle-class and disproportionately less to the poor. The psychological-mindedness, introspectiveness, striving for personal growth, and motivation for therapy, important to psychotherapy, are part of the middle-class values shared by the therapist and his middle-class patient. Although, as we saw in Chapter 16, evidence does not support the simple assumption that psychotherapy is ineffective with poorer clients, it remains true that it is more difficult. When dealing with the poor, therapists and patients often speak different languages, sometimes literally as well as figuratively, and work toward different ends.

On his part, the lower-class person may distrust the mental health effort. Its institutions, hospitals, and clinics, are part of the white, affluent establishment, as are most of its practitioners. As Reiff, Riessman, and others have pointed out, the poor person often sees his problems differently than does the middle-class client. Psychological distress, he feels, is less due to his personal inadequacies than to the harsh conditions imposed on him. His problems do not reside within, but arise from without. He is oriented to action, expects to see things done, and has little patience for talk. The middle-class patient, like his therapist, sees himself handicapped by neurotic symptoms which cause pain and limit effectiveness; self-understanding and increased personal freedom are the proper goals of therapy. By contrast, the lower-class person suffers more from helplessness in the face of debilitating social stresses and his lack of competence to deal with them. Reiff (1966) aptly notes that, as they see themselves, disturbed middle-class patients are *victims of their own selves* while lower-class patients see themselves as *victims of circumstances*. For the former, *self-actualization* may be a proper goal; for the latter, *self-determination* is more realistic and meaningful (Reiff, 1966a). Intervention, to be maximally useful to the poor client, must be designed to facilitate new social competencies as well as release existing ones from neurotic inhibitions.

Not only in the field of mental health, but in health services generally, black Americans and other minorities have great unmet needs, the more so when they are viewed in the light of the health advances in the majority population. Thus, while rates of infant and maternal mortality have fallen in the United States over the past fifty years in all segments of the population, the discrepancy between blacks and whites increases. Before 1920, blacks had 79 percent more infants stillborn than whites; by 1963, according to a National Health Survey, it was 320 percent higher (English, 1967). Correspondingly, the postnatal mortality rate among black infants was 80 percent higher than for Caucasians in 1915–1919; by

1963, it was 180 percent higher. Medical services are usually less adequate and they tend to demean their poor clients. From his experiences in the public clinics and hospitals of New York City, Alonzo Yerby once expressed the hope that America could so organize its health system that all people would have "equal access to health services as good as we can make them, and that the poor will no longer be forced to barter their dignity for their health" (quoted by J. T. English, 1967). Community mental health services are intended as a step toward this end.

THE MENTAL HOSPITAL

Another major impetus to the emergence of community psychology was the sorry state of the large state mental hospitals by the end of World War II. Socially oriented clinicians have tried (1) to improve the conditions of life within the hospital in order to make it more therapeutic and less custodial; (2) to develop alternate forms of community-based care to avert the need for hospitalization entirely; or (3) at least to so alter hospital practices—for example, by providing facilities for partial hospitalization—so as to facilitate reintegration into community life after briefer and more limited hospitalizations.

When William Tuke founded the Retreat in York, England, in 1792 he wanted it to be "a quiet haven in which the sheltered bark might find the means of reparation and safety." In the early days of the American republic, such notions guided the thinking of humane men who established asylums (in their original meaning) in which people could escape the stress of life and emerge ready again for productive social life. They believed that the mentally ill if treated humanely and urged to greater responsibility and self-control were capable of resuming normal lives in society; a point of view which has been called "moral treatment" (Bockoven, 1963). By the mid-nineteenth century, however, American society changed radically, and with it faith in moral treatment declined. Waves of new immigrants were swelling urban populations and straining the resources of psychiatric hospitals. In increasing numbers, patients tended to be of poor peasant background, more usually Catholic than Protestant, and otherwise socially unlike both earlier patient populations and the managers and staffs of the hospitals of the time. In consequence, social historians note (e.g. Grob, 1967), mental illness came to be viewed more pessimistically, and hospitals became more centers for custodial care than for moral treatment. Although there have been many efforts to reform mental hospitals, particularly early in the present century, overall there was lessened belief in what Albert Deutsch (1949) has called the "cult of curability." Small asylums grew into vast, overcrowded and understaffed state hospitals, often located far from population centers, and so poorly supported that basic necessities of food, clothing, and shelter were often lacking. In some private hospitals and the best of the state institutions more humane and therapeutic care was of course available. But for the bulk of the American population, the state hospital was the only available resource. These, by the time of World War II, had become "the shame of the states" (Deutsch, 1948).

The pathological effects of hospitalization itself have become increasingly evident in clinical and sociological studies. Whatever his psychological state on admission, the social system of the hospital imposes on its inmates a "sick role" in terms of which they accept and internalize staff and community expectations as to their inadequacy and, in fact, become less competent to manage their own lives

(Goffman, 1961). Pathetic evidence of this phenomenon is revealed in both English (Wing and Brown, 1970) and American (Braginsky, Braginsky, and Ring, 1969) studies which show that the longer one is in a hospital, the more reluctant and fearful one is of leaving it. Various authors have used different terms, such as "institutionalism," "chronicity," and "social breakdown syndrome" (Gruenberg, 1967; Zusman, 1967), but they connote the same fact, that life under the conditions of a "total institution" (Goffman, 1961) involves degradation and mortification likely to produce rather than alleviate regressive behavior and pathological symptoms. Indeed, many of the behaviors of patients can be viewed as adaptive as they attempt, to the best of their abilities, to cope with a stressful environment. The system itself promotes and maintains pathology.

In actuality, there have been considerable gains in reducing the duration and effects of hospitalization. According to NIMH statistics, the state hospital population went from 559,000 in 1955 to 275,955 in 1972, and the trend continues downward, despite the U.S. population rise over these years (B. Brown, 1973). It has been estimated that there will be only one-quarter of the number of hospitalized schizophrenics in the coming years as there were in the past. Admission rates have not changed markedly; the difference in hospital census figures is largely due to shorter hospital stays. This is mainly the result from the widespread use of psychoactive drugs (mainly phenothiazines) over the past two decades. These drugs reduce extreme affects, agitation, and disruptive behaviors, making patients more accessible to psychological therapies and generally more responsible for their behavior. They allow more humane care, reducing the need for restraint and locked wards, and lead to quicker discharge from the hospital.

Socially oriented clinicians have contributed to the well-being of severely disturbed patients by efforts to (1) make the hospital environment more therapeutic for those already hospitalized (milieu therapy, token economy wards, activity programs); and (2) keep patients out of hospitals through providing community-based alternatives (community mental health program, halfway houses, rehabilitation, self-help organizations).

Milieu therapy derives from early European experiments aimed at making the mental hospital less an institution of incarceration and more a community for therapeutic social living. The colony at Gheel has over centuries provided a model for the care of a psychotic population. In this small Belgian town, patients live and work, moving freely among the local inhabitants who accept them in an extended family. In Scotland, England, Holland, and Scandinavia, many hospitals have done away with locked wards and encouraged patients toward active involvement in the life and government of the hospital. "Therapeutic milieu" programs were developed, particularly in English hospitals (M. Jones, 1953; 1961; 1968; see also discussion in Chapter 15). Following their example, American clinicians have been studying ways in which the social system of the hospital can be so altered as to produce an environment which sustains rather than destroys the personal integrity of patients (e.g., Greenblatt, Levinson, and Williams, 1957; Greenblatt, York, and Brown, 1955; Fairweather, 1964). The more recent development of token economy programs also have as their purpose the facilitation of prosocial behavior by altering the social reinforcement contingencies in hospital wards (Krasner, 1971; see Chapter 14).

By contrast, the goal of the community mental health movement is—at its most ambitious—to keep people with disabling psychological problems entirely out of hospitals. Ultimately, this is to be achieved through prevention but more immediately and realistically by the development of alternate means of dealing with crisis and by providing alternate institutions (e.g., day and night hospitals, halfway houses) more closely tied to community life. Implicit is the assumption that the hospital, certainly the large, isolated public institutions, is inherently bad and that psychiatric care should be shifted from the hospital to community settings. Despite the most fervent hopes, it seems unlikely that a time will ever come when some portion of the patient population will not need the special resources of a hospital. Hence, there is continued need for improving inpatient care while seeking alternatives to hospitalization. Recent history has shown that the admirable goal of "emptying the hospitals" can too readily be perverted by state administrations more concerned with budgets than with human welfare. State hospitals have been closed, or their services sharply reduced, and their problems shifted to communities without sufficient resources. The closing of the Agnews State Hospital in California, for example, led to a sharp increase in the flophouse population of San Jose, with attendant increase in crime and other social problems. As a long-term aim, however, doing away with custodial hospitalization, which has been a major impetus of the community psychology movement, remains a necessary goal.

COMMUNITY PSYCHOLOGY AND THE ZEITGEIST

The rise of community psychology is an expression of the "spirit of the times," in society generally as well as in professional thinking. We have already noted some of the social forces which brought the community movement into being, namely, concern with the poor and underprivileged, with the limited contribution of professionals to growing problems, with the evils of hospitalization and inequitable care, and the apparent losing battle with population growth and spreading psychological distress. All of these seem to be part of a more general value complex becoming more salient in these times. They reflect a movement toward a new *humanitarianism* and *democratization* of society, as the profound and disturbing problems resulting from urbanization, racism, violence, and other facets of current life become manifest. Within the mental health and behavioral sciences, it is reflected in changing conceptions of psychosocial issues and a search for more active engagement in the endeavor of improving society and bettering the lot of its members.

Federal legislation in the early 1960s emphasized the commitment of the government to better the lives of all citizens. The spirit of the times is captured in the "Declaration of Policy" which precedes the "Full Opportunity and Social Accounting Act" (Senate Bill 843):

> Section II. In order to promote the general welfare, the Congress declares that it is the continuing policy and responsibility of the Federal Government . . . to promote and encourage such conditions as will give every American the opportunity to live in decency and dignity, and to provide a clear and precise picture of whether such conditions are promoted and encouraged in such areas as health, education, training, rehabilitation, housing, vocational opportunities, the arts and humanities, and special assistance for the mentally ill and retarded, the deprived, the abandoned, and the criminal, and by measuring progress in meeting such needs.

Not only were efforts to be made to upgrade the social and economic status of the poor, powerless, and alienated but also to increase their dignity and participation in the democratic process. In the ghettos, in the slums, on university campuses, and in psychiatric hospitals and prisons as well, there has been an insistent emphasis on self-determination and increased civil rights. In the new humanitarian spirit, regulations have been enacted to guard against the dangers of involuntary commitment in mental hospitals and to protect human subjects in behavioral and medical research, only to mention two matters close to our professional concerns. The intertwined efforts to reduce inequity and increase quality found expression in concerns with poverty, urban blight, consumer rights, environmental improvement, educational reform, and the improvement of welfare and mental health services.

At the same time, American society has been shaken by enormous problems. Crime rates have risen, blacks and youth have been in revolt, and an unjust and unpopular war profoundly distressed numerous Americans. In the face of the greatest affluence, and striking technological and scientific advances, vast numbers of Americans live in poverty. Pollution and blight lower the quality of life for all. Nor has the trend to increased humanitarianism and democratization moved steadily forward. There have been periods of backlash and the loss of social gains. After the Kennedy-Johnson era, more conservative administrations have limited the commitment to social legislation and programs, witnessed, for example, by reduced support for education, welfare, and community mental health programs both in the federal and state governments. However, the *Zeitgeist*, if slowed, lives on.

Both as citizens and as professionals, behavioral scientists have been responsive to this atmosphere. "Professional preciousness" (Sarason et al., 1966) has been reduced, as behavioral scientists are more willing to put aside the more academic concerns in order to contribute, as possible, to the solution of social problems. A select committee created by the National Academy of Sciences and the National Science Foundation reviewing the current state of the behavioral sciences, strongly favored increased movement toward a field of applied behavioral science (Hilgard, Riecken, and Viederman, 1969). They suggested that universities should develop new "Schools of Applied Behavioral Science," to train new professionals with the knowledge and change-oriented skills needed to make impact on social problems. Many social and behavioral scientists are arguing vigorously that their fields cannot stand aside from social realities, nor should they try to maintain a value-free, "scientific" detachment. Like atomic scientists after World War II, they are concerned that their knowledge be used for good rather than evil. Among clinical psychologists are many who see the community orientation as the best route to providing the greatest help to the greatest number of people in need.

The History of the Community Movement

The community movement emerged in the 1960s from the professional and social climate we have just reviewed, but its roots run deep in the history of psychiatry and clinical psychology (Rosen, 1968; Brand, 1968; M. Levine and A. Levine, 1970). When Clifford Beers published *A Mind that Found Itself* in 1908, professional and public attention was called sharply to the sorry condition of hospitalized mental patients. Shortly thereafter, a national organization was formed which evolved into the National Association for Mental Hygiene (NAMH), which worked for hospital reform and preventive programs. The term "mental hygiene" itself, it is interesting to note, was used as early as 1843 by William Sweetser, an American physician, in much the same meaning intended later by the NAMH. Adolph Meyer, a leading American psychiatrist early in this century, pressed for socially oriented attacks on mental health problems. He noted that "communities have to learn what they *produce* in the way of mental problems and waste of human opportunities, and with such knowledge they will rise from mere charity and mending, or hasty propaganda, to well balanced early care, prevention and general gain of health" (quoted by Brand, 1968).

By the end of World War II, mental health professionals and the federal government were ready for more definitive actions toward the improvement of mental health in the general population. An alarmingly large number of otherwise healthy young men had been rejected from service for psychiatric reasons; many who served succumbed to the stresses of military life and combat. The hospital system was clearly inadequate; the manpower shortage was increasingly evident. Viewing the postwar state of psychiatry, William C. Menninger, who had been chief psychiatrist of the U.S. Army during the war, wondered if psychiatry could give up its preoccupation with the end results of mental disease and work ". . . to discover how it can contribute to the problems of the average man and to the large social issues in which he is involved" (W. Menninger, 1948, p. xiii). Professionals and policy makers were ready for a new look at mental health problems and procedures.

In 1955, Congress passed the Mental Health Study Act which established the Joint Commission on Mental Illness and Health to survey comprehensively the care of the mentally ill in the United States and to recommend future directions and programs. A broad base of professional and citizen groups were represented in the Joint Commission. Studies were undertaken on positive concepts of mental health, hospital care, social programs, research, manpower, and mental health economics, among others. The final report, in 1961, was titled *Action for Mental Health.* It spoke out for the promotion of positive mental health, increased research and manpower, public education, and striving for prevention. But the major emphasis was on the need to alter hospital systems in order to make them more therapeutic and less custodial. Specifically, it was suggested that hospitals no longer be built with more than 1,000 beds and that they should be closer to where people live and where professionals study and work. They condemned the oversized, understaffed hospital located far from the heart of the city.

After receiving the Joint Commission's report, President John F. Kennedy presented a ringing appeal to the Congress. In significant ways, it went beyond the Joint Commission's proposals, although the essential ideas were included. Note that the president added "mental retardation" to "mental health" in the title of his message, an area which had been neglected by the Joint Commission.

Kennedy called for "bold, new approaches." He proposed "a national mental health program to assist in the inauguration of a wholly new emphasis and approach to care for the mentally ill." The traditional neglect of the psychologically disabled was to be replaced by forceful and far-reaching programs. Specifically, these were to be aimed at prevention, wherever possible, early diagnosis and comprehensive care, reducing hospital populations, and developing community-based programs. The many mental health workers who felt that the Joint Commission report was too timid and conservative in its conclusions were heartened by the Kennedy message. The proposed "comprehensive community mental health centers" were seen as a potential vehicle for far-reaching changes. At the same time, others felt that the President's proposals did not go far enough in the direction of encouraging the social change necessary for prevention; community mental health centers seemed a compromise with professional conservatism (Duhl and Leopold, 1968).

The Comprehensive Community Mental Health Center

Late in 1963, Congress passed the "Community Mental Health Centers Act" which provided up to two-thirds of the funds for the construction of comprehensive mental health centers in communities. Two years later, supplementary legislation provided additional funds for staffing needs. In order to qualify for these funds, states had to draw up long-range plans thoroughly surveying needs and resources, delineating the areas to be served, and the priorities for implementation. It was required that community members participate in the planning. Each center was expected to serve a "catchment area" of not less than 75,000 nor more than 200,000 people. Thus, in thinly populated rural areas one center might serve one or more counties, while in a metropolitan area a number of centers would be within a single city.

The term "comprehensive" was intended to have a double meaning—*all* mental health services would be available to *all* people. A critical part of the federal legislation is that it requires centers to provide five "essential" services, in order to qualify for federal funds. Another five were named as desirable, but not essential. The essential services are: (1) inpatient care; (2) outpatient treatment; (3) partial hospitalization, i.e., day or night hospitalization, with the patient going home or to work in the other hours; (4) twenty-four-hour emergency services; and (5) consultation and education to community agencies and to professional personnel. The desirable but not essential services were: (6) diagnostic services; (7) rehabilitation and aftercare; (8) training; (9) research; and (10) evaluation.

The concept of the community mental health center in the 1963 act had the desirable consequence of moving psychiatric care from isolated hospitals to community-based centers which more usually were located in general hospitals. Moreover, it provided emergency help, readily and locally available, and encouraged consultation, aftercare services, training, and research. On the whole, however, it kept mental health services anchored in medical institutions, by the requirement that they provide inpatient care along with other services, and under medical control. Later interpretations, however, have indicated that the directorship of a center should be based on clinical competence not on disciplinary affiliation (Yolles, 1966); some centers are now under the direction of psychologists. Professional issues aside, however, fear was expressed that community mental health centers might be new wine in old bottles, dominated by traditional concepts of health, disease and treatment. In an early study, sponsored by the American Psychiatric Association, Glasscote, Sanders, Forstenzer and Foley

(1964) surveyed 11 centers then in existence. The prevailing treatment was individual psychotherapy. It seemed as if little creative thought had been given to the problems of indigent and minority groups and the problems of children were slighted. Psychologists did primarily diagnostic evaluations or functioned as individual therapists. There was little evidence of consultation or other approaches more directly focused on community processes. Although the picture had changed some by 1969, a follow-up survey (Glasscote, Sussex, Cumming and Smith, 1969) showed that many centers still seemed to be working as much in a clinical as a community mode.

In 1966, the American Psychological Association issued a position paper criticizing current trends and proposing guidelines for the future development of community mental health centers (M. B. Smith and Hobbs, 1966). On the whole, the Smith and Hobbs proposals affirmed the tenets of community psychology and cautioned against the crystallization of centers in a medical model. Specifically, they called for (1) more explicit recognition of social determinants and the corresponding need for more system-oriented intervention; (2) community control; (3) greater concern with people-and-programs and less with bricks-and-stones issues in the building of centers; (4) flexibility, experimentation, and innovation, including freedom from the categorical insistence that each center provide the five essential services which necessarily casts them in a hospital-clinic format; (5) greater concern with the problems of the poor, services for children, and for those groups likely to fall between current programs, e.g., the aged, delinquent, mentally retarded, addicts, and alcoholics; (6) higher priorities for training, research, and program evaluation; (7) greater ingenuity in the use of professional manpower and recruitment of nonprofessional workers; (8) giving responsibility in terms of competence rather than disciplinary identification; and (9) readiness to change organization and program in terms of the unique problems of each community.

During the 1960s, community mental health centers were created all over the country. Many were in the spirit of the Smith-Hobbs recommendations; others were essentially extensions of preexisting mental health services. The development of new centers was hampered by problems local communities had in raising matching funds and in recruiting qualified professionals from the limited pool available. With the change of administration in 1968, cutbacks in federal appropriations further limited growth. As of 1974, there were 540 centers funded through the Community Mental Health Centers Act (Committee on Labor and Public Welfare, U.S. Senate, 1974), far short of the 2,000 predicted for 1975 in the enthusiasm of the Kennedy era.

Some centers, particularly those serving poor and minority communities, have been bedeviled by tensions between community people and professional administrators, which has sometimes erupted into destructive conflict. In principle, "community control" is an admirable expression of participatory democracy. In actuality, however, it sometimes serves as a battleground for the power struggle between, on the one extreme, professionals defending their privilege and power against the intrusion of meddling laymen and, on the other, some community people who would enhance their egos and pocketbooks by wresting control from them. The Lincoln Hospital Center, which served one of New York City's Puerto Rican and black ghettos, was a pioneering and respected program which nearly died in such a struggle (Kaplan and Roman, 1973). It pioneered in the training and utilization of nonprofessional workers (Reiff and Riessman, 1964). In time, however, these nonprofessionals came to see themselves as underpaid and given too little voice in the Center's decision-making. At the height of the conflict, they seized the Center building and ejected the professional director and most of the staff. For a while, the Center was closed, as the hospital and city withdrew support. It was later reorganized and continues to function.

In contrast, the Westside Community Mental Center of San Francisco weathered and was strengthened in early conflicts between community and professional interests. This Center was originally founded by a group of cooperating clinics, hospitals and social agencies which provide, in different settings, a wide variety of services to a multiracial population in a catchment area which includes many poor and minority members, but also some affluent, white neighborhoods. A Community Board, with the minority groups importantly represented, has considerable responsibility in determining the Center's service program, staffing, and research. It works harmoniously with the professional staff, respecting their values and needs though, whenever necessary, calling attention insistently to those of the community. A notable regard in which Westside differed from Lincoln Hospital is that, from the outset, there was a significant number of black staff in responsible roles who could bridge professional and community needs.

The comprehensive community mental health center is by now an established institution, although perhaps less vital in the total mental health picture than was originally intended. In some centers, innovative methods have been developed and tested, although it is worth noting that most of the innovative research and development in community psychology has taken place in university departments, hospitals, and clinics. A survey of the accomplishments and difficulties of community mental health centers conducted by a Ralph Nader task force paints a fairly dismal picture (Chu and Trotter, 1972). This report alleges that commendable goals are rarely achieved in practice. Overall, the Nader investigators claim that centers have not contributed importantly to reduced hospitalization; they are frequently not accessible, financially, geographically or psychologically to those who need them most; they frequently do not service indigent people or those who are most disturbed, and hence tend to perpetuate a two-class system of care (one for the rich, another for the poor); citizen involvement in decision-making and administration is more a hope than an actuality; they mainly offer traditional clinical services, some of dubious relevance to local needs. In all, the Nader group views the centers as too "medical" in outlook and organization, and as falling short of realizing the tenets of community psychology described earlier in this chapter. While defenders contend that these conclusions are too sweeping, they do agree that much of the criticism is deserved.

The Concept of Prevention

THE PUBLIC HEALTH ORIENTATION

Community psychology has been inspired by the example of public health medicine in the conquest of disease. While clinical medicine focuses on the treatment of the sick individual, public health medicine is aimed at reducing the incidence and prevalence of disease in the population.* Much of the success in combating major diseases has occurred through public health means; in comparison, the gains of clinical medicine are minor (Dubos, 1961). Logically, if one could avert disease rather than cure it when it occurs, there would be greater relief from human suffering. Programs of inoculation, sanitation, health education, and various kinds of environmental interventions have effectively removed the threat of e.g., typhoid, malaria, and polio, while reducing infant mortality and increasing longevity greatly. For many mental health workers, public health provides a frame of reference as well as an inspiration for their efforts (e.g., Eisenberg, 1962; Caplan, 1964).

Public health intervention may occur at three distinct points. (1) The state of the individual can be so altered as to increase his *resistance* to disease agents. Examples are readily available for those conditions for which antibodies have been developed which provide immunization against a disease; (2) The probability of *contact* with the disease agent is reduced or its virulence is lowered. Control of contagious diseases involves quarantine, wearing of face masks, disinfecting exposed tissue, and the like; (3) The *environment* conducive to the development of the disease agent can be changed in order to destroy the disease agent. The classic illustration involves the draining of swamps in which the anopheles mosquito, carrier of malaria, is propagated. Ideally, the etiology of the disease should be known in order to develop rational and effective preventive interventions. In fact, however, simple empirical observations, sometimes even involving fallacious hypotheses, have led to effective treatments. Thus, Jenner noticed that people who had cowpox seemed to be immune to smallpox, a much worse disease. By giving people small doses of cowpox he developed his vaccine for smallpox, long before the cause or mechanism of the disease was understood.

Public health workers distinguish between primary, secondary, and tertiary prevention. *Primary prevention* is aimed at reducing the possibility of the disease in a susceptible population (population-at-risk), as might happen with the development of a new vaccine. The goal is to prevent people from becoming ill in the first instance. *Secondary prevention* attempts to reduce the duration, prevalence, or contagiousness of the disease in those already ill. Emphasis is on early detection and early treatment. Urging people to have periodic X-rays in order to note at the earliest moment developing tuberculosis or cancer, or the admonition that one should see a dentist twice a year, are familiar instances of secondary prevention programs. *Tertiary prevention* seeks to reduce the consequences of a disease among those who have already had it. This might involve, for example, providing an amputee with an artificial limb, teaching him new job skills and helping him overcome a sense of inferiority so that he can resume a productive life. Although analogies are risky, and boundaries are indistinct, community psychologists have used these terms to characterize preventive approaches in the realm of mental health.

* The terms "incidence" and "prevalence" are widely used in public health to describe two related but independent concepts. Incidence refers to the number of people who *become* ill in a particular time period; prevalence describes the number of people who *are* ill at that time. Thus, the incidence of psychosis might be measured by the number of admissions to psychiatric hospitals. Prevalence would be indicated by the number of people in hospitals. The difference between the two rates is largely a function of the duration of the disease. If the disease is one from which people recover very quickly, then incidence and prevalence are very close.

PRIMARY PREVENTION

Many in the mental health fields have been understandably skeptical about the possibility of primary prevention. The Joint Commission on Mental Health and Mental Illness concluded simply: ". . . . primary prevention of mental illness has remained largely an article of scientific faith rather than an applicable scientific truth" (*Action for Mental Health,* 1961, p. 70). In reply René Dubos said at a meeting of the National Association for Mental Health in 1962 (quoted by Sanford, 1965):

> The Final Report of the Joint Commission on Mental Health and Mental Illness states that humane treatment and rehabilitation of the mentally ill is the great, unfinished business of the mental health movement. But the great unfinished business really is to do something about the social, psychological and other circumstances leading to this condition [p. 1378].

That is the challenge of primary prevention, which as Dubos indicates elsewhere "must be undertaken since no major disease in the history of mankind has ever been conquered by therapeutic and rehabilitative methods alone, but ultimately only through prevention" (Dubos, 1961). At this point, our knowledge of the causation of emotional disorders is both limited and gross, as are our techniques and power to effect change, particularly at the broader social levels. However, guiding ideas have been proposed for developing methods oriented to prevention.

In his conceptual model of "preventive psychiatry," Caplan (1964) starts with the basic assumption that all human beings need "supplies" appropriate to their level of development. Deficiencies in these supplies can lead to psychological disorders just as insufficient food or the wrong foods can result in malnutrition. Supplies of three kinds are needed for healthy psychological development, which Caplan labels physical, psychosocial, and sociocultural. Physical supplies include food, shelter, protection from harm, and sensory stimulation, among others. Psychosocial supplies are those received through interaction with others, and include emotional and intellectual stimulation, love and affection, participation in satisfying social encounters, and the like. If the individual does not hold the respect of others or if they manipulate him toward their own ends, emotional disorders may result. Finally, the term sociocultural supplies is used to characterize those social forces which determine the status of the individual and the expectations of others for him. In advantaged social groups, individuals have greater input of such supplies, which predicts healthier personality development. In disadvantaged groups, or in times of rapid social change, traditional social supports may be undermined and psychological distress is more likely.

Another factor of importance in Caplan's scheme is the central role of crisis resolution. Life crises, whether accidental or developmental, both endanger existing adaptation and can lead to mental disorders or provide opportunity for further growth and development. Hence, helping individuals overcome crisis situations is a critical part of primary intervention. Concepts and methods of "crisis intervention," deriving from Caplan's view, have figured importantly in community psychology programs, and will be discussed in some detail in the next chapter.

Both in order to provide the necessary supplies and to strengthen crisis coping abilities, Caplan notes that primary prevention efforts are possible both at the level of "social action" and at that of "interpersonal action." The former consists mainly of efforts to influence legislative and social programs serving welfare, health, or educational needs in the larger society; interpersonal actions are intended to influence individuals, families, and community groups through more direct, face-to-face interventions. These involve not only helping with people in need (as in crisis intervention) but also indirect actions on their behalf through consultation with "community caretakers," such as teachers, doctors, and political leaders, who are important to the lives of many in the community. Because of its importance in community psychology, we will consider concepts and methods of consultation in more detail in the next chapter.

What kinds of things can be done to foster primary prevention? In general, both the potential interventions as well as the potential distress-producing factors can be conceptualized as residing at the level of the larger society, the community, the face-to-face group, or the individual.

In the Larger Society. Any social program which increases the quality of life, fosters education, social welfare, or improved medical care, or increases job opportunities, in principle provides needed physical, psychosocial, and sociocultural supplies. Thus, improved prenatal medical care for slum mothers should reduce the number of children born psychologically and neurologically defective (Eisenberg, 1962c). Similarly, urban renewal programs can provide a psychologically as well as physically healthier environment, if attention is given to the human issues, the needs for social contact, stimulation, and recreation as well as bricks-and-stone matters (Fried, 1964b). To this end, mental health specialists have consulted with urban planners in the design of new cities (e.g., Lemkau, 1969). Social programs intended to protect family integrity can have important consequences, for the family is a central source of psychosocial supplies for the growing child. Thus, legislation that would allow young mothers to work part-time, have adequate day-care facilities, or time off to spend with the child could importantly influence the well-being of both child and mother. Similarly, changes in welfare regulations that would have the effect of encouraging, rather than as now discouraging, both parents to live with a dependent child might also foster early development. At a broader level, sociocultural needs are served through reducing job and housing discrimination, increasing educational and job-training opportunities, and protecting civil rights. Educational programs such as "Headstart," intended to overcome educational handicaps in deprived children can lead to increased social competence and heightened self-esteem.

In this realm it is important to note, the direct power of psychologists to effect changes is distinctly limited, for they depend on political processes beyond their control. The greatest contribution of psychologists and other behavioral scientists is often through research and consultation, as occurred at the time of the Supreme Court ruling on school segregation. Groups of concerned psychologists and psychiatrists, affiliated with the Society for the Psychological Study of Social Issues and the Group for the Advancement of Psychiatry, assembled all available evidence on the effects of segregated schooling on white and black children. The upshot of their analyses was that segregation resulted in poorer education for both races. The Court used these findings in reaching its decision. Increasingly, behavioral scientists and mental health specialists are being called on to provide needed facts and to advise policy makers in many areas of social legislation.

In the Community. Many efforts of the psychologist in the community can be conceived as contributing to primary prevention. Community leaders are educated to the needs for physical, psychosocial, and sociocultural supplies in various segments of the population. Similarly, programs of mental health education are launched intending to alter public attitudes and instill values more favorable to positive mental health (see Chapter 18). Community psychologists consult with urban planners in the development of facilities for recreation and housing and with community caretakers at all levels to assure that their services maximally serve the psychological needs of the people. Thus, social agencies may be encouraged to better coordinate their services so that many of the problems which people have are not neglected. Consultation with important community agencies, such as the police, is undertaken so that their work can be reconceived in terms of serving psychosocial needs. In his project, Bard and his collaborators (e.g., 1967, 1969, 1973; Zacker and Bard, 1973) have demonstrated that community psychologists training and working with police teams can make them effective agents of crisis intervention with troubled families.

Much of the effort of community psychology has focused on altering the social processes of school systems in order to make them better environments for emotional growth (e.g., Sarason et al, 1966; Sarason, 1972; 1974). At their most ambitious these efforts attempt to change basic patterns of communication and organization and attitudes of teachers and administrators, to create a more growth-inspiring environment for school children. More modest efforts involve consultation with teachers to enable them to recognize and cope with emerging psychological problems of children. These efforts, more in the nature of secondary than primary prevention, are thought by many to represent a more productive direction for community psychology. Thus, Cowen et al (1973, p. 13) say "Although primary prevention in schools is an attractive ideal, it is both abstract and futuristic. Accordingly, there is need to develop theoretically less ambitious, but practically more feasible, approaches that will facilitate young children's school adjustment." Whatever their direction and rationale, however, school programs provide a major focus of community psychological activity, for it is in school that a major portion of psychological growth takes place. Any effort to make the educational setting more productive of personality development, as well as traditional learning, is to be applauded.

Finally, community psychologists work with community groups themselves to overcome feelings of apathy and powerlessness and increase their capacity for collective action so that they can better serve their own needs. Work in "community organization" which involves the identification and encouragement of leadership and the facilitation of group process and communication and similar processes is often akin to the work of organizational psychology in business, government, and other formal organizations and makes use of similar techniques.

The Family and Small Group. Character is formed and psychological problems develop primarily within the family which has the fundamental role in providing necessary psychosocial supplies. Intervention may involve parent-education programs, prenatal instruction, and various forms of family therapy and family-crisis intervention. Sometimes such programs can best be based in well-baby clinics or other pediatric services to bring them to families who would not seek the help of a "psychiatric clinic," or they may be adjunctive to the school or even police or probation departments. The critical task is to help in redirecting parental efforts before serious problems emerge with their children.

Particularly in work with adolescents, there is increasing recognition of the peer group as a primary socializing agency. Consequently, programs directed toward the control of delinquency and drug abuse as well as less extreme problems of adolescent development have focused on the peer group. Some of these are found within existing institutions, for example, Boy Scouts or church groups, while others involve the development of essentially new social enterprises such as Project Community (Soskin, Ross, and Korchin, 1971). In this project, a membership organization was created for high-school aged disaffected youth in Berkeley which gave them their own "place" in which they could discover new modes of social interaction with peers and young adults, engage in self-exploratory and quasi-therapeutic group activities and in "workshops" in which they learn about themselves and facets of their world usually ignored by the schools. A gratifying consequence of participation was a drop in drug usage and apparent increases in social trust, motivation and a sense of purpose and direction in otherwise foundering young people.

The Individual. The main purpose of individual-centered interventions is to strengthen the person's ability to cope with life crises. They may involve either direct contact with the person in the crisis, which is similar to short-term, focused psychotherapy (see Chapter 18), or they may include consultation with caretakers, families, or friends who are directly involved with the person. This is conceived as a preventive measure by Caplan because he sees the time of crisis as a unique opportunity for fostering adaptive coping in the face of future stress. He also calls attention, however, to the fact that some crises occur in many lives at predictable points and therefore allow for anticipatory crisis intervention. Special attention should be given to such "developmental crises" as starting school, getting married, becoming pregnant, becoming physically ill, or retiring. Programs can be worked out for many people simultaneously who share these experiences and intervention can occur in such settings as college dormitories, prenatal clinics, divorce courts, personnel offices, and the like. By lessening the stress of the on-coming crisis, primary prevention is served.

SECONDARY PREVENTION

The aim of secondary prevention is to reduce the prevalence of emotional disorders through early diagnosis and prompt, effective treatment. The essential assumption is that incipient problems can be detected through early signs and that interventions at that point can head off greater problems in the future. Evidence for the effectiveness of early detection and treatment have been found in a number of realms (e.g., Caplan, 1961; Sanford, 1965; Eisenberg, 1962c, 1962d). Thus, it was found in the military services during the Korean War that treatment quickly given as close to the battle lines as possible significantly reduced the need for later treatment and hospitalization of psychiatric casualties (Glass, 1963). Such evidence, it might be argued, simply asserts that prompt recognition of a problem and early treatment is simply good clinical practice, and indeed it is.

What is distinctive about secondary prevention programs is that they involve (1) widespread screening testing of people who are not seeking help or may even be asymptomatic at the moment and (2) techniques for bringing them quickly to appropriate clinical services. The screening devices are usually both briefer and different from the techniques used in conventional clinical practice, of the kind discussed in Part III. The essential hope is that problems can be spotted before they become serious and when relatively less costly or intensive methods can be used to deal with them.

Schools provide a unique setting for secondary, like for primary, prevention activities. For many years, programs have been underway in different communities designed to identify early problems of school-aged children (e.g., Allinsmith and Goethals, 1962; Zax and Cowen, 1969; Glidewell and Swallow, 1968; M. Levine and Graziano, 1972; Cowen et al., 1973). These projects usually involve training teachers to recognize early signs of behavioral disturbance of the sort that might warrant referral to a mental health agency. Sometimes, interview or questionnaires are given to the parents. In addition, brief, quickly administered, and easily scored screening tests of considerable utility have been developed (Bower, 1969; Cowen et al., 1973).

However successful screening programs might be, they achieve little if appropriate intervention does not then follow. The distressed individual, or his family or community caretakers, should be prepared to seek appropriate help. Secondary prevention, therefore, necessarily involves public information programs toward three distinct though related purposes: first, they should inform about the signs of incipient conditions; second, they should give information about available resources, what is available, where, at what cost, etc.; third, they should attempt to combat prejudices against seeking help, misconceptions about what mental health professionals do, and the like. It was found in a national survey that over two thirds of those who felt they needed psychological help sought the services of a clergyman or a physician rather than of a mental health clinician (Gurin, Veroff, and Feld, 1960). Perhaps the choice was not inappropriate and they found help for their problems, but it may be that earlier contact with a clinician would have served better. One purpose of education is to clarify the circumstances under which one should seek clinical psychological help rather than spiritual or medical assistance, and such education should as much be directed toward clergymen, physicians, and other caretakers as to the public itself. In most communities, there is at the least great confusion as to the variety of helping agencies available and great resistance to using them.

If early detection has been effective, and people want and know where to seek early help, helping agencies must then be prepared to give quick and appropriate service, if the overall program of secondary prevention is to be successful. Too often, clinics are tied up in complex procedures and red tape which greatly delays treatment or even completely discourages prospective clients. To be of greatest help, services should be readily available, close to the patient's home, and well publicized. The development of twenty-four-hour "walk-in clinics" and emergency services, as part of the community mental health center, or of "hotlines" and other rapid referral services has helped greatly in making care immediately available. Ideally, both facets of secondary prevention—early detection and immediate intervention should occur within the same setting, so that the process can flow smoothly and continuously. This is possible and has been done in such organizations as schools, military units, and colleges, but it is less easy in other settings.

TERTIARY PREVENTION

The task of tertiary prevention is to limit the aftereffects of mental illness and hospitalization and to restore patients to effective functioning in the community. Just as secondary prevention focuses on people in danger of becoming emotionally disturbed, tertiary prevention is concerned with the one who has *been* disturbed and is now recovered or recovering. There are three major areas of emphasis in tertiary prevention.

Rehabilitation. Rehabilitative services work to restore the former patient's self-confidence and his social and vocational competence. They aim to make him a self-respecting and respectworthy citizen of the community, able to resume family, work, and social roles or take on new ones. Rehabilitation often includes therapeutic counseling, aimed at strengthening the patient's readiness to confront social challenges and possible social rebuff. At the same time, there is specific training in job-related skills that can prepare the former patient for a new occupation or to be better prepared to resume an old one. Rehabilitation centers serve not only former psychiatric hospital patients but also the somewhat parallel problems of the blind, deaf, amputees, and others recovering from severe illnesses. For such efforts to be meaningful and effective, they must be integrated with earlier hospital care. In the past, large, distant, custodial institutions made little contact with rehabilitative agencies. As mental health services become more community-oriented, within-hospital treatment and after-hospital rehabilitation should become more integrated and continuous. The psychotherapy and occupational therapy in the hospital should be geared to the problems the patient will confront when he leaves the hospital.

Changing Community Attitudes. One of the major problems faced by the patient leaving a psychiatric hospital is the distrust, rejection, and stigmatization he may face in the community. Unlike the medical patient, the former psychiatric patient, like recently released prisoners or former drug addicts, is likely to be received with distrust and fear. People too readily assume that the former patient can become dangerous to himself and others and they are reluctant to admit him to their homes or offices. Patients find it hard to get good jobs, or in general, to be treated with self-respect. A major purpose of mental health education, as we will discuss in Chapter 18, is to develop more rational and humane attitudes toward those who have suffered severe mental disturbances.

Partial Hospitalization and Other Alternatives to Hospital Care. All too often, patients continue to stay in hospitals simply because they have no where else to go and long after there is any clinical justification. They may have no families or their families are unwilling to put up with them; they may lack the courage or skills to face the competitive outside world. For many, leaving the hospital means drifting into a skid-row existence of slow deterioration. Ideally, intermediate institutions are needed which allow the patient to make the transition to community life in limited steps. Until now, the choice has been basically between inpatient hospitalization or independent living, perhaps with some outpatient therapeutic and rehabilitative service. Transitional institutions, such as night or day hospitals and halfway houses or hostels for those needing partial but not full hospital care are being developed and are effective substitutes for psychiatric hospitalization. Day, night, and weekend hospitals are alternate modes of partial hospitalization which give the patient a retreat or home and/or a place for therapeutic activities while at the same time allowing him to work or go to school, maintain contact with family and friends, and otherwise participate more fully in the life of the community. As a historic aside, it is interesting to note that the first day hospital for mental patients was started in Moscow in 1934, though apparently more for practical than therapeutic reasons (B. M. Kramer, 1962). Anyone with administrative interests realizes that the same physical plant and staff can serve a larger number of people if each one uses it on a partial basis. The better justification for partial hospitalization is that it does not separate the patient from his community.

Concern with posthospitalization rehabilitation for the mentally ill in the United States is relatively recent. There were few facilities before 1950. By contrast, in Europe and particularly in England, there is a much longer and more developed interest in psychiatric rehabilitation. A notable example is the so-called Marlborough experiment under the direction of Joshua Bierer (1964) which has inspired many American community mental health workers.

In 1938, Bierer formed a "therapeutic social club" which was followed in short order by a day hospital, a night hospital, an aftercare rehabilitation center, a self-governed community hostel, "neurotics nomine," and a weekend hospital. Together, they became a program of comprehensive care. "The primary goal of the experiment was to enable the patient to change his role from that of a passive object of treatment, etc., and to become, instead, an active participant and collaborator in the treatment process" (Bierer, 1964, p. 223). The therapeutic social club started within the hospital and involved membership dues, special rooms, and recreational facilities. Meetings were held, including some with the hospital staff, which developed social activities, discussion groups, games and painting groups, as well as group therapeutic and psychodramatic activities. Membership included people of all types, "cockneys and patients with very cultured backgrounds . . . brilliant scientists and . . . mentally retarded patients." In time, as patients were discharged, the clubs continued outside of the hospital and, as reported in 1964, some had been in existence for over twenty years. They apparently became focuses on group identification and sources of social support for their members long after they needed hospital care.

The day, night, and weekend hospital services developed by the Marlborough workers made earlier discharge possible from the full-time hospital services. The aftercare rehabilitation center they developed was similar in type to the "sheltered workshops" used in physical rehabilitation, in which people develop skills in a controlled environment that makes less demands of them than an ordinary shop or factory. The self-governed community hostel represented still another mechanism for serving a basic need of former patients, namely, decent and congenial housing within their means. A house was rented and the patients themselves established a living unit which they supported and ran by their own efforts. The hostel was a source of pride and accomplishment, which fostered cohesiveness in the group. Contrast this with the all-too-common experience of patients who move from the back wards of hospitals to the back rooms of anonymous slum hotels. Providing adequate halfway houses and other transitional settings for patients not yet ready to reenter conventional social life is a major challenge to the field (Raush and Raush, 1968).

Neurotics Nomine, developed and sponsored by Bierer in the Marlborough experiment, was another type of patient alumni organization. The patients in these groups took on themselves the task of helping others in mental hospitals, by visiting, counseling, and giving emotional and social support to fellow sufferers. More elaborate forms of the same sort of organization can be seen in groups such as Alcoholics Anonymous, Recovery, Inc., and Synanon in the United States. These can be very effective ways of maintaining the social adjustment and self-respect of their members, while being of distinct help to others in distress.

CHAPTER 18

Principles and Methods of Community Intervention

In this chapter, we will consider four major techniques of community intervention—crisis intervention, consultation, education and attitude change, and the use of nonprofessional workers—that figure prominently in the work of community psychology. *Crisis intervention,* which provides short-term, focused help to people in crisis states, has been conceived as an important way of averting later, more damaging mental disorders. *Consultation* is the principal method by which attempts are made to alter, at either the interpersonal or social-system level, the forces acting upon people presently or potentially in distress. In an important sense, consultation is to the community orientation what psychotherapy is to the therapeutic orientation. *Mental health education,* intended either to alter public attitudes toward the psychologically distressed or to encourage more health-enhancing behaviors, is a long standing concern of the mental hygiene movement which has found renewed vitality in community psychology. The trend toward the greater utilization of *nonprofessionals* is a critical part of the community approach, conceived either as a way of increasing the manpower pool generally or of bringing in people with unique and distinctive qualities not shared with professional helpers. Consultation and education are sometimes spoken of as "indirect" community mental health services, for they may influence but they do not directly involve the target client himself. Crisis intervention and nonprofessionals, by contrast, are directly involved with the client in need. In each of these realms we will see reflected the general tenets of community psychology discussed early in the last chapter.

CRISIS INTERVENTION

The Concept of Crisis

A truism, but an important one, is that life proceeds through a succession of human crises, some developmental and some accidental. Movement from one maturational phase to another necessarily involves transitional stages where established behavior patterns are no longer adequate to new demands and challenges. The skilled crawler is the stumbling toddler before he can become the successful walker. Psychosocial growth, as Erikson (1951, 1959) has described it, confronts the growing person with a sequence of developmental tasks. The successful resolution of each establishes necessary character traits of the mature person, including trust, autonomy, and identity, among others. Successful resolution of developmental crises (as well as accidental crises, which we will consider in a moment) also has the nonspecific effect of increasing the personality's resources for crisis-management itself. Defensive and coping mechanisms grow out of previous crisis experiences and make the individual more adept in future ones.

Maturation thus involves a sequence of *developmental crises,* marked by such events as weaning, entering school, menstruation, marriage, finding a vocation, menopause, and retirement. Developmental crises, at least within particular cultures, occur in predictable sequence. Culture, however, critically affects the extent and manner in which such life changes are stressful. For example, Margaret Mead pointed out years ago (1928) that the emotional crises of adolescence might be particular to our culture that invests coming of age sexually with great importance; by comparison the Samoan adolescent moves smoothly from childhood to adulthood in a permissive culture which allows early entry into heterosexual roles. Moreover, cultures change in time and what is true in one era may be different in the next, which can account for generation-gap conflicts. Currently, this seems true in the area of adolescent sexuality where parents remain American while their children have become more Samoan. Similarly, the crisis of vocational choice would hardly exist in a stable primitive culture or in a society where roles are ascribed by tradition or inheritance rather than achieved through one's own efforts.

Along with such developmental crises, there are in each life *accidental crises,* also inevitable but less predictable. Sudden illness, the loss of a job, the death of a loved one, happen without opportunity for prior emotional or practical preparation; so too, more dramatic events, such as earthquakes, fire, or other disasters which affect the lives of entire communities. Nor is crisis limited to noxious events; promotion to a "better job," with new demands and responsibilities, may be psychologically as threatening as the loss of a valued position. There are poignant stories of formerly happy but poor men who lived in misery after winning a lottery. What is critical is the impact of the new situation, its psychological meanings and connotation of threat, the social setting within which it occurs, and the personality and coping resources of the individual; all of these in complex interaction determine the extent and intensity of stress responses. L. Rapoport (1962) has described three interrelated conditions that produce the crisis state: (1) there is a hazardous event which threatens the individual; (2) the threat is more damaging if it is symbolically linked to earlier stresses that resulted in increased vulnerability or conflicts; and (3) the person is unable to respond with adequate coping mechanisms. "Stress" and "crisis" cannot readily be separated conceptually, although some writers have attempted distinctions. Both terms refer to a condition that disrupts former adaptation and involves states in which there is threat capable of overwhelming the coping resources of the individual; therefore, emergency mechanisms are called into play. The consequence may be either effective functioning or disintegration and symptom formation (Basowitz, Persky, Korchin, and Grinker, 1955; Janis, 1958; R. S. Lazarus, 1966).

Life crises are a major reason why people seek psychotherapy. Typically, some stressful event overwhelms coping capacities or reinstates earlier conflicts, and the distressed person seeks psychological help. Focusing on the precipitating stress has been found to be an effective therapeutic technique which can establish the groundwork for continued psychotherapy oriented to more extensive character reorganization (Kalis et al., 1961). In many cases, of course, people pass through crisis states without seeking mental health professionals; they may turn instead to lawyers, doctors, vocational or marital counselors, or even to friends and relatives. Crisis is universal and crisis intervention is everybody's business.

Clinicians have rightfully pointed out that they have always been involved in crisis intervention, but it is only in the recent past that there has been focal concern among mental health workers with the crisis state and its clinical management, an emphasis of considerable importance in community mental health thinking. This has arisen largely from the work of Lindemann, Caplan, and their colleagues in the Boston area (Lindemann, 1944, 1956; Caplan, 1961, 1964; Parad, 1965).

A critical event in this development was the tragic fire in the Coconut Grove nightclub in Boston in 1943. The many dead and dying were taken to nearby hospitals. Erich Lindemann, a psychiatrist on the staff of the Massachusetts General Hospital, interviewed relatives at that time and on later occasions to help them in their grief (Cobb and Lindemann, 1943). From this experience, he formulated a concept of the grief reaction and conceived the fundamentals of crisis intervention methods (Lindemann, 1944, 1956). These principles were given fuller expression in Lindemann's Wellesley Human Relations Service, which was an important forerunner and prototype of modern community mental health centers. Crisis theory and intervention methods were further developed in the writings of Gerald Caplan (e.g., 1961, 1964) and his colleagues and students (Parad, 1965).

Crisis Intervention

Caplan sees crisis intervention as one of the principal techniques of primary prevention. In and of itself, a crisis is not a "mental illness," but it may be a critical premorbid event within which there are the seeds of subsequent pathology. Early intervention in the crisis state itself may thus avert later, more damaging consequences. Of equal importance is the parallel proposition that working with people in crises may also provide opportunity for positive growth as well as simply restoring a former equilibrium.

In crises, there is heightened confusion and painful affects but also, Caplan proposes, greater susceptibility to suggestion and desire for help. The suggestibility and openness to change, if only to relieve the intolerable anxiety and uncertainty, may induce people to seek psychological help, even though they may earlier have denied persistent problems to which the present crisis is related. Crises thus bring to light enduring psychological problems and they can be the point of entry for subsequent therapeutic intervention. The challenge of crisis intervention lies in the fact that it occurs in a time when people are maximally open to change, for better or for worse.

Some other general qualities of crisis should be noted (Caplan, 1964; L. Rapoport, 1962).

1. The crisis state tends to be *temporally self-limiting,* usually running from one to six weeks. Beyond that time, some kind of resolution, perhaps inadequate, occurs, either because new events have altered the situation or because continuing distress is intolerable and defensive mechanisms have come into play to deny or disguise it. An important consequence of this for clinical practice is that it limits the time available for effective intervention.

2. There tend to be parallel changes in the individual's *feeling and cognitive states.* Tension and helplessness characterize the early phase, which is accompanied by confusion so that alternative solutions cannot be conceived nor evaluated. In the ideal resolution, there is both reduction of affect and increase in the capacity for conceptualization and action.

3. If partially or wholly unresolved, crises *tend to return.* Those which depend on rare events, such as extreme illness or disaster, may occur only once in a lifetime. However, crises more common to social life depend as much on the susceptibility of the involved person as on external events. Thus, the family which cannot deal with the acting-out behavior of an adolescent and which goes into crisis when, for example, the boy or girl is arrested, will surely find other situations for similar crisis reactions. Moreover, earlier crises can affect the nature of later ones. This can occur in one of two ways: either crisis effects can cumulate, so that later crises can be more intense, though triggered by objectively similar events, or, contrariwise, there can be a growing desensitization and less intense crisis reactions. This phenomenon, as evident in national as in familial crises, has the unhappy consequence of allowing apathy to grow so that successive crises come to be seen as "normal" and beyond concern. We simply do not know under which conditions there is incremental and, under which, decremental crisis response. The phenomenon itself warrants further study. However, in the treatment of the particular case, the individual's history of crisis and crisis coping becomes an important focus of assessment.

Necessary Conditions for Crisis Intervention Programs

Providing for people in psychological crises is a major theme in community mental health. Since crisis intervention tends to be brief, more people can be served by a limited staff. Moreover, crisis services reach sections of the population who neither know, value, nor seek conventional psychotherapy. In the crisis state people both seek relief from immediate distress and ways of dealing with intolerable situations, although they may not be psychologically minded nor motivated toward personality change. By the standards of psychotherapy, the goals of crisis intervention are limited, but their potential extended impact is great.

Effective crisis intervention programs require important changes in clinic practice. These have been slow to develop. Thus, McGee (1968) notes: "Despite a broadened outlook toward crisis intervention, our overall orientation in this area is related to a fairly traditional model having to do with intake and psychotherapy, among other things. The typical stance of a mental health agency is to wait until the individual in crisis appears for help. Once this occurs his problem is evaluated, and he is offered some form of psychotherapy. As yet, approaches to crisis intervention do not sufficiently emphasize the concepts of outreach and consultation" (McGee, 1968, p. 323). He proposes that clinics make greater efforts to reach out to people in need, partly through consultation and education in the community. Organizing a good crisis unit—indeed, any community-oriented service—requires special attention to matters of location, availability, setting, staff mobility, and functions, among others, that are of lesser importance in traditional clinics. A number of these matters will now be considered.

CLOSENESS TO THE COMMUNITY

The facility should be geographically and psychologically close to the community it serves. It should be known and respected by potential clients and significant others in their social environment. Under conditions of stress, no one is inclined to travel distances to seek help nor to be happy in alien settings. This is particularly true for the lower-class person whose psychological life-space is more limited and for whom travel outside of the immediate neighborhood may be frightening. The facility should not only be located in the neighborhood, but as much as possible be staffed by people from the neighborhood and/or familiar with its ways. The black client is likely to be more responsive to a setting which has a significant number of black staff. Communication as well as the morale of the foreign-born client depends on the availability of people who speak his language.

The nature of the larger institution with which the clinic is affiliated significantly affects the likelihood that clients will seek its services. Although fine "walk-in" clinics have been developed within large metropolitan hospitals and on university campuses (see Tanenbaum, 1966, for a good account of this development), each of these settings evokes attitudes which may be barriers to the poor and uneducated. The hospital connotes illness and death and, in its psychiatric wing, insanity and incarceration; the university, intellectuality and experimentation, with limited regard for human welfare. In urban slums, "storefront" clinics have been developed to make them immediately accessible, geographically and psychologically, to the resident population.

An incident in San Francisco's Chinatown shows how proximity and community integration might discourage as well as encourage the use of clinics. A group of Chinese-American mental health workers, associated with various agencies in the larger community, voluntarily developed a unit in the heart of Chinatown in which short-term psychotherapy is offered by Chinese staff in the various Chinese dialects as well as in English. They reasoned that realistic language problems, the cohesiveness of the community, its concern with its own problems, and cultural resistance to taking them to the outside world, would encourage many to go to their own clinic where they might resist involvement with "Caucasian" agencies. Indeed they were correct; many did. But others did not, and because of the same cultural factors. The new clinic was everybody's business. Who came and went, and to a fair degree, what went on, was widely known in this close community. Shame of being identified as a patient and a desire for privacy kept them away or led some to seek referrals to agencies where they could be more anonymous. The general principle that systems for the delivery of mental health services must be congruent with community values remains true; the specific principle that services should be in and of the community is shown here to require more subtle interpretation.

Thus far, we have considered the importance of having a facility physically and socially close to its community as a condition for effective crisis intervention. But there is another aspect of the issue of *proximity*, i.e., closeness to the place where *crises are likely to occur,* and where intervention can occur in the natural setting of the crisis without shifting to another scene. An example of this kind of program is provided by one of the projects of the Harvard Laboratory of Community Psychiatry which was concerned with the crisis surrounding the birth of a premature baby, and which involved contact with the mother while she was still in the obstetric ward, after she returned home, but while the infant remained in the nursery, and after the infant came home (Kaplan and Mason, 1960). Each of these phases had its particular psychological issues: first, recognizing without inappropriate denial the possibility of the baby's death, and dealing with the accompanying feelings of self-blame and inadequacy; second, sustaining hope for survival and preparing necessary care, during the separation; and, third, establishing a mothering relationship after the disruption of the premature birth and separation, and perhaps coping with possible congenital abnormalities.

A number of aspects of such a project should be noted: (1) The work is anchored in the setting, in this case an obstetric service, in which clinicians are known and immediately available. No "referral" is necessary, and consultation is right at hand for nurses and physicians; (2) With experience, more subtle signs of crises can be recognized and more appropriate actions taken; and (3) In the same process, clinical research of importance to the further understanding of crisis states can be conducted. For example, what kinds of emotional reaction, in which sequence, over what time, occur? What personality and social conditions dispose to more or less intense reactions? Since a number of similar people are undergoing similar experiences, a natural experiment exists; answering such questions builds a firmer understanding of the particular crisis and its management, which together with other comparable experiments contributes to better conceptualization of crisis behavior generally.

IMMEDIATE AVAILABILITY OF SERVICE

Delay between the onset of a crisis and contact with the crisis service must be minimized. Ideally, clinical workers are available on a twenty-four-hour basis to see patients as emergencies arise. Unlike conventional clinic practice, crisis services cannot allow delays due to the mechanics of making appointments, waiting for an available hour, or administrative processing. Immediate action is needed and intermediate stages have to be minimized or eliminated. Crisis services are often "walk-in clinics" which require no prior appointment. Suicide prevention services do a great part of their work on the telephone (Shneidman, 1972). The principle in all these cases is to be there when the patient needs help.

MOBILITY

Crisis intervention requires that staff leaves the confines of the clinic for the community. This may involve accompanying police, family members, ministers, or other caretakers to the scene of crises. The clinician cannot wait passively for people in need to come to him. Many will never arrive, others will come too late. Crisis-oriented clinicians should also participate in the work of settings where problems cluster, for example, by consulting to schools or medical services. The clinic itself remains a base, and a necessary one for many kinds of therapeutic transactions, but its boundaries should be flexible. It should be easy for those in need to come in and easy for staff to go out. In the apt phrase of a Berkeley colleague, it should be a "clinic without walls."

FLEXIBILITY AND VERSATILITY OF PROFESSIONAL ROLES

It follows from these considerations that traditional staff roles have to be seriously reconceptualized and reorganized. In the crisis-oriented center, the work of all disciplines converge. There is neither time nor need for separate and extensive medical, psychiatric or psychological evaluation, full social histories, or extended casework or psychotherapy; functions allocated among members of the "psychiatric team" in the past. All must be adept in rapid assessment, brief therapeutic intervention and consultation, and in knowledge of community resources and of methods effecting needed change. Some professionally distinct functions remain; medically trained psychiatrists are called on to administer psychoactive drugs necessary for relieving intense emotions; psychologists face the challenge of adapting and developing rapid and focused assessment techniques. At least, greater coordination of the discrete functions of the different professionals is required; ideally, they should be able to work interchangeably in the common tasks of crisis intervention.

Activities which seem trivial or "nonprofessional" may be of considerable importance and require the most thoughtful professional attention. Thus, the telephone call or walk-in request for information, usually conceived as a first and preliminary step to psychotherapy and delegated to a receptionist, may be of great importance in dealing with crisis patients. The expert, on-the-spot judgment of a trained clinician is required, for the future success of the entire intervention may depend on it. It is a commonplace observation that many people in acute distress make only this first contact and, if not immediately engaged, disappear from view.

In other regards, professional functions have to change as well. Clinicians have to travel outside of the clinic, be prepared to give information and advice, help directly with immediate social problems or collaborate actively with community caretakers and other helping agencies in their solution. Amenities such as regularly scheduled appointments and the fifty-minute hour may be lost. For those accustomed to the ways of conventional clinics, the work of crisis intervention involves important organizational changes and altered professional activities.

The Technique of Crisis Intervention

At the present time, crisis intervention is possible in various ways, for no single model has emerged. Current practice involves adaptations of short-term psychotherapeutic and social casework techniques, particularly of the sort characterized as ego-supportive, here-and-now oriented, problem-centered, or reality-oriented. Protagonists of crisis methods argue that they are not just less (or one phase of) psychotherapy, and that the goal does not involve gaining understanding of conflicts—particularly those which are unconsciously rooted—nor are historical exploration, corrective emotional experiences, transference, and character reconstruction important to the process. What is involved can be inferred from various accounts, although the particular process would obviously vary with the nature of the crisis, the social circumstances within which it occurs, the severity of the evoked reactions, and the particular personality involved. In addition to direct work with the patient, crisis intervention commonly involves consultation with relevant others and direct efforts to alter the social environment.

Some general properties of the clinical process in crisis intervention can be sketched. The immediate goals are (1) to relieve present distress, notably anxiety, confusion, and hopelessness; (2) to restore the patient's previous functioning; and (3) to help him, his family, and significant others learn what personal actions are possible and what community resources exist. Secondary, and more extended, goals would include (4) understanding the relation of the present crisis to past experiences and persistent psychological problems, and (5) developing new attitudes, behavior, and coping techniques that might be more effective in future crises.

Initially, the clinical transaction focuses on the crisis itself and its immediately precipitating events. By reconsidering the stressful events, new contexts and understanding can emerge. The accompanying painful affects can be reduced, in part by venting feelings and in part by coming to see them as understandable stress reactions. In later phases, the emphasis shifts to problem-solving efforts. Previous life events, particularly those which were successfully managed, are explored to bring out the patient's coping resources which might again be utilized or adapted in the present instance. Necessary information and advice is given, but hopefully in an effort to serve rather than undercut the patient's own efforts at self-determination. Alternate solutions are visualized, new behaviors rehearsed, and future consequences considered. Along with the dominant focus on the present dilemma, there is a strong future orientation in this form of therapy.

The relation between clinician and patient, central to any therapeutic process, cannot evolve slowly over time as in conventional psychotherapy. It must be built rapidly on the basis of the patient's helplessness and confusion and his readiness to invest trust and hope in the clinician. Such attitudes are encouraged by the therapist, who readily communicates his confidence, competence, and authority. The clinician is necessarily more active and directive than he might be in longer-term psychotherapy. Under such conditions, there is the realistic possibility of inducing a complementary regressive role in the patient, in which he gains relief but loses independence by turning his problems and fate over to the therapist. There is a paradox and danger here, for the relation is based on the patient's helplessness and the therapist's authority, though its purpose is to encourage self-respect and self-determination. If possible, such danger is averted by continued focus on the problem-to-be-solved, the limited time available, and the patient's own competence and capacity for autonomy. There is little discussion of the relation itself and transference elements are minimized. Unlike conventional psychotherapy, the end is constantly in view. Termination is explicitly expected and dealt with. Under these conditions, the more forceful and active role of the therapist is less likely to infantilize the patient.

Typically, crisis-oriented therapy involves six to eight contact hours. Unlike conventional practice, such sessions are more loosely scheduled and may be of variable length. Patients often seen conjointly with family members or friends. Indeed, in an experiment in one Walk-in Clinic, groups of three to six entirely unrelated patients were seen by three professionals on the first occasion in a group session (Tanenbaum, 1966). These people though strangers to each other were able to verbalize their concerns as readily as comparable patients in individual sessions. They seem to gain support and to experience relief from the presence of others in distress.

Anticipatory Crisis Intervention

On-coming crises can often be foreseen, and there is the challenging possibility of developing programs for "anticipatory crisis intervention" before people are actually in distress (Caplan, 1964). Where it can be predicted that individuals or groups are likely to be exposed to a psychologically threatening situation, advance counseling can be made available. In such a process, likely occurrences are described in detail, potentially threatening aspects analyzed, probably emotional distress considered; all to the end of reducing the novelty and shock value and of increasing the knowledge and competence required for effective action in the actual situation. Through rehearsal and vicarious experience, processes similar to what Janis (1958) has called "emotional innoculation" can occur.

There is nothing essentially new in the notion of anticipatory crisis intervention. In many familiar ways, people are prepared for the demands of new experiences. Colleges, military services, and industrial organizations run orientation programs for new members. Indeed, all of education has been called, more or less accurately, "preparation for life." Closer to our present concern are courses in sex education or premarital counseling intended to prepare young people for the challenges of maturity. Similarly, programs for expectant parents are another familiar effort to help people handle new life responsibilities. Physicians and nurses run classes for young couples which focus on the care, feeding, and medical problems of infants which, at the same time, address psychological issues of parenthood. In company with others, prospective parents acquire information and techniques necessary for infant care, while at the same time learning about common uncertainties and common concerns. As in group therapy, sharing anxieties helps reduce them. Diapering a rubber doll rather than a live baby eases the later task. In significant ways, prenatal courses can avert some of the problems which might otherwise surround and follow the birth of a child.

Caplan's Peace Corps project illustrates an effort at anticipatory crisis intervention utilizing the skills and specialized knowledge of clinicians (Caplan, 1964). In the early 1960s, many young Americans were being trained for new tasks in distant lands, often under primitive conditions, where typically they knew little of the language or culture. For many, it was a first experience abroad. In their new roles, they often had to function in relative isolation and to depend on their own resources, without accustomed social supports. "Culture shock" was predictable as they interacted with people who lived by different rules and values. Pamphlets were written for the volunteers and group discussion held to review the demands on them and their potential reactions. They were warned of the effects of isolation, homesickness, and alienation, and of the difficulties of being under constant scrutiny, and of living under new role and authority relations. Possible actions to relieve tensions and feelings of inadequacy were reviewed. These efforts, Caplan believes, contributed to the generally high morale and effective functioning of the Peace Corps volunteers in the field.

The Current Status of Crisis Intervention

At this point, crisis intervention is more an orientation and way of thinking than a systematic body of theory, knowledge, and practice. To date, there have been few systematic studies of process, outcome or follow-up to show how these brief transactions affect people in distress and whether or not they have enduring effects. Clinicians involved in the process are enthusiastic and preliminary reports suggest that crisis-oriented brief therapy in community mental health centers can avert hospitalization for some patients.

Decker and Stubblebine (1972) showed that the number of psychiatric hospitalizations were significantly reduced following the institution of a crisis intervention service compared to the preceding period. Moreover, after brief crisis services, subsequent hospitalization, if required, was significantly shorter, and the likelihood of later hospitalization was also significantly reduced. On the other hand, in a controlled study of patients given crisis treatment compared to those randomly assigned to a waiting list, Gottschalk, Fox, and Bates (1973) found no significant difference in a variety of indices of psychiatric improvement; both groups improved and to about the same extent over a six-week test period. People thus seem to recover from crisis states with or without treatment, though progress may be more rapid and less painful with some intervention. Gottschalk and his co-workers did not find, however, that those patients who were less disturbed initially, less alienated, and less disorganized, and who were more motivated toward satisfying human relations were likely to improve more with crisis treatment.

Crisis intervention is not a simple or unitary system; instead, it borrows from different therapeutic approaches. Critical questions are left unanswered: Are there desirable or necessary therapist qualities? Are these the same or different than those required for longer-term therapy? Is it possible that the skills and knowledge of the expert psychotherapist might indeed block effective action in the brief, reality-oriented encounter? Or, because of its brevity, is greater clinical knowledge and skill required for brief crisis therapy? What is most critical in the process—the relationship, the actions taken, or the atmosphere of hope? Are there kinds of patients or problems for which these techniques are ill-advised? Questions such as these point up the need for detailed studies of the process and effects of this promising but largely unproven technique. There is some uncertainty as to what is meant by crisis, even among staff members of the Harvard Laboratory of Community Psychiatry, which has been the source of much of the current thinking in the field (Bloom, 1963).

Studies of life stress and developmental crises have expanded the knowledge necessary for the further development of crisis intervention methods. Such methods have been explored in such situations as the birth of a premature infant, entry into college, surgery and debilitating disease, death of a loved one, entry into marriage and marital and family crises, among others (Parad, 1965). Students of crisis intervention have been concerned with theory and research in ego psychology, particularly that which calls attention to adaptive and coping capacities in normal development as well as under stress (e.g., R. W. White, 1963; Haan, 1969; Coelho, Hamburg, and Adams, 1974). The continued evolution of theory and knowledge in these realms, combined with more precise delineation of intervention methods and study of their effects, will surely continue and lead to a firmer base for crisis theory and practice.

CONSULTATION

Definition

Consultation is emerging as one of the major techniques in community psychology. In one or another form, consultation is as old as clinical practice itself; it is an inevitable by-product of specialization in any area. In essence, the consultative process involves one person (the consultee), who has a problem but lacks the knowledge or skill for its solution, turning to another (the consultant), who has the requisite ability to aid in its solution. One common meaning of consultation refers to the arrangement in which a problem is turned over to a consultant who then takes responsibility for its solution. We are not concerned with this meaning here. We will be dealing with the case in which a consultant aids the consultee who, however, retains responsibility for subsequent actions, whether in the care of particular clients or in the management of a program or organization. For this reason, the consultant is said to provide an *indirect* service to the person or organization in need, for he works through someone who continues to provide *direct* services.

The importance of consultation derives from the fact that the potential contribution of skilled professionals is multiplied. A greater number of clients can be helped through counsel given to mental health professionals, administrators, community caretakers, or nonprofessional aides than could possibly be done by the same professional giving direct service to each of the same clients. At the same time, the quality of service is improved, as the consultee develops new skills and knowledge in his work with the consultant.

In the early development of community mental health services in Massachusetts during the 1950s, consultation was accorded a prominent position (Hallock and Vaughan, 1956); it has become one of the central functions expected of community mental health centers under federal legislation. From the perspective of clinical services, consultation not only extends the reach of working clinicians but it can as well serve an educative function. The consultee can work more effectively with future clients, applying the principles learned in consultation with earlier clients.

In addition to extending and improving clinical services, consultation figures as importantly in program development and planning, mental health research, and effecting changes in community organization and institutions. Mental health consultants in schools or factories may help create settings more productive of psychological help; consultation with community leaders or government officials may result in far-reaching social changes. In each of these cases, distinctive skills and experience are required of the consultant, but they have in common sharing of his knowledge with a much larger population than he could serve directly. As consultation has become more valued, particularly as an instrument of preventive intervention in community psychology, there has been increased concern with discovering the unique qualities of this form of interpersonal intervention which is both similar to, yet importantly different from, such activities as psychotherapy, clinical supervision, education, or administration (Altrocchi, 1972; Caplan, 1970; Mannino and Shore, 1972).

Types

Caplan (1963, 1964, 1970) has distinguished four classes of mental health consultation:

CLIENT-CENTERED CASE CONSULTATION

This is the familiar case of referral to a specialist who provides direct service to the client. A clinician with particular expertise may be asked, by the consultee or the client himself, to examine the patient, make recommendations for further treatment, or himself take over responsibility for the subsequent clinical care. The important relation is between the consultant and the patient; the interaction between consultant and the referring clinician, although important, is secondary.

CONSULTEE-CENTERED CASE CONSULTATION

Here the focus is on the consultee's difficulties in working with a particular patient or patients. The focus may be as narrow as the treatment of a particular case, or as broad as the consultee's understanding or management of many patients of a similar kind, but in either case, the focus is upon the work of the consultee, to which the particular clinical issues are secondary. The consultee is often a fellow mental health professional, but he could as well be a community caretaker, nonprofessional, or in some other fashion involved with the client. Although he may see the patient on a particular occasion, the consultant remains essentially outside of the clinical relation.

PROGRAM-CENTERED ADMINISTRATIVE CONSULTATION

Here, like in client-centered case consultation, the focus of concern is with the program itself, rather than the consultee's problem in it. At the extreme, a consultant may be called in to provide specific technical help, such as advising on the construction of a new building, suggesting alternate designs or analyses in research, reviewing staff organization, providing information on community resources, or in any of numerous other ways, giving specific help to the program. His role is instrumental to the work of the consultee and his organization.

CONSULTEE-CENTERED ADMINISTRATIVE CONSULTATION

Here, like in consultee-centered case consultation, the focus is on the work of the consultee in regard to his program. The consultee's understanding of the situation, previous efforts, knowledge, and attitudes that would facilitate or block the solution of problems, are the center of concern; the particularities of the program are secondary.

In actuality, it may be difficult to maintain the distinction between a consultee-centered mode and a client or program-centered mode of consultation. Often, it is a matter of relative emphasis and frequently the relation moves from one mode to the other. The distinction is important, however, because there are different contracts, expectations, and consequently, behaviors appropriate to the different consultation models. Consultation of the consultee-centered kind is most likely to fulfill the dual purpose of consultation: on the one hand to contribute to the solution of the patient's (or program's) problems, while at the same time developing the capacity of the consultee to solve future problems.

General Characteristics

There are a number of general characteristics of the consultation process. These are not specific to mental health consultation, but exist as well in any realm where issues of human relations are central. Indeed, basic concepts of considerable importance to community psychology emerged from the work of social psychologists concerned with effecting change in industrial, educational, and comparable organizations (Lippitt, Watson and Westley, 1958; Argyris, 1964; Bennis, 1966).

1. The relationship is *voluntary*. Because of his presumed expertise, the consultee invites the consultant's help with a particular problem. The consultant accepts the arrangement, if he feels he can be of any help. Either party is free to terminate the relation, although in actuality each may be constrained by feelings of commitment, embarrassment, or reluctance to offend. However, since the consultee remains responsible for subsequent work with the patient (or program, or organization) he retains the freedom to accept or ignore the counsel of the consultant.

2. The consultant is an *outsider*. He is not subject to the authority structure of the consultee's organization. He is not concerned with promotion or status, nor with continuing relations with others in the organization, either superiors or subordinates. His concern while there is only with the problem and the consultee's work, and the effort to solve one and improve the other. His authority derives only from his expertise which confers upon him a degree of objectivity. Like the child in the fairy tale, he can speak out when the emperor has no clothes. Not being in or of the organization, he has a degree of detachment which allows him to see and interpret things which may not be noted by those working within the organization. By the same token, however, he is obliged to understand the peculiar organizational problems which limit the work of the consultee. Ignorance or arrogance can make the consultant's contribution less than worthless.

3. The relationship is *time-limited*, in the view of both parties. Unlike psychotherapy, which can be conceived as timeless and in which problems emerge in their own time and order, consultation has a clear onset and termination. Because of this, understanding the phases of consultation is of considerable importance. They have been the focus of much thought by workers in the field. There may, of course, be recurrent consultations over a period of time which involve the same consultee and consultant, but each unit has its own focus and duration. There is not continuous involvement in the on-going work of the consultee.

4. Consultation is *problem-focused*. Even in the consultee-centered model, it is the work of the consultee, and not his character, personal problems, or personal life, which should properly concern the consultant. Here too, there is an important distinction between psychotherapy and consultation. Indeed, the consultant must scrupulously avoid therapeutic involvement in the personal life of his consultees. The boundary between personal and work problems is at best a slim one, and consultants must necessarily draw on clinical skills and, in some degree, address the emotional problems of the consultee in order to help him in his work with his clients. The principle of problem-focus and the avoidance of personal involvement is important as a guideline; great skill is needed in its proper interpretation. For this reason, the consultant needs the skills of a wise therapist; pre-

cisely so that he will not cross over into therapy. However, the clinically trained consultant, who simply transposes his psychotherapeutic role or clinical supervisory role to the consulting situation, violates the consultation contract and risks alienating the consultee.

From these considerations, it can be seen that consultation differs importantly from other interpersonal processes such as education, supervision, psychotherapy, or administration, while sharing qualities with each of them. While knowledge is conveyed, it rarely depends on the formal technique of education. Nor is there focus on information as such, but rather upon the consultee's understanding and capacity to utilize that knowledge. Unlike psychotherapy, consultation is time-limited, problem- rather than personality-centered, and has as its immediate goal increasing the effectiveness of the consultee to function independently. Like psychotherapy, however, it depends upon an interpersonal relationship, characterized by trust and respect, and necessarily is concerned with personal barriers to learning or with work difficulties. Unlike supervision, consultation does not imply responsibility for the client's welfare. Unlike administration, there is no authority relationship, nor is the consultant responsible for the ultimate work of the consultee. However, like in all these processes, the goal is the increased effectiveness of the consultee. Ideally, good consultation should lead to changes in the consultee or his organization assuring what Lippitt (1959) called "a continuity of creative changeability." This consists of staff attitudes, social atmosphere, and an orientation to problem-solving which encourages them to analyze, understand, and as necessary, alter their own functioning in the future.

The Consultant's Functions

Altrocchi (1972) reviews the various functions which the consultant can serve. First among these is his role in the *teaching and training of consultees,* in which he functions as both a technical expert and a resource person. He brings to the attention of consultees results of appropriate research, the literature of the field, experience with comparable problems in other settings, knowledge about the functioning of other agencies, techniques that have been developed elsewhere, and other material of relevance to the work of the consultee. Secondly, he serves as a *communication facilitator,* either among consultees within an agency or between agencies or between the consultee, the agency, and the larger community. By virtue of his more extended view of work in the field and of other resources, a consultant is often in a position to bring together previously isolated workers or agencies. In one experiment with group consultation in a small community, a number of workers from different agencies were seen simultaneously in group sessions (Altrocchi et al., 1965). They found that this procedure reduced barriers to effective communication among agencies, reduced competition and mutual fear, and encouraged collaboration. Related is a third role, that of *human-relations mediator* (Cohen, 1966). As an outsider, the consultant can often see and help resolve internal conflicts and frustrations in the organization which limit the work of the consultee. It is commonplace for consultants to discover that the problem posed originally is relatively unimportant in the context of larger issues which concern and constrain the consultee. Thus, a psychologist may be asked by a teacher to discuss his work with a particularly difficult student. In short order, it becomes clear that his effectiveness as a teacher with any of his children is greatly limited by his resentment of administrative policies, feelings of lack of support from relevant administrators, conflicts with fellow teachers, or similar matters. The consultant may have to focus on these issues and, acting as a mediator, may help to resolve them. However, there is the real danger of his being pushed into the role of referee or into a quasi-administrative role for which he has no authority. Finally, a major function of the consultant is to catalyze, inspire, and facilitate the development of ideas.

Phases in the Consultation Process

The process of consultation moves through a sequence of stages, each of which poses particular problems. Gibb (1959) has distinguished entry, diagnosis, data collection, relation, boundary definition, resource development, decision-making, and finally, termination; others (e.g., Altrocchi, 1972) have similarly marked off the major stages of consultation. Some of the issues and problems in each stage will be discussed now.

ENTRY

The initial stage involves the establishment of the relation between consultant and consultee upon which the rest of the process depends. Entry, Glidewell notes (1959), is a special instance of the general problem of incorporating an outsider into any social system, whether for consultation or other reasons. Inevitably, there is uncertainty on the part of the consultee as to the consultant's role, perhaps fear that he may prove an embarrassment, and reveal inadequacies of the consultee, both to himself and to the others in the organization. Simultaneously, there may be exaggerated hope, and a readiness to ascribe both omniscience and omnipotence to the consultant. In this first phase, a clearly understood contract has to evolve and, with it, trust established. The consultant makes clear the terms under which he works; as noted, that the relation is voluntary, time-limited, and problem-oriented. Assurance is given that the consultee's privacy will be respected and information will be kept confidential. Techniques involved in consultation are described, or if possible, illustrated. The limits of the consultant's competence and authority must be made clear. At the same time, however, the attributes which make him worthy of being a consultant must be equally clear. Neither excessive modesty nor omniscience becomes the consultant; neither excessive humility nor resistance, the consultee. All of these attitudes are possible, and the initial phase involves avoiding a tangle of inappropriate postures which can entirely defeat the consultation process.

Problems reside at many levels—the personal insecurity of the consultee, an atmosphere of evaluation in the organization, the desire of administrators or colleagues to know and use information gained in consultation, among others. In the first stage, it is critically important for the consultant to truly understand why consultation was requested, what the focal problem is, and why he was chosen. Often enough, the manifest motives may not be the real ones, and there can be "hidden agendas." Understanding the situation may involve some honest soul-searching on the consultant's part. He must be able to answer for himself the questions "Why am I here?" "What can I do to help?" "Do I have appropriate knowledge and skills?" (Lippitt, 1959).

Entry is facilitated to the extent that the consultee has had the principal responsibility for initiating the arrangement. If it resulted mainly from the consultant's efforts or derived from administrative decision, entry is made more difficult. A particular problem exists where, from the consultant's viewpoint, the consultee has apparently sought his help voluntarily, although in actuality it resulted from explicit or implicit pressure from an administrative superior. The early discovery of such facts is important to the continuing relationship. At the same time, there needs to be clear sanction for consultation from those with authority in the consultee's system.

But however clear prior agreements seem to be, the consultant must be continuously attentive to the effects of earlier expectations, unverbalized concerns, personal distortions, and misinterpretations. Acceptance of the humanness of the consultee, respect for his professional and organizational position, and appropriate warmth and support facilitate the development of a relationship in this first phase. At the same time, as in psychotherapy, excessive sympathy can lead to denial of the problem and false cures.

DEFINING THE PROBLEM

With the basic relationship established, attention moves to defining and analyzing the problem in hand. The consultee's phrasing of the problem and his diagnosis of the issues involved must remain central and be respected by the consultant, though he remains alert to related and perhaps more pervasive issues which lurk behind the problem as presented. Over time, a common perception of the real issues has to emerge. But it suffices little for the consultant to say bluntly "That's not the problem at all, what really concerns you is . . ." Time and successive redefinitions of the issues are required. In the course of this, apparently irrelevant considerations may be introduced. Of particular concern are those related to the personal life or social relations of the consultee. Although as a general rule, the consultant should not engage himself with the clearly personal problems, past history, or nonwork-related aspects of the consultee's life, in actuality the boundary is difficult to maintain, particularly where the personal problem interacts with the work difficulty. This particular case Caplan (1964, 1970) has called "theme interference" and is an important focus of consultation in his system.

ANALYZING ALTERNATE ACTIONS

Following diagnosis of the problem, the task moves to a search for alternate solutions. A necessary first step, often overlooked, is to discover what in fact the consultee has done in the past and with what consequence. The diagnostic question "What do *you* think is the problem?" has to be paralleled in this phase by the question "What have *you* done so far?" In fact, the consultee may have anticipated the consultant's solution and found that it did not work. Other previous efforts may have been unsuccessful but indicate future directions. But whatever they consisted of, ignoring the consultee's own efforts reveals a disrespect for him and creates a barrier to further collaboration.

Jointly with the consultee, alternate further actions are considered. Their feasibility, possible impact and side effects, likely costs and benefits, and other considerations are discussed. Because of his broader frame of reference and greater knowledge, the consultant can guide the vicarious trial and error involved in this process. Throughout, he must create the conditions for free communication, creative cognition, and freedom to explore ideas. One can visualize the numerous ways in which an inept consultant can reduce a collaborative problem-solving activity to a one-way transmission of authoritarian dictates. Depending only on the tone of voice, the sentence "In my experience, it won't work" can either provide usable data for joint investigation or it may be the death of further collaboration.

The consultee may lack specific knowledge, which the consultant can supply or help him discover. He may lack appropriate skill or experience, and the consultant can help in their development; or, there may be barriers within the person or in his work situation which must be altered before appropriate action can be taken. In any of these realms, the consultant can extend the effectiveness of the consultee. But again, it must be emphasized that final actions have to be consonant with the consultee's motives, abilities, and status. A particular proposal might work, if only the consultant himself were responsible. But he is not. This is the essential fact of consultation.

DEALING WITH BARRIERS TO UNDERSTANDING OR ACTION

The consultee's understanding of a problem and decisions as to action may be limited by nonrational factors deriving from psychological problems within the consultee or in the consultee organization. Caplan (1964, 1970) has emphasized the importance of "theme interference," which occurs when personal problems intrude into the consultee's work. In such cases, the consultee may not lack appropriate knowledge or skills, but he is unable to use these in working with a particular client or problem. Professional objectivity may be limited and appropriate empathy replaced by overidentification and personal involvement; perception and judgment may be distorted. The consultee may experience undue emotional tension in working with the particular case. "The consultee usually ascribes his discomfort to his difficulties with the patient onto whose case he displaces feelings of anxiety, hostility and shame, and oppression, which can be seen by the consultant to be partly or even primarily originating in his personal life or in his involvement with the social-system problems of his institution" (Caplan, 1964, p. 223).

Often the consultee is not conscious of the relation between his personal problems and his difficulty with the client. It is important, Caplan believes, that the consultant not attempt to make this link conscious. He should remain focused on the problem of the client under discussion. Still, he must be attuned to the symptoms by which theme interference manifests itself, such as excessive emotional response, distortion, and particularly stereotyping, oversimplification of the issues, pessimism as to outcome, and the other ways in which the consultee shows a lack of objectivity in viewing the issues or consequences of the client's case.

Theme interference, and the consultant's approach to it, is illustrated by Caplan in an episode involving a teacher and a ten-year-old girl. The teacher expressed little hope for the girl whom he saw as mentally retarded. All his efforts to teach her had failed and he was convinced that she was to become a social outcast unless he could somehow get her to improve her school performance. At the same time, he was insensitive to her assets which included social popularity and considerable nonverbal skill. He was fully convinced that she would be badly used and that an unhappy ending was inevitable. His view of the problem was essentially: "This girl is mentally retarded. Mentally retarded people inevitably fail in life and are exploited by more intelligent people. Therefore, this girl is doomed, despite everything I will do to rescue her."

In discussions with the consultant, it emerged that the teacher himself was uncertain about his ability to achieve in a new school and insecure with a hard-driving principal who demanded high standards. In his own history, which emerged incidentally, was the fact that he had been slow to learn and had only begun to improve at the age of ten.

Despite this knowledge, the consultant focused on the client's situation. He did not challenge the consultee's contention that the girl was backward. Instead, he questioned the assumption that this necessarily would lead to an unhappy end. The consultant encouraged review of her assets and focused on the question of whether one could reasonably suppose that intelligent people would exploit her. In this way, hope as to the girl's future was communicated in the effort to reduce the teacher's feeling of hopelessness. At the same time, the consultant did not argue his initial premise ("This is a retarded girl") or bring into the discussion the teacher's own history or values. In later work, Caplan and his co-workers expanded and further developed their concepts of theme interference reduction as a major function in mental health consultation.

However, it is not only forces within the individual that block appropriate understanding or action, but conceptually similar ones in the social system of the consultee. Organizations have collective beliefs and values, biases and routinized procedures, which may limit objectivity and professional effectiveness; and just as the consultant has to tread softly with regard to the consultee's personal neurosis, so must he deal with the "institutional neurosis." Students of group dynamics have for a long time been attentive to issues of communication, authority, and other aspects of a social organization that constrain the actual freedom of choice of the consultee and which, in turn, may have to be dealt with by indirection rather than confrontation, in analogy to the case of theme interference in the consultee himself.

TERMINATION

The final phase is concerned with the termination of the originally agreed arrangement. Ideally, it should occur when both parties feel that the process has come to a natural end. Inevitably, however, negative feelings can intrude, including disappointment, incompleteness, or desertion, among others. Some degree of dependence may have evolved and a desire on the part of the consultee to continue in a warm, protected relation. Interplay with the consultant may have been intellectually stimulating, socially pleasant, or status-producing, and he is reluctant to give it up. From the other side, working with the consultee may have engaged the vanity as well as professional interest of the consultant and he might wish to continue the relation. Particularly if it is effective, the period of consultation can jar accustomed habits and ways of thinking, both in the consultee and in his organization. At the end, they may be challenged and stimulated but perhaps also uncomfortable or resentful. As in other realms of psychological intervention, increased effectiveness not mutual satisfaction is the goal and the success of consultation should be measured in those terms. Where both occur, all parties have a gratifying bonus.

Consultation with Groups

Consultation with groups of consultees proved to be effective; in some ways, superior to individual consultation (Altrocchi, Spielberger, and Eisdorfer, 1965; Tobiessen and Shoi, 1971). Groups might include workers in the same agency or different agencies, or even unrelated caretakers, parents, or others who share concern with common problems. There is an obvious economy in working with several people simultaneously. At the same time, there is less opportunity to explore individual problems. Group consultation compared to individual, shares many of the qualities which distinguish seminar and tutorial teaching or group and individual psychotherapy.

A major advantage lies in the utilization of the group process itself for educative and social-change purposes. In the group, commonly held views and shared problems emerge more readily and the likelihood of idiosyncratic personal problems emerging is reduced. Communication and human-relations skills are sharpened. On the negative side, coordination and scheduling problems arise. Personal problems do enter, and there is the danger that the group of fellow consultees may mishandle them. Insecure people are likely to hold back, dominant ones to take over. In the period of entry, greater attention need be given to developing group cohesiveness and other qualities of effective group functioning. While requiring concerned attention, these issues are challenges to the development of a promising method.

THE NONPROFESSIONAL IN COMMUNITY PSYCHOLOGY

Why Nonprofessionals?

The use of people without formal training or credentials as workers in mental health programs has become an increasingly important trend in community psychology. In this section, we will review efforts in this direction, noting the work settings, kinds of people involved, the functions served, and discuss some issues of selection, training, and supervision and some of the problems in this emerging field.

Four somewhat related arguments have been used to justify the training and use of nonprofessionals.

INCREASE OF WORKERS

It increases the sheer number of available helpers. Added to the body of professional workers, nonprofessionals can relieve professional time, provide additional services, allow more patients to be seen, and so on. If there were sufficient professionals, nonprofessionals might not be necessary, according to this argument. But there are not, and hence they are necessary. The emphasis is on more. This position responds to the chronic shortage of trained manpower.

UNUSUAL QUALITIES OF WORKERS

Nonprofessionals can add different and unique qualities to the manpower pool, and their training could be justified even if there were no manpower shortage. Particularly in serving lower-class and minority communities, there are cultural barriers between the professional, mainly middle-class white, and the population he serves. "Indigenous nonprofessionals," drawn from the community and sharing its culture, have helped bridge these barriers in community mental health programs (Reiff and Riessman, 1965). Similarly, former delinquents, criminals, drug addicts, alcoholics, and mental patients have all contributed to work with patients who have similar problems. Parents have been trained to work with their disturbed children, either as behavior therapists (Wahler, Winkel, Peterson, and Morrison, 1965) or in a form of client-centered play therapy called "filial therapy" (Andronico, Fidler, Guerney, Jr., and Guerney, 1967; Fidler, Guerney, Jr., Andronico, and Guerney, 1969). In this latter approach, six to eight mothers are simultaneously trained as therapists. They then work with their children under the guidance of a psychologist. This approach recalls the classic case of "Little Hans" which inspired Freud's theory of the Oedipus complex (Freud, 1909). However, despite this historic event and some later experiments in which psychoanalysts treated children through their parents, psychoanalysis evolved into the system of therapy most dependent on the direct involvement of a highly trained professional. In all of these illustrations of nonprofessionals in the work of mental health, it is their unique attributes which recommend them, whether derived from class or race, personal problems, or family status.

PSYCHOLOGICAL GROWTH AND COMPETENCE OF THE WORKER

A third argument shifts the emphasis from the client to the worker himself and justifies nonprofessional training in terms of its potential for facilitating psychological growth and social competence of the worker himself. This is a major theme in the "new careers" programs in poverty communities. As the worker develops skills and responsibility for the welfare of others, he becomes a more effective, satisfied, and valuable citizen himself. The underlying psychological principle is, of course, an old and familiar one. Being a helper helps the helper; the teacher learns when teaching. Participants in Alcoholics Anonymous, Synanon, Recovery Inc., and similar groups run by deviants for fellow sufferers, support positive growth in themselves. Riessman (1965) has termed this the "helper therapy" principle, and sees it as being particularly important in the case of ghetto workers. However, volunteer work performed by the more favored also serves the altruistic needs of people to serve those less fortunate. Housewives, retired persons, and college students working in helping programs have found that this experience enriched their own lives (Rioch, 1967; Cowen, Liebowitz, and Liebowitz, 1968; Holzberg, Knapp, and Turner, 1967; Goodman, 1972a).

RECRUITMENT INTO PROFESSIONAL CAREERS

Nonprofessional service can be an effective basis for recruitment into professional careers. In the past, particularly in volunteer programs for college students, the recruitment theme was prominent. Such experience gives students the opportunity to learn directly about problems of mental health, and to test their fitness for and interest in a clinical career. Indeed, many clinicians date their career decision from a summer's work in a mental hospital.

Broadly speaking, "nonprofessionals" includes many kinds of people, working in different roles, in different settings, with differing degrees of involvement, and with different career ends. Most generally, what they have in common is that they are not professional; they do not have the training, degrees, titles, or social recognition. They may be students, high school or college, or school dropouts. They may be adolescents, mature women, or elderly people. They may be socially like or unlike professionals; socially like or unlike clients served. Work is done in hospitals or clinics, community mental health programs or action programs, in schools, nurseries or day-care centers, out in the neighborhood or in the home. In their jobs, they may be paid or unpaid, full- or part-time, and involved for weeks or for years. Many illustrative programs and extensive discussions of issues in the selection, training and use of nonprofessionals can be found in Cowen, Gardner, and Zax, 1967; Guerney, 1969; Grosser, Henry, and Kelly, 1969; Sobey, 1970; Rappaport, Chinsky, and Cowen, 1971; and Zax and Specter, 1974.

What Can Nonprofessionals Contribute?

The roles played by nonprofessionals can be roughly classified in three categories: (1) those which *subserve* the work of professionals; for example, administering and scoring particular psychological tests, which are then interpreted and reported by a clinician; (2) those which are *adjunctive to* professional functions; for example, serving as a companion to hospital patients; and (3) those which *parallel,* at least in part, professional functions; for example, doing psychotherapy with particular patients. In traditional settings the nonprofessional is generally cast in a subserving or adjunctive role. Thus, students in mental hospitals have been trained to give some psychological tests, to assist in surveying case records or analyzing research data, or they have provided companionship for patients, functioning somewhat like psychiatric aides. On the other hand, programs which have developed independently of the medical model more typically emphasize adjunctive or even parallel roles to those of professionals. With relatively brief training, and sometimes little supervision, they work directly with patients as, for example, homemaker aides or even as therapists. Needless to say, there is considerable uncertainty and even more contention as to what actions nonprofessionals can take, particularly as they begin to duplicate the traditional functions of the professional.

An important ideological issue underlies this controversy. Does effective intervention require the formal training, knowledge of a field, professional identity and the other trained skills and experience which only the certified professional possesses? Or, rather, might not native endowments and personal characteristics be more vital in a helping relation? Surely, most clinicians would agree on the importance of such personal attributes, but in the context, not the absence, of professional qualifications. The most enthusiastic defenders of nonprofessionals tip the balance in the other direction, arguing that personal qualities and human skills are of the greatest importance.

Research by Poser (1966) can be cited in support of this argument. In a well-designed study, he compared the effectiveness of undergraduate college girls with that of mental health professionals (mainly psychiatrists and social workers) in group therapy with hospitalized schizophrenic patients. Groups consisted of ten patients each and met daily for over a hundred sessions. There were thirteen student-led groups, fifteen conducted by professionals, and in addition sixty-three untreated patients; a total of 343 patients was studied. Measures were made before and after the course of therapy on a variety of psychological indicators. The overall findings were clear: Patients who were treated, whether by staff or students, improved significantly more than those who were not treated. However, the student-treated patients fared somewhat better than those seen by professionals. In interpreting this finding, Poser suggests that the interest and enthusiasm which the girls brought to their work may have been the decisive factor; in reviewing his study, Rioch (1966) concurs in this judgment. Bergman and Doland (1974) similarly found that college student volunteers significantly contributed to the clinical improvement of chronic hospitalized patients. In other work, Carkhuff and Truax (1965a, 1965b) have demonstrated the effectiveness of lay counselors. Such findings suggest that nonprofessionals can contribute greatly, even in areas close to the core functions of professional clinicians.

In actuality, however, nonprofessionals have functioned mainly in ancillary activities, some close and others further from the usual work of clinicians. Thus, Sobey (1970) in surveying 185 NIMH-supported programs found that nonprofessionals were used in such direct services as tutoring, providing companionship, caretaking help, and in activity-group therapy, while professionals in these agencies retained responsibility for diagnostic interviewing and therapy. In his survey of programs supported by the Labor Department, mainly involving poverty workers, Grosser (1969) found that they were used even less in direct services and instead were mainly employed in clerical, minor administrative, transport and comparable jobs in helping agencies. Along with the growing interest in nonprofessional workers, there remains uncertainty, however, as to how and where they can be used and about the necessary selection and training. We will consider some of these issues later after looking at some illustrative nonprofessional programs.

Illustrative Nonprofessional Programs

STUDENT VOLUNTEERS IN MENTAL HOSPITALS

College students contributing to the workings of psychiatric hospitals provide one of the oldest models of nonprofessional involvement in mental health activities. In some cases, they have contributed directly to patient care, in others, they have more served institutional needs (B. S. Brown and Ishiyama, 1968). They may administer and score psychological tests, assist recreational and occupational therapists, and help in research. They may serve as companions to patients or they may have little contact with patients, doing office work or even helping in the maintenance of the hospital plant. Too often, the assigned tasks do not meaningfully engage the talents or motivation of the students.

One of the more thoughtfully organized and best evaluated programs for students was developed at the Connecticut Valley Hospital in Middletown (Holzberg, Knapp, and Turner, 1967). Holzberg and his colleagues built on the earlier experiences of Harvard students in a Massachusetts hospital (Umbarger, Dalsimer, Morrison, and Breggin, 1962). There were three major objectives to the Connecticut "companion program:" (1) to give patients an important social relationship; (2) simultaneously, to provide a rewarding intellectual and emotional experience for the student; and (3) to improve the morale of overburdened and frustrated hospital personnel. As a "companion," the student was to serve more as a friend than as a therapist. Mitchell (1966) has suggested the name "amica-therapy" to describe a helping relation of this sort.

Each student was paired with a hospital patient, with whom he explored the hospital, talked, visited in the community, and otherwise did whatever seemed natural and appropriate under staff guidance. The companions and their staff mentors met in regular group sessions to discuss their experiences; supervisory advice was available at all times. There were minimum selection criteria for students entering the program, although subsequent study showed them to be notably humane and concerned young people. In follow-up, the experience was found to have salutary effects on the students. Similarly, there is evidence that patients gained in the encounter, judged from students' ratings and the patients' own self-evaluations. Summing up, Holzberg, Knapp, and Turner (1967) conclude:

> It seems to us that the companion program has brought together two individuals who normally would have a rare or transient encounter—the patient often lost in despair and retired from life; the student, a younger person at the height of social idealism, courage and optimism. What has emerged thus far in our work is that the relationship between these two has had many beneficial consequences for both. The patient seems to borrow some of the optimism and courage of his Companion, and the Companion gains wisdom and charity which is personally enlarging. Above and beyond this, it has opened another channel of communication between the hospital and its patients, and the outside community [p. 108].

MATURE WOMEN AS MENTAL HEALTH COUNSELORS

Margaret Rioch and her co-workers set out to solve two social problems at the same time: to develop "second careers" for mature, intelligent women, whose families no longer needed their full-time attention, and to increase the availability of low-cost care, by preparing them as psychotherapists for outpatient clinic work with adolescents and adults (Rioch, 1967; Rioch, Elkes, Flint, Usdansky, Newman, and Silber, 1963). Eight women were carefully selected from over fifty serious and highly motivated applicants, through interviews, written autobiographies, and observation in a group situation. The eight chosen were educated, middle-class mothers, whose average age was in the low forties. Over a two-year period, they trained in a part-time program which was intensive if somewhat narrow by professional standards. It centered on learning psychotherapy, and included (1) from the beginning, therapeutic practice under supervision; (2) observation of individual, family, and group therapy; and (3) lectures and seminars on psychotherapy theory and practice, personality development, psychodynamics, and psychopathology, among other subjects. Eleven psychologists, psychoanalysts, psychiatrists, and social workers participated, though Rioch estimates that their composite time was perhaps the equivalent of two full-time teachers. Exacting evaluation and follow-up was built into the program. Three highly qualified psychiatrists interviewed the trainees at the end of the second year, and rated their recorded interviews and case reports as being of high quality. Independently, Golann, Breiter, and Magoon (1966) compared the clinical skill of Rioch's trainees with that of hospital volunteers, medical students, and psychiatric residents at different year levels. All of the subjects were asked to view a film of a psychiatrist interviewing a woman patient and to make judgments as to the patient's background, current status, personality dynamics, and prognosis. The ratings of each group of subjects were correlated with those of five experienced members of a psychiatric faculty. It was found that the Rioch trainees did not score as well as the more advanced residents, though they did significantly better than the volunteers and first-year medical students. On the whole, they were at about the level of senior medical students and first-year psychiatric residents.

After graduation from the training program, all of the women obtained positions in mental health agencies. In a three-year follow-up study they were found to be functioning very effectively (Magoon and Golann, 1966).

Building on this initial project, Rioch and Lourie developed a second training program, this time directed toward training mature women to work with mothers of disturbed children. Again, it was found that the necessary skills could be developed, although in this realm it was more difficult to find appropriate positions (Lourie, 1968).

Rioch's work is considerably more ambitious than most experiments with nonprofessionals. While distinctly shorter and more focused than graduate education, her program still involved considerable time and skilled teaching, for which, fortunately, she had an excellent faculty, who would have graced any graduate program in clinical psychology or psychiatry. Although still costly, she presents an innovative model for streamlined training for a familiar and important clinical role, that of psychotherapist. As important, she has demonstrated that an available but neglected "manpower" resource can be utilized both to the advantage of people with psychological problems and to those who want to help them.

COLLEGE STUDENTS AS COMPANION-THERAPISTS TO TROUBLED BOYS

To provide help for young boys in the community itself, rather than in a clinical setting, Goodman (1972a) trained college students who then worked as paid companion-therapists. Prospective companions were recruited through advertisements in the campus newspaper. Selection involved a number of personality tests and interviews but depended most centrally on a newly devised role-playing and group assessment procedure in which applicants revealed their understanding (empathy), acceptance-warmth, openness (self-disclosure), and other traits believed important to the therapist (the procedure will be discussed in some further detail later in this chapter). Training consisted mainly of group sensitivity sessions but also included workshops, lectures, and demonstrations.

Surveying the total population of fifth- and sixth-grade boys in Berkeley, California, Goodman found a large number who had psychological problems, as judged by peers, teachers, and parents. For purposes of the study, those with "quiet problems" (isolation, withdrawal, depression) were distinguished from those with "outgoing problems" (hostility, aggression). Of the families who volunteered to participate in the companionship-therapy program, eighty-eight boys were selected and paired with a companion; an additional seventy-four, who could not be treated, were studied as control subjects.

The companions worked with the boys in unstructured interactions in the home, playground, and elsewhere in the community. They spent one to four hours at a time, two or three times per week with the boys. On the average, the companion-boy pairs spent a total of 141 hours together—talking, walking, sight-seeing, working on hobbies, listening to music or watching TV, and the like, with the particular activity usually chosen by the boy. As the relationship ripened, the two more often discussed deep, personal feelings.

Overall, the companionship program had modest positive effects, when the treated group was compared to the controls. In part, the outcome findings are not more dramatic because the control boys also tended to improve over the same period, though not quite to the same extent as the participants. The participants showed more reduction in their presenting problems, as reported by the parents and the boys themselves, and were also judged generally better able to get along with others. Less evidence of change was found in teacher and peer ratings. Both the boys and their parents, however, expressed great satisfaction with the experience.

When one looks more closely at particular subgroups of boys, and particular boy-companion pairings, the conditions under which this intervention is most effective becomes clearer. The boys who gained most, when compared to appropriate comparison groups, were (1) black boys working with white companions; (2) those whose companions were "outgoing" rather than "quiet"; (3) those who had longer if less frequent visits; and (4) perhaps most interesting, those who were initially most troubled. At the other extreme, those who gained least were (1) quiet boys coupled with quiet companions; (2) boys counseled by companions who tended to be more rigid or depressed; and (3) boys working with companions who were atypically old as undergraduates (twenty-three to thirty-five years). Thus, as we might have predicted from the earlier review of psychotherapy research, outcome depends on qualities of the boy, the companion, and the interaction between them. It is clear, however, that this form of intervention has distinct promise for helping troubled youngsters. Goodman's model of companionship therapy and his methods of selection and training, are now being applied in many settings; research to make it more effective continues.

Finally, as in the studies of college volunteers in hospitals, Goodman found that the experience benefitted the companion as well as the boy. Compared to matched undergraduates, the companions tended to sharpen interests in children's behavior and problems and their motivation for a helping career. In their own interpersonal behavior, they became more assertive, autonomous, and less defensive. Those who worked with black youngsters developed a keener interest in black culture and intergroup relations. Most of them had joined the project with "the need for converting pent-up ideals into some humanitarian action," and found their expectations met. In all, the companions furthered their own development in several important ways; they learned more about intimacy, savored autonomy and responsibility, and sharpened career goals.

THE INDIGENOUS NONPROFESSIONAL AND PROBLEMS OF POVERTY COMMUNITIES

Indigenous nonprofessionals can serve as a bridge between mental health agencies and their home communities. At the same time, the worker himself gains through holding a self-respecting and socially useful job, perhaps for the first time in his life. With this latter purpose primarily in mind, a group at Howard University recruited young blacks, between seventeen and twenty-one years of age, from the poorest areas of Washington, D.C., for training as "human service aides" (Fishman, Klein, MacLennan, Mitchell, Pearl, and Walker, 1965). All were school dropouts, many had police records and poor histories of employment. The intent was to develop in them the necessary identity and motivation, general human-relation skills, and necessary knowledge to work with people needing help. They were trained, and later employed, as aides in recreation and child-care programs, schools, youth programs, and mental health centers, to be counselors in the welfare department, and to aid in research in poverty-program studies.

Regardless of their later assignments, a central activity for all trainees consisted of participation in "core groups." In these sessions, discussion centered on the values and attitudes which trainees brought with them. While some of these might be adaptive to life on the streets in the culture of poverty, they might be inappropriate to the helping role. Translating the feelings and experience of their outside lives in general human-relations principles better geared to meaningful responsibility for the well-being of others was the major task of the core group. In addition, each trainee was involved in specific units to develop skills in the particular areas in which he was to work. As appropriate, he was exposed to discussions on child development, interviewing techniques, or school practices. But a major part of the training consisted of on-the-job experience and supervision. This was built in from the outset, and gave a meaningful base for both core-group and skill-training activities.

In a number of respects the program was successful. These young people worked out well as aides in a variety of helping settings. From their own self-reports, personality testing, and observation of their work, there was little direct evidence of personality change but marked improvement was found in their social functioning. They worked steadily and productively; none were involved in criminal acts or arrested (MacLennan, Klein, Pearl and Fishman, 1966; W. L. Klein, 1967).

The Lincoln Hospital mental health program in New York City has given central attention to the training and use of nonprofessionals (Reiff and Riessman, 1965; Riessman, 1967; Peck, Kaplan, and Roman, 1966; Riessman, 1965; and Kaplan and Roman, 1973). The program is conceived in a social action ideology which emphasizes the importance of direct involvement with human problems within the local neighborhood. The most critical need of the poor, as Reiff (1966) has emphasized, requires solving basic social and economic problems (e.g., housing and jobs), developing self-determination and adequate coping skills.

Indigenous nonprofessionals were involved in such tasks as providing housing information, organizing neighborhood-improvement groups, and helping families be more competent in homemaking and child care. They functioned as "community-action aides," facilitating contacts among institutions such as schools, churches, and civil-rights groups. Finally, they took on the important role of "expeditor" to inform about and bring people into more effective relations with available community services and agencies.

Much thought was given to the particular problems of training indigenous nonprofessionals (Riessman, 1967). Recruitment must be simple and direct, involving minimum delay or processing of applicants. The built-in ambiguities of the new role must be reduced wherever and however possible. One technique suggested is to encourage the formation of unions or other worker organizations to give focus to their new identity. Just because the worker comes from the community does not necessarily mean that he is unambivalently identified with it. Along with sympathy and concern for his people, the nonprofessional may also see himself as different or superior and view his peers with "pity, annoyance, or anger." They may share the positive qualities of the resident population, but also have the negative traits of moral indignation, punitiveness, suspiciousness, and other such qualities which can interfere with the solving of community problems. They may be competitive with professionals who, in turn, can be overly concerned with preserving their "indigenous" and their "nonprofessional" status. Years after Reiff discussed these concerns, the revolution of the nonprofessionals at Lincoln Hospital, mentioned in the preceeding chapter, brought these problems into sharp focus.

THE SPECIAL ASSETS OF THE NONPROFESSIONAL

The nonprofessional has some unique qualities which may be special assets to his work. Because of the newness of his job, lack of professional knowledge, identity, and role constraints, the nonprofessional may have considerable enthusiasm and involvement, fresh points of view, role flexibility, and less social distance, all of which may serve his clients well.

Along with understandable anxiety, the nonprofessional starts with enthusiasm and a keen desire to be helpful. Both Poser and Rioch, we noted earlier, see the success of Poser's students (see p. 522) as reflecting this enthusiastic involvement. Indeed, Rioch wonders whether, if they were kept to the job for some years, the fresh enthusiasm might not wear down as the work became more routine and less rewarding. However, particularly with hospital patients, for whom life has a gray sameness and hopelessness, injecting humane interest, youthful enthusiasm and sympathetic concern may well be therapeutic and inspire constructive changes in the patient.

A related fact, noted by Rioch, is that the nonprofessional brings "fresh points of view, flexible attitudes, and sometimes new methods into the field." Being innocent, he is less burdened by the stereotypes as well as the knowledge of the field. He is free to try new approaches and may discover new techniques, which would not occur to the professional because of his sophistication. In actuality, however, a review of therapeutic proposals made by student volunteers in hospitals shows most of them to be variations of traditional themes (B. S. Brown and Ishiyama, 1968). The students' freshness is also helpful to staff morale and may produce new ideas in the professionals themselves.

The nonprofessional may do things for which the professional may not only lack time but also sees as outside his professional role. He can socialize freely with a patient and become intimately involved in his life. Particularly in community programs with multi-problem families, reducing social distance may be important. Eating and drinking with the client, helping diaper the baby, helping the family find the welfare office and negotiate its procedures can lay a foundation from which the client's trust develops. Proceeding from there, the worker can better understand his problems and the client can learn new adaptive behaviors.

Selection and Training of Nonprofessionals

On the whole, there seems to be good self-selection of candidates for nonprofessional mental health roles. Goodman, Holzberg, Cowen, and others working with college students all report that the great majority of volunteers are stable, service-oriented people with considerable interpersonal sensitivity and skill. They are not, as might be feared, simply seeking excitement or unconsciously looking for opportunities to work out their own neurotic problems. However, in most programs, there is explicit screening for grossly disturbed people.

In addition, there is frequently a formal assessment phase which involves interviews, psychological tests, and observation. The focal concern is almost invariably with personal attributes, rather than formal training, background, or experience. The most frequently sought characteristics are warmth, compassion, general human-relations skills, a lack of personal defensiveness, and what might generally be considered "positive mental health." As the particular demands and work requirements of particular projects become recognized, more precise criteria evolve. Thus, Reiff and Riessman (1965) sought indigenous workers who were not only concerned to better their community but who also seemed personally capable of learning and had a readiness to communicate with professionals across class lines. In a school project, Zax and Cowen (1967) selected housewives who seemed to have personal warmth, interest in children, a successful history of raising of their own children, and a "noncrusading" orientation toward the school system.

An ingenious method has been devised by Goodman (1972a, 1972b) to assess "psychotherapeutic talent" among applicants for a nonprofessional helping project. It attempts to operationalize and measure some of the personal qualities felt to be important for any therapist by client-centered theorists (see Chapter 14). The procedure is called the "Group Assessment of Interpersonal Traits (GAIT)." It involves having seven or eight applicants perform interpersonal tasks while observing, rating, and describing each other. In each five-minute period, one participant acts as a "discloser," describing an interpersonal concern, while another serves as an "understander," whose task is to comprehend his feelings. At the end, the understander tries to recapitulate the discloser's problem and the discloser rereads his original statement, so that all can judge whether they concur. The procedure is repeated until everyone has had a turn as a discloser and as an understander. At this point, applicants are asked to rate each other on scales describing such traits as understanding, openness, acceptance, and rigidity. Thus, each person has been judged as he faces the difficult task of revealing a personal aspect of himself before strangers and as he attempts to understand the feelings of another in a brief time, asking few questions, and being generally nonjudgmental. The scores yielded by the GAIT have been found to be fairly reliable, to relate sensibly to other personality measures, and, more important, to predict later field performance with emotionally troubled boys. The procedure is coming to be used in a number of projects to select nonprofessional workers.

Personality attributes, rather than intellectual skills, experience, or training, are most highly valued in prospective nonprofessional workers. Indeed, some psychologists involved in such programs convey the prejudice that native sensitivities might even be damaged rather than facilitated by formal training—it would be like sending Grandma Moses to art school! "The selected nonprofessionals are assumed to be individuals who, by personality, life experience, or whatever, have a good deal to offer others; it would be unwise to tamper excessively with their styles and natural reflexes by teaching them the 'right' way to do things" (Cowen, 1967, p. 425). Unlike professional education, acceptance certainly does not depend on demonstrated intellectual or academic accomplishments. As an aside, it is worth noting that educators in the helping disciplines often stress the importance of similar human qualities, but these are usually of secondary concern in the actual selection of candidates for professional degrees.

In training nonprofessionals, consideration is given to both sharpening nonspecific human-relations skills and to the learning of psychological techniques of particular relevance to the particular role. The former is often achieved through some form of group training, similar in conception and form to T-group or sensitivity-group training. The more specific skills are mostly taught through supervised practice, sometimes accompanied by seminars and reading. On the whole, however, classroom learning is deemphasized in favor of experiential learning. In programs involving minority workers in poverty communities some have suggested a "job-first, training-next" approach, in order to consolidate commitment to the role and direct understanding of the work involved before any effort is made to sharpen the worker's human or technical skills (Reiff and Riessman, 1965).

Changes in the Nonprofessional Himself

Riessman's "helper-therapy" principle seems broadly applicable (1965). He reviews evidence that young children given the task of teaching still younger ones learn more themselves. In experimental situations, subjects asked to convince others of a point of view became more firmly committed to it. Considerable evidence is accumulating to show the advantages to the helper of helping others.

College students have been found to change for the better after nonprofessional experience. Hospital companions, compared to student volunteers in other social services showed increased knowledge and positive attitudes toward mental illness by the end of their experience (Holzberg, Knapp, and Turner, 1967). There was also a healthy "stirring up" of their values. They were more interested in religious and social values, as shown by the Allport-Vernon-Lindsay Scale of Values, and more nurturant and intraceptive as measured by the Edwards' Personal Preference Inventory. They became morally more tolerant, particularly of sexual and aggressive behavior, and scored higher on measures of self-acceptance. An interesting finding was that MMPI anxiety scores increased; this is interpreted, probably correctly, as reflecting greater introspectiveness on the part of the companion students. Other studies with college student volunteers yield parallel findings. Goodman (1972) reports that his student volunteers became more interested in the behavior of children, in working with troubled people, and in their own interaction with friends, compared to comparable students who were not in the program. Cowen, Zax, and Laird (1966) studied the effects of volunteer work with emotionally disturbed children in public elementary schools. Here, they found an interesting pattern of changes, from before to after the experience. Initially overidealistic and enthusiastic evaluation of schools, teachers, mental health workers, and other aspects of the setting and project went down while simultaneously, the volunteers' evaluation of children went up. The youngsters were judged as more active, less ineffective, warmer, more cooperative, and more friendly as time went by. In this project, as in Holzberg's and Goodman's, participation often led to a decision for a mental-health career. For the college student, participation in a helping service fosters personal growth and engenders more informed and humane values. For the indigenous worker, it is hoped, the effects are even more profound. In the long run, society benefits; more immediately, help is given to people in need.

Problems in the Use of Nonprofessionals

The limited experience with nonprofessionals, and the few evaluative studies that have been reported, point up the clear promise of nonprofessional programs but also a number of inherent problems. Before the full contribution of nonprofessionals can be realized, a number of important issues have to be clarified.

PROBLEMS OF THE NONPROFESSIONAL ROLE

The role of the nonprofessional is ambiguous. In some ways, he is a staff member, in other regards he may be closer to the patient group (as in poverty programs) or he may be uncertain and vacillate in his identification (like students in mental hospitals). The nonprofessional can feel depreciated and exploited, as indeed he sometimes is, for most settings distinguish higher-level (professional) and lower-level (nonprofessional) functions, whatever their value. There can be ready identification with the client group and polarization against the professionals.

His interest, enthusiasm, and lack of experience, in some ways assets, can create friction in the agency. The nonprofessional is too inclined to expect magical changes in his clients and hence too readily discouraged by setbacks. In a suicide prevention center, but probably elsewhere as well, it was observed that nonprofessionals can take overwork much better than underwork (Heilig, Farberow, and Litman, 1968). Less familiar with the rhythms of agency life, and less inclined to accommodate to it, he can irritate staff members.

However, the nonprofessional may not only set himself off from the professional, but he may identify with him as well. A critical issue arises from the fact that nonprofessional work often inspires a desire to continue in a helping role, with greater status, income, and professional standing. This is no problem, and indeed may be a desired outcome, for the college student who is free to pursue a career in psychology, social work, or psychiatry. But for the "new careers" people, whether uneducated slum dwellers, middle-aged housewives, or others, upward striving and professional aspirations can, in the present state of affairs, be a serious frustration. In time, professional education may provide opportunities for talented people who have proven themselves in "new careers" programs, but as of now few exist.

Similarly, opportunities for more responsible and better paid employment of the trained nonprofessional are limited. Civil service regulations and agency standards do not provide sufficient appropriate jobs. Rioch was very cognizant of this issue, and expended much thought and effort to develop appropriate positions for her mental health counselors. At the same time, she had to count on their intrinsic satisfaction in their work, their lack of conventional career ambition, and the availability of a husband's income to support them if they were denied the symbols and substance of job status. Clearly, if larger numbers of trained nonprofessionals in continuing jobs are to be utilized, there must be serious reorganization of helping services, with new roles and opportunities for advancement.

PROBLEMS RELATED TO THE BACKGROUND AND PERSONAL QUALITIES OF THE NONPROFESSIONAL

Many of the advantages of "nonprofessionalness" can also be liabilities. Enthusiasm, freshness, and involvement can lead the worker into excessive and potentially harmful behaviors, as can his insecurity and lack of experience. Concerned identification with the patient may foster personal growth and self-esteem, but it also allows the projection of the worker's own problems on to the patient. Detachment, necessary to full understanding of the patient's needs, may be lost.

Precisely the qualities which make the indigenous worker valuable can limit his work as well (Riessman, 1965). For example, sharing the cultural tendency to externalize personal problems can make him insensitive to recognizing the client's responsibility for action in his own behalf. There is the danger, already noted, of negative as well as positive identification. The ghetto dweller, now in a responsible position just like the former addict or the black policeman, can set himself off from his peers and be more harshly critical of them than the detached professional. Innocence is both good and bad; so too, is enthusiasm; so too, is sharing the client's culture. Where and how these attributes can be used to the advantage of the client, and the conditions under which their potentially harmful effects can be averted, are still open issues. Indeed, they are part of the still larger and as yet unresolved questions: What qualities in the helper matter for effecting positive change in the client? To what extent do they involve intellectual or personality competence, knowledge or human-relations skills, native or trainable?

PROBLEMS RELATED TO PROFESSIONAL VALUES

Full and dispassionate understanding of the pros and cons of nonprofessional work is hampered by professional attitudes which are protective of vested interests, and reflect fear for prestige, social status, or income. We may see value in subservient or adjunctive roles, but we are reluctant to recognize nonprofessionals in parallel functions. Commenting on the Poser study, Rioch (1966) notes: "If we have invested long years of hard work in achieving a high professional status, including many courses that were dull and many examinations that were nerve wracking and we are told that some bit of a girl with no training can do the job just as well or better than we can, it is natural that we should try to find some objections" (p. 291). To discover what and how nonprofessionals can contribute, free and nondefensive inquiry is needed. In the same process, there is the opportunity to discover more about the helping process itself and perhaps to lay aside some professional myths.

As nonprofessionals become more involved in direct service, the role of the professional necessarily shifts more toward training and supervision, which may not be congenial to many clinicians who would rather treat patients directly than work through others. There is concern, often warranted, about entrusting the care of patients to untutored and inexperienced people.

The nonprofessional often comes into direct conflict with lower-level staff, particularly in mental hospitals. The college student volunteer, for example, can represent an immediate and realistic threat to the status, livelihood and self-esteem of the usually uneducated psychiatric aide who performs similar functions. Tension between student volunteers and hospital employees is destructive to the morale of both and hardly beneficial to patients. Introducing nonprofessionals into a mental health agency has to take careful account of the interests and attitudes of existing staff.

PROBLEMS IN PROGRAM ORGANIZATION, TRAINING, AND CAREER DEVELOPMENT

Thus far, nonprofessional training has taken place primarily in service-oriented settings and much less frequently in the teaching settings where professionals are trained. The emphasis is generally on serving immediate community needs; there is proportionately less interest in developing career programs. For the full potential of nonprofessionals to be realized, universities and other professional training centers will have to lend their resources and reputation to the enterprise (Lief, 1966). However, the trend in the mental health fields has been toward longer and more intensive training; in psychology, for example, graduate departments emphasize doctoral rather than masters' level training, and there is even greater reluctance to sponsor practice-oriented programs at the bachelor level. At the same time, there is a surplus of well-qualified applicants for full professional training in all of the mental health fields. Consequently, with limited resources available and the resistance of academic leaders, it is unlikely that universities will be prepared to divert much effort into nonprofessional (or lower-level professional) programs, except as an incidental activity. If larger numbers of nonprofessionals are to be trained, new teaching institutions may have to be developed.

Finally, job opportunities and secure career lines have to be created. Presently, many programs depend on special funding from the federal government or foundations in research or demonstration grants. Regularly funded positions, with clear job specifications and opportunities for advancement have to be developed, if nonprofessionals are to be used in more than a transient role.

MENTAL HEALTH EDUCATION

Goals and Problems

Mental health education is intended to serve two broad though related purposes: (1) to educate the public and its leaders about the nature of mental disorders and methods of treatment, to convey the magnitude of the problem, and to mobilize action toward *improving the care and treatment* of the mentally disturbed. The plea is for interest and compassion rather than stigmatization and rejection; (2) to improve the mental health of the community by *encouraging preventive activities*. Professional associations, citizen's groups and governmental agencies engage in educational activities toward these ends. Mental health education is one of the essential functions expected of community mental health centers under federal support. The effort to inform and change public attitudes is an important theme of community psychology.

The twin goals of improving care and fostering prevention go back to the founding in 1909 of the National Committee for Mental Hygiene, forerunner of the present National Association for Mental Health. Clifford W. Beers, a former hospital patient, enlisted as cofounders such distinguished people as William James and Adolph Meyer, the leading psychologist and psychiatrist of the day. Out of indignation at his own ill treatment, Beers was passionately dedicated to improving care for other patients. However, his professional collaborators were even more interested in the possibility of preventing mental illness, inspired by the public health successes in the control of contagious diseases through immunization and sanitation. While no comparable methods existed, then or now, they had faith that public education (in realms such as child guidance, eugenics, and birth control) and early treatment might limit the later incidence of gross psychological disturbances.

Public education has been a vital tool in the control of medical disease. Educational programs serve primary, secondary, and tertiary prevention ends, as suggested in the slogans "Don't smoke," "Get a chest X-ray yearly," or "Hire the handicapped." Such programs have helped overcome the social stigmas which blocked the recognition and treatment of a variety of diseases, such as venereal diseases and cancer. In addition to encouraging health-enhancing activities, public relations campaigns seek to influence public attitudes and social policy and to raise funds for medical research and training. Organized medical groups (e.g., AMA), voluntary health organizations (e.g., American Heart Association), and governmental agencies (e.g., U.S. Public Health Service) sponsor educational programs. The message may be direct or more subtly woven into the fabric of education. It may be conveyed by lectures or films, newspaper or magazine articles, comic strips, TV programs or spot advertisements. The best talents and techniques of communication experts are used. They are apparently quite successful in informing and changing attitudes as well as encouraging particular health-related activities. Educational efforts have proved their value in increasing the health of the American public.

In principle, education would seem to be as important and potentially valuable in the field of mental health. Actually, the situation is considerably different. There have been formidable barriers to effective educational programs and mixed feelings among mental health professionals as to their potential effectiveness. No simple information can be communicated to guide the layman in the recognition of emotional disorders nor facilitate his understanding of their course or treatment. Similarly, there are few simple prescriptions which, if followed, would assure positive mental health. At best, we can hope to foster understanding and compassion, to reduce some of the fear and ignorance which surrounds mental illness, and at the same time, to encourage modes of behavior more likely to foster sound psychological development. These, in general, have been the aims of mental health education.

A major problem lies in the fact that psychotics are rejected and stigmatized. The mentally ill person is feared as irrational and dangerous to the security of the community. More subtly, he may stimulate the fear that we might ourselves act out impulses which we sense but fortunately are able to control in ourselves. Whether seen as originating in sin, bad genes, or damaging early experiences, the psychotic is an outsider whose existence the public would as soon deny, and often literally does. Despite growing psychological-mindedness and humanitarian values, there are still few who would say sincerely as William James did early in the century, "There but for the grace of God, go I."

In the past, a central theme in mental health education has been the effort to convince a reluctant public that the mentally ill are sick in the same sense as the physically sick, and should therefore be treated with the same humane regard. Such efforts have not, in the main, succeeded, according to the Joint Commission on Mental Illness and Health (1961), because they have not sufficiently appreciated the profundity of the social rejection theme nor dealt with the fact that mental illness *is* different. The Joint Commission report notes: "(1) people (including physicians and other professionals) find it difficult to think about and recognize psychological illness as illness or to see sickness as having psychological forms, and (2) the mentally ill as a class lack in capacity to evoke sympathy, which is to say that they are overburdened with liabilities as persons and as patients" (p. 82). In future public information programs, the Joint Commission urged more modest goals, which recognize the difference between mental and medical patients, while working to overcome the pattern of rejection, defeatism, and exaggeration in public attitudes. The objectives as well as methods of mental health education are being reevaluated by specialists in the field (e.g., National Assembly on Mental Health Education, 1960; J. A. Davis, 1965; Adelson and Lurie, 1972).

What Do People Know and Believe About Mental Illness?

For most Americans, "mental illness" means only the most gross emotional disorders, those in which there is irrational and dangerous behavior for which there is no "reasonable" explanation. Unlike professionals, they do not visualize a spectrum of adjustment, ranging from optimal psychological functioning at one pole to another of gross psychological disability. Instead, thinking is more categorical—e.g., some people are crazy, most are not—nor is intervention viewed as necessary or valuable except at the extreme.

Such attitudes have been revealed in a number of public opinion surveys which made use of an ingenious technique developed by Shirley Star (1955, 1957) of the National Opinion Research Center (NORC). In 1950, NORC interviewed 3,500 respondents in a nationally representative sample. Six case descriptions were developed with the help of mental health professionals. They describe a paranoid schizophrenic, simple schizophrenic, chronic anxiety neurotic, alcoholic and an adolescent behavior disorder. Respondents were asked whether the person described had a problem at all, what was wrong, what might have caused it, whether it was mental illness, and how serious it was. Here are two of the descriptions:

> *Paranoid Schizophrenic.* I'm thinking of a man—let's call him Frank Jones—who is very suspicious; he doesn't trust anybody, and he's sure that everybody is against him. Sometimes he thinks people he sees on the street are talking about him or following him around. A couple of times now, he has beaten up men who didn't even know him, because he thought they were plotting against him. The other night he began to curse his wife terribly; then he hit her and threatened to kill her, because, he said, she was working against him too, just like everyone else.

> *Compulsive Phobic.* Here is a different sort of girl—let's call her Mary White. She seems happy and cheerful; she's pretty, has a good enough job, and is engaged to marry a nice young man. She has loads of friends; everybody likes her, and she's always busy and active. However, she just can't leave the house without going back to see whether she left the gas stove lit or not. And she always goes back again just to make sure she locked the door. And one other thing about her: she's afraid to ride up and down in an elevator; she just won't go any place where she has to ride in an elevator to get there.

Only Frank Jones, the paranoid schizophrenic, had more than a majority (75 percent) call him mentally ill. In the other five instances, the proportions ranged from 7 to 34 percent. Indeed, one-sixth of the total sample did not consider any of the six cases as representing mental illness. When commenting on the symptoms of the six people, respondents saw them as reflecting understandable reactions to every-day problems, or short-lived responses to life's stress, which either would disappear of their own accord or could be helped by some encouragement and suggestion. In Mary White's case, for example, the majority felt there was nothing at all wrong with her, and that indeed her life was good. Very few considered her "mentally ill." Her fears were seen as probably resulting from actual, frightening events in the past, and were therefore readily understandable. In fact, respondents readily admitted similarly groundless fears in themselves, of the same sort as Mary's.

In subsequent studies, the same situations were used with other samples (e.g., Cumming and Cumming, 1957; Nunnally, 1961; Lemkau and Crocetti, 1962; Dohrenwend, Bernard, and Kolb, 1962). Generally, the pattern of findings was similar to Star's. Overall, these surveys show that the readiness to identify the illustrative cases as needing psychological help increases with education and social class. The more educated and affluent layman thinks more like the mental health professional.

When not asked to comment on specific cases, but rather to respond to general questions, most respondents say that they believe that psychotics can recover, though they recognize that treatment facilities may be inadequate. The public knows of the existence of special facilities and of specially trained professionals; however, psychiatrists and psychologists are rarely correctly distinguished. Underneath what seem to be generally favorable attitudes, there is a persistent pattern of denial and rejection.

This was best revealed in the effort of the Cummings to study and change attitudes in a small Canadian community (Cumming and Cumming, 1957). Their own educational program not only had no effect, but it aroused antagonism in the community; an experience which convinced them of the profundity of the need to deny and segregate the problems of the emotionally disturbed from every-day concern. As the Cummings see it, the dual processes of denial and isolation serve the social purpose of preserving the integrity of the community by ejecting the alien, frightening, and unpredictable from within it. "In summary, the social response to mental illness seems to be: first, denial of mental illness; second, isolation of the affected person in a hospital when mental illness can no longer be denied, with concomitant rationalization of this isolation with beliefs that the hospital is a wonderful place, capable of curing mental illness, if it can be cured at all, which is doubtful, and, finally, insulation of the whole vexing problem by a secondary denial that a problem exists insofar as it needs solving by ordinary citizens" (pp. 122–123). "While the motive for isolation in mental illness is no doubt the treatment of the ill, the latent function is the reaffirmation of the solidarity of the social system in which norms are not villated—the *solidarity of the sane*" (p. 127). The Cummings aptly titled their book *Closed Ranks*.

Studies of the content of mass media show them to give a generally distorted picture of mental health problems (Nunnally, 1961). Someone is characterized as a "former mental patient" when a crime is being reported; rarely if ever in the context of heroism or accomplishment. A person in entertainment or the arts may speak about being in psychotherapy but is not likely to mention hospital care. A wise politician avoids both topics. Newspaper accounts typically overemphasize bizarre and violent behaviors. Nunnally found little specific content intended to present the views of mental conditions and treatments as they are understood by professionals. Professionals themselves are often made to appear sinister or foolish; the patient is better helped by a kindly friend. "The homespun philosopher of the 'soap opera,' with his trite homilies, becomes the therapist *par excellence*" (Clausen, 1971, p. 45).

In general, the Nunnally studies show people to be more *uninformed* than *misinformed;* a situation which bodes well for education since it is easier to supply new information than to contend with rooted misbeliefs. People are unsure of their views, want more information, look to experts for advice and assurance, and, above all, want their doubts stilled. Hence, Nunnally notes, mental health messages will be accepted if the concepts are clear, the material interesting, and the source is authoritative, but also if "the message makes the reader feel *secure* by sounding certain, by providing solutions, by presenting an understandable explanation, and by reducing anxiety in other ways." At the same time, Nunnally found many negative attitudes toward those with psychological problems. The mentally ill are regarded with distrust, fear, and dislike; people are threatened by their unpredictability. Since they are more unpredictable, psychotics are held in lower repute than neurotics. A small but significant tendency was found for more educated people to be less negative in their attitudes. Similarly, Nunnally found that younger and better informed physicians tended to be more sympathetic then older colleagues. However, even among trained and educated groups there is a high order of rejection; more so among those in business, less so among educational leaders (Dohrenwend, Bernard, and Kolb, 1962).

The Practice of Mental Health Education

Practice in this realm can be considered in terms of three components: technique, target group, and content (National Assembly on Mental Health Education, 1960; Adelson and Lurie, 1972).

TECHNIQUE

A major thrust in mental health education in recent years is the greater utilization of group processes for developing understanding of mental health issues. From the work on group dynamics and the related efforts in the "dynamics of planned change" (e.g., Lippit, Watson, and Wesley, 1958; Bennis and Shepard, 1961) in the Lewinian tradition, there is increasing recognition of the potential of voluntary group interaction as a vehicle for problem-solving and attitude change in the mental health realm as well as other aspects of social life (Adelson and Lurie, 1972). Where people participate themselves in the educational process, rather than being "educated at," change is likely to be quicker and more permanent. Hence, a major effort of mental health educators involves group discussions in which the educator is more a resource person than a lecturer. In this regard, it can be noted that consultation, though considered as a separate topic, can be conceived in much the same framework and is actually a major technique for providing mental health education.

The mass media, however, remain the primary route for reaching the public at large. Television, newspapers, and magazines carry reports on mental health programs and developments. Problems of neurosis and psychotherapy have become familiar on many TV dramatic programs, as have concerns with drug abuse, delinquency, alcoholism, and other social problems. Various kinds of mental health programs are pictured, such as crisis clinics, suicide prevention, and community mental health centers. All of this reduces the strangeness and fearsomeness of the work of mental health, though there is always the danger of oversimplified and glamorized notions being transmitted in the interest of dramatic appeal.

Lectures to organized groups (whether to the Lions Club or an eighth-grade class), demonstrations, and films are important ways of communicating mental health information. Movies have been produced for many special audiences and are often shown along with discussions led by a professional. Mental health associations and professional groups have speakers bureaus which provide speakers on request.

CONTENT

What is taught relates both to the technique used and to the needs of the target group, as well as the goals of the mental health educator. Thus, if the purpose is to strengthen support for mental health facilities in the community, and the audience is composed of community leaders, then presentations may include mental health statistics, cost-benefit accounting, or limitations of present resources, much of which might be presented in printed form or in a lecture with discussion. With a parents' group, the focus is more likely to be on matters of child development and their import for later mental health; a more participatory format would likely be required if any substantial change in attitudes and later action is to be expected. In order to be effective, an educator must not only have a broad knowledge of psychopathology, development, intervention methods, social problems, and understanding of the organization and facilities of mental health, but also have the knowledge and skills of communication and group processes, required of a fine teacher or consultant.

TARGET GROUP

In any community there are numerous potential target groups. Adelson and Lurie (1972) suggest three major groups who should be given the highest priorities in mental health education.

1. Those Vulnerable to Emotional Disorder. This includes children and their families, groups going through any developmental crisis, such as starting in a new school or career, those facing special stresses, such as illness or loss of a job, and those under long-term stress, such as inadequate housing, chronic unemployment, and the like. In these cases, the primary purpose of education is to help these groups to deal with their own problems.

2. Those Holding Power in the Community. Whether local, statewide, or national, those belonging to the power structure are important targets since the fate of the mental health enterprise, whether a local community clinic or a national research program, depends on their understanding and good will. For other reasons, however, the powerless and deprived are also of concern, for increased un-

derstanding on their part can lead to their taking a more vital part in the development of services best suited to their needs.

3. Those with Care-taking Functions. Teachers, ministers, physicians, and the police need mental health information because they are involved, in more or less direct ways, with the problems of vulnerable people.

In a lengthy review, Adelson and Lurie (1972) detail the particular forms of education which are provided for those in the educational system, health system, religious organizations, industry, and government, at all levels. Within each of these systems, the pattern of educator-participants-topic-technique that might be used differs importantly. The kind of program set up for pediatricians concerned to understand the behavior problems of children might involve lectures by a child psychiatrist; by contrast, a meeting for industrial executives to encourage them to hire former patients would probably require both factual presentations by someone who understands the problems of industrial production and sensitivity-group sessions to work through emotional resistances.

In the community approach, educational efforts are the concern of all mental health professionals but they require in addition the special talents and training of "mental health educators" (E. E. Goldston, 1968). Like colleagues in the older field of health education, mental health educators have particular expertise in educational methods, communications, and media. By sharing their knowledge with psychiatrists and psychologists, they can sharpen their educational efforts; at the same time, they can take primary responsibility for public information programs and presentations to particular target groups. To discharge these functions well, they should not only be broadly informed in the general field of mental health, and have special training in communications, public relations and social psychology, but should also be well versed in problems of community organization and planned change. Specialty training for mental health education is now being carried on in a number of schools of Public Health.

The Effectiveness of Mental Health Education

Reviewing the experimental literature on mental health education, J. A. Davis (1965) concludes that no simple overall conclusion as to its effectiveness can be reached. Many of the published studies concern student groups, though some evaluate programs addressed to adult audiences. In many cases, positive effects were found in experiments involving exposure to written material, lectures or group discussion, but in others no effects or negative findings emerged, which led Davis to the conclusion that successful and unsuccessful programs could not readily be distinguished. What does seem true, however, is that the effectiveness of the educational effort varies with the particular facet of behavior which the experimenter attempts to change, along a continuum from beliefs and attitudes to subjective states and practices. Virtually all studies of change in information showed positive results; at the other extreme, studies of change in practices tended to yield uniformly negative results. Little is known about the effects on personal and subjective feelings of happiness, effectiveness, and the like: "A key assumption of existing mental health education programs that mass exposure to books, pamphlets, movies, and so on, has a positive effect on subjective states—has not been and should be studied" (J. A. Davis, 1965, p. 137). A great problem in mental health education intended to affect the behavior as well as the beliefs of the recipient lies less in the medium or in resistance to attitude change as such, than in the nature of the message, what is (or can be) told that would be of value. Thus, education for prevention, Davis notes, has a much less firm base than education for knowledge or attitude change.

Available principles are few and often can be stated only in fairly abstract terms, which provide little guidance for personal action. The educator in the field of cancer control, for example, can deliver the simple message that smoking can be detrimental to your health, but mental health educators have few such straightforward messages to deliver. Inadequate mothering can lead to psychological disturbance in the child, but this can hardly be translated into a directive for action of the sort "if your child is to be psychologically sound, be an adequate mother!" Thus far, mental health education can better serve attitude change toward the goal of improving the understanding and care of the mentally ill than it can be used for altering the feelings and actions of the recipient so as to assure his or his family's better mental health.

Because of the lack of more complete and more specific working principles, the Joint Commission of Mental Illness and Health took the conservative position: "We should avoid the risk of false promise in 'education for better mental health' and focus on the more modest goals of disseminating such information about mental illness as the public needs and wants in order to recognize psychological forms of illness and to arrive at an informed opinion of its responsibility toward the mentally ill" (1961, p. 277).

Informed public opinion is an important goal in itself. People are understandably curious to learn what is known about human psychology and psychologists are obliged to share their knowledge. Regardless of whether such knowledge may or may not lead to greater peace of mind, it is important that it be available as a basis for informed opinion on public questions. Moreover, as J. A. Davis (1965) notes, making psychological knowledge available serves three additional purposes: (1) having information reassures. The Nunnally studies showed how unsure people were in matters pertaining to mental health, and how eager they were for authoritative and factual material. Getting information, even if incomplete, reduced their fears; (2) information provides standards for evaluating oneself. We often judge our own situation in relation to what we believe that of others to be. To the extent that we lack correct information, we can misjudge; and (3) information can inoculate against the shock of oncoming stress, as we noted in our earlier discussion of anticipatory crisis intervention. The unexpected and unknown is more threatening than the known, even when there are few specific things that can be done to avert it.

Thus, even if the more extravagant hopes of mental hygiene cannot be realized, public information campaigns are entirely justified. In areas of great personal and social interest, people should have access to all information that might extend their knowledge of themselves and their society and which might allow them to make more informed contributions to public policy.

Influencing Child Rearing

The importance of early childhood for later psychological development, both healthy and disordered, makes understandable the prominence given to parent education in prevention-oriented mental health education. Efforts in the field of parent education are worth considering, for they reveal some of the problems as well as promise in the task of educating toward better mental health.

In part, parent education involves providing relatively straightforward information about feeding and child care, clothing, playthings, weaning, and toilet training, that the parent wants and needs to know, and that experts can impart. Extending beyond this realm, however, is the effort to influence those general parental attitudes and behaviors believed to determine psychological growth. Here the task is one of inducing appropriate actions in the parent, so that he in turn can exert more beneficial influences on the child. While we can give usable information about child care, guiding parent-child interactions rests on much less secure knowledge. In this realm, it is much less clear what educational methods are suitable and how sound the knowledge is which we can convey.

Much of what mental health workers know about effects of parental behavior on child growth results from the study of problem children and disturbed adults, and emphasizes the negative in human experience. "We have developed a long list of parental ills: emotional deprivation, overt rejection, covert rejection, cold mechanical handling, overprotection and absorption of the child's life, capricious punishment, severe and crushing discipline. Experts are voluble in telling parents what not to do. On the positive side, the message has been thin and perhaps a touch sentimental: the atmosphere of the home must be one of unconditional love, acceptance, permissiveness, democracy; the climate must always be warm" (R. W. White, 1964, p. 583).

Vagueness is understandable because the conditions leading to healthy development are often less dramatic than those related to pathology. It is easier to characterize gross emotional deprivation than proper loving. Moreover, the fact is that normal emotional development has not been sufficiently studied to know in detail what goes into healthy growth. We lack sufficient understanding of how experiences of later childhood, adolescence, and adulthood itself can redirect the course of growth and neutralize the effects of adverse early circumstances. It is a commonplace observation, supported by empirical studies, that many presently effective and happy adults had childhoods filled with presumably pathogenic influences. But they did not come to clinics and were not the focus of clinician's concerns.

As we learn more about healthy development and of determinants of successful coping, information communicated to parents will likely carry more positive messages. In the past, however, advice more often consisted of "don'ts" than "do's"—and "do's" were often negative "don'ts!" In consequence, White notes, mental health messages are communicated in alarming forms. The implicit theme is that children can be ruined by parents, by acts of which the parent might not even be conscious, and that the child could subsequently be salvaged only by intensive psychotherapy. Such an approach, which amounts to intimidating and berating rather than helping parents, can do more harm than good.

White discusses two matters of particular note. On the one hand, a mental health message delivered in anxiety-producing terms can, indeed, produce anxiety. "Clearly the production of anxiety in parents will defeat the purpose of reducing it in their children. Teaching which makes parents hesitant, self-conscious, and fearful of doing the wrong thing, cannot be expected to bring children a feeling of security" (R. W. White, 1964, p. 585). Hilde Bruch, White also notes, has called attention to an equally sinister possibility. Parents are given the "illusion of omnipotence." They are led to believe that their every act has been shown scientifically to influence the child. Thus they are encouraged to "manipulate him into becoming a perfect adult." Necessary spontaneity and relaxed pleasure in the child's own accomplishments are damaged.

Despite these problems, the content and methods of parent education are becoming considerably more subtle and effective (Brim, 1959). Rather than anxiety-provoking admonitions, better conceived educational efforts start with the recognition that the parents' behaviors are deep-rooted products of their own values and character. Authoritarian pronouncements and direct attack accomplish little and may indeed worsen the situation. Instead, the parent's own concerns and motives must be respected, and time and opportunity given for working through his own self-understanding. This may more readily occur in parent group discussions than through lectures or printed material. Hereford (1963) demonstrated the value of participatory parent discussion groups for changing both parent attitudes and their children's behavior. Parents became more insightful into the causation of the child's behavior and feelings; they could communicate more effectively; they developed greater trust; in turn, their children were better accepted by classmates. Parent education programs of the more recent past have put increasing emphasis on understanding the complexities of growth, developmental states in maturation, and on the sources of competent as well as disturbed behavior. Although parent education is not likely to be the panacea promised by early protagonists of mental hygiene, it is likely to have an important role in mental health education.

CHAPTER 19

Theory and Research in Community Psychology

The community approach is still new and as yet lacks a firm base of theory and research. Much of the work being done reflects the vitality of concerned mental health workers trying to serve urgent social needs. Mainly, however, these are pragmatic efforts, building on clinical judgment and experience and an intuitive appreciation of critical problems. But the systematic study of social behavior and of community-oriented intervention required for rational program development has lagged behind. Leaders in the field have urged greater attention to the creation of relevant theory and the accumulation of relevant research evidence, particularly in this formative period when innovative, and frequently expensive, programs are being launched. In the original Community Mental Health Centers Act of 1963, the Federal Government encouraged research as one of the ten suggested functions of the new centers; in other ways as well, the National Institute of Mental Health has supported much relevant research. In its position paper, the American Psychological Association urged that greater prominence be given to research in the new centers (M. B. Smith and Hobbs, 1966). The need is recognized widely and a fair amount of financial support is available. It remains the task of the community psychologist to apply scientific concepts and skills to broaden and deepen the base of community psychology.

However, the particular kind of research needed may be strange to many psychologists. Psychologists have been trained mainly in experimental, correlational, or clinical methods of investigating psychological processes in the individual person; they are less well prepared for the study of the social forces that act on humans to facilitate or hinder psychosocial adaptation. To gain such knowledge, man must be studied in his real life situations rather than in laboratory or clinical settings. The techniques of the sociologist and anthropologist and of the ecologist and epidemiologist, have to be used as well as those more traditional in psychology. Some research endeavors, for example program evaluation, are more familiar for they parallel familiar research tasks, such as outcome research in psychotherapy. Many, however, require that the community psychologist learn techniques borrowed from other disciplines or that he create methods directly applicable to his unique problems.

In this chapter, we will survey some of the concepts and findings in the realms of epidemiology, ecology, systems theory, and program evaluation which can contribute to the further growth of community psychology. At the end, we will take a broad look at the field to assess its accomplishments and problems.

Ecology

WHAT IS ECOLOGY?

In Lewin's famous formulation, behavior is viewed as determined by the interaction of a person and his environment. Although few would deny this principle, in actuality psychologists have mainly emphasized the qualities of the person to the relative neglect of those of the environment in their efforts to understand human behavior, whether adaptive or disturbed. In recent years, however, there has been a growing realization that the total setting in which behavior occurs needs to be understood. An ecological point of view is emerging of considerable potential importance to community psychological interventions. Psychologists are looking toward ecology, field biology, and ethology, and to older applications in anthropology, sociology, and medical ecology, for principles applicable to their problems.

Ecology, as a biological science, is concerned with the mutual relatedness of species in their physical and biological environments. A home aquarium illustrates the workings of an ecological system (ecosystem). For each to survive, there must be a balanced exchange of oxygen and carbon dioxide between fish and plants. Too many fish, incompatible species, too much or too little light, extremes of temperature, overfeeding or otherwise polluting the water, can destroy the delicate balance of life in the aquarium. Fish and plants die, or growth may be stunted and reproduction hampered. In all, the continuity of the ecosystem depends on the continuous balance of biological and environmental factors. Continuity does not require complete stability but rather change within tolerable limits. In nature, over time, ecosystems evolve into new organizations, as species die out, adapt, or change.

Man's capacity to change his own ecology, for good or for bad, has become an increasing concern to thoughtful people everywhere. Mankind has radically altered the natural environments within which the human species had lived for millennia in balance with other animals, plants, and the physical world. To provide a predictable supply of desirable foods, man developed agriculture. Its consequence has been soil depletion, deforestation, and erosion. Improved medical care increases longevity and physical well-being, but it contributes to population increase and overcrowding. More homes mean less forest; more comfortable transportation leads to air pollution; more manufactured goods lead to depletion of natural resources. As material needs of food and shelter are better served, esthetic needs for quiet, beauty, and open space are frustrated. Efforts to improve the quality of life may reduce the habitability of man's world. No wonder that concern with ecology is so widespread. Nor is it limited to the relation between human life and the physical and biological environment; it extends too to the social institutions within which man lives.

The core emphases of ecology include: (1) a focus on *adaptation,* the capacity of organisms to cope, survive, and grow within their environments; (2) the *interdependence* of living and nonliving elements, which together define an ecosystem; (3) *system change,* over time, as some species prosper while others die or change, as the system moves from one to another mode of organization; and (4) a methodological emphasis on the *naturalistic study* of biological (and, in our case, psychological and social) phenomena rather than on laboratory research. In various ways, these themes are echoed in the emergent fields of "environmental psychology" (Craik, 1970; Ittelson, Proshansky, Rivlin, and Winkel, 1974), "ecological psychology" (Barker, 1968, 1969), "social ecology" (Moos and Insel, 1974), and an ecological orientation to community mental health (J. G. Kelly, 1966, 1968). Thus, Moos and Insel (1974, p. ix) state: "Social ecology may be viewed as the multidisciplinary study of the impact that physical and social environments have on human beings. It is concerned with the assessment and development of optimum human milieus."

THE ECOLOGICAL APPROACH TO COMMUNITY MENTAL HEALTH PROBLEMS

The ecological orientation calls particular attention to three distinct types of issues (J. G. Kelly, 1966):

1. The *interrelation of social or organizational systems* in the community. The underlying assumption is that change in the operation of any one service will affect the operation of all others. Thus, increased admission to a mental health facility may indicate a rise in community-wide stress, but it may also reflect decreased opportunities to find help elsewhere. The relation among organizational systems, and their impact on human behavior, has been a growing concern of those social psychologists, largely concerned with business and industrial organizations, whose work has come to be known as "organizational psychology" (Leavitt and Bass, 1964). The relevance of this field for mental health is becoming better understood (Kahn, 1968).

2. A second major emphasis is on the *relation between the physical environment and individual behavior*. Illustrative are studies of the effects of weather and geography, overcrowding, and the reactions to urban structures and design (Moos and Insel, 1974). Human ecology has made the study of the physical environment more salient in psychology. From the standpoint of community mental health, this orientation points up the value of collaboration between psychologists and other behavioral scientists with workers in engineering, architecture, and city planning toward the design of more satisfying and healthier environments.

3. A third issue concerns the *relation of the individual to his immediate social environment*. A general finding, for example, which emerges from research in ecological psychology—e.g., in studies of animal behavior—is that

group size significantly affects individual adaptation. Whether in high schools or in bee colonies, it has been noted that in the smaller social group there are fewer status differentials, less expression of maladaptive behavior, and higher work output per unit than in larger groups. Such findings provide information of relevance to the design of community psychological programs.

THE EFFECTS OF CROWDING

Ecological studies, both of human and animal behavior, have shown the importance of spatial variables in determining behavior. They can increase our understanding of the psychological effects of population density and overcrowding and contribute to the design of more psychologically healthy environments.

Some years ago, a Swiss animal psychologist noted that species of wild animals behaved as if there were two concentric circles around them (Hediger, 1950, 1955). Farther out, one line defines a "flight distance"; nearer in, there is a "critical distance." If an enemy crosses the outer line, the animal moves back until a safe distance has been restored. If the enemy advances further, and retreat cannot be made, the animal prepares for fight and attacks when the critical distance is trespassed. These boundaries differ between species and are modified in captivity, but they tend to be consistent within species. Animal trainers make use of this knowledge. At the circus, you probably have seen groups of lions or tigers who, at the command of the trainer, position themselves on stools of varying height. To achieve this, the trainer advances on the animal requiring it to move back. If horizontal space is not available, the animal will move upwards in the effort to maintain a safe distance. Knowing the critical distances involved, the trainer will move back at the precise moment. In this way, the lions or tigers are "taught" to mount the stools and maintain their positions on command.

Human behavior similarly varies with the distance between people. Edward T. Hall (1959, 1966) has pioneered a field of study he calls "proxemics" to describe these relations. He notes that there are a series of invisible concentric circles around a person which define zones of *intimate, personal, social,* and *public* behaviors. These vary between cultures, but Hall finds them to be remarkably constant within each. Thus, in the United States, the zone of intimacy extends to 18 inches. Within this distance, there is love making and fighting and direct contact of the body and the eyes. Speech is more often whispering than full vocalization.

By contrast, the personal zone runs from eighteen inches to four feet. Here, there are conversations, friendships, and psychotherapy. Touching is possible; it may or may not occur, depending on circumstances. Voices are moderately loud, and individual identities are in interplay. Should one participant move into the other's intimate zone it may be experienced as sexual or hostile intrusion by the other. From four to twelve feet, in the United States, is the zone of social distance. Here, impersonal business and casual social contacts occur. It is the distance between an executive and his subordinate at the other side of his desk or between a student and his professor in an office or in a small seminar. Public distances begin at approximately twelve feet. Here, there is no longer personal involvement. One speaks louder, and usually in a more formal and prepared way. Conversation and discussion give way to lecturing.

Much of our behavior, Hall claims, is conditioned by these distances. Visualize your feeling when you are forced into a spatial relation which does not coincide with your psychological need. In many prison visiting rooms, the prisoner and his wife are kept at a "social" distance when their need is for intimate exchange. On the other hand, city living often forces us into intimate contact with total strangers, as on a New York subway in rush hours. We defend against coerced intimacy by, for example, avoiding eye contact, thus not acknowledging the presence of the other even as we are literally wedged together. Because of their population density, the Japanese have evolved barriers around the self so impenetrable that people can move in immense masses in large and crowded cities as though each individual were alone. To the outsider, they appear rude and unconcerned with the comfort of others as they jostle and collide; to the Japanese, they thus maintain privacy and reduce social stimulation under physical conditions which would be intolerable to most Westerners. In the Japanese hotel, as in their homes, walls are often made of paper and sounds penetrate readily, but apparently only to the Western ear. For the Japanese themselves, it is as if they were literally deaf to the sounds of strangers on the other side.

Such observations call attention to the enormous differences among cultures in the dimensions of the various proxemic zones. Hall notes, for example, that Arabs seem to have smaller zones than Westerners. Thus, in an impersonal social encounter, the Arab may move within the European's personal or intimate zone, which discomforts the European, who in turn moves away to what seems to him a more appropriate distance. This, in turn, leaves the Arab at an uncomfortable public distance. Even within Western Europe, such differences are notable. Some years ago, when working in Italy, I was surprised at the physical closeness of parent and child, friends of the same sex, and even business associates, who to my eyes seemed to be in the attitude of lovers. Viewed from a dozen yards, two friends walking arm in arm down the street fuse into a single silhouette. In the middle of the year, I visited Norway, fortunately at the time of their major ski games. Because of the high cost of seats, many parents kept small children on their knees, though not resting against their chests. Thus, despite the cold, one could look down a row of benches and see space between parent and child. From my American perspective, the Norwegians seemed too distant, as the Italians had seemed too close. It is completely predictable that the Norwegian visitor in Italy might feel intruded upon; the Italian visitor in Norway might feel coldly rejected, as each seeks his own distances.

Findings such as these increase our understanding of human relations in terms of previously neglected variables. They have been amplified in studies by psychiatrists, psychologists, and architects and have become importantly applicable to the design of mental health services. Hospitals, clinics, and other agencies need to be constructed to serve the space-related needs of people. Thinking about "treatment" is too often limited to the specific intervention, psychological or medical, without sufficient thought to the social and physical environment within which it occurs. A hospital, for example, with rows of identical beds, minimal private storage, locked windows and doors, and floors and furniture chosen for ease of maintenance rather than comfort or attractiveness, can contribute more to the continuance than the cure of psychosis. Ego integration and a sense of purpose and personal value depend on opportunities for privacy, intimate spaces, personally selected and tasteful furnishings, all of which may be absent in custodial settings. In line with the emergent concern with social ecology, greater attention is being given by clinical investigators to the assessment and change of treatment environments in order to make them more health producing (Moos, 1974).

The damaging effects of overcrowding in a population of rats were dramatically demonstrated in a series of experiments by Calhoun (1962). In these experiments, the animals were given sufficient food and water, but the population density was raised well above the level of the rats' natural habitat. When a critical level was reached, Calhoun observed a variety of pathological behaviors: there was increased mortality, especially among the young; fertility rates were reduced; young were neglected by their mothers; aggressive and destructive behaviors appeared; there were sexual aberrations and other "psychotic" behaviors. Established patterns of social organization disappeared to be replaced by unstable and hostile behavior. Overall, the population became sickly and many died. In later studies, other investigators showed that other animals, ranging from monkeys to fish, are also adversely affected by population density, although the particular disturbances reported differ among species.

Overcrowding also seems to have a serious impact on human behavior, although the relation between crowding and pathology is more complex for human than for animal populations. Building on the Calhoun findings, Galle, Gove, and McPherson (1972) compared various indices of population density with those of social pathology as they covaried among the seventy-five community areas of Chicago for which social statistics are kept. The particular pathologies they considered were *mortality rate* (age-adjusted death rate), *fertility rate* (number of births per 100,000 per year), *ineffectual parental care* (indexed by use of public assistance), *juvenile delinquency rate* (as a measure of aggressiveness in the community), and *psychiatric disorders* (measured by admissions to mental hospitals). Since all of these indices are known to vary with ethnicity (race) and social class, these variables were separately measured. The essential question they asked was whether there was a correlation between density and social pathology, even when the effects of race and class are controlled. They found, indeed, that density, as indexed by the number of persons per room in the area, related significantly to the various indices of social pathology (though, strangely, least well to hospital admissions) even when the effects of race and class are eliminated. Interestingly, the relation between fertility and density was reversed from that reported in animal studies; in areas of greatest density there is higher, rather than lower, birth rates. The findings are provocative and suggest that social scientists have to consider overcrowding when attempting to explain disturbed behaviors. At the same time, the findings are limited by the fact that they are based on cross-sectional ecological data (i.e., rates for a city district) and cause-effect relations may not be so clear at an individual level. Moreover, though statistically distinct social variables, race and class are so highly related to measures of density as well as to those of social pathology that it is most difficult to identify accurately their separate effects. In all, however, the study suggests that overcrowding may have serious consequences on human behavior.

Facile generalization about crowding effects should be tempered by the realization that social psychological mechanisms develop which permit people to accommodate to restricted space. Thus, Hong Kong, with one of the world's densest urban populations, has a relatively low rate of emotional disturbances (R. Mitchell, 1971). Similarly, the "Chinatown" communities in major American cities, though usually densely populated, generally have lower incidence of social pathology than less dense areas inhabited by other ethnic groups. The Japanese, who for centuries had population densities only now being approached in the Western world, have developed cultural mechanisms, as noted earlier, to accommodate to the limited space of their island home. In all, however, density as such seems to be an important source of human misery. Even if it were possible to house, feed, and provide medical care for all people, a basic threat in the overpopulation which faces the world in the foreseeable future is that it will reduce the space of free movement of individuals and thereby the quality of human life.

ECOLOGICAL PSYCHOLOGY: THE STUDY OF BEHAVIOR IN NATURAL SOCIAL ENVIRONMENTS

The ecological orientation calls attention to the importance of studying psychological functioning of animals or of men as it is revealed in their natural habitats. For decades, the foundation of scientific psychology has been the laboratory experiment. A number of determining variables (independent variables) are controlled so that the particular effects of an experimentally manipulated "treatment" can be precisely and quantitatively evaluated as it affects measured dependent variables. Ideally, conditions should be so controlled that the effects of the factor being studied can be conclusively known; unwanted sources of variance are systematically reduced. While the laboratory experiment may be the most elegant and precise research design, it is still limited. For one thing, factors which are not preconceived, measured, and controlled may be precluded from consideration; for another, the range of possible behavior is reduced to those which can occur in the laboratory under experimental conditions.

In many areas of psychology, there is growing recognition that broadly based psychological knowledge must involve research in many modes, including correlational, clinical, and naturalistic studies as well as experimental studies. Influenced in fair measure by the thinking of the ecologists and animal ethologists, many psychologists are attempting to restore naturalistic studies to their proper importance. Such studies are valuable not only for the generation of initial hypotheses, but for the understanding of processes which cannot be duplicated in the laboratory. The experimental method is geared to hypothesis testing; naturalistic and clinical methods to the discovery and delineation of relevant phenomena. Ideally, they supplement each other, but in the past the striving for precision and control led to a devaluation of the process of discovery through nonexperimental approaches. In the volume edited by Willems and Raush (1969) some of the concepts and methods of naturalistic research are discussed, and typical programs of naturalistic animal and human research are described.

Classic research in ecological psychology has been done by Barker and his co-workers (e.g., 1965, 1968; Barker and Wright, 1951, 1955; Barker and Gump, 1964). Since 1947, they have been studying people as they move freely about in the "behavior settings" of a small Kansas town. Like naturalistic students of animal behavior, who spend many hours patiently sitting in the bush unobserved and observing, they have carefully described the actual behaviors of people in the many settings of their small town. They have called attention to the varieties of environmental circumstances that significantly contribute to the determination of human behavior. "The environment is seen to consist of highly structured, improbable arrangements of objects and events which coerce behavior in accordance with their dynamic patterning. We found, in short, that we could predict some aspects of children's behavior more adequately from knowledge of the behavior characteristics of the drug stores, arithmetic classes, and basketball games they inhabited than from knowledge of the behavior tendencies of particular children" (Barker, 1968, p. 4).

KELLY'S STUDIES OF COPING IN THE HIGH SCHOOL ENVIRONMENT

Inspired by the work of Barker and by the animal ethologists and ecologists, J. G. Kelly (1968, 1969) used the ecological analogy to conceptualize and study the conditions under which individuals are effective and function well in different social environments and, by implication, the conditions that must be understood in order to develop effective community psychological interventions. It is worth looking closely at his study of behavior in high school environments as an illustration of ecological research of relevance to community psychology.

Adaptation of teenagers to the high school environment, Kelly reasoned, should reflect the interplay of personality factors and the structure of the social environment. Because different environments generate different role structures, norms and values, personality traits which might be functional in one setting can hinder adaptation in another. Similarly, types of mental health problems which might be found in contrasting social settings should differ and, it follows, preventive or therapeutic interventions would then have to be differently conceived. To investigate such propositions, Kelly compared a *fluid* with a *constant* high school environment. On the personality side, he studied the coping styles represented in exploratory behavior, i.e., the preference for novel experience. Methodologically, the research involved both naturalistic observation of free behavior in the school environments and personality assessment of the participants.

Two high schools were studied in Columbus, Ohio, one of which could be said to have a fluid and the other a constant environment, as defined by the amount of turnover in the student body. In the fluid school, 42 percent of the students changed within a year; in the constant school, there was less than 10 percent turnover.

Over a four-week period, observers were placed in the hallways and cafeterias and in the principal's office. Information gained in field observation was amplified in interviews done in small groups; in all, 120 students were sampled in each school. Compared to the constant school, observers in the hallways of the fluid school noted that students had more varied clothing; there was more noise, gesture, and movement; and the composition of groups kept changing from day to day. While hallway conversations in the constant environment tended to consist mainly of low-level commentary, in the fluid school there were either intense, aggressive interchanges or no apparent communication between students. Behavior in the cafeteria paralleled that observed in the corridors. Student interplay was louder and more diversified in the fluid school. By contrast, in the cafeteria of the constant environment there was more subgroup discussion and less table-hopping and between-table communication. Similarly, in three-minute observation periods, there were between one and fifteen entrances into the principal's office by students and teachers in the constant school but between thirty and one hundred ten in the fluid environment.

Beyond these visible and consistent differences between the two schools, interviews revealed further contrasts in social organization. The constant environment was more of a closed and homogeneous society. It was unresponsive to newcomers, who were either ignored or ridiculed. Entry was difficult, except for those who had visible competencies or skills needed in the school and who were willing to become absorbed and dominated by the society. In the fluid setting, newcomers were welcomed by informal committees, who explored their interests and needs and gave information freely.

The schools differed even in their physical structure. In the fluid school, hallways and ceilings were almost twice as wide and high as in the constant school. As one might imagine, observation was easier and less obtrusive in the fluid than in the constant school. In the fluid environment, the principal was also more available to students than in the constant school.

In the constant environment, leadership opportunities were specific to defined status positions. In the fluid environment, by contrast, many alternate channels were open. Kelly speculates that in the constant environment psychological difficulties would more likely occur in individuals who go against the institutional values, while in the fluid environment they would be more related to individual isolation and identity diffusion.

Differences in students' preference for exploratory behavior, conceived as a coping style, were studied through the use of a thirty-item paper-and-pencil inventory. Exploration was defined as "preferences for trying out alternative behaviors and sampling diverse social situations in the high schools" (J. G. Kelly, 1968, p. 84).

It was predicted that students with high preferences for exploration would more likely emerge as adaptive members in the fluid school than in the constant one; by contrast, high explorers might fall into maladaptive roles in the constant environment. Support for this hypothesis was found in the fact that high explorers, compared to those low on this trait, were more commonly nominated as deviants by their peers in the constant environment. Thus, the settings provide different types of adaptive roles, to which persons with one or another coping style are more likely to fit. High explorers would be best suited to such psychological tasks as assessing alternatives, proposing changes, or defining new activities, which are devalued if not rejected in the constant setting; the more conforming, if less inquisitive, teenager would be better adapted to that environment. The Kelly studies point up the value of the simultaneous investigation of environmental and individual qualities to better understand the conditions under which adaptive or disturbed behavior occurs. What is adaptive in one ecosystem may be pathological in another. So too, interventions which may be effective in one setting may fail in another.

Epidemiology of Mental Health

THE FIELD OF EPIDEMIOLOGY

"Epidemiology is the study of the distribution and determinants of disease frequency in man" (MacMahon and Pugh, 1970, p. 1). It addresses such questions as: How many people now have this disease? More or less than last month, last year? What kind of people fall ill? Are they older or younger? Richer or poorer? More apt to be men or women? More likely to be living in one fashion than another? and so on. Epidemiology has had a long and important history in public health medicine; application to the field of mental health is more recent. Epidemiology is not, as the term suggests, limited to the study of epidemics or of communicable diseases but rather is concerned with any disorder. By studying the conditions which affect the distribution of a disease in a population, epidemiologists attempt to uncover the characteristics and causes of the disease and the effectiveness of attempted treatments. An early and dramatic illustration of the value of the epidemiological approach occurred during a cholera epidemic in London early in the last century. John Snow discovered that the victims lived close to a particular well from which they drew their drinking water. It seemed that something related to the well was causing the disease, although at the time nothing was known about the bacterial agent involved. When the well handle was removed and people could no longer drink the water, the number of cholera cases went down radically. In more recent times, epidemiological research has illuminated pellagra and lung cancer, in the one case discovering its relation to dietary deficiences in the southern United States and in the other the linkage to cigarette smoking. The epidemiology study of mental disorders, it is hoped, can similarly facilitate the work of the mental health field.

SOME EPIDEMIOLOGICAL CONCEPTS

Epidemiology has developed statistical methods to describe the rates, duration, and severity of disease in populations and their relation to conditions of the physical, biological, and social environment. The *incidence rate* is defined by the number of persons contracting the disease in a particular period of time. The *prevalence rate* describes the number of people who have the disease at any particular time. The difference between these rates is a function of the *duration* of the disease. For very short-acting conditions (say, the common cold) incidence and prevalence are quite similar; with longer-lasting conditions (say, schizophrenia) prevalence rates will clearly exceed incidence rates. The distinction is important because the circumstances determining each of these rates may be different, although the two taken together describe the overall health of the population.

If two populations, distinguishable in some other regard, differ in one or another of these statistics, the explanation can be sought in terms of the ways they differ. Traditionally, public health workers have examined differences in the host, an agent of disease, or the environment. *Host* characteristics might include age, sex, physical condition (e.g., overweight), behaviors (e.g., smoking), race or social class, which might dispose persons toward a disease. *Agent,* in medical epidemiology, usually refers to pathogenic bacteria or viruses. Finally, the *environment* in which the population lives may contain factors conducive to the development or continuation of diseases, in terms of factors as diverse as climate or altitude, diet, or cultural norms. Study of environmental factors may bring to light ecological determinants which might have eluded clinical notice. This was illustrated by a study in London during a period of particularly intense fog in December of 1952 which showed that the death rate rose sharply along with the increasing concentration of air pollutants (MacMahon and Pugh, 1970; see Figure 19.1). Individual physicians working with their patients could not readily see the

FIGURE 19.1

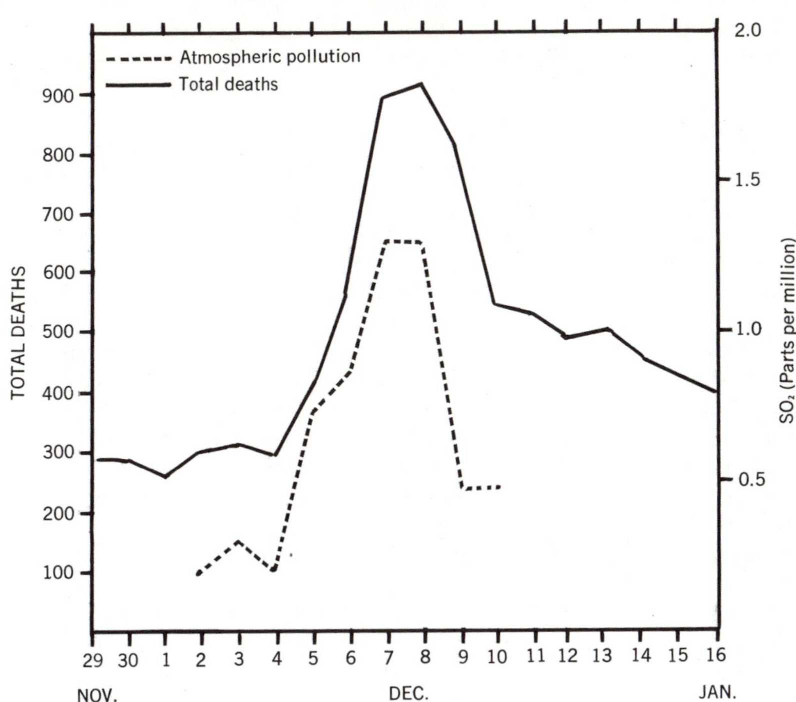

Atmospheric pollution (parts per million of sulfur dioxide) and number of deaths per day in London, November 29 to December 16, 1952.*

From MacMahon, B., & Pugh, T. F. *Epidemiology: Principles and methods.* Boston: Little, Brown, 1970, p. 4. Reprinted by permission.

damaging effects of air pollution, for people did not die of "bad air" but rather of heart conditions and other medical diseases. Only the accumulation of epidemiological data revealed the nature and extent of the problem. Similarly, epidemiological study of the incidence of ulcer attacks among accountants in the United States shows a distinct peaking at the time of year that income tax returns must be filed, which illustrates the effects of social stress on that condition.

Note, in these illustrations, that epidemiological research is best able to reveal empirical associations and to suggest hypotheses that then need to be pursued in clinical and experimental studies before the mechanism of the disease is known. To know what in the water supply causes cholera required years of further research; that something in the water caused the disease and that preventive action could be taken even without ultimate knowledge of the disease mechanism was demonstrated in Snow's pioneering work. Epidemiologists sometimes distinguish between *descriptive* and *analytic* epidemiology. The former consists of large-scale surveys describing incidence and prevalence of a disease along with numerous patient and environmental characteristics. Such studies can generate hypotheses as to the nature of the disease and suggest potential preventive and therapeutic programs. From such data, analytic epidemiology involves more controlled investigation of specific populations, agents, or environments to test the hypotheses developed earlier. Whether descriptive or analytic, however, epidemiological research usually has to be supplemented by research in other modes.

THE USES OF EPIDEMIOLOGY

Seven distinct uses of the epidemiological method have been described by Morris (1957), that are as applicable to the understanding and treatment of mental as to physical disorders (Gruenberg, 1968; Cooper and Morgan, 1973). These include: (1) discerning historical trends which indicate increase or decrease in particular conditions; (2) diagnosing the state of health in a community to aid in planning health programs; (3) discovering individual risks of particular conditions, particularly from age-related incidence rates but also in terms of other individual characteristics such as weight, smoking habits, and the like; (4) enlarging the clinical picture by discovering attributes of cases not in treatment and therefore inaccessible to clinicians; (5) possibly identifying new clinical syndromes by discovering phenotypically different cases arising from the same circumstances, (6) evaluating the effectiveness of health services in a community, and (7) aiding in the search for the causes of disorder.

Thus, both long-term and short-term purposes can be served by epidemiological study; on the one hand, it can help clarify the nature and determinants of emotional problems and, on the other, be immediately useful in the design and evaluation of helping programs. A good deal of work has gone on, some of which will be surveyed shortly, searching for social correlates of psychological dysfunctioning, which in the long run serves the development of community psychology. At the same time, community surveys which assess the mental health needs of the local population are of immediate value in designing new programs and developing innovative methods. Similar epidemiological data are useful in the evaluation of program results; effective programs should show discernible effects on the psychological well-being of the community.

The usefulness of an epidemiological approach to program evaluation is illustrated by Cooper and Morgan (1973) with reference to a study of the effect of a British suicide prevention program (Bagley, 1968). Since 1953, in Britain, the "Samaritan movement" has encouraged potentially suicidal persons to make telephone contact with their voluntary helping service which operates on a twenty-four-hour basis. To test its effectiveness, Bagley selected fifteen towns in England and Wales where the Samaritan groups had operated for at least two years before the latest available suicide statistics. Control towns were selected to match these in essential social characteristics, except for the fact that they had not developed Samaritan services. Since the first group of control towns showed a surprising 19 percent rise in suicides over the test period, a second set of control towns was added. The incidence of suicide in the Samaritan towns was noted before and after the start of the program and compared to the figures at comparable points in time for the control towns. Suicide significantly declined in those towns which had Samaritan programs compared to those which did not (see Table 19.1). Whether this is solely due to the Samaritan program is not clear, for the possibility exists that underlying social factors might possibly have led to both the founding of a program and a later drop in suicide rate. Still, a definite relation has been demonstrated that argues for continuing the program and studying it further.

TABLE 19.1.
Suicide Rates per 100,000 Population in a Group of British Towns with Samaritan Schemes and in Matched Control Towns †

	SAMARITAN TOWNS	CONTROL TOWN	
		FIRST	SECOND
Average Rate Before Samaritan Scheme	13.03	12.56	13.05
Average Rate After Samaritan Scheme	12.27	15.05	14.00
Overall Percentage Change	−5.84	+19.84 *	+7.23 *

* $p < 0.05$.
† From Cooper, B., & Morgan, H. G. *Epidemiological Psychiatry*. Springfield, Ill.: Charles C. Thomas, 1973. Reprinted by permission.

WHAT SHOULD BE COUNTED?

Ideally, a complete epidemiological survey should result in a full and accurate count of the number of cases of a clearly defined disease assessed by valid and reliable measures in an entire population. The value of the survey is lessened to the extent that the disease entity is poorly defined, measures are crude, subjective or indirect, or if any portion of the population is inaccessible. Those cases which are untreated as well as those which come to professional attention should be recorded, if the extent of the disease rather than just the availability of services is to be studied. Those considerations are as relevant for the study of the simplest medical conditions as for the complex problems of social and psychological pathology which concern the mental health professions.

Whatever condition is being studied, most readily available is information about treated cases as recorded in hospital, clinic, and practitioner statistics. However, a study that deals only with treated cases loses one of the major applications of epidemiology, that is, to discover the nature and extent of the disease in the population ("true prevalence") including, therefore, those cases which do not come to clinicians' attention, and to discover the reasons why they do not. Defining a "disease" as something treated by a physician is not only circular but it defeats the public health mission of epidemiology. Hence, to survey the health status of a population as thoroughly as possible, epidemiologists seek, in addition to clinical records, data from insurance company medical examinations, routine physical examinations done in schools, factories, or military units, and periodic examinations of health-plan clients. Moreover, information may be sought directly in field surveys; for example, testing the eyesight or hearing of school children or offering chest X-rays in mobile units, may serve secondary-prevention-program purposes as well as providing epidemiological data.

Epidemiological studies of psychological conditions depend, mainly, on two types of data: (1) hospital or clinic statistics and (2) direct evaluation of psychiatric symptoms or other aspects of psychological functioning in the community, to include untreated as well as treated cases. Both types of studies are beset by theoretical and methodological problems, which will be considered briefly as we look at some of the findings of studies in both modes. Studies based on clinical statistics are limited by the following considerations:

1. The number and type of people treated may be more a reflection of available resources than of the true prevalence of the problem. Where better hospitals are readily available, hospitalization rates are higher. For example, the hospitalization rate in New York State is approximately three and a half times as high as that of New Mexico (Maltzberg, 1959). While this may reflect genuine differences in social stress, it more likely indicates the greater public concern and higher mental health budgets in the industrial northeast compared to southern and southwestern states.

2. Seeking and receiving treatment is determined by many social factors. Attitudes toward mental illness, readiness to seek professional help, tolerance for deviancy, and the like, differ greatly among subgroups and affect the degree to which they seek treatment. Over or underutilization of available resources may more indicate public attitudes in the area than real differences in the prevalence of psychological problems.

3. Hospital practices and record keeping differ enormously. The criteria for admission and for discharge, as well as the type and quality of clinical care, differ greatly. The amount and kind of information recorded, the meticulousness of record keeping and its reliability, similarly differ among clinical centers, and change over time.

4. Records of patients treated in nonpsychiatric centers and by private practitioners are rarely available. Surveys of admission and treatment statistics most commonly are based on state psychiatric hospitals and Veterans Administration hospital records; less commonly, do they use private hospital statistics. Representation of the many thousands of people treated in community agencies and by private practitioners is usually quite incomplete.

In principle, field surveys in which there is direct examination of all people should avert some of these difficulties. However, such surveys face other problems:

1. Sampling and selectivity of respondents. Some people are simply less accessible. However complete the sample, some groups are systematically underrepresented, such as unemployed and transient people, those in certain occupations, and those living in isolated areas. People differ too in their willingness to be interviewed.

2. Training field interviewers to obtain accurate and reliable information is difficult. Rarely is it possible to use experienced clinicians in field surveys, though they may be used to rate information brought back by specially trained field interviewers.

3. Brief and relatively objective assessment techniques have to be developed to substitute the complicated assessment used in clinical practice. Thus far, different surveys have fashioned procedures for their own purposes, usually in the form of structured interviews. There has been little standardization, which would allow comparison between surveys.

Above all, in field surveys as in clinical practice, there is considerable disagreement as to the criteria of diagnosis. Whether or not a person is declared to be "emotionally disturbed" or "mentally ill" depends mainly on one's concept of psychological impairment. Any estimate of "true prevalence" requires consistent and shared concepts as to the nature of mental illness. As we have seen, hospitalization rates can hardly be taken as index of community mental health. At the same time, estimates of prevalence based on assessment in the community vary greatly depending on the criteria used; estimates have ranged from 1 to 60 percent of the population requiring care in the United States (B. P. Dohrenwend and B. S. Dohrenwend, 1965, 1974). For urban Americans, however, estimates converge on the prediction that about one person in twelve will be hospitalized for mental illness at some time during his life.

STUDIES OF HOSPITAL ADMISSION RATES

Studies of hospital admission rates show both stability and change over time. In a classic study, Goldhamer and Marshall (1953) found that the relative number of diagnosably mentally ill persons did not change appreciably over a hundred-year-period in Massachusetts. They compared the statistics of the almhouses, hospitals, and other institutions from 1840 to 1850 with those of the state hospitals of a century later, and found that approximately equal proportions of the state's population were institutionalized in the two periods. This finding is often cited by those arguing that mental illness is biological in origin, since there is no important increase paralleling the increasing complexity of social life over the past century. It should be recognized that Massachusetts was already a relatively urbanized and industrialized state by 1840. The Goldhamer-Marshall findings have also served cynics who argue that they show how little progress has been made in the understanding and treatment of mental disorders. Change in hospitalization rates do, however, emerge more clearly in more recent studies.

Detailed statistical analyses of state-hospital populations reveal interesting trend figures of potential value in planning community programs (M. Kramer, 1967). In the ten years from 1945 to 1955, the resident population of state hospitals rose by about 2 percent per year. From that point to 1963, there was a steady decline of about 1 percent per year. This decrease reflects a genuine shortening of hospital stay and a proportionate increase in discharges, rather than a reduction in admission rates or an increase in the number of deaths. Indeed, the admission rate over the second decade increased steadily at an average of 7.4 percent per year. The greatest drop in hospital residents occurred in the thirty-five-to-forty-four age group, closely followed by those in the forty-five-to-fifty-four and sixty-five-and-above groups. In sharp contrast, there has been marked increase in the number of people below twenty-four years, and particularly among those younger than fifteen years, in the hospitals. Thus, from 1950 to 1963, in Kramer's analysis, there was a fivefold increase in the number of males under fifteen years in hospitals, though the number in the general population only increased 1.4 times. Such findings point up the existence of a youth problem and the need for developing community prevention and treatment programs.

The Kramer review highlights the relation between marital status and hospitalization. Not only in U.S. statistics but also in studies performed in England and Wales, Norway, and Australia, among other countries, married people are significantly less likely to be found in hospitals than those who are single, separated, divorced, or widowed. If admitted, they stay for shorter times. Thus, in a 1960 survey of thirteen states studied intensively by the NIMH Office of Biometry, the admission rate for patients with functional psychoses, above fifteen years of age, was 22.8 per 100,000 for married people compared to 70.5 for those never married, 64.7 for those widowed, and 117.8 for those separated or divorced. The same disparities are found among marital groups in the use of outpatient clinical services. What accounts for the relation between marital status and hospitalization can only be inferred. One line of explanation is that married people are less likely to be hospitalized, even if they are as disturbed as unmarried people, because the family gives them a home and social supports. By this logic, it could be supposed that the true incidence and prevalence of mental disorders might not differ, but that married people have alternatives to hospitalization. An alternate explanation supposes instead that married people may actually be mentally healthier. Persons who can make and sustain marriages might be expected to have greater psychological strengths and to be able to cope with the demands of living. Or, alternatively, it might also be supposed that living in a family environment cushions the stresses of the outside world. Whatever the explanation, however, the fact itself is intrinsically interesting both as it aids in the search for psychosocial determinants and as a consideration in the development of mental health programs.

Studies of hospitalization statistics also reveal the important role of race and class. Hospital populations contain disproportionate numbers of poor and minority people. In a later section, we will return to this issue in the analysis of studies based on field surveys as well as clinical statistics.

PSYCHIATRIC CASE REGISTERS

To be of greatest value, either in research or community mental health planning, statistical records provided by mental health facilities should yield full and accurate information about the number of patients admitted, discharged, the lengths of stay, patient diagnoses, and their psychological and social characteristics. As far as possible, diagnostic criteria should be identical and record-keeping coordinated among institutions. With notable exceptions, few areas have such complete and coordinated record systems. What is needed, many mental health researchers and planners argue, are psychiatric case registers which contain complete information about the characteristics and care of each patient.

Available statistics are usually "event statistics" rather than "person statistics" (M. Kramer, 1967). They describe particular events, such as admissions or discharges, rather than characterizing the careers of individual patients. Thus, if there were three hospitals in a particular town, each might report that it admitted 100 people during a particular year. But there would be no way of knowing whether these were 300 different people, or perhaps the same hundred checking in and out of the three hospitals. Obviously, the estimate of prevalence of mental disturbance in that community would be rather different in the one case than in the other.

Psychiatric case registers are an important technique for centrally coordinating information about patients in a given area (Baldwin, 1972). Each facility, including if at all possible private practitioners, regularly reports information about each patient treated to a central agency. Thus, information about the psychiatric career of each person in the community can be collected in one place, indicating the facilities used, diagnoses, lengths of treatment or hospitalization, condition on discharge, follow-up information, and as much psychological and social data as can be assembled and reported. A notable example of such a community register was developed in a collaborative project between professionals in Maryland and the National Institute of Mental Health (Bahn, Gorwitz, and Kramer,

1964). Although new in this country, psychiatric case registers have been in effect for many years as part of the public health and social welfare systems of Scandinavian countries, Great Britain, and Holland.

Such registers serve many research and administrative purposes. They can provide accounts of individuals receiving services, determine admission rates on individual bases, and show the relation of diagnosis and treatment to age, sex, race, residence, and other patient characteristics. Patterns of patient mobility, as they move from place to place and are served by different institutions, can be studied. Consistency of diagnoses over time can be investigated, along with follow-up studies of patients after periods of hospitalization. They are of obvious value in the study of social correlates of mental disorders and treatment, and of equal value in the investigation of genetic factors. To be maximally useful, a careful reporting system has to be worked out and monitored continuously. There has to be a sufficiently large staff to facilitate the collection, coding, processing, and analyzing of such data.

The existence of such registers raises the specter of social abuse, as does any central information bank which retains personal information on identifiable people. Through long tradition, hospital, clinic, and practitioner records have been treated as confidential, and not to be transmitted or revealed to anyone, even in the patient's interest, without his explicit consent. A case register, however, is a step removed from clinical records, and requires that safeguards be built in to assure that the information contained in them not be used to the patient's disadvantage. It is obvious that employers, credit agencies, and others who might be interested in a particular person's psychiatric history should not have access to such files. But whether, and under what conditions, the information should be available to the police, governmental agencies, or even to mental health institutions is a more subtle and more difficult question. Because of their obvious value to mental health planning, treatment, and research, more extensive and centralized registers will undoubtedly be developed; the ethical dangers in their use or misuse have to be carefully weighed against their advantages, and clear protection against their abuse has to be developed.

SOCIAL CORRELATES OF MENTAL DISORDERS

Evidence for the role of social factors in psychopathology has been sought in epidemiological surveys based both on case statistics and on direct assessment of pathology in the general population. Modern research in the area starts with the classic study of Faris and Dunham (1939) working within the social ecological framework of Chicago sociology of the time, which has inspired similar investigations in many other cities. They searched out the addresses of all Chicago residents admitted to private and public hospitals between 1922 and 1934 and calculated the rates of various psychiatric conditions for each area of the city. Admission rates were highest for residents of the central city, which then as now was the section marked by greatest population density, mobility, unstable homes, and the lowest socioeconomic level. Rates declined as one moved toward the more stable and affluent neighborhoods in the periphery of the city. By and large, this pattern characterized patients diagnosed as schizophrenic; no characteristic ecological pattern emerged for manic depressive and senile patients.

Over the years, controversy has raged over whether these findings, which have generally been duplicated in other metropolitan areas, truly indicate that the conditions of inner-city life produce mental illness or whether they merely reflect a drifting in of people already sick. Some have argued that schizophrenia, whatever its ultimate cause, leads to a deteriorated life style, inability to work and lead an organized social life, so that schizophrenics are likely to drift downward socially and to end up living in slums or skid-row housing. Direct evidence of a downward drift socially would help resolve the controversy, but the evidence is contradictory: Hollingshead and Redlich (1958) show that schizophrenics have much the same social status as their parents; E. M. Goldberg and Morrison (1963) show that they have moved to a lower socioeconomic class. Faris and Dunham themselves inclined more toward a social causation than a drift hypothesis, as have many subsequent social theorists. It is also interesting to note that in a smaller and more homogeneous community, Hagerstown, Maryland, without the social and ecological extremes of Chicago, Clausen and Kohn (1959) report no significant differences for the rate of hospitalization for schizophrenia between the center city and outlying districts.

Hollingshead and Redlich (1958) studied social class differences in the incidence and prevalence of mental disease in New Haven. They used not only hospital and clinic statistics, but obtained rather complete information from private practitioners as well. They found that the prevalence of schizophrenia and the likelihood of hospitalization were distinctly higher in the lower social classes. Moreover, hospitalization tended to be longer. Thus, the first admission rate did not differ among social classes as much as the duration of hospital stay; therefore, the resident population of the hospitals showed disproportionately greater numbers of lower-class clients. By contrast, clinic and private practice statistics revealed the reverse, proportionately more upper-class than lower-class patients were treated on an outpatient basis. Generally, therefore, lower-class patients were more likely to be diagnosed as schizophrenic and to be hospitalized; upper-class patients were more likely to receive psychotherapy in outpatient settings. Ten years later, Myers and Bean (1968) found essentially the same relation between social class, psychopathology, and treatment in a follow-up study. Of the original patients studied by Hollingshead and Redlich, the higher the social class the less likely was the patient to have remained in the hospital or to be readmitted later.

In order to study the relation of social factors and psychopathology in the entire population, the Midtown Manhattan survey was undertaken in 1950 (Srole, Langner, Michael, Opler, and Rennie, 1962; Langner and Michael, 1963). A representative sample of about 1,700 persons in an area of New York City were selected. Each of these was interviewed by a mental health professional in an effort to approximate the kind of clinical information which might be gained in a psychiatric facility. The interview inquired into the person's background and history, whether he had been treated for psychological disorders, whether there were manifestations of psychosomatic conditions, emotional distress or anxiety, depression, feelings of inadequacy, and the like or of psychological dysfunctions, such as memory difficulties or confusion. Family, work, and social adjustment was probed. The entire interview was carefully recorded.

All information describing the respondent's history and symptoms, however with indications of social class carefully concealed, were given to a staff of psychiatrists. Their main task was to rate the respondent along a scale of psychological health-impairment, in terms of six categories: well, mild symptom formation, moderate symptom formation, marked symptom formation, severe symptom formation, and incapacitated. The latter three categories were grouped as "impaired." The reliability of these ratings was high.

A striking outcome of the study, which was widely noted in the newspapers of the time, was that almost one-quarter (23.4 percent) of those interviewed were rated "impaired." At the other extreme, less than one-fifth of the sample were rated as "well." Moreover, substantial relation was reported between social status and this index of mental health. Only 12.5 percent of the highest social group was rated as "impaired," as against 47.3 percent of the lowest group. Equally impressive was the fact that one-fifth of the impaired subjects in the upper group were receiving outpatient therapy, compared to less than 1 percent of the lowest social class. They also found that correlations with father's social class tended to be about as high as those with the respondent's own social position, thus providing no support for a "drift hypothesis." The major findings converge with those of studies based on treatment statistics in showing the decided relation of social class with emotional distress, though raising other issues of measurement and conceptualization. Why are "impairment" rates so high, when in actuality most of the people were carrying on life tasks with reasonable adequacy? A failing in this and comparable psychiatric surveys lies in the emphasis on symptoms and impairment without sufficient attention to sources of psychological strength and competence. Other limitations in survey methodology have been noted by Clausen (1968) and Dohrenwend and Dohrenwend (1969, 1974).

Over the same period as the Midtown Manhattan study, the Leightons and their co-workers have been carrying out a large-scale study of a rural Canadian population (Stirling County) which also involved direct assessment of psychiatric status (e.g., Leighton, A. H., 1959; Leighton, D. C., Harding, Macklin, Macmillan, and Leighton, A. H., 1963). In field interviews, they attempted to identify people who "if thoroughly studied by psychiatrists would be diagnosed as suffering from one or more or the specific psychiatric conditions described in the [American Psychiatric Association Diagnostic] Manual" (Leighton, D. C. et al., 1963, p. 118). As in the Midtown study, estimates of psychiatric impairment were high; 57 percent of the population were judged as potential psychiatric cases in one estimate.

The Leightons' Stirling County study was undertaken to test the central hypothesis that life under conditions of social disorganization would result in poorer mental health. They therefore contrasted communities differing in their levels of social integration, as defined by various sociological indices, and found the predicted relation. The least integrated communities did have the greatest number of diagnosable cases of psychopathology. Community integration, in their findings, is more important than indices such as age, sex, and occupational status in predicting pathology. They do find, however, that persons with high social status, within each community, have fewer psychiatric symptoms.

Surveying forty-four studies which have attempted to assess the "true prevalence" of psychological disorders in community populations, the Dohrenwends reach the overall conclusion that ". . . their most consistent result is an inverse relation between social class and the reported rate of psychological disorder" (B. P. Dohrenwend and B. S. Dohrenwend, 1969, p. 165). They go on, however, to note that "this relationship can be explained with equal plausibility as evidence of social causation, with the environmental pressures associated with low social status causing psychopathology, or, by contrast, as evidence of social selection, with pre-existing psychological disorder leading to low social status. The latter interpretation is compatible with the position that genetic factors are more important than social environmental factors in etiology" (p. 165). In their most recent review, the Dohrenwends (1974) note the growing evidence for genetic factors in the origin of schizophrenia (e.g., D. Rosenthal and Kety, 1968) derived from epidemiological studies of families, twins, and adopted children. Consequently, there is still no definitive answer as to the relative balance of social versus genetic determinants in the development of schizophrenia, although the association between social class and schizophrenia, along with other forms of psychopathology, remains strong. Moreover, the data in hand still do not allow one to choose decisively between a social-stress and a social-selection explanation of this relation.

Definitive studies, which overcome some of the methodological limitations of existing epidemiological research, are still badly needed. Ultimately, fuller understanding of the causation of mental disorders will require the convergence of studies of a clinical, experimental, and correlational kind along with epidemiological and ecological research. In this section, we have considered some of the uses of epidemiological methods which, if they fall short of giving decisive evidence about the etiology of mental disorders, can still contribute greatly to the quest. At the same time, they can, as noted earlier, help in the task of assessing community needs and problems and in the design and evaluation of community mental health services.

General Systems Theory

THE STUDY OF ORGANIZED SYSTEMS

Communities consist of interlocking networks of human, social, and environmental systems, where change in any part depends on and is reflected in change in other sectors. The approaches to the study of the functioning of organized systems developed in general systems theory may be of value, therefore, to community psychology, particularly in the planning and evaluation of community-wide services. The essence of the general systems approach is that it focuses on system properties as such, the interrelations among parts of a single system and the interrelations of the particular system with related systems. Thinking in this mode encourages both concern with man-environment relations and the multidisciplinary collaboration necessary to study them (Roen, 1971). While many communiy psychologists are using some of the concepts and language of a systems approach (e.g., Murrell, 1974), the specific application of systems analytic methods is only slowly coming into use.

General systems theory derives from the views of Ludwig von Bertalanffy (e.g., 1968) in theoretical biology. Since organisms are organized systems transacting with their environments, he points to the need to study the organizational properties as such with consequent lessening of attention of specific and isolated biological functions. He emphasizes the importance of "open systems," with their input and output relations to the surrounding environment, rather than the "closed" or steady-state systems that more generally concerned conventional biology. A number of specific approaches have evolved within general systems theory to describe the properties of systems, physical and social as well as biological. The more important include cybernetics, information theory, decision theory, game theory, and computer simulation.

Cybernetics calls particular attention to the feedback chains involved in system regulation. A familiar example is the home thermostat, which senses change in the environmental temperature and turns the furnace on and off accordingly. *Information theory,* related to cybernetics, focuses on the study and quantification of the information transmitted and received in the functioning of systems. *Decision theory* studies the processes underlying rational choices within human organizations, as for example in programming the operation of a business. *Game theory* is related to decision theory, but is concerned particularly with the quantitative analysis of the competitive strategies of two or more antagonists trying to maximize gains and minimize losses. Finally, *computer simulation* involves the effort to program computers to mimic a particular phenomenon so that it can be studied in its simulated activities more conveniently than in its real condition. An application, noted in Chapter 11, is the study of clinical diagnosis through simulation of the decision-making processes of psychological assessment.

These approaches have contributed to the solution of problems of engineering, economics, business administration, and planning. Specific specialties have evolved, such as: systems engineering, which studies the planning, design, construction, and evaluation of, for example, factory production methods; the related field of human engineering which focuses on man-machine relations to maximize efficiency and productivity; operations research, more broadly concerned with the interplay of men, machines, money, and materials; and what has even more generally been called "systems analysis," applicable to broad-scaled studies of economic processes or city planning.

APPLICATION TO MENTAL HEALTH PROBLEMS

Only in the recent past have the ideas of the general systems approach been applied to mental health problems. Hutcheson and Krause (1969) note the need for rational planning of community mental health which they believe can be facilitated by the application of systems-analytic principles and methods. More rational policy decisions can be made if such methods are used to describe the mental health system and to evaluate the costs and consequences of changing it in particular ways. The approach represents an orderly way of looking at a problem from all its angles in order to find the best operating solution in terms of the realistic constraints which exist.

Hutcheson and Krause point out that the systems-analytic approach has a number of interrelated tasks: (1) to decide on the goal or mission of the program which is to be studied by systems analysis; (2) to describe the system boundaries and the subsystems which make it up; (3) to discover how system change occurs and the factors underlying such change; (4) to develop a model—mathematical or graphic in most instances—which considers all elements of the system, those which are stable as well as those which change over time; (5) to use the model to generate theoretical changes of different kinds and to see what possible outcomes might result from different sets of changes; (6) to select the most desirable outcome, based on previously decided goals, and then to carry out in reality the activities described in the model to reach this goal, and (7) to cut costs, clarify issues, and avoid waste by experimentally manipulating the analytic models, in order to discover the most practical and efficient way of achieving desired ends before intervening in the actual situation.

Systems analyses are most readily conducted in areas where the goals are clear and relevant variables are known and readily quantified, as for example plotting the best strategy for increasing business profits in dollar terms. In the mental health field, by contrast, objectives can be put only in general terms, variables are not readily known nor isolated, and quantification is difficult. Consequently, Hutcheson and Krause propose that early efforts to apply systems-analytic methods might best address problems of limited scope, say, the mental health problems and services of a small, geographically limited or isolated region, with a relatively homogeneous population. As an ingenious approach to quantification, they suggest using as a measure time spent by people in various activities rather than money. With such a measure, the input-output analyses used in economic studies could be performed. However, even if a first approach is to be of limited scope, it is necessary for the analyst investigating a community mental health situation to take proper account of the many interacting variables. Thus, attention cannot just be limited to symptomatic behaviors but consideration must also be given to other evidences of social distress and dysfunctioning. Unemployment rates, crime rates, and other social indicators must be simultaneously studied for they interlock with mental health issues. At the first level, Hutcheson and Krause also point out, the goals of the potential program should be framed not only from the point of view of mental health specialists but from the standpoint of community values, since the community may have to participate in their implementation. Studying a community of limited size and complexity, moreover, has the additional advantage in allowing greater freedom in instituting, varying, and evaluating interventions than would be possible in larger and more socially complex cities.

At present, complete systems-analytic studies are understandably rare, though they seem clearly relevant to community mental health. Most efforts have been limited to the first few stages or goals of the analytic process—discovering boundaries, assembling relevant data, reducing the number of alternative solutions. More sophisticated steps, such as developing mathematical models, simulating and testing solutions, and the like, require greater understanding than now exists of the relations among systems and the discovery and quantification of the appropriate units for analysis. Efforts along these lines are being made, though many seem to critics to involve excessive simplification of "real life" issues. The approach is promising, however, and will likely be used in future mental health planning and programming as it now is in other social sciences, engineering, and business fields.

Evaluation Research

THE NEED

Ultimately, community programs have to face the question "Does it work?" The overall effectiveness of programs in reaching intended objectives should properly concern community psychologists and those they serve. More differentiated questions follow: "What portions of the population are helped most? With what problems? In which ways? Are there unforeseen costs? Which aspects of the program are most effective? Which are essential, which superfluous? Can it be streamlined, made more economical? These questions parallel the issues of outcome and process research on psychotherapy which we examined in Chapter 16, and they involve many of the same conceptual, methodological, and practical problems. Any intervention, at the individual or community level, in psychology, medicine, or any other field, must be thoroughly evaluated before being put into general practice. Few would disagree with this principle.

Actually, however, research rarely precedes application and even after programs are established evaluation research is often a secondary and neglected activity in community psychology programs (Bloom, 1972). There are many reasons for this.

1. Those who create and operate community programs are often not greatly interested in research, nor greatly skilled in its methodology. Though the practicing psychologist should ideally be committed to a scientist-practitioner role, in actuality most psychologists are temperamentally disposed either to practice or research, less commonly to the fusion of the two. Hence, program evaluation is often viewed as a task for a research specialist, separate from the functions of those who develop and operate the program. Indeed, the community psychologist, who is heavily invested in program development, may not even be the best one to carry out its evaluation. To be effective, he has to believe in what he is doing, and he may not have the detachment to objectively assess the success of his own efforts. In any case, however, the separation of program and research responsibilities makes it more likely that research evaluation will not be built into community programs from the outset and that it will continue to be neglected as the program progresses.

2. Client needs and social necessity dictate that something be done now, whether on the basis of previous experience, inspired hunches, or calculated risks. Gathering and analyzing data require time and effort deflected from service programs. To gain sufficient certainty about probable effects before taking action may delay potentially valuable help indefinitely.

3. Community people and their leaders are understandably impatient with research which delays action programs, deploys valuable resources from helping services, and which seems more to serve scientific curiosity than their immediate needs. They too wish to see better services, but they may not see the relevance of research or understand its operations, and they remain cynical about its ability to improve their lot.

4. Similarly, government and foundations concerned with community mental health are often more enthusiastic about paying the costs of a promising, if untried, new approach than those involved in evaluating an on-going program. In the legislation establishing community mental health centers, research was included among the ten major functions, but within the five considered "desirable but not essential." The enthusiasm of its proponents and the faith that help will be given to those in need can get new projects funded. Evaluation, by contrast, is costly and less glamorous. At best, research may document the effectiveness of the project whose value may already have been accepted on faith; at worst, it may shatter the illusions of those committed to the program.

5. Evaluation research can intrude on the service program. Overburdened professionals may resent being asked to make special observations, ratings, or

reports. They may also fear for the comfort of their clients who may be asked to participate in tests and procedures of no immediate benefit to them. Professional roles, and even personal integrity, may be threatened by the critical inquiries of the researcher.

6. Good evaluation research is intrinsically difficult and complex, and inadequate efforts may be properly resented by program administrators and participants. Efforts to simplify the research task may make the evaluation meaningless. On the other hand, the requirements for proper evaluation may seem so formidable as to be put off indefinitely by action-oriented agencies.

THE DESIGN OF PROGRAM EVALUATION STUDIES

In principle, program evaluation can easily be described. In practice, however, there are difficulties at each stage. Four major steps are involved (Bloom, 1972):

1. Specify the objectives of the program.
2. Define relevant parameters, such as the target population, the disorder to be treated, the criteria measuring it, and the criteria for determining attainment of the program objectives.
3. Specify the techniques to be used in attaining the objectives.
4. Collect relevant information to answer questions such as: How well and to what extent have the intended techniques been used with the target population? To what extent have the objectives been attained? What other changes have occurred in the community in consequence of the program? What implications are there with regard to modifying objectives or techniques? What are the costs and can they be reduced?

At the first level, it is rarely possible to specify objectives precisely, for most mental health programs have many purposes, some more explicit, others more implicit. Nor do they arrange in a neat hierarchy, in terms of relative importance or long-term versus short-term ends. The objectives as seen by the staff, the administration, supporting agencies, and the public may differ importantly. Objectives shift over time. All of these issues have to be unscrambled in the first stage of program evaluation research if accomplishments, in terms of defined goals, are to be assessed. Other problems exist, even as this first formidable step is taken. To determine success of the program, objectives have to be converted into observable and measurable criteria. Then it has to be shown that the program itself, rather than extraneous causes, lead to desired changes in these outcome criteria. Ideally, this should involve comparisons with matched control groups who have not received the program services, but this is often difficult or impossible to do. An admirable example, noted earlier in this chapter, was the British study comparing suicide rates in towns which did and did not provide a suicide-prevention program. Where matched group controls are not possible, study of "before" and "after" changes in the treated population can give valuable information about the possible impact of the program, though leaving uncertain whether they might not have occurred without the intervention. In short, program-evaluation research suffers all the challenges and difficulties of any research, magnified by the complexity of the situation within which it is done.

Measures of Effectiveness. Reported evaluation studies differ in the kinds of information used to assess program success. Commonly included are statistics as to the usage of the service. Staff can point with pride at increasing caseloads, for this does indicate popular acceptance, an early and by no means trivial aim in any program. But they do not tell whether the program is achieving its more central goal of, for example, reducing delinquency in the community. Popularity, unfortunately, does not mean quality. To claim success for the program, it must be shown that relevant behaviors have changed.

The literature also contains evaluation reports which, Bloom (1972) notes, might better be called "program descriptions." They present a narrative account of the history and current functioning of the program. This may be a necessary introduction to true evaluation, though it cannot substitute for it. Particularly in the phase before program components have stabilized, the development of an explicit research design is impractical, and recording the early experiences of the project may be particularly useful. Too often, however, project staff immersed in the day-to-day activities keep scanty records of their trials and errors. A continuous and detailed diary of the ups and downs of the program, describing the problems faced and decisions made, written at the time, tells far more than later retrospective accounts and can be of considerable use in guiding others entering the field.

More explicit evaluation studies have made use of information obtained from the clients of the service, the judgment of experts about their condition, and measures of social indicators at the community level. A number of evaluative reports are based largely on the reports of clients as to the benefits they received from the service; clinic patients feel better after receiving crisis care and school teachers report that they are better able to cope with aggressive students after receiving consultation. Such reports are important, but they raise many questions of interpretation and validity. Wherever possible, they should be coupled with independently measurable indices of changes in the relevant behaviors of the clients. Is the crisis patient now better able to hold a job? Have there been fewer episodes of aggressive outbursts in the class after the teachers received consultation? Such data are more difficult to generate, but they are necessary to extend self-report measures.

Another criterion used in evaluation reports is the judgments of the service staff or of outside professional experts as to change in the clients. To the extent that outside evaluators not invested in the program's fate are used and relatively explicit and objective judgment criteria exist and can be rated reliably, such judgments can be of great value in evaluation studies. These conditions are often difficult to arrange, and clinical judgment, just as patient report, may be of limited value in evaluation studies.

Still another evaluation approach involves shifting attention from the treated client to the community itself, and assessing program impact in terms of objective community data which do not require either client or clinician judgment. A community mental health center program may be said to be successful if the admission rate for a nearby mental hospital goes down; school consultation works if the drop-out rate falls; a suicide prevention program has had impact if the suicide rate declines. While the study of social statistics reduces some of the methodological problems involved in direct assessment of the clients served, other matters emerge. Above all, social indicators have to be chosen which relate meaningfully to program objectives. Reliable and valid social data, in quantified form, must exist. Reporting practices must remain constant over time.

Major program evaluation studies often use combinations of these methods and approaches, for they complement each other. Thus, a complete evaluation study may involve direct assessment of the client, using test and behavioral measures as well as self-report, expert judgment, and social and epidemiological indicators of change in the community. The specific criteria used have ultimately to be decided in terms of their relevance to particular program objectives. Programs aimed at reducing suicide or juvenile delinquency, for example, can more readily use social statistics, while one intended to facilitate the emotional growth of preschoolers would more likely depend on observing or testing the children or having them evaluated by child clinicians or teachers. The particular criteria used in seven major mental health evaluation programs are reviewed by Bloom (1972).

Other Aspects of Program Evaluation. Program evaluation is most effective if it is an integral part of a service program. Planning for evaluation should begin at the very beginning of the program, not as is too often the case, added on later. A chronic frustration of researchers in clinical and community agencies is the lack of consistently kept records as to clients seen, services rendered, accounts of progress, and the like. Often, new data-collection systems have to be developed for the specific purposes of evaluation to substitute for inadequate, existing files. Having the investigator participate in the original design of the program and particularly plan the methods for collecting and storing potentially relevant case data, can minimize later problems. This is not to suggest that the evaluation study should be designed and launched at the outset, in terms of its final design. Early in any program, there is an inevitable and necessary uncertainty, and procedures have to be changed as experience grows, lest the project be frozen in its tracks. Premature commitment to a research design can stifle the creative freedom needed for program development. What is necessary from the outset, however, is an "investigative attitude" on the part of the director and staff so that they are tuned to issues of consequence to later research. Thus, records should be kept in ways that will allow future research to abstract necessary information. If a particular person is to be brought in as an evaluation researcher, he or she should share from the beginning in the conceptualization and design of the program as well as being responsible for its later evaluation.

Such a researcher should be someone sympathetic to the aims of the program and compatible with the staff. Ideally, the research person should have clinical or community intervention experience himself in the realm of the project, although he may not have a service role in the particular case. Tension between research and service staff, mutual misunderstandings of purposes and ways of thinking, and the like have undercut many evaluation projects. While each has his area of expertise, mutual respect and basic understanding are necessary.

While the concern of evaluation research is, ultimately, the overall value of the program, also included are preliminary and short-term studies many of which have to be done before the major study is undertaken. These include gathering background data on the target population, surveying preexisting practices in the field, and developing, testing, and validating outcome measures, among others. Just as the program itself needs time to evolve before reaching the form in which it can be studied in a formal design, the research component too requires time for the shaping of hypotheses, development of instruments, and like tasks. Preliminary studies may involve limited measures, concern only parts of the target populations, and consist of short-term follow up of the clients studied; all of this toward the sharpening of ideas and methods for the major evaluation.

A full-scale evaluation study is a long-term endeavor. To discover whether a program has made a significant impact may require continued study long after the enterprise began and perhaps even after it is terminated. Contact with a large portion of the subject population must be maintained, which may be difficult with some social groups and in some communities. In the same vein, continuity of the research staff is required. The researchers involved must be dedicated to the project and willing to commit years of their careers to it, for evaluation studies, just as longitudinal studies in developmental psychology, can be damaged by staff turnover. Evaluation research tends, therefore, to be costly and frustrating to those who seek quick answers. Programs are sometimes altered or abandoned before there is sufficient opportunity to judge their true merit.

Program evaluation requires research-oriented community psychologists who are both motivated to serve community needs and able to use scientific methods. To a fair extent, as we noted earlier, this involves learning the concepts and methods of other disciplines, such as epidemiology, ecology, and survey research, in order to develop research models more compatible with the problems at hand than are traditional in psychological research. Training community psychologists capable of making research contributions may require changes in graduate training. Too often, the schism between the values and activities of research and those of practice, which exists in many training programs, forces many students to choose between two professional life styles. Since community research cannot exist apart from community practice, Baler (1967) argues that training institutions are obliged to discourage one sided identities in their students. To accomplish this, Baler and other community psychologists (e.g., Iscoe and Spielberger, 1970) suggest that community practicum experiences and field research experiences should be developed which can bring the practice and research aspects of the field into closer contact.

A Critical Evaluation of Community Psychology

In concluding these chapters on community psychology, let us take a broad and critical look at the field in order to put this new and promising approach into a balanced perspective. Earlier, the hopes and aspirations of the field, along with its principles and methods, were considered in some detail. In this section, therefore, we will attend more to critical objections and reservations that have been raised against the community approach. First, however, let us consider some of its accomplishments.

THE CONTRIBUTION OF COMMUNITY PSYCHOLOGY

The community orientation has inspired reconceptualization of core concepts in the mental health field. Insistence on the importance of social and environmental factors, both in determining and changing psychological dysfunctioning, has encouraged clinicians to look not only at the woes of the individual patient but at the social surroundings in which they occur. From this perspective, both inadequacies in the concepts of mental illness and possible new strategies for its treatment can be visualized. Ways of better serving the larger population, and particularly those portions previously neglected, become more evident. The community movement has served as a gadfly to the mental health professions, challenging established myths. It has inspired explorations in the outreach of services, efforts to alter human problems more quickly and efficiently, and also to create more psychologically healthy settings. Programs using the concepts and methods of consultation, crisis intervention and short-term therapy, and nonprofessional helpers in new roles have been launched and appear promising.

The goals of the community movement are many, ranging from the primary prevention of mental disorders to improving the care of the presently disturbed. Whether community interventions can truly serve prevention remains a moot and argued issue, as we will discuss shortly. What is more evident, however, is the impact of the community movement on the organization and delivery of mental health services (Zusman, 1970). Settings in which patients are treated are changing. Large state hospitals have been decentralized or reorganized into units each serving people from a particular geographic area. Psychiatric units are being developed in local, general hospitals. Thus, there is more contact between the community and the hospitals, which helps reduce the dehumanizing conditions which existed in large, bureaucratic, and impersonal hospitals in the past. Moreover, within the hospitals, programs of milieu therapy, token economies, and patient government further contribute to their being more therapeutic and less custodial institutions. Because of federal legislation, mental health agencies concerned mainly with outpatient services have increased their scope to include emergency services, partial hospitalization, rehabilitative services, and other facilities which, on the whole, have provided better service closer to home and to a wider range of patients.

In the effort to serve the largest possible number of people, methods of crisis intervention and brief therapy have been developed. For some patients at least, these have turned out to be methods of choice rather than simply stopgap substitutes for intensive psychotherapy. With such methods and the commitment to serve all in need, waiting lists have become a thing of the past in many clinics. At the same time, continuity of care has been strengthened as more effective links are developed among helping agencies. The work of clinics, hospitals, halfway houses, and rehabilitation centers has become better coordinated and patients can make the necessary transitions among them more easily. As clinicians have become more concerned with the larger framework of the patient's life, collaboration with welfare, health, employment, and educational services has increased. Thus, the care of patients is less fragmented.

These are substantial achievements but they are, by and large, within the framework of traditional mental health practice. The more distinctive contributions of the community approach still have to be made. Community and social interventions, intended for prevention rather than treatment, are still more promises than accomplished facts. Social experiments by community psychologists have been few in number and mainly in the nature of "demonstration projects." An approach is conceived and its value tested in a particular setting. Left for later research, however, is the closer examination of the particular processes which may have determined the outcome. It also remains to be shown that the new approach can be incorporated into a different and larger context, under somewhat changed conditions, and be of value to more people. Thus, the value of consultation with teachers toward the end of reducing subsequent behavior problems in their students may be suggested in one school intervention project. But success in this setting may depend on particularly persuasive investigators, a particularly receptive school system, or children of particular sorts. To spell out these contingencies and to discover what facets of the program might have lasting value obviously requires time and further effort. That community psychological projects have not advanced much beyond the initial demonstration stage is more a commentary on the newness of the field than any lack of will on the part of community psychologists.

DO WE KNOW ENOUGH TO TALK SERIOUSLY ABOUT PREVENTION?

Prevention is the broadest, most ambitious, and potentially most important goal of community psychology; it is also the area in which community psychology is most vulnerable to criticism. Critics have pressed a number of related questions: Do we know enough about the causation of mental disorders? Whatever our knowledge, do we have the methods and power to effect preventive changes? In the attempt, are we running the risk of extending beyond the realm of our training and competence? Are we cognizant of the broader social and ethical issues involved? Finally, in the quest for prevention, will we neglect therapeutic concepts and interventions of value? Will we throw out the baby with the bath water? These issues will be considered in this and the remaining sections of this chapter, for they bring out major problems and potential shortcomings in the community approach.

The Joint Commission on Mental Illness and Health (1961), as we noted in Chapter 17, was unimpressed with the history of the mental hygiene movement and remained skeptical about future efforts at prevention.

> Even if we could agree on what kind of men and women we wanted to produce, we could not predict the outcome in a given family due to the multiplicity of uncontrolled variables . . . Thus, primary prevention of mental illness has remained largely an article of scientific faith rather than an applicable scientific truth [p. 70].

Their main concern was that we lack the knowledge to launch effective preventive programs as well as clear criteria and consensus as to the desired state of positive emotional functioning we would wish to obtain. Available evidence, mainly from the child guidance movement and from mental health education, suggests that they have not reduced the incidence of severe breakdowns. Moreover, in the quest for prevention, the Joint Commission fears, the mental health professions may neglect the urgent problems of providing care for the already mentally disturbed. These concerns are echoed in the critiques of later writers (e.g., Dunham, 1965; Kubie, 1968; Mechanic, 1969; Halleck, 1969; and Zusman, 1970) in varying forms.

At its most ambitious, Dunham (1965) notes, community psychiatry asserts that it is society rather than the individual which should be considered the patient. While the importance of sociocultural factors in molding individual personality has been recognized for some time, we still know too little about the social etiology of mental disorders to have a firm base for social intervention. Without sufficient knowledge, and with little understanding of how social change is effected, Dunham questions the ability of ambitious community psychiatrists and psychologists to devise effective techniques.

> What are the possible techniques that can be developed to treat the "collectivity?" Why do psychiatrists think that it is possible to treat the "collectivity" when there still exists a marked uncertainty with respect to the treatment and cure of the individual case? What causes the psychiatrist to think that if he advances certain techniques for treating the "collectivity," they will have community acceptance?—Does the psychiatrist know how to organize a community along mentally hygienic lines and if he does, what evidence does he have that such an organization will be an improvement over the existing organization? In what institutional setting or in what cultural milieu would the psychiatrist expect to begin in order to move toward more healthy social relationships in the community? These are serious questions and I raise them with reference to the notion that the community is the patient [p. 306].

In the same spirit, Bower (1973) chides community psychologists.

> . . . implicit in the concept of community psychology is preventive intervention at the community level. Bennett (1965) defines it as "The community itself is being taught to collaborate in creating health-giving environments." Teaching communities ought to be quite a trick. I'm for an ounce of prevention against sixteen ounces of cure any day but what does a community psychologist prevent and why? How is the community being taught to create health-giving environments and where can we observe such teaching and learning? [pp. 13–14].

Community psychiatry, Dunham (1965) argues further, may only be the most recent move in the quest for a realm in which psychiatry can feel useful and important. Frustrated in their efforts to cure psychoses, psychiatrists moved into the practice of psychotherapy of people with lesser problems; with dubious success in that area, they now seek to make their mark at the community level. In this sense, community psychiatry is the "latest therapeutic bandwagon" and Dunham is cynical about the motivation of those who jump on it. While pleased at the prospect of hospital psychiatrists and office practitioners coming into closer contact with the real life and problems of the community, he believes that they must not desert their traditional task of working with the severely mentally ill. While attempting to be an agent of social change, the clinician risks losing the unique skills of diagnosis and therapy upon which his professional and ultimately his social contribution rests.

Responsible community psychologists and psychiatrists recognize, as do their critics, that a sufficient base of established knowledge still does not exist. But they note too that there is rarely enough knowledge to act with complete confidence. This is true in any field, but more true in the human-helping sciences. Faced with people seriously in need, they will have to decide whether trying a new approach is worth the potential risk and operate as wisely as possible on the basis of available knowledge. To try and to fail is no disgrace. This does not, of course, deny the lack of knowledge nor the need to search for more. However, the more extravagant claims of the "third revolution" have earned criticisms such as Dunham's and Bower's. Fired with enthusiasm and messianic zeal, community psychology is in danger of rushing off in all directions, developing programs doomed to failure, and perhaps doing harm in the process. What is sorely needed, in this time, is more temperate rhetoric and a sincere commitment to extending the knowledge base for community interventions. Both program evaluation and basic research are critically needed.

DO WE HAVE THE POWER?

Even if the interplay between social processes and psychopathology were better understood, do we have the power to bring about desired social changes? In his critique, Dunham (1965) challenges community psychiatry: "If a psychiatrist thinks that he can organize the community to move it toward a more healthy state, I suggest that he run for some public office. This would certainly add to his experience and give him some conception as to whether or not the community is ready to be moved in the direction that he regards as mentally hygienic" (p. 306). In the professional role, the power to change social policy is limited; at best, the community psychologist can work through consultation to affect the thinking of elected representatives and policy makers, on the one hand, and the public, on the other.

Not only in the realm of social action, but also in the area Caplan has called "interpersonal action," providing environmental and social supports for persons facing crises, the mental health worker is limited in his potency. In his criticism of Caplan's view of preventive psychiatry Mechanic (1969) states:

> There is much of value in Caplan's ideas, but his strong advocacy and lack of qualification undermine their credibility. It is true, as Caplan notes, that the death of a mother may be a harmful influence on a small child and that it is helpful if the father remarries a warm, understanding woman (1964, p. 27). It is not clear, however, how the psychiatrist is to achieve this laudatory goal. Indeed, the greatest weakness of Caplan's entire framework is his failure to specify in any clear fashion the techniques by which mental health professionals are to achieve the many goals he advocates [p. 100].

Whether mental health professionals should, in actuality, develop a more political role and seek greater power has been argued at length. For example, Halleck (1969) has expressed concern that the community orientation would tend to draw psychiatrists into the arena of political decision-making for which they have few qualifications and often little interest. If the clinician views his clients as victims of social evils, he cannot help but risk his traditional neutrality and be forced to take political stands. At the extreme lies the danger that he will become an agent of social control in the manner of the Soviet psychiatrists who willingly hospitalize political dissidents for the good, as they see it, of the state. Protection against this danger lies in the preservation of the clinical tradition in which the clinician works only in the service of his patient, whose interests, rather than those of society, he represents. On the other hand, others have argued for greater rather than less politicization, although on different premises. Concern only for the distressed individual, they assert, limits us to repairing social casualties rather than working to alter the conditions which caused them. As atomic scientists have spoken out politically regarding the military use of their creative efforts, so must community mental health specialists work to alter the social processes which vitally affect their clients.

Whatever one's position, it is clear that if mental health professionals enter into social action they cannot act foolishly or unprofessionally. A case in point was a national mail survey of psychiatrists who were asked to judge the mental health of a candidate for the presidency in 1964. A surprisingly large number of psychiatrists ventured opinions, though none had personally examined the man. A more recent incident which concerned many psychologists was the recommendation of the president of the American Psychological Association advocating the development of psychologically active drugs to be given to society's leaders in order to reduce the liklihood of war, racism, and other social ills (K. B. Clark, 1971). To avoid such abuses of professional expertise, psychologists and psychiatrists have a great obligation to limit their actions to areas of trained competence. If they extend beyond them, they become obliged to add new knowledge and skills and to be constantly alert to their potential impact, negative as well as positive. How and when they should engage in social action remains controversial, but that it should be done responsibly is entirely clear.

THE THREAT TO CIVIL RIGHTS

Preventive programs are necessarily conceived for the well-being of the larger population rather than to serve the needs of individuals. Intrinsic is a potential conflict between social control and individual freedom. Public health measures such as water fluoridation and polio inoculation have been resisted because they compel individuals to be treated whether they want to or not. Americans generally resist controls, even where they seem to have obvious benefits. Note, for example, the current problems of passing gun control legislation, requiring seat belts to be used in cars, or limiting the level of air pollutants. Yet, every organized society must exert controls and limit the freedom of individuals if it is to protect the well-being, health, and safety of all. Once resisted, we now accept compulsory education, fair employment practices, vaccination and quarantine, dog and car licensing, and numerous other measures as necessary social restraints.

Fear has been expressed that preventive community mental health programs may intrude on personal privacy and the rights of individuals to live their lives in their own fashion. Halleck (1969), as noted earlier, points to the danger that community psychiatry could be used by the powerful in society to control social or political deviants. As concepts of mental illness expand, they can come to include not only behaviors which are troublesome to the individual but also those which offend the power elite. An essential principle in a democracy is that the individual be allowed the greatest possible freedom to live as he chooses. The voluntary contract of the therapeutic model is most consonant with this ideal; only as one needs and desires treatment, should one have it. Involuntary treatment, incarceration, or other restraints on personal liberties should be resorted to only when there is unequivocal danger to the individual or to the public good.

The dilemma for community mental health is illustrated by an event which occurred in a small American city. Working with the police, the local mental health agency developed a preventive program aimed at reducing family conflict, broken homes, and the attendant stress on children. If a family fight came to police attention, marriage or family counselors were brought in to help resolve family problems. On one occasion, neighbors called the police because of loud and angry noises in a nearby house. The police came and quieted the family down; the next day they were visited by a counselor. The family went to court claiming that their rights had been violated. The court took the position that if a crime had been committed then they should be punished under the law, but if not, then they had to be allowed to live in any manner they pleased. The community had no right to attempt to change their life style in the name of mental health.

In their consideration of objections to community programs on civil rights grounds, Zax and Specter (1974) point to two safeguards in American society. First, American abhorrence of coercion and traditional resistance to controls, which lie deep in popular values as well as in the law, will keep Americans from permitting practices which might be more docilely accepted in more regulated societies. Second, preventive programs are built on a base of popular support.

> Thus, from our viewpoint, the notion of a community psychology would be impossible were it not for the fact that, because of a variety of social problems, need is felt for it at a grass roots level. By contrast, those who are most concerned about the possible abridgement of personal freedom imposed by community psychology . . . seem to assume that the impetus for developing community programs derives from *above*. . . . If this were truly the case, the movement would certainly founder in a society that jealously guards its traditional freedoms. Furthermore, community programs generally require the active participation of the citizenry if they are to survive [Zax and Specter, 1974, pp. 325–326].

These are important strengths in our system but they should not be exaggerated. As Zax and Specter point out elsewhere in their book, community participation and/or control of program development and operation is by no means a simple notion and the history of the community movement has often involved conflicts between community people and professional caretakers. In one sense, of course, success must depend on community acceptance, as in any business venture. No product or service will be bought by unwilling consumers. However, program aims, concepts, and methods, and certainly financial support, do in largest measure derive from above. Programs are conceived by professionals and sustained by government funds. While community participation and community values provide important safeguards, it is equally important that those who create and manage programs be constantly vigilant to their responsibility to protect civil liberties in their zeal to enhance community mental health.

FURTHER PROBLEMS IN THE COMMUNITY APPROACH

Some of the principles of community psychology lack firm foundation in established evidence. They sometimes contain partial truths which can conceal hidden dangers, while asserting reasonably sounding themes. Consequently, when interpreted too literally and applied in overzealous fashion, there is the real danger of throwing away the baby with the bathwater—the accomplishments of traditional approaches can be lost in the effort to overcome their deficiencies. Brief note can now be taken of some specific problems, some of which were considered in earlier contexts.

The Danger in Secondary Prevention. The hope of secondary prevention—early identification and early treatment—rests on the twin assumptions that it is possible to correctly identify children-at-risk for later emotional problems and that treatment given at an early stage will avert later problems more effectvely than leaving the child untreated. Both of these assumptions rest on shaky evidence. While children identified as vulnerable were more likely than those not identified to be found later in psychiatric registers of treated cases, still only 19 percent of the identified group came to the attention of psychiatrists (Cowen, Pederson, Babigan, Izzo, and Trost, 1973). Similarly, review of a wide variety of early intervention programs, ranging from Headstart to those aimed more specifically at emotional disturbances, reveals that they have not fulfilled their initial promises (Caldwell, 1974). The value of secondary prevention methods is still to be demonstrated.

There is, however, a visible danger in such programs. Case finding, it has been suggested, may be case making. Children identified early as being at risk and given special attention may become victims of labeling. They may suffer rejection from their peers and be treated as fragile by well-meaning adults; in the process self-confidence and competence may be undermined. True, we do not know how pervasive and damaging labeling effects may be, though some theorists see them as crucial sources of pathology. Whatever the actual danger, the risks of labeling have to be offset against the potential advantages of secondary prevention.

Hospitalization and Community-Centered Care. The need to avoid hospitalization and to provide care in the patient's home community are virtual axioms of the community movement and, on the whole, admirable principles. Yet, Kubie's (1968) critique of community psychiatry points up potential difficulties in these notions. He sees as a fallacy the belief that "because bad hospitals are bad for patients, any hospitalization is bad for them and should be avoided if possible or made as short as possible" (p. 263). Hospital stays have been shortened, as hospitals discharge patients to communities which have no place for them. Excessive strain may be put on families with consequent damaging effects on the patient himself. Hospitals have developed "revolving doors" as they discharge and readmit the same patients. The evils of long-term custodial hospitalization are well enough documented, but the present trend to curtailing hospital facilities and shortening stays may be damaging to those patients who can only be treated over a long period in an inpatient setting.

Kubie (1968) also questions the related assumption that treatment is best when given closest to home. The assumption, he believes, "ignores elementary common sense and familiar clinical experience." If the patient became ill while in intimate contact with family and friends, or going to school, or working: "Why should one assume that this is where to help him find the road back to health?" (Kubie, 1968, p. 262). He notes further: ". . . . in the launching of treatment, whether of the neuroses or of the psychoses, it is almost the rule that it is not merely helpful but actually essential to lift the patient out of his familiar settings" (p. 262). One can question the universality of such a rule but it does call into question the generality of the opposing principle that treatment is best if closest to home. The fact is that the patient's social-environmental conditons may either sustain pathology and block therapy or support adaptation and reintegration into the community, perhaps both in different phases of the treatment process. For present purposes, we need note only that the assumption that community-centered care is automatically to be preferred is at least a limited generalization. Mental health resources for the future will have to provide, therefore, refuge for those patients overwhelmed by community stress and opportunities for long-term as well as short-term care.

The Place of Psychotherapy. Crisis intervention and other short-term psychological interventions are, as noted earlier, important contributions of the community movement. The contention that they obviate the need for intensive psychotherapy, however, does not follow. Without repeating the arguments for and against psychotherapy, suffice it to note that it is an effective technique for many distressed people and to be maximally effective considerable time is required. That many may be helped by short-term methods, focused behavioral techniques, and psychoactive drugs is also true. The critical task, still largely before us, is to discover what kinds of problems and people, under what circumstances, in what setting, with what kind of clinician, derive greater benefits from one or another intervention. The danger, in this time, lies in either-or polarizations which block the use of existing techniques or the development of new ones in the total mental health effort.

PART 6

THE PROFESSION OF CLINICAL PSYCHOLOGY

CHAPTER 20

Training, Roles, and Responsibilities: Present and Future

"You've Come a Long Way, Baby!"

The advertiser's slogan, intended to flatter today's woman into smoking his cigarette, might well be used to describe the clinical psychologist of the mid-1970s. Clinical psychology is reaching full maturity as a profession and as a science. It has indeed come a long way. Where once limited to testing the intelligence of children in schools or clinics, under the supervision of physicians or educators, today's clinician is an increasingly autonomous worker. Mainly a subdoctoral field originally, the doctoral degree is now the established standard, with many clinicians going on into postdoctoral training and continuing education programs. Professional organizations and state governments certify and license qualifed professionals for independent practice. The arena in which clinicians work today includes schools, universities, psychiatric clinics, inpatient hospitals, both psychiatric and general, community mental health centers and other agencies, and in private practice offices, as well as industrial, military, and governmental organizations. Psychological tests still figure in the clinician's repertory, but his professional time is more given to psychotherapy—individual and group, with families, couples, and children as well as adults—behavior modification, consultation and education, administration and supervision, social planning and community intervention, and to teaching and research. As specialization grows, clinicians become assessment experts, psychotherapists, behavior therapists, child clinicians, neuropsychologists, psychopharmacologists, and community psychologists, with subspecialties in each of these areas. Psychologists conduct research to explore personality dynamics and structure, the nature and origins of psychopathology, diagnostic methods and personality assessment, psychotherapy and behavior modification, social-system interventions, biological correlates of psychological dysfunction, and the social determinants of human problems. The clinician works in prevention, treatment, and rehabilitation programs, with patients of all degrees of distress, and in institutions of all kinds. In brief, the variety of problems, roles, and settings which we viewed briefly in the opening chapter has grown enormously over the years, as clinical psychology has become broader and more diversified.

There are probably about 60,000 psychologists at the masters and doctoral levels in the United States in 1975. A majority of these are in clinical psychology or in closely related fields. In a survey of U.S. and Canadian psychologists in 1972 (Boneau and Cuca, 1974) 33 percent described themselves as clinical psychologists. Fifty-six percent of the sample were in the human service subfields, clinical, community, counseling, and school psychology. Moreover, nearly two-thirds of all psychologists in an earlier survey saw their work as relevant to mental health problems, whether in teaching, clinical service, consultation or research (Boneau, 1968). The recent survey reveals additional facts of interest about

TABLE 20.1.
Distribution of Clinical Psychologists in Work Settings *

SETTING	PERCENTAGE OF CLINICIANS
Universities	27
Colleges	7
High schools and other schools	4
Hospitals	19
Clinics	16
Private practice	16
Government agencies	5
Research establishments	1
Business, labor, religious, and military organizations	2
Law enforcement, judicial, and correctional institutions	2
Other settings	1
Total	100

* Based on the responses of 8,447 psychologists who identified their primary field as "clinical psychology" in the 1972 APA Survey of Psychologists. I am grateful to Dr. C. Alan Boneau and Ms. Janet M. Cuca of the APA Central Office for making these data available.

American psychologists. Despite the preponderance identified with human service fields, the majority work in education institutions rather than clinics, hospitals, or private practice. Moreover, psychology is a profession of young people. Forty-three percent of those replying to the survey were under forty years of age.

Table 20.1 describes the variety of settings in which clinicians work.

The various functions and roles of clinicians are listed in Table 20.2.

TABLE 20.2.
Activities of the Clinical Psychologist *

ACTIVITY	TIME SPENT ON EACH
Research (includes basic, applied and clinical research, program evaluation, research direction, etc.)	10%
Practice and application (testing, therapy, counseling, and related activities)	58%
Teaching (formal teaching, supervision and advising)	16%
Management/Administration (meetings, program review, planning and budgeting, personnel administration)	15%
Other/nonpsychological activities	1%
Total	100%

* Based on the responses of 8,447 psychologists who identified their primary field as "clinical psychology" in the 1972 APA Survey of Psychologists. Each respondent was asked to indicate the usual proportion of his time spent in various specific activities (e.g., basic research, clinical testing, student supervision, meetings, etc.) grouped into the four categories given above. I am grateful to Dr. C. Alan Boneau and Ms. Janet M. Cuca of the APA Central Office for making these data available.

The career of the clinical psychologist starts in graduate school. Just after finishing his degree, the novice clinician is likely to spend proportionately more of his time working directly with patients than he will later in his career. In his later career the clinical psychologist often moves from clinical service toward research and teaching or toward administration, supervision, and consultation.

There are experienced clinical psychologists who, in a given week or month, might see a number of patients, supervise interns, deliver lectures to university classes and to lay and professional audiences, collect research data, write a scholarly paper, advise a local school, work with a committee of their professional organization, and consult with a government agency. In fact, however, most clinical psychologists are involved in only a fraction of such activities. Those in full-time practice may rarely do research or write; teachers and researchers may see very few patients; administrators may facilitate the work of those who treat patients, teach or do research, but themselves be little involved in such activities. As a consequence, clinicians in academic hospitals, clinics, private practice settings, or administration, though they share early training and professional activities, often grow apart and become relatively ignorant of each other's needs and concerns.

Much has been written about the persistent "identity crises" of clinical psychology. Should we be more invested in practice or research? Tied to academic psychology, or to medicine and psychiatry, or play entirely in our very own ball park? Should we be working within a "disease-treatment," "growth-actualization," or a "psychosocial-prevention" model? Value more highly dynamic, experiential, or behavioral concepts? Do research in a naturalistic or experimental mode? Lean toward the biological or the social sciences? Be scientific or humanistic? Clinical psychology has become so differentiated that any and all of these positions are defended by respectworthy colleagues, all of whom have contributions to make. The student entering the field has, I believe, the obligation to know and evaluate all of the alternatives before committing himself to one ideological framework. After that, he is on his own, like the rest of us!

Becoming a Clinical Psychologist

Let us consider the making of a clinical psychologist by looking at the typical patterns of recruitment, selection, and training. In this discussion, we will focus on the typical clinican who has achieved a PhD in an academic department. Alternate career routes are developing, and will be noted briefly, but the PhD clinician remains the standard. Let us look first at what kinds of people enter clinical psychology.

MOTIVATION AND BACKGROUND OF THE CLINICAL PSYCHOLOGIST

Copyright 1960 United Feature Syndicate, Inc.

Maybe the little boy in Peanuts is right and many of us are "just nosy." Or as one of my sons said when he was about nine or ten years old, "Dad, you and your friends are sure curious." (I never did press to find out which of the double meanings was intended!) But Henry A. Murray (1959) probably speaks for most clinicians when he describes the motives which brought him into psychology:

> It is generally assumed by the uninformed and innocent that all psychologists must have at least one "orienting attitude" in common: a stout affection for human beings coupled with a consuming interest in their emotions and evaluations, their imaginations and beliefs, their purposes and plans, their endeavors, failures and achievements. But this assumption, it appears, is not correct. A psychologist who has been constantly prodded and goaded by these propulsions, as I have been, belongs to a once small and feeble though now expanding and more capable, minority. Anyhow, this bent of empathy and curiosity toward all profound experiences of individual men and women should be set down as one of the prime determinants of several definitive decisions . . . respecting the scope of my scientific concern and of a methodology to fit. This is a crucial point because, if my interest in events of this sort had been less steadfast, I might have turned to more manageable phenomena [p. 9].

The desire to understand and to help people in distress, grounded in a "stout affection for human beings," is (or at least, should be) the central motive of the clinical psychologist.

This in turn may derive, in part at least, from the need to understand and to help oneself. With autobiographical candor, Wheelis (1958) reveals how his career in psychoanalysis represented a "quest for identity." M. Brewster Smith, who has contributed at the interface of social and clinical psychology, said candidly: "I could claim with some justification that psychology represented an ideal 'synthesis' between the 'thesis' of biology as my initial undergraduate interest and the 'antithesis' of humanistic history and my family background. But it is obvious that I was mainly drawn to psychology because of preoccupation with my own inner problems" (Smith, 1972, pp. 215–216). His statement is surely true of many psychologists, though some might not be so open in admitting it. Indeed, insensitivity to one's own inner turmoil probably limits the extent to which one can appreciate that of others.

Concern with the needs of others is of course much more than just the externalization of one's own neurotic conflicts. Studies have shown that psychologists in general, and clinicians in particular, have wide-ranging commitments to human welfare and social justice. They hold liberal political attitudes and are committed to humanistic social goals.

Material needs as well as historical accidents also figure prominently in the decision of many to enter clinical psychology. Particularly for the generation which came of age in the 1940s and 1950s, clinical psychology was an open and expanding field, with considerable opportunity for graduate training and later career positions. Many who had an early interest in medical training found entrance into medical school blocked by restrictive religious and racial quotas and the high cost of medical education as well as the small number of openings for applicants of any social background. By contrast, there was less discrimination and greater financial support in Psychology departments. Veterans Administration and NIMH stipends, as well as other fellowships and assistantships, added to the GI Bill made it possible for students of limited means to achieve professional training and status. Graduate training provided a route for upward social mobility for the lower-middle-class student (K. E. Clark, 1957; Henry, Sims, and Spray, 1971).

In their study, Henry and his colleagues obtained information from almost 7,000 psychoanalysts, psychiatrists, clinical psychologists, and psychiatric social workers, all of whom were practicing psychotherapists in Los Angeles, Chicago, and New York. The reasons given by the various groups for becoming interested in their fields are shown in Table 20.3, which reveals interesting contrasts as well as communalities among mental-health professionals. Of the four professions, clinical psychologists most emphasized their need *to understand people*—a heritage of their scientific training, but intended, I believe, in Murray's sense which, as he noted, is hardly characteristic of psychologists at large.

All respondents in the Henry study pointed both to *people* and *experiences* which influenced their decisions to enter their professions. However, compared to the others, psychologists more commonly mentioned experiences rather than people as influences. Foremost among these experiences were those related to reading and to training. When talking of people who had influenced them, psychologists more commonly named *teachers* (rather than, for example, parents, relatives, or other professionals) who exerted their influence through *intellectual stimulation* (rather than, for example, by setting goals for the student or serving as a role model).

As they differ from colleagues in the other mental health fields, clinical psychologists also contrast with their colleagues in other areas of psychology. Among psychiatrists and social workers, the clinical psychologist is likely to be the most empirical and research minded; "hard-headed" among "soft-headed" colleagues. But in the precincts of psychology, his head is proportionately the softest. He is more oriented to helping people, willing to abide ambiguity, deal with vague concepts, and to speculate in the absence of hard evidence, than his academic colleagues. Thus, K. E. Clark (1957) reports data contrasting psychologists of different types, both senior and students, on the Thorndike Psychologists' Values Inventory. Clark (1957, p. 218) concludes: "Clinicians, whether established PhD's or new graduate students are characteristically more individual oriented, more committed to the dissemination of ideas, and more attracted to global theorizing and to pioneering than are, for example, experimental psychologists, who greatly value the works of laboratory experimenters at the expense of almost any other kind of contributor." On another test clinical students scored higher than those in other areas of psychology, as one might expect, in showing greater interest in "Helping Individuals." On the Strong Vocational Interest Blank, Kriedt (1949) found clinicians differing from other specialties in having stronger artistic, teaching, literary, verbal, and social-service interests. Therapists among other psychologists did more poorly in high school mathematics and science (E. L. Kelly and Goldberg, 1959). Male psychotherapists tend to show a more "feminine" pattern of interests and values (Roe, 1969).

Though they differ among themselves, graduate students in psychology have many personality characteristics in common which distinguish them from other student and professional groups (Gough, personal communication). On the California Psychological Inventory, psychology students score consistently higher in *psychological mindedness*, *flexibility*, and *achievement via independence* and lower on *socialization* (ability to accept rules and authority) and the need to make a *good impression*. Similarly, the Adjective Check List shows them to be higher than comparison groups on *intraception* (interest in knowing oneself and others)

TABLE 20.3.

Motives for becoming interested in their general field [a] *given by psychoanalysts, psychiatrists, psychologists, and psychiatric social workers in psychotherapeutic practice. (By percentage of motivations discussed).* [b]

MOTIVATION	PSYCHOANALYST	PSYCHIATRIST	CLINICAL PSYCHOLOGIST PERCENT	PSYCHIATRIC SOCIAL WORKER	TOTAL
To Help People	17.9	8.4	12.5	22.7	15.8
To Understand People	6.3	5.9	28.9	12.0	14.4
To Gain Professional Status	12.6	12.6	7.9	7.2	9.6
To Achieve Affiliation with Others	4.2	5.9	5.9	13.7	8.1
To Meet Practical Pressures	9.5	12.6	2.6	9.0	8.1
To Gain an Identity	20.0	13.4	3.3	0.6	7.7
To Understand and Help Oneself	2.1	3.4	10.5	7.2	6.4
To Help and Understand Society	6.3	2.5	3.9	9.0	5.6
Other [c]	21.1	35.3	24.4	18.6	24.4
Total	100.0 (95)	100.0 (119)	99.9 (152)	100.0 (167)	100.1 (533)

[a] General field is, for psychoanalysts and psychiatrists—medicine, for clinical psychologists—psychology, for psychiatric social workers—social work.

[b] From Henry, W. E., Sims, J. H., and Spray, S. L. *The fifth profession*. San Francisco: Josey-Bass, 1971, p. 113. Reprinted by permission.

[c] "Other" includes twenty-five different categories of response.

and lower on *deference,* although interestingly, also lower in *affiliation* (the desire to seek and sustain many personal friendships) and *heterosexuality* (need for company of peers of the opposite sex). In all, psychology graduate students seem to be open-minded, achieving, and inward-looking, not conventionally social and somewhat nonconforming.

For psychologists of all kinds, as well as professionals in the other mental health fields, entering their professions represented a decisive step up socially (K. E. Clark, 1957; Henry, Sims, and Spray, 1971). By and large psychologists come from lower-middle-class origins. Few of the fathers of psychologists were professionals themselves; one-third of their parents had not gone beyond the eighth grade. They are largely urban, with disproportionate numbers coming from the major population centers. As in a number of other scientific and professional fields, there are relatively few Catholics and disproportionate numbers of liberal Protestants and Jews. Going along with these social characteristics, two sets of related values were found: the therapists were politically and socially liberal, and often "religious apostates" rather than "religious adherents," generally not practicing the faith of their forebears.

Though perhaps differing in extent, Henry, Sims, and Spray's conclusions are supported by a far more extensive study of all PhD's awarded in the United States (Hardy, 1974). Scholarly and scientific doctorates are far more commonly obtained by people who come from liberal Protestant (e.g., Unitarians and Quakers) and secularized Jewish background than from Catholic or fundamentalistic and traditional Protestant sects. Hardy proposes that these differences reflect a composite of philosophical and religious values. Compared to those groups which produce fewer scientists and scholars, the more productive groups, he proposes, are characterized by *naturalism* (vs. a view of the world as unknowable and incomprehensible), *intrinsic valuation of learning and knowledge* (vs. suspicion of learning and education), *dignity of man* (vs. disparagement of man), *personal dedication* (vs. sense of indirection), *equalitarianism* (vs. authoritarianism), *antitraditional* (vs. traditional, respect for past), *centered on near future* (vs. centered on present and distant future, the next life).

As in all professions, ethnic minorities and women are grossly underrepresented in psychology compared to their numbers in the general population. While blacks comprise 11 percent of the total U.S. population, only 2 percent of the faculty and students in clinical training programs were black in 1971 (Boxley and Wagner, 1971). Two years later, however, there was a significant increase in black and other minority students, although no appreciable increase in black faculty (Padilla, Boxley, and Wagner, 1973). In the past, black psychologists were trained mainly in smaller and less-distinguished departments, more commonly to the masters than to the doctoral degree, and thereafter taught in small, black colleges mainly in the Southeast (Wispé, et al., 1969). George Albee estimates that of the 3,767 PhD's granted in psychology by the ten most prestigious universities from 1920 to 1966, only eight were awarded to blacks. Spanish-speaking people, American Indians, and Asian-Americans are even more underrepresented in American psychology.

About one quarter of American psychologists are women (Boneau and Cuca, 1974). In the main, they hold lower-status and lower-paying positions than men (Astin and Bayer, 1972; Boneau and Cuca, 1974). Though many women have sought careers in psychology, they find it increasingly difficult to progress up the career ladder. Thus, while 45 percent of undergraduate psychology majors are women, only 38 percent of the graduate students are women, and only 24 percent of doctorates go to women students; women account for only 10 percent of faculty positions, and more commonly are to be found in lower ranks and in smaller, less prestigious colleges (APA, 1973a; Astin and Bayer, 1972). Although careers in clinical practice are generally more available, many of the same problems exist in clinical centers as in academic settings. Fortunately, a major effort is now under way to give greater opportunity to nonwhites and women in graduate training and subsequent careers in psychology, though in the minds of many, progress is still too limited and too slow.

GRADUATE STUDIES

Most psychologists develop their interest in the field during undergraduate years, but the basic learning and socialization of the psychologist takes place in graduate school. Although studies in clinical and abnormal psychology were part of graduate education from the beginning, it was not until the late 1940s and early 1950s that more formally organized "clinical training programs" evolved. At that time, the APA developed standards and a system of accreditation to assure government agencies, the public, and student applicants that "approved programs" met basic standards of psychologists themselves. As of 1975, there were 101 fully approved programs for granting doctoral degrees in clinical psychology in the U. S. and Canada.

On the average, students spend about five years in doctoral programs, more or less depending on the demands of the program and the energy of the student. The first few years typically involve courses and seminars in general, developmental, and social psychology and in research methodology and statistics, as well as subjects closer to the core concerns of clinical students, such as personality, psychopathology, clinical assessment methods and theory, and psychotherapy and community intervention. This is followed by more specialized clinical courses, practicum experiences, and research. A year-long, full-time internship in an approved clinical agency is often required, although many programs allow an equivalent amount of clinical experience to be gained in part-time appointments over a number of years.

Clinical faculties usually encourage student efforts to expand human-relations skills and personality competence through personal psychotherapy or sensitivity training, but psychotherapy is not usually required in graduate training. Typically, however, students themselves feel the need and seek out therapeutic experiences on their own.

Graduate programs differ considerably in their orientations and emphases. Some emphasize more child clinical or community psychology, or behavior modification, or individual adult psychotherapy; some put relatively more importance on internship experiences, others on research; some require more nonclinical courses, others fewer. Increasingly, programs are becoming more and more distinguished by virtue of a behavioral, community, or psychodynamic emphasis. The student considering graduate work would do well to inquire into the specific orientation, requirements, and program of each school. The APA publishes annually a booklet entitled *Graduate Study in Psychology*, which can help guide the applicant.

CLINICAL INTERNSHIP

"The prolonged and intimate exposure to the struggles of the individual patient is the *sine qua non* of the student's evolution toward human and clinical maturity." Though writing about psychiatric training, most clinical psychology faculty would agree heartily with Kubie (1968) as to the cardinal importance of direct experience with people in distress. In the internship, under the guidance of clinical supervisors, the student's understanding of the concepts and theories of personality, pathology, and psychotherapy comes alive as he sharpens clinical understanding and skills necessary for intervening in human lives.

Internships are typically taken in independent clinical training centers or in on-campus psychological clinics or psychological service centers controlled by the clinical faculty. Independent agencies are evaluated by the APA, as are graduate departments, and lists of APA-approved internship centers are published annually in the *American Psychologist*. These are generally older, well-established psychiatric hospitals and clinics, with mature supervisors and a tradition of training, which can offer students varied experience in the practice of clinical intervention. In the Boulder model of clinical training, work toward the degree in clinical psychology was conceived as a partnership between the university department and the clinical center, with the student spending three or more years in the former and one in the latter.

A departmental clinic has the obvious advantage of being closer to home and of keeping the student involved with the same faculty in all facets of clinical training, whether the emphasis is on theory, research, or clinical practice. In principle, the various stages in graduate training will be more continuous and the transitions between them smoother than if the education of the student goes on in different settings, with differing staffs, orientations, and philosophies. Since most internship centers are directed and staffed mainly by psychiatrists and other physicians, some have argued vigorously (e.g., Albee, 1966, 1968b, 1970) that for clinical psychology to reach its full potential as an autonomous profession, psychology students should train with other psychologists in a psychological setting. Such settings may, however, lack the resources, variety of patients, range of staff interests and abilities, of the independent clinical center; staying close to home may deprive students of the range of experience as well as the opportunity to learn the thinking of colleagues of other professions. The better clinical graduate programs, in my judgment, combine the best of both alternatives. They have a strong and well-staffed psychological clinic as an integral part of the university program and they place students judiciously in the best available hospitals and clinics in the field.

POSTDOCTORAL TRAINING AND CONTINUING EDUCATION

After completing a doctoral program, the new clinical psychologist is prepared to take on the responsibilities of a professional position, at least at a journeyman level. There are usually opportunities for staff development and the young clinician is expected to learn on the job. However, many feel the need for more explicit training, which may take place in a one- or two-year appointment as a *postdoctoral fellow* or in *continuing education* programs.

A number of postdoctoral programs have developed over the years, mainly in independent clinical centers (e.g., Menninger Foundation, Michael Reese Hospital in Chicago, or the Reiss-Davis Clinic in Los Angeles) or in university psychiatry departments (e.g., at the University of Oregon, University of Colorado) or occasionally in university psychology departments (e.g., at New York University, Adelphi University, and the State University of New York, Stony Brook). Alexander (1965) describes the variety of programs available at that time. The report of a 1972 conference on postdoctoral education in clinical psychology gives a more recent overview of the field (Wiener, 1973).

Such postdoctoral programs are designed to provide advanced or specialized training for people who have completed a doctorate in clinical psychology along with the required predoctoral internship. They are not intended to substitute for the predoctoral internship or coursework normally found in the graduate curriculum. The ideal candidate is the psychologist already qualified to practice in the general field but who wants to strengthen or extend his competence in a particular area. Surveying alumni of most of the major postdoctoral programs, S. Smith (1973) finds, however, that many were motivated to repair deficiencies in graduate training as well as to extend into new areas of competence. All found such training a valuable "career moratorium" during which they could consolidate interests and grow, both professionally and personally.

Continuing education, in one form or another, is an intrinsic part of professional life. Along with their daily work, psychologists usually read journals and books, attend clinical conferences, hear lectures by authorities in different areas, attend professional meetings, and the like. More explicit training goes on in APA Postdoctoral Institutes which are held for a number of days at the time of the annual meetings. These are led by authorities in particular areas trying to give a brief overview of their field. Comparable workshops and seminars are sponsored under the auspices of hospitals, universities, and independent growth centers. In the main, however, graduate departments and clinical centers, even those involved in postdoctoral fellowship programs, have not provided much opportunity for further learning for psychologists in practice, particularly those in private practice. Compared to the continuing-education programs of medicine, law, or engineering which attempt to keep their practitioners aware of new developments, psychology has lagged behind.

SUBDOCTORAL CLINICIANS

In the early days of clinical psychology, relatively few practitioners held doctoral degrees. Following World War II, however, psychologists worked toward establishing the PhD as the basic degree of the clinician. Many universities which had previously offered both masters and doctoral degrees phased out their masters programs, except to give the MA as a terminal degree to those leaving graduate work. Colleges offering only the masters degree most often intended to provide only part of the training required of a psychologist, and advised their students to enter a PhD program after completing a masters degree. Job descriptions were rewritten so that a PhD was required for entry-level positions in federal and many state agencies. Voting membership in the APA similarly requires a doctoral degree. When states developed certification and licensing acts, the doctoral degree was usually set as a basic requirement. During the transition, older psychologists who had practiced for years with masters degrees could be certified under "grandfather" clauses, but the overall trend was toward the firm establishment of clinical psychology as a doctoral-level profession.

In the immediate postwar years, this course may have been necessary and wise. Clinical psychology had to develop standards of training and practice and to gain dignity in the eyes of other professionals and public administrators. There was a keen desire to distinguish a scientist-professional, capable of autonomous functioning and contribution, from a technician who could work only under the direction of a fully qualified person of another profession. Psychologists smarted at the thought of being "ancillary" to psychiatry or being described as a "paramedical" specialty. Perhaps most important, however, resources of the time were limited and it was necessary to use them to develop people who could take leadership roles in the future education of clinicians, while contributing maximally to clinical research and practice. By the mid-1950s, it seemed as if the subdoctoral clinician had been legislated out of psychology. The story of psychology's concern with masters-level training has been well told by Woods (1971).

By now, however, the situation has changed in some regards. It has become clear that doctoral programs cannot produce sufficient graduates to serve the many mental health needs of the American people. Moreover, many of the functions of the clinician, many now believe, can be carried on by people of lesser training. Thus, at the Chicago Conference on Professional Training (Hoch, Ross, and Winder, 1966) the legitimacy and potential contribution of masters-level "psychological technicians" was affirmed, though not without ambivalence and controversy. The concept was reaffirmed, more enthusiastically, at the 1973 Vail conference on training patterns. Most clinicians and university faculty members would probably prefer to define as a "psychologist" only people who hold a doctorate. However, there is greater willingness to see developed special educational programs for psychological workers who can, for example, administer tests, perform certain forms of intervention, or work with children in school settings under the general supervision of a doctoral psychologist. Such programs are not likely to be developed in PhD-granting departments which are reluctant to divert limited resources into lower-level professional training. The task, more likely, will fall to the colleges and universities which offer the masters degree as their highest degree. In 1971, forty-eight such institutions could be counted in the thirteen western states alone, which together offered eighty-four different psychological masters programs. Of these, twenty-five were in general experimental psychology, nineteen were in clinical psychology, thirteen in school psychology, six were in industrial psychology, while the rest were in diverse other areas. Though a number see themselves as providing general education or a base for later doctoral studies, many of these programs have accepted the role of preparing people for masters level careers.

Most likely, the coming years will see the planned development of masters-level training programs specifically intended to educate people capable of doing responsible and needed work in mental health and human-service agencies. It is harder to predict the particular shape(s) such programs will take and the extent to which the dominant doctoral clinician, professional associations, and licensing agencies will accept such subdoctoral clinicians. Meanwhile, it is well to realize that perhaps three times as many students graduate yearly with a masters than with a doctoral degree. Moreover, sizeable numbers of workers at the masters level are actually employed in hospitals and clinics, and are regarded as psychologists by their administrators and the public. A bare majority of psychologists now working in psychiatric clinics and hospitals have doctorates, nor is the proportion likely to grow in the future (Arnhoff and Jenkins, 1969). There is clear need for more explicit training and recognition for subdoctoral psychologists who will likely have a continuing if not increasing role in the future of the field.

Professional Identity, Responsibilities, and Problems

PROFESSIONAL ORGANIZATIONS

The American Psychological Association, founded in 1892, is the organizational home of the majority of American psychologists; like many families it is beset by internal conflicts and sibling rivalries though often presenting a unified face to the outside world. In 1975, it had a total membership of over 40,000. At its annual convention, numerous research reports, lectures, and symposia are offered. The APA publishes sixteen psychological journals, covering virtually all of the fields of psychology. Through its committees and boards, the organization deals with the scientific, educational, and professional concerns of its members, whether related to developing a code of research ethics, proposals regarding insurance coverage for private practitioners, or standards for accrediting graduate programs.

The APA presently includes 33 divisions, reflecting the specialized interests of different psychologists. Each of the divisions has its own officers and committees and is represented on the APA Council of Representatives which governs the larger organization. At the annual convention, each division develops its own portion of the total program. The Division of Clinical Psychology (Division 12) is the APA's largest division. Other divisions to which sizeable numbers of clinicians belong include Personality and Social Psychology, School Psychology, Counseling Psychology, Community Psychology, Psychotherapy, State Psychological Affairs, Humanistic Psychology, and Mental Retardation, though it is fair to predict that some clinicians belong to every single one of the 33 divisions as different facets of their interests dictate.

There are inevitable strains in an organization that tries to represent all of contemporary psychology and whose purpose is to "advance psychology as a *science* and as a means of *promoting human welfare*." Although the great majority of members, regardless of specialty and institutional setting, are content to identify with a single organization concerned with the needs of all parties, sizeable minorities feel that the APA has moved too far in one or another direction. Many university psychologists in nonclinical fields feel that the APA should properly be a learned society, whose major concerns should be the publication of journals and the sponsorship of scientific meetings. As they see it, the dues are excessive because of the APA's involvement in accreditation, licensure, and other "professional" matters. At the other extreme, many clinicians, particularly those in private practice, feel not only that these are necessary and legitimate activities, but that the APA should be even more vitally involved in working toward more favorable conditions for psychologists in, for example, federal legislation related to prepaid health insurance, community mental health centers, and related matters. One proposal, currently under consideration, is that the APA split into two or more relatively autonomous societies, which might remain together in a loose federation. Each of these new organizations would have its own officers and bylaws and develop its own dues structure, activities, and convention program to represent better the particular scientific or professional concerns of those who voluntarily elect to join. At this point, it is probably true that the majority of members are deeply attached to the concept of a unitary field and would prefer seeing the APA, conflicts and all, be the single organization representing the scientific and professional needs of all psychologists.

Such conflicts are not new in the history of American psychology. From 1895 on, some psychologists wanted their professional concerns recognized. In 1917 an American Association of Clinical Psychologists was founded, which in 1919 was incorporated into the APA as a Section on Clinical Psychology. Again in 1930 the Association of Consulting Psychologists (originally formed in New York in 1921) expanded nationally and eventually became part of the American Association for Applied Psychology (AAAP), when it was organized in 1937. In 1945, in an era of postwar optimism and growth, the AAAP merged with the APA to form the present APA intended to represent psychology as both science and profession.

The concerns of psychologists are represented by regional, state, and local psychological associations, as well as by APA. In addition, there are many scientific and professional associations which cut across disciplinary lines to serve as forums for exchanging ideas in a particular realm. Thus, a clinician might, for example, belong to the American Orthopsychiatric Association, American Psychosomatic Society, Association for the Advancement of Behavior Therapy, International Association of Group Therapy, or any of numerous others. With no effort whatever, a psychologist could spend much of his waking hours in the work of professional organizations, their conventions, and committee meetings.

MAINTAINING PROFESSIONAL STANDARDS

A responsible profession establishes standards to attest to the knowledge, skill, and integrity of its members, ultimately to protect the well-being of the public. On the wall of a professional's office there are often displayed a university diploma, the diploma of a professional accrediting group, and a state license to practice the profession, each of which indicates a degree of accomplishment and competence.

Board Certification. The competence of professional psychologists is certified by the American Board of Professional Psychology (ABPP); until 1968, it was called the American Board of Examiners in Professional Psychology (Morrow, 1969). It was founded as an independent organization in 1947 in the belief that professional competence was not proved simply by APA membership or by a university degree. ABPP certifies in four fields, clinical psychology, counseling psychology, industrial and organizational psychology, and school psychology. As of now, there are about 2,400 ABPP diplomates, about 1,600 of them in clinical psychology. Periodically, a directory is published and distributed to inform organizations and individuals of the names and fields of psychologists deemed most worthy to practice.

The ABPP examination is an oral one conducted by five diplomates. It is based in part on clinical protocols submitted by the candidate to illustrate his usual clinical practice. The panel tries to ascertain the candidate's knowledge and skill as well as his awareness of theoretical and research issues and his sensitivity to the ethical implications of his work. Part of the examination consists of observing the candidate as he interacts with a patient in a clinical encounter. Should the candidate fail all or part of the examination, he is given another chance to take it at a later date. Once awarded, the diploma can be revoked if the person acts unethically, according to the standards of the APA and of the Board.

State Certification and Licensure. A second approach to establishing standards of professional practice involves having legal requirements set under state statutes for the practice of psychological services. In most parts of the United States, until about twenty-five years ago, there was no legal definition of the qualifications or the practice of psychologists. Consequently, anyone could hang out a shingle declaring himself to be a psychologist and sell whatever he did to a vulnerable public. Consequently, psychologists worked long and hard to have laws drafted in each state that either set up requirements for practice or limited the use of the title "psychologist" to appropriately qualified people.

In general, there are two forms of legislative regulation: *certification* and *licensing*. A certification law guarantees that the title "psychologist" or "certified psychologist" can only be used by someone who has met particular standards. These standards may differ between states, in some cases requiring a PhD and in others none, but an examination is almost always required. What is certified is the title not the practice of psychology. In other words, others could still do the same things as a certified psychologist but they could not call themselves psychologists.

By contrast, *licensure* is more inclusive and defines a profession in terms of the functions as well as qualifications of the licensed professional. Others, who do not hold the license, are prohibited by law from doing the work as well as using the title of the profession. The best known instance, of course, is that of medicine. Medical practice acts start with a definition of practice and restrict the right to engage in these practices to physicians. Licensing is, therefore, more restrictive than certification. By 1974, forty-seven states and the District of Columbia had statutory licensing or certification laws; the states without such laws are Vermont, South Dakota, and Missouri. Although state requirements differ, most ask for the doctoral degree, one or two years of experience, and the passing of a written and/or oral examination. If the candidate is an ABPP diplomate, or was previously certified in another state with similar requirements, some states waive the examination. Standards of reciprocity are being worked on between the states. It is estimated that there are now 22,500 licensed or certified psychologists in the United States (Dörken and Whiting, 1974).

The purpose of a psychology licensing act is, broadly, to protect the public and assure standards for professional practice. Thus, the California law opens with the statement: "The Legislature finds and declares that the practice of psychology affects the public health, safety, and welfare and is to be subject to regulation and control in the public interest to protect the public from the unauthorized and unqualified practice of psychology and from unprofessional conduct by persons licensed to practice psychology." To this end, the state has developed an agency which administers licensing examinations and which can revoke licenses if they are abused.

There has been considerable opposition to the legislative efforts of psychologists by psychiatric and other medical groups. The core of the conflict usually revolves around the independent practice of psychotherapy; psychiatrists have little issue with psychologists performing therapy in hospitals or clinics, psychological testing, or research. Medical psychiatrists often hold that psychologists practicing psychotherapy should be supervised by physicians who are qualified to recognize and attend to any medical problem that might arise. For this reason, as well as less admirable motives of professional pride and economic self-interest, medical groups have often fought vigorously against legislation for psychologists. On the whole, certification acts are more acceptable to them than licensing.

Fortunately, the tensions between psychiatrists and psychologists have become reduced over the years as more and better qualified psychologists have gone into practice. The responsible psychologist recognizes the psychosomatic unity of the human body, i.e., that physiological processes can induce psychological states, and psychological conditions alter physiological states, and that intervention at either level can affect functioning at the other. Thus, psychologists often collaborate with physicians and call in medical consultation as necessary. At the same time, responsible psychiatrists recognize that most of the human problems with which they and clinical psychologists deal are rooted in psychosocial conditions and can be altered through psychosocial interventions. Both parties are coming to understand that there is no necessary reason to view psychotherapy as a facet of medical practice. Advancing human well-being is the proper work of many professions, in overlapping as well as distinct functions, each of which contributes to the solution of mental health problems (which are too large for all taken together!). As psychiatrists have relaxed their insistence on dominating and controlling the work of psychologists, and psychologists their defensive counterattacks, much of the conflict between the professions has been reduced, to the ultimate benefit of society. Competition continues, of course, but in less virulent form than in earlier years. In the field of psychotherapy, for example, more and more people realize that competence and integrity are defined by the unique personal attributes, knowledge and experience of the particular therapist rather than by the degree or license he holds.

ETHICAL STANDARDS

Over many years, psychologists have been concerned to articulate ethical standards governing their scientific, academic, and professional activities. In 1953, the first major statement of the *Ethical Standards of Psychologists* was published by the APA; the present code is a modified and simplified version (APA, 1953, 1963). The principles were derived, in part, from the examination of many critical incidents volunteered by the membership. Nineteen principles were enunciated covering such areas as responsibility, competence, moral and legal standards, client welfare, confidentiality, interprofessional relations, test security and interpretation, research precautions, publication credit and responsibility toward organizations. Along with the standards themselves, a casebook has been published to provide graphic illustrations of what is intended in the code (APA, 1967).

Here are some of the major principles of particular relevance to clinicians, to give some sense of the ethical concerns of psychologists (APA, 1963):

> *Principle 3. Moral and Legal Standards.* The psychologist in the practice of his profession shows sensible regard for the social codes and moral expectations of the community in which he works, recognizing that violations of accepted moral and legal standards on his part may involve his clients, students, or colleagues in damaging personal conflicts, and impugn his own name and the reputation of his profession.

Principle 5. Public Statements. Modesty, scientific caution, and due regard for the limits of present knowledge characterize all statements of psychologists who supply information to the public, either directly or indirectly.

Principle 6. Confidentiality. Safeguarding information about an individual that has been obtained by the psychologist in the course of his teaching, practice, or investigation is a primary obligation of the psychologist. Such information is not communicated to others unless certain important conditions are met. (These are detailed in subsections.)

Principle 7. Client Welfare. The psychologist respects the integrity and protects the welfare of the person or group with whom he is working. (Subordinate principles include: maintaining responsibility for a referred patient until another clinician can take over; terminating a clearly nonbeneficial clinical relationship; in an interprofessional conflict, having primary concern for the client rather than the profession; etc.)

Principle 10. Announcement of Services. A psychologist adheres to professional rather than commercial standards in making known his availability for professional services. (This involves not advertising, soliciting clients, using testimonials, and making extravagant claims.)

Principle 14. Test Interpretation. Test scores, like test materials, are released only to persons who are qualified to interpret and use them properly,

Principle 16. Research precautions. The psychologist assumes obligations for the welfare of his research subjects, both animal and human.

The underlying philosophy of these ethical principles is stated in the preamble:

The psychologist believes in the dignity and worth of the individual human being. He is committed to increasing man's understanding of himself and others. While pursuing this endeavor, he protects the welfare of any person who may seek his service or of any subject, human or animal, that may be the object of his study. He does not use his professional position or relationships, nor does he knowingly permit his own services to be used by others, for purposes inconsistent with these values. While demanding for himself freedom of inquiry and communication, he accepts the responsibility this freedom confers; for competence where he claims it, for objectivity in the report of his findings, and for consideration of the best interests of his colleagues and of society.

Both in general statements and in case illustrations, the ethical code expresses moral precepts with which all psychologists would surely agree. Whether they are realized in practice, however, does not depend on how clearly or eloquently they are stated or even on punishment for their violation—the ultimate threat is dropping a transgressor from APA membership and informing all other members of the association of this fact. For centuries, philosophers and wise men have noted that morality cannot truly be legislated. Neither laws nor punishments make a society or a profession moral. Laws are obeyed only to the extent that they express publicly what is deeply held in the individual conscience. The conscience of a professional derives from early socializing experiences and the examples he internalizes and it is on these that we must depend. Ethical codes are published to remind professionals of their obligations while informing others of our values. The well-socialized and self-disciplined psychologist hardly has to go to the library to discover whether he should or should not falsify research data or abuse a client. And the very few who are tempted are not likely to be deterred by the prospect of losing APA membership or even a state license, no more than a prospective murderer is deterred by the threat of imprisonment or death.

ETHICAL PROBLEMS

It is easy enough to agree on ethical precepts when put in absolute terms, as in the biblical commandments "Thou shalt not kill. . . . steal . . . etc." But agonizing decisions are put to us when two equally valuable principles are pitted against each other. Thus, a recent court case in California exposed the conflict between protecting the confidence of a patient and possibly averting harm to a third person; a case in which both professionals and legal authorities differed. A patient told his therapist that he intended to kill his girlfriend under such convincing circumstances that the therapist contacted the police and recommended emergency psychiatric detention of the patient. The therapist's superior wrote to the police overruling this suggestion, and demanded that the original therapist's letter be destroyed to preserve the confidentiality of the patient's record. Unhappily, the patient did then murder his girlfriend. Subsequently, the girl's family sued the director of psychotherapy, his institution, and the police, claiming that they could have saved her life. A lower court dismissed the suit, and a higher court sustained the action, though the judges split 2 to 1. The majority opinion held that psychotherapists are not legally required to take police action when a patient makes homicidal threats. As reported by the San Francisco *Sunday Examiner and Chronicle* (July 15, 1973, Section A, p. 3), one of the majority judges stated that:

> . . . it was "doubtful" whether the public good would be served by requiring psychotherapists to "sound a public or private alarm" whenever a patient reveals murderous intentions.

The newspaper account goes on to note the opinion of the same judge with regard to the principle of "privileged communication" which therapists deem essential and which is protected by law in California and most other states.

> "Little imagination is required," he noted, "to recognize the offense against psychotherapist-patient privilege" which would result from the rule sought by the plaintiffs. Psychiatrists would be legally compelled to divulge their patients' confidential communications of thoughts or purpose of violence. They would no longer be "able to assure patients that the confidences would be protected." And patients in great need of psychiatric help would tend to avoid doctors in the certain knowledge that disclosure of their ideas and aims or aggression would result in immediate incarceration.

In a dissenting opinion, however, another judge held that the circumstances had established "a duty to warn the victim of the patient's demented ire."

More recently, the California Supreme Court overthrew the earlier decision, and agreed with the dissenting judge that psychotherapists do have an obligation to protect potential victims of patients' intent to do harm. Many California clinicians are understandably disturbed, although it is still too early to gauge the impact of this ruling.

Here, then, are the issues and the opinions. What would you have done if you were the psychotherapist? If you were a judge?

ETHICS OF RESEARCH WITH HUMAN SUBJECTS

During recent years, there has been growing concern among scientists, governmental officials, and the public over the possible harm to people serving as subjects in biomedical or psychosocial research. In part, this reflects the inerradicable memory of the "doctors of infamy" who performed life-destroying experiments in Nazi concentration camps. Unfortunately, however, there have also been distressing abuses much closer to home, however few, yet sufficient to keep alive in the minds of concerned citizens the danger to human dignity and well-being from callous or unethical research. The U.S. Department of Health, Education and Welfare has adopted a policy of evaluating all requests for research support not only for their scientific merit but also for their ethical treatment of human subjects. Universities and hospitals have set up staff committees to review the ethics of research in their settings. Some scientific organizations, the APA included, have published ethical codes for human research and developed their own regulatory procedures.

Most scientists resent external regulation in the belief that complete freedom of inquiry is the life blood of science. There is strong distaste for bureaucratic regulatory machinery, whether run by government, lay administrators, or even fellow scientists. There is the strong, and justifiable, fear that external regulation, whether in the name of human welfare, fiscal accountability, or any other motive, can stifle research creativity and the spirit of adventure, forcing research into narrow, safe, and acceptable molds. At the same time, scientists are keenly aware that the size, complexity, and cost of modern science makes it a matter of public concern and that there are realistic dangers to human well-being in many realms of research. Because of their prevailing liberal ideology, scientists probably more so than the average citizen participate in the humanistic spirit of the times, which is coming to the fore in efforts to give more humane care to inmates of prisons and asylums, to make police methods more just, extend opportunity to the poor, protect consumers, assure civil rights and—as part of the same social spirit, I believe—protect the rights, dignity, and well-being of human subjects. The great problem lies in working out ways of balancing the freedom and responsibility of scientists, of guarding against abuse without damaging the progress or spirit of science.

In psychology, there is less danger of physical harm than in many other areas of biomedical research. But there are many opportunities for psychological damage in studies which deceive, frustrate, or otherwise visit indignities on subjects. A problem which has concerned many is the extent to which experimentation, particularly in personality and social psychology, involves deception ("this is an intelligence test and the scores will be given to the dean" to arouse anxiety). Not only are we lying, but we expect people to be candid with us, which may be a contradictory expectation (Kelman, 1967). The more deception is used, the more likely we are to engender suspicion and get dubious scientific results in further experiments. As Kelman notes, it is often possible if more costly, to find naturally occurring states, rather than trying to produce them experimentally, and in the process we can preserve our credibility. The reputation we have developed, in some quarters at least, was brought home forcefully to a colleague of mine in a poignant incident. Just before entering a lecture hall, he heard the first newscast of President Kennedy's assassination. Before starting his lecture, he told the class the tragic news—only to be met with laughter and "Okay, so what's the experiment?!"

An APA committee collected and analyzed case illustrations of ethical problems in research and drafted *Ethical Principles in the Conduct of Research with Human Participants* (APA, 1973b). The ten major principles are briefly summarized below:

1. The investigator, in planning the study, is personally responsible for its ethical acceptability. After weighing scientific and humane values, should he feel the need to deviate from any of these principles, he incurs the obligation to seek ethical advice and to take more stringent measures to protect the rights of participants.
2. Responsibility for ethical research practice is the investigator's, who is accountable for the work of his assistants and students, who, however, must also themselves be responsible for their actions.
3. The participants should be informed of all aspects of the research which might influence their decision to participate. Failure to make full disclosure gives added emphasis to the investigator's responsibility to protect the dignity and welfare of the research participant.
4. Openness and honesty are essential. Should the methodology necessitate concealment or deception, the investigator is required to ensure that the participant understand the reason for such action.
5. The investigator must respect the participant's right not to participate or to discontinue participation at any time. Special vigilance is necessary if the investigator is in a position of power over the participant.
6. Ethical research begins with a clear and fair contract. The investigator is obliged to honor all promises and commitments.
7. The ethical investigator protects participants from physical and mental discomfort, harm, and danger. The investigator is required to inform the participant of any risks, secure consent before proceeding, and take all possible precautions to minimize distress. Procedures likely to cause serious and lasting harm should not be used.
8. After data are collected, the investigator should provide participants with a full clarification of the study and remove any misconceptions that may have arisen. Should scientific or humane values require delay, the investigator is especially obligated to assure that there are no damaging consequences.
9. Where the research procedure may result in undesirable consequences, the investigator has the responsibility to detect and correct them, including, where relevant, long-term aftereffects.
10. Information gained about research participants is confidential, and every effort should be made to protect it.

These principles expand and extend the brief reference to research in the 1953 APA Code of Ethics. They are in line with current scientific and public concern and address specific issues raised in the DHEW guidelines, such as informed consent, confidentiality, protection against physical and mental harm, clear and honest contracts, and the like. Inevitably, there are shadowy areas—when and how much deception is acceptable? How much risk? Even with special vigilance, how can we be sure that we are not exploiting those in our power? We should be concerned about aftereffects, but for how long? What about subjects legally or psychologically unable to consent for themselves? Even with parental or guardian consent, what are our obligations to children or psychotics themselves?

A paradox in considerations of research ethics lies in the fact that we are as likely (perhaps, more) to sin because of the noblest of scientific motives than because of base human frailties. Gaining research knowledge is virtually a moral imperative to psychologists and other scientists. Mankind is bettered, we believe fervently, as our knowledge of man grows. Working toward such important ends, it is all too easy to justify less virtuous means. Suppose a subject suffers some pain, isn't that a small price to pay for scientific knowledge? (Perhaps, but it is for the subject to decide not the investigator.) It is far easier to rationalize shoddy treatment of people in the cause of science than in the pursuit of personal profit, yet no more right.

The new APA research-ethics principles, as the earlier code of ethics, depends finally on the individual conscience of psychologists and the collective values we hold and teach. It is sometimes true, as the code indicates, that scientific and humane considerations can be opposed, and the investigator has to make difficult decisions. It is mighty hard, for example, to respect fully the "individual's freedom . . . to discontinue participation at any time" in a study where costly repeat testing is being done over a fairly long period of time. More commonly, however, scientific and humane considerations converge in the study of human psychology, which depends so heavily on the voluntary and whole-hearted collaboration of human beings. In the final analysis, the considerate treatment of research subjects may be as justifiable on pragmatic as on moral grounds. Whatever the particular case, however, respecting the rights, dignity, and welfare of the research subject, just as those of the clinical patient, is a primary obligation of the psychologist.

PROBLEMS OF PROFESSIONALISM

Professionalism, sociologists agree, rests on three interrelated concepts, specialized expertise, autonomy, and service. Together they define one's convictions as to the ideal conditions under which one's work should be performed.

First is the belief that *specialized expertise,* knowledge, and skill is necessary to carry out one's tasks in the profession. A corollary is the conviction that such expertise can only be gained in particular types of educational and training experiences conducted by qualified professionals; these are necessary in order to enter the profession. The work of a profession is not to be done by amateurs, whatever their native skills or self-education. Standards of accomplishment are judged by senior coprofessionals, who award diplomas, certificates, and licenses.

Autonomy in the use of that competence is an important ideal of professionalism. The professional may seek consultation, but ultimately he must be responsible for his work. Thus, the dean may not tell the professor what to teach and what to study (academic freedom, a precious ideal of the teaching profession), nor will the surgeon allow the hospital administrator to direct his scalpel. Autonomy is sought not only in the pursuit of duties, but in establishing standards for their performance and for admitting new members to the profession.

The moral basis for both of these concepts however lies in the ideal of *service.* The professional's claim for restricting practice to those qualified by his standards and his demand for self-determination rest on the belief that in this way the public will best be served. Along with supporting claims to exclusive expertise and autonomy, the ideal of service also imposes responsibilities. The professional is committed to the highest standards of excellence and reliability in his work. Though he may earn his living at this work, the quality of the service he provides should stand ahead of personal profit.

As clinical psychology develops as a profession, it is necessary to remind ourselves of the negative as well as the positive side of professionalism. On the one hand, there are the desirable standards of professional practice and conduct, of the kind discussed earlier. Efforts are made to monitor the work of coprofessionals to the greatest advantage of the clients they serve. Standards of training and accreditation are set to insure that the best possible professionals will be available in the future. At best, a sense of dedication and self-sacrifice is instilled so that the professional has a "calling" rather than just a set of marketable skills.

Though all professions claim concern with individual welfare and the good of society, their actions sometimes suggest that they are more motivated by the pursuit of status, prestige, power or economic self-advantage, perhaps even to the detriment of their clients and society. They become vested interests, protecting themselves against the encroachments of others. Higher and more unrealistic standards may be set for admitting new members. The potential contributions of others in their realms are depreciated, as they become exclusive clubs of the elite. Those untrained and unaccredited are looked down upon, even including the client himself. To doctor oneself is treated with derision, if not forbidden by law. Necessary autonomy can become freedom from accountability, except perhaps to one's coprofessionals whose esteem is valued above that of the clients served. To the public, the profession can seem to be "guild-minded" and commercial, limiting and rigidifying its practice in its own, rather than the public's, advantage.

The history of medicine shows both faces of professionalism. Until early in this century, there were minimal standards for the teaching and practice of medicine and health care was correspondingly poor. After the famed Flexner report, organized medicine set high and firm standards for medical education and numerous substandard "medical schools" were closed. In time, medical practices acts and the development of specialty boards further assured that only the most competent would be allowed to practice. Yet, in the same process, premedical and medical curricula became inflexible. A valuable approach to the treatment of polio was slow in gaining medical recognition because it was proposed by Sister Kenny who, after all, was "only a nurse." Closer to home, American medicine preempted psychoanalysis, despite the wishes of its founder. The American Medical Association (AMA) became a powerful lobby and force against social change. Vast sums have been spent on propagandizing and lobbying against legislation for national health insurance and other public-health oriented threats to the private practice model.

Many psychologists, though aware of the advantages of professionalism are fearful of its dangers. They are concerned that the APA will become increasingly involved in attempts to influence legislation, following the example of the AMA. Similarly, the question of whether we have not overemphasized the psychologists of the PhD level and excluded the MA psychologists in a time of social need and limited production of doctoral psychologists, has troubled many. Although the history of the past twenty-five years has been one of increased professionalization, one can wonder if the process has not gone too far. Indeed, some hold that the concepts and methods of psychology might best serve public needs if they are freely shared rather than filtered through specially trained and accredited professionals. A recent president of the APA advised that psychology be "given away" if it is to be most valuable to society (Miller, 1969).

There are no simple solutions to gaining the advantages while avoiding the dangers of professionalism. Cognizant of the problem, the APA issued a statement suggesting what psychologists might do to be members of a "good profession" (APA, 1968, pp. 199–200).

As members of a good profession, psychologists:

1. Guide their practice and policies by a sense of social responsibility.
2. Devote more of their energies to serving the public interest than to "guild" functions and to building ingroup strength.
3. Represent accurately to the public their demonstrable competence.
4. Develop and enforce a code of ethics primarily to protect the client and only secondarily to protect themselves.
5. Identify their unique pattern of competencies and focus their efforts to carrying out those functions for which they are best equipped.
6. Engage in cooperative relations with other professions having related or overlapping competencies and common purposes.
7. Seek an adaptive balance among efforts devoted to research, teaching, and application.
8. Maintain open channels of communication among "discoverers," teachers, and appliers of knowledge.
9. Avoid nonfunctional entrance requirements into the profession, such as those based on race, nationality, creed, or arbitrary personality considerations.
10. Insure that their training is meaningfully related to the subsequent functions of the profession.
11. Guard against premature espousal of any technique or theory as a final solution to substantive problems.
12. Strive to make their services accessible to all persons seeking such services, regardless of social and financial considerations.

Clinical Psychology as a Science and Profession

The distinction between science and profession is at best tenuous. No profession serves adequately if its practitioners continue to apply methods of the past without critical evaluation of their merits and continuous efforts to gain new knowledge on which to base improved service in the future. Just applying existing knowledge reduces the professional to a technician. Thus, the scientist-professional formulation of 1947, rooted much deeper in the history of psychology, remains generally sound today. It is of course true that each clinician's identity need not straddle the hyphen, but the field as a whole must embrace the two aspects. Too much emphasis has been placed on research doing as the measure of the psychologist; insufficient on research thinking, the ability to examine critically and conceptually each act of practice. This attitude, as much as published studies, marks the good clinician. But published research is necessary to firm the base of knowledge, now so limited, needed for effective practice. Moreover, much of the necessary research must be done by clinicians under the pressure of unanswered questions raised in their work with patients.

One of the great myths in our field is that there is pure and applied science, and that clinical psychology applies the knowledge gained in general psychology. This is simply not so, for the problems themselves as well as appropriate research methodologies are often of little interest to other psychologists. In this sense, Angyal's (1941) statement about psychiatry applies as well to contemporary clinical psychology, namely, that it is the "application of a science that doesn't exist." A science of clinical psychology must be the work of clinicians, in harmonious collaboration with other psychologists and other behavioral and biological scientists.

A hard and fast line is too often drawn between pure and applied psychology. In fact, few fields of psychology do not have necessary and worthwhile applications, and systematic scientific knowledge grows from the effort to solve applied problems. The relation between clinical and general psychology is sometimes visualized as similar to that between medicine and physiology or between engineering and physics, namely, an applied technology drawing its basic principles from a pure science. The analogy is deceptive. Not only in psychology, but in these older and more established fields there is no simple distinction between the pure and the applied. Improving medical practice depends on medical research; physiology, as such, contributes little. The theory and knowledge on which bridges are built is developed by engineering scientists; they do not exist in physics. Moreover, the science of physics has grown through the experiences gained in solving engineering problems (Scriven, 1969).

At the present time, there are pressures from both sides to separate clinical psychology from the remainder of psychology. From academia comes the argument that the PhD is a degree for teachers and researchers, and university departments cannot accommodate the interests of those concerned with practice. In turn, many clinicians feel that the university department is too constricting and that only in a professional school of clinical psychology can the proper needs of clinical training be met. Still others argue for a new form of doctorate, which would not involve a research thesis. Paralleling these arguments is the question of whether a single psychological association can contain both parties and serve the legitimate needs of "scientists" and "professionals." The arguments wax, often hotly.

Were general and clinical psychology to become further estranged there would be genuine loss to both sides. On the one hand, clinical psychology needs the methods and theory of the general field of psychology. What has made clinical psychology unique among the mental health disciplines lies in its tradition of scientific inquiry and objective measurement. Clinical psychologists have had an uncontested role in mental health research, in large part out of the methodological competence developed in PhD programs. The knowledge gained from the study of special fields such as social, developmental, psychometric, motivation, and personality psychology is of obvious relevance to clinical work. But no less relevant are the findings of perception, memory, learning, and cognition generally, and of physiological and comparative psychology, in providing the conceptual framework for the thinking of the clinician. New university departments, professional schools, or degree programs could, of course, include substantial emphases in these areas of psychology, but more likely they would be reduced in favor of the more distinctly clinical aspects of the field. The professional school might, as often argued, give greater opportunity for the maturation of clinical skills, professional identity, and the development of what I earlier called the "clinical attitude." While all this would be only to the good, clinical psychology would suffer if clinicians lost the heritage of the science of psychology.

At the same time, psychology needs clinical psychology to provide it with hypotheses and phenomena for study and to challenge its ingenuity in doing research of clinical relevance. Even a cursory view of contemporary psychology shows how profoundly it has been influenced by concepts and concerns of clinicians. Dream research, psychopharmacology, experimental psychopathology, the study of anxiety, defense, frustration, and stress are all clear examples of areas which came into being in direct response to clinical concerns. The study of motivation, group dynamics, psychophysiology, emotion, neuropsychology and for that matter fields such as perception, learning, and attention have depended importantly on concepts and findings originating in the clinical field. The fields of personality assessment and personality research overlap enormously with clinical assessment and the study of personality dynamics within the clinical framework. Even in research methodology, the clinical method (gaining knowledge, as Lightner Witmer said in the 1890's, from "individuals one at a time") provides alternative and enrichment to the experimental approach. Particularly as psychology matures away from its "scientistic" biases, and reinstates more of the spirit of G. Stanley Hall and William James, its interplay with the clinical field becomes more vital.

The Future of Clinical Psychology

Clinical psychology has come a long way. Where is it going? Both social need and the demand for clinicians' services are likely to grow, even in the face of social and institutional constraints. Clinical psychology will surely grow into an increasingly more diversified field. New models of training are emerging. Prediction is always chancy, but social and professional forces are already in evidence which will shape the future course of clinical psychology. These are both external and internal to the profession itself. On the one hand, there are trends in society at large, as well as governmental policies and legislation, that will determine both the need and the support for clinical services. On the other hand, there are intellectual and scientific trends within psychology itself, and in the mental health fields generally, which will shape the values, concepts, and methods of the clinician. Some of these are briefly reviewed in the remainder of this chapter.

FORCES THAT WILL SHAPE CLINICAL PSYCHOLOGY

Cultural factors. Ultimately, as noted earlier, the fate of clinical psychology rests on the widely held belief in the perfectibility of human nature through informed interventions, whether education, psychotherapy, or encounter. In turn, this rests on the equally profound assumption that human well-being or distress results, in fair measure, from psychosocial conditions acting on people from earliest life on. Though long-standing themes in the American culture, they have become intensified as part of a new humanism. There is growing concern with the quality of life and personal freedom, dignity, and opportunity for all people. Society looks to psychology for help in the solution of personal and social problems.

Along with growing education and affluence, more and more Americans have become psychological-minded, not only in the sense of seeing psychological causes for human behavior, but also in terms of fascination with human relationships and man's inner life. Concern with technological and material things has receded, in many quarters, in favor of an insistent need to understand the psychological world of man. Particularly is this true among youth; in large parts of the youth culture there is a new spiritualism that in part converges with, and in part goes beyond, scientific psychology. A visible sign of this trend lies in the fact that psychology has become the most popular undergraduate major in American universities. Now and for years to come, psychology is in the happy situation of being sought by many of the best young minds who in earlier years might have favored careers in science, technology, government, or business.

Social factors. While the incidence of gross psychotic conditions may, as some have proposed, be relatively independent of social forces, the vast majority of problems for which people seek help relate directly to the pressures of modern social life. As one scans the long-term trends, it is clear that most of these will persist and grow. Among the most relevant are: population growth and density, geographical and social mobility, technological progress, increase in the variety of goods and services, more specialized and limited occupational roles, increased leisure, greater urbanization and suburbanization, reduced access to the natural world, more rapid communication, greater government control, and increasing danger of devastating war. Paralleling these, we have seen the breakdown of traditional social values and institutions, the reduced role of family and church, loss of subcultural differences, and increased alienation, deviance, and individual anxiety. Even desirable changes have their distress-producing facets. Increased opportunity for minorities and women casts them in a world of strife and competition for which they still lack ample preparation. Mass production raised the standard of living and made luxuries more available but it also produced dull, demoralizing jobs. Whether desirable or not, change is accelerating at such rapid rate as to tax our capacities for adaptation; we are all victims of "future shock" (Toffler, 1970). Society, it appears, conspires to keep clinicians in business.

Governmental support. At the same time, government support for mental health wavers. Thirty years ago, the federal government contributed notably to launching and supporting modern clinical psychology. Up through the 1960s, considerable amounts of federal funds supported clinical training programs, research in many areas of psychology, and many of the institutional needs of universities and clinical centers. In the recent past, however, there has been some reversal of governmental policy and a distinct reduction in the support of health, education, and welfare. At state and local levels, there is also less support for mental health facilities and educational institutions. Universities are finding it more difficult to raise necessary funds. Inevitably, these conditions have led to reduced size of graduate programs, lessened support for students and fewer career opportunities in all fields. It is impossible to say whether this condition will continue or whether the more affluent days of the 1960s will be partly restored. My own hope is that the long-term cultural and social trends, noted above, will be sufficiently compelling to turn government policy back toward greater concern with matters of health, science, education, and human welfare.

Institutional factors. Although partly dependent on governmental support and public interest, the place of clinical psychology in the university depends more on the attitudes of academic colleagues. There has been persistent ideological conflict between those who see psychology as primarily a scientific field and those who see it as spanning practice as well as scientific values. While each year new university graduate programs in clinical psychology have been launched, some graduate departments which formerly had clinical programs discontinued them. Without doubt, the large number of universities which have a clinical training program will continue their commitment to this area. At the same time, the reservations of many academic psychologists about the proper place of professional psychology in the liberal arts curriculum will lead, in the future as in the past, to the relative underrepresentation of the clinical area in the curriculum; there are not now, nor likely to be in the foreseeable future, as many clinical faculty, courses offered, or openings for students as student interest and, I believe, social need would require.

NEW DIRECTIONS IN CLINICAL TRAINING

Alternatives are developing, however, to the basic model of clinical training, i.e., the PhD program of a university Psychology Department in the scientist-professional framework. This model holds the support of most academic clinical psychologists (Thelen and Ewing, 1970), though vigorous arguments have been advanced for more frankly professional training (Rothenburg and Matulef, 1969). Although all earlier APA conferences on clinical training had endorsed the PhD scientist-professional concept, at the conference in Vail in 1973, the conferees accepted the "professional" model as a viable alternative. Supplementing the dominant PhD model, programs have already been launched involving *alternate degrees, new institutional settings* (e.g., a professional school, either within or outside of a university), or at the extreme, a *new profession.*

A New Degree. The Psychology Department of the University of Illinois offers, in addition to the PhD, a Doctor of Psychology (PsyD) to students particularly concerned with professional practice. There is considerable overlap in course work but relatively greater emphasis on practicum and internship placements. A research dissertation is not required. Graduates of the program have moved into good clinical positions and are apparently satisfied with their education (Peterson, 1969, 1971).

The Professional School. To free clinical psychology from the ideological and organizational constraints of an academic department, arguments have been advanced for relocating clinical psychology into an existing or new professional school (e.g., Coffey, 1970). Such a setting, it is argued, could take the professional roles of faculty and aspirations of students more seriously and be able to provide more flexible practicum facilities, clinical faculty appointments, reward for professional rather than simply scientific achievement, and other needs of professional education. In some universities, doctoral programs have been developed under the aegis of the Medical School, usually in the Department of Psychiatry where there is likely to be a concentration of psychologists.

An alternative is an entirely new professional school, committed only to psychological service and science. At Adelphi University in 1973 and at Rutgers University in 1974 such schools have been launched; at Rutgers, the PsyD degree is offered. The faculty includes part-time clinical appointments; their offices and clinics serve as field-training stations for students.

A more radical departure is an entirely independent professional school, not connected with a university, specifically established for the training of professional psychologists and staffed by professional psychologists. This has happened in California where, under the auspices of the state psychological association, a California School of Professional Psychology was founded which now has campuses in four cities (Pottharst, 1970; Dörken, 1975). Clinicians are trained in a PhD program and lower degrees are offered to people seeking work in mental health fields. In 1975, there are over 600 students; 800 are anticipated in 1976 when the four units will have reached their full capacity (Nicholas Cummings, personal communication). About a third of these are doctoral candidates. Comparable schools are being considered in other states.

A New Profession. Still more extreme is the proposal that the work of mental health requires a new professional, neither clinical psychologist, psychiatrist, or psychiatric social worker, but a composite of the relevant portions of each profession. The new professional would be specifically trained in the knowledge, skills, and attitudes necessary for clinical service (usually phrased in terms of psychotherapy) without being burdened by the unnecessary and irrelevant demands of the parent fields of medicine or psychology (Kubie, 1954; Holt, 1971; Blatt, 1973; Abroms and Greenfield, 1973). The first program was started in 1973. It involves collaboration between the University of California (Berkeley and San Francisco campuses) and the Psychiatry Department of the Mount Zion Hospital in San Francisco. A new doctoral program and degree are being developed.

These various developments are likely to prosper and expand so that in the future sizeable numbers of clinicians will have been trained outside the home and tradition of academic psychology. Uncomfortable as that has sometimes been, it gave a unique flavor to the scientist-professional clinician, which distinguished him from other mental health professionals and allowed him to make unique contributions to the problems of mental health. The new training models will surely produce large numbers of professionals, badly needed in today's society, probably of high quality, judging from the effort and enthusiasm going into the new programs. But whether they will be as good—or better, as some propose—than traditionally trained clinicians remains to be seen.

THE CLINICIAN OF THE FUTURE

Twenty years ago Sarason (1954) opened his book *The Clinical Interaction* with the statement "Clinical psychology is no longer an area of specialization which can be described within the confines of a book. . . . When one remembers that clinical psychology as we know it today is largely a phenomenon of the last decade, one can only be amazed by the rate of its growth and the problems it has come to encompass" (p. 1). This was true of the field in 1954, more true today, and likely to be even truer twenty years hence. No single conception can encompass the evolving field. In the future, there will surely be a *family of clinical psychologies,* some with new names but all held together, I hope, by basic concerns and shared values.

In whichever direction one looks, diversity and differentiation are growing. Future clinicians will not only hold PhD's from university departments but other doctorates from other institutions. There will be careers for subdoctoral psychologists and various types of nonprofessionals, doing some of the work of present-day clinicians. The human problems with which clinicians now deal range from the enduring and grossly disabling to the minor problems of human life. Some dysfunctions derive directly from medical conditions, others reflect distortions of psychological development and personal experience, and still others relate more directly to the conditions of social life. Correspondingly, but not in a one-to-one way, interventions range from drugs to the many forms of individual psychological therapy to family, group, and organizational interventions to social action. Nor is the trend any more distinct in one direction than the other. In the same era, there has been a resurgence of interest in the biology of emotional disorder and the concomitant development of more specific and rational drug methods, and vigorous development of community interventions, and at the same time heightening concern with, and diversification of, psychotherapeutic and behavior-therapeutic methods. Correspondingly, clinicians work within the conceptual frameworks of biological psychology, psychoanalytic, behavioral, and humanistic-existential psychologies, and social and community psychology. The range of clients with which clinicians work grows apace, and includes children, students, adults, the aged, workers, and executives, the poor and racial minorities as well as the affluent and educated, the physically handicapped, mentally retarded, brain damaged, and medically ill, as well as those with more strictly psychological problems. Not least, the settings in which clinicians of the future will work include schools and universities, community agencies and organizations, and streets and homes as well as clinics and hospitals.

The methods and techniques of clinical psychology continue to expand, whether new testing approaches, therapeutic or research methods, or applications of new technology. Psychology has already been greatly influenced by audio and video recording, teaching machines, biofeedback and other psychophysiological equipment, as well as the many applications of computers. High-speed computers can perform the most difficult statistical analyses, but computers can also store and retrieve vast amounts of clinical information in psychiatric registers. They can administer and interpret tests and conduct clinical interviews. Far ranging developments in the biological sciences cannot help but influence psychology, though neither we nor society at large have yet grasped their full impact. Some of the more important are in the areas of genetic engineering, transplantation of nervous tissue and other organs, methods for the direct stimulation of the brain, and the development of new chemicals for altering brain functions and psychological states.

These many trends in clinical psychology support the simple proposition that workers in the field will function in many modes. In the future, there will not be "standard, all-purpose" clinicians with roughly the same training doing roughly the same kind of jobs. The new clinician is likely to be more of a specialist and less of a generalist, though hopefully with enough breadth and wisdom as not to deserve the jibe that "a specialist is one who knows everything about his field except its relative unimportance." One psychologist will elect to study and train autistic children in a hospital setting, another to practice behavior therapy with phobic adults in private practice, and a third to work with psychosocial methods to increase the social competencies of former drug addicts in an inner-city rehabilitation program, to name but three of many alternatives. One thing is certain. There will be many alternatives.

The future clinician will, therefore, be able to choose among many options.

He will be able to develop his interests and skills, and eventually enter a professional career in an area of his own choosing. For some while, training programs are likely to be less differentiated than professional roles, for each faculty intends to cover a broad area they view as "clinical psychology." But even now considerable choice exists in terms of emphases and curriculum, as well as type of degree and setting. Later opportunities for field experiences and job placements are likely to be even broader. Economic and political realities will, of course, limit personal choice, in the future as in the past. In all, however, clinicians will have considerable individual freedom to choose the kinds of clients, problems, techniques, and settings with which to work.

Traditionally, the functions of the clinical psychologist consisted of assessment, therapy, and research. Working in a psychiatric clinic or hospital, the clinician was expected to test patients on referral from psychiatric colleagues, see some patients himself in individual or group therapy, and spend part of his time in research of general theoretical or applied value. Assessment and research were the most distinctive features of the psychologist's role, for therapy was shared with other mental health professionals. Today, there is less emphasis on assessment and more on therapy, though measurement and research still remain the psychologist's more unique contributions to the work of mental health. By now, however, psychologists have extended into so many different functions, both in and outside of psychiatric settings that it is no longer possible to specify the functions of the clinical psychologist. Instead, we can try to picture a number of alternate role models which clinicians now hold and which are likely to continue in the future. These include:

—*Medical psychologists,* working in general hospitals or clinics with medical, neurological, and surgical patients, or in rehabilitation with similar problems, doing psychopharmacological research and evaluation.
—*Pediatric psychologists* work with children's medical problems.
—*Clinicians in psychiatric centers,* doing assessment and therapy with severely disturbed patients, administering wards, conducting milieu therapy, or token economy programs.
—*Child clinicians,* concerned with the particular emotional emotional problems of the developing child, in clinic, hospital, or schools.
—*Clinicians specializing in the problems of adolescents,* working in counseling centers, student mental health units, or in youth-culture rap centers, community delinquency programs, etc.
—*Gerontological clinicians,* particularly concerned with the problems of the aged, both in normal life development and in degenerative diseases, working either in clinical or community contexts.
—*Private practitioners,* specializing in individual, group, or family psychotherapy, of any sort.
—*Community/clinical psychologists,* working in community agencies or community mental health centers, either in direct services (e.g., crisis intervention) or in consultation with other social institutions (e.g., schools, police, etc.).
—*Research clinical psychologists,* working either on problems of general theoretical importance, e.g., personality dynamics, psychopathology, or small-group processes or on problems of more immediate clinical relevance, such as assessment or therapeutic methods.
—*Evaluation researchers,* studying the work of an agency, impact of a program, needs in a community still requiring servicing; they may use epidemiological techniques as well as those of outcome research.

—*Consultants to schools,* the setting in which preventive interventions are most likely to be fruitful; work with teachers and administrators to develop a psychological atmosphere most productive for personal growth and learning.
—*Consultants to large organizations,* industrial, labor, educational, or governmental; they may use methods of small-group dynamics and organizational psychology.
—*Teachers,* either of future clinicians at the graduate level or of younger students seeking general understanding of human experience and functioning.
—*Administrators,* of clinical, educational or community agency or program; plan or coordinate large-scale service or research efforts; contribute to policy making at institutional or governmental level; work with professional organizations.

These brief "job descriptions" hardly do justice to the variety of functions within each of these roles, as they now exist or as they are likely to evolve in the future. For example, the good clinical teacher, as a necessary part of his professional life, does research and sees patients clinically; he may also consult with schools or organizations and contribute to the work of clinical or community agencies, as well as serve on administrative committees. Similarly, the hospital clinician may do research, teach at a local college, and consult.

Particularly as the subfields of clinical psychology become more separate and specialized, it is important to recall the obligations all of us have to the larger community which sustains our work. At one level, as noted earlier, we should be committed to acting in a socially responsible way, putting public needs above guild advantages, making service as widely available as possible. We should live by ethical professional codes, seek to correctly represent and work within, while attempting to extend, our competence. We should guard against premature foreclosure on theories or techniques, try to make our training relate meaningfully to subsequent functions, and extend opportunity without discrimination to all who would enter the profession. Furthermore we have the obligation to share our knowledge of human behavior with all people, either because, like us, they are curious or because they can use it to better their own lives.

Because of the realization that we, along with all other mental health workers, are only a small force working with relatively weak methods to combat monumental problems, it is incumbent on us to use our resources as effectively as possible. In one part, this highlights a pressing need for evaluation research and for research clarifying the sources of psychological deformities and the conditions of change, thus to be able to develop more effective methods of intervention. The same realization, moreover, must lead us to view our work in a broad social context and to seek ways of maximizing its impact. The work of the clinician is usually seen as ministering to psychological casualties, but the challenge is to contribute to the prevention of emotional distress. For one thing, this requires extensive planning in collaboration with other professionals, policy makers, and the public itself, toward the end of identifying sources of stress and the resources available for dealing with them. Psychologists should be in the forefront of the effort to develop broad-scaled social programs to increase psychological well-being. Difficult decisions have to be made as to the helping services needed and the ways in which they can best be deployed, particularly in the balance between public and private services. Beyond planning, however, a second requirement is that we stay alert to new ways of enhancing psychological competence. *Are there ways in which we can help individuals and groups to help themselves?* If we can catalyze self-maintaining positive changes, we have contributed to the ideal of prevention; we may be able to raise the level of effectiveness for many beyond those we see as patients. The task, it seems to me, is to discover sources of competence and problem-solving as they naturally occur in individuals, families, and communities, and discover what can be done to enhance them. It means orienting to the healthy rather than just the pathological, to the resources people have for working through difficulties and optimizing opportunities. At this point, suggested solutions can be vague or grandiose. What must be recommended, however, is that clinical psychologists stay alert to the challenge.

In Chapter 2, clinical psychology was defined in terms of a "clinical attitude." What most distinguishes the psychological clinician, it was suggested there, is a way of thinking, an orientation toward human beings, rather than a particular subject matter, special techniques or a professional role. The clinician wants to study and understand the individual in psychological distress in order to help him. Relevant information is gained, in the clinical process itself, in the transactions between the clinician and the patient. Central to the work of the clinician is the need "to do something about it," to facilitate the adaptation of the patient. However fascinating knowledge is in its own right, it is sought by the clinician in order to help better the lot of the patient. Furthermore, the clinical approach is necessarily personalogical, for the clinician must deal with individual lives in their complexities as patients struggle to adapt and grow. Processes in the person or in the environment, of his physiological nature or his social situation, are most relevant as they come to focus in, and have meaning for, the particular person.

Can such a definition continue to describe and guide our work as clinical psychology becomes more diverse? As some move toward biological and others toward social factors in the quest for the sources of human distress? As interventions center as much on the functioning of biological and social systems as on the experiences of the individual? I believe it can and should. Ultimately, many sciences and professions will have to contribute if human well-being is to be advanced. But the particular contribution of psychological clinicians rests, most critically, on their unique perspective—participating with unique individuals in their adaptive struggles in order to understand and to help them.

REFERENCES

Abroms, G. M., & Greenfield, N. S. A new mental health profession. *Psychiatry,* 1973, *36,* 10–22.

Ackerman, N. W. *The psychodynamics of family life.* New York: Basic Books, 1958.

Ackerman, N. W. *Treating the troubled family.* New York: Basic Books, 1966.

Ackerman, N. W. *Family therapy in transition.* New York: Little, Brown, 1970.

Ackerman, N. W., Lieb, J., & Pearce, J. K. (Eds.). *Family therapy in transition.* Boston: Little, Brown, 1970.

Adelson, D., & Lurie, L. Mental health education: Research and practice. In S. E. Golann & C. Eisdorfer (Eds.), *Handbook of community mental health.* New York: Appleton-Century-Crofts, 1972.

Adorno, T. W., Frenkel-Brunswik, E., Levinson, D. J., & Sanford, R. N. *The authoritarian personality.* New York: Harper & Row, 1950.

Ainsworth, M. D. Problems of validation. In B. Klopfer, M. D. Ainsworth, W. G. Klopfer, & R. R. Holt (Eds.), *Developments in the Rorschach technique and theory.* Vol. I. Yonkers-on-Hudson, N.Y.: World Book Company, 1954.

Albee, G. W. *Mental health manpower trends.* New York: Basic Books, 1959.

Albee, G. W. Psychological center. In E. L. Hoch, A. O. Ross, & C. L. Winder (Eds.), *Professional preparation of clinical psychologists.* Washington, D.C.: American Psychological Association, 1966.

Albee, G. W. Psychological point of view. Paper presented at American Psychiatric Association annual meeting, May 13, 1968, Boston, Mass. (a)

Albee, G. W. Conceptual models and manpower requirements in psychology. *American Psychologist,* 1968, *23,* 317–320. (b)

Albee, G. W. Models, myths, and manpower. *Mental Hygiene,* 1968, *52,* 163–180. (c)

Albee, G. W. The uncertain future of clinical psychology. *American Psychologist,* 1970, *25,* 1071–1080.

Alexander, F. The principle of flexibility. In F. Alexander & T. M. French (Eds.), *Psychoanalytic therapy.* New York: Ronald Press, 1946.

Alexander, F., & French, T. M. (Eds.) *Psychoanalytic therapy.* New York: Ronald Press, 1946.

Alexander, I. E. Postdoctoral training in clinical psychology. In B. B. Wolman (Ed.), *Handbook of clinical psychology.* New York: McGraw-Hill, 1965.

Allinsmith, W., & Goethals, G. W. *The role of schools in mental health.* New York: Basic Books, 1962.

Allison, J., Blatt, S. J., & Zimet, C. N. *The interpretation of psychological tests.* New York: Harper & Row, 1968.

Allport, G. W. *Personality: A psychological interpretation.* New York: Holt, 1937.

Allport, G. W. The use of personal documents in psychological science. *Social Science Research Council Bulletin*, 1942, No. 9.

Allport, G. W. *Becoming*. New Haven: Yale University Press, 1955.

Allport, G. W. Personality: Normal and abnormal. *Sociological Review*, 1958, *6*, 167–180.

Allport, G. W. *Pattern and growth in personality*. New York: Holt, Rinehart & Winston, 1961. (a)

Allport, G. W. Comment on earlier chapters. In R. May (Ed.), *Existential psychology*. New York: Random House, 1961. (b)

Allport, G. W. The general and the unique in psychological science. *Journal of Personality*, 1962, *30*, 405–422.

Altrocchi, J. Mental health consultation. In S. E. Golann & C. Eisdorfer (Eds.), *Handbook of community mental health*. New York: Appleton-Century-Crofts, 1972.

Altrocchi, J., Spielberger, C. D., & Eisdorfer, C. Mental health consultation with groups. *Community Mental Health Journal*, 1965, *1*, 127–134.

American Psychiatric Association. *A Diagnostic and statistical manual of mental disorders*. Washington, D.C.: American Psychiatric Association, 1968.

American Psychiatric Association. *Task force report: Automation and data processing in psychiatry*. Washington, D.C.: American Psychiatric Association, 1971.

American Psychological Association. Committee on Training in Clinical Psychology. Recommended graduate training programs in clinical psychology. *American Psychologist*, 1947, *2*, 539–558.

American Psychological Association. *Ethical standards of psychologists*. Washington, D.C.: American Psychological Association, 1953.

American Psychological Association. Ethical standards of psychologists. *American Psychologist*, 1963, *18*, 56–60.

American Psychological Association. *Case book on ethical standards of psychologists*. Washington, D.C.: American Psychological Association, 1967.

American Psychological Association. Psychology as a profession. *American Psychologist*, 1968, *23*, 195–200.

American Psychological Association. Report of the Task Force on the status of women in psychology. *American Psychologist*, 1973, *28*, 611–616. (a)

American Psychological Association. *Ethical principles in the conduct of research with human participants*. Washington, D.C.: American Psychological Association, 1973. (b)

American Psychological Association. *Standards for educational and psychological tests and manuals*. Washington, D.C.: American Psychological Association, 1974.

Anastasi, A. *Psychological testing* (3rd ed.). New York: Macmillan, 1968.

Anderson, H. H., & Anderson, G. L. (Eds.). *An introduction to projective techniques*. New York: Prentice-Hall, 1951.

Andronico, M. P., Fidler, J., Guerney, B. G., Jr., & Guerney, L. F. The combination of didactic and dynamic elements in filial therapy. *International Journal of Group Psychotherapy*, 1967, *17*, 10–17.

Angyal, A. *Foundations for a science of personality*. New York: The Commonwealth Fund, 1941.

Apfelbaum, B., & Apfelbaum, C. Encountering encounter groups: A reply to Koch and Haigh. *Journal of Humanistic Psychology*, 1973, *13*, 53–67.

Appelbaum, S. A., & Siegal, R. S. Half-hidden influences on psychological testing and practice. *Journal of Projective Techniques and Personality Assessment*, 1965, *29*, 128–133.

Argyris, C. *Integrating the individual and the organization*. New York: Wiley, 1964.

Arnhoff, F. N. Realities and mental health manpower. *Mental Hygiene*, 1968, *52*, 181–189.

Arnhoff, F. N. Social consequences of policy toward mental illness. *Science*, 1975, *188*, 1277–1281.

Asch, S. E. Forming impressions of personality. *Journal of Abnormal and Social Psychology*, 1946, *41*, 258–290.

Astin, H. D., & Bayer, A. E. Sex discrimination in academe. *Educational Record*, 1972, *53*, 101–118.

Atkinson, J. W. (Ed.). *Motives in fantasy, action and society.* Princeton, N.J.: Van Nostrand, 1958.

Atthowe, J. W., & Krasner, L. A preliminary report of the application of contingent reinforcement procedures (token economy) on a "chronic psychiatric ward." *Journal of Abnormal Psychology,* 1968, 73, 37–43.

Averill, J. R., & Opton, E. M. Psychophysiological assessment rationale and problems. In P. McReynolds (Ed.), *Advances in psychological assessment.* Palo Alto, Calif.: Science and Behavior Books, 1968.

Ayllon, T., & Azrin, N. *The token economy: A motivational system for therapy and rehabilitation.* New York: Appleton-Century-Crofts, 1968.

Babigian, H. M., Gardner, E. A., Miles, H. C., & Romano, J. Diagnostic consistency and change in a follow-up study of 1215 patients. *American Journal of Psychiatry,* 1965, *121,* 895–901.

Bach, G. R. *Intensive group psychotherapy.* New York: Ronald Press, 1954.

Bach, G. R. The marathon group: Intensive practice of intimate interaction. *Psychological Reports,* 1966, *18,* 995–1002.

Bach, G. R. Marathon group dynamics: II. Dimensions of helpfulness: Therapeutic aggression. *Psychological Reports,* 1967, 20, 1147–1158.

Bach, G. R., & Wyden, P. *The intimate enemy.* New York: Morrow, 1969.

Bachrach, A. J., & Quigley, W. A. Direct methods of treatment. In I. A. Berg & L. A. Pennington (Eds.), *Introduction to clinical psychology* (3rd ed.). New York: Ronald, 1966.

Back, K. W. *Beyond words: The story of sensitivity training and the encounter movement.* New York: Russell Sage Foundation, 1972.

Back, K. W. Intervention techniques: Small groups. *Annual Review of Psychology,* 1974, 25, 367–388.

Bagley, C. The evaluation of a suicide prevention scheme by an ecological method. *Social Science and Medicine,* 1968, 2, 1–14.

Bahn, A. K., Gorwitz, K., & Kramer, M. *A cross-sectional picture of psychiatric care in an entire state.* (Psychiatric Studies and Projects, Vol. II, No. 3). Washington, D.C.: American Psychiatric Association, 1964.

Bakan, D. *On method.* San Francisco: Jossey-Bass, 1968.

Baker, F., & Schulberg, H. C. The development of a community mental health ideology scale. *Community Mental Health Journal,* 1967, 3, 216–225.

Baldwin, J. A. Community mental health information systems: A psychiatric case register as a data bank. In S. E. Golann & C. Eisdorfer (Eds.), *Handbook of community mental health.* New York: Appleton-Century-Crofts, 1972.

Baler, L. A. Training for research in community mental health. *Community Mental Health Journal,* 1967, 3, 250–253.

Bales, R. F. *Interaction process analysis: A method for the study of small groups.* Reading, Mass.: Addison-Wesley, 1950.

Bandura, A. Psychotherapy as a learning process. *Psychological Bulletin,* 1961, 58, 143–159.

Bandura, A. *Principles of behavior modification.* New York: Holt, Rinehart & Winston, 1969.

Bandura, A. Psychotherapy based upon modeling principles. In A. E. Bergin & S. L. Garfield (Eds.), *Handbook of psychotherapy and behavior change: An empirical analysis.* New York: Wiley, 1971.

Bandura, A., Blanchard, E. B., & Ritter, B. The relative efficacy of desensitization and modeling approaches for inducing behavioral, affective, and attitudinal changes. *Journal of Personality and Social Psychology,* 1969, *13,* 173–199.

Bard, M. Family intervention police teams as a community mental health resource. *Journal of Criminal Law, Criminology and Police Science,* 1969, 60, 247–250.

Bard, M. The unique potentials of the police in interpersonal conflict management. *International Journal of Group Tensions,* 1973, *3,* 68–75.

Bard, M., & Berkowitz, B. Training police as specialists in family crisis intervention: A community psychology action program. *Community Mental Health Journal,* 1967, *3,* 315–317.

Barker, R. G. Explorations in ecological psychology. *American Psychologist,* 1965, *20,* 1–14.

Barker, R. G. *Concepts and methods for studying the environment of human behavior.* Stanford, Calif.: Stanford University Press, 1968.

Barker, R. G. Wanted: An eco-behavioral science. In E. P. Willems & H. L. Raush (Eds.), *Naturalistic viewpoints in psychological research.* New York: Holt, Rinehart & Winston, 1969.

Barker, R. G., & Gump, P. *Big school, small school.* Stanford, Calif.: Stanford University Press, 1964.

Barker, R. G., & Wright, H. F. *One boy's day.* New York: Harper & Row, 1951.

Barker, R. G., & Wright, H. F. *Midwest and its children.* New York: Harper & Row, 1955.

Barrett-Lennard, G. T. Dimensions of therapist response as causal factors in therapeutic change. *Psychological Monographs,* 1962, *76* (Whole No. 562).

Barron, F. An ego-strength scale which predicts response to psychotherapy. *Journal of Consulting Psychology,* 1953, *17,* 327–333. (a)

Barron, F. Some test correlates of response to psychotherapy. *Journal of Consulting Psychology,* 1953, *17,* 235–241. (b)

Barten, H. H. *Brief therapies.* New York: Behavioral Publications, 1971.

Bartlett, F. C. *Remembering: A study in experimental and social psychology.* Cambridge, England: Cambridge University Press, 1932.

Basowitz, H., Korchin, S. J., Oken, D., Goldstein, N. S., & Gussack, N. S. Anxiety and performance changes with minimal dose of epinephrine. *Archives of Neurology and Psychiatry,* 1956, *76,* 98–108.

Basowitz, H., Persky, H., Korchin, S. J., & Grinker, R. R. *Anxiety and stress.* New York: McGraw-Hill, 1955.

Bateson, C., Jackson D. D., Haley, J., & Weakland, J. H. Toward a theory of schizophrenia. *Behavioral Science,* 1956, *1,* 251–264.

Battle, C. C., Imber, S. D., Hoehn-Saric, R., Stone, A. R., Nash, C., & Frank, J. D. Target complaints as criteria of improvement. *American Journal of Psychotherapy,* 1966, *20,* 184–192.

Baum, O. E., Felzer, S. B., D'Zmura, T., & Schumaker, E. Psychotherapy, dropouts, and lower socio-economic patients. *American Journal of Orthopsychiatry,* 1966, *38,* 629–635.

Beach, F., & Jaynes, J. Effects of early experience upon the behavior of animals. *Psychological Bulletin,* 1954, *51,* 239–262.

Beall, L. The "corrupt" contract: Problems in conjoint therapy with parents and children. *American Journal of Orthopsychiatry,* 1972, *42,* 77–81.

Beck, S. J. The science of personality: nomothetic or idiographic? *Psychological Review,* 1953, *60,* 353–359.

Beck, S. J. *The 6 schizophrenias: Reaction patterns in children and adults.* New York: American Orthopsychiatric Association, 1954.

Bednar, R. L., & Lawlis, G. F. Empirical research in group psychotherapy. In A. E. Bergin & S. L. Garfield (Eds.), *Handbook of psychotherapy and behavior change: An empirical analysis.* New York: Wiley, 1971.

Beels, C., & Ferber, A. What family therapists do. In A. Ferber, M. Mendelsohn & A. Napier (Eds.), *The book of family therapy.* New York: Science House, 1972.

Bell, J. E. *Family group therapy.* Public Health Monograph #64, Department of Health, Education and Welfare. Washington, D.C.: U.S. Government Printing Office, 1961.

Bell, N. W., & Spiegel, J. P. Social psychiatry: Vagaries of a term. *Archives of General Psychiatry,* 1966, *14,* 337–345.

Bellak, L. Community psychiatry: The third psychiatric revolution. In L. Bellak (Ed.), *Handbook of community psychiatry.* New York: Grune & Stratton, 1964.

Bellak, L., & Small, L. *Emergency psychotherapy and brief psychotherapy.* New York: Grune & Stratton, 1965.

Bellak, L., & Smith, M. B. An experimental exploration of the psychoanalytic process. *Psychoanalytic Quarterly,* 1956, *25,* 385–414.

Beller, E. K. *Clinical process.* Glencoe, Ill.: Free Press, 1962.

Bender, I. E., & Hastorf, A. H. On measuring generalized empathic ability (social sensitivity). *Journal of Abnormal and Social Psychology,* 1953, *48,* 503–506.

Bender, L. *A visual motor Gestalt test and its clinical use.* New York: American Orthopsychiatric Association, 1938.

Benedict, R. *Patterns of culture.* Boston: Houghton Mifflin, 1934.

Bennett, C. C. Community psychology: Impressions of the Boston conference on the education of psychologists for community mental health. *American Psychologist,* 1965, *20,* 832–835.

Bennett, C. C., Anderson, L. S., Cooper, S., Hassol, L., Klein, D. C., & Rosenblum, G. (Eds.) *Community psychology: A report of the Boston Conference on the Education for Psychologists in Community Mental Health.* Boston: Boston University Press, 1966.

Bennis, W. G. *Changing organizations.* New York: McGraw-Hill, 1966.

Bennis, W. G., & Shepard, H. A theory of group development. In W. G. Bennis, K. D. Benne, & R. Chin (Eds.), *The planning of change.* New York: Holt, Rinehart & Winston, 1961.

Berg, I. A. The unimportance of test item content. In B. M. Bass and I. A. Berg (Eds.), *Objective approaches to personality assessment.* Princeton: Van Nostrand, 1959.

Berger, M. M. (Ed.) *Video tape techniques in psychiatric training and treatment.* New York: Brunner/Mazel, 1970.

Bergin, A. E. Some implications of psychotherapy research for therapeutic practice. *Journal of Abnormal Psychology,* 1966, *71,* 235–246.

Bergin, A. E. The evaluation of therapeutic outcomes. In A. E. Bergin & S. L. Garfield (Eds.), *Handbook of psychotherapy and behavior change: An empirical analysis.* New York: Wiley, 1971.

Bergin, A. E., & Strupp, H. H. *Changing frontiers in the science of psychotherapy.* Chicago: Aldine-Atherton, 1972.

Bergman, J., & Doland, D. The effectiveness of college students as therapeutic agents with chronic hospitalized patients. *American Journal of Orthopsychiatry,* 1974, *44,* 92–101.

Berne, E. *Transactional analysis in psychotherapy.* New York: Grove Press, 1961.

Berne, E. *Games people play.* New York: Grove Press, 1964.

Berne, E. *Principles of group treatment.* New York: Oxford University Press, 1966.

von Bertalanffy, L. *Organismic psychology and systems theory.* Worcester, Mass.: Clark University Press, 1968.

Bettleheim, B. Individual and mass behavior in extreme situations. *Journal of Abnormal and Social Psychology,* 1943, *38,* 417–452.

Betz, B. J. Experiences in research in psychotherapy with schizophrenic patients. In H. H. Strupp & L. Luborsky (Eds.), *Research in psychotherapy.* Vol. II. Washington, D.C.: American Psychological Association, 1962.

Bierer, J. The Marlborough experiment. In L. Bellak (Ed.), *Handbook of community psychiatry.* New York: Grune & Stratton, 1964.

Bieri, J. Cognitive complexity-simplicity and predictive behavior. *Journal of Abnormal and Social Psychology,* 1955, *51,* 263–268.

Bieri, J., Atkins, A. L., Briar, S., Leaman, R. L., Miller, H., & Tripoldi, T. *Clinical and social judgment.* New York: Wiley, 1966.

Bindman, A. J. Mental health consultation: Theory and practice. *Journal of Consulting Psychology,* 1959, *23,* 473–482.

Bindrim, P. A report on a nude marathon. *Psychotherapy: Theory, Research, and Practice,* 1968, *5,* 180–188.

Bingham, W. V. D., & Moore, B. V. *How to interview*. New York: Harper, 1924.

Bion, W. R. *Experiences in groups*. New York: Basic Books, 1959.

Birdwhistell, R. L. *Introduction to kinesics*. Louisville, Kentucky: University of Louisville Press, 1952.

Blatt, S. J. Prospectives on postdoctoral training: The need for interdisciplinary multidimensional training in mental health. In I. B. Weiner (Ed.), *Postdoctoral education in clinical psychology*. Topeka, Kansas: The Menninger Foundation, 1973.

Blatt, S. J., & Allison, J. The intelligence test in personality assessment. In A. I. Rabin (Ed.), *Projective techniques in personality assessment*. New York: Springer, 1968.

Block, J. *The Q-sort method in personality assessment and psychiatric research*. Springfield, Ill.: Charles C. Thomas, 1961.

Block, J. *The challenge of response sets*. New York: Appleton-Century-Crofts, 1965.

Bloom, B. L. Definitional aspects of the crisis concept. *Journal of Consulting Psychology*, 1963, *27*, 498–502.

Bloom, B. L. Mental health program evaluation. In S. E. Golann & C. Eisdorfer (Eds.), *Handbook of community mental health*. New York: Appleton-Century-Crofts, 1972.

Bloom, B. L. The domain of community psychology. *American Journal of Community Psychology*, 1973, *1*, 8–11.

Blum, G. S. *The Blacky pictures: a technique for the exploration of personality dynamics*. New York: Psychological Corporation, 1950.

Board, F. A. Patients' and physicians' judgements of outcome of psychotherapy in an outpatient clinic: A questionnaire investigation. *Archives of General Psychiatry*, 1959, *1*, 185–196.

Bockoven, J. S. Moral treatment in American psychiatry. *Journal of Nervous and Mental Diseases*, 1956, *124*, 167–183, and 292–304.

Bowlby, J. *Maternal care and mental health*. Geneva, Switzerland: World Health Organization, 1952.

Bolgar, H. The case study method. In B. B. Wolman (Ed.), *Handbook of clinical psychology*. New York: McGraw-Hill, 1965.

Boneau, C. A. Psychology's manpower: Report on the 1966 National Register of Scientific and Technical Personnel. *American Psychologist*, 1968, *23*, 325–334.

Boneau, C. A., & Cuca, J. H. An overview of psychology's manpower: Characteristics and salaries from the 1972 APA survey. *American Psychologist*, 1974, *29*, 821–840.

Boomer, D. S. Speech disturbances and body movement in interviews. *Journal of Nervous and Mental Diseases*, 1963, *136*, 263–266.

Bordin, E. S. Free association: An experimental analogue of the psychoanalytic situation. In L. A. Gottschalk & A. H. Auerbach (Eds.), *Methods of research in psychotherapy*. New York: Appleton-Century-Crofts, 1966.

Bowen, M. The use of family therapy in clinical practice. *Comprehensive Psychiatry*, 1966, *7*, 345–374.

Bower, E. M. *Early identification of emotionally handicapped children in school* (2nd ed.). Springfield, Ill.: Charles C. Thomas, 1969.

Bower, E. M. Community psychology and community schools. In W. L. Claiborn & R. Cohen (Eds.), *School intervention*. New York: Behavioral Publications, 1973.

Boxley, R., & Wagner, N. N. Clinical training programs and minority groups: A survey. *Professional Psychology*, 1971, *2*, 75–81.

Bradford, D., & Aronson, E. *A Theory of t-group training*. (In preparation).

Bradford, L. P., Gibb, J. R., & Benne, K. D. (Eds.). *T-group theory and laboratory method: Innovation in education*. New York: Wiley, 1964.

Brady, J. P. Behavior therapy: Fad or psychotherapy of the future. In R. D. Rubin, J. D. Henderson, D. K. Tomroy, & J. P. Brady (Eds.). *Advances in Behavior Therapy, 1970*. New York: Academic Press, 1970.

Braginsky, B. M., Braginsky, D., & Ring, K. *Methods of madness: The mental hospital as a last resort*. New York: Holt, Rinehart & Winston, 1969.

Brand, J. L. The United States: A historical perspective. In R. H. Williams & L. D. Ozarin (Eds.), *Community mental health.* San Francisco: Jossey-Bass, 1968.

Breger, L. Psychological testing: treatment and research implications. *Journal of Consulting and Clinical Psychology,* 1968, *32,* 179–181.

Breger, L., & McGaugh, J. L. Critique and reformulation of "learning theory" approaches to psychotherapy and neurosis. *Psychological Bulletin,* 1965, *63,* 338–358.

Breuer, J., & Freud, S. *Studies on hysteria.* New York: Basic Books, 1957. (Standard Edition, Vol. 2. London: Hogarth Press, 1955). (Original, 1895).

Brim, O. G., Jr. *Education for child rearing.* New York: Free Press, 1959.

Bronfenbrenner, U., Harding, J., & Gallwey, M. The measurement of skill in social perception. In D. C. McClelland, A. L. Baldwin, U. Bronfenbrenner, & F. L. Strodtbeck (Eds.), *Talent and society.* Princeton: Van Nostrand, 1958.

Brotemarkle, R. A. Fifty years of clinical psychology: Clinical psychology, 1896–1946. *Journal of Consulting Psychology,* 1947, *11,* 1–4.

Brown, B. A national view of mental health. *American Journal of Orthopsychiatry,* 1973, *43,* 700–705.

Brown, B. S., & Ishiyama, T. Some reflections on the role of students in the mental hospital. *Community Mental Health Journal,* 1968, *4,* 509–518.

Bugental, J. F. T. *The search for authenticity: An existential-analytic approach to psychotherapy.* New York: Holt, Rinehart & Winston, 1965.

Bugental, J. F. T. The humanistic ethic: The individual in psychotherapy as a societal change agent. *Journal of Humanistic Psychology,* 1971, *11,* 11–25.

Bühler, C. *Values in psychotherapy.* New York: The Free Press of Glencoe, 1962.

Bühler, C. Basic theoretical concepts of humanistic psychology. *American Psychologist,* 1971, *26,* 378–386.

Bühler, C., & Allen, M. *Introduction to humanistic psychology.* Monterey, Calif.: Brooks/Cole, 1972.

Burdock, E. I., & Hardesty, A. S. *Structured clinical interview (SCI).* New York: Springer, 1969.

Buros, O. K. *The seventh mental measurements yearbook.* Highland Park, N.J.: Gryphon Press, 1972.

Buros, O. K. (Ed.) *Tests in print* II. Highland Park, N.J.: Gryphon Press, 1974.

Buros, O. K. (Ed.) *Personality tests and reviews II.* Highland Park, N.J.: Gryphon Press, 1975.

Burrows, T. The group method of analysis. *Psychoanalytic Review,* 1927, *19,* 268–280.

Caldwell, B. A decade of early intervention programs: What we have learned. *American Journal of Orthopsychiatry,* 1974, *44,* 491–496.

Calhoun, J. Population density and social pathology. *Scientific American,* 1962, *206,* 139–146.

Campbell, D. T., & Fiske, D. W. Convergent and discriminant validation by the multitrait-multimethod matrix. *Psychological Bulletin,* 1959, *56,* 81–105.

Campbell, D. T., & Stanley, J. C. *Experimental and quasi-experimental designs for research.* Chicago: Rand McNally, 1963.

Campbell, J. P., & Dunnette, M. D. Effectiveness of t-group experiences on managerial training and development. *Psychological Bulletin,* 1968, *70,* 73–104.

Cannell, C. F., & Kahn, R. L. Interviewing. In G. Lindzey & E. Aronson (Eds.), *The handbook of social psychology.* Vol. 3. (2nd ed.) Cambridge, Mass.: Addison-Wesley, 1969.

Cannon, W. B. *Wisdom of the body.* New York: Norton, 1939.

Caplan, G. (Ed.) *Prevention of mental disorders in children.* New York: Basic Books, 1961.

Caplan, G. Types of mental health consultation. *American Journal of Orthopsychiatry,* 1963, *33,* 470–481.

Caplan, G. *Principles of preventive psychiatry.* New York: Basic Books, 1964.

Caplan, G. *The theory and practice of mental health consultation.* New York: Basic Books, 1970.

Caracena, P. F. Elicitation of dependency expressions in the initial stage of psychotherapy. *Journal of Counseling Psychology,* 1962, *9,* 329–334.

Carkhuff, R. R., Barnett, W. L., Jr., & McCall, J. N. *The counselor's handbook: Scale and profile interpretations of the MMPI.* Urbana, Ill.: R. W. Parkinson & Associates, 1965.

Carkhuff, R. R., & Pierce, R. Differential effects of therapist race and social class upon patient depth of self-exploration in the initial clinical interview. *Journal of Consulting Psychology,* 1967, *31,* 632–634.

Carkhuff, R. R., & Truax, C. B. Lay mental health counseling: The effects of lay group counseling. *Journal of Consulting Psychology,* 1965, *29,* 426–431. (a)

Carkhuff, R. R., & Truax, C. B. Training in counseling and psychotherapy: An evaluation of an integrated didactic and experiential approach. *Journal of Consulting Psychology,* 1965, *29,* 333–336. (b)

Carlson, D. A., Coleman, J. B., Errera, P., & Harrison, R. W. Problems in treating the lower class psychotic. *Archives of General Psychiatry,* 1965, *13,* 269–274.

Carson, R. C. A and B therapist "types": A possible critical variable in psychotherapy. *Journal of Nervous and Mental Diseases,* 1967, *144,* 47–54.

Carson, R. C., & Heine, R. W. Similarity and success in therapeutic dyads. *Journal of Consulting Psychology,* 1962, *26,* 38–43.

Carson, R. C., & Llewellyn, C. E., Jr. Similarity in the therapeutic dyads: A reevaluation. *Journal of Consulting Psychology,* 1966, *30,* 458.

Cartwright, D. S. Note on "changes in psychoneurotic patients with and without psychotherapy." *Journal of Consulting Psychology,* 1956, *20,* 403–404.

Cartwright, D. S., Kirtner, W. L., & Fiske, D. W. Method factors in changes associated with psychotherapy. *Journal of Abnormal and Social Psychology,* 1963, *66,* 164–175.

Cartwright, D. S., & Zander, A. (Eds.). *Group dynamics: Research and theory.* Evanston, Ill.: Row, Peterson, 1962.

Cattell, R. B. *Description and measurement of personality.* Yonkers, N.Y.: World, 1946.

Cattell, R. B. *The scientific analysis of personality.* Baltimore: Penguin, 1965.

Cattell, R. B., & Stice, G. F. *Handbook for the sixteen personality factor questionnaire.* Champaign, Ill.: Institute for Personality and Ability Testing, 1957.

Cautela, J. R. Treatment of compulsive behavior by covert sensitization. *Psychological Record,* 1966, *16,* 33–41.

Chartier, G. M. A-B therapist variable: Real or imagined? *Psychological Bulletin,* 1971, *75,* 22–33.

Chassan, J. B. *Research design in clinical psychology and psychiatry.* New York: Appleton-Century-Crofts, 1967.

Chessick, R. D. *How psychotherapy heals.* New York: Science House, 1969.

Chu, F. D., & Trotter, S. *The mental health complex. Part I: Community mental health centers.* (Part I of the task force report on the National Institute of Mental Health.) Washington, D.C.: Center for Study of Responsive Law, 1972.

Clark, K. B. The pathos of power: A psychological perspective. *American Psychologist,* 1971, *26,* 1047–1057.

Clark, K. E. *America's psychologists.* Washington, D.C.: American Psychological Association, 1957.

Clark, R. A. The projective measurement of experimentally induced levels of sexual motivation. *Journal of Experimental Psychology,* 1952, *44,* 391–399.

Clausen, J. A. Values, norms, and the health called "mental"; purposes and feasibility of assessment. In S. B. Sells (Ed.), *The definition and measurement of mental health.* Washington, D.C.: United States Public Health Service, 1968.

Clausen, J. A. Mental disorders. In R. K. Merton & R. Nisbet (Eds.), *Contemporary social problems* (3rd ed.). New York: Harcourt, Brace & World, 1971.

Clausen, J. A., & Kohn, M. L. Relation of schizophrenia to the social structure of a small city. In B. Pasamanick (Ed.), *Epidemiology of mental disorder.* Washington, D.C.: American Association for the Advancement of Science, 1959.

Clemes, S., & D'Andrea, V. J. Patients' anxiety as a function of expectation and degree of initial interview ambiguity. *Journal of Consulting Psychology,* 1965, *29,* 397–404.

Cline, V. B. Ability to judge personality assessed with a stress interview and sound film technique. *Journal of Abnormal and Social Psychology,* 1955, *50,* 183–187.

Cline, V. B. Interpersonal Perception. In B. A. Maher (Ed.), *Progress in experimental personality research.* Vol. I. New York: Academic Press, 1964.

Cline, V. B., & Richards, J. M., Jr. Accuracy of interpersonal perception—a general trait? *Journal of Abnormal and Social Psychology,* 1960, *60,* 1–7.

Cobb, S., & Lindemann, E. Symposium on the management of Coconut Grove burns at Massachusetts General Hospital: Neuropsychiatry observations. *Annals of Surgery,* 1943, *117,* 814–824.

Coelho, G. V., Hamburg, D. A., & Adams, J. E. (Eds.). *Coping and adaptation.* New York: Basic Books, 1974.

Coffey, H. S. The school of psychology model. *American Psychologist,* 1970, *25,* 434–436.

Cohen, L. D. Consultation as a method of mental health intervention. In L. E. Apt & B. J. Reiss (Eds.), *Progress in clinical psychology.* New York: Grune & Stratton, 1966.

Colby, K. M., Watt, J. B., & Gilbert, J. P. A computer method of psychotherapy: Preliminary communication. *Journal of Nervous and Mental Disease,* 1966, *142,* 148–152.

Cole, N. J., Branch, C. H., & Allison, R. B. Some relationships between social class and the practice of dynamic psychotherapy. *American Journal of Psychiatry,* 1962, *118,* 1004–1012.

Combs, A. W., & Snygg, D. *Individual behavior.* New York: Harper & Row, 1959.

Committee on Labor and Public Welfare, U.S. Senate. Health Services Act of 1974, A report of the committee, submitted September 5, 1974. Report No. 93–1137.

Cook, M. *Interpersonal perception.* Middlesex, England: Penguin, 1971.

Cooper, B., & Morgan, H. G. *Epidemiological psychiatry.* Springfield, Ill.: Charles C Thomas, 1973.

Cowen, E. L. Emergent approaches to mental health problems: An overview and direction for future work. In E. L. Cowen, E. A. Gardner, & M. Zax (Eds.). *Emergent approaches to mental health problems.* New York: Appleton-Century-Crofts, 1967.

Cowen, E. L. Social and community interventions. *Annual Review of Psychology,* 1973, *24,* 423–472.

Cowen, E. L., Dorr, D., Clarfield, S., Kreling, B., McWilliams, S. A., Pokracki, F., Pratt, D. M., Terrell, D., & Wilson, A. The AML: A quick-screening device for early identification of school mal-adaptation. *American Journal of Community Psychology,* 1973, *1,* 12–35.

Cowen, E. L., Gardner, E. A., & Zax, M. (Eds.). *Emergent approaches to mental health problems.* New York: Appleton-Century-Crofts, 1967.

Cowen, E. L., Leibowitz, E., & Leibowitz, G. The utilization of retired people as mental health aids in the schools. *American Journal of Orthopsychiatry,* 1968, *38,* 900–909.

Cowen, E. L., Pederson, A., Babigian, H., Izzo, L., & Trost, M. A. Long term follow-up of early detected vulnerable children. *Journal of Consulting and Clinical Psychiatry,* 1973, *41,* 438–446.

Cowen, E. L., Zax, M., & Laird, J. D. A college student volunteer program in the elementary school setting. *Community Mental Health Journal,* 1966, *2,* 319–328.

Craik, K. H. Environmental psychology. In K. H. Craik, B. Kleinmuntz, R. Rosnow, R. Rosenthal, J. A. Cheyne, & R. Walters (Eds.), *New directions in psychology 4.* New York: Holt, Rinehart & Winston, 1970.

Craik, K. H. Environmental psychology. *Annual Review of Psychology,* 1973, *24,* 402–422.

Cronbach, L. J. Two disciplines of psychology. *American Psychologist,* 1957, *12,* 671–684.

Cronbach, L. J. *Essentials of psychological testing* (3rd ed.). New York: Harper & Row, 1970.

Cronbach, L. J., & Gleser, G. C. *Psychological tests and personnel decisions* (2nd ed.). Urbana: University of Illinois Press, 1965.

Cronbach, L. J., & Meehl, P. E. Construct validity in psychological tests. *Psychological Bulletin,* 1955, *52,* 281–302.

Crow, W. J. The effect of training upon accuracy and variability in interpersonal perception. *Journal of Abnormal and Social Psychology,* 1957, *55,* 355–359.

Crow, W. J., & Hammond, K. R. The generality of accuracy and response sets in interpersonal perception. *Journal of Abnormal and Social Psychology,* 1957, *54,* 384–390.

Crutchfield, R. S. Conformity and character. *American Psychologist,* 1955, *10,* 191–198.

Cumming, E., & Cumming, J. *Closed ranks: An experiment in mental health education.* Cambridge, Mass.: Harvard University Press, 1957.

Dahlstrom, W. G., Welsh, G. S., & Dahlstrom, L. E. *An MMPI handbook. Volume I: Clinical interpretation* (Rev. ed.). Minneapolis: University of Minnesota Press, 1972.

Dahlstrom, W. G., Welsh, G. S., & Dahlstrom, L. E. *An MMPI handbook. Volume II: Research applications.* (Rev. ed.) Minneapolis: University of Minnesota Press, 1975.

Darwin, C. *The expression of the emotions in man and animals.* London: Murray, 1872.

Davis, J. A. *Education for positive mental health: A review of existing research and recommendations for future studies.* Chicago: Aldine, 1965.

Davis, K. Mental hygiene and the class structure. *Psychiatry,* 1938, *1,* 55–65.

Davison, G. C. Systematic desensitization as a counterconditioning process. *Journal of Abnormal Psychology,* 1968, *73,* 91–99.

Davison, G. C. A procedural critique of "Desensitization and the experimental reduction of threat." *Journal of Abnormal Psychology,* 1969, *74,* 86–87.

Davitz, J. R. *The communication of emotional meaning.* New York: McGraw-Hill, 1964.

DeCharms, R., Levy, J., & Wertheimer, M. A note on attempted evaluations of psychotherapy. *Journal of Clinical Psychology,* 1954, *10,* 233–235.

Decker, J. B., & Stubblebine, J. M. Crisis intervention and prevention of psychiatric disability: A follow-up study. *American Journal of Psychiatry,* 1972, *129,* 725–729.

Denker, P. G. Results of treatment of psychoneuroses by the general practitioner. *New York State Journal of Medicine,* 1946, *46,* 2164–2166.

Derogatis, L. R., Lipman, R. S., Rickels, J., Uhlenhuth, E. H., & Covi, L. The Hopkins Symptom Checklist (HSCL): A measure of primary symptom dimensions. In P. Pichot (Ed.), *Psychological measurements in psychopharmocology: Modern problems in pharmacopsychiatry.* Vol. 7. Basel, Switzerland: S. Krager, 1974.

Deutsch, A. *The shame of the states.* New York: Harcourt, Brace, 1948.

Deutsch, A. *The mentally ill in America* (2nd ed.). New York: Columbia University Press, 1949.

Diamond, M. C., Law, F., Rhodes, H., Lindner, B., Rosenzweig, M. R., Krech, D., & Bennett, E. L. Increases in cortical depth and glia numbers in rats subjected to enriched environments. *Journal of Comparative Neurology,* 1966, *128,* 117–126.

DiMascio, A. A., Boyd, R. W., Greenblatt, M., & Solomon, H. C. The psychiatric interview: A socio-physiologic study. *Diseases of the Nervous System,* 1955, *16,* 2–7.

DiMascio, A. A., & Suter, E. Psychological observations in psychiatric interviews. *Journal of Nervous and Mental Disease,* 1954, *120,* 413–414.

Dittmann, A. T. Kinesic research and therapeutic processes. In P. Knapp (Ed.), *Expression of the emotions in man.* New York: International Universities Press, 1963.

Dittman, A. T., & Wynne, L. C. Linguistic techniques and the analysis of emotionality in interviews. *Journal of Abnormal and Social Psychology,* 1961, *63,* 201–204.

Dohrenwend, B. P., Bernard, V. W., & Kolb, L. C. The orientations of leaders in an urban area toward problems of mental illness. *American Journal of Psychiatry,* 1962, *118,* 683–691.

Dohrenwend, B. P., & Dohrenwend, B. S. The problem of validity in field studies of psychological disorder. *Journal of Abnormal Psychology,* 1965, *70,* 52–69.

Dohrenwend, B. P., & Dohrenwend, B. S. *Social status and psychological disorder.* New York: Wiley, 1969.

Dohrenwend, B. P., & Dohrenwend, B. S. Social and cultural influences on psychopathology. *Annual Review of Psychology,* 1974, 25, 417–452.

Dollard, J., Doob, L. W., Miller, N. E., Mowrer, O. H., & Sears, R. R. *Frustration and aggression.* New Haven: Yale University Press, 1939.

Dollard, J., & Miller, N. E. *Personality and psychotherapy.* New York: McGraw-Hill, 1950.

Dollard, J., & Mowrer, O. H. A method of measuring tension in written documents. *Journal of Abnormal and Social Psychology,* 1947, 42, 3–32.

Dörken, H. Private professional sector innovations in higher education: The California School of Professional Psychology. *Journal of Community Psychology,* 1975, 3, 15–21.

Dörken, H., & Whiting, J. F. Psychologists as health-service providers. *Professional Psychology,* 1974, 5, 309–319.

Dreger, R. M., Lewis, P. M., Rich, T. A., Miller, K. S., Reid, M. P., Overlade, D. C., Taffel, C., & Fleming, E. L. Behavioral classification project. *Journal of Consulting Psychology,* 1964, 28, 1–13.

Drever, J. *A dictionary of psychology.* (Revised by Harvey Wallerstein.) Baltimore, Md.: Penguin, 1964.

Dubos, R. *Mirage of health.* Garden City, N.Y.: Doubleday, Anchor Books, 1959.

Duffy, E. *Activation and behavior.* New York: Wiley, 1962.

Duhl, L. J., & Leopold, R. L. Mental health and political process: Introduction. In L. J. Duhl & R. L. Leopold (Eds.), *Mental health and urban social policy.* San Francisco: Jossey-Bass, 1968.

Dumont, M. P. *The absurd healer: Perspectives of a community psychiatrist.* New York: Science House, 1968.

Duncker, K. On problem-solving. *Psychological Monographs,* 1945, 58 (No. 5).

Dunham, H. W. Current status of ecological research in mental disorder. *Social Forces,* 1947, 25, 321–326.

Dunham, H. W. Community psychiatry: The newest therapeutic bandwagon. *Archives of General Psychiatry,* 1965, 12, 303–313.

Durkin, H. E. *The group in depth.* New York: International Universities Press, 1964.

Ebel, R. L. Must all tests be valid? *American Psychologist,* 1964, 19, 640–647.

Edwards, A. L. The relationship between the judged desirability of a trait and the probability that the trait will be endorsed. *Journal of Applied Psychology,* 1953, 37, 90–93.

Edwards, A. L. *The social desirability variable in personality assessment and research.* New York: Dryden, 1957.

Edwards, A. L. *Edwards' Personal Preference Schedule.* New York: Psychological Corporation, 1959.

Eisenberg, L. Possibility for a preventive psychiatry. *Pediatrics,* 1962, 30, 815–828. (a)

Eisenberg, L. If not now, when? *American Journal of Orthopsychiatry,* 1962, 32, 781–793. (b)

Eisenberg, L. Preventive psychiatry. *Annual Review of Medicine,* 1962, 13, 343–360. (c)

Eisenberg, L. The sins of the fathers: Urban decay and social pathology. *American Journal of Orthopsychiatry,* 1962, 32, 5–17. (d)

Ekman, P. Body position, facial expression, and verbal behavior during interviews. *Journal of Abnormal and Social Psychology,* 1964, 68, 295–301.

Ekman, P. Studies in non-verbal behavior. Paper read at NATO Symposium on Non-verbal Communication, Oxford, 1969.

Ekman, P., & Friesen, W. V. Non-verbal behavior in psychotherapy research. In J. M. Shlien (Ed.), *Research in psychotherapy,* Vol. 3. Washington, D.C.: American Psychological Association, 1968.

Ekman, P., & Friesen, W. V. *Unmasking the face.* Englewood Cliffs, N.J.: Prentice-Hall, 1975.

Ekman, P., Sorenson, F. R., & Friesen, W. V. Pancultural elements in facial displays of emotion. *Science,* 1969, *164,* 86–88.

Elizur, A. Content analysis of the Rorschach with regard to anxiety and hostility. *Rorschach Research Exchange and Journal of Projective Techniques,* 1949, *13,* 247–284.

Engel, G. L. *Psychological development in health and disease.* Philadelphia: Saunders, 1962.

Engel, G. L. Sudden death and the "medical model" in psychiatry. *Canadian Psychiatric Association Journal,* 1970, *15,* 527–538.

Engel, M. *Psychopathology in childhood.* New York: Harcourt Brace Jovanovich, 1972.

Engel, M., & Blatt, S. J. Clinical inference in psychological assessment. Paper presented at the meeting of the American Psychological Association, Philadelphia, 1963.

English, H. B., & English, A. C. *A comprehensive dictionary of psychological and psychoanalytical terms.* New York: Longmans, Green, 1958.

English, J. T. Perspectives on preventive services. In B. L. Bloom & D. P. Buck (Eds.), *Preventive services in mental health programs.* Boulder, Colo.: Western Interstate Commission for Higher Education, 1967.

Enright, J. B. An introduction to Gestalt techniques. In J. Fagan & I. L. Sheperd (Eds.), *Gestalt therapy now.* Palo Alto, Calif.: Science and Behavior Books, 1970.

Enright, J. B. On the playing fields of Synanon. In L. Blank, G. B. Gottsegen, & M. G. Gottsegen (Eds.), *Confrontation: Encounters in self and interpersonal awareness.* New York: Macmillan, 1971.

Erikson, E. H. Identity and the life cycle. *Psychological Issues,* 1959, *1,* 18–164.

Erikson, E. H. *Childhood and society* (Rev. ed.). New York: Norton, 1963.

Eron, L. D. A normative study of the Thematic Apperception Test. *Psychological Monographs,* 1950, *64,* (9, Whole No. 315).

Escalona, S. *Roots of individuality.* Chicago: Aldine, 1968.

Escalona, S., & Heider, G. *Prediction and outcome.* New York: Basic Books, 1959.

Exner, J. E., Jr. *The Rorschach systems.* New York: Grune & Stratton, 1969.

Eysenck, H. J. The effects of psychotherapy: An evaluation. *Journal of Consulting Psychology,* 1952, *16,* 319–324.

Eysenck, H. J. A reply to Luborsky's note. *British Journal of Psychology,* 1954, *45,* 132–133.

Eysenck, H. J. The effects of psychotherapy: A reply. *Journal of Abnormal and Social Psychology,* 1955, *50,* 147–148.

Eysenck, H. J. *The structure of human personality* (2nd ed.). London: Methuen, 1960. (a)

Eysenck, H. J. Classification and the problem of diagnosis. In H. J. Eysenck (Ed.), *Handbook of abnormal psychology.* London: Sir Isaac Pitman, 1960. (b)

Eysenck, H. J. The outcome problem in psychotherapy: A reply. *Psychotherapy: Theory, Research, and Practice,* 1964, *1,* 97–100.

Eysenck, H. J. The effects of psychotherapy. *International Journal of Psychiatry,* 1965, *1,* 99–142.

Eysenck, H. J. *The effects of psychotherapy.* New York: International Science Press, 1966.

Eysenck, H. J. New ways in psychotherapy. *Psychology Today,* 1967, *1,* 39–47. (a)

Eysenck, H. J. The non-professional psychotherapist. *International Journal of Psychiatry,* 1967, 3, 150–153. (b)

Eysenck, H. J. A note on "Factors influencing the outcome of psychotherapy." *Psychological Bulletin,* 1972, *78,* 403–405.

Eysenck, H. J., & Beech, R. Counterconditioning and related methods. In A. E. Bergin & S. L. Garfield (Eds.), *Handbook of psychotherapy and behavior change: An empirical analysis.* New York: Wiley, 1971.

Ezriel, H. A psychoanalytic approach to group treatment. *British Journal of Medical Psychology,* 1950, *23,* 59–74.

Fairweather, G. W. *Social psychology in treating mental illness.* New York: Wiley, 1964.

Fairweather, G. W., Sanders, D. H., Cressler, D. L., & Maynard, H. *Community life for the mentally ill.* Chicago: Aldine, 1969.

Faris, R. E. L., & Dunham, H. W. *Mental disorders in urban areas.* Chicago: University of Chicago Press, 1939.

Farnsworth, K., Lewis, E., & Walsh, J. Counseling outcome criteria and the question of dimensionality. *Journal of Clinical Psychology,* 1971, 27, 144–145.

Feldman, M. P., & MacCulloch, M. J. The application of anticipatory avoidance learning in the treatment of homosexuality. I: Theory, technique, and preliminary results. *Behaviour Research and Therapy,* 1965, 2, 165–183.

Fenichel, O. *The psychoanalytic theory of neurosis.* New York: Norton, 1945.

Fenichel, O. *Ten years of the Berlin Psychoanalytic Institute, 1920–1930.*

Ferber, A., Mendelsohn, M., & Napier, A. (Eds.) *The book of family therapy.* New York: Science House, 1972.

Feshbach, S., & Singer, R. D. The effects of fear arousal and suppression of fear upon social perception. *Journal of Abnormal and Social Psychology,* 1957, 55, 283–288.

Fidler, J. W., Guerney, B. G., Jr., Andronico, M. P., & Guerney, L. F. Filial therapy as a logical extension of current trends in psychotherapy. In B. G. Guerney, Jr. (Ed.), *Psychotherapeutic agents: New roles for non-professionals, parents, and teachers.* New York: Holt, Rinehart & Winston, 1969.

Fiedler, F. E. The concept of an ideal therapeutic relationship. *Journal of Consulting Psychology,* 1950, *14,* 239–245. (a)

Fiedler, F. E. A comparison of therapeutic relationships in psychoanalytic, non-directive, and Adlerian therapy. *Journal of Consulting Psychology,* 1950, *14,* 436–445. (b)

Fiedler, F. E. Factor analyses of psychoanalytic, non-directive, and Adlerian therapeutic relationships. *Journal of Consulting Psychology,* 1951, *15,* 32–38.

Finney, J. C. Methodological problems in a programmed composition of psychological test reports. Paper presented at the meeting of the American Psychological Association, New York, September, 1965.

Fisher, S., & Cleveland, S. E. *Body image and personality.* Princeton, N.J.: Van Nostrand, 1958.

Fishman, J. R., Klein, W. L., MacLennan, B. W., Mitchell, L., Pearl, A., & Walker, W. *Training for new careers.* (President's Committee on Juvenile Delinquency and Youth Crime.) Washington, D.C.: U.S. Government Printing Office, 1965.

Fiske, D. W., Hunt, H. F., Luborsky, L., Orne, M. T., Parloff, M. B., Reiser, M. F., & Tuma, A. H. The planning of research on effectiveness of psychotherapy. *Archives of General Psychiatry,* 1970, 22, 22–32.

Fiske, D. W., & Pearson, P. H. Theory and techniques of personality measurement. *Annual Review of Psychology,* 1970, *21,* 49–86.

Folkins, C. H., Evans, K. L., Opton, E. M., Jr., & Lazarus, R. S. A reply to Davison's critique. *Journal of Abnormal Psychology,* 1969, 74, 88–89.

Folkins, C. H., Lawson, K. D., Opton, E. M., Jr., & Lazarus, R. S. Desensitization and the experimental reduction of threat. *Journal of Abnormal Psychology,* 1968, 73, 100–113.

Ford, D. H., & Urban, H. B. *Systems of Psychotherapy.* New York: Wiley, 1963.

Frank, G. H. The role of the family in the development of psychopathology. *Psychological Bulletin,* 1965, 64, 191–205.

Frank, J. D. Some determinants, manifestations and effects of cohesion in therapy groups. *International Journal of Group Psychotherapy,* 1957, 7, 53–62.

Frank, J. D. Problems of controls in psychotherapy as exemplified by the Psychotherapy Research Project of the Phipps Psychiatric Clinic. In E. A. Rubinstein & M. B. Parloff (Eds.), *Research in psychotherapy.* Vol. II. Washington, D.C.: American Psychological Association, 1959.

Frank, J. D. Discussion of H. J. Eysenck's "the effects of psychotherapy." *International Journal of Psychiatry,* 1965, 1, 288–290.

Frank, J. D. *Persuasion and healing* (Rev. ed.). Baltimore, Maryland: The Johns Hopkins University Press, 1973.

Frank, J. D., & Ascher, E. The corrective emotional experience in group therapy. *American Journal of Psychiatry,* 1951, *108,* 126–131.

Frank, J. D., Gliedman, L. H., Imber, S. D., Nash, E. H., Jr., & Stone, A. R. Why patients leave psychotherapy. *Archives of Neurology and Psychiatry,* 1957, 77, 283–299.

Frank, L. K. Projective methods for the study of personality. *Journal of Psychology,* 1939, *8,* 389–413.

Frankl, V. E. Paradoxical intention: a logotherapeutic technique. *American Journal of Psychotherapy,* 1960, *14,* 520–535.

Frankl, V. E. *Man's search for meaning* (Rev. ed.). New York: Washington Square Press, 1963.

Frankl, V. E. *The doctor and the soul* (2nd ed.). New York: Knopf, 1965.

Frankl, V. E. *Psychotherapy and existentialism: selected papers on logotherapy.* New York: Washington Square Press, 1967.

Freeman, G. L. Toward a psychiatric plimsoll mark: Physiological recovery quotients in experimentally induced frustration. *Journal of Psychology,* 1939, *8,* 247–252.

Freeman, T. Psycho-analytic psychotherapy in the National Health Service. *British Journal of Psychiatry,* 1967, *11,* 321–327.

Freud, A. *The ego and the mechanisms of defense.* New York: International Universities Press, 1946. (Original, 1936).

Freud, S. *The interpretation of dreams.* Standard Edition, Vols. 4 & 5. London: Hogarth Press, 1953. (Original, 1900).

Freud, S. *Fragment of an analysis of a case of hysteria.* Standard Edition, Vol. 7. London: Hogarth Press, 1953. (Original, 1905).

Freud, S. *Analysis of a phobia in a five-year-old boy.* Standard Edition, Vol. 10. London: Hogarth Press, 1955. (Original, 1909).

Freud, S. *The dynamics of transference.* Standard Edition, Vol. 12. London: Hogarth Press, 1955. (Original, 1912).

Freud, S. *The question of lay analysis.* Standard Edition, Vol. 20. London: Hogarth Press, 1959. (Original, 1926).

Freud, S. *Civilization and its discontents.* Standard Edition, Vol. 21. London: Hogarth Press, 1961. (Original, 1930).

Freud, S. *Analysis terminable and interminable.* Standard Edition, Vol. 23. London: Hogarth Press, 1964. (Original, 1937).

Fried, M. Effects of social change on mental health. *American Journal of Orthopsychiatry,* 1964, *34,* 3–28. (a)

Fried, M. Social problems and psychopathology. In L. J. Duhl (Ed.), *Urban American and the planning of mental health services* (Rev. ed.). New York: Group for the Advancement of Psychiatry, 1964. (b)

Friedman, H. Perceptual regression in schizophrenia: An hypothesis suggested by the use of the Rorschach test. *Journal of Genetic Psychology,* 1952, *81,* 63–98.

Friedman, H. Perceptual regression in schizophrenia. An hypothesis suggested by the use of the Rorschach test. *Journal of Projective Techniques,* 1953, *17,* 171–185.

Fromm-Reichmann, F. *Principles of intensive psychotherapy.* Chicago: University of Chicago Press, 1950.

Galagher, E. B., Sharaf, M. R., & Levinson, D. J. The influence of patient and therapist in determining the use of psychotherapy in a hospital setting. *Psychiatry,* 1965, *28,* 297–310.

Galdston, I. Speech before American Academy of Psychoanalysis. Reported in Roche Report, *Frontiers of Psychiatry,* April 15, 1971.

Galle, O. R., Gove, W. R., & McPherson, J. M. Population density and pathology: What are the relations for man? *Science,* 1972, *176,* 23–30.

Garfield, S., & Bergin, A. E. Personal therapy, outcome and some therapist variables. *Psychotherapy: Theory, Research and Practice,* 1971, *8,* 251–253.

Geertsma, R. H., & Mackie, J. B. (Eds.) *Studies in self-cognition: Techniques of videotape self-observation in the behavioral sciences.* Baltimore, Md.: Williams & Wilkins, 1969.

Ghiselli, E. E. *Theory of psychological measurement.* New York: McGraw-Hill, 1964.

Gibb, J. R. The role of the consultant. *Journal of Social Issues,* 1959, *15,* 1–4.

Gibb, J. R. Sensitivity training as a medium for personal growth and improved interpersonal relationships. *Interpersonal Development* 1970, *1,* 6–31.

Gibb, J. R. The effects of human relations training. In A. E. Bergin & S. L. Garfield, *Handbook of psychotherapy and behavior change: An empirical analysis.* New York: Wiley, 1971.

Gibb, J. R., & Lippitt, R. (Issue editors). Consulting with groups and organizations. *Journal of Social Issues,* 1959, *15,* 1–76.

Gilberstadt, H., & Duker, J. *A handbook for clinical and actuarial MMPI interpretation.* Philadelphia: Saunders, 1965.

Gilbert, D. C., & Levinson, D. J. Ideology, personality, and institutional policy in the mental hospital. *Journal of Abnormal and Social Psychology,* 1956, *53,* 263–271.

Gill, M. M. (Ed.) *The collected papers of David Rapaport.* New York: Basic Books, 1967.

Gill, M. M., Newman, R., & Redlich, F. C. *The initial interview in psychiatric practice.* New York: International Universities Press, 1954.

Glass, A. J. Military psychiatry. In A. Deutsch (Ed.), *The encyclopedia of mental health.* New York: Watts, 1963.

Glasscote, R. M., Sanders, D., Forstenzer, H. M., & Foley, A. R. (Eds.), with an introduction by William E. Barton. *The community mental health center: An analysis of existing models.* Washington, D.C.: American Psychiatric Association, 1964.

Glasscote, R. M., Sussex, J. N., Cumming, E., & Smith, L. *The community mental health center: An interim appraisal.* Washington, D.C.: American Psychiatric Association, 1969.

Glidewell, J. C. (Issue editor.) Mental health in the classroom. *Journal of Social Issues,* 1959, *15,* 1–65.

Glidewell, J. C., & Swallow, C. S. *The prevalence of maladjustment in elementary schools.* Chicago: University of Chicago Press, 1968.

Goffman, E. *The presentation of self in everyday life.* Garden City, N.Y.: Doubleday, 1959.

Goffman, E. *Asylums: Essays on the social situation of mental patients and other inmates.* New York: Doubleday, 1961.

Goin, M. K., Yamamoto, J., & Silverman, J. Therapy congruent with class-linked expectation. *Archives of General Psychiatry,* 1965, *13,* 133–137.

Golann, S. E. *Coordinate index reference guide to community mental health.* New York: Behavioral Publications, 1969.

Golann, S. E., Brieter, D. E., & Magoon, T. M. A filmed interview applied to the evaluation of mental health counselors. *Psychotherapy: Theory, Research, Practice,* 1966, *3,* 21–24.

Goldberg, E. M., & Morrison, S. L. Schizophrenia and social class. *British Journal of Psychiatry,* 1963, *109,* 785–802.

Goldberg, L. R. Diagnosticians vs. diagnostic signs: The diagnosis of psychoses vs. neuroses from the MMPI. *Psychological Monographs,* 1965, *79* (9, Whole No. 602).

Goldberg, L. R. Seer over sign: The first "good" example? *Journal of Experimental Research in Personality,* 1968, *3,* 168–171.

Goldberg, L. R. Man versus model of man: A rationale, plus some evidence for a method of improving on clinical inferences. *Psychological Bulletin,* 1970, *73,* 422–432.

Goldberg, L. R., & Slovic, P. Importance of test item content: An analysis of a corollary of the deviation hypothesis. *Journal of Counseling Psychology,* 1967, *14,* 462–472.

Golden, M. Some effects of combining psychological tests on clinical inferences. *Journal of Consulting Psychology,* 1964, *28,* 440–446.

Goldfarb, W. Emotional and intellectual consequences of psychologic deprivation in infancy. In P. Hoch & J. Zubin (Eds.), *Psychopathology of childhood*. New York: Grune & Stratton 1955.

Goldfried, M. R., & Kent, R. N. Traditional versus behavioral assessment: A comparison of methodological and theoretical assumptions. *Psychological Bulletin*, 1972, *77*, 409–420.

Goldfried, M. R., Stricker, G., & Weiner, I. B. *Rorschach handbook of clinical and research applications*. Englewood Cliffs, N.J.: Prentice-Hall, 1971.

Goldhamer, H., & Marshall, A. *Psychosis and civilization*. Glencoe, Ill.: Free Press, 1953.

Goldschmid, M. L., Stein, D. D., Weissman, H. N., & Sorrells, J. A survey of the training and practices of clinical psychologists. *The Clinical Psychologist*, 1969, *12*, 89–107.

Goldstein, A. P. *Therapist-patient expectancies in psychotherapy*. New York: Pergamon, 1962.

Goldstein, A. P. *Structured learning therapy: Toward a psychotherapy for the poor*. New York: Academic Press, 1973.

Goldstein, A. P., Heller, K., & Sechrest, L. B. *Psychotherapy and the psychology of behavior change*. New York: Wiley, 1966.

Goldstein, K. *The organism*. New York: American Book Company, 1939.

Goldston, S. E. (Ed.) *Concepts of community psychiatry: A framework for training*. (U.S. Public Health Service Publication No. 1319). Washington, D.C.: U.S. Government Printing Office, 1965.

Goldston, S. E. Mental health education in a community mental health center. *American Journal of Public Health*, 1968, *58*, 693–699.

Goodman, G. *Companionship therapy*. San Francisco: Jossey-Bass, 1972. (a)

Goodman, G. Systematic selection of psychotherapeutic talent: Group assessment of interpersonal traits. In S. E. Golann & C. Eisdorfer, *Handbook of community mental health*. New York: Appleton-Century-Crofts, 1972. (b)

Gottschalk, L. A. (Ed.) *Comparative psycholinguistic analysis of two psychotherapeutic interviews*. New York: International Universities Press, 1961.

Gottschalk, L. A., & Auerbach, A. H. (Eds.) *Methods of research in psychotherapy*. New York: Appleton-Century-Crofts, 1966.

Gottschalk, L. A., Fox, R. A., & Bates, D. E. A study of prediction and outcome in a mental health crisis clinic. *American Journal of Psychiatry*, 1973, *130*, 1107–1111.

Gottschalk, L. A., & Gleser, G. C. *The measurement of psychological states through the content analysis of verbal behavior*. Berkeley: University of California Press, 1969.

Gottschalk, L. A., & Pattison, E. Psychiatric perspectives on t-groups and the laboratory movement: An overview. *American Journal of Psychiatry*, 1969, *126*, 823–839.

Gough, H. G. A sociological theory of psychopathy. *American Journal of Sociology*, 1948, *53*, 359–366.

Gough, H. G. Clinical versus statistical prediction in psychology. In L. Postman (Ed.), *Psychology in the making: Histories of selected research problems*. New York: Knopf, 1962.

Gough, H. G. *California psychological inventory: manual*. Palo Alto, Calif.: Consulting Psychologists Press, 1957 (Rev. 1964).

Gough, H. G. *Adjective check list manual*. Palo Alto, Calif.: Consulting Psychologists Press, 1965.

Gough, H. G. Conceptual analysis of psychological test scores and other diagnostic variables. *Journal of Abnormal Psychology*, 1965, *70*, 294–302.

Gough, H. G. Some reflections on the meaning of psychodiagnosis. *American Psychologist*, 1971, *26*, 160–167.

Gough, H. G., & Petersen, D. R. The identification and measurement of predispositional factors in crime and delinquency. *Journal of Consulting Psychology*, 1952, *16*, 207–212.

Gould, R. E. Dr. Strangeclass: Or how I stopped worrying about the theory and began treating the blue-collar worker. *American Journal of Orthopsychiatry*, 1967, *37*, 78–86.

Greenblatt, M., Levinson, D. J., & Williams, R. H. (Eds.). *The patient and the mental hospital*. New York: Free Press of Glencoe, 1957.

Greenblatt, M., York, R., & Brown, E. L. *From custodial to therapeutic care in mental hospitals.* New York: Russell Sage, 1955.

Greenson, R. R. *The technique and practice of psychoanalysis.* Vol. I. New York: International Universities Press, 1967.

Greenspoon, J. The reinforcing effect of two spoken sounds on the frequency of two responses. *American Journal of Psychology,* 1955, *68,* 409–416.

Greist, J. H., Klein, M. H., & Van Cura, L. J. A computer interview for psychiatric patient target symptoms. *Archives of General Psychiatry,* 1973, *29,* 247–253.

Grinker, R. R., Sr. (Ed.). *Toward a unified theory of human behavior.* New York: Basic Books, 1956.

Grinker, R. R., Sr., MacGregor, H., Selan, K., Klein, A., & Kohrman, J. *Psychiatric social work: A transactional case book.* New York: Basic Books, 1961.

Grinker, R. R., Sr., Miller, J., Sabshin, M., Nunn, R., & Nunnally, J. C. *The phenomena of depressions.* New York: Hoeber, 1961.

Grinker, R. R., Sr., Werbel, B., & Drye, R. *The borderline syndrome: A behavioral study of ego functions.* New York: Basic Books, 1968.

Grob, G. H. *The state and the mentally ill: A history of Worcester State Hospital.* Chapel Hill, N.C.: University of North Carolina Press, 1966.

Grosser, C. Manpower development programs. In C. Grosser, W. E. Henry, & J. G. Kelly (Eds.), *Non-professionals in the human services.* San Francisco: Jossey-Bass, 1969.

Grosser, C., Henry, W. E., & Kelly, J. G. (Eds.). *Non-professionals in the human services.* San Francisco: Jossey-Bass, 1969.

Group for the Advancement of Psychiatry. Reports in psychotherapy: Initial interviews. In Group for the Advancement of Psychiatry, *Clinical Psychiatry.* New York: Group for the Advancement of Psychiatry, 1967.

Group for the Advancement of Psychiatry. *The field of family therapy.* (Report No. 78.) New York: Group for the Advancement of Psychiatry, 1970.

Gruenberg, E. M. The social breakdown syndrome—some origins. *American Journal of Psychiatry,* 1967, *123,* 1481–1489.

Gruenberg, E. M. Mental disorders: epidemiology. In *International Encyclopedia of the Social Sciences.* Vol. 10. New York: Macmillan and The Free Press, 1968.

Guerney, B. G., Jr. Filial therapy: Description and rationale. *Journal of Consulting Psychology,* 1964, *28,* 304–310.

Guerney, B. G., Jr. (Ed.). *Psychotherapeutic agents: New roles for non-professionals, parents, and teachers.* New York: Holt, Rinehart & Winston, 1966.

Guertin, W. H., Frank, G. H., & Rabin, A. I. Research with the Wechsler-Bellevue Intelligence Scale: 1950–1955. *Psychological Bulletin,* 1956, *53,* 235–257.

Guertin, W. H., Rabin, A. I., Frank, G. H., & Ladd, C. E. Research with the Wechsler Intelligence Scales for adults: 1955–1960. *Psychological Bulletin,* 1962, *59,* 1–26.

Guertin, W. H., Ladd, C. E., Frank, G. H., Rabin, E. I., & Hiester, O. S. Research with the Wechsler Intelligence Scales for adults: 1960–1965. *Psychological Bulletin,* 1969, *72,* 385–409.

Guilford, J. P. *Personality.* New York: McGraw-Hill, 1959.

Guilford, J. P., & Zimmerman, W. S. *The Guilford-Zimmerman Temperament Survey: Manual of instructions and interpretations.* Beverly Hills, Calif.: Sheridan Supply Company, 1949.

Gurin, G., Veroff, J., & Feld, S. *Americans view their mental health.* New York: Basic Books, 1960.

Haan, N. A proposed model of ego functioning: Coping and defense mechanisms in relationship to IQ change. *Psychological Monographs,* 1963, 77 (8 Whole No. 571).

Haan, N. A tripartite model of ego functioning values and clinical and research applications. *The Journal of Nervous and Mental Disease,* 1969, *148,* 14–30.

Haase, W. The role of socio-economic class in examiner bias. In F. Riessman, J. Cohen, & A. Pearl (Eds.), *Mental health of the poor.* New York: Free Press, 1964.

Haggard, E. A., Hicken, J. R., & Isaacs, K. S. Some effects of recording and filming on the psychotherapeutic process. *Psychiatry,* 1965, *28,* 169–191.

Haley, J. *Strategies of psychotherapy.* New York: Grune & Stratton, 1963.

Haley, J. *Changing families: A family therapy reader.* New York: Grune & Stratton, 1971.

Haley, J., & Hoffman, L. (Eds.) *Techniques of family therapy.* New York: Basic Books, 1967.

Hall, C. S., & Van De Castle, R. L. *The content analysis of dreams.* New York: Appleton-Century-Crofts, 1966.

Hall, E. T. *The silent language.* Garden City, N.Y.: Doubleday, 1959.

Hall, E. T. *The hidden dimension.* Garden City, N.Y.: Doubleday, 1966.

Halleck, S. L. Community psychiatry: Some troubling questions. In L. M. Roberts, S. L. Halleck, & M. B. Loeb (Eds.), *Community psychiatry.* Garden City, N.Y.: Doubleday, Anchor Books, 1969.

Hallock, A. C. K., & Vaughan, W. T. Community organization: A dynamic component of community mental health practice. *American Journal of Orthopsychiatry,* 1956, *26,* 691–706.

Hardy, K. R. Social origins of American scientists and scholars. *Science,* 1974, *185,* 497–506.

Harper, R. A. *Psychoanalysis and psychotherapy: 36 systems.* Englewood Cliffs, N.J.: Prentice-Hall, 1959.

Harris, R. E. Discussant's remarks. In M. M. Katz, J. O. Cole, & W. E. Barton (Eds.), *The role and methodology of classification in psychiatry and psychopathology.* Washington, D.C.: U.S. Government Printing Office, 1968.

Harris, T. *I'm O.K., you're O.K.: A practical guide to transactional analysis.* New York: Harper & Row, 1967.

Harrison, R. Thematic apperceptive methods. In B. B. Wolman (Ed.), *Handbook of clinical psychology.* New York: Wiley, 1965.

Hartmann, H. Psychoanalysis and the concept of health. *International Journal of Psychoanalysis,* 1939, 20, 308–321.

Harway, N. I., Dittmann, A. T., Raush, H. L., Bordin, E. S., & Rigler, D. The measurement of depth of interpretation. *Journal of Consulting Psychology,* 1955, *19,* 247–253.

Hathaway, S. R. A study of human behavior: The clinical psychologist. *American Psychologist,* 1958, *13,* 255–265.

Hathaway, S. R. MMPI: Professional use by professional people. *American Psychologist,* 1964, *19,* 204–210.

Hathaway, S. R., & McKinley, J. C. A multiphasic personality schedule (Minnesota): I. Construction of the schedule. *Journal of Psychology,* 1940, *10,* 249–254.

Hathaway, S. R., & McKinley, J. C. *Minnesota Multiphasic Personality Inventory manual.* New York: Psychological Corporation, 1951.

Hathaway, S. R., & Meehl, P. E. *An atlas for the clinical use of the MMPI.* Minneapolis: University of Minnesota Press, 1951.

Hathaway, S. R., & Monachesi, E. D. *An atlas of juvenile MMPI profiles.* Minneapolis: University of Minnesota Press, 1961.

Haylett, C. H., & Rapoport, L. Mental health consultation. In L. Bellak (Ed.), *Handbook of community psychiatry.* New York: Grune & Stratton, 1964.

Hediger, H. *Wild animals in captivity.* London: Butterworth, 1950.

Hediger, H. *Studies of the psychology and behavior of captured animals in zoos and circuses.* London: Butterworth, 1955.

Heider, F. *The psychology of interpersonal relations.* New York: Wiley, 1958.

Heider, F., & Simmel, M. An experimental study of apparent behavior. *American Journal of Psychology,* 1944, 57, 243–259.

Heilig, S. M., Farberow, N. L., & Litman, R. E. The role of non-professional volunteers in a suicide prevention center. *Community Mental Health Journal,* 1968, 4, 287–295.

Heine, R. W., & Trosman, H. Initial expectations of the doctor-patient interaction as a factor in continuance in psychotherapy. *Psychiatry,* 1960, *23,* 275–278.

Heller, K., & Goldstein, A. P. Client dependency and therapist expectancy as relationship maintaining variables in psychotherapy. *Journal of Consulting Psychology,* 1961, *25,* 371–375.

Henry, W. E. *The analysis of fantasy.* New York: Wiley, 1956.

Henry, W. E., & Shlien, J. M. Affective complexity and psychotherapy: Some comparisons of time-limited and unlimited treatment. *Journal of Projective Techniques,* 1958, *22,* 153–162.

Henry, W. E., Sims, J. H., & Spray, S. L. *The fifth profession: Becoming a psychotherapist.* San Francisco: Jossey-Bass, 1971.

Hereford, C. F. *Changing parental attitudes through group discussion.* Austin: University of Texas Press, 1963.

Hersch, C. The discontent explosion in mental health. *American Psychologist,* 1968, *23,* 497–506.

Hersch, C. From mental health to social action: Clinical psychology in historical perspective. *American Psychologist,* 1969, *24,* 909–916.

Hess, E. *Imprinting in birds.* Science, 1964, *146,* 1128–1139.

Hilgard, E. R., Riecken, H. R., & Viederman, S. *The behavioral and social sciences: Outlook and needs.* New York: Prentice-Hall, 1969.

Hill, S. R., Goetz, F. C., Fox, H. M., Murawski, B. T., Krakauer, L. J., Reifenstein, R. W., Gray, S. J., Reddy, W. J., Headberg, S. E., St. Marc, J. R., & Thorn, G. W. Studies on adrenocortical and psychological response to stress in man. *AMA Archives of Internal Medicine,* 1956, *97,* 269–298.

Hobbs, N. Mental health's third revolution. *American Journal of Orthopsychiatry,* 1964, *34,* 1–20.

Hoch, E., Ross, A. O., & Winder, C. L. (Eds.). *Professional preparation of clinical psychologists.* Washington, D.C.: American Psychological Association, 1966.

Hoehn-Saric, R., Frank, J. D., Imber, S. D., Nash, E. H., Jr., Stone, A. R., & Battle, C. C. Systematic preparation of patients for psychotherapy: I. Effects on therapy behavior and outcome. *Journal of Psychiatric Research,* 1964, *2,* 267–281.

Hoffman, P. J. The paramorphic representation of clinical judgment. *Psychological Bulletin,* 1960, *57,* 116–131.

Hoffman, R. S. The varieties of psychotherapeutic experience. *Journal of Irreproducible Results,* 1973, *19,* 76–77.

Hollingshead, A. B., & Redlich, F. C. Schizophrenia and social structure. *American Journal of Psychiatry,* 1954, *110,* 695–701.

Hollingshead, A. B., & Redlich, F. C. *Social class and mental illness: A community study.* New York: Wiley, 1958.

Holt, R. R. Formal aspects of the TAT: A neglected resource. *Journal of Projective Techniques,* 1958, *22,* 163–172.

Holt, R. R. Individuality and generalization in the psychology of personality. *Journal of Personality,* 1962, *30,* 377–404.

Holt, R. R. Diagnostic testing: Present status and future prospects. *Journal of Nervous and Mental Disease,* 1967, *144,* 444–465.

Holt, R. R. Editor's foreword. In R. R. Holt (Ed.), revised edition of D. Rapaport, M. M. Gill, & R. Schafer (Eds.), *Diagnostic psychological testing.* New York: International Universities Press, 1968.

Holt, R. R. *Assessing personality.* New York: Harcourt, Brace, Jovanovich, 1969.

Holt, R. R. Yet another look at clinical and statistical prediction: or is clinical psychology worthwhile? *American Psychologist,* 1970, *25,* 337–349.

Holt, R. R., Summary and prospect: The dawn of a new profession. In R. R. Holt (Ed.), *New horizon for psychotherapy.* New York: International Universities Press, 1971.

Holt, R. R., & Havel, J. A method for assessing primary and secondary process in the

Rorschach. In M. A. Rickers-Ovsiankiana (Ed.), *Rorschach psychology.* New York: Wiley, 1960.

Holt, R. R., & Luborsky, L. *Personality patterns of psychiatrists.* Vols. I & II. New York: Basic Books, 1958.

Holtzman, W. H. Can the computer supplant the clinician? *Journal of Clinical Psychology,* 1960, *16,* 119–122.

Holzberg, J. D. Reliability re-examined. In M. A. Rickers-Ovsiankiana (Ed.), *Rorschach psychology.* New York: Wiley, 1960.

Holzberg, J. D., Knapp, R. H., & Turner, J. L. College students as companions to the mentally ill. In E. L. Cowen, E. A. Gardner, & M. Zax (Eds.), *Emergent approaches to mental health problems.* New York: Appleton-Century-Crofts, 1967.

Horwitz, L. *Clinical prediction in psychotherapy.* New York: Jason Aronson, 1974.

Howard, K. I., & Orlinsky, D. E. Psychotherapeutic processes. *Annual Review of Psychology,* 1972, *23,* 615–668.

Huber, J. T. *Report writing in psychology and psychiatry.* New York: Harper & Row, 1961.

Hughes, R. The effects of sex, age, race and social history of therapist and client on psychotherapy outcome. Unpublished doctoral dissertation, University of California, Berkeley, 1972.

Hutcheson, B. R., & Krause, E. A. Systems analysis and mental health services. *Community Mental Health Journal,* 1969, 5, 29–45.

Hutt, M. L. A clinical study of "consecutive" and "adaptive" testing with the revised Stanford-Binet. *Journal of Consulting Psychology,* 1947, *11,* 93–103.

Hyman, R., & Breger, L. Discussion of H. J. Eysenck, the effects of psychotherapy. *International Journal of Psychiatry,* 1965, *1,* 317–322.

Hyman, H. H., Cobb, W. J., Feldman, J. J., Hart, C. W., & Stember, G. H. *Interviewing in social research.* Chicago: University of Chicago Press, 1954.

Imber, S. D., Gliedman, L. H., Nash, E. H., Jr., & Stone, A. R. Suggestibility, social class and the acceptance of psychotherapy. *Journal of Clinical Psychology,* 1956, *12,* 341–344.

Imber, S. D., Nash, E. H., Jr., & Stone, A. R. Social class and duration of psychotherapy. *Journal of Clinical Psychology,* 1955, *11,* 281–284.

Isaacs, K. S., & Haggard, E. A. Some methods used in the study of affect in psychotherapy. In L. A. Gottschalk & A. H. Auerbach (Eds.), *Methods of research in psychotherapy.* New York: Appleton-Century-Crofts, 1966.

Iscoe, I., & Spielberger, C. E. (Eds.) *Community psychology: Perspectives in training and research.* New York: Appleton-Century-Crofts, 1970.

Ittelson, W. H., Proshansky, H. M., Rivlin, L. G., & Winkel, G. H. *An introduction to environmental psychology.* New York: Holt, Rinehart & Winston, 1974.

Jackson, D. D. The question of family homeostasis. *Psychiatric Quarterly Supplement,* 1959, *31,* 79–90.

Jackson, D. D., & Weakland, J. H. Conjoint family therapy: Some considerations on theory, technique, and results. *Psychiatry,* 1961, *24,* 30–45.

(Jackson, J. H.), Taylor, J. (Ed.) *Selected writings of John Hughlings Jackson.* London: Hodder & Stoughton, 1931. 2 vols.

Jacobson, E. *Progressive relaxation.* Chicago: University of Chicago Press, 1938.

Jahoda, M. *Current concepts of positive mental health.* New York: Basic Books, 1958.

Janis, I. L. Emotional inoculation: Theory and research on effects of preparatory communications. In *Psychoanalysis and the Social Sciences.* New York: International Universities Press, 1958. (a)

Janis, I. L. *Psychological stress.* New York: Wiley, 1958. (b)

Jecker, J. D., Maccoby, N., & Breitrose, H. S. Improving accuracy in interpreting non-verbal cues of comprehension. *Psychology in the Schools,* 1965, 2, 239–244.

Joint Commission on Mental Illness and Health. *Action for mental health.* New York: Basic Books, 1961.
Jones, E. E. Social class and psychotherapy: A critical review of the research. *Psychiatry,* 1974, 37, 307–320.
Jones, M. *The therapeutic community.* New York: Basic Books, 1953.
Jones, M. Intra and extramural community psychiatry. *American Journal of Psychiatry,* 1961, *117,* 784–787.
Jones, M. *Social psychiatry in practice: The idea of the therapeutic community.* Middlesex, England: Penguin, 1968.
Jones, M. C. The elimination of children's fears. *Journal of Experimental Psychology,* 1924, 7, 383–390.
Jung, C. G. *Psychological types.* New York: Harcourt, 1933. (Original German, 1921.)

Kadushin, C. *Why people go to psychiatrists.* New York: Atherton, 1969.
Kagan, J., & Mussen, P. H. Dependency themes on the TAT and group conformity. *Journal of Consulting Psychology,* 1956, 20, 29–32.
Kahn, R. L. Implications of organizational research for community mental health. In J. W. Carter, Jr. (Ed.), *Research contributions from psychology to community mental health.* New York: Behavioral Publications, 1968.
Kahn, R. L., & Cannell, C. F. *The dynamics of interviewing.* New York: Wiley, 1957.
Kahn, R. L., Pollack, M., & Fink, M. Social factors in the selection of therapy in a voluntary mental hospital. *Journal of the Hillside Hospital,* 1957, 6, 216–228.
Kalis, B. L., Harris, M. R., Prestwood, A. R., & Freeman, E. H. Precipitating stress as a focus in psychotherapy. *Archives of General Psychiatry,* 1961, 5, 219–226.
Kanfer, F. H., & Phillips, J. S. *Learning foundations of behavior therapy.* New York: Wiley, 1970.
Kanfer, F. H., & Saslow, G. Behavioral analysis: An alternative to diagnostic classification. *Archives of General Psychiatry,* 1965, *12,* 529–538.
Kaplan, D. M., & Mason, E. A. Maternal reactions to premature birth viewed as an acute emotional disorder. *American Journal of Orthopsychiatry,* 1960, 30, 539–552.
Kaplan, S., & Roman, M. *Organization and delivery of mental health services in the ghetto: The Lincoln Hospital experience.* New York: Praeger, 1973.
Keen, E. *Three faces of being: Toward an existential clinical psychology.* New York: Appleton-Century-Crofts, 1970.
Keith-Spiegel, P., & Spiegel, D. E. Perceived helpfulness of others as a function of compatible intelligence levels. *Journal of Counseling Psychology,* 1967, *14,* 61–62.
Kelley, H. H. The warm-cold variable in first impressions of people. *Journal of Personality,* 1950, *18,* 431–439.
Kelly, E. L. Clinical psychology: The postwar decade. In W. Dennis (Ed.), *Current trends in psychological theory.* Pittsburgh: University of Pittsburgh Press, 1961.
Kelly, E. L., & Fiske, D. W. *The prediction of performance in clinical psychology.* Ann Arbor: University of Michigan Press, 1951.
Kelly, E. L., & Goldberg, L. R. Correlates of later performance and specialization in psychology: Follow up study of the trainees assessed in the VA Selection Research Project. *Psychological Monographs,* 1959, 73, (12, Whole No. 482).
Kelly, G. A. *The psychology of personal constructs.* New York: Norton, 1955 (2 vols).
Kelly, G. A. The theory and technique of assessment. *Annual Review of Psychology,* 1958, 9, 323–352.
Kelly, J. G. Ecological constraints on mental health services. *American Psychologist,* 1966, *21,* 535–539.
Kelly, J. G. Toward an ecological conception of preventive interventions. In J. W. Carter (Ed.), *Research contributions from psychology to community mental health.* New York: Behavioral Publications, 1968.
Kelly, J. G. Naturalistic observations in contrasting social environments. In E. P. Willems &

H. L. Raush (Eds.), *Naturalistic viewpoints in psychological research.* New York: Holt, Rinehart & Winston, 1969.

Kelman, H. C. The problem of deception in social psychological experiments. *Psychological Bulletin,* 1967, *67,* 1–11.

Keniston, K. *The uncommitted: Alienated youth in American society.* New York: Harcourt, Brace, Jovanovich, 1965.

Keniston, K. *Young radicals: Notes on committed youth.* New York: Harcourt, Brace, Jovanovich, 1968.

Kent, G. H., & Rosanoff, A. J. A study of association in insanity. *American Journal of Insanity,* 1910, *67,* 37–96, 317–390.

Kernberg, O. F., Burstein, E. D., Coyne, L., Appelbaum, A., Horwitz, L., & Voth, H. Psychotherapy and psychoanalysis: Final report of the Menninger Foundation's Psychotherapy Research Project. *Bulletin of the Menninger Clinic,* 1972, *36,* iii–275.

Kiesler, D. J. Some myths of psychotherapy research and the search for a paradigm. *Psychological Bulletin,* 1966, *65,* 110–136.

Kiesler, D. J. Experimental designs in psychotherapy research. In A. E. Bergin & S. L. Garfield (Eds.), *Handbook of psychotherapy and behavior change: An empirical analysis.* New York: Wiley, 1971.

Kiesler, D. J. *The process of psychotherapy.* Chicago: Aldine, 1973.

Klein, G. S. The clinical perspective for personality research. *Journal of Abnormal and Social Psychology,* 1949, *44,* 42–49.

Klein, G. S. Credo for a "clinical psychologist:" A personal reflection. *Bulletin of the Menninger Clinic,* 1963, *27,* 61–73.

Klein, G. S. Is psychoanalysis relevant? Paper presented at the meeting of the American Psychological Association, Miami, 1970.

Klein, M. H., Mathieu, P. L., Gendlin, E. T., & Kiesler, D. J. *The experiencing scale: A research and training manual.* Madison: Wisconsin Psychiatric Institute, Bureau of Audio-Visual Instruction, 1970. 2 vols.

Klein, W. L. The training of human service aides. In E. L. Cowen, E. A. Gardner, & M. Zax (Eds.), *Emergent approaches to mental health problems.* New York: Appleton-Century-Crofts, 1967.

Kleinmuntz, B. MMPI decision rules for the identification of college maladjustment: A digital computer approach. *Psychological Monographs,* 1963, *77,* 14, (Whole No. 577).

Kleinmuntz, B. *Personality measurements: An introduction.* Homewood, Ill.: Dorsey, 1967.

Kleinmuntz, B. (Ed.) *Clinical information processing by computer.* New York: Holt, Rinehart & Winston, 1969.

Kleinmuntz, B. Personality test interpretation by computer and clinician in J. N. Butcher (Ed.). *MMPI: Research developments and clinical applications.* New York: McGraw-Hill, 1969.

Klineberg, O. *Social psychology.* New York: Holt, 1940.

Klopfer, B., & Davidson, H. H. *The Rorschach technique: An introductory manual.* New York: Harcourt, Brace & World, 1942.

Kluckhohn, C., & Murray, H. A. Personality formation: The determinants. In C. Kluckhohn, H. A. Murray, & D. M. Schneider (Eds.), *Personality in nature, society, and culture* (2nd ed.). New York: Knopf, 1953.

Koch, S. Epilogue. In S. Koch (Ed.), *Psychology, A study of a science.* Vol. 5. New York: McGraw-Hill, 1959.

Koch, S. Psychology can not be a coherent science. *Psychology Today,* 1969, *3,* 14, 64–68.

Koch, S. The image of man implicit in encounter group theory. *Journal of Humanistic Psychology,* 1971, *11,* 109–128.

Koffka, K. *Principles of gestalt psychology.* New York: Harcourt, Brace, 1935.

Kohlberg, L. Stage and sequence: Cognitive-developmental approach to socialization. In

D. A. Goslin (Ed.), *Handbook of socialization theory and research.* Chicago: Rand McNally, 1969.

Korchin, S. J. Form perception and ego functioning. In M. A. Rickers-Ovsiankiana (Ed.), *Rorschach psychology.* New York: Wiley, 1960.

Korchin, S. J. A stout affection. (Review of R. W. White (Ed.) *The study of lives: Essays on personality in honor of Henry A. Murray.* New York: Atherton, 1963). *Contemporary Psychology,* 1964, 9, 193–196.

Korchin, S. J. Some psychological determinants of stress behavior. In S. Z. Klausner (Ed.), *The quest for self-control.* New York: Free Press, 1965.

Korchin, S. J., & Heath, H. Somatic experience in the anxiety state: Some sex and personality correlates of "autonomic feedback." *Journal of Consulting Psychology,* 1961, 25, 398–404.

Korchin, S. J., Mitchell, H. E., & Meltzoff, J. A critical evaluation of the Thompson Thematic Apperception Test. *Journal of Projective Techniques,* 1950, *14,* 445–452.

Korman, A. K. The prediction of managerial performance: A review. *Personnel Psychology,* 1968, *21,* 295–322.

Kostlan, A. A method for the empirical study of psychodiagnosis. *Journal of Consulting Psychology,* 1954, *18,* 83–88.

Kramer, B. M. *Day hospital: A study of partial hospitalization in psychiatry.* New York: Grune & Stratton, 1962.

Kramer, M. Epidimiology, biostatistics, and mental health planning. In R. R. Monroe, G. D. Klee, & E. G. Brody (Eds.), *Psychiatric epidemiology and mental health planning.* (Psychiatric Research Report No. 22). Washington, D.C.: American Psychiatric Association, 1967.

Krasner, L. The therapist as a social reinforcement machine. In H. H. Strupp & L. Luborsky (Eds.), *Research in psychotherapy. Vol. II.* Washington, D.C.: American Psychological Association, 1962.

Krasner, L. Verbal conditioning and psychotherapy. In L. Krasner & L. P. Ullman (Eds.), *Research in behavior modification.* New York: Holt, Rinehart & Winston, 1965.

Krasner, L. The operant approach in behavior therapy. In A. E. Bergin & S. L. Garfield (Eds.), *Handbook of psychotherapy and behavior change: An empirical analysis.* New York: Wiley, 1971. (a)

Krasner, L. Behavior therapy. *Annual Review of Psychology,* 1971, 22, 483–532. (b)

Krasner, L., & Kornreich, M. Psychosomatic illness and projective tests. *Journal of Projective Techniques,* 1954, *18,* 353–367.

Krasner, L., & Ullmann, L. P. (Eds.). *Research in behavior modification.* New York: Holt, 1965.

Krech, D. Behavior and neurophysiology. In M. H. Marx (Ed.), *Theories in contemporary psychology.* New York: Macmillan, 1964.

Krech, D., Crutchfield, R. S., & Livson, N. *Elements of psychology* (3rd ed.). New York: Knopf, 1974.

Kretschmer, E. *Physique and character.* New York: Harcourt, Brace, 1925.

Kriedt, P. H. Vocational interests of psychologists. *Journal of Applied Psychology,* 1949, 33, 482–488.

Kris, E. On preconscious mental processes. *Psychoanalytic Quarterly,* 1950, *19,* 540–560.

Kroeber, T. C. The coping functions of the ego mechanisms. In R. W. White (Ed.), *The study of lives.* New York: Atherton, 1963.

Kubie, L. S. The fundamental nature of the distinction between normality and neurosis. *Psychoanalytic Quarterly,* 1954, 23, 164–204.

Kubie, L. S. Pitfalls of community psychiatry. *Archives of General Psychiatry,* 1968, *18,* 257–266.

Kushner, M. Faradic aversive controls in clinical practice. In C. Neuringer & J. L. Michael (Eds.), *Behavior modification in clinical psychology.* New York: Appleton-Century-Crofts, 1970.

Lacey, J. I. Psychophysiological approaches to the evaluation of psychotherapeutic process and outcome. In E. A. Rubinstein & M. B. Parloff (Eds.), *Research in psychotherapy. Vol. 1.* Washington, D.C.: American Psychological Association, 1959.

Lacey, J. I., Bateman, D. E., & Van Lehn, R. Autonomic response specificity and Rorschach color responses. *Psychosomatic Medicine,* 1952, *14,* 256–260.

Landis, C. A. A statistical evaluation of psychotherapeutic methods. In L. E. Hinsie (Ed.), *Concepts and problems of psychotherapy.* New York: Columbia University Press, 1937.

Lang, P. J. The application of psychophysiological methods to the study of psychotherapy and behavior modification. In A. E. Bergin & S. L. Garfield (Eds.), *Handbook of psychotherapy and behavior change.* New York: Wiley, 1971.

Langer, J. *Theories of development.* New York: Holt, Rinehart & Winston, 1969.

Langner, T., & Michael, S. *Life stress and mental health.* New York: Free Press of Glencoe, 1963.

Lanyon, R. I., & Goodstein, L. D. *Personality assessment.* New York: Wiley, 1971.

Laqueur, H. P. Mechanisms of change in multiple family therapy. In C. J. Sager & H. S. Kaplan, *Progress in group and family therapy.* New York: Brunner/Mazel, 1972.

Lazarus, A. A. Crucial procedural factors in desensitization therapy. *Behaviour Research and Therapy,* 1964, 2, 65–70.

Lazarus, A. A. *Behavior therapy and beyond.* New York: McGraw-Hill, 1971.

Lazarus, A. A., & Davidson, G. C. Clinical innovation in research and practice. In A. E. Bergin & S. L. Garfield, *Handbook of psychotherapy and behavior change: An empirical analysis.* New York: Wiley, 1971.

Lazarus, R. S. *Psychological stress and the coping process.* New York: McGraw-Hill, 1966.

Leary, T., & Gill, M. The dimensions and a measure of the process of psychotherapy: A system for the analysis of the content of clinical evaluations and patient-therapist verbalizations. In E. A. Rubinstein & M. B. Parloff (Eds.), *Research in psychotherapy.* Washington, D.C.: American Psychological Association, 1959.

Leavitt, H. J., & Bass, P. M. Organizational psychology. *Annual Review of Psychology,* 1964, *15,* 371–398.

Lee, S. D. Social class bias in the diagnosis of mental illness. *Dissertation Abstracts,* 1968, *28,* 4758–4759.

Leifer, R. *In the name of mental health: The social functions of psychiatry.* New York: Science Books, 1969.

Leifer, R. The medical model as ideology. *International Journal of Psychiatry,* 1970, 9, 13–21.

Leighton, A. H. *My name is legion.* New York: Basic Books, 1959.

Leighton, D. C., Harding, J. S., Macklin, D. B., Macmillan, A. M., & Leighton, A. H. *The character of danger.* New York: Basic Books, 1963.

Leitenberg, H. Use of a single case methodology in psychotherapy research. *Journal of Abnormal Psychology,* 1973, 82, 87–101.

Lemkau, P. V. The planning project for Columbia. In M. F. Shore & F. V. Mannino (Eds.). *Mental health and the community: Problems, programs, and strategies.* New York: Behavioral Publications, 1969.

Lemkau, P. V., & Crocetti, G. M. An urban population's opinion and knowledge about mental illness. *American Journal of Psychiatry,* 1962, *118,* 692–700.

Lennard, H. L., & Bernstein, A. *The anatomy of psychotherapy: Systems of communication and expectation.* New York: Columbia University Press, 1960.

Lennard, H. L., & Bernstein, A. *Pattern in human interaction.* San Francisco: Jossey-Bass, 1969.

Lennard, H. L., Epstein, L. J., Bernstein, A., & Ransom, D. C. *Mystification and drug misuse: Hazards in using psychoactive drugs.* San Francisco: Jossey-Bass, 1971.

Levine, D. When to test: The social context of psychological testing. In A. I. Rabin (Ed.), *Projective techniques in personality assessment.* New York: Springer, 1968.

Levine, M. Some postulates of community psychology practice. In *The psycho-educational clinic.* Community Mental Health Monograph, Department of Mental Health, Commonwealth of Massachusetts, 1969, *4,* 209–224.

Levine, M., & Graziano, A. M. Intervention programs in elementary schools. In S. E. Golann & C. Eisdorfer (Eds.), *Handbook of community mental health.* New York: Appleton-Century-Crofts, 1972.

Levine, M., & Levine, A. *A social history of helping services.* New York: Appleton-Century-Crofts, 1970.

Levine, M., & Spivack, G. *Rorschach index of repressive style.* Springfield, Ill.: Charles C. Thomas, 1965.

Levinson, B. M. Traditional Jewish cultural values and performance on the Wechsler tests. *Journal of Educational Psychology,* 1959, *50,* 177–181.

Levinson, B. M. The WAIS quotient of sub-cultural deviation. *Journal of Genetic Psychology,* 1963, *103,* 123–131.

Levinson, D. J., Sharaf, M. R., & Gilbert, D. C. Intraception: Evolution of a concept. In G. J. DiRenzo (Ed.), *Concepts, theory, and explanation in the behavioral sciences.* New York: Random House, 1966.

Levitsky, A., & Perls, F. S. The rules and games of Gestalt therapy. In J. Fagan & I. L. Sheperd (Eds.), *Gestalt therapy now.* Palo Alto, Calif.: Science and Behavior Books, 1970.

Levitt, E. E. Psychotherapy research and the expectation-reality discrepancy. *Psychotherapy: Theory, Research, and Practice,* 1966, *3,* 163–166.

Levy, L. H. *Psychological interpretation.* New York: Holt, Rinehart & Winston, 1963.

Levy, L. H., & Orr, T. B. The social psychology of Rorschach validity research. *Journal of Abnormal and Social Psychology,* 1959, *58,* 79–83.

Lewin, K. Environmental forces in child behavior and development. In C. Murchison (Ed.), *A handbook of child psychology.* Worcester, Mass.: Clark University Press, 1931.

Lewin, K., Lippitt, R., & White, R. K. Patterns of aggressive behavior in experimentally created "social climates." *Journal of Social Psychology,* 1939, *10,* 271–299.

Lewis, H. B. *Shame and guilt in neurosis.* New York: International Universities Press, 1971.

Lewisohn, P. M., Nichols, R. C., Pulos, L., Lomont, J. F., Nickel, H. J., & Siskind, G. The reliability and validity of quantified judgements from psychological tests. *Journal of Clinical Psychology,* 1963, *19,* 64–73.

Lichtenberg, P., Kohrman, R., & MacGregor, H. *Motivation for child psychiatry treatment.* New York: Russell & Russell, 1960.

Lichtenstein, E. Personality similarity and therapeutic success: A failure to replicate. *Journal of Consulting Psychology,* 1966, *30,* 282.

Lieberman, M. A., Yalom, I. D., & Miles, M. B. *Encounter groups: First facts.* New York: Basic Books, 1973.

Lieberman, R. P. Behavioral approaches to family and couples therapy. *American Journal of Orthopsychiatry,* 1970, *40,* 106–118.

Lief, H. I. Sub-professional training in mental health. *Archives of General Psychiatry,* 1966, *15,* 660–664.

Lin, Tsung-yi. Community mental health services: A world view. In R. H. Williams & L. D. Ozarin (Eds.). *Community mental health.* San Francisco: Jossey-Bass, 1968.

Lindemann, E. (Eds.). Symptamatology and management of acute grief. *American Journal of Psychiatry,* 1944, *101,* 141–148.

Lindemann, E. The meaning of crisis in individual and family living. *Teachers' College Record,* 1956, *57,* 310–315.

Lindzey, G. Thematic apperception test: Interpretative assumptions and related empirical evidence. *Psychological Bulletin,* 1952, *49,* 1–25.

Lindzey, G. *Projective techniques and cross-cultural research.* New York: Appleton-Century-Crofts, 1961.

Lindzey, G. Seer versus sign. *Journal of Experimental Research in Personality,* 1965, *1,* 17–26.

Lindzey, G., Bradford, J., Tejessy, C., & Davids, A. Thematic apperception test: An interpretive lexicon. *Journal of Clinical Psychology Monograph Supplement,* 1959, No. 12.

Lindzey, G., & Kalnins, D. Thematic apperception test: Some evidence bearing on the "hero assumption." *Journal of Abnormal and Social Psychology,* 1958, *57,* 76–83.

Lingoes, J. C. Review of the MMPI. In O. K. Buros (Ed.), *Sixth mental measurements yearbook.* Highland Park, N.J.: Gryphon Press, 1965.

Linton, R. *Culture and mental disorders.* Springfield, Ill.: Charles C Thomas, 1956.

Lippitt, R. Dimensions of the consultant's job. *Journal of Social Issues,* 1959, *15,* 5–12.

Lippitt, R., Watson, J., & Westley, B. *The dynamics of planned change.* New York: Harcourt, Brace, 1958.

Lippmann, W. *Public opinion.* New York: Harcourt, Brace, 1922.

Loevinger, J. Theories of ego development. In L. Breger (Ed.), *Clinical-cognitive psychology: Models and integrations.* Englewood Cliffs, N.J.: Prentice-Hall, 1969.

London, P. *The modes and morals of psychotherapy.* New York: Holt, Rinehart & Winston, 1964.

Lorr, M., & Klett, C. J. Cross-cultural comparison of psychotic syndromes. *Journal of Abnormal Psychology,* 1969, *74,* 531–543. (a)

Lorr, M., & Klett, C. J. Psychotic behavior types: A cross-cultural comparison. *Archives of General Psychiatry,* 1969, *20,* 592–597. (b)

Lorr, M., Klett, C. J., & Cave, R. Higher level psychotic syndromes. *Journal of Abnormal Psychology,* 1967, *72,* 74–77.

Lorr, M., Klett, C. J., & McNair, D. M. *Syndromes of psychosis.* New York: Macmillan, 1963.

Lourie, R. S. Child development counselors: lessons from their training and use. (U.S. Public Health Service Publication No. 1743). In *Mental Health Reports.* Washington, D.C.: U.S. Government Printing Office, 1968.

Louttit, C. M., & Browne, C. G. Psychometric instruments in psychological clinics. *Journal of Consulting Psychology,* 1947, *11,* 49–54.

Lovaas, O. I., Freitag, G., Gold, V. J., & Kassorla, I. C. Experimental studies in childhood schizophrenia: Analysis of self-destructive behavior. *Journal of Experimental Child Psychology,* 1965, *2,* 67–84.

Loveland, N. T., Singer, M. T., & Wynne, L. C. The family Rorschach: A new method for studying family interaction. *Family Process,* 1963, *2,* 187–215.

Lubin, B., & Lubin, A. W. Patterns of psychological services in the U.S.: 1959–1969. *Professional Psychology,* 1972, *3,* 63–65.

Lubin, B., Wallis, R. R., & Paine, C. Patterns of psychological test usage in the United States: 1935–1969. *Professional Psychology,* 1971, *2,* 70–74.

Luborsky, L. A note on Eysenck's article, "The effects of psychotherapy: An evaluation." *British Journal of Psychology,* 1954, *45,* 129–131.

Luborsky, L. Psychotherapy. *Annual Review of Psychology,* 1959, *10,* 317–344.

Luborsky, L. Another reply to Eysenck. *Psychological Bulletin,* 1972, *78,* 406–408.

Luborsky, L., Chandler, M., Auerbach, A. H., Cohen, J., & Bachrach, H. M. Factors influencing the outcome of psychotherapy: A review of quantitative research. *Psychological Bulletin,* 1971, *75,* 145–185.

Luborsky, L., Singer, B., & Luborsky, L. Comparative studies of psychotherapies: Is it true that "Everyone has won and all must have prizes"? *Archives of General Psychiatry,* 1975, *32,* 995–1008.

Lusted, L. B. *Introduction to medical decision making.* Springfield, Ill.: Charles C. Thomas, 1968.

Lynd, H. *On shame and the search for identity.* New York: Harcourt, Brace, 1958.

Macfarlane, J. W., & Tuddenham, R. D. Problems in the validation of projective techniques. In H. H. Anderson & G. L. Anderson (Eds.), *An introduction to projective techniques.* New York: Prentice-Hall, 1951.

MacGregor, R., Ritchie, A. M., Serrano, A. C., & Schuster, F. P. *Multiple impact therapy with families*. New York: McGraw-Hill, 1964.
MacKinnon, D. W. IPAR's contribution to the conceptualization and study of creativity. In I. A. Taylor & J. W. Getzells (Eds.), *Perspectives in creativity*. Chicago: Aldine, 1975.
MacKinnon, R. A., & Michels, R. *The psychiatric interview in clinical practice*. Philadelphia: W. B. Saunders, 1971.
MacLennan, B. W., Klein, W. L., Pearl, A., & Fishman, J. R. Training for new careers. *Community Mental Health Journal*, 1966, *2*, 135–141.
MacLeod, R. B. The phenomenological approach to social psychology. *Psychological Review*, 1947, *54*, 193–210.
MacMahon, B., & Pugh, T. F. *Epidimiology: Principles and methods*. Boston: Little, Brown & Company, 1970.
Magoon, T. M., & Golann, S. Nontraditionally trained women as mental health counselors/psychotherapists. *Personnel and Guidance Journal*, 1966, *44*, 788–793.
Mahl, G. F. Disturbances and silences in the patient's speech in psychotherapy. *Journal of Abnormal and Social Psychology*, 1956, *53*, 1–15.
Mahl, G. F. Gestures and body movements in interviews. In J. M. Shlien (Ed.), *Research in psychotherapy*. Vol. 3. Washington, D.C.: *American Psychological Association*, 1968.
Malan, D. H. *A study of brief psychotherapy*. Springfield, Ill.: Charles C. Thomas, 1963.
Malan, D. H. The outcome problem in psychotherapy research: A historical review. *Archives of General Psychiatry*, 1973, *29*, 719–729.
Malmo, R. B. Activation: A neuropsychological dimension. *Psychological Review*, 1959, *66*, 367–386.
Malzberg, B. Important statistical data about mental illness. In S. Arieti (Ed.), *American handbook of psychiatry*. Vol. I. New York: Basic Books, 1959.
Mann, J. *Encounter: A weekend with intimate strangers*. New York: Grossman, 1970.
Mannino, F. V., & Shore, M. F. Research in mental health consultation. In S. E. Golann & C. Eisdorfer (Eds.), *Handbook of community mental health*. New York: Appleton-Century-Crofts, 1972.
Marks, P. A., & Seeman, W. *An atlas for use with MMPI: Actuarial description of abnormal personality*. Baltimore: Williams & Wilkins, 1963.
Masling, J. The influence of situational and interpersonal variables in projective testing. *Psychological Bulletin*, 1960, *57*, 65–85.
Masling, J. Role-related behavior of the subject and psychologist and its effect upon psychological data. In D. Levine (Ed.), *Nebraska Symposium on Motivation*. Lincoln: University of Nebraska Press, 1966.
Maslow, A. H. *Motivation and personality*. New York: Harper, 1954.
Maslow, A. H. *Toward a psychology of being*. Princeton, N.J.: Van Nostrand, 1962. (2nd ed., 1968).
Maslow, A. H. Self-actualization and beyond. In J. F. T. Bugental (Ed.), *Challenges of humanistic psychology*. New York: McGraw-Hill, 1967.
Mason, B., & Ammons, R. B. Note on social class and the Thematic Apperception Test. *Perceptual and Motor Skills*, 1956, *6*, 88.
Masters, W. H., & Johnson, V. E. *Human sexual response*. Boston: Little, Brown, 1966.
Masters, W. H., & Johnson, V. E. *Human sexual inadequacy*. Boston: Little, Brown, 1970.
Matarazzo, J. D. The interview. In B. B. Wolman (Ed.), *Handbook of clinical psychology*. New York: McGraw-Hill, 1965. (a)
Matarazzo, J. D. A postdoctoral residency program in clinical psychology. *American Psychologist*, 1965, *20*, 432–439. (b)
Matarazzo, J. D. *Wechsler's measurement and appraisal of adult intelligence*. (5th and Enlarged Edition.) Baltimore: Williams & Wilkins, 1972.
Matarazzo, J. D., & Wiens, A. N. *The interview: Research on its anatomy and structure*. Chicago: Aldine, 1972.
May, P. R. A. For better or worse? Psychotherapy and variance change: A critical review of the literature. *Journal of Nervous and Mental Disease*, 1971, *152*, 184–192.

May, R. The origins and significance in the existential movement in psychology. In R. May, E. Angel, & H. F. Ellenberger (Eds.), *Existence: A new dimension in psychiatry and psychology.* New York: Basic Books, 1958.

May, R. The emergence of existential psychology. In R. May (Ed.), *Existential psychology.* New York: Random House, 1961.

May, R., Angel, E., Ellenberger, E., & Ellenberger, H. F. (Eds.). *Existence: A new dimension in psychiatry and psychology.* New York: Basic Books, 1958.

Mayman, M. Style, focus, language and content of an ideal psychological test report. *Journal of Projective Techniques,* 1959, *23,* 453–458.

Mayman, M., Schafer, R., & Rapaport, D. Interpretation of the Wechsler Bellevue Intelligence Scale and personality appraisal. In H. H. Anderson & G. L. Anderson (Eds.), *An introduction to projective techniques.* New York: Prentice-Hall, 1951.

McClelland, D. C. *The achieving society.* Princeton, N.J.: Van Nostrand, 1961.

McClelland, D. C., Atkinson, J. W., Clark, R. A., & Lowell, E. L. *The achievement motive.* New York: Appleton-Century-Crofts, 1953.

McGee, T. F. Some basic considerations in crisis intervention. *Community Mental Health Journal,* 1968, *4,* 319–325.

McNair, D. M., Callahan, D. M., & Lorr, M. Therapist "types" and patient response to psychotherapy. *Journal of Consulting Psychology,* 1962, *26,* 425–429.

McNair, D. M., Lorr, M., & Callahan, D. M. Patient and therapist influences on quitting psychotherapy. *Journal of Consulting Psychology,* 1963, *27,* 10–17.

McNair, D. M., Lorr, M., Young, H. H., Roth, I., & Boyd, R. W. A three-year follow-up of psychotherapy patients. *Journal of Clinical Psychology,* 1964, *20,* 258–264.

Mead, M. *Coming of age in Samoa.* New York: Morrow, 1928.

Mechanic, D. Mental health and social policy. Englewood Cliffs, N.J.: Prentice-Hall, 1969.

Meehl, P. E. The dynamics of "structured" personality tests. *Journal of Clinical Psychology,* 1945, *1,* 296–303.

Meehl, P. E. *Clinical versus statistical prediction.* Minneapolis: University of Minnesota Press, 1954.

Meehl, P. E. The cognitive activity of the clinician. *American Psychologist,* 1960, *15,* 19–27.

Meehl, P. E. Schizotaxia, schizotypy, schizophrenia. *American Psychologist,* 1962, *17,* 827–838.

Meehl, P. E. Seer over sign: the first good example. *Journal of Experimental Research in Personality,* 1965, *1,* 27–32.

Meehl, P. E., & Rosen, A. Antecedent probability and the efficiency of psychometric signs, patterns or cutting scores. *Psychological Bulletin,* 1955, *52,* 194–216.

Megargee, E. I. *The California Psychological Inventory handbook.* San Francisco: Jossey-Bass, 1971.

Meltzoff, J., & Kornreich, M. *Research in psychotherapy.* New York: Atherton, 1970.

Meltzoff, J., Singer, J. L., & Korchin, S. J. Motor inhibition and Rorschach movement responses: A test of the sensory-tonic theory *Journal of Personality,* 1953, *21,* 400–410.

Mendelsohn, G. A. Effects of client personality and client-counselor similarity on the duration of counseling: A replication and extension. *Journal of Counseling Psychology,* 1966, *13,* 228–234.

Mendelsohn, G. A., & Geller, M. H. Effects of counselor-client similarity on the outcome of counseling. *Journal of Counseling Psychology,* 1963, *10,* 71–77.

Mendelsohn, G. A., & Geller, M. H. Structure of client attitudes toward counseling and their relation to client-counselor similarity. *Journal of Consulting Psychology,* 1965, *29,* 63–72.

Mendelsohn, G. A., & Geller, M. H. Similarity, missed sessions, and early termination. *Journal of Counseling Psychology,* 1967, *14,* 210–215.

Menninger, K. A., Mayman, M., & Pruyser, P. *A manual for psychiatric case study.* (Rev. ed.) New York: Grune & Stratton, 1962.

Menninger, K. A., Mayman, M., & Pruyser, P. *The vital balance.* New York: Viking, 1963.

Menninger, W. *Psychiatry in a troubled world.* New York: Macmillan, 1948.

Minuchin, S. *Families and family therapy.* Cambridge, Mass.: Harvard University Press, 1974.
Mischel, W. *Personality and assessment.* New York: Wiley, 1968.
Mischel, W. *Introduction to personality* (2nd ed.) Holt, Rinehart & Winston, 1975.
Mishler, E. G., & Waxler, N. E. Family interaction processes and schizophrenia: A review of current theories. *International Journal of Psychiatry,* 1966, 2, 375–413.
Mitchell, R. E. Some social implication of high density housing. *American Sociological Review,* 1971, *36,* 18–29.
Mitchell, W. E. Amicatherapy: Theoretical perspectives and an example of practice. *Community Mental Health Journal,* 1966, 2, 307–314.
Moos, R. H. *Evaluating treatment environments.* New York: Wiley, 1974.
Moos, R. H., & Insel, P. M. (Eds.). *Issues in social ecology: Human milieus.* Palo Alto, Calif.: National Press Books, 1974.
Moreno, J. L. *Psychodrama.* Beacon, N.Y.: Beacon House, 1946.
Moreno, J. L. *Who shall survive?* Beacon, N.Y.: Beacon House, 1953.
Moreno, J. L. Psychodrama. In S. Arieti (Ed.), *American handbook of psychiatry.* Vol. II. New York: Basic Books, 1959.
Morgan, C. D., & Murray, H. A. A method for investigating fantasies: the thematic apperception test. *Archives of Neurology and Psychiatry,* 1935, *34,* 289–306.
Morris, J. N. *Uses of epidimiology.* Baltimore: Williams & Wilkins, 1957.
Mowrer, O. H. Sin: The lesser of two evils. *American Psychologist,* 1960, *15,* 301–304.
Mowrer, O. H., & Mowrer, W. A. Enuresis: A method for its study and treatment. *American Journal of Orthopsychiatry,* 1938, *8,* 436–447.
Murphy, L. B., & Collaborators. *The widening world of childhood.* New York: Basic Books, 1962.
Murray, E. J. A content-analysis method for studying psychotherapy. *Psychological Monographs,* 1956, 70 (113, Whole No. 420).
Murray, E. J., & Jacobson, L. I. The nature of learning in traditional and behavioral psychotherapy. In A. E. Bergin & S. L. Garfield (eds.). *Handbook of psychotherapy and behavior change: An empirical analysis.* New York: Wiley, 1971.
Murray, H. A. The effect of fear upon estimates of the maliciousness of other personalities. *Journal of Social Psychology,* 1933, *4,* 310–329.
Murray, H. A. *Explorations in personality.* New York: Oxford University Press, 1938.
Murray, H. A. *Thematic Apperception Test manual.* Cambridge, Mass.: Harvard University Press, 1943.
Murray, H. A. Preparations for the scaffold of a comprehensive system. In S. Koch (Ed.), *Psychology: A study of a science.* Vol. 3: *Formulations of the person and the social context.* New York: McGraw-Hill, 1959.
Murrell, S. A. *Community psychology and social systems.* New York: Behavioral Publications, 1973.
Murstein, B. I. *Theory and research on projective techniques (emphasizing the TAT).* New York: Wiley, 1963.
Murstein, B. I. Normative written TAT responses for a college sample. *Journal of Personality Assessment,* 1972, *36,* 109–147.
Murstein, B. I., & Pryer, R. S. The concept of projection: A review. *Psychological Bulletin,* 1959, *56,* 353–374.
Myers, J. K., & Bean, L. L. *A decade later.* New York: Wiley, 1968.

Naranjo, C. Present-centeredness: Technique, prescription, and ideal. In J. Fagan & I. L. Sheperd (Eds.), *Gestalt therapy now.* Palo Alto, Calif.: Science and Behavior Books, 1970.
Nash, E. A., Jr., Hoehn-Saric, R., Battle, C. C., Stone, A. R., Imber, S. B., & Frank, J. D. Systematic preparation of patients for short-term psychotherapy. II. Relation to characteristics of patient, therapist, and the psychotherapeutic process. *Journal of Nervous and Mental Disease,* 1965, *140,* 374–383.

Nathan, P. E. *Cues, decisions, and diagnosis: A systems-analytic approach to the diagnosis of psychopathology.* New York: Academic Press, 1967.

National Assembly on Mental Health Education. *Mental health education: A critique.* Philadelphia: Pennsylvania Mental Health, 1960.

Neisser, U. *Cognitive psychology.* New York: Appleton-Century-Crofts, 1966.

Newton, G., & Levine, S. (Eds.). *Early experience and behavior.* Springfield, Ill.: Charles C. Thomas, 1968.

Nunnally, J. C., Jr. *Popular conceptions of mental health.* New York: Holt, Rinehart & Winston, 1961.

Nunnally, J. C., Jr. *Psychometric theory.* New York: McGraw-Hill, 1967.

Offer, D., & Sabshin, M. *Normality: Theoretical and clinical aspects of mental health.* New York: Basic Books, 1966.

Orlinsky, D. E., & Howard, K. I. The good therapy hour: Experiential correlates of patients' and therapists' evaluations of therapy sessions. *Archives of General Psychiatry,* 1967, *16,* 621–632.

Overall, P., & Aronson, H. Expectations of psychotherapy in patients of lower socioeconomic class. *American Journal of Orthopsychiatry,* 1963, *33,* 421–430.

Padilla, E. R., Boxley, R., & Wagner, N. N. The desegregation of clinical psychology training. *Professional Psychology,* 1973, *4,* 259–264.

Parad, H. J. (Ed.). *Crisis intervention: Selected readings.* New York: Family Service Association of America, 1965.

Parloff, M. B. Goals in psychotherapy: Mediating and ultimate. In A. R. Mahrer (Ed.), *The goals of psychotherapy.* New York: Appleton-Century-Crofts, 1967.

Parloff, M. B. Analytic group psychotherapy. In J. Marmor (Ed.), *Modern psychoanalysis.* New York: Basic Books, 1968.

Parloff, M. B. Group therapy and the small-group field: An encounter. *International Journal of Group Psychotherapy,* 1970, *20,* 267–304.

Parloff, M. B., Goldstein, N., & Iflund, B. Communication of values and therapeutic change. *Archives of General Psychiatry,* 1960, *2,* 300–304.

Parloff, M. B., Iflund, B., & Goldstein, N. Communication of "therapy values" between therapist and schizophrenic patients. *Journal of Nervous and Mental Disease,* 1958, *130,* 193–199.

Parloff, M. B., Kelman, H. C., & Frank, J. D. Comfort, effectiveness, and self-awareness as criteria of improvement in psychotherapy. *American Journal of Psychiatry,* 1954, *111,* 343–351.

Parry, H., & Crossley, H. Validity of responses to survey questions. *Public Opinion Quarterly,* 1950, *14,* 61–80.

Patterson, C. H. *Theories of counseling and psychotherapy.* (2nd ed.) New York: Harper & Row, 1973.

Patterson, G. R. *Families: Applications of social learning to family life.* Champaign, Ill.: Research Press, 1971.

Patterson, G. R., McNeal, S., Hawkins, N., & Phelps, R. Reprogramming the social environment. *Journal of Child Psychology and Psychiatry,* 1967, *8,* 180–195.

Paul, G. L. *Insight versus desensitization in psychotherapy: An experiment in anxiety reduction.* Stanford: Stanford University Press, 1966.

Paul, G. L. Strategy of outcome research in psychotherapy. *Journal of Consulting Psychology,* 1967, *31,* 109–118.

Pearson, J. S., & Swenson, W. M. *A user's guide to the Mayo Clinic automated MMPI program.* New York: Psychological Corporation, 1967.

Peck, H. B., Kaplan, F. R., & Roman, M. Prevention, treatment, and social action: A strategy of intervention in a disadvantaged urban area. *American Journal of Orthopsychiatry,* 1966, *36,* 57–69.

Pepitone, A., & Reichling, G. Group cohesiveness and the expression of hostility. *Human Relations,* 1955, *8,* 827–337.

Perls, F. S. *Ego, hunger and aggression.* London: Allen and Unwin, 1947.

Perls, F. S. *Gestalt therapy verbatim.* Lafayette, Calif.: Real People Press, 1969. (a)

Perls, F. S. *In and out of the garbage pail.* Palo Alto, Calif.: Science and Behavior Books, 1969. (b)

Perls, F. S. Four lectures. In J. Fagan & I. L. Sheperd (Eds.), *Gestalt therapy now.* Palo Alto, Calif.: Science and Behavior Books, 1970.

Perls, F. S., Hefferline, R. F., & Goodman, P. *Gestalt therapy.* New York: Julian Press, 1951.

Peterson, D. R. Attitudes concerning the Doctor of Psychology program. *Professional Psychology,* 1969, *1,* 44–47.

Peterson, D. R. Status of the Doctor of Psychology program. *Professional Psychology,* 1971, 2, 271–275.

Phares, E. J., & Campbell, J. P. Sensitivity training in industry: Issues and research. In L. E. Abt & B. F. Riess (Eds.), *Progress in clinical psychology.* Vol. 9: *Clinical psychology in industrial organization.* New York: Grune & Stratton, 1971.

Phillips, L., & Smith, J. G. *Rorschach interpretation: Advanced technique.* New York: Grune & Stratton, 1953.

Piaget, J. *The origins of intelligence in children.* New York: International Universities Press, 1952.

Piaget, J. Piaget's theory. In P. H. Mussen (Ed.), *Carmichael's manual of child psychology.* New York: Wiley, 1970.

Piers, G., & Singer, M. *Shame and guilt.* Springfield, Ill.: Charles C Thomas, 1953.

Piotrowski, Z. A. The Rorschach inkblot method. In B. B. Wolman (Ed.), *Handbook of clinical psychology.* New York: Wiley, 1965.

Pittenger, R. E., Hockett, C. F., & Danehy, J. J. *The first five minutes: A sample of microscopic interview analysis.* Ithaca, N.Y.: Paul Martineau, 1960.

Polanyi, M. *Personal knowledge: Towards a post-critical philosophy.* (Rev. ed.) New York: Harper Torchbooks, 1964.

Pollack, I. W., & Kiev, A. Spatial orientations and psychotherapy: An experimental study of perception. *Journal of Nervous and Mental Disease,* 1963, *137,* 93–97.

Poser, E. G. The effects of therapists' training on group therapeutic outcome. *Journal of Consulting Psychology,* 1966, 30, 283–289.

Pottharst, K. E. To renew vitality and provide a challenge in training—The California School of Professional Psychology. *Professional Psychology,* 1970, *1,* 123–130.

Rabin, A. I. *Projective techniques in personality assessment.* New York: Springer, 1968.

Rachman, S. *The effects of psychotherapy.* Oxford: Pergamon Press, 1971.

Rachman, S., & Teasdale, J. *Aversion therapy and behavior disorders and analysis.* Coral Gables, Fla.: University of Miami Press, 1969.

Raimy, V. C. (Ed.). *Training in clinical psychology.* Englewood Cliffs, N.J.: Prentice-Hall, 1950.

Rapaport, D. The theory of ego autonomy: A generalization. *Bulletin of the Menninger Clinic,* 1958, 22, 13–35.

Rapaport, D., Gill, M. M., & Schafer, R. *Diagnostic psychological testing.* (Revised and edited by R. R. Holt.) New York: International Universities Press, 1968. (Original edition, 2 vols., 1945).

Rapoport, L. The state of crisis: Some theoretical considerations. *Social Service Review,* 1962, *36,* 211–217.

Rappaport, J., Chinsky, J. M., & Cowen, E. L. *Innovations in helping chronic patients.* New York: Academic Press, 1971.

Raush, H. L., & Raush, C. L. *The halfway house movement.* New York: Appleton-Century-Crofts, 1968.

Razin, A. M. A-B variable in psychotherapy: A critical review. *Psychological Bulletin,* 1971, 75, 1–21.

Reich, W. *Character-analysis.* (3rd ed.) New York: Orgone Institute Press, 1949.

Reichenbach, H. *Experience and prediction: An analysis of the foundations and the structure of knowledge.* Chicago: University of Chicago Press, 1938.

Reiff, R. The ideological and technological implications of clinical psychology. In C. C. Bennett, L. S. Anderson, S. Cooper, L. Hassol, D. C. Klein, & G. Rosenblum (Eds.), *Community Psychology.* Boston: Boston University, 1966. (a)

Reiff, R. Mental health manpower and institutional change. *American Psychologist,* 1966, *21,* 540–548. (b)

Reiff, R., & Reissman, F. The indigenous nonprofessional:A strategy of change in commu*nity action and community mental health programs.* New York: National Institute of Labor Education, 1964.

Reiff, R., & Riessman, F. The indigenous non-professional: A strategy of change in community action and community mental health programs. *Community Mental Health Journal,* 1965, Monograph No. 1, 3–32.

Reik, T. *Listening with the third ear.* New York: Farrar, Strauss, 1948.

Reisman, J. M. *The development of clinical psychology.* New York: Appleton-Century-Crofts, 1966.

Reisman, J. M. *Toward the integration of psychotherapy.* New York: Wiley-Interscience, 1971.

Rickers-Ovsiankiana, M. (Ed.) *Rorschach psychology.* (Rev. ed.) New York: Wiley, 1976.

Riessman, F. The "helper therapy" principle. *Social Work,* 1965, *10,* 27–32.

Riessman, F. Strategies and suggestions in training non-professionals. *Community Mental Health Journal,* 1967, *3,* 103–110.

Riessman, F., Cohen, J., & Pearl, A. (Eds.). *Mental health of the poor.* New York: Free Press, 1964.

Riessman, F., & Scribner, S. The underutilization of mental health services by workers and low income groups: Cause and cures. *American Journal of Psychiatry,* 1965, *121,* 798–801.

Rioch, M. J. Changing concepts in the training of psychotherapists. *Journal of Consulting Psychology,* 1966, *30,* 290–292.

Rioch, M. J. Pilot projects in training mental health counselors. In E. L. Cowen, E. A. Gardner, & M. Zax (Eds.), *Emergent approaches to mental health problems.* New York: Appleton-Century-Crofts, 1967.

Rioch, M. J., Elkes, C., Flint, A. A., Usdansky, B. S., Newman, R. G., & Silber, E. National Institute of Mental Health pilot study in training of mental health counselors. *American Journal of Orthopsychiatry,* 1963, *33,* 678–689.

Robbins, L. L., & Wallerstein, R. S. The research strategy and tactics of the Psychotherapy Research Project of the Menninger Foundation and the problem of controls. In E. A. Rubinstein & M. B. Parloff (Eds.), *Research in psychotherapy.* Vol. 1. Washington, D.C.: American Psychological Association, 1959.

Roberts, R. R., Jr., & Renzaglia, G. A. The influence of tape recording on counseling. *Journal of Counseling Psychology,* 1965, *12,* 10–16.

Roe, A. Individual motivation and personal factors in career choice. In F. N. Arnhoff, E. A. Rubinstein, & J. C. Speisman (Eds.), *Manpower for Mental Health.* Chicago: Aldine, 1969.

Roe, A., Gustad, J. W., Moore, B. V., Ross, S., & Skodak, M. (Eds.). *Graduate education in psychology.* Washington, D.C.: American Psychological Association, 1959.

Roen, S. R. Evaluative research and community mental health. In A. E. Bergin & S. L. Garfield, *Handbook of psychotherapy and behavior change: An empirical analysis.* New York: Wiley, 1971.

Rogers, C. R. *Counseling and psychotherapy.* Boston: Houghton-Mifflin, 1942.

Rogers, C. R. *Client-centered therapy.* Boston: Houghton-Mifflin, 1951.

Rogers, C. R. The necessary and sufficient conditions of therapeutic personality change. *Journal of Consulting Psychology,* 1957, *21,* 95–103.

Rogers, C. R. A theory of therapy, personality, and interpersonal relationships as developed in the client-centered framework. In S. Koch (Ed.), *Psychology: A study of a science.* Vol. 3: *Formulations of the person and the social context.* New York: McGraw-Hill, 1959.

Rogers, C. R. *On becoming a person.* Boston: Houghton-Mifflin, 1961.

Rogers, C. R. Client-centered therapy. In S. Arieti (Ed.), *American handbook of psychiatry.* Vol. 3. New York: Basic Books, 1966.

Rogers, C. R. Interpersonal relationships: Year 2000. *Journal of Applied Behavioral Science,* 1968, *4,* 265–280.

Rogers, C. R. *Carl Rogers on encounter groups.* New York: Harper & Row, 1970.

Rogers, C. R., & Dymond, R. (Eds.). *Psychotherapy and personality change.* Chicago: University of Chicago Press, 1954.

Rogers, C. R., Gendlin, E. T., Kiesler, D. J., & Truax, C. B. *The therapeutic relationship and its impact.* Madison: University of Wisconsin Press, 1967.

Rorschach, H. *Psychodiagnostics.* Berne, Switzerland: Huber, 1942.

Rosen, G. *Madness in society: Chapters in the historical sociology of mental illness.* London: Routledge & Kegan Paul, 1968.

Rosenbaum, M., Friedlander, J., & Kaplan, S. M. Evaluation of results of psychotherapy. *Psychosomatic Medicine,* 1956, *18,* 113–132.

Rosenthal, D. Changes in some moral values following psychotherapy. *Journal of Consulting Psychology,* 1955, *19,* 431–436.

Rosenthal, D., & Frank, J. D. The fate of psychiatric clinic outpatients assigned to psychotherapy. *Journal of Nervous and Mental Disease,* 1958, *127,* 330–343.

Rosenthal, D., & Kety, S. S. (Eds.). *The transmission of schiozphrenia.* New York: Pergamon, 1968.

Rosenthal, R. *Experimental effects in behavioral research.* New York: Appleton-Century-Crofts, 1966.

Rosenthal, R. Covert communication in the psychological experiment. *Psychological Bulletin,* 1967, *67,* 356–367.

Rosenwald, G. C. Psychodiagnosis and its discontents: A contribution to the understanding of professional identity and compromise. *Psychiatry,* 1963, *26,* 222–240.

Rosenzweig, S. Levels of behavior in psychodiagnosis with special reference to the Picture-Frustration Study. *American Journal of Orthopsychiatry,* 1950, 20, 63–72.

Rosenzweig, S. A transvaluation of psychotherapy—a reply to Hans Eysenck. *Journal of Abnormal and Social Psychology,* 1954, *49,* 298–304.

Rosenzweig, S. The place of the individual and of idiodynamics in psychology: A dialogue. *Journal of Individual Psychology,* 1958, *14,* 3–21.

Ross, A. O. *Psychological disorders of children: A behavioral approach to theory, research, & therapy.* New York: McGraw-Hill, 1974.

Rossi, J. J., & Filstead, W. J. *The therapeutic community.* New York: Behavioral Publications, 1973.

Rothenberg, P. J., & Matulef, N. J. Toward professional training. *Professional Psychology,* 1969, *1,* 32–37.

Rotter, J. B. *Social learning and clinical psychology.* New York: Prentice-Hall, 1954.

Rotter, J. B. Generalized expectancies for internal versus external control of reinforcement. *Psychological Monographs,* 1966, 80 (Whole No. 609).

Rubenstein, E. A., & Lorr, M. A comparison of terminators and remainers in out-patient psychotherapy. *Journal of Clinical Psychology* 1956, *12,* 345–349.

Ruesch, J., & Bateson, G. *Communication: The social matrix of psychiatry.* New York: Norton, 1951.

Ruess, A. L. Some cultural and personality aspects of mental retardation. *American Journal of Mental Deficiency,* 1958, *63,* 50–59.

Ryan, W. (Ed.). *Distress in the city.* Cleveland: Case Western Reserve University Press, 1969.

Sabshin, M. The anti-community mental health "movement." *American Journal of Psychiatry,* 1969, *125,* 41–48.

Sager, C. J., & Kaplan, H. S. *Progress in group and family therapy.* New York: Brunner/Mazel, 1972.

Sainsbury, P. Gestural movement during psychiatric interview. *Psychosomatic Medicine,* 1955, *17,* 458–469.

Salter, A. *Conditioned reflex therapy.* New York: Farrar, Strauss, 1949.

Sandifer, M. G., Jr., Pettus, C., & Quade, D. A study of psychiatric diagnosis. *Journal of Nervous and Mental Disease,* 1964, *139,* 350–356.

Sanford, N. The prevention of mental illness. In B. B. Wolman (Ed.), *Handbook of clinical psychology.* New York: McGraw-Hill, 1965.

Sanua, V. D. Sociocultural factors in families of schizophrenics: A review of the literature. *Psychiatry,* 1961, *24,* 246–265.

Sapolsky, A. Relationship between patient-doctor compatibility, mutual perception, and outcome of treatment. *Journal of Abnormal Psychology,* 1965, *70,* 70–76.

Sarason, S. B. *The clinical interaction.* New York: Harper, 1954.

Sarason, S. B. *The creation of settings and the future societies.* San Francisco: Jossey-Bass, 1972.

Sarason, S. B. *The psychological sense of community: Prospects for a community psychology.* San Francisco: Jossey-Bass, 1974.

Sarason, S. B., Levine, M., Goldenberg, I. I., Cherlin, D. L., & Bennett, E. M. *Psychology in community settings: Clinical, educational, vocational, social aspects.* New York: Wiley, 1966.

Sarbin, T. R. A contribution to the study of actuarial and individual methods of prediction. *American Journal of Sociology,* 1943, *48,* 593–602.

Sarbin, T. R. The logic of prediction in psychology. *Psychological Review,* 1944, *51,* 210–228.

Sarbin, T. R. The scientific status of the mental illness metaphor. In S. C. Plog & R. B. Edgerton (Eds.), *Changing perspectives in mental illness.* New York: Holt, Rinehart & Winston, 1969.

Sarbin, T. R., Taft, R., & Bailey, D. E. *Clinical inference and cognitive theory.* New York: Holt, Rinehart & Winston, 1960.

Sargent, H. D. Intrapsychic change: Methodological problems in psychotherapy research. *Psychiatry,* 1961, *24,* 93–108.

Satir, V. *Conjoint family therapy* (Rev. ed.). Palo Alto, Calif.: Science and Behavior Books, 1967.

Sattler, J. M. Racial "experimenter effects" in experimentation, testing, interviewing, and psychotherapy. *Psychological Bulletin,* 1970, *73,* 137–160.

Sawyer, J. Measurement *and* prediction, clinical *and* statistical. *Psychological Bulletin,* 1966, *66,* 178–200.

Schachter, S., & Singer, J. Cognitive, social and physiological determinants of emotional state. *Psychological Review,* 1962, *69,* 379–399.

Schafer, R. *The clinical application of psychological tests: Diagnostic summaries and case studies.* New York: International Universities Press, 1948.

Schafer, R. *Psychoanalytic interpretation in Rorschach testing.* New York: Grune & Stratton, 1954.

Schafer, R. How was this story told? *Journal of Projective Techniques,* 1958, *22,* 181–210.

Schafer, R. Generative empathy in the treatment situation. *Psychoanalytic Quarterly,* 1959, *28,* 342–373.

Schaffer, L., & Myers, J. K. Psychotherapy and social stratification: An empirical study of practice in a psychiatric outpatient clinic. *Psychiatry,* 1954, *17,* 83–93.

Scheerer, M. Problems of performance analysis in the study of personality. *Annals of New York Academy of Science,* 1946, *46,* 655–678.

Scheff, T. J. *Being mentally ill.* Chicago: Aldine, 1966.

Scheflen, A. E. The significance of posture in communications systems. *Psychiatry,* 1964, *27,* 316–333.

Schilder, P. Results and problems of group psychotherapy in severe neurosis. *Mental Hygiene,* 1939, *23,* 87–98.

Schmidt, H., & Fonda, C. The reliability of psychiatric diagnoses: A new look. *Journal of Abnormal and Social Psychology,* 1956, *52,* 262–267.

Schofield, W. *Psychotherapy: The purchase of friendship.* Englewood Cliffs, N.J.: Prentice-Hall, 1964.

Schon, D. A. Foreword. In L. J. Duhl & R. L. Leopold (Eds.), *Mental health and urban social policy.* San Francisco: Jossey-Bass, 1968.

Schonfield, J., Stone, A. R., Hoehn-Saric, R., Imber, S. D., & Pande, S. K. Patient-therapist convergence and measures of improvement in short-term psychotherapy. *Psychotherapy: Theory, Research, and Practice,* 1969, 6, 267–273.

Schutz, W. C. *Joy.* New York: Grove Press, 1967.

Scodel, A., & Mussen, P. Social perception of authoritarians and non-authoritarians. *Journal of Abnormal and Social Psychology,* 1953, *48,* 81–88.

Scriven, M. Psychology without a paradigm. In L. Breger (Ed.), *Clinical-cognitive psychology: Models and integrations.* Englewood Cliffs, N.J.: Prentice-Hall, 1969.

Selye, H. *The stress of life.* New York: McGraw-Hill, 1956.

Shakow, D., & Rapaport, D. The influence of Freud on American psychology. *Psychological Issues,* 1964, *4,* Monograph No. 13.

Shanan, J., & Moses, R. The readiness to offer psychotherapy: Its relationship to social background and formulation of complaint. *Archives of General Psychiatry,* 1961, *4,* 202–212.

Shapiro, A. K. The placebo effect in the history of medical treatment—implications for psychiatry. *American Journal of Psychiatry,* 1959, *116,* 298–304.

Shapiro, A. K. Placebo effects in medicine, psychotherapy, and psychoanalysis. In A. E. Bergin and S. L. Garfield (Eds.), *Handbook of psychotherapy and behavior change: An empirical analysis.* New York: Wiley, 1971.

Shapiro, D. *Neurotic styles.* New York: Basic Books, 1965.

Sharaf, M., & Levinson, D. J. Patterns of ideology and role-definition among psychiatric residents. In M. Greenblatt, D. J. Levinson, & R. H. Williams (Eds.), *The patient and the mental hospital.* New York: The Free Press of Glencoe, 1957.

Sheldon, W. H., & Stevens, S. S. *The varieties of temperament.* New York: Harper, 1942.

Sheldon, W. H., Stevens, S. S., & Tucker, B. *The varieties of human physique.* New York: Harper, 1940.

Sherman, A. R. Real-life exposure as a primary therapeutic factor in the desensitization treatment of fear. *Journal of Abnormal Psychology,* 1972, *79,* 19–28.

Shlien, J. M., Mosak, H. H., & Dreikurs, R. Effect of time limits: A comparison of two psychotherapies. *Journal of Counseling Psychology,* 1962, *9,* 31–34.

Shneidman, E. S. Projective techniques. In B. B. Wolman (Ed.), *Handbook of clinical psychology.* New York: Wiley, 1965.

Shneidman, E. S. Prevention of suicide: A challenge for community science. In S. E. Golann & C. Eisdorfer (Eds.), *Handbook of community mental health.* New York: Appleton-Century-Crofts, 1972.

Shoben, E. J., Jr. Psychotherapy as a problem in learning theory. *Psychological Bulletin,* 1949, *46,* 366–392.

Shoben, E. J., Jr. Toward a concept of the normal personality. *American Psychologist,* 1957, *12,* 183–189.

Shostrom, E. L. Group therapy: Let the buyer beware. *Psychology Today,* 1969, *2,* 37–40.

Shrauger, S., & Altrocchi, J. The personality of the perceiver as a factor in person perception. *Psychological Bulletin,* 1964, *62,* 289–308.

Siegal, R. S., & Rosen, I. C. Character style and anxiety tolerance: A study in intrapsychic change. In H. H. Strupp & L. Luborsky, *Research in psychotherapy, Vol. II.* Washington, D.C.: American Psychological Association, 1962.

Siegman, A. W., & Pope, B. An empirical scale for the measurement of therapist specificity in the initial psychiatric interview. *Psychological Reports,* 1962, *11,* 515–520.

Sifneos, P. E. *Short-term psychotherapy and emotional crisis.* Cambridge, Mass.: Harvard University Press, 1972.

Singer, J. L. The experience type: some behavioral correlates and theoretical implications. In M. A. Rickers-Ovsiankiana (Ed.), *Rorschach psychology.* New York: Wiley, 1960.

Singer, J. L. Research applications of projective methods. In A. I. Rabin (Ed.), *Projective techniques in personality assessment.* New York: Springer, 1968.

Singer, J. L. *The inner world of daydreaming.* New York: Harper & Row, 1975.

Singer, M. T., & Wynne, L. C. Thought disorder and family relations of schizophrenics. IV. Results and implications. *Archives of General Psychiatry,* 1965, *12,* 201–212.

Slavson, S. R. Group therapy. *Mental Hygiene,* 1940, *24,* 36–49.

Slavson, S. R. *A textbook in analytic group psychotherapy.* New York: International Universities Press, 1964.

Smith, A. *Supermoney.* New York: Random House, 1972.

Smith, M. B. "Mental health" reconsidered: A special case of the problem of values in psychology. *American Psychologist,* 1961, *16,* 299–306.

Smith, M. B. Competence and "mental health": Problems in conceptualizing human effectiveness. In S. B. Sells (Ed.), *The definition and measurement of mental health: A symposium.* Washington, D.C.: National Center for Mental Health Statistics, 1968.

Smith, M. B. Toward humanizing social psychology. In T. S. Krawiec (Ed.), *The psychologist.* Vol. I. New York: Oxford University Press, 1972.

Smith, M. B. On self-actualization: A transambivalent examination of a focal theme in Maslow's psychology. *Journal of Humanistic Psychology,* 1973, *13,* 17–33.

Smith, M. B., Bruner, J. S., & White, R. W. *Opinions and personality.* New York: Wiley, 1956.

Smith, M. B., & Hobbs, N. The community and community mental health center. *American Psychologist,* 1966, *21,* 499–509.

Smith, S. A retrospective assessment of postdoctoral training: Results of a survey. In I. B. Weiner (Ed.), *Postdoctoral education in clinical psychology.* Topeka, Kansas: The Menninger Foundation, 1973.

Snyder, W. U. *The psychotherapy relationship.* New York: Macmillan, 1961.

Sobey, F. *The non-professional revolution in mental health.* New York: Columbia University Press, 1970.

Soskin, W. F. Frames of reference in personality assessment. *Journal of Clinical Psychology,* 1954, *10,* 107–114.

Soskin, W. F. Influence of four types of data on diagnostic conceptualization in psychological testing. *Journal of Abnormal and Social Psychology,* 1959, *58,* 69–78.

Soskin, W. F., Ross, N., & Korchin, S. J. The origin of Project Community: Innovating a social institution for adolescents. *Seminars in Psychiatry,* 1971, *3,* 271–287.

Speck, R. V., & Attneave, C. L. Social network intervention. In J. Haley (Ed.), *Changing families.* New York: Grune & Stratton, 1971.

Speisman, J. C. Depth of interpretation and verbal resistance in psychotherapy. *Journal of Consulting Psychology,* 1959, *23,* 93–99.

Spitzer, R. L., & Endicott, J. DIAGNO: A computer program for psychiatric diagnosis. *Archives of General Psychiatry,* 1968, *18,* 746–756.

Spitzer, R. L., & Endicott, J. An integrated group of forms for automated psychiatric case records: A progress report. *Archives of General Psychiatry,* 1971, *24,* 540–547.

Spitzer, R. L., Endicott, J., & Cohen, G. *The Psychiatric Status Schedule. Technique for evaluating social and role functioning and mental status.* New York: New York State Psychiatric Institute and Biometrics Research, 1967.

Srole, L. Social psychiatry: A case of the Babel syndrome. In J. Zubin, & F. A. Freyhan (Eds.), *Social psychiatry.* New York: Grune & Stratton, 1968.

Srole, L., Langner, T. S., Michael, S. T., Opler, M. K., & Rennie, T. A. C. *Mental health in the metropolis.* Vol. I. New York: McGraw-Hill, 1962.

Stampfl, T. G., & Levis, D. J. Essentials of implosive therapy: A learning-theory-based psychodynamic behavioral therapy. *Journal of Abnormal Psychology,* 1967, *72,* 496–503.

Stanton, A. H., & Schwartz, M. S. *The mental hospital.* New York: Basic Books, 1954.

Star, S. A. The public's ideas about mental illness. Chicago: National Opinion Research Center, 1955. (Mimeo) (Also presented to a meeting of The National Association for Mental Health, 1955.)

Star, S. A. The place of psychiatry in popular thinking. Paper read at the annual meeting of the American Association for Public Opinion Research, 1957.

Stein, K. B. Psychotherapy patients as research subjects: Problems in cooperativeness, representativeness, and generalizability. *Journal of Consulting and Clinical Psychology,* 1971, *37,* 99–105.

Stein, M. I. *The Thematic Apperception Test.* (Rev. ed.) Cambridge, Mass.: Addison-Wesley, 1955.

Stephens, J. H., & Astrup, C. Treatment outcome in "process" and "non-process" schizophrenics treated by "A" and "B" types of therapists. *Journal of Nervous and Mental Disease,* 1965, *140,* 449–456.

Stephenson, W. *The study of behavior.* Chicago: University of Chicago Press, 1953.

Stern, G. G., Stein, M. I., & Bloom, B. S. *Methods in personality assessment.* New York: Free Press, 1956.

Stevenson, I. The psychiatric interview. In S. Arieti (Ed.), *American handbook of psychiatry.* Vol. I. New York: Basic Books, 1959.

Stevenson, I., & Sheppe, W. M., Jr. The psychiatric examination. In S. Arieti (Ed.), *American handbook of psychiatry.* Vol. I. New York: Basic Books, 1959.

Stoller, F. H. Marathon group therapy. In G. N. Gazda (Ed.), *Innovations to group psychotherapy.* Springfield, Ill.: Charles C Thomas. 1968. (a)

Stoller, F. H. Accelerated interaction: A time-limited approach based on the brief intensive group. *International Journal of Group Psychotherapy,* 1968, *18,* 220–235. (b)

Stone, A., Frank, J. D., Nash, E., & Imber, S. An intensive five-year follow-up study of treated psychiatric outpatients. *Journal of Nervous and Mental Disease,* 1961, *133,* 410–422.

Stone, G. C., Gage, N. L., & Leavitt, G. S. Two kinds of accuracy in predicting another's responses. *Journal of Social Psychology,* 1957, *45,* 245–254.

Strauss, A., Schatzman, L., Bucher, R., Ehrlich, D., & Sabshin, M. *Psychiatric ideologies and institutions.* New York: Free Press, 1964.

Streitfeld, H. S. The Aureon encounter: An organic process. In L. Blank, G. B. Gottsegen, & M. G. Gottsegen, *Confrontation: Encounters in self and interpersonal awareness.* New York: Macmillan, 1971.

Strother, C. R. (Ed.). *Psychology and mental health.* Washington, D.C.: American Psychological Association, 1956.

Strupp, H. H. A multidimensional analysis of technique in brief psychotherapy. *Psychiatry,* 1957, *20,* 387–397. (a)

Strupp, H. H. A multidimensional system for analyzing psychotherapeutic technique. *Psychiatry,* 1957, *20,* 293–306. (b)

Strupp, H. H. The performance of psychoanalytic and client-centered therapists in an initial interview. *Journal of Consulting Psychology,* 1958, *22,* 265–274.

Strupp, H. H. *Psychotherapists in action.* New York: Grune & Stratton, 1960.

Strupp, H. H. The outcome problem in psychotherapy revisited. *Psychotherapy: Theory, Research, and Practice,* 1963, *1,* 1–13.

Strupp, H. H. *Psychotherapy and the modification of abnormal behavior.* New York: McGraw-Hill, 1971.

Strupp, H. H., & Bergin, A. E. Some empirical and conceptual bases for coordinated research in psychotherapy: A critical review of issues, trends, and evidence. *International Journal of Psychiatry,* 1969, 7 (Whole No. 2).

Strupp, H. H., Chassan, J. B., & Ewing, J. A. Toward the longitudinal study of the psychotherapeutic process. In L. A. Gottschalk & A. H. Auerbach (Eds.), *Methods of research in psychotherapy.* New York: Appleton-Century-Crofts, 1966.

Strupp, H. H., Wallach, M. S., Wogan, M., & Jenkins, J. W. Psychotherapists' assessment of former patients. *Journal of Nervous and Mental Disease,* 1963, *137,* 222–230.

Strupp, H. H., & Williams, J. V. Some determinants of clinical evaluations of different psychiatrists. *Archives of General Psychiatry,* 1960, 2, 434–440.

Stuart, R. B. Operant interpersonal treatment for marital discord. *Journal of Consulting and Clinical Psychology,* 1969, *33,* 675–682.

Sullivan, H. S. *Conceptions of modern psychiatry.* Washington, D.C.: The William Alanson White Psychiatric Foundation, 1947.

Sullivan, H. S. *The interpersonal theory of psychiatry.* New York: Norton, 1953.

Sullivan, H. S. *The psychiatric interview.* New York: Norton, 1954.

Sundberg, N. D. The practice of psychological testing in clinical services in the U.S. *American Psychologist,* 1961, *16,* 79–83.

Sundberg, N. D., & Tyler, L. E. *Clinical psychology.* New York: Appleton-Century-Crofts, 1962.

Sutherland, J. D. Notes on psychoanalytic group psychotherapy. *Psychiatry,* 1952, *15,* 111–117.

Szasz, T. S. The myth of mental illness. *American Psychologist,* 1960, *15,* 113–118.

Szasz, T. S. *The myth of mental illness: Foundations of a theory of personal conduct.* New York: Harper-Hoeber, 1961.

Taft, R. The ability to judge people. *Psychological Bulletin,* 1955, *52,* 1–23.

Tagiuri, R. Person perception. In G. Lindzey & E. Aronson (Eds.), *The handbook of social psychology.* Vol. III. (2nd ed.) Reading, Mass.: Addison-Wesley, 1969.

Tallent, N. On individualizing the psychologist's clinical evaluation. *Journal of Clinical Psychology,* 1958, *14,* 243–245.

Tannebaum, G. The walk-in clinic. In S. Arieti (Ed.), *American handbook of psychiatry.* Vol. III. New York: Basic Books, 1966.

Terestman, N., Miller, D., & Weber, J. Blue collar workers at the psychoanalytic clinic. *American Journal of Psychiatry,* 1974, *131,* 261–266.

Thelen, M. H., & Ewing, D. R. Roles, functions, and training in clinical psychology: A survey of academic clinicians. *American Psychologist,* 1970, *25,* 550–554.

Thurstone, L. L. *Thurstone Temperament Schedule.* Chicago: Science Research Associates, 1949.

Tobiessen, J., & Shai, A. A comparison of individual and group mental health consultation with teachers. *Community Mental Health Journal,* 1971, *7,* 218–226.

Tomkins, S. S. The limits of material obtainable in the single case study by daily administration of the Thematic Apperception Test. *Psychological Bulletin,* 1942, *39,* 490.

Tomkins, S. S. An analysis of the use of electric shock with human subjects. *Journal of Psychology,* 1943, *15,* 285–297.

Tomkins, S. S. *The Thematic Apperception Test: The theory and technique of interpretation.* New York: Grune & Stratton, 1947.

Tomkins, S. S. Discussion of Dr. Holt's paper. In J. Kagan & G. S. Lesser (Eds.), *Contemporary issues in thematic apperceptive methods.* Springfield, Ill.: Charles C. Thomas, 1961.

Tomkins, S. S. *Affect, imagery, consciousness.* New York: Springer, Vol. 1, 1962; Vol. II, 1963.

Tomkins, S. S. Left and right: A basic dimension of ideology and personality. In R. W. White (Ed.), *The study of lives.* New York: Atherton, 1963.

Toomey, L. C., & Rickers-Ovsiankiana, M. A. Tabular comparison of Rorschach scoring systems. In M. A. Rickers-Ovsiankiana (Ed.), *Rorschach psychology.* New York: Wiley, 1960.

Truax, C. B. Reinforcement and non-reinforcement in Rogerian psychotherapy. *Journal of Abnormal Psychology,* 1966, *71,* 1–9.

Truax, C. B., & Carkhuff, R. R. Experimental manipulation of therapeutic conditions. *Journal of Consulting Psychology,* 1965, *29,* 119–124.

Truax, C. B., & Carkhuff, R. R. *Toward effective counseling and psychotherapy.* Chicago: Aldine, 1967.

Truax, C. B., & Mitchell, K. M. Research on certain therapist interpersonal skills in relation to process and outcome. In A. E. Bergin & S. L. Garfield (Eds.), *Handbook of psychotherapy and behavior change: An empirical analysis.* New York: Wiley, 1971.

Truax, C. B., Wargo, D. G., Frank, J. D., Imber, S. D., Battle, C. C., Hoehn-Saric, R., Nash, E. H., & Stone, A. R. Therapist empathy, genuineness and warmth and patient therapeutic outcome. *Journal of Consulting Psychology,* 1966, *30,* 395–401.

Truax, C. B. & Wittner, J. Patient non-personal reference during psychotherapy and psychotherapeutic outcome. *Journal of Clinical Psychology,* 1971, *27,* 300–302.

Umbarger, C. C., Dalsimer, J. S., Morrison, A. P., & Breggin, P. R. *College students in a mental hospital.* New York: Grune & Stratton, 1962.

van Kaam, A. *Existential foundations of psychology.* Pittsburgh: Duquesne University Press, 1966.

Vernon, P. E. *Personality assessment.* London: Methuen, 1963.

Veroff, J. Thematic Apperception in a nationwide sample survey. In J. Kagan & G. S. Lesser (Eds.), *Contemporary issues in thematic apperceptive methods.* Springfield, Ill.: Charles C Thomas, 1961.

von Mering, O., & King, S. H. *Remotivating the Mental Patient,* N.Y.: Russell Sage Foundation, 1957.

Wahler, R. G., Winkel, G. H., Peterson, R. F., & Morrison, D. C. Mothers as behavior therapists for their own children. *Behavior Research and Therapy,* 1965, *3,* 113–124.

Walker, R. S., & Walsh, J. A. As others see us? The Medieval Multi-Purpose Inquiry. *Perceptual and Motor Skills,* 1969, *28,* 414.

Wallerstein, R. S., & Sampson, H. Issues in research in the psychoanalytic process. *International Journal of Psycho-analysis,* 1971, *52,* 11–50.

Wapner, S. An organismic-developmental approach to the study of perceptual and other cognitive operations. In C. Scheerer (Ed.), *Cognition.* New York: Harper & Row, 1964.

Wapner, S., & Werner, H. An experimental approach to body perception from the organismic-developmental point of view. In S. Wapner & H. Werner (Eds.), *The body percept.* New York: Random House, 1965.

Warr, P. B., & Knapper, C. *The perception of people and events.* London: Wiley, 1968.

Waskow, I. E., & Parloff, M. B. (Eds.). *Psychotherapy change measures.* Washington, D.C.: U.S. Government Printing Office, 1975.

Watson, E. D., & Kanter, S. S. Some influences of an experimental situation on the psychotherapeutic process. *Journal of Nervous and Mental Disease,* 1954, *120,* 414–415.

Watson, J. B. *Behaviorism.* New York: Norton, 1924.

Watson, J. B., & Rayner, R. Conditioned emotional reactions. *Journal of Experimental Psychology*, 1920, *3*, 1–14.

Watson, R. I. *The clinical method in psychology*. New York: Harper, 1951.

Watson, R. I. A brief history of clinical psychology. *Psychological Bulletin*, 1953, 50, 321–346.

Weaver, W. Science and complexity. *American Scientist*, 1948, *36*, 536–544.

Wechlser, D. *The measurement and appraisal of adult intelligence* (4th ed.). Baltimore: Williams & Wilkins, 1958.

Wechsler, H., Solomon, L., & Kramer, B. M. *Social psychology and mental health*. New York: Holt, Rinehart & Winston, 1970.

Wegrocki, H. J. A critique of cultural and statistical concepts of abnormality. *Journal of Abnormal and Social Psychology*, 1939, *34*, 166–178.

Weinberg, S. K. Psychiatric sociology: the sociology of mental disorders. In S. K. Weinberg (Ed.). *Sociology of mental disorders: Analysis and readings in psychiatric sociology*. Chicago: Aldine, 1967.

Weiner, I. B. (Ed.). *Postdoctoral education in clinical psychology*. Topeka, Kansas: The Menninger Foundation, 1973.

Weitzman, B. Behavior therapy and psychotherapy. *Psychological Review*, 1967, *74*, 300–317.

Welkowitz, J., Cohen, J., & Ortmeyer, D. Value system similarity: Investigation of patient-therapist dyads. *Journal of Consulting Psychology*, 1967, *31*, 48–55.

Wellner, A. M. Survey of psychology services in state mental hospitals. *American Psychologist*, 1968, *23*, 377–380.

Wells, F. L., & Ruesch, J. *mental examiners' handbook* (2nd ed.). New York: Psychological Corporation, 1945.

Wenar, C. *The reliability of developmental histories—summary and evaluation of evidence*. Philadelphia: University of Pennsylvania School of Medicine, 1963 (Mimeo).

Werner, H. *Comparative psychology of mental development*. New York: International Universities Press, 1948.

Wheelis, A. *The quest for identity*. New York: Norton, 1958.

Whitaker, D. S., & Lieberman, M. A. *Psychotherapy through the group process*. New York: Atherton, 1964.

White, A. M., Fichtenbaum, L., & Dollard, J. Evaluation of silence in initial interviews with psychiatric clinic patients. *Journal of Nervous and Mental Disease*, 1964, *139*, 550–557.

White, R. W. Interpretation of imaginative productions. In J. McV. Hunt (Ed.), *Personality and the behavior disorders*. New York: Ronald Press, 1944.

White, R. W. Motivation reconsidered: The concept of competence. *Psychological Review*, 1959, *66*, 297–333.

White, R. W. Ego and reality in psychoanalytic theory. *Psychological Issues*, 1963, *3*, No. 3, Monograph No. 11. (a)

White, R. W. (Ed.). *The study of lives: Essays on personality in honor of Henry A. Murray. New York: Atherton*, 1963. (b)

White, R. W. *The abnormal personality*. (3rd ed.). New York: Ronald, 1964.

White, R. W. *Lives in Progress* (2nd ed.). New York: Holt, Rinehart & Winston, 1966.

Whitehorn, J. C., & Betz, B. J. A study of psychotherapeutic relationships between physicians and schizophrenic patients. *American Journal of Psychiatry*, 1954, *111*, 321–331.

Whitehorn, J. C., & Betz, B. J. Further studies of the doctor as a crucial variable in the outcome of treatment with schizophrenic patients. *American Journal of Psychiatry*, 1960, *117*, 215–223.

Wiggins, N. L., & Hoffman, P. J. Three models of clinical judgment. *Journal of Abnormal Psychology*, 1968, *73*, 70–77.

Wilkins, W. Desensitization: Social and cognitive factors underlying the effectiveness of Wolpe's procedure. *Psychological Bulletin*, 1971, *76*, 311–317.

Wilkins, W. Desensitization: Getting it together with Davison and Wilson. *Psychological Bulletin*, 1972, *78*, 32–37.

Wilkins, W. Expectancy of therapeutic gain: An empirical and conceputal critique. *Journal of Consulting and Clinical Psychology,* 1973, 40, 69–77.

Willems, E. P., & Raush, H. L. (Eds.). *Naturalistic viewpoints in psychological research.* New York: Holt, Rinehart & Winston, 1969.

Williams, G. J., & Gordon, S. *Clinical child psychology: Current practices and future perspectives.* New York: Behavioral Publications, 1974.

Wing, J. K., & Brown, G. W. *Institutionalism and schizophrenia: A comparative study of three mental hospitals, 1960–1968.* New York: Cambridge University Press, 1970.

Wispé, L. G., & Parloff, M. B. Impact of psychotherapy on the productivity of psychologists. *Journal of Abnormal Psychology,* 1965, *70,* 188–193.

Wispé, L. G., Ash, P., Awkard, J., Hicks, L. H., Hoffman, M., & Porter, J. The Negro psychologists in America. *American Psychologist,* 1969, *24,* 142–150.

Witkin, H. A., Dyk, R. B., Faterson, H. F., Goodenough, D. R., & Karp, S. A. *Psychological differentiation.* New York: Wiley, 1962.

Witkin, H. A., Lewis, H. B., Hertzman, M., Machover, K., Meissner, P., & Wapner, S. *Personality through perception.* New York: Harper, 1954.

Wittenborn, J. B. The dimensions of psychosis. *Journal of Nervous and Mental Disease,* 1967, *134,* 117–128.

Wittson, C. L., & Hunt, W. A. The predictive value of the brief psychiatric interview. *American Journal of Psychiatry,* 1951, *107,* 582–585.

Wolff, W. M. Private practice research. *Journal of Consulting and Clinical Psychology,* 1970, *34,* 281–286.

Wolberg, L. R. *The technique of psychotherapy* (2nd ed.). New York: Grune & Stratton, 1967. 2 vols.

Wolpe, J. *Psychotherapy by reciprocal inhibition.* Stanford, Calif.: Stanford University Press, 1958.

Wolpe, J. The systematic desensitization treatment of neurosis. *Journal of Nervous and Mental Disease,* 1961, *132,* 189–203.

Wolpe, J. *The practice of behavior therapy.* New York: Pergamon, 1969.

Wolpe, J., & Lazarus, A. A. *Behavior therapy techniques.* New York: Pergamon, 1966.

Woods, P. J. A history of APA's concern with the master's degree: Or "discharged with thanks." *American Psychologist,* 1971, *26,* 696–707.

Wyatt, F. What is clinical psychology? In A. Z. Guiora & M. A. Brandwin (Eds.). *Perspectives in clinical psychology.* Princeton, N.J.: Van Nostrand, 1968.

Wylie, R. *The self-concept: Review of methodological considerations and measuring instruments.* Vol. 1. (Rev. ed.) Lincoln: University of Nebraska Press, 1974.

Wynne, L. C. Some indications and contraindications for exploratory family therapy. In I. Boszormenyi-Nagy & J. Framo (Eds.), *Intensive family therapy.* New York: Harper & Row, 1965.

Wynne, L. C., Ryckoff, I. M., Day, J., & Hirsch, S. I. Pseudomutuality in the family relations of schizophrenics. *Psychiatry,* 1958, *21,* 205–220.

Yalom, I. D. *The theory and practice of group psychotherapy* (2nd ed.). New York: Basic Books, 1975.

Yalom, I. D., & Rand, K. Compatibility and cohesiveness in therapy groups. *Archives of General Psychiatry,* 1966, *13,* 267–276.

Yamamoto, J., & Goin, M. Social class factors relevant for psychiatric treatment. *Journal of Nervous and Mental Disease,* 1966, *142,* 332–339.

Yates, A. J. *Behavior therapy.* New York: Wiley, 1970.

Yates, A. J. *Theory and practice in behavior therapy.* New York: Wiley, 1975.

Yolles, S. F. The role of the psychologist in comprehensive community mental health centers: The National Institute of Mental Health view. *American Psychologist,* 1966, *21,* 37–41.

Zacker, J., & Bard, M. Effects of conflict management training on police performance. *Journal of Applied Psychology*, 1973, *58*, 202–208.

Zax, M. & Cowen, E. L. Early identification and prevention of emotional disturbance in a public school. In E. L. Cowen, E. A. Gardner, & M. Zax (Eds.). *Emergent approaches to mental health problems*. New York: Appleton-Century-Crofts, 1967.

Zax, M., & Cowen, E. L. Research on early detection and prevention of emotional dysfunction in young school children in C. D. Spielberger (Ed.). *Current topics in clinical and community psychology*. Vol. 1. New York: Academic Press, 1969.

Zax, M. & Specter, G. A. *An introduction to community psychology*. New York: Wiley, 1974.

Zigler, E., & Phillips, L. Psychiatric diagnosis: A critique. *Journal of Abnormal and Social Psychology*, 1961, *3*, 607–618.

Zilbach, J. J., Bergel, E., & Gass, C. The role of the young child in family therapy. In C. J. Sager & H. S. Kaplan (Eds.), *Progress in group and family therapy*. New York: Brunner/Mazel, 1972.

Zilboorg, G., & Henry, G. W. *A history of medical psychology*. New York: Norton, 1941.

Zubin, J. Tests, construction and methodology. In R. E. Harris, J. G. Miller, G. A. Muench, L. J. Stone, H-L. Teuber, & J. Zubin (Eds.). *Recent advances in diagnostic psychological testing*. Springfield, Ill.: Charles C. Thomas, 1950.

Zubin, J., Eron, L. D., & Schumer, F. *An experimental approach to projective techniques*. New York: Wiley, 1965.

Zuk, G. The side-taking function in family therapy. *American Journal of Orthopsychiatry*, 1969, *38*, 553–559.

Zusman, J. Some explanations of the changing appearance of psychotic patients: Antecedents of the social breakdown syndrome concept. *International Journal of Psychiatry*, 1967, *3*, 216–237.

Zusman, J. Community psychiatry in 1970—some successes and failures. *Psychiatric Quarterly*, 1970, *44*, 687–705.

INDEX